THE McGRAW-HILL
INTRODUCTION TO
Literature

THE McGRAW-HILL
INTRODUCTION TO
Literature

GILBERT H. MULLER

The City University of New York
LaGuardia

JOHN A. WILLIAMS

Rutgers University

McGraw-Hill Book Company

New York   St. Louis   San Francisco   Auckland
Bogotá   Hamburg   Johannesburg   London   Madrid
Mexico   Montreal   New Delhi   Panama   Paris
São Paulo   Singapore   Sydney   Tokyo   Toronto

THE McGRAW-HILL INTRODUCTION TO LITERATURE

Copyright © 1985 by McGraw-Hill, Inc. All rights reserved. Printed in the United States of America. Except as permitted under the United States Copyright Act of 1976, no part of this publication may be reproduced or distributed in any form or by any means, or stored in a data base or retrieval system, without the prior written permission of the publisher.

1234567890 DOCDOC 8987654

ISBN 0-07-043989-3

See Acknowledgments on pages 1052-1058.
Copyrights included on this page by reference.

Library of Congress Cataloging in Publication Data

Muller, Gilbert H., date
The McGraw-Hill introduction to literature.

1. Literature—Collections.   I. Williams, John Alfred,
date   . II. Title.
PN6014.M74   1985   808   84-10037
ISBN 0-07-043989-3

This book was set in ITC Bookman Light by Black Dot, Inc. (ECU).
The editors were Phillip A. Butcher and David Dunham;
the designer was Robin Hessel;
the production supervisor was Joe Campanella.
R. R. Donnelley & Sons Company was printer and binder.

The cover painting titled *The Girl I Left Behind Me*
was done by Eastman Johnson.
Cover photograph by
Sotheby Parke-Bernet/Agent: Art Resource, NY.

CONTENTS

PREFACE   XV

 PART 1 *FICTION*

INTRODUCTION

1 SUBJECT AND THEME: LIFE AND DEATH   6

Edgar Allan Poe   THE CASK OF AMONTILLADO   8
Anton Chekhov   *Gooseberries*   THE BET *life prison vs death penalty*   15
Franz Kafka   A HUNGER ARTIST   20
Ralph Ellison   KING OF THE BINGO GAME   27
Shirley Jackson   THE LOTTERY   34

2 PLOT AND THEME: MARRIAGE   42

Stephen Crane   THE BRIDE COMES TO YELLOW SKY   45
Bernard Malamud   THE MAGIC BARREL *cruelties in a wife*   54
Doris Lessing   FLIGHT   67

3 CHARACTER AND THEME: CRIME AND PUNISHMENT   72

Leo Tolstoy   GOD SEES THE TRUTH, BUT WAITS   75
Guy de Maupassant   *compare*   THE PIECE OF STRING   81
Flannery O'Connor   A GOOD MAN IS HARD TO FIND   86

4 POINT OF VIEW AND THEME: SELF-DISCOVERY   **99**

Nathaniel Hawthorne	YOUNG GOODMAN BROWN	102
James Joyce	ARABY	112
Joyce Carol Oates	STALKING	117

5 MOOD AND THEME: CASTE AND CLASS   **124**

William Faulkner	DRY SEPTEMBER	126
Arna Bontemps	A SUMMER TRAGEDY	135
Eudora Welty	A WORN PATH	143

6 TONE AND THEME: THE GRAND ILLUSIONS OF WAR   **150**

Luigi Pirandello	WAR	152
Hernando Téllez	JUST LATHER, THAT'S ALL	155
Ray Bradbury	AUGUST 2026: THERE WILL COME SOFT RAINS	159

7 SYMBOLISM AND THEME: HUMAN SEXUALITY   **164**

Katherine Anne Porter	ROPE	166
John Steinbeck	THE CHRYSANTHEMUMS	171
Kay Boyle	ASTRONOMER'S WIFE	188

8 AN ANTHOLOGY OF SHORT FICTION   **185**

Edgar Allan Poe	THE BLACK CAT	185
Mark Twain	THE NOTORIOUS JUMPING FROG OF CALAVERAS COUNTY	192
Alphonse Daudet	THE LAST LESSON	197
Sarah Orne Jewett	A CHANGE OF HEART	201
Kate Chopin	A RESPECTABLE WOMAN	207
Joseph Conrad	THE LAGOON	211
Charles Waddell Chesnutt	HOW DASDY CAME THROUGH	221
Anton Chekhov	GOOSEBERRIES	225
Sherwood Anderson	HANDS	233
D. H. Lawrence	THE ROCKING-HORSE WINNER	238
Katherine Mansfield	MISS BRILL	249
Dorothy Parker	THE STANDARD OF LIVING	253
James Thurber	THE CATBIRD SEAT	258
Jorge Luis Borges	THE SOUTH	265
Ernest Hemingway	THE KILLERS	270
Isaac Bashevis Singer	OLD LOVE	278
Richard Wright	THE MAN WHO WAS ALMOST A MAN	288
Eudora Welty	POWERHOUSE	298
Carson McCullers	THE JOCKEY	307
Grace Paley	A CONVERSATION WITH MY FATHER	311
James Baldwin	THE MAN CHILD	315
Ursula K. Le Guin	A TRIP TO THE HEAD	328

PART 2 POETRY

INTRODUCTION

9 SUBJECT AND THEME: LOVE ... 339

William Shakespeare	LET ME NOT TO THE MARRIAGE OF TRUE MINDS	341
Anne Bradstreet	TO MY DEAR AND LOVING HUSBAND	342
Andrew Marvell	TO HIS COY MISTRESS	343
Emily Dickinson	WILD NIGHTS—WILD NIGHTS!	346
Adrienne Rich	I COME HOME FROM YOU	347

10 DENOTATION, CONNOTATION, AND THEME: IMAGES OF WOMEN ... 350

Aphra Behn	THE DEFIANCE	353
Elizabeth Barrett Browning	IF THOU MUST LOVE ME	354
Emily Dickinson	SHE ROSE TO HIS REQUIREMENT	356
Gwendolyn Brooks	A SONG IN THE FRONT YARD	357
Nikki Giovanni	MOTHERS	359

11 METAPHOR AND THEME: WAR ... 362

Richard Lovelace	TO LUCASTA, GOING TO THE WARS	364
Wilfred Owen	DULCE ET DECORUM EST	366
Babette Deutsch	DISASTERS OF WAR: GOYA AT THE MUSEUM	367
Langston Hughes	WITHOUT BENEFIT OF DECLARATION	369
Sylvia Plath	DADDY	371

12 PERSONIFICATION AND APOSTROPHE: NATURE ... 375

Alfred, Lord Tennyson	THE OAK	378
Walt Whitman	I SAW IN LOUISIANA A LIVE-OAK GROWING	380
Robert Frost	TREE AT MY WINDOW	382
May Swenson	HEARING THE WIND AT NIGHT	384
Denise Levertov	THE VICTORS	386

13 IMAGERY AND THEME: THE SEASONS ... 388

William Shakespeare	WINTER	391
John Keats	TO AUTUMN	392
Wallace Stevens	THE SNOW MAN	394
William Carlos Williams	SPRING AND ALL	396
Ann Stanford	THE BLACKBERRY THICKET	398

14 SYMBOLISM AND THEME: DEATH — 400

George Herbert	CHURCH-MONUMENTS	403
John Keats	WRITTEN IN DISGUST OF VULGAR SUPERSTITION	405
Emily Dickinson	THERE'S A CERTAIN SLANT OF LIGHT	406
Robert Frost	STOPPING BY WOODS ON A SNOWY EVENING	407
Anne Sexton	THE FURY OF FLOWERS AND WORMS	409

15 TONE AND THEME: POETRY — 411

William Shakespeare	SINCE BRASS, NOR STONE, NOR EARTH, NOR BOUNDLESS SEA	413
Anne Bradstreet	THE AUTHOR TO HER BOOK	414
Archibald MacLeish	ARS POETICA	416
Nikki Giovanni	POETRY	417
Victor Hernandez Cruz	TODAY IS A DAY OF GREAT JOY	419

16 IRONY, SATIRE, PARADOX, AND THEME: THE STATE — 421

Percy Bysshe Shelley	OZYMANDIAS	424
Claude McKay	AMERICA	425
E. E. Cummings	NEXT TO OF COURSE GOD	426
W. H. Auden	THE UNKNOWN CITIZEN	428
Denise Levertov	WHAT WERE THEY LIKE?	430

17 SOUND AND THEME: THE SPORTING LIFE — 432

John Donne	THE BAIT	435
Robert Burns	MY HEART'S IN THE HIGHLANDS	437
A. E. Housman	TO AN ATHLETE DYING YOUNG	438
Phyllis McGinley	REFLECTIONS OUTSIDE OF A GYMNASIUM	440
May Swenson	ANALYSIS OF BASEBALL	442

18 RHYTHM, METER, AND THEME: THE SEA — 445

Andrew Marvell	BERMUDAS	447
William Wordsworth	NEAR DOVER	449
Matthew Arnold	DOVER BEACH	451
Judith Wright	THE SURFER	453
Derek Walcott	NEARING LA GUAIRA	454

19 THE SONNET AND THEME: GOD — 457

John Donne	HOLY SONNET 14	459
John Milton	WHEN I CONSIDER HOW MY LIGHT IS SPENT	460
Elizabeth Barrett Browning	CONSOLATION	462

Countee Cullen   YET DO I MARVEL   463

Gwendolyn Brooks   FIRSTLY INCLINED TO TAKE WHAT
IT IS TOLD   465

GOD WORKS IN A MYSTERIOUS WAY   465

20 POETIC STRUCTURE AND THEME: THE CITY   **467**

Jonathan Swift   A DESCRIPTION OF A CITY SHOWER   469

William Blake   LONDON   472

Ezra Pound   IN A STATION OF THE METRO   473

Chad Walsh   PORT AUTHORITY TERMINAL: 9 A.M.
MONDAY   475

Margaret Atwood   THE CITY PLANNERS   477

21 AN ANTHOLOGY OF POETRY   **479**

Sir Thomas Wyatt   THEY FLEE FROM ME   479

Henry Howard   TO HIS LADY   481

Edmund Spenser   SONNET 75: ONE DAY I WROTE HER
NAME UPON THE STRAND   482

Sir Walter Raleigh   THE NYMPH'S REPLY TO THE
SHEPHERD   483

Sir Philip Sidney   WITH HOW SAD STEPS, O MOON   485

Christopher Marlowe   THE PASSIONATE SHEPHERD TO
HIS LOVE   486

William Shakespeare   SHALL I COMPARE THEE TO A
SUMMER'S DAY?   487

Thomas Campion   THAT TIME OF YEAR THOU MAYST
IN ME BEHOLD   488

THERE IS A GARDEN IN HER FACE   489

John Donne   SONG (Go and Catch a Falling Star)   491

HOLY SONNET 7   492

Ben Jonson   TO CELIA   494

ON MY FIRST SON   495

ON MY FIRST DAUGHTER   495

STILL TO BE NEAT   496

Robert Herrick   TO THE VIRGINS, TO MAKE MUCH
OF TIME   497

DELIGHT IN DISORDER   499

John Milton   HOW SOON HATH TIME   500

ON THE LATE MASSACRE IN
PIEDMONT   501

Sir John Suckling   SONG: WHY SO PALE AND WAN,
FOND LOVER?   502

Anne Bradstreet   IN MEMORY OF MY DEAR
GRAND-CHILD   503

BEFORE THE BIRTH OF ONE OF
HER CHILDREN   505

Katherine Philips   AGAINST LOVE   506

John Dryden   WHY SHOULD A FOOLISH
MARRIAGE VOW   507

Aphra Behn	SONG: A THOUSAND MARTYRS I HAVE MADE	509
Anne Finch	TRAIL ALL YOUR PIKES	510
Alexander Pope	ON A CERTAIN LADY AT COURT	511
Lady Mary Wortley Montagu	IN ANSWER TO A LADY WHO ADVISED RETIREMENT	512
Phillis Wheatley	TO THE RIGHT HONORABLE WILLIAM, EARL OF DARTMOUTH	514
William Blake	THE LAMB	516
	THE TYGER	517
	THE GARDEN OF LOVE	518
Robert Burns	GREEN GROW THE RASHES, O	519
William Wordsworth	COMPOSED UPON WESTMINSTER BRIDGE, SEPTEMBER 3, 1802	520
	IT IS A BEAUTEOUS EVENING	522
Samuel Taylor Coleridge	KUBLA KHAN	523
George Gordon, Lord Byron	SHE WALKS IN BEAUTY	525
	ON THIS DAY I COMPLETE MY THIRTY-SIXTH YEAR	526
Percy Bysshe Shelley	STANZAS WRITTEN IN DEJECTION, NEAR NAPLES	528
	TO A SKYLARK	530
John Keats	ODE ON A GRECIAN URN	534
	BRIGHT STAR	536
Elizabeth Barrett Browning	WHEN OUR TWO SOULS STAND UP ERECT AND STRONG	537
Edgar Allan Poe	TO HELEN	538
Alfred, Lord Tennyson	ULYSSES	539
Robert Browning	MY LAST DUCHESS	542
Emily Bronte	REMEMBRANCE	544
Walt Whitman	A NOISELESS PATIENT SPIDER	546
	CAVALRY CROSSING A FORD	547
	THE DALLIANCE OF THE EAGLES	548
Matthew Arnold	TO MARGUERITE-CONTINUED	548
Emily Dickinson	I LIKE TO SEE IT LAP THE MILES	550
	BECAUSE I COULD NOT STOP FOR DEATH	551
	A LIGHT EXISTS IN SPRING	552
Christina Rossetti	IN AN ARTIST'S STUDIO	553
Thomas Hardy	THE DARKLING THRUSH	555
	CHANNEL FIRING	556
Gerard Manley Hopkins	PIED BEAUTY	558
A. E. Housman	BREDON HILL	559
William Butler Yeats	LEDA AND THE SWAN	562
	SAILING TO BYZANTIUM	563
E. A. Robinson	RICHARD CORY	564
Amy Lowell	THE TAXI	566
Robert Frost	THE ROAD NOT TAKEN	567
	ONCE BY THE PACIFIC	568
	THE OVEN BIRD	569

Contents

Wallace Stevens	ANECDOTE OF THE JAR	570
	SUNDAY MORNING	571
Carl Sandburg	THE HARBOR	575
William Carlos Williams	TO WAKEN AN OLD LADY	576
	THIS IS JUST TO SAY	577
Sara Teasdale	BARTER	577
Elinor Wylie	PURITAN SONNET	579
D. H. Lawrence	PIANO	580
Ezra Pound	A VIRGINAL	582
	THE RIVER-MERCHANT'S WIFE: A LETTER	582
H. D.	PEAR TREE	584
Robinson Jeffers	HURT HAWKS	585
Marianne Moore	POETRY	587
Edith Sitwell	TRIO FOR TWO CATS AND A TROMBONE	589
T. S. Eliot	THE LOVE SONG OF J. ALFRED PRUFROCK	591
John Crowe Ransom	CAPTAIN CARPENTER	596
Claude McKay	OUTCAST	598
Edna St. Vincent Millay	WILD SWANS	600
Wilfred Owen	ANTHEM FOR DOOMED YOUTH	601
E. E. Cummings	IN JUST—	602
	PITY THIS BUSY MONSTER, MANUNKIND	603
Jean Toomer	GEORGIA DUSK	605
Babette Deutsch	NATURAL LAW	606
Louise Bogan	CASSANDRA	607
Melvin B. Tolson	A LEGEND OF VERSAILLES	609
Sterling A. Brown	SOUTHERN ROAD	610
Langston Hughes	EVENIN' AIR BLUES	612
	THE NEGRO SPEAKS OF RIVERS	613
	HARLEM	614
Stevie Smith	THE WEAK MONK	615
Countee Cullen	INCIDENT	616
Kay Boyle	FOR MARIANNE MOORE'S BIRTHDAY	617
Phyllis McGinley	PORTRAIT OF GIRL WITH COMIC BOOK	618
W. H. Auden	MUSÉE DES BEAUX ARTS	620
Theodore Roethke	ROOT CELLAR	622
	I KNEW A WOMAN	623
Stephen Spender	AN ELEMENTARY SCHOOL CLASSROOM IN A SLUM	624
Elizabeth Bishop	FILLING STATION	626
Josephine Miles	HOUSEWIFE	628
Robert Hayden	THOSE WINTER SUNDAYS	629
Muriel Rukeyser	THE LOST ROMANS	630
Dylan Thomas	FERN HILL	632
John Berryman	THE BALL POEM	634

Randall Jarrell	THE DEATH OF THE BALL TURRET GUNNER	636
Judith Wright	EXTINCT BIRDS	637
Margaret Walker	POPPA CHICKEN	638
Robert Lowell	CHILDREN OF LIGHT	641
	AFTER THE SURPRISING CONVERSIONS	642
Lawrence Ferlinghetti	IN GOYA'S GREATEST SCENES	644
Richard Wilbur	THE DEATH OF A TOAD	646
James Dickey	THE PERFORMANCE	647
Denise Levertov	THE ACHE OF MARRIAGE	649
Carolyn Kizer	AMUSING OUR DAUGHTERS	651
Maxine Kumin	TOGETHER	652
A. R. Ammons	THE CITY LIMITS	655
Allen Ginsberg	A SUPERMARKET IN CALIFORNIA	655
W. D. Snodgrass	THE CAMPUS ON THE HILL	657
David Wagoner	A VALEDICTORY TO STANDARD OIL OF INDIANA	659
James Wright	A BLESSING	661
John Ashbery	CITY AFTERNOON	663
Anne Sexton	THE BLACK ART	664
	THE SUN	665
Adrienne Rich	THE PARTING: I	667
	AUGUST	668
	PEELING ONIONS	669
Thom Gunn	ON THE MOVE	670
Gary Snyder	NOT LEAVING THE HOUSE	673
Sylvia Plath	POINT SHIRLEY	674
Etheridge Knight	HARD ROCK RETURNS TO PRISON FROM THE HOSPITAL FOR THE CRIMINAL INSANE	677
Amiri Baraka	IN MEMORY OF RADIO	679
Sonia Sanchez	POEM AT THIRTY	681
June Jordan	POEM FROM THE EMPIRE STATE	683
James Welch	THE ONLY BAR IN DIXON	684
Leslie Silko	WHERE MOUNTAIN LION LAY DOWN WITH DEER	685

PART **3 DRAMA**

INTRODUCTION

22 SUBJECT AND THEME: MOTHERS AND SONS   **694**

John Millington Synge	RIDERS TO THE SEA	696
Langston Hughes	SOUL GONE HOME	706

23 COMEDY, TRAGEDY, AND THEME: LOVE AND WAR   711

Aristophanes   LYSISTRATA   714
William Shakespeare   OTHELLO   750

24 PLOT AND THEME: HUMAN DESTINY   851

Sophocles   OEDIPUS REX   853
Arthur Miller   DEATH OF A SALESMAN   892

25 CHARACTER AND THEME: WOMEN AND REBELLION   961

Henrik Ibsen   A DOLL'S HOUSE   964
Alice Childress   WINE IN THE WILDERNESS   1017

GLOSSARY OF LITERARY TERMS   1043

ACKNOWLEDGMENTS   1052

INDEXES   1059
     INDEX OF AUTHORS AND TITLES
     INDEX OF LITERARY METHODS AND TECHNIQUES

PREFACE

The McGraw-Hill Introduction to Literature is a dynamic and diversified anthology for college students enrolled in literature and composition courses. It contains 45 stories, 200 poems, and 8 plays of American and international appeal. Designed with an eye to both the uniqueness and the universality of outstanding literature, this text offers in its twenty-five chapters a unified and eminently teachable approach to meaning, form, technique, and values in fiction, poetry, and drama. If literature, as Paul Valery declared, is "the art of playing on the minds of others," then what we have attempted to create in this anthology is an appreciation of the strategies and themes by which first-rate authors capture and engage the imagination, intellect, and emotions of a broad range of readers.

The organization of *The McGraw-Hill Introduction to Literature* reflects organically the prime ways in which the teaching of literature actually is done—by genre, subject, theme, and technique. However, instead of fragmenting these approaches, we combine them in order to show how readers experience the thrill and meaning of a text through the author's handling of the key elements of his or her craft. The anthology contains three traditional main sections, each with a prefatory essay: Fiction, Poetry, and Drama. While these three genres are not the only forms of literature, what we call literature is most often expressed through them. Within each of these three major sections there are self-contained chapters —excellent modules for instruction—arranged around literary selections that share a common theme and reveal the application of an isolated technique. These chapters on theme and technique contain concise introductory essays, essential biographies for all authors, and complete exercises for discussion and writing. Each distinct chapter, by isolating within the genre a specific technique in relationship to theme, asserts the primacy of method in the author's discovery, exploration, and evaluation of a subject, and offers a comparative frame for exploring the ways in which writers treat a common theme. Many themes—for instance war, images of women, love and marriage—overlap two or three genres; shared techniques like tone and symbolism also appear more than once, contributing to the unity of the text and offering versatile ways of reinforcing concepts.

The extensive chronological anthologies at the end of the fiction and poetry sections enhance the teacher's flexibility in fitting *The McGraw-Hill Introduction to Literature* to personal, pedagogical, and classroom expectations. Through these refined organizational strategies, we offer teachers holistic yet flexible materials for instruction, and direct students toward the shared methods and themes—and thus the universality of—all fine literature.

Teachers will immediately recognize the literary excellence of many of the classical and contemporary authors and selections in this anthology, and will be intrigued perhaps by their unique positioning within and across chapters. Included are Shakespeare and Dickinson, Hemingway and Joyce Carol Oates, Sophocles and Ibsen, Langston Hughes and Sylvia Plath, Tolstoy and Borges— scores of major writers and those chestnuts that we look forward to teaching in a variety of literature and composition courses. Yet in *The McGraw-Hill Introduction to Literature* there are also writers and works that are lesser known but still of high rank and of considerable interest. We think that teachers will be delighted to discover or rediscover Katherine Philips and Judith Wright, Charles Chesnutt and Hernando Téllez, Sterling Brown and Leslie Silko. In fact, this anthology offers a broader range of women, ethnic, and international authors than any comparable text, and thus anticipates, we believe, both a truly American and a pluralistic literature.

In keeping with our attempt to offer a pluralistic anthology and to address the needs and expectations of a varied group of students, we offer detailed apparatus for every story, poem, and play in *The McGraw-Hill Introduction to Literature.* Questions for discussion and questions for writing, organized in separate sections, appear after each selection. The questions range from the simple to the complex. All questions encourage students not only to understand and appreciate literature, but also to use the skills essential for critical thought—to develop and refine abilities to analyze, compare, classify, and define concepts, and to defend critical positions. The recommended writing projects for each selection also are geared to short paragraphs, essays, and longer comparative papers. Consequently this anthology will be very useful in composition courses where "writing through literature" is stressed, as well as in introductory and more specialized literature courses. An extensive glossary provides students with basic definitions helpful in discussing and writing about literature. Moreover, two indexes help students to locate information in this anthology. This apparatus is supported by an all-inclusive instructor's guide offering assistance in the exploration of all materials in the anthology.

In preparing *The McGraw-Hill Introduction to Literature*, we have sought the eloquence, formal brilliance, and plain human interest of writers from the United States and abroad, from the fifth century B.C. to the 1980s, who can tell us and our students something about our common estate. "I am quite at a loss," wrote Henry James, "to imagine anything that people might like or dislike." We trust that students will enjoy enough of this anthology to make literature meaningful for them. Through male and female authors we express the faith that good literature best reflects the human condition, for better or worse, to a far greater extent than films or television. Even these media, so easy to absorb if not delight, could not exist without the written word.

We would like to express our thanks for the many useful comments and suggestions provided by colleagues who reviewed this text during the course of its development, especially to Herman L. Asarnow, University of Portland; James L.

Battersby, Ohio State University; Warren B. Benson, West Valley College; Dennis R. Gabriel, Cuyahoga Community College, Western Campus; John Hanes, Duquesne University; Rosalie Hewitt, Northern Illinois University; Perry Lentz, Kenyon College; Dan McLeod, San Diego State University; Gratia Murphy, Youngstown State University; Frank Ross, Eastern Michigan University; J. Chesley Taylor, Washington State University; and Suzanne Wolkenfeld. We would also like to thank Richard Bliss, Ed Cohen, and George Lee of Stanford University for their assistance in developing the anthology of poetry (Chapter 21), and David Groff for his work on the Glossary of Literary Terms. Special appreciation is extended to Dr. Jack Lynch of Montclair State College for his superlative work on the instructor's manual.

Gilbert H. Muller

John A. Williams

P A R T 1 R T

FICTION

Fiction began as storytelling, perhaps at night around warming campfires or anywhere else that people gathered. In those times the stories were sung or told in verse. Fiction comes directly from the ancient oral tradition.

Sometimes there were storytelling or story-singing contests, as in the classical age of Greek letters, when poet-playwrights read their works, more in verse than not, to audiences gathered for the festivals of Dionysus, which ran from autumn through spring each year.

These early stories usually were about figures or events familiar to particular groups, and such stories often became well known. Eventually, embellishments on the standard tales (as they were then called) were applauded and encouraged. New characters with new characteristics appeared; new conflicts requiring other than the usual solutions were portrayed.

However much adorned, the stories that have lived the longest may symbolize basic human concerns that have remained unchanged. The story of Prometheus is a good example.

We know the Prometheus story well as it has come down from the Greeks. Prometheus, pitying human beings, steals fire from the gods and brings it to earth, thus enriching human life with warmth and light. The same basic story is told in many variations all over the world. However, the heroes who steal from the gods or from other powerful beings range from ordinary mortals like King Arthur of England (securing Excalibur) to Rama of India (pulling his bow) to crafty animals (lizards, birds, or insects). At their core, though, such stories· are essentially Promethean. And in all these variations, the item obtained by the hero may symbolize fire; we cannot always be sure. In "Jack and the Beakstalk," for example, the object stolen is not fire, but the hen that lays the golden eggs; and Jack kills the giant, who has proved to be not evil, but only rich.

Apparently, it is only in the story of Prometheus that the hero is punished by the more powerful beings. In the other stories these beings exact no retribution.

Clearly, a story can have as many variations as it has storytellers, and we all tend to be storytellers, given enough encouragement. Saying "Can you top this?" or telling a fish story is as old as humanity itself. Stories may be viewed as conduits through which are passed history, cultural values, knowledge, and entertainment.

The short story and the novel (which may be considered a longer, more complicated story) are the major forms of fiction used today. The novella, or short novel, is a transitional form between the short story and the novel. The three forms evolved from the earlier tale, fable, legend, and myth.

Contemporary fiction, whether short or long, suffers from (or just possibly is enriched by) a preponderance of definitions, many of which are imposed upon the works by persons other than the creators of them. There are times when it is important to let the writers themselves say what fiction is or is not and what it should do or should not do. Nevertheless, if reading a work of fiction makes us believe in its content and its characters, then the work should be considered successful; for fiction is intended first to find believers, and belief must precede any other reaction to the work. A work of fiction usually possesses character, plot, point of view, theme, and, sometimes, symbols and setting. The way language is used to establish each of these elements helps to create within us a reaction to the work. The choice of language often helps to tell us what fiction is.

For example, Thomas Berger in his novel *Killing Time* (1972) says, "A work of fiction is a construction of language and otherwise a lie." "Constructions of language" shape civilization. (Lies are told for no other reason than to be believed.) Ursula Le Guin's "A Trip to the Head" (page 328) perhaps exemplifies Berger's view, but then we confront E. L. Doctorow's opinion, "There is no fiction or nonfiction as we commonly understand the distinction." Continuing, we discover that Nobel laureate Isaac Bashevis Singer's view is, "At best, art can be nothing more than a means of forgetting the human disaster for a while," which Henry Bendiner does in Singer's "Old Love" (page 278). Singer's lies, then, are "white," and his "constructions of language" are illusions.

Other explanations of "fiction" abound. Flannery O'Connor holds that the written word has more meaning than the spoken, a fact that gives fiction more importance, perhaps more moral force, than speech. For Herman Melville, fiction offers more reality "than life itself can show." In any event, it is clear that fiction is a statement by a writer about a real or imaginary world, past, present, or future; it is a response to the enormous pulsations of the universe by a writer who is part of it. How do we or should we respond to such a statement? Do we feel pleasure? Should fiction make us pause to reflect?

The question of what fiction does or should do, if anything, draws relatively clear opinions from fiction writers. "It has," says Singer, "the magical power of merging causality with purpose, doubt with faith, the passions of the flesh with the yearnings of the soul. . . . The zeal for messages has made many writers forget that storytelling is the raison d'être of artistic prose."

We think this means that good fiction, without having a discernible "message," can fulfill a deep moral need for the reader, just as a writer may feel a moral compulsion to create fiction. Flannery O'Connor seems to support this stance: "It is the nature of fiction not to be good for much else unless it is good in itself." This statement seems to imply that it is possible for fiction not to have any value other than that of being good fiction—possessing an intrinsic worth, with all other factors being extraneous.

Time and again writers stress the need, first of all, to tell a story, a good story. William Faulkner, also a Nobel laureate, said that "the primary job of any writer is to tell you a story, a story out of human experience—I mean by that, universal, mutual experience, the anguishes and troubles and griefs of the human heart, which is universal, without regard to race or time or condition. He wants to tell you something which has seemed to him so true, so moving, either comic or tragic, that it's worth repeating."

Fiction can be a shared experience—a sharing of statements, observations, and moods. The writer invites you into his or her created, ordered world so you can view your life from a new perspective.

Former *Esquire* and *Saturday Evening Post* fiction editor Rust Hills believes that contemporary fiction "has much to tell us about how we live, presents a kind of complex truth about ourselves and our society that can be found neither in the analyses and statistics of the psychologists and sociologists nor in the recently popular 'new reportage' . . . when we try to understand any past civilization we turn first to Art." Fiction may provide us with knowledge where before there was ignorance.

Telling a good story is considered by many to be a primary function of fiction, but telling a truthful story seems to be equally important. According to Joseph Conrad, all art "may be defined as a single-minded attempt to render the highest kind of justice to the visible universe, by bringing light to the truth, manifold and one, underlying its every aspect. . . ."

Conrad's opinion raises a problem. Is the writer's truth more truthful than anyone else's? Not necessarily; his truth merges with that of the reader. Truth is joined, made "manifold and one," and that characteristic, along with others, makes for good fiction.

Finally, Grace Paley feels that fiction writing bears with it certain moral responsibilities, saying, "Everyone, real or invented, deserves the open destiny of life." We are once again faced with the fact that good fiction may awake in readers a sense of moral thought and action and that the action considered often is that of creating a story.

Most people feel that there is a novel within them waiting for an opportunity to get out, and perhaps that is as it should be. If we return to Flannery O'Connor for a guide to the materials of fiction, we find: "The fact is that the materials of the fiction writer are the humblest. Fiction is about everything human and we are made of dust. . . ."

No one has ever been able to say for sure where even the "humblest" materials come from, how they are gathered and fashioned into the shape of a story or novel. We simply do not know. Yet we do recognize, in one way or another, the ability of a good writer of fiction to take the most ordinary materials and render them into extraordinary works.

Edgar Allan Poe writes, "Either history affords [the writer] a thesis—or one is suggested by an incident of the day—or at best, the author sets himself to work in the combination of striking events to form merely the basis of his narrative—designing, generally, to fill in with description, dialogue or authorial command, whatever crevices of fact or action may, from page to page, render themselves apparent."

Somewhere in the creative process, Poe is saying, is an experience the writer has had which he or she desires to share with others. This view is shared by Leo Tolstoy: "Art is a human activity consisting in this, that one man consciously by means of certain external signs, hands on to others feelings he has lived through, and that others are infected by these feelings and also experience them. . . ."

Often the writer tries to share *uncommon* experience in order to extend our knowledge. Certainly Ernest Hemingway was such a writer. Hemingway, indeed, implies that Dostoevsky's greatness was a result of extreme hardship: "Dostoevsky was made by being sent to Siberia." It was also Hemingway's opinion, shared by a number of writers, including James Joyce and Richard Wright, that writers "are forged in injustice as a sword is forged."

The idea that fiction is based on personal experience, which then seeks universal acceptance, refers, of course, to only one method by which fiction is created. The most widely held opinion is that fiction is created from a mixture of fact and fancy. However, Thomas Wolfe writes, "a man must use the materials and experience of his own life if he is to create anything of substantial value." Assuming that this opinion has merit, how should the telling of experiences be shaped?

Although fiction comes in several forms, our basic concern in this text is with the short story, which was created and defined in the United States early in the nineteenth century. While the short prose narrative—the tale—goes back to the eighth century B.C., Edgar Allan Poe is said to have first recognized the genre of the short story in Nathaniel Hawthorne's *Twice-Told Tales* in 1842. The term "story," as opposed to "tale," is believed to have originated in the Henry James collection *Daisy Miller: A Study; and Other Stories*, which was published in 1883.

Of Hawthorne's short stories Poe wrote that the form belonged "to the loftiest region of art." As to the mechanics of creating the story, Poe added that "having conceived with deliberate care a certain unique or single *effect* to be wrought out, he [the writer] then invents such incidents—he combines such events as may best aid him in establishing his preconceived effects." Furthermore, "if his very initial sentence tend not to the outbringing of this effect, then he has failed in his first step. In the whole composition there should be no word written, of which the tendency, direct or indirect, is not to the pre-established design."

Poe's rules influenced the rise both of the short story and of poetic forms in the United States and abroad. How do these rules stand up after 140 years? Isaac Bashevis Singer states: "Unlike the novel, which can absorb and even forgive lengthy discussions, flashbacks, and loose construction, the short story must aim directly at its climax. It must possess uninterrupted tension and suspense. Also, brevity is its very essence. The short story must have a definite plan. . . ."

Both Poe and Singer eschew didactic elements in the short story, but it often happens that such elements find their way into a work even in the conceptual stage. Given many writers' concern for truth and justice, didactic sections may perhaps be excused. One definition of "didactic," it is worth noting, is "morally instructive."

Short story writers now are legion, and they have, like the form, contributed much to literature from the early stages of the industrial revolution to today's age of super-technology. It is often said, and it is probably true, that most people in most modern societies find themselves with diminishing time to read. Novels are longer and demand more time and thought from us; short stories may demand more consideration for shorter periods of time and perhaps have not quite so much labyrinthian plot. The short story may be perfect for our age.

As an integral part of literature, the short story, like the novel, must first of all tell us a story. The various interpretations of the story, the question of which philosophy it might propound, and whether the author succeeded—all such considerations come long after the facts of creation and publication. It may happen that as literature becomes more and more just another product of the entertainment factory, the labels attached to literature may come to bear more weight than the works themselves. We, of course, hope this will not happen.

By whatever means a story is created and however it is structured, whether it imitates life, expresses it, affects it, or projects it, language ultimately makes the story work. Language is the final mold of all the other elements of fiction— language shows what it is and what it does, reveals how it was created, and gives it the ultimate form it demands. Perhaps a contemporary editor of fiction best stated the value of language: "Given a choice between a work of short fiction with a solid story and mediocre language, and a work with elegant language and not much of a story, I'd take the first." He added, however, "I am sure that a first-rate story would rather be seen in an elegant limousine than in a battered Jeep." Language creates character, action, mood, tone, symbols, and so on. Concepts do not. Everything in the world, as a highly fluent chimpanzee in Bernard Malamud's novel *God's Grace* (1982) declares, might very well be the genesis of a story, but it takes language for the telling. In good fiction, in all great literature, it is language that we see, feel, and hear. Language is both the wrapper on the package and one of the gifts inside it.

1

SUBJECT AND THEME:
LIFE AND DEATH

"Cut a good story anywhere," wrote Anton Chekhov, "and it will bleed." Chekhov's observation reflects brilliantly the organic connection between subject (or content) and form in short fiction and, indeed, in all literature. A good story is like the finely molded and tuned body of a champion sprinter: flesh shaped to frame and given swift purpose; form and content that should not be altered. In each short story the writer shapes content and organizes and refines material in order to produce through a fusion of content and form an interpretation of life. It is this wedding of content (notably characters and events) and form (technique, style) that gives a story its main meaning, or theme.

A theme is a distillation of everything that happens in a story's human drama. Whereas the subject is simply the topic of the tale (that is, what the story is overtly about), our understanding of the theme grows from our perception and evaluation of the story—it is our understanding of what the work says about the subject. For instance, we might say that the subject of Edgar Allan Poe's "The Cask of Amontillado" is revenge. (Other topics could be advanced as the main subject of this complex tale.) However, stating the theme of this story would take more than one word; normally at least a sentence and, in a very real sense, often an entire essay might be required. A sentence like the following might qualify as a statement of the theme: "The desire for revenge can obsess and consume a person's life." Sadly, when we thus extract subject and theme from a story, without considering the questions of *how* and *why* they emerge, we reduce the quality of the tale, and we lose sight of that special genius that writers can sometimes bring to their subjects. "I would be unable to write about anything that did not seem to me both unique and universal," declares Joyce Carol Oates. To justify the abstraction of subject and theme from a story, we must also seek out the formal patterns and stylistic devices used by the author to communicate the subject and the theme.

The nature of a writer's subject influences the stylistic and other technical decisions that he or she will make in order to give a story both form and meaning. Robert Louis Stevenson (author of *Treasure Island* and of several superb short stories) stated that "with each new subject . . . the true artist will vary his method and change the point of attack." In other words, each new subject or subjects—love, war, youth, marriage, revenge, or a combination of topics—dictate the correct strategies and approaches. Each aspect of style and technique—imagery, plot, characterization, point of view, symbolism, mood, tone, and so forth—is a way of getting at the subject of the tale and of shaping its meaning. Ultimately, of course, all the elements of a story are involved in the creation of meaning. "The whole story is the meaning," stated Flannery O'Connor, who used decidedly unusual points of attack to convey her subjects and themes to an audience that she described wryly as blind, hard of hearing, and in need of technical shocks. In considering theme, we should examine the whole story or, for purposes of special analysis, certain aspects of the tale.

We like to search for themes in literature because they make works meaningful and relevant. However, we want to explore theme in a balanced and intelligent way, remembering that all the elements in a story contribute to the illumination of meaning. Writers themselves are usually interested in meaning; they search for the "truth" about how we think, feel, act, and perceive. At the same time, they generally do not want to preach, moralize, or convey a message. "For messages," stated the American writer of detective fiction James M. Cain, "I use Western Union." Theme in most good fiction is conveyed not through stating a moral or a didactic point, but rather in a key imaginative insight or a *series* of such insights into the human condition.

Just as there is typically a series of insights in a short story, there may be more than one subject and, as a consequence, more than one theme. Complex stories—for instance, Franz Kafka's "A Hunger Artist"—may have multiple subjects and meanings that have been engineered consciously by an author who wants to mystify. Kafka delights in obscuring his subject, forcing readers to ponder the perplexing nature of the modern condition. What, you will have to ask yourself when you read "A Hunger Artist," is the subject of the tale? Is the subject art, religion, or historical or social processes? And what theme or themes are generated by these topics? Indeed, *is* there a theme? For we have to admit that theme does not always function as a unifying element in short fiction. A story can simply be a slice of life; a striving for special effects (as in Poe and much supernatural fiction); a premium on suspense and intrigue, as in detective and espionage fiction; or a willful attempt to destroy traditional concepts of content and form, as in much contemporary "antifiction."

Some stories handle theme intensively, while others blur theme, create multiple themes, or ignore theme entirely. Stories, after all, come in many shapes and sizes. The short story writer Hortense Calisher might be correct when she says that the short story "is an apocalypse served in a very small cup." Yet we never know for sure what the outcome of all this fire and brimstone will be. Fortunately, there is more often than not an explosion of meaning in the tightly compressed world of short fiction. In the spirit of Henry James, a writer will, according to the "subject," "method," and "point of attack," produce fiction that deals either with the attitudes and conventions of society and the age; with moments of intellectual or moral crisis; with individual feelings and emotions; or with the realms of the mind and the poetic imagination. Even in the current era of experimentation and acute artistic self-consciousness, a fiction writer's natural impulse is to give shape and meaning to his or her art.

One of the significant themes of modern fiction is the conflict between illusion and reality. All the stories in this section, varied as their content might be, deal with this theme either explicitly or implicitly. And each writer pushes this theme toward the grandest of all themes in literature, for all five stories deal with matters of life and death. All five stories also use a common motif, or pattern, centering on bets, wagers, and games of chance. Life itself seems to be a game of chance, a contest in which the protagonists have to distinguish between illusion and reality. In these works by Poe, Chekhov, Kafka, Jackson, and Ellison, we see that the writers do not reduce their stories to single, prescriptive themes. Nor do they necessarily provide messages, morals, or answers. As Chekhov declared, the artist "must set the question, not solve it." These authors ask not one question, but a series of questions: Why is life the way that it is? What human (and inhuman) impulses and motivations govern our lives? What are the critical events in the human drama? What details offer clues to an understanding of human nature? These are some of the essential questions that fiction writers traditionally ask, and they are the questions that we seek to answer in any consideration of subject and theme.

Edgar Allan Poe

THE CASK OF AMONTILLADO

Edgar Allan Poe (1809–1849), who invented the modern detective story and contributed to the early development of both short fiction and science fiction, is a unique figure in American literary history. Born Edgar Poe in Boston, he was orphaned in 1811 by the death of his mother; subsequently he was taken in by the John Allans of Richmond, Virginia, and rechristened Edgar Allan Poe. The scandal of his drinking and gambling at the University of Virginia ultimately alienated Poe from Allan and hastened his departure from college life. After a brief education at West Point, shortened again by his debauchery and gambling, Poe in 1836 married his cousin Virginia Clemm, who was then 13. Thereafter, Poe's life became a constant struggle to support his family; he wrote stories and poems and was an editor, journalist, and reviewer. His wife died in 1847. Two years later, Poe was found unconscious in a Baltimore street; he died on December 7, 1849. Poe's influence as a poet, critic, and short story writer has been significant. His best stories—"The Fall of the House of Usher," "William Wilson," "The Purloined Letter," and "The Cask of Amontillado," among others—did much to establish that unity of effect that Poe espoused as the hallmark of modern short fiction. Poe, of course, specialized in what he termed in Tales of the Grotesque and Arabesque *(1840) the "terrors of the soul." In the following story, we enter a bizarre and tangled world of revenge, madness, and murder; we must pay careful attention to the mind of the teller of the tale if we are to detect its true meaning.*

The thousand injuries of Fortunato I had borne as I best could, but when he ventured upon insult, I vowed revenge. You, who so well know the nature of my soul, will not suppose, however, that I gave utterance to a threat. *At length* I would be avenged; this was a point definitively settled—but the very definitiveness with which it was resolved precluded the idea of risk. I must not only punish, but punish with impunity. A wrong is unredressed when retribution overtakes its redresser. It is equally unredressed when the avenger fails to make himself felt as such to him who has done the wrong.

It must be understood that neither by word nor deed had I given Fortunato cause to doubt my good will. I continued, as was my wont, to smile in his face, and he did not perceive that my smile *now* was at the thought of his immolation.

He had a weak point—this Fortunato—although in other regards he was a man to be respected and even feared. He prided himself on his connoisseurship in wine. Few Italians have the true virtuoso spirit. For the most part their enthusiasm is adopted to suit the time and opportunity to practice imposture upon the British and Austrian *millionaires.* In painting and gemmary Fortunato, like his countrymen, was a quack, but in the matter of old wines he was sincere. In this respect I did not differ from him materially; I was skillful in the Italian vintages myself, and bought largely whenever I could.

It was about dusk one evening during the supreme madness of the carnival season, that I encountered my friend. He accosted me with excessive warmth, for he had been drinking much. The man wore motley. He had on a tight-fitting parti-striped dress, and his head was surmounted by the conical cap and bells. I was so pleased to see him, that I thought I should never have done wringing his hand.

I said to him—"My dear Fortunato, you are luckily met. How remarkably well you are looking to-day! But I have received a pipe of what passes for Amontillado, and I have my doubts."

"How?" said he, "Amontillado?" A pipe? Impossible! And in the middle of the carnival?"

"I have my doubts," I replied, "and I was silly enough to pay the full Amontillado price without consulting you in the matter. You were not to be found, and I was fearful of losing a bargain."

"Amontillado!"

"I have my doubts."

"Amontillado!"

"And I must satisfy them."

"Amontillado!"

"As you are engaged, I am on my way to Luchesi. If any one has a critical turn, it is he. He will tell me"———

"Luchesi cannot tell Amontillado from Sherry."

"And yet some fools will have it that his taste is a match for your own."

"Come let us go."

"Whither?"

"To your vaults."

"My friend, no; I will not impose upon your good nature. I perceive you have an engagement. Luchesi"—

"I have no engagement; come."

"My friend, no. It is not the engagement, but the severe cold with which I perceive you are afflicted. The vaults are insufferably damp. They are encrusted with nitre."

"Let us go, nevertheless. The cold is merely nothing. Amontillado! You have been imposed upon; and as for Luchesi, he cannot distinguish Sherry from Amontillado."

Thus speaking, Fortunato possessed himself of my arm. Putting on a mask of black silk, and drawing a *roquelaure* closely about my person, I suffered him to hurry me to my palazzo.

There were no attendants at home; they had absconded to make merry in honor of the time. I had told them that I should not return until the morning, and had given them explicit orders not to stir from the house. These orders were sufficient, I well knew, to insure their immediate disappearance, one and all, as soon as my back was turned.

I took from their sconces two flambeaux, and giving one to Fortunato, bowed him through several suites of rooms to the archway that led into the vaults. I passed down a long and winding staircase requesting him to be cautious as he followed. We came at length to the foot of the descent, and stood together on the damp ground of the catacombs of the Montresors.

The gait of my friend was unsteady, and the bells upon his cap jingled as he strode.

"The pipe," said he.

"It is farther on," said I; "but observe the white webwork which gleams from these cavern walls."

He turned towards me, and looked into my eyes with two filmy orbs that distilled the rheum of intoxication.

"Nitre?" he asked, at length.

"Nitre," I replied. "How long have you had that cough!"

"Ugh! ugh! ugh!—ugh! ugh! ugh!—ugh! ugh! ugh!— ugh! ugh! ugh!—ugh! ugh! ugh!"

My poor friend found it impossible to reply for many minutes.

"It is nothing," he said, at last.

"Come," I said with decision, "we will go back; your health is precious. You are rich, respected, admired, beloved; you are happy, as once I was. You are a man to be missed. For me it is no matter. We will go back; you will be ill, and I cannot be responsible. Besides, there is Luchesi"————

"Enough," he said; "the cough is a mere nothing; it will not kill me. I shall not die of a cough."

"True—true," I replied; "and, indeed, I had no intention of alarming you unnecessarily—but you should use all proper caution. A draught of this Medoc will defend us from the damps."

Here I knocked off the neck of a bottle which I drew from a long row of its fellows that lay upon the mould.

"Drink," I said, presenting him the wine.

He raised it to his lips with a leer. He paused and nodded to me familiarly, while his bells jingled.

"I drink," he said, "to the buried that repose around us."

"And I to your long life."

He again took my arm and we proceeded.

"These vaults," he said, "are extensive."

"The Montresors," I replied, "were a great and numerous family."

"I forget your arms."

"A huge human foot d'or, in a field azure; the foot crushes a serpent rampant whose fangs are embedded in the heel."

"And the motto?"

"Nemo me impune lacessit."

"Good!" he said.

The wine sparkled in his eyes and the bells jingled. My own fancy grew warm with the Medoc. We had passed through walls of piled bones, with casks and puncheons intermingling, into the inmost recesses of the catacombs. I paused again, and this time I made bold to seize Fortunato by an arm above the elbow.

"The nitre!" I said; "see, it increases. It hangs like moss upon the vaults. We are below the river's bed. The drops of moisture trickle among the bones. Come, we will go back ere it is too late. Your cough"————

"It is nothing," he said; "let us go on. But first, another draught of the Medoc."

I broke and reached him a flagon of De Grave. He emptied it at a breath. His eyes flashed with a fierce light. He laughed and threw the bottle upwards with a gesticulation I did not understand.

I looked at him in surprise. He repeated the movement—a grotesque one.

"You do not comprehend?" he said.

"Not I," I replied.

"Then you are not of the brotherhood."

"How?"

"You are not of the masons."

"Yes, yes," I said, "yes, yes."

"You? Impossible! A mason?"

"A mason," I replied.

"A sign," he said.

"It is this," I answered, producing a trowel from beneath the folds of my *roquelaure.*

"You jest," he exclaimed, recoiling a few paces. "But let us proceed to the Amontillado."

"Be it so," I said, replacing the tool beneath the cloak, and again offering him my arm. He leaned upon it heavily. We continued our route in search of the Amontillado. We passed through a range of low arches, descended, passed on, and descending again, arrived at a deep crypt, in which the foulness of the air caused our flambeaux rather to glow than flame.

At the most remote end of the crypt there appeared another less spacious. Its walls had been lined with human remains piled to the vault overhead, in the fashion of the great catacombs of Paris. Three sides of this interior crypt were still ornamented in this manner. From the fourth the bones had been thrown down, and lay promiscuously upon the earth, forming at one point a mound of some size. Within the wall thus exposed by the displacing of the bones, we perceived a still interior recess, in depth about four feet, in width three, in height six or seven. It seemed to have been constructed for no especial use within itself, but formed merely the interval between two of the colossal supports of the roof of the catacombs, and was backed by one of their circumscribing walls of solid granite.

It was in vain that Fortunato, uplifting his dull torch, endeavored to pry into the depths of the recess. Its termination the feeble light did not enable us to see.

"Proceed," I said; "herein is the Amontillado. As for Luchesi"—

"He is an ignoramus," interrupted my friend, as he stepped unsteadily forward, while I followed immediately at his heels. In an instant he had reached the extremity of the niche, and finding his progress arrested by the rock, stood stupidly bewildered. A moment more and I had fettered him to the granite. In its surface were two iron staples, distant from each other about two feet, horizontally. From one of these depended a short chain, from the other a padlock. Throwing the links about his waist, it was but the work of a few seconds to secure it. He was too much astounded to resist. Withdrawing the key I stepped back from the recess.

"Pass your hand," I said, "over the wall; you cannot help feeling the nitre. Indeed it is *very* damp. Once more let me *implore* you to return. No? Then I must positively leave you. But I must first render you all the little attentions in my power."

"The Amontillado!" ejaculated my friend, not yet recovered from his astonishment.

"True," I replied, "the Amontillado."

As I said these words I busied myself among the pile of bones of which I have before spoken. Throwing them aside, I soon uncovered a quantity of building stone and mortar. With these materials and with the aid of my towel, I began vigorously to wall up the entrance of the niche.

I had scarcely laid the first tier of the masonry when I discovered that the intoxication of Fortunato had in a great measure worn off. The earliest indication I had of this was a low moaning cry from the depth of the recess. It was *not* the cry of a drunken man. There was then a long and obstinate silence. I laid the second tier, and the third, and the fourth; and then I heard the furious vibrations of the chain. The noise lasted for several minutes, during which, that I might hearken to it with the more satisfaction, I ceased my labors and sat down upon the bones. When at last the clanking subsided, I resumed the trowel, and finished without interruption the fifth, the sixth, and the seventh tier. The wall was now nearly upon a level with my breast. I again paused, and holding the flambeaux over the mason-work, threw a few feeble rays upon the figure within.

A succession of loud and shrill screams, bursting suddenly from the throat of the chained form, seemed to thrust me violently back. For a brief moment I hesitated—I trembled. Unsheathing my rapier, I began to grope with it about the recess; but the thought of an instant reassured me. I placed my hand upon the solid fabric of the catacombs, and felt satisfied. I re-approached the wall. I replied to the yells of him who clamored. I re-echoed—I aided—I surpassed them in volume and in strength. I did this, and the clamorer grew still.

It was now midnight, and my task was drawing to a close. I had completed the eighth, the ninth and the tenth tier. I had finished a portion of the last and the eleventh; there remained but a single stone to be fitted and plastered in. I struggled with its weight; I placed it partially in its destined position. But now there came from out the niche a low laugh that erected the hairs upon my head. It was succeeded by a sad voice, which I had difficulty in recognizing as that of the noble Fortunato. The voice said—

"Ha! ha! ha! he! he!—a very good joke indeed—an excellent jest. We will have many a rich laugh about it at the palazzo—he! he! he!—over our wine—he! he! he!"

"The Amontillado!" I said.

"He! he! he!—he! he! he!—yes, the Amontillado. But is it not getting late? Will not they be awaiting us at the palazzo, the Lady Fortunato and the rest? Let us be gone."

"Yes," I said, "let us be gone."

"For the love of God, Montresor!"

"Yes," I said, "for the love of God!"

But to these words I hearkened in vain for a reply. I grew impatient. I called aloud—

"Fortunato!"

No answer. I called again—

"Fortunato!"

No answer still. I thrust a torch through the remaining aperture and let it fall within. There came forth in return only a jingling of the bells. My heart grew sick—on account of the dampness of the catacombs. I hastened to make an end of my labor. I forced the last stone into its position; I plastered it up. Against the new masonry I re-erected the old rampart of bones. For the half of a century no mortal has disturbed them.

In pace requiescat!

QUESTIONS

1. What is Montresor's theory of revenge? What are some of the "thousand injuries" he has suffered at the hands of Fortunato?

2. What is the setting of the story? How does it contribute to the revenge motif? to the theme of illusion and reality?

3. Why does Montresor consider himself superior to Fortunato?

4. Why does Montresor grow sick at heart? Why does he retell the story almost half a century after the event? To whom is he telling the story?

5. What is the theme of the story?

6. Is Poe actually interested in stating a theme for this story, or is he simply interested in creating special effects that we traditionally associate with a "tale of terror"? Defend your answer.

7. How does Poe's presentation of personality conform to modern psychology's consideration of personality?

TOPICS FOR WRITING

1. Analyze Poe's exploration of human psychology in the story. Link Poe's psychological investigations to the theme that emerges from our understanding of Montresor's behavior.

2. Evaluate Poe's treatment of gothic conventions (see glossary) in the tale. Assess the probability of a theme emerging from a gothic short story.

3. Write a brief paper on the contribution of the setting to the subject and theme of the story.

Anton Chekhov

THE BET

Anton Chekhov (1860–1904), the grandson of a serf, was born in Taganrog, Russia, and studied medicine at Moscow University. He received his medical degree in 1884, the same year that his first collection of short stories was published. Chekhov wrote hundreds of stories and sketches early in his career, gaining a literary reputation and a measure of financial independence that enabled him to make writing rather than the practice of medicine his major priority. Chekhov's greatest work in both short fiction and drama came in the last years of a life drastically shortened by tuberculosis. The plays of this last period—The Seagull (1896), Uncle Vanya (1899), The Three Sisters (1901), and The Cherry Orchard (1904)—were masterpieces that established Chekhov as a great modern dramatist. Chekhov's masterpieces of short fiction are equally outstanding, a delicate mixture of comedy, pathos, and tragedy in the author's depiction of humanity. He was termed an "artist of life" by his contemporary Tolstoy. In "The Bet" Chekhov investigates the very large subject of what we know about existence. In this story, a young lawyer, accepting a bet, risks "imprisonment for life" in order to find answers to key existential questions.

The Bet

I

It was a dark autumn night. The old banker was walking up and down his study and remembering how, fifteen years before, he had given a party one autumn evening. There had been many clever men there, and there had been interesting conversations. Among other things they had talked of capital punishment. The majority of the guests, among whom were many journalists and intellectual men, disapproved of the death penalty. They considered that form of punishment out of date, immoral, and unsuitable for Christian States. In the opinion of some of them the death penalty ought to be replaced everywhere by imprisonment for life.

"I don't agree with you," said their host the banker. "I have not tried either the death penalty or imprisonment for life, but if one may judge *à priori,* the death penalty is more moral and more humane than imprisonment for life. Capital punishment kills a man at once, but lifelong imprisonment kills him slowly. Which executioner is the more humane, he who kills you in a few minutes or he who drags the life out of you in the course of many years?"

"Both are equally immoral," observed one of the guests, "for they both have the same object—to take away life. The State is not God. It has not the right to take away what it cannot restore when it wants to."

Among the guests was a young lawyer, a young man of five-and-twenty. When he was asked his opinion, he said:

"The death sentence and the life sentence are equally immoral, but if I had to choose between the death penalty and imprisonment for life, I would certainly choose the second. To live anyhow is better than not at all."

A lively discussion arose. The banker, who was younger and more nervous in those days, was suddenly carried away by excitement; he struck the table with his fist and shouted at the young man:

"It's not true! I'll bet you two millions you wouldn't stay in solitary confinement for five years."

"If you mean that in earnest," said the young man, "I'll take the bet, but I would stay not five but fifteen years."

"Fifteen? Done!" cried the banker. "Gentlemen, I stake two millions!"

"Agreed! You stake your millions and I stake my freedom!" said the young man.

And this wild, senseless bet was carried out! The banker, spoilt and frivolous, with millions beyond his reckoning, was delighted at the bet. At supper he made fun of the young man, and said:

"Think better of it, young man, while there is still time. To me two millions are a trifle, but you are losing three or four of the best years of your life. I say three or four, because you won't stay longer. Don't forget either, you unhappy man, that voluntary confinement is a great deal harder to bear than compulsory. The thought that you have the right to step out in liberty at any moment will poison your whole existence in prison. I am sorry for you."

And now the banker, walking to and fro, remembered all this, and asked himself: "What was the object of that bet? What is the good of that man's losing fifteen years of his life and my throwing away two millions? Can it prove that the death penalty is better or worse than imprisonment for life? No, no. It was all nonsensical and meaningless. On my part it was the caprice of a pampered man, and on his part simple greed for money. . . ."

Then he remembered what followed that evening. It was decided that the young man should spend the years of his captivity under the strictest supervision in one of the lodges in the banker's garden. It was agreed that for fifteen years he should not be free to cross the threshold of the lodge, to see human beings, to hear the human voice, or to receive letters and newspapers. He was allowed to have a musical instrument and books, and was allowed to write letters, to drink wine, and to smoke. By the terms of the agreement, the only relations he could have with the outer world were by a little window made purposely for that object. He might have anything he wanted—books, music, wine, and so on—in any quantity he desired by writing an order, but could only receive them through the window. The agreement provided for every detail and every trifle that would make his imprisonment strictly solitary, and bound the young man to stay there *exactly* fifteen years, beginning from twelve o'clock of November 14, 1870, and ending at twelve o'clock of November 14, 1885. The slightest attempt on his part to break the conditions, if only two minutes before the end, released the banker from the obligation to pay him two millions.

For the first year of his confinement, as far as one could judge from his brief notes, the prisoner suffered severely from loneliness and depression. The sounds of the piano could be heard continually day and night from his lodge. He refused wine and tobacco. Wine, he wrote, excites the desires, and desires are the worst foes of the prisoner; and besides, nothing could be more dreary than drinking good wine and seeing no one. And tobacco spoilt the air of his room. In the first year the books he sent for were principally of a light character; novels with a complicated love plot, sensational and fantastic stories, and so on.

In the second year the piano was silent in the lodge, and the prisoner asked only for the classics. In the fifth year music was audible again, and the prisoner asked for wine. Those who watched him through the window said that all that year he spent doing nothing but eating and drinking and lying on his bed, frequently yawning and angrily talking to himself. He did not read books. Sometimes at night he would sit down to write; he would spend hours writing, and in the morning tear up all that he had written. More than once he could be heard crying.

In the second half of the sixth year the prisoner began zealously studying languages, philosophy, and history. He threw himself eagerly into these studies— so much so that the banker had enough to do to get him the books he ordered. In the course of four years some six hundred volumes were procured at his request. It was during this period that the banker received the following letter from his prisoner:

"My dear Jailer, I write you these lines in six languages. Show them to people who know the languages. Let them read them. If they find not one mistake I implore you to fire a shot in the garden. That shot will show me that my efforts have not been thrown away. The geniuses of all ages and of all lands speak different languages, but the same flame burns in them all. Ah, if you only knew what unearthly happiness my soul feels now from being able to understand them!" The prisoner's desire was fulfilled. The banker ordered two shots to be fired in the garden.

Then after the tenth year, the prisoner sat immovably at the table and read nothing but the Gospel. It seemed strange to the banker that a man who in four years had mastered six hundred learned volumes should waste nearly a year over one thin book easy of comprehension. Theology and histories of religion followed the Gospels.

In the last two years of his confinement the prisoner read an immense quantity of books quite indiscriminately. At one time he was busy with the natural sciences, then he would ask for Byron or Shakespeare. There were notes in which he demanded at the same time books on chemistry, and a manual of medicine, and a novel, and some treatise on philosophy or theology. His reading suggested a man swimming in the sea among the wreckage of his ship, and trying to save his life by greedily clutching first at one spar and then at another.

II

The old banker remembered all this, and thought:

"To-morrow at twelve o'clock he will regain his freedom. By our agreement I ought to pay him two millions. If I do pay him, it is all over with me: I shall be utterly ruined."

Fifteen years before, his millions had been beyond his reckoning; now he was afraid to ask himself which were greater, his debts or his assets. Desperate gambling on the Stock Exchange, wild speculation, and the excitability which he could not get over even in advancing years, had by degrees led to the decline of his fortune, and the proud, fearless, self-confident millionaire had become a banker of middling rank, trembling at every rise and fall in his investments. "Cursed bet!" muttered the old man, clutching his head in despair. "Why didn't the man die? He is only forty now. He will take my last penny from me, he will marry, will enjoy life, will gamble on the Exchange; while I shall look at him with envy like a beggar, and hear from him every day the same sentence: 'I am indebted to you for the happiness of my life, let me help you!' No, it is too much! The one means of being saved from bankruptcy and disgrace is the death of that man!"

It struck three o'clock, the banker listened; everyone was asleep in the house, and nothing could be heard outside but the rustling of the chilled trees. Trying to make no noise, he took from a fireproof safe the key of the door which had not been opened for fifteen years, put on his overcoat, and went out of the house.

It was dark and cold in the garden. Rain was falling. A damp cutting wind was racing about the garden, howling and giving the trees no rest. The banker strained his eyes, but could see neither the earth nor the white statues, nor the lodge, nor the trees. Going to the spot where the lodge stood, he twice called the watchman. No answer followed. Evidently the watchman had sought shelter from the weather, and was now asleep somewhere either in the kitchen or in the greenhouse.

"If I had the pluck to carry out my intention," thought the old man, "suspicion would fall first upon the watchman."

He felt in the darkness for the steps and the door, and went into the entry of the lodge. Then he groped his way into a little passage and lighted a match. There was not a soul there. There was a bedstead with no bedding on it, and in the corner there was a dark cast-iron stove. The seals on the door leading to the prisoner's rooms were intact.

When the match went out the old man, trembling with emotion, peeped through the little window. A candle was burning dimly in the prisoner's room. He was sitting at the table. Nothing could be seen but his back, the hair on his head, and his hands. Open books were lying on the table, on the two easy-chairs, and on the carpet near the table.

Five minutes passed and the prisoner did not once stir. Fifteen years' imprisonment had taught him to sit still. The banker tapped at the window with his finger, and the prisoner made no movement whatever in response. Then the banker cautiously broke the seals off the door and put the key in the keyhole. The rusty lock gave a grating sound and the door creaked. The banker expected to hear at once footsteps and a cry of astonishment, but three minutes passed and it was as quiet as ever in the room. He made up his mind to go in.

At the table a man unlike ordinary people was sitting motionless. He was a skeleton with the skin drawn tight over his bones, with long curls like a woman's, and a shaggy beard. His face was yellow with an earthy tint in it, his cheeks were hollow, his back long and narrow, and the hand on which his shaggy head was propped was so thin and delicate that it was dreadful to look at it. His hair was already streaked with silver, and seeing his emaciated, aged-looking face, no one would have believed that he was only forty. He was asleep. . . . In front of his bowed head there lay on the table a sheet of paper on which there was something written in fine handwriting.

"Poor creature!" thought the banker, "he is asleep and most likely dreaming of the millions. And I have only to take this half-dead man, throw him on the bed, stifle him a little with the pillow, and the most conscientious expert would find no sign of a violent death. But let us first read what he has written here. . . ."

The banker took the page from the table and read as follows:

"To-morrow at twelve o'clock I regain my freedom and the right to associate with other men, but before I leave this room and see the sunshine, I think it necessary to say a few words to you. With a clear conscience I tell you, as before God, who beholds me, that I despise freedom and life and health, and all that in your books is called the good things of the world.

"For fifteen years I have been intently studying earthly life. It is true I have not seen the earth nor men, but in your books I have drunk fragrant wine, I have sung songs, I have hunted stags and wild boars in the forests, have loved women. . . . Beauties as ethereal as clouds, created by the magic of your poets and geniuses, have visited me at night, and have whispered in my ears wonderful tales that have set my brain in a whirl. In your books I have climbed to the peaks of Elburz and Mont Blanc, and from there I have seen the sun rise and have watched it at evening flood the sky, the ocean, and the mountain-tops with gold and crimson. I have watched from there the lightning flashing over my head and cleaving the storm-clouds. I have seen green forests, fields, rivers, lakes, towns. I have heard the singing of the sirens, and the strains of the shepherds' pipes; I have touched the wings of comely devils who flew down to converse with me of God. . . . In your books I have flung myself into the bottomless pit, performed miracles, slain, burned towns, preached new religions, conquered whole kingdoms. . . .

"Your books have given me wisdom. All that the unresting thought of man has created in the ages is compressed into a small compass in my brain. I know that I am wiser than all of you.

"And I despise your books, I despise wisdom and the blessings of this world. It is all worthless, fleeting, illusory, and deceptive, like a mirage. You may be proud, wise, and fine, but death will wipe you off the face of the earth as though you were no more than mice burrowing under the floor, and your posterity, your history, your immortal geniuses will burn or freeze together with the earthly globe.

"You have lost your reason and taken the wrong path. You have taken lies for truth, and hideousness for beauty. You would marvel if, owing to strange events of some sorts, frogs and lizards suddenly grew on apple and orange trees instead of fruit, or if roses began to smell like a sweating horse; so I marvel at you who exchange heaven for earth. I don't want to understand you.

"To prove to you in action how I despise all that you live by, I renounce the two millions of which I once dreamed as of paradise and which now I despise. To deprive myself of the right to the money I shall go out from here five hours before the time fixed, and so break the compact. . . ."

When the banker had read this he laid the page on the table, kissed the strange man on the head, and went out of the lodge, weeping. At no other time, even when he had lost heavily on the Stock Exchange, had he felt so great a contempt for himself. When he got home he lay on his bed, but his tears and emotion kept him for hours from sleeping.

Next morning the watchmen ran in with pale faces, and told him they had seen the man who lived in the lodge climb out of the window into the garden, go to the gate, and disappear. The banker went at once with the servants to the lodge and made sure of the flight of his prisoner. To avoid arousing unnecessary talk, he took from the table the writing in which the millions were renounced, and when he got home locked it up in the fireproof safe.

QUESTIONS

1. What ethical issue are the members of the party discussing at the outset of the story? What are some additional philosophical problems that arise in the course of the narrative? What answer, if any, does the conclusion provide for the initial question that was posed?

2. Trace the stages of existence that the young lawyer passes through during his imprisonment. What is the general nature of this progression? Why does he renounce his claim to the two million when he could have won it easily?

3. How does the banker change in the course of the story? How does this change contrast with the changes in the lawyer? Why does the banker let the lawyer depart? What has the banker learned from the bet?

4. In 1890, Chekhov visited the penal colony on the Russian island of Sakhalin, and subsequently he wrote a penetrating and compassionate account of life there. What attitudes toward imprisonment can you detect in Chekhov's presentation of the subject in "The Bet"? What, ultimately, do you think Chekhov's theme is in the story?

TOPICS FOR WRITING

1. Classify the stages in the lawyer's quest for knowledge about life, and assess the final conclusions reached by the lawyer.

2. Is life imprisonment preferable to capital punishment? Write an evalua-tion of Chekhov's answer to this question in "The Bet."

Franz Kafka

A HUNGER ARTIST

*Franz Kafka (1883–1924) was born in Prague, Czechoslova-kia. He received a law degree from the German University in Prague in 1906 and worked subsequently in the Austrian civil service. Kafka devoted his life to writing, but at the time of his death, he directed his friend and literary executor, Max Brod, to burn all his manuscripts. Instead Brod saw Kafka's novels—*The Trial *(1925),* The Castle *(1926), and* Amerika *(1927)—and many of his short stories through production. Kafka's fiction projects a distinctive tone of the uncanny—of life and reality that tend to shift away from our ability to understand them. Typically, Kafka's protagonists embark on quests for meaning but are frustrated and ulti-mately alienated by the process. In many ways, Kafka's fiction captures the absurdities of modern life and the futility of seeking any lasting meaning in the twentieth century. His stories in English can be found in* The Great Wall of China *(1933),* A Franz Kafka Miscellany *(1940),* The Penal Colony *(1948),* Parables and Paradoxes *(1963), and* The Complete Stories *(1976). In "A Hunger Artist," Kafka pre-sents one of his most celebrated alienated heroes, a figure whose obsessive and bizarre behavior places him in opposi-tion to society, culture, and himself.*

During these last decades the interest in professional fasting has markedly diminished. It used to pay very well to stage such great performances under one's own management, but today that is quite impossible. We live in a different world now. At one time the whole town took a lively interest in the hunger artist; from day to day of his fast the excitement mounted; everybody wanted to see him at least once a day; there were people who bought season tickets for the last few days and sat from morning till night in front of his small barred cage; even in the nighttime there were visiting hours, when the whole effect was heightened by torch flares; on fine days the cage was set out in the open air, and then it was the children's special treat to see the hunger artist; for their elders he was often just a joke that happened to be in fashion, but the children stood open-mouthed, holding each other's hands for greater security, marveling at him as he sat there pallid in black tights, with his ribs sticking out so prominently, not even on a seat but down among straw on the ground, sometimes giving a courteous nod, answering questions with a constrained smile, or perhaps stretching an arm through the bars so that one might feel how thin it was, and then again withdrawing deep into himself, paying no attention to anyone or anything, not even to the all-important striking of the clock that was the only piece of furniture in his cage, but merely staring into vacancy with half shut eyes, now and then taking a sip from a tiny glass of water to moisten his lips.

Besides casual onlookers there were also relays of permanent watchers selected by the public, usually butchers, strangely enough, and it was their task to watch the hunger artist day and night, three of them at a time, in case he should have some secret recourse to nourishment. This was nothing but a formality, instituted to reassure the masses, for the initiates knew well enough that during his fast the artist would never in any circumstances, not even under forcible compulsion, swallow the smallest morsel of food; the honor of his profession forbade it. Not every watcher, of course, was capable of understanding this, there were often groups of night watchers who were very lax in carrying out their duties and deliberately huddled together in a retired corner to play cards with great absorption, obviously intending to give the hunger artist the chance of a little refreshment, which they supposed he could draw from some private hoard. Nothing annoyed the artist more than such watchers; they made him miserable; they made his fast seem unendurable; sometimes he mastered his feebleness sufficiently to sing during their watch for as long as he could keep going, to show them how unjust their suspicions were. But that was of little use; they only wondered at his cleverness in being able to fill his mouth even while singing. Much more to his taste were the watchers who sat close up to the bars, who were not content with the dim night lighting of the hall but focused him in the full glare of the electric pocket torch given them by the impresario. The harsh light did not trouble him at all, in any case he could never sleep properly, and he could always drowse a little, whatever the light, at any hour, even when the hall was thronged with noisy onlookers. He was quite happy at the prospect of spending a sleepless night with such watchers; he was ready to exchange jokes with them, to tell them stories out of his nomadic life, anything at all to keep them awake and demonstrate to them again that he had no eatables in his cage and that he was fasting as not one of them could fast. But his happiest moment was when the morning came and an enormous breakfast was brought them, at his expense, on which they flung themselves with the keen appetite of healthy men after a weary night of wakefulness. Of course there were people who argued that this breakfast was an unfair attempt to bribe the watchers, but that was going rather too far, and when they were invited to take on a night's vigil without a breakfast, merely for the sake of the cause, they made themselves scarce, although they stuck stubbornly to their suspicions.

Such suspicions, anyhow, were a necessary accompaniment to the profession of fasting. No one could possibly watch the hunger artist continuously, day and night, and so no one could produce first-hand evidence that the fast had really been rigorous and continuous; only the artist himself could know that, he was therefore bound to be the sole completely satisfied spectator of his own fast. Yet for other reasons he was never satisfied; it was not perhaps mere fasting that had brought him to such skeleton thinness that many people had regretfully to keep away from his exhibitions, because the sight of him was too much for them, perhaps it was dissatisfaction with himself that had worn him down. For he alone knew, what no other initiate knew, how easy it was to fast. It was the easiest thing in the world. He made no secret of this, yet people did not believe him; at the best they set him down as modest, most of them, however, thought he was out for publicity or else was some kind of cheat who found it easy to fast because he had discovered a way of making it easy, and then had the impudence to admit the fact, more or less. He had to put up with all that, and in the course of time had got used to it, but his inner dissatisfaction always rankled, and never yet, after any term of fasting—this must be granted to his credit—had he left the cage of his own free will. The longest period of fasting was fixed by his impresario at forty days, beyond that term he was not allowed to go, not even in great cities, and there was good reason for it, too. Experience had proved that for about forty days the interest of the public could be stimulated by a steadily increasing pressure of advertisement, but after that the town began to lose interest, sympathetic support began notably to fall off; there were of course local variations as between one town and another or one country and another, but as a general rule forty days marked the limit. So on the fortieth day the flower-bedecked cage was opened, enthusiastic spectators filled the hall, a military band played, two doctors entered the cage to measure the results of the fast, which were announced through a megaphone, and finally two young ladies appeared, blissful at having been selected for the honor, to help the hunger artist down the few steps leading to a small table on which was spread a carefully chosen invalid repast. And at this very moment the artist always turned stubborn. True, he would entrust his bony arms to the outstretched helping hands of the ladies bending over him, but stand up he would not. Why stop fasting at this particular moment, after forty days of it? He had held out for a long time, an illimitably long time; why stop now, when he was in his best fasting form, or rather, not yet quite in his best fasting form? Why should he be cheated of the fame he would get for fasting longer, for being not only the record hunger artist of all time, which presumably he was already, but for beating his own record by a performance beyond human imagination, since he felt that there were no limits to his capacity for fasting? His public pretended to admire him so much, why should it have so little patience with him; if he could endure fasting longer, why shouldn't the public endure it? Besides, he was tired, he was comfortable sitting in the straw, and now he was supposed to lift himself to his full height and go down to a meal the very thought of which gave him a nausea that only the presence of the ladies kept him from betraying, and even that with an effort. And he looked up into the eyes of the ladies who were apparently so friendly and in reality so cruel, and shook his head, which felt too heavy on its strengthless neck. But then there happened yet again what always happened. The impresario came forward, without a word—for the band made speech impossible—lifted his arms in the air above the artist, as if inviting Heaven to look down upon its creature here in the straw, this suffering martyr, which indeed he was, although in quite another sense; grasped him round the emaciated waist, with exaggerated caution, so that the frail condition he was in might be appreciated; and committed him to the care of the blenching ladies, not without secretly giving him a shaking so that his legs and body tottered and swayed. The artist now submitted completely; his head lolled on his breast as if it had landed there by chance; his body was hollowed out; his legs in a spasm of self-preservation clung close to each other at the knees, yet scraped on the ground as if it were not really solid ground, as if they were only trying to find solid ground; and the whole weight of his body, a feather-weight after all, relapsed onto one of the ladies, who, looking round for help and panting a little—this post of honor was not at all what she had expected it to be—first stretched her neck as far as she could to keep her face at least free from contact with the artist, when finding this impossible, and her more fortunate companion not coming to her aid but merely holding extended on her own trembling hand the little bunch of knucklebones that was the artist's, to the great delight of the spectators burst into tears and had to be replaced by an attendant who had long been stationed in readiness. Then came the food, a little of which the impresario managed to get between the artist's lips, while he sat in a kind of half-fainting trance, to the accompaniment of cheerful patter designed to distract the public's attention from the artist's condition; after that, a toast was drunk to the public, supposedly prompted by a whisper from the artist in the impresario's ear; the band confirmed it with a mighty flourish, the spectators melted away, and no one had any cause to be dissatisfied with the proceedings, no one except the hunger artist himself, he only, as always.

So he lived for many years, with small regular intervals of recuperation, in visible glory, honored by the world, yet in spite of that troubled in spirit, and all the more troubled because no one would take his trouble seriously. What comfort could he possibly need? What more could he possibly wish for? And if some good-natured person, feeling sorry for him, tried to console him by pointing out that his melancholy was probably caused by fasting, it could happen, especially when he had been fasting for some time, that he reacted with an outburst of fury and to the general alarm began to shake the bars of his cage like a wild animal. Yet the impresario had a way of punishing these outbreaks which he rather enjoyed putting into operation. He would apologize publicly for the artist's behavior, which was only to be excused, he admitted, because of the irritability caused by fasting; a condition hardly to be understood by well-fed people; then by natural transition he went on to mention the artist's equally incomprehensible boast that he could fast for much longer than he was doing; he praised the high ambition, the good will, the great self-denial undoubtedly implicit in such a statement; and then quite simply countered it by bringing out photographs, which were also on sale to the public, showing the artist on the fortieth day of a fast lying in bed almost dead from exhaustion. This perversion of the truth, familiar to the artist though it was, always unnerved him afresh and proved too much for him. What was a consequence of the premature ending of his fast was here presented as the cause of it! To fight against this lack of understanding, against a whole world of nonunderstanding, was impossible. Time and again in good faith he stood by the bars listening to the impresario, but as soon as the photographs appeared he always let go and sank with a groan back on to his straw, and the reassured public could once more come close and gaze at him.

A few years later when the witnesses of such scenes called them to mind, they often failed to understand themselves at all. For meanwhile the aforementioned change in public interest had set in; it seemed to happen almost overnight; there may have been profound causes for it, but who was going to bother about that; at any rate the pampered hunger artist suddenly found himself deserted one fine day by the amusement seekers, who went streaming past him to other more favored attractions. For the last time the impresario hurried him over half Europe to discover whether the old interest might still survive here and there; all in vain; everywhere, as if by secret agreement, a positive revulsion from professional fasting was in evidence. Of course it could not really have sprung up so suddenly as all that, and many premonitory symptoms which had not been sufficiently remarked or suppressed during the rush and glitter of success now came retrospectively to mind, but it was now too late to take any countermeasures.

Fasting would surely come into fashion again at some future date, yet that was no comfort for those living in the present. What, then, was the hunger artist to do? He had been applauded by thousands in his time and could hardly come down to showing himself in a street booth at village fairs, and as for adopting another profession, he was not only too old for that but too fanatically devoted to fasting. So he took leave of the impresario, his partner in an unparalleled career, and hired himself to a large circus; in order to spare his own feelings he avoided reading the conditions of his contract.

A large circus with its enormous traffic in replacing and recruiting men, animals and apparatus can always find a use for people at any time, even for a hunger artist, provided of course that he does not ask too much, and in this particular case anyhow it was not only the artist who was taken on but his famous and long-known name as well, indeed considering the peculiar nature of his performance, which was not impaired by advancing age, it could not be objected that here was an artist past his prime, no longer at the height of his professional skill, seeking a refuge in some quiet corner of a circus; on the contrary, the hunger artist averred that he could fast as well as ever, which was entirely credible, he even alleged that if he were allowed to fast as he liked, and this was at once promised him without more ado, he could astound the world by establishing a record never yet achieved, a statement which certainly provoked a smile among the other professionals, since it left out of account the change in public opinion, which the hunger artist in his zeal conveniently forgot.

He had not, however, actually lost his sense of the real situation and took it as a matter of course that he and his cage should be stationed, not in the middle of the ring as a main attraction, but outside, near the animal cages, on a site that was after all easily accessible. Large and gaily painted placards made a frame for the cage and announced what was to be seen inside it. When the public came thronging out in the intervals to see the animals, they could hardly avoid passing the hunger artist's cage and stopping there for a moment, perhaps they might even have stayed longer had not those pressing behind them in the narrow gangway, who did not understand why they should be held up on their way toward the excitements of the menagerie, made it impossible for anyone to stand gazing quietly for any length of time. And that was the reason why the hunger artist, who had of course been looking forward to these visiting hours as the main achievement of his life, began instead to shrink from them. At first he could hardly wait for the intervals; it was exhilarating to watch the crowds come streaming his way, until only too soon—not even the most obstinate self-deception, clung to almost consciously, could hold out against the fact—the conviction was borne in upon him that these people, most of them, to judge from their actions, again and again, without exception, were all on their way to the menagerie. And the first sight of them from the distance remained the best. For when they reached his cage he was at once deafened by the storm of shouting and abuse that arose from the two contending factions, which renewed themselves continuously, of those who wanted to stop and stare at him—he soon began to dislike them more than the others—not out of real interest but only out of obstinate self-assertiveness, and those who wanted to go straight on to the animals. When the first great rush was past, the stragglers came along, and these, whom nothing could have prevented from stopping to look at him as long as they had breath, raced past with long strides, hardly even glancing at him, in their haste to get to the menagerie in time. And all too rarely did it happen that he had a stroke of luck, when some father of a family fetched up before him with his children, pointed a finger at the hunger artist and explained at length what the phenomenon meant, telling stories of earlier years when he himself had watched similar but much more thrilling performances, and the children, still rather uncomprehending, since neither inside nor outside school had they been sufficiently prepared for this lesson—what did they care about fasting?—yet showed by the brightness of their intent eyes that new and better times might be coming. Perhaps, said the hunger artist to himself many a time, things would be a little better if his cage were set not quite so near the menagerie. That made it too easy for people to make their choice, to say nothing of what he suffered from the stench of the menagerie, the animals' restlessness by night, the carrying past of raw lumps of flesh for the beasts of prey, the roaring at feeding times, which depressed him continually. But he did not dare to lodge a complaint with the management; after all, he had the animals to thank for the troops of people who passed his cage, among whom there might always be one here and there to take an interest in him, and who could tell where they might seclude him if he called attention to his existence and thereby to the fact that, strictly speaking, he was only an impediment on the way to the menagerie.

A small impediment, to be sure, one that grew steadily less. People grew familiar with the strange idea that they could be expected, in times like these, to take an interest in a hunger artist, and with this familiarity the verdict went out against him. He might fast as much as he could, and he did so; but nothing could save him now, people passed him by. Just try to explain to anyone the art of fasting! Anyone who has no feeling for it cannot be made to understand it. The fine placards grew dirty and illegible, they were torn down; the little notice board telling the number of fast days achieved, which at first was changed carefully every day, had long stayed at the same figure, for after the first few weeks even this small task seemed pointless to the staff; and so the artist simply fasted on and on, as he had once dreamed of doing, and it was no trouble to him, just as he had always foretold, but no one counted the days, no one, not even the artist himself, knew what records he was already breaking, and his heart grew heavy. And when once in a time some leisurely passer-by stopped, made merry over the old figure on the board and spoke of swindling, that was in its way the stupidest lie ever invented by indifference and inborn malice, since it was not the hunger artist who was cheating; he was working honestly, but the world was cheating him of his reward.

Many more days went by, however, and that too came to an end. An overseer's eye fell on the cage one day and he asked the attendants why this perfectly good cage should be left standing there unused with dirty straw inside it; nobody knew, until one man, helped out by the notice board, remembered about the hunger artist. They poked into the straw with sticks and found him in it. "Are you still fasting?" asked the overseer. "When on earth do you mean to stop?" "Forgive me, everybody," whispered the hunger artist; only the overseer, why had his ear to the bars, understood him. "Of course," said the overseer, and tapped his forehead with a finger to let the attendants know what state the man was in, "we forgive you." "I always wanted you to admire my fasting," said the hunger artist. "We do admire it," said the overseer, affably. "But you shouldn't admire it," said the hunger artist. "Well, then we don't admire it," said the overseer, "but why shouldn't we admire it?" "Because I have to fast, I can't help it," said the hunger artist. "What a fellow you are," said the overseer, "and why can't you help it?" "Because," said the hunger artist, lifting his head a little and speaking, with his lips pursed, as if for a kiss, right into the overseer's ear, so that no syllable might be lost, "because I couldn't find the food I liked. If I had found it, believe me, I should have made no fuss and stuffed myself like you or anyone else." These were his last words, but in his dimming eyes remained the firm though no longer proud persuasion that he was still continuing to fast.

"Well, clear this out now!" said the overseer, and they buried the hunger artist, straw and all. Into the cage they put a young panther. Even the most insensitive felt it refreshing to see this wild creature leaping around the cage that had so long been dreary. The panther was all right. The food he liked was brought him without hesitation by the attendants; he seemed not even to miss his freedom; his noble body, furnished almost to the bursting point with all that it needed, seemed to carry freedom around with it too; somewhere in his jaws it seemed to lurk; and the joy of life streamed with such ardent passion from his throat that for the onlookers it was not easy to stand the shock of it. But they braced themselves, crowded round the cage, and did not want ever to move away.

QUESTIONS

1. Who is the hunger artist? What might he symbolize (see sections 7 and 14)? How does our understanding of the symbolic nature of the hunger artist affect our statement of the story's theme?

2. Why does the narrator of the story state at the outset that "we live in a different world now"? What statement is Kafka making about society and about history? What is the fasting man's relationship to society? Why does the public prefer the panther to the hunger artist at the end of the story?

3. What is the importance of the "impresario" in the story?

4. What point does Kafka want to make at the end of the story when he has the hunger artist admit that he would never have fasted if he had found the food he liked?

5. What does the hunger artist's cage symbolize?

6. Compare and contrast the hunger artist with the lawyer in Chekhov's "The Bet" (page 14).

7. Kafka once intruded on a friend who was sleeping and unintentionally wakened him. The author slowly backed out of his friend's room, telling the startled individual to imagine that Kafka was simply a figure in a dream. How does this anecdote illuminate the setting and mood of the action in "A Hunger Artist"?

TOPICS FOR WRITING

1. Analyze the plight of the artist in Kafka's "A Hunger Artist."

2. Write a comparative analysis of the stories by Chekhov and Kafka.

3. The hunger artist dies before he realizes that he has broken the record. Comment briefly on this fact and its bearing on the theme of the story.

4. Does the artist "create" illusions or see more deeply into reality? How does this question bear on central meanings in Kafka's story?

Ralph Ellison

KING OF THE BINGO GAME

Ralph Ellison (1914–   ) was born in Oklahoma City and attended Tuskegee Institute, where he studied music. Like the protagonist in his celebrated novel, Invisible Man *(1956), Ellison moved to New York, working with the Federal Writers Project and subsequently editing* Negro Quarterly. *He has taught at numerous colleges, including the University of Chicago and Yale University.* Invisible Man, *Ellison's only published novel and already a contemporary classic, portrays in vivid and often grotesque detail the crises in the black experience in America. This subject is also the thematic center of Ellison's collection of essays,* Shadow and Act *(1964). In "King of the Bingo Game," Ellison combines realistic and grotesque elements to illuminate the extreme fate of the black man in America and to reflect philosophically on the general state of American culture.*

The woman in front of him was eating roasted peanuts that smelled so good that he could barely contain his hunger. He could not even sleep and wished they'd hurry and begin the bingo game. There, on his right, two fellows were drinking wine out of a bottle wrapped in a paper bag, and he could hear soft gurgling in the dark. His stomach gave a low, gnawing growl. "If this was down South," he thought, "all I'd have to do is lean over and say, 'Lady, gimme a few of those peanuts, please ma'am,' and she'd pass me the bag and never think nothing of it." Or he could ask the fellows for a drink in the same way. Folks down South stuck together that way; they didn't even have to know you. But up here it was different. Ask somebody for something, and they'd think you were crazy. Well, I ain't crazy. I'm just broke, 'cause I got no birth certificate to get a job, and Laura 'bout to die 'cause we got no money for a doctor. But I ain't crazy. And yet a pinpoint of doubt was focused in his mind as he glanced toward the screen and saw the hero steathily entering a dark room and sending the beam of a flashlight along a wall of bookcases. This is where he finds the trapdoor, he remembered. The man would pass abruptly through the wall and find the girl tied to a bed, her legs and arms spread wide, and her clothing torn to rags. He laughed softly to himself. He had seen the picture three times, and this was one of the best scenes.

On his right the fellow whispered wide-eyed to his companion, "Man, look ayonder!"

"Damn!"

"Wouldn't I like to have her tied up like that . . ."

"Hey! That fool's letting her loose!"

"Aw, man, he loves her."

"Love, or no love!"

The man moved impatiently beside him, and he tried to involve himself in the scene. But Laura was on his mind. Tiring quickly of watching the picture he looked back to where the white beam filtered from the projection room above the balcony. It started small and grew large, specks of dust dancing in its whiteness as it reached the screen. It was strange how the beam always landed right on the screen and didn't mess up and fall somewhere else. But they had it all fixed. Everything was fixed. Now suppose when they showed that girl with her dress torn the girl started taking off the rest of her clothes, and when the guy came in he didn't untie her but kept her there and went to taking off his own clothes? *That* would be something to see. If a picture got out of hand like that those guys up there would go nuts. Yeah, and there'd be so many folks in here you couldn't find a seat for nine months! A strange sensation played over his skin. He shuddered. Yesterday he'd seen a bedbug on a woman's neck as they walked out into the bright street. But exploring his thigh through a hole in his pocket he found only goose pimples and old scars.

The bottle gurgled again. He closed his eyes. Now a dreamy music was accompanying the film and train whistles were sounding in the distance, and he was a boy again walking along a railroad trestle down South, and seeing the train coming, and running back as fast as he could go, and hearing the whistle blowing, and getting off the trestle to solid ground just in time, with the earth trembling beneath his feet, and feeling relieved as he ran down the cinderstrewn embankment onto the highway, and looking back and seeing with terror that the train had left the track and was following him right down the middle of the street, and all the white people laughing as he ran screaming. . . .

"Wake up there, buddy! What the hell do you mean hollering like that? Can't you see we trying to enjoy this here picture?"

He stared at the man with gratitude.

"I'm sorry, old man," he said. "I musta been dreaming."

"Well, here, have a drink. And don't be making no noise like that, damn!"

His hands trembled as he tilted his head. It was not wine, but whiskey. Cold rye whiskey. He took a deep swoller, decided it was better not to take another, and handed the bottle back to its owner.

"Thanks, old man," he said.

Now he felt the cold whiskey breaking a warm path straight through the middle of him, growing hotter and sharper as it moved. He had not eaten all day, and it made him light-headed. The smell of the peanuts stabbed him like a knife, and he got up and found a seat in the middle aisle. But no sooner did he sit than he saw a row of intense-faced young girls, and got up again, thinking, "You chicks musta been Lindy-hopping somewhere." He found a seat several rows ahead as the lights came on, and he saw the screen disappear behind a heavy red and gold curtain; then the curtain rising, and the man with the microphone and a uniformed attendant coming on the stage.

He felt for his bingo cards, smiling. The guy at the door wouldn't like it if he knew about his having *five* cards. Well, not everyone played the bingo game; and even with five cards he didn't have much of a chance. For Laura, though, he had to have faith. He studied the cards, each with its different numerals, punching the free center hole in each and spreading them neatly across his lap; and when the lights faded he sat slouched in his seat so that he could look from his cards to the bingo wheel with but a quick shifting of his eyes.

Ahead, at the end of the darkness, the man with the microphone was pressing a button attached to a long cord and spinning the bingo wheel and calling out the number each time the wheel came to rest. And each time the voice rang out his finger raced over the cards for the number. With five cards he had to move fast. He became nervous; there were too many cards, and the man went too fast with his grating voice. Perhaps he should just select one and throw the others away. But he was afraid. He became warm. Wonder how much Laura's doctor would cost? Damn that, watch the cards! And with despair he heard the man call three in a row which he missed on all five cards. This way he'd never win . . .

When he saw the rows of holes punched across the third card, he sat paralyzed and heard the man call three more numbers before he stumbled forward, screaming.

"Bingo! Bingo!"

"Let that fool up there," someone called.

"Get up there, man!"

He stumbled down the aisle and up the steps to the stage into a light so sharp and bright that for a moment it blinded him, and he felt that he had moved into the spell of some strange, mysterious power. Yet it was as familiar as the sun, and he knew it was the perfectly familiar bingo.

The man with the microphone was saying something to the audience as he held out his card. A cold light flashed from the man's finger as the card left his hand. His knees trembled. The man stepped closer, checking the card against the numbers chalked on the board. Suppose he had made a mistake? The pomade on the man's hair made him feel faint, and he backed away. But the man was checking the card over the microphone now, and he had to stay. He stood tense, listening.

"Under the O, forty-four, the man chanted. "Under the I, seven. Under the G, three. Under the B, ninety-six. Under the N, thirteen!"

His breath came easier as the man smiled at the audience.

"Yes sir, ladies and gentlemen, he's one of the chosen people!"

The audience rippled with laughter and applause.

"Step right up to the front of the stage."

He moved slowly forward, wishing that the light was not so bright.

"To win tonight's jackpot of $36.90 the wheel must stop between the double zero, understand?"

He nodded, knowing the ritual from the many days and nights he had watched the winners march across the stage to press the button that controlled the spinning wheel and receive the prizes. And now he followed the instructions as though he'd crossed the slippery stage a million prize-winning times.

The man was making some kind of joke, and he nodded vacantly. So tense had he become that he felt a sudden desire to cry and shook it away. He felt vaguely that his whole life was determined by the bingo wheel; not only that which would happen now that he was at last before it, but all that had gone before, since his birth, and his mother's birth and the birth of his father. It had always been there, even though he had not been aware of it, handing out the unlucky cards and numbers of his days. The feeling persisted, and he started quickly away. I better get down from here before I make a fool of myself, he thought.

"Here, boy," the man called. "You haven't started yet."

Someone laughed as he went hesitantly back.

"Are you all reet?"

He grinned at the man's jive talk, but no words would come, and he knew it was not a convincing grin. For suddenly he knew that he stood on the slippery brink of some terrible embarrassment.

"Where are you from, boy?" the man asked.

"Down South."

"He's from down South, ladies and gentlemen," the man said. "Where from? Speak right into the mike."

"Rocky Mont," he said. "Rock' Mont, North Car'lina."

"So you decided to come down off that mountain to the U.S.," the man laughed. He felt that the man was making a fool of him, but then something cold was placed in his hand, and the lights were no longer behind him.

Standing before the wheel he felt alone, but that was somehow right, and he remembered his plan. He would give the wheel a short quick twirl. Just a touch of the button. He had watched it many times, and always it came close to double zero when it was short and quick. He steeled himself; the fear had left, and he felt a profound sense of promise, as though he were about to be repaid for all the things he'd suffered all his life. Trembling, he pressed the button. There was a whirl of lights, and in a second he realized with finality that though he wanted to, he could not stop. It was as though he held a high-powered line in his naked hand. His nerves tightened. As the wheel increased its speed it seemed to draw him more and more into its power, as though it held his fate; and with it came a deep need to submit, to whirl, to lose himself in its swirl of color. He could not stop it now. So let it be.

The button rested snugly in his palm where the man had placed it. And now he became aware of the man beside him, advising him through the microphone, while behind the shadowy audience hummed with noisy voices. He shifted his feet. There was still that feeling of helplessness within him, making part of him desire to turn back, even now that the jackpot was right in his hand. He squeezed the button until his fist ached. Then, like the sudden shriek of a subway whistle, a doubt tore through his head. Suppose he did not spin the wheel long enough? What could he do, and how could he tell? And then he knew, even as he wondered, that as long as he pressed the button, he could control the jackpot. He and only he could determine whether or not it was to be his. Not even the man with the microphone could do anything about it now. He felt drunk. Then, as though he had come down from a high hill and into a valley of people, he heard the audience yelling.

"Come down from there, you jerk!"

"Let somebody else have a chance . . ."

"Ole Jack thinks he done found the end of the rainbow . . ."

The last voice was not unfriendly, and he turned and smiled dreamily into the yelling mouths. Then he turned his back squarely on them.

"Don't take too long, boy," a voice said.

King of the Bingo Game

He nodded. They were yelling behind him. Those folks did not understand what had happened to him. They had been playing the bingo game day in and night out for years, trying to win rent money or hamburger change. But not one of those wise guys had discovered this wonderful thing. He watched the wheel whirling past the numbers and experienced a burst of exaltation: This is God! This is the really truly God! He said it aloud, "This is God!"

He said it with such absolute conviction that he feared he would fall fainting into the footlights. But the crowd yelled so loud that they could not hear. Those fools, he thought. I'm here trying to tell them the most wonderful secret in the world, and they're yelling like they gone crazy. A hand fell upon his shoulder.

"You'll have to make a choice now, boy. You've taken too long."

He brushed the hand violently away.

"Leave me alone, man. I know what I'm doing!"

The man looked surprised and held on to the microphone for support. And because he did not wish to hurt the man's feelings he smiled, realizing with a sudden pang that there was no way of explaining to the man just why he had to stand there pressing the button forever.

"Come here," he called tiredly.

The man approached, rolling the heavy microphone across the stage.

"Anybody can play this bingo game, right?" he said.

"Sure, but . . ."

He smiled, feeling inclined to be patient with this slick looking white man with his blue shirt and his sharp gabardine suit.

"That's what I thought," he said. "Anybody can win the jackpot as long as they get the lucky number, right?"

"That's the rule, but after all . . ."

"That's what I thought," he said. "And the big prize goes to the man who knows how to win it?"

The man nodded speechlessly.

"Well then, go on over there and watch me win like I want to. I ain't going to hurt nobody," he said, "and I'll show you how to win. I mean to show the whole world how it's got to be done."

And because he understood, he smiled again to let the man know that he held nothing against him for being white and impatient. Then he refused to see the man any longer and stood pressing the button, the voices of the crowd reaching him like sounds in distant streets. Let them yell. All the Negroes down there were just ashamed because he was black like them. He smiled inwardly, knowing how it was. Most of the time he was ashamed of what Negroes did himself. Well, let them be ashamed for something this time. Like him. He was like a long thin black wire that was being stretched and wound upon the bingo wheel; wound until he wanted to scream; wound, but this time himself controlling the winding and the sadness and the shame, and because he did, Laura would be all right. Suddenly the lights flickered. He staggered backwards. Had something gone wrong? All this noise. Didn't they know that although he controlled the wheel, it also controlled him, and unless he pressed the button forever and forever and ever it would stop, leaving him high and dry, dry and high on this hard high slippery hill and Laura dead? There was only one chance; he had to do whatever the wheel demanded. And gripping the button in despair, he discovered with surprise that it imparted a nervous energy. His spine tingled. He felt a certain power.

Now he faced the raging crowd with defiance, its screams penetrating his eardrums like trumpets shrieking from a juke-box. The vague faces glowing in the bingo lights gave him a sense of himself that he had never known before. He was running the show, by God! They had to react to him, for he was their luck. This is *me*, he thought. Let the bastards yell. Then someone was laughing inside him, and he realized that somehow he had forgotton his own name. It was a sad, lost feeling to lose your name, and a crazy thing to do. That name had been given him by the white man who had owned his grandfather a long lost time ago down South. But maybe those wise guys knew his name.

"Who am I?" he screamed.

"Hurry up and bingo, you jerk!"

They didn't know either, he thought sadly. They didn't even know their own names, they were all poor nameless bastards. Well, he didn't need that old name; he was reborn. For as long as he pressed the button he was The-man-who-pressed-the-button-who-held-the-prize-who-was-the-King-of-Bingo. That was the way it was, and he'd have to press the button even if nobody understood, even though Laura did not understand.

"Live!" he shouted.

The audience quieted like the dying of a huge fan.

"Live, Laura, baby. I got holt of it now, sugar. Live!"

He screamed it, tears streaming down his face. "I got nobody but YOU!"

The screams tore from his very guts. He felt as though the rush of blood to his head would burst out in baseball seams of small red droplets, like a head beaten by police clubs. Bending over he saw a trickle of blood splashing the toe of his shoe. With his free hand he searched his head. It was his nose. God, suppose something has gone wrong? He felt that the whole audience had somehow entered him and was stamping its feet in his stomach and he was unable to throw them out. They wanted the prize, that was it. They wanted the secret for themselves. But they'd never get it; he would keep the bingo wheel whirling forever, and Laura would be safe in the wheel. But would she? It had to be, because if she were not safe the wheel would cease to turn; it could not go on. He had to get away, *vomit* all, and his mind formed an image of himself running with Laura in his arms down the tracks of the subway just ahead of an A train, running desperately *vomit* with people screaming for him to come out but knowing no way of leaving the tracks because to stop would bring the train crushing down upon him and to attempt to leave across the other tracks would mean to run into a hot third rail as high as his waist which threw blue sparks that blinded his eyes until he could hardly see.

He heard singing and the audience was clapping its hands.

Shoot the liquor to him, Jim boy!
Clap-clap-clap
Well a-calla the cop
He's blowing his top!
Shoot the liquor to him, Jim, boy!

Bitter anger grew within him at the singing. They think I'm crazy. Well let 'em laugh. I'll do what I got to do.

He was standing in an attitude of intense listening when he saw that they were watching something on the stage behind him. He felt weak. But when he turned he saw no one. If only his thumb did not ache so. Now they were applauding. And for a moment he thought that the wheel had stopped. But that was impossible, his thumb still pressed the button. Then he saw them. Two men in uniform beckoned from the end of the stage. They were coming toward him, walking in step, slowly, like a tap-dance team returning for a third encore. But their shoulders shot forward, and he backed away, looking wildly about. There was nothing to fight them with. He had only the long black cord which led to a plug somewhere back stage, and he couldn't use that because it operated the bingo wheel. He backed slowly, fixing the men with his eyes as his lips stretched over his teeth in a tight, fixed grin; moved toward the end of the stage and realizing that he couldn't go much further, for suddenly the cord became taut and he couldn't afford to break the cord. But he had to do something. The audience was howling. Suddenly he stopped dead, seeing the men halt, their legs lifted as in an interrupted step of a slow-motion dance. There was nothing to do but run in the other direction and he dashed forward, slipping and sliding. The men fell back, surprised. He struck out violently going past.

"Grab him!"

He ran, but all too quickly the cord tightened, resistingly, and he turned and ran back again. This time he slipped them, and discovered by running in a circle before the wheel he could keep the cord from tightening. But this way he had to flail his arms to keep the men away. Why couldn't they leave a man alone? He ran, circling.

"Ring down the curtain," someone yelled. But they couldn't do that. If they did the wheel flashing from the projection room would be cut off. But they had him before he could tell them so, trying to pry open his fist, and he was wrestling and trying to bring his knees into the fight and holding on to the button, for it was his life. And now he was down, seeing a foot coming down, crushing his wrist cruelly, down, as he saw the wheel whirling serenely above.

"I can't give it up," he screamed. Then quietly, in a confidential tone, "Boys, I really can't give it up."

It landed hard against his head. And in the blank moment they had it away from him, completely now. He fought them trying to pull him up from the stage as he watched the wheel spin slowly to a stop. Without surprise he saw it rest at double-zero.

"You see," he pointed bitterly.

"Sure, boy, sure, it's O.K.," one of the men said smiling.

And seeing the man bow his head to someone he could not see, he felt very, very happy; he would receive what all the winners received.

But as he warmed in the justice of the man's tight smile he did not see the man's slow wink, nor see the bow-legged man behind him step clear of the swiftly descending curtain and set himself for a blow. He only felt the dull pain exploding in his skull, and he knew even as it slipped out of him that his luck had run out on the stage.

QUESTIONS

1. Why does Ellison create a nameless central character in the story (a technique also employed in *Invisible Man*)? What is the significance of the statement, "Somehow he had forgotton his own name"? What do we know about him, his background, his hopes and fears?

2. What does the bingo game mean to the protagonist? Why does it make him "king"? What is the significance of the fact that the needle comes to rest on the double-zero toward the end of the story?

3. Why does Ellison take an ordinary, realistic setting and turn it into a nightmarish world? What broad theme about the American experience is Ellison attempting to convey through this interaction of character and environment?

4. What statement does Ellison make about man's fate in the story?

TOPICS FOR WRITING

1. Investigate the theme of fate in the story.

2. Briefly analyze the causes of the protagonist's psychological and emotional state.

3. Does the central character in this story "see" or understand existence, or does he exist in a world of illusions? Investigate this question and the theme deriving from it.

Shirley Jackson

THE LOTTERY

Shirley Jackson (1919–1965) was born in San Francisco and educated at Syracuse University. She married the literary critic Stanley Edgar Hyman; they lived in Bennington, Vermont, where her husband taught at Bennington College. Jackson is the heiress of Poe in her talent for tales and novels of Gothic horror. What distinguishes her from Poe is her ability to modernize Gothic conventions, locating in apparently "normal" contemporary events and situations a highly convincing realm of shock, violence, and terror. Her novels include Life Among the Savages (1945), Hangsman (1951), The Bird's Nest (1954), The Haunting of Hill House (1959), and We Have Always Lived in the Castle (1962). Jackson's short fiction is collected in The Lottery (1944) and The Magic of Shirley Jackson (1966). In the well-known title story from her first collection, a commonplace celebration evolves slowly toward a bizarre and terrifying conclusion.

The Lottery

The morning of June 27th was clear and sunny, with the fresh warmth of a full-summer day; the flowers were blossoming profusely and the grass was richly green. The people of the village began to gather in the square, between the post office and the bank, around ten o'clock; in some towns there were so many people that the lottery took two days and had to be started on June 26th, but in this village, where there were only about three hundred people, the whole lottery took less than two hours, so it could begin at ten o'clock in the morning and still be through in time to allow the villagers to get home for noon dinner.

The children assembled first, of course. School was recently over for the summer, and the feeling of liberty sat uneasily on most of them; they tended to gather together quietly for a while before they broke into boisterous play, and their talk was still of the classroom and the teacher, of books and reprimands. Bobby Martin had already stuffed his pockets full of stones, and the other boys soon followed his example, selecting the smoothest and roundest stones; Bobby and Harry Jones and Dickie Delacroix—the villagers pronounced this name "Dellacroy"—eventually made a great pile of stones in one corner of the square and guarded it against the raids of the other boys. The girls stood aside, talking among themselves, looking over their shoulders at the boys, and the very small children rolled in the dust or clung to the hands of their older brothers or sisters.

Soon the men began to gather, surveying their own children, speaking of planting and rain, tractors and taxes. They stood together, away from the pile of stones in the corner, and their jokes were quiet and they smiled rather than laughed. The women, wearing faded house dresses and sweaters, came shortly after their menfolk. They greeted one another and exchanged bits of gossip as they went to join their husbands. Soon the women, standing by their husbands, began to call to their children, and the children came reluctantly, having to be called four or five times. Bobby Martin ducked under his mother's grasping hand and ran, laughing, back to the pile of stones. His father spoke up sharply, and Bobby came quickly and took his place between his father and his oldest brother.

The lottery was conducted—as were the square dances, the teenage club, the Halloween program—by Mr. Summers, who had time and energy to devote to civic activities. He was a round-faced, jovial man and he ran the coal business, and people were sorry for him, because he had no children and his wife was a scold. When he arrived in the square, carrying the black wooden box, there was a murmur of conversation among the villagers, and he waved and called, "Little late today, folks." The postmaster, Mr. Graves, followed him, carrying a three-legged stool, and the stool was put in the center of the square and Mr. Summers set the black box down on it. The villagers kept their distance, leaving a space between themselves and the stool, and when Mr. Summers said, "Some of you fellows want to give me a hand?" there was a hesitation before two men, Mr. Martin and his oldest son, Baxter, came forward to hold the box steady on the stool while Mr. Summers stirred up the papers inside it.

The original paraphernalia for the lottery had been lost long ago, and the black box now resting on the stool had been put into use even before Old Man Warner, the oldest man in town, was born. Mr. Summers spoke frequently to the villagers about making a new box, but no one liked to upset even as much tradition as was represented by the black box. There was a story that the present box had been made with some pieces of the box that had preceded it, the one that had been constructed when the first people settled down to make a village here. Every year, after the lottery, Mr. Summers began talking again about a new box, but every year the subject was allowed to fade off without anything's being done. The black box grew shabbier each year; by now it was no longer completely black but splintered badly along one side to show the original wood color, and in some places faded or stained.

Mr. Martin and his oldest son, Baxter, held the black box securely on the stool until Mr. Summers had stirred the papers thoroughly with his hand. Because so much of the ritual had been forgotten or discarded, Mr. Summers had been successful in having slips of paper substituted for the chips of wood that had been used for generations. Chips of wood, Mr. Summers had argued, had been all very well when the village was tiny, but now that the population was more than three hundred and likely to keep on growing, it was necessary to use something that would fit more easily into the black box. The night before the lottery, Mr. Summers and Mr. Graves made up the slips of paper and put them in the box, and it was then taken to the safe of Mr. Summers' coal company and locked up until Mr. Summers was ready to take it to the square next morning. The rest of the year, the box was put away, sometimes one place, sometimes another; it had spent one year in Mr. Graves's barn and another year underfoot in the post office, and sometimes it was set on a shelf in the Martin grocery and left there.

There was a great deal of fussing to be done before Mr. Summers declared the lottery open. There were the lists to make up—of heads of families, heads of households in each family, members of each household in each family. There was the proper swearing-in of Mr. Summers by the postmaster, as the official of the lottery; at one time, some people remembered, there had been a recital of some sort, performed by the official of the lottery, a perfunctory, tuneless chant that had been rattled off duly each year; some people believed that the official of the lottery used to stand just so when he said or sang it, others believed that he was supposed to walk among the people, but years and years ago this part of the ritual had been allowed to lapse. There had been, also, a ritual salute, which the official of the lottery had had to use in addressing each person who came up to draw from the box, but this also had changed with time, until now it was felt necessary only for the official to speak to each person approaching. Mr. Summers was very good at all this; in his clean white shirt and blue jeans, with one hand resting carelessly on the black box, he seemed very proper and important as he talked interminably to Mr. Graves and the Martins.

Just as Mr. Summers finally left off talking and turned to the assembled villagers, Mrs. Hutchinson came hurriedly along the path to the square, her sweater thrown over her shoulders, and slid into place in the back of the crowd. "Clean forgot what day it was," she said to Mrs. Delacroix, who stood next to her, and they both laughed softly. "Thought my old man was out back stacking wood," Mrs. Hutchinson went on, "and then I looked out the window and the kids was gone, and then I remembered it was the twenty-seventh and came a-running." She dried her hands on her apron, and Mrs. Delacroix said, "You're in time, though. They're still talking away up there."

Mrs. Hutchinson craned her neck to see through the crowd and found her husband and children standing near the front. She tapped Mrs. Delacroix on the arm as a farewell and began to make her way through the crowd. The people separated good-humoredly to let her through; two or three people said, in voices just loud enough to be heard across the crowd, "Here comes your Missus, Hutchinson," and "Bill, she made it after all." Mrs. Hutchinson reached her husband, and Mr. Summers, who had been waiting, said cheerfully, "Thought we were going to have to get on without you, Tessie." Mrs. Hutchinson said, grinning, "Wouldn't have me leave m'dishes in the sink, now, would you, Joe?," and soft laughter ran through the crowd as the people stirred back into position after Mrs. Hutchinson's arrival.

"Well, now," Mr. Summers said soberly, "guess we better get started, get this over with, so's we can go back to work. Anybody ain't here?"

"Dunbar," several people said. "Dunbar, Dunbar."

Mr. Summers consulted his list. "Clyde Dunbar," he said. "That's right. He's broke his leg, hasn't he? Who's drawing for him?"

"Me, I guess," a woman said, and Mr. Summers turned to look at her. "Wife draws for her husband," Mr. Summers said. "Don't you have a grown boy to do it for you, Janey?" Although Mr. Summers and everyone else in the village knew the answer perfectly well, it was the business of the official of the lottery to ask such questions formally. Mr. Summers waited with an expression of polite interest while Mrs. Dunbar answered.

"Horace's not but sixteen yet," Mrs. Dunbar said regretfully. "Guess I gotta fill in for the old man this year."

"Right," Mr. Summers said. He made a note on the list he was holding. Then he asked, "Watson boy drawing this year?"

A tall boy in the crowd raised his hand. "Here," he said. "I'm drawing for m'mother and me." He blinked his eyes nervously and ducked his head as several voices in the crowd said things like "Good fellow, Jack," and "Glad to see your mother's got a man to do it."

"Well," Mr. Summers said, "guess that's everyone. Old Man Warner make it?"

"Here," a voice said, and Mr. Summers nodded.

A sudden hush fell on the crowd as Mr. Summers cleared his throat and looked at the list. "All ready?" he called. "Now, I'll read the names—heads of families first—and the men come up and take a paper out of the box. Keep the paper folded in your hand without looking at it until everyone has had a turn. Everything clear?"

The people had done it so many times that they only half listened to the directions; most of them were quiet, wetting their lips, not looking around. Then Mr. Summers raised one hand high and said, "Adams." A man disengaged himself from the crowd and came forward. "Hi, Steve," Mr. Summers said, and Mr. Adams said, "Hi, Joe." They grinned at one another humorlessly and nervously. Then Mr. Adams reached into the black box and took out a folded paper. He held it firmly by one corner as he turned and went hastily back to his place in the crowd, where he stood a little apart from his family, not looking down at his hand.

"Allen," Mr. Summers said. "Anderson. . . . Bentham."

"Seems like there's no time at all between lotteries any more," Mrs. Delacroix said to Mrs. Graves in the back row. "Seems like we got through with the last one only last week."

"Time sure goes fast," Mrs. Graves said.

"Clark. . . . Delacroix."

"There goes my old man," Mrs. Delacroix said. She held her breath while her husband went forward.

"Dunbar," Mr. Summers said, and Mrs. Dunbar went steadily to the box while one of the women said, "Go on, Janey," and another said, "There she goes."

"We're next," Mrs. Graves said. She watched while Mr. Graves came around from the side of the box, greeted Mr. Summers gravely, and selected a slip of paper from the box. By now, all through the crowd there were men holding the small folded papers in their large hands, turning them over and over nervously. Mrs. Dunbar and her two sons stood together, Mrs. Dunbar holding the slip of paper.

"Harburt. . . . Hutchinson."

"Get up there, Bill," Mrs. Hutchinson said, and the people near her laughed.

"Jones."

"They do say," Mr. Adams said to Old Man Warner, who stood next to him, "that over in the north village they're talking of giving up the lottery."

Old Man Warner snorted. "Pack of crazy fools," he said. "Listening to the young folks, nothing's good enough for *them.* Next thing you know, they'll be wanting to go back to living in caves, nobody work any more, live *that* way for a while. Used to be a saying about 'Lottery in June, corn be heavy soon.' First thing you know, we'd all be eating stewed chickweed and acorns. There's *always* been a lottery," he added petulantly. "Bad enough to see young Joe Summers up there joking with everybody."

"Some places have already quit lotteries," Mrs. Adams said.

"Nothing but trouble in *that,*" Old Man Warner said stoutly. "Pack of young fools."

"Martin." And Bobby Martin watched his father go forward. "Overdyke. . . . Percy."

"I wish they'd hurry," Mrs. Dunbar said to her older son. "I wish they'd hurry."

"They're almost through," her son said.

"You get ready to run tell Dad," Mrs. Dunbar said.

Mr. Summers called his own name and then stepped forward precisely and selected a slip from the box. Then he called, "Warner."

"Seventy-seventh year I been in the lottery," Old Man Warner said as he went through the crowd. "Seventy-seventh time."

"Watson." The tall boy came awkwardly through the crowd. Someone said, "Don't be nervous, Jack," and Mr. Summers said, "Take your time, son."

"Zanini."

After that, there was a long pause, a breathless pause, until Mr. Summers, holding his slip of paper in the air, said, "All right, fellows." For a minute, no one moved, and then all the slips of paper were opened. Suddenly, all the women began to speak at once, saying, "Who is it?," "Who's got it?," "Is it the Dunbars?," "Is it the Watsons?" Then the voices began to say, "It's Hutchinson. It's Bill," "Bill Hutchinson's got it."

"Go tell your father," Mrs. Dunbar said to her older son.

People began to look around to see the Hutchinsons. Bill Hutchinson was standing quiet staring down at the paper in his hand. Suddenly, Tessie Hutchinson shouted to Mr. Summers, "You didn't give him time enough to take any paper he wanted. I saw you. It wasn't fair."

"Be a good sport, Tessie," Mrs. Delacroix called, and Mrs. Graves said, "All of us took the same chance."

"Shut up, Tessie," Bill Hutchinson said.

"Well, everyone," Mr. Summers said, "that was done pretty fast, and now we've got to be hurrying a little more to get done in time." He consulted his next list. "Bill," he said, "You draw for the Hutchinson family. You got any other households in the Hutchinsons?"

"There's Don and Eva," Mrs. Hutchinson yelled. "Make *them* take their chance!"

"Daughters draw with their husbands' families, Tessie," Mr. Summers said gently. "You know that as well as anyone else."

"It wasn't *fair*," Tessie said.

"I guess not, Joe," Bill Hutchinson said regretfully. "My daughter draws with her husband's family, that's only fair. And I've got no other family except the kids."

"Then, as far as drawing for families is concerned, it's you," Mr. Summers said in explanation, "and as far as drawing for households is concerned, that's you, too. Right?"

"Right," Bill Hutchinson said.

"How many kids, Bill?" Mr. Summers asked formally.

"Three," Bill Hutchinson said. "There's Bill, Jr., and Nancy, and little Dave. and Tessie and me."

"All right, then," Mr. Summers said. "Harry, you got their tickets back?"

Mr. Graves nodded and held up the slips of paper. "Put them in the box, then," Mr. Summers directed. "Take Bill's and put it in."

"I think we ought to start over," Mrs. Hutchinson said, as quietly as she could. "I tell you it wasn't *fair*. You didn't give him time enough to choose. *Every*body saw that."

Mr. Graves had selected the five slips and put them in the box, and dropped all the papers but those onto the ground, where the breeze caught them and lifted them off.

"Listen, everybody," Mrs. Hutchinson was saying to the people around her.

"Ready, Bill?" Mr. Summers asked, and Bill Hutchinson, with one quick glance around at his wife and children, nodded.

"Remember," Mr. Summers said, "take the slips and keep them folded until each person has taken one. Harry, you help little Dave." Mr. Graves took the hand of the little boy, who came willingly with him up to the box. "Take a paper out of the box, Davy," Mr. Summers said. Davy put his hand into the box and laughed. "Take just *one* paper," Mr. Summers said. "Harry, you hold it for him." Mr. Graves took the child's hand and removed the folded paper from the tight fist and held it while little Dave stood next to him and looked up at him wonderingly.

"Nancy next," Mr. Summers said. Nancy was twelve, and her school friends breathed heavily as she went forward, switching her skirt, and took a slip daintily from the box. "Bill, Jr.," Mr. Summers said, and Billy, his face red and his feet over-large, nearly knocked the box over as he got a paper out. "Tessie," Mr. Summers said. She hesitated for a minute, looking around defiantly, and then set her lips and went up to the box. She snatched a paper out and held it behind her.

"Bill," Mr. Summers said, and Bill Hutchinson reached into the box and felt around, bringing his hand out at last with the slip of paper in it.

The crowd was quiet. A girl whispered, "I hope it's not Nancy," and the sound of the whisper reached the edges of the crowd.

"It's not the way it used to be," Old Man Warner said clearly. "People ain't the way they used to be."

"All right," Mr. Summers said. "Open the papers. Harry, you open little Dave's."

Mr. Graves opened the slip of paper and there was a general sigh through the crowd as he held it up and everyone could see that it was blank. Nancy and Bill,

Jr., opened theirs at the same time, and both beamed and laughed, turning around to the crowd and holding their slips of paper above their heads.

"Tessie," Mr. Summers said. There was a pause, and then Mr. Summers looked at Bill Hutchinson, and Bill unfolded his paper and showed it. It was blank.

"It's Tessie," Mr. Summers said, and his voice was hushed. "Show us her paper, Bill."

Bill Hutchinson went over to his wife and forced the slip of paper out of her hand. It had a black spot on it, the black spot Mr. Summers had made the night before with the heavy pencil in the coal-company office. Bill Hutchinson held it up, and there was a stir in the crowd.

"All right, folks," Mr. Summers said. "Let's finish quickly."

Although the villagers had forgotten the ritual and lost the original black box, they still remembered to use stones. The pile of stones the boys had made earlier was ready; there were stones on the ground with the blowing scraps of paper that had come out of the box. Mrs. Delacroix selected a stone so large she had to pick it up with both hands and turned to Mrs. Dunbar. "Come on," she said. "Hurry up."

Mrs. Dunbar had small stones in both hands, and she said, gasping for breath, "I can't run at all. You'll have to go ahead and I'll catch up with you."

The children had stones already, and someone gave little Davy Hutchinson a few pebbles.

Tessie Hutchinson was in the center of a cleared space by now, and she held her hands out desperately as the villagers moved in on her. "It isn't fair," she said. A stone hit her on the side of the head.

Old Man Warner was saying, "Come on, come on, everyone." Steve Adams was in the front of the crowd of villagers, with Mrs. Graves beside him.

"It isn't fair, it isn't right," Mrs. Hutchinson screamed, and then they were upon her.

QUESTIONS

1. What clues or foreshadowing devices (see glossary) does Jackson provide that hint at a violent conclusion? At what point do you sense that Mrs. Hutchinson will be the victim?

2. What do we know about the setting for the story? Why doesn't Jackson locate the village in a specific geographic area? How is her method similar to that of Kafka in "A Hunger Artist" (page 20)?

3. Whereas Poe in "The Cask of Amontillado" (page 8) concentrates on individual psychology, Jackson in her story is far more interested in group psychology. What is her attitude toward mass behavior? toward group belief in rituals? toward group belief in tradition?

4. What is the overall theme of the story? How does the violence at the end of the tale contribute to the theme?

5. What makes the conclusion convincing? What does Jackson want to tell us about ourselves?

TOPICS FOR WRITING

1. Examine Jackson's presentation of myth, ritual, and tradition in "The Lottery." Be certain to state, analyze, and evaluate the theme that emerges from these subjects.

2. Compare and contrast the presentation of human psychology in "The Cask of Amontillado" (page 8) and "The Lottery."

3. Analyze the devices that Jackson uses to arrive at her shocking conclusion. Evaluate her success in making an improbable ending seem possible to us.

4. How do the five writers in this section treat matters of life and death? Evaluate a concept that they raise—that life is a bet, a wager, a game of chance. How does this concept relate to the general theme of illusion and reality?

5. Classify and analyze the types of violence found in the five stories.

6. Examine the theme of imprisonment and entrapment in the stories.

2

PLOT AND THEME: MARRIAGE

Plot is the planned arrangement of actions and events in a narrative; actions and events are causally related, and they progress through a variety of conflicts and opposing forces to a climax and resolution. Because the events in a story are planned, they differ from the myriad random and casual events of real life. Henry James once declared that life is splendid waste, "all inconclusion and confusion." By contrast, life embedded in narrative art is splendid economy—what James termed "all discrimination and selection," a fine focusing of life. What happens in a narrative as lives and events unfold is not wasteful, but rather selected, arranged, and patterned according to an author's purpose in creating plot.

Plot might be an artificial arrangement of life, but it is plot that gives a narrative its power, uniqueness, and excellence. It is the basis of narrative art:

the shaping of human experience so that we can understand it; the reflection of the author's perceptions and powers of invention; the vehicle through which the artist offers his or her vision of life and the world. And it is plot that gives a story its charm and beauty, as E. M. Forster stressed in his discussion of plot in *Aspects of the Novel:*

> The plot-maker expects us to remember: we expect him to leave no loose ends. Every action or word ought to count; it ought to be economical and spare; even when complicated it should be organic and free from dead matter. And over it, as it unfolds, will hover the memory of the reader (that dull glow of the mind of which intelligence is the bright advancing edge) and will constantly rearrange and reconsider, seeing new clues, new chains of cause and effect, and the final sense (if the plot has been a fine one) will not be of clues or chains, but of something which might have been shown by the novelist right away, only, if he had shown it straight away it would never have become beautiful.

Forster's assessment, which applies to both the novel and short fiction, suggests the subtle ordering and interplay of elements and the meticulous artistry involved in the writer's shaping of plot.

The arrangement and interplay of elements to form plot may assume numerous patterns in fiction, but modern critics have focused on a five-part sequence of events or thoughts to illustrate a conventional plot. This sequence includes (1) the *beginning* or *exposition*, which among other things introduces an unstable element that sets the plot in motion; (2) *rising action*, a series of events—each event causing the one that follows—which heighten the conflict; (3) the *climax*, the critical or most intense moment in the narrative; (4) *falling action*, a typically brief period in which there is less intensity of effect and an unraveling (what the French term *denouement*) of the conflict; and (5) the ending, or *resolution*, of the conflict.

We can visualize this conventional plot pattern in terms of the accompanying pyramid—a diagram first proposed by the nineteenth-century German critic Gustav Freytag.

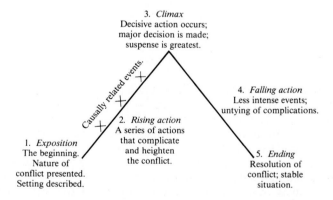

3. *Climax*
Decisive action occurs;
major decision is made;
suspense is greatest.

Causally related events.

2. *Rising action*
A series of actions
that complicate
and heighten
the conflict.

4. *Falling action*
Less intense events;
untying of complications.

1. *Exposition*
The beginning.
Nature of
conflict presented.
Setting described.

5. *Ending*
Resolution of
conflict; stable
situation.

Freytag used this diagram to analyze five-part dramatic tragedy, but the scheme has had widespread utility in the analysis of plot in fiction. In fact, a great part of the pleasure that we experience in the reading of fiction derives from our perception of the rhythm of the narrative as it moves from stage to stage in the plot. We delight in discovering how conflicts arise and develop; how one event causes another in a heightening series of conflicts; how characters caught in these conflicts engage in choices that make the climax and resolution seem almost inevitable. Finally, if the ending is a successful one, we gain satisfaction from the stable situation that emerges—whether it is happy, tragic, mysterious, or whatever—at the conclusion of the tale.

Central to this overview of plot is *conflict*, the opposition of forces. The contemporary American poet, novelist, and critic Robert Penn Warren has put the matter bluntly: "No conflict, no story." Elizabeth Bowen, a modern English short story writer and novelist, is more figurative than Warren, terming conflict a type of combustion. "There must be combustion. Plot depends for its movement on internal combustion." Conflict is at the root of the unstable situation at the start of the plot. Plot itself will pattern this conflict, but it is conflict that translates character and ideas into action. Without conflict, plot cannot exist.

We normally view conflict as the struggle of forces in relation to characters, for conflict at least in part is embodied in characters. When the main character (the protagonist) is fighting or struggling against someone (the antagonist) or something (a nonhuman force can also be the antagonist) outside himself or herself, we term this variety of conflict *external*. When the struggle, or opposition of forces, takes place inside the minds of characters, this type of conflict is *internal*. Thus characters may be involved in a variety of struggles: against other people; against society; against nature; against opposing forces within themselves; against fate or destiny. Seldom do we find a single type of conflict in a good short story. Conflict in short fiction is often subtle and complex, composed of various forces in opposition. To appreciate a complex tale, we have to locate the dramatic center of conflict, from which all other internal and external conflicts—indeed the very contours of plot—seem to radiate. By focusing on a central conflict, we can detect interrelationships among other struggles and elements in the story.

From the viewpoint of the author, plot can be artificial and formulaic or aesthetically valuable, one of fiction's "finer growths," as Forster termed it. Writers of detective stories, mysteries, romances, and espionage thrillers tend to work off standard varieties of plot formulas. Plot can also be exceedingly improbable, melodramatic, or coincidental—as with Fielding in *Tom Jones*, or Dickens in much of his fiction. Yet at its best, plot is, as Thomas Hardy declared, an organism: "to a masterpiece in story there appertains a beauty of shape, no less than to a masterpiece in pictorial or plastic art, capable of giving to the trained mind an equal pleasure." Plot involves not just mechanical workmanship but also serious and imaginative artistic response, a distinguished effort to creatively impose form on content. George Eliot might have lamented "the vulgar coercion of conventional plot" on her fiction. Nevertheless, Eliot and other great writers move beyond conventional plot to discover new varieties and to discover and reveal what the conflicts inherent in their plots might mean—what personal, psychological, social and political, and philosophical revelations they can make about life.

Let us imagine—as Stephen Crane, Bernard Malamud, and Doris Lessing must have in the fiction appearing in this section—that the author wants to write a story about marriage. Part of the process of writing such a story would involve the discovery of conflicts and determination of their interrelationship. How to begin these conflicts and end them are always twin agonies, as George Eliot admitted: "Beginnings are always troublesome. Conclusions are the weak points of most authors, but some of the fault lies in the very nature of conclusion, which is at best a negation." And between the beginning and conclusion there is the very large business of organizing and resolving main and minor conflicts, placing protagonists and antagonists in correct relationships, selecting episodes and scenes to dramatize the conflicts, and much more. In developing plot, the author must also select from well-established plotting techniques and occasionally invent new ones: the use of foreshadowing (suggesting or hinting at the resolution beforehand); flashback (creating earlier episodes within the overall progression of action in the plot); and subplots, double plots, and multiple plots. The process whereby authors invent, select, and design all these elements is rarely known to us. What we can perceive is the shape of the narrative—the synthesized product of creativity and craft—the final story itself. And embedded in the story is a plot, the structure of the tale, which permits us to evaluate the quality of the writer's work, the unity of effect, and the way he or she illuminates an idea or theme.

In Crane's "The Bride Comes to Yellow Sky," Malamud's "The Magic Barrel," and Lessing's "Flight," we discover meaning through an identification and understanding of the conflicts raised by marriage. These writers do not categorically state the meaning of these conflicts, but instead reveal it through plot. They develop their subject in unique ways, creating plots that offer brilliantly structured impressions of characters in conflict, but struggling always toward that perfect resolution that is more attainable, perhaps, in fiction than in real life.

Stephen Crane

THE BRIDE COMES TO YELLOW SKY

Stephen Crane (1871–1900), born in Newark, New Jersey, and educated at Lafayette College and Syracuse University, is a pivotal figure in American fiction, poetry, and journalism—an artist who helped to shape the modern age in literature. Although he died before the age of 29, Crane did more than any other American author to assimilate the

*European modes of naturalism, impressionism, and socio-
logical realism into our national literature. His novel* Mag-
gie: A Girl of the Streets *(1893) offended the contemporary
public with its harsh portrayal of slum life and of a young
woman whose life ends in prostitution and death. His short
novel about the Civil War,* The Red Badge of Courage *(1895),
won for Crane broader and more approving recognition and
today is considered a masterpiece of war fiction. Always
living in poverty, embroiled in scandal, and suffering from
tuberculosis, Crane led a flamboyant life, settling finally
with his mistress in England in 1897. He died in Baden-
weiler, Germany, in 1900. Crane's short stories, renowned
for their ironic realism and impressionistic detail, are collected in* The Open Boat and Other Tales of Adventure *(1898),*
The Monster and Other Stories *(1899),* Whilomville Stories
(1900), and Wounds in the Rain: War Stories *(1900). In "The
Bride Comes to Yellow Sky," Crane works with both a
conventional and a more experimental plot structure in
order to permit the lives of his central characters to converge in the violent landscape of the Wild West.*

I

The great Pullman was whirling onward with such dignity of motion that a glance
from the window seemed simply to prove that the plains of Texas were pouring
eastward. Vast flats of green grass, dull-hued spaces of mesquite and cactus, little
groups of frame houses, woods of light and tender trees, all were sweeping into
the east, sweeping over the horizon, a precipice.

A newly married pair had boarded this coach at San Antonio. The man's face
was reddened from many days in the wind and sun, and a direct result of his new
black clothes was that his brick-colored hands were constantly performing in a
most conscious fashion. From time to time he looked down respectfully at his
attire. He sat with a hand on each knee, like a man waiting in a barber's shop. The
glances he devoted to other passengers were furtive and shy.

The bride was not pretty, nor was she very young. She wore a dress of blue
cashmere, with small reservations of velvet here and there, and with steel buttons
abounding. She continually twisted her head to regard her puff sleeves, very stiff,
straight, and high. They embarrassed her. It was quite apparent that she had
cooked, and that she expected to cook, dutifully. The blushes caused by the
careless scrutiny of some passengers as she had entered the car were strange to
see upon this plain, underclass countenance, which was drawn in placid, almost
emotionless lines.

They were evidently very happy. "Ever been in a parlor car before?" he asked,
smiling with delight.

"No," she answered, "I never was. It's fine, ain't it?"

"Great! And then after a while we'll go forward to the diner, and get a big
layout. Finest meal in the world. Charge a dollar."

"Oh, do they?" cried the bride. "Charge a dollar? Why, that's too much—for
us—ain't it, Jack?"

"Not this trip, anyhow," he answered bravely. "We're going to go the whole
thing."

Later he explained to her about the trains. "You see, it's a thousand miles from one end of Texas to the other; and this train runs right across it, and never stops but four times." He had the pride of an owner. He pointed out to her the dazzling fittings of the coach; and in truth her eyes opened wider as she contemplated the sea-green figured velvet, the shining brass, silver, and glass, the wood that gleamed as darkly brilliant as the surface of a pool of oil. At one end, a bronze figure sturdily held a support for a separated chamber, and at convenient places on the ceiling were frescos in olive and silver.

To the minds of the pair, their surroundings reflected the glory of their marriage that morning in San Antonio; this was the environment of their new estate; and the man's face in particular beamed with an elation that made him appear ridiculous to the Negro porter. This individual at times surveyed them from afar with an amused and superior grin. On other occasions, he bullied them with skill in ways that did not make it exactly plain to them that they were being bullied. He subtly used all the manners of the most unconquerable kind of snobbery. He oppressed them; but of this oppression they had small knowledge, and they speedily forgot that infrequently a number of travelers covered them with stares of derisive enjoyment. Historically there was supposed to be something infinitely humorous in their situation.

"We are due in Yellow Sky at three forty-two," he said, looking tenderly into her eyes.

"Oh, are we?" she said, as if she had not been aware of it. To evince surprise at her husband's statement was part of her wifely amiability. She took from a pocket a little silver watch; and as she held it before her, and stared at it with a frown of attention, the new husband's face shone.

"I bought it in San Anton' from a friend of mine," he told her gleefully.

"It's seventeen minutes past twelve," she said, looking up at him with a kind of shy and clumsy coquetry. A passenger, noting this play, grew excessively sardonic, and winked at himself in one of the numerous mirrors.

At last they went to the dining car. Two rows of Negro waiters, in glowing white suits, surveyed their entrance with the interest, and also the equanimity, of men who had been forewarned. The pair fell to the lot of a waiter who happened to feel pleasure in steering them through their meal. He viewed them with the manner of a fatherly pilot, his countenance radiant with benevolence. The patronage, entwined with the ordinary deference, was not plain to them. And yet, as they returned to their coach, they showed in their faces a sense of escape.

To the left, miles down a long, purple slope, was a little ribbon of mist where moved the keening Rio Grande. The train was approaching it at an angle, and the apex was Yellow Sky. Presently it was apparent that, as the distance from Yellow Sky grew shorter, the husband became commensurately restless. His brick-red hands were more insistent in their prominence. Occasionally he was even rather absentminded and faraway when the bride leaned forward and addressed him.

As a matter of truth, Jack Potter was beginning to find the shadow of a deed weigh upon him like a leaden slab. He, the town marshal of Yellow Sky, a man known, liked, and feared in his corner, a prominent person, had gone to San Antonio to meet a girl he believed he loved, and there, after the usual prayers, had actually induced her to marry him, without consulting Yellow Sky for any part of the transaction. He was now bringing his bride before an innocent and unsuspecting community.

Of course, people in Yellow Sky married as it pleased them, in accordance with a general custom; but such was Potter's thought of his duty to his friends, or of their idea of his duty, or of an unspoken form which does not control men in these matters, that he felt he was heinous. He had committed an extraordinary crime. Face to face with this girl in San Antonio, and spurred by his sharp impulse, he had gone headlong over all the social hedges. At San Antonio he was like a man hidden in the dark. A knife to sever any friendly duty, any form, was easy to his hand in that remote city. But the hour of Yellow Sky—the hour of daylight—was approaching.

He knew full well that his marriage was an important thing to his town. It could only be exceeded by the burning of the new hotel. His friends could not forgive him. Frequently he had reflected on the advisability of telling them by telegraph, but a new cowardice had been upon him. He feared to do it. And now the train was hurrying him toward a scene of amazement, glee, and reproach. He glanced out of the window at the line of haze swinging slowly in toward the train.

Yellow Sky had a kind of brass band, which played painfully, to the delight of the populace. He laughed without heart as he thought of it. If the citizens could dream of his prospective arrival with his bride, they would parade the band at the station and escort them, amid cheers and laughing congratulations, to his adobe home.

He resolved that he would use all the devices of speed and plainscraft in making the journey from the station to his house. Once within that safe citadel, he could issue some sort of vocal bulletin, and then not go among the citizens until they had time to wear off a little of their enthusiasm.

The bride looked anxiously at him. "What's worrying you, Jack?"

He laughed again. "I'm not worrying, girl; I'm only thinking of Yellow Sky."

She flushed in comprehension.

A sense of mutual guilt invaded their minds and developed a finer tenderness. They looked at each other with eyes softly aglow. But Potter often laughed the same nervous laugh; the flush upon the bride's face seemed quite permanent.

The traitor to the feelings of Yellow Sky narrowly watched the speeding landscape. "We're nearly there," he said.

Presently the porter came and announced the proximity of Potter's home. He held a brush in his hand, and with all his airy superiority gone, he brushed Potter's new clothes as the latter slowly turned this way and that way. Potter fumbled out a coin and gave it to the porter, as he had seen others do. It was a heavy and muscle-bound business, as that of a man shoeing his first horse.

The porter took their bag, and as the train began to slow, they moved forward to the hooded platform of the car. Presently the two engines and their long string of coaches rushed into the station of Yellow Sky.

"They have to take water here," said Potter, from a constricted throat and in mournful cadence, as one announcing death. Before the train stopped, his eye had swept the length of the platform, and he was glad and astonished to see there was none upon it but the station agent, who, with a slightly hurried and anxious air was walking toward the water tanks. When the train had halted, the porter alighted first, and placed in position a little temporary step.

"Come on, girl," said Potter hoarsely. As he helped her down, they each laughed on a false note. He took the bag from the Negro, and bade his wife cling to his arm. As they slunk rapidly away, his hangdog glance perceived that they were unloading the two trunks, and also that the station agent, far ahead near the baggage car, had turned and was running toward him, making gestures. He laughed, and groaned as he laughed, when he noted the first effect of his marital bliss upon Yellow Sky. He gripped his wife's arm firmly to his side, and they fled. Behind them the porter stood, chuckling fatuously.

II

The California express on the Southern Railway was due at Yellow Sky in twenty-one minutes. There were six men at the bar of the Weary Gentleman saloon. One was a drummer who talked a great deal and rapidly; three were Texans who did not care to talk at that time; and two were Mexican sheepherders, who did not talk as a general practice in the Weary Gentleman saloon. The barkeeper's dog lay on the boardwalk that crossed in front of the door. His head was on his paws, and he glanced drowsily here and there with the constant vigilance of a dog that is kicked on occasion. Across the sandy street were some vivid green grass plots, so wonderful in appearance, amid the sands that burned near them in a blazing sun, that they caused a doubt in the mind. They exactly resembled the grass mats used to represent lawns on the stage. At the cooler end of the railway station, a man without a coat sat in a tilted chair and smoked his pipe. The fresh-cut bank of the Rio Grande circled near the town, and there could be seen beyond it a great, plum-colored plain of mesquite.

Save for the busy drummer and his companions in the saloon, Yellow Sky was dozing. The newcomer leaned gracefully upon the bar, and recited many tales with the confidence of a bard who has come upon a new field.

"—and at the moment that the old man fell downstairs with the bureau in his arms, the old woman was coming up with two scuttles of coal, and of course—"

The drummer's tale was interrupted by a young man who suddenly appeared in the open door. He cried, "Scratchy Wilson's drunk, and has turned loose with both hands." The two Mexicans at once set down their glasses and faded out of the rear entrance of the saloon.

The drummer, innocent and jocular, answered, "All right, old man. S'pose he had? Come in and have a drink, anyhow."

But the information had made such an obvious cleft in every skull in the room that the drummer was obliged to see its importance. All had become instantly solemn. "Say," said he, mystified, "what is this?" His three companions made the introductory gesture of eloquent speech; but the young man at the door forestalled them.

"It means, my friend," he answered, as he came into the saloon, "that for the next two hours this town won't be a health resort."

The barkeeper went to the door, and locked and barred it; reaching out of the window, he pulled in heavy wooden shutters, and barred them. Immediately a solemn, chapel-like gloom was upon the place. The drummer was looking from one to another.

"But say," he cried, "what is this, anyhow? You don't mean there is going to be a gun fight?"

"Don't know whether there'll be a fight or not," answered one man grimly, "but there'll be some shootin'—some good shootin'."

The young man who had warned them waved his hand. "Oh, there'll be a fight fast enough, if anyone wants it. Anybody can get a fight out there in the street. There's a fight just waiting."

The drummer seemed to be swayed between the interest of a foreigner and a perception of personal danger.

"What did you say his name was?" he asked.

"Scratchy Wilson," they answered in chorus.

"And will he kill anybody? What are you going to do? Does this happen often? Does he rampage around like this once a week or so? Can he break in that door?"

"No; he can't break down that door," replied the barkeeper. "He's tried it three times. But when he comes, you'd better lay down on the floor, stranger. He's dead sure to shoot at it, and a bullet may come through."

Thereafter the drummer kept a strict eye upon the door. The time had not yet been called for him to hug the floor, but as a minor precaution, he sidled near to the wall. "Will he kill anybody?" he said again.

The men laughed low and scornfully at the question.

"He's out to shoot, and he's out for trouble. Don't see any good in experiment-in' with him."

"But what do you do in a case like this? What do you do?"

A man responded, "Why, he and Jack Potter—"

"But," in chorus the other men interrupted, "Jack Potter's in San Anton'."

"Well, who is he? What's he got to do with it?"

"Oh, he's the town marshal. He goes out and fights Scratchy when he gets on one of these tears."

"Wow!" said the drummer, mopping his brow. "Nice job he's got."

The voices had toned away to mere whisperings. The drummer wished to ask further questions, which were born of an increasing anxiety and bewilderment; but when he attempted them, the men merely looked at him in irritation and motioned him to remain silent. A tense, waiting hush was upon them. In the deep shadows of the room, their eyes shone as they listened for sounds from the street. One man made three gestures at the barkeeper; and the latter, moving like a ghost, handed him a glass and a bottle. The man poured a full glass of whisky, and set down the bottle noiselessly. He gulped the whisky in a swallow, and turned again toward the door in immovable silence. The drummer saw that the barkeeper, without a sound, had taken a Winchester from beneath the bar. Later he saw this individual beckoning to him, so he tiptoed across the room.

"You better come with me back of the bar."

"No, thanks," said the drummer, perspiring. "I'd rather be where I can make a break for the back door."

Whereupon the man of bottles made a kindly but peremptory gesture. The drummer obeyed it, and finding himself seated on a box with his head below the level of the bar, balm was laid upon his soul at sight of various zinc and copper fittings that bore a resemblance to armor plate. The barkeeper took a seat comfortably upon an adjacent box.

"You see," he whispered, "this here Scratchy Wilson is a wonder with a gun—a perfect wonder; and when he goes on the war trail, we hunt our holes—naturally. He's about the last one of the old gang that used to hang out along the river here. He's a terror when he's drunk. When he's sober he's all right—kind of simple—wouldn't hurt a fly—nicest fellow in town. But when he's drunk—whoo!"

There were periods of stillness. "I wish Jack Potter was back from San Anton'," said the barkeeper. "He shot Wilson up once—in the leg—and he would sail in and pull out the kinks in this thing."

Presently they heard from a distance the sound of a shot, followed by three wild yowls. It instantly removed a bond from the men in the darkened saloon. There was a shuffling of feet. They looked at each other. "Here he comes," they said.

III

A man in a maroon-colored flannel shirt, which had been purchased for purposes of decoration, and made principally by some Jewish women on the East Side of New York, rounded a corner and walked into the middle of the main street of Yellow Sky. In either hand the man held a long, heavy, blue-black revolver. Often he yelled, and these cries rang through a semblance of a deserted village, shrilly flying over the roofs in a volume that seemed to have no relation to the ordinary vocal strength of a man. It was as if the surrounding stillness formed the arch of a tomb over him. These cries of ferocious challenge rang against walls of silence. And his boots had red tops with gilded imprints, of the kind beloved in winter by little sledding boys on the hillsides of New England.

The man's face flamed in a rage begot of whisky. His eyes, rolling, and yet keen for ambush, hunted the still doorways and windows. He walked with the creeping movement of the midnight cat. As it occurred to him, he roared menacing information. The long revolvers in his hands were as easy as straws; they were moved with an electric swiftness. The little fingers of each hand played sometimes in a musician's way. Plain from the low collar of the shirt, the cords of his neck straightened and sank, straightened and sank, as passion moved him. The only sounds were his terrible invitations. The calm adobes preserved their demeanor at the passing of this small thing in the middle of the street.

There was no offer of fight—no offer of fight. The man called to the sky. There were no attractions. He bellowed and fumed and swayed his revolvers here and everywhere.

The dog of the barkeeper of the Weary Gentleman saloon had not appreciated the advance of events. He yet lay dozing in front of his master's door. At sight of the dog, the man paused and raised his revolver humorously. At sight of the man, the dog sprang up and walked diagonally away, with a sullen head, and growling. The man yelled, and the dog broke into a gallop. As it was about to enter an alley, there was a loud noise, a whistling, and something spat the ground directly before it. The dog screamed, and wheeling in terror, galloped headlong in a new direction. Again there was a noise, a whistling, and sand was kicked viciously before it. Fearstricken, the dog turned and flurried like an animal in a pen. The man stood laughing, his weapons at his hips.

Ultimately the man was attracted by the closed door of the Weary Gentleman saloon. He went to it, and hammering with a revolver, demanded drink.

The door remaining imperturbable, he picked a bit of paper from the walk, and nailed it to the framework with a knife. He then turned his back contemptuously upon this popular resort, and walking to the opposite side of the street and spinning there on his heel quickly and lithely, fired at the bit of paper. He missed it by a half inch. He swore at himself, and went away. Later he comfortably fusilladed the windows of his most intimate friend. The man was playing with this town; it was a toy for him.

But still there was no offer of fight. The name of Jack Potter, his ancient antagonist, entered his mind, and he concluded that it would be a glad thing if he should go to Potter's house, and by bombardment induce him to come out and fight. He moved in the direction of his desire, chanting Apache scalp music.

When he arrived at it, Potter's house presented the same still front as had the other adobes. Taking up a strategic position, the man howled a challenge. But this house regarded him as might a great stone god. It gave no sign. After a decent wait, the man howled further challenges, mingling with them wonderful epithets.

Presently there came the spectacle of a man churning himself into deepest rage over the immobility of a house. He fumed at it as the winter wind attacks a prairie cabin in the North. To the distance there should have gone the sound of a tumult like the fighting of two hundred Mexicans. As necessity bade him, he paused for breath or to reload his revolvers.

IV

Potter and his bride walked sheepishly and with speed. Sometimes they laughed together shamefacedly and low.

"Next corner, dear," he said finally.

They put forth the efforts of a pair walking bowed against a strong wind. Potter was about to raise a finger to point the first appearance of the new home when, as they circled the corner, they came face to face with a man in a maroon-colored shirt, who was feverishly pushing cartridges into a large revolver. Upon the instant the man dropped his revolver to the ground and, like lightning, whipped another from its holster. The second weapon was aimed at the bridegroom's chest.

There was a silence. Potter's mouth seemed to be merely a grave for his tongue. He exhibited an instinct to at once loosen his arm from the woman's grip, and he dropped the bag to the sand. As for the bride, her face had gone as yellow as old cloth. She was a slave to hideous rites, gazing at the apparitional snake.

The two men faced each other at a distance of three paces. He of the revolver smiled with a new and quiet ferocity.

"Tried to sneak up on me," he said. "Tried to sneak up on me!" His eyes grew more baleful. As Potter made a slight movement, the man thrust his revolver venomously forward. "No; don't you do it, Jack Potter. Don't you move a finger toward a gun just yet. Don't you move an eyelash. The time has come for me to settle with you, and I'm goin' to do it my own way, and loaf along with no interferin'. So if you don't want a gun bent on you, just mind what I tell you."

Potter looked at his enemy. "I ain't got a gun on me, Scratchy," he said. "Honest, I ain't." He was stiffening and steadying, but yet somewhere at the back of his mind a vision of the Pullman floated: the sea-green figured velvet, the shining brass, silver, and glass, the wood that gleamed as darkly brilliant as the surface of a pool of oil—all the glory of the marriage; the environment of the new estate. "You know I fight when it comes to fighting, Scratchy Wilson; but I ain't got a gun on me. You'll have to do all the shootin' yourself."

His enemy's face went livid. He stepped forward, and lashed his weapon to and fro before Potter's chest. "Don't you tell me you ain't got no gun on you, you whelp. Don't tell me no lie like that. There ain't a man in Texas ever seen you without no gun. Don't take me for no kid." His eyes blazed with light, and his throat worked like a pump.

"I ain't takin' you for no kid," answered Potter. His heels had not moved an inch backward. "I'm takin' you for a damn fool. I tell you I ain't got a gun, and I ain't. If you're goin' to shoot me up, you better begin now; you'll never get a chance like this again."

So much enforced reasoning had told on Wilson's rage; he was calmer. "If you ain't got a gun, why ain't you got a gun?" he sneered. "Been to Sunday school?"

"I ain't got a gun because I've just come from San Anton' with my wife. I'm married," said Potter. "And if I'd thought there was going to be any galoots like you prowling around when I brought my wife home, I'd had a gun, and don't you forget it."

"Married!" said Scratchy, not at all comprehending.

"Yes, married. I'm married," said Potter distinctly.

"Married?" said Scratchy. Seemingly for the first time, he saw the drooping, drowning woman at the other man's side. "No!" he said. He was like a creature allowed a glimpse of another world. He moved a pace backward, and his arm, with the revolver, dropped to his side. "Is this the lady?" he asked.

"Yes; this is the lady," answered Potter.

There was another period of silence.

"Well," said Wilson at last, slowly, "I s'pose it's all off now."

"It's all off if you say so, Scratchy. You know I didn't make the trouble." Potter lifted his valise.

"Well, I 'low it's off, Jack," said Wilson. He was looking at the ground. "Married!" He was not a student of chivalry; it was merely that in the presence of this foreign condition he was a simple child of the earlier plains. He picked up his starboard revolver, and placing both weapons in their holsters, he went away. His feet made funnel-shaped tracks in the heavy sand.

QUESTIONS

1. Summarize the action in each of the four sections of the story. What is the "double" plot? How do the four parts fit together to form the outline of the plot?

2. What types of conflict do you encounter in the plot?

3. Discuss the plot in terms of the Freytag "triangle" (see page 43).

4. What are the functions of the porter, the waiters, the passengers, and the patrons of the Weary Gentleman saloon?

5. How does the setting of the story contribute to the conflict? Why does Crane render the setting so vividly? What is the relationship of setting to plot and theme?

6. What is the function of chance or coincidence in the plot? Does Crane rely too heavily on coincidental action? Justify your answer.

7. What is the theme of the story?

TOPICS FOR WRITING

1. Several critics have maintained that this is not simply a story about the conflict between the newly married sheriff and a drunken gunfighter but about a conflict in values and in the course of American civilization itself. What do you think they are getting at? What, for example, is Crane saying about the Western experience? Find evidence to support your assertions.

2. Write a short essay on the impact of marriage on human behavior in "The Bride Comes to Yellow Sky."

3. Write an essay on plot and theme in the story.

Bernard Malamud

THE MAGIC BARREL

Bernard Malamud (1914–   ), noted American short story writer and novelist, was born in Brooklyn, New York, the setting of a significant portion of his fiction. He was educated at City College and Columbia University, and for many years he has taught at Bennington College in Vermont. Malamud has a rare talent for depicting human situations in tragicomic ways. In fact, it is the element of the bizarre or absurd in the lives of his characters that alleviates their potential tragedies and offers them curious moral and spiritual victories. Malamud's novels include The Natural *(1952),* The Assistant *(1957),* A New Life *(1961),* The Fixer *(1966; winner of the Pulitzer Prize),* Dubin's Lives *(1979), and* God's Grace *(1982). His stories have been collected in* The Magic Barrel *(1958; winner of the National Book Award),* Idiots First *(1963),* Pictures of Fidelman *(1969), and* Rembrandt's Hat *(1973). In "The Magic Barrel," Malamud offers us a rabbinical student whose search for a young bride who will get him a better congregation turns into a comic journey toward that most serious of subjects—salvation itself.*

Not long ago there lived in uptown New York, in a small, almost meager room, though crowded with books, Leo Finkle, a rabbinical student in the Yeshivah University. Finkle, after six years of study, was to be ordained in June and had been advised by an acquaintance that he might find it easier to win himself a congregation if he were married. Since he had no present prospects of marriage, after two tormented days of turning it over in his mind, he called in Pinye Salzman, a marriage broker whose two-line advertisement he had read in the *Forward*.

The matchmaker appeared one night out of the dark fourth-floor hallway of the graystone rooming house where Finkle lived, grasping a black, strapped portfolio that had been worn thin with use. Salzman, who had been long in the business, was of slight but dignified build, wearing an old hat, and an overcoat too short and tight for him. He smelled frankly of fish, which he loved to eat, and although he was missing a few teeth, his presence was not displeasing, because of an amiable manner curiously contrasted with mournful eyes. His voice, his lips, his wisp of beard, his bony fingers were animated, but gave him a moment of repose and his mild blue eyes revealed a depth of sadness, a characteristic that put Leo a little at ease although the situation, for him, was inherently tense.

He at once informed Salzman why he had asked him to come, explaining that his home was in Cleveland, and that but for his parents, who had married comparatively late in life, he was alone in the world. He had for six years devoted himself almost entirely to his studies, as a result of which, understandably, he had found himself without time for a social life and the company of young women. Therefore he thought it the better part of trial and error—of embarrassing fumbling—to call in an experienced person to advise him on these matters. He remarked in passing that the function of the marriage broker was ancient and honorable, highly approved in the Jewish community, because it made practical the necessary without hindering joy. Moreover, his own parents had been brought together by a matchmaker. They had made, if not a financially profitable marriage—since neither had possessed any worldly goods to speak of—at least a successful one in the sense of their everlasting devotion to each other. Salzman listened in embarrassed surprise, sensing a sort of apology. Later, however, he experienced a glow of pride in his work, an emotion that had left him years ago, and he heartily approved of Finkle.

The two went to their business. Leo had led Salzman to the only clear place in the room, a table near a window that overlooked the lamp-lit city. He seated himself at the matchmaker's side but facing him, attempting by an act of will to suppress the unpleasant tickle in his throat. Salzman eagerly unstrapped his portfolio and removed a loose rubber band from a thin packet of much-handled cards. As he flipped through them, a gesture and sound that physically hurt Leo, the student pretended not to see and gazed steadfastly out the window. Although it was still February, winter was on its last legs, signs of which he had for the first time in years begun to notice. He now observed the round white moon, moving high in the sky through a cloud menagerie, and watched with half-open mouth as it penetrated a huge hen, and dropped out of her like an egg laying itself. Salzman, though pretending through eyeglasses he had just slipped on to be engaged in scanning the writing on the cards, stole occasional glances at the young man's distinguished face, noting with pleasure the long, severe scholar's nose, brown eyes heavy with learning, sensitive yet ascetic lips, and a certain, almost hollow quality of the dark cheeks. He gazed around at shelves upon shelves of books and let out a soft, contented sigh.

When Leo's eyes fell upon the cards, he counted six spread out in Salzman's hand.

"So few?" he asked in disappointment.

"You wouldn't believe me how much cards I got in my office," Salzman replied. "The drawers are already filled to the top, so I keep them now in a barrel, but is every girl good for a new rabbi?"

Leo blushed at this, regretting all he had revealed of himself in a curriculum vitae he had sent to Salzman. He had thought it best to acquaint him with his strict standards and specifications, but in having done so, felt he had told the marriage broker more than was absolutely necessary.

He hesitantly inquired, "Do you keep photographs of your clients on file?"

"First comes family, amount of dowry, also what kind promises," Salzman replied, unbuttoning his tight coat and settling himself in the chair. "After comes pictures, rabbi."

"Call me Mr. Finkle. I'm not yet a rabbi."

Salzman said he would, but instead called him doctor, which he changed to rabbi when Leo was not listening too attentively.

Salzman adjusted his horn-rimmed spectacles, gently cleared his throat and read in an eager voice the contents of the top card:

"Sophie P. Twenty-four year. Widow one year. No children. Educated high school and two years college. Father promises eight thousand dollars. Has wonderful wholesale business. Also real estate. On the mother's side comes teachers, also one actor. Well known on Second Avenue."

Leo gazed up in surprise. "Did you say a widow?"

"A widow don't mean spoiled, rabbi. She lived with her husband maybe four months. He was a sick boy she made a mistake to marry him."

"Marrying a widow has never entered my mind."

"This is because you have no experience. A widow, especially if she is young and healthy like this girl, is a wonderful person to marry. She will be thankful to you the rest of her life. Believe me, if I was looking now for a bride, I would marry a widow."

Leo reflected, then shook his head.

Salzman hunched his shoulders in an almost imperceptible gesture of disappointment. He placed the card down on the wooden table and began to read another:

"Lily H. High school teacher. Regular. Not a substitute. Has savings and new Dodge car. Lived in Paris one year. Father is successful dentist thirty-five years. Interested in professional man. Well Americanized family. Wonderful opportunity.

"I knew her personally," said Salzman. "I wish you could see this girl. She is a doll. Also very intelligent. All day you could talk to her about books and theyater and what not. She also knows current events."

"I don't believe you mentioned her age?"

"Her age?" Salzman said, raising his brows. "Her age is thirty-two years."

Leo said after a while, "I'm afraid that seems a little too old."

Salzman let out a laugh. "So how old are you, rabbi?"

"Twenty-seven."

"So what is the difference, tell me, between twenty-seven and thirty-two? My own wife is seven years older than me. So what did I suffer?—Nothing. If Rothschild's a daughter wants to marry you, would you say on account her age, no?"

"Yes," Leo said dryly.

Salzman shook off the no in the yes. "Five years don't mean a thing. I give you my word that when you will live with her for one week you will forget her age. What does it mean five years—that she lived more and knows more than somebody who is younger? On this girl, God bless her, years are not wasted. Each one that it comes makes better the bargain."

"What subject does she teach in high school?"

"Languages. If you heard the way she speaks French, you will think it is music. I am in the business twenty-five years, and I recommend her with my whole heart. Believe me, I know what I'm talking, rabbi."

"What's on the next card?" Leo said abruptly.

Salzman reluctantly turned up the third card:

"Ruth K. Nineteen years. Honor student. Father offers thirteen thousand cash to the right bridegroom. He is a medical doctor. Stomach specialist with marvelous practice. Brother in law owns own garment business. Particular people."

Salzman looked as if he had read his trump card.

"Did you say nineteen?" Leo asked with interest.

"On the dot."

"Is she attractive?" He blushed. "Pretty?"

Salzman kissed his finger tips. "A little doll. On this I give you my word. Let me call the father tonight and you will see what means pretty."

But Leo was troubled. "You're sure she's that young?"

"This I am positive. The father will show you the birth certificate."

"Are you positive there isn't something wrong with her?" Leo insisted.

"Who says there is wrong?"

"I don't understand why an American girl her age should go to a marriage broker."

A smile spread over Salzman's face.

"So for the same reason you went, she comes."

Leo flushed. "I am pressed for time."

Salzman, realizing he had been tactless, quickly explained. "The father came, not her. He wants she should have the best, so he looks around himself. When we will locate the right boy he will introduce him and encourage. This makes a better marriage than if a young girl without experience takes for herself. I don't have to tell you this."

"But don't you think this young girl believes in love?"

Leo spoke uneasily.

Salzman was about to guffaw but caught himself and said soberly, "Love comes with the right person, not before."

Leo parted dry lips but did not speak. Noticing that Salzman had snatched a glance at the next card, he cleverly asked, "How is her health?"

"Perfect," Salzman said, breathing with difficulty. "Of course, she is a little lame on her right foot from an auto accident that it happened to her when she was twelve years, but nobody notices on account she is so brilliant and also beautiful."

Leo got up heavily and went to the window. He felt curiously bitter and upbraided himself for having called in the marriage broker. Finally, he shook his head.

"Why not?" Salzman persisted, the pitch of his voice rising.

"Because I detest stomach specialists."

"So what do you care what is his business? After you marry her do you need him? Who says he must come every Friday night in your house?"

Ashamed of the way the talk was going, Leo dismissed Salzman, who went home with heavy, melancholy eyes.

Though he had felt only relief at the marriage broker's departure, Leo was in low spirits the next day. He explained it as arising from Salzman's failure to produce a suitable bride for him. He did not care for his type of clientele. But when Leo found himself hesitating whether to seek out another matchmaker, one more polished than Pinye, he wondered if it could be—his protestations to the contrary, and although he honored his father and mother—that he did not, in essence, care for the matchmaking institution? This thought he quickly put out of mind yet found himself still upset. All day he ran around in the woods—missed an important appointment, forgot to give out his laundry, walked out of a Broadway cafeteria without paying and had to run back with the ticket in his hand; had even not recognized his landlady in the street when she passed with a friend and courteously called out, "A good evening to you, Doctor Finkle." By nightfall, however, he had regained sufficient calm to sink his nose into a book and there found peace from his thoughts.

Almost at once there came a knock on the door. Before Leo could say enter, Salzman, commercial cupid, was standing in the room. His face was gray and meager, his expression hungry, and he looked as if he would expire on his feet. Yet the marriage broker managed, by some trick of the muscles, to display a broad smile.

"So good evening. I am invited?"

Leo nodded, disturbed to see him again, yet unwilling to ask the man to leave.

Beaming still, Salzman laid his portfolio on the table. "Rabbi, I got for you tonight good news."

"I've asked you not to call me rabbi. I'm still a student."

"Your worries are finished. I have for you a first-class bride."

"Leave me in peace concerning this subject." Leo pretended lack of interest.

"The world will dance at your wedding."

"Please, Mr. Salzman, no more."

"But first must come back my strength," Salzman said weakly. He fumbled with the portfolio straps and took out of the leather case an oily paper bag, from which he extracted a hard, seeded roll and a small, smoked white fish. With a quick motion of his hand he stripped the fish out of its skin and began ravenously to chew. "All day in a rush," he muttered.

Leo watched him eat.

"A sliced tomato you have maybe?" Salzman hesitantly inquired.

"No."

The marriage broker shut his eyes and ate. When he had finished he carefully cleaned up the crumbs and rolled up the remains of the fish, in the paper bag. His spectacled eyes roamed the room until he discovered, amid some piles of books, a one-burner gas stove. Lifting his hat he humbly asked, "A glass tea you got, rabbi?"

Conscience-stricken, Leo rose and brewed the tea. He served it with a chunk of lemon and two cubes of lump sugar, delighting Salzman.

After he had drunk his tea, Salzman's strength and good spirits were restored.

"So tell me, rabbi," he said amiably, "you considered some more the three clients I mentioned yesterday?"

"There was no need to consider."

"Why not?"

"None of them suits me."

"What then suits you?"

Leo let it pass because he could give only a confused answer.

Without waiting for a reply, Salzman asked, "You remember this girl I talked to you—the high school teacher?"

"Age thirty-two?"

But, surprisingly, Salzman's face lit in a smile. "Age twenty-nine."

Leo shot him a look. "Reduced from thirty-two?"

"A mistake," Salzman avowed. "I talked today with the dentist. He took me to his safety deposit box and showed me the birth certificate. She was twenty-nine years last August. They made her a party in the mountains where she went for her vacation. When her father spoke to me the first time I forgot to write the age and I told you thirty-two, but now I remember this was a different client, a widow."

"The same one you told me about? I thought she was twenty-four?"

"A different. Am I responsible that the world is filled with widows?"

"No, but I'm not interested in them, nor for that matter, in school teachers."

Salzman pulled his clasped hands to his breast. Looking at the ceiling he devoutly exclaimed, "Yiddishe kinder, what can I say to somebody that he is not interested in high school teachers? So what then you are interested?"

Leo flushed but controlled himself.

"In what else will you be interested," Salzman went on, "if you not interested in this fine girl that she speaks four languages and has personally in the bank ten thousand dollars? Also her father guarantees further twelve thousand. Also she has a new car, wonderful clothes, talks on all subjects, and she will give you a first-class home and children. How near do we come in our life to paradise?"

"If she's so wonderful, why wasn't she married ten years ago?"

"Why?" said Salzman with a heavy laugh. "—Why? Because she is *partikiler*. This is why. She wants the *best*."

Leo was silent, amused at how he had entangled himself. But Salzman had aroused his interest in Lily H., and he began seriously to consider calling on her. When the marriage broker observed how intently Leo's mind was at work on the facts he had supplied, he felt certain they would soon come to an agreement.

Late Saturday afternoon, conscious of Salzman, Leo Finkle walked with Lily Hirschorn along Riverside Drive. He walked briskly and erectly, wearing with distinction the black fedora he had that morning taken with trepidation out of the dusty hat box on his closet shelf, and the heavy black Saturday coat he had thoroughly whisked clean. Leo also owned a walking stick, a present from a distant relative, but quickly put temptation aside and did not use it. Lily, petite and not unpretty, had on something signifying the approach of spring. She was au courant, animatedly, with all sorts of subjects, and he weighed her words and found her surprisingly sound—score another for Salzman, whom he uneasily sensed to be somewhere around, hiding perhaps high in a tree along the street, flashing the lady signals with a pocket mirror; or perhaps a cloven-hoofed Pan, piping nuptial ditties as he danced his invisible way before them, strewing wild buds on the walk and purple grapes in their path, symbolizing fruit of a union, though there was of course still none.

Lily startled Leo by remarking, "I was thinking of Mr. Salzman, a curious figure, wouldn't you say?"

Not certain what to answer, he nodded.

She bravely went on, blushing. "I for one am grateful for his introducing us. Aren't you?"

He courteously replied, "I am."

"I mean," she said with a little laugh—and it was all in good taste, or at least gave the effect of being not in bad—"do you mind that we came together so?"

He was not displeased with her honesty, recognizing that she meant to set the relationship aright, and understanding that it took a certain amount of experience in life, and courage, to want to do it quite that way. One had to have some sort of past to make that kind of beginning.

He said that he did not mind. Salzman's function was traditional and honorable—valuable for what it might achieve, which, he pointed out, was frequently nothing.

Lily agreed with a sigh. They walked on for a while and she said after a long silence, again with a nervous laugh, "Would you mind if I asked you something a little bit personal? Frankly, I find the subject fascinating." Although Leo shrugged, she went on half embarrassedly, "How was it that you came to your calling? I mean was it a sudden passionate inspiration?"

Leo, after a time, slowly replied, "I was always interested in the Law."

"You saw revealed in it the presence of the Highest?"

He nodded and changed the subject. "I understand that you spent a little time in Paris, Miss Hirschorn?"

"Oh, did Mr. Salzman tell you, Rabbi Finkle?" Leo winced but she went on, "It was ages ago and almost forgotten. I remember I had to return for my sister's wedding."

And Lily would not be put off. "When," she asked in a trembly voice, "did you become enamored of God?"

He stared at her. Then it came to him that she was talking not about Leo Finkle, but of a total stranger, some mystical figure, perhaps even passionate prophet that Salzman had dreamed up for her—no relation to the living or dead. Leo trembled with rage and weakness. The trickster had obviously sold her a bill of goods, just as he had him, who'd expected to become acquainted with a young lady of twenty-nine, only to behold, the moment he laid eyes upon her strained and anxious face, a woman past thirty-five and aging rapidly. Only his self control had kept him this long in her presence.

"I am not," he said gravely, "a talented religious person," and in seeking words to go on, found himself possessed by shame and fear. "I think," he said in a strained manner, "that I came to God not because I loved Him, but because I did not."

This confession he spoke harshly because its unexpectedness shook him.

Lily wilted. Leo saw a profusion of loaves of bread go flying like ducks high over his head, not unlike the winged loaves by which he had counted himself to sleep last night. Mercifully, then, it snowed, which he would not put past Salzman's machinations.

He was infuriated with the marriage broker and swore he would throw him out of the room the minute he reappeared. But Salzman did not come that night, and when Leo's anger had subsided, an unaccountable despair grew in its place. At first he thought this was caused by his disappointment in Lily, but before long it became evident that he had involved himself with Salzman without a true knowledge of his own intent. He gradually realized—with an emptiness that seized him with six hands—that he had called in the broker to find him a bride because he was incapable of doing it himself. This terrifying insight he had derived as a result of his meeting and conversation with Lily Hirschorn. Her probing questions had somehow irritated him into revealing—to himself more than her—the true nature of his relationship to God, and from that it had come upon him, with shocking force, that apart from his parents, he had never loved anyone. Or perhaps it went the other way, that he did not love God so well as he might, because he had not loved man. It seemed to Leo that his whole life stood starkly revealed and he saw himself for the first time as he truly was—unloved and loveless. This bitter but somehow not fully unexpected revelation brought him to a point of panic, controlled only by extraordinary effort. He covered his face with his hands and cried.

The week that followed was the worst of his life. He did not eat and lost weight. His beard darkened and grew ragged. He stopped attending seminars and almost never opened a book. He seriously considered leaving the Yeshivah, although he was deeply troubled at the thought of the loss of all his years of study—saw them like pages torn from a book, strewn over the city—and at the devastating effect of this decision upon his parents. But he had lived without knowledge of himself, and never in the Five Books and all the Commentaries—mea culpa—had the truth been revealed to him. He did not know where to turn, and in all this desolating loneliness there was no *to whom*, although he often thought of Lily but not once could bring himself to go downstairs and make the call. He became touchy and irritable, especially with his landlady, who asked him all manner of personal questions; on the other hand, sensing his own disagreeableness, he waylaid her on the stairs and apologized abjectly, until mortified, she ran from him. Out of this, however, he drew the consolation that he was a Jew and that a Jew suffered. But gradually, as the long and terrible week drew to a close, he regained his composure and some idea of purpose in life: to go on as planned. Although he was imperfect, the ideal was not. As for his quest of a bride, the thought of continuing afflicted him with anxiety and heartburn, yet perhaps with this new knowledge of himself he would be more successful than in the past. Perhaps love would now come to him and a bride to that love. And for this sanctified seeking who needed a Salzman?

The marriage broker, a skeleton with haunted eyes, returned that very night. He looked, withal, the picture of frustrated expectancy—as if he had steadfastly waited the week at Miss Lily Hirschorn's side for a telephone call that never came.

Casually coughing, Salzman came immediately to the point: "So how did you like her?"

Leo's anger rose and he could not refrain from chiding the matchmaker: "Why did you lie to me, Salzman?"

Salzman's pale face went dead white, the world had snowed on him.

"Did you not state that she was twenty-nine?" Leo insisted.

"I give you my word—"

"She was thirty-five, if a day. *At least* thirty-five."

"Of this don't be too sure. Her father told me—"

"Never mind. The worst of it was that you lied to her."

"How did I lie to her, tell me?"

"You told her things about me that weren't true. You made me out to be more, consequently less than I am. She had in mind a totally different person, a sort of semi-mystical Wonder Rabbi."

"All I said, you was a religious man."

"I can imagine."

Salzman sighed. "This is my weakness that I have," he confessed. "My wife says to me I shouldn't be a salesman, but when I have two fine people that they would be wonderful to be married, I am so happy that I talk too much." He smiled wanly. "This is why Salzman is a poor man."

Leo's anger left him. "Well, Salzman, I'm afraid that's all."

The marriage broker fastened hungry eyes on him.

"You don't want any more a bride?"

"I do," said Leo, "but I have decided to seek her in a different way. I am no longer interested in an arranged marriage. To be frank, I now admit the necessity of premarital love. That is, I want to be in love with the one I marry."

"Love?" said Salzman, astounded. After a moment he remarked, "For us, our love is our life, not for the ladies. In the ghetto they—"

"I know, I know," said Leo. "I've thought of it often. Love, I have said to myself, should be a by-product of living and worship rather than its own end. Yet for myself I find it necessary to establish the level of my need and fulfill it."

Salzman shrugged but answered, "Listen, rabbi, if you want love, this I can find for you also. I have such beautiful clients that you will love them the minute your eyes see them."

Leo smiled unhappily. "I'm afraid you don't understand."

But Salzman hastily unstrapped his portfolio and withdrew a manila packet form it.

"Pictures," he said, quickly laying the envelope on the table.

Leo called after him to take the pictures away, but as if on the wings of the wind, Salzman had disappeared.

March came. Leo had returned to his regular routine. Although he felt not quite himself yet—lacked energy—he was making plans for a more active social life. Of course it would cost something, but he was an expert in cutting corners; and when there were no corners left he would make circles rounder. All the while Salzman's pictures had lain on the table, gathering dust. Occasionally as Leo sat studying, or enjoying a cup of tea, his eyes fell on the manila envelope, but he never opened it.

The days went by and no social life to speak of developed with a member of the opposite sex—it was difficult, given the circumstances of his situation. One morning Leo toiled up the stairs to his room and stared out the window at the city. Although the day was bright his view of it was dark. For some time he watched the people in the street below hurrying along and then tuned with a heavy heart to his little room. On the table was the packet. With a sudden relentless gesture he tore it open. For a half-hour he stood by the table in a state of excitement, examining the photographs of the ladies Salzman had included. Finally, with a deep sigh he put them down. There were six, of varying degrees of attractiveness, but look at them long enough and they all became Lily Hirschorn: all past their prime, all starved behind bright smiles, not a true personality in the lot. Life, despite their frantic yoohooings, had passed them by; they were pictures in a briefcase that stank of fish. After a while, however, as Leo attempted to return the photographs into the envelope, he found in it another, a snapshot of the type taken by a machine for a quarter. He gazed at it a moment and let out a cry.

Her face deeply moved him. Why, he could at first not say. It gave him the impression of youth—spring flowers, yet age—a sense of having been used to the bone, wasted; this came from the eyes, which were hauntingly familiar, yet absolutely strange. He had a vivid impression that he had met her before, but try as he might he could not place her although he could almost recall her name, as if he had read it in her own handwriting. No, this couldn't be; he would have remembered her. It was not, he affirmed, that she had an extraordinary beauty—no, though her face was attractive enough; it was that *something* about her moved him. Feature for feature, even some of the ladies of the photographs could do better; but she leaped forth to his heart—had *lived*, or wanted to—more than just wanted, perhaps regretted how she had lived—had somehow deeply suffered: it could be seen in the depths of those reluctant eyes, and from the way the light enclosed and shone from her, and within her, opening realms of possibility: this was her own. Her he desired. His head ached and eyes narrowed with the intensity of his gazing, then as if an obscure fog had blown up in the mind, he experienced fear of her and was aware that he had received an impression, somehow, of evil. He shuddered, saying softly, it is thus with us all. Leo brewed some tea in a small pot and sat sipping it without sugar, to calm himself. But before he had finished drinking, again with excitement he examined the face and found it good: good for Leo Finkle. Only such a one could understand him and help him seek whatever he was seeking. She might, perhaps, love him. How she had happened to be among the discards in Salzman's barrel he could never guess, but he knew he must urgently go find her.

Leo rushed downstairs, grabbed up the Bronx telephone book, and searched for Salzman's home address. He was not listed, nor was his office. Neither was he in the Manhattan book. But Leo remembered having written down the address on a slip of paper after he had read Salzman's advertisement in the "personals" column of the *Forward*. He ran up to his room and tore through his papers, without luck. It was exasperating. Just when he needed the matchmaker he was nowhere to be found. Fortunately Leo remembered to look in his wallet. There on a card he found his name written and a Bronx address. No phone number was listed, the reason—Leo now recalled—he had originally communicated with Salzman by letter. He got on his coat, put a hat on over his skull cap and hurried to the subway station. All the way to the far end of the Bronx he sat on the edge of his seat. He was more than once tempted to take out the picture and see if the girl's face was as he remembered it, but he refrained, allowing the snapshot to remain in his inside coat pocket, content to have her so close. When the train pulled into the station he was waiting at the door and bolted out. He quickly located the street Salzman had advertised.

The building he sought was less than a block from the subway, but it was not an office building, nor even a loft, nor a store in which one could rent office space. It was a very old tenement house. Leo found Salzman's name in pencil on a soiled tag under the bell and climbed three dark flights to his apartment. When he knocked, the door was opened by a thin, asthmatic, gray-haired woman, in felt slippers.

"Yes?" she said, expecting nothing. She listened without listening. He could have sworn he had seen her, too, before but knew it was an illusion.

"Salzman—does he live here? Pinye Salzman," he said, "the matchmaker?"

She stared at him a long minute. "Of course."

He felt embarrassed. "Is he in?"

"No." Her mouth, though left open, offered nothing more.

"The matter is urgent. Can you tell me where his office is?"

"In the air." She pointed upward.

"You mean he has no office?" Leo asked.

"In his socks."

He peered into the apartment. It was sunless and dingy, one large room divided by a half-open curtain, beyond which he could see a sagging metal bed. The near side of the room was crowded with rickety chairs, old bureaus, a three-legged table, racks of cooking utensils, and all the apparatus of a kitchen. But there was no sign of Salzman or his magic barrel, probably also a figment of the imagination. An odor of frying fish made Leo weak to the knees.

"Where is he?" he insisted. "I've got to see your husband."

At length she answered, "So who knows where he is? Every time he thinks a new thought he runs to a different place. Go home, he will find you."

"Tell him Leo Finkle."

She gave no sign she had heard.

He walked downstairs, depressed.

But Salzman, breathless, stood waiting at his door.

Leo was astounded and overjoyed. "How did you get here before me?"

"I rushed."

"Come inside."

They entered. Leo fixed tea, and a sardine sandwich for Salzman. As they were drinking he reached behind him for the packet of pictures and handed them to the marriage broker.

Salzman put down his glass and said expectantly, "You found somebody you like?"

"Not among these."

The marriage broker turned away.

"Here is the one I want." Leo held forth the snapshot.

Salzman slipped on his glasses and took the picture into his trembling hand. He turned ghastly and let out a groan.

"What's the matter?" cried Leo.

"Excuse me. Was an accident this picture. She isn't for you."

Salzman frantically shoved the manila packet into his portfolio. He thrust the snapshot into his pocket and fled down the stairs.

Leo, after momentary paralysis, gave chase and cornered the marriage broker in the vestibule. The landlady made hysterical outcries but neither of them listened.

"Give me back the picture, Salzman."

"No." The pain in his eyes was terrible.

"Tell me who she is then."

"This I can't tell you. Excuse me."

He made to depart, but Leo, forgetting himself, seized the matchmaker by his tight coat and shook him frenziedly.

"Please," sighed Salzman. *"Please."*

Leo ashamedly let him go. "Tell me who she is," he begged. "It's very important for me to know."

"She is not for you. She is a wild one—wild, without shame. This is not a bride for a rabbi."

"What do you mean wild?"

"Like an animal. Like a dog. For her to be poor was a sin. This is why to me she is dead now."

"In God's name, what do you mean?"

"Her I can't introduce to you," Salzman cried.

"Why are you so excited?"

"Why, he asks," Salzman said, bursting into tears. "This is my baby, my Stella, she should burn in hell."

Leo hurried up to bed and hid under the covers. Under the covers he thought his life through. Although he soon fell asleep he could not sleep her out of his mind. He woke, beating his breast. Though he prayed to be rid of her, his prayers went unanswered. Through days of torment he endlessly struggled not to love her; fearing success, he escaped it. He then concluded to convert her to goodness, himself to God. The idea alternately nauseated and exalted him.

He perhaps did not know that he had come to a final decision until he encountered Salzman in a Broadway cafeteria. He was sitting alone at a rear table, sucking the bony remains of a fish. The marriage broker appeared haggard, and transparent to the point of vanishing.

Salzman looked up at first without recognizing him. Leo had grown a pointed beard and his eyes were weighted with wisdom.

"Salzman," he said, "love has at last come to my heart."

"Who can love from a picture?" mocked the marriage broker.

"It is not impossible."

"If you can love her, then you can love anybody. Let me show you some new clients that they just sent me their photographs. One is a little doll."

"Just her I want," Leo murmured.

"Don't be a fool, doctor. Don't bother with her."

"Put me in touch with her, Salzman," Leo said humbly. "Perhaps I can be of service."

Salzman had stopped eating and Leo understood with emotion that it was now arranged.

Leaving the cafeteria, he was, however, afflicted by a tormenting suspicion that Salzman had planned it all to happen this way.

Leo was informed by letter that she would meet him on a certain corner, and she was there one spring night, waiting under a street lamp. He appeared, carrying a small bouquet of violets and rosebuds. Stella stood by the lamp post, smoking. She wore white with red shoes, which fitted his expectations, although in a troubled moment he had imagined the dress red, and only the shoes white. She waited uneasily and shyly. From afar he saw that her eyes—clearly her father's—were filled with desperate innocence. He pictured, in her, his own redemption. Violins and lit candles revolved in the sky. Leo ran forward with flowers outthrust.

Around the corner, Salzman, leaning against a wall, chanted prayers for the dead.

QUESTIONS

1. What are the key shifts of time in the story? How do these shifts serve to advance the conflicts in the story?

2. What does Leo learn about himself from his contact with the various women in the story? Why does he want a bride? Why is he dissatisfied with the prospective brides offered by Salzman? Why does he become obsessed with Stella? What attracts him to Salzman's daughter?

3. What is the importance of dialogue in the story? Who is characterized best by dialogue? Why?

4. Who is Salzman? What are his motives? In what ways is he a mysterious figure in the story? Why does Malamud depict him as something of a trickster?

5. How does the quest motif serve to structure the various plot elements in the story?

6. What complications govern the plot of the story? What is the climax? Where is the resolution?

7. What is the significance of the conclusion of the story? How do you interpret this ending? Why, for example, does Leo carry a bouquet of flowers? Why are Stella's dress and shoes the right color combination for Leo? Why does Salzman chant prayers for the dead? Establish the theme of the story in relation to your responses to these questions.

TOPICS FOR WRITING

1. Trace the process whereby Leo Finkle comes to an understanding about life, love, and himself. Demonstrate the way in which Malamud plots this quest for understanding.

2. Carefully assess the relationship of Salzman to the plot of the story. Why is he both a real and a marvelous figure?

3. The story begins in a manner reminiscent of traditional fairy tales: "Not long ago. . . ." Compare Malamud's story to the plot elements that you normally associate with a fairy tale.

Doris Lessing

FLIGHT

Doris Lessing (1919–   ) was born in Kermanshah, Iran, and moved at an early age to a large farm in Southern Rhodesia. Escaping the loneliness and isolation of African farm life, she moved to Salisbury at the age of 18, entering quickly into artistic and political life there, joining the Communist party, and marrying the first of two husbands. (Both marriages ended in divorce.) She left Africa for London in 1949, and in 1950 she published her first novel, The Grass Is Singing. *Her fiction since then, increasingly experimental in mode, has focused on the violence and political disorders of modern life and especially on the plight of contemporary women. Lessing's novels include* A Proper Marriage *(1954),* Retreat to Innocence *(1956),* A Ripple from the Storm *(1958),* The Golden Notebook *(1962),* Briefing for a Descent into Hell *(1971), and the tetralogy* Canopus in Argos: Archives *(1981). Her stories, many of the best drawn from her African experience, have been collected in* This Was the Old Chief's Country *(1951),* The Habit of Loving *(1957),* A Man and Two Women *(1963),* African Stories *(1963), and* Stories *(1978). In "Flight," Lessing plots her story around the short period of time in which an old man must come to terms with the marriage of a granddaughter and with his relationship to his daughter.*

Above the old man's head was the dovecote, a tall wire-netted shelf on stilts, full of strutting, preening birds. The sunlight broke on their gray breasts into small rainbows. His ears were lulled by their crooning; his hands stretched up toward his favorite, a homing pigeon, a young plump-bodied bird, which stood still when it saw him and cocked a shrewd bright eye.

"Pretty, pretty, pretty," he said, as he grasped the bird and drew it down, feeling the cold coral claws tighten around his finger. Content, he rested the bird lightly on his chest and leaned against a tree, gazing out beyond the dovecote into the landscape of a late afternoon. In folds and hollows of sunlight and shade, the dark red soil, which was broken into great dusty clods, stretched wide to a tall horizon. Trees marked the course of the valley; a stream of rich green grass the road.

His eyes traveled homeward along this road until he saw his granddaughter swinging on the gate underneath a frangipani tree. Her hair fell down her back in a wave of sunlight; and her long bare legs repeated the angles of the frangipani stems, bare, shining brown stems among patterns of pale blossoms.

She was gazing past the pink flowers, past the railway cottage where they lived, along the road to the village.

His mood shifted. He deliberately held out his wrist for the bird to take flight, and caught it again at the moment it spread its wings. He felt the plump shape strive and strain under his fingers; and, in a sudden access of troubled spite, shut the bird into a small box and fastened the bolt. "Now you stay there," he muttered and turned his back on the shelf of birds. He moved warily along the hedge, stalking his granddaughter, who was now looped over the gate, her head loose on her arms, singing. The light happy sound mingled with the crooning of the birds, and his anger mounted.

"Hey!" he shouted, and saw her jump, look back, and abandon the gate. Her eyes veiled themselves, and she said in a pert, neutral voice, "Hullo, Grandad." Politely she moved toward him, after a lingering backward glance at the road.

"Waiting for Steven, hey?" he said, his fingers curling like claws into his palm.

"Any objection?" she asked lightly, refusing to look at him.

He confronted her, his eyes narrowed, shoulders hunched, tight in a hard knot of pain that included the preening birds, the sunlight, the flowers, herself. He said, "Think you're old enough to go courting, hey?"

The girl tossed her head at the old-fashioned phrase and sulked, "Oh, Grandad!"

"Think you want to leave home, hey? Think you can go running around the fields at night?"

Her smile made him see her, as he had every evening of this warm end-of-summer month, swinging hand in hand along the road to the village with that red-handed, red-throated, violent-bodied youth, the son of the postmaster. Misery went to his head and he shouted angrily: "I'll tell your mother!"

"Tell away!" she said, laughing, and went back to the gate.

He heard her singing, for him to hear:

"I've got you under my skin,
I've got you deep in the heart of . . ."

"Rubbish," he shouted. "Rubbish. Impudent little bit of rubbish!"

Growling under his breath, he turned toward the dovecote, which was his refuge from the house he shared with his daughter and her husband and their children. But now the house would be empty. Gone all the young girls with their laughter and their squabbling and their teasing. He would be left, uncherished and alone, with that square-fronted, calm-eyed woman, his daughter.

He stopped, muttering, before the dovecote, resenting the absorbed, cooing birds.

From the gate the girl shouted: "Go and tell! Go on, what are you waiting for?"

Obstinately he made his way to the house, with quick, pathetic, persistent glances of appeal back at her. But she never looked around. Her defiant but anxious young body stung him into love and repentance. He stopped. "But I never meant. . . ." he muttered, waiting for her to turn and run to him. "I didn't mean. . . ."

She did not turn. She had forgotten him. Along the road came the young man Steven, with something in his hand. A present for her? The old man stiffened as he watched the gate swing back and the couple embrace. In the brittle shadows of the frangipani tree his granddaughter, his darling, lay in the arms of the postmaster's son, and her hair flowed back over his shoulder.

"I see you!" shouted the old man spitefully. They did not move. He stumped into the little whitewashed house, hearing the wooden veranda creak angrily under his feet. His daughter was sewing in the front room, threading a needle held to the light.

He stopped again, looking back into the garden. The couple were now sauntering among the bushes, laughing. As he watched he saw the girl escape from the youth with a sudden mischievous movement and run off through the flowers with him in pursuit. He heard shouts, laughter, a scream, silence.

"But it's not like that at all," he muttered miserably. "It's not like that. Why can't you see? Running and giggling, and kissing and kissing. You'll come to something quite different."

He looked at his daughter with sardonic hatred, hating himself. They were caught and finished, both of them, but the girl was still running free.

"Can't you *see*?" he demanded of his invisible granddaughter, who was at that moment lying in the thick green grass with the postmaster's son.

His daughter looked at him and her eyebrows went up in tired forbearance.

"Put your birds to bed?" she asked, humoring him.

"Lucy," he said urgently. "Lucy. . . ."

"Well, what is it now?"

"She's in the garden with Steven."

"Now you just sit down and have your tea."

He stumped his feet alternately, thump, thump, on the hollow wooden floor and shouted: "She'll marry him. I'm telling you, she'll be marrying him next!"

His daughter rose swiftly, brought him a cup, set him a plate.

"I don't want any tea. I don't want it, I tell you."

"Now, now," she crooned. "What's wrong with it? Why not?"

"She's eighteen. Eighteen!"

"I was married at seventeen, and I never regretted it."

"Liar," he said. "Liar. Then you should regret it. Why do you make your girls marry? It's you who do it. What do you do it for? Why?"

"The other three have done fine. They've three fine husbands. Why not Alice?"

"She's the last," he mourned. "Can't we keep her a bit longer?"

"Come, now, Dad. She'll be down the road, that's all. She'll be here every day to see you."

"But it's not the same." He thought of the other three girls, transformed inside a few months from charming, petulant, spoiled children into serious young matrons.

"You never did like it when we married," she said. "Why not? Every time, it's the same. When I got married you made me feel like it was something wrong. And my girls the same. You get them all crying and miserable the way you go on. Leave Alice alone. She's happy." She sighed, letting her eyes linger on the sunlit garden. "She'll marry next month. There's no reason to wait."

"You've said they can marry?" he said incredulously.

"Yes, Dad. Why not?" she said coldly and took up her sewing.

His eyes stung, and he went out on to the veranda. Wet spread down over his chin, and he took out a handkerchief and mopped his whole face. The garden was empty.

From around the corner came the young couple; but their faces were no longer set against him. On the wrist of the postmaster's son balanced a young pigeon, the light gleaming on its breast.

"For me?" said the old man, letting the drops shake off his chin. "For me?"

"Do you like it?" The girl grabbed his hand and swung on it. "It's for you, Grandad. Steven brought it for you." They hung about him, affectionate, concerned, trying to charm away his wet eyes and his misery. They took his arms and directed him to the shelf of birds, one on each side, enclosing him, petting him, saying wordlessly that nothing would be changed, nothing could change, and that they would be with him always. The bird was proof of it, they said, from their lying happy eyes, as they thrust it on him. "There, Grandad, it's yours. It's for you."

They watched him as he held it on his wrist, stroking its soft, sun-warmed back, watching the wings lift and balance.

"You must shut it up for a bit," said the girl intimately, "until it knows this is its home."

"Teach your grandmother to suck eggs," growled the old man.

Released by his half-deliberate anger, they fell back, laughing at him. "We're glad you like it." They moved off, now serious and full of purpose, to the gate, where they hung, backs to him, talking quietly. More than anything could, their grown-up seriousness shut him out, making him alone; also, it quietened him, took the sting out of their tumbling like puppies on the grass. They had forgotten him again. Well, so they should, the old man reassured himself, feeling his throat clotted with tears, his lips trembling. He held the new bird to his face, for the caress of its silken feathers. Then he shut it in a box and took out his favorite.

"*Now* you can go," he said aloud. He held it poised, ready for flight, while he looked down the garden toward the boy and the girl. Then, clenched in the pain of loss, he lifted the bird on his wrist and watched it soar. A whirr and a spatter of wings, and a cloud of birds rose into the evening from the dovecote.

At the gate Alice and Steven forgot their talk and watched the birds.

On the veranda, that woman, his daughter, stood gazing, her eyes shaded with a hand that still held her sewing.

It seemed to the old man that the whole afternoon had stilled to watch his gesture of self-command, that even the leaves of the trees had stopped shaking.

Dry-eyed and calm, he let his hands fall to his sides and stood erect, staring up into the sky.

The cloud of shining silver birds flew up and up, with a shrill cleaving of wings, over the dark ploughed land and the darker belts of trees and the bright folds of grass, until they floated high in the sunlight, like a cloud of motes of dust.

They wheeled in a wide circle, tilting their wings so there was flash after flash of light, and one after another they dropped from the sunshine of the upper sky to shadow, one after another, returning to the shadowed earth over trees and grass and field, returning to the valley and the shelter of night.

The garden was all a fluster and a flurry of returning birds. Then silence, and the sky was empty.

The old man turned, slowly, taking his time; he lifted his eyes to smile proudly down the garden at his granddaughter. She was staring at him. She did not smile. She was wide-eyed and pale in the cold shadow, and he saw the tears run shivering off her face.

QUESTIONS

1. Now much time elapses in the story? What are the specific actions of the grandfather during this time? What is the relationship of the first episode involving the old man and his birds to the last one?

2. What are the conflicts in the story?

3. Why does Lessing devote so much attention to a description of the setting? How does presentation of setting influence theme?

4. What is the significance of the birds in the story? What do they symbolize?

5. How does the relationship between the grandfather, his daughter, and his granddaughter serve to define the theme of the story? What specifically is the theme?

6. What does the final episode tell us about the relationships among the key figures?

TOPICS FOR WRITING

1. Analyze the importance of the birds in "Flight" to the plot and theme of the story.

2. Classify the varieties of conflict in the story, showing how they evolve and are resolved in terms of the action and theme.

3. Compare and contrast the plots of the three stories in this section.

3

CHARACTER AND THEME: CRIME AND PUNISHMENT

Characters are the people in narratives. We generally know their sex, body features, age, jobs, education, status in society, and family background. In other words, we know their outward form and behavior. Their physical appearance and social background are part of the way that authors handle characterization—the creation, presentation, and development of character in fiction.

Yet character is also a way of being; it determines how a person acts. As such, the writer must go beyond outward appearances that tell us who characters are. The author must reveal the inner qualities that motivate people and that make finely realized characters so memorable for readers. Many of the greatest novels include in their titles the names of such memorable characters: *Don Quixote, Tom Jones, Madame Bovary, Huckleberry Finn, Anna Karenina, The Great*

Gatsby, Lolita. These narratives explore and illuminate the inner development of character, the mental and emotional states of character, the ethical and moral traits of character, the essence of character. In short, the great writer has a rare ability, as Samuel Johnson observed of Samuel Richardson, to "dive into the recesses of the human heart."

In real life, we rarely get as close to the recesses of the human heart as novelists and short story writers do. People in life tend to hide their essential beings, to be unpredictable at times, to defy our best interpretations of them. These facts underscore an essential difference between actual people and invented characters, for the purpose of the author is not to conceal but to reveal character and to fix it for us so that we can understand it. Nevertheless, there are similarities in the ways we attempt to understand real and fictional characters. We do talk about people on an everyday basis, analyzing, criticizing, and comparing them. We try to discover what lies beneath their looks, dress, speech, mannerisms, social gestures, actions, and viewpoints. Sociology and psychology, among other things, have taught us much about the exploration of human nature. In a sense, then, we know how to "create" people, and in doing so we come close to perhaps the greatest mystery in the art of fiction—the ability of the author to breathe life into characters who are, after all, mere constructs of words.

How do we gain insight into the mystery of fictional characterization? When Guy de Maupassant at the outset of his classic tale "The Piece of String" moves swiftly and economically toward a description of characters who form an entire society in just a few paragraphs, we begin to see how the great short story writers can convince us, as E. M. Forster wrote, that there is "life within the pages of a book." Maupassant is adept at presenting a panorama of social types in his short fiction. He also has a genius for focusing—in a manner typical of compressed short story art—on key characters who sustain the *felt* existence of a larger world or society. Characters in the hands of a major figure like Maupassant are brought to life by the author's ability to see them vividly, to describe them, to place them in the right relationship to a problem or conflict, and to set them in action.

It is hard to separate character from action in any discussion of fiction. Henry James stressed the interrelationship of these elements when he asked, "What is character but the determination of incident? What is incident but the illustration of character." In a similar vein, F. Scott Fitzgerald posted on the wall of the room in which he wrote, "Character is action." Of course, James admitted that the *starting point* of fiction is probably character. We become interested in action and plot only to the extent that we are absorbed by character—by those figures drawn nominally from "reality" who speak to us about the conflicts, problems, pleasures, possibilities, and mysteries of existence.

Authors, too, are absorbed by their characters. Anthony Trollope in his *Autobiography* declared that the writer of fiction "desires to make his readers so intimately acquainted with his characters that the creations of his brain should be to them speaking, moving, living, human creatures. This he can never do unless he knows those fictitious personages himself, and he can never know them well unless he can live with them in the full reality of established intimacy." Similarly, Joseph Conrad wrote of being haunted by his characters, considering them the companions of his imagination. From a slightly different but nevertheless "intimate" perspective, Turgenev spoke of watching his characters develop.

"If I watch them long enough I see them come together, I see them *placed,* I see them engaged in this or that act and in this or that difficulty. How they look and move and speak and behave, always in the setting I have found for them, is my account of them." There is, then, an elusive genius behind character creation—a genius based on imaginative identification and powers of perception. At the same time, we can detect in this set of observations by three great writers certain clues to the ways we "see" and learn about fictional characters.

Basically we learn about people in fiction through *direct* or *indirect* characterization. With direct characterization, the author literally tells us what a character is like. When Tolstoy writes in "God Sees the Truth, but Waits" that Aksyonof "was a handsome, fair-haired, curly-headed fellow, full of fun, and very fond of singing," he is telling us about some of the outer and inner qualities of his character. He employs direct characterization—a procedure far more common in eighteenth- and nineteenth-century fiction than in modern fiction, although the method still is apparent today. More typically, however, modern fiction writers explore characters through indirect methods: what characters do, what they say, how they dress, what they look like, what they think, and what they say and think about one another. When presented with indirect characterization, readers must catch and interpret clues about personality, identify traits, and discover characters' inner motivations.

Regardless of the method of characterization, the author's invented people will be static or dynamic, flat or fully rounded. As a general rule, we can say that a static character—one who doesn't change in the course of the narrative—is relatively flat, or one-dimensional, while a dynamic character who does change is round, or fully dimensional. The terms "flat" and "round" were proposed by E. M. Forster, who in *Aspects of the Novel* (1927) distinguished between flat character types (easily recognized and easily remembered because they are unchanging and unalterable) and round characters. "The test of round character," wrote Forster, "is whether it is capable of surprising in a convincing way. If it never surprises, it is flat. If it does not convince, it is flat pretending to be round. It has the incalculability of life about it."

In practice, and notably in the practice of short fiction, there is often a fusion of static and dynamic, flat and round, properties of characterization. The short story character tends toward giving symbolic and even archetypal impressions that are essentially flat in effect. In fact, the main characters, or protagonists, in the stories by Tolstoy, Maupassant, and Flannery O'Connor in this section start almost as caricatures—people with a dominant trait that excludes all others. Yet gradually we also sense subtly the shifts in being and attitudes forced on these characters either by antagonists ("villains" in the strict sense, or countervailing characters), altered situations, or reduced circumstances. We sense the mystery and irrationality of human nature, the extremes of psychological processes, even the loss of identity—a peculiarly modern feature of short fiction. From formed and predictable characterization, we move across a field or spectrum of possibility in human behavior and response. Characters grow in complexity as we await the consequences of their choices.

The central characters in the stories that follow confront issues of crime and punishment, as well as the contradictions of justice. They are types (as even the most fully rounded short story characters tend to be) whose motivations, preoccupations, and obsessions become clear to us as we follow the evolving conflicts in the stories. They are rare and beautifully realized figures, conveying sometimes in the barest outlines the primal mystery of personality that every great short story writer attempts to probe. With characterization, the short story writer tries to capture and convey an entire life—sometimes an entire world—in a highly compressed form.

Leo Tolstoy

GOD SEES THE TRUTH, BUT WAITS

Leo Tolstoy (1828–1910), conceivably the greatest nine-teenth-century novelist, was born at Yasnaya Polyana, Russia, of aristocratic parents. Like the central character in the following story, Tolstoy was drunken and riotous in his youth; again like his protagonist, he came to believe in Christian salvation in his later years. Tolstoy began to write while he was an artillery officer during the Crimean War. After the war and after travels in Europe, where he viewed (much to his distaste) bourgeois life in Paris, Tolstoy re-turned to Russia. There he wrote his two great novels, War and Peace *(1869) and* Anna Karenina *(1877). Thereafter, Tolstoy entered a prolonged and deepening period of dissat-isfaction with his work and despair over the condition of contemporary civilization. His later works, typically* What Men Live By *(1881),* The Death of Ivan Ilych *(1866), and* Resurrection *(1899), reflect the spiritual and highly moralis-tic nature of his final production. In "God Sees the Truth, but Waits," Tolstoy traces the unpredictable fate of a human being who, persecuted much of his adult life, ultimately finds inner peace.*

In the town of Vladímir lived a young merchant named Iván Dmítritch Aksyónof. He had two shops and a house of his own.

Aksyónof was a handsome, fair-haired, curly-headed fellow, full of fun, and very fond of singing. When quite a young man he had been given to drink, and was riotous when he had had too much; but after he married he gave up drinking, except now and then.

One summer Aksyónof was going to the Nízhny Fair, and as he bade good-bye to his family his wife said to him, "Iván Dmítritch, do not start to-day; I have had a bad dream about you."

Aksyónof laughed, and said, "You are afraid that when I get to the fair I shall go on the spree."

His wife replied: "I do not know what I am afraid of; all I know is that I had a bad dream. I dreamt you returned from the town, and when you took off your cap I saw that your hair was quite grey."

Leo Tolstoy

Aksyónof laughed. "That's a lucky sign," said he. "See if I don't sell out all my goods, and bring you some presents from the fair."

So he said good-bye to his family, and drove away.

When he had travelled half-way, he met a merchant whom he knew, and they put up at the same inn for the night. They had some tea together, and then went to bed in adjoining rooms.

It was not Aksyónof's habit to sleep late, and, wishing to travel while it was still cool, he aroused his driver before dawn, and told him to put in the horses.

Then he made his way across to the landlord of the inn (who lived in a cottage at the back), paid his bill, and continued his journey.

When he had gone about twenty-five miles, he stopped for the horses to be fed. Aksyónof rested awhile in the passage of the inn, then he stepped out into the porch, and, ordering a *samovár* to be heated, got out his guitar and began to play.

Suddenly a *tróyka* drove up with tinkling bells, and an official alighted, followed by two soldiers. He came to Aksyónof and began to question him, asking him who he was and whence he came. Aksyónof answered him fully, and said, "Won't you have some tea with me?" But the official went on cross-questioning him and asking him, "Where did you spend last night? Were you alone, or with a fellow-merchant? Did you see the other merchant this morning? Why did you leave the inn before dawn?"

Aksyónof wondered why he was asked all these questions, but he described all that had happened, and then added, "Why do you cross-question me as if I were a thief or a robber? I am travelling on business of my own, and there is no need to question me."

Then the official, calling the soldiers, said, "I am the police-officer of this district, and I question you because the merchant with whom you spent last night has been found with his throat cut. We must search your things."

They entered the house. The soldiers and the police-officer unstrapped Aksyónof's luggage and searched it. Suddenly the officer drew a knife out of a bag, crying, "Whose knife is this?"

Aksyónof looked, and seeing a blood-stained knife taken from his bag, he was frightened.

"How is it there is blood on this knife?"

Aksyónof tried to answer, but could hardly utter a word, and only stammered: "I—I don't know—not mine."

Then the police-officer, said, "This morning the merchant was found in bed with his throat cut. You are the only person who could have done it. The house was locked from inside, and no one else was there. Here is this blood-stained knife in your bag, and your face and manner betray you! Tell me how you killed him, and how much money you stole?"

Aksyónof swore he had not done it; that he had not seen the merchant after they had had tea together, that he had no money except eight thousand roubles of his own, and that the knife was not his. But his voice was broken, his face pale, and he trembled with fear as though he were guilty.

The police-officer ordered the soldiers to bind Aksyónof and to put him in the cart. As they tied his feet together and flung him into the cart, Aksyónof crossed himself and wept. His money and goods were taken from him, and he was sent to the nearest town and imprisoned there. Enquiries as to his character were made in Vladímir. The merchants and other inhabitants of that town said that in former days he used to drink and waste his time, but that he was a good man.

Then the trial came on: he was charged with murdering a merchant from Ryazán, and robbing him of twenty thousand roubles.

His wife was in despair, and did not know what to believe. Her children were all quite small; one was a baby at her breast. Taking them all with her, she went to the town where her husband was in gaol. At first she was not allowed to see him; but, after much begging, she obtained permission from the officials, and was taken to him. When she saw her husband in prison-dress and in chains, shut up with thieves and criminals, she fell down, and did not come to her senses for a long time. Then she drew her children to her, and sat down near him. She told him of things at home, and asked about what had happened to him. He told her all, and she asked, "What can we do now?"

"We must petition the Tsar not to let an innocent man perish."

His wife told him that she had sent a petition to the Tsar, but that it had not been accepted.

Aksyónof did not reply, but only looked downcast.

Then his wife said, "It was not for nothing I dreamt your hair had turned grey. You remember? You should not have started that day." And passing her fingers through his hair, she said: "Ványa dearest, tell your wife the truth; was it not you who did it?"

"So you, too, suspect me!" said Aksyónof, and, hiding his face in his hands, he began to weep. Then a soldier came to say that the wife and children must go away; and Aksyónof said good-bye to his family for the last time.

When they were gone, Aksyónof recalled what had been said, and when he remembered that his wife also had suspected him, he said to himself, "It seems that only God can know the truth; it is to Him alone we must appeal, and from Him alone expect mercy."

And Aksyónof wrote no more petitions; gave up all hope, and only prayed to God.

Aksyónof was condemned to be flogged and sent to the mines. So he was flogged with a knout, and when the wounds made by the knout were healed, he was driven to Siberia with other convicts.

For twenty-six years Aksyónof lived as a convict in Siberia. His hair turned white as snow, and his beard grew long, thin, and grey. All his mirth went; he stooped; he walked slowly, spoke little, and never laughed, but he often prayed.

In prison Aksyónof learnt to make boots, and earned a little money, with which he bought *The Lives of the Saints.* He read this book when there was light enough in the prison; and on Sundays in the prison-church he read the lessons and sang in the choir; for his voice was still good.

The prison authorities liked Aksyónof for his meekness, and his fellow-prisoners respected him: they called him 'Grandfather,' and 'The Saint.' When they wanted to petition the prison authorities about anything, they always made Aksyónof their spokesman, and when there were quarrels among the prisoners they came to him to put things right, and to judge the matter.

No news reached Aksyónof from his home, and he did not even know if his wife and children were still alive.

One day a fresh gang of convicts came to the prison. In the evening the old prisoners collected round the new ones and asked them what towns or villages they came from, and what they were sentenced for. Among the rest Aksyónof sat down near the new-comers, and listened with downcast air to what was said.

Leo Tolstoy

One of the new convicts, a tall, strong man of sixty, with a closely-cropped gray beard, was telling the others what he had been arrested for.

"Well, friends," he said, "I only took a horse that was tied to a sledge, and I was arrested and accused of stealing. I said I had only taken it to get home quicker, and had then let it go; besides, the driver was a personal friend of mine. So I said, 'It's all right'". "No," said they, "you stole it." But how or where I stole it they could not say. I once really did something wrong, and ought by rights to have come here long ago, but that time I was not found out. Now I have been sent here for nothing at all. . . . Eh, but it's lies I'm telling you; I've been to Siberia before, but I did not stay long."

"Where are you from?" asked some one.

"From Valdímir. My family are of that town. My name is Makár, and they also call me Semyónitch."

Aksyónof raised his head and said: "Tell me, Semyónitch, do you know anything of the merchants Aksyónof, of Vladímir? Are they still alive?"

"Know them? Of course I do. The Aksyónofs are rich, though their father is in Siberia: a sinner like ourselves, it seems! As for you, Gran'dad, how did you come here?"

Aksyónof did not like to speak of his misfortune. He only sighed, and said, "For my sins I have been in prison these twenty-six years."

"What sins?" asked Makár Semyónitch.

But Aksyónof only said, "Well, well—I must have deserved it!" He would have said no more, but his companions told the new-comer how Aksyónof came to be in Siberia: how some one had killed a merchant, and had put a knife among Aksyónof's things, and Aksyónof had been unjustly condemned.

When Makár Semyónitch heard this, he looked at Aksyónof, slapped his own knee, and exclaimed, "Well, this is wonderful! Really wonderful! But how old you've grown, Gran'dad!"

The others asked him why he was so surprised, and where he had seen Aksyónof before; but Makár Semyónitch did not reply. He only said: "It's wonderful that we should meet here, lads!"

Those words made Aksyónof wonder whether this man knew who had killed the merchant; so he said, "Perhaps, Semyónitch, you have heard of that affair, or maybe you've seen me before?"

"How could I help hearing? The world's full of rumours. But it's long ago, and I've forgotten what I heard."

"Perhaps you heard who killed the merchant?" asked Aksyónof.

Makár Semyónitch laughed, and replied, "It must have been him in whose bag the knife was found! If some one else hid the knife there, 'He's not a thief till he's caught,' as the saying is. How could any one put a knife into your bag while it was under your head? It would surely have woke you up?"

When Aksyónof heard these words, he felt sure this was the man who had killed the merchant. He rose and went away. All that night Aksyónof lay awake. He felt terribly unhappy, and all sorts of images rose in his mind. There was the image of his wife as she was when he parted from her to go to the fair. He saw her as if she were present; her face and her eyes rose before him; he heard her speak and laugh. Then he saw his children, quite little, as they were at that time: one with a little cloak on, another at his mother's breast. And then he remembered himself as he used to be—young and merry. He remembered how he sat playing the guitar in the porch of the inn where he was arrested, and how free from care he had been. He saw, in his mind, the place where he was flogged, the executioner, and the people standing around; the chains, the convicts, all the twenty-six years of his prison life, and his premature old age. The thought of it all made him so wretched that he was ready to kill himself.

"And it's all that villain's doing!" thought Aksyónof. And his anger was so great against Makár Semyónitch that he longed for vengeance, even if he himself should perish for it. He kept repeating prayers all night, but could get no peace. During the day he did not go near Makár Semyónitch, nor even look at him.

A fortnight passed in this way. Aksyónof could not sleep at nights, and was so miserable that he did not know what to do.

One night as he was walking about the prison he noticed some earth that came rolling out from under one of the shelves on which the prisoners slept. He stopped to see what it was. Suddenly Makár Semyónitch crept out from under the shelf, and looked up at Aksyónof with frightened face. Aksyónof tried to pass without looking at him, but Makár seized his hand and told him that he had dug a hole under the wall, getting rid of the earth by putting it into his high-boots, and emptying it out every day on the road when the prisoners were driven to their work.

"Just you keep quiet, old man, and you shall get out too. If you blab they'll flog the life out of me, but I will kill you first."

Aksyónof trembled with anger as he looked at his enemy. He drew his hand away, saying, "I have no wish to escape, and you have no need to kill me; you killed me long ago! As to telling of you—I may do so or not, as God shall direct."

Next day, when the convicts were led out to work, the convoy soldiers noticed that one or other of the prisoners emptied some earth out of his boots. The prison was searched, and the tunnel found. The Governor came and questioned all the prisoners to find out who had dug the hole. They all denied any knowledge of it. Those who knew, would not betray Makár Semyónitch, knowing he would be flogged almost to death. At last the Governor turned to Aksyónof, whom he knew to be a just man, and said:

"You are a truthful old man; tell me, before God, who dug the hole?"

Makár Semyónitch stood as if he were quite unconcerned, looking at the Governor and not so much as glancing at Aksyónof. Aksyónof's lips and hands trembled, and for a long time he could not utter a word. He thought, "Why should I screen him who ruined my life? Let him pay for what I have suffered. But if I tell, they will probably flog the life out of him, and maybe I suspect him wrongly. And, after all, what good would it be to me?"

"Well, old man," repeated the Governor, "tell us the truth: who has been digging under the wall?"

Aksyónof glanced at Makár Semyónitch, and said, "I cannot say, your honour. It is not God's will that I should tell! Do what you like with me; I am in your hands."

However much the Governor tried, Aksyónof would say no more, and so the matter had to be left.

That night, when Aksyónof was lying on his bed and just beginning to doze, some one came quietly and sat down on his bed. He peered through the darkness and recognized Makár.

"What more do you want of me?" asked Aksyónof. "Why have you come here?"

Makár Semyónitch was silent. So Aksyónof sat up and said, "What do you want? Go away, or I will call the guard!"

Makár Semyónitch bent close over Aksyónof, and whispered, "Iván Dmítritch, forgive me!"

"What for?" asked Aksyónof.

"It was I who killed the merchant and hid the knife among your things. I meant to kill you too, but I heard a noise outside; so I hid the knife in your bag and escaped out of the window."

Aksyónof was silent, and did not know what to say. Makár Semyónitch slid off the bed-shelf and knelt upon the ground. "Iván Dmítritch," said he, "forgive me! For the love of God, forgive me! I will confess that it was I who killed the merchant, and you will be released and can go to your home."

"It is easy for you to talk," said Aksyónof, "but I have suffered for you these twenty-six years. Where could I go to now? . . . My wife is dead, and my children have forgotten me. I have nowhere to go. . . ."

Makár Semyónitch did not rise, but beat his head on the floor. "Iván Dmítritch, forgive me!" he cried. "When they flogged me with the knout it was not so hard to bear as it is to see you now . . . yet you had pity on me, and did not tell. For Christ's sake forgive me, wretch that I am!" And he began to sob.

When Aksyónof heard him sobbing he, too, began to weep.

"God will forgive you!" said he. "Maybe I am a hundred times worse than you." And at these words his heart grew light, and the longing for home left him. He no longer had any desire to leave the prison, but only hoped for his last hour to come.

In spite of what Aksyónof had said, Makár Semyónitch confessed his guilt. But when the order for his release came, Aksyónof was already dead.

QUESTIONS

1. Why does Tolstoy mention at the outset of the story that Aksyónof had been riotous and drunken in youth and that as a merchant he was "full of fun and very fond of singing"?

2. What is Tolstoy's purpose in rendering Aksyónof's character in such economical and basic terms? What does he gain from the method? What, if anything, does he lose?

3. Aksyónof acts guilty when confronted by the police officer. Is his behavior plausible at this point? Why or why not?

4. Describe Aksyónof's wife. What is her role in the story? What is the importance of her dream?

5. Why does Aksyónof come to the conclusion that he deserved to be imprisoned? What does Tolstoy seem to be saying at this point? Is he criticizing worldly justice or defending the idea of God's justice, or is he doing something else?

6. How does Dmitrich Aksyónof achieve salvation? What is the nature of this salvation? How does it relate to the title of the story?

7. What theme finally emerges from the tale?

TOPICS FOR WRITING

1. Analyze character and theme in the story.

2. Briefly analyze Tolstoy's handling of conflict in the story. What is the source of the conflict in the life of the central character?

Guy de Maupassant

THE PIECE OF STRING

Guy de Maupassant (1850–1893), considered with Chekhov to be one of the two greatest nineteenth-century short story writers, was born at Château de Miromesnil in France to an affluent Norman family. Following a rather tempestuous youth and service in the French army during the Franco-Prussian War, Maupassant settled in Paris, where he associated with notable writers of the era—Flaubert, Turgenev, Zola, Daudet. Apprenticing himself to Flaubert, he published as his first work "Boule de suif" ("Ball of Fat") in 1880 to instant acclaim. In the next decade, Maupassant wrote more than three hundred stories, in addition to novels, plays, and travel sketches. Maupassant's native Normandy provided him with much of the inspiration for his finest stories, which in tone tend to be comic-pessimistic accounts of the foibles of French culture. His pessimism grew much more pronounced toward the end of his life, as the syphilis he had contracted in childhood drove him to madness and a premature death in a sanitarium. One of the superlative short story craftsmen, Maupassant in "The Piece of String" reveals the economical characterization, deft depiction of setting, and subtle irony for which he is famous.

It was market day, and over all the roads round Goderville the peasants and their wives were coming towards the town. The men walked easily, lurching the whole body forward at every step. Their long legs were twisted and deformed by the slow, painful labors of the country: by bending over to plow, which is what also makes their left shoulders too high and their figures crooked; and by reaping corn, which obliges them for steadiness' sake to spread their knees too wide. Their starched blue blouses, shining as though varnished, ornamented at collar and cuffs with little patterns of white stitch-work, and blown up big around their bony bodies, seemed exactly like balloons about to soar, but putting forth a head, two arms, and two feet.

Some of these fellows dragged a cow or a calf at the end of a rope. And just behind the animal, beating it over the back with a leaf-covered branch to hasten its pace, went their wives, carrying large baskets from which came forth the heads of chickens or of ducks. These women walked with steps far shorter and quicker than the men; their figures, withered and upright, were adorned with scanty little shawls pinned over their flat bosoms; and they enveloped their heads each in a white cloth, close fastened round the hair and surmounted by a cap.

Now a char-à-banc passed by, drawn by a jerky-paced nag. It shook up strangely the two men on the seat. And the woman at the bottom of the cart held fast to its sides to lessen the hard joltings.

In the market-place at Goderville was a great crowd, a mingled multitude of men and beasts. The horns of the cattle, the high and long-napped hats of wealthy peasants, the head-dresses of the women, came to the surface of that sea. And voices clamorous, sharp, shrill, made a continuous and savage din. Above it a huge burst of laughter from the sturdy lungs of a merry yokel would sometimes sound, and sometimes a long bellow from a cow tied fast to the wall of a house.

It all smelled of the stable, of milk, of hay, and of perspiration; giving off that half human, half animal odor which is peculiar to the men of the fields.

Maître Hauchecorne, of Bréauté, had just arrived at Goderville, and was taking his way towards the square, when he perceived on the ground a little piece of string. Maître Hauchecorne, economical like all true Normans, reflected that everything was worth picking up which could be of any use; and he stooped down—but painfully, because he suffered with rheumatism. He took the bit of thin cord from the ground, and was carefully preparing to roll it up when he saw Maître Malandain the harnessmaker on his doorstep, looking at him. They had once had a quarrel about a halter, and they had remained angry, bearing malice on both sides. Maître Hauchecorne was overcome with a sort of shame at being seen by his enemy looking in the dirt so for a bit of string. He quickly hid his find beneath his blouse; then in the pocket of his breeches; then pretended to be still looking for something on the ground which he did not discover; and at last went off towards the market-place, with his head bent forward, and a body almost doubled in two by rheumatic pains.

He lost himself immediately in the crowd, which was clamorous, slow, and agitated by interminable bargains. The peasants examined the cows, went off, came back, always in great perplexity and fear of being cheated, never quite daring to decide, spying at the eye of the seller, trying ceaselessly to discover the tricks of the man and the defect in the beast.

The women, having placed their great baskets at their feet, had pulled out the poultry, which lay upon the ground, tied by the legs, with eyes scared, with combs scarlet.

They listened to propositions, maintaining their prices, with a dry manner, with an impassive face; or suddenly, perhaps, deciding to take the lower price which was offered, they cried out to the customer, who was departing slowly:—

"All right: I'll let you have them, Maît' Anthime."

Then, little by little, the square became empty; and when the Angelus struck midday, those who lived at a distance poured into the inns.

At Jourdain's, the great room was filled with eaters, just as the vast court was filled with vehicles of every sort,—wagons, gigs, char-à-bancs, tilburies, tilt-carts which have no name, yellow with mud, misshapen, pieced together, raising their shafts to heaven like two arms, or it may be with their nose in the dirt and their rear in the air.

Just opposite to where the diners were at table, the huge fireplace, full of clear flame, threw a lively heat on the backs of those who sat along the right. Three spits were turning, loaded with chickens, with pigeons, and with joints of mutton; and a delectable odor of roast meat, and of gravy gushing over crisp brown skin, took wing from the hearth, kindled merriment, caused mouths to water.

All the aristocracy of the plow were eating there, at Maît' Jourdain's, the innkeeper's,—a dealer in horses also, and a sharp fellow who had made a pretty penny in his day.

The dishes were passed round, were emptied, with jugs of yellow cider. Every one told of his affairs, of his purchases and his sales. They asked news about the crops. The weather was good for green stuffs, but a little wet for wheat.

All of a sudden the drum rolled in the court before the house. Every one, except some of the most indifferent, was on his feet at once and ran to the door, to the windows, with his mouth still full, and his napkin in his hand.

When the public crier had finished his tattoo, he called forth in a jerky voice, making his pauses out of time:—

"Be it known to the inhabitants of Goderville, and in general to all—persons present at the market, that there has been lost this morning, on the Beuzeville road, between—nine and ten o'clock, a pocket-book of black leather, containing five hundred francs and business papers. You are requested to return it—to the mayor's office at once, or to Maître Fortuné Houlbrèque of Manneville. There will be fifty francs reward."

Then the man departed. They heard once more at a distance the dull beatings on the drum, and the faint voice of the crier.

Then they began to talk of this event, reckoning up the chances which Maître Houlbrèque had of finding or of not finding his pocket-book again.

And the meal went on.

They were finishing their coffee when the corporal of gendarmes appeared on the threshold.

He asked:—

"Is Maître Hauchecorne, of Bréautè, here?"

Maître Hauchecorne, seated at the other end of the table, answered:—

"Here I am."

And the corporal resumed:—

"Maître Hauchecorne, will you have the kindness to come with me to the mayor's office? M. le Laire would like to speak to you."

The peasant, surprised and uneasy, gulped down his little glass of cognac, got up, and—even worse bent over than in the morning, since the first steps after a rest were always particularly difficult—started off, repeating:—

"Here I am, here I am."

And he followed the corporal.

The mayor was waiting for him, seated in an arm-chair. He was the notary of the place, a tall, grave man of pompous speech.

"Maître Hauchecorne," said he, "this morning, on the Beuzeville road, you were seen to pick up the pocket-book lost by Maître Houlbrèque of Manneville."

The countryman, speechless, gazed at the mayor; frightened already by this suspicion, which rested on him he knew not why.

"I—I picked up that pocket-book?"

"Yes, you."

"I swear I didn't even know nothing about it at all."

Guy de Maupassant

"You were seen."

"They saw me—me? Who is that who saw me?"

"M. Malandain, the harness-maker."

Then the old man remembered, understood, and reddening with anger:—

"Ah! he saw me, did he, the rascal? He saw me picking up this string here, M'sieu' le Maire."

And fumbling at the bottom of his pocket, he pulled out of it the little end of string.

But the mayor incredulously shook his head:—

"You will not make me believe, Maître Mauchecorne, that M. Malandain, who is a man worthy of credit, has mistaken this string for a pocket-book."

The peasant, furious, raised his hand and spit as if to attest his good faith, repeating:—

"For all that, it is the truth of the good God, the blessed truth, M'sieu' le Maire. There! on my soul and my salvation I repeat it."

The mayor continued:—

"After picking up the thing in question, you even looked for some time in the mud to see if a piece of money had not dropped out of it."

The good man was suffocated with indignation and with fear.

"If they can say—! If they can say such lies as that to slander an honest man! If they can say—!"

He might protest, he was not believed.

He was confronted with M. Malandain, who repeated and sustained his testimony. They abused one another for an hour. At his own request, Maître Hauchecorne was searched. Nothing was found on him.

At last the mayor, much perplexed, sent him away, warning him that he would inform the public prosecutor and ask for orders.

The news had spread. When he left the mayor's office, the old man was surrounded, interrogated with a curiosity which was serious or mocking as the case might be, but into which no indignation entered. And he began to tell the story of the string. They did not believe him. They laughed.

He passed on, buttonholed by every one, himself buttonholing his acquaintances, beginning over and over again his tale and his protestations, showing his pockets turned inside out to prove that he had nothing.

They said to him:—

"You old rogue, *va!*"

And he grew angry, exasperated, feverish, in despair at not being believed; and always telling his story.

The night came. It was time to go home. He set out with three of his neighbors, to whom he pointed out the place where he had picked up the end of string; and all the way he talked of his adventure.

That evening he made the round in the village of Bréauté, so as to tell every one. He met only unbelievers.

He was ill of it all night long.

The next day, about one in the afternoon, Marius Paumelle, a farm hand of Maître Breton, the market-gardener at Ymauville, returned the pocket-book and its contents to Maître Houlbrèque of Manneville.

This man said that he had indeed found it on the road; but not knowing how to read, he had carried it home and given it to his master.

The news spread to the environs. Maître Hauchecorne was informed. He put

The Piece of String

himself at once upon the go, and began to relate his story as completed by the dénouement. He triumphed.

"What grieved me," said he, "was not the thing itself, do you understand; but it was the lies. There's nothing does you so much harm as being in disgrace for lying."

All day he talked of his adventure; he told it on the roads to the people who passed; at the cabaret to the people who drank; and the next Sunday, when they came out of church. He even stopped strangers to tell them about it. He was easy now, and yet something worried him without his knowing exactly what it was. People had a joking manner while they listened. They did not seem convinced. He seemed to feel their tittle-tattle behind his back.

On Tuesday of the next week he went to market at Goderville, prompted entirely by the need of telling his story.

Malandain, standing on his door-step, began to laugh as he saw him pass. Why?

He accosted a farmer of Criquetot, who did not let him finish, and giving him a punch in the pit of his stomach, cried in his face:—

"Oh you great rogue, *va!*" Then turned his heel upon him.

Maître Hauchecorne remained speechless, and grew more and more uneasy. Why had they called him "great rogue"?

When seated at table in Jourdain's tavern he began again to explain the whole affair.

A horse-dealer of Montivilliers shouted at him:—

"Get out, get out, you old scamp: I know all about your string!"

Hauchecorne stammered:—

"But since they found it again, the pocket-book—!"

But the other continued:—

"Hold your tongue, daddy: there's one who finds it and there's another who returns it. And no one the wiser."

The peasant was choked. He understood at last. They accused him of having had the pocket-book brought back by an accomplice, by a confederate.

He tried to protest. The whole table began to laugh.

He could not finish his dinner, and went away amid a chorus of jeers.

He went home ashamed and indignant, choked with rage, with confusion; the more cast down since from his Norman cunning, he was perhaps capable of having done what they accused him of, and even if boasting of it as a good trick. His innocence dimly seemed to him impossible to prove, his craftiness being so well known. And he felt himself struck to the heart by the injustice of the suspicion.

Then he began anew to tell of his adventure, lengthening his recital every day, each time adding new proofs, more energetic protestations, and more solemn oaths which he thought of, which he prepared in his hours of solitude, his mind being entirely occupied by the story of the string. The more complicated his defense, the more artful his arguments, the less he was believed.

"Those are liars' proofs," they said behind his back.

He felt this; it preyed upon his heart. He exhausted himself in useless efforts.

He was visibly wasting away.

The jokers now made him tell "the story of the piece of string" to amuse them, just as you make a soldier who has been on a campaign tell his story of the battle. His mind, struck at the root, grew weak.

About the end of December he took to his bed.

He died early in January, and in the delirium of the death agony he protested his innocence, repeating:—

"A little bit of string—a little bit of string—see, here it is, M'sieu' le Maire."

QUESTIONS

1. How does Maupassant describe the peasants at the start of the story? What is his purpose in revealing them in deformed or distorted postures? Why does he combine the animal with the human?

2. What is your first impression of Maître Hauchecorne? Where is there foreshadowing of events to come?

3. How does the vivid scene at Jourdain's, of which Hauchecorne is a part, contrast with subsequent events? In what way is the scene involving Hauchecorne's response to the accusations of the mayor similar to the situation in Tolstoy's tale (page 75)?

4. What is the cause of Hauchecorne's increasing desire to tell his story? Why is his fate psychologically convincing? Does his death seem credible to you? Why or why not?

5. What meaning does this story have? How does the theme compare with that in "God Sees the Truth, but Waits" (page 75)?

TOPICS FOR WRITING

1. A critic has written, "Maupassant does not analyze his characters. He takes little interest in the reason why." Evaluate this observation with reference to "The Piece of String."

2. Compare and contrast character development and theme in the stories by Tolstoy (page 75) and Maupassant.

Flannery O'Connor

A GOOD MAN IS HARD TO FIND

Flannery O'Connor (1925–1964) was born in Savannah, Georgia. She attended Georgia State College for Women, where her fondness for drawing cartoons and caricatures hinted at some of her future fiction methods. Awarded a fellowship to the Writers Workshop of the University of Iowa, she received an MFA in creative writing in 1947. Following a brief stay in New York and Connecticut, O'Connor returned to Georgia, living on her mother's farm in Milledgeville. In 1950, she learned that she had the same disease— disseminated lupus—that had killed her father; the last fourteen years of her life involved a painful battle with that illness. O'Connor translates her own suffering into her fiction, as well as her commitment to a transcending Catholic faith. Her novels and stories reflect a distinctive mixture of Christian values and the grotesque. O'Connor once declared that her "subject in fiction is the action of grace in territory held largely by the devil." The devil's territory—our contemporary world—is a landscape populated by grotesque figures—like the Misfit in the following story—who are engaged in violent and destructive action. O'Connor wrote two novels, Wise Blood *(1951) and* The Violent Bear It Away *(1960). Her short stories, three of which won O. Henry first prizes, are collected in* A Good Man Is Hard to Find *(1955) and* Everything That Rises Must Converge *(1965). In the title story from her first collection, O'Connor with deft comic talent transforms a family vacation into a grotesque confrontation with evil and grace.*

The grandmother didn't want to go to Florida. She wanted to visit some of her connections in east Tennessee and she was seizing every chance to change Bailey's mind. Bailey was the son she lived with, her only boy. He was sitting on the edge of his chair at the table, bent over the orange sports section of the *Journal.* "Now look here, Bailey," she said, "see here, read this," and she stood with one hand on her thin hip and the other rattling the newspaper at his bald head. "Here this fellow that calls himself The Misfit is aloose from the Federal Pen and headed toward Florida and you read here what it says he did to these people. Just you read it. I wouldn't take my children in any direction with a criminal like that aloose in it. I couldn't answer to my conscience if I did."

Bailey didn't look up from his reading so she wheeled around then and faced the children's mother; a young mother in slacks, whose face was as broad and innocent as a cabbage and was tied around with a green headkerchief that had two points on the top like rabbit's ears. She was sitting on the sofa, feeding the baby his apricots out of a jar. "The children have been to Florida before," the old lady said. "You all ought to take them somewhere else for a change so they would see different parts of the world and be broad. They never have been to east Tennessee."

The children's mother didn't seem to hear her, but the eight-year-old boy, John Wesley, a stocky child with glasses, said, "If you don't want to go to Florida, why dontcha stay at home?" He and the little girl, June Star, were reading the funny papers on the floor.

"She wouldn't stay at home to be queen for a day," June Star said without raising her yellow head.

"Yes, and what would you do if this fellow, The Misfit, caught you?" the grandmother asked.

"I'd smack his face," John Wesley said.

"She wouldn't stay at home for a million bucks," June Star said. "Afraid she'd miss something. She has to go everywhere we go."

"All right, Miss," the grandmother said. "Just remember that the next time you want me to curl your hair."

June Star said her hair was naturally curly.

The next morning the grandmother was the first one in the car, ready to go. She had her big black valise that looked like the head of a hippopotamus in one corner, and underneath it she was hiding a basket with Pitty Sing, the cat, in it. She didn't intend for the cat to be left alone in the house for three days because he would miss her too much and she was afraid he might brush against one of the gas burners and accidentally asphyxiate himself. Her son, Bailey, didn't like to arrive at a motel with a cat.

She sat in the middle of the back seat with John Wesley and June Star on either side of her. Bailey and the children's mother and the baby sat in the front and they left Atlanta at eight forty-five with the mileage on the car at 55890. The grandmother wrote this down because she thought it would be interesting to say how many miles they had been when they got back. It took them twenty minutes to reach the outskirts of the city.

The old lady settled herself comfortably, removing her white cotton gloves and putting them up with her purse on the shelf in front of the back window. The children's mother still had on slacks and still had her head tied up in a green kerchief, but the grandmother had on a navy blue straw sailor hat with a bunch of white violets on the brim and a navy blue dress with a small white dot in the print. Her collar and cuffs were white organdy trimmed with lace and at her neckline she had pinned a purple spray of cloth violets containing a sachet. In case of an accident, anyone seeing her dead on the highway would know at once that she was a lady.

She said she thought it was going to be a good day for driving, neither too hot nor too cold, and she cautioned Bailey that the speed limit was fifty-five miles an hour and that the patrolmen hid themselves behind bill-boards and small clumps of trees and sped out after you before you had a chance to slow down. She pointed out interesting details of the scenery: Stone Mountain, the blue granite that in some places came up to both sides of the highway; the brilliant red clay banks slightly streaked with purple; and the various crops that made rows of green lack-work on the ground. The trees were full of silver-white sunlights and the meanest of them sparkled. The children were reading comic magazines and their mother had gone back to sleep.

"Let's go through Georgia fast so we won't have to look at it much," John Wesley said.

"If I were a little boy," said the grandmother, "I wouldn't talk about my native state that way. Tennessee has the mountains and Georgia has the hills."

"Tennessee is just a hillbilly dumping ground," John Wesley said, "and Georgia is a lousy state too."

"You said it," June Star said.

"In my time," said the grandmother, folding her thin veined fingers, "children were more respectful of their native states and their parents and everything else. People did right then. Oh look at the cute little pickaninny!" she said and pointed to a Negro child standing in the door of a shack. "Wouldn't that make a picture, now?" she asked and they all turned and looked at the little Negro out of the back window. He waved.

"He didn't have any britches on," June Star said.

"He probably didn't have any," the grandmother explained. "Little niggers in the country don't have things like we do. If I could paint, I'd paint that picture," she said.

The children exchanged comic books.

The grandmother offered to hold the baby and the children's mother passed him over the front seat to her. She set him on her knee and bounced him and told him about the things they were passing. She rolled her eyes and screwed up her mouth and stuck her leathery thin face into his smooth bland one. Occasionally he gave her a faraway smile. They passed a large cotton field with five or six graves fenced in the middle of it, like a small island. "Look at the graveyard!" the grandmother said, pointing it out. "That was the old family burying ground. That belonged to the plantation."

"Where's the plantation?" John Wesley asked.

"Gone With the Wind," said the grandmother. "Ha. Ha."

When the children finished all the comic books they had brought, they opened the lunch and ate it. The grandmother ate a peanut butter sandwich and an olive and would not let the children throw the box and the paper napkins out the window. When there was nothing else to do they played a game by choosing a cloud and making the other two guess what shape it suggested. John Wesley took one the shape of a cow and June Star guessed a cow and John Wesley said, no, an automobile, and June Star said he didn't play fair, and they began to slap each other over the grandmother.

The grandmother said she would tell them a story if they would keep quiet. When she told a story, she rolled her eyes and waved her head and was very dramatic. She said once when she was a maiden lady she had been courted by a Mr. Edgar Atkins Teagarden from Jasper, Georgia. She said he was a very good-looking man and a gentleman and that he brought her a watermelon every Saturday afternoon with his initials cut in it, E. A. T. Well, one Saturday, she said, Mr. Teagarden brought the watermelon and there was nobody at home and he left it on the front porch and returned in his buggy to Jasper, but she never got the watermelon, she said, because a nigger boy ate it when he saw the initials, E. A. T.! This story tickled John Wesley's funny bone and he giggled and giggled but June Star didn't think it was any good. She said she wouldn't marry a man that just brought her a watermelon on Saturday. The grandmother said she would have done well to marry Mr. Teagarden because he was a gentleman and had bought Coca-Cola stock when it first came out and that he had died only a few years ago, a very wealthy man.

They stopped at The Tower for barbecued sandwiches. The Tower was a part-stucco and part-wood filling station and dance hall set in a clearing outside of Timothy. A fat man named Red Sammy Butts ran it and there were signs stuck here and there on the building and for miles up and down the highway saying, TRY RED SAMMY'S FAMOUS BARBECUE. NONE LIKE FAMOUS RED SAMMY'S! RED SAM! THE FAT BOY WITH THE HAPPY LAUGH. A VETERAN! RED SAMMY'S YOUR MAN!

Red Sammy was lying on the bare ground outside The Tower with his head under a truck while a gray monkey about a foot high, chained to a small chinaberry tree, chattered nearby. The monkey sprang back into the tree and got on the highest limb as soon as he saw the children jump out of the car and run toward him.

Inside, The Tower was a long dark room with a counter at one end and tables at the other and dancing space in the middle. They all sat down at a broad table next to the nickelodeon and Red Sam's wife, a tall burnt-brown woman with hair and eyes lighter than her skin, came and took their order. The children's mother put a dime in the machine and played "The Tennessee Waltz," and the grandmother said that tune always made her want to dance. She asked Bailey if he would like to dance but he only glared at her. He didn't have a naturally sunny disposition like she did and trips made him nervous. The grandmother's brown eyes were very bright. She swayed her head from side to side and pretended she was dancing in her chair. June Star said play something she could tap to so the children's mother put in another dime and played a fast number and June Star stepped out onto the dance floor and did her tap routine.

"Ain't she cute?" Red Sam's wife said, leaning over the counter. "Would you like to come be my little girl?"

"No, I certainly wouldn't," June Star said. "I wouldn't live in a broken-down place like this for a million bucks!" and she ran back to the table.

"Ain't she cute?" the woman repeated, stretching her mouth politely.

"Aren't you ashamed?" hissed the grandmother.

Red Sam came in and told his wife to quit lounging on the counter and hurry up with these people's order. His khaki trousers reached just to his hip bones and his stomach hung over them like a sack of meal swaying under his shirt. He came over and sat down at a table nearby and let out a combination sigh and yodel. "You can't win," he said. "You can't win," and he wiped his sweating red face off with a gray handkerchief. "These days you don't know who to trust," he said. "Ain't that the truth?"

"People are certainly not nice like they used to be," said the grandmother.

"Two fellers come in here last week," Red Sammy said, "driving a Chrysler. It was an old beat-up car but it was a good one and these boys looked all right to me. Said they worked at the mill and you know I let them fellers charge the gas they bought? Now why did I do that?"

"Because you're a good man!" the grandmother said at once.

"Yes'm, I suppose so," Red Sam said as if he were struck with this answer.

His wife brought the orders, carrying the five plates all at once without a tray, two in each hand and one balanced on her arm. "It isn't a soul in this green world of God's that you can trust," she said. "And I don't count nobody out of that, not nobody," she repeated, looking at Red Sammy.

"Did you read about that criminal, The Misfit, that's escaped?" asked the grandmother.

"I wouldn't be a bit surprised if he didn't attack this place right here," said the woman. "If he hears about it being here, I wouldn't be none surprised to see him. If he hears it's two cent in the cash register, I wouldn't be a tall surprised if he. . . ."

"That'll do," Red Sam said. "Go bring these people their Co'-Colas," and the woman went off to get the rest of the order.

"A good man is hard to find," Red Sammy said. "Everything is getting terrible. I remember the day you could go off and leave your screen door unlatched. Not no more."

He and the grandmother discussed better times. The old lady said that in her opinion Europe was entirely to blame for the way things were now. She said the way Europe acted you would think we were made of money and Red Sam said it was no use talking about it, she was exactly right. The children ran outside into the white sunlight and looked at the monkey in the lacy chinaberry tree. He was busy catching fleas on himself and biting each one carefully between his teeth as if it were a delicacy.

They drove off again into the hot afternoon. The grandmother took cat naps and woke up every few minutes with her own snoring. Outside of Toombsboro she woke up and recalled an old plantation that she had visited in this neighborhood once when she was a young lady. She said the house had six white columns across the front and that there was an avenue of oaks leading up to it and two little wooden trellis arbors on either side in front where you sat down with your suitor after a stroll in the garden. She recalled exactly which road to turn off to get to it. She knew that Bailey would not be willing to lose any time looking at an old house, but the more she talked about it, the more she wanted to see it once again and find out if the little twin arbors were still standing. "There was a secret panel in this house," she said craftily, not telling the truth but wishing that she were, "and the story went that all the family silver was hidden in it when Sherman came through but it was never found. . . ."

"Hey!" John Wesley said. "Let's go see it! We'll find it! We'll poke all the wood work and find it! Who lives there? Where do you turn off at? Hey Pop, can't we turn off there?"

"We never have seen a house with a secret panel!" June Star shrieked. "Let's go to the house with the secret panel! Hey, Pop, can't we go see the house with the secret panel!"

"It's not far from here, I know," the grandmother said. "It wouldn't take over twenty minutes."

Bailey was looking straight ahead. His jaw was as rigid as a horseshoe. "No," he said.

The children began to yell and scream that they wanted to see the house with the secret panel. John Wesley kicked the back of the front seat and June Star hung over her mother's shoulder and whined desperately into her ear that they never had any fun even on their vacation, that they could never do what THEY wanted to do. The baby began to scream and John Wesley kicked the back of the seat so hard that his father could feel the blows in his kidney.

"All right!" he shouted and drew the car to a stop at the side of the road. "Will you all shut up? Will you all just shut up for one second? If you don't shut up, we won't go anywhere."

"It would be very educational for them," the grandmother murmured.

"All right," Bailey said, "but get this. This is the only time we're going to stop for anything like this. This is the one and only time."

"The dirt road that you have to turn down is about a mile back," the grandmother directed. "I marked it when we passed."

"A dirt road," Bailey groaned.

After they had turned around and were headed toward the dirt road, the grandmother recalled other points about the house, the beautiful glass over the front doorway and the candle lamp in the hall. John Wesley said that the secret panel was probably in the fireplace.

"You can't go inside this house," Bailey said. "You don't know who lives there."

"While you all talk to the people in front, I'll run around behind and get in a window," John Wesley suggested.

"We'll all stay in the car," his mother said.

They turned onto the dirt road and the car raced roughly along in a swirl of pink dust. The grandmother recalled the times when there were no paved roads and thirty miles was a day's journey. The dirt road was hilly and there were sudden washes in it and sharp curves on dangerous embankments. All at once they would be on a hill, looking down over the blue tops of trees for miles around, then the next minute, they would be in a red depression with the dust-coated trees looking down on them.

"This place had better turn up in a minute," Bailey said, "or I'm going to turn around."

The road looked as if no one had traveled on it in months.

"It's not much farther," the grandmother said and just as she said it, a horrible thought came to her. The thought was so embarrassing that she turned red in the face and her eyes dilated and her feet jumped up, upsetting her valise in the corner. The instant the valise moved, the newspaper top she had over the basket under it rose with a snarl and Pitty Sing, the cat, sprang onto Bailey's shoulder.

The children were thrown to the floor and their mother, clutching the baby, was thrown out the door onto the ground; the old lady was thrown into the front seat. The car turned over once and landed right-side-up in a gulch on the side of the road. Bailey remained in the driver's seat with the cat—gray-striped with a broad white face and an orange nose—clinging to his neck like a caterpillar.

As soon as the children saw they could move their arms and legs, they scrambled out of the car, shouting, "We've had an ACCIDENT!" The grandmother was curled up under the dashboard, hoping she was injured so that Bailey's wrath would not come down on her all at once. The horrible thought she had had before the accident was that the house she had remembered so vividly was not in Georgia but in Tennessee.

Bailey removed the cat from his neck with both hands and flung it out the window against the side of a pine tree. Then he got out of the car and started looking for the children's mother. She was sitting against the side of the red gutted ditch, holding the screaming baby, but she only had a cut down her face and a broken shoulder. "We've had an ACCIDENT" the children screamed in a frenzy of delight.

"But nobody's killed," June Star said with disappointment as the grandmother limped out of the car, her hat still pinned to her head but the broken front brim standing up at a jaunty angle and the violet spray hanging off the side. They all sat down in the ditch, except the children, to recover from the shock. They were all shaking.

"Maybe a car will come along," said the children's mother hoarsely.

"I believe I have injured an organ," said the grandmother, pressing her side, but no one answered her. Bailey' s teeth were clattering. He had on a yellow sport shirt with bright blue parrots designed in it and his face was as yellow as the shirt. The grandmother decided that she would not mention that the house was in Tennessee.

The road was about ten feet above and they could see only the tops of the trees on the other side of it. Behind the ditch they were sitting in there were more woods, tall and dark and deep. In a few minutes they saw a car some distance away on top of a hill, coming slowly as if the occupants were watching them. The grandmother stood up and waved both arms dramatically to attract their attention. The car continued to come on slowly, disappeared around a bend and appeared again, moving even slower, on top of the hill they had gone over. It was a big black battered hearselike automobile. There were three men in it.

It came to a stop just over them and for some minutes, the driver looked down with a steady expressionless gaze to where they were sitting, and didn't speak. Then he turned his head and muttered something to the other two and they got out. One was a fat boy in black trousers and a red sweat shirt with a silver stallion embossed on the front of it. He moved around on the right side of them and stood staring, his mouth partly open in a kind of loose grin. The other had on khaki pants and a blue striped coat and a gray hat pulled down very low, hiding most of his face. He came around slowly on the left side. Neither spoke.

The driver got out of the car and stood by the side of it, looking down at them. He was an older man than the other two. His hair was just beginning to gray and he wore silver-rimmed spectacles that gave him a scholary look. He had a long creased face and didn't have on any shirt or undershirt. He had on blue jeans that were too tight for him and was holding a black hat and a gun. The two boys also had guns.

"We've had an ACCIDENT!" the children screamed.

The grandmother had the peculiar feeling that the bespectacled man was someone she knew. His face was as familiar to her as if she had known him all her life but she could not recall who he was. He moved away from the car and began to come down the embankment, placing his feet carefully so that he wouldn't slip. He had on tan and white shoes and no socks, and his ankles were red and thin. "Good afternoon," he said. "I see you all had you a little spill."

"We turned over twice!" said the grandmother.

"Oncet," he corrected. "We see it happen. Try their car and see will it run, Hiram," he said quietly to the boy with the gray hat.

"What you got that gun for?" John Wesley asked. "Whatcha gonna do with that gun?"

"Lady," the man said to the children's mother, "would you mind calling them children to sit down by you? Children make me nervous. I want all you all to sit down right together there where you're at."

"What are you telling us what to do for?" June Star asked.

Behind them the line of woods gaped like a dark open mouth. "Come here," said their mother.

"Look here now," Bailey began suddenly, "we're in a predicament! We're in. . . ."

The grandmother shrieked. She scrambled to her feet and stood staring. "You're The Misfit!" she said. "I recognized you at once!"

"Yes'm," the man said, smiling slightly as if he were pleased in spite of himself to be known, "but it would have been better for all of you, lady, if you hadn't of reckernized me."

Bailey turned his head sharply and said something to his mother that shocked even the children. The old lady began to cry and The Misfit reddened.

"Lady," he said, "don't you get upset. Sometimes a man says things he don't mean. I don't reckon he meant to talk to you thataway."

"You wouldn't shoot a lady, would you?" the grandmother said and removed a clean handkerchief from her cuff and began to slap at her eyes with it.

The Misfit pointed the toe of his shoe into the ground and made a little hole and then covered it up again. "I would hate to have to," he said.

"Listen," the grandmother almost screamed, "I know you're a good man. You don't look a bit like you have common blood. I know you must come from nice people!"

"Yes mam," he said, "finest people in the world." When he smiled he showed a row of strong white teeth. "God never made a finer woman than my mother and my daddy's heart was pure gold," he said. The boy with the red sweat shirt had come around behind them and was standing with his gun at his hip. The Misfit squatted down on the ground. "Watch them children, Bobby Lee," he said. "You know they make me nervous." He looked at the six of them huddled together in front of him and he seemed to be embarrassed as if he couldn't think of anything to say. "Ain't a cloud in the sky," he remarked, looking up at it. "Don't see no sun but don't see no cloud neither."

"Yes, it's a beautiful day," said the grandmother. "Listen," she said, "you shouldn't call yourself The Misfit because I know you're a good man at heart. I can just look at you and tell."

"Hush!" Bailey yelled. "Hush! Everybody shut up and let me handle this!" He was squatting in the position of a runner about to sprint forward but he didn't move.

"I pre-chate that, lady," The Misfit said and drew a little circle in the ground with the butt of his gun.

"It'll take a half a hour to fix this here car," Hiram called, looking over the raised hood of it.

"Well, first you and Bobby Lee get him and that little boy to step over yonder with you," The Misfit said, pointing to Bailey and John Wesley. "The boys want to ask you something," he said to Bailey. "Would you mind stepping back in them woods there with them?"

"Listen," Bailey began, "we're in a terrible predicament! Nobody realizes what this is," and his voice cracked. His eyes were as blue and intense as the parrots in his shirt and he remained perfectly still.

The grandmother reached up to adjust her hat brim as if she were going to the woods with him but it came off in her hand. She stood staring at it and after a second she let it fall on the ground. Hiram pulled Bailey up by the arm as if he were assisting an old man. John Wesley caught hold of his father's hand and Bobby Lee followed. They went off toward the woods and just as they reached the dark edge, Bailey turned and supporting himself against a gray naked pine trunk, he shouted, "I'll be back in a minute, Mamma, wait on me!"

"Come back this instant!" his mother shrilled but they all disappeared into the woods.

"Bailey Boy!" the grandmother called in a tragic voice but she found she was looking at The Misfit squatting on the ground in front of her. "I just know you're a good man," she said desperately. "You're not a bit common!"

"Nome, I ain't a good man," The Misfit said after a second as if he had considered her statement carefully, "but I ain't the worst in the world neither. My daddy said I was a different breed of dog from my brothers and sisters. 'You know,' Daddy said, 'it's some that can live their whole life out without asking about it and it's others has to know why it is, and this boy is one of the latters. He's going to be into everything!'" He put on his black hat and looked up suddenly and then away deep into the woods as if he were embarrassed again. "I'm sorry, I don't have on a shirt before you ladies," he said, hunching his shoulders slightly. "We buried our clothes that we had on when we escaped and we're just making do until we can get better. We borrowed these from some folks we met," he explained.

"That's perfectly all right," the grandmother said. "Maybe Bailey has an extra shirt in his suitcase."

"I'll look and see terrectly," The Misfit said.

"Where are they taking him?" the children's mother screamed.

"Daddy was a card himself," The Misfit said. "You couldn't put anything over on him. He never got in trouble with the Authorities though. Just had the knack of handling them."

"You could be honest too if you'd only try," said the grandmother. "Think how wonderful it would be to settle down and live a comfortable life and not have to think about somebody chasing you all the time."

The Misfit kept scratching in the ground with the butt of his gun as if he were thinking about it. "Yes'm, somebody is always after you," he murmured.

The grandmother noticed how thin his shoulder blades were just behind his hat because she was standing up looking down on him. "Do you ever pray?" she asked.

He shook his head. All she saw was the black hat wiggle between his shoulder blades. "Nome," he said.

There was a pistol shot from the woods, followed closely by another. Then silence. The old lady's head jerked around. She could hear the wind move through the tree tops like a long satisifed insuck of breath. "Bailey Boy!" she called.

"I was a gospel singer for a while," The Misfit said. "I been most everything. Been in the arm service, both land and sea, at home and abroad, been twict married, been an undertaker, been with the railroads, plowed Mother Earth, been in a tornado, seen a man burnt alive oncet," and he looked up at the children's mother and the little girl who were sitting close together, their faces white and their eyes glass; "I even seen a woman flogged," he said.

"Pray, pray," the grandmother began, "pray, pray. . . ."

"I never was a bad boy that I remember of," The Misfit said in an almost dreamy voice, "but somewheres along the line I done something wrong and got sent to the penitentiary. I was buried alive," and he looked up and held her attention to him by a steady stare.

"That's when you should have started to pray," she said. "What did you do to get sent to the penitentiary that first time?"

"Turn to the right, it was a wall," The Misfit said, looking up again at the cloudless sky. "Turn to the left, it was a wall. Look up it was a ceiling, look down it was a floor. I forget what I done, lady. I set there and set there, trying to remember what it was I done and I ain't recalled it to this day. Oncet in a while, I would think it was coming to me, but it never come."

"Maybe they put you in by mistake," the old lady said vaguely.

"Nome," he said. "It wasn't no mistake. They had the papers on me."

"You must have stolen something," she said.

The Misfit sneered slightly. "Nobody had nothing I wanted," he said. "It was a head-doctor at the penitentiary said what I had done was kill my daddy but I known that for a lie. My daddy died in nineteen ought nineteen of the epidemic flu and I never had a thing to do with it. He was buried in the Mount Hopewell Baptist churchyard and you can go there and see for yourself."

"If you would pray," the old lady said, "Jesus would help you."

"That's right," The Misfit said.

"Well then, why don't you pray?" she asked trembling with delight suddenly.

"I don't want no hep," he said. "I'm doing all right by myself."

Bobby Lee and Hiram came ambling back from the woods. Bobby Lee was dragging a yellow shirt with bright blue parrots in it.

"Throw me that shirt, Bobby Lee," The Misfit said. The shirt came flying at him and landed on his shoulder and he put it on. The grandmother couldn't name what the shirt reminded her of. "No, lady," The Misfit said while he was buttoning it up, "I found out the crime don't matter. You can do one thing or you can do another, kill a man or take a tire off his car, because sooner or later you're going to forget what it was you done and just be punished for it."

The children's mother had begun to make heaving noises as if she couldn't get her breath. "Lady," he asked, "would you and that little girl like to step off yonder with Bobby Lee and Hiram and join your husband?"

"Yes, thank you," the mother said faintly. Her left arm dangled helplessly and she was holding the baby, who had gone to sleep, in the other. "Hep that lady up, Hiram," The Misfit said as she struggled to climb out of the ditch, "and Bobby Lee, you hold onto that little girl's hand."

"I don't want to hold hands with him," June Star said. "He reminds me of a pig."

The fat boy blushed and laughed and caught her by the arm and pulled her off into the woods after Hiram and her mother.

Alone with The Misfit, the grandmother found that she had lost her voice. There was not a cloud in the sky nor any sun. There was nothing around her but woods. She wanted to tell him that he must pray. She opened and closed her mouth several times before anything came out. Finally she found herself saying, "Jesus, Jesus," meaning, Jesus will help you, but the way she was saying it, it sounded as if she might be cursing.

"Yes'm," The Misfit said as if he agreed. "Jesus thrown everything off balance. It was the same case with Him as with me except He hadn't committed any crime and they could prove I had committed one because they had the papers on me. Of course," he said, "they never shown me my papers. That's why I sign myself now. I said long ago, you get you a signature and sign everything you do and keep a copy of it. Then you'll know what you done and you can hold up the crime to the punishment and see do they match and in the end you'll have something to prove you ain't been treated right. I call myself The Misfit," he said, "because I can't make what all I done wrong fit what all I gone through in punishment."

There was a piercing scream from the woods, followed closely by a pistol report. "Does it seem right to you, lady, that one is punished a heap and another ain't punished at all?"

"Jesus!" the old lady cried. "You've got good blood! I know you wouldn't shoot a lady! I know you come from nice people! Pray! Jesus, you ought not to shoot a lady. I'll give you all the money I've got!"

"Lady," The Misfit said, looking beyond her far into the woods, "there never was a body that give the undertaker a tip."

There were two more pistol reports and the grandmother raised her head like

A Good Man Is Hard to Find

a parched old turkey hen crying for water and called, "Bailey Boy, Baily Boy!" as if her heart would break.

"Jesus was the only One that ever raised the dead," The Misfit continued, "and He shouldn't have done it. He thrown everything off balance. If He did what He said, then it's nothing for you to do but throw away everything and follow Him, and if He didn't then it's nothing for you to do but enjoy the few minutes you got left the best way you can—by killing somebody or burning down his house or doing some other meanness to him. No pleasure but meanness," he said and his voice had become almost a snarl.

"Maybe He didn't raise the dead," the old lady mumbled, not knowing what she was saying and feeling so dizzy that she sank down in the ditch with her legs twisted under her.

"I wasn't there so I can't say He didn't," The Misfit said. "I wisht I had of been there," he said, hitting the ground with his fist. "It ain't right I wasn't there because if I had of been there I would of known. Listen lady," he said in a high voice, "if I had of been there I would of known and I wouldn't be like I am now." His voice seemed about to crack and the grandmother's head cleared for an instant. She saw the man's face twisted close to her own as if he were going to cry and she murmured, "Why, you're one of my babies. You're one of my own children!" She reached out and touched him on the shoulder. The Misfit sprang back as if a snake had bitten him and shot her three times through the chest. Then he put his gun down on the ground and took off his glasses and began to clean them.

Hiram and Bobby Lee returned from the woods and stood over the ditch, looking down at the grandmother who half sat and half lay in a puddle of blood with her legs crossed under her like a child's and her face smiling up at the cloudless sky.

Without his glasses, The Misfit's eyes were red-rimmed and pale and defenseless-looking. "Take her off and throw her where you thrown the others," he said, picking up the cat that was rubbing itself against his leg.

"She was a talker, wasn't she?" Bobby Lee said, sliding down the ditch with a yodel.

"She would of been a good woman," The Misfit said, "if it had been somebody there to shoot her every minute of her life."

"Some fun!" Bobby Lee said.

"Shut up, Bobby Lee," The Misfit said. "It's no real pleasure in life."

QUESTIONS

1. What methods does O'Connor use to create a memorable family portrait in the first few paragraphs of the story? How realistic is the character depiction? Where does she employ comedy, exaggeration, and distortion?

2. How do the family members contrive to create their own fate?

3. Why does O'Connor make the action of the story so memorably violent?

4. The two key characters in the story are the grandmother and The Misfit. How is the grandmother characterized? What traditional values does she repre-

sent? What is the author's attitude toward the grandmother? Cite evidence to support your statement.

5. Who exactly is The Misfit? In what ways is he a misfit? Is he more than a criminal or psychopath? Explain. Why is he preoccupied with Jesus? Why does he kill the grandmother and all the members of her family?

6. How does the title of the story point toward the theme? What statement is O'Connor making about goodness and evil in modern times? About crime and punishment? About justice?

TOPICS FOR WRITING

1. O'Connor once declared in an interview that the short story "has an extra dimension and I think this extra dimension comes about when the writer puts us in the middle of some human action and shows it as it is illuminated and outlined by mystery." Write an essay applying this statement to character, action, and theme in "A Good Man Is Hard to Find."

2. Analyze the comic-grotesque method of character development in the story, showing how it contributes to a definition of the theme.

3. Compare and contrast the interrelationship of character, religion, and theme in the stories by Tolstoy (page 75) and O'Connor.

4. Explore the theme of crime and punishment and its impact on the lives of the characters in the three stories in this section.

4

POINT OF VIEW
AND THEME:
SELF-DISCOVERY

Point of view is the position or vantage point from which the author presents the action of the story. It is the point from which the writer decides to tell the tale. "The whole intricate question of method," writes Percy Lubbock in *The Craft of Fiction* (1921), "I take to be governed by the question of point of view—the question of the relation in which the author stands to the story." Through point of view, we are permitted to see from a special narrative perspective the actions, events, and characters that an author creates. Thus point of view is one of the most important technical considerations for fiction writers, because it directly influences all other elements in a tale.

Although the history of fiction reveals numerous ways of disclosing information through different narrative perspectives, criticism traditionally has focused on three major types of point of view: (1) *omniscient*, where the author sees and knows everything, moving across space and time, commenting on character and action, an all-knowing, godlike creator; (2) *first person*, in which the author allows one character to tell the story, thereby limiting himself or herself to what can be seen, heard, felt, thought, or known by that single character; and (3) *third person*, in which actions, thoughts, and perceptions are filtered in the third person (signaled by the pronouns "he," "she," "it," and "they") through the mind of one character or the minds of several characters. By selecting one point of view or by combining points of view, the author attempts to persuade the reader, who hears a special "voice" operating in the story, to accept the world that is being created in fiction and to view the life forces inherent in the tale from a special perspective.

Writers of fiction—from Homer to Chaucer to Joyce—have always been alert to the need to create a special angle of vision in order to produce an authentic, or believable, world and to illuminate that world. In the early history of both the novel and short fiction, authors would often call attention to the fact that they were telling the tale, and indeed this form of omniscience is one of the oldest points of view, stemming perhaps from the oral tradition. Many of the greatest eighteenth- and nineteenth-century novels—Fielding's *Tom Jones*, Sterne's *Tristram Shandy*, Hawthorne's *The Scarlet Letter*, George Eliot's *The Mill on the Floss*, Tolstoy's *Anna Karenina*—use this omniscient method. For example, Tolstoy writes in one of the most famous opening paragraphs in fiction: "Happy families are all alike; every unhappy family is unhappy in its own way." In *Anna Karenina*, we hear Tolstoy, the demigod, telling us *his* story, giving us *his* views from the outset of the narrative.

We also sense omniscience or authorial intrusion in Nathaniel Hawthorne's "Young Goodman Brown," presented in this section. At times, Hawthorne limits the omniscience to the mind of the protagonist, but he also reserves the right to be omniscient, or all-knowing; he even editorializes, or comments on the action, notably at the end of the tale. In fact, after reading this mysterious, temptingly symbolic story, we might very well wish that Hawthorne had editorialized even more in order to resolve some of the ambiguities raised by the narrative.

However, as fiction moved toward the twentieth century, it became increasingly unfashionable for authors to adopt a baldly omniscient point of view. James in his prefaces criticized some of his literary contemporaries for authorial intrusion—for inserting themselves into the action and commenting on it. In modern fiction, we do not see and hear the author as directly as we once did. The author, in the words of James Joyce, vanishes: "The artist, like the God of creation, remains within or behind or beyond his handiwork, invisible, refined out of existence, indifferent, paring his fingernails." Of course, there is *always* an implied author in the tale (a point that Wayne Booth posits brilliantly in *The Rhetoric of Fiction*), but typically the voice of the author, his or her second self, assumes a muted presence in modern fiction.

The common aim of many modern fiction writers is to achieve invisibility by utilizing a variety of points of view that we might think of as corresponding to different lenses for a camera. Each change of lens alters the relationship between the form and the subject. Typically, the storyteller will hide behind one of several first-person or third-person lenses, or points of view. With the first-person point of view, the narrator speaks from the "I" frame of reference. Actually the first-person point of view is not a peculiarly modern type; it derives from fictional memoirs, such as Goldsmith's *Vicar of Wakefield*, and from epistolary fiction, such as Richardson's *Clarissa*, and it prevails in such first-person masterpieces as *Jane Eyre, Huckleberry Finn*, and *Great Expectations*. Speaking from the "I" vantage point, the imaginary author can project himself or herself as a participant in the action, an observer of the action, or both an observer and a participant. The speaker can be a major or minor character in the story. The advantage of this first-person point of view, which is evident in another story in this section, James Joyce's "Araby," is that a special immediacy and intimacy—a confessional quality—can be achieved. (Joyce also plots this tale in order to achieve at the end a special effect that he termed an *epiphany*, an intense moment of self-awareness or revelation.) However, there are also significant limitations to the first-person point of view. James, for one, spoke of the "terrible fluidity of self-revelation" with the first-person narrator. Moreover, the narrator cannot see into the minds of others; special angles or perspectives on events cannot be created easliy; events that the narrator has not witnessed cannot be recounted reliably. In fact, the very reliability of the first-person narrator can be called into question. Authors, of course, strive to solve these problems. For instance, they often employ the device of a story within a story in order to achieve a more balanced perspective, a framing technique favored by James in *The Turn of the Screw* and by Conrad in *Heart of Darkness*.

Authors can avoid some of the problems posed by first-person point of view (but at the same time raise new issues for themselves) by selecting a third-person point of view. This third-person point of view can be limited or unlimited. With a limited third-person point of view, the action is filtered through the mind or consciousness of only one character. This is the case in Joyce Carol Oates' "Stalking," the third story in this section. As readers, we know only what the central consciousness thinks and does; we cannot enter into the mind of any other character. This is a popular strategy for modern short story authors and novelists, for they can present "reality" from a consistent perspective. If we perceive reality from a single perspective, we are inclined as readers to detect a resemblance between what we see in fiction and the way we view the world. In addition, with the limited third-person point of view, the inner experiences of one individual tend to unify the world of the tale. Therefore, from this narrative perspective the illusion is created that we are sharing the thoughts, feelings, and perceptions of a character who is confronting the world from a clear angle of vision.

If authors desire a greater perspective on action and events, they can resort to a multiple or unlimited third-person point of view. Here they enter the minds of two or more characters. The scope of the lens is broad; in fact, it can amount for all practical purposes to a form of omniscience. The method can lead to an erosion of the illusion of reality, and thus the short story writer must possess considerable skill in order to move successfully from one consciousness to another without destroying either the unity of the tale or the impression that what is happening is real rather than contrived.

A final variety of third-person point of view arises when authors refuse to enter the mind of any character, achieving what we term an *objective*, or *dramatic*, third-person point of view. In this situation, a writer views characters as we would view other people in normal life. These figures are like characters on the street or figures in a play. We can interpret them only through their actions and words, their behavior and dress, and what others say the street or figures in a play are. The effect created by an objective point of view is very special, as a story that appears later in this anthology, Hemingway's "The Killers" (page 270), reveals.

Each type of point of view has its special functions, powers, and limitations. Great writers can either stay within the limits of these modes, mining them successfully, or combine modes. Melville in *Moby Dick*, Dickens in *Bleak House*, and Faulkner in *The Sound and the Fury* work marvelously with mixed modes, "bouncing" us, as Forster said, from one type of point of view to another. Writers also invent new techniques to enrich point of view, as when Joyce, Faulkner, and Virginia Woolf employ "stream of consciousness" methods that put us next to the highly associative thought processes of their characters.

As you read the stories in this section and other stories in the anthology, ask yourself why the author has selected a certain point of view. Who tells the story? Is he or she reliable or unreliable, and why? What are the advantages and disadvantages of point of view in a specific tale? Are there any special features to the point of view? What effects does point of view have on character, language, and setting? Finally, how does point of view contribute to the development of the story's theme? The stories in this chapter deal with discoveries that young protagonists make about the nature of the world and about their alienation from the world. These characters live for us through point of view and other techniques. They live with or without authorial intrusion, apart from the author's real self. "We must," declared Flaubert, "by an effort of mind, go over to our characters, as it were, not make them come over to us." Point of view accomplishes this transformation. With a successful short story, the lens selected by the author always conveys the best and most illuminating perspective on character and action, subject and theme.

Nathaniel Hawthorne

YOUNG GOODMAN BROWN

Nathaniel Hawthorne (1804–1869) was born in Salem, Massachusetts. Salem had been the setting for the infamous witchcraft trials of 1692, and one of Hawthorne's ancestors had been a presiding judge. This sense of family guilt, linked to the burden of Puritan history, would temper some of Hawthorne's greatest work. Following graduation from Bowdoin College in Maine in 1825, Hawthorne returned to Salem and entered into a relatively isolated twelve-year period of writing that culminated in the publication of Twice-Told Tales in 1837. But it was not until 1850, after a felicitous marriage, an experiment in utopian living at Brook Farm, and a move to the Old Manse in Concord, that Hawthorne achieved fame with the publication of The Scarlet Letter. *This novel, along with* The House of the Seven Gables *(1851) and his finest short fiction, centers on sin, evil, guilt, and the mysterious—almost supernatural—workings of these forces in human affairs. In the story that follows, Hawthorne reveals through point of view and other techniques the shifting patterns of perception in young Goodman Brown as the protagonist moves from innocence to experience.*

Young Goodman Brown came forth at sunset into the street at Salem village; but put his head back, after crossing the threshold, to exchange a parting kiss with his young wife. And Faith, as the wife was aptly named, thrust her own pretty head into the street, letting the wind play with the pink ribbons of her cap while she called to Goodman Brown.

"Dearest heart," whispered she, softly and rather sadly, when her lips were close to his ear, "prithee put off your journey until sunrise and sleep in your own bed to-night. A lone woman is troubled with such dreams and such thoughts that she's afeard of herself sometimes. Pray tarry with me this night, dear husband, of all nights in the year."

"My love and my Faith," replied young Goodman Brown, "of all nights in the year, this one night must I tarry away from thee. My journey, as thou callest it, forth and back again, must needs be done 'twixt now and sunrise. What, my sweet, pretty wife, dost thou doubt me already, and we but three months married?"

"Then God bless you!" said Faith, with the pink ribbons; "and may you find all well when you come back."

"Amen!" cried Goodman Brown. "Say thy prayers, dear Faith, and go to bed at dusk, and no harm will come to thee."

So they parted; and the young man pursued his way until, being about to turn the corner by the meeting-house, he looked back and saw the head of Faith still peeping after him with a melancholy air, in spite of her pink ribbons.

"Poor little Faith!" thought he, for his heart smote him. "What a wretch am I to leave her on such an errand! She talks of dreams, too. Methought as she spoke there was trouble in her face, as if a dream had warned her what work is to be done to-night. But no, no; 't would kill her to think it. Well, she's a blessed angel on earth; and after this one night I'll cling to her skirts and follow her to heaven."

With this excellent resolve for the future, Goodman Brown felt himself justified in making more haste on his present evil purpose. He had taken a dreary road, darkened by all the gloomiest trees of the forest, which barely stood aside to let the narrow path creep through, and closed immediately behind. It was all as lonely as could be; and there is this peculiarity in such a solitude, that the traveller knows not who may be concealed by the innumerable trunks and the thick boughs overhead; so that with lonely footsteps he may yet be passing through an unseen multitude.

"There may be a devilish Indian behind every tree," said Goodman Brown to himself; and he glanced fearfully behind him as he added, "What if the devil himself should be at my very elbow!"

His head being turned back, he passed a crook of the road, and, looking forward again, beheld the figure of a man, in grave and decent attire, seated at the foot of an old tree. He arose at Goodman Brown's approach and walked onward side by side with him.

"You are late, Goodman Brown," said he. "The clock of the Old South was striking as I came through Boston, and that is full fifteen minutes agone."

"Faith kept me back a while," replied the young man, with a tremor in his voice, caused by the sudden appearance of his companion, though not wholly unexpected.

It was now deep dusk in the forest, and deepest in that part of it where these two were journeying. As nearly as could be discerned, the second traveller was about fifty years old, apparently in the same rank of life as Goodman Brown, and bearing a considerable resemblance to him, though perhaps more in expression than features. Still they might have been taken for father and son. And yet, though the elder person was as simply clad as the younger, and as simple in manner too, he had an indescribable air of one who knew the world, and who would not have felt abashed at the governor's dinner table or in King William's court, were it possible that his affairs should call him thither. But the only thing about him that could be fixed upon as remarkable was his staff, which bore the likeness of a great black snake, so curiously wrought that it might almost be seen to twist and wriggle itself like a living serpent. This, of course, must have been an ocular deception, assisted by the uncertain light.

"Come, Goodman Brown," cried his fellow-traveler, "this is a dull pace for the beginning of a journey. Take my staff, if you are so soon weary."

"Friend," said the other, exchanging his slow pace for a full stop, "having kept covenant by meeting thee here, it is my purpose now to return whence I came. I have scruples touching the matter thou wot'st of."

"Sayest thou so?" replied he of the serpent, smiling apart. "Let us walk on, nevertheless, reasoning as we go; and if I convince thee not thou shalt turn back. We are but a little way in the forest yet."

"Too far! too far!" exclaimed the goodman, unconsciously resuming his walk. "My father never went into the woods on such an errand, nor his father before him. We have been a race of honest men and good Christians since the days of the martyrs; and shall I be the first of the name of Brown that ever took this path and kept"—

"Such company, thou wouldst say," observed the elder person, interpreting his pause. "Well said, Goodman Brown! I have been as well acquainted with your family as with ever a one among the Puritans; and that's no trifle to say. I helped your grandfather, the constable, when he lashed the Quaker woman so smartly through the streets of Salem; and it was I that brought your father a pitchpine knot, kindled at my own hearth, to set fire to an Indian village, in King Philip's war. They were my good friends, both; and many a pleasant walk have we had along this path, and returned merrily after midnight. I would fain be friends with you for their sake."

"If it be as thou sayest," replied Goodman Brown, "I marvel they never spoke of these matters; or, verily, I marvel not, seeing that the least rumor of the sort would have driven them from New England. We are a people of prayer, and good works to boot, and abide no such wickedness."

"Wickedness or not," said the traveller with the twisted staff, "I have a very general acquaintance here in New England. The deacons of many a church have drunk the communion wine with me; the selectmen of divers towns make me their chairman; and a majority of the Great and General Court are firm supporters of my interest. The governor and I, too—But these are state secrets."

"Can this be so?" cried Goodman Brown, with a stare of amazement at his undisturbed companion. "Howbeit, I have nothing to do with the governor and council; they have their own ways, and are no rule for a simple husbandman like me. But, were I to go on with thee, how should I meet the eye of that good old man, our minister, at Salem village? Oh, his voice would make me tremble both Sabbath day and lecture day."

Thus far the elder traveller had listened with due gravity; but now burst into a fit of irrepressible mirth, shaking himself so violently that his snake-like staff actually seemed to wriggle in sympathy.

"Ha! ha! ha!" shouted he again and again; then composing himself, "Well, go on, Goodman Brown, go on; but, prithee, don't kill me with laughing."

"Well, then, to end the matter at once," said Goodman Brown, considerably nettled, "there is my wife, Faith. It would break her dear little heart; and I'd rather break my own."

"Nay, if that be the case," answered the other, "e'en go thy ways, Goodman Brown. I would not for twenty old women like the one hobbling before us that Faith should come to any harm."

As he spoke he pointed his staff at a female figure on the path, in whom Goodman Brown recognized a very pious and exemplary dame, who had taught him his catechism in youth, and was still his moral and spiritual adviser, jointly with the minister and Deacon Gookin.

"A marvel, truly, that Goody Cloyse should be so far in the wilderness at nightfall," said he. "But with your leave, friend, I shall take a cut through the woods until we have left this Christian woman behind. Being a stranger to you, she might ask whom I was consorting with and whither I was going."

"Be it so," said his fellow-traveller. "Betake you the woods, and let me keep the path."

Accordingly the young man turned aside; but took care to watch his companion, who advanced softly along the road until he had come within a staff's length of the old dame. She, meanwhile, was making the best of her way, with singular speed for so aged a woman, and mumbling some indistinct words—a prayer, doubtless—as she went. The traveller put forth his staff and touched her withered neck with what seemed the serpent's tail.

"The devil!" screamed the pious old lady.

"Then Goody Cloyse knows her old friend?" observed the traveller, confronting her and leaning on his writhing stick.

"Ah, forsooth, and is it your worship indeed?" cried the good dame. "Yea, truly is it, and in the very image of my old gossip, Goodman Brown, the grandfather of the silly fellow that now is. But—would your worship believe it?—my broomstick hath strangely disappeared, stolen, as I suspect, by that unhanged witch, Goody Cory, and that, too, when I was all anointed with the juice of smallage, and cinquefoil, and wolf's bane"—

"Mingled with fine wheat and the fat of a new-born babe," said the shape of old Goodman Brown.

"Ah, your worship knows the recipe," cried the old lady, cackling aloud. "So, as I was saying, being all ready for the meeting, and no horse to ride on, I made up my mind to foot it; for they tell me there is a nice young man to be taken into communion to-night. But now your good worship will lend me your arm, and we shall be there in a twinkling."

"That can hardly be," answered her friend. "I may not spare you my arm, Goody Cloyse; but here is my staff, if you will."

So saying, he threw it down at her feet, where, perhaps, it assumed life, being one of the rods which its owner had formerly lent to the Egyptian magi. Of this fact, however, Goodman Brown could not take cognizance. He had cast up his eyes in astonishment, and, looking down again, beheld neither Goody Cloyse nor the serpentine staff, but this fellow-traveller alone, who waited for him as calmly as if nothing had happened.

"That old woman taught me my catechism," said the young man; and there was a world of meaning in this simple comment.

They continued to walk onward, while the elder traveller exhorted his companion to make good speed and persevere in the path, discoursing so aptly that his arguments seemed rather to spring up in the bosom of his auditor than to be suggested by himself. As they went, he plucked a branch of maple to serve for a walking stick, and began to strip it of the twigs and little boughs, which were wet with evening dew. The moment his fingers touched them they became strangely withered and dried up as with a week's sunshine. Thus the pair proceeded, at a good free pace, until suddenly, in a gloomy hollow of the road, Goodman Brown sat himself down on the stump of a tree and refused to go any farther.

"Friend," said he, stubbornly, "my mind is made up. Not another step will I budge on this errand. What if a wretched old woman do choose to go to the devil when I thought she was going to heaven: is that any reason why I should quit my dear Faith and go after her?"

"You will think better of this by and by," said his acquaintance, composedly. "Sit here and rest yourself a while; and when you feel like moving again, there is my staff to help you along."

Without more words, he threw his companion the maple stick, and was as speedily out of sight as if he had vanished into the deepening gloom. The young man sat a few moments by the roadside, applauding himself greatly, and thinking with how clear a conscience he should meet the minister in his morning walk, nor shrink from the eye of good old Deacon Gookin. And what calm sleep would be his that very night, which was to have been spent so wickedly, but so purely and sweetly now, in the arms of Faith! Amidst these pleasant and praiseworthy meditations, Goodman Brown heard the tramp of horses along the road, and deemed it advisable to conceal himself within the verge of the forest, conscious of the guilty purpose that had brought him thither, though now so happily turned from it.

On came the hoof tramps and the voices of the riders, two grave old voices, conversing soberly as they drew near. These mingled sounds appeared to pass along the road, within a few yards of the young man's hiding-place; but, owing doubtless to the depth of the gloom at that particular spot, neither the travellers nor their steeds were visible. Though their figures brushed the small boughs by the wayside, it could not be seen that they intercepted, even for a moment, the faint gleam from the strip of bright sky athwart which they must have passed. Goodman Brown alternately crouched and stood on tiptoe, pulling aside the branches and thrusting forth his head as far as he durst without discerning so much as a shadow. It vexed him the more, because he could have sworn, were such a thing possible, that he recognized the voices of the minister and Deacon

Gookin, jogging along quietly, as they were wont to do, when bound to some ordination of ecclesiastical council. While yet within hearing, one of the riders stopped to pluck a switch.

"Of the two, reverend sir," said the voice like the deacon's, "I had rather miss an ordination dinner than to-night's meeting. They tell me that some of our community are to be here from Falmouth and beyond, and others from Connecticut and Rhode Island, besides several of the Indian powwows, who, after their fashion, know almost as much deviltry as the best of us. Moreover, there is a goodly young woman to be taken into communion."

"Mighty well, Deacon Gookin!" replied the solemn old tones of the minister. "Spur up, or we shall be late. Nothing can be done, you know, until I get on the ground."

The hoofs clattered again; and the voices, talking so strangely in the empty air, passed on through the forest, where no church had ever been gathered or solitary Christian prayed. Whither, then, could these holy men be journeying so deep into the heathen wilderness? Young Goodman Brown caught hold of a tree for support, being ready to sink down on the ground, faint and overburdened with the heavy sickness of his heart. He looked up to the sky, doubting whether there really was a heaven above him. Yet there was the blue arch, and the stars brightening it.

"With heaven above and Faith below, I wlll yet stand firm against the devil!" cried Goodman Brown.

While he still gazed upward into the deep arch of the firmament and had lifted his hands to pray, a cloud, though no wind was stirring, hurried across the zenith and hid the brightening stars. The blue sky was still visible, except directly overhead, where this black mass of cloud was sweeping swiftly northward. Aloft in the air, as if from the depths of the cloud, came a confused and doubtful sound of voices. Once the listener fancied that he could distinguish the accents of towns-people of his own, men and women, both pious and ungodly, many of whom he had met at the communion table, and had seen others rioting at the tavern. The next moment, so indistinct were the sounds, he doubted whether he had heard aught but the murmur of the old forest, whispering without a wind. Then came a stronger swell of those familiar tones, heard daily in the sunshine at Salem village, but never until now from a cloud of night. There was one voice, of a young woman, uttering lamentations, yet with an uncertain sorrow, and entreating for some favor, which, perhaps, it would grieve her to obtain; and all the unseen multitude, both saints and sinners, seemed to encourage her onward.

"Faith!" shouted Goodman Brown, in a voice of agony and desperation; and the echoes of the forest mocked him, crying, "Faith! Faith!" as if bewildered wretches were seeking her all through the wilderness.

The cry of grief, rage, and terror was yet piercing the night, when the unhappy husband held his breath for a response. There was a scream, drowned immediately in a louder murmur of voices, fading into far-off laughter, as the dark cloud swept away, leaving the clear and silent sky above Goodman Brown. But something fluttered lightly down through the air and caught on the branch of a tree. The young man seized it, and beheld a pink ribbon.

"My Faith is gone!" cried he, after one stupefied moment. "There is no good on earth; and sin is but a name. Come, devil; for to thee is this world given."

And, maddened with despair, so that he laughed loud and long, did Goodman

Brown grasp his staff and set forth again, at such a rate that he seemed to fly along the forest path rather than to walk or run. The road grew wilder and drearier and more faintly traced, and vanished at length, leaving him in the heart of the dark wilderness, still rushing onward with the instinct that guides mortal man to evil. The whole forest was peopled with frightful sounds—the creaking of the trees, the howling of wild beasts, and the yell of Indians; while sometimes the wind tolled like a distant church bell, and sometimes gave a broad roar around the traveller, as if all Nature were laughing him to scorn. But he was himself the chief horror of the scene, and shrank not from its other horrors.

"Ha! ha! ha!" roared Goodman Brown when the wind laughed at him. "Let us hear which will laugh loudest. Think not to frighten me with your deviltry. Come witch, come wizard, come Indian powwow, come devil himself, and here comes Goodman Brown. You may as well fear him as he fear you."

In truth, all through the haunted forest there could be nothing more frightful than the figure of Goodman Brown. On he flew among the black pines, brandishing his staff with frenzied gestures, now giving vent to an inspiration of horrid blasphemy, and now shouting forth such laughter as set all the echoes of the forest laughing like demons around him. The fiend in his own shape is less hideous than when he rages in the breast of man. Thus sped the demoniac on his course, until, quivering among the trees, he saw a red light before him, as when the felled trunks and branches of a clearing have been set on fire, and throw up their lurid blaze against the sky, at the hour of midnight. He paused, in a lull of the tempest that had driven him onward, and heard the swell of what seemed a hymn, rolling solemnly from a distance with the weight of many voices. He knew the tune; it was a familiar one in the choir of the village meeting-house. The verse died heavily away, and was lengthened by a chorus, not of human voices, but of all the sounds of the benighted wilderness pealing in awful harmony together. Goodman Brown cried out, and his cry was lost to his own ear by its unison with the cry of the desert.

In the interval of silence he stole forward until the light glared full upon his eyes. At one extremity of an open space, hemmed in by the dark wall of the forest, arose a rock, bearing some rude, natural resemblance either to an altar or a pulpit, and surrounded by four blazing pines, their tops aflame, their stems untouched, like candles at an evening meeting. The mass of foliage that had overgrown the summit of the rock was all on fire, blazing high into the night and fitfully illuminating the whole field. Each pendent twig and leafy festoon was in a blaze. As the red light arose and fell, a numerous congregation alternately shone forth, then disappeared in shadow, and again grew, as it were, out of the darkness, peopling the heart of the solitary woods at once.

"A grave and dark-clad company," quoth Goodman Brown.

In truth they were such. Among them, quivering to and fro between gloom and splendor, appeared faces that would be seen next day at the council board of the province, and others which, Sabbath after Sabbath, looked devoutly heavenward, and benignantly over the crowded pews, from the holiest pulpits in the land. Some affirm that the lady of the governor was there. At least there were high dames well known to her, and wives of honored husbands, and widows, a great multitude, and ancient maidens, all of excellent repute, and fair young girls, who trembled lest their mothers should espy them. Either the sudden gleams of light flashing over the obscure field bedazzled Goodman Brown, or he recognized a score of the church members of Salem village famous for their especial sanctity. Good old Deacon Gookin had arrived, and waited at the skirts of that venerable saint, his revered pastor. But irreverently consorting with these grave, reputable, and pious people, these elders of the church, these chaste dames and dewy virgins, there were men of dissolute lives and women of spotted fame, wretches given over to all mean and filthy vice, and suspected even of horrid crimes. It was strange to see that the good shrank not from the wicked, nor were the sinners abashed by the saints. Scattered also among their pale-faced enemies were the Indian priests, or powwows, who had often scared their native forest with more hideous incantations than any known to English witchcraft.

"But where is Faith?" thought Goodman Brown; and, as hope came into his heart, he trembled.

Another verse of the hymn arose, a slow and mournful strain, such as the pious love, but joined to words which expressed all that our nature can conceive of sin, and darkly hinted at far more. Unfathomable to mere mortals is the lore of fiends. Verse after verse was sung; and still the chorus of the desert swelled between like the deepest tone of a mighty organ; and with the final peal of that dreadful anthem there came a sound, as if the roaring wind, the rushing streams, the howling beasts, and every other voice of the unconcerted wilderness were mingling and according with the voice of guilty man in homage to the prince of all. The four blazing pines threw up a loftier flame, and obscurely discovered shapes and visages of horror on the smoke wreaths above the impious assembly. At the same moment the fire on the rock shot redly forth and formed a glowing arch above its base, where now appeared a figure. With reverence be it spoken, the figure bore no slight similitude, both in garb and manner, to some grave divine of the New England churches.

"Bring forth the converts!" cried a voice that echoed through the field and rolled into the forest.

At the word, Goodman Brown stepped forth from the shadow of the trees and approached the congregation, with whom he felt a loathful brotherhood by the sympathy of all that was wicked in his heart. He could have well-nigh sworn that the shape of his own dead father beckoned him to advance, looking downward from a smoke wreath, while a woman, with dim features of despair, threw out her hand to warn him back. Was it his mother? But he had no power to retreat one step, nor to resist, even in thought, when the minister and good old Deacon Gookin seized his arms and led him to the blazing rock. Thither came also the slender form of a veiled female, led between Goody Cloyse, that pious teacher of the catechism, and Martha Carrier, who had received the devil's promise to be queen of hell. A rampant hag was she. And there stood the proselytes beneath the canopy of fire.

"Welcome, my children," said the dark figure, "to the communion of your race. Ye have found thus young your nature and your destiny. My children, look behind you!"

They turned; and flashing forth, as it were, in a sheet of flame, the fiend worshippers were seen; the smile of welcome gleamed darkly on every visage.

"There," resumed the sable form, "are all whom ye have reverenced from youth. Ye deemed them holier than yourselves, and shrank from your own sin, contrasting it with their lives of righteousness and prayerful aspirations heavenward. Yet here are they all in my worshipping assembly. This night it shall be granted you to know their secret deeds: how hoary-bearded elders of the church have whispered wanton words to the young maids of their households; how many a woman, eager for widows' weeds, has given her husband a drink at bedtime and let him sleep his last sleep in her bosom; how beardless youths have made haste to inherit their fathers' wealth; and how fair damsels—blush not, sweet ones—have dug little graves in the garden, and bidden me, the sole guest, to an infant's funeral. By the sympathy of your human hearts for sin ye shall scent out all the places—whether in church, bed-chamber, street, field, or forest—where crime has been committed, and shall exult to behold the whole earth one stain of guilt, one mighty blood spot. Far more than this. I shall be yours to penetrate, in every bosom, the deep mystery of sin, the fountain of all wicked arts, and which inexhaustibly supplies more evil impulses than human power—than my power at its utmost—can make manifest in deeds. And now, my children, look upon each other."

They did so; and, by the blaze of the hell-kindled torches, the wretched man beheld his Faith, and the wife her husband, trembling before that unhallowed altar.

"Lo, there ye stand, my children," said the figure, in a deep and solemn tone, almost sad with its despairing awfulness, as if his once angelic nature could yet mourn for our miserable race. "Depending upon one another's hearts, ye had still hoped that virtue were not all a dream. Now are ye undeceived. Evil is the nature of mankind. Evil must be your only happiness. Welcome again, my children, to the communion of your race."

"Welcome," repeated the fiend worshippers, in one cry of despair and triumph.

And there they stood, the only pair, as it seemed, who were yet hesitating on the verge of wickedness in this dark world. A basin was hollowed, naturally, in the rock. Did it contain water, reddened by the lurid light? or was it blood? or, perchance, a liquid flame? Herein did the shape of evil dip his hand and prepare to lay the mark of baptism upon their foreheads, that they might be partakers of the mystery of sin, more conscious of the secret guilt of others, both in deed and thought, than they could now be of their own. The husband cast one look at his pale wife, and Faith at him. What polluted wretches would the next glance show them to each other, shuddering alike at what they disclosed and what they saw!

"Faith! Faith!" cried the husband, "look up to heaven, and resist the wicked one."

Whether Faith obeyed he knew not. Hardly had he spoken when he found himself amid calm night and solitude, listening to a roar of the wind which died heavily away through the forest. He staggered against the rock, and felt it chill and damp; while a hanging twig, that had been all on fire, besprinkled his cheek with the coldest dew.

The next morning young Goodman Brown came slowly into the street of Salem village, staring around him like a bewildered man. The good old minister was taking a walk along the graveyard to get an appetite for breakfast and meditate his sermon, and bestowed a blessing, as he passed, on Goodman Brown. He shrank from the venerable saint as if to avoid an anathema. Old Deacon Gookin was at domestic worship, and the holy words of his prayer were heard through the open window. "What God doth the wizard pray to?" quoth Goodman Brown. Goody Cloyse, that excellent old Christian, stood in the early sunshine at her own lattice, catechizing a little girl who had brought her a pint of morning's milk. Goodman Brown snatched away the child as from the grasp of the fiend himself. Turning the corner by the meeting-house, he spied the head of Faith, with the pink ribbons, gazing anxiously forth, and bursting into such joy at sight of him that she skipped along the street and almost kissed her husband before the whole village. But Goodman Brown looked sternly and sadly into her face, and passed on without a greeting.

Had Goodman Brown fallen asleep in the forest and only dreamed a wild dream of a witch-meeting?

Be it so if you will; but, alas! it was a dream of evil omen for young Goodman Brown. A stern, a sad, a darkly meditative, a distrustful, if not a desperate man did he become from the night of that fearful dream. On the Sabbath day, when the congregation were singing a holy psalm, he could not listen because an anthem of sin rushed loudly upon his ear and drowned all the blessed strain. When the minister spoke from the pulpit with power and fervid eloquence, and, with his hand on the open Bible, of the sacred truths of our religion, and of saint-like lives and triumphant deaths, and of future bliss or misery unutterable, then did Goodman Brown turn pale, dreading lest the roof should thunder down upon the gray blasphemer and his hearers. Often, awaking suddenly at midnight, he shrank from the bosom of Faith; and at morning or eventide, when the family knelt down at prayer, he scowled and muttered to himself, and gazed sternly at his wife, and turned away. And when he had lived long, and was borne to his grave a hoary corpse, followed by Faith, an aged woman, and children and grandchildren, a goodly procession, besides neighbors not a few, they carved no hopeful verse upon his tombstone, for his dying hour was gloom.

QUESTIONS

1. How do we know from the very first paragraph that Hawthorne employs the omniscient point of view in the story? Locate other examples of authorial intrusion in the story. Where does Hawthorne editorialize? Why does he employ this method? What is the effect?

2. What is the nature of Young Goodman Brown's journey? Why does he go into the woods? Does Hawthorne treat Brown's frame of mind from a consistent point of view? Explain.

3. What is the relationship between Brown's frame of mind and the supernatural elements in the tale? Who is the stranger "with the twisted staff"? How do the stranger, Deacon Gookin, Goody Cloyse, and the minister function in the story? How do they influence the protagonist's mental and emotional state? Why does point of view facilitate the interpenetration of the psychological and supernatural realms?

4. What do the names of Young Goodman Brown and Faith signify in terms of the theme of the story? Explain the effect of Faith's pink ribbons. Why does the husband reject Faith's joyfulness at his return? What is the nature of his alienation?

5. What is the effect of the last three paragraphs in the story? What mysteries do they create? How do these paragraphs affect our interpretation of the tale?

TOPICS FOR WRITING

1. Write an analysis of Hawthorne's editorializing techniques in the story and his reason for employing the method.

2. Analyze the way Hawthorne develops his psychological profile of Young Goodman Brown, emphasizing the relationship of point of view to this portrait.

3. Evaluate the theme of alienation in the story.

James Joyce

ARABY

James Joyce (1882–1941) was born in Dublin, Ireland, a city and a country standing at the center of his literary universe. Living much of his adult life in self-imposed exile, Joyce produced a series of works in fiction, progressively more experimental in technique and vision, that established him as one of the great literary modernists of the twentieth century: Dubliners (1914), A Portrait of the Artist as a Young Man (1916), Ulysses (1922), and Finnegan's Wake (1939). Joyce was a brilliant, daring, and provocative stylist, willing to break new literary ground and to assault popular taste and conventions, notably in his treatment of human sexuality—a habit that resulted in the censorship of his masterpiece, Ulysses, for more than a decade. In "Araby," from Joyce's cycle of stories, Dubliners, we see this interest in human sexual response from a unique, interior perspective. In the story, we enter the consciousness of the narrator in order to trace with him a delicate process of youthful quest and revelation.

North Richmond Street, being blind, was a quiet street except at the hour when the Christian Brothers School set the boys free. An uninhabited house of two stories stood at the blind end, detached from its neighbors in a square ground. The other houses of the street, conscious of decent lives within them, gazed at one another with brown imperturbable faces.

The former tenant of our house, a priest, had died in the back drawing-room. Air, musty from having been long enclosed, hung in all the rooms, and the waste room behind the kitchen was littered with old useless papers. Among these, I found a few paper-covered books, the pages of which were curled and damp: *The Abbott,* by Walter Scott, *The Devout Communicant* and *The Memoirs of Vidocq.* I liked the last best because its leaves were yellow. The wild garden behind the house contained a central apple-tree and a few straggling bushes under one of which I found the late tenant's rusty bicycle-pump. He had been a very charitable priest; in his will he had left all his money to institutions and the furniture of his house to his sister.

When the short days of winter came dusk fell before we had well eaten our dinners. When we met in the street the houses had grown somber. The space of sky above us was the color of ever-changing violet and towards it the lamps of the street lifted their feeble lanterns. The cold air stung us and we played till our bodies glowed. Our shouts echoed in the silent street. The career of our play brought us through the dark muddy lanes behind the houses where we ran the gauntlet of the rough tribes from the cottages, to the back doors of the dark dripping gardens where odors arose from the ashpits, to the dark odorous stables where a coachman smoothed and combed the horse or shook music from the buckled harness. When we returned to the street light from the kitchen windows had filled the areas. If my uncle was seen turning the corner we hid in the shadow until we had seen him safely housed. Or if Mangan's sister came out on the doorstep to call her brother in to his tea we watched her from our shadow peer up and down the street. We waited to see whether she would remain or go in and, if she remained, we left our shadow and walked up to Mangan's steps resignedly. She was waiting for us, her figure defined by the light from the half-opened door. Her brother always teased her before he obeyed and I stood by the railings looking at her. Her dress swung as she moved her body and the soft rope of her hair tossed from side to side.

Every morning I lay on the floor in the front parlor watching her door. The blind was pulled down to within an inch of the sash so that I could not be seen. When she came out on the doorstep my heart leaped. I ran to the hall, seized my books and followed her. I kept her brown figure always in my eye and, when we came near the point at which our ways diverged, I quickened my pace and passed her. This happened morning after morning. I had never spoken to her, except for a few casual words, and yet her name was like a summons to all my foolish blood.

Her image accompanied me even in places the most hostile to romance. On Saturday evenings when my aunt went marketing I had to go to carry some of the parcels. We walked through the flaring streets, jostled by drunken men and bargaining women, amid the curses of laborers, the shrill litanies of shopboys who stood on guard by the barrels of pigs' cheeks, the nasal chanting of street-singers, who sang a *come-all-you* about O'Donovan Rossa, or a ballad about the troubles in our native land. These noises converged in a single sensation of life for me: I imagined that I bore my chalice safely through a throng of foes. Her name sprang to my lips at moments in strange prayers and praises which I myself did not understand. My eyes were often full of tears (I could not tell why) and at times a flood from my heart seemed to pour itself out into my bosom. I thought little of the future. I did not know whether I would ever speak to her or not or, if I spoke to her, how I could tell her of my confused adoration. But my body was like a harp and her words and gestures were like fingers running upon the wires.

One evening I went into the back drawing-room in which the priest had died. It was a dark rainy evening and there was no sound in the house. Through one of the broken panes I heard the rain impinge upon the earth, the fine incessant needles of water playing in the sodden beds. Some distant lamp or lighted window gleamed below me. I was thankful that I could see so little. All my senses seemed to desire to veil themselves and, feeling that I was about to slip from them, I pressed the palms of my hands together until they trembled, murmuring: *"Oh love! O love!"* many times.

At last she spoke to me. When she addressed the first words to me I was so confused that I did not know what to answer. She asked me was I going to *Araby*. I forgot whether I answered yes or no. It would be a splendid bazaar, she said she would love to go.

"And why can't you?" I asked.

While she spoke she turned a silver bracelet round and round her wrist. She could not go, she said, because there would be a retreat that week in her convent. Her brother and two other boys were fighting for their caps and I was alone at the railings. She held one of the spikes, bowing her head towards me. The light from the lamp opposite our door caught the white curve of her neck, lit up her hair that rested there and, falling, lit up the hand upon the railing. It fell over one side of her dress and caught the white border of a petticoat, just visible as she stood at ease.

"It's well for you," she said.

"If I go," I said, "I will bring you something."

What innumerable follies laid waste my waking and sleeping thoughts after that evening! I wished to annihilate the tedious intervening days. I chafed against the work of school. At night in my bedroom and by day in the classroom her image came between me and the page I strove to read. The syllables of the word *Araby* were called to me through the silence in which my soul luxuriated and cast an Eastern enchantment over me. I asked for leave to go to the bazaar on Saturday night. My aunt was surprised and hoped it was not some Freemason affair. I answered few questions in class. I watched my master's face pass from amiability to sternness; he hoped I was not beginning to idle. I could not call my wandering thoughts together. I had hardly any patience with the serious work of life which, now that it stood between me and my desire, seemed to me child's play, ugly monotonous child's play.

On Saturday morning I reminded my uncle that I wished to go to the bazaar in the evening. He was fussing at the hallstand, looking for the hat-brush, and answered me curtly:

"Yes, boy, I know."

As he was in the hall I could not go into the front parlor and lie at the window. I left the house in bad humor and walked slowly towards the school. The air was pitilessly raw and already my heart misgave me.

When I came home to dinner my uncle had not yet been home. Still it was early. I sat staring at the clock for some time and, when its ticking began to irritate me, I left the room. I mounted the staircase and gained the upper part of the house. The high cold empty gloomy rooms liberated me and I went from room to room singing. From the front window I saw my companions playing below in the street. Their cries reached me weakened and indistinct and, leaning my forehead against the cool glass, I looked over at the dark house where she lived. I may have stood there for an hour, seeing nothing but the brown-clad figure cast by my imagination, touched discreetly by the lamplight at the curved neck, at the hand upon the railings and at the border below the dress.

Araby

When I came downstairs again I found Mrs. Mercer sitting at the fire. She was an old garrulous woman, a pawnbroker's widow, who collected used stamps for some pious purpose. I had to endure the gossip of the tea-table. The meal was prolonged beyond an hour and still my uncle did not come. Mrs. Mercer stood up to go: she was sorry she couldn't wait any longer, but it was after eight o'clock and she did not like to be out late, as the night air was bad for her. When she had gone I began to walk up and down the room, clenching my fists. My aunt said:

"I'm afraid you may put off your bazaar for this night of Our Lord."

At nine o'clock I heard my uncle's latchkey in the halldoor. I heard him talking to himself and heard the hallstand rocking when it had received the weight of his overcoat. I could interpret these signs. When he was midway through his dinner I asked him to give me the money to go to the bazaar. He had forgotten.

"The people are in bed and after their first sleep now," he said.

I did not smile. My aunt said to him energetically:

"Can't you give him the money and let him go? You've kept him late enough as it is."

My uncle said he was very sorry he had forgotten. He said he believed in the old saying: "All work and no play makes Jack a dull boy." He asked me where I was going and, when I had told him a second time he asked me did I know *The Arab's Farewell to his Steed*. When I left the kitchen he was about to recite the opening lines of the piece to my aunt.

I held a florin tightly in my hand as I strode down Buckingham Street towards the station. The sight of the streets thronged with buyers and glaring with gas recalled to me the purpose of my journey. I took my seat in a third-class carriage of a deserted train. After an intolerable delay the train moved out of the station slowly. It crept onward among ruinous houses and over the twinkling river. At Westland Row Station a crowd of people pressed to the carriage doors; but the porters moved them back, saying that it was a special train for the bazaar. I remained alone in the bare carriage. In a few minutes the train drew up beside an improvised wooden platform. I passed out on to the road and saw by the lighted dial of a clock that it was ten minutes to ten. In front of me was a large building which displayed the magical name.

I could not find any sixpenny entrance and, fearing that the bazaar would be closed, I passed in quickly through a turnstile, handing a shilling to a weary-looking man. I found myself in a big hall girdled at half its height by a gallery. Nearly all the stalls were closed and the greater part of the hall was in darkness. I recognized a silence like that which pervades a church after a service. I walked into the center of the bazaar timidly. A few people were gathered about the stalls which were still open. Before a curtain, over which the words *Café Chantant* were written in colored lamps, two men were counting money on a salver. I listened to the fall of the coins.

Remembering with difficulty why I had come I went over to one of the stalls and examined porcelain vases and flowered tea-sets. At the door of the stall a young lady was talking and laughing with two young gentlemen. I remarked their English accents and listened vaguely to their conversation.

"O, I never said such a thing!"

"O, but you did!"

"O, but I didn't!"

"Didn't she say that?"

"Yes. I heard her."

"O, there's a . . . fib!"

Observing me the young lady came over and asked me did I wish to buy something. The tone of her voice was not encouraging; she seemed to have spoken to me out of a sense of duty. I looked humbly at the great jars that stood like eastern guards at either side of the dark entrance to the stall and murmured:

"No, thank you."

The young lady changed the position of one of the vases and went back to the two young men. They began to talk of the same subject. Once or twice the young lady glanced at me over her shoulder.

I lingered before her stall, though I knew my stay was useless, to make my interest in her wares seem the more real. Then I turned away slowly and walked down the middle of the bazaar. I allowed the two pennies to fall against the sixpence in my pocket. I heard a voice call from one end of the gallery that the light was out. The upper part of the hall was now completely dark.

Gazing up into the darkness I saw myself as a creature driven and derided by vanity; and my eyes burned with anguish and anger.

QUESTIONS

1. At what point in the story do we learn that "Araby" has been placed in a first-person point of view? What is the value of having an "I" narrator who is both a child in terms of the action and an adult who is reflecting on the action?

2. What advantages does Joyce gain from casting many of the narrator's observations in romantic terms? Cite examples of romantic statements and imagery. What bearing does this language have on the theme?

3. What is the importance of Mangan's sister? What perspective does the "I" narrator develop toward her?

4. How does the uncle function in the story? What other details reinforce the world that the uncle represents? How conscious of this world is the narrator? Explain.

5. The Irish short fiction writer and critic Sean O'Faolain has stated that a story "must lead toward its point of illumination." In a similar vein, Joyce termed this point of illumination or revelation an *epiphany*. What is the point of illumination in "Araby"? How does it dictate the final theme?

6. How effective is point of view in advancing the theme of the story? Explain.

TOPICS FOR WRITING

1. Write an analysis of the "I" narrator as child and the "I" narrator as adult in "Araby."

2. Write an essay on the romantic quest in Joyce's story. Link the quest to the boy's sexual awakening and to the epiphany at the end.

3. Compare and contrast the psychological and emotional states of Young Goodman Brown (page 102) and the boy in "Araby." Look carefully at the nature of their quests and at the nature of their self-discoveries.

Joyce Carol Oates

STALKING

Joyce Carol Oates (1938–   ), one of the most prolific contemporary short story writers and novelists, was born in Lockport, New York, a locale that figures prominently in her fiction. Also a poet, playwright, and critic, Oates was educated at Syracuse University, the University of Wisconsin, and Rice University. She has been a college teacher during much of her varied and spectacular career, serving currently as writer-in-residence at Princeton University. Oates's fiction reveals a broad range of technique and subject matter. Essentially the author is interested in the psychological and sociological forces in people's lives; her fiction often concentrates on professional types or on representatives of certain classes in American society. Her novels include A Garden of Earthly Delights (1967), Them (1969), and Bellefleur (1980). Her short stories, including nine O. Henry Award winners, have established her as one of the most significant innovators in the genre. In "Stalking," selected from Marriages and Infidelities and Other Stories (1972), Oates creates a unique consciousness—a severely disturbed girl—who is alienated by a hostile and deadening environment.

The Invisible Adversary is fleeing across a field.

Gretchen, walking slowly, deliberately, watches with her keen unblinking eyes the figure of the Invisible Adversary some distance ahead. The Adversary has run boldly in front of all that traffic—on long spiky legs brisk as colts' legs—and jumped up onto a curb of new concrete, and now is running across a vacant field. The Adversary glances over his shoulder at Gretchen.

Bastard, Gretchen thinks.

Saturday afternoon. November. A cold gritty day. Gretchen is out stalking. She has hours for her game. Hours. She is dressed for the hunt, her solid legs crammed into old blue jeans, her big, square, strong feet jammed into white leather boots that cost her mother forty dollars not long ago, but are now scuffed and filthy with mud. Hopeless to get them clean again, Gretchen doesn't give a damn. She is wearing a dark green corduroy jacket that is worn out at the elbows and the rear, with a zipper that can be zipped swiftly up or down, attached to a fringed leather strip. On her head nothing, though it is windy today.

She has hours ahead.

Cars and trucks and buses from the city and enormous interstate trucks hauling automobiles pass by on the highway; Gretchen waits until the way is nearly clear, then starts out. A single car is approaching. *Slow down, you bastard,* Gretchen thinks; and like magic he does.

Following the footprints of the Invisible Adversary. There is no sidewalk here yet, so she might as well cut right across the field. A gigantic sign announces the site of the new Pace & Fischbach Building, an office building of fifteen floors to be completed the following year. The land around here is all dug up and muddy; she can see the Adversary's footsteps leading right past the gouged-up area . . . and there he is, smirking back at her, pretending panic.

I'll get you. Don't worry, Gretchen thinks carefully.

Because the Adversary is so light-footed and invisible, Gretchen doesn't make any effort to be that way. She plods along as she does at school, passing from classroom to classroom, unhurried and not even sullen, just unhurried. She knows she is very visible. She is thirteen years old and weighs one hundred and thirty-five pounds. She's only five feet three—stocky, muscular, squat in the torso and shoulders, with good strong legs and thighs. She could be good at gym, if she bothered; instead, she just stands around, her face empty, her arms crossed and her shoulders a little slumped. If forced, she takes part in the games of volleyball and basketball, but she runs heavily, without spirit, and sometimes bumps into other girls, hurting them. *Out of my way,* she thinks; at such times her face shows no expression.

And now? . . . The Adversary is peeking out at her from around the corner of a gas station. Something flickers in her brain. *I see you,* she thinks, with quiet excitement. The Adversary ducks back out of sight. Gretchen heads in his direction, plodding through a jumbled, bulldozed field of mud and thistles and debris that is mainly rocks and chunks of glass. The gas station is brand new and not yet opened for business. It is all white tile, white concrete, perfect plate-glass windows with white-washed X's on them, a large driveway and eight gasoline pumps, all proudly erect and ready for business. But the gas station has not opened since Gretchen and her family moved here—about six months ago. Something must have gone wrong. Gretchen fixes her eyes on the corner where the Adversary was last seen. He can't escape.

One wall of the gas station's white tile has been smeared with something like tar. Dreamy, snakelike, thick twistings of black. Black tar. Several windows have been broken. Gretchen stands in the empty driveway, her hands jammed into her pockets. Traffic is moving slowly over here. A barricade has been set up that directs traffic out onto the shoulder of the highway, on a narrow, bumpy, muddy lane that loops out and back again onto the pavement. Cars move slowly, carefully. Their bottoms scrape against the road. The detour signs are great rectangular things, bright yellow with black zigzag lines. SLOW. DETOUR. In the two center lanes of the highway are bulldozers not being used today, and gigantic concrete pipes to be used for storm sewers. Eight pipes. They are really enormous; Gretchen's eyes crinkle with awe, just to see them.

She remembers the Adversary.

There he is—headed for the shopping plaza. *He won't get away in the crowds,* Gretchen promises herself. She follows. Now she is approaching an area that is more completed, though there are still no sidewalks and some of the buildings are brand-new and yet unoccupied, vacant. She jumps over a concrete ditch that is stained with rust-colored water and heads up a slight incline to the service drive of the Federal Savings Bank. The drive-in tellers' windows are all dark today, behind their green-tinted glass. The whole bank is dark, closed. Is this the bank her parents go to now? It takes Gretchen a minute to recognize it.

Now a steady line of traffic, a single lane, turns onto the service drive that leads to the shopping plaza. BUCKINGHAM MALL. 101 STORES. Gretchen notices a few kids her own age, boys or girls, trudging in jeans and jackets ahead of her, through the mud. They might be classmates of hers. Her attention is captured again by the Invisible Adversary, who has run all the way up to the Mall and is hanging around the entrance of the Cunningham Drug Store, teasing her.

You'll be sorry for that, you bastard, Gretchen thinks with a smile.

Automobiles pass her slowly. The parking lot for the Mall is enormous, many acres. A city of cars on a Saturday afternoon. Gretchen sees a car that might be her mother's, but she isn't sure. Cars are parked slanted here, in lanes marked LOT K, LANE 15; LOT K. LANE 16. The signs are spheres, bubbles, perched up on long slender poles. At night they are illuminated.

Ten or twelve older kids are hanging around the drugstore entrance. One of them is sitting on top of a mailbox, rocking it back and forth. Gretchen pushes past them—they are kidding around, trying to block people—and inside the store her eye darts rapidly up and down the aisles, looking for the Invisible Adversary.

Hiding here? Hiding?

She strolls along, cunning and patient. At the cosmetics counter a girl is showing an older woman some liquid make-up. She smears a small oval onto the back of the woman's hand, rubs it in gently. "That's Peach Pride," the girl says. She has shimmering blond hair and eyes that are penciled to show a permanent exclamatory interest. She does not notice Gretchen, who lets one hand drift idly over a display of marked-down lipsticks, each for only $1.59.

Gretchen slips the tube of lipstick into her pocket. Neatly. Nimbly. Ignoring the Invisible Adversary, who is shaking a finger at her, she drifts over to the newsstand, looks at the magazine covers without reading them, and edges over to another display. Packages in a cardboard barrel, out in the aisle. Big bargains. Gretchen doesn't even glance in the barrel to see what is being offered . . . she just slips one of the packages in her pocket. No trouble.

She leaves by the other door, the side exit. A small smile tugs at her mouth.

The Adversary is trotting ahead of her. The Mall is divided into geometric areas, each colored differently: the Adversary leaves the blue pavement and is now on the green. Gretchen follows. She notices the Adversary going into a Franklin Joseph store.

Gretchen enters the store, sniffs in the perfumy, overheated smell, sees nothing that interests her on the counters or at the dress racks, and so walks right to the back of the store, to the Ladies Room. No one inside. She takes the tube of lipstick out of her pocket, opens it, examines the lipstick. It has a tart, sweet smell. A very light pink: *Spring Blossom.* Gretchen goes to the mirror and smears the lipstick onto it, at first lightly, then coarsely: part of the lipstick breaks and falls into a hair-littered sink. Gretchen goes into one of the toilet stalls and tosses the tube into the toilet bowl. She takes handfuls of toilet paper and crumbles them into a ball and throws them into the toilet. Remembering the package from the drugstore, she takes it out of her pocket—just toothpaste. She throws it, cardboard package and all, into the toilet bowl, then, her mind glimmering with an idea, she goes to the apparatus that holds the towel—a single cloth towel on a roll—and tugs at it until it comes loose, then pulls it out hand over hand, patiently, until the entire towel is out. She scoops it up and carries it to the toilet. She pushes it in and flushes the toilet.

The stuff doesn't go down, so she tries again. This time it goes part-way down before it gets stuck.

Gretchen leaves the rest room and strolls unhurried through the store. The Adversary is waiting for her outside—peeking through the window—wagging a finger at her. *Don't you wag no finger at me,* she thinks, with a small tight smile. Outside, she follows him at a distance. Loud music is blaring around her head. It is rock music, piped out onto the colored squares and rectangles of the Mall, blown everywhere by the November wind, but Gretchen hardly hears it.

Some boys are fooling around in front of the record store. One of them bumps into Gretchen and they all laugh as she is pushed against a trash can. "Watch it, babe!" the boy sings out. Her leg hurts. Gretchen doesn't look at them but, with a cold, swift anger, her face averted, she knocks the trash can over onto the sidewalk. Junk falls out. The can rolls. Some women shoppers scurry to get out of the way and the boys laugh.

Gretchen walks away without looking back.

She wanders through Sampson Furniture, which has two entrances. In one door and out the other, as always: it is a ritual with her. Again she notices the sofa that is like the sofa in their family room at home covered with black and white fur, real goatskin. All over the store there are sofas, chairs, tables, beds. A jumble of furnishings. People stroll around them, in and out of little displays, displays meant to be living rooms, dining rooms, bedrooms, family rooms. . . . It makes Gretchen's eyes squint to see so many displays: like seeing the inside of a hundred houses. She slows down, almost comes to a stop. Gazing at a living-room display on a raised platform. Only after a moment does she remember why she is here—whom she is following—and she turns to see the Adversary beckoning to her.

She follows him outside again. He goes into Dodi's Boutique and, with her head lowered so that her eyes seem to move to the bottom of her eyebrows, pressing up against her forehead, Gretchen follows him. *You'll regret this,* she thinks. Dodi's Boutique is decorated in silver and black. Metallic strips hang down from a dark ceiling, quivering. Salesgirls dressed in pants suits stand around with nothing to do except giggle with one another and nod their heads in time to the music amplified throughout the store. It is music from a local radio station. Gretchen wanders over to the dress rack, for the hell of it. Size 14. "The time is now 2:35," a radio announcer says cheerfully. "The weather is 32 degrees with a chance of showers and possible sleet tonight. You're listening to WCKK, Radio Wonderful. . . ." Gretchen selects several dresses and a salesgirl shows her to a dressing room.

"Need any help?" the girl asks. She has long swinging hair and a high-shouldered, indifferent, bright manner.

"No," Gretchen mutters.

Alone, Gretchen takes off her jacket. She is wearing a navy blue sweater. She zips one of the dresses open and it falls off the flimsy plastic hanger before she can catch it. She steps on it, smearing mud onto the white wool. *The hell with it.* She lets it lie there and holds up another dress, gazing at herself in the mirror.

She has untidy, curly hair that looks like a wig set loosely on her head. Light brown curls spill out everywhere, bouncy, a little frizzy, a cascade, a tumbling of curls. Her eyes are deep set, her eyebrows heavy and dark. She has a stern, staring look, like an adult man. Her nose is perfectly formed, neat and noble. Her upper lip is long, as if it were stretched to close with difficulty over the front teeth. She wears no make-up, her lips are perfectly colorless, pale, a little chapped, and they are usually held tight, pursed tightly shut. She has a firm, rounded chin. Her facial structure is strong, pensive, its features stern and symmetrical as a statue's, blank, neutral, withdrawn. Her face is attractive. But there is a blunt, neutral, sexless stillness to it, as if she were detached from it and somewhere else, uninterested.

She holds the dress up to her body, smooths it down over her breasts, staring.

After a moment she hangs the dress up again, and runs down the zipper so roughly that it breaks. The other dress she doesn't bother with. She leaves the dressing room, putting on her jacket.

At the front of the store the salesgirl glances at her . . . "—Didn't fit?—"

"No," says Gretchen.

She wanders around for a while, in and out of Carmichael's, the Mall's big famous store, where she catches sight of her mother on an escalator going up. Her mother doesn't notice her. She pauses by a display of "winter homes." Her family owns a home like this, in the Upper Peninsula, except theirs is larger. This one comes complete for only $5330: PACKAGE ERECTED ON YOUR LOT—YEAR-ROUND HOME FIBER GLASS INSULATION—BEAUTIFUL ROUGH-SAWN VERTICAL B.C. CEDAR SIDING WITH DEEP SIMULATED SHADOW LINES FOR A RUGGED EXTERIOR.

Only 3:15. For the hell of it, Gretchen goes into the Big Boy restaurant and orders a ground-round hamburger with French fries. Also a Coke. She sits at the crowded counter and eats slowly, her jaws grinding slowly, as she glances at her reflection in the mirror directly in front of her—her mop of hair moving almost imperceptibly with the grinding of her jaws—and occasionally she sees the Adversary waiting outside, coyly. *You'll get yours,* she thinks.

She leaves the Big Boy and wanders out into the parking lot, eating from a bag of potato chips. She wipes her greasy hands on her thighs. The afternoon has turned dark and cold. Shivering a little, she scans the maze of cars for the Adversary—yes, there he is—and starts after him. He runs ahead of her. He runs through the parking lot, waits teasingly at the edge of a field, and as she approaches he runs across the field, trotting along with a noisy crowd of four or five loose dogs that don't seem to notice him.

Gretchen follows him through that field, trudging in the mud, and through another muddy field, her eyes fixed on him. Now he is at the highway—hesitating there—now he is about to run across in front of traffic—now, now—now he darts out—

Now! He is struck by a car! His body knocked backward, spinning backward. Ah, now, *now how does it feel?* Gretchen asks.

He picks himself up. Gets to his feet. Is he bleeding? Yes, bleeding! He stumbles across the highway to the other side, where there is a sidewalk. Gretchen follows him as soon as the traffic lets up. He is staggering now, like a drunken man. *How does it feel? Do you like it now?*

The Adversary staggers along the sidewalk. He turns onto a side street, beneath an archway. *Piney Woods.* He is leading Gretchen into the Piney Woods subdivision. Here the homes are quite large, on artificial hills that show them to good advantage. Most of the homes are white colonials with attached garages. There are no sidewalks here, so the Adversary has to walk in the street, limping like an old man, and Gretchen follows him in the street, with her eyes fixed on him.

Are you happy now? Does it hurt? Does it?

She giggles at the way he walks. He looks like a drunken man. He glances back at her, white-faced, and turns up a flagstone walk . . . goes right up to a big white colonial house. . . .

Gretchen follows him inside. She inspects the simulated brick of the foyer: yes, there are blood spots. He is dripping blood. Entranced, she follows the splashes of blood into the hall, to the stairs . . . forgets her own boots, which are muddy . . . but she doesn't feel like going back to wipe her feet. The hell with it.

Nobody seems to be home. Her mother is probably still shopping, her father is out of town for the weekend. The house empty. Gretchen goes into the kitchen, opens the refrigerator, takes out a Coke, and wanders to the rear of the house, to the family room. It is two steps down from the rest of the house. She takes off her jacket and tosses it somewhere. Turns on the television set. Sits on the goatskin sofa and stares at the screen: a rerun of a Shotgun Steve show, which she has already seen.

If the Adversary comes crawling behind her, groaning in pain, weeping, she won't even bother to glance at him.

QUESTIONS

1. What is unusual about the limited third-person point of view in the story? Who is the Invisible Adversary?

2. What do we learn about Gretchen's emotional and mental state in the course of the story?

3. Why does Oates create the action in the present tense, filtering it through the mind of the protagonist? What advantages does she gain from using this method?

4. What is the relationship of Gretchen's mental state and the setting and society to which she is exposed?

5. There seems to be a point to the journeys embarked on by the characters in "Young Goodman Brown" and "Araby." What is the point of Gretchen's journey? What theme emerges from the episodes that govern her trip?

6. How does the ending resolve (at least temporarily) the conflict in the story? Is the ending consistent with the point of view established in the tale? Explain.

TOPICS FOR WRITING

1. Analyze the conscious and unconscious life of Gretchen in "Stalking."

2. Evaluate the impact of society on Gretchen's mental and emotional state.

3. Examine the dual perspectives created by point of view in "Araby" (page 112) and "Stalking."

4. Evaluate the theme of alienation in these stories, concentrating on the fact that all three central characters are relatively young and that they make striking discoveries about themselves and their world.

5. Analyze the motif of the journey in the three stories in this section. Try to show how point of view serves to magnify the importance of each journey.

$$\boxed{5}$$

MOOD AND THEME:
CASTE AND CLASS

Mood is the emotional aura or quality that we detect in a story, a distinctive yet intangible feeling that pervades a literary work. It derives from atmospheric setting (time, weather, landscape, place), characters, plot, and style. Because precision, and sometimes brevity, are so important in a short story, mood must be quickly and firmly established, for it reveals the author's attitude toward the conditions that he or she expresses in the narrative. Mood, as J. Volkelt wrote, "may be the basic experience in the creation and appreciation of art." We remember mood long after we have forgotten a story's details.

Mood is often equated with atmosphere, and this can be useful. More accurately, however, atmosphere is concerned with the setting in which a scene takes place. Atmosphere grows from a physical area—a palace room, perhaps, or a Bowery flophouse. It grows also from time in a given place: from the historical moment of Chekhov's Russia, the seasonal rhythms of some of Faulkner's greatest stories, the clock time of Hemingway's "The Killers," even calendar time. Atmosphere and mood, at times used interchangeably, are conceived to elicit specific emotional responses from the reader.

Mood, which supports theme and is to be found in every story, can be reflected in such a simple element as the title of a story. Note carefully the titles of the stories in this section to see how well they reflect mood and meaning. In the fiction of Edgar Allan Poe and Nathaniel Hawthorne, the dark, brooding moods are primary clues to the meaning of their stories.

Although mood is often described as being dark or light, gay or melancholy (in Greek the stem *melan* means "black"), among many other descriptions, it could not exist without the careful use of language. In "Winter Dreams" (1926) F. Scott Fitzgerald establishes mood in the second paragraph of the story while at the same time creating atmosphere:

> In the fall when the days became crisp and gray, and the long Minnesota winter shut down like the white lid of a box, Dexter's skis moved over the snow that hid the fairways of the golf course. At these times the country gave him a feeling of profound melancholy.

The author has set time, place, and feeling.

Willa Cather's "Paul's Case" (1905), in contrast, provides us with different moods for the different characters who are involved in the same situation:

> It was Paul's afternoon to appear before the faculty of the Pittsburgh High School to account for his various misdemeanors. He had been suspended a week ago, and his father had called at the Principal's office and confessed his perplexity about his son. Paul entered the faculty room suave and smiling.

The father is puzzled but Paul seems not to understand the gravity of his situation. Using a brief flashback, the author not only establishes mood and atmosphere, but conflict between characters as well.

With Fitzgerald, the mood indicates that the conflict may not be between characters, but between characters and things. The selection from Cather shows that mood can emanate from a character or from what a character may say or do. Thus, when Bontemps in "A Summer Tragedy" describes his character:

> Old Jeff Patton, the black share farmer, fumbled with his bow tie.

we are struck by the incongruity of a sharecropper putting on a bow tie, and the indication is that something significant is about to happen. A mood of anticipation and apprehension arises because of the contradictions that grow out of the language.

It should be clear from the examples that description is a key element in the creation of mood and atmosphere that work because the author has set off in us signals lying dormant within our personal experiences, whether lived or learned.

For example, we know that William Faulkner wrote almost exclusively about the South and its history. Let this be signal number 1 since Southern history is a part of the American experience. Faulkner also stirs up the physical and psychological reaction most people have to long periods of excessive heat; such periods set us on edge and make us irritable. This is signal number 2. In Faulkner's South, the joining in fact or fancy of a white woman and a black man was an event filled with the most dreaded consequences, and thus we have a third signal. They create mood and atmosphere, theme, and a sense of heavy foreboding:

> Through the bloody September twilight, aftermath of sixty-two rainless days, it had gone like a fire in dry grass—the rumor, the story, whatever it was. Something about Miss Minnie Cooper and a Negro.

The language itself is a flag snapping in dangerously high winds: "bloody" and "like a fire in dry grass." We advance into the story with the sense, if not the knowledge, of danger.

If "Dry September" had been set outside the South, its impact might not have been quite as powerful, nor its mood so awesome. Faulkner's South, like Richard Wright's, was an overtly violent place. For Welty, too, the "Southern mood" hums with the unceasing potential for conflict. While the conflict, the violence, is there for Bontemps as well, his creation of mood is delicate by comparison. What he achieves is the creation of an impersonal violence that is in its way just as effective, just as Southern in mood, as Faulkner's and Welty's.

William Faulkner

DRY SEPTEMBER

William Faulkner (1897–1962), 1949 winner of the Nobel Prize in literature, was born in New Albany, Mississippi. His family moved to Oxford in 1902, and Faulkner attended the University of Mississippi there. He drew extensively on his family history and the people of the region he would come to make famous in his novels as Yoknapatawpha County. The interrelated problems of race and class are recurring themes in Faulkner's work. These were, Malcolm Cowley said, "the tragic fable of Southern history." From his first novel, Soldier's Pay *(1926), to* The Reivers *(1962), Faulkner's stories and novels, some of them difficult to comprehend at first reading, have been lyrical, interior, and brimming with characters and symbolism. In "Dry September" many of the constants in Faulkner's work appear—race, class, pride, and self-loathing. The protests against racism are ineffective because the system fosters deeply racist motivations and rewards while it punishes. In "Dry September" the black man—the Negro— is as much a symbol as Minnie Cooper, who in the early autumn of her years is also a tolerated outcast. John McLendon, both protector and debaser of women, is yet another complex Faulknerian symbol.*

I

Through the bloody September twilight, aftermath of sixty-two rainless days, it had gone like a fire in dry grass—the rumor, the story, whatever it was. Something about Miss Minnie Cooper and a Negro. Attacked, insulted, frightened: none of them, gathered in the barber shop on that Saturday evening where the ceiling fan stirred, without freshening it, the vitiated air, sending back upon them in recurrent surges of stale pomade and lotion, their own stale breath and odors, knew exactly what had happened.

"Except it wasn't Will Mayes," a barber said. He was a man of middle age; a thin, sand-colored man with a mild face, who was shaving a client. "I know Will Mayes. He's a good nigger. And I know Miss Minnie Cooper, too."

"What do you know about her?" a second barber said.

"Who is she?" the client said. "A young girl?"

"No," the barber said. "She's about forty, I reckon. She aint married. That's why I dont believe—"

"Believe, hell!" a hulking youth in a sweat-stained silk shirt said. "Wont you take a white woman's word before a nigger's?"

"I don't believe Will Mayes did it," the barber said. "I know Will Mayes."

"Maybe you know who did it, then. Maybe you already got him out of town, you damn niggerlover."

"I dont believe anybody did anything. I dont believe anything happened. I leave it to you fellows if them ladies that get old without getting married dont have notions that a man cant—"

"Then you are a hell of a white man," the client said. He moved under the cloth. The youth had sprung to his feet.

"You dont?" he said. "Do you accuse a white woman of lying?"

The barber held the razor poised above the half-risen client. He did not look around.

"It's this durn weather," another said. "It's enough to make a man do anything. Even to her."

Nobody laughed. The barber said in his mild, stubborn tone: "I aint accusing nobody of nothing. I just know and you fellows know how a woman that never—"

"You damn niggerlover!" the youth said.

"Shut up, Butch," another said. "We'll get the facts in plenty of time to act."

"Who is? Who's getting them?" the youth said. "Facts, hell! I—"

"You're a fine white man," the client said. "Aint you?" In his frothy beard he looked like a desert rat in the moving pictures. "You tell them, Jack," he said to the youth. "If there aint any white men in this town, you can count on me, even if I aint only a drummer and a stranger."

"That's right, boys," the barber said. "Find out the truth first. I know Will Mayes."

"Well, by God!" the youth shouted. "To think that a white man in this town—"

"Shut up, Butch," the second speaker said, "We got plenty of time."

The client sat up. He looked at the speaker. "Do you claim that anything excuses a nigger attacking a white woman? Do you mean to tell me you are a white man and you'll stand for it? You better go back North where you came from. The South dont want your kind here."

"North what?" the second said. "I was born and raised in this town."

"Well, by God!" the youth said. He looked about with a strained, baffled gaze, as if he was trying to remember what it was he wanted to say or to do. He drew his sleeve across his sweating face. "Damn if I'm going to let a white woman—"

"You tell them, Jack," the drummer said. "By God, if they—"

The screen door crashed open. A man stood in the door, his feet apart and his heavy-set body poised easily. His white shirt was open at the throat; he wore a felt hat. His hot, bold glance swept the group. His name was McLendon. He had commanded troops at the front in France and had been decorated for valor.

"Well," he said, "are you going to sit there and let a black son rape a white woman on the streets of Jefferson?"

Butch sprang up again. The silk of his shirt clung flat to his heavy shoulders. At each armpit was a dark halfmoon. "That's what I been telling them! That's what I—"

"Did it really happen?" a third said. "This aint the first man scare she ever had, like Hawkshaw says. Wasn't there something about a man on the kitchen roof, watching her undress, about a year ago?"

"What?" the client said. "What's that?" The barber had been slowly forcing him back into the chair; he arrested himself reclining, his head lifted, the barber still pressing him down.

McLendon whirled on the third speaker. "Happen? What the hell difference does it make? Are you going to let the black sons get away with it until one really does it?"

"That's what I'm telling them!" Butch shouted. He cursed, long and steady, pointless.

"Here, here," a fourth said. "Not so loud. Dont talk so loud."

"Sure," McLendon said; "no talking necessary at all. I've done my talking. Who's with me?" He poised on the balls of his feet, roving his gaze.

The barber held the drummer's face down, the razor poised. "Find out the facts first, boys. I know Willy Mayes. It wasn't him. Let's get the sheriff and do this thing right."

McLendon whirled upon him his furious, rigid face. The barber did not look away. They looked like men of different races. The other barbers had ceased also above their prone clients. "You mean to tell me," McLendon said, "that you'd take a nigger's word before a white woman's? Why, you damn niggerloving—"

The third speaker rose and grasped McLendon's arm; he too had been a soldier, "Now, now. Let's figure this thing out. Who knows anything about what really happened?"

"Figure out hell!" McLendon jerked his arm free. "All that're with me get up from there. The ones that aint—" He roved his gaze, dragging his sleeve across his face.

Three men rose. The drummer in the chair sat up. "Here," he said, jerking at the cloth about his neck; "get this rag off me. I'm with him. I dont live here, but by God, if our mothers and wives and sisters—" He smeared the cloth over his face and flung it to the floor. McLendon stood in the floor and cursed the others. Another rose and moved toward him. The remainder sat uncomfortable, not looking at one another, then one by one they rose and joined him.

The barber picked the cloth from the floor. He began to fold it neatly. "Boys, dont do that. Will Mayes never done it. I know."

"Come on," McLendon said. He whirled. From his hip pocket protruded the butt of a heavy automatic pistol. They went out. The screen door crashed behind them reverberant in the dead air.

The barber wiped the razor carefully and swiftly, and put it away, and ran to the rear, and took his hat from the wall. "I'll be back as soon as I can," he said to the other barbers. "I cant let—" He went out, running. The two other barbers followed him to the door and caught it on the rebound, leaning out and looking up the street after him. The air was flat and dead. It had a metallic taste at the base of the tongue.

"What can he do?" the first said. The second one was saying "Jees Christ, Jees Christ" under his breath. "I'd just as lief be Will Mayes as Hawk, if he gets McLendon riled."

"Jees Christ, Jees Christ," the second whispered.

"You reckon he really done it to her?" the first said.

II

She was thirty-eight or thirty-nine. She lived in a small frame house with her invalid mother and a thin, sallow, unflagging aunt, where each morning between ten and eleven she would appear on the porch in a lace-trimmed boudoir cap, to sit swinging in the porch swing until noon. After dinner, she lay down for a while, until the afternoon began to cool. Then, in one of the three or four new voile dresses which she had each summer, she would go downtown to spend the afternoon in the stores with the other ladies, where they would handle the goods and haggle over the prices in cold, immediate voices, without any intention of buying.

She was of comfortable people—not the best in Jefferson, but good people enough—and she was still on the slender side of ordinary looking, with a bright, faintly haggard manner and dress. When she was young she had had a slender, nervous body and a sort of hard vivacity which had enabled her for a time to ride upon the crest of the town's social life as exemplified by the high school party and church social period of her contemporaries while still children enough to be unclassconscious.

She was the last to realize that she was losing ground; that those among whom she had been a little brighter and louder flame than any other were beginning to learn the pleasure of snobbery—male—and retaliation—female. That was when her face began to wear that bright, haggard look. She still carried it to parties on shadowy porticoes and summer lawns, like a mask or a flag, with that bafflement of furious repudiation of truth in her eyes. One evening at a party she heard a boy and two girls, all schoolmates, talking. She never accepted another invitation.

She watched the girls with whom she had grown up as they married and got homes and children, but no man ever called on her steadily until the children of the other girls had been calling her "aunty" for several years, the while their mothers told them in bright voices about how popular Aunt Minnie had been as a girl. Then the town began to see her driving on Sunday afternoons with the cashier in the bank. He was a widower of about forty—a high-colored man, smelling always faintly of the barber shop or of whisky. He owned the first automobile in town, a red runabout; Minnie had the first motoring bonnet and veil the town ever saw. Then the town began to say: "Poor Minnie." "But she is old enough to take care of herself," others said. That was when she began to ask her old schoolmates that their children call her "cousin" instead of "aunty."

It was twelve years now since she had been relegated into adultery by public opinion, and eight years since the cashier had gone to a Memphis bank, returning for one day each Christmas, which he spent at an annual bachelors' party at a hunting club on the river. From behind their curtains the neighbors would see the party pass, and during the over-the-way Christmas day visiting they would tell her about him, about how well he looked, and how they heard that he was prospering in the city, watching with bright, secret eyes her haggard, bright face. Usually by that hour there would be the scent of whisky on her breath. It was supplied her by a youth, a clerk at the soda fountain: "Sure; I buy it for the old gal. I reckon she's entitled to a little fun."

Her mother kept to her room altogether now; the gaunt aunt ran the house. Against that background Minnie's bright dresses, her idle and empty days, had a quality of furious unreality. She went out in the evenings only with women now, neighbors, to the moving pictures. Each afternoon she dressed in one of the new dresses and went downtown alone, where her young "cousins" were already strolling in the late afternoons with their delicate, silken heads and thin, awkward arms and conscious hips, clinging to one another or shrieking and giggling with paired boys in the soda fountain when she passed and went on along the serried store fronts, in the doors of which the sitting and lounging men did not even follow her with their eyes any more.

III

The barber went swiftly up the street where the sparse lights, insect-swirled, glared in rigid and violent suspension in the lifeless air. The day had died in a pall of dust; above the darkened square, shrouded by the spent dust, the sky was as clear as the inside of a brass bell. Below the east was a rumor of the twice-waxed moon.

When he overtook them McLendon and three others were getting into a car parked in an alley. McLendon stooped his thick head, peering out beneath the top. "Changed your mind, did you?" he said. "Damn good thing; by God, tomorrow when this town hears about how you talked tonight—"

"Now, now," the other ex-soldier said. "Hawkshaw's all right. Come on, Hawk; jump in."

"Will Mayes never done it, boys," the barber said. "If anybody done it. Why, you all know well as I do there aint any town where they got better niggers than us. And you know how a lady will kind of think things about men when there aint any reason to, and Miss Minnie anyway—"

"Sure, sure," the soldier said. "We're just going to talk to him a little; that's all."

"Talk hell!" Butch said. "When we're through with the—"

Dry September

"Shut up, for God's sake!" the soldier said. "Do you want everybody in town—"

"Tell them, by God!" McLendon said. "Tell every one of the sons that'll let a white woman—"

"Let's go; let's go: here's the other car." The second car slid squealing out of a cloud of dust at the alley mouth. McLendon started his car and took the lead. Dust lay like fog in the street. The street lights hung nimbused as in water. They drove on out of town.

A rutted lane turned at right angles. Dust hung above it too, and above all the land. The dark bulk of the ice plant, where the Negro Mayes was night watchman, rose against the sky. "Better stop here, hadn't we?" the soldier said. McLendon did not reply. He hurled the car up and slammed to a stop, the headlights glaring on the blank wall.

"Listen here, boys," the barber said; "if he's here, dont that prove he never done it? Dont it? If it was him, he would run. Dont you see he would?" The second car came up and stopped. McLendon got down; Butch sprang down beside him. "Listen, boys," the barber said.

"Cut the lights off!" McLendon said. The breathless dark rushed down. There was no sound in it save their lungs as they sought air in the parched dust in which for two months they had lived; then the diminishing crunch of McLendon's and Butch's feet, and a moment later McLendon's voice:

"Will! . . . Will!"

Below the east the wan hemorrhage of the moon increased. It heaved above the ridge, silvering the air, the dust, so that they seemed to breathe, live, in a bowl of molten lead. There was no sound of nightbird nor insect, no sound save their breathing and a faint ticking of contracting metal about the cars. Where their bodies touched one another they seemed to sweat dryly, for no more moisture came. "Christ!" a voice said; "let's get out of here."

But they didn't move until vague noises began to grow out of the darkness ahead; then they got out and waited tensely in the breathless dark. There was another sound: a blow, a hissing expulsion of breath and McLendon cursing in undertone. They stood a moment longer, then they ran forward. They ran in a stumbling clump, as though they were fleeing something. "Kill him, kill the son," a voice whispered. McLendon flung them back.

"Not here," he said. "Get him into the car." "Kill him, kill the black son!" the voice murmured. They dragged the Negro to the car. The barber had waited beside the car. He could feel himself sweating and he knew he was going to be sick at the stomach.

"What is it, captains?" the Negro said. "I aint done nothing. 'Fore God, Mr. John." Someone produced handcuffs. They worked busily about the Negro as though he were a post, quiet, intent, getting in one another's way. He submitted to the handcuffs, looking swiftly and constantly from dim face to dim face. "Who's here, captains?" he said, leaning to peer into the faces until they could feel his breath and smell his sweaty reek. He spoke a name or two. "What you all say I done, Mr. John?"

McLendon jerked the car door open. "Get in!" he said.

The Negro did not move. "What you all going to do with me, Mr. John? I aint done nothing. White folks, captains, I aint done nothing: I swear 'fore God." He called another name.

"Get in!" McLendon said. He struck the Negro. The others expelled their breath in a dry hissing and struck him with random blows and he whirled and cursed them, and swept his manacled hands across their faces and slashed the barber upon the mouth, and the barber struck him also. "Get him in there," McLendon said. They pushed at him. He ceased struggling and got in and sat quietly as the others took their places. He sat between the barber and the soldier, drawing his limbs in so as not to touch them, his eyes going swiftly and constantly from face to face. Butch clung to the running board. The car moved on. The barber nursed his mouth with his handkerchief.

"What's the matter, Hawk?" the soldier said.

"Nothing," the barber said. They regained the highroad and turned away from town. The second car dropped back out of the dust. They went on, gaining speed; the final fringe of houses dropped behind.

"Goddamn, he stinks!" the soldier said.

"We'll fix that," the drummer in front beside McLendon said. On the running board Butch cursed into the hot rush of air. The barber leaned suddenly forward and touched McLendon's arm.

"Let me out, John," he said.

"Jump out, niggerlover," McLendon said without turning his head. He drove swiftly. Behind them the sourceless lights of the second car glared in the dust. Presently McLendon turned into a narrow road. It was rutted with disuse. It led back to an abandoned brick kiln—a series of reddish mounds and weed- and vine-choked vats without bottom. It had been used for pasture once, until one day the owner missed one of his mules. Although he prodded carefully in the vats with a long pole, he could not even find the bottom of them.

"John," the barber said.

"Jump out, then," McLendon said, hurling the car along the ruts. Beside the barber the Negro spoke:

"Mr. Henry."

The barber sat forward. The narrow tunnel of the road rushed up and past. Their motion was like an extinct furnace blast: cooler, but utterly dead. The car bounded from rut to rut.

"Mr. Henry," the Negro said.

The barber began to tug furiously at the door. "Look out, there!" the soldier said, but the barber had already kicked the door open and swung onto the running board. The soldier leaned across the Negro and grasped at him, but he had already jumped. The car went on without checking speed.

The impetus hurled him crashing through dust-sheathed weeds, into the ditch. Dust puffed about him, and in a thin, vicious crackling of sapless stems he lay choking and retching until the second car passed and died away. Then he rose and limped on until he reached the highroad and turned toward town, brushing at his clothes with his hands. The moon was higher, riding high and clear of the dust at last, and after a while the town began to glare beneath the dust. He went on, limping. Presently he heard cars and the glow of them grew in the dust behind him and he left the road and crouched again in the weeds until they passed. McLendon's car came last now. There were four people in it and Butch was not on the running board.

They went on; the dust swallowed them; the glare and the sound died away. The dust of them hung for a while, but soon the eternal dust absorbed it again. The barber climbed back onto the road and limped on toward town.

IV

As she dressed for supper on that Saturday evening, her own flesh felt like fever. Her hands trembled among the hooks and eyes, and her eyes had a feverish look, and her hair swirled crisp and crackling under the comb. While she was still dressing the friends called for her and sat while she donned her sheerest underthings and stockings and a new voile dress. "Do you feel strong enough to go out?" they said, their eyes bright too, with a dark glitter. "When you have had time to get over the shock, you must tell us what happened. What he said and did; everything."

In the leafed darkness, as they walked toward the square, she began to breathe deeply, something like a swimmer preparing to dive, until she ceased trembling, the four of them walking slowly because of the terrible heat and out of solicitude for her. But as they neared the square she began to tremble again, walking with her head up, her hands clenched at her sides, their voices about her murmurous, also with that feverish, glittering quality of their eyes.

They entered the square, she in the center of the group, fragile in her fresh dress. She was trembling worse. She walked slower and slower, as children eat ice cream, her head up and her eyes bright in the haggard banner of her face, passing the hotel and the coatless drummers in chairs along the curb looking around at her: "That's the one: see? The one in pink in the middle." "Is that her? What did they do with the nigger? Did they—?" "Sure. He's all right." "All right, is he?" "Sure. He went on a little trip." Then the drug store, where even the young men lounging in the doorway tipped their hats and followed with their eyes the motion of her hips and legs when she passed.

They went on, passing the lifted hats of the gentlemen, the suddenly ceased voices, deferent, protective. "Do you see?" the friends said. Their voices sounded like long, hovering sighs of hissing exultation. "There's not a Negro on the square. Not one."

They reached the picture show. It was like a miniature fairyland with its lighted lobby and colored lithographs of life caught in its terrible and beautiful mutations. Her lips began to tingle. In the dark, when the picture began, it would be all right; she could hold back the laughing so it would not waste away so fast and so soon. So she hurried on before the turning faces, the undertones of low astonishment, and they took their accustomed places where she could see the aisle against the silver glare and the young men and girls coming in two and two against it.

The lights flicked away; the screen flowed silver, and soon life began to unfold, beautiful and passionate and sad, while still the young men and girls entered, scented and sibilant in the half dark, their paired backs in silhouette delicate and sleek, their slim, quick bodies awkward, divinely young, while beyond them the silver dream accumulated, inevitably on and on. She began to laugh. In trying to suppress it, it made more noise than ever; heads began to turn. Still laughing, her friends raised her and led her out, and she stood at the curb, laughing on a high, sustained note, until the taxi came up and they helped her in.

They removed the pink voile and the sheer underthings and the stockings, and put her to bed, and cracked ice for her temples, and sent for the doctor. He was hard to locate, so they ministered to her with hushed ejaculations, renewing the ice and fanning her. While the ice was fresh and cold she stopped laughing and lay still for a time, moaning only a little. But soon the laughing welled again and her voice rose screaming.

"Shhhhhhhhhhh! Shhhhhhhhhhhhhhh!" they said, freshening the ice-pack, smoothing her hair, examining it for gray; "poor girl!" Then to one another: "Do you suppose anything really happened?" their eyes darkly aglitter, secret and passionate. "Shhhhhhhhhh! Poor girl! Poor Minnie!"

V

It was midnight when McLendon drove up to his neat new house. It was trim and fresh as a birdcage and almost as small, with its clean, green-and-white paint. He locked the car and mounted the porch and entered. His wife rose from a chair beside the reading lamp. McLendon stopped in the floor and stared at her until she looked down.

"Look at that clock," he said, lifting his arm, pointing. She stood before him, her face lowered, a magazine in her hands. Her face was pale, strained, and weary-looking. "Haven't I told you about sitting up like this, waiting to see when I come in?"

"John," she said. She laid the magazine down. Poised on the balls of his feet, he glared at her with his hot eyes, his sweating face.

"Didn't I tell you?" He went toward her. She looked up then. He caught her shoulder. She stood passive, looking at him.

"Don't, John. I couldn't sleep . . . The heat; something. Please, John. You're hurting me."

"Didn't I tell you?" He released her and half struck, half flung her across the chair, and she lay there and watched him quietly as he left the room.

He went on through the house, ripping off his shirt, and on the dark, screened porch at the rear he stood and mopped his head and shoulders with the shirt and flung it away. He took the pistol from his hip and laid it on the table beside the bed, and sat on the bed and removed his shoes, and rose and slipped his trousers off. He was sweating again already, and he stooped and hunted furiously for the shirt. At last he found it and wiped his body again, and, with his body pressed against the dusty screen, he stood panting. There was no movement, no sound, not even an insect. The dark world seemed to lie stricken beneath the cold moon and the lidless stars.

QUESTIONS

1. What mood is created by Faulkner's opening sentence?

2. Draw a symbolic comparison between the time of the year and Minnie Cooper's age and marital status.

3. Why is mood intensified by the conversations in the barber shop?

4. How has Minnie's life contributed to the rumor that she has been "attacked, insulted, frightened"?

5. What does McLendon represent? Why is he the character who uses the word "rape"?

6. Why do those who were originally hesitant join McLendon after all?

7. Why is the Negro addressed as such by the narrative voice, though he is known to the men who've abducted him?

8. What is the contradiction between the way McLendon behaves on Minnie's behalf and the way he behaves with his wife?

9. What themes are present in this story?

10. How do the townspeople view Minnie before the incident? After the incident?

TOPICS FOR WRITING

1. Explain the class structure in this town and the impact of class and caste on events.

2. Evaluate Minnie Cooper's psychological need for attention.

3. Analyze setting, atmosphere, and mood in this story and their relationship to events. How does the vivid description (termed *imagery*) contribute to atmosphere? What patterns to the imagery do you detect?

4. Explain the consistency of mood in the two sections dealing directly with Minnie Cooper, and analyze the way mood shifts in the other three sections.

Arna Bontemps

A SUMMER TRAGEDY

Long a close friend of Langston Hughes, Arna Wendell Bontemps (1902–1973) was born in Alexandria, Louisiana. A courtly man, he served Fisk University in Nashville as librarian and assistant to the president for much of his life. Bontemps and Hughes collaborated on many collections and other works. "He sought," says Charles Nichols, "the source and shape of his creative work in his own roots—the deep South of Louisiana and Alabama. The stark, laconic, poignant stories he wrote in the early 1930's are in the realistic mode of American regionalism." The South was the place Bontemps returned to after his graduation from Pacif-

> *ic Union College in 1924, and two years later he won the Alexander Pushkin Poetry Prize. He became as well an essayist, a playwright, a short story writer, a novelist, and the author of many children's books, on some of which he collaborated with Hughes, Jack Conroy, and Countee Cullen. Bontemps was one of several writers to emerge from the Harlem Renaissance (1925–1929). Perhaps his most important novel was* Black Thunder *(1936), a forerunner to William Styron's 1967 novel* The Confessions of Nat Turner. *Bontemps'* The Poetry of the Negro, 1746–1970 *(with Hughes; first published in 1949) has since been revised. "A Summer Tragedy" is deceptive in its simplicity. Ironic symbols are everywhere in the story, framing the mood of timorous resignation—or is it determination? Like Paul Laurence Dunbar, Bontemps uses the dialect of the people within a defined place and time.*

Old Jeff Patton, the black share farmer, fumbled with his bow tie. His fingers trembled and the high stiff collar pinched his throat. A fellow loses his hand for such vanities after thirty or forty years of simple life. Once a year, or maybe twice if there's a wedding among his kinfolks, he may spruce up; but generally fancy clothes do nothing but adorn the wall of the big room and feed the moths. That had been Jeff Patton's experience. He had not worn his stiff-bosomed shirt more than a dozen times in all his married life. His swallow-tailed coat lay on the bed beside him, freshly brushed and pressed, but it was as full of holes as the overalls in which he worked on weekdays. The moths had used it badly. Jeff twisted his mouth into a hideous toothless grimace as he contended with the obstinate bow. He stamped his good foot and decided to give up the struggle.

"Jennie," he called.

"What's that, Jeff?" His wife's shrunken voice came out of the adjoining room like an echo. It was hardly bigger than a whisper.

"I reckon you'll have to he'p me wid this heah bow tie, baby," he said meekly. "Dog if I can hitch it up."

Her answer was not strong enough to reach him, but presently the old woman came to the door, feeling her way with a stick. She had a wasted, dead-leaf appearance. Her body, as scrawny and gnarled as a string bean, seemed less than nothing in the ocean of frayed and faded petticoats that surrounded her. These hung an inch or two above the tops of her heavy unlaced shoes and showed little grotesque piles where the stockings had fallen down from her negligible legs.

"You oughta could do a heap mo' wid a thing like that'n me— beingst as you got yo' good sight."

"Looks like I oughta could," he admitted. "But ma fingers is gone democrat on me. I get all mixed up in the looking glass an' can't tell wicha way to twist the devilish thing."

Jennie sat on the side of the bed and old Jeff Patton got down on one knee while she tied the bow knot. It was a slow and painful ordeal for each of them in this position. Jeff's bones cracked, his knee ached, and it was only after a half dozen attempts that Jennie worked a semblance of a bow into the tie.

"I got to dress maself now," the old woman whispered. "These is ma old shoes an' stockings, and I ain't so much as unwrapped ma dress."

"Well, don't worry 'bout me no mo', baby," Jeff said. "That 'bout finishes me. All I gotta do now is slip on that old coat 'n ves' an' I'll be fixed to leave."

Jennie disappeared again through the dim passage into the shed room. Being blind was no handicap to her in that black hole. Jeff heard the cane placed against the wall beside the door and knew that his wife was on easy ground. He put on his coat, took a battered top hat from the bedpost and hobbled to the front door. He was ready to travel. As soon as Jennie could get on her Sunday shoes and her old black silk dress, they would start.

Outside the tiny log house, the day was warm and mellow with sunshine. A host of wasps were humming with busy excitement in the trunk of a dead sycamore. Gray squirrels were searching through the grass for hickory nuts and blue jays were in the trees, hopping from branch to branch. Pine woods stretched away to the left like a black sea. Among them were scattered scores of log houses like Jeff's, houses of black share farmers. Cows and pigs wandered freely among the trees. There was no danger of loss. Each farmer knew his own stock and knew his neighbor's as well as he knew his neighbor's children.

Down the slope to the right were the cultivated acres on which the colored folks worked. They extended to the river, more than two miles away, and they were today green with the unmade cotton crop. A tiny thread of a road, which passed directly in front of Jeff's place, ran through these green fields like a pencil mark.

Jeff, standing outside the door, with his absurd hat in his left hand, surveyed the wide scene tenderly. He had been forty-five years on these acres. He loved them with the unexplained affection that others have for the countries to which they belong.

The sun was hot on his head, his collar still pinched his throat, and the Sunday clothes were intolerbly hot. Jeff transferred the hat to his right hand and began fanning with it. Suddenly the whisper that was Jennie's voice came out of the shed room.

"You can bring the car round front whilst you's waitin'," it said feebly. There was a tired pause; then it added, "I'll soon be fixed to go."

"A'right, baby," Jeff answered. "I'll get it in a minute."

But he didn't move. A thought struck him that made his mouth fall open. The mention of the car brought to his mind, with new intensity, the trip he and Jennie were about to take. Fear came into his eyes; excitement took his breath. Lord, Jesus!

"Jeff . . . O Jeff," the old woman's whisper called.

He awakened with a jolt. "Hunh, baby?"

"What you doin'?"

"Nuthin. Jes studyin'. I jes been turnin' things round'n round in ma mind."

"You could be gettin' the car," she said.

"Oh yes, right away, baby."

He started round to the shed, limping heavily on his bad leg. There were three frizzly chickens in the yard. All his other chickens had been killed or stolen recently. But the frizzly chickens had been saved somehow. That was fortunate indeed, for these curious creatures had a way of devouring "Poison" from the yard and in that way protecting against conjure and black luck and spells. But even the frizzly chickens seemed now to be in a stupor. Jeff thought they had some ailment; he expected all three of them to die shortly.

The shed in which the old T-model Ford stood was only a grass roof held up by four corner poles. It had been built by tremulous hands at a time when the little rattletrap car had been regarded as a peculiar treasure. And, miraculously, despite wind and downpour it still stood.

Jeff adjusted the crank and put his weight upon it. The engine came to life with a sputter and bang that rattled the old car from radiator to taillight. Jeff hopped into the seat and put his foot on the accelerator. The sputtering and banging increased. The rattling became more violent. That was good. It was good banging, good sputtering and rattling, and it meant that the aged car was still in running condition. She could be depended on for this trip.

Again Jeff's thought halted as if paralyzed. The suggestion of the trip fell into the machinery of his mind like a wrench. He felt dazed and weak. He swung the car out into the yard, made a half turn and drove around to the front door. When he took his hands off the wheel, he noticed that he was trembling violently. He cut off the motor and climbed to the ground to wait for Jennie.

A few minutes later she was at the window, her voice rattling against the pane like a broken shutter.

"I'm ready, Jeff."

He did not answer, but limped into the house and took her by the arm. He led her slowly through the big room, down the step and across the yard.

"You reckon I'd oughta lock the do'?" he asked softly.

They stopped and Jennie weighed the question. Finally she shook her head.

"Ne' mind the do'," she said. "I don't see no cause to lock up things."

"You right," Jeff agreed. "No cause to lock up."

Jeff opened the door and helped his wife into the car. A quick shudder passed over him. Jesus! Again he trembled.

"How come you shaking so?" Jennie whispered.

"I don't know," he said.

"You mus' be scairt, Jeff."

"No, baby, I ain't scairt."

He slammed the door after her and went around to crank up again. The motor started easily. Jeff wished that it had not been so responsive. He would have liked a few more minutes in which to turn things around in his head. As it was, with Jennie chiding him about being afraid, he had to keep going. He swung the car into the little pencil-mark road and started off toward the river, driving very slowly, very cautiously.

Chugging across the green countryside, the small battered Ford seemed tiny indeed. Jeff felt a familiar excitement, a thrill, as they came down the first slope to the immense levels on which the cotton was growing. He could not help reflecting that the crops were good. He knew what that meant, too; he had made forty-five of them with his own hands. It was true that he had worn out nearly a dozen mules, but that was the fault of old man Stevenson, the owner of the land. Major Stevenson had the odd notion that one mule was all a share farmer needed to work a thirty-acre plot. It was an expensive notion, the way it killed mules from overwork, but the old man held to it. Jeff thought it killed a good many share farmers as well as mules, but he had no sympathy for them. He had always been strong, and he had been taught to have no patience with weakness in men. Women or children might be tolerated if they were puny, but a weak man was a curse. Of course, his own children—

Jeff's thought halted there. He and Jennie never mentioned their dead children any more. And naturally he did not wish to dwell upon them in his mind.

Before he knew it, some remark would slip out of his mouth and that would make Jennie feel blue. Perhaps she would cry. A woman like Jennie could not easily throw off the grief that comes from losing five grown children within two years. Even Jeff was still staggered by the blow. His memory had not been much good recently. He frequently talked to himself. And, although he had kept it a secret, he knew that his courage had left him. He was terrified by the least unfamiliar sound at night. He was reluctant to venture far from home in the daytime. And that habit of trembling when he felt fearful was now far beyond his control. Sometimes he became afraid and trembled without knowing what had frightened him. The feeling would just come over him like a chill.

The car rattled slowly over the dusty road. Jennie sat erect and silent, with a little absurd hat pinned to her hair. Her useless eyes seemed very large, very white in their deep sockets. Suddenly Jeff heard her voice, and he inclined his head to catch the words.

"Is we passed Delia Moore's house yet?" she asked.

"Not yet," he said.

"You must be drivin' mighty slow, Jeff."

"We might just as well take our time, baby."

There was a pause. A little puff of steam was coming out of the radiator of the car. Heat wavered above the hood. Delia Moore's house was nearly half a mile away. After a moment Jennie spoke again.

"You ain't really scairt, is you, Jeff?"

"Nah, baby, I ain't scairt."

"You know how we agreed—we gotta keep on goin'."

Jewels of perspiration appeared on Jeff's forehead. His eyes rounded, blinked, becamed fixed on the road.

"I don't know," he said with a shiver. "I reckon it's the only thing to do."

"Hm."

A flock of guinea fowls, pecking in the road, were scattered by the passing car. Some of them took to their wings; others hid under bushes. A blue jay, swaying on a leafy twig, was annoying a roadside squirrel. Jeff held an even speed till he came near Delia's place. Then he slowed down noticeably.

Delia's house was really no house at all, but an abandoned store building converted into a dwelling. It sat near a crossroads, beneath a single black cedar tree. There Delia, a cattish old creature of Jennie's age, lived alone. She had been there more years than anybody could remember, and long ago had won the disfavor of such women as Jennie. For in her young days Delia had been gayer, yellower and saucier than seemed proper in those parts. Her ways with menfolks had been dark and suspicious. And the fact that she had had as many husbands as children did not help her reputation.

"Yonder's old Delia," Jeff said as they passed.

"What she doin'?"

"Jes sittin' in the do'," he said.

"She see us?"

"Hm," Jeff said. "Musta did."

That relieved Jennie. It strengthened her to know that her old enemy had seen her pass in her best clothes. That would give the old she-devil something to chew her gums and fret about, Jennie thought. Wouldn't she have a fit if she didn't find out? Old evil Delia! This would be just the thing for her. It would pay her back for being so evil. It would also pay her, Jennie thought, for the way she used to grin at Jeff—long ago when her teeth were good.

The road became smooth and red, and Jeff could tell by the smell of the air that they were nearing the river. He could see the rise where the road turned and ran along parallel to the stream. The car chugged on monotonously. After a long silent spell, Jennie leaned against Jeff and spoke.

"How many bale o' cotton you think we got standin'?" she said.

Jeff wrinkled his forehead as he calculated.

"'Bout twenty-five, I reckon."

"How many you make las' year?"

"Twenty-eight," he said. "How come you ask that?"

"I's jes thinkin'," Jennie said quietly.

"It don't make a speck o' difference though," Jeff reflected. "If we get much or if we get little, we still gonna be in debt to old man Stevenson when he gets through counting up agin us. It's took us a long time to learn that."

Jennie was not listening to these words. She had fallen into a trance-like meditation. Her lips twitched. She chewed her gums and rubbed her gnarled hands nervously. Suddenly she leaned forward, buried her face in the nervous hands and burst into tears. She cried aloud in a dry cracked voice that suggested the rattle of fodder on dead stalks. She cried aloud like a child, for she had never learned to suppress a genuine sob. Her slight old frame shook heavily and seemed hardly able to sustain such violent grief.

"What's the matter, baby?" Jeff asked awkwardly. "Why you cryin' like all that?"

"I's jes thinkin'," she said.

"So you the one what's scairt now, hunh?"

"I ain't scairt, Jeff. I's jes thinkin' 'bout leavin' eve'thing like this—eve'thing we been used to. It's right sad-like."

Jeff did not answer, and presently Jennie buried her face again and cried.

The sun was almost overhead. It beat down furiously on the dusty wagon-path road, on the parched roadside grass and the tiny battered car. Jeff's hands, gripping the wheel, became wet with perspiration; his forehead sparkled. Jeff's lips parted. His mouth shaped a hideous grimace. His face suggested the face of a man being burned. But the torture passed and his expression softened again.

"You mustn't cry, baby," he said to his wife. "We gotta be strong. We can't break down."

Jennie waited a few seconds, then said, "You reckon we oughta do it, Jeff? You reckon we oughta go 'head an' do it, really?"

Jeff's voice choked; his eyes blurred. He was terrified to hear Jennie say the thing that had been in his mind all morning. She had egged him on when he had wanted more than anything in the world to wait, to reconsider, to think things over a little longer. Now she was getting cold feet. Actually there was no need of thinking the question through again. It would only end in making the same painful decision once more. Jeff knew that. There was no need of fooling around longer.

"We jes as well to do like we planned," he said. "They ain't nothin' else for us now—it's the bes' thing."

Jeff thought of the handicaps, the near impossibility, of making another crop with his leg bothering him more and more each week. Then there was always the chance that he would have another stroke, like the one that had made him lame. Another one might kill him. The least it could do would be to leave him helpless. Jeff gasped—Lord, Jesus! He could not bear to think of being helpless, like a baby, on Jennie's hands. Frail, blind Jennie.

The little pounding motor of the car worked harder and harder. The puff of steam from the cracked radiator became larger. Jeff realized that they were climbing a little rise. A moment later the road turned abruptly and he looked down upon the face of the river.

"Jeff."

"Hunh?"

"Is that the water I hear?"

"Hm. Tha's it."

"Well, which way you goin' now?"

"Down this-a way," he said. "The road runs 'long 'side o' the water a lil piece."

She waited a while calmly. Then she said, "Drive faster."

"A'right, baby," Jeff said.

The water roared in the bed of the river. It was fifty or sixty feet below the level of the road. Between the road and the water there was a long smooth slope, sharply inclined. The slope was dry, the clay hardened by prolonged summer heat. The water below, roaring in a narrow channel, was noisy and wild.

"Jeff."

"Hunh?"

"How far you goin'?"

"Jes a lil piece down the road."

"You ain't scairt, is you, Jeff?"

"Nah, baby," he said trembling. "I ain't scairt."

"Remember how we planned it, Jeff. We gotta do it like we said. Brave-like."

"Hm."

Jeff's brain darkened. Things suddenly seemed unreal, like figures in a dream. Thoughts swam in his mind foolishly, hysterically, like little blind fish in a pool within a dense cave. They rushed, crossed one another, jostled, collided, retreated and rushed again. Jeff soon became dizzy. He shuddered violently and turned to his wife.

"Jennie, I can't do it. I can't." His voice broke pitifully.

She did not appear to be listening. All the grief had gone from her face. She sat erect, her unseeing eyes wide open, strained and frightful. Her glossy black skin had become dull. She seemed as thin, as sharp and bony, as a starved bird. Now, having suffered and endured the sadness of tearing herself away from beloved things, she showed no anguish. She was absorbed with her own thoughts, and she didn't even hear Jeff's voice shouting in her ear.

Jeff said nothing more. For an instant there was light in his cavernous brain. The great chamber was, for less than a second, peopled by characters he knew and loved. They were simple, healthy creatures, and they behaved in a manner that he could understand. They had quality. But since he had already taken leave of them long ago, the remembrance did not break his heart again. Young Jeff Patton was among them, the Jeff Patton of fifty years ago who went down to New Orleans with a crowd of country boys to the Mardi Gras doings. The gay young crowd, boys with candy-striped shirts and rouged-brown girls in noisy silks, was like a picture in his head. Yet it did not make him sad. On that very trip Slim

Burns had killed Joe Beasley—the crowd had been broken up. Since then Jeff Patton's world had been the Greenbriar Plantation. If there had been other Mardi Gras carnivals, he had not heard of them. Since then there had been no time; the years had fallen on him like waves. Now he was old, worn out. Another paralytic stroke (like the one he had already suffered) would put him on his back for keeps. In that condition, with a frail blind woman to look after him, he would be worse off than if he were dead.

Suddenly Jeff's hands became steady. He actually felt brave. He slowed down the motor of the car and carefully pulled off the road. Below, the water of the stream boomed, a soft thunder in the deep channel. Jeff ran the car onto the clay slope, pointed it directly toward the stream and put his foot heavily on the accelerator. The little car leaped furiously down the steep incline toward the water. The movement was nearly as swift and direct as a fall. The two old black folks, sitting quietly side by side, showed no excitement. In another instant the car hit the water and dropped immediately out of sight.

A little later it lodged in the mud of a shallow place. One wheel of the crushed and upturned little Ford became visible above the rushing water.

QUESTIONS

1. What kind of community do Jeff and Jennie live in?

2. Who is Major Stevenson and how does share farming work?

3. Why are the Pattons in debt to Major Stevenson?

4. Why are the Pattons dressing up as the story opens? What does their dressing up tell you about them?

5. How has the author, without saying so, developed the great love Jeff and Jennie have for each other?

6. What point of view is used in "A Summer Tragedy"? Why is it effective?

7. What kind of mood has Bontemps established? How does he establish it?

8. What themes are touched on?

TOPICS FOR WRITING

1. Examine the tragic irony of share farming with a mule and then driving off in a product of the industrial revolution. What is Bontemps saying about the social and economic forces in people's lives?

2. Explore the contradictions inherent in the title of the story. Analyze the words "summer" and "tragedy" in the context of the narrative, and demonstrate how they are the controlling terms for the mood of the story.

3. Analyze the many foreshadowing devices (see glossary) in this story and show how they influence the mood of the tale.

Eudora Welty

A WORN PATH

*Eudora Welty (1909–   ) was born in Jackson, Mississippi,
where she began an education that was completed at the
University of Wisconsin and at Columbia University. During
the Depression, she worked for the WPA as a publicist; later
she became an advertising copywriter. She also wrote for
radio. Welty, who has a keen eye for description, once
thought about becoming a painter. Instead, she became a
writer, her work first appearing in 1936; a collection of
stories,* A Curtain of Green, *was published five years later.
Among her novels are* Delta Wedding *(1946),* The Ponder
Heart *(1954), and* The Optimist's Daughter *(1972). Though
sometimes considered a Southern regionalist in the tradition of Robert Penn Warren, Faulkner, and John Crowe
Ransom, Welty's main interest is in character—what the
character thinks, feels, and sees, how the character adapts
to the world in which she or he lives. In this sense she is
closer to the Chekhovian tradition than to the American
realist writers. "A Worn Path" is a journey into a character
who cunningly endures on her own terms.*

It was December—a bright frozen day in the early morning. Far out in the country
there was an old Negro woman with her head tied in a red rag, coming along a
path through the pinewoods. Her name was Phoenix Jackson. She was very old
and small and she walked slowly in the dark pine shadows, moving a little from
side to side in her steps, with the balanced heaviness and lightness of a
pendulum in a grandfather clock. She carried a thin, small cane made from an
umbrella, and with this she kept tapping the frozen earth in front of her. This
made a grave and persistent noise in the still air, that seemed meditative like the
chirping of a solitary little bird.

She wore a dark striped dress reaching down to her shoe tops, and an equally
long apron of bleached sugar sacks, with a full pocket: all neat and tidy, but every
time she took a step she might have fallen over her shoe-laces, which dragged
from her unlaced shoes. She looked straight ahead. Her eyes were blue with age.
Her skin had a pattern all its own of numberless branching wrinkles and as
though a whole little tree stood in the middle of her forehead, but a golden color
ran underneath, and the two knobs of her cheeks were illuminated by a yellow
burning under the dark. Under the red rag her hair came down on her neck in the
frailest of ringlets, still black, and with an odor like copper.

Now and then there was a quivering in the thicket. Old Phoenix said, "Out of
my way, all you foxes, owls, beetles, jack rabbits, coons, and wild animals! . . .
Keep out from under these feet, little bob-whites. . . . Keep the big wild hogs out
of my path. Don't let none of those come running my direction. I got a long way."
Under her small black-freckled hand her cane, limber as a buggy whip, would
switch at the brush as if to rouse up any hiding things.

On she went. The woods were deep and still. The sun made the pine needles
almost too bright to look at, up where the wind rocked. The cones dropped as

light as feathers. Down in the hollow was the mourning dove—it was not too late for him.

The path ran up a hill. "Seem like there is chains about my feet, time I get this far," she said, in the voice of argument old people keep to use with themselves. "Something always take a hold of me on this hill—pleads I should stay."

After she got to the top she turned and gave a full, severe look behind her where she had come. "Up through pines," she said at length. "Now down through oaks."

Her eyes opened their widest, and she started down gently. But before she got to the bottom of the hill a bush caught her dress.

Her fingers were busy and intent, but her skirts were full and long, so that before she could pull them free in one place they were caught in another. It was not possible to allow the dress to tear. "I in the thorny bush," she said. "Thorns, you doing your appointed work. Never want to let folks pass—no sir. Old eyes thought you was a prettly little *green* bush."

Finally, trembling all over, she stood free, and after a moment dared to stoop for her cane.

"Sun so high!" she cried, leaning back and looking, while the thick tears went over her eyes. "The time getting all gone here."

At the foot of this hill was a place where a log was laid across the creek.

"Now comes the trial," said Phoenix.

Putting her right foot out, she mounted the log and shut her eyes. Lifting her skirt, levelling her cane fiercely before her, like a festival figure in some parade, she began to march across. Then she opened her eyes and she was safe on the other side.

"I wasn't as old as I thought," she said.

But she sat down to rest. She spread her skirts on the bank around her and folded her hands over her knees. Up above her was a tree in a pearly cloud of mistletoe. She did not dare to close her eyes, and when a little boy brought her a little plate with a slice of marble-cake on it she spoke to him. "That would be acceptable," she said. But when she went to take it there was just her own hand in the air.

So she left that tree, and had to go through a barbed-wire fence. There she had to creep and crawl, spreading her knees and stretching her fingers like a baby trying to climb the steps. But she talked loudly to herself: she could not let her dress be torn now, so late in the day, and she could not pay for having her arm or her leg sawed off if she got caught fast where she was.

At last she was safe through the fence and risen up out in the clearing. Big dead trees, like black men with one arm, were standing in the purple stalks of the withered cotton field. There sat a buzzard.

"Who you watching?"

In the furrow she made her way along.

"Glad this not the season for bulls," she said, looking sideways, "and the good Lord made his snakes to curl up and sleep in the winter. A pleasure I don't see no two-headed snake coming around that tree, where it come once. It took a while to get by him, back in the summer."

She passed through the old cotton and went into a field of dead corn. It whispered and shook and was taller than her head. "Through the maze now," she said, for there was no path.

Then there was something tall, black, and skinny there, moving before her.

At first she took it for a man. It could have been a man dancing in the field. But she stood still and listened, and it did not make a sound. It was as silent as a ghost.

"Ghost," she said sharply, "who be you the ghost of? For I have heard of nary death close by."

But there was no answer—only the ragged dancing in the wind.

She shut her eyes, reached out her hand, and touched a sleeve. She found a coat and inside that an emptiness, cold as ice.

"You scarecrow," she said. Her face lighted. "I ought to be shut up for good," she said with laughter. "My senses is gone. I too old. I the oldest people I ever know. Dance, old scarecrow," she said, "while I dancing with you."

She kicked her foot over the furrow, and with mouth drawn down, shook her head once or twice in a little strutting way. Some husks blew down and whirled in streamers about her skirts.

Then she went on, parting her way from side to side with the cane, through the whispering field. At last she came to the end, to a wagon track where the silver grass blew between the red ruts. The quail were walking around like pullets, seeming all dainty and unseen.

"Walk pretty," she said. "This the easy place. This the easy going."

She followed the track, swaying through the quiet bare fields, through the little strings of trees silver in their dead leaves, past cabins silver from weather, with the doors and windows boarded shut, all like old women under a spell sitting there. "I walking in their sleep," she said, nodding her head vigorously.

In a ravine she went where a spring was silently flowing through a hollow log. Old Phoenix bent and drank. "Sweet-gum makes the water sweet," she said, and drank more. "Nobody know who made this well, for it was here when I was born."

The track crossed a swampy part where the moss hung as white as lace from every limb. "Sleep on, alligators, and blow you bubbles." Then the track went into the road.

Deep, deep the road went down between the high green-colored banks. Overhead the live-oaks met, and it was as dark as a cave.

A black dog with a lolling tongue came up out of the weeds by the ditch. She was meditating, and not ready, and when he came at her she only hit him a little with her cane. Over she went in the ditch, like a little puff of milk-weed.

Down there, her senses drifted away. A dream visited her, and she reached her hand up, but nothing reached down and gave her a pull. So she lay there and presently went to talking. "Old woman," she said to herself, "that black dog come up out of the weeds to stall you off, and now there he sitting on his fine tail, smiling at you."

A white man finally came along and found her—a hunter, a young man, with his dog on a chain.

"Well, Granny!" he laughed. "What are you doing there?"

"Lying on my back like a June-bug waiting to be turned over, mister," she said, reaching up her hand.

He lifted her up, gave her a swing in the air, and set her down, "Anything broken, Granny?"

"No sir, them old dead weeds is springy enough," said Phoenix, when she had got her breath. "I thank you for your trouble."

"Where do you live, Granny?" he asked, while the two dogs were growling at each other.

"Away back yonder, sir, behind the ridge. You can't even see it from here."

"On your way home?"

"No, sir, I going to town."

"Why, that's too far! That's as far as I walk when I come out myself, and I get something for my trouble." He patted the stuffed bag he carried, and there hung down a little closed claw. It was one of the bob-whites, with its beak hooked bitterly to show it was dead. "Now you go on home, Granny!"

"I bound to go to town, mister," said Phoenix. "The time come around."

He gave another laugh, filling the whole landscape. "I know you old colored people! Wouldn't miss going to town to see Santa Claus!"

But something held Old Phoenix very still. The deep lines in her face went into a fierce and different radiation. Without warning, she had seen with her own eyes a flashing nickel fall out of the man's pocket onto the ground.

"How old are you, Granny?" he was saying.

"There is no telling, mister," she said, "no telling."

Then she gave a little cry and clapped her hands and said, "Git on away from here, dog! Look! Look at that dog!" She laughed as if in admiration. "He ain't scared of nobody. He a big black dog." She whispered, "Sic him!"

"Watch me get rid of that cur," said the man. "Sic him, Pete! Sic him!"

Phoenix heard the dogs fighting, and heard the man running and throwing sticks. She even heard a gunshot. But she was slowly bending forward by that time, further and further forward, the lids stretched down over her eyes, as if she were doing this in her sleep. Her chin was lowered almost to her knees. The yellow palm of her hand came out from the fold of her apron. Her fingers slid down and along the ground under the piece of money with the grace and care they would have in lifting an egg from under a sitting hen. The she slowly straightened up, she stood erect, and the nickel was in her apron pocket. A bird flew by. Her lips moved. "God watching me the whole time. I come to stealing."

The man came back, and his own dog panted about them. "Well, I scared him off that time," he said, and then he laughed and lifted his gun and pointed it at Phoenix.

She stood straight and faced him.

"Doesn't the gun scare you?" he said, still pointing it.

"No, sir, I seen plenty go off closer by, in my day, and for less than what I done," she said, holding utterly still.

He smiled, and shouldered the gun. "Well, Granny," he said, "you must be a hundred years old, and scared of nothing. I'd give you a dime if I had any money with me. But you take my advice and stay home, and nothing will happen to you."

"I bound to go on my way, mister," said Phoenix. She inclined her head in the red rag. Then they went in different directions, but she could hear the gun shooting again and again over the hill.

She walked on. The shadows hung from the oak trees to the road like curtains. Then she smelled wood-smoke, and smelled the river, and she saw a steeple and the cabins on their steep steps. Dozens of little black children whirled around her. There ahead was Natchez shining. Bells were ringing. She walked on.

In the paved city it was Christmas time. There were red and green electric lights strung and crisscrossed everywhere, and all turned on in the daytime. Old Phoenix would have been lost if she had not distrusted her eyesight and depended on her feet to know where to take her.

She paused quietly on the sidewalk where people were passing by. A lady came along in the crowd, carrying an armful of red-, green-, and silver-wrapped presents; she gave off perfume like the red roses in hot summer, and Phoenix stopped her.

"Please, missy, will you lace up my shoe?" She held up her foot.

"What do you want, Grandma?"

"See my shoe," said Phoenix. "Do all right for out in the country, but wouldn't look right to go in a big building."

"Stand still then, Grandma," said the lady. She put her packages down on the sidewalk beside her and laced and tied both shoes tightly.

"Can't lace 'em with a cane," said Phoenix. "Thank you, missy. I doesn't mind asking a nice lady to tie up my shoe, when I gets out on the street."

Moving slowly and from side to side, she went into the big building and into a tower of steps, where she walked up and around and around until her feet knew to stop.

She entered a door, and there she saw nailed up on the wall the document that had been stamped with the gold seal and framed in the gold frame, which matched the dream that was hung up in her head.

"Here I be," she said. There was a fixed and ceremonial stiffness over her body.

"A charity case, I suppose," said an attendant who sat at the desk before her.

But Phoenix only looked above her head. There was sweat on her face, the wrinkles in her skin shone like a bright net.

"Speak up, Grandma," the woman said. "What's your name? We must have your history, you know. Have you been here before? What seems to be the trouble with you?"

Old Phoenix only gave a twitch to her face as if a fly were bothering her.

"Are you deaf?" cried the attendant.

But then the nurse came in.

"Oh, that's just old Aunt Phoenix," she said. "She doesn't come for herself— she has a little grandson. She makes these trips just as regular as clockwork. She lives away back off the Old Natchez Trace." She bent down. "Well, Aunt Phoenix, why don't you just take a seat? We won't keep you standing after your long trip." She pointed.

The old woman sat down, bolt upright in the chair.

"Now, how is the boy?" asked the nurse.

Old Phoenix did not speak.

"I said, how is the boy?"

But Phoenix only waited and stared straight ahead, her face very solemn and withdrawn into rigidity.

"Is his throat any better?" asked the nurse. "Aunt Phoenix, don't you hear me? Is your grandson's throat any better since the last time you came for the medicine?"

With her hands on her knees, the old woman waited, silent, erect and motionless, just as if she were in armour.

"You mustn't take up our time this way, Aunt Phoenix," the nurse said. "Tell us quickly about your grandson, and get it over. He isn't dead, is he?"

At last there came a flicker and then a flame of comprehension across her face, and she spoke.

"My grandson. It was my memory had left me. There I sat and forgot why I made my long trip."

"Forgot?" The nurse frowned. "After you came so far?"

Then Phoenix was like an old woman begging a dignified forgiveness for waking up frightened in the night. "I never did go to school, I was too old at the Surrender," she said in a soft voice. "I'm an old woman without an education. It was my memory fail me. My little grandson, he is just the same, and I forgot it in the coming."

"Throat never heals, does it?" said the nurse, speaking in a loud, sure voice to Old Phoenix. By now she had a card with something written on it, a little list. "Yes. Swallowed lye. When was it—January—two-three years ago—"

Phoenix spoke unasked now. "No, missy, he not dead, he just the same. Every little while his throat begin to close up again, and he not able to swallow. He not get his breath. He not able to help himself. So the time come around, and I go on another trip for the soothingmedicine."

"All right. The doctor said as long as you came to get it, you could have it," said the nurse. "But it's an obstinate case."

"My little grandson, he sit up there in the house all wrapped up, waiting by himself," Phoenix went on. "We is the only two left in the world. He suffer and it don't seem to put him back at all. He got a sweet look. He going to last. He wear a little patch quilt and peep out holding his mouth open like a little bird. I remembers so plain now. I not going to forget him again, no, the whole enduring time. I could tell him from all the others in creation."

"All right." The nurse was trying to hush her now. She brought her a bottle of medicine. "Charity," she said, making a check mark in a book.

Old Phoenix held the bottle close to her eyes and then carefully put it into her pocket.

"I thank you," she said.

"It's Christmas time, Grandma," said the attendant. "Could I give you a few pennies out of my purse?"

"Five pennies is a nickel," said Phoenix stiffly.

"Here's a nickel," said the attendant.

Phoenix rose carefully and held out her hand. She received the nickel and then fished the other nickel out of her pocket and laid it beside the new one. She stared at her palm closely, with her head on one side.

Then she gave a tap with her cane on the floor.

"This is what come to me to do," she said. "I going to the store and buy my child a little windmill they sells, made out of paper. He going to find it hard to believe there such a thing in the world. I'll march myself back where he waiting, holding it straight up in this hand."

She lifted her free hand, gave a little nod, turned round, and walked out of the doctor's office. Then her slow step began on the stairs, going down.

QUESTIONS

1. What mood does the title convey? How do the season and the rural setting create atmosphere?

2. Why does everyone call Phoenix Jackson "Granny," "Grandma," or "Aunt Phoenix," when it is quite clear none are related to her?

3. What is the symbolic meaning of the Phoenix, and how would it apply to this story?

4. What themes does this story deal with?

5. What is the ironic relationship between the "charity" medicine and Phoenix's obviously rich history?

6. Why has she stolen the hunter's nickel and more or less demanded another from the attendant in the clinic?

TOPICS FOR WRITING

1. Write an essay on Phoenix Jackson, on the animals she thinks about or sees, and on her relationship with them. How does this relationship influence the mood of the story?

2. "A Worn Path" was the favorite story heard by students in a Jackson freedom school in 1964. Why, do you think, did they like this tale? What contribution did the story's mood make to their enjoyment?

3. Compare Phoenix Jackson to Jeff and Jennie Patton in "A Summer Tragedy" (page 135).

4. Eudora Welty wrote of "A Worn Path": "What I hoped would come clear was that in the whole surround of this story, the world it threads through, the only certain thing at all is the worn path. The habit of love cuts through confusion and stumbles or continues its way out of difficulty, it remembers the way even when it forgets, for a dumb-founded moment, its reason for being. The path is the thing that matters." Relate the "mood" of this statement to the mood of the tale.

TONE AND THEME: THE GRAND ILLUSIONS OF WAR

Tone is what we seem to hear in a story: anger, sadness, delight, satire, and so on. We are directed to these emotions and attitudes by the author; it is his or her voice that we are really listening to, his or her state of mind we are perceiving, his or her attitude toward the subject. Tone not only lends emphasis to theme, but also creates its own levels of tension and conflict, which are orchestrated by the author's choice of and placement of words.

We can find tone in dialogue, when it is present, as well as in narrative. Dialogue also, of course, moves the action of a story (certainly of a play) and is in great part what makes up a character.

The following stories use the ironic tone, which has long been used in literature, beginning with the Greeks; probably, its origins are oral. Irony is used to convey meanings that are different from or opposite to the apparent sense of certain words and images; it is the incongruity between appearance and reality.

Certain well-known obscenities, for example, may, by virtue of the tone of voice, be used as words of praise instead of damnation or disgust. By the same token, words of endearment, depending upon the situation in which they are spoken, may convey instead contempt.

There are different kinds of irony that are used in both drama and fiction; irony has also been a useful tool for poets (Chaucer), essayists (Swift), and many others.

Perhaps the best example of *dramatic irony*, or *tragic irony*, is to be found in Sophocles's *Oedipus Rex* (pages 853–891), wherein the protagonist unknowingly creates the structure for his own undoing. This might also be called *irony of fate*, which is to say that the protagonist gets what he deserves or what the gods or fate believes he deserves.

In *verbal irony* the words, by design or not, conceal the real meaning and produce incongruity. This kind of irony can be found in all writing, but it is most prominent in drama. The handkerchief scene in *Othello* (Act III, Scene 4) is an example (pages 806–807).

Othello: Give me your hand. This hand is moist, my lady.
Desdemona: It yet hath felt no age nor known no sorrow.
Othello: This argues fruitfulness and liberal heart,
    Hot, hot, and moist. This hand of yours requires
    A sequester from liberty, fasting and prayer,
    Much castigation, exercise devout;
    For here's a young and sweating devil here
    That commonly rebels. 'Tis a good hand,
    A frank one.
Desdemona: You may, indeed, say so;
    For 'twas that hand that gave away my heart.
Othello: A liberal hand: the hearts of old gave hands;
    But our new heraldry is hands, not hearts.

The above exchange is close to being mockery, another form of irony. Both are forms of word play, which is used to move action and blur the perception between what is real and what isn't. Polite banter *(Asteism)* and innuendo are also related to word play.

Irony may also encompass *self-effacement;* there are examples of this in "Just Lather, That's All." *Understatement* is also used in ironic expression; and *low-rating*, or *ranking*, is a contemporary relative of irony often used by comics whose night-club dissertations on individuals and society offer so much barbed amusement.

Paradox, an apparent contradiction that may, however, be a truthful statement, is also related to irony, but it is *satire* that assumes, even in its relationship to irony, a position of importance all its own, as we see in Pirandello's "War." The "censure of humanity has been the dominant quality of satire," according to Shipley. Satire, an expression of criticism of human frailty and folly, was used by Cervantes, Rabelais, Swift, Voltaire, Lewis, and others. Such censure is designed to improve human institutions.

War lends itself easily to the use of irony in all its forms. In the first of the stories in this section, we see a group of people on a train talking about their sons fighting on the front during World War I. In the second there are only two characters, and the kind of war being fought is vastly different from Pirandello's. In the third, "August 2026: There Will Come Soft Rains," there are no characters at all—an arrangement that becomes ironic, but, one hopes not prophetic, in itself.

While irony is the literary weapon of the underdog, the persona who poses as the antagonist in order to become the protagonist (bombast and bravado are usually traits found in the *real* antagonist, almost never in the hero), we should remember that irony may be in the voice and outlook of the author. (See *Lysistrata*, pages 714–748.)

Irony finds for us another reality, one we can live with, but it also serves the purpose of pointing up the reality from which we so often flee.

Luigi Pirandello

WAR

The 1934 recipient of the Nobel Prize in literature, Luigi Pirandello (1867–1936) was born in Girgenti, Italy, and was educated at Palermo, Rome, and the University of Bonn, in Germany. He was a professor of Italian literature at the Normal College for Women in Rome for approximately thirty years. Perhaps best known as a playwright, Pirandello did not begin writing for the stage until he was 46. Prior to that time, he gained a considerable reputation as a novelist and short story writer. His most famous play, Six Characters in Search of an Author, *was published in 1921. His fiction works include* The Late Mattia Pascal *(1904) and* One, None and a Hundred Thousand *(1926). Pirandello's stories, numbering in the hundreds, have been published in English under the titles* Horse in the Moon *(1932),* Better Think Twice about It *(1935), and* The Medals and Other Stories *(1939). Pirandello's works usually have a major theme, voiced by a character in his story "Deathwatch": "I'm not suffering on my account, or on your account. I'm suffering because life is what it is."*

The passengers who had left Rome by the night express had had to stop until dawn at the small station of Fabriano in order to continue their journey by the small old-fashioned "local" joining the main line with Sulmona.

At dawn, in a stuffy and smoky second-class carriage in which five people had already spent the night, a bulky woman in deep mourning, was hoisted in—almost like a shapeless bundle. Behind her—puffing and moaning, followed her husband—a tiny man, thin and weakly, his face death-white, his eyes small and bright and looking shy and uneasy.

Having at last taken a seat he politely thanked the passengers who had helped his wife and who had made room for her; then he turned round to the woman trying to pull down the collar of her coat and politely inquired:

"Are you all right, dear?"

The wife, instead of answering, pulled up her collar again to her eyes, so as to hide her face.

"Nasty world," muttered the husband with a sad smile.

And he felt it his duty to explain to his traveling companions that the poor woman was to be pitied for the war was taking away from her her only son, a boy of twenty to whom both had devoted their entire life, even breaking up their home at Sulmona to follow him to Rome where he had to go as a student, then, allowing him to volunteer for war with an assurance, however, that at least for six months he would not be sent to the front and now, all of a sudden, receiving a wire saying that he was due to leave in three days' time and asking them to go and see him off.

The woman under the big coat was twisting and wriggling, at times growling like a wild animal, feeling certain that all those explanations would not have aroused even a shadow of sympathy from those people who—most likely—were in the same plight as herself. One of them, who had been listening with particular attention, said:

"You should thank God that your son is only leaving now for the front. Mine has been sent there the first day of the war. He has already come back twice wounded and been sent back again to the front."

"What about me? I have two sons and three nephews at the front," said another passenger.

"Maybe, but in our case it is our *only* son," ventured the husband.

"What difference can it make? You may spoil your only son with excessive attentions, but you cannot love him more than you would all your other children if you had any. Paternal love is not like bread that can be broken into pieces and split amongst the children in equal shares. A father gives *all* his love to each one of his children without discrimination, whether it be one or ten, and if I am suffering now for my two sons, I am not suffering half for each of them but double. . . ."

"True . . . true . . ." sighed the embarrassed husband, "but suppose (of course we all hope it will never be your case) a father has two sons at the front and he loses one of them, there is still one left to console him . . . while . . ."

"Yes," answered the other, getting cross, "a son left to console him but also a son left for whom he must survive, while in the case of the father of an only son if the son dies the father can die too and put an end to his distress. Which of the two positions is the worse? Don't you see how my case would be worse than yours?"

"Nonsense," interrupted another traveler, a fat, red-faced man with bloodshot eyes of the palest gray.

He was panting. From his bulging eyes seemed to spurt inner violence of an uncontrolled vitality which his weakened body could hardly contain.

"Nonsense," he repeated, trying to cover his mouth with his hand so as to hide the two missing front teeth. "Nonsense. Do we give life to our children for our own benefit?"

The other travelers stared at him in distress. The one who had had his son at the front since the first day of the war sighed: "You are right. Our children do not belong to us, they belong to the Country. . . ."

"Bosh," retorted the fat traveler. "Do we think of the Country when we give life to our children? Our sons are born because . . . well, because they must be born and when they come to life they take our own life with them. This is the truth. We belong to them but they never belong to us. And when they reach twenty they are exactly what we were at their age. We too had a father and mother, but there were so many other things as well . . . girls, cigarettes, illusions, new ties . . . and the Country, of course, whose call we would have answered—when we were twenty—even if father and mother had said no. Now, at our age, the love of our Country is still great, of course, but stronger than it is the love for our children. Is there any one of us here who wouldn't gladly take his son's place at the front if he could?"

There was a silence all round, everybody nodding as to approve.

"Why then," continued the fat man, "shouldn't we consider the feelings of our children when they are twenty? Isn't it natural that at their age they should consider the love for their Country (I am speaking of decent boys, of course) even greater than the love for us? Isn't it natural that it should be so, as after all they must look upon us as upon old boys who cannot move any more and must stay at home? If Country exists, if Country is a natural necessity like bread, of which each of us must eat in order not to die of hunger, somebody must go to defend it. And our sons go, when they are twenty, and they don't want tears, because if they die, they died inflamed and happy (I am speaking, of course, of decent boys). Now, if one dies young and happy, without having the ugly sides of life, the boredom of it, the pettiness, the bitterness of disillusion . . . what more can we ask for him? Everyone should stop crying: everyone should laugh, as I do . . . or at least thank God—as I do—because my son, before dying, sent me a message saying that he was dying satisfied at having ended his life in the best way he could have wished. That is why, as you see, I do not even wear mourning. . . ."

He shook his light fawn coat as to show it; his livid lip over his missing teeth was trembling, his eyes were watery and motionless and soon after he ended with a shrill laugh which might well have been a sob.

"Quite so . . . Quite so . . ." agreed the others.

The woman who, bundled in a corner under her coat, had been sitting and listening had—for the last three months—tried to find in the words of her husband and her friends something to console her in her deep sorrow, something that might show her how a mother should resign herself to send her son not even to death but to a probable danger of life. Yet not a word had she found amongst the many which had been said . . . and her grief had been greater in seeing that nobody—as she thought—could share her feelings.

But now the words of the traveler amazed and almost stunned her. She suddenly realized that it wasn't the others who were wrong and could not understand her but herself who could not rise up to the same height of those fathers and mothers willing to resign themselves, without crying, not only to the departure of their sons but even to their death.

She lifted her head, she bent over from her corner trying to listen with great attention to the details which the fat man was giving to his companions about the way his son had fallen as a hero, for his King and his Country, happy and without regrets. It seemed to her that she had stumbled into a world she had never dreamt of, a world so far unknown to her and she was so pleased to hear everyone joining in congratulating that brave father who could so stoically speak of his child's death.

Then suddenly, just as if she had heard nothing of what had been said and almost as if waking up from a dream, she turned to the old man, asking him:

"Then . . . is your son really dead?"

Everybody stared at her. The old man, too, turned to look at her, fixing his great, bulging, horribly watery light gray eyes, deep in her face. For some little time he tried to answer, but words failed him. He looked and looked at her, almost as if only then—at that silly, incongruous question—he had suddenly realized at last that his son was really dead . . . gone forever . . . forever. His face contracted, became horribly distorted, then he snatched in haste a handkerchief from his pocket and, to the amazement of everyone, broke into harrowing, heart-rending, uncontrollable sobs.

QUESTIONS

1. What is Pirandello's attitude toward war in this story? How do you know?

2. What is the ironic intent indicated by the phrase "decent boys"?

3. How is patriotism being used here as a protective device? Is Pirandello's tone satiric or not? Explain.

4. Is the fat man successful with his argument that "Country" is more important to 20-year-olds than anything else? Explain.

TOPICS FOR WRITING

1. Explain why the fat man breaks down and cries at the end of the story.

2. What comic elements exist in this story? For example, how does comedy creep into Pirandello's depiction of character and his creation of dialogue? Explain how this comic tone is juxtaposed against a tragic element. How successful is the tragic irony at the end of the tale?

Hernando Téllez

JUST LATHER,
THAT'S ALL

Hernando Téllez (1908–1966) was born in Bogotá, Colombia, where for much of his life he was involved in the literary and journalistic life of the city. At 17 he joined the staff of the weekly Mundo al Día. *Two years later, German Arciniegas started a magazine,* Universidad, *with Téllez's help. The formation of this publication helped to draw the intellectuals of his generation into what they called* Los Nuevos *("the*

*New Ones"). The group succeeded the writers and journal-
ists of an earlier generation of Colombian—more precisely,
Bogotan—fiction, nonfiction, and poetry writers. Arciniegas
and Alberto Lleras Camargo, who headed El Tiempo, which
Téllez joined in 1929, were leading figures in the New Ones.
Active in national politics, Téllez in 1937 was designated
the consul in Marseille, France. He returned to Colombia
shortly before World War II and took up the post of subdirec-
tor of another publication, El Liberal. He was a senator from
1944 to 1947, and in 1959 he was appointed ambassador to
UNESCO in Paris. "The prose of Téllez," wrote Richard
Latcham, editor of Stories of the Hispanic American, "is
distinguished for the qualities of spirtual contention and
noble power exactly synthesized and shaded." In addition to
his editorial and diplomatic activities, Téllez published In-*
quietud del mundo *(*The Restless of the World; *1943);* Baga-
telas *(1944);* Diario *(1946);* Luces en el bosque *(Lights in the
Woods; *1946);* Cenizas para el viento y otras historias *(Ashes
to the Wind and Other Stories; *1950), from which "Just
Lather, That's All" ("Espuma y nada más") is taken;*
Literatura *(Literature; *1951);* Literatura y sociedad *(1956);
and* Confesión de parte *(In the Name of Confession; *1966).*

He said nothing when he entered. I was passing the best of my razors back and forth on a strop. When I recognized him I started to tremble. But he didn't notice. Hoping to conceal my emotion, I continued sharpening the razor. I tested it on the meat of my thumb, and then held it up to the light. At that moment he took off the bullet-studded belt that his gun holster dangled from. He hung it up on a wall hook and placed his military cap over it. Then he turned to me, loosening the knot of his tie, and said, "It's hot as hell. Give me a shave." He sat in the chair.

I estimated he had a four-day beard. The four days taken up by the latest expedition in search of our troops. His face seemed reddened, burned by the sun. Carefully, I began to prepare the soap. I cut off a few slices, dropped them into the cup, mixed in a bit of warm water, and began to stir with the brush. Immediately the foam began to rise. "The other boys in the group should have this much beard, too." I continued stirring the lather.

"But we did all right, you know. We got the main ones. We brought back some dead, and we've got some others still alive. But pretty soon they'll all be dead."

"How many did you catch?" I asked.

"Fourteen. We had to go pretty deep into the woods to find them. But we'll get even. Not one of them comes out of this alive, not one."

He leaned back on the chair when he saw me with the lather-covered brush in my hand. I still had to put the sheet on him. No doubt about it, I was upset. I took a sheet out of a drawer and knotted it around my customer's neck. He wouldn't stop talking. He probably thought I was in sympathy with his party.

"The town must have learned a lesson from what we did the other day," he said.

"Yes," I replied, securing the knot at the base of his dark, sweaty neck.

"That was a fine show, eh?"

"Very good," I answered, turning back for the brush. The man closed his eyes with a gesture of fatigue and sat waiting for the cool caress of the soap. I had never had him so close to me. The day he ordered the whole town fo file into the patio of the school to see the four rebels hanging there, I came face to face with him for an instant. But the sight of the mutilated bodies kept me from noticing the face of the man who had directed it all, the face I was now about to take into my hands. It was not an unpleasant face, certainly. And the beard, which made him seem a bit older than he was, didn't suit him badly at all. His name was Torres. Captain Torres. A man of imagination, because who else would have thought of hanging the naked rebels and then holding target practice on certain parts of their bodies? I began to apply the first layer of soap. With his eyes closed, he continued. "Without any effort I could go straight to sleep," he said, "but there's plenty to do this afternoon." I stopped the lathering and asked with a feigned lack of interest: "A firing squad?" "Something like that, but a little slower." I got on with the job of lathering his beard. My hands started trembling again. The man could not possibly realize it, and this was in my favor. But I would have preferred that he hadn't come. It was likely that many of our faction had seen him enter. And an enemy under one's roof imposes certain conditions. I would be obliged to shave that beard like any other one, carefully, gently, like that of any customer, taking pains to see that no single pore emitted a drop of blood. Being careful to see that the little tufts of hair did not lead the blade astray. Seeing that his skin ended up clean, soft, and healthy, so that passing the back of my hand over it I couldn't feel a hair. Yes, I was secretly a rebel, but I was also a conscientious barber, and proud of the preciseness of my profession. And this four-days' growth of beard was a fitting challenge.

I took the razor, opened up the two protective arms, exposed the blade and began the job, from one of the sideburns downward. The razor responded beautifully. His beard was inflexible and hard, not too long, but thick. Bit by bit the skin emerged. The razor rasped along, making its customary sound as fluffs of lather mixed with bits of hair gathered along the blade. I paused a moment to clean it, then took up the strop again to sharpen the razor, because I'm a barber who does things properly. The man, who had kept his eyes closed, opened them now, removed one of his hands from under the sheet, felt the spot on his face where the soap had been cleared off, and said, "Come to the school today at six o'clock." "The same thing as the other day?" I asked horrified. "It could be better," he replied. "What do you plan to do?" "I don't know yet. But we'll amuse ourselves." Once more he leaned back and closed his eyes. I approached him with the razor poised. "Do you plan to punish them all?" I ventured timidly. "All." The soap was drying on his face. I had to hurry. In the mirror I looked toward the street. It was the same as ever: the grocery store with two or three customers in it. Then I glanced at the clock: two-twenty in the afternoon. The razor continued on its downward stroke. Now from the other sideburn down. A thick, blue beard. He should have let it grow like some poets or priests do. It would suit him well. A lot of people wouldn't recognize him. Much to his benefit, I thought, as I attempted to cover the neck area smoothly. There, for sure, the razor had to be handled masterfully, since the hair, although softer, grew into little swirls. A curly beard. One of the tiny pores could be opened up and issue forth its pearl of blood. A good barber such as I prides himself on never allowing this to happen to a client. And this was a first-class client. How many of us had he ordered shot? How many of us had he ordered mutilated? It was better not to think about it. Torres did not know that I was his enemy. He did not know it nor did the rest. It was a secret shared by very few, precisely so that I could inform the revolutionaries of what Torres was doing in the town and of what he was planning each time he undertook a

Hernando Téllez

rebel-hunting excursion. So it was going to be very difficult to explain that I had him right in my hands and let him go peacefully—alive and shaved.

The beard was now almost completely gone. He seemed younger, less burdened by years than when he had arrived. I suppose this always happens with men who visit barber shops. Under the stroke of my razor Torres was being rejuvenated—rejuvenated because I am a good barber, the best in the town, if I may say so. A little more lather here, under his chin, on his Adam's apple, on this big vein. How hot it is getting! Torres must be sweating as much as I. But he is not afraid. He is a calm man, who is not even thinking about what he is going to do with the prisoners this afternoon. On the other hand I, with this razor in my hands, stroking and re-stroking this skin, trying to keep blood from oozing from these pores, can't even think clearly. Damn him for coming, because I'm a revolutionary and not a murderer. And how easy it would be to kill him. And he deserves it. Does he? No! What the devil! No one deserves to have someone else make the sacrifice of becoming a murderer. What do you gain by it? Nothing. Others come along and still others, and the first ones kill the second ones and they the next ones and it goes on like this until everything is a sea of blood. I could cut this throat just so, zip! zip! I wouldn't give him time to complain and since he has his eyes closed he wouldn't see the glistening knife blade or my glistening eyes. But I'm trembling like a real murderer. Out of his neck a gush of blood would spout onto the sheet, on the chair, on my hands, on the floor. I would have to close the door. And the blood would keep inching along the floor, warm, ineradicable, uncontainable, until it reached the street, like a little scarlet stream. I'm sure that one solid stroke, one deep incision, would prevent any pain. He wouldn't suffer. But what would I do with the body? Where would I hide it? I would have to flee, leaving all I have behind, and take refuge far away, far, far away. But they would follow until they found me. "Captain Torres' murderer. He slit his throat while he was shaving him—a coward." And then on the other side. "The avenger of us all. A name to remember. (And here they would mention my name.) He was the town barber. No one knew he was defending our cause."

And what of all this? Murderer or hero? My destiny depends on the edge of this blade. I can turn my hand a bit more, press a little harder on the razor, and sink it in. The skin would give way like silk, like rubber, like the strop. There is nothing more tender than human skin and blood is always there, ready to pour forth. A blade like this doesn't fail. It is my best. But I don't want to be a murderer, no sir. You came to me for a shave. And I perform my work honorably. . . . I don't want blood on my hands. Just lather, that's all. You are an executioner and I am only a barber. Each person has his own place in the scheme of things. That's right. His own place.

Now his chin had been stroked clean and smooth. The man sat up and looked into the mirror. He rubbed his hands over his skin and felt it fresh, like new.

"Thanks," he said. He went to the hanger for his belt, pistol and cap. I must have been very pale; my shirt felt soaked. Torres finished adjusting the buckle, straightened his pistol in the holster and after automatically smoothing down his hair, he put on the cap. From his pants pocket he took out several coins to pay me for my services. And he began to head toward the door. In the doorway he paused for a moment, and turning to me he said:

"They told me that you'd kill me. I came to find out. But killing isn't easy. You can take my word for it." And he headed on down the street.

QUESTIONS

1. Why does the barber tremble as the story opens? Why does the barber tremble a second time? What change in emotion has occurred? Why?

2. Why does Torres remind the barber of "the other day" as he settles into the chair? What is the author's attitude toward Torres? Cite evidence to support your claim.

3. Who or what does the barber represent? Does the author approve or disapprove of the barber? Support your answer.

4. How does the barber rationalize his inability to kill Torres?

5. What is the ironic meaning of the title of the story?

6. How do mood and point of view contribute to the tone of this tale?

TOPICS FOR WRITING

1. Analyze the types of irony in the story—the ironic title, the irony of situation, verbal irony, the ironic reversal at the end of the narrative, perhaps even tragic irony. Toward what end, purpose, or theme does Téllez direct the irony?

2. Explore the contradictions and tensions involved in the difference between being a revolutionary and being a murderer. What tone does the author adopt in exploring this conflict? What is his final statement?

Ray Bradbury

AUGUST 2026: THE WILL COME SOFT RAINS

Ray Douglas Bradbury (1920–   ) was born in Waukegan, Illinois, a small city some 40 miles north of Chicago. He began publishing his stories in 1941, and several have been selected for the Best American Short Stories *and* O. Henry Prize Stories *collections. Bradbury arranges his highly moralistic stories in science-fiction settings that often possess allegorical meanings for the present. He has written also for the stage, radio, and film. Among the most popular of his many works are* Dark Carnival *(1947),* The Martian Chronicles *(1950),* Fahrenheit 451 *(1953), and* A Medicine for Melan-

choly (1959). In "August 2026: There Will Come Soft Rains,"
Bradbury offers a haunting, ironic vision of the future, and
the irony is deepened by his selection of the Sara Teasdale
poem. Teasdale, a gifted lyric poet, committed suicide in
1933. In this story Bradbury juxtaposes the eternal—
children, balls, dogs, the comfortable and familiar—against
the technologically destructive new and unknown. Brad-
bury's irony here is heightened by the use of understate-
ment.

In the living room the voice-clock sang, *Tick-tock, seven o'clock, time to get up,*
time to get up. seven o'clock! as if it were afraid that nobody would. The morning
house lay empty. The clock ticked on, repeating and repeating its sounds into the
emptiness. *Seven-nine, breakfast time, seven-nine!*

In the kitchen the breakfast stove gave a hissing sigh and ejected from its
warm interior eight pieces of perfectly browned toast, eight eggs sunnyside up,
sixteen slices of bacon, two coffees, and two cool glasses of milk.

"Today is August 4, 2026," said a second voice from the kitchen ceiling, "in
the city of Allendale, California." It repeated the date three times for memory's
sake. "Today is Mr. Featherstone's birthday. Today is the anniversary of Tilita's
marriage. Insurance is payable, as are the water, gas, and light bills."

Somewhere in the walls, relays clicked, memory tapes glided under electric
eyes.

Eight-one, tick-tock, eight-one o'clock, off to school, off to work, run, run,
eight-one! But no doors slammed, no carpets took the soft tread of rubber heels.
It was raining outside. The weather box on the front door sang quietly: "Rain,
rain, go away; rubbers, raincoats for today . . ." And the rain tapped on the empty
house, echoing.

Outside, the garage chimed and lifted its door to reveal the waiting car. After
a long wait the door swung down again.

At eight-thirty the eggs were shriveled and the toast was like stone. An
aluminum wedge scraped them into the sink, where hot water whirled them
down a metal throat which digested and flushed them away to the distant sea.
The dirty dishes were dropped into a hot washer and emerged twinkling dry.

Nine-fifteen, sang the clock, *time to clean.*

Out of warrens in the wall, tiny robot mice darted. The rooms were acrawl
with the small cleaning animals, all rubber and metal. They thudded against
chairs, whirling their mustached runners, kneading the rug nap, sucking gently
at hidden dust. Then, like mysterious invaders, they popped into their burrows.
Their pink electric eyes faded. The house was clean.

Ten o'clock. The sun came out from behind the rain. The house stood alone
in a city of rubble and ashes. This was the one house left standing. At night the
ruined city gave off a radioactive glow which could be seen for miles.

Ten-fifteen. The garden sprinklers whirled up in golden founts, filling the soft
morning air with scatterings of brightness. The water pelted windowpanes,
running down the charred west side where the house had been burned evenly free
of its white paint. The entire west face of the house was black, save for five places.
Here the silhouette in paint of a man mowing a lawn. Here, as in a photograph, a
woman bent to pick flowers. Still farther over, their images burned on wood in
one titanic instant, a small boy, hands flung into the air higher up, the image of a
thrown ball, and opposite him a girl, hands raised to catch a ball which never
came down.

The five spots of paint—the man, the woman, the children, the ball—remained. The rest was a thin charcoaled layer.

The gentle sprinkler rain filled the garden with falling light.

Until this day, how well the house had kept its peace. How carefully it had inquired, "Who goes there? What's the password?" and, getting no answer from lonely foxes and whining cats, it had shut up its windows and drawn shades in an old-maidenly preoccupation with self-protection which bordered on a mechanical paranoia.

It quivered at each sound, the house did. If a sparrow brushed a window the shade snapped up. The bird, startled, flew off! No, not even a bird must touch the house!

The house was an altar with ten thousand attendants, big, small, servicing attending, in choirs. But the gods had gone away, and the ritual of the religion continued senselessly, uselessly.

Twelve noon.

A dog whined, shivering, on the front porch.

The front door recognized the dog voice and opened. The dog, once huge and fleshy, but now gone to bone and covered with sores, moved in and through the house, tracking mud. Behind it whirred angry mice, angry at having to pick up mud, angry at inconvenience.

For not a leaf fragment blew under the door but what the wall panel flipped open and the copper scrap rats flashed swiftly out. The offending dust, hair, or paper, seized in miniature steel jaws, was raced back to the burrow. There, down tubes which fed into the cellar, it was dropped into the sighing vent of an incinerator which sat like evil Baal in a dark corner.

The dog ran upstairs, hysterically yelping to each door, at last realizing, as the house realized, that only silence was here.

It sniffed the air and scratched the kitchen door. Behind the door, the stove was making pancakes which filled the house with a rich baked odor and the scent of maple syrup.

The dog frothed at the mouth, lying at the door, sniffing, its eyes turned to fire. It ran wildly in circles, biting at its tail, spun in a frenzy, and died. It lay in the parlor for an hour.

Two o'clock, sang a voice.

Delicately sensing decay at last, the regiments of mice hummed out as softly as blown gray leaves in an electrical wind.

Two-fifteen.

The dog was gone.

In the cellar, the incinerator glowed suddenly and a whirl of sparks leaped up the chimney.

Two thirty-five.

Bridge tables sprouted from patio walls. Playing cards fluttered onto pads in a shower of pips. Martinis manifested on an oaken bench with egg-salad sandwiches. Music played.

But the tables were silent and the cards untouched.

At four o'clock the tables folded like great butterflies back through the paneled walls.

Four-thirty.

The nursery walls glowed.

Animals took shape: yellow giraffes, blue lions, pink antelopes, lilac panthers cavorting in crystal substance. The walls were glass. They looked out upon color and fantasy. Hidden films clocked through well-oiled sprockets, and the walls lived. The nursery floor was woven to resemble a crisp, cereal meadow. Over this ran aluminum roaches and iron crickets, and in the hot still air butterflies of delicate red tissue wavered among the sharp aroma of animal spoors! There was the sound like a great matted yellow hive of bees within a dark bellows, the lazy bumble of a purring lion. And there was the patter of okapi feet and the murmur of a fresh jungle rain, like other hoofs, falling upon the summer-starched grass. Now the walls dissolved into distances of parched weed, mile on mile, and warm endless sky. The animals drew away into thorn brakes and water holes.

It was the children's hour.

Five o'clock. The bath filled with clear hot water.

Six, seven, eight o'clock. The dinner dishes manipulated like magic tricks, and in the study a *click.* In the metal stand opposite the hearth where a fire now blazed up warmly, a cigar popped out, half an inch of soft gray ash on it, smoking, waiting.

Nine o'clock. The beds warmed their hidden circuits, for nights were cool here.

Nine-five. A voice spoke from the study ceiling:

"Mrs. McClellan, which poem would you like this evening?"

The house was silent.

The voice said at last, "Since you express no preference, I shall select a poem at random." Quiet music rose to back the voice. "Sara Teasdale. As I recall, your favorite. . . .

> There will come soft rains and the smell of the ground,
> And swallows circling with their shimmering sound;
>
> And frogs in the pools singing at night,
> And wild plum trees in tremulous white;
>
> Robins will wear their feathery fire,
> Whistling their whims on a low fence-wire;
>
> And not one will know of the war, not one
> Will care at last when it is done.
>
> Not one would mind, neither bird nor tree,
> If mankind perished utterly;
>
> And Spring herself, when she woke at dawn
> Would scarcely know that we were gone.

The fire burned on the stone hearth and the cigar fell away into a mound of quiet ash on its tray. The empty chairs faced each other between the silent walls, and the music played.

At ten o'clock the house began to die.

The wind blew. A falling tree bough crashed through the kitchen window. Cleaning solvent, bottled, shattered over the stove. The room was ablaze in an instant!

"Fire!" screamed a voice. The house lights flashed, water pumps shot water from the ceilings. But the solvent spread on the linoleum, licking, eating, under the kitchen door, while the voices took it up in chorus: "Fire, fire, fire!"

The house tried to save itself. Doors sprang tightly shut, but the windows were broken by the heat and the wind blew and sucked upon the fire.

The house gave ground as the fire in ten billion angry sparks moved with flaming ease from room to room and then up the stairs. While scurrying water rats squeaked from the walls, pistoled their water, and ran for more. And the wall sprays let down showers of mechanical rain.

But too late. Somewhere, sighing, a pump shrugged to a stop. The quenching rain ceased. The reserve water supply which had filled baths and washed dishes for many quiet days was gone.

The fire crackled up the stairs. It fed upon Picassos and Matisses in the upper halls, like delicacies, baking off the oily flesh, tenderly crisping the canvases into black shavings.

QUESTIONS

1. What tone is quickly established in this story?

2. Which similarities exist between life now in the United States and life in the future United States, as described here?

3. How is theme carried forth in this story without characters? How does it differ in this respect from the other two stories in this section?

4. Why does Bradbury use the Teasdale poem?

5. The three stories in this section each possess a different point of view. Describe each. Contrast and compare them.

TOPICS FOR WRITING

1. Write a paper on how the indecision on the part of the barber in Téllez's story—an individual lack of action—may indirectly relate to what has happened in the Bradbury story.

2. Draw a relationship between the Teasdale poem and what has occurred in the story, bearing in mind the irony of the perpetual coming of spring and the inability of the most advanced civilizations to guarantee that they will also endure.

3. There are several levels of irony in this story. Write an essay on the robot mice and what it means that humankind here has eliminated even the real ones, yet cannot save itself.

7

SYMBOLISM
AND THEME:
HUMAN SEXUALITY

A symbol is something that represents something else by convention, habit, resemblance, or association. Symbols in literature have specific referents.

The word "symbol" is derived from the Greek *symbolaeon* and was originally political and not literary. *Symbolaeon* described a group of words that made up a treaty or a contract. The problem was that each of the contractees attached different ideas to the words they agreed to approve. Inasmuch as the symbols a writer uses may mean different things to different people, the problem of understanding symbols still exists. But they are, as D. H. Lawrence defines them, "organic units of consciousness with a life of their own, and you can never explain them away, because their value is dynamic, emotional, belonging to the sense-consciousness of the body and soul, and not simply mental. An allegorical image has meaning."

Perhaps we can simplify the definition to correspond with the one in the first paragraph of this section: symbolism can be defined as the representation of a reality on one level of reference by a corresponding reality on another. "It is easier," Plato wrote, "to say what a thing is like than what it is," so we think of someone "running like the wind," which is only to say, very fast.

There are times when the major symbol of a story may be found in the title, which may also supply the theme. We recognize symbols by the position of importance they hold in a story, and by their frequent recurrence, either in the narrative or in dialogue. The author *intends* for the reader to understand the symbols he or she uses, for they may be the clue to understanding the story itself.

We all understand certain common symbols—rainbows, daybreak, a cross, a flag, and others—but symbols are drawn from nearly every field of human endeavor and have come into literary use from many sources and at different times. The lotus flower, for example, may symbolize perfect form or perfect state of being to Asian readers, but not necessarily to British readers. Steel may symbolize automobiles to a reader in Detroit, but may symbolize an ax to a reader in central Africa.

In addition to the widely understood symbols, there are cultural, national, religious, and psychological symbols. Whatever the origin of a symbol, if it finds its way into the English language, it enriches literature and, naturally, extends the number and kinds of symbols that can be used.

Jean Toomer's *Cane* (1923) explored symbolism through the dream of a character, Esther:

> Another dream comes. There is no fire department. There are no heroic men. The fire starts. The loafers on the corner form a circle, chew their tobacco faster, and squirt juice just as fast as they can chew. Gallons on top of gallons they squirt upon the flames. The air reeks with the stench of scorched tobacco juice. Women, fat, chunky Negro women, lean scrawny white women, pull their skirts up above their heads and display the most ludicrous underclothes. The women scoot in all directions from the danger zone. She alone is left to take the baby in her arms. But what a baby! Black, singed, woolly, tobacco-juice baby—ugly as sin. Once held to her breast, miraculous thing: its breath is sweet and its lips can nibble. She loves it frantically.

The symbols here have to do with sex, race, and desire; they also relate to Esther's madness. We have only to think of the language Toomer has used: fire (and there is no fire department to quench the flames); the men forming a circle, chewing tobacco so they can squirt juice, (brown) tobacco juice, scorched tobacco juice, tobacco-juice baby: the women raising their dresses, but only Esther is left to take (bear) the baby, which is transformed because she alone is capable of creating that transformation.

The conscious infusion of psychological symbols was taking place at the time Toomer was writing, but it is important to remember that symbolism is not meant to intimidate the reader; rather it is used to add depth to the story and theme.

Allegory, related to symbolism, while often used in a religious context, is a representation of things or ideas that themselves hold deeper meaning. The story of Prometheus is an example of allegory. Metaphor, another relative of symbolism, is a figure of speech in which one thing is substituted for another. Hamlet, in considering whether or not "To take up arms against a sea of troubles," utters a Shakespearean metaphor.

The stories in this section (as in many others),   symbol and theme in their titles. In each, the dominant symb   ly to convey several meanings, all of which relate to the theme

Steinbeck's "The Chrysanthemums" uses a f   r symbol to build on theme. While flowers have always been pr   objects, rope has not. Yet Porter's "Rope" provides us with a diff   ion, through symbolic use, of what rope is and does than is usu

Perhaps more commonplace than rope are plun   ers, found in Boyle's "Astronomer's Wife." Astronomers and tele   quite so ordi-nary, but both plumber and star-gazer employ to   ortant to the successful use of symbolism in the story.

Although symbolism is the literary tool most ur   here, note also the presence of irony, tone, and mood, the uses of   ew, character, subject, and theme. When symbols do exist (and F   nor was one of many writers who warned against our tendency to   up too thin" by hunting for symbols everywhere), they add yet and   n to the techni-cally complex world of short fiction.

Katherine Anne Porter

ROPE

Katherine Anne Porter (1890–   ) was born in Indian Creek, Texas. She was educated in convent schools in that state and in Louisiana. She worked as a reporter and later traveled in Mexico and Europe; she moved to New York City in 1937. Porter's work began to appear in 1924, and Flowering Judas (1930) pulled her earliest work together in one volume. A novella, Hacienda (1934), was followed by Pale Horse, Pale Rider (1939), which contained a second novella, Noon Wine. Between 1960 and 1962, she published another novella, a collection of stories, and the novel Ship of Fools, which had been twenty years in the writing. Porter deals with characters who are "in disharmony with their environ-ment," says critic Leo Gurko. In "Rope" she builds on dishar-mony from a single symbolic object, and in the building reveals the characters, their weaknesses, and ultimately their strengths.

On the third day after they moved to the country he came walking back from the village carrying a basket of groceries and a twenty-four-yard coil of rope. She came out to meet him, wiping her hands on her green smock.. Her hair was tumbled, her nose scarlet with sunburn; he told her that already she looked like a born country woman. His gray flannel shirt stuck to him, his heavy shoes were dusty. She assured him he looked like a rural character in a play.

Had he brought the coffee? She had been waiting all day long for coffee. They had forgot it when they ordered at the store the first day.

Gosh, no, he hadn't. Lord, now he'd have to go back. Yes, he would if it killed him. He thought, though, he had everything else. She reminded him it was only because he didn't drink coffee himself. If he did he would remember it quick enough. Suppose they ran out of cigarettes? Then she saw the rope. What was that for? Well, he thought it might do to hang clothes on, or something. Naturally she asked him if he thought they were going to run a laundry? They already had a fifty-foot line hanging right before his eyes. Why, hadn't he noticed it, really? It was a blot on the landscape to her.

He thought there were a lot of things a rope might come in handy for. She wanted to know what, for instance. He thought for a few seconds, but nothing occurred. They could wait and see, couldn't they? You need all sorts of strange odds and ends around a place in the country. She said, yes, that was so; but she thought just at that time, when every penny counted, it seemed funny to buy more rope. That was all. She hadn't meant anything else. She hadn't just seen, not at first, why he felt it was necessary.

Well, thunder, he had bought it because he wanted to, and that was all there was to it. She thought that was reason enough, and couldn't understand why he hadn't said so, at first. Undoubtedly it would be useful, twenty-four yards of rope, there were hundreds of things, she couldn't think of any at the moment, but it would come in. Of course. As he had said, things always did in the country.

But she was a little disappointed about the coffee, and oh, look, look, look at the eggs! Oh, my, they're all running! What had he put on top of them? Hadn't he known eggs mustn't be squeezed? Squeezed, who had squeezed them, he wanted to know. What a silly thing to say. He had simply brought them along in the basket with the other things. If they got broke it was the grocer's fault. He should know better than to put heavy things on top of eggs.

She believed it was the rope. That was the heaviest thing in the pack; she saw him plainly when he came in from the road, the rope was a big package on top of everything. He desired the whole wide world to witness that this was not a fact. He had carried the rope in one hand and the basket in the other, and what was the use of her having eyes if that was the best they could do for her?

Well, anyhow, she could see one thing plain: no eggs for breakfast. They'd have to scramble them now, for supper. It was too damned bad. She had planned to have steak for supper. No ice, meat wouldn't keep. He wanted to know why she couldn't finish breaking the eggs in a bowl and set them in a cool place.

Cool place! If he could find one for her, she'd be glad to set them there. Well, then, it seemed to him they might very well cook the meat at the same time they cooked the eggs and then warm up the meat for tomorrow. The idea simply choked her. Warmed-over meat, when they might as well have had it fresh. Second-best and scraps and makeshifts, even to the meat! He rubbed her shoulder a little. It doesn't really matter so much, does it, darling? Sometimes when they were playful, he would rub her shoulder and she would arch and purr. This time she hissed and almost clawed. He was getting ready to say that they could surely manage somehow when she turned on him and said, if he told her they could manage somehow she would certainly slap his face.

He swallowed the words red hot, his face burned. He picked up the rope and started to put it on the top shelf. She would not have it on the top shelf, the jars and tins belonged there; positively she would not have the top shelf cluttered up with a lot of rope. She had borne all the clutter she meant to bear in the flat in town, there was space here at least and she meant to keep things in order.

Well, in that case, he wanted to know what the hammer and nails were doing up there? And why had she put them there when she knew very well he needed that hammer and those nails upstairs to fix the window sashes. She simply slowed down everything and made double work on the place with her insane habit of changing things around and hiding them.

She was sure she begged his pardon and if she had had any reason to believe he was going to fix the sashes this summer she would have left the hammer and nails right where he put them; in the middle of the bedroom floor where they could step on them in the dark. And now if he didn't clear the whole mess out of there she would throw them down the well.

Oh, all right, all right—could he put them in the closet? Naturally not, there were brooms and mops and dustpans in the closet, and why couldn't he find a place for his rope outside her kitchen? Had he stopped to consider there were seven rooms in the house and only one kitchen?

He wanted to know what of it? And did she realize she was making a complete fool of herself? And what did she take him for, a three-year-old idiot? The whole trouble with her was she needed something weaker than she was to heckle and tyrannize over. He wished now they had a couple of children she could take it out on. Maybe he'd get some rest.

Her face changed at this, she reminded him he forgot the coffee and had bought a worthless piece of rope. And when she thought of all the things they actually needed to make the place even decently fit to live in, well, she would cry, that was all. She looked so forlorn, so lost and despairing he couldn't believe it was only a piece of rope that was causing all the racket. What was the matter?

Oh, would he please hush and go away, and stay away, if he could, for five minutes. By all means, yes, he would. He'd stay away indefinitely if she wished. Lord, yes, there was nothing he'd like better than to clear out and never come back. She couldn't for the life of her see what was holding him, then. It was a swell time. Here she was, stuck, miles from a railroad, with a half-empty house on her hands, and not a penny in her pocket, and everything on earth to do; it seemed the moment for him to get out from under. She was surprised he hadn't stayed in town as it was until she had come out and done the work and got things straightened out. It was his usual trick.

It appeared to him that this was going a little far. Just a touch out of bounds, if she didn't mind his saying so. Why had he stayed in town the summer before? To do a half-dozen extra jobs to get the money he had sent her. That was it. She knew perfectly well they couldn't have done it otherwise. She had agreed with him at the time. And that was the only time, so help him, he had ever left her to do anything by herself.

Oh, he could tell that to his great-grandmother. She had her notion of what had kept him in town. Considerably more than a notion, if he wanted to know. So, she was going to bring all that up again, was she? Well, she could just think what she pleased. He was tired of explaining. It may have looked funny but he had simply got hooked in, and what could he do? It was impossible to believe that she was going to take it seriously. Yes, yes, she knew how it was with a man: if he was left by himself a minute, some woman was certain to kidnap him. And naturally he couldn't hurt her feelings by refusing!

Well, what was she raving about? Did she forget she had told him those two weeks alone in the country were the happiest she had known for four years? And how long had they been married when she said that? All right, shut up! If she thought that hadn't stuck in his craw.

She hadn't meant she was happy because she was away from him. She meant she was happy getting the devilish house nice and ready for him. That was what she meant, and now look! Bringing up something she had said a year ago simply to justify himself for forgetting her coffee and breaking the eggs and buying a wretched piece of rope they couldn't afford. She really thought it was time to drop the subject, and now she wanted only two things in the world. She wanted him to get that rope from underfoot, and go back to the village and get her coffee, and if he could remember it, he might bring a metal mitt for the skillets, and two more curtain rods, and if there were any rubber gloves in the village, her hands were simply raw, and a bottle of milk of magnesia from the drugstore.

He looked out at the dark blue afternoon sweltering on the slopes, and mopped his forehead and sighed heavily and said, if only she could wait a minute for *anything*, he was going back. He had said so, hadn't he, the very instant they found he had overlooked it?

Oh, yes, well . . . run along. She was going to wash windows. The country was so beautiful. She doubted they'd have a moment to enjoy it. He meant to go, but he could not until he had said that if she wasn't such a hopeless melancholiac she might see that this was only for a few days. Couldn't she remember anything pleasant about the other summers? Hadn't they ever had any fun? She hadn't time to talk about it, and now would he please not leave that rope lying around for her to trip on? He picked it up, somehow it had toppled off the table, and walked out with it under his arm.

Was he going this minute? He certainly was. She thought so. Sometimes it seemed to her he had second sight about the precisely perfect moment to leave her ditched. She had meant to put the mattresses out to sun, if they put them out this minute they would get at least three hours, he must have heard her say that morning she meant to put them out. So of course he would walk off and leave her to do it. She supposed he thought the exercise would do her good.

Well, he was merely going to get her coffee. A four-mile walk for two pounds of coffee was ridiculous, but he was perfectly willing to do it. The habit was making a wreck of her, but if she wanted to wreck herself there was nothing he could do about it. If he thought it was coffee that was making a wreck of her, she congratulated him: he must have an easy conscience.

Conscience or no conscience, he didn't see why the mattresses couldn't very well wait until tomorrow. And, anyhow, were they living *in* the house, or were they going to let the house ride them to death? She paled at this, her face grew livid about the mouth, she looked quite dangerous, and reminded him that housekeeping was no more her work than it was his: she had other work to do as well, and when did he think she was going to find time to do it at this rate?

Was she going to start on that again? She knew as well as he did that his work brought in the regular money, hers was only occasional, if they depended on what *she* made—and she might as well get straight on this question once for all!

That was positively not the point. The question was, when both of them were working on their own time, was there going to be a division of the housework, or wasn't there? She merely wanted to know, she had to make her plans. Why, he thought that was all arranged. It was understood that he was to help. Hadn't he always, in summer?

Hadn't he, though? Oh, just hadn't he? And when, and where, and doing what? Lord, what an uproarious joke!

It was such a very uproarious joke that her face turned slightly purple, and she screamed with laughter. She laughed so hard she had to sit down, and finally a rush of tears spurted from her eyes and poured down into the lifted corners of her mouth. He dashed toward her and dragged her up to her feet and tried to pour water on her head. The dipper hung by a string on a nail and he broke it loose. Then he tried to pump water with one hand while she struggled in the other. So he gave it up and shook her instead.

She wrenched away, crying out for him to take his rope and get out, she had simply given him up; and ran. He heard her high-heeled bedroom slippers clattering and stumbling on the stairs.

He went out around the house and into the lane; he suddenly realized he had a blister on his heel and his shirt felt as if it were on fire. Things broke so suddenly you didn't know where you were. She could work herself into a fury about simply nothing. She was terrible, not an ounce of reason. You might as well talk to a sieve as that woman when she got going. Darned if he'd spend his life humoring her! Well, what to do now? He would take back the rope and exchange it for something else. Things accumulated, things were mountainous, you couldn't move them or sort them out or get rid of them. They just lay and rotted around. He'd take it back. Why should he? He wanted it. What was it anyhow? A piece of rope. Imagine anybody caring more about a piece of rope than about a man's feelings. What earthly right had she to say a word about it? He remembered all the useless, meaningless things she bought for herself: Why? because I wanted it, that's why! He stopped and selected a large stone by the road. He would put the rope behind it. He would put it in the toolbox when he got back. He'd heard enough about it to last him a lifetime.

When he came back she was leaning against the post box beside the road waiting. It was pretty late, the smell of broiled steak floated nose high in the cooling air. Her face was young and smooth and fresh-looking. Her unmanageable funny black hair was all on end. She waved to him from a distance, and he speeded up. She called out that supper was ready and waiting, was he starved?

You bet he was starved. Here was the coffee. He waved it at her. She looked at his other hand. What was that he had there?

Well, it was the rope again. He stopped short. He had meant to exchange it but forgot. She wanted to know why he should exchange it, if it was something he really wanted. Wasn't the air sweet now, and wasn't it fine to be here?

She walked beside him with one hand hooked into his leather belt. She pulled and jostled him a little as he walked, and leaned against him. He put his arm clear around her and patted her stomach. They exchanged wary smiles. Coffee, coffee for the Ootsum-Wootums! He felt as if he were bringing her a beautiful present.

He was a love, she firmly believed, and if she had had her coffee in the morning, she wouldn't have behaved so funny. . . . There was a whippoorwill still coming back, imagine, clear out of season, sitting in the crab-apple tree calling all by himself. Maybe his girl stood him up. Maybe she did. She hoped to hear him once more, she loved whippoorwills. . . . He knew how she was didn't he?

Sure, he knew how she was.

QUESTIONS

1. From whose point of view is "Rope" told? Why?

2. Using the verbs "fray" and "bind," indicate the symbolic uses of the rope in the story.

3. After the initial argument about the rope, how many other trivial discussions derive from it and why?

4. Do the man and woman represent symbolic types of personality? Explain.

5. What theme emerges from this story?

TOPICS FOR WRITING

1. Explore the reasons why the author uses no dialogue in the story and the symbolic intent in telling the story this way.

2. Describe as many uses of rope as you can think of and relate these to the theme of "Rope."

John Steinbeck

THE CHRYSANTHEMUMS

John Steinbeck (1902–1968) was born in Salinas, California, and much of his fiction is located in Monterey County, where he spent the greater part of his life. He held a variety of jobs after attending Stanford University: marine biologist, chemist, seaman, hod carrier, newsman. It was from those experiences that he came to understand the working person who stands astride so many of his works. Steinbeck's first book, published in 1929, was a biography of a buccaneer, Sir Henry Morgan. His novels include Tortilla Flat (1935), In Dubious Battle (1936), Of Mice and Men (1937), and The Grapes of Wrath (1939). Many other novels, nonfiction books, and short stories are included in the considerable body of work that gained for him the Nobel Prize in literature in

1962. In "The Chrysanthemums" Elisa Allen, childless and much alone while her husband cares for their ranch, tries to share her world, inhabited mainly with the flowers she grows, with a passing stranger. Joseph Henry Jackson said of Steinbeck, and this story is an example: "He earnestly wishes to make people understand one another, and he is able, like Blake, to 'seek love in the pity of others.'"

The high grey-flannel fog of winter closed off the Salinas Valley from the sky and from all the rest of the world. On every side it sat like a lid on the mountains and made of the great valley a closed pot. On the broad, level land floor the gang plows bit deep and left the black earth shining like metal where the shares had cut. On the foothill ranches across the Salinas River, the yellow stubble fields seemed to be bathed in pale cold sunshine, but there was no sunshine in the valley now in December. The thick willow scrub along the river flamed with sharp and positive yellow leaves.

It was a time of quiet and of waiting. The air was cold and tender. A light wind blew up from the southwest so that the farmers were mildly hopeful of a good rain before long: but fog and rain do not go together.

Across the river, on Henry Allen's foothill ranch there was little work to be done, for the hay was cut and stored and the orchards were plowed up to receive the rain deeply when it should come. The cattle on the higher slopes were becoming shaggy and rough-coated.

Elisa Allen, working in her flower garden, looked down across the yard and saw Henry, her husband, talking to two men in business suits. The three of them stood by the tractor shed, each man with one foot on the side of the little Fordson. They smoked cigarettes and studied the machine as they talked.

Elisa watched them for a moment and then went back to her work. She was thirty-five. Her face was lean and strong and her eyes were as clear as water. Her figure looked blocked and heavy in her gardening costume, a man's black hat pulled low down over her eyes, clod-hopper shoes, a figured print dress almost completely covered by a big corduroy apron with four big pockets to hold the snips, the trowel and scratcher, the seeds and the knife she worked with. She wore heavy leather gloves to protect her hands while she worked.

She was cutting down the old year's chrysanthemum stalks with a pair of short and powerful scissors. She looked down toward the men by the tractor shed now and then. Her face was eager and mature and handsome; even her work with the scissors was over-eager, over-powerful. The chrysanthemum stems seemed too small and easy for her energy.

She brushed a cloud of hair out of her eyes with the back of her glove, and left a smudge of earth on the cheek in doing it. Behind her stood the neat white farm house with red geraniums close-banked around it as high as the windows. It was a hard-swept looking little house, with hard-polished windows, and a clean mud-mat on the front steps.

Elisa cast another glance toward the tractor shed. The strangers were getting into their Ford coupe. She took off a glove and put her strong fingers down into the forest of new green chrysanthemum sprouts that were growing around the old roots. She spread the leaves and looked down among the close-growing stems. No aphids were there, no sowbugs or snails or cutworms. Her terrier fingers destroyed such pests before they could get started.

Elisa started at the sound of her husband's voice. He had come near quietly, and he leaned over the wire fence that protected her flower garden from cattle and dogs and chickens.

"At it again," he said. "You've got a strong new crop coming."

Elisa straightened her back and pulled on the gardening glove again. "Yes. They'll be strong this coming year." In her tone and on her face there was a little smugness.

"You've got a gift with things," Henry observed. "Some of those yellow chrysanthemums you had this year were ten inches across. I wish you'd work out in the orchard and raise some apples that big."

Her eyes sharpened. "Maybe I could do it, too. I've a gift with things, all right. My mother had it. She could stick anything in the ground and make it grow. She said it was having planters' hands that knew how to do it."

"Well, it sure works with flowers," he said.

"Henry, who were those men you were talking to?"

"Why, sure, that's what I came to tell you. They were from the Western Meat Company. I sold those thirty head of three-year-old steers. Got nearly my own price, too."

"Good," she said. "Good for you."

"And I thought," he continued, "I thought how it's Saturday afternoon, and we might go to Salinas for dinner at a restaurant, and then to a picture show—to celebrate, you see."

"Good," she repeated. "Oh, yes. That will be good."

Henry put on his joking tone. "There's fights tonight. How'd you like to go to the fights?"

"Oh, no," she said breathlessly. "No, I wouldn't like fights."

"Just fooling, Elisa. We'll go to a movie. Let's see. It's two now. I'm going to take Scotty and bring down those steers from the hill. It'll take us maybe two hours. We'll go in town about five and have dinner at the Cominos Hotel. Like that?"

"Of course I'll like it. It's good to eat away from home."

"All right, then. I'll go get up a couple of horses."

She said, "I'll have plenty of time to transplant some of these sets, I guess."

She heard her husband calling Scotty down by the barn. And a little later she saw the two men ride up the pale yellow hillside in search of the steers.

There was a little square sandy bed kept for rooting the chrysanthemums. With her trowel she turned the soil over and over, and smoothed it and patted it firm. Then she dug ten parallel trenches to receive the sets. Back at the chrysanthemum bed she pulled out the little crisp shoots, trimmed off the leaves of each one with her scissors and laid it on a small orderly pile.

A squeak of wheels and plod of hoofs came from the road. Elisa looked up. The country road ran along the dense bank of willows and cottonwoods that bordered the river, and up this road came a curious vehicle, curiously drawn. It was an old spring-wagon, with a round canvas top on it like the cover of a prairie schooner. It was drawn by an old bay horse and a little grey-and-white burro. A big stubble-bearded man sat between the cover flaps and drove the crawling team. Underneath the wagon, between the hind wheels, a lean and rangy mongrel dog walked sedately. Words were painted on the canvas in clumsy, crooked letters. "Pots, pans, knives, sisors, lawn mores. Fixed." Two rows of articles, and the

John Steinbeck

triumphantly definitive "Fixed" below. The black paint had run down in little sharp points beneath each letter.

Elisa, squatting on the ground, watched to see the crazy, loose-jointed wagon pass by. But it didn't pass. It turned into the farm road in front of her house, crooked old wheels skirling and squeaking. The rangy dog darted from between the wheels and ran ahead. Instantly the two ranch shepherds flew out at him. Then all three stopped, and with stiff and quivering tails, with taut straight legs, with ambassadorial dignity, they slowly circled, sniffing daintily. The caravan pulled up to Elisa's wire fence and stopped. Now the newcomer dog, feeling outnumbered, lowered his tail and retired under the wagon with raised hackles and bared teeth.

The man on the wagon seat called out. "That's a bad dog in a fight when he gets started."

Elisa laughed. "I see he is. How soon does he generally get started?"

The man caught up her laughter and echoed it heartily. "Sometimes not for weeks and weeks," he said. He climbed stiffly down, over the wheel. The horse and the donkey drooped like unwatered flowers.

Elisa saw that he was a very big man. Although his hair and beard were greying, he did not look old. His worn black suit was wrinkled and spotted with grease. The laughter had disappeared from his face and eyes the moment his laughing voice ceased. His eyes were dark and they were full of the brooding that gets in the eyes of teamsters and of sailors. The calloused hands he rested on the wire fence were cracked, and every crack was a black line. He took off his battered hat.

"I'm off my general road, ma'am," he said. "Does this dirt road cut over across the river to the Los Angeles highway?"

Elisa stood up and shoved the thick scissors in her apron pocket. "Well, yes, it does, but it winds around and then fords the river. I don't think your team could pull through the sand."

He replied with some asperity, "It might surprise you what them beasts can pull through."

"When they get started?" she asked.

He smiled for a second. "Yes. When they get started."

"Well," said Elisa, "I think you'll save time if you go back to the Salinas road and pick up the highway there."

He drew a big finger down the chicken wire and made it sing. "I ain't in any hurry, ma'am. I go from Seattle to San Diego and back every year. Takes all my time. About six months each way. I aim to follow nice weather."

Elisa took off her gloves and stuffed them in the apron pocket with the scissors. She touched the under edge of her man's hat, searching for fugitive hairs. "That sounds like a nice kind of a way to live," she said.

He leaned confidentially over the fence. "Maybe you noticed the writing on my wagon. I mend pots and sharpen knives and scissors. You got any of them things to do?"

"Oh, no," she said quickly. "Nothing like that." Her eyes hardened with resistance.

"Scissors is the worst thing," he explained. "Most people just ruin scissors trying to sharpen 'em, but I know how. I got a special tool. It's a little bobbit kind of thing, and patented. But it sure does the trick."

"No. My scissors are all sharp."

"All right, then. Take a pot," he continued earnestly, "a bent pot, or a pot with a hole. I can make it like new so you don't have to buy no new ones. That's a saving for you."

"No," she said shortly. "I tell you I have nothing like that for you to do."

His face fell to an exaggerated sadness. His voice took on a whining undertone. "I ain't had a thing to do today. Maybe I won't have no supper tonight. You see I'm off my regular road. I know folks on the highway clear from Seattle to San Diego. They save their things for me to sharpen up because they know I do it so good and save them money."

"I'm sorry," Elisa said irritably. "I haven't anything for you to do."

His eyes left her face and fell to searching the ground. They roamed about until they came to the chrysanthemum bed where she had been working. "What's them plants, ma'am?"

The irritation and resistance melted from Elisa's face. "Oh, those are chrysanthemums, giant whites and yellows. I raise them every year, bigger than anybody around here."

"Kind of a long-stemmed flower? Looks like a quick puff of colored smoke?" he asked.

"That's it. What a nice way to describe them."

"They smell kind of nasty till you get used to them," he said.

"It's a good bitter smell," she retorted, "not nasty at all."

He changed his tone quickly. "I like the smell myself."

"I had ten-inch blooms this year," she said.

The man leaned farther over the fence. "Look. I know a lady down the road a piece, has got the nicest garden you ever seen. Got nearly every kind of flower but no chrysanthemums. Last time I was mending a copper-bottom washtub for her (that's a hard job but I do it good), she said to me, 'If you ever run acrost some nice chrysanthemums I wish you'd try to get me a few seeds.' That's what she told me."

Elisa's eyes grew alert and eager. "She couldn't have known much about chrysanthemums. You can raise them from seed, but it's much easier to root the little sprouts you see there."

"Oh," he said. "I s'pose I can't take none to her, then."

"Why yes you can," Elisa cried. "I can put some in damp sand, and you can carry them right along with you. They'll take root in the pot if you keep them damp. And then she can transplant them."

"She'd sure like to have some, ma'am. You say they're nice ones?"

"Beautiful," she said. "Oh, beautiful." Her eyes shone. She tore off the battered hat and shook out her dark pretty hair. "I'll put them in a flower pot, and you can take them right with you. Come into the yard."

While the man came through the picket gate Elisa ran excitedly along the geranium-bordered path to the back of the house. And she returned carrying a big red flower pot. The gloves were forgotten now. She kneeled on the ground by the starting bed and dug up the sandy soil with her fingers and scooped it into the bright new flower pot. Then she picked up the little pile of shoots she had prepared. With her strong fingers she pressed them into the sand and tamped around them with her knuckles. The man stood over her. "I'll tell you what to do," she said. "You remember so you can tell the lady."

"Yes, I'll try to remember."

"Well, look. These will take root in about a month. Then she must set them out, about a foot apart in good rich earth like this, see?" She lifted a handful of dark soil for him to look at. "They'll grow fast and tall. Now remember this. In July tell her to cut them down, about eight inches from the ground."

"Before they bloom?" he asked.

"Yes, before they bloom." Her face was tight with eagerness. "They'll grow right up again. About the last of September the buds will start."

She stopped and seemed perplexed, "It's the budding that takes the most care," she said hesitantly. "I don't know how to tell you." She looked deep into his eyes, searchingly. Her mouth opened a little, and she seemed to be listening. "I'll try to tell you," she said. "Did you ever hear of planting hands?"

"Can't say I have, ma'am."

"Well, I can only tell you what it feels like. It's when you're picking off the buds you don't want. Everything goes right down into your fingertips. You watch your fingers work. They do it themselves. You can feel how it is. They pick and pick the buds. They never make a mistake. They're with the plant. Do you see? Your fingers and the plant. You can feel that, right up your arm. They know. They never make a mistake. You can feel it. When you're like that you can't do anything wrong. Do you see that? Can you understand that?"

She was kneeling on the ground looking up at him. Her breast swelled passionately.

The man's eyes narrowed. He looked away self-consciously. "Maybe I know," he said. "Sometimes in the night in the wagon there—"

Elisa's voice grew husky. She broke in on him. "I've never lived as you do, but I know what you mean. When the night is dark—why, the stars are sharp-pointed, and there's quiet. Why, you rise up and up! Every pointed star gets driven into your body. It's like that. Hot and sharp and—lovely."

Kneeling there, her hand went out toward his legs in the greasy black trousers. Her hesitant fingers almost touched the cloth. Then her hand dropped to the ground. She crouched low like a fawning dog.

He said, "It's nice, just like you say. Only when you don't have no dinner, it ain't."

She stood up then, very straight, and her face was ashamed. She held the flower pot out to him and placed it gently in his arms. "Here. Put it in your wagon, on the seat, where you can watch it. Maybe I can find something for you to do."

At the back of the house she dug in the can pile and found two old and battered aluminum saucepans. She carried them back and gave them to him. "Here, maybe you can fix these."

His manner changed. He became professional. "Good as new I can fix them." At the back of his wagon he set a little anvil, and out of an oily tool box dug a small machine hammer. Elisa came through the gate to watch him while he pounded out the dents in the kettles. His mouth grew sure and knowing. At a difficult part of the work he sucked his under-lip.

"You sleep right in the wagon?" Elisa asked.

"Right in the wagon, ma'am. Rain or shine I'm dry as a cow in there."

"It must be nice," she said. "It must be very nice. I wish women could do such things."

"It ain't the right kind of a life for a woman."

Her upper lip raised a little, showing her teeth. "How do you know? How can you tell?" she said.

"I don't know ma'am," he protested. "Of course I don't know. Now here's your kettles, done. You don't have to buy no new ones."

"How much?"

"Oh, fifty cents'll do. I keep my prices down and my work good. That's why I have all them satisfied customers up and down the highway."

Elisa brought him a fifty-cent piece from the house and dropped it in his hand. "You might be surprised to have a rival some time. I can sharpen scissors, too. And I can beat the dents out of little pots. I could show you what a woman might do."

He put his hammer back in the oily box and shoved the little anvil out of sight. "It would be a lonely life for a woman, ma'am, and a scarey life, too, with animals creeping under the wagon all night." He climbed over the single-tree, steadying himself with a hand on the burro's white rump. He settled himself in the seat, picked up the lines. "Thank you kindly, ma'am," he said. "I'll do like you told me; I'll go back and catch the Salinas road."

"Mind," she called, "if you're long in getting there, keep the sand damp."

"Sand, ma'am? . . . Sand? Oh, sure. You mean round the chrysanthemums. Sure I will." He clucked his tongue. The beasts leaned luxuriously into their collars. The mongrel dog took his place between the back wheels. The wagon turned and crawled out the entrance road and back the way it had come, along the river.

Elisa stood in front of her wire fence watching the slow progress of the caravan. Her shoulders were straight, her head thrown back, her eyes half-closed, so that the scene came vaguely into them. Her lips moved silently, forming the words "Good-bye—good-bye." Then she whispered, "That's a bright direction. There's a glowing there." The sound of her whisper startled her. She shook herself free and looked about to see whether anyone had been listening. Only the dogs had heard. They lifted their heads toward her from their sleeping in the dust, and then stretched out their chins and settled asleep again. Elisa turned and ran hurriedly into the house.

In the kitchen she reached behind the stove and felt the water tank. It was full of hot water from the noonday cooking. In the bathroom she tore off her soiled clothes and flung them into the corner. And then she scrubbed herself with a little block of pumice, legs and thighs, loins and chest and arms, until her skin was scratched and red. When she had dried herself she stood in front of a mirror in her bedroom and looked at her body. She tightened her stomach and threw out her chest. She turned and looked over her shoulder at her back.

After a while she began to dress, slowly. She put on her newest underclothing and her nicest stockings and the dress which was the symbol of her prettiness. She worked carefully on her hair, pencilled her eyebrows and rouged her lips.

Before she was finished she heard the little thunder of hoofs and the shouts of Henry and his helper as they drove the red steers into the corral. She heard the gate bang shut and set herself for Henry's arrival.

His step sounded on the porch. He entered the house calling "Elisa, where are you?"

"In my room, dressing. I'm not ready. There's hot water for your bath. Hurry up. It's getting late."

When she heard him splashing in the tub, Elisa laid his dark suit on the bed, and shirt and socks and tie beside it. She stood his polished shoes on the floor beside the bed. Then she went to the porch and sat primly and stiffly down. She looked toward the river road where the willow-line was still yellow with frosted leaves so that under the high grey fog they seemed a thin band of sunshine. This was the only color in the grey afternoon. She sat unmoving for a long time. Her eyes blinked rarely.

Henry came banging out of the door, shoving his tie inside his vest as he came. Elisa stiffened and her face grew tight. Henry stopped short and looked at her. "Why—why, Elisa. You look so nice!"

"Nice? You think I look nice? What do you mean by 'nice?'"

Henry blundered on. "I don't know. I mean you look different, strong and happy."

"I am strong? Yes, strong. What do you mean 'strong?'"

He looked bewildered. "You're playing some kind of a game," he said helplessly. "It's a kind of a play. You look strong enough to break a calf over your knee, happy enough to eat it like watermelon."

For a second she lost her rigidity. "Henry! Don't talk like that. You didn't know what you said." She grew complete again. "I'm strong," she boasted. "I never knew before how strong."

Henry looked down toward the tractor shed, and when he brought his eyes back to her, they were his own again. "I'll get out the car. You can put on your coat while I'm starting."

Elisa went into the house. She heard him drive to the gate and idle down his motor, and then she took a long time to put on her hat. She pulled it here and pressed it there. When Henry turned the motor off she slipped into her coat and went out.

The little roadster bounced along on the dirt road by the river, raising the birds and driving the rabbits into the brush. Two cranes flapped heavily over the willow-line and dropped into the river-bed.

Far ahead on the road Elisa saw a dark speck. She knew.

She tried not to look as they passed it, but her eyes would not obey. She whispered to herself sadly. "He might have thrown them off the road. That wouldn't have been much trouble, not very much. But he kept the pot," she explained. "He had to keep the pot. That's why he couldn't get them off the road."

The roadster turned a bend and she saw the caravan ahead. She swung full around toward her husband so she could not see the little covered wagon and the mismatched team as the car passed them.

In a moment it was over. The thing was done. She did not look back. She said loudly, to be heard above the motor, "It will be good, tonight, a good dinner."

"Now you're changed again," Henry complained. He took one hand from the wheel and patted her knee. "I ought to take you in to dinner oftener. It would be good for both of us. We get so heavy out on the ranch."

"Henry," she asked, "could we have wine at dinner?"

"Sure we could. Say! That will be fine."

She was silent for a little while; then she said, "Henry, at those prize fights, do the men hurt each other very much?"

"Sometimes a little, not often. Why?"

"Well, I've read how they break noses, and blood runs down their chests. I've read how the fighting gloves get heavy and soggy with blood."

He looked around at her. "What's the matter, Elisa? I didn't know you read things like that." He brought the car to a stop, then turned to the right over the Salinas River bridge.

"Do any women ever go to the fights?" she asked.

"Oh, sure, some. What's the matter, Elisa? Do you want to go? I don't think you'd like it, but I'll take you if you really want to go."

She relaxed limply in the seat. "Oh, no. No. I don't want to go. I'm sure I don't." Her face was turned away from him. "It will be enough if we can have wine. It will be plenty." She turned up her coat collar so he could not see that she was crying weakly—like an old woman.

QUESTIONS

1. What does the stranger quickly perceive about Elisa?

2. Is Henry Allen truly interested in her flowers? Does he mean it when he suggests she might use her skills to improve the apples? What is the nature of the Allen's relationship?

3. What do the setting, the characters, and the flowers symbolize?

4. Why does Elisa change her mind and give the stranger pots to mend?

5. What theme is present when she feels the need to brag about her own ability to sharpen scissors?

6. Why does the stranger discard Elisa's plants?

TOPICS FOR WRITING

1. Analyze the quality of desperation Elisa brings to her care of the chrysanthemums—and why.

2. Explore the world of sexuality in this story, and the symbolic properties Steinbeck brings to his treatment of it.

Kay Boyle

ASTRONOMER'S WIFE

*Born close to the turn of the century, Kay Boyle (1903–   )
left her hometown, St. Paul, Minnesota, for study in Ohio
from 1917 to 1919. She was a steady and frequent contribu-
tor to the little magazines that flourished at the close of
World War I. Boyle lived in Europe, mainly France, for long
periods of time, and much of her fiction is set overseas. The
1936 and 1941 winner of the O. Henry Award for short
fiction, Boyle has also gained great prominence as a poet.
The poetic touch is easily discernible in her fiction. Her
early work in fiction was considered to be, in the mode of
Henry James, highly psychological. She is also adept at the
use of symbolism, as might be suspected. Her first novel,*
Wedding Day, *was published in 1931 and was followed five
years later by* The White Horses of Vienna and Other Stories.
*These brought her considerable attention and established
her as a writer who touched the world with a woman's
sensibilities.* The Crazy Hunter *(1940);* American Citizen, *a
poem (1944);* 1939 *(1948);* Generation without Farewell
(1959); The Seagull on the Step: Three Short Novels *(1958);
and* Testament for my Students, *a collection of poems (1970),
are among her notable works, which also include* Thirty
Stories *(1946) and* Fifty Stories *(1980). In "Astronomer's
Wife" Mrs. Ames chooses for the moment between a man
literally in the world and a man who peers out of it. In
addition to the symbolism, Boyle's sense of poetry is obvious.*

There is an evil moment on awakening when all things seem to pause. But for
women, they only falter and may be set in action by a single move: a lifted hand
and the pendulum will swing, or the voice raised and through every room the
pulse takes up its beating. The astronomer's wife felt the interval gaping and at
once filled it to the brim. She fetched up her gentle voice and sent it warily down
the stairs for coffee, swung her feet out upon the oval mat, and hailed the
morning with her bare arms' quivering flesh drawn taut in rhythmic exercise:
left, left, left my wife and fourteen children, right, right, right in the middle of the
dusty road.

The day would proceed from this, beat by beat, without reflection, like every
other day. The astronomer was still asleep, or feigning it, and she, once out of
bed, had come into her own possession. Although scarcely ever out of sight of the
impenetrable silence of his brow, she would be absent from him all the day in
being clean, busy, kind. He was a man of other things, a dreamer. At times he lay
still for hours, at others he sat upon the roof behind his telescope, or wandered
down the pathway to the road and out across the mountains. This day, like any
other, would go on from the removal of the spot left there from dinner on the
astronomer's vest to the severe thrashing of the mayonnaise for lunch. That man
might be each time the new arching wave, and woman the undertow that sucked
him back, were things she had been told by his silence were so.

In spite of the earliness of the hour, the girl had heard her mistress's voice
and was coming up the stairs. At the threshold of the bedroom she paused, and
said: "Madame, the plumber is here."

The astronomer's wife put on her white and scarlet smock very quickly and buttoned it at the neck. Then she stepped carefully around the motionless spread of water in the hall.

"Tell him to come right up," she said. She laid her hands on the bannisters and stood looking down the wooden stairway. "Ah, I am Mrs. Ames," she said softly as she saw him mounting. "I am Mrs. Ames," she said softly, softly down the flight of stairs. "I am Mrs. Ames," spoken soft as a willow weeping. "The professor is still sleeping. Just step this way."

The plumber himself looked up and saw Mrs. Ames with her voice hushed, speaking to him. She was a youngish woman, but this she had forgotten. The mystery and silence of her husband's mind lay like a chiding finger on her lips. Her eyes were gray, for the light had been extinguished in them. The strange dim halo of her yellow hair was still uncombed and sideways on her head.

For all of his heavy boots, the plumber quieted the sound of his feet, and together they went down the hall, picking their way around the still lake of water that spread as far as the landing and lay docile there. The plumber was a tough, hardy man; but he took off his hat when he spoke to her and looked her fully, almost insolently in the eye.

"Does it come from the wash-basin," he said, "or from the other . . .?"

"Oh, from the other," said Mrs. Ames without hesitation.

In this place the villas were scattered out few and primitive, and although beauty lay without there was no reflection of her face within. Here all was awkward and unfit; a sense of wrestling with uncouth forces gave everything an austere countenance. Even the plumber, dealing as does a woman with matters under hand, was grave and stately. The mountains round about seemed to have cast them into the shadow of great dignity.

Mrs. Ames began speaking of their arrival that summer in the little villa, mourning each event as it followed on the other.

"Then, just before going to bed last night," she said, "I noticed something was unusual."

The plumber cast down a folded square of sack-cloth on the brimming floor and laid his leather apron on it. Then he stepped boldly onto the heart of the island it shaped and looked long into the overflowing bowl.

"The water should be stopped from the meter in the garden," he said at last.

"Oh, I did that," said Mrs. Ames, "the very first thing last night. I turned it off at once, in my nightgown, as soon as I saw what was happening. But all this had already run in."

The plumber looked for a moment at her red kid slippers. She was standing just at the edge of the clear, pure-seeming tide.

"It's no doubt the soil lines," he said severely. "It may be that something has stopped them, but my opinion is that the water seals aren't working. That's the trouble often enough in such cases. If you had a valve you wouldn't be caught like this."

Mrs. Ames did not know how to meet this rebuke. She stood, swaying a little, looking into the plumber's blue relentless eye.

"I'm sorry—I'm sorry that my husband," she said, "is still—resting and cannot go into this with you. I'm sure it must be very interesting. . . ."

"You'll probably have to have the traps sealed," said the plumber grimly, and at the sound of this Mrs. Ames' hand flew in dismay to the side of her face. The plumber made no move, but the set of his mouth as he looked at her seemed to soften. "Anyway, I'll have a look from the garden end," he said.

"Oh, do," said the astronomer's wife in relief. Here was a man who spoke of action and object as simply as women did! But however hushed her voice had been, it carried clearly to Professor Ames who lay, dreaming and solitary, upon his bed. He heard their footsteps come down the hall, pause, and skip across the pool of overflow.

"Katherine!" said the astronomer in a ringing tone. "There's a problem worthy of your mettle!"

Mrs. Ames did not turn her head, but led the plumber swiftly down the stairs. When the sun in the garden struck her face, he saw there was a wave of color in it, but this may have been anything but shame.

"You see how it is," said the plumber, as if leading her mind away. "The drains run from these houses right down the hill, big enough for a man to stand upright in them, and clean as a whistle too." There they stood in the garden with the vegetation flowering in disorder all about. The plumber looked at the astronomer's wife. "They come out at the torrent on the other side of the forest beyond there," he said.

But the words the astronomer had spoken still sounded in her in despair. The mind of man, she knew, made steep and sprightly flights, pursued illusion, took foothold in the nameless things that cannot pass between the thumb and finger. But whenever the astronomer gave voice to the thoughts that soared within him, she returned in gratitude to the long expanses of his silence. Desert-like they stretched behind and before the articulation of his scorn.

Life, life is an open sea, she sought to explain it in sorrow, and to survive women cling to the floating débris on the tide. But the plumber had suddenly fallen upon his knees in the grass and had crooked his fingers through the ring of the drains' trap-door. When she looked down she saw that he was looking up into her face, and she saw too that his hair was as light as gold.

"Perhaps Mr. Ames," he said rather bitterly, "would like to come down with me and have a look around?"

"Down?" said Mrs. Ames in wonder.

"Into the drains," said the plumber brutally. "They're a study for a man who likes to know what's what."

"Oh, Mr. Ames," said Mrs. Ames in confusion. "He's still—still in bed, you see."

The plumber lifted his strong, weathered face and looked curiously at her. Surely it seemed to him strange for a man to linger in bed, with the sun pouring yellow as wine all over the place. The astronomer's wife saw his lean cheeks, his high, rugged bones, and the deep seams in his brow. His flesh was as firm and clean as wood, stained richly tan with the climate's rigor. His fingers were blunt, but comprehensible to her, gripped in the ring and holding the iron door wide. The backs of his hands were bound round and round with ripe blue veins of blood.

"At any rate," said the astronomer's wife, and the thought of it moved her lips to smile a little, "Mr. Ames would never go down there alive. He likes going up," she said. And she, in her turn, pointed, but impudently, towards the heavens. "On the roof. Or on the mountains. He's been up on the tops of them many times."

"It's a matter of habit," said the plumber, and suddenly he went down the trap. Mrs. Ames saw a bright little piece of his hair still shining, like a star, long after the rest of him had gone. Out of the depths, his voice, hollow and dark with foreboding, returned to her. "I think something has stopped the elbow," was what he said.

This was speech that touched her flesh and bone and made her wonder. When her husband spoke of height, having no sense of it, she could not picture it nor hear. Depth or magic passed her by unless a name were given. But madness in a daily shape, as elbow stopped, she saw clearly and well. She sat down on the grasses, bewildered that it should be a man who had spoken to her so.

She saw the weeds springing up, and she did not move to tear them up from life. She sat powerless, her senses veiled, with no action taking shape beneath her hands. In this way some men sat for hours on end, she knew, tracking a single thought back to its origin. The mind of man could balance and divide, weed out, destroy. She sat on the full, burdened grasses, seeking to think, and dimly waiting for the plumber to return.

Whereas her husband had always gone up, as the dead go, she knew now that there were others who went down, like the corporeal being of the dead. That men were then divided into two bodies now seemed clear to Mrs. Ames. This knowledge stunned her with its simplicity and took the uneasy motion from her limbs. She could not stir, but sat facing the mountains' rocky flanks, and harking in silence to lucidity. Her husband was the mind, this other man the meat, of all mankind.

After a little, the plumber emerged from the earth: first the light top of his head, then the burnt brow, and then the blue eyes fringed with whitest lash. He braced his thick hands flat on the pavings of the garden-path and swung himself completely from the pit.

"It's the soil lines," he said pleasantly. "The gases," he said as he looked down upon her lifted face, "are backing up the drains."

"What in the world are we going to do?" said the astronomer's wife softly. There was a young and strange delight in putting questions to which true answers would be given. Everything the astronomer had ever said to her was a continuous query to which there could be no response.

"Ah, come, now," said the plumber, looking down and smiling. "There's a remedy for every ill, you know. Sometimes it may be that," he said as if speaking to a child, "or sometimes the other thing. But there's always a help for everything a-miss."

Things come out of herbs and make you young again, he might have been saying to her; or the first good rain will quench any drought; or time of itself will put a broken bone together.

"I'm going to follow the ground pipe out right to the torrent," the plumber was saying. "The trouble's between here and there and I'll find it on the way. There's nothing at all that can't be done over for the caring," he was saying, and his eyes were fastened on her face in insolence, or gentleness, or love.

The astronomer's wife stood up, fixed a pin in her hair, and turned around towards the kitchen. Even while she was calling the servant's name, the plumber began speaking again.

"I once had a cow that lost her cud," the plumber was saying. The girl came out on the kitchen-step and Mrs. Ames stood smiling at her in the sun.

"The trouble is very serious, very serious," she said across the garden. "When Mr. Ames gets up, please tell him I've gone down."

She pointed briefly to the open door in the pathway, and the plumber hoisted his kit on his arm and put out his hand to help her down.

"But I made her another in no time," he was saying, "out of flowers and things and what-not."

"Oh," said the astronomer's wife in wonder as she stepped into the heart of the earth. She took his arm, knowing that what he said was true.

QUESTIONS

1. What kind of man does Mr. Ames seem to be?

2. What in the story indicates a tolerance on the part of Mrs. Ames for the marriage?

3. Mrs. Ames and the plumber seem to be in some ways alike. Explain how.

4. There are times when the point of view shifts from Mrs. Ames to the plumber. Why is this so?

5. Much of the conversation between the plumber and Mrs. Ames is symbolic. Of what?

6. What is the theme of this story? How does the symbolism reveal it?

TOPICS FOR WRITING

1. Write a paper comparing Mrs. Ames to Elisa in the Steinbeck story (page 171) and to the wife in the Porter story (page 166).

2. The location of "The Chrysanthemums," "Rope," and "Astronomer's Wife" is crucial to the way the characters behave. Where do they live? In what way or ways are these settings symbolic landscapes?

3. Write an essay on the symbolic role each of the husbands in these stories plays. How are they similar? How are they dissimilar?

4. Draw a comparison between the strangers who appear in the Steinbeck and Boyle stories and the symbolic tale summarized by the song "Some Day My Prince Will Come."

8

AN ANTHOLOGY OF SHORT FICTION

Edgar Allan Poe

THE BLACK CAT

*Edgar Allan Poe (1809–1849), presented earlier in this an-
thology (page 8), was the first notable theoretician of the
short story as a form. He made basic observations about the
short story, defining it in his famous 1842 review of Hawthorne's Twice-Told Tales in terms of our ability to read it in
a single sitting. Moreover, Poe offered more refined critical
notions about short fiction—concepts that often applied to
his own tales. He believed in isolating "single effects" for
narrative focus, seeking "combinations of event, or tone, as
shall best aid me in construction of the effect." Poe's effects
were never far from the realm of the grotesque and of
supernatural horror, as "The Black Cat" illustrates. With
this story, we are in a realm similar to that in "The Cask of
Amontillado." Again, a tormented narrator takes us into a
violent, morbid, and supernatural realm in which he confronts the terrors of his own soul.*

For the most wild, yet most homely narrative which I am about to pen, I neither expect nor solicit belief. Mad indeed would I be to expect it, in a case where my very senses reject their own evidence. Yet, mad am I not—and very surely do I not dream. But tomorrow I die, and to-day I would unburthen my soul. My immediate purpose is to place before the world, plainly, succinctly, and without comment, a series of mere household events. In their consequences, these events have terrified—have tortured—have destroyed me. Yet I will not attempt to expound them. To me, they have presented little but Horror—to many they will seem less terrible than *baroques*. Hereafter, perhaps, some intellect may be found which will reduce my phantasm to the common-place—some intellect more calm, more logical, and far less excitable than my own, which will perceive, in the circumstances I detail with awe, nothing more than an ordinary succession of very natural causs and effects.

From my infancy I was noted for the docility and humanity of my disposition. My tenderness of heart was even so conspicuous as to make me the jest of my companions. I was especially fond of animals, and was indulged by my parents with a great variety of pets. With these I spent most of my time, and never was so happy as when feeding and caressing them. This peculiarity of character grew with my growth, and, in my manhood, I derived from it one of my principal sources of pleasure. To those who have cherished an affection for a faithful and sagacious dog, I need hardly be at the trouble of explaining the nature or the intensity of the gratification thus derivable. There is something in the unselfish and self-sacrificing love of a brute, which goes directly to the heart of him who has had frequent occasion to test the paltry friendship and gossamer fidelity of mere *Man*.

I married early, and was happy to find in my wife a disposition not uncongenial with my own. Observing my partiality for domestic pets, she lost no opportunity of procuring those of the most agreeable kind. We had birds, gold fish, a fine dog, rabbits, a small monkey, and *a cat*.

This latter was a remarkably large and beautiful animal, entirely black, and sagacious to an astonishing degree. In speaking of his intelligence, my wife, who at heart was not a little tinctured with superstition, made frequent allusion to the ancient popular notion, which regarded all black cats as witches in disguise. Not that she was ever *serious* upon this point—and I mention the matter at all for no better reason than that it happens, just now, to be remembered.

Pluto—this was the cat's name—was my favorite pet and playmate. I alone fed him, and he attended me wherever I went about the house. It was even with difficulty that I could prevent him from following me through the streets.

Our friendship lasted, in this manner, for several years, during which my general temperament and character—through the instrumentality of the Fiend Intemperance—had (I blush to confess it) experienced a radical alteration for the worse. I grew, day by day, more moody, more irritable, more regardless of the feelings of others. I suffered myself to use intemperate language to my wife. At length, I even offered her personal violence. My pets, of course, were made to feel the change in my disposition. I not only neglected, but ill-used them. For Pluto, however, I still retained sufficient regard to restrain me from maltreating him, as I made no scruple of maltreating the rabbits, the monkey, or even the dog, when by accident, or through affection, they came in my way. But my disease grew upon me—for what disease is like Alcohol!—and at length even Pluto, who was now becoming old, and consequently somewhat peevish—even Pluto began to experience the effects of my ill temper.

One night, returning home, much intoxicated, from one of my haunts about town, I fancied that the cat avoided my presence. I seized him; when, in his fright at my violence, he inflicted a slight wound upon my hand with his teeth. The fury of a demon instantly possessed me. I knew myself no longer. My original soul seemed, at once, to take its flight from my body; and a more than fiendish malevolence, gin-nurtured, thrilled every fibre of my frame. I took from my waistcoat-pocket a pen-knife, opened it, grasped the poor beast by the throat, and deliberately cut one of its eyes from the socket! I blush, I burn, I shudder, while I pen the damnable atrocity.

When reason returned with the morning—when I had slept off the fumes of the night's debauch—I experienced a sentiment half of horror, half of remorse, for the crime of which I had been guilty; but it was, at best, a feeble and equivocal feeling, and the soul remained untouched. I again plunged into excess, and soon drowned in wine all memory of the deed.

In the meantime the cat slowly recovered. The socket of the lost eye presented, it is true, a frightful appearance, but he no longer appeared to suffer any pain. He went about the house as usual, but, as might be expected, fled in extreme terror at my approach. I had so much of my old heart left, as to be at first grieved by this evident dislike on the part of a creature which had once so loved me. But this feeling soon gave place to irritation. And then came, as if to my final and irrevocable overthrow, the spirit of PERVERSENESS. Of this spirit philosophy takes no account. Yet I am not more sure that my soul lives, than I am that perverseness is one of the primitive impulses of the human heart—one of the indivisible primary faculties, or sentiments, which give direction to the character of Man. Who has not, a hundred times, found himself committing a vile or a silly action, for no other reason than because he knows he should *not?* Have we not a perpetual inclination, in the teeth of our best judgment, to violate that which is *Law,* merely because we understand it to be such? This spirit of perverseness, I say, came to my final overthrow. It was this unfathomable longing of the soul *to vex itself*—to offer violence to its own nature—to do wrong for the wrong's sake only—that urged me to continue and finally to consummate the injury I had inflicted upon the unoffending brute. One morning, in cool blood, I slipped a noose about its neck and hung it to the limb of a tree;—hung it with the tears streaming from my eyes, and with the bitterest remorse at my heart;—hung it *because* I knew that it had loved me, and *because* I felt it had given me no reason of offence;—hung it *because* I knew that in so doing I was committing a sin—a deadly sin that would so jeopardize my immortal soul as to place it—if such a thing were possible—even beyond the reach of the infinite mercy of the Most Merciful and Most Terrible God.

On the night of the day on which this cruel deed was done, I was aroused from sleep by the cry of fire. The curtains of my bed were in flames. The whole house was blazing. It was with great difficulty that my wife, a servant, and myself, made our escape from the conflagration. The destruction was complete. My entire worldly wealth was swallowed up, and I resigned myself thenceforward to despair.

I am above the weakness of seeking to establish a sequence of cause and effect, between the disaster and the atrocity. But I am detailing a chain of facts—and wish not to leave even a possible link imperfect. On the day succeeding the fire, I visited the ruins. The walls, with one exception, had fallen in. This exception was found in a compartment wall, not very thick, which stood about the middle of the house, and against which had rested the head of my bed. The plastering had here, in great measure, resisted the action of the fire—a fact which I attributed to its having been recently spread. About this wall a dense crowd were collected, and many persons seemed to be examining a particular portion of it with very minute and eager attention. The words "strange!" "singular!" and other similar expressions, excited my curiosity. I approached and saw, as if graven in *bas relief* upon the white surface, the figure of a gigantic *cat*. The impression was given with an accuracy truly marvellous. There was a rope about the animal's neck.

When I first beheld this apparition—for I could scarcely regard it as less—my wonder and my terror were extreme. But at length reflection came to my aid. The cat, I remembered, had been hung in a garden adjacent to the house. Upon the alarm of fire, this garden had been immediately filled by the crowd—by some one of whom the animal must have been cut from the tree and thrown, through an open window, into my chamber. This had probably been done with the view of arousing me from sleep. The falling of other walls had compressed the victim of my cruelty into the substance of the freshly-spread plaster; the lime of which, with the flames, and the *ammonia* from the carcass, had then accomplished the portraiture as I saw it.

Although I thus readily accounted to my reason, if not altogether to my conscience, for the startling fact just detailed, it did not the less fail to make a deep impression upon my fancy. For months I could not rid myself of the phantasm of the cat; and, during this period, there came back into my spirit a half-sentiment that seemed, but was not, remorse. I went so far as to regret the loss of the animal, and to look about me, among the vile haunts which I now habitually frequented, for another pet of the same species, and of somewhat similar appearance, with which to supply its place.

One night as I sat, half stupified, in a den of more than infamy, my attention was suddenly drawn to some black object, reposing upon the head of one of the immense hogsheads of Gin, or of Rum, which constituted the chief furniture of the apartment. I had been looking steadily at the top of this hogshead for some minutes, and what now caused me surprise was the fact that I had not sooner perceived the object thereupon. I approached it, and touched it with my hand. It was a black cat—a very large one—fully as large as Pluto, and closely resembling him in every respect but one. Pluto had not a white hair upon any portion of his body; but this cat had a large, although indefinite splotch of white, covering nearly the whole region of the breast.

Upon my touching him, he immediately arouse, purred loudly, rubbed against my hand, and appeared delighted with my notice. This, then, was the very creature of which I was in search. I at once offered to purchase it of the landlord; but this person made no claim to it—knew nothing of it—had never seen it before.

I continued my caresses, and, when I prepared to go home, the animal evinced a disposition to accompany me. I permitted it to do so; occasionally stooping and patting it as I proceeded. When it reached the house it domesticated itself at once, and became immediately a great favorite with my wife.

The Black Cat

For my own part, I soon found a dislike to it arising within me. This was just the reverse of what I had anticipated; but I know not how or why it was—its evident fondness for myself rather disgusted and annoyed. By slow degrees, these feelings of disgust and annoyance rose into the bitterness of hatred. I avoided the creature; a certain sense of shame, and the remembrance of my former deed of cruelty, preventing me from physically abusing it. I did not, for some weeks, strike, or otherwise violently ill use it; but gradually—very gradually—I came to look upon it with unutterable loathing, and to flee silently from its odious presence, as from the breath of a pestilence.

What added, no doubt, to my hatred of the beast, was the discovery, on the morning after I brought it home, that, like Pluto, it also had been deprived of one of its eyes. This circumstance, however, only endeared it to my wife, who, as I have already said, possessed, in a high degree, that humanity of feeling which had once been my distinguishing trait, and the source of many of my simplest and purest pleasures.

With my aversion to this cat, however, its partiality for myself seemed to increase. It followed my footsteps with a pertinacity which it would be difficult to make the reader comprehend. Whenever I sat, it would crouch beneath my chair, or spring upon my knees, covering me with its loathsome caresses. If I arose to walk it would get between my feet and thus nearly throw me down, or, fastening its long and sharp claws in my dress, clamber, in this manner, to my breast. At such times, although I longed to destroy it with a blow, I was yet withheld from so doing, partly by a memory of my former crime, but chiefly—let me confess it at once—by absolute *dread* of the beast.

This dread was not exactly a dread of physical evil—and yet I should be at a loss how otherwise to define it. I am almost ashamed to own—yes, even in this felon's cell, I am almost ashamed to own—that the terror and horror with which the animal inspired me, had been heightened by one of the merest chimaeras it would be possible to conceive. My wife had called my attention, more than once, to the character of the mark of white hair, of which I have spoken, and which constituted the sole visible difference between the strange beast and the one I had destroyed. The reader will remember that this mark, although large, had been originally very indefinite; but, by slow degrees—degrees nearly imperceptible, and which for a long time my Reason struggled to reject as fanciful—it had, at length, assumed a rigorous distinctness of outline. It was now the representation of an object that I shudder to name—and for this, above all, I loathed, and dreaded, and would have rid myself of the monster *had I dared*—it was now, I say, the image of a hideous—of a ghastly thing—of the GALLOWS!—oh, mournful and terrible engine of Horror and of Crime—of Agony and of Death!

And now was I indeed wretched beyond the wretchedness of mere Humanity. And *a brute beast*—whose fellow I had contemptuously destroyed—*a brute beast* to work out for *me*—for me a man, fashioned in the image of the High God—so much of insufferable wo! Alas! neither by day nor by night knew I the blessing of Rest any more! During the former the creature left me no moment alone; and, in the latter, I started, hourly, from dreams of unutterable fear, to find the hot breath of *the thing* upon my face, and its vast weight—an incarnate Night-Mare that I had no power to shake off—incumbent eternally upon my *heart!*

Beneath the pressure of torments such as these, the feeble remnant of the good within me succumbed. Evil thoughts became my sole intimates—the darkest and most evil of thoughts. The moodiness of my usual temper increased to hatred of all things and of all mankind; while, from the sudden, frequent, and ungovernable outbursts of a fury to which I now blindly abandoned myself, my uncomplaining wife, alas! was the most usual and the most patient of sufferers.

One day she accompanied me, upon some household errand, into the cellar of the old building which our poverty compelled us to inhabit. The cat followed me down the steep stairs, and, nearly throwing me headlong, exasperated me to madness. Uplifting an axe, and forgetting, in my wrath, the childish dread which had hitherto stayed my hand, I aimed a blow at the animal which, of course, would have proved instantly fatal had it descended as I wished. But this blow was arrested by the hand of my wife. Goaded, by the interference, into a rage more than demoniacal, I withdrew my arm from her grasp and buried the axe in her brain. She fell dead upon the spot, without a groan.

This hideous murder accomplished, I set myself forthwith, and with entire deliberation, to the task of concealing the body. I knew that I could not remove it from the house, either by day or by night, without the risk of being observed by the neighbors. Many projects entered my mind. At one period I thought of cutting the corpse into minute fragments, and destroying them by fire. At another, I resolved to dig a grave for it in the floor of the cellar. Again, I deliberated about casting it in the well in the yard—about packing it in a box, as if merchandize, with the usual arrangements, and so getting a porter to take it from the house. Finally I hit upon what I considered a far better expedient than either of these. I determined to wall it up in the cellar—as the monks of the middle ages are recorded to have walled up their victims.

For a purpose such as this the cellar was well adapted. Its walls were loosely constructed, and had lately been plastered throughout with a rough plaster, which the dampness of the atmosphere had prevented from hardening. Moreover, in one of the walls was a projection, caused by a false chimney, or fireplace, that had been filled up, and made to resemble the rest of the cellar. I made no doubt that I could readily displace the bricks at this point, insert the corpse, and wall the whole up as before, so that no eye could detect anything suspicious.

And in this calculation I was not deceived. By means of a crow-bar I easily dislodged the bricks, and, having carefully deposited the body against the inner wall, I propped it in that position, while, with little trouble, I re-laid the whole structure as it originally stood. Having procured mortar, sand, and hair, with every possible precaution, I prepared a plaster which could not be distinguished from the old, and with this I very carefully went over the new brick-work. When I had finished, I felt satisfied that all was right. The wall did not present the slightest appearance of having been disturbed. The rubbish on the floor was picked up with the minutest care. I looked around triumphantly, and said to myself—"Here at least, then, my labor has not been in vain."

My next step was to look for the beast which had been the cause of so much wretchedness; for I had, at length, firmly resolved to put it to death. Had I been able to meet with it, at the moment, there could have been no doubt of its fate; but it appeared that the crafty animal had been alarmed at the violence of my previous anger, and forebore to present itself in my present mood. It is impossible to

The Black Cat

describe, or to imagine, the deep, the blissful sense of relief which the absence of the detested creature occasioned in my bosom. It did not make its appearance during the night—and thus for one night at least, since its introduction into the house, I soundly and tranquilly slept; aye, *slept* even with the burden of murder upon my soul!

The second and the third day passed, and still my tormentor came not. Once again I breathed as a free-man. The monster, in terror, had fled the premises forever! I should behold it no more! My happiness was supreme! The guilt of my dark deed disturbed me but little. Some few inquiries had been made, but these had been readily answered. Even a search had been instituted—but of course nothing was to be discovered. I looked upon my future felicity as secured.

Upon the fourth day of the assassination, a party of the police came, very unexpectedly, into the house, and proceeded again to make rigorous investigation of the premises. Secure, however, in the inscrutability of my place of concealment, I felt no embarrassment whatever. The officers bade me accompany them in their search. They left no nook or corner unexplored. At length, for the third or fourth time, they descended into the cellar. I quivered not in a muscle. My heart beat calmly as that of one who slumbers in innocence. I walked the cellar from end to end. I folded my arms upon my bosom, and roamed easily to and fro. The police were thoroughly satisfied and prepared to depart. The glee at my heart was too strong to be restrained. I burned to say if but one word, by way of triumph, and to render doubly sure their assurance of my guiltlessness.

"Gentlemen," I said at last, as the party ascended the steps, "I delight to have allayed your suspicions. I wish you all health, and a little more courtesy. By the bye, gentlemen, this—this is a very well constructed house." [In the rabid desire to say something easily, I scarcely knew what I uttered at all.]—"I may say an *excellently* well constructed house. These walls—are you going, gentlemen?—these walls are solidly put together;" and here, through the mere phrenzy of bravado, I rapped heavily, with a cane which I held in my hand, upon that very portion of the brick-work behind which stood the corpse of the wife of my bosom.

But may God shield and deliver me from the fangs of the Arch-Fiend! No sooner had the reverberation of my blows sunk into silence, than I was answered by a voice from within the tomb!—by a cry, at first muffled and broken, like the sobbing of a child, and then quickly swelling into one long, loud, and continuous scream, utterly anomalous and inhuman—a howl—a wailing shriek, half of horror and half of triumph, such as might have arisen only out of hell, conjointly from the throats of the damned in their agony and of the demons that exult in the damnation.

Of my own thoughts it is folly to speak. Swooning, I staggered to the opposite wall. For one instant the party upon the stairs remained motionless, through extremity of terror and of awe. In the next, a dozen stout arms were toiling at the wall. It fell bodily. The corpse, already greatly decayed and clotted with gore, stood erect before the eyes of the spectators. Upon its head, with red extended mouth and solitary eye of fire, sat the hideous beast whose craft had seduced me into murder, and whose informing voice had consigned me to the hangman. I had walled the monster up within the tomb!

QUESTIONS

1. A typical device at the start of a Poe short story is the declaration by the narrator that he is not mad. We see this strategy in "The Black Cat" and in another famous story by Poe, "The Tell-Tale Heart." In "The Black Cat," can we accept this declaration? If so, how then do we explain his killing of Pluto and his wife?

2. What are the specific "effects" that Poe creates in the story? What methods does he rely on to produce these effects?

3. The style of language used by the narrator is rather complex. How does this complexity of style reinforce effects and also contribute to the psychological profile of the speaker? What do we in fact know about the character's motives?

4. Why does Poe emphasize the supernatural aspects of the two cats?

5. Does this story have a moral or thesis, or is Poe interested exclusively in producing effects? Explain.

TOPICS FOR WRITING

1. Discuss the various techniques used by Poe to achieve special moods or effects in "The Black Cat."

2. Present a psychological analysis, or "case study," of the narrator in the story.

3. Compare and contrast point of view, setting, and mood in "The Black Cat" and "The Cask of Amontillado" (page 8).

Mark Twain

THE NOTORIOUS JUMPING FROG OF CALAVERAS COUNTY

Mark Twain (1835–1910), the celebrated pen name of Samuel Langhorne Clemens, was born in Florida, Missouri, and raised in Hannibal, a river town that he would immortalize in The Adventures of Tom Sawyer *(1876),* Life on the Mississippi *(1883), and* The Adventures of Huckleberry Finn *(1885). As journeyman printer, riverboat pilot, and journalist, Twain as a young man gained the experience and mastered the prose techniques that would serve as the foundation of his later work. In San Francisco, Twain began a career as a lecturer that would ultimately make him an international celebrity—a symbol of the New World. Rich, famous, and happily married, a revered author of many popular literary successes, Twain saw his world crumble with bankruptcy from bad investments and the successive deaths of loved ones in his immediate family. These reversals occasioned a considerable amount of pessimism in Twain's later work. However, he is still best known to us as one of America's greatest comic geniuses. A master of a broad range of comic devices, many of them drawn from frontier humor, Twain in much of his fiction created pictures of comical humanity, susceptible to numerous foibles. In fact, much of Twain's wisdom derives from his conviction that humanity is down-right foolish. In "The Notorious Jumping Frog of Calaveras County," Twain retells a California yarn, displaying a remarkable variety of comic techniques and a zest for native American humor.*

In compliance with the request of a friend of mine, who wrote me from the East, I called on good-natured, garrulous old Simon Wheeler, and inquired after my friend's friend, Leonidas W. Smiley, as requested to do, and I hereunto append the result. I have a lurking suspicion that *Leonidas W.* Smiley is a myth; that my friend never knew such a personage; and that he only conjectured that if I asked old Wheeler about him, it would remind him of his infamous *Jim* Smiley, and he would go to work and bore me to death with some exasperating reminiscence of him as long and as tedious as it should be useless to me. If that was the design, it succeeded.

I found Simon Wheeler dozing comfortably by the bar-room stove of the dilapidated tavern in the decayed mining camp of Angel's, and I noticed that he was fat and bald-headed, and had an expression of winning gentleness and simplicity upon his tranquil countenance. He roused up, and gave me good day. I told him that a friend of mine had commissioned me to make some inquiries about a cherished companion of his boyhood named *Leonidas W.* Smiley—*Rev. Leonidas W.* Smiley, a young minister of the Gospel, who he had heard was at one time a resident of Angel's Camp. I added that if Mr. Wheeler could tell me anything about this Rev. Leonidas W. Smiley, I would feel under many obligations to him.

Simon Wheeler backed me into a corner and blockaded me there with his chair, and then sat down and reeled off the monotonous narrative which follows this paragraph. He never smiled, he never frowned, he never changed his voice from the gentle-flowing key to which he tuned his initial sentence, he never betrayed the slightest suspicion of enthusiasm; but all through the interminable narrative there ran a vein of impressive earnestness and sincerity, which showed me plainly that, so far from his imagining that there was anything ridiculous or funny about his story, he regarded it as a really important matter, and admired its two heroes as men of transcendent genius in *finesse.* I let him go on in his own way, and never interrupted him once.

"Rev. Leonidas W. H'm, Reverend Le—well, there was a feller here once by the name of *Jim* Smiley, in the winter of '49—or maybe it was the spring of '50—I don't recollect exactly, somehow, though what makes me think it was one or the other is because I remember the big flume warn't finished when he first come to the camp; but anyway, he was the curiousest man about always betting on anything that turned up you ever see, if he could get anybody to bet on the other side; and if he couldn't he'd change sides. Any way that suited the other man would suit *him*—any way just so's he got a bet, *he* was satisfied. But still he was lucky, uncommon lucky; he most always come out winner. He was always ready and laying for a chance; there couldn't be no solit'ry thing mentioned but that feller'd offer to bet on it, and take ary side you please, as I was just telling you. If there was a horse-race, you'd find him flush or you'd find him busted at the end of it; if there was a dog-fight, he'd bet on it; if there was a cat-fight, he'd bet on it; if there was a chicken-fight, he'd bet on it; why, if there was two birds setting on a fence, he would bet you which one would fly first; or if there was a camp-meeting, he would be there reg'lar to bet on Parson Walker, which he judged to be the best exhorter about here, and so he was too, and a good man. If he even see a straddle-bug start to go anywheres, he would bet you how long it would take him to get to—to wherever he was going to, and if you took him up, he would foller that straddle-bug to Mexico but what he would find out where he was bound for and how long he was on the road. Lots of the boys here has seen that Smiley, and can tell you about him. Why, it never made no difference to *him*—he'd bet on *any*thing—the dangdest feller. Parson Walker's wife laid very sick once, for a good while, and it seemed as if they warn't going to save her; but one morning he come in, and Smiley up and asked him how she was, and he said she was considerable better—thank the Lord for his inf'nite mercy—and coming on so smart that with the blessing of Prov'dence she'd get well yet; and Smiley, before he thought, says, 'Well, I'll resk two-and-a-half she don't anyway.'

"Thish-yer Smiley had a mare—the boys called her the fifteen-minute nag, but that was only in fun, you know, because of course she was faster than that—and he used to win money on that horse, for all she was so slow and always had the asthma, or the distemper, or the consumption, or something of that kind. They used to give her two or three hundred yards' start and then pass her under way; but always at the fag end of the race she'd get excited and desperate like, and come cavorting and straddling up, and scattering her legs around limber, sometimes in the air, and sometimes out to one side among the fences, and kicking m-o-r-e dust and raising m-o-r-e racket with her coughing and sneezing and blowing her nose—and *always* fetch up at the stand just about a neck ahead, as near as you could cipher it down.

"And he had a little small bull-pup, that to look at him you'd think he warn't worth a cent but to set around and look ornery and lay for a chance to steal something. But as soon as money was up on him he was a different dog; his under-jaw'd begin to stick out like the fo'castle of a steamboat, and his teeth would uncover and shine like the furnaces. And a dog might tackle him and bully-rag him, and bite him, and throw him over his shoulder two or three times, and Andrew Jackson—which was the name of the pup—Andrew Jackson would never let on but what *he* was satisfied, and hadn't expected nothing else—and the bets being doubled and doubled on the other side all the time, till the money was all up; and then all of a sudden he would grab that other dog jest by the j'int of his hind leg and freeze to it—not chaw, you understand, but only just grip and hang on till they throwed up the sponge, if it was a year. Smiley always come out winner on that pup, till he harnessed a dog once that didn't have no hind legs, because they'd been sawed off in a circular saw, and when the thing had gone along far enough, and the money was all up, and he come to make a snatch for his pet holt, he see in a minute how he'd been imposed on, and how the other dog had him in the door, so to speak, and he 'peared surprised, and then he looked sorter discouraged-like, and didn't try no more to win the fight, and so he got shucked out bad. He give Smiley a look, as much as to say his heart was broke, and it was *his* fault, for putting up a dog that hadn't no hind legs for him to take holt of, which was his main dependence in a fight, and then he limped off a piece and laid down and died. It was a good pup, was that Andrew Jackson, and would have made a name for hisself if he'd lived, for the stuff was in him and he had genius—I know it, because he hadn't no opportunities to speak of, and it don't stand to reason that a dog could make such a fight as he could under them circumstances if he hadn't no talent. It always makes me feel sorry when I think of that last fight of his'n, and the way it turned out.

"Well, thish-yer Smiley had rat-tarriers, and chicken cocks, and tomcats and all them kind of things, till you couldn't rest, and you couldn't fetch nothing for him to bet on but he'd match you. He ketched a frog one day, and took him home, and said he cal'lated to educate him; and so he never done nothing for three months but set in his back yard and learn that frog to jump. And you bet you he *did* learn him, too. He'd give him a little punch behind, and the next minute you'd see that frog whirling in the air like a doughnut—see him turn one summerset, or maybe a couple, if he got a good start, and come down flat-footed and all right, like a cat. He got him up so in the matter of ketching flies, and kep' him in practice so constant, that he'd nail a fly every time as fur as he could see him. Smiley said all a frog wanted was education, and he could do 'most anything—and I believe him. Why, I've seen him set Dan'l Webster down here on this floor—Dan'l Webster was the name of the frog—and sing out, 'Flies, Dan'l, flies!' and quicker'n you could wink he'd spring straight up and snake a fly off'n the counter there, and flop down on the floor ag'in as solid as a gob of mud, and fall to scratching the side of his head with his hind foot as indifferent as if he hadn't no idea he'd been doin' any more'n any frog might do. You never see a frog so modest and straightfor'ard as he was, for all he was so gifted. And when it come to fair and square jumping on a dead level, he could get over more ground at one straddle than any animal of his breed you ever see. Jumping on a dead level was his strong suit, you understand; and when it come to that, Smiley would ante up money on him as long as he had a red. Smiley was monstrous proud of his frog, and well he might be, for fellers that had traveled and been everywheres all said he laid over any frog that ever *they* see.

"Well, Smiley kep' the beast in a little lattice box, and he used to fetch him down-town sometimes and lay for a bet. One day a feller—a stranger in the camp, he was—come acrost him with his box and says:

"'What might it be that you've got in the box?'

"And Smiley says, sorter indifferent-like, 'It might be a parrot, or it might be a canary, maybe, but it ain't—it's only just a frog.'

"And the feller took it, and looked at it careful, and turned it round this way and that, and says, 'H'm—so 'tis. Well, what's *he* good for?'

"'Well,' Smiley says, easy and careless, 'he's good enough for *one* thing, I should judge—he can outjump any frog in Calaveras County.'

"The feller took the box again, and took another long, particular look, and give it back to Smiley , and says, very deliberate, 'Well,' he says, 'I don't see no p'ints about that frog that's any better'n any other frog.'

"'Maybe you don't,' Smiley says. 'Maybe you understand frogs and maybe you don't understand 'em; maybe you've had experience, and maybe you ain't only a amature, as it were. Anyways, I've got *my* opinion, and I'll resk forty dollars that he can outjump any frog in Calaveras County.'

Mark Twain

"And the feller studied a minute, and then says, kinder sad-like, 'Well, I'm only a stranger here, and I ain't got no frog; but if I had a frog, I'd bet you.'

"And then Smiley says, 'That's all right—that's all right—if you'll hold my box a minute, I'll go and get you a frog.' And so the feller took the box, and put up his forty dollars along with Smiley's, and set down to wait.

"So he set there a good while thinking and thinking to himself, and then he got the frog out and prized his mouth open and took a teaspoon and filled him full of quail-shot—filled him pretty near up to his chin—and set him on the floor. Smiley he went to the swamp and slopped around in the mud for a long time, and finally he ketched a frog, and fetched him in, and give him to this feller, and says:

"'Now, if you're ready, set him alongside of Dan'l, with his fore paws just even with Dan'l's, and I'll give the word.' Then he says, 'One—two—three—*git!*' and him and the feller touched up the frogs from behind, and the new frog hopped off lively, but Dan'l give a heave, and hysted up his shoulders—so—like a Frenchman, but it warn't no use—he couldn't budge; he was planted as solid as a church, and he couldn't no more stir than if he was anchored out. Smiley was a good deal surprised, and he was disgusted too, but he didn't have no idea what the matter was, of course.

"The feller took the money and started away; and when he was going out at the door, he sorter jerked his thumb over his shoulder—so—at Dan'l, and says again, very deliberate, 'Well,' he says, 'I don't see no p'ints about that frog that's any better'n any other frog.'

"Smiley he stood scratching his head and looking down at Dan'l a long time, and at last he says, 'I do wonder what in the nation that frog throw'd off for—I wonder if there ain't something the matter with him—he 'pears to look mighty baggy, somehow.' And he ketched Dan'l by the nap of the neck, and hefted him, and says, 'Why blame my cats if he don't weigh five pound!' and turned him upside down and he belched out a double handful of shot. And then he see how it was, and he was the maddest man—he set the frog down and took out after that feller, but he never ketched him. And—"

[Here Simon Wheeler heard his name called from the front yard, and got up to see what was wanted.] And turning to me as he moved away, he said: "Just set where you are, stranger, and rest easy—I ain't going to be gone a second."

But, by your leave, I did not think that a continuation of the history of the enterprising vagabond *Jim* Smiley would be likely to afford me much information concerning the Rev. *Leonidas W.* Smiley, and so I started away.

At the door I met the sociable Wheeler returning, and he buttonholed me and recommenced:

"Well, thish-yer Smiley had a yaller one-eyed cow that didn't have no tail, only just a short stump like a bannanner, and—"

However, lacking both time and inclination, I did not wait to hear about the afflicted cow, but took my leave.

QUESTIONS

1. Why does Twain use two first-person narrators in this story? What is the relationship between these two narrators? How do they differ?

2. How does the second narrator, Simon Wheeler, create Jim Smiley as a comic character?

3. What elements of comic exaggeration, drawn from the tradition of the tall tale, do you find in this yarn?

4. Why does Smiley shift the focus of his tale so much? Is there a method or end that controls these shifts? How do the shifts contribute to the comic tone?

5. In "How to Tell a Story," an essay that he wrote in 1895, Twain declared that a humorous story "may wander anywhere it pleases and not arrive at any point." How does this observation apply to this story?

6. Does Twain's tall tale have a theme? Explain.

TOPICS FOR WRITING

1. Analyze the peculiarly American elements of Twain's humor in "The Notorious Jumping Frog of Calaveras County."

2. Compare the two narrators in the story.

Alphonse Daudet

THE LAST LESSON

Alphonse Daudet (1840–1897), French novelist and short fiction writer, is famous for his simple, lucid narrative style; he remains today a popular short story author in France and overseas. Daudet was born in Nimes, in the southern part of the nation, and the Midi is the setting for some of his finest caricatures of French life. He went to Paris in 1857 and lived there for the rest of his life, achieving a place among the major writers of his generation. At his best as a novelist of manners in such works as Jack (1876) and Sapho (1884), Daudet combines careful attention to realistic detail with a sophisticated moral sense. His gifts as a short story writer are even finer and more subtle. In the following story, Daudet combines a graceful, natural style with mature ethical observation. "The Last Lesson," one of his most famous stories, is a gently ironic and at the same time patriotic tale of a schoolboy who learns too late the value of his native language.

That morning it was quite late before I started for school, and I was terribly afraid I should be scolded, for Monsieur Hamel had told us that he would question us upon participles, and I did not know the first thing about them. For a moment I thought of escaping from school and roving through the fields.

The day was so warm, so clear! The blackbirds were whistling on the

Alphonse Daudet

outskirts of the woods. In Rippert Meadow, behind the sawmill, the Prussians were drilling. All these things were far more attractive to me than the rule for the use of participles. But I mustered up strength to resist temptation, and hurried on to school.

As I reached the town hall, I saw a group of people; they loitered before the little grating, reading the placards posted upon it. For two years every bit of bad news had been announced to us from that grating. There we read what battles had been lost, what requisitions made; there we learned what orders had issued from headquarters. And though I did not pause with the rest, I wondered to myself, "What can be the matter now?"

As I ran across the square, Wachter, the blacksmith, who, in company with his apprentice, was absorbed in reading the notice, exclaimed,—

"Not so fast, child! You will reach your school soon enough!"

I believed he was making game of me, and I was quite out of breath when I entered Monsieur Hamel's small domain.

Now, at the beginning of the session there was usually such an uproar that it could be heard as far as the street. Desks were opened and shut, lessons recited at the top of our voices, all shouting together, each of us stopping his ears that he might hear better. Then the master's big ruler would descend upon his desk, and he would say,—

"Silence!"

I counted upon making my entrance in the midst of the usual babel and reaching my seat unobserved, but upon this particular morning all was hushed. Sabbath stillness reigned. Through the open window I could see that my comrades had already taken their seats; I could see Monsieur Hamel himself, passing back and forth, his formidable iron ruler under his arm.

I must open that door. I must enter in the midst of that deep silence. I need not tell you that I grew red in the face, and terror seized me.

But, strangely enough, as Monsieur Hamel scrutinized me, there was no anger in his gaze. He said very gently,—

"Take your seat quickly, my little Franz. We were going to begin without you."

I climbed over the bench, and seated myself. But when I had recovered a little from my fright, I noticed that our master had donned his beautiful green frock-coat, his finest frilled shirt, and his embroidered black silk calotte, which he wore only on inspection days, or upon those occasions when prizes were distributed. Moreover, an extraordinary solemnity had taken possession of my classmates. But the greatest surprise of all came when my eye fell upon the benches at the farther end of the room. Usually they were empty, but upon this morning the villagers were seated there, solemn as ourselves. There sat old Hauser, with his three-cornered hat, there sat the venerable mayor, the aged carrier, and other personages of importance. All of our visitors seemed sad, and Hauser had brought with him an old primer, chewed at the edges. It lay wide open upon his knees, his big spectacles reposing upon the page.

While I was wondering at all these things, Monsieur Hamel had taken his seat, and in the same grave and gentle tone in which he had greeted me, he said to us,—

"My children, this is the last day I shall teach you. The order has come from Berlin that henceforth in the schools of Alsace and Lorraine all instruction shall be given in the German tongue only. Your new master will arrive to-morrow.

The Last Lesson

To-day you hear the last lesson you will receive in French, and I beg you will be most attentive."

My "last" French lesson! And I scarcely knew how to write! Now I should never learn. My education must be cut short. How I grudged at that moment every minute I had lost, every lesson I had missed for the sake of hunting birds' nests or making slides upon the Saar! And those books which a moment before were so dry and dull, so heavy to carry, my grammar, my Bible-history, seemed now to wear the faces of old friends, whom I could not bear to bid farewell. It was with them as with Monsieur Hamel, the thought that he was about to leave, that I should see him no more, made me forget all the blows of his ruler, and the many punishments I had received.

Poor man! It was in honor of that last session that he was arrayed in his finest Sunday garb, and now I began to understand why the villagers had gathered at the back of the class-room. Their presence at such a moment seemed to express a regret that they had not visited that school-room oftener; it was their way of telling our master they thanked him for his forty years of faithful service, and desired to pay their respects to the land whose empire was departing.

I was busied with these reflections when I heard my name called. It was now my turn to recite. Ah! what would I not have given then, had I been able to repeat from beginning to end that famous rule for the use of participles loudly, distinctly, and without a single mistake; but I became entangled in the first few words, and remained standing at my seat, swinging from side to side, my heart swelling. I dared not raise my head. Monsieur Hamel was addressing me.

"I shall not chide thee, my little Franz; thy punishment will be great enough. So it is! We say to ourselves each day, 'Bah! I have time enough. I will learn to-morrow.' And now see what results. Ah, it has ever been the greatest misfortune of our Alsace that she was willing to put off learning till To-morrow! And now these foreigners can say to us, and justly, 'What! you profess to be Frenchmen, and can neither speak nor write your own language?' And in all this, my poor Franz, you are not the chief culprit. Each of us has something to reproach himself with.

"Your parents have not shown enough anxiety about having you educated. They preferred to see you spinning, or tilling the soil, since that brought them in a few more sous. And have I nothing with which to reproach myself? Did I not often send you to water my garden when you should have been at your tasks? And if I wished to go trout-fishing, was my conscience in the least disturbed when I gave you a holiday?"

One topic leading to another, Monsieur Hamel began to speak of the French language, saying it was the strongest, clearest, most beautiful language in the world, which we must keep as our heritage never allowing it to be forgotten, telling us that when a nation has become enslaved, she holds the key which shall unlock her prison as long as she preserves her native tongue.

Then he took a grammar, and read our lesson to us, and I was amazed to see how well I understood. Everything he said seemed so simple, so easy! I had never, I believe, listened to any one as I listened to him at that moment, and never before had he shown so much patience in his explanations. It really seemed as if the poor man, anxious to impart everything he knew before he took leave of us, desired to strike a single blow that might drive all his knowledge into our heads at once.

The lesson was followed by writing. For this occasion Monsieur Hamel had prepared some copies that were entirely new, and upon these were written in a beautiful round hand, *"France, Alsace! France, Alsace!"*

These words were as inspiring as the sight of the tiny flags attached to the rod of our desks. It was good to see how each one applied himself, and how silent it was! Not a sound save the scratching of pens as they touched our papers. Once, indeed, some cockchafers entered the room, but no one paid the least attention to them, not even the tiniest pupil; for the youngest were absorbed in tracing their straight strokes as earnestly and conscientiously as if these too were written in French! On the roof of the schoolhouse the pigeons were cooing softly, and I thought to myself as I listened, "And must they also be compelled to sing in German?"

From time to time, looking up from my page, I saw Monsieur Hamel, motionless in his chair, his eyes riveted upon each object about him, as if he desired to fix in his mind, and forever, every detail of his little school. Remember that for forty years he had been constantly at his post, in that very school-room, facing the same playground. Little had changed. The desks and benches were polished and worn, through long use; the walnut-trees in the playground had grown taller; and the hop-vine he himself had planted curled its tendrils about the windows, running even to the roof. What anguish must have filled the poor man's heart, as he thought of leaving all these things, and heard his sister moving to and fro in the room overhead, busied in fastening their trunks! For on the morrow they were to leave the country, never to return. Nevertheless his courage did not falter; not a single lesson was omitted. After writing came history, and then the little ones sang their *"Ba, Be, Bi, Bo, Bu,"* together. Old Hauser, at the back of the room, had put on his spectacles, and, holding his primer in both hands, was spelling out the letters with the little ones. He too was absorbed in his task; his voice trembled with emotion, and it was so comical to hear him that we all wanted to laugh and to cry at the same moment. Ah! never shall I forget that last lesson!

Suddenly the church clock struck twelve, and then the Angelus was heard.

At the same moment, a trumpet-blast under our window announced that the Prussians were returning from drill. Monsieur Hamel rose in his chair. He was very pale, but never before had he seemed to me so tall as at that moment.

"My friends—" he said, "my friends—I—I—"

But something choked him. He could not finish his sentence.

Then he took a piece of chalk, and grasping it with all his strength, wrote in his largest hand,—

"VIVE LA FRANCE!"

He remained standing at the blackboard, his head resting against the wall. He did not speak again, but a motion of his hand said to us,—

"That is all. You are dismissed."

QUESTIONS

1. The historical background of this story touches on the Franco-Prussian War. What can we infer about the aftermath of the war from the context of the story? How does this historical background dictate the tone of the narrative?

2. A critic of Daudet as a short story writer has written that he "was perhaps

the first to apply this form of literary art to a passing phase of thought, to a momentary emotion, and to incidents that are psychological in character, rather than anecdotic." Apply this observation to "The Last Lesson."

3. What varieties of situational irony do you encounter in the story?

4. How does the theme of the tale relate to the subject of language and culture?

TOPICS FOR WRITING

1. At Daudet's grave, his friend and celebrated contemporary Émile Zola declared, "The least page he has ever written will preserve the vibration of his soul as long as our language shall exist." Based on your reading of "The Last Lesson," do you agree or disagree with Zola's high evaluation, and why?

2. Compare and contrast style and tone in "The Last Lesson" and Maupassant's "The Piece of String" (pages 81–86). What conclusions can you draw about the diverging attitudes toward life expressed by these two French authors?

3. Analyze Daudet's handling of setting and mood in the story.

Sarah Orne Jewett

A CHANGE OF HEART

Sarah Orne Jewett (1849–1909), whose work Henry James called a "beautiful little quantum of achievement," was born and raised in Maine, and New England village life is the setting and subject of the bulk of her fiction. Often ill and out of school in childhood, she accompanied her father, who was a doctor, on his country rounds, absorbing much of the local color that later would go into her fiction. By the age of 20, she had published stories in the Atlantic Monthly, *and in her lifetime she would write close to 150 tales. Her collections of short fiction include* A White Heron and Other Stories *(1886),* Tales of New England *(1890), and* The Country of the Pointed Firs *(1896). Jewett is strongest in her ability to realistically and sympathetically describe the insular lives of her characters and their confrontations with universal problems—isolation, love, aging—often set, as in the following story, against the backdrop of the New England landscape and the changing seasons.*

Sarah Orne Jewett

I

Sally Martin sat by her favorite kitchen window sewing a little and looking off over the sunny spring fields. All winter through the bare trees she could see the next house farther down the hill, but now the budding orchard had suddenly made a thick screen. After many defeated glances neighborward she was too conscious of being cut off from companionship and social pleasures, and folded up the blue gingham apron which she had been hemming, and took her shawl from the nail behind the door. There was a look of anticipation on her face; she had evidently found herself dull company for once. She brought a deep wicker basket, brown with age, from a closet, and going down cellar filled it with russet apples, and then locked the door after her and went her way.

The grass was green by the roadside, and she walked in the foot-path at its edge, feeling the ground under foot with much pleasure and stopping once to look at some bluebirds in a maple tree. One always feels young again with the spring, and this year the snow and mud had lingered late and kept her much indoors.

Sally Martin had not much to look forward to except continued poverty and anxiety, but she was one of the persons who have imagination, that enchanter's wand, which would have kept her satisfied with life, except for one regret which could never be quite put behind her or be forgotten.

It was a day for youth and pleasure, and when she was out in the open air her face grew serene and childlike; she stopped to listen to the bluebirds and watched their pretty color in the gray branches, then she walked on down the hill with her golden russets. The widespread lower country and the hills beyond it were blue with the soft spring haze. Her neighbor's house stood not far away, at a little distance from the road, and the narrow lane into which she soon turned was prettier than ever that spring, with its sheltered turf as soft as velvet, and an early dandelion or two shining against the fence. The old apple trees leaned their long boughs over it so that they almost met, and in later summer they would be hung thick with wisps of hay and straw from the high-heaped loads that went by to the barn. This was a huge building, like an unwieldy elephant in the landscape, while the house was low and small, with a tiny pointed porch and a door that had three panes of glass at top. When you stood in the entry within you could scarcely get room to shut the door behind you, and were at close quarters with an old colored wood-cut of General Washington, which greeted strangers with an impartial air of dignity. On the right another door opened into the Bascoms' living room, which surprised one in so small a house with its size and cheerfulness. The windows looked both north and south, and there were plenty of bright braided rugs on the clean floor.

"I saw you comin' up the lane, Sally, and I don't know whenever I was more pleased," said Mrs. Bascom, who was a lame woman and could not rise to greet her friends except in spirit. "Now bring that little rocking-chair right over here close to me, and let's have a good talk. It's so pretty looking out o' my window. I'm all alone, the folks have gone to the village, shoppin'. David he found his old plough wouldn't do him this year, and Cynthi' she's always ready an' willin', so they started right off after an early dinner. I'm braidin' up my rags as usual; I couldn't seem to do anything else just because I felt so busy. There's everything to be done this time of year, ain't there?"

"I waked up feelin' all of a bustle, too, and I soon come down to hemmin' me a blue gingham apron that I don't need one bit," confessed Sally. "I expect it's the spring workin' in us, though there ain't no leaves to show for it. I guess the trees themselves must feel just the same."

The two good women smiled, and Sally reached over and took a handful of the dark woolen strips and began to braid in company.

"I brought your folks some o' my apples," she said presently. "I'm on the last barrel, but they never were nicer this time of year. They wilt right away quick as you bring 'em up from the cellar, but you shall have more as long as they last."

"I call 'em a great treat; our apples have been gone some time and the last of 'em were very poor. There ain't such a keepin' cellar in town as yours; it seems to give everything a good taste."

"Grandfather always used to say that it cost him most as much to dig it right out of the rock there as it did to build the house above it," said Sally. "You know 'twas for that little glimpse of the sea you only get right there, and he couldn't bear to set his house anywhere else. Three sides o' the cellar is sound rock; I don't know's you remember, it's so many years since you was able to get down."

"I recall all those things I used to be in the habit o' seeing as if it were yesterday," said Mrs. Bascom. "I find my thoughts such good company that I don't miss goin' about as much as everybody expects. Everybody knows just where to find me, and so they come to me; folks like to feel a certainty when they make some effort to come."

"I don't know but what I should have been disappointed pretty bad to-day myself," said Sally. "I seemed to miss seeing the house as I sat there to my window sewing. The trees and bushes have budded out amazin' since yesterday. I kind of missed you and felt lonesome. I expect I can see the lower light for some nights yet, till the leaves really come, and Cynthi's light I can see all the year round in her window up-stairs. I can't seem to go to bed till she does," and they both laughed.

"You and Cynthi' used to make signals when you was girls, don't you remember, wavin' things and movin' your lamps?"

" 'Twas kind o' convenient, really. We used to be havin' our plots together, and we had ways o' askin' things an' answerin' yes and no. I seem to forget a good deal of it now," explained Sally.

"You're just as much of a girl as ever you were," said the elder woman looking up with an affectionate and an appreciative smile.

"Well, I did feel as if I wanted to stop and make a dam by the side of the road there where the water runs out under the stone wall," and Sally smiled in her turn.

"Spring is spring, ain't it? Always just as new every year." Mrs. Bascom gave a long look out across the lovely April country. Suddenly her expression changed. "Why, I can see the gable o' Isaac Bolton's new house. I knew he was raising yesterday, but I never thought to look. There over the knoll, to the right of the woods, you can just see the top of it."

"Why yes," said Sally, looking eagerly and then going back to her rocking-chair again. She was blushing and her eyes looked very bright. She seemed to make an effort to speak, but no words came.

Mrs. Bascom also made an effort to look away for some time, and pretended to be busy with her work. At last she laid her hands in her lap.

"Sally," she asked, as a mother might speak to her child, "don't you really think you are foolish? I feel as if you were most as near to me as my own Cynthia;

truth is I can say things right out to you sometimes that I can't to her, much as I love her. Isaac's a good man and faithful; I don't know what he's building that house for, but I don't believe he'll ever want anybody for his wife but you."

"I heard he was engaged to be married to somebody in Pelham," answered Sally stiffly, but with no resentment. "I haven't seen him to speak with for eight months—not since last August, when I happened to meet him here in the yard."

"You done very wrong then, Sally, my dear," said Mrs. Bascom with dignity. "He was glad of the chance to see you and all ready to be friendly, and you passed him right by after you said, 'How do you do,' an' something about the weather. I set right here where I be now, an' I see his face work like a child's that has a real task to keep from cryin'. All these years now you've held on to that grudge, an' 'twas all foolishness. Your Gran'ther Walker's narrow stubbedness keeps you from givin' in, while he's made every effort he could. Sometimes I've thought you didn't love him, an' he was better off to let you have your way about it, but, truth is, you'd deny yourself an' go through the world without happiness, rather than feel you was the one to give in."

"It's all true," said Sally humbly. "I've tried to beat down that hard feelin', but I can't, Mis' Bascom. I own up to you as if you was my own mother; somethin' freezes right up in me. I wish folks hadn't made such a talk about it." She covered her face with her hands and began to cry.

"There, there, dear; 'twill all come right one of these days," said Mrs. Bascom soothingly. "I never meant to work you all up just as we was havin' such a pleasant visit together."

"Somehow or 'nother I'm so contented livin' just as I be, if it only wa'n't for that," said Sally drying her eyes, but not changing the subject. "I never could think of anybody else as I have of Isaac. I'm glad you spoke right out, Mis' Bascom. I've wished you would a good many times."

"You an' Isaac an' Cynthi' used to have such good times together when he was still livin' here"—Mrs. Bascom braided away intently and did not look up as she spoke—"an' since all this has happened he's often talked to me very free and said it troubled him to know you had so little means while he was well off, and you with no brother nor nobody to look after you in winter time, an' all that."

"I've got along all right," insisted Sally with dangerous spirit, then she softened again. "You see how it is, Mis' Bascom, it's too late now and we've got to leave it as it is. I expect it's poor old grandfather's setness, as you say." Her face was pathetic and childish as she spoke. "You're always real good."

"Well, I don't know's I be," said the placid old friend. "I've had very hard feelings about being laid on the shelf so early, while I was full of spirit to work, and we'd just built that great barn and had all our plans about running a creamery. The farm's so good for grazin', and 'twould been easier for my husband, but Cynthia wa'n't able to continue without me. He never complains, but in a few years we should have been forehanded and paid what we owed, instead o' only adding to it." She looked out across the green yard at the barn, the building of which had proved to be such a mistake, and sighed. "I'm going to tell you, too, that we weren't married very young ourselves, Mr. Bascom and I, and 'twas partly owing to my indulgin' just such feelin's as yours, though the occasion was different."

"Why, Mis' Bascom!" exclaimed Sally with deep sympathy.

"Yes, dear, I give you warnin' out of my own experience," and the elder woman looked grave and kindly. "I've been tryin' ever since to make up for real injustice to the good man I loved best in the world. And you can be sure of this thing, Sally, the wrong road never leads to the right place."

It was very still in the wide kitchen; one of the windows was open and the bluebirds were chirping in the orchard. There was a far-away sound of frogs. The old tortoise-shell cat which had been asleep on a cushioned chair came across the floor gaping, and when she saw Sally she hopped up into that friendly neighbor's lap. Sally fondled her a little and laughed at the loud purring that at once began. Her cheeks were a little flushed. "I heard ever so many robins this morning," she said, as if she were afraid of the silence, and her hostess nodded. "If it keeps to this weather we shall have the golden robins comin' right along. I do long to get them here in the spring. Then I really feel as if the winter's gone for good."

Sally rose to go after a little while, in spite of kind protestations from Mrs. Bascom. They both longed to say something more, but neither ventured. Sally, who had grown prim and undemonstrative with every year, came back after her hand was on the door latch, and kissed Mrs. Bascom affectionately.

"There, there, Sally!" said the old woman affectionately. "Don't get worked up! I only want you to think over things before it's too late. I expect you and Isaac'll be happy yet, but don't push him away too far; he's got pride too."

II

As Sally Martin went up the road she wished that she were still sitting with her old neighbor. For almost the first time there was something lonely-looking and repellent, something cold and heartless about her own little house as she unlocked the door and went in. She missed the motherliness she had just left, and the sun no longer shone into her own kitchen. She sat down without taking off her shawl.

After all it was too late now to change her manners to Isaac Bolton or to let him know that her love had always been his. Everybody had spoken of his approaching marriage, and the new house was the surest proof. Mrs. Bascom had treated the story lightly, but perhaps she did not know, or had not been told because she was certain not to approve. Sally knew that her old neighbor had always been her friend. A crisis seemed to have come into her life. Isaac Bolton had been an orphan boy brought up by his uncle and aunt; beside the tract of fine valley land joining the Bascom farm, on which he was putting the new house, he had a good property in money. Sally knew that he would have stayed on with the Bascoms and been a great help to them, if the neighborhood to herself had not grown so difficult and unpleasant. Since then he must often have felt homeless. For herself, too, not far beyond thirty, strong and fond of hard work, it was a poor sort of life to live on year after year in her little house, pinching out a living from a bit of ledgy land and the tiniest of incomes. Isaac was large-hearted and manly, though quick-tempered enough, as she had known. She saw things differently now, the old habits of her mind, the self-pity that had clung so long to a grievance had worn themselves away and left only regret behind on that spring afternoon. It was too late now, she could not do anything, she had lost all right to the man whom she loved and who had so long loved her. She remembered, as she had so many times before, that when she saw him last his coat needed mending, and that

Sarah Orne Jewett

he had grown to look older and even a little gray. She remembered now the sweet, wistful look in his eyes, and how quickly they had clouded over when she with a beating heart had treated him so coldly.

III

Sally Martin still sat by her window in the late afternoon. She had taken up her sewing again, but her eyes looked as if she had been crying. Every few minutes she glanced down the long road to see Mr. Bascom and Cynthia when they came back; that seemed the only interest to which one might still look forward. At last the wagon came in sight and she wondered what the father and daughter would have to tell. To her surprise they passed their own lane's end and came on up the hill, driving fast. Cynthia would not take time just now to come past the house unless for something important—she was late already—and Sally's heart was filled with apprehension.

They turned out of the road, and still sitting by her window she saw Cynthia get out of the wagon, after a word with her father. In both faces was a look of sorrow and shock, and she sprang to her feet as her friend came into the kitchen.

"Oh, Sally, Sally!" said Cynthia, "Isaac got awfully hurt this afternoon. He fell from the house frame, and the doctor can't tell yet whether there is much chance for him. They stopped us as we came by, and they've got him in a little shed until he can be moved to our house—he's got nowhere else to turn. He saw me, and told somebody he had got to speak to me, and when I got to him all he could whisper was that I must come and tell you, and I said I would. He didn't ask you to come, only to let you know."

The two friends faced each other. Sally looked gray and old and stern, but Cynthia had come to an end of her self-control and began to cry. "What will poor mother say?" her voice faltered. "She thinks everything of Isaac and she'll want to get to him, and feel so bad that she can't."

All the color rushed back to Sally's face, and a lovely self-forgetfulness shone in her eyes. She suddenly looked young again and even happy. "Go right home as fast as you can," she said. "I'm going to ask your father to take me right down to Isaac's place. Tell your mother I'll take care of him. I'm going to Isaac now just as fast as I can."

Later still in the twilight, Sally Martin found her way among the new timbers of Isaac's house to the little tool-shed where he lay. Most of the neighbors had gone. The doctor was still there, and he spoke cheerfully as she came near.

"No, there are no bones broken after all, 'twas only the breath knocked out of him," said the doctor. "You'll be laid up for awhile, but I believe you'll do well, Isaac. Now who is there to leave him with? I must be off and it's going to be a damp spring night, he mustn't stay here any longer. Move him carefully."

"I'm right here, Doctor," said old Mr. Bascom, who loved Isaac like a son. "I'll take him right home with me if he's ready to go. I've got the long wagon, you know."

As for Sally, she had gone straight to her lover's side—where he lay weak and pale on the pile of coats and shavings; she was kneeling by him with a sweet and quiet face, and Isaac's hand was fast in hers. Somehow their happiness seemed all the lovelier because it had come at last in the spring.

QUESTIONS

1. Analyze the local-color elements—character types, scenery, dialects, manners, and customs—that Jewett introduces into the tale. How do these elements contribute to the realism of the tale?

2. Evaluate as carefully and fully as possible the relationship between Sally Martin and Mrs. Bascom.

3. Why does Jewett plot the action in three sections?

4. How is nature used symbolically in "A Change of Heart"? Why is the title a clue to Jewett's method?

5. Do you think that Jewett is successful in controlling tone at the end of the story? How would you respond to assertions that claim the conclusion is too sentimental?

6. What is the theme of the story, and how significant is it?

TOPICS FOR WRITING

1. Explore the relationship of the New England setting to character and action in "A Change of Heart."

2. Evaluate the appropriateness and effectiveness of the happy ending in the story.

Kate Chopin

A RESPECTABLE WOMAN

Kate Chopin (1851–1904) was born in St. Louis, Missouri. At the age of 20, she married a man from New Orleans, and she lived there until her husband's premature death caused her to return to St. Louis and assume in 1887 a career in writing. Chopin gained a national reputation in the 1890s for her local-color tales about Louisiana, which appeared in such leading journals as The Atlantic *and* Vogue. *These stories were collected in* Bayou Folk *(1894) and* A Night in Acadie *(1897). She wrote nearly one hundred sketches and stories during the decade. In 1899, she published a novel,* The Awakening. *Termed by one critic an American* Madame Bovary, *this novel about a passionate and independent woman was severely criticized by reviewers and even banned in Chopin's native city. She wrote very little following the controversy over* The Awakening. *In "A Respectable Woman," Chopin displays a willingness to touch on issues of sexual morality and the power of human sexuality. In her willingness to create assertive heroines, she treated characters in a fresh and open manner.*

Mrs. Baroda was a little provoked to learn that her husband expected his friend, Gouvernail, up to spend a week or two on the plantation.

They had entertained a good deal during the winter; much of the time had also been passed in New Orleans in various forms of mild dissipation. She was looking forward to a period of unbroken rest, now, and undisturbed tête-a-tête with her husband, when he informed her that Gouvernail was coming up to stay a week or two.

This was a man she had heard much of but never seen. He had been her husband's college friend; was now a journalist, and in no sense a society man or "a man about town," which were, perhaps, some of the reasons she had never met him. But she had unconsciously formed an image of him in her mind. She pictured him tall, slim, cynical; with eye-glasses, and his hands in his pockets; and she did not like him. Gouvernail was slim enough, but he wasn't very tall nor very cynical; neither did he wear eye-glasses nor carry his hands in his pockets. And she rather liked him when he first presented himself.

But why she liked him she could not explain satisfactorily to herself when she partly attempted to do so. She could discover in him none of those brilliant and promising traits which Gaston, her husband, had often assured her that he possessed. On the contrary, he sat rather mute and receptive before her chatty eagerness to make him feel at home and in face of Gaston's frank and wordy hospitality. His manner was as courteous toward her as the most exacting woman could require; but he made no direct appeal to her approval or even esteem.

Once settled at the plantation he seemed to like to sit upon the wide portico in the shade of one of the big Corinthian pillars, smoking his cigar lazily and listening attentively to Gaston's experience as a sugar planter.

"This is what I call living," he would utter with deep satisfaction, as the air that swept across the sugar field caressed him with its warm and scented velvety touch. It pleased him also to get on familiar terms with the big dogs that came about him, rubbing themselves sociably against his legs. He did not care to fish, and displayed no eagerness to go out and kill grosbecs when Gaston proposed doing so.

Gouvernail's personality puzzled Mrs. Baroda, but she liked him. Indeed, he was a lovable, inoffensive fellow. After a few days, when she could understand him no better than at first, she gave over being puzzled and remained piqued. In this mood she left her husband and her guest, for the most part, alone together. Then finding that Gouvernail took no manner of exception to her action, she imposed her society upon him, accompanying him in his idle strolls to the mill and walks along the batture. She persistently sought to penetrate the reserve in which he had unconsciously enveloped himself.

"When is he going—your friend?" she one day asked her husband. "For my part, he tires me frightfully."

"Not for a week yet, dear. I can't understand; he gives you no trouble."

"No. I should like him better if he did; if he were more like others, and I had to plan somewhat for his comfort and enjoyment."

Gaston took his wife's pretty face between his hands and looked tenderly and laughingly into her troubled eyes. They were making a bit of toilet sociably together in Mrs. Baroda's dressing-room.

"You are full of surprises, ma belle," he said to her. "Even I can never count upon how you are going to act under given conditions." He kissed her and turned to fasten his cravat before the mirror.

"Here you are," he went on, "taking poor Gouvernail seriously and making a commotion over him, the last thing he would desire or expect."

"Commotion!" she hotly resented. "Nonsense! How can you say such a thing? Commotion, indeed! But, you know, you said he was clever."

"So he is. But the poor fellow is run down by overwork now. That's why I asked him here to take a rest."

"You used to say he was a man of ideas," she retorted, unconciliated. "I expected him to be interesting, at least. I'm going to the city in the morning to have my spring gowns fitted. Let me know when Mr. Gouvernail is gone; I shall be at my Aunt Octavie's."

That night she went and sat alone upon a bench that stood beneath a live oak tree at the edge of the gravel walk.

She had never known her thoughts or her intentions to be so confused. She could gather nothing from them but the feeling of a distinct necessity to quit her home in the morning.

Mrs. Baroda heard footsteps crunching the gravel; but could discern in the darkness only the approaching red point of a lighted cigar. She knew it was Gouvernail, for her husband did not smoke. She hoped to remain unnoticed, but her white gown revealed her to him. He threw away his cigar and seated himself upon the bench beside her; without a suspicion that she might object to his presence.

"Your husband told me to bring this to you, Mrs. Baroda," he said, handing her a filmy, white scarf with which she sometimes enveloped her head and shoulders. She accepted the scarf from him with a murmur of thanks, and let it lie in her lap.

He made some commonplace observation upon the baneful effect of the night air at that season. Then as his gaze reached out into the darkness, he murmured, half to himself:

"'Night of south winds—night of the large few stars!
Still nodding night——'"

She made no reply to this apostrophe to the night, which indeed, was not addressed to her.

Gouvernail was in no sense a diffident man, for he was not a self-conscious one. His periods of reserve were not constitutional, but the result of moods. Sitting there beside Mrs. Baroda, his silence melted for the time.

He talked freely and intimately in a low, hesitating drawl that was not unpleasant to hear. He talked of the old college days when he and Gaston had been a good deal to each other; of the days of keen and blind ambitions and large intentions. Now there was left with him, at least, a philosophic acquiescence to the existing order—only a desire to be permitted to exist, with now and then a little whiff of genuine life, such as he was breathing now.

Her mind only vaguely grasped what he was saying. Her physical being was for the moment predominant. She was not thinking of his words, only drinking in the tones of his voice. She wanted to reach out her hand in the darkness and touch him with the sensitive tips of her fingers upon the face or the lips. She wanted to draw close to him and whisper against his cheek—she did not care what—as she might have done if she had not been a respectable woman.

The stronger the impulse grew to bring herself near him, the further, in fact, did she draw away from him. As soon as she could do so without an appearance of too great rudeness, she rose and left him there alone.

Before she reached the house, Gouvernail had lighted a fresh cigar and ended his apostrophe to the night.

Mrs. Baroda was greatly tempted that night to tell her husband—who was also her friend—of this folly that had seized her. But she did not yield to the temptation. Beside being a respectable woman she was a very sensible one; and she knew there are some battles in life which a human being must fight alone.

When Gaston arose in the morning, his wife had already departed. She had taken an early morning train to the city. She did not return till Gouvernail was gone from under her roof.

There was some talk of having him back during the summer that followed. That is, Gaston greatly desired it; but this desire yielded to his wife's strenuous opposition.

However, before the year ended, she proposed, wholly from herself, to have Gouvernail visit them again. Her husband was surprised and delighted with the suggestion coming from her.

"I am glad, chère amie, to know that you have finally overcome your dislike for him; truly he did not deserve it."

"Oh," she told him, laughingly, after pressing a long, tender kiss upon his lips, "I have overcome everything! you will see. This time I shall be very nice to him."

QUESTIONS

1. How is setting used to control the mood and direction of this story?

2. What advantages does the author gain from limiting the third-person point of view to the consciousness of Mrs. Baroda?

3. Chopin writes at the beginning of the story that Mrs. Baroda "had unconsciously formed an image" of Gouvernail in her mind. Why does Chopin stress unconscious impressions at the outset of the tale?

4. What ironies do you detect in the story?

5. Analyze the tone of "A Respectable Woman." Does Chopin moralize, or does she employ a relatively amoral tone? How does tone influence the theme? Does the theme strike you as new or traditional? Explain.

TOPICS FOR WRITING

1. Trace the process of Mrs. Baroda's emerging consciousness in "A Respectable Woman."

2. Compare and contrast images of women in "A Respectable Woman" and in "A Change of Heart" by Sarah Orne Jewett (page 201).

Joseph Conrad

THE LAGOON

Joseph Conrad (1857–1924), christened Jozef Teodor Konrad Nalecz Korzeniowski, was born in Berdycezew, Poland. He was raised in the Polish Ukraine and in Russia, where his parents had been exiled. After his parents' death, Conrad at the age of 17 joined the French merchant navy. From 1874 to 1894, Conrad sailed around the globe, traveling to exotic places like the one described in "The Lagoon," surviving two shipwrecks, and ultimately obtaining a captain's commission in the British merchant marine. Conrad had started to write fiction before the end of his naval career, basing his tales on the impressionistic settings and highly charged human dramas that he had witnessed during his voyages to Africa, the Far East, South America, and Australia. Writing in his third language (Polish and French were his first two), Conrad evolved a distinctive style in English and a unique approach to fiction that made him a celebrated figure. He is the author of Lord Jim *(1900);* Youth *(1902); his masterpiece,* Nostromo *(1904);* The Secret Agent *(1907);* Under Western Skies *(1910); and* Victory *(1915), among other works. In "The Lagoon," the first story that he published, Conrad sets his tale in the Malay Archipelago, attempting to locate that "heart of darkness" which would animate so many of his future stories.*

The white man, leaning with both arms over the roof of the little house in the stern of the boat, said to the steersman—

"We will pass the night in Arsat's clearing. It is late."

The Malay only grunted, and went on looking fixedly at the river. The white man rested his chin on his crossed arms and gazed at the wake of the boat. At the end of the straight avenue of forests cut by the intense glitter of the river, the sun appeared unclouded and dazzling, poised low over the water that shone smoothly like a band of metal. The forests, sombre and dull, stood motionless and silent on each side of the broad stream. At the foot of big, towering trees, trunkless nipa palms rose from the mud of the bank, in bunches of leaves enormous and heavy, that hung unstirring over the brown swirl of eddies. In the stillness of the air every tree, every leaf, every bough, every tendril of creeper and every petal of minute blossoms seemed to have been bewitched into an immobility perfect and final. Nothing moved on the river but the eight paddles that rose flashing regularly, dipped together with a single splash; while the steersman swept right and left with a periodic and sudden flourish of his blade describing a glinting semicircle above his head. The churned-up water frothed alongside with a confused murmur. And the white man's canoe, advancing upstream in the short-lived disturbance of its own making, seemed to enter the portals of a land from which the very memory of motion had forever departed.

The white man, turning his back upon the setting sun, looked along the empty and broad expanse of the sea-reach. For the last three miles of its course the wandering, hesitating river, as if enticed irresistibly by the freedom of an open horizon, flows straight into the sea, flows straight to the east—to the east that harbours both light and darkness. Astern of the boat the repeated call of some bird, a cry discordant and feeble, skipped along over the smooth water and lost itself, before it could reach the other shore, in the breathless silence of the world.

The steersman dug his paddle into the stream, and held hard with stiffened arms, his body thrown forward. The water gurgled aloud; and suddenly the long straight reach seemed to pivot on its centre, the forests swung in a semicircle, and the slanting beams of sunset touched the broadside of the canoe with a fiery glow, throwing the slender and distorted shadows of its crew upon the streaked glitter of the river. The white man turned to look ahead. The course of the boat had been altered at right-angles to the stream, and the carved dragon-head of its prow was pointing now at a gap in the fringing bushes of the bank. It glided through, brushing the overhanging twigs, and disappeared from the river like some slim and amphibious creature leaving the water for its lair in the forests.

The narrow creek was like a ditch: tortuous, fabulously deep; filled with gloom under the thin strip of pure and shining blue of the heaven. Immense trees soared up, invisible behind the festooned draperies of creepers. Here and there, near the glistening blackness of the water, a twisted root of some tall tree showed amongst the tracery of small ferns, black and dull, writhing and motionless, like an arrested snake. The short words of the paddlers reverberated loudly between the thick and sombre walls of vegetation. Darkness oozed out from between the trees, through the tangled maze of the creepers, from behind the great fantastic and unstirring leaves; the darkness, mysterious and invincible; the darkness scented and poisonous of impenetrable forests.

The men poled in the shoaling water. The creek broadened, opening out into a wide sweep of a stagnant lagoon. The forests receded from the marshy bank, leaving a level strip of bright green, reedy grass to frame the reflected blueness of the sky. A fleecy pink cloud drifted high above, trailing the delicate colouring of its image under the floating leaves and the silvery blossoms of the lotus. A little house, perched on high piles, appeared black in the distance. Near it, two tall nibong palms, that seemed to have come out of the forests in the background, leaned slightly over the ragged roof, with a suggestion of sad tenderness and care in the droop of their leafy and soaring heads.

The steersman, pointing with his paddle, said, "Arsat is there. I see his canoe fast between the piles."

The polers ran along the sides of the boat glancing over their shoulders at the end of the day's journey. They would have preferred to spend the night somewhere else than on this lagoon of weird aspect and ghostly reputation. Moreover, they disliked Arsat, first as a stranger, and also because he who repairs a ruined house, and dwells in it, proclaims that he is not afraid to live amongst the spirits that haunt the places abandoned by mankind. Such a man can disturb the course of fate by glances or words; while his familiar ghosts are not easy to propitiate by casual wayfarers upon whom they long to wreak the malice of their human master. White men care not for such things, being unbelievers and in league with the Father of Evil, who leads them unharmed through the invisible dangers of this world. To the warnings of the righteous they oppose an offensive pretence of disbelief. What is there to be done?

So they thought, throwing their weight on the end of their long poles. The big canoe glided on swiftly, noiselessly, and smoothly, towards Arsat's clearing, till, in a great rattling of poles thrown down, and the loud murmurs of "Allah be praised!" it came with a gentle knock against the crooked piles below the house.

The boatmen with uplifted faces shouted discordantly, "Arsat! O Arsat!" Nobody came. The white man began to climb the rude ladder giving access to the bamboo platform before the house. The juragan of the boat said sulkily, "We will cook in the sampan, and sleep on the water."

"Pass my blankets and the basket," said the white man, curtly.

He knelt on the edge of the platform to receive the bundle. Then the boat shoved off, and the white man, standing up, confronted Arsat, who had come out through the low door of his hut. He was a man young, powerful, with broad chest and muscular arms. He had nothing on but his sarong. His head was bare. His big, soft eyes stared eagerly at the white man, but his voice and demeanour were composed as he asked, without any words of greeting—

"Have you medicine, Tuan?"

"No," said the visitor in a startled tone. "No. Why? Is there sickness in the house?"

"Enter and see," replied Arsat, in the same calm manner, and turning short round, passed again through the small doorway. The white man, dropping his bundles, followed.

In the dim light of the dwelling he made out on a couch of bamboos a woman stretched on her back under a broad sheet of red cotton cloth. She lay still, as if dead; but her big eyes, wide open, glittered in the gloom, staring upwards at the slender rafters, motionless and unseeing. She was in a high fever, and evidently unconscious. Her cheeks were sunk slightly, her lips were partly open, and on the young face there was the ominous and fixed expression—the absorbed, contemplating expression of the unconscious who are going to die. The two men stood looking down at her in silence.

"Has she been long ill?" asked the traveller.

"I have not slept for five nights," answered the Malay, in a deliberate tone. "At first she heard voices calling her from the water and struggled against me who held her. But since the sun of to-day rose she hears nothing—she hears not me. She sees nothing. She sees not me—me!"

He remained silent for a minute, then asked softly—

"Tuan, will she die?"

"I fear so," said the white man, sorrowfully. He had known Arsat years ago, in a far country in times of trouble and danger, when no friendship is to be despised. And since his Malay friend had come unexpectedly to dwell in the hut on the lagoon with a strange woman, he had slept many times there, in his journeys up and down the river. He liked the man who knew how to keep faith in council and how to fight without fear by the side of his white friend. He liked him—not so much perhaps as a man likes his favourite dog—but still he liked him well enough to help and ask no questions, to think sometimes vaguely and hazily in the midst of his own pursuits, about the lonely man and the long-haired woman with audacious face and triumphant eyes, who lived together hidden by the forests—alone and feared.

The white man came out of the hut in time to see the enormous conflagration of sunset put out by the swift and stealthy shadows that, rising like a black and impalpable vapour above the tree-tops, spread over the heaven, extinguishing the crimson glow of floating clouds and the red brilliance of departing daylight. In a few moments all the stars came out above the intense blackness of the earth and the great lagoon gleaming suddenly with reflected lights resembled an oval patch of night sky flung down into the hopeless and abysmal night of the wilderness. The white man had some supper out of the basket, then collecting a few sticks that lay about the platform, made up a small fire, not for warmth, but for the sake of the smoke, which would keep off the mosquitos. He wrapped himself in the blankets and sat with his back against the reed wall of the house, smoking thoughtfully.

Arsat came through the doorway with noiseless steps and squatted down by the fire. The white man moved his outstretched legs a little.

"She breathes," said Arsat in a low voice, anticipating the expected question. "She breathes and burns as if with a great fire. She speaks not; she hears not—and burns!"

He paused for a moment, then asked in a quiet, incurious tone—

"Tuan . . . will she die?"

The white man moved his shoulders uneasily and muttered in a hesitating manner—

"If such is her fate."

"No, Tuan," said Arsat, calmly. "If such is my fate. I hear, I see, I wait. I remember . . . Tuan, do you remember the old days? Do you remember my brother?"

"Yes," said the white man. The Malay rose suddenly and went in. The other, sitting still outside could hear the voice in the hut. Arsat said: "Hear me! Speak!" His words were succeeded by a complete silence. "O Diamelen!" he cried, suddenly. After that cry there was a deep sigh. Arsat came out and sank down again in his old place.

They sat in silence before the fire. There was no sound within the house, there was no sound near them; but far away on the lagoon they could hear the voices of the boatmen ringing fitful and distinct on the calm water. The fire in the bows of the sampan shone faintly in the distance with a hazy red glow. Then it died out. The voices ceased. The land and the water slept invisible, unstirring and mute. It was as though there had been nothing left in the world but the glitter of stars streaming, ceaseless and vain, through the black stillness of the night.

The white man gazed straight before him into the darkness with wide-open eyes. The fear and fascination, the inspiration and the wonder of death—of death near, unavoidable, and unseen, soothed the unrest of his race and stirred the most indistinct, the most intimate of his thoughts. The ever-ready suspicion of evil, the gnawing suspicion that lurks in our hearts, flowed out into the stillness round him—into the stillness profound and dumb, and made it appear untrust-worthy and infamous, like the placid and impenetrable mask of an unjustifiable violence. In that fleeting and powerful disturbance of his being the earth enfolded in the starlight peace became a shadowy country of inhuman strife, a battle-field of phantoms terrible and charming, august or ignoble, struggling ardently for the possession of our helpless hearts. An unquiet and mysterious country of inextin-guishable desires and fears.

A plaintive murmur rose in the night; a murmur saddening and startling, as if the great solitudes of surrounding woods had tried to whisper into his ear the wisdom of their immense and lofty indifference. Sounds hesitating and vague floated in the air round him, shaped themselves slowly into words; and at last flowed on gently in a murmuring stream of soft and monotonous sentences. He stirred like a man waking up and changed his position slightly. Arsat, motionless and shadowy, sitting with bowed head under the stars, was speaking in a low and dreamy tone—

". . . for where can we lay down the heaviness of our trouble but in a friend's heart? A man must speak of war and of love. You, Tuan, know what war is, and you have seen me in time of danger seek death as other men seek life! A writing may be lost; a lie may be written; but what the eye has seen is truth and remains in the mind!"

"I remember," said the white man, quietly. Arsat went on with mournful composure—

"Therefore I shall speak to you of love. Speak in the night. Speak before both night and love are gone—and the eye of day looks upon my sorrow and my shame; upon my blackened face; upon my burnt-up heart."

A sigh, short and faint, marked an almost imperceptible pause, and then his words flowed on, without a stir, without a gesture.

"After the time of trouble and war was over and you went away from my country in the pursuit of your desires, which we, men of the islands, cannot understand, I and my brother became again, as we had been before, the sword-bearers of the Ruler. You know we were men of family, belonging to a ruling race, and more fit than any to carry on our right shoulder the emblem of power. And in the time of prosperity Si Dendring showed us favour, as we, in time of sorrow, had showed to him the faithfulness of our courage. It was a time of peace. A time of deer-hunts and cock-fights; of idle talks and foolish squabbles between men whose bellies are full and weapons are rusty. But the sower watched the young rice-shoots grow up without fear, and the traders came and went, departed lean and returned fat into the river of peace. They brought news, too. Brought lies and truth mixed together, so that no man knew when to rejoice and when to be sorry. We heard from them about you also. They had seen you here and had seen you there. And I was glad to hear, for I remembered the stirring times, and I always remembered you, Tuan, till the time came when my eyes could see nothing in the past, because they had looked upon the one who is dying there—in the house."

He stopped to exclaim in an intense whisper, "O Mara bahia! O Calamity!" then went on speaking a little louder:

"There's no worse enemy and no better friend than a brother, Tuan, for one brother knows another, and in perfect knowledge is strength for good or evil. I loved my brother. I went to him and told him that I could see nothing but one face, hear nothing but one voice. He told me: 'Open your heart so that she can see what is in it—and wait. Patience is wisdom. Inchi Midah may die or our Ruler may throw off his fear of a woman!' . . . I waited! . . . You remember the lady with the veiled face, Tuan, and the fear of our Ruler before her cunning and temper. And if she wanted her servant, what could I do? But I fed the hunger of my heart on short glances and stealthy words. I loitered on the path to the bath-houses in the daytime, and when the sun had fallen behind the forest I crept along the jasmine hedges of the women's courtyard. Unseeing, we spoke to one another through the scent of flowers, through the veil of leaves, through the blades of long grass that stood still before our lips; so great was our prudence, so faint was the murmur of our great longing. The time passed swiftly . . . and there were whispers amongst women—and our enemies watched—my brother was gloomy, and I began to think of killing and of a fierce death. . . . We are of a people who take what they want—like you whites. There is a time when a man should forget loyalty and respect. Might and authority are given to rulers, but to all men is given love and strength and courage. My brother said, 'You shall take her from their midst. We are two who are like one.' And I answered, 'Let it be soon, for I find no warmth in sunlight that does not shine upon her.' Our time came when the Ruler and all the great people went to the mouth of the river to fish by torchlight. There were hundreds of boats, and on the white sand, between the water and the forests, dwellings of leaves were built for the households of the Rajahs. The smoke of cooking-fires was like a blue mist of the evening, and many voices rang in it joyfully. While they were making the boats ready to beat up the fish, my brother came to me and said, 'To-night!' I looked to my weapons, and when the time came our canoe took its place in the circle of boats carrying the torches. The lights blazed on the water, but behind the boats there was darkness. When the shouting began and the excitement made them like mad we dropped out. The water swallowed our fire, and we floated back to the shore that was dark with only here and there the glimmer of embers. We could hear the talk of slave-girls amongst the sheds. Then we found a place deserted and silent. We waited there. She came. She came running along the shore, rapid and leaving no trace, like a leaf driven by the wind into the sea. My brother said gloomily, 'Go and take her; carry her into our boat.' I lifted her in my arms. She panted. Her heart was beating against my breast. I said, 'I take you from those people. You came to the cry of my heart, but my arms take you into my boat against the will of the great!' 'It is right,' said my brother. 'We are men who take what we want and can hold it against many. We should have taken her in daylight.' I said, 'Let us be off'; for since she was in my boat I began to think of our Ruler's many men. 'Yes. Let us be off,' said my brother. 'We are cast out and this boat is our country now—and the sea is our refuge.' He lingered with his foot on the shore, and I entreated him to hasten, for I remembered the strokes of her heart against my breast and thought that two men cannot withstand a hundred. We left, paddling downstream close to the bank; and as we passed by the creek where they were fishing, the great shouting had ceased, but the murmur of voices was loud like the humming of insects flying at noonday. The boats floated, clustered together, in the red light of torches, under a black roof of smoke; and men talked of their sport. Men that boasted, and praised, and jeered—men that would have been our friends in the morning, but on that night were already our enemies. We paddled swiftly past. We had no more friends in the country of our birth. She sat in the middle of the canoe with covered face; silent as she is now; unseeing as she is now—and I had no regret at what I was leaving because I could hear her breathing close to me—as I can hear her now."

He paused, listened with his ear turned to the doorway, then shook his head and went on:

"My brother wanted to shout the cry of challenge—one cry only—to let the people know we were freeborn robbers who trusted our arms and the great sea. And again I begged him in the name of our love to be silent. Could I not hear her breathing close to me? I knew the pursuit would come quick enough. My brother loved me. He dipped his paddle without a splash. He only said, 'There is half a man in you now—the other half is in that woman. I can wait. When you are a whole man again, you will come back with me here to shout defiance. We are sons of the same mother.' I made no answer. All my strength and all my spirit were in my hands that held the paddle—for I longed to be with her in a safe place beyond the reach of men's anger and of women's spite. My love was so great, that I thought it could guide me to a country where death was unknown, if I could only escape from Inchi Midah's fury and from our Ruler's sword. We paddled with haste, breathing through our teeth. The blades bit deep into the smooth water. We passed out of the river; we flew in clear channels amongst the shallows. We skirted the black coast; we skirted the sand beaches where the sea speaks in whispers to the land; and the gleam of white sand flashed back past our boat, so swiftly she ran upon the water. We spoke not. Only once I said, 'Sleep, Diamelen, for soon you may want all your strength.' I heard the sweetness of her voice, but I never turned my head. The sun rose and still we went on. Water fell from my face like rain from a cloud. We flew in the light and heat. I never looked back, but I knew that my brother's eyes, behind me, were looking steadily ahead, for the boat went as straight as a bushman's dart, when it leaves the end of the sumpitan. There was no better paddler, no better steersman than my brother. Many times, together, we had won races in that canoe. But we never had put out our strength as we did then—then, when for the last time we paddled together! There was no braver or stronger man in our country than my brother. I could not spare the strength to turn my head and look at him, but every moment I heard the hiss of his breath getting louder behind me. Still he did not speak. The sun was high. The heat clung to my back like a flame of fire. My ribs were ready to burst, but I could no longer get enough air into my chest. And then I felt I must cry out with my last breath, 'Let us rest!' . . . 'Good!' he answered; and his voice was firm. He was strong. He was brave. He knew not fear and no fatigue . . . My brother!"

A murmur powerful and gentle, a murmur vast and faint; the murmur of trembling leaves, of stirring boughs, ran through the tangled depths of the forests, ran over the starry smoothness of the lagoon, and the water between the piles lapped the slimy timber once with a sudden splash. A breath of warm air touched the two men's faces and passed on with a mournful sound—a breath loud and short like an uneasy sigh of the dreaming earth.

Arsat went on in an even, low voice.

"We ran our canoe on the white beach of a little bay close to a long tongue of

Joseph Conrad

land that seemed to bar our road; a long wooded cape going far into the sea. My brother knew that place. Beyond the cape a river has its entrance, and through the jungle of that land there is a narrow path. We made a fire and cooked rice. Then we lay down to sleep on the soft sand in the shade of our canoe, while she watched. No sooner had I closed my eyes than I heard her cry of alarm. We leaped up. The sun was halfway down the sky already, and coming in sight in the opening of the bay we saw a prau manned by many paddlers. We knew it at once; it was one of our Rajah's praus. They were watching the shore,and saw us. They beat the gong, and turned the head of the prau into the bay. I felt my heart become weak within my breast. Diamelen sat on the sand and covered her face. There was no escape by sea. My brother laughed. He had the gun you had given him, Tuan, before you went away, but there was only a handful of powder. He spoke to me quickly: 'Run with her along the path. I shall keep them back, for they have no firearms, and landing in the face of a man with a gun is certain death for some. Run with her. On the other side of that wood there is a fisherman's house—and a canoe. When I have fired all the shots I will follow. I am a great runner, and before they can come up we shall be gone. I will hold out as long as I can, for she is but a woman—that can neither run nor fight, but she has your heart in her weak hands.' He dropped behind the canoe. The prau was coming. She and I ran, and as we rushed along the path I heard shots. My brother fired—once—twice—and the booming of the gong ceased. There was silence behind us. That neck of land is narrow. Before I heard my brother fire the third shot I saw the shelving shore, and I saw the water again; the mouth of a broad river. We crossed a grassy glade. We ran down to the water. I saw a low hut above the black mud, and a small canoe hauled up. I heard another shot behind me. I thought, 'That is his last charge.' We rushed down to the canoe; a man came running from the hut, but I leaped on him, and we rolled together in the mud. Then I got up, and he lay still at my feet. I don't know whether I had killed him or not. I and Diamelen pushed the canoe afloat. I heard yells behind me, and I saw my brother run across the glade. Many men were bounding after him, I took her in my arms and threw her into the boat, then leaped in myself. When I looked back I saw that my brother had fallen. He fell and was up again, but the men were closing round him. He shouted, 'I am coming!' The men were close to him. I looked. Many men. Then I looked at her. Tuan, I pushed the canoe! I pushed it into deep water. She was kneeling forward looking at me, and I said, 'Take your paddle,' while I struck the water with mine. Tuan, I heard him cry. I heard him cry my name twice; and I heard voices shouting, 'Kill! Strike!' I never turned back. I heard him calling my name again with a great shriek, as when life is going out together with the voice—and I never turned my head. My own name! . . . My brother! Three times he called—but I was not afraid of life. Was she not there in that canoe? And could I not with her find a country where death is forgotten—where death is unknown!"

The white man sat up. Arsat rose and stood, an indistinct and silent figure above the dying embers of the fire. Over the lagoon a mist drifting and low had crept, erasing slowly the glittering images of the stars. And now a great expanse of white vapour covered the land; it flowed cold and gray in the darkness, eddied in noiseless whirls round the tree-trunks and about the platform of the house, which seemed to float upon a restless and impalpable illusion of a sea. Only far away the tops of the trees stood outlined on the twinkle of heaven, like a sombre and forbidding shore—a coast deceptive, pitiless and black.

Arsat's voice vibrated loudly in the profound peace.

"I had her there! I had her! To get her I would have faced all mankind. But I had her—and——"

His words went out ringing into the empty distances. He paused, and seemed to listen to them dying away very far—beyond help and beyond recall. Then he said quietly—

"Tuan, I loved my brother."

A breath of wind made him shiver. High above his head, high above the silent sea of mist the drooping leaves of the palms rattled together with a mournful and expiring sound. The white man stretched his legs. His chin rested on his chest, and he murmured sadly without lifting his head—

"We all love our brothers."

Arsat burst out with an intense whispering violence—

"What did I care who died? I wanted peace in my own heart."

He seemed to hear a stir in the house—listened—then stepped in noiselessly. The white man stood up. A breeze was coming in fitful puffs. The stars shone paler as if they had retreated into the frozen depths of immense space. After a chill gust of wind there were a few seconds of perfect calm and absolute silence. Then from behind the black and wavy line of the forests a column of golden light shot up into the heavens and spread over the semicircle of the eastern horizon. The sun had risen. The mist lifted, broke into drifting patches, vanished into thin flying wreaths; and the unveiled lagoon lay, polished and black, in the heavy shadows at the foot of the wall of trees. A white eagle rose over it with a slanting and ponderous flight, reached the clear sunshine and appeared dazzlingly brilliant for a moment, then soaring higher, became a dark and motionless speck before it vanished into the blue as if it had left the earth forever. The white man, standing gazing upwards before the doorway, heard in the hut a confused and broken murmur of distracted words ending with a loud groan. Suddenly Arsat stumbled out with outstretched hands, shivered, and stood still for some time with fixed eyes. Then he said—

"She burns no more."

Before his face the sun showed its edge above the tree-tops rising steadily. The breeze freshened; a great brilliance burst upon the lagoon, sparkled on the rippling water. The forests came out of the clear shadows of the morning, became distinct, as if they had rushed nearer—to stop short in a great stir of leaves, of nodding boughs, of swaying branches. In the merciless sunshine the whisper of unconscious life grew louder, speaking in an incomprehensible voice round the dumb darkness of that human sorrow. Arsat's eyes wandered slowly, then stared at the rising sun.

"I can see nothing," he said half aloud to himself.

"There is nothing," said the white man, moving to the edge of the platform and waving his hand to his boat. A shout came faintly over the lagoon and the sampan bagan to glide towards the abode of the friend of ghosts.

"If you want to come with me, I will wait all the morning," said the white man, looking away upon the water.

"No, Tuan," said Arsat, softly. "I shall not eat or sleep in this house, but I must first see my road. Now I can see nothing—see nothing! There is no light and no peace in the world; but there is death—death for many. We are sons of the same mother—and I left him in the midst of enemies; but I am going back now."

He drew a long breath and went on in a dreamy tone:

"In a little while I shall see clear enough to strike—to strike. But she has died, and . . . now . . . darkness."

He flung his arms wide open, let them fall along his body, then stood still with unmoved face and stony eyes, staring at the sun. The white man got down into his canoe. The polers ran smartly along the sides of the boat, looking over their shoulders at the beginning of a weary journey. High in the stern, his head muffled up in white rags, the juragan sat moody, letting his paddle trail in the water. The white man, leaning with both arms over the grass roof of the little cabin, looked back at the shining ripple of the boat's wake. Before the sampan passed out of the lagoon into the creek he lifted his eyes. Arsat had not moved. He stood lonely in the searching sunshine; and he looked beyond the great light of a cloudless day into the darkness of a world of illusions.

QUESTIONS

1. Perhaps the most distinctive aspect of Conrad's style in "The Lagoon" is the rich, imagistic, highly impressionistic description of the setting. What mood is created by this description? How does this mood inform some of the ideas raised by the story? What is the significance of the pattern of imagery dealing with light and dark? What might the river and the lagoon symbolize?

2. What does Arsat seek in his escape to the lagoon? Why, at the end of the story, is he left gazing "into the darkness of a world of illusions"?

3. What is significant about the fact that a white man journeys up the river to the lagoon? Is the white man a fully developed character? Explain. How does his place in the frame of the story relate to the inner tale that Arsat tells?

4. Why is this a story about the primal forces that govern human lives? What forces among these are treated by Conrad in the story?

5. Is there any way for us to determine from the context of the story whether or not Arsat was correct in abandoning his brother to certain death in order to save Diamelen? Explain. Why does Arsat vow to return to the land of the Ruler at the end of the story?

6. What, ultimately, is "The Lagoon" about? What are the difficulties in trying to establish a single theme for this story?

TOPICS FOR WRITING

1. Analyze in detail the significance of the setting in "The Lagoon." Be certain to deal with patterns of imagery, with possible symbolic overtones to the river and the lagoon, and with the way that mood influences theme.

2. Explore the ways in which "The Lagoon" is about universal themes in human existence—life and death, love, courage, loyalty, and so forth.

3. Is "The Lagoon" a romantic or a realistic story? Defend your position.

Charles Waddell Chesnutt

HOW DASDY CAME THROUGH

Charles Waddell Chesnutt (1858–1932), considered the first major black American short story writer and novelist, was born in Cleveland, Ohio, but was raised largely in Fayetteville, North Carolina. He went to school there, and was then employed as a teacher and subsequently as a principal. He also studied law and passed his bar examinations in 1887, ultimately opening his own office in Cleveland as a court reporter. Around this time, he also began publishing his short stories in the Atlantic Monthly. *His collection of stories based on folk traditions was published in* The Conjure Woman *(1899). Chesnutt's other well-known books are* The House Behind the Cedars *(1900) and* The Marrow of Tradition *(1901). A pioneer at portraying the lives of black people in short fiction and at outlining black-white relationships, Chesnutt has a rare comic talent and an ability to transcribe the folkways and vernacular of his characters. In the following story, Chesnutt pokes gentle fun at the institutions of courtship, class, marriage, and religion in showing how his major character triumphs over her adversaries.*

"What's de matter wid yer, Dasdy?" asked Aunt Zilpha, looking up from the washtub at her good-looking daughter.

"Dey ain't nuthin' de matter wid me," replied Dasdy, slamming her iron viciously on the ironing board, where a limp mass of snowy linen was gradually assuming form and substance under her skillful hand.

Aunt Zilpha rubbed away for several minutes, and then asked another question:

"Is yer gwine ter chu'ch ter-night, Dasdy?"

"I dunno as I is," replied Dasdy (short for Desdemona) gloomily.

"Better g'long, honey," continued Aunt Zilpha. "Elder Smith gwine to preach ter-night."

Dasdy worked away vigorously at the ironing board. Presently she said: "'Lizah Davis had on dat new silk dress and velvet bonnet las' night."

"Wonder whar dat gal got de money ter buy a silk dress?" asked Aunt Zilpha, contemptuously; "it mus' be dis here cheap silk."

"I 'spect it's secondhand," remarked Dasdy, as she changed her iron. "She never had no silk dress 'fo' she went to C'lumbia. She say her sister give 'er dat dress—but I dunno."

"Did 'Dolphus ax yer to go to ch'uch wid 'im ary night dis week?" asked Aunt Zilpha, after a pause.

"No, he's be'n gwine wid dat 'Lizah Davis all de week. She was shoutin' las' night."

"Umph!" grunted Aunt Zilpha, "dat's all 'pocrisy—dat gal ain't got no religion." She wrung out a few more pieces, and then continued:

"Better g'long to chu'ch, honey. Good religion better dan sweethearts."

There was a great revival in progress at the Mt. Gilead Baptist Church, the chief tabernacle of worship for the colored people of Patesville. The interest had been kept up for six weeks, and was still unabated, and the number of conversions and additions to the church was something unprecedented. The elder in charge had not been able to do half the work, and preachers had come from distant towns to assist him. Meetings were held nightly, and on Sundays five times a day—beginning at sunrise and ending only at midnight. In fact the religious enthusiasm of the colored people at Patesville, who constituted half the population, was at fever heat.

Adolphus Sampson was among the earliest converts. Adolphus was head waiter at the Clarendon House, the leading hotel of the town, and being yellow and rather goodlooking, was very popular among the young women who were willing to fulfill their duty to society by getting married.

Before the revival began 'Dolphus had for a long time kept company with Dasdy Williams, one of the best-looking of the girls that attended the Baptist church. He had hesitated a little at one time between Dasdy and 'Lizah Davis, another dusky belle. But Dasdy was more attractive in person and could earn more money as a laundress than 'Lizah as a nurse, and 'Dolphus' susceptible heart had prudently succumbed to this combination of attractions.

But now everything was changed. Soon after the revival 'Dolphus had been converted, and his zeal for religion had temporarily overshadowed his fondness for Dasdy's company. She was still a sinner, and the callow saint was fond of trying his new wings. He found Dasdy a poor listener to that kind of conversation —she preferred the old style. A slight coolness had thus sprung up between the lovers, when 'Lizah Davis appeared upon the scene with all the prestige of a visit to Columbia, and with the additional charms conferred by a new silk dress and a velvet bonnet. Moreover, she was converted during the second week of the revival and 'Dolphus hence found in her a sympathetic listener, and enjoyed at the same time the somewhat worldly satisfaction of going to church with the best-dressed girl in the congregation.

Of course this was gall and wormwood to Dasdy. She was in love with 'Dolphus and did not at all approve of the turn affairs had taken. The condition of her mind at this time predisposed her to sentimental impressions. A powerful sermon by Elder Smith affected her considerably, and one evening she left her seat in church and went forward to the mourners' bench. The next day the impressions of the evening before seemed to have passed away entirely. Dasdy tried to think of her sins, but the figure of 'Dolphus intruded itself persistently, and instead of reflecting on her own shortcomings, she could not keep her mind from the meanness of 'Lizah Davis, who had stolen her lover. At night Dasdy did not feel the least inclination to go forward when the mourners were invited up to the front seats. But curious eyes were watching her, and consistency required that she should not give up soon.

While she hesitated 'Dolphus came into the church at the right door and 'Lizah Davis at the left, resplendent in her new dress and bonnet; they had evidently come to church together.

Dasdy struggled for a moment between two powerful emotions—love for 'Dolphus, which made her feel like crying, and hatred for the other girl, which made her feel like tearing her eyes out.

Then another motive for going to the mourners' bench suggested itself: If she could only get religion 'Dolphus might come back to her; and she liked to think of

Brother 'Dolphus bending over her at the mourners' bench, encouraging her in tones of love and religion combined. Yielding to the impulse of this idea, she went forward and knelt at the front seat. Now it happened that during the whole evening 'Dolphus had not come near her. There was a large congregation and many mourners; and 'Dolphus did not know she was at the mourners' bench for some time, and then could not reach her for the crowd of women standing around.

Dasdy prayed mechanically, but her heart was not in it; and she went home in a worse frame of mind than that in which she had gone to church. The next day she had the conversation with her mother, and this good old woman persuaded her to go to church and continue her prayers.

At eight o'clock Dasdy got ready for church. She put on her plainest dress, and a starched gingham sunbonnet instead of her Sunday hat. Her face wore an expression which indicated some determined purpose. As she left the house her mother said:

"Try to get through dis week, Dasdy. De big baptizin' gwine ter come off next Sunday, an' ef I was you I rudder be baptized at a big baptizin'."

"I feel dat I'm gwine ter git through dis night," said Dasdy firmly.

The church was crowded that night, and the enthusiasm ran high. Dasdy did not go forward at the first call; but when 'Lizah Davis came in and took her seat in front of the pulpit, just behind the last of the benches reserved for mourners, Dasdy's eyes glistened with something which was not a tear or yet religious feeling. She went forward and knelt a short distance from 'Lizah's seat. Prayers and hymns followed each other in rapid succession. By and by somebody started one of the popular and stirring revival songs. During this hymn Dasdy was observed to slip from the seat where she was kneeling and fall to the floor, where she lay at full length, with half closed eyes, moaning and groaning, with occasional writhings and spasmodic movements of the limbs.

"Sister Dasdy Williams under conviction," ran round the room. A circle was formed about her, a special prayer was offered, and a special hymn sung for her benefit. One or two sisters knelt beside her and poured exhortations into her ears. Others in the background exchanged opinions as to whether she would get through that evening or not. Dasdy through her half-shut eyes saw 'Lizah Davis join the circle about her. Then her movements became more violent.

"I b'leeve she's comin' through," said one sister, breathlessly, looking over the shoulder of the woman in front of her.

"I knowed she'd git through in time fur de big baptizin'," whispered another young woman, sarcastically, pressing forward into the circle. The spectators in the gallery were leaning over toward the crowd below. Suddenly Dasdy sprang to her feet, her face beaming. Uttering a loud shout she jumped straight up and down for a dozen times.

"Glory!" she cried; "oh, so happy! praise de Lamb!" She threw her arms out sidewise. One hand struck a sister on the nose, and the crimson tide proceeding from that organ compelled her to retire. Then as a backward movement in the circle indicated a disposition on the part of the more timid to seek safety, Dasdy sprang in the direction of 'Lizah Davis, and seizing her new velvet bonnet, swung it once or twice on high; then, still shouting and as though unconscious of what she did, dropped it to the floor and trampled it under foot. Another hat shared the same fate. Half a dozen officious women grasped her arms and tried to hold her. Meanwhile 'Lizah, with an angry look, was trying to get her bonnet. Dasdy slipped down between the encircling arms of those who held her, and reaching out caught the overskirt of 'Lizah's silk dress.

Rip! r-r-r-ip! went the fragile fabric—it was cheap silk—and as 'Lizah attempted to escape, the fastenings of the overskirt gave way at the waist, and the devoted garment fell under the feet of the women who tried to hold the still writhing Dasdy. 'Lizah finally escaped with the fragments of her finery, and with feelings far different from what a religious meeting should have inspired, forced a passage through the crowded aisles and hastened homeward, to weep scalding tears of rage and grief. Her bonnet was entirely ruined, and the silk dress never entirely recovered its pristine splendor.

Dasdy was baptized the following Sunday, and established her reputation for piety by the fine exhibitions of shouting she gave on that occasion. Her designs on Adolphus were successful; she had added one more to the long list of those who have stolen the livery of heaven to serve their own selfish ends; those who believe that all is fair in love may perhaps find excuse for her. The Sunday after the baptizing she appeared at church in a new blue silk dress, with satin trimmings, and a hat gorgeous in the wealth of feathers and ribbons that adorned it. The susceptible but inconstant 'Dolphus could not resist this new combination of gorgeousness and sanctity, and returned to his former allegiance. And from the following announcement which recently appeared in the local newspaper, it may be inferred that the course of true love ran thenceforth smoothly to its proper goal: "Last Wednesday evening the efficient and scholarly head waiter of the Clarendon House led to hymeneal altar the lovely and accomplished Miss Desdemona Brown, one of our most popular young society ladies. The ceremony was performed at Mt. Gilead Baptist Church by Elder Smith, and the happy pair left the following morning for a two weeks' bridal tour, after which they will reside temporarily with the bride's mother. Mr. Sampson will still continue to preside over the Clarendon dining room."

QUESTIONS

1. What does the title of the story signify?

2. What point of view does Chesnutt employ? Where do you sense that the author is editorializing?

3. Analyze the satiric tone of the story. What subjects is Chesnutt looking at in a comic manner? What does he say about these subjects?

4. How are Chesnutt's comic techniques reflected in his method of narrative action and character development?

5. What are Chesnutt's principal ways of creating local color in his depiction of the world of this story?

6. In what way or ways does this story draw on the same traditions that Twain exploits in "The Notorious Jumping Frog of Calaveras County" (page 192)?

7. What is the theme of the story?

TOPICS FOR WRITING

1. Evaluate Chesnutt's attitude toward class, courtship, marriage, and religion in "How Dasdy Came Through."

2. Examine the ways that Chesnutt, Twain (page 192), and Jewett (page 201), handle local-color elements in their stories.

Anton Chekhov

GOOSEBERRIES

Anton Chekhov (1860–1904), whose biography appears earlier in this anthology (page 14), once declared to his friend and fellow writer Maxim Gorky, "What an absurd, clumsy country our Russia is!" No story better reveals Chekhov's ambivalent feelings about his country than his masterpiece "Gooseberries." This story is a subtle and brilliantly plotted tale about the dreams, obsessions, and illusions that we all entertain about ourselves and our position in society. It is a story without heroes, without monumental episodes, without overwhelming conflicts, without a clear ending—in short, a typical Chekhov tale. Instead, Chekhov places characters from various walks of life together, lets them interact, and without resolving anything, leaves us with the same sense of perplexity and wonder about human nature (and perhaps the world) that one individual experiences at the end of the story. Yet at the conclusion of the tale, we also sense that the life of the soul—and of Russia itself—has been revealed to us by a major literary artist.

The sky had been covered with rain-clouds ever since the early morning; it was a still day, cool and dull, one of those misty days when the clouds have long been lowering overhead and you keep thinking it is just going to rain, and the rain holds off. Ivan Ivanich, the veterinary surgeon, and Burkin, the high-school teacher, had walked till they were tired, and the way over the fields seemed endless to them. Far ahead they could just make out the windmill of the village of Mironositskoye, and what looked like a range of low hills at the right extending well beyond the village, and they both knew that this range was really the bank of the river, and that further on were meadows, green willow-trees, country-estates; if they were on the top of these hills, they knew they would see the same boundless fields and telegraph-posts, and the train, like a crawling caterpillar in the distance, while in fine weather even the town would be visible. On this still day, when the whole of nature seemed kindly and pensive, Ivan Ivanich and Burkin felt a surge of love for this plain, and thought how vast and beautiful their country was.

"The last time we stayed in Elder Prokofy's hut," said Burkin, "you said you had a story to tell me."

"Yes. I wanted to tell you the story of my brother."

Ivan Ivanich took a deep breath and lighted his pipe as a preliminary to his narrative, but just then the rain came. Five minutes later it was coming down in torrents and nobody could say when it would stop. Ivan Ivanich and Burkin stood still, lost in thought. The dogs, already soaked, stood with drooping tails, gazing at them wistfully.

"We must try and find shelter," said Burkin. "Let's go to Alekhin's. It's quite near."

"Come on, then."

They turned aside and walked straight across the newly reaped field, veering to the right till they came to a road. Very soon poplars, an orchard, and the red roofs of barns came into sight. The surface of the river gleamed, and they had a view of an extensive reach of water, a windmill and a whitewashed bathing-shed. This was Sofyino, where Alekhin lived.

The mill was working, and the noise made by its sails drowned the sound of the rain; the whole dam trembled. Horses, soaking wet, were standing near some carts, their heads drooping, and people were moving about with sacks over their heads and shoulders. It was wet, muddy, bleak, and the water looked cold and sinister. Ivan Ivanich and Burkin were already experiencing the misery of dampness, dirt, physical discomfort, their boots were caked with mud, and when, having passed the mill-dam, they took the upward path to the landowner's barns, they fell silent, as if vexed with one another.

The sound of winnowing came from one of the barns; the door was open, and clouds of dust issued from it. Standing in the doorway was Alekhin himself, a stout man of some forty years, with longish hair, looking more like a professor or an artist than a landed proprietor. He was wearing a white shirt greatly in need of washing, belted with a piece of string, and long drawers with no trousers over them. His boots, too, were caked with mud and straw. His eyes and nose were ringed with dust. He recognised Ivan Ivanich and Burkin, and seemed glad to see them.

"Go up to the house, gentlemen," he said, smiling. "I'll be with you in a minute."

It was a large two-storey house. Alekhin occupied the ground floor, two rooms with vaulted ceilings and tiny windows, where the stewards had lived formerly. They were poorly furnished, and smelled of rye-bread, cheap vodka, and harness. He hardly ever went into the upstairs rooms, excepting when he had guests. Ivan Ivanich and Burkin were met by a maid-servant, a young woman of such beauty that they stood still involuntarily and exchanged glances.

"You have no idea how glad I am to see you here, dear friends," said Alekhin, overtaking them in the hall. "It's quite a surprise! Pelageya," he said, turning to the maid, "find the gentlemen a change of clothes. And I might as well change, myself. But I must have a wash first, for I don't believe I've had a bath since the spring. Wouldn't you like to go and have a bathe while they get things ready here?"

The beauteous Pelageya, looking very soft and delicate, brought them towels and soap, and Alekhin and his guests set off for the bathing-house.

"Yes, it's a long time since I had a wash," he said, taking off his clothes. "As you see I have a nice bathing-place, my father had it built, but somehow I never seem to get time to wash."

He sat on the step, soaping his long locks and his neck, and all round him the water was brown.

"Yes, you certainly . . ." remarked Ivan Ivanich, with a significant glance at his host's head.

"It's a long time since I had a wash . . ." repeated Alekhin, somewhat abashed, and he soaped himself again, and now the water was dark blue, like ink.

Ivan Ivanich emerged from the shed, splashed noisily into the water, and began swimming beneath the rain spreading his arms wide, making waves all round him and the white water-lilies rocked on the waves he made. He swam into the very middle of the river and then dived, a moment later came up at another place and swam further, diving constantly, and trying to touch the bottom. "Ah, my God" he kept exclaiming in his enjoyment. "Ah, my God . . ." He swam up to the mill, had a little talk with some peasants there and turned back, but when he got to the middle of the river, he floated, holding his face up to the rain. Burkin and Alekhin were dressed and ready to go, but he went on swimming and diving.

"God! God!" he kept exclaiming. "Dear God!"

"Come out!" Burkin shouted to him.

They went back to the house. And only after the lamp was lit in the great drawing-room on the upper floor, and Burkin and Ivan Ivanich, in silk dressing-gowns and warm slippers, were seated in arm-chairs, while Alekhin, washed and combed, paced the room in his new frock-coat, enjoying the warmth, the cleanliness, his dry clothes and comfortable slippers, while the fair Pelageya, smiling benevolently, stepped noiselessly over the carpet with her tray of tea preserves, did Ivan Ivanich embark upon his yarn, and the ancient dames, young ladies and military gentlemen looking down at them severely from their gilded frames, as if they, too, were listening.

"There were two of us brothers," he began. "Ivan Ivanich (me), and my brother Nikolai Ivanich, two years younger than myself. I went in for learning and became a veterinary surgeon, but Nikolai started working in a government office when he was only nineteen. Our father, Chimsha-Himalaisky, was educated in a school for the sons of private soldiers, but was later promoted to officer's rank, and was made a hereditary nobleman and given a small estate. After his death the estate had to be sold for debts, but at least our childhood was passed in the freedom of the countryside, where we roamed the fields and the woods like peasant children, taking the horses to graze, peeling bark from the trunks of lime-trees, fishing, and all that sort of thing. And anyone who has once in his life fished for perch, or watched the thrushes fly south in the autumn, rising high over the village on clear, cool days, is spoilt for town life, and will long for the countryside for the rest of his days. My brother pined in his government office. The years passed and he sat in the same place every day, writing out the same documents and thinking all the time of the same thing—how to get back to the country. And these longings of his gradually turned into a definite desire, into a dream of purchasing a little estate somewhere on the bank of a river or the shore of a lake.

"He was a meek, good-natured chap, I was fond of him, but could feel no sympathy with the desire to lock oneself up for life in an estate of one's own. They say man only needs six feet of earth. But it is a corpse, and not man, which needs these six feet. And now people are actually saying that it is a good sign for our intellectuals to yearn for the land and try to obtain country-dwellings. And yet these estates are nothing but those same six feet of earth. To escape from the town, from the struggle, from the noise of life, to escape and hide one's head on a country-estate, is not life, but egoism, idleness, it is a sort of renunciation, but renunciation without faith. It is not six feet of earth, not a country-estate, that man needs, but the whole globe, the whole of nature, room to display his qualities and the individual characteristics of his soul.

"My brother Nikolai sat at his office-desk, dreaming of eating soup made from his own cabbages, which would spread a delicious smell all over his own yard, of eating out of doors, on the green grass, of sleeping in the sun, sitting for hours on a bench outside his gate, and gazing at the fields and woods. Books on agriculture and all those hints printed on calendars were his delight, his favourite spiritual nourishment. He was fond of reading newspapers, too, but all he read in them was advertisements of the sale of so many acres of arable and meadowland, with residence attached, a river, an orchard, a mill, and ponds fed by springs. His head was full of visions of garden paths, flowers, fruit, nesting-boxes, carp-ponds, and all that sort of thing. These visions differed according to the advertisements he came across, but for some reason gooseberry bushes invariably figured in them. He could not picture to himself a single estate or picturesque nook that did not have gooseberry bushes in it.

"'Country life has its conveniences,' he would say. 'You sit on the verandah, drinking tea, with your own ducks floating on the pond, and everything smells so nice, and . . . and the gooseberries ripen on the bushes.'

"He drew up plans for his estate, and every plan showed the same features: a) the main residence, b) the servants' wing, c) the kitchen-garden, d) gooseberry bushes. He lived thriftily, never ate or drank his fill, dressed any-how, like a beggar, and saved up all his money in the bank. He became terribly stingy. I could hardly bear to look at him, and whenever I gave him a little money, or sent him a present on some holiday, he put that away, too. Once a man gets an idea into his head, there's no doing anything with him.

"The years passed, he was sent to another gubernia, he was over forty, and was still reading advertisements in the papers, and saving up. At last I heard he had married. All for the same purpose, to buy himself an estate with gooseberry bushes on it, he married an ugly elderly widow, for whom he had not the slightest affection, just because she had some money. After his marriage he went on living as thriftily as ever, half-starving his wife, and putting her money in his own bank account. Her first husband had been a post-master, and she was used to pies and cordials, but with her second husband she did not even get enough black bread to eat. She began to languish on this diet and three years later yielded up her soul to God. Of course my brother did not for a moment consider himself guilty of her death. Money, like vodka, makes a man eccentric. There was a merchant in our town who asked for a plate of honey on his deathbed and ate up all his bank-notes and lottery tickets with the honey, so that no one else should get them. And one day when I was examining a consignment of cattle at a railway station, a drover fell under the engine and his leg was severed from his body. We carried him all bloody into the waiting-room, a terrible sight, and he did nothing but beg us to look for his leg, worrying all the time—there were twenty rubles in the boot, and he was afraid they would be lost."

"You're losing the thread," put in Burkin.

Ivan Ivanich paused for a moment, and went on: "After his wife's death my brother began to look about for an estate. You can search for five years, of course, and in the end make a mistake and buy something quite different from what you dream of. My brother Nikolai bought three hundred acres, complete with gentleman's house, servants' quarters, and a park, on a mortgage to be paid through an agent, but there were neither an orchard, gooseberry bushes, nor a pond with ducks on it. There was a river, but it was as dark as coffee, owing to the fact that there was a brick-works on one side of the estate, and bone-kilns on the other. Nothing daunted, however, my brother Nikolai Ivanich ordered two dozen gooseberry bushes and settled down as a landed proprietor.

"Last year I paid him a visit. I thought I would go and see how he was getting on there. In his letters my brother gave his address as Chumbaroklova Pustosh or Himalaiskoye. I arrived at Himalaiskoye in the afternoon. It was very hot. Everywhere were ditches, fences, hedges, rows of fir-trees, and it was hard to drive into the yard and find a place to leave one's carriage. As I went a fat ginger-coloured dog, remarkably like a pig, came out to meet me. It looked as if it would have barked if it were not so lazy. The cook, who was also fat and like a pig, came out of the kitchen, barefoot, and said her master was having his after-dinner rest. I made my way to my brother's room, and found him sitting up in bed, his knees covered by a blanket. He had aged, and grown stout and flabby. His cheeks, nose and lips protruded—I almost expected him to grunt into the blanket.

"We embraced and wept—tears of joy, mingled with melancholy—because we had once been young and were now both grey-haired and approaching the grave. He put on his clothes and went out to show me over his estate.

"'Well, how are you getting on here?' I asked.

"'All right, thanks be, I'm enjoying myself.'

"He was no longer the poor, timid clerk, but a true proprietor, a gentleman. He had settled down, and was entering with zest into country life. He ate a lot, washed in the bath-house, and put on flesh. He had already got into litigation with the village commune, the brick-works and the bone-kilns, and took offence if the peasants failed to call him 'Your Honour'. He went in for religion in a solid, gentlemanly way, and there was nothing casual about his pretentious good works. And what were these good works? He treated all the diseases of the peasants with bicarbonate of soda and castor-oil, and had a special thanksgiving service held on his name-day, after which he provided half a pail of vodka, supposing that this was the right thing to do. Oh, those terrible half pails! Today the fat landlord hauls the peasants before the Zemstvo representative for letting their sheep graze on his land, tomorrow, on the day of rejoicing, he treats them to half a pail of vodka, and they drink and sing and shout hurrah, prostrating themselves before him when they are drunk. Any improvement in his conditions, anything like satiety or idleness, develops the most insolent complacency in a Russian. Nikolai Ivanich, who had been afraid of having an opinion of his own when he was in the government service, was now continually coming out with axioms, in the most ministerial manner: 'Education is essential, but the people are not ready for it yet', 'corporal punishment is an evil, but in certain cases it is beneficial and indispensable'.

"'I know the people and I know how to treat them,' he said. 'The people love me. I only have to lift my little finger, and the people will do whatever I want.'

"And all this, mark you, with a wise, indulgent smile. Over and over again he repeated: 'We the gentry', or 'speaking as a gentleman', and seemed to have quite forgotten that our grandfather was a peasant, and our father a common soldier. Our very surname—Chimsha-Himalaisky—in reality so absurd, now seemed to him a resounding, distinguished, and euphonious name.

"But it is of myself, and not of him, that I wish to speak. I should like to describe to you the change which came over me in those few hours I spent on my brother's estate. As we were drinking tea in the evening, the cook brought us a full plate of gooseberries. These were not gooseberries bought for money, they came from his own garden, and were the first fruits of the bushes he had planted. Nikolai Ivanich broke into a laugh and gazed at the gooseberries in tearful silence for at least five minutes. Speechless with emotion, he popped a single gooseberry into his mouth, darted at me the triumphant glance of a child who has at last gained possession of a longed-for toy, and said:

"'Delicious!'

"And he ate them greedily, repeating over and over again:

"'Simply delicious! You try them.'

"They were hard and sour, but, as Pushkin says: 'The lie which elates us is dearer than a thousand sober truths.' I saw before me a really happy man, one whose dearest wish had come true, who had achieved his aim in life, got what he wanted, and was content with his lot and with himself. There had always been a tinge of melancholy in my conception of human happiness, and now, confronted by a happy man, I was overcome by a feeling of sadness bordering on desperation. This feeling grew strongest of all in the night. A bed was made up for me in the room next to my brother's bedroom, and I could hear him moving about restlessly, every now and then getting up to take a gooseberry from the plate. How many happy, satisfied people there are, after all, I said to myself. What an overwhelming force! Just consider this life—the insolence and idleness of the strong, the ignorance and bestiality of the weak, all around intolerable poverty, cramped dwellings, degeneracy, drunkenness, hypocrisy, lying. . . . And yet peace and order apparently prevail in all those homes and in the streets. Of the fifty thousand inhabitants of a town, not one will be found to cry out, to proclaim his indignation aloud. We see those who go to the market to buy food, who eat in the day-time and sleep at night, who prattle away, marry, grow old, carry their dead to the cemeteries. But we neither hear nor see those who suffer, and the terrible things in life are played out behind the scenes. All is calm and quiet, only statistics, which are dumb, protest: so many have gone mad, so many barrels of drink have been consumed, so many children died of malnutrition. . . . And apparently this is as it should be. Apparently those who are happy can only enjoy themselves because the unhappy bear their burdens in silence, and but for this silence happiness would be impossible. It is a kind of universal hypnosis. There ought to be a man with a hammer behind the door of every happy man, to remind him by his constant knocks that there are unhappy people, and that happy as he himself may be, life will sooner or later show him its claws, catastrophe will overtake him—sickness, poverty, loss—and nobody will see it, just as he now neither sees nor hears the misfortunes of others. But there is no man with a hammer, the happy man goes on living and the petty vicissitudes of life touch him lightly, like the wind in an aspen-tree, and all is well.

"That night I understood that I, too, was happy and content," continued Ivan Ivanich, getting up. "I, too, while out hunting, or at the dinner table, have held forth on the right way to live, to worship, to manage the people. I, too, have declared that without knowledge there can be no light, that education is essential, but that bare literacy is sufficient for the common people. Freedom is a blessing, I have said, one can't get on without it, any more than without air, but we must wait. Yes, that is what I said, and now I ask: In the name of what must we wait?" Here Ivan Ivanich looked angrily at Burkin. "In the name of what must we wait, I ask you? What is there to be considered? Don't be in such a hurry, they tell me, every idea materialises gradually, in its own time. But who are they who say this? What is the proof that it is just? You refer to the natural order of things, to the logic of facts, but according to what order, what logic do I, a living, thinking individual, stand on the edge of a ditch and wait for it to be gradually filled up, or choked with silt, when I might leap across it or build a bridge over it? And again, in the name of what must we wait? Wait, when we have not the strength to live, though live we must and to live we desire!

"I left my brother early the next morning, and ever since I have found town life intolerable. The peace and order weigh on my spirits, and I am afraid to look into windows, because there is now no sadder spectacle for me than a happy family seated around the tea-table. I am old and unfit for the struggle, I am even incapable of feeling hatred. I can only suffer inwardly, and give way to irritation and annoyance, at night my head burns from the rush of thoughts, and I am unable to sleep. . . . Oh, if only I were young!"

Ivan Ivanich began pacing backwards and forwards, repeating:

"If only I were young still!"

Suddenly he went up to Alekhin and began pressing first one of his hands, and then the other.

"Pavel Konstantinich," he said in imploring accents. "Don't *you* fall into apathy, don't *you* let your conscience be lulled to sleep! While you are still young, strong, active, do not be weary of well-doing. There is no such thing as happiness, nor ought there to be, but if there is any sense or purpose in life, this sense and purpose are to be found not in our own happiness, but in something greater and more rational. Do good!"

Ivan Ivanich said all this with a piteous, imploring smile, as if he were asking for something for himself.

Then they all three sat in their arm-chairs a long way apart from one another, and said nothing. Ivan Ivanich's story satisfied neither Burkin nor Alekhin. It was not interesting to listen to the story of a poor clerk who ate gooseberries, when from the walls generals and fine ladies, who seemed to come to life in the dark, were looking down from their gilded frames. It would have been much more interesting to hear about elegant people, lovely women. And the fact that they were sitting in a drawing-room in which everything—the swathed chandeliers, the arm-chairs, the carpet on the floor—proved that the people now looking out of the frames had once moved about here, sat in the chairs, drunk tea, where the fair Pelageya was now going noiselessly to and fro, was better than any story.

Alekhin was desperately sleepy. He had got up early, at three o'clock in the morning, to go about his work on the estate, and could now hardly keep his eyes open. But he would not go to bed, for fear one of his guests would relate something interesting after he was gone. He could not be sure whether what Ivan Ivanich had just told them was wise or just, but his visitors talked of other things besides grain, hay, or tar, of things which had no direct bearing on his daily life, and he liked this, and wanted them to go on. . . .

"Well, time to go to bed," said Burkin, getting up. "Allow me to wish you a good night."

Alekhin said good night and went downstairs to his own room, the visitors remaining on the upper floor. They were allotted a big room for the night, in which were two ancient bedsteads of carved wood, and an ivory crucifix in one corner. There was a pleasant smell of freshly laundered sheets from the wide, cool beds which the fair Pelageya had made up for them.

Ivan Ivanich undressed in silence and lay down.

"Lord have mercy on us, sinners," he said, and covered his head with the sheet.

There was a strong smell of stale tobacco from his pipe, which he put on the table, and Burkin lay awake a long time, wondering where the stifling smell came from.

The rain tapped on the window-panes all night.

QUESTIONS

1. There is an unusual framing device in this story—an inner tale and an outer tale. What is the relationship of the inner tale told by Ivan to the outer tale that traces the day's activities?

2. Why does Ivan want to tell the story of his brother? Where does the subject first come up? How does Chekhov inject irony into the story through Ivan's own tale? Is Ivan a reliable storyteller? Explain.

3. Analyze carefully the characters of Ivan, Burkin, Alekhin, and Nikolai. How do they form a microcosm of Russian life and thought? What is Chekhov saying about Russia in the story?

4. What is the role of Pelageya in the tale?

5. What do the gooseberries symbolize?

6. What theme emerges from the action and the conflicts in the story?

7. Why is Burkin disturbed by Ivan's story at the end of Chekhov's tale? How do you explain the inconclusiveness of the story?

TOPICS FOR WRITING

1. "The Russian is a strange being," Chekhov once observed. Apply the author's statement to his depiction of character and action in "Gooseberries."

2. Examine the connections and relationships between the outer and inner stories in "Gooseberries."

3. Compare and contrast Chekhov's vision of humanity in "The Bet" (page 14) and in "Gooseberries."

Sherwood Anderson

HANDS

Sherwood Anderson (1876–1941) was born in Camden, Ohio. He had a sporadic education, finally dropping out of school at the age of 14. Anderson held a variety of jobs before enlisting in the Army during the Spanish-American War. Afterward, he managed a paint factory in Ohio, but quit in order to pursue a career as a writer. Anderson found his way into the Chicago Renaissance group, associating with Carl Sandburg, Theodore Dreiser, and others. His early fiction was not successful, but with the publication of his cycle of stories Winesburg, Ohio *in 1919, Anderson won instant acclaim. At his best, Anderson depicts in his short fiction the frustration, repression, and alienation caused by provincial Midwestern life. His short stories are collected in* Triumph of the Egg *(1921),* Horses and Men *(1923), and* Death in the Woods and Other Stories *(1933). In "Hands," Anderson renders an interesting and sympathetic portrait of one of the many psychological cripples and lost souls who populate his Winesburg universe.*

Upon the half decayed veranda of a small frame house that stood near the edge of a ravine near the town of Winesburg, Ohio, a fat little old man walked nervously up and down. Across a long field that had been seeded for clover but that had produced only a dense crop of yellow mustard weeds, he could see the public highway along which went a wagon filled with berry pickers returning from the fields. The berry pickers, youths and maidens, laughed and shouted boisterously. A boy clad in a blue shirt leaped from the wagon and attempted to drag after him one of the maidens, who screamed and protested shrilly. The feet of the boy in the road kicked up a cloud of dust that floated across the face of the departing sun.

Over the long field came a thin girlish voice. "Oh, you Wing Biddlebaum, comb your hair, it's falling into your eyes," commanded the voice to the man, who was bald and whose nervous little hands fiddled about the bare white forehead as though arranging a mass of tangled locks.

Wing Biddlebaum, forever frightened and beset by a ghostly band of doubts, did not think of himself as in any way a part of the life of the town where he had lived for twenty years. Among all the people of Winesburg but one had come close to him. With George Willard, son of Tom Willard, the proprietor of the New Willard House, he had formed something like a friendship. George Willard was the reporter on the *Winesburg Eagle* and sometimes in the evenings he walked out along the highway to Wing Biddlebaum's house. Now as the old man walked up and down on the veranda, his hands moving nervously about, he was hoping that George Willard would come and spend the evening with him. After the wagon containing the berry pickers had passed, he went across the field through the tall mustard weeds and climbing a rail fence peered anxiously along the road to the town. For a moment he stood thus, rubbing his hands together and looking up and down the road, and then, fear overcoming him, ran back to walk again upon the porch on his own house.

In the presence of George Willard, Wing Biddlebaum, who for twenty years had been the town mystery, lost something of his timidity, and his shadowy personality, submerged in a sea of doubts, came forth to look at the world. With the young reporter at his side, he ventured in the light of day into Main Street or strode up and down on the rickety front porch of his own house, talking excitedly. The voice that had been low and trembling became shrill and loud. The bent figure straightened. With a kind of wriggle, like a fish returned to the brook by the fisherman, Biddlebaum the silent began to talk, striving to put into words the ideas that had been accumulated by his mind during long years of silence.

Wing Biddlebaum talked much with his hands. The slender expressive fingers, forever active, forever striving to conceal themselves in his pockets or behind his back, came forth and became the piston rods of his machinery of expression.

The story of Wing Biddlebaum is a story of hands. Their restless activity, like unto the beating of the wings of an imprisoned bird, had given him his name. Some obscure poet of the town had thought of it. The hands alarmed their owner. He wanted to keep them hidden away and looked with amazement at the quiet inexpressive hands of other men who worked beside him in the fields, or passed, driving sleepy teams on country roads.

When he talked to George Willard, Wing Biddlebaum closed his fists and beat with them upon a table or on the walls of his house. The action made him more comfortable. If the desire to talk came to him when the two were walking in the fields, he sought out a stump or the top board of a fence and with his hands pounding busily talked with renewed ease.

The story of Wing Biddlebaum's hands is worth a book in itself. Sympathetically set forth it would tap many strange, beautiful qualities in obscure men. It is a job for a poet. In Winesburg the hands had attracted attention merely because of their activity. With them Wing Biddlebaum had picked as high as a hundred and forty quarts of strawberries in a day. They became his distinguishing feature, the source of his fame. Also they made more grotesque an already grotesque and elusive individuality. Winesburg was proud of the hands of Wing Biddlebaum in the same spirit in which it was proud of Banker White's new stone house and Wesley Moyer's bay stallion, Tony Tip, that had won the two-fifteen trot at the fall races in Cleveland.

As for George Willard, he had many times wanted to ask about the hands. At times an almost overwhelming curiosity had taken hold of him. He felt that there must be a reason for their strange activity and their inclination to keep hidden away and only a growing respect for Wing Biddlebaum kept him from blurting out the questions that were often in his mind.

Once he had been on the point of asking. The two were walking in the fields on a summer afternoon and had stopped to sit upon a grassy bank. All afternoon Wing Biddlebaum had talked as one inspired. By a fence he had stopped and beating like a giant woodpecker upon the top board had shouted at George Willard, condemning his tendency to be too much influenced by the people about him. "You are destroying yourself," he cried. "You have the inclination to be alone and to dream and you are afraid of dreams. You want to be like others in town here. You hear them talk and you try to imitate them."

On the grassy bank Wing Biddlebaum had tried again to drive his point home. His voice became soft and reminiscent, and with a sigh of contentment he launched into a long rambling talk, speaking as one lost in a dream.

Out of the dream Wing Biddlebaum made a picture for George Willard. In the picture men lived again in a kind of pastoral golden age. Across a green open country came clean-limbed young men, some afoot, some mounted upon horses. In crowds the young men came to gather about the feet of an old man who sat beneath a tree in a tiny garden and who talked to them.

Wing Biddlebaum became wholly inspired. For once he forgot the hands. Slowly they stole forth and lay upon George Willard's shoulders. Something new and bold came into the voice that talked. "You must try to forget all you have learned," said the old man. "You must begin to dream. From this time on you must shut your ears to the roaring of the voices."

Pausing in his speech, Wing Biddlebaum looked long and earnestly at George Willard. His eyes glowed. Again he raised the hands to caress the boy and then a look of horror swept over his face.

With a convulsive movement of his body, Wing Biddlebaum sprang to his feet and thrust his hands deep into his trousers pockets. Tears came to his eyes. "I must be getting along home. I can talk no more with you," he said nervously.

Without looking back, the old man had hurried down the hillside and across a meadow, leaving George Willard perplexed and frightened upon the grassy slope. With a shiver of dread the boy arose and went along the road toward town. "I'll not ask him about his hands," he thought, touched by the memory of the terror he had seen in the man's eyes. "There's something wrong, but I don't want to know what it is. His hands have something to do with his fear of me and of everyone."

And George Willard was right. Let us look briefly into the story of the hands. Perhaps our talking of them will arouse the poet who will tell the hidden wonder story of the influence for which the hands were but fluttering pennants of promise.

In his youth Wing Biddlebaum had been a school teacher in a town in

Pennsylvania. He was not then known as Wing Biddlebaum, but went by the less euphonic name of Adolph Myers. As Adolph Myers he was much loved by the boys of his school.

Adolph Myers was meant by nature to be a teacher of youth. He was one of those rare, little-understood men who rule by a power so gentle that it passes as a lovable weakness. In their feeling for the boys under their charge such men are not unlike the finer sort of women in their love of men.

And yet that is but crudely stated. It needs the poet there. With the boys of his school, Adolph Myers had walked in the evening or had sat talking until dusk upon the schoolhouse steps lost in a kind of dream. Here and there went his hands, caressing the shoulders of the boys, playing about the tousled heads. As he talked his voice became soft and musical. There was a caress in that also. In a way the voice and the hands, the stroking of the shoulders and the touching of the hair were a part of the schoolmaster's effort to carry a dream into the young minds. By the caress that was in his fingers he expressed himself. He was one of those men in whom the force that creates life is diffused, not centralized. Under the caress of his hands doubt and disbelief went out of the minds of the boys and they began also to dream.

And then the tragedy. A half-witted boy of the school became enamored of the young master. In his bed at night he imagined unspeakable things and in the morning went forth to tell his dreams as facts. Strange, hideous accusations fell from his loose-hung lips. Through the Pennsylvania town went a shiver. Hidden, shadowy doubts that had been in men's minds concerning Adolph Myers were galvanized into beliefs.

The tragedy did not linger. Trembling lads were jerked out of bed and questioned. "He put his arms about me," said one. "His fingers were always playing in my hair," said another.

One afternoon a man of the town, Henry Bradford, who kept a saloon, came to the schoolhouse door. Calling Adolph Myers into the school yard he began to beat him with his fists. As his hard knuckles beat down into the frightened face of the schoolmaster, his wrath became more and more terrible. Screaming with dismay, the children ran here and there like disturbed insects. "I'll teach you to put your hands on my boy, you beast," roared the saloon keeper, who, tired of beating the master, had begun to kick him about the yard.

Adolph Myers was driven from the Pennsylvania town in the night. With lanterns in their hands a dozen men came to the door of the house where he lived alone and commanded that he dress and come forth. It was raining and one of the men had a rope in his hands. They had intended to hang the schoolmaster, but something in his figure, so small, white, and pitiful, touched their hearts and they let him escape. As he ran away into the darkness they repented of their weakness and ran after him, swearing and throwing sticks and great balls of soft mud at the figure that screamed and ran faster and faster into the darkness.

For twenty years Adolph Myers had lived alone in Winesburg. He was but forty but looked sixty-five. The name of Biddlebaum he got from a box of goods seen at a freight station as he hurried through an eastern Ohio town. He had an aunt in Winesburg, a black-toothed old woman who raised chickens, and with her he lived until she died. He had been ill for a year after the experience in Pennsylvania, and after his recovery worked as a day laborer in the fields, going timidly about and striving to conceal his hands. Although he did not understand what had happened he felt that the hands must be to blame. Again and again the fathers of the boys had talked of the hands. "Keep your hands to yourself," the saloon keeper had roared, dancing with fury in the schoolhouse yard.

Upon the veranda of his house by the ravine, Wing Biddlebaum continued to walk up and down until the sun had disappeared and the road beyond the field was lost in the grey shadows. Going into his house he cut slices of bread and spread honey upon them. When the rumble of the evening train that took away the express cars loaded with the day's harvest of berries had passed and restored the silence of the summer night, he went again to walk upon the veranda. In the darkness he could not see the hands and they became quiet. Although he still hungered for the presence of the boy, who was the medium through which he expressed his love of man, the hunger became again a part of his loneliness and his waiting. Lighting a lamp, Wing Biddlebaum washed the few dishes soiled by his simple meal and, setting up a folding cot by the screen door that led to the porch, prepared to undress for the night. A few stray white bread crumbs lay on the cleanly washed floor by the table; putting the lamp upon a low stool he began to pick up the crumbs, carrying them to his mouth one by one with unbelievable rapidity. In the dense blotch of light beneath the table, the kneeling figure looked like a priest engaged in some service of his church. The nervous expressive fingers, flashing in and out of the light, might well have been mistaken for the fingers of the devotee going swiftly through decade after decade of his rosary.

QUESTIONS

1. Why does Anderson begin the story with the scene of the berry pickers, boys and girls, in the field?

2. Why is an omniscient point of view employed in the story? What is the effect?

3. Explain what the author means when he writes, "The story of Wing Biddlebaum is a story of hands." Do you accept this authorial intrusion? Why or why not?

4. Anderson alludes to Wing as a "grotesque." Define this term. What makes Wing a grotesque character?

5. Why is Wing so fearful? What are the causes of his repressed and solitary state?

6. What is the role of George Willard in the story?

7. What is the tone of the story? What is the theme?

8. Speaking of "Hands," Anderson wrote, "It was and is a very beautiful story." Would you agree or disagree with the author's own evaluation of his story? Explain.

TOPICS FOR WRITING

1. Develop a psychological portrait of Wing Biddlebaum.

2. Analyze the significance of Wing's hands and what they suggest about the grotesque nature of his condition.

3. Assess Anderson's depiction of society and social values and attitudes in "Hands."

D. H. Lawrence

THE ROCKING-HORSE WINNER

David Herbert Lawrence (1885–1930), the son of a coalminer and a former schoolteacher, was born in Eastwood, Notting-hamshire, England. Raised in England's industrial midlands and exposed to fierce tensions within his family life, Lawrence used these twin realities to achieve his first literary recognition with Sons and Lovers *(1913). Thereafter, his daring, inventive, and prolific literary production; his iconoclastic personal life; and his idiosyncratic search for pure alternatives to the crassness and dehumanization of English industrial and social life made Lawrence an international literary figure. Prior to World War I, Lawrence eloped to Europe with the wife of a Nottingham University professor. He returned to England during the war years and thereafter spent the rest of his life searching intermittently in Italy, Mexico, Australia, and the mountains of New Mexico for a perfect, "organic" life. He died of tuberculosis in the south of France. Lawrence's achievement as an author of novels, short stories, travel books, essays, and poetry establishes him as a great modern writer. Among the significant publications of his works are* The Rainbow *(1915),* Twilight in Italy *(1916),* Women in Love *(1920),* Studies in Classic American Literature *(1923),* Lady Chatterly's Lover *(1928),* The Complete Stories *(1961), and* Complete Poems *(1964). Lawrence is renowned for his grim dissection of English class life, for his subtle depiction of contemporary anxieties and alienation, and for his shrewd probing of human psychology. In "The Rocking-Horse Winner," one of his short fiction masterpieces, Lawrence combines his major themes concerning contemporary life to render the story of a young boy who attempts tragically to triumph over society and over destiny itself.*

There was a woman who was beautiful, who started with all the advantages, yet she had no luck. She married for love, and the love turned to dust. She had bonny children, yet she felt they had been thrust upon her, and she could not love them. They looked at her coldly, as if they were finding fault with her. And hurriedly she felt she must cover up some fault in herself. Yet what it was that she must cover up she never knew. Nevertheless, when her children were present, she always felt the centre of her heart go hard. This troubled her, and in her manner she was all the more gentle and anxious for her children, as if she loved them very much. Only she herself knew that at the centre of her heart was a hard little place that could not feel love, no, not for anybody. Everybody else said of her: "She is such a good mother. She adores her children." Only she herself, and her children themselves, knew it was not so. They read it in each other's eyes.

There were a boy and two little girls. They lived in a pleasant house, with a garden, and they had discreet servants, and felt themselves superior to anyone in the neighbourhood.

Although they lived in style, they felt always an anxiety in the house. There was never enough money. The mother had a small income, and the father had a small income, but not nearly enough for the social position which they had to keep up. The father went in to town to some office. But though he had good prospects, these prospects never materialized. There was always the grinding sense of the shortage of money, though the style was always kept up.

At last the mother said: "I will see if *I* can't make something." But she did not know where to begin. She racked her brains, and tried this thing and the other, but could not find anything successful. The failure made deep lines come into her face. Her children were growing up, they would have to go to school. There must be more money, there must be more money. The father, who was always very handsome and expensive in his tastes, seemed as if he never *would* be able to do anything worth doing. And the mother, who had a great belief in herself, did not succeed any better, and her tastes were just as expensive.

And so the house came to be haunted by the unspoken phrase: *There must be more money! There must be more money!* The children could hear it all the time, though nobody said it aloud. They heard it at Christmas, when the expensive and splendid toys filled the nursery. Behind the shining modern rocking-horse, behind the smart doll's-house, a voice would start whispering: "There *must* be more money! There *must* be more money!" And the children would stop playing, to listen for a moment. They would look into each other's eyes, to see if they had all heard. And each one saw in the eyes of the other two that they too had heard. "There *must* be more money! There *must* be more money!"

It came whispering from the springs of the still-swaying rocking-horse, and even the horse, bending his wooden, champing head, heard it. The big doll, sitting so pink and smirking in her new pram, could hear it quite plainly, and seemed to be smirking all the more self-consciously because of it. The foolish puppy, too, that took the place of the teddy-bear, he was looking so extraordinarily foolish for no other reason but that he heard the secret whisper all over the house: "There *must* be more money!"

Yet nobody ever said it aloud. The whisper was everywhere, and therefore no one spoke it. Just as no one ever says: "We are breathing!" in spite of the fact that breath is coming and going all the time.

"Mother," said the boy Paul one day, "why don't we keep a car of our own? Why do we always use uncle's, or else a taxi?"

"Because we're the poor members of the family," said the mother.

"But why *are* we, mother?"

"Well—I suppose," she said slowly and bitterly, "it's because your father has no luck."

The boy was silent for some time.

"Is luck money, mother?" he asked rather timidly.

"No, Paul. Not quite. It's what causes you to have money."

"Oh!" said Paul vaguely. "I thought when Uncle Oscar said *filthy lucker,* it meant money."

"*Filthy lucre* does mean money," said the mother. "But it's lucre, not luck."

"Oh!" said the boy. "Then what *is* luck, mother?"

"It's what causes you to have money. If you're lucky you have money. That's why it's better to be born lucky than rich. If you're rich, you may lose your money. But if you're lucky, you will always get more money."

"Oh! Will you? And is father not lucky?"

"Very unlucky, I should say," she said bitterly.

The boy watched her with unsure eyes.

"Why?" he asked.

"I don't know. Nobody ever knows why one person is lucky and another unlucky."

"Don't they? Nobody at all? Does *nobody* know?"

"Perhaps God. But He never tells."

"He ought to, then. And aren't you lucky either, mother?"

"I can't be, if I married an unlucky husband."

"But by yourself, aren't you?"

"I used to think I was, before I married. Now I think I am very unlucky indeed."

"Why?"

"Well—never mind! Perhaps I'm not really," she said.

The child looked at her, to see if she meant it. But he saw, by the lines of her mouth, that she was only trying to hide something from him.

"Well, anyhow," he said stoutly, "I'm a lucky person."

"Why?" said his mother, with a sudden laugh.

He stared at her. He didn't even know why he had said it.

"God told me," he asserted, brazening it out.

"I hope He did, dear!" she said, again with a laugh, but rather bitter.

"He did, mother!"

"Excellent!" said the mother, using one of her husband's exclamations.

The boy saw she did not believe him; or, rather, that she paid no attention to his assertion. This angered him somewhat, and made him want to compel her attention.

He went off by himself, vaguely, in a childish way, seeking for the clue to "luck." Absorbed, taking no heed of other people, he went about with a sort of stealth, seeking inwardly for luck. He wanted luck, he wanted it, he wanted it. When the two girls were playing dolls in the nursery, he would sit on his big rocking-horse, charging madly into space, with a frenzy that made the little girls peer at him uneasily. Wildly the horse careered, the waving dark hair of the boy tossed, his eyes had a strange glare in them. The little girls dared not speak to him.

When he had ridden to the end of his mad little journey, he climbed down and stood in front of his rocking-horse, staring fixedly into its lowered face. Its red mouth was slightly open, its big eye was wide and glassy-bright.

"Now!" he would silently command the snorting steed. "Now, take me to where there is luck! Now take me!"

And he would slash the horse on the neck with the little whip he had asked Uncle Oscar for. He *knew* the horse could take him to where there was luck, if only he forced it. So he would mount again, and start on his furious ride, hoping at last to get there. He knew he could get there.

"You'll break your horse, Paul!" said the nurse.

"He's always riding like that! I wish he'd leave off!" said his elder sister Joan.

But he only glared down on them in silence. Nurse gave him up. She could make nothing of him. Anyhow he was growing beyond her.

One day his mother and his Uncle Oscar came in when he was on one of his furious rides. He did not speak to them.

"Hallo, you young jockey! Riding a winner?" said his uncle.

"Aren't you growing too big for a rocking-horse? You're not a very little boy any longer, you know," said his mother.

But Paul only gave a blue glare from his big, rather close-set eyes. He would speak to nobody when he was in full tilt. His mother watched him with an anxious expression on her face.

At last he suddenly stopped forcing his horse into the mechanical gallop, and slid down.

"Well, I got there!" he announced fiercely, his blue eyes still flaring, and his sturdy long legs straddling apart.

"Where did you get to?" asked his mother.

"Where I wanted to go," he flared back at her.

"That's right, son!" said Uncle Oscar. "Don't you stop till you get there. What's the horse's name?"

"He doesn't have a name," said the boy.

"Gets on without all right?" asked the uncle.

"Well, he has different names. He was called Sansovino last week."

"Sansovino, eh? Won the Ascot. How did you know his name?"

"He always talks about horse-races with Bassett," said Joan.

The uncle was delighted to find that his small nephew was posted with all the racing news. Bassett, the young gardener, who had been wounded in the left foot in the war and had got his present job through Oscar Cresswell, whose batman he had been, was a perfect blade of the "turf." He lived in the racing events, and the small boy lived with him.

Oscar Cresswell got it all from Bassett.

"Master Paul comes and asks me, so I can't do more than tell him, sir," said Bassett, his face terribly serious, as if he were speaking of religious matters.

"And does he ever put anything on a horse he fancies?"

"Well—I don't want to give him away—he's a young sport, a fine sport, sir. Would you mind asking him himself? He sort of takes a pleasure in it, and perhaps he'd feel I was giving him away, sir, if you don't mind."

Bassett was serious as a church.

D. H. Lawrence

The uncle went back to his nephew and took him off for a ride in the car.

"Say, Paul, old man, do you ever put anything on a horse?" the uncle asked.

The boy watched the handsome man closely.

"Why, do you think I oughtn't to?" he parried.

"Not a bit of it! I thought perhaps you might give me a tip for the Lincoln."

The car sped on into the country, going down to Uncle Oscar's place in Hampshire.

"Honour bright?" said the nephew.

"Honour bright, son!" said the uncle.

"Well, then, Daffodil."

"Daffodil! I doubt it, sonny. What about Mirza?"

"I only know the winner," said the boy. "That's Daffodil."

"Daffodil, eh?"

There was a pause. Daffodil was an obscure horse comparatively.

"Uncle!"

"Yes, son?"

"You won't let it go any further, will you? I promised Bassett."

"Bassett be damned, old man! What's he got to do with it?"

"We're partners. We've been partners from the first. Uncle, he lent me my first five shillings, which I lost. I promised him, honour bright, it was only between me and him; only you gave me that ten-shilling note I started winning with, so I thought you were lucky. You won't let it go any further, will you?"

The boy gazed at his uncle from those big, hot, blue eyes, set rather close together. The uncle stirred and laughed uneasily.

"Right you are, son! I'll keep your tip private. Daffodil, eh? How much are you putting on him?"

"All except twenty pounds," said the boy. "I keep that in reserve."

The uncle thought it a good joke.

"You keep twenty pounds in reserve, do you, you young romancer? What are you betting, then?"

"I'm betting three hundred," said the boy, gravely. "But it's between you and me, Uncle Oscar! Honour bright?"

The uncle burst into a roar of laughter.

"It's between you and me all right, you young Nat Gould," he said, laughing. "But where's your three hundred?"

"Bassett keeps it for me. We're partners."

"He won't go quite as high as I do, I expect. Perhaps he'll go a hundred and fifty."

"What, pennies?" laughed the uncle.

"Pounds," said the child, with a surprised look at his uncle. "Bassett keeps a bigger reserve than I do."

Between wonder and amusement Uncle Oscar was silent. He pursued the matter no further, but he determined to take his nephew with him to the Lincoln races.

"Now, son," he said, "I'm putting twenty on Mirza, and I'll put five for you on any horse you fancy. What's your pick?"

"Daffodil, uncle."

"No, not the fiver on Daffodil!"

"I should if it was my own fiver," said the child.

"Good! Good! Right you are! A fiver for me and a fiver for you on Daffodil."

The child had never been to a race-meeting before, and his eyes were blue fire. He pursed his mouth tight, and watched. A Frenchman just in front had put his money on Lancelot. Wild with excitement, he flayed his arms up and down, yelling *Lancelot! Lancelot!"* in his French accent.

Daffodil came in first, Lancelot second, Mirza third. The child, flushed and with eyes blazing, was curiously serene. His uncle brought him four five-pound notes, four to one.

"What am I to do with these?" he cried, waving them before the boy's eyes.

"I suppose we'll talk to Bassett," said the boy. "I expect I have fifteen hundred now; and twenty in reserve; and this twenty."

His uncle studied him for some moments.

"Look here, son!" he said. "You're not serious about Bassett and that fifteen hundred, are you?"

"Yes, I am. But it's between you and me, uncle. Honour bright!"

"Honour bright all right, son! But I must talk to Bassett."

"If you'd like to be a partner, uncle, with Bassett and me, we could all be partners. Only, you'd have to promise, honour bright, uncle, not to let it go beyond us three. Bassett and I are lucky, and you must be lucky, because it was your ten shillings I started winning with. . . ."

Uncle Oscar took both Bassett and Paul into Richmond Park for an afternoon, and there they talked.

"It's like this, you see, sir," Bassett said. "Master Paul would get me talking about racing events, spinning yarns, you know, sir. And he was always keen on knowing if I'd made or if I'd lost. It's about a year since, now, that I put five shillings on Blush of Dawn for him—and we lost. Then the luck turned, with that ten shillings he had from you, that we put on Singhalese. And since that time, it's been pretty steady, all things considering. What do you say, Master Paul?"

"We're all right when we're sure," said Paul. "It's when we're not quite sure that we go down."

"Oh, but we're careful then," said Bassett.

"But when are you *sure?*" smiled Uncle Oscar.

"It's Master Paul, sir," said Bassett, in a secret, religious voice. "It's as if he had it from heaven. Like Daffodil, now, for the Lincoln. That was as sure as eggs."

"Did you put anything on Daffodil?" asked Oscar Cresswell.

"Yes, sir. I made my bit."

"And my nephew?"

Bassett was obstinately silent, looking at Paul.

"I made twelve hundred, didn't I Bassett? I told uncle I was putting three hundred on Daffodil."

"That's right," said Bassett, nodding.

"But where's the money?" asked the uncle.

"I keep it safe locked up, sir. Master Paul he can have it any minute he likes to ask for it."

"What, fifteen hundred pounds?"

"And twenty! And *forty,* that is, with the twenty he made on the course."

"It's amazing!" said the uncle.

"If Master Paul offers you to be partners, sir, I would, if I were you; if you'll excuse me," said Bassett.

D. H. Lawrence

Oscar Cresswell thought about it.

"I'll see the money," he said.

They drove home again, and sure enough, Bassett came round to the garden-house with fifteen hundred pounds in notes. The twenty pounds reserve was left with Joe Glee, in the Turf Commission deposit.

"You see, it's all right, uncle, when I'm *sure!* Then we go strong, for all we're worth. Don't we, Bassett?"

"We do that, Master Paul."

"And when are you sure?" said the uncle, laughing.

"Oh, well, sometimes I'm *absolutely* sure, like about Daffodil," said the boy; "and sometimes I have an idea; and sometimes I haven't even an idea, have I, Bassett? Then we're careful, because we mostly go down."

"You do, do you! And when you're sure, like about Daffodil, what makes you sure, sonny?"

"Oh, well, I don't know," said the boy uneasily. "I'm sure, you know, uncle; that's all."

"It's as if he had it from heaven, sir," Bassett reiterated.

"I should say so!" said the uncle.

But he became a partner. And when the Leger was coming on, Paul was "sure" about Lively Spark, which was a quite inconsiderable horse. The boy insisted on putting a thousand on the horse, Bassett went for five hundred, and Oscar Cresswell two hundred. Lively Spark came in first, and the betting had been ten to one against him. Paul had made ten thousand.

"You see," he said, "I was absolutely sure of him."

Even Oscar Cresswell had cleared two thousand.

"Look here, son," he said, "this sort of thing makes me nervous."

"It needn't, uncle! Perhaps I shan't be sure again for a long time."

"But what are you going to do with your money?" asked the uncle.

"Of course," said the boy, "I started it for mother. She said she had no luck, because father is unlucky, so I thought if *I* was lucky, it might stop whispering."

"What might stop whispering?"

"Our house. I *hate* our house for whispering."

"What does it whisper?"

"Why—why"—the boy fidgeted—"why, I don't know. But it's always short of money, you know, uncle."

"I know it, son, I know it."

"You know people send mother writs, don't you, uncle?"

"I'm afraid I do," said the uncle.

"And then the house whispers, like people laughing at you behind your back. It's awful, that is! I thought if I was lucky . . ."

"You might stop it," added the uncle.

The boy watched him with big blue eyes, that had an uncanny cold fire in them, and he said never a word.

"Well, then!" said the uncle. "What are we doing?"

"I shouldn't like mother to know I was lucky," said the boy.

"Why not, son?"

"She'd stop me."

"I don't think she would."

"Oh!"—and the boy writhed in an odd way—"I *don't* want her to know, uncle."

The Rocking-Horse Winner

"All right, son! We'll manage it without her knowing."

They managed it very easily. Paul, at the other's suggestion, handed over five thousand pounds to his uncle, who deposited it with the family lawyer, who was then to inform Paul's mother that a relative had put five thousand pounds into his hands, which sum was to be paid out a thousand pounds at a time, on the mother's birthday, for the next five years.

"So she'll have a birthday present of a thousand pounds for five successive years," said Uncle Oscar. "I hope it won't make it all the harder for her later."

Paul's mother had her birthday in November. The house had been "whispering" worse than ever lately, and, even in spite of his luck, Paul could not bear up against it. He was very anxious to see the effect of the birthday letter, telling his mother about the thousand pounds.

When there were no visitors, Paul now took his meals with his parents, as he was beyond the nursery control. His mother went into town nearly every day. She had discovered that she had an odd knack of sketching furs and dress materials, so she worked secretly in the studio of a friend who was the chief "artist" for the leading drapers. She drew the figures of ladies in furs and ladies in silk and sequins for the newspaper advertisements. This young woman artist earned several thousand pounds a year, but Paul's mother only made several hundreds, and she was again dissatisfied. She so wanted to be first in something, and she did not succeed, even in making sketches for drapery advertisements.

She was down to breakfast on the morning of her birthday. Paul watched her face as she read her letters. He knew the lawyer's letter. As his mother read it, her face hardened and became more expressionless. Then a cold, determined look came on her mouth. She hid the letter under the pile of others, and said not a word about it.

"Didn't you have anything nice in the post on your birthday, mother?" said Paul.

"Quite moderately nice," she said, her voice cold and absent.

She went away to town without saying more.

But in the afternoon Uncle Oscar appeared. He said Paul's mother had had a long interview with the lawyer, asking if the whole five thousand could not be advanced at once, as she was in debt.

"What do you think, uncle?" said the boy.

"I leave it to you, son."

"Oh, let her have it, then! We can get some more with the other," said the boy.

"A bird in the hand is worth two in the bush, laddie!" said Uncle Oscar.

"But I'm sure to *know* for the Grand National; or the Lincolnshire; or else the Derby. I'm sure to know for *one* of them," said Paul.

So Uncle Oscar signed the agreement, and Paul's mother touched the whole five thousand. Then something very curious happened. The voices in the house suddenly went mad, like a chorus of frogs on a spring evening. There were certain new furnishings, and Paul had a tutor. He was *really* going to Eton, his father's school, in the following autumn. There were flowers in the winter, and a blossoming of the luxury Paul's mother had been used to. And yet the voices in the house, behind the sprays of mimosa and almond blossom, and from under the piles of iridescent cushions, simply trilled and screamed in a sort of ecstasy: "There *must* be more money! Oh-h-h; there *must* be more money Oh, now, now-w! Now-w-w—there *must* be more money!—more than ever! More than ever!"

D. H. Lawrence

It frightened Paul terribly. He studied away at his Latin and Greek with his tutors. But his intense hours were spent with Bassett. The Grand National had gone by: he had not "known," and had lost a hundred pounds. Summer was at hand. He was in agony for the Lincoln. But even for the Lincoln he didn't "know," and he lost fifty pounds. He became wild-eyed and strange, as if something were going to explode in him.

"Let it alone, son! Don't you bother about it!" urged Uncle Oscar. But it was as if the boy couldn't really hear what his uncle was saying.

"I've got to know for the Derby! I've got to know for the Derby!" the child reiterated, his big blue eyes blazing with a sort of madness.

His mother noticed how overwrought he was.

"You'd better go to the seaside. Wouldn't you like to go now to the seaside, instead of waiting? I think you'd better," she said, looking down at him anxiously. her heart curiously heavy because of him.

But the child lifted his uncanny blue eyes.

"I couldn't possibly go before the Derby, mother!" he said. "I couldn't possibly!"

"Why, you curious child, what makes you care about this house so much, not? You can still go from the seaside to see the Derby with your Uncle Oscar, if that's what you wish. No need for you to wait here. Besides, I think you care too much about these races. It's a bad sign. My family has been a gambling family, and you won't know till you grow up how much damage it has done. But it has done damage. I shall have to send Bassett away, and ask Uncle Oscar not to talk racing to you, unless you promise to be reasonable about it; go away to the seaside and forget it. You're all nerves!"

"I'll do what you like, mother, so long as you don't send me away till after the Derby," the boy said.

"Send you away from where? Just from this house?"

"Yes," he said, gazing at her.

"Why, you curious child, what makes you care about this house so much, suddenly? I never knew you loved it."

He gazed at her without speaking. He had a secret within a secret, something he had not divulged, even to Bassett or to his Uncle Oscar.

But his mother, after standing undecided and a little bit sullen for some moments, said:

"Very well, then! Don't go to the seaside till after the Derby if you don't wish it. But promise me you won't let your nerves go to pieces. Promise you won't think so much about horse-racing and events, as you call them!"

"Oh, no," said the boy casually. "I won't think much about them, mother. You needn't worry. I wouldn't worry, mother, if I were you."

"If you were me and I were you," said his mother, 'I wonder what we *should* do!"

"But you know you needn't worry, mother, don't you?" the boy repeated.

"I should be awfully glad to know it," she said wearily."

"Oh, well, you *can*, you know. I mean, you *ought* to know you needn't worry," he insisted.

"Ought I? Then I'll see about it," she said.

Paul's secret of secrets was his wooden horse, that which had no name. Since he was emancipated from a nurse and a nursery-governess, he had had his rocking-horse removed to his own bedroom at the top of the house.

"Surely, you're too big for a rocking-horse!" his mother had remonstrated.

"Well, you see, mother, till I can have a *real* horse, I like to have *some* sort of animal about," had been his quaint answer.

"Do you feel he keeps you company?" she laughed.

"Oh, yes! He's very good, he always keeps me company, when I'm there," said Paul.

So the horse, rather shabby, stood in an arrested prance in the boy's bedroom.

The Derby was drawing near, and the boy grew more and more tense. He hardly heard what was spoken to him, he was very frail, and his eyes were really uncanny. His mother had sudden strange seizures of uneasiness about him. Sometimes, for half-an-hour, she would feel a sudden anxiety about him that was almost anguish. She wanted to rush to him at once, and know he was safe.

Two nights before the Derby, she was at a big party in town, when one of her rushes of anxiety about her boy, her first-born, gripped her heart till she could hardly speak. She fought with the feeling, might and main, for she believed in common-sense. But it was too strong. She had to leave the dance and go downstairs to telephone to the country. The children's nursery-governess was terribly surprised and startled at being rung up in the night.

"Are the children all right, Miss Wilmot?"

"Oh, yes, they are quite all right."

"Master Paul? Is he all right?"

"He went to bed as right as a trivet. Shall I run up and look at him?"

"No," said Paul's mother reluctantly. "No! Don't trouble. It's all right. Don't sit up. We shall be home fairly soon." She did not want her son's privacy intruded upon.

"Very good," said the governess.

It was about one o'clock when Paul's mother and father drove up to their house. All was still. Paul's mother went to her room and slipped off her white fur cloak. She had told her maid not to wait up for her. She heard her husband downstairs, mixing a whisky-and-soda.

And then, because of the strange anxiety at her heart, she stole upstairs to her son's room. Noiselessly she went along the upper corridor. Was there a faint noise? What was it?

She stood, with arrested muscles, outside his door, listening. There was a strange, heavy, and yet not loud noise. Her heart stood still. It was a soundless noise, yet rushing and powerful. Something huge, in violent, hushed motion. What was it? What in God's name was it? She ought to know. She felt that she knew the noise. She knew what it was.

Yet she could not place it. She couldn't say what it was. And on and on it went, like a madness.

Softly, frozen with anxiety and fear, she turned the door-handle.

The room was dark. Yet in the space near the window, she heard and saw something plunging to and fro. She gazed in fear and amazement.

Then suddenly she switched on the light, and saw her son, in his green pyjamas, madly surging on the rocking-horse. The blaze of light suddenly lit him up, as he urged the wooden horse, and lit her up, as she stood, blonde, in her dress of pale green and crystal, in the doorway.

"Paul!" she cried. "Whatever are you doing?"

"It's Malabar!" he screamed, in a powerful, strange voice. "It's Malabar!"

D. H. Lawrence

His eyes blazed at her for one strange and senseless second, as he ceased urging his wooden horse. Then he fell with a crash to the ground, and she, all her tormented motherhood flooding upon her, rushed to gather him up.

But he was unconscious, and unconscious he remained, with some brain-fever. He talked and tossed, and his mother sat stonily by his side.

"Malabar! It's Malabar! Bassett, Bassett, I *know!* It's Malabar!"

So the child cried, trying to get up and urge the rocking-horse that gave him his inspiration.

"What does he mean by Malabar?" asked the heart-broken mother.

"I don't know," said the father stonily.

"What does he mean by Malabar?" she asked her brother Oscar.

"It's one of the horses running for the Derby," was the answer.

And, in spite of himself, Oscar Cresswell spoke to Bassett, and himself put a thousand on Malabar: at fourteen to one.

The third day of the illness was critical: they were waiting for a change. The boy, with his rather long, curly hair, was tossing ceaselessly on the pillow. He neither slept nor regained consciousness, and his eyes were like blue stones. His mother sat, feeling her heart had gone, turned actually into a stone.

In the evening, Oscar Cresswell did not come, but Bassett sent a message, saying could he come up for one moment, just one moment? Paul's mother was very angry at the intrusion, but on second thought she agreed. The boy was the same. Perhaps Bassett might bring him to consciousness.

The gardener, a shortish fellow with a little brown moustache, and sharp little brown eyes, tip-toed into the room, touched his imaginary cap to Paul's mother, and stole to the bedside, staring with glittering, smallish eyes, at the tossing, dying child.

"Master Paul!" he whispered. "Master Paul! Malabar came in first all right, a clean win. I did as you told me. You've made over seventy thousand pounds, you have; you've got over eighty thousand. Malabar came in all right, Master Paul."

"Malabar! Malabar! Did I say Malabar, mother? Did I say Malabar? Do you think I'm lucky, mother? I knew Malabar, didn't I? Over eighty thousand pounds! I call that lucky, don't you, mother? Over eighty thousand pounds! I knew, didn't I know I knew! Malabar came in all right. If I ride my horse till I'm sure, then I tell you, Bassett, you can go as high as you like. Did you go for all you were worth, Bassett?"

"I went a thousand on it, Master Paul."

"I never told you, mother, that if I can ride my horse, and, *get there*, then I'm absolutely sure—oh absolutely! Mother, did I ever tell you? I *am* lucky!"

"No, you never did," said the mother.

But the boy died in the night.

And even as he lay dead, his mother heard her brother's voice saying to her: "My God, Hester, you're eighty-odd thousand to the good, and a poor devil of a son to the bad. But, poor devil, he's best gone out of a life where he rides his rocking-horse to find a winner."

QUESTIONS

1. There is a significant amount of exposition—or background information—at the start of the story. What is its significance? How does it temper the tone of the story?

2. Paul and his mother discuss the concept of "luck" at the beginning of the story. What is the mother's definition of luck? What is Paul's initial response to his mother's definition? How does this response shape his tragic fate? Throughout the story, what are some of the conflicting concepts of luck raised by Lawrence?

3. How does Lawrence depict the mother and father in the story? What is his attitude toward them and their class aspirations?

4. How do you explain the "whispering" in the house? Is the whispering a genuine supernatural element, a sign of Paul's psychological state, or possibly both? How does the whispering affect the mood of the story?

5. What is the importance of Uncle Oscar and Bassett in the story?

6. Do the mother's anxieties over Paul toward the end of the story seem to be consistent with her character? Explain.

7. State the theme of the story.

TOPICS FOR WRITING

1. Lawrence has often been accused of being a didactic author—a writer who likes to preach, instruct, and moralize. Analyze this tone and its relative success in "The Rocking-Horse Winner."

2. Examine the concept of "luck" as presented by Lawrence in the story.

3. Analyze the "supernatural" mood in the tale and Lawrence's success in connecting it to Paul's psychological state.

4. Assess the significance of the rocking-horse as a major symbol in the story.

Katherine Mansfield

MISS BRILL

Katherine Mansfield (1888–1923) was born Kathleen Beauchamp in Wellington, New Zealand. When 9 years old, she won first prize in English composition with a story called "A Sea Voyage." At 14 Mansfield was sent to England for her education, and there she edited the Queens College magazine. After college, she reluctantly went home, but soon returned to England, where she moved in a literary circle composed of D. H. Lawrence, Aldous Huxley, Virginia Woolf, and John Middleton Murry, whom she later married. In a German Pension, a series of reminiscences, and Women at the Store *(1911) were her first two published works, but it was "Bliss" (1920) that established her reputation. Mansfield published subsequent collections entitled* The Garden Party *(1922) and* The Dove's Nest *(1923). After her sudden death, Murry published three volumes of her work, including* The Short Stories of Katherine Mansfield *(1937). Her husband wrote that Mansfield should be considered as having been more influenced by English poets than by English writers of fiction: "Her affinities are rather with the English poets than the English prose-writers. There is no English prose-writer to whom she can be related." In "Miss Brill" something of the Victorian era lingers on.*

Although it was so brilliantly fine—the blue sky powdered with gold and great spots of light like white wine splashed over the Jardins Publiques—Miss Brill was glad that she had decided on her fur. The air was motionless, but when you opened your mouth there was just a faint chill, like a chill from a glass of iced water before you sip, and now and again a leaf came drifting—from nowhere, from the sky. Miss Brill put up her hand and touched her fur. Dear little thing! It was nice to feel it again. She had taken it out of its box that afternoon, shaken out the moth-powder, given it a good brush, and rubbed the life back into the dim little eyes. "What has been happening to me?" said the sad little eyes. Oh, how sweet it was to see them snap at her again from the red eiderdown! . . . But the nose, which was of some black composition, wasn't at all firm. It must have had a knock, somehow. Never mind—a little dab of black sealing-wax when the time came—when it was absolutely necessary. . . . Little rogue! Yes, she really felt like that about it. Little rogue biting its tail just by her left ear. She could have taken it off and laid it on her lap and stroked it. She felt a tingling in her hands and arms, but that came from walking, she supposed. And when she breathed, something light and sad—no, not sad, exactly—something gentle seemed to move in her bosom.

There were a number of people out this afternoon, far more than last Sunday. And the band sounded louder and gayer. That was because the Season had begun. For although the band played all the year round on Sundays, out of season it was never the same. It was like some one playing with only the family to listen; it didn't care how it played if there weren't any strangers present. Wasn't the conductor wearing a new coat, too? She was sure it was new. He scraped with his foot and flapped his arms like a rooster about to crow, and the bandsmen sitting in the green rotunda blew out their cheeks and glared at the music. Now there came a little "flutey" bit—very pretty!—a little chain of bright drops. She was sure it would be repeated. It was; she lifted her head and smiled.

Only two people shared her "special" seat: a fine old man in a velvet coat, his hands clasped over a huge carved walking-stick, and a big old woman, sitting upright, with a roll of knitting on her embroidered apron. They did not speak. This was disappointing, for Miss Brill always looked forward to the conversation. She had become really quite expert, she thought, at listening as though she didn't listen, at sitting in other people's lives just for a minute while they talked round her.

She glanced, sideways, at the old couple. Perhaps they would go soon. Last Sunday, too, hadn't been as interesting as usual. An Englishman and his wife, he wearing a dreadful Panama hat and she button boots. And she'd gone on the whole time about how she ought to wear spectacles; she knew she needed them; but that it was no good getting any; they'd be sure to break and they'd never keep on. And he'd been so patient. He'd suggested everything—gold rims, the kind that curved round your ears, little pads inside the bridge. No, nothing would please her. "They'll always be sliding down my nose!" Miss Brill had wanted to shake her.

The old people sat on the bench, still as statues. Never mind, there was always the crowd to watch. To and fro, in front of the flower-beds and the band rotunda, the couples and groups paraded, stopped to talk, to greet, to buy a handful of flowers from the old beggar who had his tray fixed to the railings. Little children ran among them, swooping and laughing; little boys with big white silk bows under their chins, little girls, little French dolls, dressed up in velvet and lace. And sometimes a tiny staggerer came suddenly rocking into the open from under the trees, stopped, stared, as suddenly sat down "flop," until its small high-stepping mother, like a young hen, rushed scolding to its rescue. Other people sat on the benches and green chairs, but they were nearly always the same, Sunday after Sunday, and—Miss Brill had often noticed—there was something funny about nearly all of them. They were odd, silent, nearly all old, and from the way they stared they looked as though they'd just come from dark little rooms or even—cupboards!

Behind the rotunda the slender trees with yellow leaves down drooping, and through them just a line of sea, and beyond the blue sky with gold-veined clouds.

Tum-tum-tum tiddle-um! tum tiddley-um tum ta! blew the band.

Two young girls in red came by and two young soldiers in blue met them, and they laughed and paired and went off arm-in-arm. Two peasant women with funny straw hats passed, gravely, leading beautiful smoke-coloured donkeys. A cold, pale nun hurried by. A beautiful woman came along and dropped her bunch of violets, and a little boy ran after to hand them to her, and she took them and threw them away as if they'd been poisoned. Dear me! Miss Brill didn't know whether to admire that or not! And now an ermine toque and a gentleman in grey met just in front of her. He was tall, stiff, dignified, and she was wearing the ermine toque she'd bought when her hair was yellow. Now everything, her hair, her face, even her eyes, was the same colour as the shabby ermine, and her hand, in its cleaned glove, lifted to dab her lips, was a tiny yellowish paw. Oh, she was so pleased to see him—delighted! She rather thought they were going to meet that afternoon. She described where she'd been—everywhere, here, there, along by the sea. The day was so charming—didn't he agree? And wouldn't he, perhaps? . . . But he shook his head, lighted a cigarette, slowly breathed a great deep puff into her face, and, even while she was still talking and laughing, flicked the match away and walked on. The ermine toque was alone; she smiled more brightly than ever. But even the band seemed to know what she was feeling and played more softly, played tenderly, and the drum beat, "The Brute! The Brute!" over and over. What would she do? What was going to happen now? But as Miss Brill wondered, the ermine toque turned, raised her hand as though she'd seen some one else, much nicer, just over there, and pattered away. And the band changed again and played more quickly, more gaily than ever, and the old couple on Miss Brill's seat got up and marched away, and such a funny old man with long whiskers hobbled along in time to the music and was nearly knocked over by four girls walking abreast.

Oh, how fascinating it was! How she enjoyed it! How she loved sitting here, watching it all! It was like a play. It was exactly like a play. Who could believe the sky at the back wasn't painted? But it wasn't till a little brown dog trotted on solemn and then slowly trotted off, like a little "theatre" dog, a little dog that had been drugged, that Miss Brill discovered what it was that made it so exciting. They were all on the stage. They weren't only the audience, not only looking on; they were acting. Even she had a part and came every Sunday. No doubt somebody would have noticed if she hadn't been there; she was part of the performance after all. How strange she'd never thought of it like that before! And yet it explained why she made such a point of starting from home at just the same time each week—so as not to be late for the performance—and it also explained why she had quite a queer, shy feeling at telling her English pupils how she spent her Sunday afternoons. No wonder! Miss Brill nearly laughed out loud. She was on the stage. She thought of the old invalid gentleman to whom she read the newspaper four afternoons a week while he slept in the garden. She had got quite used to the frail head on the cotton pillow, the hollowed eyes, the open mouth and the high pinched nose. If he'd been dead she mighn't have noticed for weeks; she wouldn't have minded. But suddenly he knew he was having the paper read to him by an actress! "An actress!" The old head lifted; two points of light quivered in the old eyes. "An actress—are ye?" And Miss Brill smoothed the newspaper as though it were the manuscript of her part and said gently: "Yes, I have been an actress for a long time."

The band had been having a rest. Now they started again. And what they played was warm, sunny, yet there was just a faint chill—a something, what was it?—not sadness—no, not sadness—a something that made you want to sing. The tune lifted, lifted, the light shone; and it seemed to Miss Brill that in another moment all of them, all the whole company, would begin singing. The young ones, the laughing ones who were moving together, they would begin, and the men's voices, very resolute and brave, would join them. And then she too, she too, and the others on the benches—they would come in with a kind of accompaniment—something low, that scarcely rose or fell, something so beautiful—moving. . . . And Miss Brill's eyes filled with tears and she looked smiling at all the other members of the company. Yes, we understand, we understand, she thought—though what they understood she didn't know.

Just at that moment a boy and a girl came and sat down where the old couple had been. They were beautifully dressed; they were in love. The hero and heroine, of course, just arrived from his father's yacht. And still soundlessly singing, still with that trembling smile, Miss Brill prepared to listen.

"No, not now," said the girl. "Not here, I can't."

"But why? Because of that stupid old thing at the end there?" asked the boy. "Why does she come here at all—who wants her? Why doesn't she keep her silly old mug at home?"

"It's her fu-fur which is so funny," giggled the girl. "It's exactly like a fried whiting."

"Ah, be off with you!" said the boy in an angry whisper. Then: "Tell me, ma petite chérie—"

"No, not here," said the girl. "Not *yet*."

On her way home she usually bought a slice of honey-cake at the baker's. It was her Sunday treat. Sometimes there was an almond in her slice, sometimes not. It made a great difference. If there was an almond it was like carrying home a tiny present—a surprise—something that might very well not have been there. She hurried on the almond Sundays and struck the match for the kettle in quite a dashing way.

But to-day she passed the baker's by, climbed the stairs, went into the little dark room—her room like a cupboard—and sat down on the red eiderdown. She sat there for a long time. The box that the fur came out of was on the bed. She unclasped the necklet quickly; quickly, without looking, laid it inside. But when she put the lid on she thought she heard something crying.

QUESTIONS

1. How often does Miss Brill visit the Public Gardens?

2. Why does she visit them?

3. In imagining herself to be part of a theater company, what is Miss Brill doing?

4. At which point in the story do we realize that Miss Brill is not quite as young as her thoughts led us to believe?

5. Why does she not stop at the baker's?

6. Why are her fur and honey-cake important to her?

TOPICS FOR WRITING

1. Discuss the similarities between Miss Brill and Minnie Cooper in Faulkner's "Dry September" (pages 126–135).

2. Evaluate Miss Brill and her fur and the woman wearing the ermine toque, bearing in mind the following questions: Does Miss Brill, in a flash, recognize herself? Is this the theater of the personal? Does Miss Brill expect something like this—without the rejection—to happen to her? And how does this scene relate to the music being played by the band?

Dorothy Parker

THE STANDARD OF LIVING

Poet, short story writer, and playwright, Dorothy Parker (1893–1967) wrote work laced heavily with the sardonic and with irony. Born in West End, New Jersey, she began writing as a poet. Later, she became a drama critic for Vanity Fair, *but was fired after three years because of the toughness of her reviews. Thereafter, she wrote reviews frequently for* The

*New Yorker. Known for her wit, Parker is said to have
remarked that a popular actress had run "the whole gamut
of emotions from A to B." Her verse,* Enough Rope *(1926,
1933) and* Sunset Gun *(1928), preceded her first stories,*
Lament for the Living *(1938), and the later collection,* Here
Lies *(1939). Parker disliked cruelty, pretension, and weakness. In "The Standard of Living," Annabel and Midge,
ordinary working girls who dream of better things through
the game they play, confront reality and become angered by
it. They do not discard their dream, but retreat into it.*

Annabel and Midge came out of the tea room with the arrogant slow gait of the
leisured, for their Saturday afternoon stretched ahead of them. They had
lunched, as was their wont, on sugar, starches, oils, and butter-fats. Usually they
ate sandwiches of spongy new white bread greased with butter and mayonnaise;
they ate thick wedges of cake lying wet beneath ice cream and whipped cream and
melted chocolate gritty with nuts. As alternates, they ate patties, sweating beads
of inferior oil, containing bits of bland meat bogged in pale, stiffening sauce; they
ate pastries, limber under rigid icing, filled with an indeterminate yellow sweet
stuff, not still solid, not yet liquid, like salve that has been left in the sun. They
chose no other sort of food, nor did they consider it. And their skin was like the
petals of wood anemones, and their bellies were as flat and their flanks as lean as
those of young Indian braves.

Annabel and Midge had been best friends almost from the day that Midge had
found a job as stenographer with the firm that employed Annabel. By now,
Annabel, two years longer in the stenographic department, had worked up to the
wages of eighteen dollars and fifty cents a week; Midge was still at sixteen dollars.
Each girl lived at home with her family and paid half her salary to its support.

The girls sat side by side at their desks, they lunched together every noon,
together they set out for home at the end of the day's work. Many of their evenings
and most of their Sundays were passed in each other's company. Often they were
joined by two young men, but there was no steadiness to any such quartet; the
two young men would give place, unlamented, to two other young men, and
lament would have been inappropriate, really, since the newcomers were scarcely
distinguishable from their predecessors: Invariably the girls spent the fine idle
hours of their hot-weather Saturday afternoons together. Constant use had not
worn ragged the fabric of their friendship.

They looked alike, though the resemblance did not lie in their features. It was
in the shape of their bodies, their movements, their style, and their adornments.
Annabel and Midge did, and completely, all that young office workers are
besought not to do. They painted their lips and their nails, they darkened their
lashes and lightened their hair, and scent seemed to shimmer from them. They
wore thin, bright dresses, tight over their breasts and high on their legs, and
tilted slippers, fancifully strapped. They looked conspicuous and cheap and
charming.

Now, as they walked across to Fifth Avenue with their skirts swirled by the
hot wind, they received audible admiration. Young men grouped lethargically
about newsstands awarded them murmurs, exclamations, even—the ultimate
tribute—whistles. Annabel and Midge passed without the condescension of
hurrying their pace; they held their heads higher and set their feet with exquisite
precision, as if they stepped over the necks of peasants.

The Standard of Living

Always the girls went to walk on Fifth Avenue on their free afternoons, for it was the ideal ground for their favorite game. The game could be played anywhere, and, indeed, was, but the great shop windows stimulated the two players to their best form.

Annabel had invented the game; or rather she had evolved it from an old one. Basically, it was no more than the ancient sport of what-would-you-do-if-you-had-a-million dollars? But Annabel had drawn a new set of rules for it, had narrowed it, pointed it, made it stricter. Like all games, it was the more absorbing for being more difficult.

Annabel's version went like this: You must suppose that somebody dies and leaves you a million dollars, cool. But there is a condition to the bequest. It is stated in the will that you must spend every nickel of the money on yourself.

There lay the hazard of the game. If, when playing it, you forgot, and listed among your expenditures the rental of a new apartment for your family, for example, you lost your turn to the other player. It was astonishing how many—and some of them among the experts, too—would forfeit all their innings by such slips.

It was essential, of course, that it be played in passionate seriousness. Each purchase must be carefully considered and, if necessary, supported by argument. There was no zest to playing wildly. Once Annabel had introduced the game to Sylvia, another girl who worked in the office. She explained the rules to Sylvia and then offered her the gambit "What would be the first thing you'd do?" Sylvia had not shown the decency of even a second of hesitation. "Well," she said, "the first thing I'd do, I'd go out and hire somebody to shoot Mrs. Gary Cooper, and then . . ." So it is to be seen that she was no fun.

But Annabel and Midge were surely born to be comrades, for Midge played the game like a master from the moment she learned it. It was she who added the touches that made the whole thing cozier. According to Midge's innovations, the eccentric who died and left you the money was not anybody you loved, or, for the matter of that, anybody you even knew. It was somebody who had seen you somewhere and had thought, "That girl ought to have lots of nice things. I'm going to leave her a million dollars when I die." And the death was to be neither untimely nor painful. Your benefactor, full of years and comfortably ready to depart, was to slip softly away during sleep and go right to heaven. These embroideries permitted Annabel and Midge to play their game in the luxury of peaceful consciences.

Midge played with a seriousness that was not only proper but extreme. The single strain on the girls' friendship had followed an announcement once made by Annabel that the first thing she would buy with her million dollars would be a silver-fox coat. It was as if she had struck Midge across the mouth. When Midge recovered her breath, she cried that she couldn't imagine how Annabel could do such a thing—silver-fox coats were common! Annabel defended her taste with the retort that they were not common, either. Midge then said that they were so. She added that everybody had a silver-fox coat. She went on, with perhaps a slight loss of head, to declare that she herself wouldn't be caught dead in silver fox.

For the next few days, though the girls saw each other as constantly, their coversation was careful and infrequent, and they did not once play their game. Then one morning, as soon as Annabel entered the office, she came to Midge and said that she had changed her mind. She would not buy a silver-fox coat with any part of her million dollars. Immediately on receiving the legacy, she would select a coat of mink.

Midge smiled and her eyes shone. "I think," she said, "you're doing absolutely the right thing."

Now, as they walked along Fifth Avenue, they played the game anew. It was one of those days with which September is repeatedly cursed; hot and glaring, with slivers of dust in the wind. People drooped and shambled, but the girls carried themselves tall and walked a straight line, as befitted young heiresses on their afternoon promenade. There was no longer need for them to start the game at its formal opening. Annabel went direct to the heart of it.

"All right," she said. "So you've got this million dollars. So what would be the first thing you'd do?"

"Well, the first thing I'd do," Midge said, "I'd get a mink coat." But she said it mechanically, as if she were giving the memorized answer to an expected question.

"Yes," Annabel said, "I think you ought to. The terribly dark kind of mink." But she, too, spoke as if by rote. It was too hot; fur, no matter how dark and sleek and supple, was horrid to the thoughts.

They stepped along in silence for a while. Then Midge's eye was caught by a shop window. Cool, lovely gleamings were there set off by chaste and elegant darkness.

"No," Midge said, "I take it back. I wouldn't get a mink coat the first thing. Know what I'd do? I'd get a string of pearls. Real pearls."

Annabel's eyes turned to follow Midge's.

"Yes," she said, slowly. "I think that's a kind of a good idea. And it would make sense, too. Because you can wear pearls with anything."

Together they went over to the shop window and stood pressed against it. It contained but one object—a double row of great, even pearls clasped by a deep emerald around a little pink velvet throat.

"What do you suppose they cost?" Annabel said.

"Gee, I don't know," Midge said. "Plenty, I guess."

"Like a thousand dollars?" Annabel said.

"Oh, I guess like more," Midge said. "On account of the emerald."

"Well, like ten thousand dollars?" Annabel said.

"Gee, I wouldn't even know," Midge said.

The devil nudged Annabel in the ribs. "Dare you to go in and price them," she said.

"Like fun!" Midge said.

"Dare you," Annabel said.

"Why, a store like this wouldn't even be open this afternoon," Midge said.

"Yes, it is so, too," Annabel said. "People just came out. And there's a doorman on. Dare you."

"Well," Midge said. "But you've got to come too."

They tendered thanks, icily, to the doorman for ushering them into the shop. It was cool and quiet, a broad, gracious room with paneled walls and soft carpet. But the girls wore expressions of bitter disdain, as if they stood in a sty.

A slim, immaculate clerk came to them and bowed. His neat face showed no astonishment at their appearance.

"Good afternoon," he said. He implied that he would never forget it if they would grant him the favor of accepting his soft-spoken greeting.

"Good afternoon," Annabel and Midge said together, and in like freezing accents.

"Is there something—?" the clerk said.

"Oh, we're just looking," Annabel said. It was as if she flung the words down from a dais.

The clerk bowed.

"My friend and myself merely happened to be passing," Midge said, and stopped, seeming to listen to the phrase. "My friend here and myself," she went on, "merely happened to be wondering how much are those pearls you've got in your window."

"Ah, yes," the clerk said. "The double rope. That is two hundred and fifty thousand dollars, Madam."

"I see," Midge said.

The clerk bowed. "An exceptionally beautiful necklace," he said. "Would you care to look at it?"

"No, thank you," Annabel said.

"My friend and myself merely happened to be passing," Midge said.

They turned to go; to go, from their manner, where the tumbrel awaited them. The clerk sprang ahead and opened the door. He bowed as they swept by him.

The girls went on along the Avenue and disdain was still on their faces.

"Honestly!" Annabel said. "Can you imagine a thing like that?"

"Two hundred and fifty thousand dollars!" Midge said. "That's a quarter of a million dollars right there!"

"He's got his nerve!" Annabel said.

They walked on. Slowly the disdain went, slowly and completely as if drained from them, and with it went the regal carriage and tread. Their shoulders dropped and they dragged their feet; they bumped against each other, without notice or apology, and caromed away again. They were silent and their eyes were cloudy.

Suddenly Midge straightened her back, flung her head high, and spoke, clear and strong.

"Listen, Annabel," she said. "Look. Suppose there was this terribly rich person, see? You don't know this person, but this person has seen you somewhere and wants to do something for you. Well, it's a terribly old person, see? And so this person dies, just like going to sleep, and leaves you ten million dollars. Now, what would be the first thing you'd do?"

QUESTIONS

1. Why are Annabel and Midge so arrogant? What does Fifth Avenue symbolize to them?

2. Which qualities make Annabel the leader? Which qualities make Midge the follower?

3. In the game they play, why must the million dollars be spent on self?

4. Why is Sylvia quickly discarded as a "game player?" What is wrong with what she would do with her million dollars?

5. What is ironic about the story when posed against the title?

TOPICS FOR WRITING

1. Describe the differences in character between Annabel and Midge and between Minnie Cooper and Miss Brill.

2. Analyze the impact of environment on character in "The Standard of Living."

3. Describe the story's tone and style. How are both related to theme?

James Thurber

THE CATBIRD SEAT

James Thurber (1894–1961) was born in Columbus, Ohio, into a family that he claimed was "hooked on" the absurd. Some of Thurber's most humorous stories and essays retell incidents during his boyhood; it was also as a boy that an accident impaired his vision in one eye. Eventually, he would lose vision in the other and become completely blind. Before this happened, however, he studied at Ohio State University and later became a reporter and illustrator in Columbus, New York, and Paris. He was on the staff of The New Yorker, but left as quickly as was graciously possible. Thurber was keenly attuned to the fears and fantasies of people. "The Secret Life of Walter Mitty" was only one of many stories that explored the theme of fear and fantasy, weakness and power. Thurber's books started to come in 1929 when he wrote Is Sex Necessary? (with E. B. White). There followed, among others, My Life and Hard Times (1933), The Middle-Aged Man on the Flying Trapeze (1935), The Male Animal (a play, with Elliot Nugent, 1940), Alarms and Diversions (1957), and a last book of essays, Lanterns and Lances (1961). "The Catbird Seat" is told with Thurber's usual humorous tone, but in it he once again explores power and weakness, deftly outlining his protagonist and antagonist. We clearly know whose side we're on, which seems to be the way Thurber wanted it.

Mr. Martin bought the pack of Camels on Monday night in the most crowded cigar store on Broadway. It was theater time and seven or eight men were buying cigarettes. The clerk didn't even glance at Mr. Martin, who put the pack in his overcoat pocket and went out. If any of the staff at F & S had seen him buy the cigarettes, they would have been astonished, for it was generally known that Mr. Martin did not smoke, and never had. No one saw him.

The Catbird Seat

It was just a week to the day since Mr. Martin had decided to rub out Mrs. Ulgine Barrows. The term "rub out" pleased him because it suggested nothing more than the correction of an error—in this case an error of Mr. Fitweiler. Mr. Martin had spent each night of the past week working out his plan and examining it. As he walked home now he went over it again. For the hundredth time he resented the element of imprecision, the margin of guesswork that entered into the business. The project as he had worked it out was casual and bold, the risks were considerable. Something might go wrong anywhere along the line. And therein lay the cunning of his scheme. No one would ever see in it the cautious, painstaking hand of Erwin Martin, head of the filing department at F & S, of whom Mr. Fitweiler had once said, "Man is fallible but Martin isn't." No one would see his hand, that is, unless it were caught in the act.

Sitting in his apartment, drinking a glass of milk, Mr. Martin reviewed his case against Mrs. Ulgine Barrows, as he had every night for seven nights. He began at the beginning. Her quacking voice and braying laugh had first profaned the halls of F & S on March 7, 1941 (Mr. Martin had a head for dates). Old Roberts, the personnel chief, had introduced her as the newly appointed special adviser to the president of the firm, Mr. Fitweiler. The woman had appalled Mr. Martin instantly, but he hadn't shown it. He had given her his dry hand, a look of studious concentration, and a faint smile. "Well," she had said, looking at the papers on his desk, "are you lifting the oxcart out of the ditch?" As Mr. Martin recalled that moment, over his milk, he squirmed slightly. He must keep his mind on her crimes as a special adviser, not on her peccadillos as a personality. This he found difficult to do, in spite of entering an objection and sustaining it. The faults of the woman as a woman kept chattering on in his mind like an unruly witness. She had, for almost two years now, baited him. In the halls, in the elevator, even in his own office, into which she romped now and then like a circus horse, she was constantly shouting these silly questions at him. "Are you lifting the oxcart out of the ditch? Are you tearing up the pea patch? Are you hollering down the rain barrel? Are you scraping around the bottom of the pickle barrel? Are you sitting in the catbird seat?"

It was Joey Hart, one of Mr. Martin's two assistants, who had explained what the gibberish meant. "She must be a Dodger fan," he had said. "Red Barber announces the Dodger games over the radio and he uses those expressions— picked 'em up down South." Joey had gone on to explain one or two. "Tearing up the pea patch" meant going on a rampage; "sitting in the catbird seat" meant sitting pretty, like a batter with three balls and no strikes on him. Mr. Martin dismissed all this with an effort. It had been annoying, it had driven him near to distraction, but he was too solid a man to be moved to murder by anything so childish. It was fortunate, he reflected as he passed on to the important charges against Mrs. Barrows, that he had stood up under it so well. He had maintained always an outward appearance of polite tolerance. "Why, I even believe you like the woman," Miss Paird, his other assistant, had once said to him. He had simply smiled.

A gavel rapped in Mr. Martin's mind and the case proper was resumed. Mrs. Ulgine Barrows stood charged with willful, blatant, and persistent attempts to destroy the efficiency and system of F & S. It was competent, material, and relevant to review her advent and rise to power. Mr. Martin had got the story from Miss Paird, who seemed always able to find things out. According to her, Mrs.

Barrows had met Mr. Fitweiler at a party, where she had rescued him from the embraces of a powerfully built drunken man who had mistaken the president of F & S for a famous retired Middle Western football coach. She had led him to a sofa and somehow worked upon him a monstrous magic. The aging gentleman had jumped to the conclusion there and then that this was a woman of singular attainments, equipped to bring out the best in him and in the firm. A week later he had introduced her into F & S as his special adviser. On that day confusion got its foot in the door. After Miss Tyson, Mr. Brundage, and Mr. Bartlett had been fired and Mr. Munson had taken his hat and stalked out, mailing his resignation later, old Roberts had been emboldened to speak to Mr. Fitweiler. He mentioned that Mr. Munson's department had been "a little disrupted" and hadn't they perhaps better resume the old system there? Mr. Fitweiler had said certainly not. He had the greatest faith in Mrs. Barrows' ideas. "They require a little seasoning, a little seasoning, is all," he had added. Mr. Roberts had given it up. Mr. Martin reviewed in detail all the changes wrought by Mrs. Barrows. She had begun chipping at the cornices of the firm's edifice and now she was swinging at the foundation stones with a pickaxe.

Mr. Martin came now, in his summing up, to the afternoon of Monday, November 2, 1942—just one week ago. On that day, at 3 P.M., Mrs. Barrows had bounced into his office. "Boo!" she had yelled. "Are you scraping around the bottom of the pickle barrel?" Mr. Martin had looked at her from under his green eyeshade, saying nothing. She had begun to wander about the office, taking it in with her great, popping eyes. "Do you really need *all* these filing cabinets?" she had demanded suddenly. Mr. Martin's heart had jumped. "Each of these files," he had said, keeping his voice even, "plays an indispensable part in the system of F & S." She had brayed at him, "Well, don't tear up the pea patch!" and gone to the door. From there she had bawled, "But you sure have got a lot of fine scrap in here!" Mr. Martin could no longer doubt that the finger was on his beloved department. Her pickaxe was on the upswing, poised for the first blow. It had not come yet; he had received no blue memo from the enchanted Mr. Fitweiler bearing nonsensical instructions deriving from the obscene woman. But there was no doubt in Mr. Martin's mind that one would be forthcoming. He must act quickly. Already a precious week had gone by. Mr. Martin stood up in his living room, still holding his milk glass. "Gentlemen of the jury," he said to himself, "I demand the death penalty for this horrible person."

The next day Mr. Martin followed his routine, as usual. He polished his glasses more often and once sharpened an already sharp pencil, but not even Miss Paird noticed. Only once did he catch sight of his victim; she swept past him in the hall with a patronizing "Hi!" At five-thirty he walked home, as usual, and had a glass of milk, as usual. He had never drunk anything stronger in his life—unless you could count ginger ale. The late Sam Schlosser, the S of F & S, had praised Mr. Martin at a staff meeting several years before for his temperate habits. "Our most efficient worker neither drinks nor smokes," he had said. "The results speak for themselves." Mr. Fitweiler had sat by, nodding approval.

Mr. Martin was still thinking about that red-letter day as he walked over to the Schrafft's on Fifth Avenue near Forty-sixth Street. He got there, as he always did, at eight o'clock. He finished his dinner and the financial page of the *Sun* at a quarter to nine, as he always did. It was his custom after dinner to take a walk. This time he walked down Fifth Avenue at a casual pace. His gloved hands felt moist and warm, his forehead cold. He transferred the Camels from his overcoat to a jacket pocket. He wondered, as he did so, if they did not represent an unnecessary note of strain. Mrs. Barrows smoked only Luckies. It was his idea to puff a few puffs on a Camel (after the rubbing-out), stub it out in the ashtray holding her lipstick-stained Luckies, and thus drag a small red herring across the trail. Perhaps it was not a good idea. It would take time. He might even choke, too loudly.

Mr. Martin had never seen the house on West Twelfth Street where Mrs. Barrows lived, but he had a clear enough picture of it. Fortunately, she had bragged to everybody about her ducky first-floor apartment in the perfectly darling three-story red-brick. There would be no doorman or other attendants; just the tenants of the second and third floors. As he walked along, Mr. Martin realized that he would get there before nine-thirty. He had considered walking north on Fifth Avenue from Schrafft's to a point from which it would take him until ten o'clock to reach the house. At that hour people were less likely to be coming in or going out. But the procedure would have made an awkward loop in the straight thread of his casualness, and he had abandoned it. It was impossible to figure when people would be entering or leaving the house, anyway. There was a great risk at any hour. If he ran into anybody, he would simply have to place the rubbing-out of Ulgine Barrows in the inactive file forever. The same thing would hold true if there were someone in her apartment. In that case he would just say that he had been passing by, recognized her charming house, and thought to drop in.

It was eighteen minutes after nine when Mr. Martin turned into Twelfth Street. A man passed him, and a man and a woman, talking. There was no one within fifty paces when he came to the house, halfway down the block. He was up the steps and in the small vestibule in no time, pressing the bell under the card that said "Mrs. Ulgine Barrows." When the clicking in the lock started, he jumped forward against the door. He got inside fast, closing the door behind him. A bulb in a lantern hung from the hall ceiling on a chain seemed to give a monstrously bright light. There was nobody on the stair, which went up ahead of him along the left wall. A door opened down the hall in the wall on the right. He went toward it swiftly, on tiptoe.

"Well, for God's sake, look who's here!" bawled Mrs. Barrows, and her braying laugh rang out like the report of a shotgun. He pushed past her like a football tackle, bumping her. "Hey, quit shoving!" she said, closing the door behind them. They were in her living room, which seemed to Mr. Martin to be lighted by a hundred lamps. "What's after you?" she said. "You're as jumpy as a goat." He found he was unable to speak. His heart was wheezing in his throat. "I—yes," he finally brought out. She was jabbering and laughing as she started to help him off with his coat. "No, no," he said. "I'll put it here." He took it off and put it on a chair near the door. "Your hat and gloves, too," she said. "You're in a lady's house." He put his hat on top of the coat. Mrs. Barrows seemed larger than he had thought. He kept his gloves on. "I was passing by," he said. "I recognized—is there anyone here?" She laughed louder than ever. "No," she said, "we're all alone. You're as white as a sheet, you funny man. Whatever *has* come over you? I'll mix you a toddy." She started toward a door across the room. "Scotch-and-soda be all right? But say, you don't drink, do you?" She turned and gave him her amused look. Mr. Martin pulled himself together. "Scotch-and-soda will be all right," he heard himself say. He could hear her laughing in the kitchen.

Mr. Martin looked quickly around the living room for the weapon. He had counted on finding one there. There were andirons and a poker and something in a corner that looked like an Indian club. None of them would do. It couldn't be that way. He began to pace around. He came to a desk. On it lay a metal paper knife with an ornate handle. Would it be sharp enough? He reached for it and knocked over a small brass jar. Stamps spilled out of it and it fell to the floor with a clatter. "Hey," Mrs. Barrows yelled from the kitchen, "are you tearing up the pea patch?" Mr. Martin gave a strange laugh. Picking up the knife, he tried its point against his left wrist. It was blunt. It wouldn't do.

When Mrs. Barrows reappeared, carrying two highballs, Mr. Martin, standing there with his gloves on, became acutely conscious of the fantasy he had wrought. Cigarettes in his pocket, a drink prepared for him—it was all too grossly improbable. It was more than that; it was impossible. Somewhere in the back of his mind a vague idea stirred, sprouted. "For heaven's sake, take off those gloves," said Mrs. Barrows. "I always wear them in the house," said Mr. Martin. The idea began to bloom, strange and wonderful. She put the glasses on a coffee table in front of a sofa and sat on the sofa. "Come over her, you odd little man," she said. Mr. Martin went over and sat beside her. It was difficult getting a cigarette out of the pack of Camels, but he managed it. She held a match for him, laughing. "Well," she said, handing him his drink, "this is perfectly marvelous. You with a drink and a cigarette."

Mr. Martin puffed, not too awkwardly, and took a gulp of the highball. "I drink and smoke all the time," he said. He clinked his glass against hers. "Here's nuts to that old windbag, Fitweiler," he said, and gulped again. The stuff tasted awful, but he made no grimace. "Really, Mr. Martin," she said, her voice and posture changing, "you are insulting our employer." Mrs. Barrows was now all special adviser to the president. "I am preparing a bomb," said Mr. Martin, "which will blow the old goat higher than hell." He had only had a little of the drink, which was not strong. It couldn't be that. "Do you take dope or something?" Mrs. Barrows asked coldly. "Heroin," said Mr. Martin. "I'll be coked to the gills when I bump that old buzzard off." "Mr. Martin!" she shouted, getting to her feet. "That will be all of that. You must go at once." Mr. Martin took another swallow of his drink. He tapped his cigarette out in the ashtray and put the pack of Camels on the coffee table. Then he got up. She stood glaring at him. He walked over and put on his hat and coat. "Not a word about this," he said, and laid an index finger against his lips. All Mrs. Barrows could bring out was "Really!" Mr. Martin put his hand on the doorknob. "I'm sitting in the catbird seat," he said. He stuck his tongue out at her and left. Nobody saw him go.

Mr. Martin got to his apartment, walking, well before eleven. No one saw him go in. He had two glasses of milk after brushing his teeth, and he felt elated. It wasn't tipsiness, because he hadn't been tipsy. Anyway, the walk had worn off all effects of the whiskey. He got in bed and read a magazine for a while. He was asleep before midnight.

Mr. Martin got to the office at eight-thirty the next morning, as usual. At a quarter to nine, Ulgine Barrows, who had never before arrived at work before ten, swept into his office. "I'm reporting to Mr. Fitweiler now!" she shouted. "If he turns you over to the police, it's no more than you deserve!" Mr. Martin gave her a look of shocked surprise. "I beg your pardon?" he said. Mrs. Barrows snorted and bounced out of the room, leaving Miss Paird and Joey staring after her. "What's the matter with that old devil now?" asked Miss Paird. "I have no idea," said Mr.

Martin, resuming his work. The other two looked at him and then at each other. Miss Paird got up and went out. She walked slowly past the closed door of Mr. Fitweiler's office. Mrs Barrows was yelling inside, but she was not braying. Miss Paird could not hear what the woman was saying. She went back to her desk.

Forty-five minutes later, Mrs. Barrows left the president's office and went into her own, shutting the door. It wasn't until half an hour later that Mr. Fitweiler sent for Mr. Martin. The head of the filing department, neat, quiet, attentive, stood in front of the old man's desk. Mr. Fitweiler was pale and nervous. He took his glasses off and twiddled them. He made a small, bruffing sound in his throat. "Martin," he said, "you have been with us more than twenty years." "Twenty-two, sir," said Mr. Martin. "In that time," pursued the president, "your work and your—uh—manner have been exemplary." "I trust so, sir," said Mr. Martin. "I have understood, Martin," said Mr. Fitweiler, "that you have never taken a drink or smoked." "That is correct, sir," said Mr. Martin. "Ah, yes." Mr. Fitweiler polished his glasses. "You may describe what you did after leaving the office yesterday, Martin," he said. Mr. Martin allowed less than a second for his bewildered pause. "Certainly, sir," he said. "I walked home. Then I went to Schrafft's for dinner. Afterward I walked home again. I went to bed early, sir, and read a magazine for a while. I was asleep before eleven." "Ah, yes," said Mr. Fitweiler again. He was silent for a moment, searching for the proper words to say to the head of the filing department. "Mrs. Barrows," he said finally, "Mrs. Barrows has worked hard, Martin, very hard. It grieves me to report that she has suffered a severe breakdown. It has taken the form of a persecution complex accompanied by distressing hallucinations." "I am very sorry, sir," said Mr. Martin. "Mrs. Barrows is under the delusion," continued Mr. Fitweiler, "that you visited her last evening and behaved yourself in an—uh—unseemly manner." He raised his hand to silence Mr. Martin's little pained outcry. "It is the nature of these psychological diseases," Mr. Fitweiler said, "to fix upon the least likely and most innocent party as the—uh—source of persecution. These matters are not for the lay mind to grasp, Martin. I've just had my psychiatrist, Dr. Fitch, on the phone. He would not, of course, commit himself, but I suggested to Mrs. Barrows, when she had completed her—uh—story to me this morning, that she visit Dr. Fitch, for I suspected a condition at once. She flew, I regret to say, into a rage, and demanded—uh—requested that I call you on the carpet. You may not know, Martin, but Mrs. Barrows had planned a reorganization of your department— subject to my approval, of course, subject to my approval. This brought you, rather than anyone else, to her mind—but again that is a phenomenon for Dr. Fitch and not for us. So, Martin, I am afraid Mrs. Barrows' usefulness here is at an end." "I am dreadfully sorry, sir," said Mr. Martin.

It was at this point that the door to the office blew open with the suddenness of a gas-main explosion and Mrs. Barrows catapulted through it. "Is the little rat denying it?" she screamed. "He can't get away with that!" Mr. Martin got up and moved discreetly to a point beside Mr. Fitweiler's chair. "You drank and smoked at my apartment," she bawled at Mr. Martin, "and you know it! You called Mr. Fitweiler an old windbag and said you were going to blow him up when you got coked to the gills on your heroin!" She stopped yelling to catch her breath and a new glint came into her popping eyes. "If you weren't such a drab, ordinary little man," she said, "I'd think you'd planned it all. Sticking your tongue out, saying you were sitting in the catbird seat, because you thought no one would believe me when I told it! My God, it's really too perfect!" She brayed loudly and hysterically, and the fury was on her again. She glared at Mr. Fitweiler. "Can't you see how he has tricked us, you old fool? Can't you see his little game?" But Mr. Fitweiler had been surreptitiously pressing all the buttons under the top of his desk and employees of F & S began pouring into the room. "Stockton," said Mr. Fitweiler, "you and Fishbein will take Mrs. Barrows to her home. Mrs. Powell, you will go with them." Stockton, who had played a little football in high school, blocked Mrs. Barrows as she made for Mr. Martin. It took him and Fishbein together to force her out of the door into the hall, crowded with stenographers and office boys. She was still screaming imprecations at Mr. Martin, tangled and contradictory imprecations. The hubbub finally died out down the corridor.

"I regret that this has happened," said Mr. Fitweiler. "I shall ask you to dismiss it from your mind, Martin." "Yes, sir," said Mr. Martin, anticipating his chief's "That will be all" by moving to the door. "I will dismiss it." He went out and shut the door, and his step was light and quick in the hall. When he entered his department he had slowed down to his customary gait, and he walked quietly across the room to the W20 file, wearing a look of studious concentration.

QUESTIONS

1. Why is Erwin Martin upset by Ulgine Barrows?

2. Why is the F & S system so important to Martin? Why is he upset with the changes that Barrows is making?

3. When do we come to understand the kind of influence Barrows wields over Fitweiler? Is it before or after Martin goes to her apartment?

4. What kind of person does Barrows symbolize? Martin? Fitweiler? Miss Paird? Joey Hart?

5. How would you describe the overall tone of this story? Ironic? Satiric? Humorous? How does Thurber create this tone?

6. Contrast Barrows with Elisa in "The Chrysanthemums" (pages 171–179).

7. Draw a comparison between the lives and work of Annabel and Midge in "The Standard of Living" (page 253) and that of Erwin Martin in Thurber's "The Catbird Seat."

TOPICS FOR WRITING

1. Write an essay on the use of manipulation in this story—which characters do it and to whom and with what results?

2. Describe as many phrases as you can remember being used by your local sportscaster. Supply reasons why they might find their way into common usage, as many of Red Barber's did. How does Thurber's use of phrases and language in general contribute to the success of the story?

3. Evaluate Thurber's attitude toward women in this story.

Jorge Luis Borges

THE SOUTH

*Jorge Luis Borges (1899–) was born in Argentina. Between 1923 and 1929 he published several volumes of poetry, which were mainly nostalgic and nationalistic (*Fervor de Buenos Aires, *1923;* Luna de enfrente, *1925;* Cuaderno de San Martin, *1929). He then began writing essays on literature, metaphysics, and language. When his eyesight began to fail, he turned to writing fictional narratives, and these established his reputation. Somewhat like Kafka, Borges weaves together the real and the surreal to create yet another reality. Among his better-known publications are* Historia de la infamia *(1935),* Ficciones *(1945, 1956)* El Aleph *(1949),* Other Inquisitions *(1952), and* Labyrinths, Stories and Essays *(1962). "The South" is typical of Borges' distinctive attempt in his fiction to explore the nature of time and reality.*

The man who landed in Buenos Aires in 1871 bore the name of Johannes Dahlmann and he was a minister in the Evangelical Church. In 1939, one of his grandchildren, Juan Dahlmann, was secretary of a municipal library on Calle Córdoba, and he considered himself profoundly Argentinian. His maternal grandfather had been that Francisco Flores, of the Second Line-Infantry Division, who had died on the frontier of Buenos Aires, run through with a lance by Indians from Catriel; in the discord inherent between his two lines of descent, Juan Dahlmann (perhaps driven to it by his Germanic blood) chose the line represented by his romantic ancestor, his ancestor of the romantic death. An old sword, a leather frame containing the daguerreotype of a blank-faced man with a beard, the dash and grace of certain music, the familiar strophes of *Martin Fierro,* the passing years, boredom and solitude, all went to foster this voluntary, but never ostentatious nationalism. At the cost of numerous small privations, Dahlmann had managed to save the empty shell of a ranch in the South which had belonged to the Flores family: he continually recalled the image of the balsamic eucalyptus trees and the great rose-colored house which had once been crimson. His duties, perhaps even indolence, kept him in the city. Summer after summer he contented himself with the abstract idea of possession and with the certitude that his ranch was waiting for him on a precise site in the middle of the plain. Late in February, 1939, something happened to him.

Blind to all fault, destiny can be ruthless at one's slightest distraction. Dahlmann had succeeded in acquiring, on that very afternoon, an imperfect copy of Weil's edition of *The Thousand and One Nights.* Avid to examine this find, he did not wait for the elevator but hurried up the stairs. In the obscurity, something brushed by his forehead: a bat, a bird? On the face of the woman who opened the door to him he saw horror engraved, and the hand he wiped across his face came away red with blood. The edge of a recently painted door which someone had forgotten to close had caused this wound. Dahlmann was able to fall asleep, but from the moment he awoke at dawn the savor of all things was atrociously poignant. Fever wasted him and the pictures in *The Thousand and One Nights* served to illustrate nightmares. Friends and relatives paid him visits and, with exaggerated smiles, assured him that they thought he looked fine. Dahlmann listened to them with a kind of feeble stupor and he marveled at their not knowing that he was in hell. A week, eight days passed, and they were like eight centuries. One afternoon, the usual doctor appeared, accompanied by a new doctor, and they carried him off to a sanitarium on the Calle Ecuador, for it was necessary to X-ray him. Dahlmann, in the hackney coach which bore them away, thought that he would, at last, be able to sleep in a room different from his own. He felt happy and communicative. When he arrived at his destination, they undressed him, shaved his head, bound him with metal fastenings to a stretcher; they shone bright lights on him until he was blind and dizzy, auscultated him, and a masked man stuck a needle into his arm. He awoke with a feeling of nausea, covered with a bandage, in a cell with something of a well about it; in the days and nights which followed the operation he came to realize that he had merely been, up until then, in a suburb of hell. Ice in his mouth did not leave the least trace of freshness. During these days Dahlmann hated himself in minute detail; he hated his identity, his bodily necessities, his humiliation, the beard which bristled upon his face. He stoically endured the curative measures, which were painful, but when the surgeon told him he had been on the point of death from septicemia, Dahlmann dissolved in tears of self-pity for his fate. Physical wretchedness and the incessant anticipation of horrible nights had not allowed him time to think of anything so abstract as death. On another day, the surgeon told him he was healing and that, very soon, he would be able to go to his ranch for convalescence. Incredibly enough, the promised day arrived.

Reality favors symmetries and slight anachronisms: Dahlmann had arrived at the sanitarium in a hackney coach and now a hackney coach was to take him to the Constitución station. The first fresh tang of autumn, after the summer's oppressiveness, seemed like a symbol in nature of his rescue and release from fever and death. The city, at seven in the morning, had not lost that air of an old house lent it by the night; the streets seemed like long vestibules, the plazas were like patios. Dahlmann recognized the city with joy on the edge of vertigo: a second before his eyes registered the phenomena themselves, he recalled the corners, the billboards, the modest variety of Buenos Aires. In the yellow light of the new day, all things returned to him.

Every Argentine knows that the South begins at the other side of Rivadavia. Dahlmann was in the habit of saying that this was no mere convention, that whoever crosses this street enters a more ancient and sterner world. From inside the carriage he sought out, among the new buildings, the iron grille window, the brass knocker, the arched door, the entranceway, the intimate patio.

At the railroad station he noted that he still had thirty minutes. He quickly recalled that in a café on the Calle Brazil (a few dozen feet from Yrigoyen's house) there was an enormous cat which allowed itself to be caressed as if it were a disdainful divinity. He entered the café. There was the cat, asleep. He ordered a cup of coffee, slowly stirred the sugar, sipped it (this pleasure had been denied him in the clinic), and thought, as he smoothed the cat's black coat, that this contact was an illusion and that the two beings, man and cat, were as good as separated by a glass, for man lives in time, in succession, while the magical animal lives in the present, in the eternity of the instant.

Along the next to the last platform the train lay waiting. Dahlmann walked through the coaches until he found one almost empty. He arranged his baggage in the network rack. When the train started off, he took down his valise and extracted, after some hesitation, the first volume of *The Thousand and One Nights.* To travel with this book, which was so much a part of the history of his ill-fortune, was a kind of affirmation that his ill-fortune had been annulled; it was a joyous and secret defiance of the frustrated forces of evil.

Along both sides of the train the city dissipated into suburbs; this sight, and then a view of the gardens and villas, delayed the beginning of his reading. The truth was that Dahlmann read very little. The magnetized mountain and the genie who swore to kill his benefactor are—who would deny it?—marvelous, but not so much more than the morning itself and the mere fact of being. The joy of life distracted him from paying attention to Scheherazade and her superfluous miracles. Dahlmann closed his book and allowed himself to live.

Lunch—the bouillon served in shining metal bowls, as in the remote summers of childhood—was one more peaceful and rewarding delight.

Tomorrow I'll wake up at the ranch, he thought, and it was as if he was two men at a time: the man who traveled through the autumn day and across the geography of the fatherland, the other one, locked up in a sanitarium and subject to methodical servitude. He saw unplastered brick houses, long and angled, timelessly watching the trains go by; he saw horsemen along the dirt roads; he saw gullies and lagoons and ranches; he saw great luminous clouds that resembled marble; and all these things were accidental, casual, like dreams of the plain. He also thought he recognized trees and crop fields; but he would not have been able to name them, for his actual knowledge of the countryside was quite inferior to his nostalgic and literary knowledge.

From time to time he slept, and his dreams were animated by the impetus of the train. The intolerable white sun of high noon had already become the yellow sun which precedes nightfall, and it would not be long before it would turn red. The railroad car was now also different; it was not the same as the one which had quit the station siding at Constitución; the plain and the hours had transfigured it. Outside, the moving shadow of the railroad car stretched toward the horizon. The elemental earth was not perturbed either by settlements or other signs of humanity. The country was vast but at the same time intimate and, in some measure, secret. The limitless country sometimes contained only a solitary bull. The solitude was perfect, perhaps hostile, and it might have occurred to Dahlmann that he was traveling into the past and not merely south. He was distracted from these considerations by the railroad inspector who, on reading his ticket, advised him that the train would not let him off at the regular station but at another: an earlier stop, one scarcely known to Dahlmann. (The man added an explanation which Dahlmann did not attempt to understand, and which he hardly heard, for the mechanism of events did not concern him.)

The train laboriously ground to a halt, practically in the middle of the plain. The station lay on the other side of the tracks; it was not much more than a siding and a shed. There was no means of conveyance to be seen, but the station chief supposed that the traveler might secure a vehicle from a general store and inn to be found some ten or twelve blocks away.

Dahlmann accepted the walk as a small adventure. The sun had already disappeared from view, but a final splendor exalted the vivid and silent plain, before the night erased its color. Less to avoid fatigue than to draw out his enjoyment of these sights, Dahlmann walked slowly, breathing in the odor of clover with sumptuous joy.

The general store at one time had been painted a deep scarlet, but the years had tempered this violent color for its own good. Something in its poor architecture recalled a steel engraving, perhaps one from an old edition of *Paul et Virginie*. A number of horses were hitched up to the paling. Once inside, Dahlmann thought he recognized the shopkeeper. Then he realized that he had been deceived by the man's resemblance to one of the male nurses in the sanitarium. When the shopkeeper heard Dahlmann's request, he said he would have the shay made up. In order to add one more event to that day and to kill time, Dahlmann decided to eat at the general store.

Some country louts, to whom Dahlmann did not at first pay any attention, were eating and drinking at one of the tables. On the floor, and hanging on to the bar, squatted an old man, immobile as an object. His years had reduced and polished him as water does a stone or the generations of men do a sentence. He was dark, dried up, diminutive, and seemed outside time, situated in eternity. Dahlmann noted with satisfaction the kerchief, the thick poncho, the long *chiripá*, and the colt boots, and told himself, as he recalled futile discussions with people from the Northern counties or from the province of Entre Rios, that gauchos like this no longer existed outside the South.

Dahlmann sat down next to the window. The darkness began overcoming the plain, but the odor and sound of the earth penetrated the iron bars of the window. The shop owner brought him sardines, followed by some roast meat. Dahlmann washed the meal down with several glasses of red wine. Idling, he relished the tart savor of the wine, and let his gaze, now grown somewhat drowsy, wander over the shop. A kerosene lamp hung from a beam. There were three customers at the other table: two of them appeared to be farm workers; the third man, whose features hinted at Chinese blood, was drinking with his hat on. Of a sudden, Dahlmann felt something brush lightly against his face. Next to the heavy glass of turbid wine, upon one of the stripes in the tablecloth, lay a spit ball of breadcrumb. That was all: but someone had thrown it there.

The men at the other table seemed totally cut off from him. Perplexed, Dahlmann decided that nothing had happened, and he opened the volume of *The Thousand and One Nights*, by way of suppressing reality. After a few moments another little ball landed on his table, and now the *peones* laughed outright. Dahlmann said to himself that he was not frightened, but he reasoned that it would be a major blunder if he, a convalescent, were to allow himself to be dragged by strangers into some chaotic quarrel. He determined to leave, and had already gotten to his feet when the owner came up and exhorted him in an alarmed voice:

"*Señor* Dahlmann, don't pay any attention to those lads; they're half high."

Dahlmann was not surprised to learn that the other man, now, knew his name. But he felt that these conciliatory words served only to aggravate the situation. Previously to this moment, the *peones'* provocation was directed against an unknown face, against no one in particular, almost against no one at all. Now it was an attack against him, against his name, and his neighbors knew it. Dahlmann pushed the owner aside, confronted the *peones*, and demanded to know what they wanted of him.

The tough with the Chinese look staggered heavily to his feet. Almost in Juan Dahlmann's face he shouted insults, as if he had been a long way off. His game was to exaggerate his drunkenness, and this extravagance constituted a ferocious mockery. Between curses and obscenities, he threw a long knife into the air, followed it with his eyes, caught and juggled it, and challenged Dahlmann to a knife fight. The owner objected in a tremulous voice, pointing out that Dahlmann was unarmed. At this point, something unforeseeable occurred.

From a corner of the room, the old ecstatic gaucho—in whom Dahlmann saw a summary and cipher of the South (his South)—threw him a naked dagger, which landed at his feet. It was as if the South had resolved that Dahlmann should accept the duel. Dahlmann bent over to pick up the dagger, and felt two things. The first, that this almost instinctive act bound him to fight. The second, that the weapon, in his torpid hand, was no defense at all, but would merely serve to justify his murder. He had once played with a poniard, like all men, but his idea of fencing and knife-play did not go further than the notion that all strokes should be directed upward, with the cutting edge held inward. *They would not have allowed such things to happen to me in the sanitarium*, he thought.

"Let's get on our way," said the other man.

They went out and if Dahlmann was without hope, he was also without fear. As he crossed the threshold, he felt that to die in a knife fight, under the open sky, and going forward to the attack, would have been a liberation, a joy, and a festive occasion, on the first night in the sanitarium, when they stuck him with the needle. He felt that if he had been able to choose, then, or to dream his death, this would have been the death he would have chosen or dreamt.

Firmly clutching his knife, which he perhaps would not know how to wield, Dahlmann went out into the plain.

QUESTIONS

1. What makes this story a metaphor of recent history?

2. At which two points in the story does Dahlmann's heritage clash with that of the indigenous people?

3. What does the translator, Gustav Weil (1808–1889), share with Dahlmann?

4. How does "The Thousand and One Nights" become the vehicle for moving between fact and fancy here?

5. What does Borges have to say concerning time and history in this story?

6. Describe the mood of this story.

7. What does Dahlmann symoblize? What do the people in the bar symbolize?

TOPICS FOR WRITING

1. "Reality favors symmetries and slight anachronisms. . . ." Write an analysis of this statement, describing what in this story is real and what may not be.

2. Analyze the relationship of various melodramatic elements in this story to the theme.

Ernest Hemingway

THE KILLERS

Ernest Miller Hemingway (1899–1961) was born in Oak Park, Illinois, and he died in Ketchum, Idaho. He was for a long time a journalist (see By-Line Ernest Hemingway, *edited by William White); in 1954 he won the Nobel Prize in literature. Even during his career as a novelist, story writer, and playwright, Hemingway reported from various parts of the world. It is sometimes difficult to note extreme differences between his dispatches and passages in his fiction, though he believed that the two kinds of writing were distinct. Following World War I, he lived in Europe, where he knew many writers, among them Gertrude Stein, F. Scott Fitzgerald, Wallace Stevens, Morley Callaghan, and Ezra Pound. In 1923 he published* Three Stories and Ten Poems, *which was followed the next year by a collection of stories,* In Our Time. The Torrents of Spring *and* The Sun Also Rises *(1926), both novels, came next.* The Sun Also Rises *established "his reputation and set him, at the age of 26, in the limelight which he both enjoyed and resented for the rest of his life," wrote critic Philip Young. A legion of works marched from Hemingway's typewriter, but some of his "middle period" stories, such as "The Killers," remain popular. This is a lean, sparely written story, rich in dialogue. It reflects a theme exemplified by Hemingway's characters who have "grace under pressure."*

The door of Henry's lunch-room opened and two men came in. They sat down at the counter.

"What's yours?" George asked them.

"I don't know," one of the men said. "What do you want to eat, Al?"

"I don't know," said Al. "I don't know what I want to eat."

Outside it was getting dark. The street-light came on outside the window.

The two men at the counter read the menu. From the other end of the counter Nick Adams watched them. He had been talking to George when they came in.

"I'll have a roast pork tenderloin with apple sauce and mashed potatoes," the first man said.

"It isn't ready yet."

"What the hell do you put it on the card for?"

"That's the dinner," George explained. "You can get that at six o'clock."

George looked at the clock on the wall behind the counter.

"It's five o'clock."

"The clock says twenty minutes past five," the second man said.

"It's twenty minutes fast."

"Oh, to hell with the clock," the first man said. "What have you got to eat?"

"I can give you any kind of sandwiches," George said. "You can have ham and eggs, bacon and eggs, liver and bacon, or a steak."

"Give me chicken croquettes with green peas and cream sauce and mashed potatoes."

"That's the dinner."

"Everything we want's the dinner, eh? That's the way you work it."

"I can give you ham and eggs, bacon and eggs, liver——"

"I'll take ham and eggs," the man called Al said. He wore a derby hat and a black overcoat buttoned across the chest. His face was small and white and he had tight lips. He wore a silk muffler and gloves.

"Give me bacon and eggs," said the other man. He was about the same size as Al. Their faces were different, but they were dressed like twins. Both wore overcoats too tight for them. They sat leaning forward, their elbows on the counter.

"Got anything to drink?" Al asked.

"Silver beer, bevo, ginger-ale," George said.

"I mean you got anything to *drink*?"

"Just those I said."

"This is a hot town," said the other. "What do they call it?"

"Summit."

"Ever hear of it?" Al asked his friend.

"No," said the friend.

"What do you do here nights?" Al asked.

"They eat the dinner," his friend said. "They all come here and eat the big dinner."

"That's right," George said.

"So you think that's right?" Al asked George.

"Sure."

"You're a pretty bright boy, aren't you?"

"Sure," said George.

"Well, you're not," said the other little man. "Is he, Al?"

"He's dumb," said Al. He turned to Nick. "What's your name?"

"Adams."

"Another bright boy," Al said. "Ain't he a bright boy, Max?"

"The town's full of bright boys," Max said.

George put the two platters, one of ham and eggs, the other of bacon and eggs, on the counter. He set down two side-dishes of fried potatoes and closed the wicket into the kitchen.

"Which is yours?" he asked Al.

"Don't you remember?"

"Ham and eggs."

"Just a bright boy," Max said. He leaned forward and took the ham and eggs. Both men ate with their gloves on. George watched them eat.

"What are *you* looking at?" Max looked at George.

"Nothing."

"The hell you were. You were looking at me."

"Maybe the boy meant it for a joke, Max," Al said.

George laughed.

"*You* don't have to laugh," Max said to him. "*You* don't have to laugh at all, see?"

"All right," said George.

"So he thinks it's all right." Max turned to Al. "He thinks it's all right. That's a good one."

"Oh, he's a thinker," Al said. They went on eating.

"What's the bright boy's name down the counter?" Al asked Max.

"Hey, bright boy," Max said to Nick. "You go around on the other side of the counter with your boy friend."

"What's the idea?" Nick asked.

"There isn't any idea."

"You better go around, bright boy," Al said. Nick went around behind the counter.

"What's the idea?" George asked.

"None of your damn business," Al said. "Who's out in the kitchen?"

"The nigger."

"What do you mean the nigger?"

"The nigger that cooks."

"Tell him to come in."

"What's the idea?"

"Tell him to come in."

"Where do you think you are?"

"We know damn well where we are," the man called Max said. "Do we look silly?"

"You talk silly," Al said to him. "What the hell do you argue with this kid for? Listen," he said to George, "tell the nigger to come out here."

"What are you going to do to him?"

"Nothing. Use your head, bright boy. What would we do to a nigger?"

George opened the slit that opened back into the kitchen. "Sam," he called. "Come in here a minute."

The door to the kitchen opened and the nigger came in. "What was it?" he asked. The two men at the counter took a look at him.

"All right, nigger. You stand right there," Al said.

Sam, the nigger, standing in his apron, looked at the two men sitting at the counter. "Yes, sir," he said. Al got down from his stool.

"I'm going back to the kitchen with the nigger and bright boy," he said. "Go on back to the kitchen, nigger. You go with him, bright boy." The little man walked after Nick and Sam, the cook, back into the kitchen. The door shut after them. The man called Max sat at the counter opposite George. He didn't look at George but looked in the mirror that ran along back of the counter. Henry's had been made over from a saloon into a lunch-counter.

"Well, bright boy," Max said, looking into the mirror, "why don't you say something?"

"What's it all about?"

"Hey, Al," Max called, "bright boy wants to know what it's all about."

"Why don't you tell him?" Al's voice came from the kitchen.

"What do you think it's all about?"

"I don't know."

"What do you think?"

Max looked into the mirror all the time he was talking.

"I wouldn't say."

"Hey, Al, bright boy says he wouldn't say what he thinks it's all about."

"I can hear you, all right," Al said from the kitchen. He had propped open the slit that dishes passed through into the kitchen with a catsup bottle. "Listen, bright boy," he said from the kitchen to George. "Stand a little further along the bar. You move a little to the left, Max." He was like a photographer arranging for a group picture.

"Talk to me, bright boy," Max said. "What do you think's going to happen?"

George did not say anything.

"I'll tell you," Max said. "We're going to kill a Swede. Do you know a big Swede named Ole Andreson?"

"Yes."

"He comes here to eat every night, don't he?"

"Sometimes he comes here."

"He comes here at six o'clock, don't he?"

"If he comes."

"We know all that, bright boy," Max said. "Talk about something else. Ever go to the movies?"

"Once in a while."

"You ought to go to the movies more. The movies are fine for a bright boy like you."

"What are you going to kill Ole Andreson for? What did he ever do to you?"

"He never had a chance to do anything to us. He never even seen us."

"And he's only going to see us once," Al said from the kitchen.

"What are you going to kill him for, then?" George asked.

"We're killing him for a friend. Just to oblige a friend, bright boy."

"Shut up," said Al from the kitchen. "You talk too goddam much."

"Well, I got to keep bright boy amused. Don't I, bright boy?"

"You talk too damn much," Al said. "The nigger and my bright boy are amused by themselves. I got them tied up like a couple of girl friends in the convent."

"I suppose you were in a convent?"

"You never know."

"You were in a kosher convent. That's where you were."

George looked up at the clock.

"If anybody comes in you tell them the cook is off, and if they keep after it, you tell them you'll go back and cook yourself. Do you get that, bright boy?"

"All right," George said. "What you going to do with us afterward?"

"That'll depend," Max said. "That's one of those things you never know at the time."

George looked up at the clock. It was a quarter past six. The door from the street opened. A street-car motorman came in.

"Hello, George" he said. "Can I get supper?"

"Sam's gone out," George said. "He'll be back in about half an hour."

"I'd better go up the street," the motorman said. George looked at the clock. It was twenty minutes past six.

"That was nice, bright boy," Max said. "You're a regular little gentleman."

"He knew I'd blow his head off," Al said from the kitchen.

"No," said Max. "It ain't that. Bright boy is nice. He's a nice boy. I like him."

At six-fifty-five George said: "He's not coming."

Two other people had been in the lunch-room. Once George had gone out to the kitchen and made a ham-and-egg sandwich "to go" that a man wanted to take with him. Inside the kitchen he saw Al, his derby hat tipped back, sitting on a stool beside the wicket with the muzzle of a sawed-off shotgun resting on the ledge. Nick and the cook were back to back in the corner, a towel tied in each of their mouths. George had cooked the sandwich, wrapped it up in oiled paper, put it in a bag, brought it in, and the man had paid for it and gone out.

"Bright boy can do everything," Max said. "He can cook and everything. You'd make some girl a nice wife, bright boy."

"Yes?" George said. "Your friend, Ole Andreson, isn't going to come."

"We'll give him ten minutes," Max said.

Max watched the mirror and the clock. The hands of the clock marked seven o'clock, and then five minutes past seven.

"Come on, Al," said Max. "We better go. He's not coming."

"Better give him five minutes," Al said from the kitchen.

In the five minutes a man came in, and George explained that the cook was sick.

"Why the hell don't you get another cook?" the man asked. "Aren't you running a lunch-counter?" He went out.

"Come on, Al," Max said.

"What about the two bright boys and the nigger?"

"They're all right."

"You think so?

"Sure. We're through with it."

"I don't like it," said Al. "It's sloppy. You talk too much."

"Oh, what the hell," said Max. "We got to keep amused, haven't we?"

"You talk too much, all the same," Al said. He came out from the kitchen. The cut-off barrels of the shotgun made a slight bulge under the waist of his too tight-fitting overcoat. He straightened his coat with his gloved hands.

"So long, bright boy," he said to George. "You got a lot of luck."

"That's the truth," Max said. "You ought to play the races, bright boy."

The two of them went out the door. George watched them, through the window, pass under the arc-light and cross the street. In their tight overcoats and derby hats they looked like a vaudeville team. George went back through the swinging-door into the kitchen and untied Nick and the cook.

"I don't want any more of that," said Sam, the cook. "I don't want any more of that."

Nick stood up. He had never had a towel in his mouth before.

"Say," he said. "What the hell?" He was trying to swagger it off.

"They were going to kill Ole Andreson," George said. "They were going to shoot him when he came in to eat."

"Ole Andreson?"

"Sure."

The cook felt the corners of his mouth with his thumbs.

"They all gone?" he asked.

"Yeah," said George. "They're gone now."

"I don't like it," said the cook. "I don't like any of it at all."

"Listen," George said to Nick. "You better go see Ole Andreson."

"All right."

"You better not have anything to do with it at all," Sam, the cook, said. "You better stay way out of it."

"Don't go if you don't want to," George said.

"Mixing up in this ain't going to get you anywhere," the cook said. "You stay out of it."

"I'll go see him," Nick said to George. "Where does he live?"

The cook turned away.

"Little boys always know what they want to do," he said.

"He lives up at Hirsch's rooming-house," George said to Nick.

"I'll go up there."

Outside the arc-light shone through the bare branches of a tree. Nick walked up the street beside the car-tracks and turned at the next arc-light down a side-street. Three houses up the street was Hirsch's rooming-house. Nick walked up the two steps and pushed the bell. A woman came to the door.

"Is Ole Andreson here?"

"Do you want to see him?"

"Yes, if he's in."

Nick followed the woman up a flight of stairs and back to the end of a corridor. She knocked on the door.

"Who is it?"

"It's somebody to see you, Mr. Andreson," the woman said.

"It's Nick Adams."

"Come in."

Nick opened the door and went into the room. Ole Andreson was lying on the bed with all his clothes on. He had been a heavyweight prizefighter and he was too long for the bed. He lay with his head on two pillows. He did not look at Nick.

"What was it?" he asked.

"I was up at Henry's," Nick said, "and two fellows came in and tied up me and the cook, and they said they were going to kill you."

It sounded silly when he said it. Ole Andreson said nothing.

"They put us out in the kitchen," Nick went on. "They were going to shoot you when you came in to supper."

Ole Andreson looked at the wall and did not say anything.

"George thought I better come and tell you about it."

"There isn't anything I can do about it," Ole Andreson said.

"I'll tell you what they were like."

"I don't want to know what they were like." Ole Andreson said. He looked at the wall. "Thanks for coming to tell me about it."

"That's all right."

Nick looked at the big man lying on the bed.

"Don't you want me to go and see the police?"

"No," Ole Andreson said. "That wouldn't do any good."

"Isn't there something I could do?"

"No. There ain't anything to do."

"Maybe it was just a bluff."

"No. It ain't just a bluff."

Ole Andreson rolled over toward the wall.

"The only thing is," he said, talking toward the wall, "I just can't make up my mind to go out. I been in here all day."

"Couldn't you get out of town?"

"No," Ole Andreson said. "I'm through with all that running around."

He looked at the wall.

"There ain't anything to do now."

"Couldn't you fix it up some way?"

"No. I got in wrong." He talked in the same flat voice. "There ain't anything to do. After a while I'll make up my mind to go out."

"I better go back and see George," Nick said.

"So long," said Ole Andreson. He did not look toward Nick. "Thanks for coming around."

Nick went out. As he shut the door he saw Ole Andreson with all his clothes on, lying on the bed looking at the wall.

"He's been in his room all day," the landlady said down-stairs. "I guess he don't feel well. I said to him: 'Mr. Andreson, you ought to go out and take a walk on a nice fall day like this,' but he didn't feel like it."

"He doesn't want to go out."

"I'm sorry he don't feel well," the woman said. "He's an awfully nice man. He was in the ring, you know."

"I know it."

"You'd never know it except from the way his face is," the woman said. They stood talking just inside the street door. "He's just as gentle."

"Well, good-night, Mrs. Hirsch," Nick said.

"I'm not Mrs. Hirsch," the woman said. "She owns the place. I just look after it for her. I'm Mrs. Bell."

"Well, good-night, Mrs. Bell," Nick said.

"Good-night," the woman said.

Nick walked up the dark street to the corner under the arc-light, and then along the car-tracks to Henry's eating-house. George was inside, back of the counter.

"Did you see Ole?"

"Yes," said Nick. "He's in his room and he won't go out."

The cook opened the door from the kitchen when he heard Nick's voice.

"I don't even listen to it," he said and shut the door.

"Did you tell him about it?" George asked.

"Sure. I told him but he knows what it's all about."

"What's he going to do?"

"Nothing."

"They'll kill him."

"I guess they will."

"He must have got mixed up in something in Chicago."

"I guess so," said Nick.

"It's a hell of a thing."

"It's an awful thing," Nick said.

They did not say anything. George reached down for a towel and wiped the counter.

"I wonder what he did?" Nick said.

"Double-crossed somebody. That's what they kill them for."

"I'm going to get out of this town," Nick said.

"Yes," said George. "That's a good thing to do."

"I can't stand to think about him waiting in the room and knowing he's going to get it. It's too damned awful."

"Well," said George, "you better not think about it."

QUESTIONS

1. The story is written from the third-person point of view; whose eyes is it actually seen through?

2. Why does Hemingway stress that the killers dress alike, look alike, and resemble a vaudeville team?

3. Why does the narrative voice use the pejorative term "nigger" since, *within* the story, it is used by the characters?

4. Why does Nick try to "swagger off" the incident?

5. Why does the cook warn Nick off, and why does Nick go anyway to warn Andreson?

TOPICS FOR WRITING

1. "The Killers" was published in 1938, when European fascism was reaching its peak. Draw a symbolic relationship between the "uniformed" killers and the passive, former heavyweight boxer Andreson.

2. Evaluate the title of this story. Are the killers really the focus? How does the ordinariness of this incident strike you? Compare *and* contrast "The Killers" with "Dry September" (pages 126–135).

Isaac Bashevis Singer

OLD LOVE

Isaac Bashevis Singer (1904–   ) was born in Radzymin, Poland, and came to the United States in 1935. He became a citizen in 1943. Singer was a journalist with the Jewish Daily Forward, writing first in Hebrew. Later, he said, "Hebrew was not a living language then," and he also wrote in Yiddish. A former rabbinical student, Singer injects elements of religion into much of his work. Since 1950 his work has been translated into English, in which language he has gained great recognition, winning the 1979 Nobel Prize in literature. Of Singer, critic Thomas Lask wrote: "We are aware of a natural story teller who moves at his own pace, confident of his powers, fertile in invention, and able to hold the reader as long as he wishes. . . ." Singer has published well over one hundred stories in collections that include Gimpel the Fool *(1957),* The Seance *(1968),* The Spinoza of Market Street *(1961), and* The Collected Stories *(1982). His novels include* The Family Moskat *(1955) and* The Slave *(1962). In addition, Singer has published several books for children, the most recent being (with Ira Moskowitz)* A Little Boy in Search of God *(1976). "The short story," Singer says, "must aim directly at its climax." "Old Love" practices what Singer preaches as the consummate "story teller's story teller."*

Harry Bendiner awoke at five with the feeling that as far as he was concerned the night was finished and he wouldn't get any more sleep. Actually, he woke up a dozen times every night. He had undergone an operation for his prostate years before, but this hadn't relieved the constant pressure on his bladder. He would sleep an hour or less, then wake up with the need to void. Even his dreams centered around this urge. He got out of bed and padded to the bathroom on shaky legs. On the way back he stepped out onto the balcony of his eleventh-story condominium. To the left he could see the skyscrapers of Miami, to the right the rumbling sea. The air had turned a bit cooler during the night, but it was still tropically tepid. It smelled of dead fish, oil, and perhaps of oranges as well. Harry stood there for a long while enjoying the breeze from the ocean on his moist forehead. Even though Miami Beach had become a big city, he imagined that he could feel the nearness of the Everglades, the smells and vapors of its vegetation and swamps. Sometimes a seagull would awake in the night, screeching. It happened that the waves threw onto the beach the carcass of a barracuda or even that of a baby whale. Harry Bendiner looked off in the direction of Hollywood. How long was it since the whole area had been undeveloped? Within a few years a wasteland had been transformed into a settlement crowded with hotels, condominiums, restaurants, supermarkets, and banks. The street lights and neon signs dimmed the stars in the sky. Cars raced along even in the middle of the night. Where were all these people hurrying to before dawn? Didn't they ever sleep? What kind of force drove them on? "Well, it's no longer my world. Once you pass eighty, you're as good as a corpse."

He leaned his hand on the railing and tried to reconstruct the dream he had been having. He recalled only that all those who had appeared in the dream were now dead—the men and the women both. Dreams obviously didn't acknowledge death. In his dreams, his three wives were still alive, and so was his son, Bill, and his daughter, Sylvia. New York, his hometown in Poland, and Miami Beach merged into one. He, Harry or Hershel, was both an adult and a cheder boy.

He closed his eyes for a moment. Why was it impossible to remember dreams? He could recall every detail of events that had happened seventy and even seventy-five years ago, but tonight's dreams dissolved like foam. Some force made sure that not a trace of them remained. A third of a person's life died before he went to his grave.

After a while Harry sat down on the plastic chaise that stood on the balcony. He looked toward the sea, to the east, where day would soon be dawning. There was a time when he went swimming the first thing in the morning, particularly during the summer months, but he no longer had the desire to do such things. The newspapers occasionally printed accounts of sharks attacking swimmers, and there were other sea creatures whose bites caused serious complications. For him it now sufficed to take a warm bath.

His thoughts turned to matters of business. He knew full well that money couldn't help him; still, one couldn't constantly brood about the fact that everything was vanity of vanities. It was easier to think about practical matters. Stocks and bonds rose or fell. Dividends and other earnings had to be deposited in the bank and marked down in an account book for tax purposes. Telephone and electric bills and the maintenance of the apartment had to be paid. One day a week a woman came to do his cleaning and press his shirts and underwear. Occasionally he had to have a suit dry-cleaned and shoes repaired. He received letters that he had to answer. He wasn't involved with a synagogue all year, but on Rosh Hashanah and Yom Kippur he had to have a place to worship, and because of this he received appeals to help Israel, yeshivas, Talmud Torahs, old-age homes, and hospitals. Each day he got a pile of "junk mail," and before he discarded it, he had to open and glance at it, at least.

Since he had resolved to live out his years without a wife or even a housekeeper, he had to arrange for his meals, and every other day he went shopping at the local supermarket. Pushing his cart through the aisles, he selected such items as milk, cottage cheese, fruit, canned vegetables, chopped meat, occasionally some mushrooms, a jar of borscht or gefilte fish. He certainly could have permitted himself the luxury of a maid, but some of the maids were thieves. And what would he do with himself if other people waited on him? He remembered a saying from the Gemara that slothfulness led to madness. Fussing over the electric stove in the kitchen, going to the bank, reading the newspaper—particularly the financial section—and spending an hour or two at the office of Merrill Lynch watching the quotations from the New York Exchange flash by on the board lifted his spirits. Recently he had had a television set installed, but he rarely watched it.

His neighbors in the condominium often inquired maliciously why he did things himself that others could do for him. It was known that he was rich. They offered him advice and asked him questions: Why didn't he settle in Israel? Why didn't he go to a hotel in the mountains during the summer? Why didn't he get married? Why didn't he hire a secretary? He had acquired the reputation of a miser. They constantly reminded him that "you can't take it with you"—as if this were some startling revelation. For this reason he stopped attending the tenants' meetings and their parties. Everyone tried in one way or another to get something out of him, but no one would have given him a penny if he needed it. A few years ago, he boarded a bus from Miami Beach to Miami and found he was two cents short of the fare. All he had with him was twenty-dollar bills. No one volunteered either to give him the two cents or to change one of his bank notes, and the driver made him get off.

The truth was, in no hotel could he feel as comfortable as he did in his own home. The meals served in hotels were too plentiful for him and not of the kind that he needed. He alone could see to it that his diet excluded salt, cholesterol, spices. Besides, plane and train rides were too taxing for a man of his delicate health. Nor did it make any sense to remarry at his age. Younger women demanded sex, and he hadn't the slightest interest in an old woman. Being what he was, he was condemned to live alone and to die alone.

A reddish glow had begun to tinge the eastern sky, and Harry went to the bathroom. He stood for a moment studying his image in the mirror—sunken cheeks, a bare skull with a few tufts of white hair, a pointed Adam's apple, a nose whose tip turned down like a parrot's beak. The pale-blue eyes were set somewhat off-center, one higher than the other, and expressed both weariness and traces of youthful ardor. He had once been a virile man. He had had wives and love affairs. He had a stack of love letters and photographs lying about somewhere.

Harry Bendiner hadn't come to America penniless and uneducated like the other immigrants. He had attended the study house in his hometown until the age of nineteen; he knew Hebrew and had secretly read newspapers and worldly books. He had taken lessons in Russian, Polish, and even German. Here in America he had attended Cooper Union for two years in the hope of becoming an engineer, but he had fallen in love with an American girl, Rosalie Stein, and married her, and her father, Sam Stein, had taken him into the construction business. Rosalie died of cancer at the age of thirty, leaving him with two small children. Even as the money came in to him so did death take from him. His son, Bill, a surgeon, died at forty-six, of a heart attack, leaving two children, neither of whom wanted to be Jewish. Their mother, a Christian, lived somewhere in Canada with another man. Harry's daughter, Sylvia, got the very same type of cancer as her mother, and at exactly the same age. Sylvia left no children. Harry refused to sire any more generations, even though his second wife, Edna, pleaded that he have a child or two with her.

Yes, the Angel of Death had taken everything from him. At first his grandchildren had called him occasionally from Canada and sent him a card for the New Year. But now he never heard from them, and he had cut them out of his will.

Harry shaved and hummed a melody—where it had come from he didn't know. Was it something he had heard on television, or a tune from Poland revived in his memory? He had no ear for music and sang everything off-key, but he had retained the habit of singing in the bathroom. His toilet took a long time. For years the pills he took to relieve constipation had had no effect, and every other day he gave himself an enema—a long and arduous process for a man in his eighties. He tried to do calisthenics in the bathtub, raising his skinny legs and splashing his hands in the water as if they were paddles. These were all measures to lengthen life, but even as Harry performed them he asked himself, "Why go on living?" What flavor did his existence possess? No, his life made no sense whatsoever—but did that of his neighbors make more sense? The condominium was full of old people, all well off, many rich. Some of the men couldn't walk, or dragged their feet; some of the women leaned on crutches. A number suffered from arthritis and Parkinson's disease. This wasn't a building but a hospital. People died, and he didn't find out about it until weeks or months afterward. Although he had been among the first tenants in the condominium, he seldom recognized anybody. He didn't go to the pool and he didn't play cards. Men and women greeted him in the elevator and at the supermarket, but he didn't know who any of them were. From time to time someone asked him, "How are you, Mr. Bendiner?" And he usually replied, "How *can* you be at my age? Each day is a gift."

This summer day began like all the others. Harry prepared his breakfast in the kitchen—Rice Krispies with skimmed milk and Sanka sweetened with saccharin. At about nine-thirty he took the elevator down to get the mail. A day didn't go by that he didn't receive a number of checks, but this day brought a bounty. The stocks had fallen, but the companies kept paying the dividends as usual. Harry got money from buildings on which he held mortgages, from rents, bonds, and all kinds of business ventures that he barely remembered. An insurance company paid him an annuity. For years he had been getting a monthly check from Social Security. This morning's yield came to over eleven thousand dollars. True, he would have to withhold a great part of this for taxes, but it still left him with some five thousand dollars for himself. While he totaled up the figures, he deliberated: Should he go to the office of Merrill Lynch and see what was happening on the Exchange? No, there was no point to it. Even if the stocks rose early in the morning, the day would end in losses. "The market is completely crazy," he mumbled to himself. He had considered it an iron rule that inflation always went along with a bullish market, not with a bearish market. But now both the dollar *and* the stocks were collapsing. Well, you could never be sure about anything except death.

Around eleven o'clock he went down to deposit the checks. The bank was a small one; all the employees knew him and said good morning. He had a safe-deposit box there, where he kept his valuables and jewelry. It so happened that all three of his wives had left him everything; none of them had made out a will. He didn't know himself exactly how much he was worth, but it couldn't be less than five million dollars. Still, he walked down the street in a shirt and trousers that any pauper could afford and a cap and shoes he had worn for years. He poked with his cane and took tiny steps. Once in a while he cast a glance backward. Maybe someone was following him. Maybe some crook had found out how rich he was and was scheming to kidnap him. Although the day was bright and the street full of people, no one would interfere if he was grabbed, forced into a car, and dragged off to some ruin or cave. No one would pay ransom for him.

After he had concluded his business at the bank, he turned back toward home. The sun was high in the sky and poured down a blazing fire. Women stood in the shade of canopies looking at dresses, shoes, stockings, brassières, and bathing suits in a store windows. Their faces expressed indecision—to buy or not to buy? Harry glanced at the windows. What could he buy there? There wasn't anything he could desire. From now until five, when he would prepare his dinner, he needed absolutely nothing. He knew precisely what he would do when he got home—take a nap on the sofa.

Thank God, no one had kidnapped him, no one had held him up, no one had broken into his apartment. The air conditioner was working and so was the plumbing in the bathroom. He took off his shoes and stretched out on the sofa.

Strange, he still daydreamed; he fantasized about unexpected successes, restored powers, masculine adventures. The brain wouldn't accept old age. It teemed with the same passions it had in his youth. Harry often said to his brain, "Don't be stupid. It's too late for everything. You have nothing to hope for any more." But the brain was so constituted that it went on hoping nonetheless. Who was it who said, A man takes his hopes into the grave?

He had dozed off and was awakened by a jangling at the door. He became alarmed. No one ever came to see him. "It must be the exterminator," he decided. He opened the door the length of the chain and saw a small woman with reddish cheeks, yellow eyes, and a high pompadour of blond hair the color of straw. She wore a white blouse.

Harry opened the door, and the woman said in a foreign-accented English, "I hope I haven't wakened you. I'm your new neighbor on the left. I wanted to introduce myself to you. My name is Mrs. Ethel Brokeles. A funny name, eh? That was my late husband's name. My maiden name is Goldman."

Harry gazed at her in astonishment. His neighbor on the left had been an old woman living alone. He remembered her name—Mrs. Halpert. He asked, "What happened to Mrs. Halpert?"

"The same as happens to everybody," the woman replied smugly.

"When did it happen? I didn't know anything about it."

"It's more than five months already."

"Come in, come in. People die and you don't even know," Harry said. "She was a nice woman . . . kept herself at a distance."

"I didn't know her. I bought the apartment from her daughter."

"Please have a seat. I don't even have anything to offer you. I have a bottle of liqueur somewhere, but—"

"I don't need any refreshments and I don't drink liqueur. Not in the middle of the day. May I smoke?"

"Certainly, certainly."

The woman sat down on the sofa. She snapped a fancy lighter expertly and lit her cigarette. She wore red nail polish and Harry noticed a huge diamond on one of her fingers.

The woman asked, "You live here alone?"

"Yes, alone."

"I'm alone, too. What can you do? I lived with my husband twenty-five years, and we didn't have a bad day. Our life together was all sunshine without a single cloud. Suddenly he passed away and left me alone and miserable. The New York climate is unhealthy for me. I suffer from rheumatism. I'll have to live out my years here."

"Did you buy the apartment furnished?" Harry asked in businesslike fashion.

"Everything. The daughter wanted nothing for herself besides the dresses and linens. She turned it all over to me for a song. I wouldn't have had the patience to go out and buy furniture and dishes. Have you lived here a long time already?"

The woman posed one question after another, and Harry answered them willingly. She looked comparatively young—no more than fifty or possibly even younger. He brought her an ashtray and put a glass of lemonade and a plate of cookies on the coffee table before her. Two hours went by, but he hardly noticed. Ethel Brokeles crossed her legs, and Harry cast glances at her round knees. She had switched to a Polish-accented Yiddish. She exuded the intimate air of a relative. Something within Harry exulted. It could be nothing else but that heaven had acceded to his secret desires. Only now, as he listened to her, did he realize how lonely he had been all these years, how oppressed by the fact that he seldom exchanged a word with anyone. Even having her for a neighbor was better than nothing. He grew youthful in her presence, and loquacious. He told her about his three wives, the tragedies that had befallen his children. He even mentioned that, following the death of his first wife, he had had a sweetheart.

The woman said, "You don't have to make excuses. A man is a man."

"I've grown old."

"A man is never old. I had an uncle in Wloclawek who was eighty when he married a twenty-year-old girl, and she bore him three children."

"Wloclawek? That's near Kowal, my hometown."

"I know. I've been to Kowal. I had an aunt there."

The woman glanced at her wristwatch. "It's one o'clock. Where are you having lunch?"

"Nowhere. I only eat breakfast and dinner."

"Are you on a diet?"

"No, but at my age—"

"Stop talking about your age!" the woman scolded him. "You know what? Come over to my place and we'll have lunch together. I don't like to eat by myself. For me, eating alone is even worse than sleeping alone."

"Really, I don't know what to say. What did I do to deserve this?"

"Come, come; don't talk nonsense. This is America, not Poland. My refrigerator is stuffed with goodies. I throw out more than I eat, may I be forgiven."

The woman used Yiddish expressions that Harry hadn't heard in at least sixty years. She took his arm and led him to the door. He didn't have to go more than a few steps. By the time he had locked his door she had opened hers. The apartment he went into was larger than his and brighter. There were pictures on the walls, fancy lamps, bric-a-brac. The windows looked out directly at the ocean. On the table stood a vase of flowers. The air in Harry's apartment smelled of dust, but here the air was fresh. "She wants something; she has some ulterior motive," Harry told himself. He recalled what he had read in the newspapers about female cheats who swindled fortunes out of men and out of other women, too. The main thing was to promise nothing, to sign nothing, not to hand over even a single penny.

She seated him at a table, and from the kitchen soon issued the bubbling sound of a percolator and the smell of fresh rolls, fruit, cheese, and coffee. For the first time in years Harry felt an appetite in the middle of the day. After a while they both sat down to lunch.

Between one bite and the next, the woman took a drag from a cigarette. She complained, "Men run after me, but when it comes down to brass tacks they're all interested only in how much money I have. As soon as they start talking about money I break up with them. I'm not poor; I'm even—knock wood—wealthy. But I don't want anyone to take me for my money."

"Thank God I don't need anyone's money," Harry said. "I've got enough even if I live a thousand years."

"That's good."

Gradually they began to discuss their finances, and the woman enumerated her possessions. She owned buildings in Brooklyn and on Staten Island; she had stocks and bonds. Based on what she said and the names she mentioned, Harry decided that she was telling the truth. She had, here in Miami, a checking account and a safe-deposit box in the very same bank as Harry. Harry estimated that she was worth at least a million or maybe more. She served him food with the devotion of a daughter or wife. She talked of what he should and shouldn't eat. Such miracles had occurred to him in his younger years. Women had met him, grown instantly intimate, and stuck with him, never to leave again. But that such a thing should happen to him at his age seemed like a dream. He asked abruptly, "Do you have children?"

"I have a daughter, Sylvia. She lives all alone in a tent in British Columbia."

"Why in a tent? My daughter's name was Sylvia, too. You yourself could be my daughter," he added, not knowing why he had said such a thing.

"Nonsense. What are years? I always liked a man to be a lot older than me. My husband, may he rest in peace, was twenty years older, and the life we had together I would wish for every Jewish daughter."

"I've surely got forty years on you," Harry said.

The woman put down her spoon. "How old do you take me for?"

"Around forty-five," Harry said, knowing she was older.

"Add another twelve years and you've got it."

"You don't look it."

"I had a good life with my husband. I could get anything out of him—the moon, the stars, nothing was too good for his Ethel. That's why after he died I became melancholy. Also, my daughter was making me sick. I spent a fortune on psychiatrists, but they couldn't help me. Just as you see me now, I stayed seven months in an institution, a clinic for nervous disorders. I had a breakdown and I didn't want to live any more. They had to watch me day and night. He was calling me from his grave. I want to tell you something, but don't misunderstand me."

"What is it?"

"You remind me of my husband. That's why—"

"I'm eighty-two," Harry said and instantly regretted it. He could have easily subtracted five years. He waited a moment, then added, "If I were ten years younger, I'd make you a proposition."

Again he regretted his words. They had issued from his mouth as if of their own volition. He was still bothered by the fear of falling into the hands of a gold digger.

The woman looked at him inquisitively and cocked an eyebrow. "Since I decided to live, I'll take you just as you are."

"How is this possible? How can it be?" Harry asked himself again and again. They spoke of getting married and of breaking through the wall that divided their two apartments to make them into one. His bedroom was next to hers. She revealed the details of her financial situation to him. She was worth about a million and a half. Harry had already told her how much he had. He asked, "What will we do with so much money?"

"I wouldn't know what to do with money myself," the woman replied, "but together, we'll take a trip around the world. We'll buy an apartment in Tel Aviv or Tiberias. The hot springs there are good for rheumatism. With me beside you, you'll live a long time. I guarantee you a hundred years, if not more."

"It's all in God's hands," Harry said, amazed at his own words. He wasn't religious. His doubts about God and His providence had intensified over the years. He often said that, after what had happened to the Jews in Europe, one had to be a fool to believe in God.

Ethel stood up and so did he. They hugged and kissed. He pressed her close and youthful urges came throbbing back within him.

She said, "Wait till we've stood under the wedding canopy."

It struck Harry that he had heard these words before, spoken in the same voice. But when? And from whom? All three of his wives had been American-born and wouldn't have used this expression. Had he dreamed it? Could a person foresee the future in a dream? He bowed his head and pondered. When he looked up he was astounded. Within those few seconds the woman's appearance had undergone a startling transformation. She had moved away from him and he hadn't noticed it. Her face had grown pale, shrunken, and aged. Her hair seemed to him to have become suddenly disheveled. She gazed at him sidelong with a dull, sad, even stern expression. Did I insult her or what? he wondered. He heard himself ask, "Is something wrong? Don't you feel well?"

"No, but you'd better go back to your own place now," she said in a voice which seemed alien, harsh, and impatient. He wanted to ask her the reason for the sudden change that had come over her, but a long-forgotten (or a never-forgotten) pride asserted itself. With women, you never knew where you stood anyhow. Still, he asked, "When will we see each other?"

"Not today any more. Maybe tomorrow," she said after some hesitation.

"Goodbye. Thanks for the lunch."

She didn't even bother to escort him to the door. Inside his own apartment again, he thought, Well, she changed her mind. He was overcome with a feeling of shame—for himself and for her, too. Had she been playing a game with him? Had malicious neighbors arranged to make a fool of him? His apartment struck him as half empty. I won't eat dinner, he decided. He felt a pressure in his stomach. "At my age one shouldn't make a fool of oneself," he murmured. He lay down on the sofa and dozed off, and when he opened his eyes again it was dark outside. Maybe she'll ring my doorbell again. Maybe I should call her? She had given him her phone number. Though he had slept, he woke up exhausted. He had letters to answer, but he put it off until morning. He went out onto the balcony. One side of his balcony faced a part of hers. They could see each other here and even converse, if she should still be interested in him. The sea splashed and foamed. There was a freighter far in the distance. A jet roared in the sky. A single star that no street lights or neon signs could dim appeared above. It's a good thing one can see at least one star. Otherwise one might forget that the sky exists altogether.

He sat on the balcony waiting for her to possibly show up. What could she be thinking? Why had her mood changed so abruptly? One minute she was as tender and talkative as a bride in love; a moment later she was a stranger.

Harry dozed off again, and when he awoke it was late in the evening. He wasn't sleepy, and he wanted to go downstairs for the evening edition of the morning paper, with the reports of the New York Exchange; instead he went to lie down on his bed. He had drunk a glass of tomato juice before and swallowed a pill. Only a thin wall separated him from Ethel, but walls possessed a power of their own. Perhaps this is the reason some people prefer to live in a tent, he thought. He assumed that his broodings would keep him from sleeping, but he quickly nodded off. He awoke with pressure on his chest. What time was it? The luminous dial on his wristwatch showed that he had slept two hours and a quarter. He had dreamed, but he couldn't remember what. He retained only the impression of nocturnal horrors. He raised his head. Was she asleep or awake? He couldn't hear even a rustle from her apartment.

He slept again and was awakened this time by the sound of many people talking, doors slamming, footsteps in the corridor, and running. He had always been afraid of a fire. He read newspaper accounts of old people burning to death in old-age homes, hospitals, hotels. He got out of bed, put on his slippers and robe, and opened the door to the hall. There was no one there. Had he imagined it? He closed the door and went out onto the balcony. No, not a trace of firemen below. Only people coming home late, going out to nightclubs, making drunken noise. Some of the condominium tenants sublet their apartments in the summer to South Americans. Harry went back to bed. It was quiet for a few minutes; then he again heard a din in the corridor and the sound of men's and women's voices. Something had happened, but what? He had an urge to get up and take another look, but he didn't. He lay there tense. Suddenly he heard a buzzing from the house phone in the kitchen. When he lifted the receiver, a man's voice said, "Wrong number." Harry had turned on the fluorescent light in the kitchen and the glare dazzled him. He opened the refrigerator, took out a jug of sweetened tea, and poured himself half a glass, not knowing whether he did this because he was thirsty or to buoy his spirits. Soon afterward he had to urinate, and he went to the bathroom.

At that moment, his doorbell rang, and the sound curtailed his urge. Maybe robbers had broken into the building? The night watchman was an old man and hardly a match for intruders. Harry couldn't decide whether to go to the door or not. He stood over the toilet bowl trembling. *These might be my final moments on earth* flashed through his mind. "God Almighty, take pity on me," he murmured. Only now did he remember that he had a peephole in the door through which he could see the hall outside. How could I have forgotten about it? he wondered. I must be getting senile.

He walked silently to the door, raised the cover of the peephole and looked out. He saw a white-haired woman in a robe. He recognized her; it was his neighbor on the right. In a second everything became clear to him. She had a paralyzed husband and something had happened to him. He opened the door. The old woman held out an unstamped envelope.

"Excuse me, Mr. Bendiner, the woman next door left this envelope by your door. Your name is on it."

"What woman?"

"On the left. She committed suicide."

Harry Bendiner felt his guts constrict, and within seconds his belly grew as tight as a drum.

"The blond woman?"

"Yes."

"What did she do?"

"Threw herself out the window."

Harry held out his hand and the old woman gave him the envelope.

"Where is she?" he asked.

"They took her away."

"Dead?"

"Yes, dead."

"My God!"

"It's already the third such incident here. People lose their minds in America."

Harry's hand shook, and the envelope fluttered as if caught in a wind. He thanked the woman and closed the door. He went to look for his glasses, which he had put on his night table. "I dare not fall," he cautioned himself. "All I need now is a broken hip." He staggered over to his bed and lit the night lamp. Yes, the eyeglasses were lying where he had left them. He felt dizzy. The walls, the curtains, the dresser, the envelope all jerked and whirled like a blurry image on television. Am I going blind or what? he wondered. He sat and waited for the dizziness to pass. He barely had the strength to open the envelope. The note was written in pencil, the lines were crooked, and the Yiddish words badly spelled. It read:

> Dear Harry, forgive me. I must go where my husband is. If it's not too much trouble, say Kaddish for me. I'll intercede for you where I'm going.
>
> Ethel

He put the sheet of paper and his glasses down on the night table and switched off the lamp. He lay belching and hiccuping. His body twitched, and the bedsprings vibrated. Well, from now on I won't hope for anything, he decided with the solemnity of a man taking an oath. He felt cold, and he covered himself with the blanket.

It was ten past eight in the morning when he came out of his daze. A dream? No, the letter lay on the table. That day Harry Bendiner did not go down for his mail. He did not prepare breakfast for himself, nor did he bother to bathe and dress. He kept on dozing on the plastic chaise on the balcony and thinking about that other Sylvia—Ethel's daughter—who was living in a tent in British Columbia. Why had she run away so far? he asked himself. Did her father's death drive her into despair? Could she not stand her mother? Or did she already at her age realize the futility of all human efforts and decide to become a hermit? Is she endeavoring to discover herself, or God? An adventurous idea came into the old man's mind: to fly to British Columbia, find the young woman in the wilderness, comfort her, be a father to her, and perhaps try to meditate together with her on why a man is born and why he must die.

QUESTIONS

1. Are aging and death the only themes present in "Old Love"? Is there another kind of love under discussion here? Explain.

2. What is indicated by the fact that Ethel once lived near Harry's hometown, Kowal?

3. What is symbolized by the two Sylvias?

4. What is implied by Harry's final thoughts in the story? How do they relate to the title?

5. Who or what does Ethel symbolize when she appears to change before Harry's eyes?

6. Describe the mood of the story. What irony also is present?

TOPICS FOR WRITING

1. Analyze Singer's complex attitude toward aging and memory in this story. In this context, what is meant by old love?

2. Singer often uses elements that are religious and mystical. Point out these elements and describe their meaning and purpose in this story.

Richard Wright

THE MAN WHO WAS
ALMOST A MAN

Richard Wright (1908–1960) was born on a cotton plantation near Natchez, Mississippi. Wright was 5 when his father, a mill worker, abandoned the family. His childhood, vividly recorded in his autobiography, Black Boy *(1945), was characterized by persistent poverty, hardship, wanderings, and, following his mother's paralysis from strokes, intermittent stays in foster homes and orphanages. After working for a time in Memphis, Wright went to Chicago in 1927, joined the Communist party, and began to write, gaining his first recognition as a short story writer. In 1940, Wright published his first and most famous novel,* Native Son. *This novel is a brutal, naturalistic account of Bigger Thomas, a young black man victimized by his own blind impulses and by white society. Wright went into exile in France in 1947 and lived there until his death. His later work, still largely neglected, includes an account of his disenchantment with communism,* The God That Failed *(1950); two mildly existentialist novels,* The Outsider *(1953) and* The Long Dream *(1958); and an analysis of emerging nations in west Africa and the end of colonialism,* Black Power *(1954). Some of Wright's stories are collected in* Uncle Tom's Children *(1938) and* Eight Men *(1961). Referring to the black American experience, Wright in* 12 Million Black Voices *(1941) declared, "The seasons of the plantation no longer dictate the lives of many of us." In the following story, the author traces the meaning of this statement in the rebellion—part conscious and part unconscious—of 17-year-old Dave Saunders, who by the end of the tale will strike out from the modern plantation toward a new but undetermined life.*

Dave struck out across the fields, looking homeward through paling light. Whut's the use talkin wid 'em niggers in the field? Anyhow, his mother was putting supper on the table. Them niggers can't understan nothing. One of these days he was going to get a gun and practice shooting, then they couldn't talk to him as though he were a little boy. He slowed, looking at the ground. Shucks, Ah ain scareda them even ef they are biggern me! Aw, Ah know whut Ahma do. Ahm going by ol Joe's sto n git that Sears Roebuck catlog n look at them guns. Mebbe Ma will lemme buy one when she gits mah pay from ol man Hawkins. Ahma beg her t gimme some money. Ahm ol ernough to hava gun. Ahm seventeen. Almost a man. He strode, feeling his long loose-jointed limbs. Shucks, a man oughta hava little gun aftah he done worked hard all day.

He came in sight of Joe's store. A yellow lantern glowed on the front porch. He mounted steps and went through the screen door, hearing it bang behind him. There was a strong smell of coal oil and mackerel fish. He felt very confident until he saw fat Joe walk in through the rear door, then his courage began to ooze.

"Howdy, Dave! Whutcha want?"

"How yuh, Mistah Joe? Aw, Ah don wanna buy nothing. Ah jus wanted t see ef yuhd lemme look at tha catlog erwhile."

"Sure! You wanna see it here?"

"Nawsuh, Ah wans t take it home wid me. Ah'll bring it back termorrow when Ah come in from the fiels."

"You plannin on buying something?"

"Yessuh."

"Your ma lettin you have your own money now?"

"Shucks. Mistah Joe, Ahm gittin t be a man like anybody else!"

Joe laughed and wiped his greasy white face with a red bandanna.

"Whut you plannin on buyin?"

Dave looked at the floor, scratched his head, scratched his thigh, and smiled. Then he looked up shyly.

"Ah'll tell yuh, Mistah Joe, ef yuh promise yuh won't tell."

"I promise."

"Waal, Ahma buy a gun."

"A gun? Whut you want with a gun?"

"Ah wanna keep it."

"You ain't nothing but a boy. You don't need a gun."

"Aw, lemme have the catlog, Mistah Joe. Ah'll bring it back."

Joe walked through the rear door. Dave was elated. He looked around at barrels of sugar and flour. He heard Joe coming back. He craned his neck to see if he was bringing the book. Yeah, he's got it. Gawddog, he's got it!

"Here, but be sure you bring it back. It's the only one I got."

"Sho, Mistah Joe."

"Say, if you wanna buy a gun, why don't you buy one from me? I gotta gun to sell."

"Will it shoot?"

"Sure it'll shoot."

"Whut kind is it?"

"Oh, it's kinda old . . . a left-handed Wheeler. A pistol. A big one."

"Is it got bullets in it?"

"It's loaded."

"Kin Ah see it?"

"Where's your money?"

"Whut yuh wan fer it?"

"I'll let you have it for two dollars."

"Just two dollahs? Shucks, Ah could buy tha when Ah git mah pay."

"I'll have it here when you want it."

"Awright, suh. Ah be in fer it."

He went through the door, hearing it slam again behind him. Ahma git some money from Ma n buy me a gun! Only two dollahs! He tucked the thick catalogue under his arm and hurried.

"Where yuh been, boy?" His mother held a steaming dish of black-eyed peas.

"Aw, Ma, Ah jus stopped down the road t talk wid the boys."

"Yuh know bettah t keep suppah waitin."

He sat down, resting the catalogue on the edge of the table.

"Yuh git up from there and git to the well n wash yosef! Ah ain feedin no hogs in mah house!"

She grabbed his shoulder and pushed him. He stumbled out of the room, then came back to get the catalogue.

"Whut this?"

"Aw, Ma, it's jusa catlog."

"Who yuh git it from?"

"From Joe, down at the sto."

"Waal, thas good. We kin use it in the outhouse."

"Naw, Ma." He grabbed for it. "Gimme ma catlog, Ma."

She held onto it and glared at him.

"Quit hollerin at me! Whut's wrong wid yuh? Yuh crazy?"

"But Ma, please. It ain mine! It's Joe's! He tol me t bring it back t im termorrow."

She gave up the book. He stumbled down the back steps, hugging the thick book under his arm. When he had splashed water on his face and hands, he groped back to the kitchen and fumbled in a corner for the towel. He bumped into a chair; it clattered to the floor. The catalogue sprawled at his feet. When he had dried his eyes he snatched up the book and held it again under his arm. His mother stood watching him.

"Now, ef yuh gonna act a fool over that ol book, Ah'll take it n burn it up."

"Naw, Ma, please."

"Waal, set down n be still!"

He sat down and drew the oil lamp close. He thumbed page after page, unaware of the food his mother set on the table. His father came in. Then his small brother.

"Whutcha got there, Dave?" his father asked.

"Jusa catlog," he answered, not looking up.

"Yeah, here they is!" His eyes glowed at blue-and-black revolvers. He glanced up, feeling sudden guilt. His father was watching him. He eased the book under the table and rested it on his knees. After the blessing was asked, he ate. He scooped up peas and swallowed fat meat without chewing. Buttermilk helped to wash it down. He did not want to mention money before his father. He would do much better by cornering his mother when she was alone. He looked at his father uneasily out of the edge of his eye.

"Boy, how come yuh don quit foolin wid tha book n eat yo suppah?"

"Yessuh."

"How you n old man Hawkins gitten erlong?"

"Suh?"

"Can't yuh hear? Why don yuh lissen? As ast yu how wuz yuh n ol man Hawkins gittin erlong?"

"Oh, swell, Pa. Ah plows mo lan than anybody over there."

"Waal, yuh oughta keep yo mind on whut yuh doin."

"Yessuh."

He poured his plate full of molasses and sopped it up slowly with a chunk of cornbread. When his father and brother had left the kitchen, he still sat and looked again at the guns in the catalogue, longing to muster courage enough to present his case to his mother. Lawd, ef Ah only had tha pretty one! He could almost feel the slickness of the weapon with his fingers. If he had a gun like that he would polish it and keep it shining so it would never rust. N Ah'd keep it loaded, by Gawd!

"Ma?" His voice was hesitant.

"Hunh?"

"Ol man Hawkins give yuh mah money yit?"

"Yeah, but ain no usa yuh thinking bout throwin nona it erway. Ahme keepin tha money sos yuh kin have cloes t go to school this winter."

He rose and went to her side with the open catalogue in his palms. She was washing dishes, her head bent low over a pan. Shyly he raised the book. When he spoke, his voice was husky, faint.

"Ma, Gawd knows Ah wans one of these."

"One of whut?" she asked, not raising her eyes.

"One of these," he said again, not daring even to point. She glanced up at the page, then at him with wide eyes.

"Nigger, is yuh gone plumb crazy?"

"Aw, Ma—"

"Git outta here! Don yuh talk to me bout no gun! Yuh a fool!"

"Ma, Ah kin buy one fer two dollahs."

"Not ef Ah knows it, yuh ain!"

"But yuh promised me one—"

"Ah don care whut Ah promised! Yuh ain nothing but a boy yit!"

"Ma, ef yuh lemme buy one Ah'll *never* ast yuh fer nothing no mo."

"Ah tol yuh t git outta here! Yuh ain gonna toucha penny of tha money fer no gun! Thas how come Ah has Mistah Hawkins t pay yo wages t me, cause Ah knows yuh ain got no sense."

"But, Ma, we needa gun. Pa ain got no gun. We needa gun in the house. Yuh kin never tell whut might happen."

"Now don yuh try to maka fool outta me, boy! Ef we did hava gun, yuh wouldn't have it!"

He laid the catalogue down and slipped his arm around her waist.

"Aw, Ma, Ah done worked hard alla summer n ain ast yuh fer nothin, is Ah, now?"

"Thas whut yuh spose t do!"

"But Ma, Ah wans a gun. Yuh kin lemme have two dollahs outta mah money. Please, Ma. I kin give it to Pa . . . Please, Ma! Ah loves yuh, Ma."

When she spoke her voice came soft and low.

"Whut yu wan wida gun, Dave? Yuh don need no gun. Yuh'll git in trouble. N ef yo pa jus thought Ah let yuh have money t buy a gun he'd hava fit."

"I'll hide it, Ma. It ain but two dollahs."

"Lawd, chil, whut's wrong wid yuh?"

"Ain nothin wrong, Ma. Ahm almos a man now. Ah wans a gun."

"Who gonna sell yuh a gun?"

"Ol Joe at the sto."

"N it don cos but two dollahs?"

"Thas all, Ma. Jus two dollahs. Please, Ma."

She was stacking the plates away; her hands moved slowly, reflectively. Dave kept an anxious silence. Finally, she turned to him.

"Ah'll let yuh git tha gun ef yuh promise me one thing."

"Whut's tha, Ma?"

"Yuh bring it straight back t me, yuh hear? It be fer Pa."

"Yessum! Lemme go now, Ma."

She stooped, turned slightly to one side, raised the hem of her dress, rolled down the top of her stocking, and came up with a slender wad of bills.

"Here," she said. "Lawd knows yuh don need no gun. But yer pa does. Yuh bring it right back t me, yuh hear? Ahma put it up. Now ef yuh don, Ahma have yuh pa lick yuh so hard yuh won fergit it."

"Yessum."

He took the money, ran down the steps, and across the yard.

"Dave! Yuuuuuh Daaaaave!"

He heard, but he was not going to stop now. "Naw, Lawd!"

The first movement he made the following morning was to reach under his pillow for the gun. In the gray light of dawn he held it loosely, feeling a sense of power. Could kill a man with a gun like this. Kill anybody, black or white. And if he were holding his gun in his hand, nobody could run over him; they would have to respect him. It was a big gun, with a long barrel and a heavy handle. He raised and lowered it in his hand, marveling at its weight.

He had not come straight home with it as his mother had asked; instead he had stayed out in the fields, holding the weapon in his hand, aiming it now and then at some imaginary foe. But he had not fired it; he had been afraid that his father might hear. Also he was not sure he knew how to fire it.

To avoid surrendering the pistol he had not come into the house until he knew that they were all asleep. When his mother had tiptoed to his bedside late that night and demanded the gun, he had first played possum; then he had told her that the gun was hidden outdoors, that he would bring it to her in the morning. Now he lay turning it slowly in his hands. He broke it, took out the cartridges, felt them, and then put them back.

He slid out of bed, got a long strip of old flannel from a trunk, wrapped the gun in it, and tied it to his naked thigh while it was still loaded. He did not go in to breakfast. Even though it was not yet daylight, he started for Jim Hawkins' plantation. Just as the sun was rising he reached the barns where the mules and plows were kept.

"Hey! That you, Dave?"

He turned. Jim Hawkins stood eying him suspiciously.

"What're yuh doing here so early?"

"Ah didn't know Ah wuz gittin up so early, Mistah Hawkins. Ah wuz fixin t hitch up ol Jenny n take her t the fiels."

"Good. Since you're so early, how about plowing that stretch down by the woods?"

"Suits me, Mistah Hawkins."

"O.K. Go to it!"

He hitched Jenny to a plow and started across the fields. Hot dog! This was just what he wanted. If he could get down by the woods, he could shoot his gun and nobody would hear. He walked behind the plow, hearing the traces creaking, feeling the gun tied tight to his thigh.

When he reached the woods, he plowed two whole rows before he decided to take out the gun. Finally, he stopped, looked in all directions, then untied the gun and held it in his hand. He turned to the mule and smiled.

"Know whut this is, Jenny? Naw, yuh wouldn know! Yuhs jusa ol mule! Anyhow, this is a gun, n it kin shoot, by Gawd!"

He held the gun at arm's length. Whut t hell, Ahma shoot this thing! He looked at Jenny again.

"Lissen here, Jenny! When Ah pull this ol trigger, Ah don wan yuh t run n acka fool now!"

Jenny stood with head down, her short ears pricked straight. Dave walked off about twenty feet, held the gun far out from him at arm's length, and turned his head. Hell, he told himself, Ah ain afraid. The gun felt loose in his fingers; he waved it wildly for a moment. Then he shut his eyes and tightened his forefinger. Bloom! A report half deafened him and he thought his right hand was torn from his arm. He heard Jenny whinnying and galloping over the field, and he found himself on his knees, squeezing his fingers hard between his legs. His hand was numb; he jammed it into his mouth, trying to warm it, trying to stop the pain. The gun lay at his feet. He did not quite know what had happened. He stood up and stared at the gun as though it were a living thing. He gritted his teeth and kicked the gun. Yuh almos broke mah arm! He turned to look for Jenny; she was far over the fields, tossing her head and kicking wildly.

"Hol on there, ol mule!"

When he caught up with her she stood trembling, walling her big white eyes at him. The plow was far away; the traces had broken. Then Dave stopped short, looking, not believing. Jenny was bleeding. Her left side was red and wet with blood. He went closer. Lawd, have mercy! Wondah did Ah shoot this mule? He grabbed for Jenny's mane. She flinched, snorted, whirled, tossing her head.

"Hol on now! Hol on."

Then he saw the hole in Jenny's side, right between the ribs. It was round, wet, red. A crimson stream streaked down the front leg, flowing fast, Good Gawd! Ah wuzn't shootin at tha mule. He felt panic. He knew he had to stop that blood, or Jenny would bleed to death. He had never seen so much blood in all his life. He chased the mule for half a mile, trying to catch her. Finally she stopped, breathing hard, stumpy tail half arched. He caught her mane and led her back to where the plow and gun lay. Then he stooped and grabbed handfuls of damp black earth and tried to plug the bullet hole. Jenny shuddered, whinnied, and broke from him.

"Hol on! Hol on now!"

He tried to plug it again, but blood came anyhow. His fingers were hot and sticky. He rubbed dirt into his palms, trying to dry them. Then again he attempted to plug the bullet hole, but Jenny shied away, kicking her heels high. He stood helpless. He had to do something. He ran at Jenny; she dodged him. He watched a red stream of blood flow down Jenny's leg and form a bright pool at her feet.

"Jenny . . . Jenny," he called weakly.

His lips trembled. She's bleeding t death! He looked in the direction of home, wanting to go back, wanting to get help. But he saw the pistol lying in the damp black clay. He had a queer feeling that if he only did something, this would not be; Jenny would not be there bleeding to death.

When he went to her this time, she did not move. She stood with sleepy, dreamy eyes; and when he touched her she gave a low-pitched whinny and knelt to the ground, her front knees slopping in blood.

"Jenny . . . Jenny . . ." he whispered.

For a long time she held her neck erect; then her head sank, slowly. Her ribs swelled with a mighty heave and she went over.

Dave's stomach felt empty, very empty. He picked up the gun and held it gingerly between his thumb and forefinger. He buried it at the foot of a tree. He took a stick and tried to cover the pool of blood with dirt—but what was the use? There was Jenny lying with her mouth open and her eyes walled and glassy. He could not tell Jim Hawkins he had shot his mule. But he had to tell something. Yeah, Ah'll tell en Jenny started gittin wil n fell on the joint of the plow. . . . But that would hardly happen to a mule. He walked across the field slowly, head down.

It was sunset. Two of Jim Hawkins' men were over near the edge of the woods digging a hole in which to bury Jenny. Dave was surrounded by a knot of people, all of whom were looking down at the dead mule.

"I don't see how in the world it happened," said Jim Hawkins for the tenth time.

The crowd parted and Dave's mother, father, and small brother pushed into the center.

"Where Dave?" his mother called.

"There he is," said Jim Hawkins.

His mother grabbed him.

"What happened, Dave? Whut yuh done?"

"Nothin."

"C mon, boy, talk," his father said.

Dave took a deep breath and told the story he knew nobody believed.

"Waal," he drawled. "Ah brung ol Jenny down here sos Ah could do mah plowin. Ah plowed bout two rows, just like yuh see." He stopped and pointed at the long rows of upturned earth. "Then somethin musta been wrong wid ol Jenny. She wouldn ack right a-tall. She started snortin n kickin her heels. Ah tried t hol her, but she pulled erway, rearin n goin in. Then when the point of the plow was stickin up in the air, she swung erroun n twisted herself back on it . . . She stuck herself n started t bleed. N fo Ah could do anything, she wuz dead."

"Did you ever hear of anything like that in all your life?" asked Jim Hawkins.

There were white and black standing in the crowd. They murmured. Dave's mother came close to him and looked hard into his face. "Tell the truth, Dave," she said.

"Looks like a bullet hole to me," said one man.

"Dave, whut yuh do wid the gun?" his mother asked.

The crowd surged in, looking at him. He jammed his hands into his pockets, shook his head slowly from left to right, and backed away. His eyes were wide and painful.

"Did he hava gun?" asked Jim Hawkins.

"By Gawd, Ah tol yuh that wuz a gun wound," said a man, slapping his thigh.

His father caught his shoulders and shook him till his teeth rattled.

"Tell whut happened, yuh rascal! Tell whut . . ."

Dave looked at Jenny's stiff legs and began to cry.

"Whut yuh do wid tha gun?" his mother asked.

"Whut wuz he doin wida gun?" his father asked.

"Come on and tell the truth." said Hawkins. "Ain't nobody going to hurt you . . ."

His mother crowded close to him.

"Did yuh shoot tha mule, Dave?"

Dave cried, seeing blurred white and black faces.

"Ahh ddinn gggo tt sshooot hher . . . Ah sssswear ffo Gawd Ahh ddin. . . . Ah wuz a-tryin t sssee ef the old gggun would sshoot—"

"Where yuh git the gun from?" his father asked.

"Ah got it from Joe, at the sto."

"Where yuh git the money?"

"Ma give it t me."

"He kept worryin me, Bob. Ah had t. Ah tol im t bring the gun right back t me . . . It was fer yuh, the gun."

"But how yuh happen to shoot that mule?" asked Jim Hawkins.

"Ah wuzn shootin at the mule, Mistah Hawkins. The gun jumped when Ah pulled the trigger . . . N fo Ah knowed anythin Jenny was there a-bleedin."

Somebody in the crowd laughed. Jim Hawkins walked close to Dave and looked into his face.

"Well, looks like you have bought you a mule, Dave."

"Ah swear fo Gawd, Ah didn go t kill the mule, Mistah Hawkins!"

"But you killed her!"

All the crowd was laughing now. They stood on tiptoe and poked heads over one another's shoulders.

"Well, boy, look like yuh done bought a dead mule! Hahaha!"

"Ain tha ershame."

"Hohohohoho."

Dave stood, head down, twisting his feet in the dirt.

"Well, you needn't worry about it, Bob," said Jim Hawkins to Dave's father. "Just let the boy keep on working and pay me two dollars a month."

"Whut yuh wan fer yo mule, Mistah Hawkins?"

Jim Hawkins screwed up his eyes.

"Fifty dollars."

"Whut yuh do wid tha gun?" Dave's father demanded.

Dave said nothing.

"Yuh wan me t take a tree n beat yuh till yuh talk!"

"Nawsuh!"

"Whut yuh do wid it?"

"Ah throwed it erway."

"Where?"

"Ah . . . Ah throwed it in the creek."

"Waal, c mon home. N firs thing in the mawnin git to tha creek n fin tha gun."

"Yessuh."

"What yuh pay fer it?"

"Two dollahs."

"Take tha gun n git yo money back n carry it t Mistah Hawkins, yuh hear? N don fergit Ahma lam you black bottom good fer this! Now march yosef on home, suh!"

Dave turned and walked slowly. He heard people laughing. Dave glared, his eyes welling with tears. Hot anger bubbled in him. Then he swallowed and stumbled on.

That night Dave did not sleep. He was glad that he had gotten out of killing the mule so easily, but he was hurt. Something hot seemed to turn over inside him each time he remembered how they laughed. He tossed on his bed, feeling his hard pillow. N Pa says he's gonna beat me . . . He remembered other beatings, and his back quivered. Naw, naw, Ah sho don wan im t beat me tha way no mo. Dam em all! Nobody ever gave him anything. All he did was work. They treat me like a mule, n then they beat me. He gritted his teeth. N Ma had t tell on me.

Well, if he had to, he would take old man Hawkins that two dollars. But that meant selling the gun. And he wanted to keep that gun. Fifty dollars for a dead mule.

He turned over, thinking how he had fired the gun. He had an itch to fire it again. Ef other men kin shoota gun, by Gawd, Ah kin! He was still, listening. Mebbe they all sleepin now. The house was still. He heard the soft breathing of his brother. Yes, now! He would go down and get that gun and see if he could fire it! He eased out of bed and slipped into overalls.

The moon was bright. He ran almost all the way to the edge of the woods. He stumbled over the ground, looking for the spot where he had buried the gun. Yeah, here it is. Like a hungry dog scratching for a bone, he pawed it up. He puffed his black cheeks and blew dirt from the trigger and barrel. He broke it and found four cartridges unshot. He looked around; the fields were filled with silence and moonlight. He clutched the gun stiff and hard in his fingers. But, as soon as he wanted to pull the trigger, he shut his eyes and turned his head. Naw, Ah can't shoot wid mah eyes closed n mah head turned. With effort he held his eyes open; then he squeezed. *Blooooom!* He was stiff, not breathing. The gun was still in his hands. Dammit, he'd done it. He fired again. *Blooooom!* He smiled. *Blooooom! Blooooom! Click, click.* There! It was empty. If anybody could shoot a gun, he could. He put the gun into his hip pocket and started across the fields.

When he reached the top of a ridge he stood straight and proud in the moonlight, looking at Jim Hawkins' big white house, feeling the gun sagging in his pocket. Lawd, ef Ah had just one mo bullet Ah'd taka shot at tha house. Ah'd like t scare ol man Hawkins jusa little . . . Jusa enough t let im know Dave Saunders is a man.

To his left the road curved, running to the tracks of the Illinois Central. He jerked his head, listening. From far off came a faint *hoooof-hoooof; hoooof-hoooof; hoooof-hoooof.* . . . He stood rigid. Two dollahs a mont. Les see now . . . Tha means it'll take bout two years. Shucks! Ah'll be dam!

He started down the road, toward the tracks. Yeah, here she comes! He stood beside the track and held himself stiffly. Here she comes, erroun the ben . . . C mon, yuh slow poke! C mon! He had his hand on his gun; something quivered in his stomach. Then the train thundered past, the gray and brown box cars rumbling and clinking. He gripped the gun tightly; then he jerked his hand out of his pocket. Ah betcha Bill wouldn't do it! Ah betcha . . . The cars slid past, steel grinding upon steel. Ahm ridin yuh ternight, so hep me Gawd! He was hot all over. He hesitated just a moment; then he grabbed, pulled atop of a car, and lay flat. He felt his pocket; the gun was still there. Ahead the long rails were glinting in the moonlight, stretching away, away to somewhere, somewhere where he could be a man . . .

QUESTIONS

1. What is the importance of the setting to the development of the major conflicts in this story? How does the setting affect Dave's motivations and behavior?

2. Why does Dave want to own a gun? What ironies does Wright develop from the central character's desire for a gun? How does the gun itself serve to define Dave's relationship to other characters in the story?

3. How do dialogue and point of view help to capture Dave's emerging personality? Why is he so rebellious? What are some of the implications of this rebelliousness? How much does he understand about the sources or causes of his revolt?

4. Explain the importance of the secondary characters in the story—notably Dave's mother and father, Jim Hawkins, Joe, and the crowd that assembles at the site of the dead mule.

5. Why does Dave hop aboard the train at the end of the story? How does the ending connect with the inadvertent killing of the mule? What might Wright be saying about our fate?

6. What is the theme of the story?

7. Does Dave become a man in the course of the tale? Defend your answer.

TOPICS FOR WRITING

1. Analyze the causes and effects of Dave's conscious and unconscious rebellions in "The Man Who Was Almost a Man."

2. Explain the social and economic world depicted by Wright in the story.

3. Explore the significance—some of it symbolic—of the gun in the tale.

4. Compare and contrast character, setting, mood, and theme in Wrights's "The Man Who Was Almost a Man" and Bontemp's "A Summer Tragedy" (pages 135–142).

Eudora Welty

POWERHOUSE

Eudora Welty (1909–   ) in her previous story herein (page 143) presented us with a character almost completely in isolation, both physical and mental. When Phoenix Jackson meets someone else, even in the city, that mood of isolation lingers. In "Powerhouse," we find once again that sense of isolation. Although the story echoes with music and crowd noises, another world exists beyond these, and Powerhouse has a slender relationship with it. Some critics have called this story "mysterious" and "mythological," but Welty herself says, "I had no wish to sound mystical, but did expect to sound mysterious now and then." In "Powerhouse" mood and tone enhance the theme.

Powerhouse is playing!

He's here on tour from the city—"Powerhouse and His Keyboard"—"Powerhouse and His Tasmanians"—think of the things he calls himself! There's no one in the world like him. You can't tell what he is. "Nigger man"?—he looks more Asiatic, monkey, Jewish, Babylonian, Peruvian, fanatic, devil. He has pale gray eyes, heavy lids, maybe horny like a lizard's, but big glowing eyes when they're open. He has African feet of the greatest size, stomping, both together, on each side of the pedals. He's not coal black—beverage colored—looks like a preacher when his mouth is shut, but then it opens—vast and obscene. And his mouth is going every minute: like a monkey's when it looks for something. Improvising, coming on a light and childish melody—*smooch*—he loves it with his mouth.

Is it possible that he could be this! When you have him there performing for you, that's what you feel. You know people on a stage—and people of a darker race—so likely to be marvelous, frightening.

This is a white dance. Powerhouse is not a show-off like the Harlem boys, not drunk, not crazy—he's in a trance; he's a person of joy, a fanatic. He listens as much as he performs, a look of hideous, powerful rapture on his face. Big arched eyebrows that never stop traveling, like a Jew's—wandering-Jew eyebrows. When he plays he beats down piano and seat and wears them away. He is in motion every moment—what could be more obscene? There he is with his great head, fat stomach, and little round piston legs, and long yellow-sectioned strong big fingers, at rest about the size of bananas. Of course you know how he sounds—you've heard him on records—but still you need to see him. He's going all the time, like skating around the skating rink or rowing a boat. It makes everybody crowd around, here in this shadowless steel-trussed hall with the rose-like posters of Nelson Eddy and the testimonial for the mind-reading horse in handwriting magnified five hundred times. Then all quietly he lays his fingers on a key with the promise and serenity of a sibyl touching the book.

Powerhouse is so monstrous he sends everybody into oblivion. When any group, any performers, come to town, don't people always come out and hover near, leaning inward about them, to learn what it is? What is it? Listen. Remember how it was with the acrobats. Watch them carefully, hear the least word, especially what they say to one another, in another language—don't let them escape you; it's the only time for hallucination, the last time. They can't stay. They'll be somewhere else this time tomorrow.

Powerhouse has as much as possible done by signals. Everybody, laughing as if to hide a weakness, will sooner or later hand him up a written request. Powerhouse reads each one, studying with a secret face: that is the face which looks like a mask—anybody's; there is a moment when he makes a decision. Then a light slides under his eyelids, and he says, "92!" or some combination of figures—never a name. Before a number the band is all frantic, misbehaving, pushing, like children in a schoolroom, and he is the teacher getting silence. His hands over the keys, he says sternly, "You-all ready? You-all ready to do some serious walking?"—waits—then, STAMP. Quiet. STAMP, for the second time. This is absolute. Then a set of rhythmic kicks against the floor to communicate the tempo. Then, O Lord! say the distended eyes from beyond the boundary of the trumpets, Hello and good-bye, and they are all down the first note like a waterfall.

This note marks the end of any known discipline. Powerhouse seems to abandon them all—he himself seems lost—down in the song, yelling up like somebody in a whirlpool—not guiding them—hailing them only. But he knows, really. He cries out, but he must know exactly. "Mercy! . . . What I say! . . . Yeah!" And then drifting, listening—"Where that skin beater?"—wanting drums, and starting up and pouring it out in the greatest delight and brutality. On the sweet pieces such a leer for everybody! He looks down so benevolently upon all our faces and whispers the lyrics to us. And if you could hear him at this moment on "Marie, the Dawn is Breaking"! He's going up the keyboard with a few fingers in some very derogatory triplet-routine, he gets higher and higher, and then he looks over the end of the piano, as if over a cliff. But not in a show-off way—the song makes him do it.

He loves the way they all play, too—all those next to him. The far section of the band is all studious, wearing glasses, every one—they don't count. Only those playing around Powerhouse are the real ones. He has a bass fiddler from Vicksburg, black as pitch, named Valentine, who plays with his eyes shut and talking to himself, very young: Powerhouse has to keep encouraging him. "Go on, go on, give it up, bring it on out there!" When you heard him like that on records, did you know he was really pleading?

He calls Valentine out to take a solo.

"What you going to play?" Powerhouse looks out kindly from behind the piano; he opens his mouth and shows his tongue, listening.

Valentine looks down, drawing against his instrument, and says without a lip movement, "'Honeysuckle Rose.'"

He has a clarinet player named Little Brother, and loves to listen to anything he does. He'll smile and say, "Beautiful!" Little Brother takes a step forward when he plays and stands at the very front, with the whites of his eyes like fishes swimming. Once when he played a low note, Powerhouse muttered in dirty praise, "He went clear downstairs to get that one!"

After a long time, he holds up the number of fingers to tell the band how many choruses still to go—usually five. He keeps his directions down to signals.

It's a bad night outside. It's a white dance, and nobody dances, except a few straggling jitterbugs and two elderly couples. Everybody just stands around the band and watches Powerhouse. Sometimes they steal glances at one another, as if to say, Of course, you know how it is with *them*—Negroes—band leaders—they would play the same way, giving all they've got, for an audience of one. . . . When somebody, no matter who, gives everything, it makes people feel ashamed for him.

Late at night they play the one waltz they will ever consent to play—by request, "Pagan Love Song." Powerhouse's head rolls and sinks like a weight between his waving shoulders. He groans, and his fingers drag into the keys heavily, holding on to the notes, retrieving. It is a sad song.

"You know what happened to me?" says Powerhouse.

Valentine hums a response, dreaming at the bass.

"I got a telegram my wife is dead," says Powerhouse, with wandering fingers.

"Uh-huh?"

His mouth gathers and forms a barbarous O while his fingers walk up straight, unwillingly, three octaves.

"Gypsy? Why how come her to die, didn't you just phone her up in the night last night long distance?"

"Telegram say—here the words: Your wife is dead." He puts 4/4 over the 3/4.

"Not but four words?" This is the drummer, an unpopular boy named Scoot, a disbelieving maniac.

Powerhouse is shaking his vast cheeks. "What the hell was she trying to do? What was she up to?"

"What name has it got signed, if you got a telegram?" Scoot is spitting away with those wire brushes.

Little Brother, the clarinet player, who cannot now speak, glares and tilts back.

"Uranus Knockwood is the name signed." Powerhouse lifts his eyes open. "Ever heard of him?" A bubble shoots out on his lip like a plate on a counter.

Valentine is beating slowly on with his palm and scratching the strings with his long blue nails. He is fond of a waltz, Powerhouse interrupts him.

"I don't know him. Don't know who he is." Valentine shakes his head with the closed eyes.

"Say it again."

"Uranus Knockwood."

"That ain't Lenox Avenue."

"It ain't Broadway."

"Ain't ever seen it wrote out in any print, even for horse racing."

"Hell, that's on a star, boy, ain't it?" Crash of the cymbals.

"What the hell was she up to?" Powerhouse shudders. "Tell me, tell me, tell me." He makes triplets, and begins a new chorus. He holds three fingers up.

"You say you got a telegram." This is Valentine, patient and sleepy, beginning again.

Powerhouse is elaborate. "Yas, the time I go out, go way downstairs along a long cor-ri-dor to where they puts us: coming back along the cor-ri-dor: steps out and hands me a telegram: Your wife is dead."

"Gypsy?" The drummer like a spider over his drums.

"Aaaaaaaaa!" shouts Powerhouse, flinging out both powerful arms for three whole beats to flex his muscles, then kneading a dough of bass notes. His eyes glitter. He plays the piano like a drum sometimes—why not?

"Gypsy? Such a dancer?"

"Why you don't hear it straight from your agent? Why it ain't come from headquarters? What you been doing, getting telegrams in the *corridor*, signed nobody?"

They all laugh. End of that chorus.

"What time is it?" Powerhouse calls. "What the hell place is this? Where is my watch and chain?"

"I hang it on you," whimpers Valentine. "It still there."

There it rides on Powerhouse's great stomach, down where he can never see it.

"Sure did hear some clock striking twelve while ago. Must be *midnight*."

"It going to be intermission," Powerhouse declares, lifting up his finger with the signet ring.

He draws the chorus to an end. He pulls a big Northern hotel towel out of the deep pocket in his vast, special-cut tux pants and pushes his forehead into it.

"If she went and killed herself!" he says with a hidden face. "If she up and jumped out that window!" He gets to his feet, turning vaguely, wearing the towel on his head.

"Ha, ha!"

"Sheik, sheik!"

"She wouldn't do that." Little Brother sets down his clarinet like a precious vase, and speaks. He still looks like an East Indian queen, implacable, divine, and full of snakes. "You ain't going to expect people doing what they says over long distance."

"Come on!" roars Powerhouse. He is already at the back door, he has pulled it wide open, and with a wild, gathered-up face is smelling the terrible night.

Powerhouse, Valentine, Scoot and Little Brother step outside into the drenching rain.

"Well, they emptying buckets," says Powerhouse in a mollified voice. On the street he holds his hands out and turns up the blanched palms like sieves.

A hundred dark, ragged, silent, delighted Negroes have come around from under the eaves of the hall, and follow wherever they go.

"Watch out Little Brother don't shrink," says Powerhouse. "You just the right size now, clarinet don't suck you in. You got a dry throat, Little Brother, you in the desert?" He reaches into the pocket and pulls out a paper of mints. "Now hold 'em in your mouth—don't chew 'em. I don't carry around nothing without limit."

"Go in that joint and have beer," says Scoot, who walks ahead.

"Beer? Beer? You know what beer is? What do they say is beer? What's beer? Where I been?"

"Down yonder where it say World Café—that do?" They are in Negrotown now.

Valentine patters over and holds open a screen door warped like a sea shell, bitter in the wet, and they walk in, stained darker with the rain and leaving footprints. Inside, sheltered dry smells stand like screens around a table covered with a red-checkered cloth, in the center of which flies hang onto an obelisk-shaped ketchup bottle. The midnight walls are checkered again with admonishing "Not Responsible" signs and black-figured, smoky calendars. It is a waiting, silent, limp room. There is a burned-out-looking nickelodeon and right beside it a long-necked wall instrument labeled "Business Phone, Don't Keep Talking." Circled phone numbers are written up everywhere. There is a worn-out peacock feather hanging by a thread to an old, thin, pink exposed light bulb, where it slowly turns around and around, whoever breathes.

A waitress watches.

"Come here, living statue, and get all this big order of beer we fixing to give."

"Never seen you before anywhere." The waitress moves and comes forward and slowly shows little gold leaves and tendrils over her teeth. She shoves up her shoulders and breasts. "How I going to know who you might be? Robbers? Coming in out of the black of night right at midnight, setting down so big at my table?"

"Boogers," says Powerhouse, his eyes opening lazily as in a cave.

The girl screams delicately with pleasure. O Lord, she likes talk and scares.

"Where you going to find enough beer to put out on this here table?"

She runs to the kitchen with bent elbows and sliding steps.

"Here's a million nickels," says Powerhouse, pulling his hand out of his pocket and sprinkling coins out, all but the last one, which he makes vanish like a magician.

Valentine and Scoot take the money over to the nickelodeon, which looks as battered as a slot machine, and read all the names of the records out loud.

"Whose 'Tuxedo Junction'?" asks Powerhouse.

"You know whose."

"Nickelodeon, I request you please to play 'Empty Bed Blues' and let Bessie Smith sing."

Silence: they hold it like a measure.

"Bring me all those nickels on back here," says Powerhouse. "Look at that! What you tell me the name of this place?"

"White dance, week night, raining, Alligator, Mississippi, long ways from home."

"Uh-huh."

"Sent for You Yesterday and Here You Come Today" plays.

The waitress, setting the tray of beer down on a back table, comes up taut and apprehensive as a hen. "Says in the kitchen, back there putting their eyes to little hole peeping out, that you is Mr. Powerhouse. . . . They knows from a picture they seen."

"They seeing right tonight, that is him." says Little Brother.

"You him?"

"That is him in the flesh," says Scoot.

"Does you wish to touch him?" asks Valentine. "Because he don't bite."

"You passing through?"

"Now you got everything right."

She waits like a drop, hands languishing together in front.

"Little-Bit, ain't you going to bring the beer?"

She brings it, and goes behind the cash register and smiles, turning different ways. The little fillet of gold in her mouth is gleaming.

"The Mississippi River's here," she says once.

Now all the watching Negroes press in gently and bright-eyed through the door, as many as can get in. One is a little boy in a straw sombrero which has been coated with aluminum paint all over.

Powerhouse, Valentine, Scoot and Little Brother drink beer, and their eyelids come together like curtains. The wall and the rain and the humble beautiful waitress waiting on them and the other Negroes watching enclose them.

"Listen!" whispers Powerhouse, looking into the ketchup bottle and slowly spreading his performer's hands over the damp, wrinkling cloth with the red squares. "Listen how it is. My wife gets missing me. Gypsy. She goes to the window. She looks out and sees you know what. Street. Sign saying Hotel. People walking. Somebody looks up. Old man. She looks down, out the window. Well? . . . *Ssssst! Plooey!* What she do? Jump out and bust her brains all over the world.".

He opens his eyes.

"That's it," agrees Valentine. "You gets a telegram."

"Sure she misses you," Little Brother adds.

"No, it's night time." How softly he tells them! "Sure. It's the night time. She say, What do I hear? Footsteps walking up the hall? That him? Footsteps go on off. It's not me. I'm in Alligator, Mississippi, she's crazy. Shaking all over. Listens till her ears and all grow out like old music-box horns but still she can't hear a thing. She says, All right! I'll jump out the window then. Got on her nightgown. I know that nightgown, and her thinking there. Says, Ho hum, all right, and jumps out the window. Is she mad at me! Is she crazy! She don't leave *nothing* behind her!"

"Ya! Ha!"

"Brains and insides everywhere, Lord, Lord."

All the watching Negroes stir in their delight, and to their higher delight he says affectionately, "Listen! Rats in here."

"That must be the way, boss."

"Only, naw, Powerhouse, that ain't true. That sound too *bad.*"

"Does? I even know who finds her," cries Powerhouse. "That no-good pussyfooted crooning creeper, that creeper that follow around after me, coming up like weeds behind me, following around after me everything I do and messing around on the trail I leave. Bets my numbers, sings my songs, gets close to my agent like a Betsybug; when I going out he just coming in. I got him now! I got my eye on him."

"Know who he is?"

"Why, it's that old Uranus Knockwood!"

"Ya! Ha!"

"Yeah, and he coming now, he going to find Gypsy. There he is, coming around that corner, and Gypsy kadoodling down, oh-oh, watch out! *Ssssst! Plooey!* See, there she is in her little old nightgown, and her insides and brains all scattered round."

A sigh fills the room.

"Hush about her brains. Hush about her insides."

"Ya! Ha! You talking about her brains and insides—old Uranus Knockwood," says Powerhouse, "look down and say Jesus! He say, Look here what I'm walking round in!"

They all burst into halloos of laughter. Powerhouse's face looks like a big hot iron stove.

"Why, he picks her up and carries her off!" he says.

"Ya! Ha!"

"Carries her *back* around the corner. . . ."

"Oh, Powerhouse!"

"You know him."

"Uranus Knockwood!"

"Yeahhh!"

"He take our wives when we gone!"

"He come in when we goes out!"

"Uh-huh!"

"He go out when we comes in!"

"Yeahhh!"

"He standing behind the door!"

"Old Uranus Knockwood."

"You know him."

"Middle-size man."

"Wears a hat."

"That's him."

"Everybody in the room moans with pleasure. The little boy in the fine silver hat opens a paper and divides out a jelly roll among his followers.

And out of the breathless ring somebody moves forward like a slave, leading a great logy Negro with bursting eyes, and says, "This here is Sugar-Stick Thompson, that dove down to the bottom of July Creek and pulled up all those drownded white people fall out of a boat. Last summer, pulled up fourteen."

"Hello," says Powerhouse, turning and looking around at them all with his great daring face until they nearly suffocate.

Sugar-Stick, their instrument, cannot speak; he can only look back at the others.

"Can't even swim. Done it by holding his breath," says the fellow with the hero.

Powerhouse looks at him seekingly.

"I his half brother," the fellow puts in.

They step back.

"Gypsy say," Powerhouse rumbles gently again, looking at *them*, "'What is the use? I'm gonna jump out so far—so far. . . .' *Ssssst—!*"

"Don't, boss, don't do it agin," says Little Brother.

"It's awful," says the waitress. "I hates that Mr. Knockwoods. All that the truth?"

"Want to see the telegram I got from him?" Powerhouse's hand goes to the vast pocket.

"Now wait, now wait, boss." They all watch him.

"It must be the real truth," says the waitress, sucking in her lower lip, her luminous eyes turning sadly, seeking the windows.

"No, babe, it ain't the truth." His eyebrows fly up, and he begins to whisper to her out of his vast oven mouth. His hand stays in his pocket. "Truth is something worse, I ain't said what, yet. It's something hasn't come to me, but I ain't saying it won't. And when it does, then want me to tell you?" He sniffs all at once, his eyes come open and turn up, almost too far. He is dreamily smiling.

"Don't, boss, don't, Powerhouse!"

"Oh!" the waitress screams.

"Go on git out of here!" bellows Powerhouse, taking his hand out of his pocket and clapping after her red dress.

The ring of watchers breaks and falls away.

"*Look* at that! Intermission is up," says Powerhouse.

He folds money under a glass, and after they go out, Valentine leans back in and drops a nickel in the nickelodeon behind them, and it lights up and begins to play "The Goona Goo." The feather dangles still.

"Take a telegram!" Powerhouse shouts suddenly up into the rain over the street. "Take a answer. Now what was that name?"

They get a little tired.

"Uranus Knockwood."

"You ought to know."

"Yas? Spell it to me."

They spell it all the ways it could be spelled. It puts them in a wonderful humor.

"Here's the answer. I got it right here. 'What in the hell you talking about? Don't make any difference: I gotcha.' Name signed: Powerhouse."

"That going to reach him, Powerhouse?" Valentine speaks in a maternal voice.

"Yas, yas."

All hushing, following him up the dark street at a distance, like old rained-on black ghosts, the Negroes are afraid they will die laughing.

Powerhouse throws back his vast head into the steaming rain, and a look of hopeful desire seems to blow somehow like a vapor from his own dilated nostrils over his face and bring a mist to his eyes.

"Reach him and come out the other side."

"That's it, Powerhouse, that's it. You got him now."

Powerhouse lets out a long sigh.

"But ain't you going back there to call up Gypsy long distance, the way you did last night in that other place? I seen a telephone. . . . Just to see if she there at home?"

There is a measure of silence. That is one crazy drummer that's going to get his neck broken some day.

"No," growls Powerhouse. "No! How many thousand times tonight I got to say No?"

He holds up his arm in the rain.

"You sure-enough unroll your voice some night, it about reach up yonder to her," says Little Brother, dismayed.

They go on up the street, shaking the rain off and on them like birds.

Back in the dance hall, they play "San" (99). The jitterbugs start up like windmills stationed over the floor, and in their orbits—one circle, another, a long stretch and a zigzag—dance the elderly couples with old smoothness, undisturbed and stately.

When Powerhouse first came back from intermission, no doubt full of beer, they said, he got the band tuned up again in his own way. He didn't strike the piano keys for pitch—he simply opened his mouth and gave falsetto howls—in A, D and so on—they tuned by him. Then he took hold of the piano, as if he saw it for the first time in his life, and tested it for strength, hit it down in the bass, played an octave with his elbow, lifted the top, looked inside, and leaned against it with all his might. He sat down and played it for a few minutes with outrageous force and got it under his power—a bass deep and coarse as a sea net—then produced something glimmering and fragile, and smiled. And who could ever remember any of the things he says? They are just inspired remarks that roll out of his mouth like smoke.

They've requested "Somebody Loves Me," and he's already done twelve or fourteen choruses, piling them up nobody knows how, and it will be a wonder if he ever gets through. Now and then he calls and shouts, "'Somebody loves me! Somebody loves me, I wonder who!'" His mouth gets to be nothing but a volcano. "I wonder who!"

"Maybe . . ." He uses all his right hand on a trill.

"Maybe . . ." He pulls back his spread fingers, and looks out upon the place where he is. A vast, impersonal and yet furious grimace transfigures his wet face.

". . . Maybe it's you!"

QUESTIONS

1. Why does the author use the present tense instead of the past tense in this story?

2. From which character's perspective is Powerhouse seen in the first four paragraphs?

3. Why does the *narrator* say, "You can't tell what he is," when it soon after becomes quite clear that Powerhouse is a black man? What is the *author* saying here?

4. What influence does Powerhouse hold over the white audience, and in what simple way does he mute that influence? Why does he do this?

5. Why does Powerhouse disclose, when his band is playing the only waltz, that a telegram has arrived announcing the death of his wife? What does this reveal about him?

6. Why must the show go on for Powerhouse? How does this attitude relate to Anderson's in Hemingway's "The Killers" (pages 270–277)?

TOPICS FOR WRITING

1. Explore the behavioral differences between the white dancers and the black observers. Why can't the blacks dance? What does the music signify?

2. Explain why there are changes in the point of view and how this influences the tone and mood of the story.

3. Analyze fully what Powerhouse symbolizes in this story, combining this material with an analysis of Phoenix Jackson in Welty's previous story herein, "A Worn Path" (pages 143–149).

Carson McCullers

THE JOCKEY

Born in Columbus, Georgia, Carson Smith McCullers (1917–1967) grew up in the South but left it to study music at Juilliard in New York. Unable to continue her studies because she lost her tuition money in a subway, McCullers moved into writing and published her first novel, The Heart Is a Lonely Hunter, *in 1940. This allegorical work, which dealt with fascism, gained wide recognition. The following year her experimental and heavily symbolic second novel,* Reflections in a Golden Eye, *was published.* The Member of the Wedding *(1946), which she also dramatized (1950), explored loneliness and isolation, situations McCullers endured personally.* The Ballad of the Sad Cafe *(1951) is a novella and collection of short stories. She not only investigated isolation, but the pursuit of love among young children and society's outcasts. These were major themes in most of her fiction.*

The jockey came to the doorway of the dining room, then after a moment stepped to one side and stood motionless, with his back to the wall. The room was crowded, as this was the third day of the season and all the hotels were full. In the dining room bouquets of August roses scattered their petals on the white table linen and from the adjoining bar came a warm, drunken wash of voices. The jockey waited with his back to the wall and scrutinized the room with pinched, crêpy eyes. He examined the room until at last his eyes reached a table in a corner diagonally across from him, at which three men were sitting. As he watched, the jockey raised his chin and tilted his head back to one side, his dwarfed body grew rigid, and his hands stiffened so that the fingers curled inward like gray claws. Tense against the wall of the dining room, he watched and waited in this way.

He was wearing a suit of green Chinese silk that evening, tailored precisely and the size of a costume for a child. The shirt was yellow, the tie striped with pastel colors. He had no hat with him and wore his hair brushed down in a stiff, wet bang on his forehead. His face was drawn, ageless, and gray. There were shadowed hollows at his temples and his mouth was set in a wiry smile. After a time he was aware that he had been seen by one of the three men he had been watching. But the jockey did not nod; he only raised his chin still higher and hooked the thumb of his tense hand in the pocket of his coat.

The three men at the corner table were a trainer, a bookie, and a rich man. The trainer was Sylvester—a large, loosely built fellow with a flushed nose and slow blue eyes. The bookie was Simmons. The rich man was the owner of a horse named Seltzer, which the jockey had ridden that afternoon. The three of them drank whiskey with soda, and a white-coated waiter had just brought on the main course of the dinner.

It was Sylvester who first saw the jockey. He looked away quickly, put down his whiskey glass, and nervously mashed the tip of his red nose with his thumb. "It's Bitsy Barlow," he said. "Standing over there across the room. Just watching us."

"Oh, the jockey," said the rich man. He was facing the wall and he half turned his head to look behind him. "Ask him over."

"God no," Sylvester said.

"He's crazy," Simmons said. The bookie's voice was flat and without inflection. He had the face of a born gambler, carefully adjusted, the expression a permanent deadlock between fear and greed.

"Well, I wouldn't call him that exactly," said Sylvester. "I've known him a long time. He was O.K. until about six months ago. But if he goes on like this, I can't see him lasting another year. I just can't."

"It was what happened in Miami," said Simmons.

"What?" asked the rich man.

Sylvester glanced across the room at the jockey and wet the corner of his mouth with his red, fleshy tongue. "A accident. A kid got hurt on the track. Broke a leg and a hip. He was a particular pal of Bitsy's. A Irish kid. Not a bad rider, either."

"That's a pity," said the rich man.

"Yeah. They were particular friends," Sylvester said. "You would always find him up in Bitsy's hotel room. They would be playing rummy or else lying on the floor reading the sports page together."

"Well, those things happen," said the rich man.

Simmons cut into his beefsteak. He held his fork prongs downward on the plate and carefully piled on mushrooms with the blade of his knife. "He's crazy," he repeated. "He gives me the creeps."

All the tables in the dining room were occupied. There was a party at the banquet table in the center, and green-white August moths had found their way in from the night and fluttered about the clear candle flames. Two girls wearing flannel slacks and blazers walked arm in arm acorss the room into the bar. From the main street outside came the echoes of holiday hysteria.

"They claim that in August Saratoga is the wealthiest town per capita in the world." Sylvester turned to the rich man. "What do you think?"

"I wouldn't know," said the rich man. "It may very well be so."

Daintily, Simmons wiped his greasy mouth with the tip of his forefinger. "How about Hollywood? And Wall Street——"

"Wait," said Sylvester. "He's decided to come over here."

The jockey had left the wall and was approaching the table in the corner. He walked with a prim strut, swinging out his legs in a half-circle with each step, his heels biting smartly into the red velvet carpet on the floor. On the way over he brushed against the elbow of a fat woman in white satin at the banquet table; he stepped back and bowed with dandified courtesy, his eyes quite closed. When he had crossed the room he drew up a chair and sat at a corner of the table, between Sylvester and the rich man, without a nod of greeting or a change in his set, gray face.

"Had dinner?" Sylvester asked.

"Some people might call it that." The jockey's voice was high, bitter, clear.

Sylvester put his knife and fork down carefully on his plate. The rich man shifted his position, turning sidewise in his chair and crossing his legs. He was dressed in twill riding pants, unpolished boots, and a shabby brown jacket—this was his outfit day and night in the racing season, although he was never seen on a horse. Simmons went on with his dinner.

"Like a spot of seltzer water?" asked Sylvester. "Or something like that?"

The jockey didn't answer. He drew a gold cigarette case from his pocket and snapped it open. Inside were a few cigarettes and a tiny gold penknife. He used the knife to cut a cigarette in half. When he had lighted his smoke he held up his hand to a waiter passing by the table. "Kentucky bourbon, please."

"Now, listen, Kid," said Sylvester.

"Don't Kid me."

"Be reasonable. You know you got to behave reasonable."

The jockey drew up the left corner of his mouth in a stiff jeer. His eyes lowered to the food spread out on the table, but instantly he looked up again. Before the rich man was a fish casserole, baked in a cream sauce and ·garnished with parsley. Sylvester had ordered eggs Benedict. There was asparagus, fresh buttered corn, and a side dish of wet black olives. A plate of French-fried potatoes was in the corner of the table before the jockey. He didn't look at the food again, but kept his pinched eyes on the centerpiece of full-blown lavender roses. "I don't suppose you remember a certain person by the name of McGuire," he said.

"Now, listen," said Sylvester.

The waiter brought the whiskey, and the jockey sat fondling the glass with his small, strong, callused hands. On his wrist was a gold link bracelet that clinked against the table edge. After turning the glass between his palms, the jockey suddenly drank the whiskey neat in two hard swallows. He set down the glass sharply. "No, I don't suppose your memory is that long and extensive," he said.

"Sure enough, Bitsy," said Sylvester. "What makes you act like this? You hear from the kid today?"

"I received a letter," the jockey said. "The certain person we were speaking about was taken out from the cast on Wednesday. One leg is two inches shorter than the other one. That's all."

Sylvester clucked his tongue and shook his head. "I realize how you feel."

"Do you?" The jockey was looking at the dishes on the table. His gaze passed from the fish casserole to the corn, and finally fixed on the plate of fried potatoes. His face tightened and quickly he looked up again. A rose shattered and he picked up one of the petals, bruised it between his thumb and forefinger, and put it in his mouth.

"Well, those things happen," said the rich man.

The trainer and the bookie had finished eating, but there was food left on the serving dishes before their plates. The rich man dipped his buttery fingers in his water glass and wiped them with his napkin.

"Well," said the jockey. "Doesn't somebody want me to pass them something? Or maybe perhaps you desire to reorder. Another hunk of beefsteak, gentlemen, or——"

"Please," said Sylvester. "Be reasonable. Why don't you go on upstairs?"

"Yes, why don't I?" the jockey said.

His prim voice had risen higher and there was about it the sharp whine of hysteria.

"Why don't I go up to my god-damn room and walk around and write some letters and go to bed like a good boy? Why don't I just——" He pushed his chair back and got up. "Oh, foo," he said. "Foo to you. I want a drink."

"All I can say is it's your funeral," said Sylvester. "You know what it does to you. You know well enough."

The jockey crossed the dining room and went into the bar. He ordered a

Manhattan, and Sylvester watched him stand with his heels pressed tight together, his body hard as a lead soldier's, holding his little finger out from the cocktail glass and sipping the drink slowly.

"He's crazy," said Simmons. "Like I said."

Sylvester turned to the rich man. "If he eats a lamb chop, you can see the shape of it in his stomach a hour afterward. He can't sweat things out of him any more. He's a hundred and twelve and a half. He's gained three pounds since we left Miami."

"A jockey shouldn't drink," said the rich man.

"The food don't satisfy him like it used to and he can't sweat it out. If he eats a lamb chop, you can watch it tooching out in his stomach and it don't go down."

The jockey finished his Manhattan. He swallowed, crushed the cherry in the bottom of the glass with his thumb, then pushed the glass away from him. The two girls in blazers were standing at his left, their faces toward each other, and at the other end of the bar two touts had started an argument about which was the highest mountain in the world. Everyone was with somebody else; there was no other person drinking alone that night. The jockey paid with a brand-new fifty-dollar bill and didn't count the change.

He walked back to the dining room and to the table at which the three men were sitting, but he did not sit down. "No, I wouldn't presume to think your memory is that extensive," he said. He was so small that the edge of the table top reached almost to his belt, and when he gripped the corner with his wiry hands he didn't have to stoop. "No, you're too busy gobbling up dinners in dining rooms. You're too——"

"Honestly," begged Sylvester. "You got to behave reasonable."

"Reasonable! Reasonable!" The jockey's gray face quivered, then set in a mean, frozen grin. He shook the table so that the plates rattled, and for a moment it seemed that he would push it over. But suddenly he stopped. His hand reached out toward the plate nearest to him and deliberately he put a few of the French-fried potatoes in his mouth. He chewed slowly, his upper lip raised, then he turned and spat out the pulpy mouthful on the smooth red carpet which covered the floor. "Libertines," he said again, and turned and walked with his rigid swagger out of the dining room.

Sylvester shrugged one of his loose, heavy shoulders. The rich man sopped up some water that had been spilled on the tablecloth, and they didn't speak until the waiter came to clear away.

QUESTIONS

1. What kind of relationship is suggested between the jockey, Bitsy Barlow, and the injured jockey, McGuire?

2. Which elements in the story suggest that a relationship exists?

3. How may the bookie, trainer, and rich man have been involved in the accident that injured McGuire?

4. Which comparisons may be drawn between the jockey and Powerhouse in the Welty story?

5. Explain the change in point of view from Barlow to the men at the table.

TOPICS FOR WRITING

1. Describe the lives of the three men as contrasted to Barlow's as they all move through the thoroughbred horse racing world.

2. Explain what makes the jockey remind us of a child.

Grace Paley

A CONVERSATION WITH MY FATHER

Born in the Bronx and schooled in New York, Grace Paley (1922–   ) taught creative writing at a number of colleges before settling in at Sarah Lawrence. Of her stories Philip Roth writes that she possesses "an understanding of loneliness, lust, selfishness, and fatigue that is splendidly comic and unladylike . . . and a style whose toughness and bumpiness arise not only out of exasperation with the language, but the daring and heart of a genuine writer of prose." Paley's stories are collected in two volumes, The Little Disturbances of Man (1959) and Enormous Changes at the Last Minute (1975), from which "A Conversation with My Father" is taken. This is a story—or two—paced by crisp dialogue in which is revealed love, determination, and the conflicting desires of the generations. "A Conversation with My Father" also sets forth Paley's personal credo as a writer: "Everyone, real or invented, deserves the open destiny of life."

My father is eighty-six years old and in bed. His heart, that bloody motor, is equally old and will not do certain jobs any more. It still floods his head with brainy light. But it won't let his legs carry the weight of his body around the house. Despite my metaphors, this muscle failure is not due to his old heart, he says, but to a potassium shortage. Sitting on one pillow, leaning on three, he offers last-minute advice and makes a request.

"I would like you to write a simple story just once more," he says, "the kind de Maupassant wrote, or Chekhov, the kind you used to write. Just recognizable people and then write down what happened to them next."

I say, "Yes, why not? That's possible." I want to please him, though I don't remember writing that way. I *would* like to try to tell such a story, if he means the kind that begins: "There was a woman . . ." followed by plot, the absolute line between two points which I've always despised. Not for literary reasons, but because it takes all hope away. Everyone, real or invented, deserves the open destiny of life.

Finally I thought of a story that had been happening for a couple of years right across the street. I wrote it down, then read it aloud. "Pa," I said, "how about this? Do you mean something like this?"

> Once in my time there was a woman and she had a son. They lived nicely, in a small apartment in Manhattan. This boy at about fifteen became a junkie, which is not unusual in our neighborhood. In order to maintain her close friendship with him, she became a junkie too. She said it was part of the youth culture, with which she felt very much at home. After a while, for a number of reasons, the boy gave it all up and left the city and his mother in disgust. Hopeless and alone, she grieved. We all visit her.

"O.K., Pa, that's it," I said, "An unadorned and miserable tale."

"But that's not what I mean," my father said. "You misunderstood me on purpose. You know there's a lot more to it. You know that. You left everything out. Turgenev wouldn't do that. Chekhov wouldn't do that. There are in fact Russian writers you never heard of, you don't have an inkling of, as good as anyone, who can write a plain ordinary story, who would not leave out what you have left out. I object not to facts but to people sitting in trees talking senselessly, voices from who knows where. . . ."

"Forget that one, Pa, what have I left out now? In this one?"

"Her looks, for instance."

"Oh. Quite handsome, I think. Yes."

"Her hair?"

"Dark, with heavy braids, as though she were a girl or a foreigner."

"What were her parents like, her stock? That she became such a person. It's interesting, you know."

"From out of town. Professional people. The first to be divorced in their county. How's that? Enough?" I asked.

"With you, it's all a joke," he said. "What about the boy's father? Why didn't you mention him? Who was he? Or was the boy born out of wedlock?"

"Yes," I said. "He was born out of wedlock."

"For Godsakes, doesn't anyone in your stories get married? Doesn't anyone have the time to run down to City Hall before they jump into bed?"

"No," I said. "In real life, yes. But in my stories, no."

"Why do you answer me like that?"

"Oh, Pa, this is a simple story about a smart woman who came to N.Y.C. full of interest love trust excitement very up to date, and about her son, what a hard time she had in this world. Married or not, it's of small consequence."

"It is of great consequence," he said.

"O.K.," I said.

"O.K. O.K. yourself," he said, "but listen. I believe you that she's good-looking, but I don't think she was so smart."

"That's true," I said. "Actually that's the trouble with stories. People start out fantastic. You think they're extraordinary, but it turns out as the work goes along, they're just average with a good education. Sometimes the other way around, the person's kind of dumb innocent, but he outwits you and you can't even think of an ending good enough."

"What do you do then?" he asked. He had been a doctor for a couple of decades and he's still interested in details, craft, technique.

"Well, you just have to let the story lie around till some agreement can be reached between you and the stubborn hero."

"Aren't you talking silly now?" he asked. "Start again," he' said. "It so happens I'm not going out this evening. Tell the story again. See what you can do this time."

"O.K.," I said. "But it's not a five-minute job." Second attempt:

Once, across the street from us, there was a fine handsome woman, our neighbor. She had a son whom she loved because she'd known him since birth (in helpless chubby infancy, and in the wrestling, hugging ages, seven to ten, as well as earlier and later). This boy, when he fell into the fist of adolescence, became a junkie. He was not a hopeless one. He was in fact hopeful, an ideologue and successful converter. With his busy brilliance, he wrote persuasive articles for his high-school newspaper. Seeking a wider audience, using important connections, he drummed into Lower Manhattan newsstand distribution a periodical called *Oh! Golden Horse!*

In order to keep him from feeling guilty (because guilt is the stony heart of nine tenths of all clinically diagnosed cancers in America today, she said), and because she had always believed in giving bad habits room at home where one could keep an eye on them, she too became a junkie. Her kitchen was famous for a while—a center for intellectual addicts who knew what they were doing. A few felt artistic like Coleridge and others were scientific and revolutionary like Leary. Although she was often high herself, certain good mothering reflexes remained, and she saw to it that there was lots of orange juice around and honey and milk and vitamin pills. However, she never cooked anything but chili, and that no more than once a week. She explained, when we talked to her, seriously, with neighborly concern, that it was her part in the youth culture and she would rather be with the young, it was an honor, than with her own generation.

One week, while nodding through an Antonioni film, this boy was severely jabbed by the elbow of a stern and proselytizing girl, sitting beside him. She offered immediate apricots and nuts for his sugar level, spoke to him sharply, and took him home.

She had heard of him and his work and she herself published, edited, and wrote a competitive journal called *Man Does Live by Bread Alone.* In the organic heat of her continuous presence he could not help but become interested once more in his muscles, his arteries, and nerve connections. In fact he began to love them, treasure them, praise them with funny little songs in *Man Does Live.* . . .

the fingers of my flesh transcend
my transcendental soul
the tightness in my shoulders end
my teeth have made me whole

To the mouth of his head (that glory of will and determination) he brought hard apples, nuts, wheat germ, and soybean oil. He said to his old friends, From now on, I guess I'll keep my wits about me. I'm going on the natch. He said he was about to begin a spiritual deep-breathing journey. How about you too, Mom? he asked kindly.

His conversion was so radiant, splendid, that neighborhood kids his age began to say that he had never been a real addict at all, only a journalist along for the smell of the story. The mother tried several times to give up what had become without her son and his friends a lonely habit. This effort only brought it to supportable levels. The boy and his girl took their electronic mimeograph and moved to the bushy edge of another borough. They were very strict. They said they would not see her again until she had been off drugs for sixty days.

At home alone in the evening, weeping, the mother read and reread the seven issues of *Oh! Golden Horse!* They seemed to her as truthful as ever. We often crossed the street to visit and console. But if we mentioned any of our children who were at college or in the hospital or dropouts at home, she would cry out, My baby! My baby! and burst into terrible, face-scarring, time-consuming tears. The End.

First my father was silent, then he said, "Number One: You have a nice sense of humor. Number Two: I see you can't tell a plain story. So don't waste time." Then he said sadly, "Number Three: I suppose that means she was alone, she was left like that, his mother. Alone. Probably sick?"

I said, "Yes."

"Poor woman. Poor girl, to be born in a time of fools, to live among fools, The end. The end. You were right to put that down. The end."

I didn't want to argue, but I had to say, "Well, it is not necessarily the end, Pa."

"Yes," he said, "what a tragedy. The end of a person."

"No, Pa," I begged him. "It doesn't have to be. She's only about forty. She could be a hundred different things in this world as time goes on. A teacher or a social worker. An ex-junkie! Sometimes it's better than having a master's in education."

"Jokes," he said. "As a writer that's your main trouble. You don't want to recognize it. Tragedy! Plain tragedy! Historical tragedy! No hope. The end."

"Oh, Pa," I said. "She could change."

"In your own life, too, you have to look it in the face." He took a couple of nitroglycerin. "Turn to five," he said, pointing to the dial on the oxygen tank. He inserted the tubes into his nostrils and breathed deep. He closed his eyes and said, "No."

I had promised the family to always let him have the last word when arguing, but in this case I had a different responsibility. That woman lives across the street. She's my knowledge and my invention. I'm sorry for her. I'm not going to leave her there in that house crying. (Actually neither would Life, which unlike me has no pity.)

Therefore: She did change. Of course her son never came home again. But right now, she's the receptionist in a storefront community clinic in the East Village. Most of the customers are young people, some old friends. The head doctor has said to her, "If we only had three people in this clinic with your experiences. . . ."

"The doctor said that?" My father took the oxygen tubes out of his nostrils and said, "Jokes. Jokes again."

"No, Pa, it could really happen that way, it's a funny world nowadays."

"No," he said. "Truth first. She will slide back. A person must have character. She does not."

"No, Pa," I said. "That's it. She's got a job. Forget it. She's in that storefront working."

"How long will it be?" he asked. "Tragedy! You too. When will you look it in the face?"

QUESTIONS

1. Why does the father believe his daughter should write stories like de Maupassant or Chekhov or Turgenev?

2. How is this in keeping with his thinking that all life's a tragedy?

3. After the first rendition of a story, why does he ask his daughter to "fill it out"?

4. Even after she complies with his wish, why is she reluctant to do more?

5. Symbolically, who does the father represent? the daughter?

TOPICS FOR WRITING

1. Describe the irony present in this story.

2. Dicuss the generational differences that appear in this story. Why does the father think the way he does? Why does the daughter feel the way she does?

3. Analyze this story as a presentation of the artistic process. What is the connection between life and art?

James Baldwin

THE MAN CHILD

*Born in Harlem, where he attended the public schools, James Baldwin (1924–   ), known mainly as a novelist, is also a playwright (*The Amen Corner, *1959, and* Blues for Mister Charlie, *1964). Baldwin, moreover, is an essayist and a short story writer. His essays began appearing in 1948, while his first novel was published in 1953.* Go Tell It on the Mountain *helped to build his reputation, which was secured by the publication of* Another Country *(1963); three addition-al novels were authored by Baldwin. His collections of essays range from* Notes of a Native Son *(1955), through* The Fire Next Time *(1963), to* The Devil Finds Work *(1976). Some of Baldwin's short stories have been collected in* Going to Meet the Man *(1956); "The Man Child" is taken from this collection. Although it has been fashionable to judge Bald-win's works only as examples of "Negro writing," he has treated the subjects of race and racism as forms of injustice. Harry L. Jones writes: "Baldwin's great strength . . . lies in*

James Baldwin

> *his creation of patterns of static reference, presenting de-*
> *scriptions or affective states of his characters." This is seen*
> *in "The Man Child," where race is not a factor, but love and*
> *jealousy are. In the story, the failed and the successful meet*
> *in a combat they do not recognize as mortal until they are in*
> *it—a constant theme in Baldwin's work.*

As the sun began preparing for her exit, and he sensed the waiting night, Eric, blond and eight years old and dirty and tired, started homeward across the fields. Eric lived with his father, who was a farmer and the son of a farmer, and his mother, who had been captured by his father on some far-off, unblessed, unbelievable night, who had never since burst her chains. She did not know that she was chained anymore than she knew that she lived in terror of the night. One child was in the churchyard, it would have been Eric's little sister and her name would have been Sophie: for a long time, then, his mother had been very sick and pale. It was said that she would never, really, be better, that she would never again be as she had been. Then, not long ago, there had begun to be a pounding in his mother's belly, Eric had sometimes been able to hear it when he lay against her breast. His father had been pleased. *I did that,* said his father, big, laughing, dreadful, and red, and Eric knew how it was done, he had seen the horses and the blind and dreadful bulls. But then, again, his mother had been sick, she had had to be sent away, and when she came back the pounding was not there anymore, nothing was there anymore. His father laughed less, something in his mother's face seemed to have gone to sleep forever.

Eric hurried, for the sun was almost gone and he was afraid the night would catch him in the fields. And his mother would be angry. She did not really like him to go wandering off by himself. She would have forbidden it completely and kept Eric under her eye all day but in this she was overruled: Eric's father liked to think of Eric as being curious about the world and as being daring enough to explore it, with his own eyes, by himself.

His father would not be at home. He would be gone with his friend, Jamie, who was also a farmer and the son of a farmer, down to the tavern. This tavern was called the Rafters. They went each night, as his father said, imitating an Englishman he had known during a war, *to destruct the Rafters, sir.* They had been destructing The Rafters long before Eric had kicked in his mother's belly, for Eric's father and Jamie had grown up together, gone to war together, and survived together—never, apparently, while life ran, were they to be divided. They worked in the fields all day together, the fields which belonged to Eric's father. Jamie had been forced to sell his farm and it was Eric's father who had bought it.

Jamie had a brown and yellow dog. This dog was almost always with him; whenever Eric thought of Jamie he thought also of the dog. They had always been there, they had always been together: in exactly the same way, for Eric, that his mother and father had always been together, in exactly the same way that the earth and the trees and the sky were together. Jamie and his dog walked the country roads together, Jamie walking slowly in the way of country people, seeming to see nothing, heads lightly bent, feet striking surely and heavily on the earth, never stumbling. He walked as though he were going to walk to the other end of the world and knew it was a long way but knew that he would be there by morning. Sometimes he talked to his dog, head bent a little more than usual and turned to one side, a slight smile playing about the edges of his granite lips; and the dog's head snapped up, perhaps he leapt upon his master, who cuffed him down lightly, with one hand. More often he was silent. His head was carried in a cloud of blue smoke from his pipe. Through this cloud, like a ship on a foggy day, loomed his dry and steady face. Set far back, at an unapproachable angle, were those eyes of his, smoky and thoughtful, eyes which seemed always to be considering the horizon. He had the kind of eyes which no one had ever looked into—except Eric, only once. Jamie had been walking these roads and across these fields, whistling for his dog in the evenings as he turned away from Eric's house, for years, in silence. He had been married once, but his wife had run away. Now he lived alone in a wooden house and Eric's mother kept his clothes clean and Jamie always ate at Eric's house.

Eric had looked into Jamie's eyes on Jamie's birthday. They had had a party for him. Eric's mother had baked a cake and filled the house with flowers. The doors and windows of the great kitchen all stood open on the yard and the kitchen table was placed outside. The ground was not muddy as it was in winter, but hard, dry, and light brown. The flowers his mother so loved and so labored for flamed in their narrow borders against the stone wall of the farmhouse; and green vines covered the grey stone wall at the far end of the yard. Beyond this wall were the fields and barns, and Eric could see, quite far away, the cows nearly motionless in the bright green pasture. It was a bright, hot, silent day, the sun did not seem to be moving at all.

This was before his mother had had to be sent away. Her belly had been beginning to grow big, she had been dressed in blue, and had seemed—that day, to Eric—younger than she was ever to seem again.

Though it was still early when they were called to table, Eric's father and Jamie were already tipsy and came across the fields, shoulders touching, laughing, and telling each other stories. To express disapproval and also, perhaps, because she had heard their stories before and was bored, Eric's mother was quite abrupt with them, barely saying, "Happy Birthday, Jamie" before she made them sit down. In the nearby village church bells rang as they began to eat.

It was perhaps because it was Jamie's birthday that Eric was held by something in Jamie's face. Jamie, of course, was very old. He was thirty-four today, even older than Eric's father, who was only thirty-two. Eric wondered how it felt to have so many years and was suddenly, secretly glad that he was only eight. For today, Jamie *looked* old. It was perhaps the one additional year which had done it, this day before their very eyes—a metamorphosis which made Eric rather shrink at the prospect of becoming nine. The skin of Jamie's face, which had never before seemed so, seemed wet today, and that rocky mouth of his was loose; loose was the word for everything about him, the way his arms and shoulders hung, the way he sprawled at the table, rocking slightly back and forth. It was not that he was drunk. Eric had seen him much drunker. Drunk, he became rigid, as though he imagined himself in the army again. No. He was old. It had come upon him all at once, today, on his birthday. He sat there, his hair in his eyes, eating, drinking, laughing now and again, and in a very strange way, and teasing the dog at his feet so that it sleepily growled and snapped all through the birthday dinner.

"Stop that," said Eric's father.

"Stop what?" asked Jamie.

"Let that stinking useless dog alone. Let him be quiet."

James Baldwin

"Leave the beast alone," said Eric's mother—very wearily, sounding as she often sounded when talking to Eric.

"Well, now," said Jamie, grinning, and looking first at Eric's father and then at Eric's mother, "it *is* my beast. And a man's got a right to do as he likes with whatever's his."

"That dog's got a right to bite you, too," said Eric's mother, shortly.

"This dog's not going to bite me," said Jamie, "he knows I'll shoot him if he does."

"That dog knows you're not going to shoot him," said Eric's father. "Then you *would* be all alone."

"All alone," said Jamie, and looked around the table. "All alone." He lowered his eyes to his plate. Eric's father watched him. He said, "It's pretty serious to be all alone at *your* age." He smiled. "If I was you, I'd start thinking about it."

"I'm thinking about it," said Jamie. He began to grow red.

"No, you're not," said Eric's father, "you're dreaming about it."

"Well, goddammit," said Jamie, even redder now, "it isn't as though I haven't tried!"

"Ah," said Eric's father, "that was a *real* dream, that was. I used to pick *that* up on the streets of town every Saturday night."

"Yes," said Jamie, "I bet you did."

"I didn't think she was as bad as all that," said Eric's mother, quietly. "*I* liked her. I was surprised when she ran away."

"Jamie didn't know how to keep her," said Eric's father. He looked at Eric and chanted: "*Jamie, Jamie, pumkin-eater, had a wife and couldn't keep her!*" At this, Jamie at last looked up, into the eyes of Eric's father. Eric laughed again, more shrilly, out of fear. Jamie said:

"Ah, yes, you can talk, you can."

"It's not my fault," said Eric's father, "if you're getting old—and haven't got anybody to bring you your slippers when night comes—and no pitter-patter of little feet—"

"Oh, leave Jamie alone," said Eric's mother, "he's *not* old, leave him alone."

Jamie laughed a peculiar, high, clicking laugh which Eric had never heard before, which he did not like, which made him want to look away and, at the same time, want to stare. "Hell, no," said Jamie, "I'm not old, I can still do all the things we used to do." He put his elbows on the table, grinning. "I haven't ever told you, have I, about the things we used to do?"

"No, you haven't," said Eric's mother, "and I certainly don't want to hear about them now."

"He wouldn't tell you anyway," said Eric's father, "he knows what I'd do to him if he did."

"Oh, sure, sure," said Jamie, and laughed again. He picked up a bone from his plate. "Here," he said to Eric, "why don't you feed my poor mistreated dog?"

Eric took the bone and stood up, whistling for the dog; who moved away from his master and took the bone between his teeth. Jamie watched with a smile and opened the bottle of whiskey and poured himself a drink. Eric sat on the ground beside the dog, beginning to be sleepy in the bright, bright sun.

"Little Eric's getting big," he heard his father say.

"Yes," said Jamie, "they grow fast. It won't be long now."

"Won't be long *what?*" he heard his father ask.

"Why, before he starts skirt-chasing like his Daddy used to do," said Jamie. There was mild laughter at the table in which his mother did not join; he heard instead, or thought he heard, the familiar, slight, exasperated intake of her breath. No one seemed to care whether he came back to the table or not. He lay on his back, staring up at the sky, wondering—wondering what he would feel like when he was old—and fell asleep.

When he awoke his head was in his mother's lap, for she was sitting on the ground. Jamie and his father were still sitting at the table; he knew this from their voices, for he did not open his eyes. He did not want to move or speak. He wanted to remain where he was, protected by his mother, while the bright day rolled on. Then he wondered about the uncut birthday cake. But he was sure, from the sound of Jamie's voice, which was thicker now, that they had not cut it yet; or if they had, they had certainly saved a piece for him.

"—ate himself just as full as he could and then fell asleep in the sun like a little animal," Jamie was saying, and the two men laughed. His father—though he scarcely ever got as drunk as Jamie did, and had often carried Jamie home from The Rafters—was a little drunk, too.

Eric felt his mother's hand on his hair. By opening his eyes very slightly he would see, over the curve of his mother's thigh, as through a veil, a green slope far away and beyond it the everlasting, motionless sky.

"—she was a no-good *bitch*," said Jamie.

"She was beautiful," said his mother, just above him.

Again, they were talking about Jamie's wife.

"Beauty!" said Jamie, furious. "Beauty doesn't keep a house clean. Beauty doesn't keep a bed warm, neither."

Eric's father laughed. "You were so—poetical—in those days, Jamie," he said. "Nobody thought you cared much about things like that. I guess she thought you didn't care, neither."

"I cared," said Jamie, briefly.

"In fact," Eric's father continued, "I *know* she thought you didn't care."

"*How* do you know?" asked Jamie.

"She told me," Eric's father said.

"What do you mean," asked Jamie, "what do you mean, she told you?"

"I mean just that. She told me."

Jamie was silent.

"In those days," Eric's father continued after a moment, "all you did was walk around the woods by yourself in the daytime and sit around The Rafters in the evenings with me."

"You two were always together then," said Eric's mother.

"Well," said Jamie, harshly, "at least that hasn't changed."

"Now, you know," said Eric's father, gently, "it's not the same. Now I got a wife and kid—and another one coming—"

Eric's mother stroked his hair more gently, yet with something in her touch more urgent, too, and he knew that she was thinking of the child who lay in the churchyard, who would have been his sister.

"Yes," said Jamie, "you really got it all fixed up, you did. You got it all—the wife, the kid, the house, and all the land."

"I didn't steal your farm from you. It wasn't my fault you lost it. I gave you a better price for it than anybody else would have done."

"I'm not blaming you. I know all the things I have to thank you for."

There was a short pause, broken, hesitantly, by Eric's mother. "What I don't understand," she said, "is why, when you went away to the city, you didn't *stay* away. You didn't really have anything to keep you here."

There was the sound of a drink being poured. Then, "No. I didn't have nothing—*really*—to keep me here. Just all the things I ever knew—all the things—*all* the things—I ever cared about."

"A man's not supposed to sit around and mope," said Eric's father, wrathfully, "for things that are over and dead and finished, things that can't *ever* begin again, that can't ever be the same again. That's what I mean when I say you're a dreamer—if you hadn't kept on dreaming so long, you might not be alone now.'

"Ah, well," said Jamie, mildly, and with a curious rush of affection in his voice, "I know you're the giant-killer, the hunter, the lover—the real old Adam, that's you. I know you're going to cover the earth. I know the world depends on men like you."

"And you're damn right," said Eric's father, after an uneasy moment.

Around Eric's head there was a buzzing, a bee, perhaps, a blue-fly, or a wasp. He hoped that his mother would see it and brush it away, but she did not move her hand. And he looked out again, through the veil of his eyelashes, at the slope and the sky, and then saw that the sun had moved and that it would not be long now before she would be going.

"—just like you already," Jamie said.

"You think my little one's like me?" Eric knew that his father was smiling—he could almost feel his father's hands.

"Looks like you, walks like you, talks like you," said Jamie.

"*And* stubborn like you," said Eric's mother.

"Ah, yes," said Jamie, and sighed. "You married the stubbornest, most determined—most selfish—man I know."

"I didn't know you felt that way," said Eric's father. He was still smiling.

"I'd have warned you about him," Jamie added, laughing, "if there'd been time."

"Everyone who knows you feels that way," said Eric's mother, and Eric felt a sudden brief tightening of the muscle in her thigh.

"Oh, *you*," said Eric's father, "I know *you* feel that way, women like to feel that way, it makes them feel important. But," and he changed to the teasing tone he took so persistently with Jamie today, "I didn't know my fine friend, Jamie, here—"

It was odd how unwilling he was to open his eyes. Yet, he felt the sun on him and knew that he wanted to rise from where he was before the sun went down. He did not understand what they were talking about this afternoon, these grown-ups he had known all his life; by keeping his eyes closed he kept their conversation far from him. And his mother's hand lay on his head like a blessing, like protection. And the buzzing had ceased, the bee, the blue-fly, or the wasp seemed to have flown away.

"—if it's a boy this time," his father said, "we'll name it after you."

"That's touching," said Jamie, "but that really won't do me—or the kid—a hell of a lot of good."

"Jamie can get married and have kids of his own any time he decides to," said Eric's mother.

"No," said his father, after a long pause, "Jamie's thought about it too long."

The Man Child

And suddenly, he laughed and Eric sat up as his father slapped Jamie on the knee. At the touch, Jamie leaped up, shouting, spilling his drink and overturning his chair, and the dog beside Eric awoke and began to bark. For a moment, before Eric's unbelieving eyes, there was nothing in the yard but noise and flame.

His father rose slowly and stared at Jamie. "What's the matter with you?"

"What's the matter with me!" mimicked Jamie, "what's the matter with me? what the hell do you care what's the matter with me! What the hell have you been riding me for all day like this? What do you want? what do you *want?*"

"I want you to learn to hold your liquor for one thing," said his father, coldly. The two men stared at each other. Jamie's face was red and ugly and tears stood in his eyes. The dog, at his legs, kept up a furious prancing and barking. Jamie bent down and, with one hand, with all his might, slapped his dog, which rolled over, howling, and ran away to hide itself under the shadows of the far grey wall.

Then Jamie stared again at Eric's father, trembling, and pushed his hair back from his eyes.

"You better pull yourself together," Eric's father said. And, to Eric's mother, "Get him some coffee. He'll be all right."

Jamie set his glass on the table and picked up the overturned chair. Eric's mother rose and went into the kitchen. Eric remained sitting on the ground, staring at the two men, his father and his father's best friend, who had become so unfamiliar. His father, with something in his face which Eric had never before seen there, a tenderness, a sorrow—or perhaps it was, after all, the look he sometimes wore when approaching a calf he was about to slaughter—looked down at Jamie where he sat, head bent, at the table. "You take things too hard," he said. "You always have. I was only teasing you for your own good."

Jamie did not answer. His father looked over to Eric, and smiled.

"Come on," he said. "You and me are going for a walk."

Eric, passing on the side of the table farthest from Jamie, went to his father and took his hand.

"Pull yourself together," his father said to Jamie. "We're going to cut your birthday cake as soon as me and the little one come back."

Eric and his father passed beyond the grey wall where the dog still whimpered, out into the fields. Eric's father was walking too fast and Eric stumbled on the uneven ground. When they had gone a little distance his father abruptly checked his pace and looked down at Eric, grinning.

"I'm sorry," he said. "I guess I said we were going for a walk, not running to put out a fire."

"What's the matter with Jamie?" Eric asked.

"Oh," said his father, looking westward where the sun was moving, pale orange now, making the sky ring with brass and copper and gold—which, like a magician, she was presenting only to demonstrate how variously they could be transformed—"Oh," he repeated, "there's nothing wrong with Jamie. He's been drinking a lot," and he grinned down at Eric, "and he's been sitting in the sun—you know, his hair's not as thick as yours," and he ruffled Eric's hair, "and I guess birthdays make him nervous. Hell," he said, "they make me nervous, too."

"Jamie's *very* old," said Eric, "isn't he?"

His father laughed. "Well, butch, he's not exactly ready to fall into the grave yet—he's going to be around awhile, is Jamie. Hey," he said, and looked down at Eric again, "you must think I'm an old man, too."

"Oh," said Eric, quickly, "I know you're not as old as Jamie."

His father laughed again. "Well, thank you, son. That shows real confidence. I'll try to live up to it."

They walked in silence for awhile and then his father said, not looking at Eric, speaking to himself, it seemed, or to the air: "No, Jamie's not so old. He's not as old as he should be."

"How old *should* he be?" asked Eric.

"Why," said his father, "he ought to be his age," and, looking down at Eric's face, he burst into laughter again.

"Ah," he said, finally, and put his hand on Eric's head again, very gently, very sadly, "don't you worry now about what you don't understand. The time is coming when you'll have to worry—but that time hasn't come yet."

Then they walked till they came to the steep slope which led to the railroad tracks, down, down, far below them, where a small train seemed to be passing forever through the countryside, smoke, like the very definition of idleness, blowing out of the chimney stack of the toy locomotive. Eric thought, resentfully, that he scarcely ever saw a train pass when he came here alone. Beyond the railroad tracks was the river where they sometimes went swimming in the summer. The river was hidden from them now by the high bank where there were houses and where tall trees grew.

"And this," said his father, "is where your land ends."

"What?" said Eric.

His father squatted on the ground and put one hand on Eric's shoulder. "You know all the way we walked, from the house?" Eric nodded. "Well," said his father, "that's your land."

Eric looked back at the long way they had come, feeling his father watching him.

His father, with a pressure on his shoulder made him turn; he pointed: "And over there. It belongs to you." He turned him again. "And that," he said, "that's yours, too."

Eric stared at his father. "Where does it end?" he asked.

His father rose. "I'll show you that another day," he said. "But it's further than you can walk."

They started walking slowly, in the direction of the sun.

"When did it get to be mine?" asked Eric.

"The day you were born" his father said, and looked down at him and smiled.

"My father," he said, after a moment, "had some of this land—and when he died, it was mine. He held on to it for me. And I did my best with the land I had, and I got some more. I'm holding on to it for you."

He looked down to see if Eric was listening. Eric was listening, staring at his father and looking around him at the great countryside.

"When I get to be a real old man," said his father, "even older than old Jamie there—you're going to have to take care of all this. When I die it's going to be yours." He paused and stopped; Eric looked up at him. "When you get to be a big man, like your Papa, you're going to get married and have children. And all this is going to be theirs."

"And when *they* get married?" Eric prompted.

"All this will belong to *their* children," his father said.

"Forever?" cried Eric.

"Forever," said his father.

They turned and started walking toward the house.

"Jamie," Eric asked at last, "how much land has *he* got?"

"Jamie doesn't have any land," his father said.

"Why not?" asked Eric.

"He didn't take care of it," his father said, "and he lost it."

"Jamie doesn't have a wife anymore, either, does he?" Eric asked.

"No," said his father. "He didn't take care of her, either."

"And he doesn't have any little boy," said Eric—very sadly.

"No," said his father. Then he grinned. "But *I* have."

"*Why* doesn't Jamie have a little boy?" asked Eric.

His father shrugged. "Some people do, Eric, some people don't."

"Will I?" asked Eric.

"Will you what?" asked his father.

"Will I get married and have a little boy?"

His father seemed for a moment both amused and checked. He looked down at Eric with a strange, slow smile. "Of course you will," he said at last. "Of course you will." And he held out his arms. "Come," he said, "climb up. I'll ride you on my shoulders home."

So Eric rode on his father's shoulders through the wide green fields which belonged to him, into the yard which held the house which would hear the first cries of his children. His mother and Jamie sat at the table talking quietly in the silver sun. Jamie had washed his face and combed his hair, he seemed calmer, he was smiling.

"Ah," cried Jamie, "the lord, the master of this house arrives! And bears on his shoulders the prince, the son, and heir!" He described a flourish, bowing low in the yard. "My lords! Behold your humble, most properly chastised servant, desirous of your—compassion, your love, and your forgiveness!"

"Frankly," said Eric's father, putting Eric on the ground, "I'm not sure that this is an improvement." He looked at Jamie and frowned and grinned. "Let's cut that cake."

Eric stood with his mother in the kitchen while she lit the candles—thirty-five, one, as they said, to grow on, though Jamie, surely, was far past the growing age—and followed her as she took the cake outside. Jamie took the great, gleaming knife and held it with a smile.

"Happy Birthday!" they cried—only Eric said nothing—and then Eric's mother said, "You have to blow out the candles, Jamie, before you cut the cake."

"It looks so pretty the way it is," Jamie said.

"Go ahead," said Eric's father, and clapped him on the back, "be a man."

Then the dog, once more beside his master, awoke, growling, and this made everybody laugh. Jamie laughed loudest. Then he blew out the candles, all of them at once, and Eric watched him as he cut the cake. Jamie raised his eyes and looked at Eric and it was at this moment, as the suddenly blood-red sun was striking the topmost tips of trees, that Eric had looked into Jamie's eyes. Jamie smiled that strange smile of an old man and Eric moved closer to his mother.

"The first piece for Eric," said Jamie, then, and extended it to him on the silver blade.

That had been near the end of summer, nearly two months ago. Very shortly after the birthday party, his mother had fallen ill and had had to be taken away. Then his father spent more time than ever at The Rafters; he and Jamie came home in the evenings, stumbling drunk. Sometimes, during the time that his mother was away, Jamie did not go home at all, but spent the night at the farm house; and once or twice Eric had awakened in the middle of the night, or near dawn, and heard Jamie's footsteps walking up and down, walking up and down, in the big room downstairs. It had been a strange and dreadful time, a time of waiting, stillness, and silence. His father rarely went into the fields, scarcely raised himself to give orders to his farm hands—it was unnatural, it was frightening, to find him around the house all day, and Jamie was there always, Jamie and his dog. Then one day Eric's father told him that his mother was coming home but that she would not be bringing him a baby brother or sister, not this time, nor in any time to come. He started to say something more, then looked at Jamie who was standing by, and walked out of the house. Jamie followed him slowly, his hands in his pockets and his head bent. From the time of the birthday party, as though he were repenting of that outburst, or as though it had frightened him, Jamie had become more silent than ever.

When his mother came back she seemed to have grown older—old; she seemed to have shrunk within herself, away from them all, even, in a kind of storm of love and helplessness, away from Eric; but, oddly, and most particularly, away from Jamie. It was in nothing she said, nothing she did—or perhaps it was in everything she said and did. She washed and cooked for Jamie as before, took him into account as much as before as a part of the family, made him take second helpings at the table, smiled good night to him as he left the house—it was only that something had gone out of her familiarity. She seemed to do all that she did out of memory and from a great distance. And if something had gone out of her ease, something had come into it, too, a curiously still attention, as though she had been startled by some new aspect of something she had always known. Once or twice at the supper table, Eric caught her regard bent on Jamie, who, obliviously, ate. He could not read her look, but it reminded him of that moment at the birthday party when he had looked into Jamie's eyes. She seemed to be looking at Jamie as though she were wondering why she had not looked at him before; or as though she were discovering, with some surprise, that she had never really liked him but also felt, in her weariness and weakness, that it did not really matter now.

Now, as he entered the yard, he saw her standing in the kitchen doorway, looking out, shielding her eyes against the brilliant setting sun.

"Eric!" she cried, wrathfully, as soon as she saw him. "I've been looking high and low for you for the last hour. You're getting old enough to have some sense of responsibility and I wish you wouldn't worry me so when you know I've not been well."

She made him feel guilty at the same time that he dimly and resentfully felt that justice was not all on her side. She pulled him to her, turning his face up toward hers, roughly, with one hand.

"You're filthy," she said, then. "Go around to the pump and wash your face. And hurry, so I can give you your supper and put you to bed."

And she turned and went into the kitchen, closing the door lightly behind her. He walked around to the other side of the house, to the pump.

On a wooden box next to the pump was a piece of soap and a damp rag. Eric picked up the soap, not thinking of his mother, but thinking of the day gone by, already half asleep: and thought of where he would go tomorrow. He moved the pump handle up and down and the water rushed out and wet his socks and shoes—this would make his mother angry, but he was too tired to care. Nevertheless, automatically, he moved back a little. He held the soap between his hands, his hands beneath the water.

He had been many places, he had walked a long way and seen many things that day. He had gone down to the railroad tracks and walked beside the tracks for awhile, hoping that a train would pass. He kept telling himself that he would give the train one more last chance to pass; and when he had given it a considerable number of last chances, he left the railroad bed and climbed a little and walked through the high, sweet meadows. He walked through a meadow where there were cows and they looked at him dully with their great dull eyes and moo'd among each other about him. A man from the far end of the field saw him and shouted, but Eric could not tell whether it was someone who worked for his father or not and so he turned and ran way, ducking through the wire fence. He passed an apple tree, with apples lying all over the ground—he wondered if the apples belonged to him, if he were still walking on his own land or had gone past it—but he ate an apple anyway and put some in his pockets, watching a lone brown horse in a meadow far below him nibbling at the grass and flicking his tail. Eric pretended that he was his father and was walking through the fields as he had seen his father walk, looking it all over calmly, pleased, knowing that everything he saw belonged to him. And he stopped and pee'd as he had seen his father do, standing wide-legged and heavy in the middle of the fields; he pretended at the same time to be smoking and talking, as he had seen his father do. Then, having watered the ground, he walked on, and all the earth, for that moment, in Eric's eyes, seemed to be celebrating Eric.

Tomorrow he would go away again, somewhere. For soon it would be winter, snow would cover the ground, he would not be able to wander off alone.

He held the soap between his hands, his hands beneath the water; then he heard a low whistle behind him and a rough hand on his head and the soap fell from his hands and slithered between his legs onto the ground.

He turned and faced Jamie, Jamie without his dog.

"Come on, little fellow," Jamie whispered. "We got something in the barn to show you."

"Oh, did the calf come yet?" asked Eric—and was too pleased to wonder why Jamie whispered.

"Your Papa's there," said Jamie. And then: "Yes. Yes, the calf is coming now."

And he took Eric's hand and they crossed the yard, past the closed kitchen door, past the stone wall and across the field, into the barn.

"But *this* isn't where the cows are!" Eric cried. He suddenly looked up at Jamie, who closed the barn door behind them and looked down at Eric with a smile.

"No," said Jamie, "that's right. No cows here." And he leaned against the door as though his strength had left him. Eric saw that his face was wet, he breathed as though he had been running.

"Let's go see the cows," Eric whispered. Then he wondered why he was whispering and was terribly afraid. He stared at Jamie, who stared at him.

"In a minute," Jamie said, and stood up. He had put his hands in his pockets and now he brought them out and Eric stared at his hands and began to move away. He asked, "Where's my Papa?"

"Why," said Jamie, "he's down at The Rafters, I guess. I have to meet him there soon."

"I have to go," said Eric. "I have to eat my supper." He tried to move to the door, but Jamie did not move. "I have to go," he repeated, and, as Jamie moved toward him the tight ball of terror in his bowels, in his throat, swelled and rose, exploded, he opened his mouth to scream but Jamie's fingers closed around his throat. He stared, stared into Jamie's eyes.

"That won't do you any good," said Jamie. And he smiled. Eric struggled for breath, struggled with pain and fright. Jamie relaxed his grip a little and moved one hand and stroked Eric's tangled hair. Slowly, wondrously, his face changed, tears came into his eyes and rolled down his face.

Eric groaned—perhaps because he saw Jamie's tears or because his throat was so swollen and burning, because he could not catch his breath, because he was so frightened—he began to sob in great, unchildish gasps. "Why do you hate my father?"

"I love your father," Jamie said. But he was not listening to Eric. He was far away—as though he were struggling, toiling inwardly up a tall, tall mountain. And Eric struggled blindly, with all the force of his desire to live, to reach him, to stop him before he reached the summit.

"Jamie," Eric whispered, "you can have the land. You can have all the land."

Jamie spoke, but not to Eric: "I don't want the land."

"I'll be your little boy," said Eric. "I'll be your little boy forever and forever and forever—and you can have the land and you can live forever! Jamie!"

Jamie had stopped weeping. He was watching Eric.

"We'll go for a walk tomorrow," Eric said, "and I'll show it to you, all of it—really and truly—if you kill my father I can be your little boy and we can have it all!"

"This land," said Jamie, "Will belong to no one."

"Please!" cried Eric, "oh, please! Please!"

He heard his mother singing in the kitchen. Soon she would come out to look for him. The hands left him for a moment. Eric opened his mouth to scream, but the hands then closed around his throat.

Mama. Mama.

The singing was further and further away. The eyes looked into his, there was a question in the eyes, the hands tightened. Then the mouth began to smile. He had never seen such a smile before. He kicked and kicked.

Mama. Mama. Mama. Mama. Mama.

Far away, he heard his mother call him.

Mama.

He saw nothing, he knew that he was in the barn, he heard a terrible breathing near him, he thought he heard the sniffling of beasts, he remembered the sun, the railroad tracks, the cows, the apples, and the ground. He thought of tomorrow—he wanted to go away again somewhere tomorrow. *I'll take you with me,* he wanted to say. He wanted to argue the question, the question he remembered in his eyes—wanted to say, *I'll tell my Papa you're hurting me.* Then terror and agony and darkness overtook him, and his breath went violently out of him. He dropped on his face in the straw in the barn, his yellow head useless on his broken neck.

Night covered the countryside and here and there, like emblems, the lights of houses glowed. A woman's voice called, "Eric! Eric!"

Jamie reached his wooden house and opened his door; whistled, and his dog came bounding out of darkness, leaping up on him; and he cuffed it down lightly, with one hand. Then he closed his door and started down the road, his dog beside him, his hands in his pockets. He stopped to light his pipe. He heard singing from The Rafters, then he saw the lights; soon, the lights and the sound of singing diminished behind him. When Jamie no longer heard the singing, he began to whistle the song that he had heard.

QUESTIONS

1. What does the term "man child" mean? Why is it used to address certain young people?

2. Does the use of the term "man child" explain the point of view from which the story is told? Explain.

3. Why is Eric's father contemptuous of Jamie? Why does he at first attempt to conceal this contempt?

4. Why is Eric's mother so resigned to Jamie's presence? What is it she and Eric see in Jamie's eyes?

5. Why is Jamie envious of Eric's father, and why, finally, is this envy taken out on Eric?

6. Can the term "man child" be accurately applied to anyone other than Eric?

TOPICS FOR WRITING

1. Compare the reasons for the murders done by Montresor in "A Cask of Amontillado" (pages 8–14) and by Jamie in "The Man Child."

2. Explore the role and presence of the mother. What function does she perform? How would the story be different without her?

3. Analyze the theme of this story.

Ursula K. Le Guin

A TRIP TO THE HEAD

Ursula K. Le Guin (1929–) was born in Berkeley, California, which she deserted for studies at Radcliffe and Columbia. "Her characters," wrote Helen Rogan of Time, *"are complex and haunting, and her writing is remarkable for its sinewy grace." In 1968, she was awarded the* Boston Globe–Hornbook *prize for excellence in juvenile fiction; in 1969, she won the Hugo award for best science-fiction novel; she also won the 1973 National Book Award and the 1974 Nebula Award for "The Day Before the Revolution." LeGuin has published a number of novels, including* Rocannon's World *(1964),* The Left Hand of Darkness *(1969), and* The Dispossessed *(1974). Le Guin is always deceptively challenging the reader's range, or capacity for translating what some consider fantasy into reality.*

"Is this Earth?" he cried, for things had changed abruptly.

"Yes, this is Earth," said the one beside him, "nor are you out of it. In Zambia men are rolling down hills inside barrels as training for space flight. Israel and Egypt have defoliated each other's deserts. The *Reader's Digest* has bought a controlling interest in the United States of America/General Mills combine. The population of the Earth is increasing by thirty billion every Thursday. Mrs Jacqueline Kennedy Onassis will marry Mao Tse-Tung on Saturday, in search of security; and Russia has contaminated Mars with bread mold."

"Why then," said he, "nothing has changed."

"Nothing much," said the one beside him. "As Jean-Paul Sartre has said in his lovable way, 'Hell is other people.'"

"To Hell with Jean-Paul Sartre. I want to know where I am."

"Well then," said the other, "tell me who you are."

"I'm."

"Well?"

"My name is."

"What?"

He stood, his eyes filling with tears and his knees with palsy, and knew he did not know his name. He was a blank, a cipher, an x. He had a body and all that, but he had no who.

They stood at the edge of a forest, he and the other one. It was a recognizable forest, though rather dingy in the leaf, and damaged at the fringes by weedkiller. A fawn was walking away from them into the forest and as it went its name fell away from it. Something looked back at them with mild eyes from the darkness of the trees before it vanished. "This is England!" cried blank, grasping the floating straw, but the other said, "England sank years ago."

"Sank?"

"Yes. Foundered. Nothing is left now but the topmost fourteen feet of Mt Snowdon, known as the New Welsh Reef."

At this blank also sank. He was crushed. "Oh," he cried on his knees, intending to ask somebody's help, but he could not remember whose help it was one asked. It began with a T, he was almost certain. He began to weep.

The other sat down on the grass beside him and presently put a hand on his shoulder, saying, "Come on now, don't take it so hard."

The kindly voice gave blank some courage. He controlled himself, dried his face on his sleeve, and looked at the other. It was like him, roughly. It was another. However, it had no name either. What good was it?

Shadow came into the eyes as Earth went round on its axis. Shadow slipped eastward and upward into the other's eyes.

"I think," blank said carefully, "that we should move out from the shadow of the, this, here." He gestured to the objects near them, large things, dark below and multitudinously green above, the names of which he could no longer remember. He wondered if each one had a name, or if they were all called by the same name. What about himself and the other, did they share a name in common, or did each have one of his own? "I have a feeling I'll remember better farther away from it, from them," he said.

"Certainly," said the other. "But it won't make as much difference as it used to."

When they came clear away from it into the sunlight, he at once remembered that it was called a forest and that they were called trees. However, he could not recall whether or not each tree had a name of its own. If they did, he did not remember any of them. Perhaps he did not know these trees personally.

"What shall I do," he said, "what shall I do?"

"Well, look here, you can call yourself whatever you please, you know. Why not?"

"But I want to know my *real* name."

"That isn't always easy. But meanwhile you could just take a label, as it were, for ease of reference and conversational purposes. Pick a name, any name!" said the other and held out a blue box named DISPOSABLE.

"No," said blank proudly, "I'll choose my own."

"Right. But don't you want a kleenex?"

Blank took a kleenex, blew his nose, and said, "I shall call myself . . ." He halted in terror.

The other watched him, mild-eyed.

"How can I say who I am when I can't say what I am?"

"How would you find out what you are?"

"If I had anything—If I did something—"

"That would make you be?"

"Of course it would."

"I never thought of that. Well, then, it doesn't matter what name you're called by; any one will do; it's what you do that counts."

Blank stood up. "I will exist," he stated firmly. "I will call myself Ralph."

Whipcord breeches fitted close on his powerful thighs, the stock rose high on his neck, sweat clung in his thick, curly hair. He tapped his boots with his riding-crop, his back to Amanda, who sat in her old grey dress in the deep shade of the pecan tree. He stood in full sunlight, hot with anger. "You're a fool," he said.

"Why Mr Ralph," came the soft lilting Southern voice, "Ah'm just a little bit stubborn."

"You realize, don't you, that Yankee as I am, I own all the land from here to Weevilville? I own this county! Your farm wouldn't make a peanut-patch for one of my darkies' kitchen gardens!"

Ursula K. Le Guin

"Indeed not. Won't you come sit down in the shade, Mr Ralph? Youah gettin' so hot out theah."

"You proud vixen," he murmured, turning. He saw her, white as a lily in her worn old dress, in the shade of the great old trees: the white lily of the garden. Suddenly he was at her feet, clasping her hands. She fluttered in his powerful grasp. "Oh Mr Ralph," she cried faintly, "what does this mean?"

"I am a man, Amanda, and you are a woman. I never wanted your land. I never wanted anything but you, my white lily, my little rebel! I want you, I want you! Amanda! Say you will be my wife!"

"Ah will," she breathed faintly, bending towards him as a white flower stoops; and their lips met in a long, long kiss. But it did not seem to help at all.

Perhaps it ought to be moved up twenty or thirty years.

"You sick bitch," he muttered, turning. He saw her, stark naked there in the shade, her back against the pecan tree, her knees up. He strode towards her unbuttoning his fly. They coupled in the centipede-infested crabgrass. He bucked like a bronco, she cried ululatingly, *Oooh! Aaah!* Coming coming coming COME WOW WOW WOW CLIMAX!

Now what?

Blank stood at a little distance from the forest and stared disconsolately at the other.

"Am I a man?" he inquired. "Are you a woman?"

"Don't ask me," the other said, morose.

"I thought surely that was the most important thing to establish!"

"Not so damned important."

"You mean it doesn't *matter* if I am a man or a woman?"

"Of course it matters. It matters to me too. It also matters which man and which woman we are or, as the case may be, are not. For instance, what if Amanda was black?"

"But sex."

"Oh, Hell," said the other with a flare of temper, "bristleworms have sex, tree-sloths have sex, Jean-Paul Sartre has sex—what does it prove?"

"Why, sex is real, I mean really real—it's having and acting in its intensest form. When a man takes a woman he proves his being!"

"I see. But what if he's a woman?"

"I was Ralph."

"Try being Amanda," the other said sourly.

There was a pause. Shadows were coming on eastward and upward from the forest over the grass. Small birds cried *jug jug, tereu.* Blank sat hunched over his knees. The other lay stretched out, making patterns with fallen pine needles, shadowed, sorrowful.

"I'm sorry," blank said.

"No harm done," the other said. "After all, it wasn't real."

"Listen," blank said, leaping up, "I know what's happened! I'm on some kind of trip. I took something, and I'm on a trip, that's it!"

It was. He was on a trip. A canoe trip. He was paddling a small canoe along a long, narrow, dark, shining stretch of water. The roof and walls were of concrete. It was pretty dark. The long lake, or stream, or sewer, slanted upward visibly. He was paddling against the current, uphill. It was hard work, but the canoe kept sliding forward upriver as silently as the black shining water moved back down. He kept his strokes quiet, the paddle entering the water silent as a knife in butter. His large black-and-pearl electric guitar lay on the forward seat. He knew there was somebody behind him, but he didn't say anything. He wasn't allowed to say anything or even look around, so if they didn't keep up that was their look-out, he couldn't be called responsible. He certainly couldn't slow down, the current might get hold of his canoe and pull it right out from under him and then where'd he be? He shut his eyes and kept paddling, silent entry, strong stroke. There was no sound behind him. The water made no sound. The cement made no sound. He wondered if he was actually going forward or only hanging still while the black water ran hellbent beneath. He would never get out to daylight. Out, out—

out. The other didn't even seem to have noticed that blank had been away on a trip, but just lay there making patterns with pine needles, and presently said, "How is your memory?"

Blank searched it to see if it had improved while he was away. There was less in it than before. The cupboard was bare. There was a lot of junk in the cellars and attics, old toys, nursery rhymes, myths, old wives' tales, but no nourishment for adults, no least scrap of possession, not a crumb of success. He searched and searched like a starving methodical rat. At last he said uncertainly, "I do remember England."

"Why surely. I expect you can even remember Omaha."

"But I mean, I remember being in England."

"Do you?" The other sat up, scattering pinestraw. "You do remember being, then! What a pity England sank."

They were silent again.

"I have lost everything."

There was a darkness in the other's eyes and on the eastern edge of the earth plunging down the steepening slopes of night.

"I'm nobody."

"At least," said the other, "you know you're human."

"Oh, what good's that? with no name, no sex, no nothing? I might as well be a bristleworm or a tree-sloth!"

"You might as well," the other agreed, "be Jean-Paul Sartre."

"I?" said blank, offended. Driven to denial by so nauseous a notion, he stood up and said, "I certainly am not Jean-Paul Sartre. I am myself." And so saying he found himself to be, in fact, himself; his name was Lewis D. Charles and he knew it as well as he knew his own name. There he was.

The forest was there, root and branch.

The other was, however, gone.

Lewis D. Charles looked in the red eye of the west and the dark eye of the east. He shouted aloud, "Come back! Please come back!"

He had gone at it all wrong, backwards. He had found the wrong name. He turned, and without the least impulse of self-preservation plunged into the pathless forest, casting himself away so that he might find what he had cast away.

Under the trees he forgot his name again at once. He also forgot what he was looking for. What was it he had lost? He went deeper and deeper into shadows, under leaves, eastward, in the forest where nameless tigers burned.

QUESTIONS

1. Who was Jean-Paul Sartre, and what philosophy did he espouse? How does that philosophy apply to "A Trip to the Head"?

2. How does the canoe trip in the story compare to the "final journey" in Greek mythology?

3. What is the subject of this story? What is the theme?

TOPICS FOR WRITING

1. What is the relationship of William Blake's poem "The Tiger" (page 517) to the last two sentences in this story?

2. Analyze and compare the mystical elements in Singer's "Old Love" (pages 278–288) and in this work by Le Guin.

3. Compare and contrast "A Trip to the Head" with Bradbury's "August 2026: There Will Come Soft Rains" (pages 159–163) in terms of the science-fiction mode.

4. Evaluate the significance of the title of this story and its relationship to the theme.

P A R T

2

R T

POETRY

Perhaps the oldest kind of literature known to humanity, poetry in its earliest stages was told or sung, but during its long and continuing evolution it has become part of the written tradition and has been used for several purposes.

Foremost among its uses has been its use as narrative to recount the history of specific groups of people. The Greek epics, the Indian vedas, the Norse sagas, and some sections of the Old Testament are a few examples of group history, a "dramatic shorthand record," wrote Robert Graves, of group history and experience in poetic narrative form.

Another early way in which poetry was used was in paying homage to the gods. We recognize form and rhythm and imagery and compression in Egyptian, Hebrew, Babylonian, and other religious recitations from all parts of the world.

Greek writers were known as poets, a title that carried both responsibility and praise, and their works in large measure were plays written in poetry, a convention at the time. The rules of playwrighting were later formalized by Aristotle in his *Poetics*.

Roman poets adopted most of the classical rules of the Greeks, but observance of these rules went into decline, more or less, to be revived during the Renaissance, mainly by the Italians and the French. However, beginning with

Geoffrey Chaucer (1340?–1400), poetry in England began a flowering that spread throughout the English-speaking world and beyond. The English language was influenced by the French, Romans, Angles and Saxons. These influences strengthened the language and helped to fine-tune imagery, enrich metaphor, and establish new and enlarge old themes that were not merely English, but universal.

During the course of these evolutions, there has been the enduring discussion about what poetry *is*. Strabo (58 B.C.–24 A.D.) believed that poetry was a mask for historical and scientific truths, such as those believed to be in Homer's works. Aristotle held the opinion that poetry was a discipline more serious than history because it represented the universal. Wordsworth felt that poetry was opposed to science, as did Coleridge, who wrote, "Poetry is not the proper antithesis to prose, but to science. Poetry is opposed to science, and prose to meter." Leigh Hunt (1784–1859), the "indicator" of the Romantic period, declared, "Poetry begins where matter of fact or of science ceases to be merely such and to exhibit a further truth, that is to say, the connection it has with the world of emotion, and its power to produce imaginative pleasure."

Science was expressed in prose, whatever its findings, whatever its rules. It was empirical, allowing for no emotion, which for many poets possessed a truth of its own. The question of what poetry is remains open; and perhaps that is the wisest way to perceive poetry: as not being static.

We presume that poetry and prose differ, but even here argument arises. Thomas Mann (1875–1955) wrote: "It is a fruitless and futile mania of the critics to insist on a distinction between the poet and the man of letters (prose writers)—it is an impossible distinction; for the boundary between the two does not lie in the product of either, but rather within the personality of the artist himself."

Similarly, Ezra Pound observed in 1918 that clearly distinguishing prose and poetry would be impossible unless one wrote "a complete treatise on the art of writing, defining each word as one would define the terms in an essay on chemistry. And on this account all essays about 'poetry' are usually not only dull but inaccurate and wholly useless."

Nevertheless, commonly accepted as basic to the difference between poetry and prose is that poetry may be written in meter, and prose is not; that poetry may use rhyme (though it is not at all times required to), while prose does not; that poetry may use rhythm, but prose normally does not. (Poetry, according to Poe, is "the rhythmical creation of beauty.") Poetry distills, compresses, and refines knowledge from bulk to universal essences through the rigorous and selective use of language. Prose, in contrast, is not necessarily concerned with distillation, compression, or refinement; prose has long been considered "ordinary language," even though the best prose may be composed of quite extraordinary language.

The poet may be like Houdini. He binds himself in the chains of a poetic form; he allows himself to be locked in the safe of tradition, where he is expected to create interaction between theme, tone, imagery, metaphor, and other poetic devices; then he is tossed into the sea of creativity. He is further expected to produce the miracle of escape, a poetic rendering of a universal truth, vision, or beauty. Poetry, when all is said and done, should surprise us as much as Houdini's escapes surprised and delighted his audiences.

Some poetry may appear to be difficult to read and understand (and some really is); like other forms of literature, it should be placed in perspective. We should know for example, when it was written, because that helps to tell us what kind of tradition it has inherited. Perhaps the title of a poem will supply the clues we need to understand its theme and subject. In any case, we should not bring more to a poem than is really there. If we anticipate, we cannot be surprised and delighted. Above all, the reader should have confidence in his or her ability to understand and enjoy poetry, whatever its form. The more familiar structures, such as the sonnet or the villanelle, may be in part the result of convention or challenge. Other forms may result from the way poets envision their work on the page. Whatever the form, in the final analysis the *content* of poetry is meant to arouse a response in us, as E. E. Cummings notes:

since feeling is first
who pays any attention
to the syntax of things
will never wholly kiss you

Nothing about a poem is as important as the way it makes us feel—usually, the way the poet *wants* us to feel. This is a reminder that imagination is the most important gift the poet can bring us, not profound meanings.

A. E. Housman wrote that poetry is "more physical than intellectual," and Robert W. Boynton expressed a similar idea, when he wrote, "Poets are the athletes of language." This form of athletics is the exercise of imagination. For Thomas MacCaulay, poetry is "the art of employing words in such a manner as to produce an illusion on the imagination," while William Carlos Williams wrote that imagination is the single force able "to refine, to clarify, to intensify the eternal moment in which we alone live." Poetic imagination may be defined as the ability to deal creatively with reality; to take what is real and experienced and, through invention, render it visible and accessible to all. Invention is synonomous with imagination. ("The essence of poetry is invention: such invention as, by producing something unexpected, surprises and delights," wrote Samuel Johnson.)

Like Houdini, who kept seeking new ways to escape new inventions for detention, poetry evolved from the confinement of conventional structure—meter, rhyme, and sometimes content—to what we now call free verse (see section 18, pages 445–447, and section 20, pages 467–469). It was imagination fired by a new kind of poet, epitomized by Walt Whitman, in a relatively new nation, that introduced free verse. This was a poetry freed from the old rules; it followed mainly the poetic need for rhythm, which it called "cadence," and relied heavily on imagery. (See section 13, pages 388–399.) Free verse gave rise to new forms that explored the universe from new perspectives; free verse imagined the ordinary to be universal.

But the new forms that were to spark the imagination in a new way were not by any means acceptable to all poets. In this collection, for example, a number of twentieth-century poets are as comfortable with the sonnet as were the sixteenth-century poets of England. W. H. Auden, who remained a disciple of the traditional structures, wrote of such devices as rhymes, meters, and stanza forms that they "are like servants. If the master [the poet] is fair enough to win their affection and firm enough to command their respect, the result is an orderly, happy household. If he is too tyrannical, they give notice; if he lacks authority, they become slovenly, impertinent, drunk and dishonest."

We should remember, however, that whatever the form and whatever the age, poetry, like other forms of literature, tells a story; but the stories poetry tells are reduced to shimmering essences. Homer told stories with his poetry; so did Shakespeare and Whitman. All the rest did and do, too. We should not forget, in addition, the legions of blues singers and other folk singers, "the singing poets," whose lyrics constitute a region of poetry still to be completely explored, but who have already inspired generations with their poetry as much as with their music.

For our part we want to know what story—for a poem exists to tell a story about something—a particular poet, with or without music, is going to tell us. Maybe his or her view of the universe is better than ours, the experiences more glorious; we know that they must at least be different. Yet, if the story-poem is good, we also know that somehow the view and the experiences must be approximately the same as ours. Then we can be delighted and surprised by the experiences and the view and rest comfortably with Gwendolyn Brooks' assessment that poetry is, in the final analysis, "life distilled."

9

SUBJECT AND THEME: LOVE

A poem, as Robert Frost once suggested, might very well begin in delight and end in wisdom, but before a poem can even be written the poet needs—if only subconsciously—to have a subject in mind. Any subject might inspire the poet. Nevertheless, we do tend to think of traditional subjects for poetry—love, death, nature, religion, and war, for example—and to place many poems in such categories; we place poems in conventional categories far more frequently than we place fiction or drama in subject groups. Moreover, poets often become identified, sometimes misleadingly or simplistically, with specific subjects. Thus Shakespeare becomes a love poet because of his sonnets; Donne a poet preoccupied with God; Rupert Brooke a war poet; Robert Frost a nature poet; Emily Dickinson and Anne Sexton poets dwelling on death.

Poetry is the most complex, intense, and condensed of literary forms, but we can respond to much of it by understanding each poem's subject. We cannot extrapolate a theme from a poem until we identify and understand the subject. Theme, discussed initially in section 1 of this text (pages 6–8), is a general statement the poet wants to make about a specific subject. Until the modern period, the subjects, themes, and forms acceptable to poetic culture were fairly uniform and conventional. However, in the twentieth century, the range of content, ideas, and forms—broadened by everything from psychoanalysis to thermodynamics to jazz—has led to a greater complexity of expression. Often technique—notably image and diction—obscures content in contemporary poetry, a phenomenon that confirms paradoxically our pressing need to know what a poem is about before we can know what it means.

Because poetry, as the American poet and critic Ivor Winters was fond of stating, is a statement in words about a human experience, we know that a poet will attempt to communicate through language some aspect of experience. In this section, for example, the poets want to communicate something about love and are speakers in their own poems. We know quite readily that love is the subject or the occasion of the poems. But we must also ask about the purpose behind the speaker's presentation of the subject. The purpose might be to offer a definition, to express an emotion, to describe something objectively, to reveal something about human nature, or to project an idea or attitude. By establishing the central purpose of the poem, we move closer to understanding its meaning, or theme. In Shakespeare's "Let me not to the marriage of true minds," the purpose is relatively clear: the poet wants to state (perhaps dogmatically) the nature of true love. Similarly, a clear purpose governs Anne Bradstreet's "To My Dear and Loving Husband"; in fact, the title of the poem conveys its purpose quite handsomely. A poet's deepest purpose, however, might seem simple when it is actually quite subtle. Andrew Marvell in "To His Coy Mistress" apparently takes as his central purpose the seduction of his mistress, but perhaps he has larger philosophical intentions to convey. If we determine that Marvell's purpose embraces not just love and sexuality but also ethics and morality, then our final understanding of the poem, growing as it does from our perception of subject, speaker, and purpose, might be at odds with other interpretations.

Diverging interpretations and evaluations of poems are commonplace, even when readers establish a consensus on the general subject, purpose, speaker, and context of the poem. Ultimately, each of us is forced back to the language of the poem for meaning. "Language," declared Shelley, "is given to us to express our ideas." Thus, to understand a poem we often have recourse to paraphrase—to restating the poem in our own words, often line by line or stanza by stanza. We also look for poetic techniques—for the methods discussed in subsequent sections of this anthology—to both help us in detecting meaning and aid us in our appreciation of the poem and the poet's craft. We seek in a poem the illumination of experience and, often, revelations about it. We turn to poets, the most intense creators of literary art, expecting from them a vision of life that contains the power to offer both delight and wisdom.

William Shakespeare

LET ME NOT TO THE MARRIAGE OF TRUE MINDS

William Shakespeare (1564–1616) is not only the greatest dramatist in English literature (see Othello, *page 750) but also one of its most memorable poets. Shakespeare composed a sequence of 154 sonnets, writing most of them prior to 1600. As William Wordsworth declared, these sonnets offer insights into Shakespeare and his art, for with them "Shakespeare unlocked his heart." The sonnet cycle by Shakespeare is a remarkably personal account in which the poet dramatizes his love for an unidentified woman, his unfortunate relationship with a young man, and the profound philosophical and psychological problems raised by this sad triangle. Yet rather than speculate on the biographical details of Shakespeare's life, it is far more important to recognize the poet's intense effort to understand the complexities of human emotions, key philosophical issues centering on love, and the nature of the world in these sonnets. In "Let me not to the marriage of true minds," sonnet 116 in the series, Shakespeare offers a concise definition of what he means by the often turbulent and paradoxical emotion of love.*

Let me not to the marriage of true minds
Admit impediments. Love is not love
Which alters when it alteration finds,
Or bends with the remover to remove:
O, no; it is an ever-fixèd mark,   5
That looks on tempests and is never shaken:
It is the star to every wandering bark,
Whose worth's unknown, although his height be taken.
Love's not Time's fool, though rosy lips and cheeks
Within his bending sickle's compass come;   10
Love alters not with his brief hours and weeks,
But bears it out even to the edge of doom.
 If this be error and upon me proved,
 I never writ, nor no man ever loved.

QUESTIONS

1. What familiar part of the standard Christian marriage ceremony does Shakespeare's first sentence echo? Why does Shakespeare use "marriage" as a key word at the outset of the poem?

2. Shakespeare employs two "negative" definitions in lines 2–4. What are they? What is their effect?

3. What two comparisons does Shakespeare draw in lines 5–8? What is the connection between "mark" and "star"? Explain the meaning of the eighth line.

4. How does Shakespeare establish the conflict between love and time in lines 8–12?

5. What is the meaning and the tone of the last two rhymed lines? State the general theme that emerges from the poem.

TOPICS FOR WRITING

1. Write an analysis of Shakespeare's philosophy of love in this poem, concentrating on the examples that the poet offers to flesh out his definition.

2. A sonnet is based on certain poetic conventions (see pages 457–459). One key convention of a Shakespearean sonnet is the division of the fourteen lines of the poem into four groups: lines 1–4, 5–8, 9–12, and 13–14. Analyze the organization of the poem according to these divisions, showing the way that Shakespeare advances his definition from stage to stage.

3. Do you agree or disagree with Shakespeare's definition of love? Write an essay explaining your position.

Anne Bradstreet

TO MY DEAR AND LOVING HUSBAND

Anne Bradstreet (1612?–1672) was born Anne Dudley in Lincolnshire, England. She married before she was 17 and joined her husband, Simon Bradstreet, in the great migra-tion to America in 1630, sailing aboard John Winthrop's ship Arabella. *Simon Bradstreet was a prominent member of the Massachusetts Bay Colony. In 1635, following several moves, the family settled in Ipswich, near Boston. In 1645, the Bradstreets moved to Andover, and it was here that Anne Bradstreet raised four of her eight chldren and wrote her finest poems. Bradstreet is known as a Puritan poet but, as one critic observes, a "worldly Puritan." She writes often from personal experience—the births, lives, and deaths of children and grandchildren; the relationship with her hus-band; the burning of their beloved house and its library, which occurred in 1666. Her best poetry is in a plain style, controlled in tone and mood, and precise in poetic state-ment. In "To My Dear and Loving Husband," Bradstreet offers a simple but moving tribute to their love and to the man who, eight years after her own death, would become governor of Massachusetts Bay Colony.*

If ever two were one, then surely we.
If ever man were lov'd by wife, then thee;
If ever wife was happy in a man,
Compare with me ye women if you can.
I prize thy love more than whole Mines of gold,   5
Or all the riches that the East doth hold.
My love is such that Rivers cannot quench,
Nor ought but love from thee, give recompense.
Thy love is such I can no way repay,
The heavens reward thee manifold, I pray.   10
Then while we live, in love lets so persever,
That when we live no more, we may live ever.

QUESTIONS

1. How does Bradstreet balance her love for Simon against his own love for her? Why does this method feed the theme of the poem?

2. Does the language of the poem strike you as overly simple and sentimental or plain but effective? Justify your answer.

3. How does the love poem broaden and deepen in scope in the last four lines?

TOPICS FOR WRITING

1. Write an essay on the way that Bradstreet controls subject and theme through the use of relatively simple language in this poem.

2. Evaluate the approaches of Shakespeare (page 341) and Bradstreet to the subject of love, explaining why you prefer one poem to the other or why both are equally successful in their own right.

Andrew Marvell

TO HIS COY MISTRESS

Andrew Marvell (1621–1678), the son of an Anglican clergy-man, studied at Cambridge University, served as an assis-tant to Milton, and was a member of Parliament from 1659 until his death. He was famous in his own time as a political satirist in both prose and poetry. However, his greatest poems express diverse attitudes, ranging from seductive Cavalier lyrics, such as "To His Coy Mistress," to deeply contemplative poems. "To His Coy Mistress" is typical of Marvell's best poetry, which focuses on human experience in this world and the difficult, often ironic choices that we must make. Although the poem is in the tradition of the seductive lyric of the Cavalier period, it also contains philosophical elements touching on time and death. Marvell balances emotion and ideas perfectly to advance his argument, or debate.

Had we but world enough, and time,
This coyness, lady, were no crime.
We would sit down, and think which way
To walk, and pass our long love's day.
Thou by the Indian Ganges' side   5
Should'st rubies find: I by the tide
Of Humber would complain. I would
Love you ten years before the Flood,
And you should, if you please, refuse
Till the conversion of the Jews,   10
My vegetable love should grow
Vaster than empires, and more slow,
An hundred years should go to praise
Thine eyes, and on thy forehead gaze:
Two hundred to adore each breast: 15
But thirty thousand to the rest;
An age at least to every part,
And the last age should show your heart.
For, lady, you deserve this state,
Nor would I love at lower rate.   20
    But at my back I always hear
Time's wingèd chariot hurrying near;
And yonder all before us lie
Deserts of vast eternity.
Thy beauty shall no more be found,   25
Nor in thy marble vault shall sound
My echoing song; then worms shall try
That long preserved virginity,
And your quaint honor turn to dust,
And into ashes all my lust.   30
The grave's a fine and private place,
But none, I think, do there embrace.
    Now therefore, while the youthful hue
Sits on thy skin like morning dew,
And while thy willing soul transpires   35
At every pore with instant fires,
Now let us sport us while we may;
And now, like am'rous birds of prey,
Rather at once our time devour,
Than languish in his slow-chapped power.   40
Let us roll all our strength, and all

Our sweetness, up into one ball;
And tear our pleasures with rough strife
Thorough the iron gates of life.
Thus, though we cannot make our sun   45
Stand still, yet we will make him run.

QUESTIONS

1. Marvell builds a cogent argument to persuade his love in this poem, employing in the first two stanzas what debaters call a *straw man* (that is, an idea that is easy to knock down). What idea does he advance and then demolish in the first stanza? What related idea does he present and then destroy in the second stanza? With these possible objections to his argument eliminated, what is left for the lady to accept in the third stanza?

2. What is the theme of the poem?

3. The term "vegetable love" in line 11 is unusual. How long does it take most vegetables to grow to maturity? What might Marvell's phrase mean in this context?

4. The imagery, or vivid description, is very effective in this poem. Examine each stanza and explain the types or patterns of description that you detect. How does the description contribute to Marvell's argument?

5. How skillful is Marvell's argument? Is the poet interested only in seducing a woman, or are deeper ideas involved? For example, why does he refer to time and death?

TOPICS FOR WRITING

1. Write a critical essay on the argumentative structure of the poem. Analyze the devices Marvell uses to advance the argument.

2. Many critics state that "To His Coy Mistress" is in the *carpe diem* tradition, in which the poet states that we should "seize the day," or do things immediately rather than postpone them. Here, Marvell relates the *carpe diem* motif to the need to enjoy love while one is still young. Evaluate the importance of this concept to your understanding of the poem.

3. Argue for or against the proposition that Marvell is not interested in love in this poem but is simply a sexist.

Emily Dickinson

WILD NIGHTS—WILD NIGHTS!

Emily Dickinson (1830–1886) was born in Amherst, Massachusetts, the second child of an important local family. She attended Amherst Academy from 1840 to 1847 and spent a year at Mount Hadley Female Seminary, but ill health often forced her to interrupt her education. Aside from brief trips to Boston, Philadelphia, and Washington, Dickinson remained in Amherst all her life, electing to keep her own soul company and becoming the "New England Nun" of popular legend. She wrote poems prolifically from 1858 to 1865, but was largely uninterested in publication, arranging her poems in packets and storing them in a box—a cache that would be discovered by her sister, Lavinia, after Emily died. Only with the publication of The Poems of Emily Dickinson in 1955 did the bulk of her poetry—some 1,775 items—become available to readers. Dickinson remarked to Thomas Wentworth Higginson when he visited her on August 16, 1870, that if she read a book and "it makes my whole body so cold no fire can warm me I know that is poetry." There is a similar chill in much of her greatest poetry, for she often deals with loneliness, loss, pain, sorrow, despair, and death. Yet Dickinson commanded many moods: she could be witty, comic, playful, irreverent. Her love lyrics are of the same order as the rest of her poetry—demanding, existing in tension with other felt emotions. The following love poem is typical of her poetic imagination, but at the same time unusual in the intensity and vividness of her passionate longing for an absent figure.

Wild Nights—Wild Nights!
Were I with thee
Wild Nights should be
Our Luxury!

Futile—the Winds—   5
To a Heart in port—
Done with the Compass—
Done with the Chart!

Rowing in Eden—
Ah, the Sea!   10
Might I but moor—Tonight—
In Thee!

QUESTIONS

1. Why does Dickinson write in the first stanza that wild nights would be a "luxury"?

2. Explain the connection between the various images in the second stanza. What is the effect?

3. How do you interpret the last stanza? Why is the image of the sea especially effective?

4. What emotions and tensions does the speaker project in the poem?

5. State the theme of "Wild Nights—Wild Nights!"

6. Commenting on Dickinson's love lyrics, the critic Denis Donoghue observes: "Many of her poems enact certain moments on the way toward love, including desire, expectation, premonition, fear. But more poems still dispose certain moments on the other side of love, as loss, despair, terror, then death." Into which category would you place "Wild Nights—Wild Nights!" and why?

TOPICS FOR WRITING

1. Compare and contrast the varieties of love expressed by Bradstreet in "To My Dear and Loving Husband" (page 343) and Dickinson in "Wild Nights—Wild Nights!"

2. Write a psychological profile of the speaker of the poem. Point to details in the poem that reveal her attitudes—emotional, intellectual, and, perhaps, sexual.

Adrienne Rich

I COME HOME FROM YOU

Adrienne Rich (1929–   ) was born in Baltimore, Maryland, and received her BA from Radcliffe College in 1951, the same year that her first book of poems, A Change of World, *was published. She has taught at several colleges and universities, including Swarthmore, Columbia, City College of New York, and Brandeis. Rich has received numerous awards for her poetry, among them two Guggenheim fellowships and the National Book Award for* Diving into the Wreck *(1973). Her other volumes include* The Diamond Cutters *(1955),* Snapshots of a Daughter-in-Law *(1963),* Necessities of Life *(1966), and* Poems: Selected and New, 1950–1974 *(1975). A determined feminist, Rich has written: "To be a woman at this time is to know extraordinary forms of anger, joy, impatience, love, and hope." In the following poem, the fourth in a series entitled "Twenty-one Love Poems," from* The Dream of a Common Language *(1978), Rich writes about both love and the absence of love in a world dominated by one especially cruel and jarring image of tortured humanity.*

I come home from you through the early light of spring
flashing off ordinary walls, the Pez Dorado,
the Discount Wares, the shoe-store. . . . I'm lugging my sack
of groceries, I dash for the elevator

where a man, taut, elderly, carefully composed   5
lets the door almost close on me.—*For god's sake hold it!*
I croak at him.—*Hysterical,*—he breathes my way.
I let myself into the kitchen, unload my bundles,
make coffee, open the window, put on Nina Simone
singing *Here comes the sun.* . . . I open the mail,   10
drinking delicious coffee, delicious music,
my body still both light and heavy with you. The mail
lets fall, a Xerox of something written by a man
aged 27, a hostage, tortured in prison:
My genitals have been the object of such a sadistic display   15
they keep me constantly awake with the pain . . .
Do whatever you can to survive.
You know, I think that men love wars . . .
And my incurable anger, my unmendable wounds
break open further with tears, I am crying helplessly,   20
and they still control the world, and you are not in my arms.

QUESTIONS

1. How is the experience of the poem framed by the "you"? What figures in the poem contrast with this "you"?

2. What are the speaker's various emotions in the poem? What is her attitude toward life?

3. The speaker mentions "Delicious coffee, delicious music/my body still heavy with you." Explain the effect of these images.

4. How does the letter "written by a man" alter the speaker's frame of mind? Why is the "sadistic display" that he alludes to especially relevant to the theme of the poem? What is the theme?

5. Who is the "they" at the end of the poem? How are "they" set in opposition to love?

6. Does the speaker project a strong image or a weak and vulnerable image of herself? Explain.

7. What evidence, if any, exists in the poem that the "you" might be a woman? Discuss.

TOPICS FOR WRITING

1. Analyze the absence of love—and yet paradoxically the importance of love—in the world that unfolds in "I come home from you."

2. Write a psychological profile of the speaker in this poem.

3. Marge Piercy has written that Rich's poems are "taut with pain and intelligence, honed by a careful clear-eyed rage and precise compassion." Use this statement to explore the qualities and strengths of "I come home from you."

4. Rich has asserted that "we are confronted with the naked and unabashed failure of patriarchal politics and patriarchal civilization." In this context, explain why "I come home from you" could be interpreted as an assault on male-dominated society.

5. What makes this poem "modern"? Define your term and relate the poem to other poems in this section.

6. Use the poems in this section to write a comparative essay on the theme of love.

10

DENOTATION, CONNOTATION, AND THEME: IMAGES OF WOMEN

"Poetry," wrote Ralph Waldo Emerson, "teaches us the enormous force of a few words." The careful selection, compression, and arrangement of language by the artist gives poetry the power to project experience vividly and memorably for the reader. Poets generally do not want to use language to convey information, argue issues, or engage in conventional forms of discourse, although these objectives might infiltrate or even dominate individual poems. Instead, they want to use the force of language to heighten our perception of some aspect of experience—to render that experience as precisely, brilliantly, and originally as possible.

Poets manipulate and control language, using a wide range of strategies—the most important of which will be examined in the next twelve chapters of this anthology. They know that words appeal to the instincts, emotions, senses, intelligence, and biases of readers, and that they must select and position words effectively in a poem in order to obtain the desired effect. "Proper words in proper places," demanded Jonathan Swift, stressing this dual commitment to the selection and placement of language in poetry. If poets take such painstaking care in choosing and ordering language, then we should not rush through a poem, quickly seeking its meaning or central experience. A poem deserves our commitment to appreciating the use of language.

In this context, we begin by recognizing that words have both denotative and connotative meanings and values. The *denotative meaning* of a word is given by the dictionary definition and is largely independent of people's emotions and personal responses to the word. Of course, ordinary words—"fall," for instance— can have multiple definitions in a dictionary. Words can also change in meaning with the passage of time.

The other realm of meaning that pertains to words is *connotation,* referring to the shades of meaning and suggestive possibilities of words. In this essentially emotional, subjective realm of language, a word like "rose" as used by Gwendolyn Brooks in a poem in this section or a word like "mothers" in a selection by Nikki Giovanni moves from the denotation of the term to a special range of meaning and suggestion that the poet wants to bring to it. Poets make conscious choices concerning the denotations and connotations of words. Poets, seeking the richest possibilities of language, might be plain or ornamental, direct or indirect, witty or serious, in style and tone. Regardless of these stylistic strategies, they must always start with the denotative and connotative power of words to convey experience and meaning.

Poets, the supreme craftsmen and craftswomen of language, invariably move beyond the bare, denotative values of words to mine the rich suggestions and associations that words hold. They work magic with the core of meaning inherent in words, transforming plain metal into a rare alloy that shimmers with emotional implication and possibility. The English writer Robert Thouless, in an essay called "Emotional Meanings," took two famous lines from John Keats's poem "The Eve of St. Agnes" and reduced them from connotative splendor to denotative neutrality in order to explore some of the ways in which we respond to language. Keats wrote:

> Full on this casement shone the wintry moon,
> And threw warm gules on Madeline's fair breast.

The beauty of these lines derives in large part from the ordering and presentation of emotionally charged words—*casement, warm gules* (the name in heraldry for red), *Madeline, fair, breast*—suggesting or creating an aura of romance. Thouless reduces these beautiful lines to bare, denotative exactness:

> Full on the window shown the wintry moon,
> Making red marks on Jane's uncolored chest.

All poetic and assuredly most connotative power goes out of language in the second version. Emotional effect has been replaced by scientific effect. Fortunately, the poet moves effectively from the power of denotative meanings to the greater power of connotative meanings in the creation of poetry that appeals to the experience of readers.

Consider, for instance, the denotative and connotative value of language in the following short poem by Aphra Behn, who was the first woman in England to earn her living exclusively as a writer.

When Maidens Are Young

When maidens are young, and in their spring,
Of pleasure, of pleasure, let'em take their full swing,
   Full swing, full swing,
And love, and dance, and play, and sing,
For Silvia, believe it, when youth is done,
There's naught but hum-drum, hum-drum, hum-drum,
There's naught but hum-drum, hum-drum, hum-drum.

In this poem, Aphra Behn is considering the youth of maidens and urging them to enjoy themselves before the cares of adult womanhood set in. This is the theme, or general meaning, of the experience that we can abstract from the poem. Yet how does the poet arrive at this statement about experience, if not through the images, ideas, and rhythms that we associate with the language? To participate in the experience of the poem, we have to ask basic questions about the way language performs in it. What did "maidens" mean to Behn in the 1670s, and what does it mean to us today? What denotations and connotations attach themselves to the word "spring"? What words convey the joys of a woman's youth? What meanings has "hum-drum" in the last two lines, and why are certain words repeated? In considering such questions, we discover that words in "When Maidens Are Young" assuredly control the experience of the poem. Aphra Behn's selection and repetition of words convey the range of maidenly pleasure, the urgency in embracing it quickly, and the certainty that it will alter to the plodding, repetitive, and irrevocably dull state of "hum-drum" adulthood in a way that no prose statement can.

All of the poems in this section—by Aphra Behn, Emily Dickinson, Elizabeth Barrett Browning, Gwendolyn Brooks, and Nikki Giovanni—offer images from the lives of women. If words are power, then the class that controls language also accumulates power. Traditionally those who have shaped literary history and especially attitudes toward the experience of poetry have been men. Here we see power in the hands of women, and the varieties of experience that they express with it. And here we also see how each poet chooses, as Adrienne Rich said of Emily Dickinson, to have it out on her own premises.

Aphra Behn

THE DEFIANCE

Aphra Behn (1640–1689), whose poem "When Maidens Are Young" appears in the introduction to this section (page 352), was born in Kent, England. She spent part of her childhood in Surinam, Guiana, an experience that provided her with the background for her best-known novel, Oroonoko (1688). She was married briefly to a Dutch merchant, who died during their marriage. In 1666, when Behn was 26, she was sent on a mission as a spy in the Netherlands for Charles II, becoming known for her exploits as "the Incomparable." However, she fell out of royal favor, spent time in debtors' prison in London, and on her release turned to writing to earn a living. Behn wrote seventeen plays, twelve histories and novels, poetry, and translations. A feminist and a decidedly unconventional figure, Aphra Behn in the following selection from Poems upon Several Occasions (1684) offers an image of a woman who knows how to sting a false suitor.

By Heaven 'tis false, I am not vain;
   And rather would the subject be
Of your indifference, or disdain,
   Than wit or raillery.

Take back the trifling praise you give,   5
   And pass it on some other fool,
Who may the injuring wit believe,
   That turns her into ridicule.

Tell her, she's witty, fair, and gay,
   With all the charms that can subdue: 10
Perhaps she'll credit what you say;
   But curse me if I do.

If your diversion you design,
   On my good-nature you have prest:
Or if you do intend it mine,   15
   You have mistook the jest.

QUESTIONS

1. From just the title of the poem, what can you tell about the tone of the language in which it is written? What does the poet mean by "defiance" in the context of the poem?

2. What are the origins of "'tis" in the first line? Consult the *Oxford English Dictionary* (OED) to answer this question.

3. Use the OED or some other unabridged dictionary to find out how Behn would have been using these words: "wit," "raillery," "design," "prest."

4. How does the poet characterize the "you" of the poem? What words serve to typify the behavior of this individual?

5. What synonyms do "disdain," "trifling," "gay," and "diversion" suggest in the poem?

6. What denotations exist for "wit"? Which is most appropriate in the context of the poem?

7. What words and phrases capture the mood of the speaker? Explain.

8. Paraphrase each stanza. Sum up the general meaning of the poem. Did you arrive at this statement of the theme through a consideration of the poet's use of denotation, connotation, or both? Explain.

TOPICS FOR WRITING

1. How does attention to denotative and connotative aspects of language lead to an appreciation of the theme of Behn's poem? One form of such attention would be to analyze the words and phrases she uses to capture the varieties of human action and reaction.

2. Contrast the speaker of the poem to the object of her defiance and to other women to whom she alludes.

Elizabeth Barrett Browning

IF THOU MUST LOVE ME, LET IT BE FOR NAUGHT

Elizabeth Barrett Browning (1806–1861), born at Durham, England, received in childhood a rich, leisurely education from her brothers' tutors. She was devoted to literature, and when she was 14 her father had published her epic poem, The Battle of Marathon. In 1819, she apparently suffered a spinal injury that left her a semi-invalid until her marriage to Robert Browning in 1846. During these years, she kept to her room in her father's London home. After she eloped with Browning and settled in Italy for the last 15 years of her life, she recovered from her infirmities and gave birth to a son, Robert, in 1849. Elizabeth Browning enjoyed great fame for her Sonnets from the Portuguese (1850) and her blank-verse novel, Aurora Leigh (1857). In Florence, at Casa Guidi, she and her husband entertained their notable friends, among them Julia Ward Howe, Margaret Fuller, Nathaniel Hawthorne, and Walter Savage Landor. She was a progressive thinker—an advocate of women's and children's rights, the abolition of slavery, and the Italian struggle for freedom from Austria. In the following sonnet, Browning outlines gently the terms on which she wants her husband's love.

If thou must love me, let it be for naught
Except for love's sake only. Do not say
"I love her for her smile—her look—her way
Of speaking gently—for a trick of thought
That falls in well with mine, and certes brought   5
A sense of pleasant ease on such a day"—
For these things in themselves, Belovéd, may
Be changed, or change for thee—and love, so wrought,
May be unwrought so. Neither love me for
Thine own dear pity's wiping my cheeks dry—   10
A creature might forget to weep, who bore
Thy comfort long, and lose thy love thereby!
But love me for love's sake, that evermore
Thou mayst love on, through love's eternity.

QUESTIONS

1. What contrast does Browning draw between lasting and potentially less permanent love? What details does she offer to explain the changing nature of love?

2. What does she mean by "love's sake" and "love's eternity"?

3. List those words in the poem that seem especially dated. Explain the meaning of each.

4. Why is the word "creature" in line 11 rich in connotations?

5. Explain the portrait of the speaker that emerges from the poem. What are we told about her beloved? Is she correct to admonish him? Justify your answer.

6. Does Browning have a sentimental or "feminine" attitude toward love? Debate this issue.

TOPICS FOR WRITING

1. Analyze Browning's vision of love and the language she uses to define it.

2. Compare and contrast this poem with Shakespeare's "Let me not to the marriage of true minds" (page 341).

3. Evaluate whether or not this poem is an example of the feminine consciousness, arguing that it can or cannot be categorized by gender. Point to the language and content of the poem to substantiate your response.

Emily Dickinson

SHE ROSE TO
HIS REQUIREMENT

*Emily Dickinson (1830–1886), introduced earlier in this
anthology (page 346), published only seven poems in her
lifetime, but today is considered, along with Walt Whitman,
one of the greatest nineteenth-century American poets. After
her death from Bright's disease, 1,775 poems were found in
her bedroom. "I am one of the bad ones," Emily Dickinson
once declared whimsically of her refusal to endorse traditional pieties and platitudes. Her rebellion extended, as the
following poem suggests, to marriage. Although Dickinson
had important men in her life—notably her companion
Benjamin Franklin Newton and the Reverend Charles
Wadsworth—she remained single. In "She rose to His Requirement," Dickinson measures curtly the sacrifices
women must make upon entering the married state.*

She rose to His Requirement—dropt
The Playthings of Her Life
To take the honorable Work
Of Woman, and of Wife—

If ought She missed in Her new Day,　　　　　　　　　　　　5
Of Amplitude, or Awe—
Or first Prospective—Or the Gold
In using, wear away,

It lay unmentioned—as the Sea
Develop Pearl, and Weed,　　　　　　　　　　　　　　　　10
But only to Himself—be known
The Fathoms they abide—

QUESTIONS

1. What two words in the first stanza mean the opposite of each other? What
words might be taken connotatively to be opposites? Why does Dickinson arrange
key words this way?

2. What equation does Dickinson draw between "Work," "Woman," and
"Wife"?

3. What is the standard definition of "honorable"? How does Dickinson use
this word in the context of the poem?

4. Explain Dickinson's use of "Amplitude," "Awe," and "Prospective" in the
second stanza. What might "Gold" refer to, and what connotations are involved?

5. List the words in the third stanza that denote the life of the sea. In what

way is a woman's mind like the sea? What idea does Dickinson want to draw from this frame of reference?

6. Who is the "Himself" in the last stanza?

7. What larger meaning concerning women and marriage emerges from the poem?

TOPICS FOR WRITING

1. Analyze Dickinson's handling of the "requirements" of women's lives, concentrating on the words she uses.

2. Compare the poem with Aphra Behn's "When Maidens Are Young" (page 352).

3. Analyze Dickinson's use of positive and negative connotations in the poem.

Gwendolyn Brooks

A SONG IN THE FRONT YARD

Gwendolyn Brooks (1917–   ) was born in Topeka, Kansas, but was raised in Chicago's South Side. As a child, Brooks was encouraged by both of her parents to write; her mother, alluding to an earlier black American poet, predicted that she would one day be the female Paul Laurence Dunbar. Brooks attended Wilson Junior College in Chicago and published her first book of poetry, A Street in Bronzeville, *in 1945. Her second book,* Annie Allen, *won the Pulitzer Prize in 1949, making Brooks the first black writer to win that award. Other volumes include* Bronzeville Boys and Girls *(1956);* The Bean Eaters *(1960);* In the Mecca *(1968);* Family Portraits *(1971); an autobiography,* Report from Part One *(1972); and a novel,* Maud Martha *(1953). A major poet, Brooks has been a prodigious supporter of younger artists and an inspiration for them. She has pioneered in depicting inner-city lives and in blending classical poetics with dialect and vernacular. In the following poem, Brooks offers a playful "song" for the lives of girls growing up. At the same time, she might be rendering a more serious personal statement about the need for women to expand the territory and field of vision of their lives.*

I've stayed in the front yard all my life.
I want a peek at the back
Where it's rough and untended and hungry weed grows.
A girl gets sick of a rose.

I want to go in the back yard now   5
And maybe down the alley,
To where the charity children play.
I want a good time today.

They do some wonderful things.
They have some wonderful fun.   10
My mother sneers, but I say it's fine
How they don't have to go in at quarter to nine.
My mother, she tells me that Johnnie Mae
Will grow up to be a bad woman.
That George'll be taken to Jail soon or late   15
(On account of last winter he sold our back gate).

But I say it's fine. Honest, I do.
And I'd like to be a bad woman, too,
And wear the brave stockings of night-black lace
And strut down the streets with paint on my face.   20

QUESTIONS

1. Why does Brooks call her poem a "song"?

2. Explain the connotations Brooks establishes for "front yard" and "back yard" in the poem. What contrast does she draw between life in the front and back yards? Why does she want to go into the back yard?

3. How does Brooks give a fresh connotation to the traditional poetic word "rose" in line 4?

4. What do these words denote in the poem: "peek," "weed," "sneers," "strut"? What do they suggest?

5. Why does Brooks repeat "wonderful" in lines 9 and 10 and "fine" in lines 11 and 17? How does "good time" exist in an unusual relationship to "bad woman"?

6. What feelings concerning the speaker are you left with after reading the poem? Does the poem deal only with the longings of a young girl? Explain.

TOPICS FOR WRITING

1. Write an analysis of the "front yard" and "back yard" of women's lives as depicted by Brooks in the poem.

2. Compare the substance and spirit of this poem with Dickinson's "She Rose to His Requirement" (page 356).

3. Analyze the level of language in the poem, stressing Brooks's use of conventional, everyday terms and rhythms.

Nikki Giovanni

MOTHERS

Nikki Giovanni (1943–   ) was born in Nashville, Tennessee, and was raised in Ohio. She received a BA in history from Fisk University in 1967 and did graduate work at the University of Pennsylvania. Giovanni was witness to the crises of the 1960s and the problems of her generation. "Blacks made the sixties," she has stated, and much of her poetry from that period deals with the need for revolutionary social change. Giovanni's more recent poetry is introspective, dealing with the basic processes of life and the struggles of the individual self. One of the most popular poets today, Giovanni has published numerous volumes of verse, including Black Judgment *(1969),* Re-Creation *(1970),* Broadside Poem of Angela Yvonne Davis *(1970),* Gemini *(1971),* My House *(1972),* The Women and the Men *(1975), and* Cotton Candy on a Rainy Day *(1978). Her work is part of the quest to define our full humanity. In the following poem, Giovanni seeks some of the connections that define her as a black woman, a mother, and a poet.*

the last time i was home
to see my mother we kissed
exchanged pleasantries
and unpleasantries pulled a warm
comforting silence around   5
us and read separate books

i remember the first time
i consciously saw her
we were living in a three room
apartment on burns avenue   10

mommy always sat in the dark
i don't know how i knew that but she did

that night i stumbled into the kitchen
maybe because i've always been
a night person or perhaps because i had wet the bed   15
she was sitting on a chair
the room was bathed in moonlight diffused through
those thousands of panes landlords who rented
to people with children were prone to put in windows

she may have been smoking but maybe not   20
her hair was three-quarters her height
which made me a strong believer in the samson myth
and very black

i'm sure i just hung there by the door
i remember thinking: what a beautiful lady   25

she was very deliberately waiting
perhaps for my father to come home
from his night job or maybe for a dream
that had promised to come by   30
"come here" she said "i'll teach you
a poem: *i see the moon*
      the moon sees me
      god bless the moon
      and god bless me"
i taught it to my son   35
who recited it for her
just to say we must learn
to bear the pleasures
as we have borne the pains

QUESTIONS

1. What is the occasion of this poem? What does the speaker learn? Define the speaker's feelings in the first stanza and in succeeding stanzas.

2. Give several denotations for "pleasantries" in line 3; then select the one that is most appropriate here.

3. Does the word "home" have positive or negative connotations for Giovanni? Justify your answer.

4. What is the poet's attitude toward "mothers"? Why does she use the plural? What is the effect of "mommy" in line 11? What details does the speaker use to depict her mother?

5. How is the speaker like her mother? Point to the details that stress this connection.

6. Why is the poem about the moon especially relevant in the context of Giovanni's poem?

TOPICS FOR WRITING

1. What does the poem reveal about the speaker and her attitude toward her mother?

2. What range of connotations does Giovanni bring to the word "mothers"?

11

METAPHOR AND THEME:
WAR

The language of poetry typically is not literal: it does not project direct statements about experience. Instead, poets utilize numerous *figures of speech*—and there are more than 200 distinct varieties—in order to render an experience indirectly and imaginatively. Figures of speech are ways of saying one thing and meaning another. Thus Robert Burns relies on figurative language when he declares, in one of the most famous stanzas in English poetry:

> O, my luve's like a red, red rose
> That's newly sprung in June.
> O, my luve is like the melodie
> That's sweetly played in tune.

We know that Burn's love is not literally a rose or a melody. But by using figurative language—in this case two similes that draw comparisions quickly—Burns invites us to picture the essence of his love through the rich train of associations that we bring to flowers and music.

Often the pictorial impact of figurative language, its power to make us "see," is generated by vivid comparisons known as *similes* and *metaphors*. Both similes and metaphors draw comparisons between things that are essentially unlike; in other words, we picture someone or something as if it were someone or something else. A poet who directly identifies the comparison by using such signals as "like," "as," and "resembles" is creating similes. With a metaphor, the comparison is expressed, indirect, or implied, rather than stated. If Burns had written, "My luve's a red, red rose" (and forms of the verb "to be" are the clearest metaphorical signals), he would have designed a metaphor. In both instances, poets seek compressed, imaginative likenesses of things drawn from logically different realms.

Metaphorical language (and here we include both metaphors and similes) permits poets to project ideas and emotions more vividly and eloquently than they could by literal statement. Often we are amazed by the power and originality of the metaphorical statement, for metaphorical language can transform experience for us, presenting it in unsuspected ways. Thus the American poet Donald Hall begins a poem, "An Airstrip in Essex, 1960," with these lines: "It is a lost road into the air/It is a desert/among sugar beets." An airstrip that resembles a lost road and a desert: note how we develop a *feeling* for the place through metaphorical language, but also how we are controlled by the metaphors in our thinking about the subject. Why is the airstrip a lost road? Why is it a desert? We apprehend the lostness and abandonment of the place, and indeed Hall goes on to reminisce on earlier events there during World War II. The poet therefore introduces metaphor to convey the subjective truth of the experience that unfolds in the rest of the poem.

In the fragments from the poems by Burns and Hall, we see how similes and metaphors can draw explicit comparisons that dominate individual lines. As a general rule, similes do not develop long or complex comparisons. Certain varieties of metaphor, however, can control not just lines but major segments of a poem, or even an entire poem. The *extended metaphor* stretches over a series of lines; while the *controlling metaphor* dominates the poem. William Shakespeare in the following sonnet uses both varieties of metaphorical language to structure the content of the poem.

> My love is as a fever, longing still
> For that which longer nurseth the disease,
> Feeding on that which doth preserve the ill,
> The uncertain sickly appetite to please.
> My reason, the physician to my love,
> Angry that his prescriptions are not kept,
> Hath left me, and I desperate now approve
> Desire is death, which physic did except.
> Past cure I am, now reason is past care,
> And frantic-mad with evermore unrest;
> My thoughts and my discourse as madmen's are,
> At random from the truth vainly expressed:
>   For I have sworn thee fair, and thought thee bright,
>   Who art as black as hell, as dark as night.

Here the controlling metaphor likens the poet's love to a fever, while a subordinate extended metaphor compares his reason to a physician. And in the last line of the couplet at the end of the sonnet, Shakespeare shifts to striking, almost vicious similes to damn the subject that has caused him so much madness.

In dealing with metaphorical language in poetry, we must expect the unexpected and recognize that the detection of likenesses is not always as easy as in our examples. At times, there are implied metaphors in poetry—comparisons that we must infer without the aid of such grammatical connectives as "like" or "is"—that test our interpretive abilities. Here, for instance, is a short lyric by Randall Jarrell entitled "The Death of the Ball Turret Gunner":

> From my mother's sleep I fell into the State,
> And I hunched in its belly till my wet fur froze.
> Six miles from earth, loosed from its dream of life,
> I woke to black flak and the nightmare fighters.
> When I died they washed me out of the turret with a hose.

Admittedly these are not the easiest lines to interpret, for the dominant metaphor is implied; it can be known only if we examine the images that attach to it. Fortunately, Jarrell in a note on his poem has given us a clue to its metaphorical meaning. Speaking of the gunner, he observed: "hunched upside-down in his little sphere, he looked like the foetus in the womb." Armed with this revelation, we are better prepared to understand the experience of war—as painful separation from life—invoked by the metaphorical language of the poem.

War is also the subject—directly or indirectly—of the poems in this section. All of the poets rely heavily on metaphorical language to capture their visions of war, ranging from the lofty idealism of Richard Lovelace, to the cold sensuousness of Wilfred Owen, to the personal betrayals sensed by Sylvia Plath. Because the subject itself is so volatile, the metaphorical statements by these poets elicit unusually sharp and precise reactions from readers. Each poem, conditioned strongly by simile and metaphor, offers a compressed, emotionally intense, and highly imaginative clarification of the effect of war and its legacy for the poet.

Richard Lovelace

TO LUCASTA, GOING TO THE WARS

Richard Lovelace (1618–1658) was born in Kent, England, the heir to a great estate. He was educated at Oxford University and moved successfully within Cavalier society, a wealthy, handsome, and witty man whose manners captured the courtly spirit of the times. Caught up in the political controversies of the age, Lovelace was imprisoned in 1642 for his anti-Parliamentary activities, and again in 1648. Lovelace's "Lucasta" poems were written to Lucy Sacheverell, his betrothed; however, when she heard, erroneously, that Lovelace had been killed while serving the French king, Charles I, she married another man. Conventional scholarship holds that Lovelace died in extreme poverty, but there is little evidence to support this position. Lovelace's finest poems appear in Lucasta *(1649). In the following poem, one of his best known, Lovelace uses the conventions of Cavalier verse to make a broader statement about love, honor, and war.*

Tell me not, Sweet, I am unkind
   That from the nunnery
Of thy chaste breast and quiet mind,
   To war and arms I fly.

True, a new mistress now I chase,   5
   The first foe in the field;
And with a stronger faith embrace
   A sword, a horse, a shield.

Yet this inconstancy is such
   As you too shall adore;   10
I could not love thee, Dear, so much,
   Loved I not Honor more.

QUESTIONS

1. What is the dramatic occasion of this poem?

2. Lovelace terms his love's "chaste breast and quiet mind" a "nunnery." What is he suggesting? Might "arms" have a double meaning? Explain.

3. Who is the "new mistress" in the second stanza? Why does this metaphor have unusual value?

4. A special type of metaphorical comparison is *metonomy*, in which the poet uses something closely related for the thing actually meant. Which words in the second stanza function this way?

5. How does Lovelace turn his "inconstancy" to honorable advantage in the last stanza? What is the paradox that he resolves? Do you think that he is serious or simply playing with language? Justify your answer.

TOPICS FOR WRITING

1. Develop a portrait of the speaker of the poem, explaining the way he uses figurative language to advance an argument and resolve a potential dilemma.

2. Is this a love poem, a poem about war, or something else? Write an interpretive essay that resolves this issue.

Wilfred Owen

DULCE ET DECORUM EST

Wilfred Owen (1893–1918), a native of Liverpool, England, and a graduate of London University, was killed on the western front just seven days before the armistice that ended World War I. He never lived to see the publication of a projected collection of verse whose subject would be, he declared in a note, "war and the pity of war." His Collected Poems *was published in 1920 by a friend and fellow poet, Siegfried Sassoon, whom Owen had met in a military hospital. Although he won the Military Cross, Owen once asked, ". . . am I not myself a conscientious objector with a very seared conscience?" His most powerful poems, which were written during his thirteen months of service in France, convey Owen's opposition to war and to the false idealism spawned by it. In "Dulce et Decorum Est," Owen offers a vivid picture of men who have been gassed and who have gone insane, who are the living dead. The poem tests the gruesome reality of war against the patriotic sentiment of Horace's lines.*

Bent double, like old beggars under sacks,
Knock-kneed, coughing like hags, we cursed through sludge,
Till on the haunting flares we turned our backs
And towards our distant rest began to trudge.
Men marched asleep. Many had lost their boots   5
But limped on, blood-shod. All went lame; all blind;
Drunk with fatigue; deaf even to the hoots
Of tired, outstripped Five-Nines that dropped behind.

Gas! Gas! Quick, boys!—An ecstasy of fumbling,
Fitting the clumsy helmets just in time,   10
But someone still was yelling out and stumbling
And flound'ring like a man in fire or lime . . .
Dim through the misty panes and thick green light,
As under a green sea, I saw him drowning.

In all my dreams, before my helpless sight,   15
He plunges at me, guttering, choking, drowning.

If in some smothering dreams you too could pace
Behind the wagon that we flung him in,
And watch the white eyes writhing in his face,
His hanging face, like a devil's sick of sin;   20
If you could hear, at every jolt, the blood
Come gargling from the froth-corrupted lungs
Obscene as cancer, bitter as the cud
Of vile, incurable sores on innocent tongues,—
My friend, you would not tell with such high zest   25
To children ardent for some desperate glory,
The old lie: *Dulce et decorum est
Pro patria mori.*

QUESTIONS

1. Why are the troops in the first line "like old beggars under sacks"? How does this simile connect with the one in line 2?

2. Are the soldiers literally drunk and deaf in line 7? Explain.

3. What extended metaphor controls the second and third stanzas? How does the simile in line 12 successfully reinforce the larger comparison?

4. Why is the gassed soldier's face likened to a devil's in line 20? How does the comparison in lines 23–24 contribute to the effectiveness of the poem?

5. Explain the relationship of the speaker to the action and to the audience. What is he saying to the reader?

6. The last lines of the poem are taken from the Latin poet Horace: "It is sweet and fitting to die for one's country." What is Owen's attitude toward this idea? How does it bear on the theme of the poem?

7. The poet Ted Hughes has written of Owens, "His work is a version of old-style prophecy." What do you think Hughes meant by this?

TOPICS FOR WRITING

1. Analyze carefully the way that metaphorical language in "Dulce et Decorum Est" captures the experience of the poem.

2. Write an essay comparing the dramatic situations in "To Lucasta, Going to the Wars" (page 365) and "Dulce et Decorum Est."

Babette Deutsch

DISASTERS OF WAR:
GOYA AT THE MUSEUM

Babette Deutsch (1895–1982) was born in New York City and began publishing poetry when she was a student at Barnard College. She served as Thorstein Veblen's secretary at the New School for Social Research and married the Russian scholar Avrahm Yarmolinsky, with whom she collaborated on a number of verse translations. Deutsch wrote poetry, criticism, novels, and children's books. She is best known as a poet, a distinctive author who combines a refined intellect with emotional involvement in social and political issues. Much of her work is assembled in Collected Poems, 1919–

Babette Deutsch

1962 (1963). "Disasters of War: Goya at the Museum" is
typical of Deutsch's best poetry—brilliant and varied in its
classical surface, tough and yet moving in its willingness to
look unsentimentally at the evils of the world.

Streets opening like wounds: Madrid's. The thresh
Of resistance ends before a tumbled wall;
    The coward and the cursing sprawl
    Brotherly, one white heap of flesh
    Char-mouthed and boneyard black.   5
A woman, dragged off, howls—a lively sack
Of loot. An infant, fallen on its back,
Scowls from the stones at the Herodian lark.
Light is the monster fattening on this dark.

If shadow takes cadavers for her chair,   10
Where fresh fires glare life lifts a wolfish snout.
    Bruised and abused by hope, the rout,
    Turning, is gunned across the square
    And scattered. Rope, knife, lead
Slice prayer short. A lolling head   15
Grins, as with toothache. Stubbornly, the dead
Thrust forward like a beggar's senseless claw.
What is scrawled there in acid? THIS I SAW.

Beyond the Madonnas and marbles, Goya's brute
Testament pits itself against the hush   20
    Of the blond halls, the urbane crush—
    Against the slat-eyed, the astute,
    Craning, against the guard, who yawns.
And pits itself in vain: this dark, these dawns,
Vomit of an old war, things the nightmare spawns   25
Are pictures at an exhibition. We
Look, having viewed too much, and cannot see.

QUESTIONS

1. We can center our analysis of this poem by understanding at the outset
certain references, notably the key reference to Goya. These references function
as *allusions*—that is, as indirect references. Any person, place, or thing—
whether imaginary or actual—can be the subject of an allusion. By consulting a
dictionary or encyclopedia, explain how the mentions of "Goya," "Disasters of
War," "Herodian," and "Madonnas" function as allusions. What is the value of
allusion in a poem?

2. Paraphrase each of the three stanzas of the poem. What is the poet looking
at? What general impression do you get of the scene? What is the dramatic
situation that all the metaphorical language refers to?

3. Identify all the similes and metaphors in the first stanza and explain the

dominant impression that they make. How do you interpret line 9, "Light is the monster fattening on this dark"?

4. What attitude is conveyed by the metaphorical language related to death in stanza 2? Why is life likened to "a wolfish snout"?

5. Are there any metaphors implicit in stanza 3? Explain. What do you understand the poet's feelings to be about the people at the exhibition? How did you arrive at this interpretation?

6. How, according to Deutsch, does Goya's art offer a commentary on the human condition, both historical and contemporary?

TOPICS FOR WRITING

1. Develop an essay entitled "Pictures at an Exhibition" in which you explore Deutsch's use of metaphorical language to make a statement about Goya's art.

2. Some critics maintain that Deutsch's poetry is too intellectual and lacking in emotion. Consider this assertion in light of "Disasters of War."

Langston Hughes

WITHOUT BENEFIT OF DECLARATION

James Langston Hughes (1902–1967) was born of black American and Cherokee ancestry in Joplin, Missouri, and raised in Kansas, Illinois, and Ohio. He was elected class poet in grammar school in Lincoln, Illinois, and again in high school in Ohio. Hughes attended Columbia University briefly and then roamed the world as a seaman, traveling to Africa and Europe before returning to the United States to complete his education at Lincoln University. Hughes then moved back to New York and settled in Harlem. Best known for his poetry and for his stories of Simple, Hughes also wrote journalism, opera librettos, plays and television scripts, and was a notable anthologist of black writing. His poetry reveals a keen ear for folk vernacular, and he is a major experimenter in verse technique in his use of music rhythms. Richard Wright observed that Hughes' poetry is "full of irony and urban imagery." It is deceptively simple and casual, but beneath the simplicity of colloquial statement there are undercurrents of humor and irony, of social criticism, and of compassion for the gallery of figures that Hughes draws. Much of Hughes' most memorable poetry

Langston Hughes

deals with the history and experience of black Americans and with the struggle against hate and oppression. Among his collections of poetry are Weary Blues *(1926),* Fine Clothes to the Jew *(1927),* The Dream Keeper *(1932),* Shakespeare in Harlem *(1942),* Fields of Wonder *(1947),* One Way Ticket *(1949),* Montage of a Dream Deferred *(1951), and* Ask Your Mama *(1961). In his last book of poetry,* The Panther and the Lash *(1967), from which this selection is extracted, Hughes captures in plain speech and lean, compact writing the protest spirit of the 1960s.*

Listen here, Joe
Don't you know
That tomorrow
You got to go
Out yonder where   5
The steel winds blow?

Listen here, kid,
It's been said
Tomorrow you'll be dead
Out there where   10
The snow is lead.

Don't ask me why.
Just go ahead and die.
Hidden from the sky
Out yonder you'll lie;   15
A medal to your family—
In exchange for
A guy.

Mama, don't cry.

QUESTIONS

1. What is meant by the title of the poem?

2. Who is the poet addressing in the poem? What is his purpose?

3. In stanza 1, why does Hughes write "steel winds"?

4. How does the metaphor in stanza 2 connect with "steel winds" in the first stanza?

5. Explain the metaphor in the third stanza, and its appropriateness in the context of the total poem.

6. Hughes wrote in his autobiography, *The Big Sea* (1940), that he learned early the uselessness of crying. How does this statement inform the last line of the poem and does it relate to the poet's general attitude toward the experience?

7. What is the effect of the short, rhymed lines and the colloquial language on the theme of the poem? How do the metaphors complement this style? Would the poem have been as effective without the metaphors? Explain.

TOPICS FOR WRITING

1. Analyze carefully the attitude that is conveyed by language in the poem, especially the metaphors, the vernacular style, and the short lines.

2. Argue for or against the proposition that Lovelace's poem (page 365) is "romantic" while Hughes's is "realistic." Make certain that you explain what you mean by these terms and that you deal with the metaphorical language in the poems.

Sylvia Plath

DADDY

Sylvia Plath (1932–1963) was born in Boston, Massachusetts, and educated at Smith College and Cambridge University. At Cambridge she met and married the English poet Ted Hughes, with whom she had two children. Her style in the first and only volume of poetry that she published in her lifetime, Colossus *(1960), is elegant and classically controlled, dominated by images and metaphors exploring the relationship between the poet and her world. Plath's later poetry, assembled notably in the posthumous volume* Ariel *(1965), reveals a preoccupation with psychic strain and death—painful warnings perhaps of her own suicide. This motif also dominates an autobiographical novel,* The Bell Jar *(1971). "Daddy," which is Plath's most famous poem, captures many of her attitudes, subjects, and themes: war, alienation, victimization, love and hate, anger, death in various forms. It centers on her fury over her father, or on the fury of daughters over fathers. Plath idolized her own father, Otto Plath, who had emigrated from Germany at the age of 16, received a doctorate from Harvard, and become in 1928 a professor of biology; he died in 1940, when Plath was 8 years old, from a neglected case of diabetes. The poem ranges far beyond so-called confessional modes to a statement about the contemporary human condition as an eternal battleground. "You cannot read it," Elizabeth Hardwick has written, "without shivering."*

Sylvia Plath

You do not do, you do not do
Any more, black shoe
In which I have lived like a foot
For thirty years, poor and white,
Barely daring to breathe or Achoo.   5

Daddy, I have had to kill you.
You died before I had time—
Marble-heavy, a bag full of God,
Ghastly statue with one grey toe
Big as a Frisco seal   10

And a head in the freakish Atlantic
Where it pours bean green over blue
In the waters off beautiful Nauset.
I used to pray to recover you.
Ach, du.   15

In the German tongue, in the Polish town
Scraped flat by the roller
Of wars, wars, wars.
But the name of the town is common.
My Polack friend   20

Says there are a dozen or two.
So I never could tell where you
Put your foot, your root,
I never could talk to you.
The tongue stuck in my jaw.   25

It stuck in a barb wire snare.
Ich, ich, ich, ich,
I could hardly speak.
I thought every German was you.
And the language obscene   30

An engine, an engine
Chuffing me off like a Jew.
A Jew to Dachau, Auschwitz, Belsen.
I began to talk like a Jew.
I think I may well be a Jew.   35

The snows of the Tyrol, the clear beer of Vienna
Are not very pure or true.
With my gypsy ancestress and my weird luck
And my Taroc pack and my Taroc pack
I may be a bit of a Jew.   40

Daddy

I have always been scared of *you*,
With your Luftwaffe, your gobbledygoo.
And your neat moustache
And your Aryan eye, bright blue.
Panzer-man, panzer-man, O You—   45

Not God but a swastika
So black no sky could squeak through.
Every woman adores a Fascist,
The boot in the face, the brute
Brute heart of a brute like you.   50

You stand at the blackboard, daddy,
In the picture I have of you,
A cleft in your chin instead of your foot
But no less a devil for that, no not
Any less the black man who   55

Bit my pretty red heart in two.
I was ten when they buried you.
At twenty I tried to die
And get back, back, back at you.
I thought even the bones will do.   60

But they pulled me out of the sack,
And they stuck me together with glue.
And then I knew what to do.
I made a model of you,
A man in black with a Meinkampf look   65

And a love of the rack and the screw.
And I said I do, I do.
So daddy, I'm finally through.
The black telephone's off at the root,
The voices just can't worm through.   70

If I've killed one man, I've killed two—
The vampire who said he was you
And drank my blood for a year,
Seven years, if you want to know.
Daddy, you can lie back now.   75

There's a stake in your fat black heart
And the villagers never liked you.
They are dancing and stamping on you.
They always *knew* it was you,
Daddy, daddy, you bastard, I'm through.   80

QUESTIONS

1. What extended metaphors control the speaker's emotional responses to her father?

2. Why in stanza 1 does the speaker declare that she has "lived like a foot"?

3. To what objects and concepts does she liken her father in stanzas 2–3?

4. Explain the shift in setting in stanza 4. Why does the speaker liken language to an "engine" and herself to a Jew? In this context, identify the German terms and allusions in the poem and explain their relevance.

5. What explicit comparison does she draw in stanza 9? How do you interpret the line in stanza 10 "Every woman adores a Fascist"?

6. How do the extended comparisons in stanzas 11–16 reinforce the dominant comparison established earlier in the poem?

7. Why must the speaker "kill" her father? Why does Plath entitle the poem "Daddy"? Must all women kill their fathers? Discuss this issue with reference to the poem.

8. Explain the relationship between the actual war alluded to in this poem and the personal and psychological wars experienced by the speaker.

TOPICS FOR WRITING

1. Speaking of *Ariel*, Robert Lowell declared: "Everything in these poems is personal, confessional, felt, but the manner of feeling is controlled hallucination, the autobiography of a fever." Relate this statement to "Daddy," examining carefully the metaphorical language.

2. Analyze the varieties of warfare introduced in the poem and the metaphors and similes used to advance the subject.

3. Sylvia Plath wrote, "I think that personal experience is very important, but certainly it shouldn't be a kind of shut-box and mirror-looking, narcissistic experience. I believe it should be *relevant*, and relevant to larger things, the bigger things such as Hiroshima and Dachau and so on." Write an essay assessing Plath's statement in the context of "Daddy."

4. Write a comparative essay on the metaphors of warfare offered by the poets in this section.

12

PERSONIFICATION AND APOSTROPHE: NATURE

One variety of figurative language is personification, which attributes human characteristics to ideas, nonhuman forms of life, and inanimate objects. As such, personification draws comparisons in special ways, tapping the world of correspondences from a clear technical perspective. It offers imaginative discoveries about experience and clarifications about the world by linking things from different realms. When poets personify beauty or wisdom, a mandolin or the moon, a tree or a flower, a cat or a toad, they call attention to those human and nonhuman connections that broaden and illuminate the universe of experience.

Personification humanizes and animates the universe for us. Its figurative comparisons are condensed, concrete, and often conventional, but also at times unique. At times, personification exists in a line or two of a poem, much like a limited or minor metaphor. The Welsh poet Dylan Thomas personifies time in these lines from "Fern Hill":

Time let me hail and climb
Golden in the heydays of his eyes.

That is fresh and inventive personification, more intriguing perhaps than this personification from "What Is Our Life?" by Sir Walter Raleigh:

Heaven the judicious sharp spectator is,
Who sits and marks still who doth act amiss.

Heaven as a spectator and judge of human behavior is a conventional comparison, but Raleigh turns it nicely; much personification does operate with conventional correspondences.

Just as individual lines of a poem might be governed by personification, so an entire poem can be dominated by the technique, as in the well-known "I Wandered Lonely as a Cloud," by William Wordsworth.

I wandered lonely as a cloud
That floats on high o'er vales and hills,
When all at once I saw a crowd,
A host, of golden daffodils,
Beside the lake, beneath the trees,
Fluttering and dancing in the breeze.

Continuous as the stars that shine
And twinkle on the milky way,
They stretched in never-ending line
Along the margin of a bay;
Ten thousand saw I at a glance,
Tossing their heads in sprightly dance.

The waves beside them danced, but they
Outdid the sparkling waves in glee;
A poet could not but be gay,
In such a jocund company;
I gazed—and gazed—but little thought
What wealth the show to me had brought:

For oft, when on my couch I lie
In vacant or in pensive mood,
They flash upon that inward eye
Which is the bliss of solitude;
And then my heart with pleasure fills,
And dances with the daffodils.

Wordsworth does not belabor the comparison of the daffodils to a joyful band of dancers. In fact, the imaginative power of the personification lies in the poet's subdued and subtle humanization of the flowers. We can visualize the daffodils as human forms in a merry procession, as well as perceive their impact on Wordsworth's emotions.

Personification is often allied to apostrophe, in which the speaker addresses someone who is absent or something that is nonhuman and generally not spoken to, but addressed as if it were alive and present. Here, for instance, is the Renaissance poet Sir Philip Sidney, addressing one of the most traditionally personified objects in world literature.

> With how sad steps, O Moon, thou climb'st the skies,
> How silently, and with how wan a face!
> What! may it be that even in heav'nly place
> That busy archer his sharp arrows tries?
> Sure, if that long-with-love-acquainted eyes
> Can judge of love, thou feel'st a lover's case.
> I read it in thy looks; thy languisht grace
> To me, that feel the like, thy state descries.
> Then, ev'n of fellowship, O Moon, tell me,
> Is constant love deem'd there but want of wit?
> Are beauties there as proud as here they be?
> Do they above love to be lov'd, and yet
> Those lovers scorn whom that love doth possess?
> Do they call virtue there ungratefulness?

The moon is personified as a stricken lover, sad and silent, pallid, and languishing over unrequited love. Sidney permits this personification to dominate the first eight lines of the sonnet before drawing another set of correspondences between lunar and terrestrial love in the last six lines. Thus the moon comes alive, not for a purely fanciful purpose, but rather to serve as a vehicle for indicting ungrateful or thoughtless worldly lovers. Moreover, Sidney in the title and twice in the poem addresses his subject intimately as "O Moon" and reinforces this human bond with "thou" and "thy." Through apostrophe, the moon and Sidney become companions in a lovers' complaint.

Apostrophe as a distinct figure of speech can also exist without personification. William Wordsworth, for instance, begins one sonnet by apostrophizing a deceased poet, "Milton thou shouldst be living at this hour." And when William Blake apostrophizes the tiger in his famous poem (which appears for further discussion on page 517), he does so without humanizing or personifying the beast.

> Tyger! Tyger! burning bright
> In the forests of the night,
> What immortal hand or eye
> Could frame thy fearful symmetry?
>
> In what distant deeps or skies
> Burnt the fire of thine eyes?
> On what wings dare he aspire?
> What the hand dare seize the fire?
>
> And what shoulder, & what art,
> Could twist the sinews of thy heart?
> And when thy heart began to beat,
> What dread hand? & what dread feet?

What the hammer? what the chain?
In what furnace was thy brain?
What the anvil? what dread grasp
Dare its deadly terrors clasp?

When the stars threw down their spears,
And water'd heaven with their tears,
Did he smile his work to see?
Did he who made the Lamb make thee?

Tyger! Tyger! burning bright
In the forests of the night,
What immortal hand or eye
Dare frame thy fearful symmetry?

Apostrophe in this instance heightens the life of the tiger, but that life (and the force behind it) is nonhuman, even as Blake anthropomorphizes the creator of the tiger and indulges in personification of the stars.

Both personification and apostrophe have the power to infuse life, objects, the natural world, and the realm of ideas with a humanizing impulse. As techniques, they bring us closer to the things of this world—in this section to landscapes dominated by trees—with compression and immediacy. Because personification and apostrophe tend to treat conventional subjects and rely on standardusage, they can seem stilted or all too familiar. Consequently, we must be prepared to evaluate the effectiveness and originality of personification and apostrophe when poets use these techniques in their verse.

Alfred, Lord Tennyson

THE OAK

Alfred, Lord Tennyson (1809–1892), born in Lincolnshire, England, began writing poetry at the age of 8. He and his brother Charles published their first book of verse, Poems by Two Brothers, *in 1827. Tennyson attended Cambridge University without taking a degree, but met there Arthur Hallam, beginning the deepest and most significant friendship of his life. Tennyson's first significant collection,* Poems, Chiefly Lyrical, *was published in 1830, but met with spotty critical reception and even ridicule. His father died in 1831; and Hallam, engaged to Tennyson's sister Emily, also died suddenly in 1833. These shocks, combined with financial difficulties, family problems (including the mental illnesses of three of his brothers), and critical disapproval of his poetry, constituted a period of crisis for Tennyson. Nevertheless, it also inspired some memorable poetry, including "Ulysses" and parts of* In Memoriam *(1850). Many of his literary friends of the 1830s and 1840s, notably Carlyle and Edward Fitzgerald, recorded their impressions of the enormously handsome Tennyson as a solitary and gloomy soul, "carrying a bit of Chaos about him," as Carlyle declared. But in 1850, Tennyson's mind and fortunes improved with the success of* In Memoriam *and his marriage to Emily Sellwood, whom he had courted for fourteen years. Befriended by Queen Victoria and appointed poet laureate, Tennyson in later life was happy, secure, and famous. His* Idylls of the King *(1859) was very successful, and by the end of his life he was the most revered Victorian poet. A technically accomplished poet, an accurate recorder of nature, and an artist famous for his "messages," Tennyson in the following lyric reveals those qualities most typical of his verse.*

Live thy Life,
   Young and old,
Like yon oak,
Bright in spring,
   Living gold;   5

Summer-rich
   Then; and then
Autumn-changed,
Soberer-hued
   Gold again.   10

All his leaves
   Fall'n at length,
Look, he stands,
Trunk and bough,
   Naked strength.   15

QUESTIONS

1. What basic comparison unifies the three stanzas of this poem?

2. At what point in the poem does Tennyson clearly introduce personification?

3. Does personification govern the entire poem or just a few lines? Explain.

4. What human characteristics are invested in the oak?

5. Besides being personified, the oak to some degree becomes a symbol. (See pages 400–403 for a discussion of symbolism.) What words in the poem encourage us to treat the oak symbolically?

6. Might this poem be considered an example of apostrophe? Justify your decision.

7. How do you assess the originality and success of the personification in the poem? How significant is the poem's theme? Explain.

TOPICS FOR WRITING

1. Analyze Tennyson's use of personification in the poem and its relationship to other varieties of figurative language in the poem.

2. Is this a good poem? Base your evaluation on a careful assessment of the poet's use of such things as personification and other figures of speech, the significance and originality of the idea, and the development of the idea.

Walt Whitman

I SAW IN LOUISIANA A LIVE-OAK GROWING

Walt Whitman (1819–1892) was born on Long Island, the Paumanok of his poems. He attended public schools in Brooklyn and started his career by working in rural schools, setting type, and serving as a writer for several newspapers. Whitman was editor of the influential Brooklyn Eagle *from 1846 to 1848; he used the newspaper's editorial page to espouse abolitionism, opposition to banks and to capital punishment, and endorsement of free soil—positions that probably hastened his dismissal. Subsequently Whitman spent three months on a Louisiana paper,* The Crescent, *and the impact of the South is reflected in "I Saw in Louisiana a Live-Oak Growing" and other poems. After his return to New York, he worked as a carpenter for his father, free-lanced, and then served as editor of* The Brooklyn Times *from 1857 to 1859; once again he was discharged for his outspoken editorial opinions on sex, abortion, prostitution, and slavery. During the Civil War, Whitman served as a volunteer nurse for the Army in Washington, and later was given a clerkship in the Indian Department, but was fired by the secretary of the interior, who labeled* Leaves of Grass *an "indecent book." Whitman published the first edition of Leaves of Grass, which contained twelve untitled poems, in 1855. At the outset of this seminal book, Whitman declared his subject: "One's-self I sing, a simple separate person/Yet utter the word Democratic, the word En Masse." Frank in its subject matter and technically experimental, Leaves of Grass is a mystical celebration of the body and the soul, the individual and the collective, all woven into a process of regeneration that frees humanity from the absoluteness of death. From the embryonic first edition with its magnificent centerpiece, "Song of Myself," Whitman would evolve a symbolic autobiography in later, expanded editions of Leaves of Grass. Stricken by paralysis, Whitman spent the last nineteen years of his life in Camden, New Jersey, generally enjoying his role as "the good gray poet." In "I Saw in Louisiana a Live-Oak Growing," Whitman addresses his true subject—the self—by seeking correspondences in nature.*

I saw in Louisiana a live-oak growing,
All alone stood it and the moss hung down from the branches,
Without any companion it grew there uttering joyous leaves of dark green,
And its look, rude, unbending, lusty, made me think of myself,
But I wonder'd how it could utter joyous leaves standing alone there without
    its friend near, for I knew I could not,   5
And I broke off a twig with a certain number of leaves upon it, and twined
    around it a little moss,
And brought it away, and I have placed it in sight in my room,
It is not needed to remind me as of my own dear friends,
(For I believe lately I think of little else than of them,)
Yet it remains to me a curious token, it makes me think of manly love;   10
For all that, and though the live-oak glistens there in Louisiana solitary in a
    wide flat space,
Uttering joyous leaves all its life without a friend a lover near,
I know very well I could not.

QUESTIONS

1. How does Whitman personify the tree? What words capture its human characteristics?

2. Why is Whitman so affected by the live-oak? In what ways is he like the tree? In what ways unlike?

3. In the context of the poem, what does Whitman mean by "manly love" (line 10)? Is there a sexual element in the poem? Explain.

4. The American poet and critic Josephine Miles (see her poem on page 628) has stated that Whitman is "more visionary, more invocative, more adjectival, more cumulative and more harmonic than any other poet in English." How well does this assessment apply to the poem? Explain. How does the fact that the poem is composed as one long sentence reinforce some of Miles's observation?

TOPICS FOR WRITING

1. Whitman stated of *Leaves of Grass*, "Who touches this book touches a man." Apply his statement to this poem, indicating the use he makes of personification and other techniques to reveal elements of himself.

2. Evaluate Whitman's success in conveying the idea of "manly love" in the poem.

3. Both Tennyson and Whitman examine the oak in order to "read" human meanings into it. Which poet is more successful in the attempt? Which poet is more original? Give reasons for your answers.

Robert Frost

TREE AT MY WINDOW

Robert Frost (1875–1963) was born in San Francisco but moved at the age of 11 with his family to the New Hampshire farm country that would become identified with some of his finest poetry. Frost graduated from Lawrence High School as valedictorian and class poet in 1892. He then attended Dartmouth College briefly, leaving to assume a variety of jobs: bobbin boy in a Lawrence mill, shoemaker, newspaper editor, schoolteacher, farmer. Frost wrote poetry in his leisure hours; he published his first poem in 1894. He married in 1895, and after years of largely unsuccessful farming Frost sold his farm and moved his family to England in 1912, risking everything to become a poet. His first book, A Boy's Will (1913) was published in England, as well as his second, North of Boston (1914), which won critical acclaim. By the time Frost returned to America in 1915, he was a successful and celebrated, if somewhat embarrassed, poet. He won four Pulitzer prizes, for New Hampshire (1923), Collected Poems (1930), A Further Range (1936), and A Witness Tree (1942). A poet of the New England soil, Frost spent the bulk of his mature career on farms in New Hampshire and Vermont, wintering later in his life at a palmetto patch he owned in Florida, and serving intermittently as poet-in-residence at Amherst, Harvard, Michigan, and Dartmouth. Honored after his fortieth year by important foundations, academies, and universities, and even by the American government, Robert Frost died at the age of eight-eight following an operation for cancer. "Tree at My Window," taken from West-running Brook (1928), is typical of Frost's best lyrics—simple, close to nature in its brilliant powers of observation, restrained in emotion and language, "native" in its idiomatic rhythms, tough in the portrayal of life and human existence.

Tree at my window, window tree,
My sash is lowered when night comes on;
But let there never be curtain drawn
Between you and me.

Vague dream-head lifted out of the ground,   5
And thing next most diffuse to cloud,
Not all your light tongues talking aloud
Could be profound.

But, tree, I have seen you taken and tossed,
And if you have seen me when I slept,   10
You have seen me when I was taken and swept
And all but lost.

That day she put our heads together,
Fate had her imagination about her,
Your head so much concerned with outer,   15
Mine with inner, weather.

QUESTIONS

1. Describe the effect of Frost's use of apostrophe in the poem.

2. Paraphrase the second stanza. Why is the tree personified as "a vague dream-head"? How do you interpret "light tongues" (line 7)?

3. What comparison does the speaker draw in the third stanza? What is the nature of the personification here?

4. Why does Frost introduce and personify fate in the last stanza?

5. What does Frost mean by "inner" and "outer" weather in lines 15–16? How does the "weather" connect with earlier elements in the poem?

6. Is there a dominant metaphor in the poem? Explain.

7. What is Frost's final relationship to nature? What is the theme of the poem?

8. Critics have pointed out that Frost's poetry often contains a hint of the dramatic. How do personification and apostrophe contribute to this dramatic effect in "Tree at My Window"?

TOPICS FOR WRITING

1. A critic, Harold Watts, has suggested that the bulk of Frost's poetry "is a dialogue in which the two speakers are Robert Frost himself and the entity which we call nature or process." Explore this dialogue in "Tree at My Window," and explain the contribution of figurative language to the establishment of dramatic effects.

2. Write a comparative essay on the personal or "confessional" quality of the poems by Whitman and Frost, concentrating on the figurative strategies that they employ to reveal (or mask) themselves.

May Swenson

HEARING THE WIND AT NIGHT

May Swenson (1919–   ) was born in Logan, Utah, and educated at Utah State University. She has lived in the New York metropolitan area since 1949, serving periodically as poet-in-residence at Purdue, the University of California at Riverside, and elsewhere. An award-winning poet and critic, Swenson is an experimental artist, seeking in her own words "to get through the curtain of things as they appear, to things as they are, and then into the larger, wilder space of things as they are becoming." She explores mysteries through riddles, and celebrates especially the sounds and colors of natural and urban landscapes, concentrating on the "thingness" (as the poet Chad Walsh observed) of the world. Her collections include Another Animal *(1954),* A Cage of Spines *(1958),* To Mix with Time *(1963),* Half Sun Asleep *(1967), and* New and Selected Things Taking Place *(1978). In this poem, Swenson offers precise images of nature that awaken insights into the surfaces and depths of the world.*

I heard the wind coming,
transferred from tree to tree.
I heard the leaves
swish, wishing to be free

to come with the wind, yet wanting to stay   5
with the boughs like sleeves.
The wind was a green ghost.
Possessed of tearing breath

the body of each tree
whined, a whipping post,   10
then straightened and resumed
its vegetable oath.

I heard the wind going,
and it went wild.
Somewhere the forest threw itself   15
into tantrum like a child.

I heard the trees tossing
in punishment or grief,
then sighing, and soughing,
soothing themselves to sleep.   20

QUESTIONS

1. What is the relationship of the wind to the trees?

2. In what ways are the trees personified in the poem?

3. Is the wind personified? Explain.

4. What is the contribution of simile and metaphor to the poem?

5. What does Swenson mean by "vegetable oath" (line 12)?

6. The poet and critic Elizabeth Bishop (see her poem on page 625) has stated: "Miss Swenson is one of the few good poets who write good poems about nature, and really about nature, not just comparing it to states of mind or society." Does her statement apply to "Hearing the Wind at Night"? Defend your answer.

7. What is the relationship of the speaker to the events in the poem?

TOPICS FOR WRITING

1. Analyze Swenson's extensive use of figurative language in the poem—notably personification, simile, and metaphor—and the way that she achieves a coherent picture of certain objects in the natural world.

2. Robert Lowell, whose own poetry appears on pages 641–643, has called Swenson "quick-eyed." Is she a more acute observer of nature than other poets in this section? In an essay, assess this issue.

3. Compare and contrast the "tree-night" poems by Swenson and Frost.

Denise Levertov

THE VICTORS

*Denise Levertov (1923–   ) was born in Ilford, Essex, Eng-
land, and served as a nurse during World War II. She came to
the United States in 1948 after her marriage to an American,
the writer Mitchell Goodman; she has been an American
citizen since 1955. Levertov acknowledges, "Marrying an
American and coming to live here whle still young was very
stimulating to me as a writer for it necessitated the finding
of new rhythms in which to write, in accordance with new
rhythms of life and speech." Influenced by William Carlos
Williams and Wallace Stevens, and profiting from contact
with other leading contemporary poets, notably Charles
Olson and Robert Duncan, Levertov seeks to capture what
she terms "authentic experience" in verse. She is the author
of more than a dozen volumes of poetry, including* With Eyes
at the Back of Our Heads *(1960),* To Stay Alive *(1971), and* Life
in the Forest *(1979). Levertov's best poetry is, in the words of
Kenneth Rexroth, "clear, sparse, immediate, and vibrant."
She celebrates the world of the senses and, as in the
following poem, invokes nature to clarify more abstract
human attitudes.*

In June the bush we call
alder was heavy, listless,
its leaves studded with galls,

growing wherever we didn't
want it. We cut it   5
savagely, hunted it from the pasture, chopped it

away from the edge of the wood.
In July, still everywhere, it appeared
wearing green berries.

Anyway it must go. It takes   10
the light and air and the good of the earth
from flowers and young trees.

But now in August
its berries are red. Do the birds
eat them? Swinging   15

clusters of red, the hedges are full of them,
red-currant red, a graceful
ornament or a merry smile.

QUESTIONS

1. Levertov has admitted to a preoccupation in her poetry with "the correspondences between things." What is the basic correspondence in the poem?

2. How do the stages of summer serve to structure the poem? What changes

occur in the alder? Are there comparative changes in the perspective of the "we" in the poem? Explain.

3. What use does Levertov make of personification? of metaphor?

4. What do you understand from the title of the poem?

5. What is the theme of the poem?

TOPICS FOR WRITING

1. Explain the shifting view of nature presented by Levertov in the poem, and the contribution of personification to the development of a theme.

2. In a 1965 interview, Levertov observed: "By meditation upon the object the form of the apparently, let us say, fluid or vague or formless object is discovered and can be transmuted into words. It's a kind of alchemy." How well is Levertov's description of the creative process revealed by "The Victors"? Explore this question by looking at the ways the poet transmutes the alders into words.

13

IMAGERY AND THEME: THE SEASONS

Poetry often helps us to visualize and experience the world by offering images or descriptive details that appeal to our senses. This collection of individual images in a poem is termed imagery; and imagery in turn may be defined as the verbal representation of sensory experience. The poet's most typical strategy in developing imagery is to concentrate on visual impressions—on things that we can see in the mind's eye. But forms of imagery based on other sense impressions—sound, taste, touch, smell—can also be employed. Imagery can even involve internal physical sensations like hunger, pain, and nausea, as well as a broad range of mental and emotional states. What we appreciate in imagery is the pictorial power of language to capture the world of sensory impressions.

Archibald MacLeish reveals the centrality of imagery to poetic art and to the nature of figurative language at the outset of his famous poem "Ars Poetica," which appears again for discussion on page 416).

A poem should be palpable and mute
As a globed fruit,

Dumb
As old medallions to the thumb,

Silent as the sleeve-worn stone
Of casement ledges where the moss has grown—

A poem should be wordless
As the flight of birds.

We can readily imagine what these lines would be like without the sequence of images that heightens the ideas posited by the poem. Indeed, part of MacLeish's intention is to contrast the flat, expository, "prosaic" statement at the start of each stanza with the heightened, metaphoric, "poetic" sensory details that govern the end of each stanza. The delight of these lines comes in large part from the coincidence of ideas and images. The "art of poetry" involves the poet's ability to invent imagery that arouses sensations in readers, thereby bringing them into intimate contact with the experience of the poem and perhaps enabling them to understand that experience better.

MacLeish's images convey the idea of what a poem "should be." Similarly, imagery conveys an understanding of things, whether that imagery is literal or figurative, denotative or connotative. Even when the poem relies heavily on imagery to project a direct impression of things, as in Japanese haiku poetry or the poetry of the twentieth-century Imagists, there is often a clear line of meaning traced through the images. One of the most famous haiku poems, by Taniguchi Buson (1715–1783), reveals again the coincidence of imagery and idea:

The piercing chill I feel:
    my dead wife's comb, in our bedroom,
        under my heel.

This is a remarkable poem, even in translation, for it captures in a series of visceral and tactile images the sense of death a husband feels for his departed wife. The chill in the first line of the poem is existential, running to the very fiber of the speaker's being. It is reinforced in the next two lines, in which the cold sense of touch serves as a correlative of death. Even the comb and the bedroom, intimate aspects of his wife's former existence, are details that serve to intensify the sensation felt by the speaker. Here, some might say that Buson captures the sensory experience of the speaker, but that "meaning" is not involved. However, we do understand the mind and feelings of the speaker, and assuredly this is meaning enough.

Many modern poets—notably Ezra Pound, William Carlos Williams, and Amy Lowell—were influenced by earlier Japanese and Chinese poetry. They learned from this verse the power of imagery, untainted by poetic statement, to capture and convey the experience of things in this world. William Carlos Williams's "The Red Wheelbarrow" is one of the best-known Imagist poems:

So much depends
upon

a red wheel
barrow

glazed with rain
water

beside the white
chickens.

The visual images in this poem are fixed and vivid, but what the poem seemingly lacks, in contrast to Buson's haiku, is a definable human mood or a readily comprehensible statement about experience. In short, the imagery seems too literal and too denotative, meaning exactly what it states, offering us a mental picture of a scene but nothing more. Yet we are drawn back to the poet's opening declaration; the poem actually begins with a declarative statement, forcing us to discover why "so much" depends upon the things that are described. In other words, we must probe the imagery once again to discover meaning, and various interpretations might develop. Perhaps Williams means that we do live in a physical world, in a world that we are able to apprehend with our senses, and that we depend on that world, for we are defined by our relationship to it.

Poets want us to sense vividly and to perceive the world through their images, often arranged in a pattern, but they also tend to call attention to the significance of the imagery. When the English poet and Catholic priest Gerard Manley Hopkins offers a catalogue of seasonal delights in "Spring," we know that other meaningful statements reinforce the pattern of imagery:

> Nothing is so beautiful as spring—
>   When weeds, in wheels, shoot long and lovely and lush;
>   Thrush's eggs look little low heavens, and thrush
> Through the echoing timber does so rinse and wring
> The ear, it strikes like lightnings to hear him sing;
>   The glassy peartree leaves and blooms, they brush
>   The descending blue; that blue is all in a rush
> With richness; the racing lambs too have fair their fling.
>
> What is all this juice and all this joy?
>   A strain of the earth's sweet being in the beginning
> In Eden garden.—Have, get, before it cloy,
>   Before it cloud, Christ, lord, and sour with sinning,
> Innocent mind and Mayday in girl and boy,
>   Most, O maid's child, thy choice and worthy the winning.

The visual and auditory images reinforce the poet's expository statement in the first line. In the second and third stanzas, Hopkins deepens the significance of the imagery and the poem by likening the pristine and pastoral spring landscape to Eden before the fall. He turns the poem into a delicate prayer for purity and innocence, which he associates with the purity of spring—a landscape and a time freed from another season "sour with sinning."

All of the poems in this section resemble Hopkin's "Spring" in that they capture specific seasonal rhythms through various patterns of imagery. However, there is a wide range of intention and effect in these poems. We can imagine or visualize the seasonal landscapes offered by the poets with varying degrees of precision. More significantly, we discover through the imagery and the sensory experience—the sights, sounds, and other sensations evoked—a carefully arranged landscape of meaning and value.

William Shakespeare

WINTER

William Shakespeare (1564–1616), introduced on page 341 and presented more fully in the drama section (page 750), is renowned for his vivid depictions of the seasons in his plays and sonnets. Often he used seasonal rhythms as reflections of the human condition, as in the opening lines of sonnet 73, a poem that appears later in full on page 488.

That time of year thou mayst in me behold
When yellow leaves, or none, or few, do hang
Upon those boughs which shake against the cold,
Bare ruin'd choirs, where late the sweet birds sang.

Here and throughout this sonnet, Shakespeare speaks of death by seeking counterparts to it in nature and the seasons. Yet Shakespeare could also create literal images of the seasons that are appealing in themselves, successful in their ability to create a mental picture in readers' and playgoers' imaginations, and presented largely for effect rather than theme. In the following song from the end of Love's Labour's Lost, Shakespeare recreates some of the sensations we associate with a winter landscape.

When icicles hang by the wall,
   And Dick the shepherd blows his nail,
And Tom bears logs into the hall,
   And milk comes frozen home in pail,
When blood is nipped and ways be foul,   5
Then nightly sings the staring owl,
"Tu-whit, tu-who!"
A merry note,
While greasy Joan doth keel the pot.

When all aloud the wind doth blow,   10
   And coughing drowns the parson's saw,
And birds sit brooding in the snow,
   And Marian's nose looks red and raw,
When roasted crabs hiss in the bowl,
Then nightly sings the staring owl,   15
"Tu-whit, tu-who!"
A merry nose,
While greasy Joan doth keel the pot.

QUESTIONS

1. In an unabridged dictionary, find meanings for these words: "nail" (line 2); "ways" (line 5); "keel" (line 10); "saw" (line 11); "crabs" (line 14).

2. List all the images of winter and winter life introduced by Shakespeare. Which have unpleasant connotations, and which pleasant? What is the final effect of the imagery?

3. Which images appeal to the sense of sight? Why is "greasy Joan" an especially evocative image?

4. Which images appeal to the sense of sound? How do you explain the "merry note" of the owl?

5. Are other types of imagery involved? Explain.

6. What is the dominant pattern of imagery in the poem?

7. What images are concrete and literal? Which images could be identified as figurative?

8. What was Shakespeare's purpose in writing this poem? Is there a theme or any subordinate meaning that you sense in the imagery? Explain.

TOPICS FOR WRITING

1. Evaluate Shakespeare's success in making us visualize the winter scene that he depicts in the poem. Focus on the varieties of imagery that he employs.

2. Must a poem contain a theme? Present evidence from Shakespeare's poem to support your position.

John Keats

TO AUTUMN

John Keats (1795–1821) was born at Finsbury, north of London, the eldest of five children. His father was killed by a fall from his horse in 1804, and when his mother remarried the same year, the children were sent to their maternal grandparents at Enfield and, later, Edmonton. In 1815, Keats went to London for medical training. He published his first poetry the following year and met many notable literary figures, including Shelley; by 1817, he had abandoned his plans for a medical career. Keats published his first collection, Poems, in 1817 and Endymion in 1818. In 1818, Keats contracted a severe sore throat during a walking tour in Scotland; he also met 18-year-old Fanny Brawne, with whom he began an affair. Keats wrote all of his major odes, including "To Autumn," in 1819; by the end of the year, his sore throat had recurred. Following hemorrhaging and an attack of blood spitting in the first half of 1820, Keats upon his doctor's advice sailed for Italy in September. The Eve of St. Agnes and Other Poems was published that year. He died on February 23, 1821, and was buried in the English ceme-

*tery at Rome. In "To Autumn," Keats writes an ode—a
special, typically elaborate and lofty form of lyric addressed
to a person or thing—to express his sentiments about
various aspects of a specific season.*

I

Season of mists and mellow fruitfulness,
  Close bosom-friend of the maturing sun;
Conspiring with him how to load and bless
  With fruit the vines that round the thatch-eves run;
To bend with apples the mossed cottage-trees,   5
  And fill all fruit with ripeness to the core;
    To swell the gourd, and plump the hazel shells
With a sweet kernel; to set budding more,
  And still more, later flowers for the bees,
  Until they think warm days will never cease,   10
    For Summer has o'er-brimmed their clammy cells.

II

Who hath not seen thee oft amid thy store?
  Sometimes whoever seeks abroad may find
Thee sitting careless on a granary floor,
  Thy hair soft-lifted by the winnowing wind;   15
Or on a half-reaped furrow sound asleep,
  Drowsed with the fume of poppies, while thy hook
    Spares the next swath and all its twinéd flowers:
And sometimes like a gleaner thou dost keep
  Steady thy laden head across a brook;   20
  Or by a cider-press, with patient look,
    Thou watchest the last oozings hours by hours.

III

Where are the songs of Spring? Ay, where are they?
  Think not of them, thou hast thy music too—
While barréd clouds bloom the soft-dying day,   25
  And touch the stubble-plains with rosy hue;
Then in a wailful choir the small gnats mourn
  Among the river sallows, borne aloft
    Or sinking as the light wind lives or dies;
And full-grown lambs loud bleat from hilly bourn;   30
  Hedge-crickets sing; and now with treble soft
  The red-breast whistles from a garden-croft;
    And gathering swallows twitter in the skies.

QUESTIONS

1. Define the following words: "thatch-eves" (line 4); "hook" (line 17); "sallows" (line 28); "bourn" (line 30); "croft" (line 32).

2. Why does Keats apostrophize autumn? What are his feelings about this season?

3. Personification as a special variety of figurative language (see pages 375–378) appears in the poem. How does Keats personify autumn in each of the three stanzas?

4. What patterns of imagery do you detect in each stanza? What is the relationship of other seasons to the development of the imagery? Why is time important in the poem?

5. In addition to visual imagery, what other types of sensory imagery appear in the poem? Cite examples and explain their effects.

6. What mood is created by the various forms of imagery in the poem?

7. To what extent can you visualize this scene? Explain. How does it compare with your ability to visualize the scene in Shakespeare's poem (page 391)?

8. Is the subject of the poem simply autumn, or does Keats introduce other subjects and ideas?

TOPICS FOR WRITING

1. Explain the way the imagery is organized in "To Autumn," stressing various types of imagery in the poem, pattern in each stanza, and final meanings and effects.

2. Analyze Keats's attitude toward beauty in the poem.

Wallace Stevens

THE SNOW MAN

Wallace Stevens (1879–1955), a major American poet, was born in Redding, Pennsylvania. He attended Harvard University and received a degree from New York University Law School. Stevens was admitted to the New York bar in 1904, and from 1916 he was associated with Hartford Accident and Indemnity Company, becoming a vice president in 1934. Few of his associates in the insurance world knew of Stevens' private penchant for jotting down poems, but he liked the blend of business and private vocations. "It gives a man character as a poet," he once observed, "to have daily contact with a job." Stevens' first book of verse, Harmonium, did not appear until 1923. Later volumes, including Ideas of Order (1935), The Man with the Blue Guitar (1937), Transport to Summer (1947), Collected Poems (1954), and Opus Posthumous (1957), secured his reputation as a "virtuoso." A poet in and of the world, singing the American landscape more persistently than any poet since Whitman, Stevens was a bold and elegant experimenter in poetics. Often he dealt with the role of the imagination or, as in the following poem, with the nature of reality. Always poetry and humanity seem to be at the center of reality, and in "The Snow Man" Stevens offers a series of striking images as an eloquent and contemplative statement about the nature of creation and our perception of it.

One must have a mind of winter
To regard the frost and the boughs
Of the pine-trees crusted with snow;

And have been cold a long time
To behold the junipers shagged with ice,   5
The spruces rough in the distant glitter

Of the January sun; and not to think
Of any misery in the sound of the wind,
In the sound of a few leaves,

Which is the sound of the land   10
Full of the same wind
That is blowing in the same bare place

For the listener, who listens in the snow,
And, nothing himself, beholds
Nothing that is not there and the nothing that is.   15

QUESTIONS

1. What does Stevens mean when he states in the opening line, "One must have a mind of winter"? Why must one have such a mind?

2. Note that this poem consists of one long, periodic sentence, whose theme is stated at the end. Interpret the last line, which offers a clue to the theme. Why is the imagery in the poem consistent with the theme and the tone?

3. Exactly who or what is the "snow man" in the title?

4. How does the auditory imagery complement the visual imagery in the poem? Are there other types of sensory imagery? Explain.

5. Point out images of color, sight, sound, and distance. What is the dominant impression?

6. Why is the poem quite unlike that by Shakespeare on winter (page 391)? Are they alike in any way?

7. Roy Harvey Pearce, in *The Continuity of American Poetry*, states that "Stevens' quest for an ultimate humanism . . . leads him toward a curious dehumanization." Comment on this remark in relation to "The Snow Man."

TOPICS FOR WRITING

1. Analyze the way in which Stevens uses imagery to reinforce abstract statement in "The Snow Man."

2. Compare and contrast the poems about winter by Shakespeare (page 391) and Stevens.

3. Robert Pack, in a book on Stevens, observes, "Stevens' acute sense of color and sound becomes a part of a larger awareness of the sensual as a principle, a force, and of physical life as the setting in which thought and imagination thrive." Apply this statement to "The Snow Man."

William Carlos Williams

SPRING AND ALL

William Carlos Williams (1883–1963), who like his friend Wallace Stevens was both a professional man and a poet, was born in Rutherford, New Jersey. He received his medical degree from the University of Pennsylvania in 1906, and from 1910 until his retirement in 1951 he was a successful pediatrician in Rutherford. Influenced by Ezra Pound when the two were at the University of Pennsylvania, and himself a major influence on such later poets as Robert Lowell and Theodore Roethke, Williams was an advocate of American images, materials, and strategies in poetry. His books include The Collected Later Poems *(1950),* The Collected Earlier Poems *(1951), and a magnificent five-volume philosophical poem about the American experience,* Paterson *(1946–1958). Williams was a poet of particulars, seeking to lift moments of reality from the actual world and transcribe them economically in poetry. "No ideas but in things," he declared. Taking his "things" from the native surroundings of the New Jersey landscape, as in the following poem, Williams is unrivaled in the clarity of his images depicting parts of the world. However, in "Spring and All" Williams also uses, in his words, "the particular to discover the universal."*

By the road to the contagious hospital
under the surge of the blue
mottled clouds driven from the
northeast—a cold wind. Beyond, the
waste of broad, muddy fields   5
brown with dried weeds, standing and fallen

Spring and All

patches of standing water
the scattering of tall trees

All along the road the reddish
purplish, forked, upstanding, twiggy   10
stuff of bushes and small trees
with dead, brown leaves under them
leafless vines—

Lifeless in appearance, sluggish
dazed spring approaches—   15

They enter the new world naked,
cold, uncertain of all
save that they enter. All about them
the cold, familiar wind—

Now the grass, tomorrow   20
the stiff curl of wildcarrot leaf

One by one objects are defined—
It quickens: clarity, outline of leaf

But now the stark dignity of
entrance—Still, the profound change   25
has come upon them: rooted, they
grip down and begin to awaken

QUESTIONS

1. What time of year is fixed by the imagery in this poem? What change is Williams describing?

2. What effect does the image of the "contagious hospital" have on the natural processes described by Williams? Can we be certain about his intention in introducing the image? Why or why not?

3. How does this poem resemble the haiku on page 389 and Williams's own "The Red Wheelbarrow" (pages 389–390)?

4. Does this poem deal exclusively with a literal description of natural processes, or does it reveal larger truths? Explain. Defend your answer by specific reference to the imagery in the poem.

5. Explain the function of color, distance, temperature, and outline of objects in fixing the landscape of the poem.

6. What role does the personification of spring in stanza 4 play in the balance and organization of the poem?

7. What patterns of imagery do you detect in the poem?

TOPICS FOR WRITING

1. Speaking of *Spring and All* (1923), critic James Breslin states, "The shifts in the outer world, as Williams' identification with the spring suggests, correspond to an inner change—and so the real subject of these poems is the re-creation of the self." Apply this statement to the title poem.

2. Demonstrate the consistency in Williams's development of images and image patterns in the poem, and the overall harmony of effect that he achieves.

3. Assess Williams's success in capturing a particular period in the change of seasons and in conveying the "universal" message that he wants to derive from it.

Ann Stanford

THE BLACKBERRY THICKET

Ann Stanford (1916–   ), an award-winning poet, translator, and anthologist of women's poetry, was born in La Habra, California. She received her BA from Stanford University and her Ph.D. from UCLA. Currently she is professor of English at California State University, Northridge. Stanford's collections include In Narrow Bound *(1943),* The White Bird *(1949),* The Weathercock *(1966),* The Descent *(1970), and* In Mediterranean Air *(1977). In "The Blackberry Thicket," Stanford uses a controlling image and lush supporting imagery to capture and hold the essence of memory.*

I stand here in the ditch, my feet on a rock in the water,
Head-deep in a coppice of thorns,
Picking wild blackberries,
Watching the juice-dark rivulet run
Over my fingers, marking the lines and the whorls,   5
Remembering stains—
The blue of mulberry on the tongue
Brown fingers after walnut husking,
And the green smudge of grass—
The earnest part   10
Of heat and orchards and sweet springing places.
Here I am printed with the earth
Always and always the earth ground into the fingers,
And the arm scratched in thickets of spiders.
Over the marshy water the cicada rustles,   15
A runner snaps sharp into place.

The Blackberry Thicket

The dry leaves are a presence,
A companion that follows up under the trees of the orchard
Repeating my footsteps. I stop to listen.
Surely not alone   20
I stand in this quiet in the shadow
Under a roof of bees.

QUESTIONS

1. What is the season? List some of the images that permit you to draw this conclusion.

2. Why is the blackberry thicket a controlling image for all the other images in the poem?

3. What is the speaker's emotional state or frame of mind? How can you tell?

4. What kinds of imagery are present in the poem? Cite examples of each. How do the images contribute to the dramatic situation?

5. Which line or lines make an abstract statement? Could this be construed as the theme of the poem? Explain.

6. What other types of figurative language exist in the poem?

TOPICS FOR WRITING

1. Show how Stanford conveys her theme through a series of related images.

2. Explain how the images in this poem create a decided atmosphere, or mood.

3. Write an essay in which you classify the types of imagery found in the poems in this section.

14

SYMBOLISM AND THEME: DEATH

We know from an earlier section (see pages 164–166) that a symbol may be defined as something that stands for other than what it is. For example, the chrysanthemums in John Steinbeck's story mean more than what they simply are; they stand for the earthy, sensuous part of the main character's personality. In a similar way, symbolism in poetry radiates beyond the thing toward other levels and varieties of meaning. Often a symbol in poetry may be readily understood because it has become a part of common cultural knowledge: a cross symbolizes Christ, a rose beauty, an American flag patriotism. Yet symbolism in poetry also can be complex and demanding, forcing us to use our best critical faculties to discuss broader meanings in objects, persons, conditions, and things.

   With a conventional poetic symbol or with symbolism that we can easily understand, we readily detect highly charged meaning in an image. This rich suggestiveness, pointing toward added meaning or value in a word, reflects the connotative power of language—the ability of words to mean more than they denote. Yet the importance of a conventional symbol is that it has a similar effect on all of us. The conventional symbol is like a sign pointing directly from the object to something else that it clearly suggests. The rose has functioned traditionally in this manner, as in Burns's "A Red, Red Rose" or the following well-known poem, "Song," by Edmund Waller:

> Go, lovely rose!
> Tell her that wastes her time and me
>   That now she knows,
> When I resemble her to thee,
> How sweet and fair she seems to be.
>
> Tell her that's young
> And shuns to have her graces spied,
>   That hadst thou sprung
> In deserts, where no men abide,
> Thou must have uncommended died.
>
> Small is the worth
> Of beauty from the light retired;
>   Bid her come forth,
> Suffer herself to be desired,
> And not blush so to be admired.
>
> Then die! that she
> The common fate of all things rare
>   May read in thee:
> How small a part of time they share
> That are so wondrous sweet and fair!

Here the fragile and transitory beauty of the rose is likened by the speaker to his beloved's beauty; and Waller apostrophizes the flower in order to advance a conventional thesis that his own rose, his beloved, should "suffer herself to be desired" before her "rare" beauty fades.

Not all symbols, however, have meanings so readily identified and understood. For one thing, poets can use even conventional symbols in special contexts that force us to reconsider or abandon traditional meanings. William Blake, especially, has a penchant for altering traditional symbolic meanings. In "The Sick Rose," he offers a strikingly new symbolic context for this overused flower:

> O rose, thou art sick
> The invisible worm
> That flies in the night
> In the howling storm
>
> Has found out thy bed
> Of crimson joy,
> And his dark secret love
> Does thy life destroy.

Why is the rose sick? And who or what is the "invisible worm"? In this poem we are forced to mediate between two major symbols in order to arrive at any interpretation. Nevertheless, it is the overall context of the poem that permits us to fix symbolic meaning. The rose—which might symbolize love, beauty, innocence, sexual purity, or this entire constellation of ideas—is being attacked by the destructive agent or force symbolized by the worm. Violation, notably of a sexual nature, is the normative or standard context, forcing us to read the poem in a despairing, potentially tragic way. Even when there is a *range* of meaning associated with a symbol, we can usually set this range and work within it in order to understand the poem.

Another problem involved in understanding poetic symbolism is that it often overlaps with or is reinforced by imagery, metaphors, and allusions. An image, for instance, can be repeated in a poem, forming a pattern of persistent symbolic meaning. The following poem by Emily Dickinson reflects the way in which image, metaphor, and symbolism blend within each other:

> 'Twas warm—at first—like Us—
> Until there crept upon
> A Chill—like frost upon a Glass—
> Till all the scene—be gone.
>
> The forehead copied Stone—
> The Fingers grew too cold
> To ache—and like a Skater's Brook—
> The busy eyes—congealed—
>
> It straightened—that was all—
> It crowded Cold to Cold—
> It multiplied indifference—
> As Pride were all it could—
>
> And even when with Cords—
> 'Twas lowered, like a Weight—
> It made no Signal, nor demurred,
> But dropped like Adamant.

In this remarkable tracing of the process whereby death encroaches upon life, Dickinson employs images of coldness and rocklike hardness to suggest death, reinforcing the image with metaphorical language. Yet it might be argued that the *degree* to which Dickinson stresses these qualities forces us to interpret the images symbolically. She is, of course, speaking very literally as well, but the importance that she invests in a particular portion of imagery makes us suspect that Dickinson also wants the poem to possess symbolic power.

Symbolism also can shade into allusion. We can have difficulty determining whether a reference to something in history, literature, or legend (either real or imaginary) is allusive or symbolic. Essentially, poets are willing to exploit both the allusive and symbolic dimensions of language in a single context. Ann Finch, Countess of Winchilsea (1661–1720), does this in her poem "Adam Pos'd":

> Cou'd our first father, at his toilsome plough,
> Thorns in his path, and labour on his brow,
> Cloath'd only in a rude, unpolish'd skin,
> Cou'd he a vain fantastick nymph have seen,
> In all her airs, in all her antick graces,
> Her various fashions, and more various faces;

How had it pos'd that skill, which late assign'd
Just appellations to each several kind!
A right idea of the sight to frame;
T' have guest from what new element she came;
T' have hit the wav'ring form, and giv'n this Thing a name.

We might argue that the poet is alluding to the biblical creation myth, to Adam in the Garden of Eden, and specifically to the creation and even naming of the primal woman, Eve. And we would be correct. Yet, "our first father" and "this Thing" are also symbolic properties of a highly conventional nature. Understanding of them does not require specialized knowledge; at the symbolic level, they are part of our cultural heritage.

When dealing with the most common and obvious poetic symbols or the most unusual and complex, we must be prepared to explain and assess a symbol's contribution to the richness of meaning in a poem. The following selections, all centering on death and on last things, are fine examples of the way in which poets employ symbolism and technical resources to vary and compress meaning.

George Herbert

CHURCH-MONUMENTS

George Herbert (1593–1633), who was born into an illustrious and pious Anglo-Welsh family, was educated at Cambridge University. He was appointed reader in rhetoric in 1618 and was public orator from 1620 to 1627. Herbert was elected to Parliament in 1624, but in 1626 he debarred himself from civil service by taking minor religious orders; he was ordained a priest in 1630. A friend of John Donne and Francis Bacon, Herbert chose "to lose himself in an humble way," serving as a pious and charitable country parson. Aware early in 1633 that he was dying of consumption, Herbert readied a copy of his book, The Temple, *for publication. The religious lyrics in this miscellany, which also includes hymns, prayers, and Church history, are varied in verse forms, but clear, concise, and natural in diction. "Church-Monuments," one of Herbert's greatest sacred poems, is a logically developed argument and a meditation in which the speaker submits himself to last things.*

While that my soul repairs to her devotion,
Here I intomb my flesh, that it betimes
May take acquaintance of this heap of dust;
To which the blast of death's incessant motion,
Fed with the exhalation of our crimes,
Drives all at last. Therefore I gladly trust   5

My body to this school, that it may learn
To spell his elements, and find his birth
Written in dusty heraldry and lines;
Which dissolution sure doth best discern,   10
Comparing dust with dust, and earth with earth.
These laugh at jet and marble put for signs,

To sever the good fellowship of dust,
And spoil the meeting. What shall point out them,
When they shall bow, and kneel, and fall down flat   15
To kiss those heaps, which now they have in trust?
Dear flesh, while I do pray, learn here thy stem
And true descent: that when thou shalt grow fat

And wanton in thy cravings, thou mayst know,
That flesh is but the glass, which holds the dust   20
That measures all our time; which also shall
Be crumbled into dust. Mark here below
How tame these ashes are, how free from lust,
That thou mayst fit thy self against thy fall.

QUESTIONS

1. How does the title help us to interpret symbols in the poem? Where is the speaker in relation to those church monuments?

2. What patterns of imagery do you detect in the poem? Does any of this imagery assume symbolic weight? For example, what do you understand from the repetition of the word "dust"?

3. Are the "soul" and the "body" personified or treated as symbols? Explain. What must the body or the flesh learn in "this school"?

4. Explain the lines "flesh is but the glass, which holds the dust/That measures all our time." What sort of figurative language is used here?

5. Why is this such a grim, almost ominous poem? Summarize your interpretation of the poem. How effective is the poem as an intricate account of death?

TOPICS FOR WRITING

1. Write an extended interpretation of Herbert's account of the experience of death in this poem and of what death tells him about life.

2. Analyze the various elements in the poem that function symbolically.

John Keats

WRITTEN IN DISGUST
OF VULGAR SUPERSTITION

John Keats (1795–1821), introduced in an earlier section (page 392), occasionally engaged in poetry-writing contests with his friend and mentor Leigh Hunt, who sponsored his first publication. The following sonnet is one distinguished product of these literary exercises. "Written in Disgust of Vulgar Superstition" is a chilling poem, dominated by Keats's revulsion over religion and containing a gentle affirmation of life. Unlike his stance in "To Autumn" (page 393), Keats here cannot make any sympathetic identification with the scene that he coldly depicts in the following poem.

The church bells toll a melancholy round,
  Calling the people to some other prayers,
  Some other gloominess, more dreadful cares,
More hearkening to the sermon's horrid sound.
Surely the mind of man is closely bound   5
  In some black spell; seeing that each one tears
  Himself from fireside joys, and Lydian airs,
And converse high of those with glory crown'd.
Still, still they toll, and I should feel a damp—
  A chill as from a tomb, did I not know   10
That they are going like an outburnt lamp;
  That 'tis their sighing, wailing ere they go
  Into oblivion;—that fresh flowers will grow,
And many glories of immortal stamp.

QUESTIONS

1. What is Keats's general attitude toward religion in the poem?

2. How do the church bells in Keats's poem become symbolic of various aspects of the human condition?

3. Explain the symbolic quality of the following words and phrases: "the sermon's horrid sound"; "black spell"; "tomb"; and "fresh flowers." Why do the "fresh flowers" contrast with other elements of the poem?

4. Explain the allusion to "Lydian airs."

5. How do other types of figurative language contribute to symbolic meanings in the poem?

6. Why is there a deathlike quality in the poem?

TOPICS FOR WRITING

1. Compare the symbolic quality of Herbert's church-monuments (page 403) to that of the church bells in Keats's poem.

2. More than one poem has dealt with the tolling of church bells. Evaluate Keats's relative success in breathing life into an old symbol.

Emily Dickinson

THERE'S A CERTAIN SLANT OF LIGHT

Emily Dickinson (1830–1886), whose life was traced on page 346, wrote some of her finest poems about the pain that is generated by specific natural movements. In this drama of natural process, death for Dickinson is the great absolute, the force that tunes her sensibility to perfect pitch. In fact, her greatest achievements tend to focus on "the Hour of Lead," as she wrote in one poem. In "There's a certain slant of light," Dickinson begins with a neutral image, but by accretion binds it into a powerful and rather sinister symbol, or "seal," as she terms it, of despair.

There's a certain slant of light,
On winter afternoons,
That oppresses, like the weight
Of cathedral tunes.

Heavenly hurt it gives us;   5
We can find no scar,
But internal difference
Where the meanings are.

None may teach it anything,
'Tis the seal, despair,—   10
An imperial affliction

Sent us of the air.

When it comes, the landscape listens,
Shadows hold their breath;
When it goes, 'tis like the distance   15
On the look of death.

QUESTIONS

1. Is the light in the first line a symbol? How does it become symbolic in the course of the poem?

2. Why does Dickinson liken the winter light to cathedral tunes? What is the relationship between the words "oppresses" and "weight"?

3. What contribution does the phrase "Heavenly hurt" make to the symbolic meaning of the poem?

4. Which important word from stanza 3 functions as a symbol?

5. Explain the dramatic force of the last stanza.

6. The critic Denis Donaghue observes, "Distance and death are cousins in many of Emily Dickinson's poems." Apply this statement to this poem and to its symbolic meanings.

TOPICS FOR WRITING

1. Analyze the way in which the winter light becomes a vehicle for the consideration of death.

2. Explain the mood that is generated by the situation in the poem.

Robert Frost

STOPPING BY WOODS ON A SNOWY EVENING

Robert Frost (1874–1963), whose ability to capture brilliantly the various contours of natural landscapes was alluded to earlier (see page 382), often invested the simplest of these landscapes with symbolic meaning. Thus in his poem "The Road Not Taken," which appears later in this anthology, the two roads symbolize not just natural paths in the woods, but also the choices we are confronted with in our lives. Similarly, in "Stopping by Woods on a Snowy Evening,"

Robert Frost

Frost offers more than a calm and vivid description of a winter scene. There might very well be a primal conflict lurking in the geography of the poem—a conflict which once again forces the poet to confront two diverging roads.

Whose woods these are I think I know.
His house is in the village though;
He will not see me stopping here
To watch his woods fill up with snow.

My little horse must think it queer   5
To stop without a farmhouse near
Between the woods and frozen lake
The darkest evening of the year.

He gives his harness bells a shake
To ask if there is some mistake.   10
The only other sound's the sweep
Of easy wind and downy flake.

The woods are lovely, dark and deep,
But I have promises to keep,
And miles to go before I sleep,   15
And miles to go before I sleep.

QUESTIONS

1. Paraphrase what happens literally in the course of this poem.

2. What do we know about the speaker in the poem? What is his relationship to the horse and to the owner of the woods?

3. What conflict does the speaker experience in the poem? How is the conflict expressed in symbolic terms?

4. How do the various images in the poem—the snow, the "darkest" winter night, the frozen lake, the "easy wind and downy flake"—form a symbolic pattern?

5. Offer a symbolic interpretation of the last stanza. How do the dark woods and the repeated image of sleep reinforce each other symbolically?

6. What is Frost saying about the relationship between life and death, between the pursuit of beauty and pursuit of other obligations?

TOPICS FOR WRITING

1. Write an essay on the imagery and symbols of death in the poem and on the theme that Frost wants to evoke.

2. Compare and contrast Frost's poem with Dickinson's (page 406) on the topic of death.

Anne Sexton

THE FURY OF FLOWERS
AND WORMS

*Anne Sexton (1928–1974) was born in Newton, Massachu-
setts. She was an indifferent student but a writer of poetry at
an early age. Sexton attended Garland Junior College in
Boston before eloping in the summer of 1948 with Alfred
"Kayo" Sexton II. In 1953, she was hospitalized for severe
depression and a suicide attempt; she subsequently began
writing poetry again, on the advice of her psychiatrist.
Sexton became a student of W. D. Snodgrass and Robert
Lowell, and through Lowell's 1958–59 poetry seminar at
Boston University she entered into a close friendship with
Sylvia Plath. To Bedlam and Part Way Back (1960), Sexton's
first poetry collection, is a confessional account of the
author's confrontations with insanity and of her personal
relationships with her family. In the spring of 1961, the
Radcliffe Institute for Independent Study named Sexton and
her friend Maxine Kumin their first scholars in poetry.
Sexton's subsequent volumes, notably All My Pretty Ones
(1962), the Pulitzer Prize–winning Live or Die (1966), and
Transformations (1971), continue to trace her psychological
conflicts and torments. On October 4, 1974, she had lunch
with Kumin and then went home and committed suicide. In
the following poem, Sexton balances confessionalism and
craft as she explores her dominant theme.*

Let the flowers make a journey
on Monday so that I can see
ten daisies in a blue vase
with perhaps one red ant
crawling to the gold center.   5
A bit of the field on my table,
close to the worms
who struggle blindly,
moving deep into their slime,
moving deep into God's abdomen,   10
moving like oil through water,
sliding through the good brown.

The daisies grow wild
like popcorn.
They are God's promise to the field.   15
How happy I am, daisies, to love you.
How happy you are to be loved
and found magical, like a secret
from the sluggish field.
If all the world picked daisies   20
wars would end, the common cold would stop,
unemployment would end, the monetary market
would hold steady and no money would float.

Listen world,
if you'd just take the time to pick   25
the white fingers, the penny heart,
all would be well.
They are so unexpected.

They are as good as salt.
If someone had brought them   30
to van Gogh's room daily
his ear would have stayed on.
I would like to think that no one would die anymore
if we all believed in daisies
but the worms know better, don't they?   35
They slide into the ear of a corpse
and listen to his great sigh.

QUESTIONS

1. Why does Sexton want the flowers to "make a journey/on Monday"?

2. How is the earth described in the poem?

3. What do the flowers, notably the daisies, symbolize in the poem?

4. Explain the symbolic function of the worms.

5. What is the relationship of the flowers to the worms? How do you explain the "fury" in the title? What triumphs, the flowers or the worms, and why?

6. What is the allusion to Van Gogh? How does it fit into the context of the poem?

TOPICS FOR WRITING

1. Analyze the symbolic conflict between the flowers and the worms in Sexton's poem.

2. Write a psychological profile of Sexton based on the images and symbols she uses in the poem.

3. What makes her a "confessional" poet?

4. Write a comparative essay on the similarities and differences among the themes of the poems in this section. Analyze especially the various symbolic stances that the poets take toward life and death.

15

TONE AND THEME: POETRY

Tone, as defined in the fiction section devoted to this topic (see pages 150–152), is the writer's attitude toward his or her subject. It is the *voice* of the writer that we hear—a voice that is intimately connected in most instances to theme and mood. This voice may be serious or playful, modest or arrogant, irreverent or devout. Tone may be constant, or it may shift from line to line or stanza to stanza in a poem. We trace in the tone of a poem the speaker's unique emotional and intellectual approach to a subject.

With certain subjects—for example, death—it is often easy for us to hear the tone or voice that illuminates the emotional context, the situation, the mood, and the speaker's frame of mind. Here are the opening lines from Ben Jonson's poem on the death of his first son (1616). The complete poem appears on page 495 of the anthology.

Farewell, thou child of my right hand and joy;
My sin was too much hope of thee, loved boy,
Seven years thou wert lent to me, and I thee pay,
Exacted by thy fate, on the just day.

We expect the tone of grief and loss in such a poem, but other tonalities are involved as well, notably the sense of sin and of fatalism that Jonson brings to the specific occasion of the poem. We hear the voice of a great poet coping with personal tragedy in natural and moving yet at the same time stately and noble language.

We seek in the language of a poem clues to its range of tone. Indeed, if we overlook or misinterpret these clues, we misjudge tone and as a consequence fail to understand the theme or complete meaning of a poem. Virtually all of the elements of poetic language come into play when we explore a poem's tonality: word choice, selection of details, connotations, figures of speech, imagery, rhythm, phrasing and construction of lines and sentences, irony, satire, and other conventions. With so many elements and techniques to contend with, we should avoid the temptation to reduce the tone of a poem to a single word—except if we use that word as a starting point for a more sophisticated analysis of the mingling of tones that we typically encounter in a poem.

Even very short lyrics can require us to be sensitive to the full range of poetic convention and literary tradition that a poet might exploit in the rendering of tone. Phillis Wheatley, who was born in Africa around 1753 and brought to Boston in 1761 as a slave, offers an interesting commingling of tones in her short poem, "On Being Brought From Africa to America":

'Twas mercy brought me from my pagan land,
Taught my benighted soul to understand
That there's a God, that there's a Saviour too:
Once I redemption neither sought nor knew.
Some view our sable race with scornful eye,
"Their colour is a diabolic dye."
Remember, Christians, Negroes, black as Cain,
May be refined, and join th' angelic train.

How do we contend with tone or *tones* in this poem? Is the tone serious in the first four lines, or is Wheatley being ironic? Indeed, could the tone of the overall poem be slightly ironic and even paradoxical? (Irony, paradox, and satire will be discussed more fully in the next chapter.) Again, is Wheatley neutral and subdued in tone in lines 5–6, or is gentle criticism of the position implied? By the end of the lyric, the tone—moralistic and mildly imperative—seems to crystalize, as Wheatley offers a homily for her "Christian" audience. Nevertheless, we can approach the problem of tone in this poem from shifting perspectives, depending largely on the voice of the poet.

One way to profitably study the question of tone is to examine poems that have a similar subject. The five poems in this section are unified by the common subject of poetry itself and of the poet's craft. Other subjects—either major or subordinate—might be involved, but the statement, or theme, emerging from all of these poems seems to be about poetry. Yet the poems assembled here are also either subtly or sharply different in tone. A careful reading and analysis of these selections should yield insights into the way that tone influences our interpretation of the subject of a poem.

William Shakespeare

SINCE BRASS, NOR STONE, NOR EARTH, NOR BOUNDLESS SEA

William Shakespeare (1564–1616), who appears earlier in this anthology (pages 341 and 391), wrote several sonnets that explore the power of poetry to preserve the transitory and mortal aspects of this world. Perhaps the most famous poem in this category is "Shall I compare thee to a summer's day?" (page 487). Another sonnet that explores this subject, complex and impressive in execution, is "Since brass, nor stone, nor earth. . . ." Here Shakespeare formulates a series of questions about time, nature, beauty, and death that lead, typically, to a statement about poetic art at the end of the poem.

Since brass, nor stone, nor earth, nor boundless sea,
But sad mortality o'er-sways their power,
How with this rage shall beauty hold a plea,
Whose action is no stronger than a flower?
O, how shall summer's honey breath hold out   5
Against the wreckful siege of battering days,
When rocks impregnable are not so stout,
Nor gates of steel so strong, but Time decays?
O fearful meditation! where, alack,
Shall Time's best jewel from Time's chest lie hid?   10
Or what strong hand can hold his swift foot back?
Or who his spoil of beauty can forbid?
  O, none, unless this miracle have might,
  That in black ink my love may still shine bright.

QUESTIONS

1. Paraphrase all of the questions that Shakespeare uses to structure the poem. Why does he employ so many questions? What is the effect of these questions on the tone of the poem?

2. What tone is created by the images of powerful elements in the first line? How does this tone compare with the image of the flower at the end of the first quatrain, or first four lines?

3. How is the content of lines 5–8 (the second quatrain in the sonnet) similar to the content of lines 1–4? Is the tone the same? Why or why not?

4. Why does the tone shift slightly in lines 9–10? How do you interpret "Time's best jewel" and "Time's chest"?

5. Characterize the tones of the last two lines. What theme emerges at the end of the poem? How does tone complement theme at this point?

TOPICS FOR WRITING

1. Write an essay exploring the question-and-answer pattern in the poem, and the effect of this pattern on the tonalities of the poem.

2. Examine the images and symbols in the poem and their contribution to tone and theme.

3. Stephen Spender once observed: "The great difficulty confronting the reader of Shakespeare's sonnets is to discriminate among the different kinds of truth they reveal." Apply his observation to the poem.

Anne Bradstreet

THE AUTHOR TO HER BOOK

Anne Bradstreet (1612?–1672), whose most famous poem, "To My Dear and Loving Husband," appears on page 343, was the first truly dedicated poet to settle in America. Bradstreet's poems were taken to London by her brother-in-law and apparently published without her consent in a volume entitled The Tenth Muse Lately Sprung Up in America *(1650). Around 1666, Bradstreet began to revise the poems and work on others for a second edition, which she did not live to see published in 1678. She wanted the following poem to serve as a preface to the authorized edition.*

Thou ill-formed offspring of my feeble brain,
Who after birth did'st by my side remain,
Till snatched from thence by friends, less wise than true,
Who thee abroad exposed to public view;
Made thee in rags, halting, to the press to trudge,   5
Where errors were not lessened, all may judge.
At thy return my blushing was not small,
My rambling brat (in print) should mother call;
I cast thee by as one unfit for light,
Thy visage was so irksome in my sight;   10

The Author to Her Book

Yet being mine own, at length affection would
Thy blemishes amend, if so I could:
I washed thy face, but more defects I saw,
And rubbing off a spot, still made a flaw.
I stretched thy joints to make thee even feet,   15
Yet still thou run'st more hobbling than is meet;
In better dress to trim thee was my mind,
But nought save homespun cloth in the house I find.
In this array, 'mongst vulgars may'st thou roam;
In critics' hands beware thou dost not come;   20
And take thy way where yet thou are not known.
If for thy Father asked, say thou had'st none;
And for thy Mother, she alas is poor,
Which caused her thus to send thee out of door.

QUESTIONS

1. What is the poet's attitude toward the "friends" who published her book without her consent?

2. Bradstreet compares her relationship to the book as similar to the relationship of a mother to a child. List some of the details she uses in this extended metaphor. What tone is fostered by the details in lines 1–10?

3. How does the poet's tone shift after line 10?

4. What comments does Bradstreet make about the poet's craft? With what tone does she render these observations?

5. What is Bradstreet's attitude toward critics?

6. Explain Bradstreet's final attitude toward her book.

TOPICS FOR WRITING

1. Write an essay that traces the shifts in tone in this poem and the techniques employed by Bradstreet to successfully balance and integrate these shifting tonalities.

2. Assess Bradstreet's attitude toward poetry and her own craft as expressed in this poem.

Archibald MacLeish

ARS POETICA

Archibald MacLeish (1892–1982), a noted American poet, playwright, educator, and public figure, was born in Glencoe, Illinois. Following three years as an attorney in Boston, MacLeish joined the expatriate community in Paris, living there from 1923 to 1928. After his return to the United States, MacLeish pursued for many years dual vocations as writer and public figure, serving as assistant secretary of state during the Roosevelt administration and also as librarian of Congress. He won Pulitzer prizes for Collected Poems *(1952) and for his Broadway success* J.B. *(1958). "Ars Poetica," which means "the art of poetry," is one of MacLeish's early poems. In this selection, MacLeish offers a memorable definition of poetry, attempting to realize stated ideas in the form of the poem itself.*

A poem should be palpable and mute
As a globed fruit,

Dumb
As old medallions to the thumb,

Silent as the sleeve-worn stone   5
Of casement ledges where the moss has grown—

A poem should be wordless
As the flight of birds.

A poem should be motionless in time
As the moon climbs,   10

Leaving, as the moon releases
Twig by twig the night-entangled trees,

Leaving, as the moon behind the winter leaves,
Memory by memory the mind—

A poem should be motionless in time   15
As the moon climbs.

A poem should be equal to:
Not true.

For all the history of grief
An empty doorway and a maple leaf.   20

For love
The leaning grasses and two lights above the sea—

A poem should not mean
But be.

QUESTIONS

1. List the five similes in stanzas 1–5. How are they unified in effect? What does MacLeish mean when he says a poem should be wordless?

2. Why does MacLeish use a refrain in stanzas 5 and 8?

3. What is the argument in stanzas 9–12? What is the relationship of the last two lines to the entire poem?

4. Why has MacLeish used so many images to convey his philosophy of poetry?

5. Characterize the tone of the poem.

TOPICS FOR WRITING

1. MacLeish makes a dogmatic statement at the end of the poem. Compare this statement with the poem itself. How effectively does MacLeish realize his ideals? Why?

2. Explain MacLeish's control of tone in the poem and the relationship of tone to imagery and theme.

Nikki Giovanni

POETRY

Nikki Giovanni (1943–   ), in her previous poem, "Mothers" (page 359), attempted indirectly to define her role as a poet. In this selection, Giovanni looks more consciously and comprehensively at the nature and purpose of poetry, offering also a personal statement about the private world of the poet.

poetry is motion graceful
as a fawn
gentle as a teardrop
strong like the eye
finding peace in a crowded room   5

Nikki Giovanni

we poets tend to think
our words are golden
though emotion speaks too
loudly to be defined
by silence   10

sometimes after midnight or just before
the dawn
we sit typewriter in hand
pulling loneliness around us
forgetting our lovers or children   15
who are sleeping
ignoring the weary wariness
of our own logic
to compose a poem
    no one understands it   20
it never says "love me" for poets are
beyond love
it never says "accept me" for poems seek not
acceptance but controversy
it only says "i am" and therefore   25
i concede that you are too
a poem is pure energy
horizontally contained
between the mind
of the poet and the ear of the reader   30
if it does not sing discard the ear
for poetry is song
if it does not delight discard
the heart for poetry is joy
if it does not inform then close   35
off the brain for it is dead
if it cannot heed the insistent message
that life is precious

which is all we poets
wrapped in our loneliness   40
are trying to say

QUESTIONS

1. How does the first stanza in this poem resemble elements in MacLeish's "Ars Poetica"? Is the tone of the two poems similar? Explain.

2. Why does Giovanni, or any poet, write poetry? What is the feeling or attitude of the speaker toward her craft?

3. What connections exist between art and life, between art and love?

4. What is the effect of the definition of poetry in stanza 4?

5. Explain the tone of this poem in the last stanza.

TOPICS FOR WRITING

1. Analyze Giovanni's motives for writing poetry and her attitude toward the poet and his or her craft.

2. MacLeish once cited the writers of his generation—notably Pound, Eliot, and Yeats—for having restored "public" speech to poetry. Assess the appropriateness of this remark for Giovanni's poem and the general effect of language on tone in "Poetry."

Victor Hernandez Cruz

TODAY IS A DAY OF GREAT JOY

Victor Hernandez Cruz (1949–   ) was born in Aguas Buenas, Puerto Rico, and grew up in New York City. He has taught at San Francisco State University and at the University of California, Berkeley. Cruz's collections of verse include Snaps *(1969),* Mainland *(1973), and* Tropicalization *(1976). "My mind," comments Cruz, "is creole and can fuse many unlikely things together: outer variety, inner unity; we are an experiment in communications." In the following selection, Cruz fuses images from unlikely realms in order to validate, in simultaneously humorous and critical tones, the potential power of poetry.*

when they stop poems
in the mail & clap
their hands & dance to
them
when women become pregnant   5
by the side of poems
the strongest sounds making
the river go along

it is a great day

as poems fall down to   10
movie crowds in restaurants
in bars

when poems start to
knock down walls to
choke politicians   15
when poems scream &
begin to break the air

that is the time of

true poets   that is
the time of greatness   20

a true poet aiming
poems & watching things
fall to the ground

it is a great day.

QUESTIONS

1. What imaginary situation does Cruz describe in the poem? What details contribute to the overall impression? What is the poet's attitude toward pregnant women, movie crowds, and politicians?

2. How do the level of language and the absence of both capitalization and punctuation help to establish the tone?

3. Explain the public functions of the "true poet." How does this attitude contrast with Giovanni's description of the function of the poet?

4. How does the term "great day" influence the tone of the poem? What is the overall tone of the poem?

5. Is the situation in the poem opposed to the actual situation in today's world? Explain.

TOPICS FOR WRITING

1. Define Cruz's attitude toward the function of poetry in the world.

2. Among the poems in this section, what explanation of poetry seems best to you? Why?

3. Describe and account for the similarities and differences in tone encountered in the poetry in this section.

16

IRONY, SATIRE, PARADOX, AND THEME: THE STATE

The contradictions of life and living provide the poet with the powerful weapons of irony, satire, and paradox; they have been used longest, it seems, against the greatest human institution, the state. Almost universal is the question: Why can't my country be better than it now is?

The writer may have led all other artists into an adversary relationship with the state—not necessarily wanting to overthrow it (though this sometimes has been true), but to help make its actions commensurate with the humanistic ideals nearly every state implants among its citizens.

Irony (from the Greek *eironeia*) has long been a major weapon because it is not what it seems to be; it possesses shades of meaning that run counter to the obvious sense of images and words. Satire (from the Latin *satira*) is criticism of human folly, individual or collective, but carries with it the hope that once folly is revealed, those guilty of it will quit being fools. Paradox (from the Greek *paradoxon*), may seem to be contradictory, but it carries certain truths. These tools and their many relatives (see section 6; pages 150–152, and the glossary) are used more precisely by poets, who imaginatively compress and distill their ideas to a far greater extent than do writers of fiction.

Tone is perhaps most discernible when the poet uses irony, satire, or paradox, for they largely reveal the author's attitude toward the subject he or she is writing about. The great Roman satirist Juvenal (A.D. 60–130) noted that "it is difficult not to write satire," given the follies of Roman society during his day, and that "indignation creates [his] verses."

Juvenal, like many poets he influenced, did not rely on understatement, a relative of irony; he used wit like a rapier, perhaps finding that understatement was deceitful, like using a dagger.

Understatement *is* used in these lines from Franz Werfel's (1890–1945) "The Bulletproof Hidalgo":

> The seared features of the Colonel revealed his regret that he was unable to deal out anything worse than death.

Shelly's irony and paradox in "Ozymandias" in no way approaches the ironic fervor—the opposite of understatement—seen in his "Song to the Men of England":

> Men of England, wherefore plough
> For the lords who lay ye low?
> Wherefore weave with toil and care
> The rich robes your tyrants wear?
>
> Wherefore feed, and clothe, and save,
> From the cradle to the grave,
> Those ungrateful drones who would
> Drain your sweat—nay, drink your blood?

While "Ozymandias" is coolly allegorical in its irony, "Song to the Men of England" seems to have been written with uncommon urgency. It might be considered a call to revolt against the state, or it might be considered hyperbole—exaggeration for reasons having little to do with credence.

If the state is a ready target for the use of irony, then the mores and habits and practices within it, sanctioned *de facto* by the state, are equally vulnerable. It seems to be true, however, that the discrepancies between what the state says it is and what it really is are the subjects mainly of the victims of those discrepancies.

It will be argued that such situations are not the stuff of art, but humanity's conflicts and its desire to be rid of conflicts often seem to be central to creativity.

Claude McKay's "America" reflects not only the racial, but also the creative, conflict when race becomes a factor in literature. This is a relatively recent phenomenon that is most often observed in the Western world. However, in Africa, South America, and Central America and in other parts of the world where people of different cultures have merged into one civilization, the phenomenon is spreading.

McKay had poetic predecessors, among them George Moses Horton (1799–1883) and Paul Laurence Dunbar (1872–1906), who sometimes used satire or irony. There were not many such poets, for black people, slave and free, in many regions of the United States were not permitted by law to learn to read and write, sometimes on pain of death. McKay's followers have been far more numerous.

One of the best satirists was Melvin B. Tolson (1898–1966), whose irony is deeply rooted in history, not in the personal, as with McKay. Both share a sense of form and rhythm. "Dark Symphony" (1940) concretely attacks the state, while "America" deals with it in the abstract:

> None in the Land can say
> To us black men Today:
> You smash stock markets with your coined blitzkriegs,
> And make a hundred million guinea pigs.
> You counterfeit our Christianity,
> And bring contempt upon Democracy.

Tolson is saying here that black men are not guilty of making the state what it is, that being victim precludes the possession and exercise of power. Cummings, in "next to of course god" supplies us with an alternate image of one of those who does have power and who wishes to retain it.

Irony and paradox and the role of the state at home and abroad provide the tools and subjects of Auden's "The Unknown Citizen," and Levertov's "What Were They Like?" In these poems the state is faceless and mute, yet clearly able to determine (hardly ever for the better) the course of our lives. Though one poem deals with war and its aftermath and the other with state bureaucracy and its red tape, the sense of individual helplessness, of being trapped in the belly of a monster, prevails.

This is not a new subject for poets; those in England who were caught up in the enthusiastic demands for liberty that resulted finally in the American, French, and Haitian revolutions often developed a healthy distrust for the state. That attitude carried into the Victorian period, with Tennyson's lightly regarded though telling poem "Charge of the Light Brigade" (1855). Here, blind obedience to the state is mocked in blood:

> Theirs is not to make reply,
> Theirs is not to reason why,
> Theirs is but to do and die.
> Into the valley of Death
>   Rode the six hundred.

Irony, satire, and paradox in poetry, drama, and fiction are used to the end that human institutions be improved. It is debatable that these weapons have been successful. Nevertheless, their continued use serves as fair warning that improvement is still much to be desired and that these well-used literary tools will be with us for some time to come.

Percy Bysshe Shelley

OZYMANDIAS

*The son of a country squire, Percy Bysshe Shelley (1792–
1822), influenced by the credos of the Enlightenment, or the
Age of Reason, revolted against his conservative upbringing. At Oxford, he wrote a pamphlet in favor of atheism and
was dismissed. He first married at 19, but that marriage
ended in disaster. Shelley married Mary Godwin in 1816. He
was a student of Greek and spent much time in Italy, where
he drowned. Shelley believed that a Platonic civilization
was possible, but that men needed pushing in that direction.
His works, often abstract and allegorical, were lyrical and
elegiac and sometimes, as with "Ozymandias," were warnings couched in irony. Among his best-known works are
"Hymn to Intellectual Beauty" (1816); "Ode to the West
Wind" (1819); "To a Skylark" (1819); and Prometheus Unbound (1819). Less emphasis, unfortunately, has been
placed on Shelley's social philosophy than on his metaphysical views.*

I met a traveler from an antique land
Who said: Two vast and trunkless legs of stone
Stand in the desert . . . Near them, on the sand,
Half sunk, a shattered visage lies, whose frown,
And wrinkled lip, and sneer of cold command,   5
Tell that its sculptor well those passions read
Which yet survive, stamped on these lifeless things,
The hand that mocked them, and the heart that fed;
And on the pedestal these words appear:
"My name is Ozymandias, king of kings: 10
Look on my works, ye Mighty, and despair!"
Nothing beside remains. Round the decay
Of that colossal wreck, boundless and bare
The lone and level sands stretch far away.

QUESTIONS

1. The "traveler from an antique land" mentioned by Shelley might not be a
person. What, then, might he symbolize?

2. "Two vast and trunkless legs" may be an ironic recapitulation of a
still-current phrase. What is that phrase and how would it apply here?

3. What statement is Shelley making about the artist and his or her work?

4. From the description in the poem, what kind of ruler was Ozymandias
likely to have been?

5. How does the poet achieve dramatic effects in the poem?

6. Explain fully the irony of the shattered statue and the words chiseled on its
pedestal.

TOPICS FOR WRITING

1. Using this poem as a basis, describe the importance of the artist in any civilization and how his or her work reflects whether that civilization was bad, good, or indifferent.

2. Analyze the way in which Shelley combines irony of situation, dramatic irony, and verbal irony in "Ozymandias."

3. Compare the description of Ozymandias' statue to those you may have seen of the pharaohs in Egypt and the gods of the temples of Angkor Wat in Cambodia. Describe what is seen in the faces of the latter that is not present in the face of Ozymandias?

Claude McKay

AMERICA

Born in Jamaica, Claude McKay (1890–1948) is believed to have been the first black American writer to publish a best-selling novel—though the quality of that novel remains in doubt. Primarily a poet, McKay was a ranking figure of the Harlem Renaissance, which was one element of the entire post–World War I renaissance of American letters. After publishing two volumes of poetry in the West Indies, McKay came to the United States in 1912. A lukewarm supporter of the new communist society in Russia, he was disillusioned after a visit there. Two additional volumes of verse, Spring in New Hampshire and Other Poems *(1920) and* Harlem Shadows *(1922), preceded his popular novels,* Home to Harlem *(the best-seller, 1922),* Banjo *(1929), and* Banana Bottom *(1933). A far better poet than novelist, McKay's lyricism often echoed the Romantic poets of England. "America," a sonnet, is direct and less lyrical than his other work. Both ironic and paradoxical, it is also a lament in the classic English sonnet form.*

Although she feeds me bread of bitterness,
And sinks into my throat her tiger's tooth,
Stealing my breath of life, I will confess
I love this cultured hell that tests my youth!
Her vigor flows like tides into my blood,   5
Giving me strength against her hate.
Her bigness sweeps my being like a flood.
Yet as a rebel fronts a king in state,

I stand within her walls with not a shred
Of terror, malice, not a word of jeer.   10
Darkly I gaze into the days ahead,
And see her might and granite wonders there,
Beneath the touch of Time's unerring hand,
Like priceless treasures sinking in the sand.

QUESTIONS

1. What connotations does "America" have for McKay?

2. Compare the final seven lines of "America" to the last seven lines of "Ozymandias" (page 424), pointing out the similarities.

3. Why does McKay call himself "a rebel"?

4. Describe the tone and theme of "America."

5. Explain why McKay cites the paradox of his love and "her hate." What does "bread of bitterness" symbolize in biblical terms?

6. What does the author mean by the phrase "cultured hell"? Explain why, for McKay, the juxtaposition of words like these adds to the depth of his ironic lament.

TOPICS FOR WRITING

1. It is implied by McKay that the same elements that brought down Ozymandias and his civilization will bring down America. Describe those elements and offer an evaluation.

2. Analyze and evaluate the paradox that McKay establishes in "America." Is "cultured hell" an apt description of America? Why or why not?

3. Explain why McKay personifies America as female and granite-walled.

E. E. Cummings

NEXT TO OF COURSE GOD

Edward Estlin Cummings (1894–1962) was mainly a poet, but also a novelist, playwright, painter, and essayist. "Of all the post–World War I writers of the renaissance of American literature, none possessed a greater lyrical gift or more imagination than E. E. Cummings," wrote Max Herzberg. Cummings himself said: "My writing consists of a pair of miscalled novels; a brace of plays, one in prose, the other in blank verse; nine books of poems; an indeterminate number of essays; an untitled volume of satire; and a ballet scenario." Cummings's first published work was his novel The Enormous Room *(1922) which was considered a modern masterpiece. The plays,* HIM *(1927) and* Santa Claus *(1946), came between the poetry. There were seven volumes between* Tulips and Chimneys *(1923) and* Poems 1923–1954 *(1954). Cummings, a gifted satirist, nevertheless maintained the rhythmic cadences of natural speech. In "next to of course god," he takes familiar lines, pushing us from one to the next until at last we are faced with the familiar politician and his familiar lines.*

"next to of course god america i
love you land of the pilgrims' and so forth oh
say can you see by the dawn's early my
country 'tis of centuries come and go
and are no more what of it we should worry   5
in every language even deafanddumb
thy sons acclaim your glorious name by gorry
by jingo by gee by gosh by gum
why talk of beauty what could be more beautiful
than these heroic happy dead   10
who rushed like lions to the roaring slaughter
they did not stop to think they died instead
then shall the voice of liberty be mute?"

He spoke. And drank rapidly a glass of water

QUESTIONS

1. How does the structure of the poem differ from the "traditional" fourteen-line sonnet? Supply the rhyme scheme. Why is it that two lines do not rhyme with any other?

2. Why is the poem composed primarily of clichés, and what kind of person is generally associated with the use of them?

3. The first thirteen lines in this poem are a single sentence. Explain what effect is gained by this strategy.

4. The nouns "pilgrim" and "sons" form the basis upon which this poem is structured. What satire does Cummings intend by using them?

5. Which lines have the most alliteration (see page 433)? In which lines are there sound changes?

6. Why would this poem not "work" without the last line? What impression is given by the lack of a period after "water"?

TOPICS FOR WRITING

1. "next to of course god" was first published in 1926. Why is it still a valid reflection of American life? Analyze and evaluate the implications of this question.

2. Compare the paradoxes present in this poem with those appearing in the poem by McKay.

W. H. Auden

THE UNKNOWN CITIZEN

Wystan Hugh Auden (1907–1973) was born in England in 1907. After college at Oxford he became a member of a group of London poets that included Stephen Spender, C. Day Lewis, Louis MacNeice, and Christopher Isherwood. This was one of the most talented collections of writers in England at that time. Auden, like many other writers of the period, saw socialism as the political system that would save the world. He fought with the Republicans during the Spanish Civil War and in 1939, after his marriage to Erika Mann, emigrated to the United States and later became a citizen. Greatly influenced by W. B. Yeats and T. S. Eliot, Auden's work was first socially concerned and then more religiously concerned. He collaborated with MacNeice on Letters from Iceland *(1937) and with Isherwood on four plays during the decade of the 1930s. A deft employer of satire, as in "The Unknown Citizen," Auden was wedged between English and American culture. His references tend to be more English, and this is true even though he lived in Greenwich Village in New York until a few years before his death. His works include* Poems *(1930),* Look, Stranger *(1936),* Spain *(1937),* The Sea and the Mirror *(1944),* For the Time Being: A Christmas Oratorio *(1944),* Selected Poetry *(1959), and* Homage to Clio *(1960).*

(TO JS/07/M/378

THIS MARBLE MONUMENT

IS ERECTED BY THE STATE)

He was found by the Bureau of Statistics to be
One against whom there was no official complaint,
And all the reports on his conduct agree
That, in the modern sense of an old-fashioned word, he was a saint.

For in everything he did he served the Greater Community.   5
Except for the War till the day he retired
He worked in a factory and never got fired,
But satisfied his employers, Fudge Motors Inc.
Yet he wasn't a scab or odd in his views,
For his Union reports that he paid his dues,   10
(Our report on his Union shows it was sound)
And our Social Psychology workers found
That he was popular with his mates and liked a drink.
The Press are convinced that he bought a paper every day
And that his reactions to advertisements were normal in every way.   15
Policies taken out in his name prove that he was fully insured,
And his Health-card shows he was once in hospital but left it cured.
Both Producers Research and High-Grade Living declare
He was fully sensible to the advantages of the Installment Plan
And had everything necessary to the Modern Man,   20
A phonograph, radio, a car and a frigidaire.
Our researchers into Public Opinion are content
That he held the proper opinions for the time of year;
When there was peace, he was for peace; when there was war, he went.
He was married and added five children to the population,   25
Which our Eugenist says was the right number for a parent of his
    generation,
And our teachers report that he never interfered with their education.
Was he free? Was he happy? The question is absurd:
Had anything been wrong, we should certainly have heard.   30

QUESTIONS

1. Characterize the tone of this poem.

2. What is the theme of "The Unknown Citizen"?

3. What famous monument in Washington forms the basis of the irony present here?

4. Why is this "report" issued by the Bureau of Statistics?

5. Which contemporary institutions found the "unknown citizen" to be of great value? Why?

6. What meaning does this poem have for the present? The future?

7. Describe the form of this poem: Is it free verse in rhyme? Or does it contain a more "traditional" structure? Explain.

TOPICS FOR WRITING

1. Describe and comment on the paradox that exists between the title and the theme of the poem and the line "Was he free? Was he happy? The question is absurd."

2. Draw a relationship between the tone and theme of Cummings's poem "next to of course god" (page 427) and this poem.

3. Analyze what Auden is saying about life and society in this poem. What is the relevance of irony, satire, and paradox to his purpose?

Denise Levertov

WHAT WERE THEY LIKE?

Denise Levertov Goodman (1923–   ), introduced earlier in this anthology (page 386), was born in England and came to the United States in 1948 as the war bride of an American GI, author Mitchell Goodman, who had stayed in Europe to study. She had displayed considerable skill as a poet while growing up and this came to fruition under the influence of poets she studied, among them William Carlos Williams, Wallace Stevens, and Robert Creeley. Levertov's work has been marked by a natural gracefulness, an inquisitive mind, and an elegant humanity that assumes the best may be in all of us. In "What Were They Like?" posed in questions and answers, she defines the humanity of the Vietnamese people and their civilization, which the military found necessary to deny in order carry on the war there. Through the use of metaphor and juxtaposed imagery, Levertov reaches beyond the war to her essential theme, which might be called the loss of love. Her collections include Overland to the Islands *(1958),* With Eyes at the Back of Our Heads *(1960),* Here and There *(1957),* Jacob's Ladder *(1961),* The Sorrow Dance *(1966; from which the following poem was taken),* Stay Alive *(1971), and* Life in the Forest *(1979). Levertov has done five other collections.*

1) Did the people of Viet Nam
    use lanterns of stone?
2) Did they hold ceremonies
    to reverence the opening of buds?
3) Were they inclined to quiet laughter?   5
4) Did they use bone and ivory,
    jade and silver, for ornament?
5) Had they an epic poem?
6) Did they distinguish between speech and singing?

1) Sir, their light hearts turned to stone.   10
    It is not remembered whether in gardens

stone lanterns illumined pleasant ways.

2) Perhaps they gathered once to delight in blossom,
    but after the children were killed
    there were no more buds.   15
3) Sir, laughter is bitter to the burned mouth.
4) A dream ago, perhaps. Ornament is for joy.
    All the bones were charred.
5) It is not remembered. Remember,
    most were peasants; their life   20
    was in rice and bamboo.
    When peaceful clouds were reflected in the paddies
    and the water buffalo stepped surely along terraces,
    maybe fathers told their sons old tales.
    When bombs smashed those mirrors   25
    there was time only to scream.
6) There is an echo yet
    of their speech which was like a song.
    It was reported their singing resembled
    the flight of moths in moonlight.   30
    Who can say? It is silent now.

QUESTIONS

1. Describe the tone and theme of "What Were They Like?"

2. How would you describe the structure of the poem?

3. What is the author's purpose in using this title?

4. In which example here is the permanence of artists' works acknowledged?

5. The first part of "What Were They Like?" is composed of questions. Who or what is answering them in the second part of the poem? Refer to Shelley's "traveler" (page 424).

6. There are several paradoxes in the second portion of the poem. Point them out and explain why they are paradoxes.

TOPICS FOR WRITING

1. Explain the importance of an epic poem to a culture. What purpose does such a work serve? Which cultures have them? Does the United States have one?

2. Describe Levertov's use of imagery in this poem and how it contributes to the ironies inherent in the author's descriptions.

3. Describe the elements in "What Were They Like?" that make it an artistic and humanitarian work.

17

SOUND AND THEME: THE SPORTING LIFE

How does a poem sound? Merry? Sad? Does a poem sound like what the poem's about? Fishing, hiking, playing baseball, cavorting in a gym?

If we have never heard Beethoven's Fifth Symphony, the opening notes hint that it is going to be exultant, more heroic even than his Third Symphony. We understand sound when it is made, but sometimes it escapes us when it is created in poetry. If we once again recall that originally poetry was written to be heard, we can then understand sound being a major component in the composition of it. "Music," Alexander Pope wrote in *An Essay on Criticism*, "resembles poetry."

Sound is strongly related to theme—that is, sound created by the poet's careful selection of certain words that possess the ability to evoke in the reader the senses of sight and sound. "Manifest in rhythm and meter," writes Joseph Shipley, "its [sound's] power is subtlest within the word."

The poems in this section have been selected for the quality of their sound. (This does not mean that the other poems have none.) Note the use of *alliteration*, which is the repetition of a *consonant* sound at the front of words or syllables; the use of *assonant* words, which resemble each other in sound; the *dissonant* words, which do not, but which create an inharmonious juxtaposition of sounds or rhythms to create special effects; and *onomatopoeiac* words, which fortify the sense of the word used. *Rhyme*, the repetition of identical or similar sounds, is used very often in poetry because it is beautiful in and of itself, because it fulfills a rhythmically constructive function, and because it defines pauses or the end of a poem. The most widely used is *end rhyme*, but *front rhyme* and *sprung rhyme* are not unusual. (See the glossary for definitions of all terms used.)

Recalling Boynton's description of poets being "the athletes of language," because "The secret of both kinds of skill, the poet's and the athlete's is coordination," perhaps we can now sense a connection with the theme of the sporting life. We begin with John Donne, who was, A. Alvarez writes, "not only one of the most supremely intelligent poets in the English language, he was also the first Englishman to write verse in a way that reflected the whole complex activity of intelligence."

Donne possessed a wit and skill many poets imitated but never equaled. Compared to Donne, they were humorless and slow; compared to Donne's sleek, precise, and compelling verse, theirs was bulky and halting, unleavened by Donne's resonance and turn of phrase. Thomas Carew (1595?–1639?), who much admired Donne's work and wrote an elegy to him, could capture the meter, but not the gracious sounds or rhythms of Donne in his "Ingrateful Beauty Threatened" (1640):

> Know Celia, since thou art so proud
>   T'was I that gave thee thy renown;
> Thou hadst in the forgotten crowd
>   Of common beauties lived unknown
> Had not my verse exhaled thy name,
> And with it imped* the wings of fame.

Robert Burns's poem "My Heart's in the Highlands," in contrast, is distinctively his, the sound created in great part by repetition and *refrain*—which is the term used to designate a phrase or stanza that is used again and again and is most often found in songs. "Repetition for effectiveness" was one of the rules of writing radio advertising copy. That rule was merely borrowed from poetry and song.

"Highlands" is in meter most like Burns's "Sweet Afton." The two poems are also similar in that most of the lines used in the opening stanzas are repeated in the closing stanzas:

> Flow gently, sweet Afton, among thy green braes!
> Flow gently, I'll sing thee a song in thy praise!
> My Mary's asleep by thy murmuring stream,
> Flow gently, sweet Afton, disturb not her dream!

*A term used in falconry; to repair the wing of a falcon by grafting to it feathers from another bird.

Flow gently, sweet Afton, among thy green braes!
Flow gently, sweet river, the theme of my lays!
My Mary's asleep by thy murmuring stream,
Flow gently, sweet Afton, disturb not her dream!

Though not much heard in recent years, "Sweet Afton" is a good example of poetry set to music, a throwback to extremely ancient days when rhythms of instrument and poem matched perfectly and when sound was of paramount importance.

A. E. Housman, however, is not quite so sure that poetry should possess "perfection." "Poetry," he says, "is not the thing said but a way of saying it." In "To an Athlete Dying Young" he speaks of death posed in steady rhythms against life. If the imagery is sharp, it may be because poets write as much of death as they do of love.

Two hundred and sixty-eight years separate the birthdates of Housman and Robert Herrick, yet they use essentially the same meter and rhythm to create a sense of loss for a person so young. R. P. Tristram Coffin and Alexander M. Witherspoon wrote in 1929: "Songs are many, but the poets who have made the world's best poems for songs are few and far apart. You can count them, almost, on the fingers of one hand: Sappho, Horace, Burns and Heine. Maybe A. E. Housman will join that company in time. But Robert Herrick (1591–1674) is already there and he is not the least of them."

The comparison of sound between Housman and Herrick therefore may be apt. The imagery in Herrick's "Upon a Child That Died" (1648) is disturbingly similar to Housman's:

Here she lies, a pretty bud,
Lately made of flesh and blood,
Who as soon fell fast asleep
As her eyes did little peep.
Give her strewings, but not stir
The earth that lightly covers her.

Phyllis McGinley and May Swenson bring us quickly back to life with less somber rhythms, fewer somber sounds, and brighter imagery. It may be exceedingly difficult to write anything new about the American national pastime—baseball—but Swenson has attempted a new analysis through a two-line form, irregular rhymes and baseball park images, sound, and language.

Her contemporary, Samuel Allen (1917–   ) has also tried to capture baseball, but through one player, not the reaction of the crowd, as Swenson does. Both use the "language of the people" rather than the "extraordinary" language allegedly assigned to poets. Allen's poem is about and dedicated to the legendary pitcher Satchell Paige. It has the ironic title "American Gothic." Paige was black.

To Satch

Sometimes I feel like I will *never* stop
Just go on forever
Til one fine mornin'

I'm gonna reach up and grab me a handfulla stars
Swing out my long lean leg
And whip three hot strikes burnin' down the heavens
And look over at God and say
How about that!

When we have little or no rhyme and little or no rhythm (that is, meter), as is true with Swenson and Allen (though there is some onomatopoeia in Swenson), we are required to *imagine* sound to accompany the images presented. In the case of baseball, that isn't difficult to do; free, or "experimental," verse draws largely upon a more or less shared familiarity with the subject. Poetry simply would not be poetry without sound.

John Donne

THE BAIT

Considered to have been the first great English metaphysical poet, John Donne (1572–1631) came from a Roman Catholic family whose ways he preferred less than those of a man about town. However, after sipping from the cup of the good life, he had a change of heart and converted to Anglicanism. He became dean of St. Paul's Cathedral in 1621. His early works were shaped by satire, irony, and eroticism and are as famous as his later poems which, with great power and grace, express his desire for a rapprochement with God. Donne's elegies, epigrams, and devotions are an extraordinary examination of sickness and considerations of death. In "The Bait," from his early period, Donne effectively uses metaphor to create a double image. His poetic skills are clearly seen here. John Donne's poems were first published two years after his death.

Come, live with me, and be my love,
And we will some new pleasures prove,
Of golden sands, and crystal brooks,
With silken lines, and silver hooks.

There will the river whisp'ring run,   5
Warm'd by thy eyes more than the sun;

John Donne

And there the enamoured fish will stay,
Begging themselves they may betray.

When thou wilt swim in that live bath,
Each fish, which every channel hath,   10
Most amorously to thee will swim,
Gladder to catch thee, than thou him.

If thou, to be so seen, beest loath
By sun or moon, thou dark'nest both;
And if mine eyes have leave to see,   15
I need not their light, having thee.

Let others freeze with angling reeds,
And cut their legs with shells and weeds,
Or treacherously poor fish beset
With strangling snares or windowy net;   20

Let coarse bold hands, from slimy nest,
The bedded fish in banks outwrest;
Or curious traitors, sleave-silk flies,
Bewitch poor fishes' wand'ring eyes.

For thee, thou need'st no such deceit,   25
For thou thyself art thine own bait;
That fish, that is not catch'd thereby,
Is wiser far, alas, than I.

QUESTIONS

1. What is the "bait" Donne is referring to?

2. What is the theme of this poem? What varieties and patterns of sound reinforce the theme?

3. How is theme introduced in the first stanza and concluded in the final stanza?

4. Donne tends to use words with very few syllables. But the words in this poem of more than two syllables are crucial to the ambivalence felt in the relationship. Which words are these?

5. What is the meaning of the line: "Or curious traitors, sleave-silk flies"?

6. To what extent is "The Bait" an erotic poem? Explain.

TOPICS FOR WRITING

1. Analyze the double image Donne employs here and the effectiveness of the language, sound, and imagery exercised in the use of it.

2. Write an essay determining whether Donne is praising or criticizing the subject of the poem. Cite the compliments and condemnations by line.

3. Choose a sport. Write a poem modeled after Donne's. Let that sport be the metaphor for a relationship between a young man and a young woman.

Robert Burns

MY HEART'S IN THE HIGHLANDS

Robert Burns (1756–1796), like his father, was a share farmer, or cotter. Often considered the greatest Scottish poet, Burns became a literary sensation when, at the age of 30, he published his first poems. Using the vernacular of his region, Burns wrote lyrical poetry on love, nature, country life, and patriotism. He had been compared to Chaucer and Byron in his use of conversational rhythms set to meter. Burns's longer works include The Cotter's Saturday Night, Tam O'Shanter, *and* The Jolly Beggars. *"To a Mouse," "Sweet Afton," and "To a Mountain Daisy," and the following poem are among his most remembered works. "My Heart's in the Highlands" with its end-line rhyme, repetition of certain words, and imagery that shifts from scene to scene, is typical of Burns's poetic portraits.*

My heart's in the Highlands, my heart is not here;
My heart's in the Highlands a-chasing the deer;
A-chasing the wild deer, and following the roe,
My heart's in the Highlands wherever I go.
Farewell to the Highlands, farewell to the North,   5
The birth-place of valor, the country of worth;
Wherever I wander, wherever I rove,
The hills of the Highlands forever I love.

Farewell to the mountains high-covered with snow;
Farewell to the straths and green valleys below;   10
Farewell to the forests and wild-hanging woods;
Farewell to the torrents and loud-pouring floods.
My heart's in the Highlands, my heart is not here;
My heart's in the Highlands a-chasing the deer;
A-chasing the wild deer, and following the roe,   15
My heart's in the Highlands, wherever I go.

QUESTIONS

1. This poem might be dedicated to what kind of outdoorsman?

2. Three words in the poem are repeated almost to excess. Which words are they and what effect do they have on the sound of the poem?

3. Discuss whether or not the repetition of certain words is a calculated attempt to create the kind of echo one might hear in the woods.

4. What is the theme of "My Heart's in the Highlands"?

5. Burns uses words of more than two syllables only twice. How strong or weak does this make the poem? Explain.

6. Why does Burns chase "the wild deer," but follow "the roe"?

TOPICS FOR WRITING

1. Describe what may be happening to the person who is leaving the Highlands. Might it be Burns himself after becoming famous who knows that his life has changed? Explain.

2. Supply examples from everyday life where repetition is traditionally used to stimulate the imagination and create a mood. Relate your evaluation to Burns's poem.

3. Analyze the sound patterns in this poem and their contribution to our sense of the poem as "song."

A. E. Housman

TO AN ATHLETE DYING YOUNG

Alfred Edward Housman (1859–1936) was above all a Latin scholar, and this influenced his career as a poet. His work reveals the influence of classical study and the traditional prosody of England. Yet he knew well the value of everyday language, but ordered it to meet his poetic demands. His works include A Shropshire Lad *(1896) and* Lost Poems *(1922).* More Poems *(1936) was published after his death. "To an Athlete Dying Young" possesses a rhythm that suggests running, and the alliteration builds an interior sound and rhythm as well. This is one of Housman's best-loved poems.*

The time you won your town the race
We chaired you through the market-place;
Man and boy stood cheering by,
And home we brought you shoulder-high.

Today, the road all runners come,   5
Shoulder-high we bring you home,
And set you at your threshold down,
Townsman of a stiller town.

Smart lad, to slip betimes away
From fields where glory does not stay,   10
And early though the laurel grows
It withers quicker than the rose.

Eyes the shady night has shut
Cannot see the record cut,
And silence sounds no worse than cheers   15
After earth has stopped the ears;

Now you will not swell the rout
Of lads that wore their honors out,
Runners whom renown outran
And the name died before the man.   20

So set, before its echoes fade,
The fleet foot on the sill of shade,
And hold to the low lintel up
The still-defended challenge-cup.

And round that early-laureled head   25
Will flock to gaze the strengthless dead
And find unwithered on its curls
The garland briefer than a girl's.

QUESTIONS

1. Describe the sound of this poem. Does the sound of it relate to the theme? How? In which lines as the theme develops?

2. Could this poetic tribute be applicable to any other young athlete? Explain.

3. How many feet are in each line of the poem? Scan it completely, marking stressed and unstressed syllables. (See pages 445–447 and the Glossary for an analysis of meter.)

4. Is it important that we do not know what the athlete died of? Why or why not?

5. What small consolation does Housman offer in the wake of the death? What imagery suggests that triumph will continue?

6. Point out the lines where Housman's alliteration is most effective and least effective.

TOPICS FOR WRITING

1. Compare the intensity of the images Housman creates in the first stanza and the solemnity of the images in the second stanza, using the term "shoulder-high" as the connection.

2. *Contrast* the imagery, sound, and theme of the first stanza and of the final stanza of the poem.

Phyllis McGinley

REFLECTIONS OUTSIDE OF A GYMNASIUM

Phyllis McGinley (1905–) was born in Ontario, Oregon. She attended the University of Utah and the University of California. McGinley was the winner of numerous poetry awards before becoming the recipient of the Pulitzer Prize for poetry in 1961. Her first collection of verse, On the Contrary, was published in 1934, and A Pocketful of Wry (1940), was her third. There followed, starting in 1954, eight children's books, and then McGinley returned to poetry. She has since divided her time between them. McGinley calls herself "a writer of light verse, articles, and literary criticism." The pungency of some of her poetry, however, renders it of greater weight than she admits. There is an almost panting, exhausted quality here, with breathless asides that provide a bouncy charm and a plaintive sound to the lost eighties.

The belles of the eighties were soft,
　They were ribboned and ruffled and gored,
With bustles built proudly aloft
　And Bosoms worn dashingly for'rd.

So, doting on bosoms and bustles,   5
   By fashion and circumstance pent,
They languished, neglecting their muscles,
   Growing flabby and plump and content,
Their most strenuous sport
   A game of croquet   10
On a neat little court
   In the cool of the day,
Or dipping with ladylike motions,
Fully clothed, into decorous oceans.

The eighties surveyed with alarm   15
   A figure long-legged and thinnish;
And they had not discovered the charm
   Of a solid-mahogany finish.
Of suns that could darken or speckle
   Their delicate skins they were wary.   20
They found it distasteful to freckle
   Or brown like a nut or a berry.
So they sat in the shade
   Or they put on a hat
And frequently stayed   25
   Fairly healthy at that
(And never lay nightlong awake
For sunburn and loveliness' sake).

When ladies rode forth, it was news,
   Though sidewise ensconced on the saddle.   30
And when they embarked in canoes
   A gentleman wielded the paddle.
They never felt urged to compete
   With persons excessively agile.
Their slippers were small on their feet   35
   And they thought it no shame to be fragile.
Could they swim? They could not.
Did they dive? They forbore it.
And nobody thought
   The less of them for it.   40

No, none pointed out how their course was absurd,
Though their tennis was feeble, their golf but a word.
When breezes were chilly, they wrapped up in flannels,
They couldn't turn cartwheels, they didn't swim channels,
They seldom climbed mountains, and, what was more shocking,   45
Historians doubt that they even went walking.
If unenergetic,
   A demoiselle dared to
Be no more athletic
   Than ever she cared to.   50

Oh, strenuous comrades and maties,
How pleasant was life in the eighties!

QUESTIONS

1. Locate examples of alliteration in "Reflections outside of a Gymnasium." What is the effect?

2. What kind of meter is used here? Does it fit the theme?

3. How would you describe the sound of the poem—witty? rueful? How does McGinley achieve this effect?

4. From this poem, what seems most to have been demanded of women in the Victorian age?

5. How can this poem be contrasted to "To an Athlete Dying Young" (page 438), with regard to sound and theme?

6. Using this poem as a basis for paradox, describe the demands now being made of and by women.

TOPICS FOR WRITING

1. Write an essay on sunbathing in the 1980s compared to sunbathing in the 1880s, paying particular attention to the second stanza of McGinley's poem.

2. Characterize the person of "Reflections outside of a Gymnasium." What sounds might that person be hearing? How old might she be? Would she be a mother? a grandmother?

3. Write a paper, using the phrase "bosoms and bustles," demonstrating that such concerns with anatomy, while they may have changed in some respects, are still very much on the minds of designers and clothes buyers.

4. How do the alliteration in "bosoms and bustles" and other sound devices reflect McGinley's approach to the lives of women?

May Swenson

ANALYSIS OF BASEBALL

May Swenson (1919–   ), introduced earlier in this anthology (page 384), was born in Logan, Utah. A graduate of Utah State, she later moved east and became editor of New Directions Press (1959–1966). Her collections of poems include Another Animal *(1954),* A Cage of Spines *(1958),* Half

Analysis of Baseball

Sun Half Sleep *(1967), and* More Poems to Solve *(1971). Swenson, a sharp observer of and commentator on American life, uses a natural rhythm and a natural language. In "Analysis of Baseball," she is both playful and serious, using one-syllable words to emphasize action and perhaps as well the comic aspects of the national pastime.* New and Selected Things Taking Place *(1978) is her most recent collection.*

It's about
the ball,
the bat,
and the mitt.
Ball hits   5
bat, or it
hits mitt.
Bat doesn't
hit ball, bat
meets it.   10
Ball bounces
off bat, flies
air, or thuds
ground (dud)
or it   15
fits mitt.

Bat waits
for ball
to mate.
Ball hates   20
to take bat's
bait. Ball
flirts, bat's
late, don't
keep the date.   25
Ball goes in
(thwack) to mitt,
and goes out
(thwack) back
to mitt.   30

Ball fits
mitt, but
not all
the time.
Sometimes   35
ball gets hit
(pow) when bat
meets it,
and sails
to a place   40
where mitt
has to quit
in disgrace.
That's about
the bases   45
loaded,
about 40,000
fans exploded.

It's about
the ball,   50
the bat,
the mitt.
the bases
and the fans.
It's done   55
on a diamond,
and for fun.
It's about
home, and it's
about run.   60

QUESTIONS

1. Describe the sound and theme of this poem.

2. Is the poem truly an analysis of baseball? Explain.

3. Where are the satirical elements in the poem?

4. Can you describe "Analysis of Baseball" in terms of the kind of verse it employs?

5. How does Swenson's poem differ in sound from "To an Athlete Dying Young" (page 439) and "My Heart's in the Highlands" (page 437)?

6. Does the cadence of the poem fit its theme? How?

TOPICS FOR WRITING

1. Compose a list of all the one-syllable words that apply to baseball. Do the same for the two- and three-syllable words that also apply to the game.

2. Write a profile of the person who wrote this poem. How many times might she have gone to a game? Does she understand the purpose of the game? the function of the players?

3. Write a comparison between this poem and "Casey at the Bat," determining which is the more exciting and why.

4. Compare "Analysis of Baseball" and its approach to John Donne's "The Bait" (page 435) and its approach. Which most effectively uses sound? Why?

5. Analyze the relationship of sound to the shortness of the lines in this poem.

18

RHYTHM, METER, AND THEME: THE SEA

Our universe is filled with rhythm. We find it in the seasonal changes, the ebb and flow of the tides, the rising and setting of the moon and sun, and the planets and stars that are most visible at regular intervals.

Our bodies, too, function as a result of rhythmic impulses sent out by the brain, which itself pulses in rhythmic waves. Sometimes we can tell who a person is not by the face—we may not be able to see the face from a distance—but by the way he or she walks; the rhythms of the walk are familiar to us.

The use of rhythm in poetry in fact may be a subconscious attempt to imitate the movements of things that control our lives. Of course the use of rhythm is also a conscious effort to emulate patterns of thought, speech, and sometimes sight.

The rhythms we find in poetry are achieved through the use of meter, and meter is produced by accentuating the sounds of certain syllables in certain words. We call this emphasis "stress" or "accent." The syllables or words that are *not* emphasized are characterized as being "unstressed" or "unaccented." If we remember that poetry was at first intended to be heard rather than read, meter and rhythm make far more sense to us. The poet, whether he or she wishes to be or not, is part of an old tradition that demands that the poet carefully select words not only for their syllabic content, but also for the power of those words to evoke in us an experience he or she wishes to share.

In traditional poetry, each line contains a number of feet, usually one to eight:

One foot	Monometer
Two feet	Dimeter
Three feet	Trimeter
Four feet	Tetrameter
Five feet	Pentameter
Six feet	Hexameter
Seven feet	Heptameter
Eight feet	Octameter

Within each foot of poetry there is usually one stressed and one or two unstressed syllables. We still use Greek terms to identify the kind of stress placed on various syllables:

Iamb (Iambic) First used by the seventh century B.C. poet Archilochus, the iamb was considered to approximate more than any other meter the rhythm and character of speech. Within a foot it is characterized by an unstressed (˘) syllable followed by a stressed (⁄) syllable.

Trochee (trochaic) Used in early Greek tragedies and later replaced by the iamb, the trochee was believed useful in heightening excitement. Within a foot it is characterized by a stressed (⁄) syllable followed by an unstressed (˘) syllable. In Greek, "trochee" means "running foot."

Anapest (Anapestic) Also widely used in Greek drama, the anapest later became a favorite of generations of English poets. In Greek, "anapest" means "struck back"; anapest is recognized by its two unstressed (˘ ˘) beats and one stressed (⁄) beat.

Dactyl (Dactylic) In Greek, "dactyl" means "finger"; this meter is intended to correspond with its three syllables to the three joints of a finger. It is composed of one stressed (⁄) beat and two unstressed (˘ ˘) beats.

Spondee (Spondaic) Rarely used today except in so-called experimental poetry, the spondee uses two stressed (⁄⁄) beats. The Greeks used it with "drinking poems."

Scansion is the method of analyzing the metrical pattern—the kind of meter and number of feet used—of a poem. To scan is to analyze and measure. For example, if we scan William Cowper's (1731–1800) "The Castaway," we can readily see that the first two lines are predominantly iambic, with one anapestic substitution. (Substitution of one foot of a predominant pattern is a key way to vary rhythm.)

Ŏb scúr/ ĕst níght/ ĭn volvéd / thĕ ský

Thĕ Ăt lán/ tĭc bíll / ŏws roáred

More than 2,600 years old, the iamb continues to be the most popular metrical pattern, possibly because, as the Greeks believed, it most closely approximates the alternating short and long (or unaccented and accented) emphasis found in everyday speech.

The poems in this section relate to the sea, and the sea represents a poetic and historical merging when we consider that from the "wine-dark sea" of Homer's *Odyssey* to the present, it has intrigued poets almost as much as love.

The sea itself may not be the primary concern of the poems, but, rather, a metaphor. Of course, for different poets, the sea possesses different rhythms. Edmund Waller (1606–1687), as a case in point, using the Bermudas much like Marvell, employs a different line, but the meter is similar:

Ber mu / das walled / with rocks / who does / not know/
That hap / py is / land where / huge lem / ons grow

By contrast, Shelley mixes trochaic and iambic patterns in a hexameter line to create excitement in his "To Night" (1821):

Swift ly / walk o'er / the west / ern wave,/Spir it / of Night!

Rhythm, which derives in large part from meter, is one of the distinctive features that separates poetry from prose. It lulls us "into the poem's mood," wrote J. M. Murry, and "our sensitivity to the poet's ideas and images is increased."

Andrew Marvell

BERMUDAS

Andrew Marvell (1621–1678), introduced earlier in this anthology (page 343), was a good friend of Richard Lovelace, with whose politics Marvell did not agree. He was one of the early lyric poets whose metaphysical views merged well with his style and themes. This becomes clear in "Bermudas," wherein he has posed civilization against nature, both overseen by God. The Bermuda islands were in the process of being settled by the British, and the story of how a shipwrecked crew had found its way there captured the imagination of English writers for several generations. Meter, rhythm, sound, and imagery, all in concert, make "Bermudas" one of Marvell's most popular poems.

Where the remote Bermudas ride
In th' ocean's bosom unespied,
From a small boat that rowed along,
The list'ning winds received this song:
    What should we do but sing his praise   5
That led us through the wat'ry maze
Unto an isle so long unknown,
And yet far kinder than our own?

Andrew Marvell

Where he the huge sea-monsters wracks,
That lift the deep upon their backs,   10
He lands us on a grassy stage,
Safe from the storms and prelates' rage.
He gave us this eternal spring
Which here enamels everything,
And sends the fowls to us in care,   15
On daily visits through the air.
He hangs in shades the orange bright,
Like golden lamps in a green night;
And does in the pomegranates close
Jewels more rich than Ormus shows.   20
He makes the figs our mouths to meet
And throws the melons at our feet,
But apples plants of such a price,
No tree could ever bear them twice.
With cedars, chosen by his hand,   25
From Lebanon, he stores the land,
And makes the hollow seas that roar
Proclaim the ambergris on shore.
He cast, of which we rather boast,
The Gospel's pearl upon our coast,   30
And in these rocks for us did frame
A temple, where to sound his name.
Oh, let our voice his praise exalt,
Till it arrive at heaven's vault;
Which thence, perhaps, rebounding, may   35
Echo beyond the Mexic Bay.
   Thus sung they in the English boat
An holy and a cheerful note,
And all the way, to guide their chime,
With falling oars they kept the time.   40

QUESTIONS

1. Scan any six lines of this poem. What is the predominant metrical pattern?

2. What is the theme of "Bermudas"?

3. How would you describe its rhythm?

4. Does the poem necessarily refer to the real Bermuda islands? If not, what are they metaphorically?

5. "Safe from storms and prelates' rage": What allusion does this make to actual English history?

6. How does Marvell's language differ from Donne's?

TOPICS FOR WRITING

1. The long middle section of this poem is composed as a prayer. Explain how and why it has the rhythm of a prayer.

2. Analyze why Marvell (and others) felt it necessary to have a remote, idyllic place as a subject for his work. Do poets still feel this compulsion? If so, why? If not, in your opinion, why not? Does the actual history and geography of the Bermudas resemble Marvell's islands? Why or why not?

3. Write a speculative paper about who the survivors in the boat may be and why they sing a hymn as they row toward "Bermudas."

William Wordsworth

NEAR DOVER

William Wordsworth (1770–1850) was born at Cockermouth, in Cumberland, England. He was a student at Cambridge until 1791. Wordsworth formed a close friendship with Samuel Taylor Coleridge, and they became luminaries of the Romantic movement. Influenced by Jean Jacques Rousseau, William Godwin, and others, Wordsworth was passionate and rebellious. Certainly he lived through times of tremendous changes: the founding of the new American republic, the French Revolution, and the emergence of the concept that the common man had a place in the scheme of things. Although at first an ardent supporter of the French Revolution, Wordsworth became sickened by the excesses of the Republicans. The revolution and the subsequent war between France and England caused upheaval, too, in Wordsworth's personal life: a lover and daughter had to be left behind in France, though Wordsworth cared for them until Annette Vallon married after Wordsworth himself married an Englishwoman. It is likely that Wordsworth, when he wrote "Near Dover" in 1802, was thinking as much of his personal life as he was of England's failures. His extensive body of work, both poetry and essays, his use of language, and his perception of great issues place him with Shakespeare and Milton. Wordsworth was poet laureate of England from 1843 until his death. "Near Dover" is a sonnet in which "the coast of France" is an ambivalent metaphor for what he thought England might have achieved, but had not at the time he wrote the poem.

Inland, within a hollow vale, I stood:
And saw, while sea was calm and air was clear,
The coast of France—the coast of France how near!
Drawn almost into frightful neighborhood,
I shrunk; for verily the barrier flood   5
Was like a lake, or river bright and fair,
A span of waters; yet what power is there!
What mightiness for evil and for good!
Even so doth God protect us if we be
Virtuous and wise. Winds blow, and waters roll,   10
Strength to the brave, and Power, and Deity;
Yet in themselves are nothing! One decree
Spake laws to *them*, and said that by the soul
Only, the Nations shall be great and free.

QUESTIONS

1. How does the sonnet form (see pages 457–459) control the meter in this poem? Are there any variations in the metrical rhythm? If so, point them out.

2. What does the "coast of France" symbolize to Wordsworth? What moment in French history is he referring to? What is his attitude toward this period in history?

3. Explain the significance of the sea imagery in the poem. What rhythms does Wordsworth want to create? Why?

4. Why does Wordsworth emphasize *them* in line 13? What is the pronoun reference?

5. Scan the rhyme scheme. How does the rhyme reinforce rhythm and meaning?

TOPICS FOR WRITING

1. Write a paper on the major events taking place in Europe at the time Wordsworth wrote this poem and on how those events influenced its composition. Be certain to explain the poet's attitude toward these events as reflected in the poem.

2. Write a careful analysis of the relationship of the punctuation in this poem to its rhythm.

Matthew Arnold

DOVER BEACH

The son of the clergyman and headmaster of Rugby, Matthew Arnold (1822–1888) was born at Laleham, England, the day before Christmas. He was educated at Winchester, Rugby, and Oxford and in 1847 was secretary to the marquis of Lansdowne. Arnold published his first collection of verse, The Strayed Pearl and Other Poems *(1849) when he was 27. His studies and teaching led him to literary criticism; in 1852 he published* Empedocles, *a poem on Wordsworth, Byron, and Goethe. His other works include* Stanzas from the Grande Chartreuse *(1855),* Merope *(1858),* Thyrsis *(1866), and* Essays in Criticism *(1865, 1888). The obligation of a critic, he wrote, is "a disinterested endeavor to learn and propagate the best that is known and thought in the world." Arnold lectured in the United States in 1883–84 and in 1886. In "Dover Beach" he uses the ocean as a metaphor for the Sea of Faith that is receding from the shorelines of the world, a fitting image for one like Arnold (and his contemporaries) caught in the Victorian period of Darwinian theory; the rediscovery of Egypt and the translation of some of the glyphs; Mill's potent work,* On Liberty; *and the cresting of the Industrial Revolution, then a century old.*

The sea is calm tonight,
The tide is full, the moon lies fair
Upon the straits; on the French coast the light
Gleams and is gone; the cliffs of England stand,
Glimmering and vast, out in the tranquil bay.   5
Come to the window, sweet is the night-air!
Only, from the long line of spray
Where the sea meets the moon-blanched land,
Listen! you hear the grating roar
Of pebbles which the waves draw back, and fling,   10
At their return, up the high strand,
Begin, and cease, and then again begin,
With tremulous cadence slow, and bring
The eternal note of sadness in.

Sophocles long ago   15
Heard it on the Aegean, and it brought
Into his mind the turbid ebb and flow
Of human misery; we
Find also in the sound a thought,
Hearing it by this distant northern sea.   20

The Sea of Faith
Was once, too, at the full, and round earth's shore
Lay like the folds of a bright girdle furled.
But now I only hear
Its melancholy, long, withdrawing roar,   25

Retreating, to the breath
Of the night-wind, down the vast edges drear
And naked shingles of the world.

Ah, love, let us be true
To one another! for the world, which seems   30
To lie before us like a land of dreams,
So various, so beautiful, so new,
Hath really neither joy, nor love, nor light,
Nor certitude, nor peace, nor help for pain;
And we are here as on a darkling plain   35
Swept with confused alarms of struggle and flight,
Where ignorant armies clash by night.

QUESTIONS

1. What mood does this poem at first evoke? How does it change? Why?

2. How does Arnold's reference to Sophocles and the Aegaean Sea contribute to the theme?

3. What kind of meter and rhythm does Arnold use?

4. What quality of the sea makes it a good metaphor for Arnold's theme? How does the "rhythm" of the sea influence the poet's theme?

5. Which armies, metaphorically speaking, is Arnold referring to?

6. What thematic similarities and differences exist between "Dover Beach" and "Near Dover," (page 449) and how may they be explained?

TOPICS FOR WRITING

1. The English port of Dover and the French port near Calais have been important in English history. Explain why Wordsworth and Arnold set their respective poems near these places.

2. Compare Arnold's concern for the presence of a religious faith and Wordsworth's concern for a more just world. Are the two mutually exclusive?

3. Write a critical assessment of "Dover Beach," discussing why it is Arnold's best-known work. Decide if the poem represents a "disinterested endeavor."

4. Examine how meter contributes to the tone of "Dover Beach."

Judith Wright

THE SURFER

He thrust his joy against the weight of the sea,
climbed through, slid under those long banks of foam—
(hawthorn hedges in spring, thorns in the face stinging).
How his brown strength drove through the hollow and coil
of green-through weirs of water! 5
Muscle of arm thrust down long muscle of water.
And swimming so, went out of sight
where mortal, masterful, frail, the gulls went wheeling
in air, as he in water, with delight.

Turn home, the sun goes down; swimmer, turn home. 10
Last leaf of gold vanishes from the sea-curve.
Take the big roller's shoulder, speed and swerve.
Come to the long beach home like a gull diving.

For on the sand the grey-wolf sea lies snarling;
cold twilight wind splits the waves' hair and shows 15
the bones they worry in their wolf-teeth. O, wind blows,
and sea crouches on sand, fawning and mouthing;
drops there and snatches again, drops and again snatches
its broken toys, its whitened pebbles and shells.

QUESTIONS

1. How do the sometimes uneven cadences of "The Surfer" contribute to its theme? its structure? its imagery?

2. What tone is conveyed through the first nine lines of this poem?

3. How is the sea portrayed in these lines?

4. In what way does the cadence in the next four lines differ from the cadences in the first nine?

5. Describe the mood of "The Surfer" in stanzas 1, 2, and 3.

TOPICS FOR WRITING

1. Provide a symbolic analysis of the poem stanza by stanza. Explain how rhythm and cadence reinforce symbolic meaning.

2. Draw a comparison between youth as depicted in "To an Athlete Dying Young" (page 438) and as depicted in "The Surfer."

Derek Walcott

NEARING LA GUAIRA

Born in Castries on the island of St. Lucia, Derek Walcott (1930–   ) graduated from the University of the West Indies, in Jamaica. Although he has lived and traveled in Europe and makes the United States his home, much of his poetry is about the Caribbean. Commenting on Walcott's first volume of poetry, Selected Poems *(1964), Robert Graves said that Walcott "handles English with a closer understanding of its inner magic than most (if not any) of his English-born contemporaries." Also the author of three plays, Walcott's poetry collections since 1964 have included* The Gulf *(1970),* Another Life *(1973),* Sea Grapes *(1976),* The Star-Apple Kingdom *(1979), and* The Fortunate Traveller *(1982). In "Nearing La Guaira," Walcott probes the rhythms and depths of the sea for an elusive philosophical meaning.*

At dead of night, the sailors sprawled on deck.
The wind shakes out its blanket overhead.
All are ribbed equally; all must shipwreck.
The breakers kiss, then bitterly separate,
There is one error flesh cannot repent
Nor motion drown, not while one moon makes white
The tossed sea and her sheet's dishevellment.

5

Like men in graves, each disappointing west,
They wait in patience for the coming east;
Farewell to that, I have made my separate peace,   10
Bitter and sleepless as the ocean's curse.
A sailor in an oil-stained vest looks down
To the sea's lace, ripped by the raging wind.
"Buenas noches, amigo, qué tal?"
"Nada, amigo, nada."   15
The stars fly from his cigarette in the wind.
A broken man, with a dead wife in mind.
"Mañana esaremos en La Guaira."
I ask him what La Guaira means, he grins,
Says it means nothing.   20

So, the next morning, nothing is green water,
Sun to the left like a starfish, the moon a washed-out shell
And on rust hills, La Guaira, strict as sorrow.
And nothing is a cornet in the plaza, nothing the Morro
Where the garbage drifts, nothing   25
The bullfight roaring for six thousand tickets,
Nothing Christ's blood forgotten
In the arena of the free cathedral.
Nothing the soldiers drilling in the square,
And the green fountain with its sacrament.   30
Señor, we have joined a different detachment.

Nothing her mouth, my east and crimson west,
Nothing our restless, separated sleep;
Nothing is bitter and is very deep.

QUESTIONS

1. What meter does Walcott mostly employ in "Nearing La Guaira"?

2. What is the theme of the poem? What clues reinforce theme?

3. What tone is established early in the poem? Why?

4. Which lines are most alliterative?

5. What is the relationship between "Nearing La Guaira" and "The Unknown Citizen" (page 428)?

6. What is meant by the lines

Like men in graves, each disappointing west,
They wait in patience for the coming east

Derek Walcott

TOPICS FOR WRITING

1. Provide a profile of the narrator of this poem. What is he? What does he do?

2. Write a description of what La Guaira symbolizes, citing other poems in which La Guaira is present but called by other names.

3. What might the ship symbolize in Walcott's poem? Provide an analysis.

4. What might all the activity on shore symbolize? Provide an analysis.

5. Explore the sea as a metaphor or symbol in the five poems in this chapter, and analyze the rhythmic and metrical patterns the poets exploit in their treatment of the sea.

19

THE SONNET AND THEME: GOD

There is an atmosphere inside a religious edifice that makes us conform to its unspoken demands. We follow the rules in these places and submit to discipline.

Poets often seem to relish discipline, so it is not strange that we have come from the flowing, imagery-filled blank verse of the Song of Solomon and the Psalms to the rigid fourteen-line sonnet with all its limitations: a sonnet must possess fourteen lines—no more, no less; it must have rhythm and meter—iambic pentameter; and it must rhyme in comformity with a traditional scheme.

From the Italian and English sonnet forms there have come, even with the limitations—challenges, some might say—new thematic approaches to writing the sonnet. (Sonnet means "little sound.") Although a short poem, the sonnet may be thematically as powerful as a longer poem, a story, or even a novel, and it may be just as satisfying. The form has lasted through seven centuries and shows no sign of falling out of favor in the late twentieth century. The sonnet reaches backward and forward, complementing past and future; John Donne probably would have admired Cullen's sonnets, as Cullen admired Keats's sonnets. Themes change, as they should, but the tradition of the form holds.

The sonnets in this section consider God and His power; there is reverence, but in some there is also irony, a gentle lamentation; there is challenge, the poet wrestling, however briefly, with the power he or she must always submit to. But the sonnet form maintains the ordained position of poet and God in good order; everything is tidy, as should be the case in disciplined writing and thought.

For the sonnet is much like the classical essay that begins with a question; after the question, the essay is all answer. The sonnet poses a problem or asks a question in its first eight lines—the *octave*—and in the next six—the *sestet*—proposes to solve the problem or to answer the question.

The sonnet underwent changes in England, although many poets continued to use the Italian form of octave and sestet. The English, following the lead of Shakespeare, often used three four-line stanzas, or *quatrains,* and resolved any question or problem in the final two lines of the sonnet, which were called the *couplet.*

Keats's "On First Looking into Chapman's Homer" is an example of the Italian sonnet:

> Much have I travell'd in the realms of gold,
> And many goodly states and kingdoms seen;
> Round many western islands have I been
> Which bards in fealty to Apollo hold.
> Oft of one wide expanse had I been told
> That deep-brow'd Homer ruled as his demesne:
> Yet did I never breathe its pure serene
> Till I heard Chapman speak out loud and bold:
> Then I felt like some watcher of the skies
> When a new planet swims into his ken;
> Or like stout Cortez, when with eagle eyes
> He stared at the Pacific—and all his men
> Look'd at each other with a wild surmise—
> Silent, upon a peak in Darien.

Coleridge's "To the Reverend W. L. Bowles" (1794) is in the English, or Elizabethan, or Shakespearean, tradition:

> My heart has thanked thee, Bowles! for those soft strains
>   Whose sadness soothes me, like the murmuring
>   Of wild-bees in the sunny showers of spring!
> For hence not callous to the mourner's pains
>
> Through youth's gay prime and thornless paths I went:
>   And when the mightier throes of mind began,
>   And drove me forth, a thought-bewildered man,
> Their mild and manliest melancholy lent
>
> A mingled charm, such as the pang consigned
>   To slumber, though the big tear it renewed;
>   Bidding a strange mysterious pleasure brood
> Over the wavy and tumultuous mind,
>
> As the great Spirit erst with plastic sweep
> Moved on the darkness of the unformed deep.

While Coleridge's sonnet has much in common with Browning's (later in this section), it is clear that the form is used by Keats to express a joy for knowledge. And if sonnets also often deal with love, requited or not, this in no way hampers its disciplined approach to more heavenly themes, which once determined, bows to structure. As a result, clear imagery, clarity of theme, and purity of language are found in the sonnet. The form demands a great deal of the poet, but it always rewards both author and reader in kind.

John Donne

HOLY SONNET 14

John Donne (1572–1631), whose friend and biographer was Isaak Walton, was born in London. On his mother's side of the family he was related to Sir Thomas More. He was educated at Oxford, Cambridge, and Lincoln's Inn. In 1596 he took part in an expedition against Cádiz and the Azores. In 1601 he married the niece of his employer, Sir Thomas Egerton, lord keeper of the great seal. Donne was summarily dismissed and imprisoned, the marriage being a violation of common and canon law. His incarceration was brief. In the later years of his life, after conversion to the Anglican Church, Donne was regarded as the most prominent minister of his day, his rather well-rounded young manhood notwithstanding. Donne introduced in his work the rhythm of the natural, speaking voice and what A. Alvarez called "the rhythm of intelligence." Although his poetry is highly technical, Donne (and his followers), wishing to appear as natural as possible, buried their technical expertise within the structures of their poems. With Donne, however, wit revealed his power and grace.

Batter my heart, three-personed God; for you
As yet but knock, breathe, shine, and seek to mend.
That I may rise and stand, o'erthrow me and bend
Your force to break, blow, burn, and make me new.
I, like an usurped town, to another due,   5
Labor to admit you, but, oh, to no end;
Reason, your viceroy in me, me should defend,
But is captived and proves weak or untrue.
Yet dearly I love you and would be lovèd fain,
But am betrothed unto your enemy: 10
Divorce me, untie or break that knot again,
Take me to you, imprison me, for I,
Except you enthrall me, never shall be free,
Nor ever chaste, except you ravish me.

QUESTIONS

What is the rhyme scheme of this sonnet?

1. What is meant by "three-personed God"?

2. Would this poem be classified as an Italian or English sonnet?

3. What theme does Donne develop in "Holy Sonnet 14"?

4. The metaphors in the first eight lines—the octave—differ from the metaphor in the sestet—the remaining six lines. How effective is each metaphor? What is their combined effect?

5. Why does the writing of a sonnet require great discipline?

TOPICS FOR WRITING

1. Summarize your life in a sonnet just like Donne's in structure.

2. Analyze the difference in language, rhythm, and structure between "The Bait" (page 435) and "Holy Sonnet 14."

3. Write an essay comparing woman as metaphor in "The Bait" and "Holy Sonnet 14."

John Milton

WHEN I CONSIDER
HOW MY LIGHT IS SPENT

John Milton (1608–1674) is considered to be one of the most important writers in the English language. He studied at Cambridge and then toured Europe, where he met Galileo. Milton wrote in Latin and English, producing in his early period such works as L'Allegro, Il Penseroso, and Lycidas before 1639, when he returned to England, just before the start of the civil war (1642–1646 and 1648–1652). Five years later Milton published Areopagitica. This defense of printing's right not to be subject to licensing, as well as The Doctrine and Discipline of Divorce (1643), placed him in opposition to official Puritan doctrines—though Milton was a Puritan himself and became, in 1649, secretary to Cromwell. Three years later Milton was blind, but he continued his massive output, liberal and often cantankerous in tone. In 1657 Andrew Marvell became his assistant and probably saved him from persecution after the Restoration (1660).

Paradise Lost (1667) fulfilled Milton's dream of producing a national epic. "When I Consider How My Light Is Spent" was published between 1652 and 1658; it is composed of fourteen lines in iambic pentameter. The pun in the poem relates Milton's literary talents to a unit of money known, during the time of Christ, as a talent. In the Gospel According to St. Matthew a servant is rebuked for not putting his talent (money) to good use.

When I consider how my light is spent
    Ere half my days, in this dark world and wide,
    And that one talent which is death to hide
    Lodged with me useless, though my soul more bent
To serve therewith my Maker, and present   5
    My true account, lest he returning chide;
    "Doth God exact day-labor, light denied?"
    I fondly ask: but Patience to prevent
That murmur, soon replies, "God doth not need
    Either man's work or his own gifts; who best   10
    Bear his mild yoke, they serve him best. His state
Is kingly. Thousands at his bidding speed
    And post o'er land and ocean without rest:
    They also serve who only stand and wait."

QUESTIONS

1. Does the rhyme scheme of this poem differ markedly from the one used by John Donne (page 459)? What is the rhyme scheme?

2. What is a pun and where is it used by Milton?

3. What double meaning does "talent" have? What double meaning does "useless" have?

4. Is there evidence of bitterness in Milton's poem? Explain.

5. Could Milton's sightlessness, oncoming or complete, be part of a pun somewhere in the poem? In what way?

6. Whose poem, Milton's or Donne's (page 459), seems to be more respectful?

TOPICS FOR WRITING

Analyze and compare Milton's and Donne's (page 459) approaches to the worship of God, taking into account tone, manner of address, and language.

1. In the sonnets of Donne and Milton, the first eight lines seem to pose a question or a problem, and the next six lines seem to resolve it. What tradition demands this structure, and how effective is this structure in conveying theme?

Elizabeth Barrett Browning

CONSOLATION

Elizabeth Barrett Browning (1806–1861), introduced earlier in this anthology (page 354), was born at Coxhoe Hall, Durham, England. She was the eldest daughter of Edward Moulton, who took the name Barrett when he succeeded to an estate. When 13 she suffered an accident that left her a semi-invalid, "a pale, small person scarcely embodied at all," as Nathaniel Hawthorne described her. In 1846 she married Robert Browning and they left England to reside in Florence, Italy. She was the author of Prometheus Bound *(translation, 1833),* The Seraphim, and Other Poems *(1838),* Poems *(1844),* Poems *(including* Sonnets from the Portuguese, *(1850),* Aurora Leigh *(1857), and other works. Her best-known work was perhaps* Sonnets from the Portuguese, *a series of love poems addressed to Browning.*

All are not taken; there are left behind
Living Belovéds, tender looks to bring
And make the daylight still a happy thing,
And tender voices, to make soft the wind.
But if it were not so—if I could find   5
No love in all the world for comforting,
Nor any path but hollowly did ring
Where "dust to dust" the love from life disjoined,
And if, before those sepulchers unmoving
I stood alone (as some forsaken lamb   10
Goes bleating up the moors in weary dearth),
Crying, "Where are ye, O my loved and loving?"—
I know a Voice would sound, "Daughter, I AM.
Can I suffice for HEAVEN and not for earth?"

QUESTIONS

1. What is the rhyme scheme of "Consolation"?

2. In which respects does the structure of the poem differ from that of Milton's sonnet?

3. How does Browning's God differ from Donne's (page 459)? from Milton's (page 460)?

4. What is the theme of "Consolation"? Is such a theme still current?

5. Would you consider the last two lines of the poem weak or strong? Explain.

TOPICS FOR WRITING

1. Write a comparative essay on the sonnet forms used by Browning and by Donne (page 459), analyzing those features that are most striking.

2. Analyze the use of poetic language in the works of Donne (page 459), Milton (page 460), and Browning. Whose language best suits the theme of the poem?

3. Contrast "Consolation" with "To an Athlete Dying Young" (page 438), exploring meter, rhythm, and the different approaches to theme.

Countee Cullen

YET DO I MARVEL

Countee Cullen (1903–1946) grew up in Harlem, the son of a minister. He studied at New York University and Harvard. He was 23 when he published his first volume of poetry, Color (1926). Like McKay, Bontemps, Hughes, and others, Cullen was involved in the Harlem Renaissance. However, his principal occupation was teaching French in the New York City schools. Cullen was also an editor of various publications. In 1927 he published Copper Sun and The Ballad of the Brown Girl. The Black Christ followed two years later. Cullen wrote two children's books and a novel, One Way to Heaven (1932). A year after his death a collection of selected poems was published, On These I Stand. Countee Cullen was greatly influenced by the works of John Keats and like him was a lyric poet. "Yet Do I Marvel" is a sonnet, a gently satiric commentary on racism using God as a fake focus. The bite comes in the final line of the poem.

I doubt not God is good, well-meaning, kind,
And did He stoop to quibble could tell why
The little buried mole continues blind,
Why flesh that mirrors Him must some day die,
Make plain the reason tortured Tantalus   5
Is baited by the fickle fruit, declare
If merely brute caprice dooms Sisyphus
To struggle up a never-ending stair.
Inscrutable His ways are, and immune
To catechism by a mind too strewn   10
With petty cares to slightly understand
What awful brain compels His awful hand.
Yet do I marvel at this curious thing:
To make a poet black, and bid him sing!

QUESTIONS

1. In structure, how does Cullen's poem differ from the sonnets of Donne (page 459), Milton (page 460), and Browning (page 462)?

2. Is Cullen's God more reasonable than the God described by Donne (page 459)? by Milton (page 460)?

3. Who was Tantalus?

4. Who was Sisyphus?

5. Until the couplet—the thirteenth and fourteenth lines—what tone and theme are present in "Yet Do I Marvel"?

6. Where is alliteration used?

7. How great a role does religion appear to have played in Cullen's life?

TOPICS FOR WRITING

1. Analyze the final two lines and their relationship to the rest of the poem. What do they mean? Why were they used? Explain fully the irony emphasized by the exclamation mark.

2. Man's relationship to God differs in the works of Milton, Donne, Browning, and Cullen. Compare these relationships, bearing in mind that Cullen's has a particular distinction.

Gwendolyn Brooks

Gwendolyn Brooks (1917–   ), introduced earlier in this anthology (page 357), was born in Topeka, Kansas, and raised on Chicago's South Side. She still lives there. Her parents liked the poetry of Paul Laurence Dunbar and encouraged Brooks to write so that one day she might become the female counterpart of Dunbar. Brooks has written of the street and of the soul, often using, as in "God works in a mysterious way," blank verse. She attended Wilson Junior College, and her first collection of poetry, A Street in Bronzeville (1945), appeared a few years later. Her second book, Annie Allen (1949), won for her the Pulitzer Prize. Her other books include Bronzeville Boys and Girls (1956), The Bean Eaters (1960); In the Mecca (1968); Family Pictures (1970); an autobiography, Report from Part One (1971); and a novel, Maud Martha (1953). Brooks worked long and earnestly with the younger black writers of Chicago who belonged to the OBACI group. Don L. Lee was one of her proteges. Like Langston Hughes, Brooks writes about inner-city life. "firstly inclined to take what it is told" and "God works in a mysterious way" constitute a double sonnet and an extension of such a poem as "The Sundays of Satin-Legs Smith," which calls upon old, interior sensibilities to recognize the spiritual element in life. Harvey Curtis Webster said of Brooks that she "has never denied her engagement in the contemporary situation or been over-obsessed by it . . . compared not to other Negro poets or other women poets but to the best of modern poets, she ranks high."

FIRSTLY INCLINED TO TAKE WHAT IT IS TOLD

Thee sacrosanct, Thee sweet, Thee crystalline,
With the full jewel wile of mightly light—
With the narcotic milk of peace for men
Who find Thy beautiful center and relate
Thy round command, Thy grand, Thy mystic good—   5
Thee like the classic quality of a star;
A little way from warmth, a little sad,
Delicately lovely to adore—
I had been brightly ready to believe.
For youth is a frail thing, not unafraid.   10
Firstly inclined to take what it is told.
Firstly inclined to lean. Greedy to give
Faith tidy and total. To a total God.
With billowing heartiness no whit withheld.

"GOD WORKS IN A MYSTERIOUS WAY"

But often now the youthful eye cuts down its
Own dainty veiling. Or submits to winds.
And many an eye that all its age had drawn its
Beam from a Book endures the impudence
Of modern glare that never heard of tact   5
Or timeliness, or Mystery that shrouds
Immortal joy: it merely can direct
Chancing feet across dissembling clods.
Out from Thy shadows, from Thy pleasant meadows,
Quickly, in undiluted light. Be glad, whose   10
Mansions are bright, to right Thy children's air.
If Thou be more than hate or atmosphere
Step forth in splendor, mortify our wolves.
Or we assume a sovereignty ourselves.

QUESTIONS

1. Which elements in these poems make them a double sonnet?

2. Describe the alliteration and use of metaphor in the first eight lines of "firstly inclined to take what it is told" and in the final six lines.

3. Describe the connection of imagery between "firstly inclined to take what it is told" and "God works in a mysterious way."

4. Why do these poems not constitute a sonnet in the traditional sense?

5. Why has Brooks divided this work into two sonnets? What is happening in the first? What is happening in the second?

6. How does the theme of this double sonnet differ from the theme of Cullen's poem?

7. Brooks and Donne (page 459) both ask the same thing of God. What?

8. "I had been brightly ready to believe." What occurrence seems to work against that belief?

9. What is the meaning of this line: "But often now the youthful eye cuts down its/Own dainty veiling"?

10. Who are the "wolves"? Who are the people who endure "the impudence/Of modern glare"?

11. There is a sense of extreme need in the poem. Who needs what and for which reasons?

TOPICS FOR WRITING

1. Analyze all the metaphors Brooks uses for God in "firstly inclined to take what it is told," and explain why she uses so many, why each possesses a special image, and what the purpose of each is.

2. Describe the counterpoint effect of the last six lines of "firstly inclined to take what it is told" and why Brooks uses them at this point. How do these same six lines create the transition to "God works in a mysterious way"?

3. The term "frail" usually implies a weakness, but here the poet's use conveys the opposite meaning. Where else in the work does she do the same thing?

4. Describe what "Beam" and "Book" symbolize here and how the second term relates to the first.

5. Who are the wolves? What are they doing? Why must they be mortified?

6. Analyze theme and structure in Brooks' double sonnet.

20

POETIC STRUCTURE AND THEME: THE CITY

Of all the regions that serve as theme, metaphorically or not, the city may be the most fascinating for the poet. The names of famous cities mark the long route of urban literature from the past to the present: Thebes, Nineveh, Tyre, Sidon, Athens, Rome, Baghdad, Paris, London, New York, Chicago . . .

From Homer's "Hundred-Gated Thebes" to Juvenal's wicked Rome, from Swift's filthy London to Melville's riotous New York to Sandburg's brawling Chicago, the city, wherever it is, continues to be an inexhaustible source for the poetic imagination, and why not? It represents constant movement, shifting moods, and cultural confrontations, but most of all, a towering challenge to the poet who, like the photographer, would freeze it in time and form while suggesting that, as Galileo said of the earth, *Eppur si muove*—yet it does move.

Into cities all over the world have poured peoples of complementing and conflicting backgrounds, bringing with them poetic sensibilities, some of which have been expressed in such music as blues, folk song, country, western, reggae, ballad, rock, and jazz. With or without music the poetry of the city sometimes laments city life, but often exalts it, and nearly every poet seems compelled to describe the people of the city and the way they live, feel, and think.

In the city the delicate haikú (written by Matsuo Basho, 1664–1694)

> This road:
> no one walks along it
> Dusk in autumn.

may meet the limerick (anonymous author)

> There once was a man from Nantucket
> Who kept all his cash in a bucket
>   But his daughter named Nan
>   Ran away with a man,
> And as for the bucket, Nantucket.

The cadenced enthusiasm of Whitman is never chilled by the "pure and lonely," which is how Robert Lowell sees New York; the New Critic poets trade themes with the poets of the Harlem Renaissance; the Beat poets mimic Langston Hughes's use of jazz in poetry. And the poets' various ethnic impulses to universality echo through city after city whether in the old world or new.

Yet, as we look at the poems in this section it becomes palpably clear that the city does move, making the poet, to the extent possible, find forms to match its moods and its unending rhythms.

Perhaps, for example, William Blake felt that his "London" required a structure different from the one used by Juvenal to describe Rome. Blake's eye sweeps through the streets of London and finds them to be just as offensive as they were a century earlier, when Swift described them in "heroic verse," a form here used with mockery. Heroic verse, normally used in French, Latin, and Greek, was for heroic themes.

But each poet feels a different rhythm of the city; for Blake the quatrain expresses division; for Swift, the forty-nine-line iambic pentameter produces a mass and perhaps a view of what 42nd Street in New York was to become 172 years later. The stanza or, in Blake's case, the quatrain, like a paragraph in fiction, may be seen as a look from another camera angle at the same subject. The stanza may also state one complete theme or idea, but be linked to related ideas and stanzas.

With Pound's "In a Station of the Metro," the master of the Imagist poets reflects the delicate depth of the haiku. There is even the echo of a sonnet here, for the poem has as many words as a sonnet has lines. Also, the problem or question (can the apparition somehow be real?) is separated from the rest by a semicolon, punctuation that both indicates completeness and does not, implying a realism that may be presented only through its metaphorical essences. The second flurry of images calls to mind nothing as much as the remains of flowers destroyed by a storm. What storm? Is that the way Pound sees the City of Light?

The structure and rhythm of Chad Walsh's "Port Authority Terminal: 9 a.m. Monday" suggests another kind of storm, one created by mindless routine. In a sense, Walsh's work reminds us of Blake's "London," but in Blake the forces of opposition are not visible; in Walsh's they are clearly drawn.

There is less linear precision in "The City Planners," a poem rooted in twentieth-century life where "urban planning" and "developmental living" have been accepted as contemporary norms. But Atwood's emphasis on images of the places where people live and what living in such places reveals about them is at the heart of this work. Suburbs are children of the city; they are for the escapee who, in the end, has not escaped the city at all.

Such themes are not yet terribly comfortable with traditional poetic structures, yielding poems that are as uneven in length as some city blocks and as diverse; but in carrying us from "August sunlight" to the "bland madness of snows," Atwood may be seeing in the city's suburbs a quiet death.

Jonathan Swift

A DESCRIPTION OF A CITY SHOWER

Born in Dublin, Jonathan Swift (1667–1745) was educated in Ireland before going to England, where he became deeply involved in politics. He also became a master of satiric prose and poetry and an important political writer for the moderate Tories. Returning to Ireland, Swift was appointed dean of St. Patrick's Cathedral in 1713 and, except for brief trips, remained in Ireland for the rest of his life. His Tale of a Tub and Battle of the Books (1704); A Modest Proposal (1729); and most famous work, Gulliver's Travels (1726), all combined to create for Swift the image of a nasty misanthrope—though he was not. In fact, he joked about the label. Swift was a true political animal, unable to refrain from the battles. Sometimes he used pen names (although most people knew they were his): "Isaac Bickerstaff," "M. B. Drapier," "Cadenus," "Presto," and "Lemuel Gulliver." Swift knew—and sometimes ridiculed—many other writers, among them Addison and Steele, Pope, Parnell, Congreve, and Gay. Swift was declared insane in 1742. "A Description of a City Shower" not only provides an image of London during Swift's time, but is also a satire on the people of the city and their habits and a swipe at the poetic structures used by Dryden and others, which Swift thought pretentious.

   Careful observers may foretell the hour
(By sure prognostics) when to dread a shower:
While rain depends, the pensive cat gives o'er
Her frolics, and pursues her tail no more.
Returning home at night, you'll find the sink   5
Strike your offended sense with double stink.
If you be wise, then go not far to dine;
You'll spend in coach hire more than save in wine.

A coming shower your shooting corns presage,
Old aches throb, your hollow tooth will rage.   10
Sauntering in coffeehouse is Dulman seen;
He damns the climate and complains of spleen.
  Meanwhile the South, rising with dabbled wings,
A sable cloud athwart the welkin flings,
That swilled more liquor than it could contain,   15
And, like a drunkard, gives it up again.
Brisk Susan whips her linen from the rope,
While the first drizzling shower is borne aslope:
Such is that sprinkling which some careless quean
Flirts on you from her mop, but not so clean: 20
You fly, invoke the gods; then turning, stop
To rail; she singing, still whirls on her mop.
Not yet the dust had shunned the unequal strife,
But, aided by the wind, fought still for life,
And wafted with its foe by violent gust,   25
Twas doubtful which was rain and which was dust.
Ah! where must needy poet seek for aid,
When dust and rain at once his coat invade?
Sole coat, where dust cemented by the rain
Erects the nap, and leaves a mingled stain.   30
  Now in contiguous drops the flood comes down,
Threatening with deluge this devoted town.
To shops in crowds the daggled females fly,
Pretend to cheapen goods, but nothing buy.
The Templar spruce, while every spout's abroach,   35
Stays till 'tis fair, yet seems to call a coach.
The tucked-up sempstress walks with hasty strides,
While streams run down her oiled umbrella's sides.
Here various kinds, by various fortunes led,
Commence acquaintance underneath a shed.   40
Triumphant Tories and desponding Whigs
Forget their feuds, and join to save their wigs.
Boxed in a chair the beau impatient sits,
While spouts run clattering o'er the roof by fits,
And ever and anon with frightful din   45
The leather sounds, he trembles from within.
So when Troy chairmen bore the wooden steed,
Pregnant with Greeks impatient to be freed
(Those bully Greeks, who, as the moderns do,
Instead of paying chairmen, run them through),   50
Laocoön struck the outside with his spear,
And each imprisoned hero quaked for fear.
  Now from all parts the swelling kennels flow,
And bear their trophies with them as they go:
Filth of all hues and odors seem to tell   55
What street they sailed from, by their sight and smell.
They, as each torrent drives with rapid force,

From Smithfield or St. Pulchre's shape their course,
And in huge confluence joined at Snow Hill ridge,
Fall from the conduit prone to Holborn Bridge.   60
Sweepings from butchers' stalls, dung, guts, and blood,
Drowned puppies, stinking sprats, all drenched in mud,
Dead cats, and turnip tops, come tumbling down the flood.

QUESTIONS

1. What mood does Swift create in this poem? How does he create it?

2. Identify and define at least three archaic words in the poem.

3. In which ways do rhyme and rhythm contribute to the structure of "A Description of a City Shower"?

4. Swift (like Cullen after him) makes tongue-in-cheek references to the Greeks. What satire is intended?

5. What tone does Swift take toward his subject?

6. Why is the shower so important a factor in bringing out what Swift perceives to be the worst in people?

7. Can you compare aspects of Swift's city to a contemporary city? Consider the behavior of the citizens.

TOPICS FOR WRITING

1. Evaluate the mood and the number of representative people described in Swift's poem.

2. Language and its meanings are always changing. Look up the words in Swift's poem you do not understand. Which ones, current then, are still in use? For example, "corn" may refer to the result of a neglected bunion.

3. Swift defined good writing style as "proper words in proper places." Write a critical review of his poem, paying special attention to this criterion.

4. The final three lines of "A Description of a City Shower" might symbolize Swift's philosophical view of what or whom? In a paper, explore whether or not this ending is a logical one for this unrelieved satire on London life. Also explore the much-discussed question of Swift's misanthropy. Is misanthropy evident here?

William Blake

LONDON

*William Blake (1757–1827) was born in London, where dur-
ing the course of his life he was a poet, an engraver, a
painter, and a mystic whose views became recognizable in
his work. It is perhaps this element of the mystical that
gives his work its lyricism and metaphysical strength. Many
of his works are based on a mythological structure created
by Blake, one that bypasses or ignores organized religion of
Blake's day. His wife once remarked, without satiric overtone or rancor, "I have very little of Mr. Blake's company; he
is always in Paradise." Blake illustrated many of his own
works, which include* Poetical Sketches by W. B. *(1783),*
Songs of Innocence *(1789),* Songs of Experience *(1794), and
the "prophetical books"—*The Book of Thel *(1789),* The Marriage of Heaven and Hell *(1790),* The Gates of Paradise *(1793),*
The Vision of the Daughters of Albion *(1793), and others. He
illustrated works by Mary Wollstonecraft, Edward Young,
and Robert Blair during the period 1791 to 1826. Blake's
"London," unlike Swift's, is humorless and grim. Perhaps
one of the clues to his vision is that across the English
Channel, the French Revolution began when the poet was at
the peak of his power.*

I wander thro' each charter'd street,
Near where the charter'd Thames does flow,
And mark in every face I meet
Marks of weakness, marks of woe.

In every cry of every Man,   5
In every Infant's cry of fear,
In every voice, in every ban,
The mind-forg'd manacles I hear.

How the Chimney-sweeper's cry
Every black'ning Church appalls;   10
And the hapless Soldier's sigh
Runs in blood down Palace walls.

But most thro' midnight streets I hear
How the youthful Harlot's curse
Blasts the new born Infant's tear,   15
And blights with plagues the Marriage hearse.

QUESTIONS

1. What kind of a city does Blake's "London" seem to be?

2. What is the theme of this poem?

3. How many feet are in each line?

4. What contribution does rhyme make to the theme? rhythm?

5. "London" moves from the general in the first stanza to the specific in the others. But what segment of the population is not included in this survey? Why not?

6. Explain the lines, "And the hapless Soldier's sigh/Runs in blood down Palace walls."

7. Which lines of the poem indicate that the future of the residents of London will be as bleak as Blake described their present?

8. Look up the term "ban" as used here. What is a ban?

TOPICS FOR WRITING

1. What does Blake mean by "charter'd streets" and "charter'd Thames"?

2. Explain what Blake means by the line "The mind-forg'd manacles I hear." Is the underlying concept still current? Does Blake really mean he "hears" them?

3. Analyze the relationship of these two lines, "How the youthful Harlot's curse/Blasts the new born Infant's tear." Is Blake describing a vicious cycle in which, from the cradle to the grave, things remain ever the same for some people?

4. Analyze the ways in which the structure and mood of Blake's London differ from those in Swift's "A Description of a City Shower."

Ezra Pound

IN A STATION OF THE METRO

Ezra Loomis Pound (1885–1972) was born in Haily, Idaho, and studied at the University of Pennsylvania and Hamilton College. He moved to Europe and became a permanent resident of Italy in 1924. His first collection of poems, A Lume Spento (1908), was published when he was 23. Pound was drawn to medieval and Renaissance literature, translating several works from those periods. He was a forceful critic and commentator and one of the guiding lights behind the Imagist movement in England and America, which involved T. E. Hulme, Hilda Doolittle, William Carlos Williams, Amy Lowell, and others. In his criticism Pound insisted on fresh, appropriate, natural language; compositions structured like music, though using free, rather than metric, verse; and clarity of metaphor and image. In addition to the

Cantos (1925, 1930, 1940, 1948, and 1956), Pound produced many poetic and prose works. He influenced the direction and work of W. B. Yeats and sought publishers for the early works of such writers as James Joyce, William Carlos Williams, T. S. Eliot, and Wyndham Lewis. He was over several years a close friend of Hilda Doolittle (H. D.), who appears under various classical names in his poems. Pound is at the center of the controversy over whether an artist's work should be kept apart from the artist's private life. Pound was arrested and detained after World War II for collaborating with the Italian fascists.

The apparition of these faces in the crowd;
Petals on a wet, black bough.

QUESTIONS

1. How would you describe the structure of this poem?

2. Does this poem contain rhythm? cadence?

3. How many words does it contain? Might this number be an allusion to the structure of a particular kind of poem? What kind of poem?

4. Why does Pound use the term "apparition" instead of "sight" or "view"?

5. What mood is created by Pound?

6. Petals are usually found on a flower. What would have happened, symbolically, for them to be on a "wet, black bough?" What is the "wet, black bough," literally?

TOPICS FOR WRITING

1. Write a description of a city scene in fourteen words.

2. Look up the definitions of "apparition." Apply one or more of them in a paper in which you analyze Pound's use of the term.

3. Blake (page 473) and Swift (page 469) see particular faces in the crowd; to Pound the faces form a collective image. Analyze what this image symbolizes.

4. Is poetry better with rhyme and meter? Why or why not? Compare Pound's and Blake's poems.

Chad Walsh

PORT AUTHORITY TERMINAL: 9 A.M. MONDAY

Born (1914–   ) in South Boston, Virginia, Chad Walsh studied at the University of Virginia and the University of Michigan. He was ordained an Episcopal priest in 1949. Walsh has taught at a number of colleges in the United States and abroad, most notably in Finland. Many of his nonfiction works have been about the interaction of modern man and modern religion. Between these he has published, among other volumes of poetry, The Unknowing (1964), and Garlands for Christmas (1965). Walsh's work is marked by a humanitarian concern and a clear vision of the problems of contemporary life. Some of his works are in traditional poetic structures into which he places contemporary themes. "Port Authority Terminal: 9 a.m. Monday" has obvious similarities to Pound's "In a Station in the Metro." Pound's poem is a small portrait; Walsh's vibrates with tensions yet to be released.

From buses beached like an invasion fleet
They fill the waiting room with striding feet.

Their faces, white, and void of hate or pity,
Move on tall bodies toward the conquered city.

Among the lesser breeds of black and brown   5
They board their taxis with an absent frown,

Each to his concrete citadel,
To rule the city and to buy and sell.

At five o'clock they ride the buses back,
Leaving their Irish to guard the brown and black.   10

At six a drink, at seven dinner's served.
At ten or twelve, depressed, undressed, unnerved,

They mount their wives, dismount, they doze and dream
Apocalyptic Negroes in a stream

Of moving torches, marching from the slums,   15
Beating a band of garbage pails for drums,

Marching, with school-age children in their arms,
Advancing on the suburbs and the farms,

To integrate the schools and burn the houses . . .
The normal morning comes, the clock arouses   20

Junior and senior executive alike.
Back on the bus, and down the usual pike.

From buses beached like an invasion fleet
They fill the waiting room with striding feet.

QUESTIONS

1. How do rhyme, rhythm, meter, and structure contribute to the theme of this poem?

2. What is the theme of "Port Authority Terminal: 9 a.m. Monday"?

3. The stanzas of the poem are identicial in form. What mood is created by this structure? What does it imply about the theme of the poem?

4. Pound created a single image with several implications. How many images does Walsh use? What is the single implication?

5. Why is there no sense of emotion in the poem? Which of Walsh's images help to create this absence?

6. How does the use of action verbs help to create the movement in and out of the city?

TOPICS FOR WRITING

1. Explore the reasons why Walsh says the white commuters "move" while the Negroes are "marching."

2. The relationship of the white commuter to the urban ethnic residents is pictured as a movement of troops. What kind of war seems to be foreseen by Walsh? Analyze and evaluate his vision of urban and suburban life.

3. The lives of the white commuters are sketched out; the lives of the "lesser breeds" are not. Why was the poem written this way?

4. Pound (page 474) creates a static image. Walsh creates, through dispassionate description, images that seem ready to evolve into other images. Is this true of Blake's (page 472) images? of Swift's (page 469)? How is Walsh's imagery specifically different from the images of the city found in other poems in this section?

Margaret Atwood

THE CITY PLANNERS

Margaret Eleanor Atwood (1939–   ) studied at the University of Toronto, in her native Canada, and at Radcliffe College, in the United States (1957–1962). She has taught at Canadian universities and is the recipient of several awards for poetry, including the E. J. Pratt, the Governor's, and the President's medals. Atwood is considered to be one of the most important contemporary writers. She is also a novelist. Among her collections of published poetry Atwood includes Double Persephone *(1961),* The Circle Game *(1967),* The Journals of Susanna Moodie *(1970), and* Power Politics *(1971). Her novels include* The Edible Woman *(1969) and* Surfacing *(1972). Atwood has also published stories and nonfiction and writes television scripts.*

Cruising these residential Sunday
streets in dry August sunlight:
what offends us is
the sanities:
the houses in pedantic rows, the planted   5
sanitary trees, assert
levelness of surface like a rebuke
to the dent in our car door.
No shouting here, or
shatter of glass; nothing more abrupt   10
than the rational whine of a power mower
cutting a straight swath in the discouraged grass.

But though the driveways neatly
sidestep hysteria
by being even, the roofs all display   15
the same slant of avoidance to the hot sky,
certain things:
the smell of spilled oil a faint

sickness lingering in the garages,
a splash of paint on brick surprising as a bruise,   20
a plastic hose poised in a vicious
coil; even the too-fixed stare of the wide windows

give momentary access to
the landscape behind or under
the future cracks in the plaster   25

when the houses, capsized, will slide
obliquely into the clay seas, gradual as glaciers
that right now nobody notices.

That is where the City Planners
with the insane faces of political conspirators   30
are scattered over unsurveyed
territories, concealed from each other,
each in his own private blizzard;

guessing directions, they sketch
transitory lines rigid as wooden borders   35
on a wall in the white vanishing air

tracing the panic of suburb
order in a bland madness of snows.

QUESTIONS

1. Is this poem more concerned with providing images than with rhyme or rhythm? How do its structure and its images relate to those of "In a Station in the Metro" (page 474)?

2. What is the theme of "The City Planners"?

3. How does the irregular structure of the stanzas lend emphasis to the theme? Does the structure fit the poem?

4. Is it disturbing that there is but one indirect reference to people here?

5. Can you fit the commuters in "Port Authority Terminal: 9 a.m. Monday" (page 475) into these homes? What would the people be like?

6. What, literally, is the future of this town?

7. What, symbolically, is the future of this town?

8. Why are the "sanities" offensive?

TOPICS FOR WRITING

1. Draw a comparison between the emptiness described in "The City Planners" and the emptiness we encounter in the Bradbury story "August 2026: There Will Come Soft Rains" (page 159). Explore the reasons for the emptiness. What causes it?

2. Explore in the poems in this section the ominous tone that arises in those places where humans live and meet. Why is the mood ominous? What does this say for urban civilization? Is there another way for humans to live?

3. Compare "The City Planners" to Auden's "The Unknown Citizen" (page 429). Explore the implications behind a seeming anonymity: who's responsible for it? is it good or bad? what does it conceal?

21

AN ANTHOLOGY
OF POETRY

Sir Thomas Wyatt

THEY FLEE FROM ME

*Sir Thomas Wyatt (1503–1542) was born in Kent and edu-
cated at Cambridge University. His life was filled with
intrigues and adventures (he was even rumored to be the
lover of Ann Boleyn). Before the age of 25, he had attracted
the notice of Henry VIII, who used him as a deputy and an
ambassador on various missions to the Continent. His
Continental travels, especially his 1527 visit to Italy, bore
unexpected fruit for English poetry—the sonnet. Wyatt and
the hotheaded earl of Surrey, Henry Howard, introduced this
verse form, which was to become one of the most important
genres in the language. In this poem, Wyatt employs vivid
imagery in order to explore the trials and fortunes of love.*

Sir Thomas Wyatt

They flee from me, that sometime did me seek,
With naked foot stalking in my chamber.
I have seen them, gentle, tame, and meek,
That now are wild, and do not remember
That sometime they put themselves in danger 5
To take bread at my hand; and now they range,
Busily seeking with a continual change.

Thankéd be fortune it hath been otherwise,
Twenty times better; but once in special,
In thin array, after a pleasant guise, 10
When her loose gown from her shoulders did fall,
And she me caught in her arms long and small,
And therewithall sweetly did me kiss
And softly said, "Dear heart, how like you this?"

It was no dream, I lay broad waking. 15
But all is turned, thorough my gentleness,
Into a strange fashion of forsaking;
And I have leave to go, of her goodness,
And she also to use newfangleness.
But since that I so kindely am servéd, 20
I fain would know what she hath deservéd.

QUESTIONS

1. Wyatt's first stanza is laden with animal imagery, implicit and explicit. How is this explainable in the context of a love affair?

2. The verbs and adjectives in stanza 1 alternate in meaning (e.g., "seek" follows "flee"; "wild" follows "gentle, tame, and meek"). What relationship does this alternation have to "fortune" in stanza 2?

3. What distinction does the speaker make between the "special" lady and his other lovers?

4. What does the poet suggest is the cause of his abandonment? Is there an irony to his explanation? Explain.

TOPICS FOR WRITING

1. Write a short essay on the final issue Wyatt raises in his poem.

2. Analyze the psychological and emotional state of the speaker in this poem. What does he reveal about himself and about his attitude toward women?

Henry Howard

TO HIS LADY

Henry Howard (1515–1547), son of the powerful duke of Norfolk, had a tumultuous youth, full of the customary pastimes of young aristocrats—vigorous games, traveling, and wenching. Along the way, he also acquired a first-rate education at the hands of private tutors. Fierce and absurdly proud, he almost had his right hand chopped off for striking a courtier; eventually, he was beheaded for suspicion of treason. With Thomas Wyatt, he helped establish the sonnet in English, and he was the first poet to publish in blank verse. "To His Lady" is a poem with the typical urbanity, clarity, and control that made him a popular writer among Elizabethans.

Set me whereas the sun doth parch the green,
 Or where his beams may not dissolve the ice,
In temperate heat, where he is felt and seen,
 With proud people, in presence sad and wise;
Set me in base, or yet in high degree,   5
 In the long night, or in the shortest day,
In clear weather, or where mists thickest be,
 In lofty youth, or when my hairs be gray;
Set me in earth, in heaven, or yet in hell,
 In hill, in dale, or in the foaming flood,   10
Thrall, or at large, alive whereso I dwell,
 Sick, or in health, in ill fame, or in good;
  Yours will I be, and with that only thought
  Comfort myself when that my hap is nought.

QUESTIONS

1. Howard's poem is one of the first of its genre in English—a sonnet. Describe the rhyme scheme and discuss what you perceive to be the limitations and the assets of such a strict form.

2. What is the force of the word "sad" in line 4?

3. Howard's sonnet relies heavily on the rhetorical device *antithesis*, the pairing of opposites. Is the device gracefully used here or does it become tedious? Explain.

4. Is the level of diction uniform? Give examples.

TOPICS FOR WRITING

1. Comment on and classify the ways in which Howard balances different types of opposites in this poem. What is the effect of this balancing, and what is its relationship to the theme?

2. Write a short report on the development of the love lyric in English by Wyatt and Howard, with special emphasis on their two poems herein.

Edmund Spenser

SONNET 75:
ONE DAY I WROTE HER NAME
UPON THE STRAND

Edmund Spenser (1552–1599) was born of middle-class parents in London and in 1569 attended Cambridge on a fellowship. Cambridge then was a hotbed of Puritan and humanist activity. He was to be profoundly influenced by each of the movements, but was simply too large a figure to become pigeonholed in either of them. By 1576 he had an MA and made his way into the employ of the lord deputy of Ireland. His first important work, The Shepherd's Calendar *(1579), was dedicated to Sir Philip Sidney in appreciation of his efforts to reinvigorate English poetry. Yet Spenser's own work is full of archaic language and rustic idioms. His most famous poem is* The Faerie Queen, *a compendium of philosophy, Arthurian myth, and allegorical polemics. He sought always to delight and instruct; Milton reverenced him as the greatest Christian poet. In this sonnet from his sequence* Amoretti *(1595), Spenser employs a popular theme in English poetry—the power of poetry to immortalize a woman's virtues.*

One day I wrote her name upon the strand,
But came the waves and washed it away:
Again I wrote it with a second hand,
But came the tide, and made my pains his prey.
"Vain man," said she, "that doest in vain assay,   5
A mortal thing so to immortalize,
For my self shall like to this decay,
And eek my name be wiped out likewise."
"Not so," quoth I, "let baser things devise
To die in dust, but you shall live by fame: 10
My verse your virtues rare shall eternalize,
And in the heavens write your glorious name.
Where whenas death shall all the world subdue,
Our love shall live, and later life renew."

QUESTIONS

1. Spenser's poem, like Wyatt's (page 480), is concerned with the durability of love. By what method does he seek to ensure its survival?

2. What is the central image of the sonnet? Is it personified? How?

3. Does the lady's attitude surprise you? Does the poet's response convince you? Point to details in the poem to support your answer.

4. Is there a pun on "second hand" in line 3? Explain.

5. Is there a religious undertone to this poem? Find terms equally at home in the realms of love, art, and faith.

TOPICS FOR WRITING

1. Analyze the relationship between love and art, between mortality and immortality, that Spenser investigates in this sonnet.

2. Write a short essay comparing the positions of Spenser and Wyatt (page 480) on the place of change in human life. Do they accept it? in the same way? Which seems more naive to you? Why?

Sir Walter Raleigh

THE NYMPH'S REPLY
TO THE SHEPHERD

Sir Walter Raleigh (1552–1618) was born in Devon. He left Oxford University without taking a degree. Like Sir Philip Sidney, Raleigh filled the pattern of an Elizabethan gentleman. World explorer, poet, historian, courtier, and the favorite of Queen Elizabeth in the 1580s, he was famous all over England. His poetry, however, was not at all flamboyant. In fact, he is considered a master of the restrained, plain style of verse, though in his hands it achieves a vigor seldom equaled. He fell out of favor with the young James I in 1603 and spent the next fifteen years in the Tower of London. He was executed in 1618. In this famous poem, a critical response to one by Christopher Marlowe (page 486), Raleigh offers a wry commentary on love and the passage of time.

If all the world and love were young,
And truth in every shepherd's tongue,
These pretty pleasures might me move
To live with thee and be thy love.

Time drives the flocks from field to fold   5
When rivers rage and rocks grow cold,
And Philomel becometh dumb;
The rest complains of cares to come.

The flowers do fade, and wanton fields
To wayward winter reckoning yields;   10
A honey tongue, a heart of gall,
Is fancy's spring, but sorrow's fall.

Thy gowns, thy shoes, thy beds of roses,
Thy cap, thy kirtle, and thy posies
Soon break, soon wither, soon forgotten—   15
In folly ripe, in reason rotten.

Thy belt of straw and ivy buds,
Thy coral clasps and amber studs,
All these in me no means can move
To come to thee and be thy love.   20

But could youth last and love still breed,
Had joys no date nor age no need,
Then these delights my mind might move
To live with thee and be thy love.

QUESTIONS

1. Marlowe's shepherd (page 486) relies heavily on images drawn from nature to woo the young lady. Her reply, however, in Raleigh's version (and there are numerous others) relies on something which transcends nature. What is it?

2. Raleigh uses a great deal of alliteration in this poem. What are some of the effects he achieves with it? Pay special attention to stanzas 2, 3, and 4.

3. The final lines of stanzas 3 and 4 contain clever puns that resonate against one another. Explain this effect.

TOPICS FOR WRITING

1. Does the lady's pragmatic reasoning convince you? Or do you favor the *carpe diem* theme of Marlowe (page 486)? Write an essay defending your position.

2. Though simple at first glance, both Marlowe's and Raleigh's poems are virtuoso performances. Write a short essay closely examining their use of assonance and alliteration, the couplet as a vehicle for argument, and the success of the plain style.

Sir Philip Sidney

WITH HOW SAD STEPS, O MOON

Sir Philip Sidney (1554–1586) was born in Penhurst, Kent, of an aristocratic family. He attended both Oxford and Cambridge, but took no degree. He traveled to France with the English ambassador in 1572 and there witnessed the St. Bartholomew's Day Massacre, an event which turned him and his countrymen firmly toward Protestantism. Sidney became the epitome of the Elizabethan gentleman—an accomplished poet, scholar, soldier, and diplomat. Perhaps his most famous work is his Defense of Poetry (1595), which was published after his death from wounds received in battle. His place in English poetry has never wavered. His prose, criticism, and poetry are all considered of the highest order. Sidney's greatest achievement in poetry is the sonnet sequence Astrophel and Stella (1582). In this well-known sonnet, Sidney speculates about the constancy of love.

With how sad steps, O Moon, thou climb'st the skies,
How silently, and with how wan a face!
What! may it be that even in heav'nly place
That busy archer his sharp arrows tries?
Sure, if that long-with-love-acquainted eyes   5
Can judge of love, thou feel'st a lover's case.
I read it in thy looks; thy languisht grace
To me, that feel the like, thy state descries.
Then, ev'n of fellowship, O Moon, tell me,
Is constant love deem'd there but want of wit?   10
Are beauties there as proud as here they be?
Do they above love to be lov'd, and yet
Those lovers scorn whom that love doth possess?
Do they call virtue there ungratefulness?

QUESTIONS

1. Why does the unsuccessful lover address the rising moon? How effective do you find Sidney's use of apostrophe, or address?

2. What is the nature of the speaker's speculations in the octave? What does he ask rhetorically in the sestet?

3. What contrasts exist in this poem?

4. How do you interpret the last line of the poem?

TOPICS FOR WRITING

1. Define what you think Sidney means by "ungratefulness" in the poem, and explain its relationship to the theme of constant love.

2. Analyze the nature and effect of the questions that Sidney uses to structure this poem.

Christopher Marlowe

THE PASSIONATE SHEPHERD TO HIS LOVE

Christopher Marlowe (1564–1593) was born the son of a Canterbury shoemaker. He attended Cambridge University on a scholarship and took his BA in 1584 and MA in 1587. Speculation abounds on his life after leaving Cambridge. Apparently he was employed by the Crown, perhaps even while a student, as some sort of messenger or spy. His literary career began with the publication of Tamburlaine *(1587). Eventually he was to produce influential translations of the classics, as well as his own* Hero and Leander *(1593). The circumstances surrounding his death at the age of 29 are unclear, but he seems to have been murdered in the midst of political intrigue. A profound psychologist in such plays as* Dr. Faustus *(1592?), he could also turn his hand to lighter affairs, as in our selection from his poetry.*

Come live with me and be my love,
And we will all the pleasures prove
That valleys, groves, hills, and fields,
Woods, or steepy mountain yields.

And we will sit upon the rocks, 5
Seeing the shepherds feed their flocks,
By shallow rivers to whose falls
Melodious birds sing madrigals.

And I will make thee beds of roses
And a thousand fragrant posies, 10
A cap of flowers, and a kirtle
Embroidered all with leaves of myrtle;

A gown made of the finest wool
Which from our pretty lambs we pull;
Fair lined slippers for the cold, 15
With buckles of the purest gold;

A belt of straw and ivy buds,
With coral clasps and amber studs:
And if these pleasures may thee move,
Come live with me, and be my love. 20

The shepherds' swains shall dance and sing
For thy delight each May morning:
If these delights thy mind may move,
Then live with me and be my love.

QUESTIONS

1. This simple song of Marlowe's has remained popular since the sixteenth century. What does the speaker offer as enticement in stanza 1? What does he avoid mentioning?

2. By stanza 3, the young lover is varying his appeal. How does he do this? What does it suggest to you?

3. He offers "a gown of finest wool" and "buckles of the purest gold" in stanza 4. Does this add to his charm or make us begin to suspect him?

4. By the end of the poem, how convincing do you find Marlowe's appeal? Why?

TOPIC FOR WRITING

Marlowe, in a few stanzas, has conjured up an earthly paradise. Does it seem reasonable to you that a poem about young love should contain images only from nature?

William Shakespeare

William Shakespeare (1564–1616), introduced earlier in the anthology (page 341), stands as the finest dramatist and, with Philip Sidney, most skillful sonneteer in the language. Just who the sonnets were addressed to has been a matter of heated controversy for centuries. Our selections open with references to the seasons and like many of Shakespeare's sonnets are concerned with love in the flux of time.

SHALL I COMPARE THEE TO A SUMMER'S DAY?

Shall I compare thee to a summer's day?
Thou art more lovely and more temperate,
Rough winds do shake the darling buds of May,
And summer's lease hath all too short a date.
Sometime too hot the eye of heaven shines,   5
And often is his gold complexion dimm'd;
And every fair from fair sometime declines,

By chance, or nature's changing course, untrimm'd;
But thy eternal summer shall not fade
Nor lose possession of that fair thou ow'st,   10
Nor shall Death brag thou wand'rest in his shade
When in eternal lines to time thou grow'st.
  So long as men can breathe or eyes can see,
  So long lives this, and this gives life to thee.

QUESTIONS

1. Shakespeare's attitude toward nature is a complex one. How would you characterize it? Does he praise or reject nature? And if not nature, what is there to admire in the beloved?

2. The phrase "eternal summer" seems to be a contradiction in terms. What might Shakespeare be referring to?

3. What do we know about the person the poem addresses?

4. Shakespeare's response to the flux of time and the stasis of death is the same: that his art shall conquer them both. Is there anything in the poem to which art itself plays a subordinate role? Explain.

TOPICS FOR WRITING

1. Write an essay exploring Shakespeare's treatment of the season in this sonnet.

2. Analyze the various images of limitation in the poem and their relationship to the theme of immortality.

3. Write a short essay placing Shakespeare's view of art's function and potential in conjunction with that of Edmund Spenser (page 482), Ben Jonson (page 494), and Robert Herrick (page 497).

THAT TIME OF YEAR
THOU MAYST IN ME BEHOLD

That time of year thou mayst in me behold
When yellow leaves, or none, or few, do hang
Upon those boughs which shake against the cold,
Bare ruined choirs where late the sweet birds sang.
In me thou see'st the twilight of such day   5
As after sunset fadeth in the west,
Which by and by black night doth take away,
Death's second self, that seals up all in rest.

In me thou see'st the glowing of such fire,
That on the ashes of his youth doth lie   10
As the deathbed whereon it must expire,
Consumed with that which it was nourished by.
  This thou perceivest, which makes thy love more strong,
  To love that well which thou must leave ere long.

QUESTIONS

1. How does the speaker portray himself in this sonnet? What is his attitude toward age and aging?

2. Explain the controlling metaphor in lines 1–4, 5–8, and 9–12. How are these metaphors related?

3. What patterns of imagery do you detect in the poem? What do the images in lines 1–4 suggest? How do the images change in lines 5–8? What tone and mood are created by the images in lines 9–12?

4. Where does personification exist in the poem? For what purpose?

5. What is the function of the couplet (lines 13–14)?

TOPICS FOR WRITING

1. Analyze the intricate use of metaphors and imagery to advance the theme in this sonnet.

2. Which of Shakespeare's two poems on the seasons in this section is more successful? Why?

Thomas Campion

THERE IS A GARDEN
IN HER FACE

Thomas Campion (1567–1620) was born in London, the son of well-to-do parents who died in his childhood. A man of many interests and talents, Campion studied at Cambridge from 1581 to 1584, but took no degree; and at Gray's Inn, but never practiced law. He obtained a medical degree, probably at Caen in 1605, and for the rest of his life practiced medicine. Poetry and music were his main preoccupations, and he was much appreciated in his own time for his productions. Campion published five collections of lute songs in his lifetime. "In these airs," he wrote, "I have chiefly aimed to couple my words and notes lovingly together." Praised in modern times by T. S. Eliot as an "accomplished master of rhymed lyric," Campion in the following song offers traditional praise of a lady's beauty.

There is a garden in her face,
Where roses and white lilies grow,
A heavenly paradise is that place,
Wherein all pleasant fruits do flow.
There cherries grow, which none may buy   5
Till "Cherry ripe!" themselves do cry.

Those cherries fairly do enclose
Of orient pearl a double row;
Which when her lovely laughter shows,
They look like rosebuds filled with snow.   10
Yet them nor peer nor prince can buy,
Till "Cherry ripe!" themselves do cry.

Her eyes like angels watch them still;
Her brows like bended bows do stand,
Threatening with piercing frowns to kill   15
All that attempt with eye or hand
Those sacred cherries to come nigh,
Till "Cherry ripe!" themselves do cry.

QUESTIONS

1. Though most madrigal writers hired poets to write verses for their songs, Campion chose to write his own. In this, perhaps his most famous, a lady is praised for her beauty. What is the religious resonance of the "roses" and "white lilies" of stanza 1? What lady is traditionally associated with these flowers?

2. Throughout the poem, images of flowers and fruit predominate. Is it, then, a fault to introduce an "orient pearl" in stanza 2? How would you explain the presence of an alien image?

3. By stanza 3, the lady has undergone a change in status. No longer merely a pleasant garden, she has been given the power to kill with a single glance those who would disturb her prerogative. Just what is this "right" of hers and how does it relate to the refrain "Cherry ripe!"?

TOPICS FOR WRITING

1. Analyze the patterns of imagery in the poem and their relationship to the theme.

2. Define and describe the attitudes toward love found in the poems by Wyatt (page 480), Howard (page 481), Spenser (page 482), Sidney (page 485), and Campion.

John Donne

John Donne (1572–1631), introduced previously in this anthology (page 435), was a lover of the poetic conceit— powerful images which capture our imagination, especially when swiftly alternated. The themes of his poetry range from the profane to the sacred, as in the selections you have been given. The poems date, respectively, from the beginning and end of his career, and both bear the stamp of his restless, ever-changing mind.

SONG (GO AND CATCH A FALLING STAR)

Go and catch a falling star,
  Get with child a mandrake root,
Tell me where all past years are,
  Or who cleft the Devil's foot,
Teach me to hear mermaids singing,   5
Or to keep off envy's stinging,
        And find
        What wind
Serves to advance an honest mind.

If thou beest borne to strange sights,   10
  Things invisible to see,
Ride ten thousand days and nights,
  Till age snow white hairs on thee,

Thou, when thou return'st, wilt tell me,
All strange wonders that befell thee, 15
   And swear
   No where
Lives a woman true, and fair.

If thou find'st one, let me know,
 Such a Pilgrimage were sweet; 20
Yet do not, I would not go,
 Though at next door we might meet;
Though she were true, when you met her,
And last till you write your letter,
   Yet she 25
   Will be
False, ere I come, to two, or three.

QUESTIONS

1. The poem begins with a series of imperatives. Is Donne being playful or serious here? Can these commands be carried out, or is their impossibility related to his deeper purpose?

2. In stanza 2, line 13, we find age treated metaphorically. What does Donne mean to suggest by his verb "snow"? Does it fit in well with the rest of the stanza? Or does it seem too ordinary or tame?

3. What makes the rhythms of this poem so choppy? What is the intention?

TOPIC FOR WRITING

Examine the method of Donne's "argument" in this poem and the various effects that he creates.

HOLY SONNET 7

At the round earth's imagined corners, blow
Your trumpets, angels; and arise, arise
From death, you numberless infinities
Of souls, and to your scattered bodies go;
All whom the flood did, and fire shall, o'erthrow, 5
All whom war, dearth, age, agues, tyrannies,
Despair, law, chance hath slain, and you whose eyes
Shall behold God, and never taste death's woe.
But let them sleep, Lord, and me mourn a space;
For, if above all these, my sins abound, 10

'Tis late to ask abundance of Thy grace
When we are there. Here on this lowly ground,
Teach me how to repent; for that's as good
As if Thou hadst sealed my pardon with Thy blood.

QUESTIONS

1. The second selection, Holy Sonnet 7, begins with yet another impossibility, or paradox—the round earth's corners. Why might Donne be attracted to paradox in a poem about the Resurrection?

2. Who is the "you" of line 7? All told, how many persons does Donne address in the poem? Do you find his frequent shifts of address bothersome? Why or why not?

3. What exactly does Donne order the "you" in line 7 to do? Why?

4. The tone, as well as the addressee, abruptly changes in line 9. How would you describe the new tone?

5. Though the tone changes, the grammatical mood remains the same—the imperative. What does this suggest about Donne's state of mind?

TOPICS FOR WRITING

1. Why does Donne select the sonnet as the form in which to address his subjects in this poem? How and why is the sonnet a "holy" one?

2. Write an essay exploring the relationship of Donne's verse to Ben Jonson's (pages 493–498). Though both were vigorous, intellectual men, they chose to express themselves in contrasting verse styles. Examine the contrast, of which Jonson remarked, "Donne himself for not being understood would perish."

Ben Jonson

Ben Jonson (1572–1637), dramatist, poet, and literary critic, was one of the greatest writers of the English Renaissance; among his contemporaries, he was more influential than Shakespeare or Donne. Born a few months after his clergyman father's death, into impoverished circumstances, Jon-

Ben Jonson

*son somehow managed to attend the most noted school of
the period—Westminster—and to study language and literature under the famous schoolmaster William Camden. No
"mouse of the scrolls," Jonson worked as a bricklayer, a
soldier (he killed an enemy in single combat), and finally as
an actor and playwright. Jonson's finest comedies are* Vol-
pone *(1606) and* The Alchemist *(1610). As a poet, Jonson
preferred the "plain," or "native," style. Throughout his life,
he looked to the masterpieces of antiquity for inspiration. In
1616 he published his* Works, *which showed a flawless
command of all the genres of the ancient world—epigram,
lyric, satire, tragedy, and comedy. His spare, graceful, laconic, and essentially classical style is reflected in the four
lyrics that follow.*

TO CELIA

Come my *Celia*, let us prove,
While we may, the sports of love;
Time will not be ours, for ever:
He, at length, our good will sever.
Spend not then his gifts in vain.   5
Sunnes, that set, may rise again:
But if once we lose this light,
'Tis, with us, perpetual night.
Why should we defer our joys?
Fame, and rumor are but toys.   10
Cannot we delude the eyes
Of a few poor houshold spys?
Or his easier ears beguile,
So removed by our wile?

QUESTIONS

1. What is the "argument" in the poem?

2. How does the rhyme scheme contribute to the development of the speaker's argument?

3. Where is the allusion to the story of Adam and Eve? What use does the
speaker put this allusion to?

4. How would you characterize the speaker of this poem, and how would you
judge his motives?

5. What examples of sight imagery appear in the poem? What is the function
of such imagery?

TOPIC FOR WRITING

Many younger writers, notably Herrick (page 497) and Suckling (page 502), considered themselves Jonson's literary "sons." How does this lyric influence the poems by Herrick and Suckling that appear in this anthology?

ON MY FIRST SON

Farewell, thou child of my right hand, and joy;
My sin was too much hope of thee, loved boy:
Seven years thou wert lent to me, and I thee pay,
Exacted by thy fate, on the just day.
O could I lose all father now! for why   5
Will man lament the state he should envy,
To have so soon 'scaped world's and flesh's rage,
And, if no other misery, yet age?
Rest in soft peace, and asked, say, "Here doth lie
Ben Jonson his best piece of poetry."   10
For whose sake henceforth all his vows be such
As what he loves may never like too much.

QUESTIONS

1. What attitude does Jonson take toward the death of his son? Cite examples to support your answers.

2. What does Jonson mean by "My sin" in line 2; by "O could I lose all father now" in line 5? Is this a simple or complex poem? Why?

3. Explain why Jonson is self-conscious about his role as a poet. Why does he inject this role into a poem that, after all, is an epitaph on his son?

4. How do meter and rhyme influence the tone of this poem?

TOPIC FOR WRITING

Evaluate the success of this poem as an example of epitaph. How does Jonson manage to control and objectify his grief?

ON MY FIRST DAUGHTER

Here lies, to each her parents' ruth,
Mary, the daughter of their youth;
Yet all heaven's gifts being heaven's due,

Ben Jonson

It makes the father less to rue.
At six months' end she parted hence   5
With safety of her innocence;
Whose soul heaven's queen, whose name she bears,
In comfort of her mother's tears,
Hath placed amongst her virgin train:
Where, while that severed doth remain,   10
This grave partakes the fleshly birth;
Which cover lightly, gentle earth!

QUESTIONS

1. Jonson's epitaph has been admired for the excellence of its diction and syntax. What might readers have found to praise in the features of the poem?

2. How could the tone be best described?

3. Is the poem pervaded by a dominant feeling, or is there a mixture of feelings expressed? Explain.

TOPIC FOR WRITING

Compare and contrast Jonson's two epitaphs, concentrating on such matters as diction, imagery, tone, mood, and rhyme.

STILL TO BE NEAT

Still to be neat, still to be drest,
As you were going to a feast;
Still to be pou'dred, still perfum'd:
Lady, it is to be presum'd,
Though arts hid causes are not found,   5
All is not sweet, all is not sound.

Give me a look, give me a face,
That makes simplicity a grace;
Robes loosely flowing, hair as free:
Such sweet neglect more taketh me,   10
Than all th'adulteries of art.
They strike mine eyes, but not my heart.

QUESTIONS

1. Contrast the images of woman in the first stanza with those in the second stanza.

2. Is this poem concerned with a lady or with art itself? Explain.

3. What does Jonson mean by "sweet neglect" in line 10?

4. What is the effect of the rhyme scheme on meaning in this poem?

TOPIC FOR WRITING

Write an essay on the themes of simplicity, clarity, and "sweet neglect" in this poem and, perhaps, in the other selections that you have by Jonson. Why did Jonson prefer these themes to the "adulteries of art"?

Robert Herrick

Robert Herrick (1591–1674) was born in London of a middle-class family. He served for ten years as an apprentice goldsmith to his uncle, Sir William Herrick. Educated at St. John's College, Cambridge, and Trinity Hall, he later accepted a clerical position and lived his life as a bachelor in Devonshire (1629–1647). In terms of his poetic style, Herrick is usually classified with the Cavaliers, poets who wrote during the reign of Charles I. Other Cavaliers included Thomas Carew, Sir John Suckling, and Richard Lovelace. Early in his career, Herrick was greatly influenced by Ben Jonson. However, poems such as "To the Virgins, to Make Much of Time" and "Delight in Disorder" reveal him to be a less didactic and more playful poet than Jonson. Herrick's major collection, Hesperides, was published in 1648 and contained over 1,200 sacred and secular poems.

TO THE VIRGINS,
TO MAKE MUCH OF TIME

Gather ye rosebuds while ye may:
   Old Time is still a-flying,
And this same flower that smiles to-day
   Tomorrow will be dying.

Robert Herrick

The glorious lamp of heaven, the sun,　　　　　　　　　　5
　　The higher he's a-getting,
The sooner will his race be run,
　　And nearer he's to setting.

That age is best which is the first,
　　When youth and blood are warmer;　　　　　　　　　10
But, being spent, the worse, and worst
　　Times, still succeed the former.

Then be not coy, but use your time,
　　And while ye may, go marry:
For having lost but once your prime,　　　　　　　　　15
　　You may for ever tarry.

QUESTIONS

1. How does Herrick use natural imagery to indicate the rapid passage of time? What is he saying about the relationship between old age and youth?

2. What is the poet's opinion of social "games," such as coyness?

3. Explain how the expression "go marry" is used as a pun in line 14.

4. Herrick repeats the word "may" three times in this poem (lines 1, 14, and 16). What multiple meanings can you find for those uses, and how do they help create the poem's thematic effects?

5. The last two lines of the poem capsulize the *carpe diem* theme (Latin for "seize the day"). Thus it can be read as a cynical warning to those who "hold out" in their lives. Do you agree or disagree with Herrick's message? Why?

TOPICS FOR WRITING

1. Investigate the *carpe diem* theme in the poem. Who is the persona of this poem? Who is he addressing, and how is he imploring them to change their lives? Point to words and phrases in the first stanza which speak of the passing of time. More generally, what is the poet saying about "wasting time"?

2. Herrick uses metaphors of sexuality and virginity to express his theme. What tone does Herrick create through his use and interpretation of these metaphors? Evaluate this tone.

DELIGHT IN DISORDER

A sweet disorder in the dress
Kindles in clothes a wantonness:
A lawn about the shoulders thrown
Into a fine distraction:
An erring lace, which here and there   5
Enthrals the crimson stomacher:
A cuff neglectful, and thereby
Ribbands to flow confusedly:
A winning wave (deserving note)
In the tempestuous petticoat: 10
A careless shoe-string, in whose tie
I see a wild civility:
Do more bewitch me than when art
Is too precise in every part.

QUESTIONS

1. An *oxymoron* is an expression that joins two contradictory terms for emphasis. For example, "sweet disorder" in line 1 is an oxymoron. What other oxymorons does Herrick use in the poem? What effects are achieved by their use? How does Herrick's use of this poetic device thematically relate to the poem?

2. Many of the terms that Herrick uses to describe women's clothing have moral or judgmental overtones. Analyze four such descriptions from the poem.

3. In this poem, Herrick employs a number of half rhymes, such as "tie" and "civility" in lines 11 and 12. What are other examples of half rhymes? How do they serve as an example of the type of art for which the poet is arguing?

TOPICS FOR WRITING

1. This poem is arranged as an argument concerning an important issue, which is revealed through a guiding metaphor controlled by an issue of lesser importance. Analyze the two issues that are discussed and the ways in which they are related. Compare this argument to the one in "To the Virgins, to Make Much of Time."

2. Do you agree or disagree with Herrick's attitudes towards the nature of women's clothes and/or art? Can these things ever be too orderly or precise?

John Milton

*John Milton (1608–1674), introduced earlier in this antholo-
gy (page 460), was born in London of an upper-middle-class
father who was employed as a notary. As a boy, Milton
attended St. Paul's School in London. He supplemented his
formal training with the voracious reading that would later
make him one of the most learned men in Europe. He took a
BA at Cambridge in 1629 and an MA in 1632. He began his
literary career in earnest with the writing of Comus in 1634.
By 1641 he was involved in the religious and political
disputes that would result in the execution of King Charles I
and the imposition of the Cromwell government, both of
which he enthusiastically supported. His greatest work is
Paradise Lost (1667), in which he sets out "to justify the
ways of God to man." This rigorous Puritan composed the
work while blind and poor. His dreams of a "new Jerusalem"
had collapsed with the ousting of Cromwell, yet he remained
at his post, at least in his own eyes a dutiful soldier of Christ
and a "priest of the imagination." The two sonnets by Milton
that appear here reveal the poet in his typical stoical
attitude toward life and dutiful relationship toward God.*

HOW SOON HATH TIME

How soon hath Time, the subtle thief of youth,
  Stolen on his wing my three-and-twentieth year!
  My hasting days fly on with full career,
  But my late spring no bud or blossom shew'th.
Perhaps my semblance might deceive the truth   5
  That I to manhood am arrived so near;
  And inward ripeness doth much less appear,
  That some more timely-happy spirits endu'th.
Yet, be it less or more, or soon or slow,
  It shall be still in strictest measure even   10
  To that same lot, however mean or high,
Toward which Time leads me, and the will of Heaven.
  All is, if I have grace to use it so,
  As ever in my great Task-Master's eye.

QUESTIONS

1. What is Milton's attitude toward time in this poem? Is it a consistent
attitude? How does it change?

2. In what ways is Milton's attitude toward free will depicted in the poem?
How does this fit in with his religious beliefs? Pay special attention to lines
9–14.

3. What is Milton's "late spring" (line 4)? How does this relate to his "semblance" (line 5)? to his "inward ripeness" (line 7)?

TOPIC FOR WRITING

How would you describe the level of diction in this poem and in its companion piece? Does it seem inflated to you? Perhaps even self-indulgent? Or suitably formal, solemn, and ritualistic? Explain how tone and mood fit the subject and theme of the poem.

ON THE LATE MASSACRE IN PIEDMONT

Avenge, O Lord, thy slaughtered saints, whose bones
  Lie scattered on the Alpine mountains cold,
  Even them who kept thy truth so pure of old
  When all our fathers worshiped stocks and stones,
Forget not: in thy book record their groans   5
  Who were thy sheep and in their ancient fold
  Slain by the bloody Piemontese that rolled
  Mother with infant down the rocks. Their moans
  The vales redoubled to the hills, and they
  To Heaven. Their martyred blood and ashes sow   10
  O'er all th' Italian fields where still doth sway
The triple tyrant: that from these may grow
  A hundredfold, who having learnt thy way
  Early may fly the Babylonian woe.

QUESTIONS

1. This sonnet has its background in the 1655 Easter Sunday massacre of 1,700 Protestants in Piedmont, northern Italy, by the soldiers of the Catholic duke of Savoy. What position does Milton, an English Puritan, take on this event?

2. Explain these religious allusions in the poem: "slaughtered saints" (line 1), "stocks and stones" (line 4), "the Triple Tyrant" (line 12), and "the Babylonian woe" (line 14).

3. This poem is not only an example of apostrophe (see page 377), it is also a prayer. In what tone does Milton cast his prayer? Point to key words that help you to establish this tone.

4. Why is this a highly original sonnet?

TOPICS FOR WRITING

1. Examine the way in which Milton evokes sympathy for the Piedmontese in this sonnet.

2. Compare and contrast Milton's handling of sonnet form in this poem and in "How soon hath Time."

Sir John Suckling

SONG:
WHY SO PALE AND WAN,
FOND LOVER?

Sir John Suckling (1609–1642), born in Norfolk and educated at Cambridge, was the child of a wealthy royal official. When his father died, the young Suckling inherited his money, which he used to lead a life of legendary revelry. His Cambridge University education equipped him for little else besides the traditional pastimes of a courtier—gaming (he invented cribbage), traveling, political maneuvering, drama, and poetry. By middle age he had overplayed his hand in the first three, and he died in pathetic circumstances in France. His poems, as the one that follows, reflect the energy and attitudes of a great rake.

Why so pale and wan, fond lover?
  Prithee, why so pale?
Will, when looking well can't move her,
  Looking ill prevail?
  Prithee, why so pale?   5

Why so dull and mute, young sinner?
  Prithee, why so mute?
Will, when speaking well can't win her,
  Saying nothing do't?
  Prithee, why so mute?   10

Quit, quit, for shame; this will not move,
  This cannot take her.
If of herself she will not love,
  Nothing can make her:
  The devil take her!   15

QUESTIONS

1. How does Suckling achieve compression and unity in each stanza? What is the nature of the poem's progression? That is, what is the sequence of motifs? Does this sequence make sense to you?

2. Katherine Philips (page 506) counseled self-possession in the face of love's agonies. What is Suckling's response to this misery? How is it different from Philip's?

3. Suckling's poem comes from a play and was put to music by the famous seventeenth-century composer William Lawes. How does the verse form fit the sentiments expressed within it? How does it fit the tone, for example? Is it better as a song than as a poem? Explain.

TOPIC FOR WRITING

Suckling's poems are directed at a courtly audience. Examine the tastes and expectations of such an audience, basing your appraisal on the poem provided.

Anne Bradstreet

Anne Bradstreet (1612?–1672), previously introduced (page 342), a mother of eight, was the first American woman to write distinguished verse. She reveals a complex emotional life in her poetry, a life much bound to the assumptions and attitudes of colonial Puritanism. Nevertheless, she is still able to touch us—as in the following poems—as an individual whose fears we can share and whose warmth we can appreciate.

IN MEMORY OF MY DEAR GRAND-CHILD ELIZABETH BRADSTREET, WHO DECEASED AUGUST, 1665, BEING A YEAR AND A HALF OLD

Farewel dear babe, my hearts too much content.
Farewel sweet babe, the pleasure of mine eye,
Farewel fair flower that for a space was lent,
Then ta'en away unto Eternity.

Blest babe why should I once bewail thy fate,   5
Or sigh thy dayes so soon were terminate;
Sith thou art settled in an Everlasting state.

By nature Trees do rot when they are grown.
And Plumbs and Apples throughly ripe do fall,
And Corn and grass are in their season mown,   10
And time brings down what is both strong and tall.
But plants new set to be eradicate,
And buds new blown, to have so short a date,
Is by His hand alone that guides nature and fate.

QUESTIONS

1. What rhyme pattern (a variation of *rime royale*) does Bradstreet employ in the poem? How does she use rhyme to link the two stanzas?

2. Cite examples of alliteration. What is the effect?

3. How does Bradstreet employ both contrast and parallelism in the two stanzas? For what purpose?

4. This poem is reprinted in its original form. What changes in language between Bradstreet's time and today do you detect?

5. Why does Bradstreet employ nature imagery?

TOPICS FOR WRITING

1. Explain how the theme of fate relates to both the child and nature in this poem.

2. Evaluate the nature of *influence* as it is reflected in this poem. Bradstreet had read Shakespeare. Are there echoes of Shakespeare in her lyric? (See Shakespeare's poems in this anthology, especially "Shall I compare thee to a summer's day?" page 487.) Again, compare Jonson's epitaphs (pages 495–496) to the one here.

BEFORE THE BIRTH OF ONE OF HER CHILDREN

All things within this fading world hath end,
Adversity doth still our joyes attend;
No tyes so strong, no friends so dear and sweet,
But with deaths parting blow is sure to meet.
The sentence past is most irrevocable,   5
A common thing, yet oh inevitable;
How soon, my Dear, death may my steps attend,
How soon't may be thy Lot to lose thy friend,
We both are ignorant, yet love bids me
These farewell lines to recommend to thee,   10
That when that knot's unty'd that made us one,
I may seem thine, who in effect am none.
And if I see not half my dayes that's due,
What nature would, God grant to yours and you;
The many faults that well you know I have,   15
Let be interr'd in my oblivious grave;
If any worth or virtue were in me,
Let that live freshly in thy memory
And when thou feel'st no grief, as I no harms,
Yet love thy dead, who long lay in thine arms: 20
And when thy loss shall be repaid with gains
Look to my little babes my dear remains.
And if thou love thy self, or loved'st me
These O protect from step Dames injury.
And if chance to thine eyes shall bring this verse,   25
With some sad sighs honour my absent Herse;
And kiss this paper for thy loves dear sake,
Who with salt tears this last Farewel did take.

QUESTIONS

1. Does it seem odd to you that an occasional poem of this sort (on birth) should begin by remarking "this fading world hath end"? Why or why not?

2. What is the "sentence" of line 5?

3. What is the "knot" of line 11? What is she asking for?

4. What debt does she refer to in line 13?

5. How does she characterize time in lines 17–22?

TOPIC FOR WRITING

Bradstreet's husband, Simon (a governor, like her father, of Massachusetts), was the subject of many of her poems. Write a short essay that examines their relationship, especially in regard to the religious context in which they lived. Use this poem and "To My Dear and Loving Husband" (page 342) as the basis for your discussion.

Katherine Philips

AGAINST LOVE

Katherine Philips (1631–1664) was the daughter of a wealthy London businessman. She was educated in Hackney, and at the age of 16 she married a prestigious man of 54. Though her husband was a strict Puritan and a supporter of Cromwell, she herself embraced more genial and open forms of religion and government. A noted translator and accomplished poet, she was widely admired throughout England as the "English Sappho" and was the founder of a literary salon that included Cowley and Vaughan. Her collected verses appeared in a pirated version in 1664. In "Against Love," Philips deals with one of the oldest themes in Western literature—the miseries of love.

Hence, Cupid! with your cheating toys,
Your real Griefs, and painted Joys,
Your Pleasure which itself destroys.
Lovers like men in fevers burn and rave,
And only what will injure them do crave.   5
Men's weakness makes Love so severe,
They give him power by their fear,
And make the shackles which they wear.
  Who to another does his heart submit;
  Makes his own Idol, and then worships it.   10
Him whose heart is all his own,
Peace and liberty does crown;
He apprehends no killing frown.
  He feels no raptures which are joys diseas'd,
  And is not much transported, but still pleas'd.   15

QUESTIONS

1. How would you describe the progression of tone? To whom are the words addressed?

2. What solution does Philips oppose to the idolizing of another person? Is this solution perilous in itself? Explain.

3. Does the unusual rhyme scheme of this poem delight you? irritate you? Does it suggest anything about the mood of the speaker? Explain.

4. What is the force of "transported" in line 15? How does it resonate against "raptures" in the preceding line? Is there humor here or simply irony?

TOPICS FOR WRITING

1. Analyze the tone of this poem and the techniques that Philips uses to achieve it.

2. Compare and contrast this poem and Herrick's poems (pages 497–499).

John Dryden

WHY SHOULD A FOOLISH MARRIAGE VOW

John Dryden (1631–1700) was born to wealthy parents in Northamptonshire and was educated at the famed Westminster School and later at Trinity College, Cambridge. In and out of public affairs most of his life, Dryden is thought to have begun his career with a minor position in the Puritan regime of Oliver Cromwell. Later in life, Dryden's sympathies changed; he became a staunch monarchist and a Roman Catholic. In 1668, he became poet laureate. His poetry, like his plays, is not at all introspective or personal. His gaze in poems like Absalom and Achitophel *(1681) and* Miscellany Poems *(1684) was turned outward, inspecting and evaluating the changing manners and morals of his day. "Why Should a Foolish Marriage Vow," which is about failed love, demonstrates the flexibility of tone, thematic variation, and technical range that helped to make Dryden the major English literary figure of the latter part of the seventeenth century.*

Why should a foolish marriage vow
  Which long ago was made,
Oblige us to each other now
  When passion is decay'd?
We lov'd, and we lov'd, as long as we cou'd,   5
  Till our love was lov'd out in us both.
But our marriage is dead, when the pleasure is fled:
  'Twas pleasure first made it an oath.

John Dryden

If I have pleasures for a friend,
   And farther love in store,   10
What wrong has he whose joys did end
   And who cou'd give no more?
'Tis a madness that he
Shou'd be jealous of me,
Or that I shou'd bar him of another: 15
For all we can gain is to give our selves pain,
When neither can hinder the other.

QUESTIONS

1. The speaker, in this case a woman, calls her marriage vow foolish. But what specifically is her evidence for her claim?

2. In terms of English history, is it surprising that a poem of the later seventeenth century should display this attitude toward marriage? Why or why not?

3. Dryden's poem is actually a song from his play *Marriage à la Mode* (1672). The last two lines of each stanza strongly suggest a common verse form of our own day. What is it, and why is its use by Dryden appropriate, even masterful?

4. What is the force of "hinder" in line 16?

5. Why does the rhythm change in the fifth line of each stanza?

6. Consider the diction of this poem/song. How might it be improved? How abused? On what do you base your conclusions?

TOPIC FOR WRITING

Evaluate the effectiveness of the speaker's argument in this poem. How logical is it? Are nonlogical factors involved? Do diction and tone reinforce the argument? Explain.

Aphra Behn

SONG:
A THOUSAND MARTYRS
I HAVE MADE

*Aphra Behn (1640–1689), introduced on page 353, was long
thought to have been born in eastern England, in Kent, but
modern scholarship has cast doubt on even the birthplace
of this puzzling woman. She may have spent her youth in
Surinam, in the West Indies, and she seems to have been
involved in espionage for the British government in Holland.
Debtors' prison was her reward when she returned to Brit-
ain, until her friends could rescue her. Upon her release, she
became the first woman to support herself solely by her
writing. Her literary reputation has fluctuated violently over
the centuries, with Victorians considering her a failure and
modern critics admiring her. In this poem, Behn offers a
unique view of love between the sexes.*

A thousand martyrs I have made,
  All sacrific'd to my desire;
A thousand beauties have betray'd,
  That languish in resistless fire.
The untam'd heart to hand I brought,   5
And fixed the wild and wandering thought.

I never vow'd nor sigh'd in vain
  But both, tho' false, were well receiv'd.
The fair are pleas'd to give us pain,
  And what they wish is soon believ'd.   10
And tho' I talk'd of wounds and smart,
Love's pleasures only touched my heart.

Alone the glory and the spoil
  I always laughing bore away;
The triumphs, without pain or toil,   15
  Without the hell, the heav'n of joy.
And while I thus at random rove
Despis'd the fools that whine for love.

QUESTIONS

1. How would you describe the tone of Behn's poem? How would you
characterize the narrator? Is there a split between the poet and the narrator?
Explain.

2. Who are "the fair" of line 9? What does this line suggest about the speaker's view of love between the sexes?

3. The word "alone" in stanza 3 has been described as the most significant word in the poem. Does this seem just to you? Explain.

TOPIC FOR WRITING

Mrs. Behn was termed in her lifetime "not a lady." How could a poem like "A Thousand Martyrs I Have Made" provide evidence for such a charge? How might we judge the poem today? Why, for example, does the contemporary critic Louise Bernikow call Behn a Bohemian and a feminist?

Anne Finch

TRAIL ALL YOUR PIKES

Anne Finch (1661–1722) was born the daughter of a South-ampton nobleman. By marriage she became the countess of Winchelsea. Her position, interests, and talent kept her in the thick of England's intellectual life, and she earned the respect and admiration of Pope and Swift, with whom she was known to banter in verse epistles. Her range is exten-sive, touching on the personal and public issues of her day, and some consider her a precursor of Romanticism. In this short poem, Finch offers a critical view of war and "Honour."

Trail all your pikes, dispirit every drum,
March in a slow procession from afar,
Ye silent, ye dejected, men of war.
Be still the hautboys, and the flute be dumb!
Display no more, in vain, the lofty banner;   5
For see where on the bier before ye lies
The pale, the fall'n, the untimely sacrifice
To your mistaken shrine, to your false idol Honour.

QUESTIONS

1. Finch's poem is skeptical of the claims of "Honour." Does this attitude seem shortsighted or deep spirited to you? Her poem seems to imply that life itself is more precious than the abstract codes men devise. Could her rejection of honor be extended to courage, loyalty, or truth? Explain.

2. What does Finch mean by the "untimely sacrifice"? Does she suggest that there could ever be a "timely" one? What do you yourself think?

TOPIC FOR WRITING

Read Richard Lovelace's "To Lucasta, Going to the Wars" (page 364) and then write a short essay contrasting his position on honor with Anne Finch's. Which do you find more appealing? more convincing?

Alexander Pope

ON A CERTAIN LADY AT COURT

Alexander Pope (1688–1744) was born into a well-to-do merchant family of London. Deformed and sickly from birth, he suffered from another handicap, which was even worse than these in the eyes of his countrymen—he was a Catholic. Since Catholics were forbidden access to most schools, he was self-educated. His literary career began early, at 12, and he was soon attracting the attention of established writers. His greatest successes included An Essay on Criticism (1711), The Rape of the Lock (1714), An Essay on Man (1733, 1734), and the Dunciad (1728, 1729, 1742). Pope was a first-rate satirist and one of the most humorous poets since Chaucer. His keen wit was never far from the surface of his poems, and even in a selection as mild as ours, it is to be found. In his cleverness, polish, and control, Pope mirrors the values of his day better than anyone else.

I know the thing that's most uncommon;
  (Envy be silent, and attend!)
I know a reasonable Woman,
  Handsome and witty, yet a Friend.

Not warp'd by Passion, aw'd by Rumour,   5
  Not grave thro' Pride, or gay thro' Folly,
An equal mixture of good Humour,
  And sensible soft Melancholy.

"Has she no faults then (Envy says) Sir?"
   Yes, she has one, I must aver;   10
When all the World conspires to praise her,
   The Woman's deaf, and does not hear.

QUESTIONS

1. An unusual feature of the poem is the final quatrain, which deviates in rhyme scheme from the preceding two. Though the deviation is subtle, it is also clear. What is this altered rhyme scheme, and, most important, what is its effect?

2. What is the force of the word "humour" in line 5?

3. Pope was considered one of the greatest wits of eighteenth-century England, and the final quatrain demonstrates how deft his touch could be; but does it seem merely glib two centuries later? Explain.

TOPICS FOR WRITING

1. This poem, published in *Works* (1751), was written for Catharine Howard, one of Queen Caroline's waiting women, afterward countess of Suffolk and mistress to George II. What is Pope telling this lady? What is his attitude toward her? Are there advice, warnings, or criticism in the poem? Explain.

2. In the eighteenth century, "wit" was prized highly. Write an extended definition of this term, applying it to Pope's poem.

Lady Mary Wortley Montagu

IN ANSWER TO A LADY
WHO ADVISED RETIREMENT

Lady Mary Wortley Montagu (1689–1762), born Mary Pierrepont, educated herself with the assistance of her uncle, a bishop of the Anglican church. In her youth she made the acquaintance of London's literary stars—Addison, Steele, Congreve, and Pope (who later attacked her virulently in one of his satires). She married Edward Wortley Montagu, a diplomat, traveled to Turkey, and brought back to England the method of inoculation to combat the dreaded smallpox. Her poetry, as was the woman herself, is straightforward and self-possessed.

In Answer to a Lady Who Advised Retirement

You little know the heart that you advise;
I view this various scene with equal eyes:
In crowded courts I find myself alone,
And pay my worship to a nobler throne.
Long since the value of this world I know,   5
Pity the madness, and despise the show:
Well as I can my tedious part I bear,
And wait for my dismission without fear.
Seldom I mark mankind's detested ways,
Not hearing censure, nor affecting praise;   10
And, unconcern'd, my future fate I trust
To that sole Being, merciful and just.

QUESTIONS

1. Do you find Lady Montagu's use of the heroic couplet well suited to her topic? Is the couplet a natural vehicle for her tone and frame of mind? How?

2. Examine the diction of this poem. Is it high or low, Latinate or Anglo-Saxon? What relationship is there between the diction and the content?

3. Exactly what does she mean by "retirement," "this various scene," and "equal eyes"?

4. Are the last two lines overly sentimental, or are they appropriate? Explain.

TOPICS FOR WRITING

1. After Pope attacked her libelously in his *Imitation of the First Satire of the Second Book of Horace*, Montagu left her husband and England, living in Europe for the next twenty-two years. What "psychological" evidence do you find in this poem that might shed light on Lady Montagu's own "retirement"?

2. Compare and contrast Montagu's vision of public life with Pope's (page 511).

Phillis Wheatley

TO THE RIGHT HONORABLE WILLIAM, EARL OF DARTMOUTH

Phillis Wheatley (1753–1784), whose poem "On Being Brought from Africa to America" appears on page 412, did not remember what part of Africa she had been taken from, nor could she recall much about her family. She arrived at the age of 7 in Boston, Massachusetts, in 1761, where John Wheatley, a minor tradesman, bought her at auction. The young girl was educated in English and Latin by her new family, and she later traveled to England with them. In 1773, her Poems on Various Subjects, Religious and Moral was published in England. Her fame had increased so much by 1776 that she was granted an audience by George Washington. She married John Peters in 1778; her last years were filled with poverty and illness. Wheatley's poetry, as in the following selection, is in the neoclassic tradition and typically personal in its glorification of freedom.

Hail, happy day, when, smiling like the morn,
Fair Freedom rose New England to adorn:
The northern clime beneath her genial ray,
Dartmouth, congratulates thy blissful sway:
Elate with hope her race no longer mourns,   5
Each soul expands, each grateful bosom burns,
While in thine hand with pleasure we behold
The silken reins, and Freedom's charms unfold.
Long lost to realms beneath the northern skies
She shines supreme, while hated faction dies: 10
Soon as appear'd the Goddess long desir'd,
Sick as the view, she languish'd and expir'd;
Thus from the splendors of the morning light
The owl in sadness seeks the caves of night.

   No more America in mournful strain   15
Of wrongs, and grievance unredress'd complain,
No longer shalt thou dread the iron chain,
Which wanton Tyranny with lawless hand
Had made, and which it meant t' enslave the land.

   Should you, my lord, while you peruse my song,   20
Wonder from whence my love of Freedom sprung,
Whence flow these wishes for the common good,
By feeling hearts alone best understood,
I, young in life, by seeming cruel fate
Was snatch'd from Afric's fancy'd happy seat: 25
What pangs excruciating must molest,
What sorrows labour in my parent's breast!
Steel'd was the soul and by no misery mov'd

That from a father seiz'd his babe belov'd.
Such, such my case. And can I then but pray   30
Others may never feel tyrannic sway?
  For favours past, great Sir, our thanks are due,
And thee we ask thy favours to renew,
Since in thy pow'r, as in thy will before,
To sooth the griefs, which thou did'st once deplore.   35
May heav'nly grace the sacred sanction give
To all thy works, and thou for ever live
Not only on the wings of fleeting Fame,
Though praise immortal crowns the patriot's name,
But to conduct to heav'n's refulgent fane,   40
May fiery courses sweep th' ethereal plain,
And bear thee upwards to that blest abode,
Where, like prophet, thou shalt find thy God.

QUESTIONS

1. How does Wheatley invoke and personify Freedom in this poem? What sort of diction does she rely on? What are its virtues and its liabilities?

2. In what stanza is the poet most intensely personal? What is the effect?

3. What is the function of mythology and religion in the poem?

TOPICS FOR WRITING

1. Evaluate Wheatley's skill in this poem in applying such aspects of neoclassic form as iambic pentameter couplets, invocation to the muse, panoramic view, elevation of language, and hyperbole.

2. Analyze the ways in which this poem reflects an awareness of current events affecting the society in which Wheatley lives. (Be certain to find out who the earl of Dartmouth was.)

William Blake

William Blake (1757–1827), introduced previously (page 472), is one of the most enigmatic of English poets. He created, out of personal visions, an elaborate mythology that expresses his dissatisfaction with traditional Christianity. T. S. Eliot called him a heretic, but acknowledged, as even his severest critics do, his power, which often achieves the sublime, as in "The Tyger." His penetrating simplicity shows through "The Lamb" and his unique personality in "The Garden of Love."

THE LAMB

Little Lamb, who made thee?
  Dost thou know who made thee?
Gave thee life & bid thee feed,
By the stream & o'er the mead;
Gave thee clothing of delight,   5
Softest clothing wooly bright;
Gave thee such a tender voice,
Making all the vales rejoice!
  Little Lamb who made thee?
  Dost thou know who made thee?   10
  Little Lamb I'll tell thee,
  Little Lamb I'll tell thee!
He is calléd by thy name,
For he calls himself a Lamb:
He is meek & he is mild,   15
He became a little child:
I a child & thou a lamb,
We are calléd by his name.
  Little Lamb God bless thee.   20
  Little Lamb God bless thee.

QUESTIONS

    1. The temptation is to dismiss this poem as doggerel. What insights are gained by resisting the temptation?

    2. Does the tone of the poem suit its theme well? Why or why not?

    3. How should we take the interpenetration of God, humankind, and the Lamb? What is Blake suggesting?

    4. Does the question-and-answer style of this poem please or displease you? Explain.

TOPIC FOR WRITING

What techniques are used by Blake to establish the Lamb as a symbol of creation?

THE TYGER

Tyger! Tyger! burning bright
In the forests of the night,
What immortal hand or eye
Could frame thy fearful symmetry?

In what distant deeps or skies   5
Burnt the fire of thine eyes?
On what wings dare he aspire?
What the hand, dare seize the fire?

And what shoulder, & what art,
Could twist the sinews of thy heart?   10
And when thy heart began to beat,
What dread hand? & what dread feet?

What the hammer? what the chain?
In what furnace was thy brain?
What the anvil? what dread grasp   15
Dare its deadly terrors clasp?

When the stars threw down their spears,
And water'd heaven with their tears,
Did he smile his work to see?
Did he who made the Lamb make thee?   20

Tyger! Tyger! burning bright
In the forests of the night,
What immortal hand or eye
Dare frame thy fearful symmetry?

QUESTIONS

1. What is the Tyger? Is it the sole subject of the poem?

2. What Christian metaphors do you find in this poem?

3. What is the effect of the series of rhetorical questions?

4. Who or what are the "stars" of line 17?

5. Milton, a fellow dissenter, had a vast influence on Blake. Does the Tyger remind you of any of Milton's characters or creations? How and in what ways?

TOPICS FOR WRITING

1. Bertrand Russell recounts that the first time he read this poem he became too dizzy to stand and nearly fainted. Was Russell's reaction ludicrous, or does the poem raise issues that are staggering? Explain.

2. "The Lamb" is from Blake's *Songs of Innocence* and "The Tyger" from *Songs of Experience*. Explain why these poems should be considered as a pair, one the reverse of the other.

THE GARDEN OF LOVE

I went to the Garden of Love
    And saw what I never had seen;
A chapel was built in the midst,
    Where I used to play on the green.

And the gates of this chapel were shut,   5
    And "Thou shalt not" writ over the door;
So I turned to the Garden of Love
    That so many sweet flowers bore;

And I saw it was filled with graves,
    And tombstones where flowers should be;   10
And priests in black gowns were walking their rounds,
    And binding with briars my joys and desires.

QUESTIONS

1. In this poem, Blake contrasts the imagery of nature and humanity's handiwork. What theme do these contrasts gradually reveal?

2. What other garden does "The Garden of Love" allude to?

3. What is "Thou shalt not" a reference to?

4. What associations linger around "binding with briars my joys and desires"?

TOPICS FOR WRITING

1. What is Blake's apparent attitude toward religion in this poem?

2. Blake's poetry is often misread and unappreciated when the reader fails to see its connection with Protestant hymns. Write an essay examining these connections and the affinities of Blake's work with music in general.

Robert Burns

GREEN GROW THE RASHES, O

Robert Burns (1759–1796), previously introduced (page 437), delighted in cultivating (like Robert Frost) the image of the "heaven-taught plowman." Like Frost, he was widely read and much more sophisticated than his verse reveals. Impulsive and irreverent, he fascinated and appalled many of his contemporaries, whose sobriety seemed to limp along well-trodden paths. Our selection, "Green Grow the Rashes, O," must have seemed to them disarmingly earthy, even pagan.

CHORUS
Green grow the rashes, O;
Green grow the rashes, O;
The sweetest hours that e'er I spend,
   Are spent among the lasses, O.

1
There's nought but care on ev'ry han',   5
   In every hour that passes, O:
What signifies the life o' man,
   An' 'twere nae for the lasses, O.

2
The war'ly race may riches chase,
   An' riches still may fly them, O;   10
An' tho' at last they catch them fast,
   Their hearts can ne'er enjoy them, O.

3
But gie me a cannie hour at e'en,
   My arms about my dearie, O,
An' war'ly cares an' war'ly men   15
   May a' gae tapsalteerie, O!

4
For you sae douce, ye sneer at this;
   Ye're nought but senseless asses, O;
The wisest man the warl' e'er saw,
   He dearly loved the lasses, O.   20

5
Auld Nature swears, the lovely dears
   Her noblest work she classes, O:
Her prentice han' she tried on man,
   An' then she made the lasses, O.

CHORUS

Green grow the rashes, O;   25
   Green grow the rashes, O;
The sweetest hours that e'er I spend,
   Are spent among the lasses, O.

QUESTIONS

1. Though the poem celebrates "sweet hours" spent "among the lasses," there is a dark side to Burns's vision as well. What forms the background to the joys of this poem?

2. What role does woman play in the poem? How pleased are you to see her depicted in this fashion? Explain.

3. Does the title have any relationship to the poem's theme?

TOPIC FOR WRITING

Burns delighted in love, nature, mirth, and song. Explain how these attitudes coalesce in this poem.

William Wordsworth

William Wordsworth (1770–1850), introduced on page 449, had a profound and lasting influence on English poetry. His prizing of simplicity of diction, his discovery of extraordinary significance in ordinary folk, and his reliance on nature as a moral touchstone are some of the novelties he made familiar, even overfamiliar, to English readers. Like Hopkins, he spied "the dearest freshness" in the hearts of the plainest things, as the following selections reveal.

COMPOSED UPON WESTMINSTER BRIDGE, SEPTEMBER 3, 1802

Earth has not anything to show more fair:
Dull would he be of soul who could pass by
A sight so touching in its majesty:
This City now doth, like a garment, wear
The beauty of the morning; silent, bare,   5

Composed upon Westminster Bridge, September 3, 1802

Ships, towers, domes, theatres, and temples lie
Open unto the fields, and to the sky;
All bright and glittering in the smokeless air.
Never did sun more beautifully steep
In his first splendour, valley, rock, or hill;   10
Ne'er saw I, never felt, a calm so deep!
The river glideth at his own sweet will:
Dear God! the very houses seem asleep;
And all that mighty heart is lying still!

QUESTIONS

1. Though he was a champion of plain diction and common speech, Words-worth often puts a "poetic" or privileged vocabulary to good use. Can you find examples of unusual words or phrases in this poem?

2. What does Wordsworth gain by his use of both "bright" and "glittering" in line 8? Might the poem have been improved by using only one such adjective? What might you substitute for Wordsworth's choices?

3. Line 4 introduces the simile of the city wearing beauty like a garment. By line 9, the sun is steeping the countryside beautifully. Do these images comple-ment each other, or is there a gap between them which is unbridgeable? If they conflict, what is the nature of the conflict? If they do not, what is the nature of their harmony?

4. Line 12 reads, "The river glideth at his own sweet will." John Ruskin would have called this an example of the pathetic fallacy. How might Wordsworth have defended this anthropomorphism?

TOPIC FOR WRITING

Analyze the ways in which Wordsworth develops the theme of this poem within the framework of the sonnet form.

William Wordsworth

IT IS A BEAUTEOUS EVENING

It is a beauteous evening, calm and free,
The holy time is quiet as a Nun
Breathless with adoration; the broad sun
Is sinking down in its tranquillity;
The gentleness of heaven broods o'er the Sea: 5
Listen! the mighty Being is awake,
And doth with his eternal motion make
A sound like thunder—everlastingly.
Dear Child! dear Girl! that walkest with me here,
If thou appear untouched by solemn thought,   10
Thy nature is not therefore less divine:
Thou liest in Abraham's bosom all the year;
And worship'st at the Temple's inner shrine,
God being with thee when we know it not.

QUESTIONS

1. What does Wordsworth mean when he describes the evening as "free"?

2. If the positions of "holy" and "quiet" in line 2 were reversed, would anything be lost or gained?

3. Is there any relationship between the "Nun" of line 2 and "Dear Child! dear Girl!" in line 9? Is there a sense of continuity between the two?

4. Who is the "we" of line 14?

5. Is there a reason why this poem is a sonnet and not some other literary form? Is the material well covered in fourteen lines that rhyme in a previously stipulated pattern?

TOPICS FOR WRITING

1. Write an essay discussing the theme of "wise passiveness" in this poem and, if you wish, in "Composed Upon Westminster Bridge."

2. Write an essay in which you agree or disagree with Wordsworth that poetry should rely upon simple diction and common syntax.

Samuel Taylor Coleridge

KUBLA KHAN

*Samuel Taylor Coleridge (1772–1834) was born in the coun-
tryside (Devonshire), but was educated in London. From
childhood on his extraordinary imaginative powers made
themselves known and were noted by others. He attended
Cambridge University, disliked its monotony, and enlisted
impulsively in the British cavalry. Though purchased out of
the army by his family and returned to Cambridge, he never
took his degree. This pattern of impulsiveness and incom-
pleteness was to recur many times in the course of his life.
He met William Wordsworth in 1795, and the two men
exercised a stabilizing and stimulating influence on one
another. Together they published Lyrical Ballads in 1798,
one of the most revolutionary documents in English literary
history. But soon the radical spirit of youth became more
circumspect, and Coleridge espoused—in philosophy, politics, and religion—conservative causes. Sensitive and volatile, he is one of the most beloved poets in English. In "Kubla
Khan" (1797), Coleridge uses exotic images to create a world
that is both wondrous and sinister. He claimed to have
composed it in a dream, as a "psychological curiosity."*

In Xanadu did Kubla Khan
A stately pleasure dome decree:
Where Alph, the sacred river, ran
Through caverns measureless to man
  Down to a sunless sea.   5
So twice five miles of fertile ground
With walls and towers were girdled round:
And there were gardens bright with sinuous rills,
Where blossomed many an incense-bearing tree;
And here were forests ancient as the hills,   10
Enfolding sunny spots of greenery.

But oh! that deep romantic chasm which slanted
Down the green hill athwart a cedarn cover!
A savage place! as holy and enchanted
As e'er beneath a waning moon was haunted   15
By woman wailing for her demon lover!
And from this chasm, with ceaseless turmoil seething,
As if this earth in fast thick pants were breathing,
A mighty fountain momently was forced:
Amid whose swift half-intermitted burst   20
Huge fragments vaulted like rebounding hail,
Or chaffy grain beneath the thresher's flail:
And 'mid these dancing rocks at once and ever
It flung up momently the sacred river.
Five miles meandering with a mazy motion   25
Through wood and dale the sacred river ran,
Then reached the caverns measureless to man,

And sank in tumult to a lifeless ocean:
And 'mid this tumult Kubla heard from far
Ancestral voices prophesying war!   30
   The shadow of the dome of pleasure
   Floated midway on the waves;
   Where was heard the mingled measure
   From the fountain and the caves.
It was a miracle of rare device,   35
A sunny pleasure dome with caves of ice!

   A damsel with a dulcimer
   In a vision once I saw:
   It was an Abyssinian maid,
   And on her dulcimer she played,   40
   Singing of Mount Abora.
Could I revive within me
Her symphony and song,
To such a deep delight 'twould win me,
That with music loud and long,   45
I would build that dome in air,
That sunny dome! those caves of ice!
And all who heard should see them there,
And all should cry, Beware! Beware!
His flashing eyes, his floating hair!   50
Weave a circle round him thrice,
And close your eyes with holy dread,
For he on honeydew hath fed,
And drunk the milk of Paradise.

QUESTIONS

1. Kipling called the first nine lines of this poem "the most magical in the English language." What accounts for their preternatural quality? For example, what is gained by the phrase "twice five miles"?

2. What can Coleridge have in mind when he describes the chasm of line 12 as "romantic"? Why is it a "savage" place?

3. How should we take the "sacred river" of line 23? Coleridge has named it for us (Alph), but what is its significance? Can it fairly be called a symbol?

4. The poem's final stanza switches from third-person narrative to first-person direct address. What reason can you give for this? Do the speaker's concerns hearken back to the matter of the first two stanzas?

TOPICS FOR WRITING

1. Some critics claim that "Kubla Khan" is about the pleasures of art and the sinister forces that threaten it. Examine the evidence in the poem that would support this interpretation.

2. Robert Graves maintains that Coleridge is the finest poet in English in rendering the state of "entrancement." What makes the imaginative force of "Kubla Khan" so intense? How does Coleridge conceive the role of imagination in the poem?

George Gordon, Lord Byron

George Gordon, Lord Byron (1788–1824), was described by a contemporary as "mad, bad, and dangerous to know." Born of aristocratic parents with titles but little wealth, Byron grew up in poverty in the Scottish city of Aberdeen. A series of coincidences left him as the sixth Lord Byron, and he completed his education at Trinity College, Cambridge. A victim of both nature (he was born with a clubfoot) and nineteenth-century medicine, he nevertheless became a fine athlete, excelling in boxing, fencing, horse racing, and swimming. Financial difficulties and personal catastrophes plagued him most of his life, which ended with him fighting and dying in faraway Greece for the thing he loved most— freedom. Byron in his lifetime enjoyed sensational popular success as the author of such romantic narratives as Childe Harold's Pilgrimage *(1812),* The Corsair *(1814), and the unfinished* Don Juan *(1818). His poems are as various as his moods, ranging from the playful to the evangelical. At his best, as in the following selections, he writes as movingly as any poet in the language.*

SHE WALKS IN BEAUTY

1

She walks in Beauty, like the night
  Of cloudless climes and starry skies;
And all that's best of dark and bright
  Meet in her aspect and her eyes: 5
Thus mellowed to that tender light
  Which Heaven to gaudy day denies.

2

One shade the more, one ray the less,
  Had half impaired the nameless grace
Which waves in every raven tress,
  Or softly lightens o'er her face;   10

George Gordon, Lord Byron

Where thoughts serenely sweet express
  How pure, how dear their dwelling-place.

3

And on that cheek, and o'er that brow,
  So soft, so calm, yet eloquent,
The smiles that win, the tints that glow,   15
  But tell of days in goodness spent,
A mind at peace with all below,
  A heart whose love is innocent!

QUESTIONS

1. Stanza 1 of Byron's poem introduces the light imagery around which the poem is built. But just what is the dominant image of light? Does the mixture of images trouble or delight you? Explain.

2. How carefully is the opening of stanza 2 thought out? Will it stand up under close scrutiny?

3. Byron uses the word "eloquent" to describe the woman. Does the word work well alongside its counterparts, "soft" and "calm"?

TOPIC FOR WRITING

Evaluate Byron's conceptions of beauty and of women in this poem. Are his ideas too romantic, sentimental, or idealized for your taste? Explain.

ON THIS DAY I COMPLETE
MY THIRTY-SIXTH YEAR

MISSOLONGHI, Jan. 22, 1824.

'Tis time this heart should be unmoved,
  Since others it hath ceased to move:
Yet, though I cannot be beloved,
    Still let me love!

My days are in the yellow leaf;   5
  The flowers and fruits of love are gone;
The worm, the canker, and the grief
    Are mine alone!

The fire that on my bosom preys
  Is lone as some volcanic isle;   10

No torch is kindled at its blaze—
    A funeral pile.

The hope, the fear, the jealous care,
  The exalted portion of the pain
And power of love, I cannot share,   15
    But wear the chain.

But 'tis not *thus*—and 'tis not *here*—
  Such thoughts should shake my soul, nor *now*,
Where glory decks the hero's bier,
    Or binds his brow.   20

The sword, the banner, and the field,
  Glory and Greece, around me see!
The Spartan, borne upon his shield,
    Was not more free.

Awake! (not Greece—she is awake!)   25
  Awake, my spirit! Think through *whom*
Thy life-blood tracks its parent lake,
    And then strike home!

Tread those reviving passions down,
  Unworthy manhood!—unto thee   30
Indifferent should the smile or frown
    Of beauty be.

If thou regrett'st thy youth, *why live?*
  The land of honourable death
Is here:—up to the field, and give   35
    Away thy breath!

Seek out—less often sought than found—
  A soldier's grave, for thee the best;
Then look around, and choose thy ground,
    And take thy rest.   40

QUESTIONS

1. This is one of the last poems that Byron wrote. What do you find that foretells his death?

2. Why does Byron declare in the first stanza, "Still let me love"? What type of love does he have in mind? Is it the same love that animates "She Walks in Beauty"? Explain.

3. What does the "fire" in stanza 3 symbolize?

4. How does Byron invoke his passion for Greece in this poem?

5. What is the theme of this poem?

6. Explain the tone—or the varieties of tone—in the poem.

TOPIC FOR WRITING

Analyze the connection between love and death that Byron explores in the poem.

Percy Bysshe Shelley

Percy Bysshe Shelley (1792–1822), introduced previously (page 424), is a poet most at home at the limits of thought, perception, and emotion. Extremes and exotica attracted him all of his life, and these preoccupations are reflected in his verse. The two selections in our text show him at his most ebullient and most despairing.

STANZAS WRITTEN IN DEJECTION, NEAR NAPLES

1

The sun is warm, the sky is clear,
  The waves are dancing fast and bright,
Blue isles and snowy mountains wear
  The purple noon's transparent might,
  The breath of the moist earth is light,   5
Around its unexpanded buds;
  Like many a voice of one delight,
The winds, the birds, the ocean floods,
The City's voice itself is soft like Solitude's.

2

I see the Deep's untrampled floor   10
  With green and purple seaweeds strown;
I see the waves upon the shore,

Like light dissolved in star-showers, thrown:
　　I sit upon the sands alone—
The lightning of the noontide ocean　　　　　　　　　　　　15
　　Is flashing round me, and a tone
　　Arises from its measured motion;
How sweet! did any heart now share in my emotion.

　　3
Alas! I have nor hope nor health,
　　Nor peace within nor calm around,　　　　　　　　　　　　20
Nor that content surpassing wealth
　　The sage in meditation found,
　　And walked with inward glory crowned—
Nor fame, nor power, nor love, nor leisure.
　　Others I see whom these surround—　　　　　　　　　　　　25
Smiling they live, and call life pleasure—
To me that cup has been dealt in another measure.

　　4
Yet now despair itself is mild,
　　Even as the winds and waters are;
I could lie down like a tired child,　　　　　　　　　　　　30
　　And weep away the life of care
　　Which I have borne and yet must bear,
Till death like sleep might steal on me,
　　And I might feel in the warm air
My cheek grow cold, and hear the sea　　　　　　　　　　　　35
Breathe o'er my dying brain its last monotony.

　　5
Some might lament that I were cold,
　　As I, when this sweet day is gone,
Which my lost heart, too soon grown old,
　　Insults with this untimely moan;　　　　　　　　　　　　40
　　They might lament—for I am one
Whom men love not—and yet regret,
　　Unlike this day, which, when the sun
　　Shall on its stainless glory set,
Will linger, though enjoyed, like joy in memory yet.　　　　45

QUESTIONS

1. What is the mood evoked in the first stanza? How is it different from the mood of the second stanza? Is there any transition between the two? Is transition necessary in a poem like this?

2. Is Shelley concerned with giving us an insight into nature or into himself in this poem? Does nature function as a foil or an analogue to the poet?

3. A good example of how complicated Shelley's imagery can be occurs in the final lines of stanza 4. How does the stanza's end relate to its beginning? Is the imagery merely confused, or does it hold up under close examination?

4. The description of one sensory perception in terms of another (*synesthesia*) is a favorite device of Shelley's. One example is the moon that "rains out her beams" in line 29. What is the effect?

TOPIC FOR WRITING

Analyze the relationships among the five parts of this poem. How does this pattern of organization serve to advance the poet's argument?

TO A SKYLARK

1
Hail to thee, blithe Spirit!
  Bird thou never wert,
That from Heaven, or near it,
  Pourest thy full heart
In profuse strains of unpremeditated art.   5

2
Higher still and higher
  From the earth thou springest
Like a cloud of fire;
  The blue deep thou wingest,
And singing still dost soar, and soaring ever singest.   10

3
In the golden lightning
  Of the sunken Sun,
O'er which clouds are bright'ning,
  Thou dost float and run;
Like an unbodied joy whose race is just begun.   15

4
The pale purple even
  Melts around thy flight;
Like a star of Heaven,
  In the broad day-light
Thou art unseen, but yet I hear thy shrill delight,   20

5

Keen as are the arrows
 Of that silver sphere,
Whose intense lamp narrows
 In the white dawn clear,
Until we hardly see, we feel that it is there.   25

6

All the earth and air
 With thy voice is loud,
As, when Night is bare,
 From one lonely cloud
The moon rains out her beams, and Heaven is overflowed.   30

7

What thou art we know not;
 What is most like thee?
From rainbow clouds there flow not
 Drops so bright to see,
As from thy presence showers a rain of melody.   35

8

Like a poet hidden
 In the light of thought,
Singing hymns unbidden,
 Till the world is wrought
To sympathy with hopes and fears it heeded not—   40

9

Like a high-born maiden
 In a palace-tower,
Soothing her love-laden
 Soul in secret hour
With music sweet as love, which overflows her bower—   45

10

Like a glow-worm golden
 In a dell of dew,
Scattering unbeholden
 Its aërial hue
Among the flowers and grass, which screen it from the view—   50

11

Like a rose embowered
 In its own green leaves,
By warm winds deflowered,
 Till the scent it gives
Makes faint with too much sweet those heavy-wingéd thieves.   55

12

Sound of vernal showers
   On the twinkling grass,
Rain-awakened flowers,
   All that ever was
Joyous, and clear, and fresh, thy music doth surpass.   60

13

Teach us, Sprite or Bird,
   What sweet thoughts are thine:
I have never heard
   Praise of love or wine
That panted forth a flood of rapture so divine.   65

14

Chorus Hymeneal,
   Or triumphant chaunt,
Matched with thine, would be all
   But an empty vaunt,
A thing wherein we feel there is some hidden want.   70

15

What objects are the fountains
   Of thy happy strain?
What fields, or waves, or mountains?
   What shapes of sky or plain?
What love of thine own kind? what ignorance of pain?   75

16

With thy clear keen joyance
   Languor cannot be—
Shadow of annoyance
   Never came near thee:
Thou lovest—but ne'er knew love's sad satiety.   80

17

Waking or asleep,
   Thou of death must deem
Things more true and deep
   Than we mortals dream,
Or how could thy notes flow in such a crystal stream?   85

18

We look before and after,
   And pine for what is not:
Our sincerest laughter
   With some pain is fraught;
Our sweetest songs are those that tell of saddest thought.   90

19

Yet if we could scorn
    Hate, and pride, and fear;
If we were things born
    Not to shed a tear,
I know not how thy joy we ever should come near.   95

20

Better than all measures
    Of delightful sound—
Better than all treasures
    That in books are found—
Thy skill to poet were, thou scorner of the ground!   100

21

Teach me half the gladness
    That thy brain must know,
Such harmonious madness
    From my lips would flow
The world should listen then—as I am listening now.   105

QUESTIONS

1. In stanza 1, Shelley praises the "unpremediatated art" of the skylark. Is it fair to characterize the poet's work in the same way, as has often been done?

2. Shelley inserts a series of stanza-similes into the body of the text (lines 36–55). Do the similes seem farfetched to you? Would the poem have profited from the excision of any of them?

3. Shelley beseeches the skylark to teach him the secret of true joy and claims "harmonious madness from my lips would flow" and capture the world's admiration. Why does Shelley express himself in this fashion? Do you believe he is justified in his unusual pairing of terms?

TOPIC FOR WRITING

Analyze the tone and mood of this poem and the way they complement the theme.

John Keats

John Keats (1795–1821), previously introduced on page 405, had his life cut short when he was 25. He sensed that his time on earth would be short, and he sought to accomplish as much as he could before he died. He wrote his five great odes in less than a month. In our selections, Keats meditates on his vulnerability and, implicity, on the power of his art to transcend that vulnerability.

ODE ON A GRECIAN URN

1

Thou still unravished bride of quietness,
  Thou foster child of silence and slow time,
Sylvan historian, who canst thus express
  A flowery tale more sweetly than our rhyme:
What leaf-fringed legend haunts about thy shape   5
    Of deities or mortals, or of both,
      In Tempe or the dales of Arcady?
   What men or gods are these? What maidens loath?
What mad pursuit? What struggle to escape?
    What pipes and timbrels? What wild ecstasy?   10

2

Heard melodies are sweet, but those unheard
  Are sweeter; therefore, ye soft pipes, play on;
Not to the sensual ear, but, more endeared,
  Pipe to the spirit ditties of no tone:
Fair youth, beneath the trees, thou canst not leave   15
  Thy song, nor ever can those trees be bare;
    Bold Lover, never, never canst thou kiss,
Though winning near the goal—yet, do not grieve;
    She cannot fade, though thou hast not thy bliss,
  Forever wilt thou love, and she be fair!   20

3

Ah, happy, happy boughs! that cannot shed
  Your leaves, nor ever bid the Spring adieu;
And, happy melodist, unwearied,
  Forever piping songs forever new;
More happy love! more happy, happy love!   25
  Forever warm and still to be enjoyed,
    Forever panting, and forever young;
All breathing human passion far above,
  That leaves a heart high-sorrowful and cloyed,
    A burning forehead, and a parching tongue.   30

4

Who are these coming to the sacrifice?
   To what green altar, O mysterious priest,
Lead'st thou that heifer lowing at the skies,
   And all her silken flanks with garlands dressed?
What little town by river or sea shore,   35
   Or mountain-built with peaceful citadel,
      Is emptied of this folk, this pious morn?
And, little town, thy streets forevermore
   Will silent be; and not a soul to tell
      Why thou art desolate, can e'er return.   40

5

O Attic shape! Fair attitude! with brede
   Of marble men and maidens overwrought,
With forest branches and the trodden weed;
   Thou, silent form, dost tease us out of thought
As doth eternity: Cold Pastoral!   45
   When old age shall this generation waste,
      Thou shalt remain, in midst of other woe
Than ours, a friend to man, to whom thou say'st,
   'Beauty is truty, truth beauty,'—that is all
      Ye know on earth, and all ye need to know.   50

QUESTIONS

1. Keats offers us an enthusiastic vision of a realm where victory and defeat, bliss and desolation, are meaningless—the realm of art. Do you value the vision as highly as Keats did, or does it seem overrated to you? Explain.

2. In what sense, if any, is it true that all we need to know on earth is that truth and beauty are synonymous? Might it not be more true if we were in the next world rather than this one?

3. What is the effect of repeating the word "happy" over and over in stanza 3? Are there multiple effects?

4. What is the tone of the last two lines?

TOPICS FOR WRITING

1. Examine the "tale" told by the urn in this ode. What details does Keats stress? What is the relationship between the urn and poetry? What functions best as "historian"? Are the "tale" and its actions completed? Why or why not?

2. Contrast the depiction of nature in this poem with a depiction of nature in Shelley (page 530), Wordsworth (page 522), or Coleridge (page 523).

John Keats

BRIGHT STAR

Bright star, would I were steadfast as thou art—
   Not in lone splendor hung aloft the night
And watching, with eternal lids apart,
   Like nature's patient, sleepless Eremite,
The moving waters at their priestlike task   5
   Of pure ablution round earth's human shores,
Or gazing on the new soft-fallen mask
   Of snow upon the mountains and the moors—
No—yet still steadfast, still unchangeable,
   Pillowed upon my fair love's ripening breast,   10
To feel forever its soft fall and swell,
   Awake forever in a sweet unrest,
Still, still to hear her tender-taken breath,
And so live ever—or else swoon to death.

QUESTIONS

1. In this reflective sonnet, some of Keats's values become apparent. Can you identify what he values most?

2. Is there a thoughtless incongruity in Keats's wish to escape mutability "upon my fair love's ripening breast"? If there is, does it mar the poem seriously? Why or why not?

3. In line 5, we find the pathetic fallacy that Ruskin disliked so much. Does the image of earth's waters washing the shore like priests performing their duties mesh well with the poem's theme? Or is consistency a minor affair in a poem like this? Explain.

TOPIC FOR WRITING

What is Keats's frame of mind in this poem? What are his moral and ethical values?

Elizabeth Barrett Browning

WHEN OUR TWO SOULS STAND UP ERECT AND STRONG

Elizabeth Barrett Browning (1806–1861), whose work appears earlier in this anthology (pages 354 and 462), addressed her poems in Sonnets from the Portuguese *to her future husband, Robert Browning. Elizabeth was dark-complexioned, and Browning often called her "my little Portuguese"; the title for the sonnet sequence probably derives from this source. The following sonnet reflects accurately the strength of their love.*

When our two souls stand up erect and strong,
Face to face, silent, drawing nigh and nigher,
Until the lengthening wings break into fire
At either curved point,—What bitter wrong
Can the earth do to us, that we should not long   5
Be here contented? Think. In mounting higher,
The angels would press on us, and aspire
To drop some golden orb of perfect song
Into our deep, dear silence. Let us stay
Rather on earth, beloved,—where the unfit,   10
Contrarious moods of men recoil away
And isolate pure spirits, and permit
A place to stand and love in for a day,
With darkness and the death-hour rounding it.

QUESTIONS

1. What key paradox exists at the center of this poem?

2. Interpret the lines, "the lengthening wings break into fire/At either curved point. . . ."

3. What is the poet's attitude toward heaven? How is it expressed?

4. Why is this an especially effective and original love sonnet?

TOPIC FOR WRITING

There is much imagery of movement in this sonnet. What types or patterns of movement do you detect? What does movement signify? How does it relate to the theme?

Edgar Allan Poe

TO HELEN

Edgar Allan Poe (1809–1849), previously introduced (page 8), was born in Boston, Massachusetts, the child of traveling actors. His father vanished and his mother died while he was still a child. The young boy was brought up by a wealthy Virginian, John Allan. Allan saw to his education both at home and abroad. His relationship with his step-father deteriorated after Poe had run up large gambling debts while at the University of Virginia. He attempted to regain his step-father's favor by enrolling at West Point, but this effort failed; he was dismissed for disobedience. Alcoholism began to sicken him. Eventually, he died under confusing circumstances, rather like Christopher Marlowe. His poetry is not thought to be as enduring as his fiction (pages 9 and 185), though in France he has always been regarded as a poetic genius. Baudelaire honored him for his craft. "To Helen" reflects a persistent theme in Poe's poetry: the struggle to attain ideal or "supernal" beauty.

Helen, thy beauty is to me
　Like those Nicean barks of yore,
That gently, o'er a perfumed sea,
　The weary, way-worn wanderer bore
　To his own native shore.　　　　　　　　　　　　　5

On desperate seas long wont to roam,
　Thy hyacinth hair, thy classic face,
Thy Naiad airs have brought me home
　To the glory that was Greece
And the grandeur that was Rome.　　　　　　　　　10

Lo, in yon brilliant window-niche
　How statue-like I see thee stand,
　The agate lamp within thy hand,
Ah! Psyche, from the regions which
　Are Holy Land!　　　　　　　　　　　　　　　15

QUESTIONS

1. Poe's poetry has been subject to widely varying evaluations and is perhaps coming into its own again. (See, for example, Guy Davenport's analysis of this poem in *A Geography of the Imagination*.) How do you evaluate the quality of the poem?

2. Do you think the classical allusions ring true? Do they seem beautiful or absurd? Is it sillier to compare one's love to "those Nicean barks of yore" than to a "red, red rose" (see Robert Burns, page 362)? Explain.

3. How would you characterize the diction in the poem? Do words like "thy," "yore," "lo," and "yon" seem appropriate to you?

4. John Ruskin called phrases like "desperate sea" *pathetic fallacies,* since they attributed feelings to inanimate objects or entities. Ruskin considered these to be artistic flaws. Was he right, or can a reasonable defense be presented for such phrases in general? In particular, what about "desperate seas"?

TOPICS FOR WRITING

1. Poe indicated that the inspiration for this poem was "the first purely ideal love of my soul," Mrs. Jane Stanard, a Richmond neighbor who died in 1824. Examine "To Helen" as a reflection of Poe's quest for the ideal. What might he remember of Mrs. Stanard, and how does this transfer into the poem?

2. Analyze the classical imagery in the poem, its meaning, purpose, and effect. (T. O. Mabbot indicates that Poe probably had three classical stories in mind: the Trojan Helen; the return of Bacchus from his peaceful conquest of the east, when he made the sea perfumed with wine; and Psyche's awakening Cupid by dropping oil from her lamp. Comment on these classical connections.)

Alfred, Lord Tennyson

ULYSSES

Alfred, Lord Tennyson (1809–1892), introduced on page 378, was the most popular poet of the Victorian age. His Poems *(1842), which contained "Ulysses," "Morte d'Arthur," and "Locksley Hall," expressed Tennyson's doubts about the increasing materialism of the period and projected a longing on the poet's part for a sustaining faith. "Ulysses," one of Tennyson's most famous poems, was written in 1833, when Tennyson was feeling the full effect of the loss of his closest friend, Arthur Hallam. Comparing two of his well-known poems, "In Memoriam" and "Ulysses," Tennyson wrote, "There is more about myself in 'Ulysses,' which was written under the sense of loss and that all had gone by, but that still life must be fought out to its end." Ulysses, king of Ithaca, is one of the heroes of the Trojan War as it is*

Alfred, Lord Tennyson

recounted in Homer's Odyssey. *Book XI of the* Odyssey *and*
Book XXVI of Dante's Inferno *offer the immediate back-*
ground for "Ulysses." In Tennyson's poem, Ulysses is about
to embark on one last voyage.

It little profits that an idle king,
By this still hearth, among these barren crags,
Match'd with an aged wife, I mete and dole
Unequal laws unto a savage race,
That hoard, and sleep, and feed, and know not me.   5
I cannot rest from travel: I will drink
Life to the lees: all times I have enjoy'd
Greatly, have suffer'd greatly, both with those
That loved me, and alone; on shore, and when
Thro' scudding drifts the rainy Hyades   10
Vext the dim sea: I am become a name;
For always roaming with a hungry heart
Much have I seen and known; cities of men
And manners, climates, councils, governments,
Myself not least, but honour'd of them all;   15
And drunk delight of battle with my peers,
Far on the ringing plains of windy Troy.
I am a part of all that I have met;
Yet all experience is an arch wherethro'
Gleams that untravell'd world, whose margin fades   20
For ever and for ever when I move.
How dull it is to pause, to make an end,
To rust unburnish'd, not to shine in use!
As tho' to breathe were life. Life piled on life
Were all too little, and of one to me   25
Little remains: but every hour is saved
From that eternal silence, something more,
A bringer of new things; and vile it were
For some three suns to store and hoard myself,
And this gray spirit yearning in desire   30
To follow knowledge like a sinking star,
Beyond the utmost bound of human thought.
   This is my son, mine own Telemachus,
To whom I leave the sceptre and the isle—
Well-loved of me, discerning to fulfil   35
This labour, by slow prudence to make mild
A rugged people, and thro' soft degrees
Subdue them to the useful and the good.
Most blameless is he, centred in the sphere
Of common duties, decent not to fail   40
In offices of tenderness, and pay
Meet adoration to my household gods,
When I am gone. He works his work, I mine.

There lies the port; the vessel puffs her sail:
There gloom the dark broad seas. My mariners,   45
Souls that have toil'd and wrought, and thought with me—
That ever with a frolic welcome took
The thunder and the sunshine, and opposed
Free hearts, free foreheads—you and I are old;
Old age hath yet his honour and his toil;   50
Death closes all: but something ere the end,
Some work of noble note, may yet be done,
Not unbecoming men that strove with Gods.
The lights begin to twinkle from the rocks.
The long day wanes: the slow moon climbs: the deep   55
Moans round with many voices. Come, my friends,
'Tis not too late to seek a newer world.
Push off, and sitting well in order smite
The sounding furrows; for my purpose holds
To sail beyond the sunset, and the baths   60
Of all the western stars, until I die.
It may be that the gulfs will wash us down:
It may be we shall touch the Happy Isles,
And see the great Achilles, whom we knew.
Tho' much is taken, much abides; and tho'   65
We are not now that strength which in old days
Moved earth and heaven; that which we are, we are,
One equal temper of heroic hearts,
Made weak by time and fate, but strong in will
To strive, to seek, to find, and not to yield.   70

QUESTIONS

1. Many critics consider "Ulysses" one of the great dramatic monologues in English poetry. What is Ulysses like? Where is he standing? To whom is he talking? Where is he going (see lines 59–64)? Why does he want to sail to the "Happy Isles"?

2. How would you characterize the speaker's mood in lines 1–5? What evidence supports your judgment? How and why does the mood shift in lines 6–11?

3. Why is there so much imagery of adventure in the poem? Cite examples and explain their significance.

4. Explain the metaphor in lines 19–22. What other examples of metaphor and simile can you find and interpret?

5. What does Ulysses want to believe? What, ultimately, does he symbolize?

TOPICS FOR WRITING

1. Analyze the interweaving of past, present, and future in "Ulysses." How does this complex time pattern relate to the theme?

2. Write a character analysis of Ulysses and the way or vision of life that he represents.

3. Summarize and evaluate the Homeric background to this poem. Define such allusions as "an aged wife" (line 3), "Troy" (line 7), "Telemachus" (line 33), "the Happy Isles" (line 63), and "Achilles" (line 64). Explain why the legend of Ulysses was so useful to Tennyson in the advancement of his theme.

Robert Browning

MY LAST DUCHESS

Robert Browning (1812–1869) was born near London, of wealthy parents, and was educated at home and at the University of London. Poetry was a childhood passion, used by Browning as a therapeutic tool to rid himself of his turbulent emotions. In September 1846, he eloped to Italy with the poet Elizabeth Barrett (see page 354). They were to live fairly happily together until her death fifteen years later. A fine, though often difficult, poet, he is most famous for his development, as in "My Last Duchess," of the dramatic monologue, in which he presents complex characters through their own voices.

FERRARA

That's my last Duchess painted on the wall,
Looking as if she were alive. I call
That piece a wonder, now: Frà Pandolf's hands
Worked busily a day, and there she stands.
Will't please you sit and look at her? I said   5
"Frà Pandolf" by design, for never read
Strangers like you that pictured countenance,
The depth and passion of its earnest glance,
But to myself they turned (since none puts by
The curtain I have drawn for you, but I)   10
And seemed as they would ask me, if they durst,
How such a glance came there; so, not the first
Are you to turn and ask thus Sir, 'twas not
Her husband's presence only, called that spot

Of joy into the Duchess' cheek: perhaps 15
Frà Pandolf chanced to say "Her mantle laps
Over my lady's wrist too much," or "Paint
Must never hope to reproduce the faint
Half-flush that dies along her throat": such stuff
Was courtesy, she thought, and cause enough 20
For calling up that spot of joy. She had
A heart—how shall I say?—too soon made glad,
Too easily impressed; she liked whate'er
She looked on, and her looks went everywhere.
Sir, 'twas all one! My favor at her breast, 25
The dropping of the daylight in the West,
The bough of cherries some officious fool
Broke in the orchard for her, the white mule
She rode with round the terrace—all and each
Would draw from her alike the approving speech, 30
Or blush, at least. She thanked men—good! but thanked
Somehow—I know not how—as if she ranked
My gift of a nine-hundred-years-old name
With anybody's gift. Who'd stoop to blame
This sort of trifling? Even had you skill 35
In speech—(which I have not)—to make your will
Quite clear to such an one, and say, "Just this
Or that in you disgusts me; here you miss,
Or there exceed the mark"—and if she let
Herself be lessoned so, nor plainly set 40
Her wits to yours, forsooth, and made excuse
—E'en then would be some stooping; and I choose
Never to stoop. Oh sir, she smiled, no doubt,
Whene'er I passed her; but who passed without
Much the same smile? This grew; I gave commands; 45
Then all smiles stopped together. There she stands
As if alive. Will't please you rise? We'll meet
The company below, then. I repeat,
The Count your master's known munificence
Is ample warrant that no just pretense 50
Of mine for dowry will be disallowed;
Though his fair daughter's self, as I avowed
At starting, is my object. Nay, we'll go
Together down, sir. Notice Neptune, though,
Taming a sea horse, thought a rarity, 55
Which Claus of Innsbruck cast in bronze for me!

QUESTIONS

1. Browning was famous for his dramatic monologues, and this is one of his best. What is the dramatic situation? How would you describe the speaker? Why do you think he values art so highly? How does he gratuitously give himself and his past actions away?

2. What was the speaker's "last duchess" like? To whom is he speaking, and what is the listener like?

3. What is the difference between these couplets and the heroic couplets of the eighteenth century? What literary effects are achieved by Browning's use of the couplet?

4. Can you explain what the speaker means when he says, "I choose never to stoop"? What is the immediate context of the remark?

5. The poem ends.as it begins, with a reference to art. What significance is there to the statue of Neptune taming a seahorse? Does Browning mean this to be taken symbolically? Explain.

TOPICS FOR WRITING

1. Analyze the way in which this dramatic monologue is structured around the gradual revelation of the speaker's personality.

2. A critic, Leonard Nathanson, writes that "the Duke performs the very act he asserts to be the most repugnant to his nature; after sacrificing his wife rather than his dignity, he sacrifices that dignity." What other instances and varieties of irony do you detect in the poem?

Emily Brontë

REMEMBRANCE

Emily Bronte (1818–1848) was born in the north of England and grew up in the company of two literary sisters, Charlotte and Anne. Her most famous work is the gothic novel Wuthering Heights (1847). Her poems were largely ignored in her own lifetime, but with the passage of time have become better appreciated, especially for their hymnlike qualities. Most of them deal, as our selection does, with the triumph of love over death.

Cold in the earth, and the deep snow piled above thee!
Far, far removed, cold in the dreary grave!
Have I forgot, my Only Love, to love thee,
Severed at last by Time's all-wearing wave?

Remembrance

Now, when alone, do my thoughts no longer hover   5
Over the mountains on Angora's shore;
Resting their wings where heath and fern-leaves cover
That noble heart for ever, ever more?

Cold in the earth, and fifteen wild Decembers
From those brown hills have melted into spring—   10
Faithful indeed is the spirit that remembers
After such years of change and suffering!

Sweet Love of youth, forgive if I forget thee
While the World's tide is bearing me along:
Sterner desires and darker hopes beset me,   15
Hopes which obscure but cannot do thee wrong.

No other Sun has lightened up my heaven;
No other Star has ever shone for me;
All my life's bliss from thy dear life was given—
All my life's bliss is in the grave with thee.   20

But when the days of golden dreams had perished
And even Despair was powerless to destroy,
Then did I learn how existence could be cherished,
Strengthened and fed without the aid of joy;

Then did I check the tears of useless passion,   25
Weaned my young soul from yearning after thine;
Sternly denied its burning wish to hasten
Down to that tomb already more than mine!

And even yet, I dare not let it languish,
Dare not indulge in Memory's rapturous pain;   30
Once drinking deep of that divinest anguish,
How could I seek the empty world again?

QUESTIONS

    1. Is there a good reason to repeat the word "far" in stanza 1? or "cold"? Are these examples of verbal inflation, mere windiness, or artistic control?

    2. How appropriate is it to speak of waves "severing" (line 4)? How might this image be sharpened? Would the poem be marred by a more explicit rendering of detail?

    3. Does the rhetorical question of stanza 2 seem overly long? How would you describe its tone? What does the word "indeed" do to the tone of stanza 3?

    4. Can you account for the sudden tense change between stanzas 5 and 6? What purpose does "But" serve there?

    5. What is a phrase like "burning wish" called? Explain its effect.

TOPIC FOR WRITING

One critic, speaking of Brontë's poems, declared: "Her imagination resembles that of Blake in power and freedom, but she lacked skill and craftsmanship." Test this remark against your own evaluation of the poem's success (or lack of it) in seeking a resolution of grief.

Walt Whitman

Walt Whitman (1819–1892), previously introduced (page 380), is the embodiment of American individualism. At once volatile and delicate, he enjoyed quoting Savanarola's phrase, "Do I contradict myself? Very well, I contradict myself. I am large; I contain multitudes." And so it seemed to his astonished contemporaries. If he was capable of roaring through the pines, as Edgar Lee Masters wrote, he was also capable of great precision in his poetic voices. Our selections find him using his fine powers of perception to capture and hold the things of nature, this world, and the spiritual realm.

A NOISELESS PATIENT SPIDER

A noiseless patient spider,
I mark'd where on a little promontory it stood isolated,
Mark'd how to explore the vacant vast surrounding,
It launch'd forth filament, filament, filament, out of itself,
Ever unreeling them, ever tirelessly speeding them.   5

And you O my soul where you stand,
Surrounded, detached, in measureless oceans of space,
Ceaselessly musing, venturing, throwing, seeking the spheres to connect them,
Till the bridge you will need be form'd, till the ductile anchor hold,
Till the gossamer thread you fling catch somewhere, O my soul.   10

QUESTIONS

1. How effective is the analogy that Whitman draws between the spider and his soul? Explain.

2. Whitman is fond of repeated words in this poem. What is the effect?

3. Each stanza is composed of a single sentence. What is the relationship of sentence structure to rhythm?

4. Why does Whitman personify his soul in the poem? Why does he use apostrophe?

TOPIC FOR WRITING

Whitman described his poetic voice as a "barbaric yawp." Explain why you think this tone is an asset or a liability in "A Noiseless, Patient Spider."

CAVALRY CROSSING A FORD

A line in long array, where they wind betwixt green islands;
They take a serpentine course—their arms flash in the sun—Hark to the
    musical clank;
Behold the silvery river—in it the splashing horses, loitering, stop to drink;
Behold the brown-faced men—each group, each person, a picture—the   5
    negligent rest on the saddles;
Some emerge on the opposite bank—others are just entering the
    ford—while,
Scarlet, and blue, and snowy white,
The guidon flags flutter gaily in the wind.   10

QUESTIONS

1. Whitman terms this poem a "picture." How does he construct it? Why could this poem be considered a forerunner of impressionism or imagism?

2. What is the purpose of this poem? Does it have a theme in a traditional sense? Why or why not?

TOPIC FOR WRITING

Define the mood that Whitman creates in the poem and the methods he uses to create it. Look at line lengths, punctuation, alliteration, imagery, and the use of the imperative, among other techniques.

Matthew Arnold

THE DALLIANCE
OF THE EAGLES

Skirting the river road (my forenoon walk, my rest),
Skyward in air a sudden muffled sound, the dalliance of the eagles,
The rushing amorous contact high in space together,
The clinching, interlocking claws, a living, fierce, gyrating wheel,
Four beating wings, two beaks, a swirling mass tight grappling,   5
In tumbling, turning, clustering loops, straight downward falling,
Till o'er the river pois'd, the twain yet one, a moment's lull,
A motionless still balance in the air, then parting, talons loosing,
Upward again on slow-firm pinions slanting, their separate diverse flight,
She hers, he his, pursuing.   10

QUESTIONS

1. Whitman uses seventeen present participles in ten lines. What positive effects does this create? What negative effects?

2. Is the word "dalliance" more salacious than one might initially think? Does it seem odd to you that this earthy poet should resort to euphemism?

3. The last word of the poem is "pursuing." Is this an accident of chronology or is Whitman making a dark statement about nature?

TOPICS FOR WRITING

1. Analyze the way that Whitman describes the "amorous contact" of the eagles in this poem.

2. Compare and contrast this poem with Yeats's "Leda and the Swan" (page 562).

Matthew Arnold

TO MARGUERITE—CONTINUED

Matthew Arnold (1822–1888), who appears earlier in this anthology (page 451), wrote a series of "Marguerite" poems. We do not know who this Marguerite was. The poems deal ostensibly with love, but we are more interested in the speaker's self-conscious relationship to Marguerite. Indeed, the persona in these poems seems more preoccupied with change and impermanence than with love. In "To Marguerite

—Continued," *one of his finest poems in this sequence,
Arnold has the lover and his beloved confront universal
alienation.*

Yes! in the sea of life enisled,
With echoing straits between us thrown,
Dotting the shoreless watery wild,
We mortal millions live *alone*.
The islands feel the enclasping flow,   5
And then their endless bounds they know.

But when the moon their hollows lights,
And they are swept by balms of spring,
And in their glens, on starry nights,
The nightingales divinely sing;   10
And lovely notes, from shore to shore,
Across the sounds and channels pour—

Oh! then a longing like despair
Is to their farthest caverns sent;
For surely once, they feel, we were   15
Parts of a single continent!
Now round us spreads the watery plain—
Oh might our marges meet again!

Who order'd, that their longing's fire
Should be, as soon as kindled, cool'd?   20
Who renders vain their deep desire?—
A God, a God their severance ruled!
And bade betwixt their shores to be
The unplumb'd, salt, estranging sea.

QUESTIONS

1. Paraphrase each of the four stanzas in this poem. How does Arnold
advance his thesis from stanza to stanza? Which famous line best states the
thesis?

2. What varieties of alliteration, rhyme, and other sound effects can you find
in the poem? What is the cumulative effect?

3. Imagery of water predominates in this poem. Cite examples and their
significance. What other patterns of imagery relate to the water motif?

4. What is Arnold's attitude toward God? Why?

TOPIC FOR WRITING

Write an essay on Arnold's vision of love in the modern world, basing it on this
poem and on "Dover Beach" (page 451).

Emily Dickinson

Emily Dickinson (1830–1886), previously introduced in the anthology (page 346), called her poetry "my letter to the World." She lived most of her life as a recluse, dying in the same house she was born in, communicating with neighbors and literary friends through charming, crafted letters and gifts of bread. Her temperament and style of life suggest a delicate, fragile awareness; yet her poetry wrestles with the problems of death and loss without fear. "Because I could not stop for Death" is a jocular encounter with death and immortality, while "A Light exists in Spring" presents a more somber, deeply felt loss. The less serious poem "I like to see it lap the miles" asks the reader to solve an extended riddle, which is perhaps more difficult for modern readers living in the jet age.

I LIKE TO SEE IT LAP THE MILES

I like to see it lap the miles,
And lick the valleys up,
And stop to feed itself at tanks;
And then, prodigious, step

Around a pile of mountains,   5
And, supercilious, peer
In shanties by the sides of roads;
And then a quarry pare

To fit its sides
And crawl between   10
Complaining all the while
In horrid, hooting stanza;
Then chase itself down hill

And neigh like Boanerges;
Then, punctual as a star,   15
Stop—docile and omnipotent—
At its own stable door.

QUESTIONS

1. What is the basic metaphor in "I like to see it lap the miles"? How is the metaphor extended in line 15? Do you think that Dickinson visualizes a complete train or just a single engine? What is gained by referring to the train as "it" throughout the poem?

2. What gives the poem a playful quality?

3. Point out instances of alliteration in the poem, and describe the effect. What other sound effects do you encounter?

4. Why does Dickinson start so many lines with the word "And"?

TOPIC FOR WRITING

Analyze the way that Dickinson develops her controlling metaphor in this poem.

BECAUSE I COULD NOT STOP FOR DEATH

Because I could not stop for Death—
He kindly stopped for me—

The Carriage held but just Ourselves—
And Immortality.

We slowly drove—He knew no haste   5
And I had put away
My labor and my leisure too,
For His Civility—

We passed the School, where Children strove
At Recess—in the Ring—   10
We passed the Fields of Gazing Grain—
We passed the Setting Sun—

Or rather—He passed Us—
The Dews drew quivering and chill—
For only Gossamer, my Gown—   15
My Tippet—only Tulle—

We paused before a House that seemed
A Swelling of the Ground—
The Roof was scarcely visible—
The Cornice—in the Ground—   20

Since then—'tis Centuries—and yet
Feels shorter than the Day
I first surmised the Horses' Heads
Were toward Eternity—

Emily Dickinson

QUESTIONS

1. Why can't the poet stop for Death? Why must a third person be present? (Remember that Dickinson is a single woman living in Victorian New England.)

2. What is Dickinson's attitude toward Death? Is she worried? indifferent? How careful are her observations? Give examples.

3. What happens to the poet's spatial sense in stanza 3? To her temporal sense in the last stanza?

4. How can Death and the poet come upon an unfamiliar house in the fifth stanza, after they have passed everything else? Why do they pause? Does Dickinson distinguish between the inside and the outside of the house? Some critics have identified the house with a tomb. Why? Do you agree?

TOPIC FOR WRITING

The poet and critic Allen Tate has said that this poem shows "love being a symbol interchangeable with death." In a short essay explain if this is an accurate reading of the poem and discuss its implication.

A LIGHT EXISTS IN SPRING

A Light exists in Spring
Not present on the Year
At any other period—
When March is scarcely here

A Color stands abroad   5
On Solitary Fields
That Science cannot overtake
But Human Nature feels.

It waits upon the Lawn,
It shows the furthest Tree   10
Upon the furthest Slope you know
It almost speaks to you.

Then as Horizons step
Or Noons report away
Without the Formula of sound   15
It passes and we stay—

A quality of loss
Affecting our Content

As Trade had suddenly encroached
Upon a Sacrament.   20

QUESTIONS

1. Explain the speaker's mood in this poem.

2. What are the pairs of opposed terms in "A Light exists in Spring"? Why are there so many?

3. What does Dickinson mean by "Formula of sound" in the fourth stanza? Why does she use the scientific term "formula"?

TOPICS FOR WRITING

1. Describe the overall effect of "A Light Exists in Spring" and the techniques used by Dickinson to achieve it.

2. Analyze Dickinson's views on nature and technology in the first and third poems.

Christina Rossetti

IN AN ARTIST'S STUDIO

Christina Rossetti (1830–1894) was born in London, twelve years after her brother, Dante Gabriel Rossetti, the poet, painter, and founder of the Pre-Raphaelite group. Throughout her life, her two abiding loves were her brother, whom she idolized, and the Anglican Church, which she celebrated in many powerful, unselfconscious devotional poems. Unlike most of the other Pre-Raphaelites, she was profoundly moral and had little sympathy for the pleasure seeking and sensuality they advocated. Twice in her life she turned down offers of marriage because of religious differences and instead devoted herself to her family and the mystical contemplation of the world. Goblin Market (1862), the first poem by any of the Pre-Raphaelites to become widely known, is an elaborate fantasy, full of images and events that suggest to many readers deep sexual repression. The following poem, "In an Artist's Studio," develops from Rossetti's complex relationship with Elizabeth Siddal, her brother's favorite model and his eventual wife.

One face looks out from all his canvases,
   One selfsame figure sits or walks or leans:
   We found her hidden just behind those screens,
That mirror gave back all her loveliness.
A queen in opal or in ruby dress,   5
   A nameless girl in freshest summer-greens,
   A saint, an angel—every canvas means
The same one meaning, neither more or less.
He feeds upon her face by day and night,
   And she with true kind eyes looks back on him,   10
Fair as the moon and joyful as the light:
   Not wan with waiting, not with sorrow dim;
Not as she is, but was when hope shone bright;
   Not as she is, but as she fills his dream.

QUESTIONS

1. What is implied by the word "we" in line 3? Why isn't the word repeated again in the poem? Does line 9 offer an agreeable image? Why is it used?

2. How does the poet's attitude toward the model differ from the artist's feelings? Does it surprise you to learn that the poet is a woman? Explain.

3. Why does Rossetti repeat "Not as she is" at the end of the poem?

TOPICS FOR WRITING

1. The Roman poet Horace wrote, "Poetry is like painting," but in this poem the two mediums seem to be contrasted. Describe the differences between the two and the relative strengths and weaknesses of each. Can one be said to be superior to the other? Support your answers.

2. Analyze the attitude of the speaker toward the model and the artist in the poem.

Thomas Hardy

Thomas Hardy (1840–1928) was born in Dorset, and it is this provincial setting (called Wessex in his novels) that provided the backdrop for all his writing. His father was a master mason and Hardy's formal education was as an architect. A literary career also tempted him, and as a young man, he read widely if erratically in classical and modern literature. Like Jude, the hero of Hardy's last novel, he taught himself ancient Greek. After practicing architecture unsuccessfully in London for several years, he returned to Dorset and began a successful career as a novelist. He wrote fourteen novels, many still read today, and at the age of 55, he turned to poetry. Hardy spent the last thirty years of his life as a prolific and almost always gloomy poet. "The Darkling Thrush," written to inaugurate the beginning of the twentieth century, strikes an uncharacteristic and perhaps ironic note of hope; while "Channel Firing," written on the eve of World War I, insists that the stupidity of militarism is a stupidity compounded by its repetition throughout English history.

THE DARKLING THRUSH

I leant upon a coppice gate
    When Frost was spectre-gray,
And Winter's dregs made desolate
    The weakening eye of day.
The tangled bine-stems scored the sky   5
    Like strings of broken lyres,
And all mankind that hounted nigh
    Had sought their household fires.

The land's sharp features seemed to be
    The Century's corpse outleant,   10
His crypt the cloudy canopy,
    The wind his death-lament.
The ancient pulse of germ and birth
    Was shrunken hard and dry,
And every spirit upon earth   15
    Seemed fervourless as I.

At once a voice arose among
    The bleak twigs overhead
In a full-hearted evensong
    Of joy illimited;   20
An aged thrush, frail, gaunt, and small,
    In blast-beruffled plume,
Had chosen thus to fling his soul
    Upon the growing gloom.

So little cause for carolings   25
    Of such ecstatic sound
Was written on terrestrial things
    Afar or nigh around,
That I could think there trembled through
    His happy good-night air   30
Some blessed Hope, whereof he knew
    And I was unaware.

QUESTIONS

1. The original title of "The Darkling Thrush" was "By the Century's Death-bed." Why did Hardy change it, and what did he gain by the change? What does the thrush symbolize?

2. Explain the mood of the poem and the way Hardy handles it. To what is Hardy referring when he says, "The weakening eye of day"?

3. What is the cumulative effect of the adjectives in the line, "An aged thrush, frail, gaunt, and small"?

4. Explain the function of personification in the poem.

TOPICS FOR WRITING

1. Analyze Hardy's vision of the twentieth century in "The Darkling Thrush."

2. Compare and contrast "The Darkling Thrush" and Dickinson's "A Light exists in Spring."

CHANNEL FIRING

That night your great guns, unawares,
Shook all our coffins as we lay,
And broke the chancel window-squares,
We thought it was the Judgment-day

And sat upright. While drearisome   5
Arose the howl of wakened hounds:
The mouse let fall the altar-crumb,
The worms drew back into the mounds,

The glebe cow drooled. Till God called, "No;
It's gunnery practice out at sea   10
Just as before you went below;
The world is as it used to be:

"All nations striving strong to make
Red war yet redder. Mad as hatters
They do no more for Christés sake 15
Than you who are helpless in such matters.

"That this is not the judgment-hour
For some of them's a blessed thing,
For if it were they'd have to scour
Hell's floor for so much threatening. . . . 20

"Ha, ha. It will be warmer when
I blow the trumpet (if indeed
I ever do; for you are men,
And rest eternal sorely need)."

So down we lay again. "I wonder, 25
Will the world ever saner be,"
Said one, "than when He sent us under
In our indifferent century!"

And many a skeleton shook his head.
"Instead of preaching forty year," 30
My neighbour Parson Thirdly said,
"I wish I had stuck to pipes and beer."

Again the guns disturbed the hour,
Roaring their readiness to avenge,
As far inland as Stourton Tower, 35
And Camelot, and starlit Stonehenge.

QUESTIONS

1. Describe the diction and tone that Hardy gives to God in "The Channel Firing." Is it sacrilegious? Is it amusing? Explain.

2. Is this a realistic poem or a fantastic one? Support your answer by reference to details in the poem.

3. Why does Hardy conclude with mention of Stourton Tower, Camelot, and Stonehenge?

4. What is anticlimactic about the sentence that continues from the first stanza to the second? Why does Hardy refer to the "mouse" and "worms" instead of other farm animals?

TOPICS FOR WRITING

1. Analyze the differences in voice and tone in "Channel Firing" in the first and last stanzas and in the rest of the poem.

2. Explain why Hardy uses black humor to promote his thesis in "Channel Firing." Would the poem have been more effective if it were written in a high, formal style throughout?

3. In the first line of one poem and in the last line of the other, Hardy uses the word "unaware." Relate the concept of unawareness to Hardy's philosophy of life as it is presented in the two poems.

Gerard Manley Hopkins

PIED BEAUTY

Gerard Manley Hopkins (1844–1889) was the eldest son in a middle-class, Anglican family. His childhood was apparently uneventful, but he blossomed intellectually at Oxford, where he studied with Walter Pater and was befriended by John (later Cardinal) Newman. With Newman's sponsorship and against the wishes of his family, he converted to Catholicism in 1866. Two years later he entered the Jesuit order and, in a dramatic gesture, burned the final copy of all his early poems. At this point in his life he feared that the aesthetic and the religious might not be reconcilable. Six years later, however, with the encouragement of his prefect, he wrote a long poem to honor five nuns drowned in a shipwreck and continued to write from then on. Hopkins spent his life as a teacher and as a priest, serving many different communities, some of which were poor and isolated. He made only halfhearted attempts to have his poetry published in his lifetime. "Pied Beauty," which is a kind of joyful prayer, celebrates the apparently minor manifestations of varied things in the world that supply evidence of the divine.

Glory be to God for dappled things—
  For skies of couple-colour as a brinded cow;
    For rose-moles all in stipple upon trout that swim;
Fresh-firecoal chestnut-falls; finches' wings;
  Landscape plotted and pieced—fold, fallow, and plough;   5
    And áll trádes, their gear and tackle and trim.

All things counter, original, spare, strange;
  Whatever is fickle, freckled (who knows how?)

With swift, slow; sweet, sour; adazzle, dim;
He fathers-forth whose beauty is past change: 10
      Praise him.

QUESTIONS

1. Why does Hopkins use the term "pied" in his title instead of a word like "varied" or "variegated"?

2. What do the images in lines 2—4 have in common?

3. Why does Hopkins include his rhetorical question in line 8?

4. In line 9, Hopkins mentions three pairs of opposites, and the members of each pair begin with similar sounds (the practice is called alliteration). Why does Hopkins do this?

5. Would the poem be more effective with the last two words omitted? Explain.

6. What is the theme of the poem?

TOPICS FOR WRITING

1. Beauty is usually thought to derive from symmetry and proportion. Explain why Hopkins praises disorder and unevenness in his poem.

2. In an unabridged dictionary, look up all the words you are unfamiliar with. Do they seem to have a common source? What does it suggest to you that many of Hopkins's terms have dropped out of common usage? What differences does this signal between our world and the world Hopkins knew?

A. E. Housman

BREDON HILL

Alfred Edward Housman (1859–1936), introduced earlier in this anthology (page 438), published only two short volumes of poetry in his lifetime. He was a scholar of Latin literature by training and a recluse by temperament. Though his classical training steeped him in the driest form of textual scholarship, he also appreciated the emotional surge of

A. E. Housman

*feeling that great poetry stimulates. If a line of true poetry
entered his head while shaving, he wrote, he could feel his
skin bristle and a shiver go up his spine. In "Bredon Hill,"
Housman's treatment of the twin themes of youthful death
and unrequited love creates the strong emotional reaction
that he valued but avoids sentimentality by its understated
tone and its use of a traditional ballad form.*

In summertime on Bredon
  The bells they sound so clear;
Round both the shires they ring them
  In steeples far and near,
  A happy noise to hear.   5

Here of a Sunday morning
  My love and I would lie,
And see the colored counties,
  And hear the larks so high
  About us in the sky.   10

The bells would ring to call her
  In valleys miles away:
"Come all to church, good people;
  Good people, come and pray."
  But here my love would stay.   15

And I would turn and answer
  Among the springing thyme,
"O, peal upon our wedding,
  And we will hear the chime,
  And come to church in time."   20

But when the snows at Christmas
  On Bredon top were strown,
My love rose up so early
  And stole out unbeknown
  And went to church alone.   25

They tolled the one bell only,
  Groom there was none to see,
The mourners followed after,
  And so to church went she,
  And would not wait for me.   30

The bells they sound on Bredon,
  And still the steeples hum,
"Come all to church, good people"—
  Oh, noisy bells, be dumb;
  I hear you, I will come.   35

QUESTIONS

1. Does the poem convey any sense of the personality of the woman or her fiancé? Why does Housman avoid making his characters distinctive, unique individuals?

2. Explain why the poet uses a place name for his title.

3. Is the mood of the poem shattered by the last two lines? Would the emotion be more poignant without them? Explain.

4. The poem is told in the first person. How would it change the poem to have it related in the third person?

TOPICS FOR WRITING

1. Housman's editors believe that he was a homosexual. Does this information change your impression of the poem? Do you think the poem any less sincere because of it? Justify your response.

2. Compare the attitudes toward death of this poem and Hardy's "Channel Firing" (page 556).

William Butler Yeats

William Butler Yeats (1865–1939), the most prolific and one of the greatest modern poets, was born in Dublin, the son of the well-known painter John Butler Yeats. His Irish Protestant family moved often between London and the Irish countryside, and Yeats grew up more Irish than Protestant, a precocious youth fascinated by poetry, philosophy, politics, folklore, and the occult. He achieved early fame as a poet and wrote extraordinary poetry his entire life. (The two selections below were both composed when Yeats was in his sixties.) In a life full of projects and accomplishments, his work in the theater and his long study of and belief in magic deserve the most attention. In 1889 he met and fell in love with the Irish radical Maud Gonne. The passion was never reciprocated. He proposed marriage to her on several occasions and at least once made the same offer to Gonne's daughter, Iseult. He finally married another woman in 1917 and, with the help of his wife, wrote A Vision, which presents

William Butler Yeats

his systematic theory of world philosophy. A Vision works out a predetermined cyclical theory of history that "Leda and the Swan" illustrates. "Sailing to Byzantium" contrasts the inevitable decline of civilization and the decay of old age with the possibility of some form of eternal consciousness.

LEDA AND THE SWAN

A sudden blow; the great wings beating still
Above the staggering girl, her thighs caressed
By the dark webs, her nape caught in his bill,
He holds her helpless breast upon his breast.

How can those terrified vague fingers push   5
The feathered glory from her loosening thighs?
And how can body, laid in that white rush,
But feel the strange heart beating where it lies?

A shudder in the loins engenders there
The broken wall, the burning roof and tower   10
And Agamemnon dead.
     Being so caught up,
So mastered by the brute blood of the air,
Did she put on his knowledge with his power
Before the indifferent beak could let her drop?   15

QUESTIONS

1. As a reader, are you expected to answer the three questions posed in "Leda and the Swan"? How would you answer them?

2. Why does Yeats write in the last line "could let her drop" rather than just "let her drop"?

3. In a book on mythology, look up the story of Leda and the story of the sacking of Troy. Are they traditionally thought to be related? What does it signify that Yeats has yoked them together?

4. How is the very form of this sonnet structured around the sexual act? What correspondences exist between the octave (first eight lines) the sestet (last six lines)?

TOPIC FOR WRITING

Analyze Yeats's approach to the rape in "Leda and the Swan." What is the relationship between power and beauty that is implied by the apparent lack of moral repulsion in the poem?

SAILING TO BYZANTIUM

I

That is no country for old men. The young
In one another's arms, birds in the trees
—Those dying generations—at their song,
The salmon-falls, the mackerel-crowded seas,
Fish, flesh, or fowl, commend all summer long   5
Whatever is begotten, born, and dies.
Caught in that sensual music all neglect
Monuments of unageing intellect.

II

An aged man is but a paltry thing,
A tattered coat upon a stick, unless   10
Soul clap its hands and sing, and louder sing
For every tatter in its mortal dress,
Nor is there singing school but studying
Monuments of its own magnificence;
And therefore I have sailed the seas and come   15
To the holy city of Byzantium.

III

O sages standing in God's holy fire
As in the gold mosaic of a wall,
Come from the holy fire, perne in a gyre,
And be the singing-masters of my soul.   20
Consume my heart away; sick with desire
And fastened to a dying animal
It knows not what it is; and gather me
Into the artifice of eternity.

IV

Once out of nature I shall never take   25
My bodily form from any natural thing,
But such a form as Grecian goldsmiths make
Of hammered gold and gold enamelling
To keep a drowsy Emperor awake;
Or set upon a golden bough to sing   30
To lords and ladies of Byzantium
Of what is past, or passing, or to come.

QUESTIONS

1. How old do you think the poet is? What is his initial feeling toward the young? Why?

2. Give some examples of what you think Yeats means by "Monuments of

unageing intellect" and by "Monuments of its own magnificence." Are there differences between the two ideas?

3. A songbird has long been a symbol for the poet. What is special about Yeats's adaptation of the symbol? Is his bird presented as ephemeral? trivial?

4. An oxymoron is a phrase which logically contradicts itself and yet has rhetorical force (such as "loving hate" and "icy fire"). Why is "artifice of eternity" close to being an oxymoron? Does it have a meaning?

TOPICS FOR WRITING

1. What is the progression of emotional states in "Sailing to Byzantium"? Describe and analyze the implied argument of the poem.

2. R. P. Blackmur states that "Yeats commonly hovered betweeen myth and philosophy . . . which is why he is not one of the greatest poets." Assess this remark in terms of the two poems presented.

E. A. Robinson

RICHARD CORY

Edward Arlington Robinson (1869–1935) was born in Head Tide and grew up in Gardiner, both barren Maine towns. He remembered his childhood as unhappy and was able to attend Harvard for only two years before the death of his father and the failure of the family business made further education impossible. He published his first volume of poetry at his own expense ($52) and soon after moved to New York to make writing his career. One of his later books of poetry came to the attention of President Theodore Roosevelt, who praised and aided Robinson. Robinson's popular reputation continued to grow during his lifetime, and today he has a firm place as a significant modern poet. Like Robert Frost, he usually writes about New England, but instead of describing a scene in nature, Robinson uses dramatic monologues to sketch New England character types: drunks, unemployed dreamers, unconventional misfits. "Richard Cory" shows the unthinking materialism of a small-town figure; the poem manages the difficult feat of revealing as much about the unnamed speaker as it does about Richard Cory.

Whenever Richard Cory went down town,
We people on the pavement looked at him:
He was a gentleman from sole to crown,
Clean favored, and imperially slim.

And he was always quietly arrayed,   5
And he was always human when he talked;
But still he fluttered pulses when he said,
'Good-morning,' and he glittered when he walked.

And he was rich—yes, richer than a king—
And admirably schooled in every grace: 10
In fine, we thought that he was everything
To make us wish that we were in his place.

So on we worked, and waited for the light,
And went without the meat, and cursed the bread;
And Richard Cory, one calm summer night,   15
Went home and put a bullet through his head.

QUESTIONS

1. Why does the narrator refer to "We people" in the second line? Does he ever speak of himself as "I" or "me"? Does the narrator have a sense of self-worth?

2. Point out word choices that imply the narrator's respect for Richard Cory. How would the poem be diminished if Robinson named his creation John Smith or Luke Havergal (a character in another Robinson sketch)?

3. Does the narrator understand the suicide of Richard Cory? Is the reader better able to comprehend it? How does this affect the reader's attitude toward the poem's narrator?

4. What is the effect of the definite articles in the last stanza, "the light . . . the meat . . . the bread"? Express the sentence's meaning in more literal language. What are the religious overtones of "the light"? Would the narrator be expected to intend those overtones?

TOPICS FOR WRITING

1. Critics have attacked the poem's surprise ending as "cheap." Do you agree? Defend or criticize the ending, and in doing so, address the issue that most people value poems that deserve to be read and studied more than once.

2. Analyze Robinson's use of irony and ironic contrast in this poem.

Amy Lowell

THE TAXI

*Like her younger contemporary T. S. Eliot, Amy Lowell
(1874–1925) was born into an illustrious Boston family. As
a child and young woman she often traveled to Europe, and
at the age of 28, she began to write poetry. Her first volume
of verse was fairly conventional, but in 1913 she met Ezra
Pound and became part of the imagist movement, which she
eventually dominated. She spent the last years of her life
writing a biographical study of the poet John Keats. Lowell's
version of imagism, which "The Taxi" demonstrates, tem-
pers the hard, objective, impersonal focus on a single image
with a more subjective caring about the emotions of love
and disappointment.*

When I go away from you
The world beats dead
Like a slackened drum.
I call out for you against the jutted stars
And shout into the ridges of the wind.   5
Streets coming fast,
One after the other,
Wedge you away from me,
And the lamps of the city prick my eyes
So that I can no longer see your face.   10
Why should I leave you,
To wound myself upon the sharp edges of the night?

QUESTIONS

1. What situation is being described in Lowell's poem? How does the taxi fit
into the scene? Do you find her description overdone or extravagant? Is this an
event that is often repeated?

2. What is interesting about lines 9–10?

3. How is the last metaphor prepared for in the rest of the poem?

4. The word "I" never appears on a line without being accompanied by "you"
or one of its forms. Why?

TOPICS FOR WRITING

1. Describe the way in which the urban setting intrudes upon the theme of
love in this poem.

2. Analyze the violence of the imagery in "The Taxi."

Robert Frost

Robert Frost (1874–1963), introduced previously in this an-thology (page 382), saw himself as having a "lover's quarrel with the world." Though his quarreling is whimsical and full of dry understatements, his poetry suggests deep sadness and danger. Frost's dark pessimism, partially redeemed by his sense of humor, emerges from the realistic scenes in nature that Frost describes in intimate and yet laconic detail. As he puts it, "I'm always saying something that's just the edge of something more." "The Road Not Taken" mourns the unchangeable past; "Once by the Pacific" envi-sions a dangerous future; and "The Oven Bird" presents the gloomy present, a time of constant diminishment.

THE ROAD NOT TAKEN

Two roads diverged in a yellow wood,
And sorry I could not travel both
And be one traveler, long I stood
And looked down one as far as I could
To where it bent in the undergrowth;   5

Then took the other, as just as fair,
And having perhaps the better claim,
Because it was grassy and wanted wear;
Though as for that the passing there
Had worn them really about the same,   10

And both that morning equally lay
In leaves no step had trodden black.
Oh, I kept the first for another day!
Yet knowing how way leads on to way,
I doubted if I should ever come back.   15

I shall be telling this with a sigh
Somewhere ages and ages hence:
Two roads diverged in a wood, and I—
I took the one less traveled by,
And that has made all the difference.   20

QUESTIONS

1. Does the speaker in "The Road Not Taken" think he has made a mistake? If not, why does he "sigh"?

2. How does the structure of the poem mimic the confusion that the speaker is explaining?

3. Explain Frost's use of symbolism in the poem. Why is the symbolism so rich in positive meanings?

4. Ivor Winters accused Frost of "mistaking whimsical impulse for moral choice" in this poem. Do you agree or disagree? Why?

TOPIC FOR WRITING

Discuss the following in response to "The Road Not Taken": Do you believe that there are decisions that can make "all the difference"? Does the speaker's view of the world coincide with your understanding of it? What kind of person would be concerned with a small matter "ages and ages hence"?

ONCE BY THE PACIFIC

The shattered water made a misty din.
Great waves looked over others coming in,
And thought of doing something to the shore
That water never did to land before.
The clouds were low and hairy in the skies,   5
Like locks blown forward in the gleam of eyes.
You could not tell, and yet it looked as if
The shore was lucky in being backed by cliff,
The cliff in being backed by continent;
It looked as if a night of dark intent   10
Was coming, and not only a night, an age.
Someone had better be prepared for rage.
There would be more than ocean-water broken
Before God's last *Put out the Light* was spoken.

QUESTIONS

1. Why isn't the title of this poem simply "By the Pacific"?

2. The rhymes in the poem are very, very exact. This creates a singsong effect. Does this make the poem more or less serious?

3. Genesis, the first book of the Bible, reads, "And God said, Let there be light, and there was light." Does Frost's version of God's last words have a similar majesty? Explain.

4. Is the speaker genuinely scared? Point out details to support your answer. Compare this poem to Dickinson's "Because I could not stop for Death" (page 551).

TOPIC FOR WRITING

Assess Frost's vision of age in this poem.

THE OVEN BIRD

There is a singer everyone has heard,
Loud, a mid-summer and a mid-wood bird,
Who makes the solid tree trunks sound again.
He says that leaves are old and that for flowers
Mid-summer is to spring as one to ten.   5
He says the early petal-fall is past,
When pear and cherry bloom went down in showers
On sunny days a moment overcast;
And comes that other fall we name the fall.
He says the highway dust is over all.   10
The bird would cease and be as other birds
But that he knows in singing not to sing.
The question that he frames in all but words
Is what to make of a diminished thing.

QUESTIONS

1. What problem does the poet create for his reader with the title "The Oven Bird" and with the assertion in the first line that "There is a singer everyone has heard"? Where in the poem does the poet resolve the problem? Why does Frost shift from "he" (the bird) to "we"?

2. What is the force of the fifth line, with its use of the ratio "one to ten"?

3. Explain how the sonnet form helps to structure the theme of the poem.

4. Is the oven bird a symbol or simply an object? Explain.

TOPICS FOR WRITING

1. Analyze mood, tone, and theme in this poem.

2. Compare and contrast "The Oven Bird" with Hardy's "The Darkling Thrush" (page 551).

3. Frost once said, "I'm always saying something that's just the edge of something more." Select one of the three poems and explain how Frost's statement applies to it.

4. Assess the vision of life projected by these three poems.

Wallace Stevens

*The business career of Wallace Stevens (1879–1955), intro-
duced earlier in the anthology (page 394), hardly suggests
that he was one of the great poets of the twentieth century.
Out of a deep reticence, he declined the prominent role
embraced by many writers of his generation. When he did
choose to speak about poetry, however, he exuberantly
insisted upon its necessity. "What makes the poet the potent
figure that he is, or was, or ought to be, is that he creates the
world to which we turn incessantly and without knowing it
and that he gives to life the supreme fictions without which
we are unable to conceive of it." "Anecdote of the Jar," an
intensely compressed, mysterious lyric, suggests that our
imagination, like the jar itself, can take dominion anywhere.
In "Sunday Morning," one of the greatest modern lyrics,
Stevens meditates on religion and art and on how both
address the inevitability of death.*

ANECDOTE OF THE JAR

I placed a jar in Tennessee,
And round it was, upon a hill.
It made the slovenly wilderness
Surround that hill.

The wilderness rose up to it,   5
And sprawled around, no longer wild.
The jar was round upon the ground
And tall and of a port in air.

It took dominion everywhere.
The jar was gray and bare.   10
It did not give of bird or brush,
Like nothing else in Tennessee.

QUESTIONS

   1. In a short lyric like "Anecdote of the Jar," each word contributes directly to
the poem's essence. How would the poem change if "jar" were changed to
"container"? to "urn"? to "bucket"? if "anecdote" were changed to "history"? to
"story"? to "parable"? if "Tennessee" were changed to "New York"? to "Florida"?
to "Rhode Island"?

   2. What are the aesthetic qualities of the jar? What is its relationship to the
wilderness?

3. What does "It did not give of bird or bush" mean to you?

4. What is the effect of the double negative in the last sentence of the poem?

5. How is the presence of the speaker handled in the poem?

TOPIC FOR WRITING

What is the theme of this poem? Refer to the poem to support your analysis.

SUNDAY MORNING

I

Complacencies of the peignoir, and late
Coffee and oranges in a sunny chair,
And the green freedom of a cockatoo
Upon a rug mingle to dissipate
The holy hush of ancient sacrifice.   5
She dreams a little, and she feels the dark
Encroachment of that old catastrophe,
As a calm darkens among water-lights.
The pungent oranges and bright, green wings
Seem things in some procession of the dead,   10
Winding across wide water, without sound.
The day is like wide water, without sound,
Stilled for the passing of her dreaming feet
Over the seas, to silent Palestine,
Dominion of the blood and sepulchre.   15

II

Why should she give her bounty to the dead?
What is divinity if it can come
Only in silent shadows and in dreams?
Shall she not find in comforts of the sun,
In pungent fruit and bright, green wings, or else   20
In any balm or beauty of the earth,
Things to be cherished like the thought of heaven?
Divinity must live within herself:
Passions of rain, or moods in falling snow;

Grievings in loneliness, or unsubdued 25
Elations when the forest blooms; gusty
Emotions on wet roads on autumn nights;
All pleasures and all pains, remembering
The bough of summer and the winter branch.
These are the measures destined for her soul. 30

III

Jove in the clouds had his inhuman birth.
No mother suckled him, no sweet land gave
Large-mannered motions to his mythy mind
He moved among us, as a muttering king,
Magnificent, would move among his hinds, 35
Until our blood, commingling, virginal,
With heaven, brought such requital to desire
The very hinds discerned it, in a star.
Shall our blood fail? Or shall it come to be
The blood of paradise? And shall the earth 40
Seem all of paradise that we shall know?
The sky will be much friendlier then than now,
A part of labor and a part of pain,
And next in glory to enduring love,
Not this dividing and indifferent blue. 45

IV

She says, "I am content when wakened birds,
Before they fly, test the reality
Of misty fields, by their sweet questionings;
But when the birds are gone, and their warm fields
Return no more, where, then, is paradise?" 50
There is not any haunt of prophecy,
Nor any old chimera of the grave,
Neither the golden underground, nor isle
Melodious, where spirits gat them home,
Nor visionary south, nor cloudy palm 55
Remote on heaven's hill, that has endured
As April's green endures; or will endure
Like her remembrance of awakened birds,
Or her desire for June and evening, tipped
By the consummation of the swallow's wings. 60

V

She says, "But in contentment I still feel
The need of some imperishable bliss."
Death is the mother of beauty; hence from her,
Alone, shall come fulfillment to our dreams
And our desires. Although she strews the leaves 65
Of sure obliteration on our paths,
The path sick sorrow took, the many paths
Where triumph rang its brassy phrase, or love

Sunday Morning

Whispered a little out of tenderness,
She makes the willow shiver in the sun   70
For maidens who were wont to sit and gaze
Upon the grass, relinquished to their feet.
She causes boys to pile new plums and pears
On disregarded plate. The maidens taste
And stray impassioned in the littering leaves.   75

        VI
Is there no change of death in paradise?
Does ripe fruit never fall? Or do the boughs
Hang always heavy in that perfect sky,
Unchanging, yet so like our perishing earth,
With rivers like our own that seek for seas   80
They never find, the same receding shores
That never touch with inarticulate pang?
Why set the pear upon those river-banks
Or spice the shores with odors of the plum?
Alas, that they should wear our colors there,   85
The silken weavings of our afternoons,
And pick the strings of our insipid lutes!
Death is the mother of beauty, mystical,
Within whose burning bosom we devise
Our earthly mothers waiting, sleeplessly.   90

        VII
Supple and turbulent, a ring of men
Shall chant in orgy on a summer morn
Their boisterous devotion to the sun,
Not as a god, but as a god might be,
Naked among them, like a savage source.   95
Their chant shall be a chant of paradise,
Our of their blood, returning to the sky;
And in their chant shall enter, voice by voice,
The windy lake wherein their lord delights,
The trees, like serafin, and echoing hills,   100
That choir among themselves long afterward.
They shall know well the heavenly fellowship
Of men that perish and of summer morn.
And whence they came and whither they shall go
The dew upon their feet shall manifest.   105

        VIII
She hears, upon that water without sound,
A voice that cries, "The tomb in Palestine
Is not the porch of spirits lingering.
It is the grave of Jesus, where he lay."
We live in an old chaos of the sun,   110
Or old dependency of day and night,
Or island solitude, unsponsored, free,

Of that wide water, inescapable.
Deer walk upon our mountains, and the quail
Whistle about us their spontaneous cries;   115
Sweet berries ripen in the wilderness;
And, in the isolation of the sky,
At evening, casual flocks of pigeons make
Ambiguous undulations as they sink,
Downward to darkness, on extended wings.   120

QUESTIONS

1. Carefully paraphrase each stanza of this poem. How do traditional expectations about Sunday morning help to structure the poem? Why is the opening so colorful?

2. Explain Stevens' views of life, death, and paradise in the poem. What theme emerges from these elements?

3. What varieties of symbolism does Stevens employ, and why?

4. How many people speak in "Sunday Morning"? Describe them. Why is there more than one voice in the poem? Why does Stevens include a female voice? What pronoun shifts do you encounter, and why?

5. Are the questions in the second part of the poem ever answered? How are they answered?

6. In the last stanza, what does the poet mean by "unsponsored"? by "free"? Why are the "undulations" of the "casual flocks of pigeons" "ambiguous"? Does the poem end positively or negatively? On an abstract or a concrete note? Explain.

TOPICS FOR WRITING

1. Twice in "Sunday Morning" Stevens insists that "Death is the mother of beauty." Write an essay exploring what Stevens means by this statement.

2. The critic Helen Vendler writes that "Sunday Morning" "offers no single doctrine but rather a choice among truths: we live either (1) in chaos, or (2) in a system of mutual dependency, or (3) in a condition of solitude, which may itself be seen as (3a) lonely or (3b) liberated, but which is in any case inescapable." Find evidence in the poem for these different positions. Is one of them given priority in any way? Are they mutually exclusive?

Carl Sandburg

THE HARBOR

Carl Sandburg (1879–1967) was born in Illinois, the son of immigrant parents. He never finished college and spent much of his early adulthood traveling the country, supporting himself by whatever jobs came his way. At one point he hoped to attend West Point, but he failed the mathematical part of the entrance exam. His first volume of poetry, Chicago Poems (1914), was unorthodox in form and effusively popularistic in mood. His later volumes drew upon American folklore and insisted upon the wisdom and vocabulary of common people. He lived to be 89, and in the last decades of his life, having the air of a sage about him, he enjoyed great popular esteem. He wrote many poems in praise of Chicago. In the following poem, he depicts Chicago's harbor, not so much because of its natural beauty, but because it represents the possibilities of mobility and travel, an exciting aspect of this country's freedom.

Passing through huddled and ugly walls
By doorways where women
Looked from their hunger-deep eyes,
Haunted with shadows of hunger-hands,
Out from the huddled and ugly walls,   5
I came sudden, at the city's edge,
On a blue burst of lake,
Long lake waves breaking under the sun
On a spray-flung curve of shore;
And a fluttering storm of gulls,   10
Masses of great gray wings
And flying white bellies
Veering and wheeling free in the open.

QUESTIONS

1. In what part of the poem are colors mentioned, and in what part are they avoided? Why? How else does Sandburg divide the two scenes he presents?

2. The phrase "free in the open" is redundant. Why does Sandburg use it?

3. Is there any evidence that the speaker is bothered by the poverty he sees? Does the poem suggest any solutions to the problems of a big city? Explain.

TOPICS FOR WRITING

1. Analyze the way that Sandburg uses contrast to structure this poem.

2. Compare and contrast visions of the city in this poem and in Lowell's "The Taxi" (page 566).

3. Sandburg has been praised and damned as a "romantic." Use "The Harbor" as a vehicle to explore this debate.

William Carlos Williams

William Carlos Williams (1883–1963), previously introduced in this anthology (page 396), favored the concrete over the abstract. He had little patience with the highly intellectual, erudite poetry of such contemporaries as Wallace Stevens and T. S. Eliot. Stevens, in turn, found Williams's work to be "antipoetic" because of its apparent casualness of arrangement and thought. Williams's poetic credo advocated "No ideas but in things." Williams's talent for evoking "things," whether it be the plums in "This Is Just to Say" or his complicated metaphor for old age in "To Waken an Old Lady," shows his affection for the simple and often overlooked details of life.

TO WAKEN AN OLD LADY

Old age is
a flight of small
cheeping birds
skimming
bare trees   5
above a snow glaze.
Gaining and failing
they are buffeted
by a dark wind—
But what?   10
On harsh weedstalks
the flock has rested,
the snow
is covered with broken
seedhusks   15
and the wind tempered
by a shrill
piping of plenty.

QUESTIONS

1. Williams's "To Waken an Old Lady" is in two parts, divided by the ambiguous question in line 10, "But what?" Describe the two scenes and their important differences. What does the question signify or signal?

2. Explain the figure of speech that relates old age to a flight of birds. Why is it apt?

3. Could the poem have ended at line 9? How does the mood of the poem change in the second half?

TOPIC FOR WRITING

Analyze imagery and theme in "To Waken an Old Lady."

THIS IS JUST TO SAY

I have eaten
the plums
that were in
the icebox

and which   5
you were probably
saving
for breakfast

Forgive me
they were delicious   10
so sweet
and so cold

QUESTIONS

1. Why does Williams eschew punctuation in "This Is Just to Say"?

2. The title of the poem makes up part of a complete sentence. Why is it appropriate as a separate unit?

3. Why is the "I" important in the poem?

4. What is the effect of the unadorned images in the poem?

TOPIC FOR WRITING

Some people will find "This Is Just to Say" trivial because it lacks academic or philosophic depth. Defend or attack this position.

Sara Teasdale

BARTER

Sara Teasdale (1884–1933) was born in St. Louis to wealthy, middle-aged parents. She started writing poetry in high school, and her first volume of poetry was published at her parents' expense in 1907. Over the next twenty years, she became one of the most widely read poets in America, best known for her love sonnets. She won the Pulitzer Prize for

Sara Teasdale

poetry in 1917 for Love Songs. *Her adult life was a constant struggle to achieve some measure of independence, first from her devoted parents and later from her loving husband. She married when she was 30 and was divorced a few years later. Her divorce would not seem unusual today, but then divorce had a hint of scandal about it that made the matter difficult for all concerned. All her life, Teasdale felt her nature divided. She could not decide if she was truly Puritan or pagan. "Barter" celebrates a joyful pagan hedonism, but the poet never quite escapes her harsh economic metaphor.*

Life has loveliness to sell—
    All beautiful and splendid things,
Blue waves whitened on a cliff,
    Climbing fire that sways and sings,
And children's faces looking up   5
Holding wonder like a cup.

Life has loveliness to sell—
    Music like a curve of gold,
Scent of pine trees in the rain,
    Eyes that love you, arms that hold,   10
And for your spirit's still delight,
Holy thoughts that star the night.

Spend all you have for loveliness,
    Buy it and never count the cost,
For one white singing hour of peace   15
    Count many a year of strife well lost,
And for a breath of ecstasy
Give all you have been or could be.

QUESTIONS

1. Reduce the poem to a prose equivalent. Why does the poet depend on examples rather than on logic to make her position clear?

2. What does Teasdale mean by "your spirit's still delight"?

3. What kinds of societies use barter as a form of economic exchange? Why does Teasdale use that particular term?

TOPICS FOR WRITING

1. Analyze the spirit of affirmation that characterizes the poem. Does Teasdale cast that spirit in acceptable terms and tones?

2. Teasdale once referred to her poetry as "a delicate fabric of bird songs." Examine the relevance of this phrase for "Barter."

Elinor Wylie

PURITAN SONNET

Elinor Wylie (1885–1928) was born in New Jersey and grew up in Philadelphia. She married in 1905 and later left her husband to be with Horace Wylie, whom she married soon after. Her first volume of poetry, Nets to Catch the Wind, *was published in 1921; she published novels and poetry until her death at 43. Though she is the contemporary of T. S. Eliot and Marianne Moore, her poetry has nothing of their revolutionary "newness" of form and expression. Her best work displays a single emotion elegantly stated, as in "Puritan Sonnet," where the traditional form expresses a feeling of historical continuity with her New England roots.*

Down to the Puritan marrow of my bones
There's something in this richness that I hate.
I love the look, austere, immaculate,
Of landscapes drawn in pearly monotones.
There's something in my very blood that owns   5
Bare hills, cold silver on a sky of slate,
A thread of water, churned to milky spate
Streaming through slanted pastures fenced with stones.

I love those skies, thin blue or snowy gray,
Those fields sparse-planted, rendering meager sheaves;   10
That spring, briefer than apple-blossom's breath,
Summer, so much too beautiful to stay,
Swift autumn, like a bonfire of leaves,
And sleepy winter, like the sleep of death.

QUESTIONS

  1. What is Puritanism in the context of the poem? What does it prepare Wylie for?

  2. What is "this richness" of line 2? Does Wylie ever mention it again? Why or why not?

  3. Do any of her descriptions and metaphors for the seasons surprise you? Do you think that they are intentionally commonplace? Explain.

  4. What type of sonnet is this? How does the form govern the progression of meaning?

TOPICS FOR WRITING

  1. Discuss Puritanism and Wylie's attitude toward existence as reflected in the poem.

2. Compare the poem to Keats's "To Autumn" (page 392). Which is the better poem? Why?

3. A critic observed of Wylie: "She seemed to write little out of mood or out of a passing emotion . . . but nearly always out of a complex thought." Apply this observation to "Puritan Sonnet."

D. H. Lawrence

PIANO

David Herbert Lawrence (1885–1930), whose story "The Rocking-Horse Winner" appears on page 238, was born the son of a miner in Eastwood, Nottinghamshire. His mother taught school, and the parental division between the earthy and the cerebral stayed with him his entire life. He was educated at the University of Nottingham and took a teaching job after graduation. He published his first collection of poems in 1909 and his first novel in 1911. In 1912, after breaking engagements to two other women, he met Frieda Weekley, and though she was married and had three children, they almost immediately decided to elope. Lawrence strongly opposed World War I, and after its conclusion, he abandoned the society of Western Europe to make "savage pilgrimages" to Sicily, Ceylon, Australia, and New Mexico. He died of tuberculosis at the age of 44. Lawrence's poetry rarely achieves the gemlike perfection of the finest lyrics. He was more concerned with creating a sense of what he called the "immediate present." "Piano," a powerfully emotional poem, captures the dynamism that Lawrence felt was more valuable than beauty or harmony.

Softly, in the dusk, a woman is singing to me;
Taking me back down the vista of years, till I see
A child sitting under the piano, in the boom of the tingling strings
And pressing the small, poised feet of a mother who smiles as she sings

In spite of myself, the insidious mastery of song   5
Betrays me back, till the heart of me weeps to belong
To the old Sunday evenings at home, with winter outside
And hymns in the cosy parlour, the tinkling piano our guide.

So now it is vain for the singer to burst into clamour
With the great black piano appassionato. The glamour   10
Of childish days is upon me, my manhood is cast
Down in the flood of remembrance, I weep like a child for the past.

QUESTIONS

1. Do you think that the woman in line 1 is actually singing to the poet? Who do you think she is?

2. Who is the child in line 3? When do you learn his identity?

3. Does "the insidious mastery of song" have positive or negative connotations? What bothers Lawrence about song? What do you think Lawrence's opinion of manhood is?

4. Are childhood days usually considered glamorous? With whom are memories of the poet's childhood associated?

5. Why does Lawrence use the verb "belong" in line 6?

TOPICS FOR WRITING

1. Discuss the relationship between the speaker and his mother that is suggested by the poem. What is the poet's attitude toward his past?

2. Write an extended definition of sentimentality in poetry—its use and abuse. Refer to "Piano" to support your assertions.

Ezra Pound

Ezra Pound (1885–1972), previously introduced in this anthology (page 473), was a revolutionary conservative. He wished to reclaim and recover the great literary achievements of all past civilizations, and at the same time, he ordered contemporary writers to "make it new." His knowledge of past literatures was immense, and his influence on the writing styles of many of his peers was strong. (During one heady period, he traded writing lessons for boxing lessons with Ernest Hemingway.) The two selections below show Pound's historical range. "A Virginal" is in the style of the medieval troubador poets, while "The River-Merchant's Wife: A Letter" is a free adaptation of a poem by Li Po (whose Japanese name is Rihaku), a Chinese poet of the eighth century. Yet both poems are more than simply literary curios, because they movingly describe states of love, its excitement and its despair, that are human universals.

Ezra Pound

A VIRGINAL

No, no! Go from me. I have left her lately.
I will not spoil my sheath with lesser brightness,
For my surrounding air hath a new lightness;
Slight are her arms, yet they have bound me straitly
And left me cloaked as with a gauze of aether;   5
As with sweet leaves; as with subtle clearness.
Oh, I have picked up magic in her nearness
To sheathe me half in half the things that sheathe her.
No, no! Go from me. I have still the flavour,
Soft as spring wind that's come from birchen bowers.   10
Green come the shoots, aye April in the branches,
As winter's wound with her sleight hand she staunches,
Hath of the trees a likeness of the savour;
As white their bark, so white this lady's hours.

QUESTIONS

1. In "A Virginal" whom is the speaker addressing? What does he want to stop?

2. What seasons are mentioned in the poem? Why are there so many references to natural processes?

3. Why is the poem called "A Virginal"?

TOPIC FOR WRITING

Analyze the argument developed by the speaker in this poem and its relationship to the sonnet form.

THE RIVER-MERCHANT'S WIFE: A LETTER

While my hair was still cut straight across my forehead
I played about the front gate, pulling flowers.
You came by on bamboo stilts, playing horse,
You walked about my seat, playing with blue plums.
And we went on living in the village of Chokan: 5
Two small people, without dislike or suspicion.

At fourteen I married My Lord you.
I never laughed, being bashful.
Lowering my head, I looked at the wall.
Called to, a thousand times, I never looked back.   10

At fifteen I stopped scowling,
I desired my dust to be mingled with yours
For ever and for ever and for ever.
Why should I climb the look out?
At sixteen you departed,   15
You went into far Ku-to-yen, by the river of swirling eddies,
And you have been gone five months.
The monkeys make sorrowful noise overhead.

You dragged your feet when you went out.
By the gate now, the moss is grown, the different mosses,   20
Too deep to clear them away!
The leaves fall early this autumn, in wind.
The paired butterflies are already yellow with August
Over the grass in the West garden;
They hurt me. I grow older.   25
If you are coming down through the narrows of the river Kiang,
Please let me know beforehand,
And I will come out to meet you
        As far as Cho-fu-Sa.

QUESTIONS

1. Why do you think the poet chose to use a letter motif in this poem? What is the persona of the letter writer? Who is being addressed?

2. What is the temporal organization of this poem? Trace the events described. At age 15, why would the river-merchant's wife stop scowling? What is the significance of the woman's addressing her husband as "My Lord you"?

3. The figurative description most clearly used as a metaphor is the "dust" in lines 12–13. Explain the meaning of these lines.

4. In what ways can line 14 be seen as a pivotal line in the poem's development?

5. How does Pound use line length and end punctuation to reflect the attitudes and emotions of the speaker of the poem? What then are the tonal and thematic effects of the long last sentence?

6. Line 19 ("You dragged your feet when you went out") reveals much about the circumstances of the husband's leaving. Discuss several possible interpretations of this image.

7. Throughout the poem, the river-merchant's wife seems quite devoted to her husband. Why does she qualify her promise to meet him—"As far as Cho-fu-Sa"?

TOPICS FOR WRITING

1. Evaluate Pound's success in imitating an earlier style of poetry. Assess the value of imitation in poetry.

2. Imagist poetry such as Pound's uses few figurative comparisons (similes, metaphors, symbols). Instead, attitudes are communicated directly through images. In "The River-Merchant's Wife: A Letter," Pound relies heavily on natural imagery, as he does in the poem "In a Station of the Metro" (page 474). Select three or four natural images from this poem and analyze how they help reveal the persona's emotional state.

3. Compare and contrast the speakers in "A Virginal" and "The River-Merchant's Wife."

H.D.

PEAR TREE

Hilda Doolittle (1886–1961) was born in Pennsylvania and, like Marianne Moore, attended college at Bryn Mawr. Because of ill health, she did not finish her degree, but she did have the good fortune to meet William Carlos Williams and Ezra Pound (to whom she was briefly engaged). Williams remembers her "provocative indifference to rule and order." She traveled to London in 1911 and renewed her friendship with Pound. With his encouragement, she began to write poems in the imagist style then popular. (Pound's "In a Station of the Metro" (page 473) and Lowell's "The Taxi" (page 566) are two other poems from this school.) Some years after World War I, she moved to Switzerland, where she lived with occasional absences until her death in 1961. She wrote long, episodic poems and some prose (including her memories of her treatment by Sigmund Freud), and carried on diligent correspondence during the later decades of her life. Like an ancient Greek priest, H.D. worships the plentitude of nature in her vision of a succulent pear tree.

Silver dust,
lifted from the earth,
higher than my arms reach,
you have mounted,
O, silver,   5
higher than my arms reach,
you front us with great mass;

no flower ever opened
so staunch a white leaf,
no flower ever parted silver   10
from such rare silver;

O, white pear,
your flower-tufts
thick on the branch
bring summer and ripe fruits   15
in their purple hearts.

QUESTIONS

1. What is suggested by the mention of the reaching arm? by the poet addressing the tree itself (in what is known as an apostrophe)?

2. Why does the speaker say the pear tree will "bring summer and ripe fruit"?

3. What does "silver dust" refer to?

4. What would be lost if the poem were only about the tree, rather than about the poet confronting the tree?

TOPICS FOR WRITING

1. Explain the relationship between the poet and the pear tree; between the poet and natural processes in general.

2. Try to account for the immediate pleasure of a poem like "Pear Tree."

Robinson Jeffers

HURT HAWKS

Robinson Jeffers (1887–1962) was born in Pittsburgh. He was educated in Switzerland, Germany, and America and, after taking an MA in literature, dabbled at the study of medicine, forestry, and law. A small bequest in 1912 left him free to write, and in 1914 he settled with his wife in Carmel,

Robinson Jeffers

on the California coast. His early poetry shows only a
modicum of talent but in 1924 he published Tamar and Other
Poems, *a wild, violent collection that constantly reiterates*
Jeffers's disdain for modern life. Other volumes on the same
pessimistic theme followed, and, though Jeffers never re-
ceived the veneration reserved for Frost or Sandburg, he
developed an intensely loyal following. Jeffers's poetry
showers contempt on human weakness and celebrates
strength which seems to be found only in the natural setting
of the rough Pacific coastline. Jeffers's strange misanthropy
leads him to have much greater sympathy for the wounded
animal in "Hurt Hawks" than he has for humanity.

I

The broken pillar of the wing jags from the clotted shoulder,
The wing trails like a banner in defeat,
No more to use the sky forever but live with famine
And pain a few days: cat nor coyote
Will shorten the week of waiting for death, there is game without talons.   5
He stands under the oak-bush and waits
The lame feet of salvation; at night he remembers freedom
And flies in a dream, the dawns ruin it.
He is strong and pain is worse to the strong, incapacity is worse.
The curs of the day come and torment him   10
At distance, no one but death the redeemer will humble that head,
The intrepid readiness, the terrible eyes.
The wild God of the world is sometimes merciful to those
That ask mercy, not often to the arrogant.
You do not know him, you communal people, or you have forgotten him;   15
Intemperate and savage, the hawk remembers him;
Beautiful and wild, the hawks, and men that are dying, remember him.

II

I'd sooner, except the penalties, kill a man than a hawk; but the great
     redtail
Had nothing left but unable misery   20
From the bone too shattered for mending, the wing that trailed under his
     talons when he moved.
We had fed him six weeks, I gave him freedom,
He wandered over the foreland hill and returned in the evening, asking for
     death,   25
Not like a beggar, still eyed with the old
Implacable arrogance. I gave him the lead gift in the twilight.
     What fell was relaxed,
Owl-downy, soft feminine feathers; but what
Soared: the fierce rush: the night-herons by the flooded river cried fear at its   30
     rising
Before it was quite unsheathed from reality.

QUESTIONS

1. Why does Jeffers refer to hawks in the plural in his title?

2. Why won't cat or coyote end the hawk's life? Explain why Jeffers breaks line 10 where he does.

3. Why does the poet shift from "we" to "I" in the fourth line of the second part?

4. Why does Jeffers use the word "unsheathed" in the last line? What do we usually think of as being unsheathed? What does Jeffers envision when he describes the hawk going "from reality"?

TOPICS FOR WRITING

1. What does Jeffers admire in the hawk? Does he create a viable philosophy of life from his admiration? What is the appeal of Jeffers's vision of life?

2. In another poem, Jeffers writes, "The flower fades to made fruit, the fruit rots to make earth,/Out of mothers, and through the spring exultances, ripeness and decadence; and home to the mother." What theory of history is implied in this passage? Does "Hurt Hawks" support a similar theory? Which period, ripeness or decadence, does Jeffers see himself living in?

3. Compare and contrast Jeffers's view with the one expressed in Yeats's "Leda and the Swan" (page 562).

Marianne Moore

POETRY

Marianne Moore (1887–1972) was born in St. Louis and educated at Bryn Mawr. After teaching at a government Indian school in Pennsylvania, she moved to New York and worked at a variety of literary jobs. Her poetry won a steady stream of awards and prizes. Though Moore's life was uncomplicated and uneventful, her poetry, while at times despairing, never expresses boredom. She lived most of her life like a "church mouse," sharing apartments with her mother. They had little money, and Moore indulged herself with two pleasures. She loved zoos and filled her poetry with exotic fauna. She was also a devotee of baseball, with its "miracles of dexterity." Moore possessed a satiric sense of

*the absurd. When the Ford Motor Company asked her to
name one of their cars, she suggested "Utopian Turtletop."
Moore hated the arrogance and cliquishness that characterizes some of modern poetry. Like T. S. Eliot, she felt that a
poet must be humble. "Poetry" begins with self-reproach,
but ends as an extended apology for poetry and a striking
demonstration of its power to make what Moore called
"piercing glances into the life of things."*

I, too, dislike it: there are things that are important beyond all this fiddle.
  Reading it, however, with a perfect contempt for it, one discovers in it
  after all, a place for the genuine.
      Hands that can grasp, eyes
        that can dilate, hair that can rise   5
           if it must, these things are important not because a

high-sounding interpretation can be put upon them but because they are
  useful. When they become so derivative as to become unintelligible, the
  same thing may be said for all of us, that we
      do not admire what   10
      we cannot understand: the bat
        holding on upside down or in quest of something to
eat, elephants pushing, a wild horse taking a roll, a tireless wolf under
  a tree, the immovable critic twitching his skin like a horse that feels
      a flea, the base–   15
  ball fan, the statistician—
      nor is it valid
        to discriminate against 'business documents and

school-books'; all these phenomena are important. One must make a
  distinction   20
  however: when dragged into prominence by half poets, the result is not
  poetry,
  nor till the poets among us can be
      literalists of
      the imagination—above   25
        insolence and triviality and can present
for inspection, 'imaginary gardens with real toads in them', shall we have
  it. In the meantime, if you demand on the one hand,
  the raw material of poetry in
      all its rawness and   30
      that which is on the other hand
        genuine, you are interested in poetry.

QUESTIONS

  1. What does Moore imply by writing "I, too" in the first line?

  2. In the final collection of Moore's poetry, she cut all of this poem except for the first two lines. Why? Do you think that editors are right in restoring the earlier version as the better one? Why or why not?

3. In the second stanza, there is a rather strange list of things. Why does Moore group them as a discrete set?

4. Why does Moore divide "baseball" by a line break in the second stanza? What is peculiar about the poem's division into stanzas?

5. What does Moore mean by "imaginary gardens with real toads in them"?

TOPICS FOR WRITING

1. What does Moore value in poetry? What are her criteria? Does she care about technique? What does she esteem in poets? Why? Discuss.

2. Select a poem that seems to meet Moore's standards of true poetry. Explain your choice.

Edith Sitwell

TRIO FOR TWO CATS AND A TROMBONE

Edith Sitwell (1887–1964) was born to a wealthy, landed British family. Along with her younger brothers Osbert and Sacheverell, she became one of the most talked about figures within twentieth-century British literary circles. Known as both a dazzling socialite and an eccentric literary light, Sitwell came to so dominate British letters that in 1954 she was created Dame Commander, Order of the British Empire, and was the first poet to be so honored. While her later poems, many inspired by her experience of World War II, often provide poignant insights on and criticisms of the Georgian society within which she lived, it is for the verbal pyrotechnics of her early works that her poetry is most remembered. Moving from her family's rural estate to the fashionable world of London in 1914, Sitwell slanted her first works in opposition to the rural disciplines and reflections of the Georgian poets. In the introduction of the anthology The Canticle of the Rose *(1949), Sitwell writes: "At the time I began to write, a change in the direction of imagery and rhymes in poetry had become necessary,*

Edith Sitwell

*owing to the rhythmical flaccidity, the verbal deadness, the
dead and expected patterns of some of the poetry immediately preceding us." "Trio for Two Cats and a Trombone"
demonstrates Sitwell's concern for verbal eccentricity by
playing the language of erudition against the "common" life
of a prostitute.*

Long steel grass—
The white soldiers pass—
The light is braying like an ass.
See
The tall Spanish jade   5
With hair black as nightshade
Worn as a cockade!
Flee
Her eyes' gasconade
And her gown's parade   10
(As stiff as a brigade).
Tee-hee!
The hard and braying light
Is zebra'd black and white,
It will take away the slight   15
And free
Tinge of the mouth-organ sound,
(Oyster-stall notes) oozing round
Her flounces as they sweep the ground.
The   20
Trumpet and the drum
And the martial cornet come
To make the people dumb—
But we
Won't wait for sly-foot night   25
(Moonlight, watered milk-white, bright)
To make clear the declaration
Of our Paphian vocation,
Beside the castanetted sea,
Where stalks Il Capitano   30
Swaggart braggadocio
Sword and moustachio—
He
Is green as a cassada
And his hair is an armada.   35
To the jade 'Come kiss me harder'
He called across the battlements as she
Heard our voices thin and shrill
As the steely grasses' thrill,
Or the sound of the onycha   40
When the phoca has the pica
In the palace of the Queen Chinee!

QUESTIONS

1. Who are the "two cats"? Why are they "cats"?

2. The poem uses a variety of hard, rigid images in its descriptions. What kind of tone do these images evoke? Why?

3. In describing the "jade," Sitwell uses a series of terms associated with the military. Is this association appropriate? What effect does it have on your understanding of the woman's activities? Why is she a "jade"?

4. What is the role of "Il Capitano" in the poem?

TOPIC FOR WRITING

Sitwell uses a series of arcane words and phrases to construct her story of the jade and the captain. As you read the poem for the first time, how did the words you didn't know affect your reading? Why did Sitwell include them? Look up the words you don't know. Does this change your understanding of the poem? How would the poem be different if it used only familiar language? Is Sitwell justified in writing as she does?

T. S. Eliot

THE LOVE SONG OF J. ALFRED PRUFROCK

Descended from a respected New England family, Thomas Stearns Eliot (1888–1965) was born in St. Louis. An outstanding student, he traveled to Europe on an academic fellowship shortly before the start of World War I. He eventually settled in London, where he quickly established himself as a radically innovative poet and an influential and often acerbic critic. He counted among his friends Virginia Woolf, James Joyce, H.D., and Ezra Pound, all important figures in the literary movement known as modernism. His first volume of poetry, Prufrock and Other Observations, *was published in 1917, but it was his long poem* The Waste Land *(1922) that established him as the leading poet writing in English between the wars and as the most prominent spokesman for what became known as the "lost generation." He wrote comparatively little lyric poetry after World War II, but instead concentrated on verse drama and on*

T. S. Eliot

literary and social criticism. His poetry and plays often show a courageous intelligence in confrontation with a deep, seemingly inescapable unhappiness, and it is this confrontation, translated into a minor key, that finds its first expression in the following poem, written when Eliot was a 23-year-old graduate student at Harvard.

S'io credessi che mia risposta fosse
a persona che mai tornasse al mondo,
questa fiamma staria senza più scosse.
Ma per ció che giammai di questo fondo
non tornó vivo alcun, s'i'odo il vero,
senza tema d'infamia ti rispondo.*

Let us go then, you and I,
When the evening is spread out against the sky
Like a patient etherised upon a table;
Let us go, through certain half-deserted streets,
The muttering retreats   5
Of restless nights in one-night cheap hotels
And sawdust restaurants with oyster-shells:
Streets that follow like a tedious argument
Of insidious intent
To lead you to an overwhelming question . . .   10
Oh, do not ask, 'What is it?'
Let us go and make our visit.

In the room the women come and go
Talking of Michelangelo.

The yellow fog that rubs its back upon the window-panes,   15
The yellow smoke that rubs its muzzle on the window-panes,
Licked its tongue into the corners of the evening,
Lingered upon the pools that stand in drains,
Let fall upon its back the soot that falls from chimneys,
Slipped by the terrace, made a sudden leap,   20
And seeing that it was a soft October night,
Curled once about the house, and fell asleep.

And indeed there will be time
For the yellow smoke that slides along the street
Rubbing its back upon the window-panes;   25
There will be time, there will be time
To prepare a face to meet the faces that you meet;
There will be time to murder and create,
And time for all the works and days of hands

---

*Epigraph: "If I thought my answer were to one who would never return to the world, this flame would shake no more; but since no one did ever return alive from this depth, if what I hear be true, without fear of infamy I answer you." (Inferno 27:61–66)

The Love Song of J. Alfred Prufrock

That lift and drop a question on your plate;   30
Time for you and time for me,
And time yet for a hundred indecisions,
And for a hundred visions and revisions,
Before the taking of a toast and tea.

In the room the women come and go   35
Talking of Michelangelo.

And indeed there will be time
To wonder, 'Do I dare?' and, 'Do I dare?'
Time to turn back and descend the stair,
With a bald spot in the middle of my hair—   40
(They will say: 'How his hair is growing thin!')
My morning coat, my collar mounting firmly to the chin,
My necktie rich and modest, but asserted by a simple pin—
(They will say: "But how his arms and legs are thin!')
Do I dare   45
Disturb the universe?
In a minute there is time
For decisions and revisions which a minute will reverse.

For I have known them all already, known them all—
Have known the evenings, mornings, afternoons,   50
I have measured out my life with coffee spoons;
I know the voices dying with a dying fall
Beneath the music from a farther room.
    So how should I presume?

And I have known the eyes already, known them all—   55
The eyes that fix you in a formulated phrase,
And when I am formulated, sprawling on a pin,
When I am pinned and wriggling on the wall,
Then how should I begin
To spit out all the butt-ends of my days and ways?   60
    And how should I presume?

And I have known the arms already, known them all—
Arms that are braceleted and white and bare
(But in the lamplight, downed with light brown hair!)
Is it perfume from a dress   65
That makes me so digress?
Arms that lie along a table, or wrap about a shawl.
    And should I then presume?
    And how should I begin?
        .   .   .   .   .

Shall I say, I have gone at dusk through narrow streets   70
And watched the smoke that rises from the pipes
Of lonely men in shirt-sleeves, leaning out of windows? . . .

T. S. Eliot

I should have been a pair of ragged claws
Scuttling across the floors of silent seas.
    . . . . .

And the afternoon, the evening, sleeps so peacefully!   75
Smoothed by long fingers,
Asleep . . . tired . . . or it malingers,
Stretched on the floor, here beside you and me.
Should I, after tea and cakes and ices,
Have the strength to force the moment to its crisis?   80
But though I have wept and fasted, wept and prayed,
Though I have seen my head (grown slightly bald) brought in upon a platter,
I am no prophet—and here's no great matter;
I have seen the moment of my greatness flicker,
And I have seen the eternal Footman hold my coat, and snicker,   85
And in short, I was afraid.

And would it have been worth it, after all,
After the cups, the marmalade, the tea,
Among the porcelain, among some talk of you and me,
Would it have been worth while,   90
To have bitten off the matter with a smile,
To have squeezed the universe into a ball
To roll it towards some overwhelming question,
To say: 'I am Lazarus, come from the dead,
Come back to tell you all, I shall tell you all'—   95
If one, settling a pillow by her head,
    Should say: 'That is not what I meant at all.
    That is not it, at all.'
And would it have been worth it, after all,
Would it have been worth while,   100
After the sunsets and the dooryards and the sprinkled streets,
After the novels, after the teacups, after the skirts that trail along the floor—
And this, and so much more?—
It is impossible to say just what I mean!
But as if a magic lantern threw the nerves in patterns on a screen: 105
Would it have been worth while
If one, settling a pillow or throwing off a shawl,
And turning toward the window, should say:
    'That is not it at all,
    That is not what I meant, at all.'   110
    . . . . .

No! I am not Prince Hamlet, nor was meant to be;
Am an attendant lord, one that will do
To swell a progress, start a scene or two,
Advise the prince; no doubt, an easy tool,   115
Deferential, glad to be of use,
Politic, cautious, and meticulous;
Full of high sentence, but a bit obtuse;
At times, indeed, almost ridiculous—
Almost, at times, the Fool.

I grow old . . . I grow old . . .   120
I shall wear the bottoms of my trousers rolled.

Shall I part my hair behind? Do I dare to eat a peach?
I shall wear white flannel trousers, and walk upon the beach.
I have heard the mermaids singing, each to each.

I do not think that they will sing to me.   125

I have seen them riding seaward on the waves
Combing the white hair of the waves blown back
When the wind blows the water white and black.

We have lingered in the chambers of the sea
By sea-girls wreathed with seaweed red and brown   130
Till human voices wake us, and we drown.

QUESTIONS

   1. Thinking about the whole poem, what can you infer about Prufrock's situation and character? What is your opinion of him as a person? Is he likable? admirable? How does your opinion of him differ from his own opinion of himself?

   2. Eliot refers to this poem as an "observation," but the poem takes the form of a dramatic monologue. In what sense is Prufrock observed and by whom? Is he judged?

   3. Is the "you" of Eliot's first line meant to represent another character in the poem? the generalized reader? Does the "you" appear again in the poem? Why does Prufrock refer to "us" in the second to last line of the poem?

   4. At the beginning of the last section, Prufrock says, "I am not Prince Hamlet, nor was meant to be." If you have read Shakespeare's play, explain how Prufrock differs from Hamlet, but also how he is in some ways similar. Eliot, speaking of Hamlet in an essay, refers to "the buffoonery of an emotion which can find no outlet in action." Does this description also apply to Prufrock?

TOPICS FOR WRITING

   1. The poem is called a "love song," but Prufrock is not singing to any individual woman. What is his attitude toward women? toward sexuality? Would you call him a misogynist?

   2. Prufrock refers to an "overwhelming question." Consider the fifteen questions asked by Prufrock in the poem. Do you find them overwhelming? Why does Prufrock ask so many questions? Do the questions become more serious as the poem progresses? What do you think Prufrock's "overwhelming question" refers to?

John Crowe Ransom

CAPTAIN CARPENTER

John Crowe Ransom (1888–1974), a minister's son, was born in Tennessee. He studied at Vanderbilt, and after taking an advanced degree at Oxford, he returned to Vanderbilt to teach. At Vanderbilt he helped form a group of southern writers (known as the Fugitives) who wished to preserve the values of the Southern agrarian society against the twin dangers of liberalism and industrialism. In 1937 he moved to Kenyon College, where for many years he edited the Kenyon Review. His later career as an eminent teacher and critic overshadows the relatively small amount of poetry that he wrote, mostly in the 1920s. As a devout Southerner, he felt the life he knew and loved was slipping away, and his poems often turn upon a noble but doomed quest. "Captain Carpenter" with its archaic ballad form and awkwardly comic diction tells the pathetic yet funny story of a man trying against all odds to live by an outmoded code of courtesy and honor.

Captain Carpenter rose up in his prime
Put on his pistols and went riding out
But had got wellnigh nowhere at that time
Till he fell in with ladies in a rout.

It was a pretty lady and all her train   5
That played with him so sweetly but before
An hour she'd taken a sword with all her main
And twined him of his nose for evermore.

Captain Carpenter mounted up one day
And rode straightway into a stranger rogue   10
That looked unchristian but be that as may
The Captain did not wait upon prologue.

But drew upon him out of his great heart
The other swung against him with a club
And cracked his two legs at the shinny part   15
And let him roll and stick like any tub.

Captain Carpenter rode many a time
From male and female took he sundry harms
He met the wife of Satan crying "I'm
The she-wolf bids you shall bear no more arms."   20

Their strokes and counters whistled in the wind
I wish he had delivered half his blows
But where she should have made off like a hind
The bitch bit off his arms at the elbows.

And Captain Carpenter parted with his ears   25
To a black devil that used him in this wise
O Jesus ere his threescore and ten years
Another had plucked out his sweet blue eyes.

Captain Carpenter got up on his roan
And sallied from the gate in hell's despite   30
I heard him asking in the grimmest tone
If any enemy yet there was to fight?

"To any adversary it is fame
If he risk to be wounded by my tongue
Or burnt in two beneath my red heart's flame   35
Such are the perils he is cast among.

"But if he can he has a pretty choice
From an anatomy with little to lose
Whether he cut my tongue and take my voice
Or whether it be my round red heart he choose."   40

It was the neatest knave that ever was seen
Stepping in perfume from his lady's bower
Who at this word put in his merry mien
And fell on Captain Carpenter like a tower.

I would not knock old fellows in the dust   45
But there lay Captain Carpenter on his back
His weapons were the old heart in his bust
And a blade shook between rotten teeth alack.

The rogue in scarlet and grey soon knew his mind
He wished to get his trophy and depart   50
With gentle apology and touch refined
He pierced him and produced the Captain's heart.

God's mercy rest on Captain Carpenter now
I thought him Sirs an honest gentleman
Citizen husband soldier and scholar enow   55
Let jangling kites eat of him if they can.

But God's deep curses follow after those
That shore him of his goodly nose and ears
His legs and strong arms at the two elbows
And eyes that had not watered seventy years.   60

The curse of hell upon the sleek upstart
That got the Captain finally on his back
And took the red red vitals of his heart
And made the kites to whet their beaks clack clack.

QUESTIONS

1. Can you relate the hero's name or title to any other aspect of the poem?

2. Can you deduce where or when the poem is set by the title, the weapons used, or the poem's narrative?

3. Examine the rhymes of the poem. Are any of them forced? Are certain word choices made simply to produce a rhyme? How do these "flaws" affect the poem? Would a deft poetic performance be inappropriate?

4. Does the narrator intrude his own value judgments at any point? What are they? How do they suggest that the poem is more serious than it first appears?

5. Do you, as a reader, identify with Captain Carpenter's plight? Why do you do so? Does the narrator express a feeling of sympathetic identification with his hero?

TOPICS FOR WRITING

1. Analyze the ideal of heroism presented in the poem. Is it consistent throughout?

2. One critic likens this poem to "a case history of absurdity." Analyze this proposition.

Claude McKay

OUTCAST

Though Claude McKay (1890–1948), previously introduced in this anthology (see page 425), taught himself much about English and European literature, as well as political theory, the strength of his poetry derives from its roots in black experience. It is no accident that McKay wrote his first two volumes of poetry in Jamaican dialect. As a black man speaking to other black men, McKay helped start a tradition of black poetry that blossomed into the Harlem Renaissance, which included Jean Toomer and Langston Hughes. McKay always mourned the loss of the African tribal customs and songs, which he had learned secondhand from his father, but in such a justly bitter poem as "Outcast," he helped reestablish a coherent black cultural tradition that might, in part, substitute for all that had been lost in transit.

Outcast

For the dim regions whence my fathers came
My spirit, bondaged by the body, longs.
Words felt, but never heard, my lips would frame;
My soul would sing forgotten jungle songs.
I would go back to darkness and to peace,   5
But the great western world holds me in fee,
And I may never hope for full release
While to its alien gods I bend my knee.
Something in me is lost, forever lost,
Some vital thing has gone out of my heart,   10
And I must walk the way of life a ghost
Among the sons of earth, a thing apart.

For I was born, far from my native clime,
Under the white man's menace, out of time.

QUESTIONS

1. What is the poet's attitude toward his fate? What alternatives, if any, does he find?

2. This is a poem almost entirely of mood. Does it contain many clear visual images? Does McKay use extensive figurative language (personification, simile, metaphor, and so on)? Explain.

3. Why is "Outcast" so poetically stark?

4. What is the "vital thing" that the poet feels he has lost? Why can't he be more specific in his description?

TOPICS FOR WRITING

1. Most poetry has a social function. It contributes to the communal order by affirming or correcting the values of the society in which it is written. Discuss the social function of McKay's poem.

2. Evaluate McKay's success in using the sonnet form to advance his thesis. Examine carefully the effect of the couplet at the end of the sonnet.

Edna St. Vincent Millay

WILD SWANS

Edna St. Vincent Millay (1892–1950) was born in Maine. As a poet, she was something of a child prodigy, writing her first poem at age 5 and submitting work regularly to St. Nicholas Magazine. She graduated from Vassar in 1917 with an established reputation for her poem "Renascence" and local infamy for her headstrong baiting of the college administrators. (She repeatedly dared the president to expel her.) She moved to Greenwich Village in New York, a safe harbor for rebellious youth, and, throughout the twenties and thirties, published regularly. In 1923 she won the Pulitzer Prize. Though deeply immersed in contemporary life, Millay's poetry often seeks to be timeless. "Wild Swans" gives no internal clues to its date of composition, and though it is about unhappiness, the poem is not peculiarly modern in its despair.

I looked in my heart while the wild swans went over.
And what did I see I had not seen before?
Only a question less or a question more;
Nothing to match the flight of wild birds flying.
Tiresome heart, forever living and dying,   5
House without air, I leave you and lock your door.
Wild swans, come over the town, come over
The town again, trailing your legs and crying!

QUESTIONS

1. Most swans, we would assume, would be wild. Why does Millay use and repeat the adjective in her poem?

2. What does "a question less or a question more" refer to? What is better about the vision of wild swans?

3. What is the "house without air"?

TOPICS FOR WRITING

1. Write a prose paraphrase of the poem. What is it that nature offers the unhappy poet in this situation?

2. With the publication of *A Few Figs and Thistles* in 1920, Millay became the prototype of the emancipated woman. What new consciousness appears in "Wild Swans"?

Wilfred Owen

ANTHEM FOR DOOMED YOUTH

Wilfred Owen (1893–1918), introduced previously in this anthology (page 366), died in the last week of the war whose horror he described so acutely. In a letter from the front, he speaks of "hideous landscapes, vile noises, foul languages . . . everything unnatural, broken, blasted; the distortion of the dead . . . the most execrable sights on earth. In poetry we call them the most glorious." Yet Owen's poetry did nothing to glorify the fighting; instead, it encouraged a healthy distrust of the slogans and beliefs that kept men at war. For Owen the only beautiful thing in war is not victory but the abbreviated physical sense of comradeship between the soldiers. Though his "Anthem for Doomed Youth" must use ironic substitutes for the traditional funeral accessories, Owen's sense of tragic bereavement is no less sincere.

What passing-bells for these who die as cattle?
  Only the monstrous anger of the guns.

  Only the stuttering rifles' rapid rattle
Can patter out their hasty orisons.
No mockeries now for them; no prayers nor bells,   5
  Nor any voice of mourning save the choirs,—
The shrill, demented choirs of wailing shells;
  And bugles calling for them from sad shires.

What candles may be held to speed them all?
  Not in the hands of boys, but in their eyes   10
Shall shine the holy glimmers of good-byes.
  The pallor of girls' brows shall be their pall;
Their flowers the tenderness of patient minds,
And each slow dusk a drawing-down of blinds.

QUESTIONS

1. To "die as cattle" is a profoundly repellent image. Why does Owen begin with it? Are other images in the poem similar? Why or why not?

2. What is the one idea behind all of Owen's examples? Why does he use so many?

3. Can you tell that Owen is a soldier, is himself one of the doomed youths? Why is Owen's achievement of impersonality so appropriate and so difficult to maintain?

4. Why does Owen end the poem with references to dusk and the lowering of blinds? What are these two things potential metaphors for?

TOPICS FOR WRITING

1. Compare the poem with the excerpt from Owen's letter quoted in the introduction. Which is more visual? Which is more moving? Why?

2. Analyze the visual and auditory imagery in the poem, and its relationship to mood and theme.

E. E. Cummings

E. E. Cummings (1894–1963), previously introduced in the anthology (page 426), had little respect for the conventions and assumptions of modern life. His home had no radio or telephone, and his poetry constantly attacks the political and economic ideologies of his day. His replacement for these systems of belief, however, is curiously old-fashioned and American. Cummings believed in individualism, physical love, and the sanctity of small children. His poem "pity this busy monster,manunkind," exemplifies Cummings's revulsion at industrial progress; "in Just—" presents a childish world of innocence violated by a strange, older intruder.

IN JUST—

in Just—
spring   when the world is mud-
Luscious the little
lame balloonman

Whistles   far   and wee   5

and eddieandbill come
running from marbles and
piracies and it's
spring

when the world is puddle-wonderful   10

the queer
old balloonman whistles
far   and   wee
and bettyandisbel come dancing

from hop-scotch and jump-rope and   15

it's

spring
and
   the
      goat-footed   20

balloonMan   whistles
far
and
wee

QUESTIONS

1. What are Cummings's feelings about spring?

2. How does the refrain of the balloon man's whistle help to structure the poem?

3. What mythological allusion is Cummings making when he tells us that the balloon man is "goat-footed"?

4. Cummings is famous for his orthographic innovations. Find words and phrases that are laid out on the page in unconventional format. What does Cummings gain by writing such things as "balloonMan" and "bettyandisbel"? Why is visual effect important in a typical Cummings poem?

TOPIC FOR WRITING

Write an essay on the structure of "in Just—," showing how the poem explores the phenomenon of spring in terms of time, space, sight, and sound.

PITY THIS BUSY
MONSTER, MANUNKIND

pity this busy monster,manunkind,

not. Progress is a comfortable disease:
your victim(death and life safely beyond)

plays with the bigness of his littleness
—electrons deify one razorblade   5
into a mountainrange;lenses extend

unwish through curving wherewhen till unwish
returns on its unself.
                    A world of made
is not a world of born—pity poor flesh   10

and trees,poor stars and stones,but never this
fine specimen of hypermagical

ultraomnipotence. We doctors know

a hopeless case if—listen:there's a hell
of a good universe next door;let's go   15

QUESTIONS

1. What three words can you decode from "manunkind"? What is the relationship among them? Why is man a monster?

2. Explain Cummings's allusions to the electron microscope and to razor blade ads. What is he saying about our relationship to the universe?

3. How does the "not" in the second line change the meaning of the first line?

4. Why does Cummings call progress a "comfortable disease"?

5. Analyze Cummings's use of negatives. What is the effect?

TOPICS FOR WRITING

1. Explain Cummings's vision of humankind in "pity this busy monster,manunkind."

2. In what sense, if any, is Cummings a "primitive"? Refer to the two poems to support your ideas.

3. The critic Helen Vendler has said that Cummings's mind "was abysmally short on ideas." What poets seem to you to be long on ideas? Discuss this alleged flaw in relationship to the two above poems.

Jean Toomer

GEORGIA DUSK

*Jean Toomer (1894–1967) was born in Washington, D.C., and
grew up in the household of his maternal grandfather, a
prominent black politician during Reconstruction, after the
Civil War. A restless student, Toomer studied five different
subjects at five different colleges and never completed his
degree. Like Carl Sandburg, he spent many years wandering
in America. He returned to Washington, D.C., and began to
publish his poetry in various literary magazines. His work
Cane (1923), which combined poetry, drama, and short
fiction, established his reputation, and he became closely
associated with other writers of the Harlem Renaissance.
Though he continued to write in his later years, much of his
work remains unpublished, marred by the distracting influence of the Russian mystic Gurdjieff. Toomer is a poet of the
land, and his best work explores the complicated interaction
of men and women with nature, as we see in the poem
"Georgia Dusk."*

The sky, lazily disdaining to pursue
  The setting sun, too indolent to hold
  A lengthened tournament for flashing gold,
Passively darkens for night's barbecue,

A feast of moon and men and barking hounds,   5
  An orgy for some genius of the South
  With blood-hot eyes and cane-lipped scented mouth,
Surprised in making folk-songs from soul sounds.

The sawmill blows its whistle, buzz-saws stop,
  And silence breaks the bud of knoll and hill,   10
  Soft settling pollen where plowed lands fulfill
Their early promise of a bumper crop.

Smoke from the pyramidal sawdust pile
  Curls up, blue ghosts of trees, tarrying low
  Where only chips and stumps are left to show   15
The solid proof of former domicile.

Meanwhile, the men, with vestiges of pomp,
  Race memories of king and caravan,
  High priests, an ostrich, and a juju-man,
Go singing through the footpaths of the swamp.   20

Their voices rise . . the pine trees are guitars,
  Strumming, pine-needles fall like sheets of rain . .
  Their voices rise . . the chorus of the cane
Is caroling a vesper to the stars . .

O singers, resinous and soft your songs   25
  Give virgin lips to cornfield concubines,
  Above the sacred whisper of the pines,
Bring dreams of Christ to dusky cane-lipped throngs.

QUESTIONS

1. What does Toomer mean by "An orgy for some genius of the South"?

2. Who are the men in the poem? How can you tell?

3. What sexual and romantic imagery do you find in the poem? Explain why it is there.

4. How does the poem change in the last stanza?

TOPICS FOR WRITING

1. Analyze the relationship between humanity and nature in the poem. How is this relationship different in other poems of nature that you have read?

2. W. E. B. DuBois, in reviewing *Cane,* asserted: "The world of black folk will some day arise and point to Jean Toomer as a writer who first dared to emancipate the colored world from the conventions of sex." Analyze this statement in the context of "Georgia Dusk."

Babette Deutsch

NATURAL LAW

Babette Deutsch (1895–1982), introduced earlier in this text (page 367), combines the many fields of her experience in her poetic encounters with the world. The poem presented here, "Natural Law," illustrates the way in which such a complex interweaving of experience—especially the experience of being a woman—can lead to questions about the difference between the nature of existence and what others want us to believe that nature to be.

If you press a stone with your finger,
Sir Isaac Newton observed,
The finger is also
Pressed by the stone.

But can a woman, pressed by memory's finger,   5
In the deep night, alone,
Of her softness move
The airy thing
That presses upon her
With the whole weight of love? This   10
Sir Isaac said nothing of.

QUESTIONS

1. The first sentence of the poem presents a description of the famous Newtonian law of the conservation of energy ("For every action there is an equal and opposite reaction"). How is this "poetic" description different from a "scientific" description? What effect does this different use of language have on the way you understand Newton's law?

2. Why does the poem's speaker ask explicitly if a *woman* fits into this Newtonian explanation of the world? How would Newton explain the "airy thing/That presses upon her"? Could he?

TOPIC FOR WRITING

The poem consists of three sentences. Compare and contrast the use of imagery, diction, and tone in each sentence. How are the sentences related? How is the poem organized? Why does it conclude with a question?

Louise Bogan

CASSANDRA

Louise Bogan (1897–1970) was born in Maine and attended Boston University for one year. She lived most of her life in New York City, where she supported herself (sometimes just barely) by writing stories, articles, translations, and book reviews for The New Republic, The Nation, The New Yorker, *and other magazines. She published her first volume of poetry in 1923. Though she wrote many things simply to pay the bills, she was a perfectionist about her poetry. She reduced the contents of her final collection,* The Blue Estuar-

Louise Bogan

ies: Poems 1923–1968, *to only 105 poems, her lifetime's work. Often her poetry depicts the situation of women and asserts the need for a separate feminine view of the world. In the dramatic monologue "Cassandra" the speaker denies herself the traditional role of motherhood for the higher, more painful calling of prophet.*

To me, one silly task is like another.
I bare the shambling tricks of lust and pride.
This flesh will never give a child its mother,—
Song, like a wing, tears through my breast, my side,
And madness chooses out my voice again,   5
Again. I am the chosen no hand saves:
The shrieking heaven lifted over men,
Not the dumb earth, wherein they set their graves.

QUESTIONS

1. Who is Cassandra in Greek mythology? Why is she an appropriate figure for woman?

2. Does the "shrieking heaven" or "dumb earth" sound attractive or pleasant? What does the phrase "earth mother" signify? How is Bogan playing off the normative concept of "earth mother"?

3. Explain the line "And madness chooses out my voice again." How is "chosen" used in the next line?

4. Is this a happy poem? Explain.

TOPICS FOR WRITING

1. Does the speaker feel involved in the world? Is her aloofness a burden or a value? Why does she think everything a "silly task"?

2. Discuss the conflicting desires for motherhood and self-fulfillment in the poem.

3. A critic, Paul Christenson, has said of Bogan: "The essential charm of her best work is the quiet, feminine perception she expresses in her strict, tightly framed forms." Test this quotation against "Cassandra." Be certain to deal with the question of "feminine perception."

Melvin B. Tolson

A LEGEND OF VERSAILLES

Melvin B. Tolson (1900–   ) was born in Moberly, Missouri. Surveying his life in an interview entitled "A Poet's Odyssey," he said: "Tennyson's protagonist says in "Ulysses," 'Much I have seen and know!' And again, 'I am a part of all that I have met. . . .'—as shoeshine boy, stevedore, soldier, janitor, packinghouse worker, cook on a railroad, waiter in a beachfront hotel, boxer, actor, football coach, director of drama, lecturer for the NAACP, organizer of sharecroppers' unions, teacher, father of Ph.D.s, poet laureate of a foreign country, painter, newspaper columnist, four-time mayor of a town, facer of mobs, I have made my way in the world since I was twelve years old." Tolson's wide experience as a black man in American culture led him to write poetry that challenged oppression wherever it occurred. Though his works are written in a very standard English (something poet and critic Alan Tate was to praise him for), his perspective is entirely one of a man marginalized by his society. "A Legend of Versailles" focuses on one historical moment in order to demonstrate Tolson's concern for the way the larger society contradicts its values with its actions.

Lloyd George and Woodrow Wilson and Clemenceau—
The Big Three: England, America, and France—
Met at Versailles. The Tiger ached to know
About the myth to end war's dominance.

"One moment, gentlemen," the Tiger said,   5
"Do you really want a lasting peace?" And then
Lloyd George assented with his shaggy head
And Woodrow Wilson, nodding, chafed his chin.

"The price of such a peace is great. We must give
Up secret cartels, spheres of power and trade;   10
Tear down our tariff walls; let lesser breeds live
As equals; scrap the empires we have made."

The gentlemen protested, "You go too far."
The Tiger shouted, "You don't mean peace, but war!"

QUESTIONS

1. The first two lines of the poem identify three political leaders with the three superpowers after World War I. Why are these countries identified with their political leaders? Are political leaders the "essence" of a nation?

2. Why is the desire to end war's dominance a "myth"? Why is it "the Tiger" that aches to know this myth? Who is the Tiger?

3. What are the conditions for peace? Why are they unacceptable?

TOPIC FOR WRITING

This poem uses an historical event—the Versailles peace conference—to make a comment on the condition of the world. How is this account different from an account you might find in a history text? in a newspaper from the time? Which is more interpretive? Which gets closer to the "truth"?

Sterling A. Brown

SOUTHERN ROAD

Sterling Brown (1901–   ) was born in Washington, D.C. He received one of the best educations of the writers in the Harlem Renaissance, graduating from Williams and earning an MA from Harvard University. Brown taught for many years at Howard University. His main contribution to scholarship has been his recording of the lyrics of blues and spirituals and his helping these forms earn standing as legitimate forms of artistic expression. His study of spirituals and the blues influences his own poetry. "Southern Road," the title poem from his first collection (1932), seems at first simply a song recorded on a chain gang, but closer inspection reveals that Brown has embroidered the primitive ballad form with a care for language and narration that makes the inhumane situation and the sense of protest more explicit and more moving.

Swing dat hammer—hunh—
Steady, bo';
Swing dat hammer—hunh—
Steady, bo';
Ain't no rush, bebby,   5
Long ways to go.

Burner tore his—hunh—
Black heart away;
Burner tore his—hunh—
Black heart away;
Got me life, bebby,   10
An' a day.

Gal's on Fifth Street—hunh—
Son done gone;
Gal's on Fifth Street—hunh—   15

Son done gone;
Wife's in de ward, bebby,
Babe's not bo'n.

My ole man died—hunh—
Cussin' me;   20
My ole man died—hunh—
Cussin' me;
Ole lady rocks, bebby,
Huh misery.

Doubleshackled—hunh—   25
Guard behin';
Doubleshackled—hunh—
Guard behin';
Ball an' chain, bebby,
On my min'.   30

White man tells me—hunh—
Damn yo' soul;
White man tells me—hunh—
Damn yo' soul;
Got no need, bebby,   35
To be tole.

Chain gang nevah—hunh—
Let me go;
Chain gang nevah—hunh—
Let me go;   40
Po' los' boy, bebby,
Evahmo'. . . .

QUESTIONS

1. What does "hunh" signal throughout the poem?

2. The repetition of the first line of each stanza mimics the device blues singers use to give themselves time to make up the next line. Why does Brown adopt this system of repetition? What mood does it create?

3. Is this a song of protest? of racial protest? Cite details from the poem to support your answer.

TOPIC FOR WRITING

Analyze the relationship of the blues, folk epics, and ballads to the form and content of "Southern Road."

Langston Hughes

As a young man, Langston Hughes (1902–1967), previously introduced in the anthology (page 369), was told, "Hide and write and study and think." He followed that advice all his life, and his poetry is more detached and analytical than angry and rebellious. He does not express the intense bitterness of a poet like Claude McKay. Hughes knew his world and understood its despair but wished to render the beauty in it as well. He found such beauty in relationships with nature and antiquity, as in the poem "The Negro Speaks of Rivers." He also discovered beauty in blues and jazz, which he recreated in "Evenin' Air Blues." Hughes might have been describing his own poetry when he explained the paradox of the blues. "The mood of the Blues is almost always despondency, but when they were sung people laugh." His most fiercely apocalyptic poem, "Harlem," gains force because so much of Hughes's other poetry is well tempered and at peace.

EVENIN' AIR BLUES

Folks, I come up North
Cause they told me de North was fine.
I come up North
Cause they told me de North was fine.
Been up here six months—   5
I'm about to lose my mind.

This mornin' for breakfast
I chawed de mornin' air.
This mornin' for breakfast
Chawed de mornin' air.   10
But this evenin' for supper,
I got evenin' air to spare.

Believe I'll do a little dancin'
Just to drive my blues away—
A little dancin''   15
To drive my blues away,
Cause when I'm dancin'
De blues forgets to stay.

But if you was to ask me
How de blues they come to be,   20
Says if you was to ask me
How de blues they come to be—
You wouldn't need to ask me:
Just look at me and see!

QUESTIONS

1. What definition of the blues does Hughes offer in this poem?

2. Compare "Evenin' Air Blues" with "Southern Road" (page 610). Explain how both benefit from the blues idiom.

3. Explain the types of humor found in the poem.

THE NEGRO SPEAKS
OF RIVERS

I've known rivers:
I've known rivers ancient as the world and older than the flow of human
    blood in human veins.

My soul has grown deep like the rivers.

I bathed in the Euphrates when dawns were young.   5
I built my hut near the Congo and it lulled me to sleep.
I looked upon the Nile and raised the pyramids above it.
I heard the singing of the Mississippi when Abe Lincoln went down to New
    Orleans, and I've seen its muddy bosom turn all golden in the sunset.

I've known rivers: 10
Ancient, dusky rivers.

My soul has grown deep like the rivers.

QUESTIONS

1. What is the historical point of the references to the Euphrates, the Congo, the Nile, and the Mississippi in "The Negro Speaks of Rivers"?

2. What does Hughes mean by "I've known rivers"? Isn't everyone familiar with rivers? What is the difference?

3. Hughes was one of the first poets to use "soul" in a special sense. What is that sense in the poem?

Langston Hughes

HARLEM

What happens to a dream deferred?
    Does it dry up
    like a raisin in the sun?
    Or fester like a sore—
    And then run?   5

    Does it stink like rotten meat?
    Or crust and sugar over—
    like a syrupy sweet?

    Maybe it just sags
    like a heavy load.   10

    Or does it explode?

QUESTIONS

1. What is the relationship between the title, "Harlem", and the rest of the poem?

2. Why does Hughes choose a raisin for his simile? Why wouldn't another fruit do as well?

3. Why does Hughes frame "Harlem" as a series of questions? How would it change the poem if it were a series of statements?

TOPICS FOR WRITING

1. Discuss the conflict between the individual and society in the three poems.

2. Kenneth Kinnamon observes of Hughes that "the three major categories of his poems relate to black music, poems of racial protest, and poems of racial affirmation." Write an essay on this topic, examining whether these poems fit these categories.

3. The critic David Daiches observed in 1949: "For Mr. Hughes, the idiom of poetry is valuable only to the degree that it pins down a situation and draws it to the attention of his readers. The ultimate meaning, the subtler vision of reality, the oblique insight into man's personality and man's fate are not for him; he has a more urgent and immediate problem, to project the living American Negro onto the page." Do you agree or disagree? Refer to the three poems to support your response.

Stevie Smith

THE WEAK MONK

Stevie Smith (1902–1971) was born Florence Margaret Smith in Tarkshire, England. Her nickname, "Stevie," refer- ring to her shortness, was taken from the name of a popular jockey at the time. Until 1953, Smith worked in a London publisher's office, after which she devoted her time to writ- ing and to broadcasts on the BBC. Known for her personal wit and charm as as well as for the wit and charm of her verse, poet and novelist Smith brought to her poetry a sense of the comic that pierced through the surface of reality. Often appearing at first irrelevant or childish because they rely on fairy tales, nursery rhymes, or childlike visions, Smith's self-illustrated poems assume a naive pose in order to probe the "agonies" of existence. Her poem "The Weak Monk," provided below, demonstrates the comic seriousness of her work by combining a light verse style with the ponderousness of theological debate.

The monk sat in his den,
He took the mighty pen
And wrote "Of God and Men."

One day the thought struck him
It was not according to Catholic doctrine;   5
His blood ran dim.

He wrote till he was ninety years old,
Then he shut the book with a clasp of gold
And buried it under the sheep fold.

He'd enjoyed it so much, he loved to plod,   10
And he thought he'd a right to expect that God
Would rescue his book alive from the sod.

Of course it rotted in the snow and rain;
No one will ever know now what he wrote of God and men.
For this the monk is to blame.   15

QUESTIONS

1. What is it that the monk is writing? Why might it violate "Catholic doctrine"?

2. Why does the book have a "clasp of gold"? Is it significant that he buries it under the "sheep fold"?

3. What is wrong with the monk's enjoyment? Why is he wrong to expect a resurrection of his work?

4. Who is blaming the monk? Who can call him weak?

TOPICS FOR WRITING

1. Smith uses a poetic form known as *terza rima*—the same form Dante used to write the *Divine Comedy*—to evoke her description of the weak monk. How is this form appropriate to her subject matter? How does it contribute to the tone and tempo of the poem? Is the triadic form appropriate to a "Christian" subject? How does a poem's "form" contribute to its "meaning"?

2. Evaluate Smith's comic vision in this poem.

Countee Cullen

INCIDENT

Countee Cullen (1903–1946), previously introduced in this anthology (page 463), wanted poetry in general and his poetry in particular to be free of social and political import. He found such aloofness impossible to maintain. "In spite of myself, I find that I am actuated by a strong sense of race consciousness. This grows upon me." His personal consciousness of race led him to be more bewildered than rebellious when faced with racial hatred or discrimination. "Incident" records a minor event that painfully reverberates in tones more sorrowful than angry.

(FOR ERIC WALROND)

Once riding in old Baltimore,
  Heart-filled, head-filled with glee,
I saw a Baltimorean
  Keep looking straight at me.

Now I was eight and very small,   5
  And he was no whit bigger,
And so I smiled, but he poked out
  His tongue, and called me, "Nigger."

I saw the whole of Baltimore
  From May until December;   10
Of all the things that happened there
  That's all that I remember.

QUESTIONS

1. Why does Cullen use such a bland title?

2. How does Cullen convey the human cost of the encounter?

3. Arna Bontemps stated that "Cullen's verses skip; those by Hughes glide." What might he have meant by this observation?

4. Does "protest poetry" become dated, or can it remain universal? What is the status of Cullen's poem?

TOPICS FOR WRITING

1. Compare this poem with Lawrence's "Piano" (page 580). How do the two attitudes toward childhood differ?

2. Investigate variations in tone in "Incident," "Outcast" (page 598), and "Evenin' Air Blues" (page 612).

Kay Boyle

FOR MARIANNE MOORE'S BIRTHDAY

Kay Boyle (1903–) was born in Minnesota, and after studying music and architecture, she settled in France with her husband, a French citizen. After her divorce, she remained in Europe working as a foreign correspondent and writing novels and short stories. She has taught at many American universities and won numerous awards for her work. Though the bulk of her work is fiction (page 180), she has said that she thinks of herself mainly as a poet. Her poem for an occasion, "For Marianne Moore's Birthday," honors another female poet (page 587) who shares Boyle's vision of the human experience.

NOVEMBER 15, 1967

I wish you triumphs that are yours already,
And also wish to say whatever I have done
Has been in admiration (imitation even)
Of all you marvelously proliferate. Once someone
Turned to me and said in lowered voice (because you too were in the room)   5

That William Carlos Williams gave to you at sight that
Singular esteem known by no other name save love. These words were
Spoken perhaps a half century ago
(In Monroe Wheeler's Eastside flat) when you
Wore amber braids around your head. And now,   10
As then, I cannot write this book or that
Without you. You have always been
Nightingale, baseball fan, librarian of my visions,
Poised on a moving ladder in the sun.

QUESTIONS

1. Why does Boyle use the loquacious expression "Singular esteem known by no other name save love"?

2. Explain the aptness of emphasizing Moore's job as a librarian and her love for baseball in the penultimate line. How does Boyle expand on the image of Moore as librarian?

TOPIC FOR WRITING

Relationships between poets are often contentious, and sometimes rivalries develop. Why is Boyle so careful to avoid any suggestion of such contentiousness? What is different about the friendship between Boyle and Moore and the usual relationship between poets?

Phyllis McGinley

PORTRAIT OF GIRL
WITH COMIC BOOK

Phyllis McGinley (1905–   ), introduced earlier (page 440), lists one of her avocations as "sticking pins into the smugger aspects of the social scene." She marks out her place in American letters as a poet of flashing wit and often searing insight. Her poetry, though usually treating "light" subjects in an oftentimes carefree and gamboling style, asserts a concern for life amidst a world that sometimes seems to forget the value of living. For as she says, "in times of ease it is the duty of . . . a writer to deflate, but in times of unrest

Portrait of Girl with Comic Book

*and fear it is perhaps his duty to celebrate, to single out
some of the values we can cherish, to talk about the few
warm things we know in the world." "Portrait of Girl with
Comic Book," like an earlier poem by McGinley (page 440),
offers a unique vision of time, age, and the experience of
being female.*

Thirteen's no age at all. Thirteen is nothing.
It is not wit, or powder on the face,
Or Wednesday matinées, or misses' clothing,
Or intellect, or grace.
Twelve has its tribal customs. But thirteen   5
Is neither boys in battered cars nor dolls,
Not *Sara Crewe,* or movie magazine,
Or pennants on the walls.

Thirteen keeps diaries and tropical fish
(A month, at most); scorns jumpropes in the spring;   10
Could not, would fortune grant it, name its wish;
Wants nothing, everything;
Has secrets from itself, friends it despises;
Admits none to the terrors that it feels;
Owns half a hundred masks but no disguises;   15
And walks upon its heels.

Thirteen's anomalous—not that, not this:
Not folded bud, or wave that laps a shore,
Or moth proverbial from the chrysalis.
Is the one age defeats the metaphor.   20
Is not a town, like childhood, strongly walled
But easily surrounded; is no city.
Nor, quitted once, can it be quite recalled—
Not even with pity.

QUESTIONS

1. The title, "Portrait of Girl with Comic Book," establishes a variety of expectations for the poem. What are they? What would a painting of this title look like? In what way is a verbal portrait the same as and/or different from a visual portrait?

2. How can thirteen be "nothing" and at the same time "own half a hundred masks but no disguises"? How does the juxtaposition of absence ("nothing") and multiplicity ("half a hundred") affect your understanding of what being thirteen is like?

3. The poem uses a variety of images and associations to evoke the experience of being thirteen. How would you organize these images? Are there consistent similarities? differences? How are they arranged throughout the poem? Is this how a thirteen-year-old would see her world?

TOPIC FOR WRITING

The speaker of the poem says, "Thirteen's anomalous—not that, not this." How do the structure, style, syntax, diction, imagery, and mood of this poem work to illustrate this statement? Is it possible for the poem to recreate parts of the experience of being thirteen even though it claims, "Nor, quitted once, can it be quite recalled"? What is the relationship between poetry and memory?

W. H. Auden

MUSÉE DES BEAUX ARTS

W. H. Auden (1907–1973), previously introduced in the anthology (page 428), was acknowledged the finest poet of his generation. Auden's early work often presents his critique of English society. He felt that the writings of Freud and Marx held the answers to many of his country's problems. His later work retreats from such systematic reduction and favors more traditional religious and individualistic values. Throughout his work he asserts that the poet is a source of wit and insightful intelligence. "Musée des Beaux Arts" points out a lesson learned from earlier artists, that suffering does not take place in a vacuum but in a world of indifference.

About suffering they were never wrong,
The Old Masters; how well they understood
Its human position; how it takes place
While someone else is eating or opening a window or just walking dully
    along;   5
How, when the aged are reverently, passionately waiting
For the miraculous birth, there always must be
Children who did not specially want it to happen, skating
On a pond at the edge of the wood:
They never forgot   10
That even the dreadful martyrdom must run its course
Anyhow in a corner, some untidy spot
Where the dogs go on with their doggy life and the torturer's horse
Scratches its innocent behind on a tree.

In Brueghel's *Icarus*, for instance: how everything turns away   15
Quite leisurely from the disaster; the ploughman may
Have heard the splash, the forsaken cry,

But for him it was not an important failure; the sun shone
As it had to on the white legs disappearing into the green
Water; and the expensive delicate ship that must have seen   20
Something amazing, a boy falling out of the sky,
Had somewhere to get to and sailed calmly on.

QUESTIONS

1. What do the "miraculous birth" and the "dreadful martyrdom" refer to? Who is Icarus? Why does Auden choose one example from Christian tradition and the other from Greek mythology?

2. What does the poet mean by the "human position" of suffering?

3. The horse scratching itself is a faintly comic image. Does it belong in the poem? Why?

4. Why does Auden personify the "expensive delicate ship"?

5. What is the relationship between the two stanzas in the poem?

TOPICS FOR WRITING

1. Does Auden mean for the reader to draw any moral or maxim from his poem? If so, what is it, and what details does Auden supply to support his generalization?

2. View a copy of Brueghel's *Icarus*. Write an essay that explores Auden's approach to the painting: how he "reads" the painting and for what reasons.

Theodore Roethke

Theodore Roethke (1908–1963), whose death on August 1, 1963, produced an acute sense of loss among such contemporaries as Lowell, Berryman, Wilbur, and Kizer, was a poet loved by colleagues, students, and friends. He was born in Saginaw, Michigan, and received his education at the University of Michigan and Harvard. As a boy, Roethke worked and played around his parents' greenhouses, among the most famous in America and the center of some of his finest poems. His career began with Open House *(1941). His second volume,* The Lost Son and Other Poems, *was published in 1948, shortly after he joined the faculty at the University of Washington. The* Waking: Poems 1933–1953 *won the*

Pulitzer Prize in 1953, and Words for the Wind: The Collected
Verse of Theodore Roethke (1958) won the National Book
Award. In 1964 he received a second National Book Award
for his posthumous volume, The Far Field. Styled by Dylan
Thomas as the "greatest reader of poetry in America,"
Roethke could enthrall an audience. "I think of myself as a
poet of love, a poet of praise," he declared. "And I wish to
read aloud." At another time he wrote, "Energy is the soul of
poetry." In "Root Cellar" and "I Knew a Woman" the beautiful
energy and intensity of life can be sensed.

ROOT CELLAR

Nothing would sleep in that cellar, dank as a ditch,
Bulbs broke out of boxes hunting for chinks in the dark,
Shoots dangled and drooped,
Lolling obscenely from mildewed crates,
Hung down long yellow evil necks, like tropical snakes.   5
And what a congress of stinks!—
Roots ripe as old bait,
Pulpy stems, rank, silo-rich,
Leaf-mold, manure, lime, piled against slippery planks.
Nothing would give up life: 10
Even the dirt kept breathing a small breath.

QUESTIONS

1. What are some of the images of darkness in the poem? What do they
suggest?

2. What is the emotional effect of the weaving of short and long lines?

3. What images have sexual connotations to them? Does the root cellar itself
function as a sexual symbol? Explain.

4. Explain Roethke's purpose in writing this poem. Does he simply create a
vivid description of the root cellar, or does the root cellar signify more to him?

TOPICS FOR WRITING

1. Analyze the sexual imagery and symbolism in the poem. What statement,
or theme, does Roethke want to draw?

2. "Root Cellar" is one of Roethke's "greenhouse" poems. What "message"
about life, energy, and the world does Roethke convey in the poem, and what
methods does he use?

I KNEW A WOMAN

I knew a woman, lovely in her bones,
When small birds sighed, she would sigh back at them;
Ah, when she moved, she moved more ways than one:
The shapes a bright container can contain!
Of her choice virtues only gods should speak,   5
Or English poets who grew up on Greek
(I'd have them sing in chorus, cheek to cheek).

How well her wishes went! She stroked my chin,
She taught me Turn, and Counter-turn, and Stand;
She taught me Touch, that undulant white skin;   10
I nibbled meekly from her proffered hand;
She was the sickle; I, poor I, the rake,
Coming behind her for her pretty sake;
(But what prodigious mowing we did make).

Love likes a gander, and adores a goose: 15
Her full lips pursed, the errant note to seize;
She played it quick, she played it light and loose;
My eyes, they dazzled at her flowing knees;
Her several parts could keep a pure repose,
Or one hip quiver with a mobile nose   20
(She moved in circles, and those circles moved).

Let seed be grass, and grass turn into hay:
I'm martyr to a motion not my own;
What's freedom for? To know eternity.
I swear she cast a shadow white as stone.   25
But who would count eternity in days?
These old bones live to learn her wanton ways:
(I measure time by how a body sways).

QUESTIONS

1. In part, this poem is about the rhythms of love. Which lines in the poem and what words and images suggest this idea?

2. Roethke sings his lady's praise or praises his lady's beauty in the traditional tones of English poetry. What metaphors and images have a traditional ring to them?

3. Roethke ends the second stanza with an extended metaphor. What is it, and what does it mean?

4. Is there any wit or humor in the poem, and if so, where? What is the effect?

5. In the last stanza, Roethke turns "metaphysical" or philosophical. What is he saying?

6. Is this a poem about love, about poetry, or about both? Explain.

TOPICS FOR WRITING

1. Roethke once wrote in his notebook, "Poetry is feeling and feeling is wonder." How does this statement illuminate the quality of "I Knew a Woman"?

2. Compare and contrast the speaker and lady in this poem with those in Wyatt's "They Flee from Me" (page 479).

Stephen Spender

AN ELEMENTARY SCHOOL CLASSROOM IN A SLUM

Stephen Spender (1909–   ) was born in London and educated at Oxford University. As novelist, playwright, essayist, and poet, he has become one of the most outspoken and concerned literary figures of our age. For most of his life he has been a professor at a variety of American and British universities, and he has produced a vast body of work that attests to his concern for oppressed individuals within contemporary society. Beginning with overtly political works on the Spanish Civil War in the 1930s, Spender gradually moved toward issues of more general social concern. "An Elementary School Classroom in a Slum" illustrates Spender's concern by focusing on the contradictions between the real prospects of the slum children and the way society represents human potential in terms of art, beauty, and geography.

Far far from gusty waves, these children's faces.
Like rootless weeds the torn hair round their paleness.
The tall girl with her weighed-down head. The paper-
seeming boy with rat's eyes. The stunted unlucky heir
Of twisted bones, reciting a father's gnarled disease,   5
His lesson from his desk. At back of the dim class,
One unnoted, sweet and young: his eyes live in a dream
Of squirrels' game, in tree room, other than this.

On sour cream walls, donations. Shakespeare's head
Cloudless at dawn, civilized dome riding all cities.   10
Belled, flowery, Tyrolese valley. Open-handed map
Awarding the world its world. And yet, for these
Children, these windows, not this world, are world,
Where all their future's painted with a fog,
A narrow street sealed in with a lead sky,   15
Far far from rivers, capes, and stars of words.

Surely Shakespeare is wicked, the map a bad example
With ships and sun and love tempting them to steal—
For lives that slyly turn in their cramped holes
From fog to endless night? On their slag heap, these children   20
Wear skins peeped through by bones and spectacles of steel
With mended glass, like bottle bits on stones.
All of their time and space are foggy slum
So blot their maps with slums as big as doom.

Unless, governor, teacher, inspector, visitor,   25
This map becomes their window and these windows
That open on their lives like crouching tombs
Break, O break open, till they break the town
And show the children to the fields and all their world
Azure on their sands, to let their tongues   30
Run naked into books, the white and green leaves open
The history theirs whose language is the sun.

QUESTIONS

1. In describing the children, Spender uses a variety of "natural" images ("waves," "weeds," "rats," and so on). Why is this a particularly effective device given the scene of the poem?

2. What do the "donations" in the classroom mean to the children? What did the donors intend them to mean?

3. How does the map of the children's world differ from the "open-handed map/Awarding the world its world"? How do maps award the world to its world?

TOPICS FOR WRITING

1. In the poem's final stanza, Spender allows for the possibility that the children might escape the "slums as big as doom." Comparing the tone and diction of this stanza to the rest of the poem, explain why such an escape is possible.

2. Spender concludes the poem with the line, "The history theirs whose language is the sun." In what way is this poem "theirs"? Does it use the "language" of the sun? Explain.

Elizabeth Bishop

FILLING STATION

Elizabeth Bishop (1911–1979) was born in Worcester, Massachusetts, and raised by grandparents and an aunt in Nova Scotia and Boston. She graduated from Vassar in 1934 and then traveled extensively in Europe, Mexico, and finally Brazil, where she settled more or less permanently in 1951. Bishop won the Pulitzer Prize in 1956 and the National Book Award in 1970; the bulk of her verse appears in The Complete Poems *(1969). Her friend Marianne Moore, whom she first met in 1934, once declared that Bishop was "spectacular in being unspectacular." Bishop is natural, deliberate, commonplace, modest, yet subtly contemplative in her best verse. However, she can also be, as she remarks of one of her favorite poets, George Herbert, "almost surrealistic" in her vivid descriptions of landscapes, objects, and people. In "Filling Station," Bishop uses precise, concrete detail and a deftly jaunty tone to capture a soft presence in the midst of harsh reality.*

Oh, but it is dirty!
—this little filling station,
oil-soaked, oil-permeated
to a disturbing, over-all
black translucency.   5
Be careful with that match!

Father wears a dirty,
oil-soaked monkey suit
that cuts him under the arms,
and several quick and saucy   10
and greasy sons assist him
(it's a family filling station),
all quite thoroughly dirty.

Do they live in the station?
It has a cement porch   15
behind the pumps, and on it
a set of crushed and grease-
impregnated wickerwork;
on the wicker sofa
a dirty dog, quite comfy.   20

Some comic books provide
the only note of color—
of certain color. They lie
upon a big dim doily
draping a taboret   25
(part of the set), beside
a big hirsute begonia.

Why the extraneous plant?
Why the taboret?
Why, oh why, the doily?   30
(Embroidered in daisy stitch
with marguerites, I think,
and heavy with gray crochet.)

Somebody embroidered the doily.
Somebody waters the plant,   35
or oils it, maybe. Somebody
arranges the rows of cans
so that they softly say:
ESSO—so—so—so
to high-strung automobiles.   40
Somebody loves us all.

QUESTIONS

1. What expectation is created by the exclamatory sequence at the start of the poem? Is the expectation fulfilled? Explain.

2. What words and images convey the dirtiness of the filling station?

3. What details in the scene contrast with the dirt and grease? Why does Bishop ask so many questions about these contrasting details?

4. How does Bishop achieve a playful, witty tone in this poem? Why does she adopt this stance? What is the tone of the last line, "Somebody loves us all"?

TOPICS FOR WRITING

1. Analyze Bishop's use of contrasting imagery in the poem to render her portrait of the filling station and to make a statement about the family that runs it.

2. Wallace Fowlie writes, "Miss Bishop's world is opulent, but in the most unexpected and most humble ways." How does this observation capture the spirit of "Filling Station"?

Josephine Miles

HOUSEWIFE

Josephine Miles (1911–   ) was born in Chicago, descend-
ed from a family which came to America aboard the May-
flower. She began writing poems at the age of 8, and in
public schools in Los Angeles, she received a rigorous
training in Latin and Greek. Subsequently Miles took an
undergraduate degree at UCLA and a doctorate at the
University of California, Berkeley; she joined the Berkeley
faculty in 1940, becoming university professor emerita in
1978. A noted scholar, especially of the metaphysical poets,
Miles in her own finest verse is simple, factual, and incisive.
Like William Carlos Williams, she seeks to render through
the national vision the commonplace occurrences of Ameri-
can life. Much of her important work is collected in Poems,
1930–1960. *In "Housewife," we sense some of the familiar*
territory in a typical Miles poem: the city landscape, the
insight into the lives of women, the matter-of-factness and
yet mystery of existence itself.

Occasional mornings when an early fog
Not yet dispersed stands in every yard
And drips and undiscloses, she is severely
Put to the task of herself.

Usually here we have view window dawns,   5
The whole East Bay at least some spaces into the room,
Puffing the curtains, and then she is out
In the submetropolitan stir.

But when the fog at the glass pauses and closes
She is put to ponder   10
A life-line, how it chooses to run obscurely
In her hand, before her.

QUESTIONS

1. Why does the fog "undisclose" the world? How is the fog personified? What
is the effect of the fog on the woman?

2. What, if anything, does the woman learn from her occasional confrontations with the fog? What do we learn about the normal pattern of her days?

3. Miles has declared of her own poetry that it projects a "strong beat of
meaning against the beat of pattern." Apply this comment to the poem.

4. What is the significance of the poem's title?

TOPICS FOR WRITING

1. Miles has said that her main themes are "human doubt and amazement." Discuss these themes in the context of "Housewife."

2. Explain the ways in which Miles takes a commonplace landscape and event in "Housewife" and transforms it into a lyrical statement about the "life-line" that confronts all of us at one time or another.

Robert Hayden

THOSE WINTER SUNDAYS

Robert Hayden (1913–1980) was born and raised in the black workingclass neighborhoods of Detroit. After attending Wayne State University, he became a professor of English literature at the University of Michigan. As a poet of the black experience, Hayden employed a wide variety of styles and forms—ranging from his early use of colloquial street language to his later, more stylized work with long poems— in order to explore the complexities of his own history. Among his major poetry collections are A Ballad of Remembrance (1962) and Selected Poems (1966). "These Winter Sundays" pauses on a particular character—the poet's father—as he was perceived both by the outside world and by his son.

Sundays too my father got up early
and put his clothes on in the blueblack cold,
then with cracked hands that ached
from labor in the weekday weather made
banked fires blaze. No one ever thanked him.   5

I'd wake and hear the cold splintering, breaking.
When the rooms were warm, he'd call,
and slowly I would rise and dress,
fearing the chronic angers of that house,

Speaking indifferently to him,   10
who had driven out the cold
and polished my good shoes as well.
What did I know, what did I know
of love's austere and lonely offices?

QUESTIONS

1. The narrator remembers his father as fluctuating between the "blueblack cold" and the fire's "blaze." How does he use this opposition between hot and cold to illustrate "love's austere and lonely offices"?

2. How does the narrator's "fearing the chronic angers of that house" and "speaking indifferently to him" affect his description of his father? What is his attitude toward his father after having "spoken" the poem?

TOPICS FOR WRITING

1. Can we read this poem as a unique rendering of the black experience in America? How does Hayden's use of imagery, diction, and syntax support your conclusion? How does the use of language organize the poem's "meaning"?

2. Analyze the way Hayden controls mood and tone in this poem in order to define his attitude toward his father.

Muriel Rukeyser

THE LOST ROMANS

Muriel Rukeyser (1913–1980) was born in New York City and educated at Vassar College and Columbia University. Her Theory of Flight *won the Yale Series of Younger Poets award in 1935. The last of twelve volumes,* Collecter Poems, *was published in 1978. In both her poetry and her daily life she sought to transform the world in which she lived from one filled with violence and oppression to one in which each individual could begin to understand his or her own (potential) abilities. Much of her poetry is expressly political. Beginning with her personal involvement in the Scottsboro trial and the Spanish Civil War and continuing through her involvement with the anti-Vietnam War movement, Rukeyser demonstrated that poetry is the ground on which the personal and political come together to change the way we think about the world. Though "The Lost Romans" is not Rukeyser's most polemical poem, it illustrates her complex use of detailed physical and sensory experience to consider how we ought to act in order to transform both ourselves and our world.*

The Lost Romans

Where are they, not those young men, not those
               young women
Who walked among the bullet-headed Romans with their
               roads, their symmetry, their iron rule—
We know the dust and bones they are gone to, those   5
               young Romans
Who stood against the bitter imperial, their young
               green life with its poems—
Where are the poems made music against the purple
Setting their own purple up for a living sign,   10
Bright fire of some forgotten future against empire,
Their poems in the beautiful Roman tongue
Sex-songs, love-poems, freedom-songs?
Not only the young, but the old and in chains,
The slaves in their singing, the fierce northern   15
               gentle blond rhythms,
The Judean cantillations, lullabies of Carthage,
Gaul with her cries, all the young Roman rebels,
Where are their songs? Who will unlock them,
Who will find them for us, in some undiscovered   20
               painted cave
For we need you, sisters, far brothers, poems
               of our lost Rome.

QUESTIONS

1. The speaker of the poem juxtaposes the "iron rule" of the Romans to the "green life with its poems" of the young. How is this opposition achieved? What kinds of images and activities are associated with each? (What is the effect of calling the Romans "bullet-headed"?)

2. Why is the speaker looking for lost "poems" and "songs"? How are these forms of communication different from others? Why is poetry a "living sign" set up against "empire"? How does poetry resist "imperial" power?

3. The opposition between Roman youth and the Roman empire established in the first 13 lines of the poem is extended to other groups in the last 10 lines. Who are these others who stand against the Romans' "bitter" power? What do they have in common with each other? with the Roman youth? What is the effect of introducing these groups with a negative ("not those young men,/ not those young women" and "Not only the young")?

TOPICS FOR WRITING

1. The poem concludes with a plea that someone find the lost poems that recount the tales of oppression that dominating cultures have excluded from their stories about their past. In what way is Rukeyser's poem itself such a poem of

oppression? Will anyone "find" these poems? Do these poems need to be written still today?

2. Compare and contrast Rukeyser's statement about the nature of poetry with that by Sexton in "The Black Art" (page 664).

Dylan Thomas

FERN HILL

Dylan Thomas (1914–1953) was born and received a grammar school education in Swansea, Wales. Deciding against attending a university, Thomas instead adopted the role of the bohemian poet, a role based in part on the style of Oscar Wilde. His first book of poems, Eighteen Poems *(1934), won him the enthusiastic acclaim of London literati, especially that of the equally flamboyant Edith Sitwell (page 589). Like Sitwell, Thomas felt the need for poetry to act, to "narrate," and as a result his verbal virtuosity often produces images of darkly suggestive obscurity. This style was seen in contrast to the arid landscapes and alienated metaphors of the early modernists, of whom T. S. Eliot (page 591), is the best example, and was claimed by some to be a turn toward a new romantic poetry. When this turn failed to materialize, however, Thomas remained a lone voice for unity amidst the modernists' roar of "fragmentation!" Emphasizing themes of unity within diversity, of wholeness encompassing contradiction, Thomas's poems create intricately woven webs of diverse images and metaphors. Thus, Thomas's poem provided here, "Fern Hill," written seven years before his death by alcoholism, uses the repeated experiences and visions of childhood joy in order to unravel the poet-persona's reflections on the unified movement of "Time."*

Now as I was young and easy under the apple boughs
About the lilting house and happy as the grass was green,
    The night above the dingle starry,
      Time let me hail and climb
    Golden in the heydays of his eyes,
And honoured among wagons I was prince of the apple towns
And once below a time I lordly had the trees and leaves
      Trail with daisies and barley
    Down the rivers of the windfall light.

5

And as I was green and carefree, famous among the barns   10
About the happy yard and singing as the farm was home,
      In the sun that is young once only,
          Time let me play and be
      Golden in the mercy of his means,
And green and golden I was huntsman and herdsman, the calves   15
Sang to my horn, the foxes on the hills barked clear and cold,
          And the sabbath rang slowly
      In the pebbles of the holy streams.

All the sun long it was running, it was lovely, the hay
Fields high as the house, the tunes from the chimneys, it was air   20
      And playing, lovely and watery
          And fire green as grass.
      And nightly under the simple stars
As I rode to sleep the owls were bearing the farm away,
All the moon long I heard, blessed among stables, the night-jars   25
      Flying with the ricks, and the horses
          Flashing into the dark.

And then to awake, and the farm, like a wanderer white
With the dew, come back, the cock on his shoulder: it was all
      Shining, it was Adam and maiden,   30
          The sky gathered again
      And the sun grew round that very day.
So it must have been after the birth of the simple light
In the first, spinning place, the spellbound horses walking warm
      Out of the whinnying green stable   35
          On to the fields of praise.

QUESTIONS

1. The poem opens with the phrase "Now as I was young," yet the "now" of the poem is obviously not the "now" of the persona recalling his youth. How does this disjunction demonstrate the way time will be represented in the poem? Give other examples of how the poem's use of language evokes different senses of time.

2. The narrator recalls the scenes of his childhood in terms of his interaction with nature. How would you characterize this interaction? Is it possible for an adult to have such a relation to the natural world? Is it possible for anyone, today?

3. After being described in the first stanza as the "prince of the apple towns" and being associated with plant life, why is the child placed so conspicuously among animals in the rest of the poem?

4. Does the narrator regret his lost youth? Explain.

TOPICS FOR WRITING

1. The poem seems to move through the cycles of the days as the persona recollects his youth. Why is this cycle particularly significant for this poem? How does it provide a context for the poem's last three lines?

2. Childhood has often been used to express a state of human innocence in which, if we could only return to it after growing up, we would be able to live with each other in harmony with nature. Is this a good model for an ideal society? How does the narrator of "Fern Hill" see childhood?

John Berryman

THE BALL POEM

John Berryman (1914–1972) was born in Oklahoma and moved to Florida when he was 10. His father committed suicide, and his mother remarried John Berryman, whose name her children adopted. Berryman studied at Columbia, attended Cambridge on a fellowship, and taught at a number of universities in America. He was married three times. Berryman ended his life at the age of 57 by jumping from a bridge. Among Berryman's collections of verse are Homage to Mistress Bradstreet *(1956),* 77 Dream Songs *(1964), and* Short Poems *(1967). Berryman's poetry is both confessional and theatrical, and the combination often borders on the neurotic. "The Ball Poem" magnifies the importance of the trivial event of a boy losing his ball, but the ball stands in place of the many other losses that Berryman suffered in his painful life.*

What is the boy now, who has lost his ball,
What, what is he to do? I saw it go
Merrily bouncing, down the street, and then
Merrily over—there it is in the water!
No use to say 'O there are other balls': 5
An ultimate shaking grief fixes the boy
As he stands rigid, trembling, staring down
All his young days into the harbour where
His ball went. I would not intrude on him,
A dime, another ball, is worthless. Now 10
He senses first responsibility
In a world of possessions. People will take balls,
Balls will be lost always, little boy,
And no one buys a ball back. Money is external.

He is learning, well behind his desperate eyes,   15
The epistemology of loss, how to stand up
Knowing what every man must one day know
And most know many days, how to stand up.
And gradually light returns to the street,
A whistle blows, the ball is out of sight,   20
Soon part of me will explore the deep and dark
Floor of the harbour . . . I am everywhere,
I suffer and move, my mind and my heart move
With all that move me, under the water
Or whistling, I am not a little boy.   25

QUESTIONS

1. Who is the boy in the poem? How do you understand the last line of the poem?

2. What does he mean by the "epistemology of loss"?

3. Where does the ball go?

4. Why is another ball "worthless"?

5. Does the poem strike you as autobiographical? Cite details to support your response.

6. The title can have two interpretations. It can mean "the poem about the ball," or it can mean "the poem that is like the ball." Expand on the second reading.

TOPICS FOR WRITING

1. Explain the relationship between the boy and the narrator. Do you think they are the same person at different times in his life? Explain.

2. Write an essay on the theme of loss in "The Ball Poem."

3. The poet and critic Ivor Winters once declared that Berryman was "frustrated by his inability to define his theme and his disinclination to understand and discipline his emotions." Agree or disagree with this judgment, using "The Ball Poem" as the basis of your argument.

Randall Jarrell

THE DEATH
OF THE BALL TURRET GUNNER

Randall Jarrell (1914–1965) was born in Nashville, Tennessee, and received degrees in psychology and English from Vanderbilt University. During World War II, he served as an air control tower operator. Noted as much for his translations and criticism as for his poetry, Jarrell in 1956 was appointed a consultant in poetry at the Library of Congress. He also served as an editor for The Nation, Partisan Review, *and* Yale Review. *Robert Lowell said that Jarrell was "the most heartbreaking . . . poet of his generation." The thematic and structural intensity of "The Death of the Ball Turret Gunner" exemplifies the relentless passion with which Jarrell viewed the world.*

From my mother's sleep I fell into the State,
And I hunched in its belly till my wet fur froze.
Six miles from earth, loosed from its dream of life,
I woke to black flak and the nightmare fighters.
When I died they washed me out of the turret with a hose.   5

QUESTIONS

1. Who is the speaker of this poem? What is the dramatic situation? Are we supposed to take the persona and the situation literally? Why?

2. Why is "State" capitalized in line 1?

3. A metaphor can work not only because of similarities of the two elements compared, but also because of their differences. What is the guiding metaphoric comparison in this poem? List images which contribute to this guiding metaphor. How does it create a frightening emotional overtone in the poem?

4. List several examples of sharp descriptive contrasts in the poem. What is the effect of these contrasts?

5. How does Jarrell condense the time sequence of this poem? What is his purpose in doing so?

6. Point to places where Jarrell uses repetition of sound in the poem. Explain how these sound devices contribute to the poem's overall tonal effect.

TOPICS FOR WRITING

1. Discuss the social or political interpretation of this poem, paying special attention to the last line.

2. The poem begins with the gunner's "fall" from his mother's sleep and ends with his remains being washed out of the plane with a hose. Analyze this

chronicle of movement through life. What does it suggest the nature of life to be? Does the gunner learn anything? What is the effect of having a first-person—dead —narrator?

Judith Wright

EXTINCT BIRDS

Judith Wright (1915–   ), introduced earlier (page 453), is an Australian poet; she locates her concerns in the history of the Australian continent: "I have I suppose been trying to expiate a deep sense of guilt over what we have done to the country, to its first inhabitants of all lands, and are increasingly doing." Using the natural landscape, the biological setting, and the aboriginal cultures as the backdrop for her poetry, Wright explores the questions and contradictions of modern existence. Death, alienation, and the power of poetry to transcend these provide dominant themes for Wright. In addition, she explicitly identifies herself as a female poet ("As a woman poet, the biological aspect of feminine experience has naturally been an important part of my work. . . .") and she has written a volume of poetry, Woman to Man, centering on the experience of childbirth. In "Extinct Birds," Wright singles out Australian romantic poet Charles Harpur in order to consider the complex relations among nature, poetry, and the finality of death.

Charles Harpur in his journals long ago
(written in hope and love, and never printed)
recorded the birds of his time's forest—
birds long vanished with the fallen forest—
described in copperplate on unread pages.　　　　　　　　　　5

The scarlet satin-bird, swung like a lamp in berries,
he watched in love, and then in hope described it.
There was a bird, blue, small, spangled like dew.
All now are vanished with the fallen forest.
And he, unloved, past hope, was buried,　　　　　　　　　　10

who helped with proud stained hands to fell the forest,
and set those birds in love on unread pages;
yet thought himself immortal, being a poet.

And is he not immortal, where I found him,
in love and hope along his careful pages?—
the poet vanished, in the vanished forest,
among his brightly tinted extinct birds?

15

QUESTIONS

1. The poem begins with the words "Charles Harpur." How does this initial use of a proper name frame the poem? How does the name stand in relation to the title?

2. What effect does the poem's talking about "unread pages" have on your reading of this page? Is your reading of Wright's poem similar to her reading of Harpur's? Why or why not?

3. What is the poet Harpur's relation to the birds? Why is it significant that he "helped with proud stained hands to fell the forest"?

TOPIC FOR WRITING

Since this poem is one in which a poet-persona discusses another poet writing poetry, we call it a *metapoetic* poem—a poem about writing poems. If we consider the poem in this light, then how are we to take the last stanza of the poem—the claim that Harpur is immortal because he can be rediscovered in poetry? Is Wright similarly making a claim for her own immortality because we are reading her works? What is the relationship between the poet and the poem? Between the poet and the source of inspiration (for Harpur, birds; for Wright, Harpur)? Why are the birds extinct?

Margaret Walker

POPPA CHICKEN

Margaret Walker (1915–   ), poet and novelist, was born in Birmingham, Alabama, and educated at Northwestern University and the University of Iowa. She won the Yale Award for Younger Poets in 1942 for her volume For My People. *Walker was then teaching at Livingston College, in North Carolina, and since that time she has held several academic posts, most recently at Jackson State University, in Mississippi. In the introduction to her prizewinning novel* Jubilee *(1966), Walker observes that hers was a "talking" family, given to anecdotes, folklore, and discussions of history, politics, and race. In "Poppa Chicken," Walker writes with*

*verbal brilliance and zest about one of her people, offering a
celebration of an individual who makes his own way in the
world. "Writers should not write exclusively for black or
white audiences," states Walker, "but most inclusively. After
all, it is the business of all writers to write about the human
condition, and all humanity must be involved in the writing
and in the reading."*

Poppa was a sugah daddy
Pimping in his prime;
All the gals for miles around
Walked to Poppa's time.

Poppa Chicken owned the town,   5
Give his women hell;
All the gals on Poppa's time
Said that he was swell.

Poppa's face was long and black;
Poppa's grin was broad.   10
When Poppa Chicken walked the streets
The gals cried Lawdy! Lawd!

Poppa Chicken made his gals
Toe his special line:
"Treat 'em rough and make 'em say   15
Poppa Chicken's fine!"

Poppa Chicken toted guns;
Poppa wore a knife.
One night Poppa shot a guy
Threat'ning Poppa's life.   20

Poppa done his time in jail
Though he got off light;
Bought his pardon in a year;
Come back out in might.

Poppa walked the streets this time,   25
Gals around his neck.
And everybody said the jail
Hurt him nary speck.

Poppa smoked his long cigars—
Special Poppa brands—   30
Rocks all glist'ning in his tie;
On his long black hands.

Poppa lived without a fear;
Walked without a rod.

Poppa cussed the coppers out;   35
Talked like he was God.

Poppa met a pretty gal;
Heard her name was Rose;
Took one look at her and soon
Bought her pretty clothes.   40

One night she was in his arms,
In walked her man Joe,
All he done was look and say,
"Poppa's got to go."

Poppa Chicken still is hot   45
Though he's old and gray,
Walking round here with his gals
Pimping every day.

QUESTIONS

1. What is the tone of this poem? Why doesn't Walker make any ethical judgment about Poppa's activities? Is she fond of Poppa? Explain.

2. What features of this poem give it a balladlike quality? What do we typically expect of the figures in ballads?

3. Point to instances of black idiom in the poem. Does this make the poem too narrow? What of Walker's intention to write inclusively about the human condition?

4. Is there a theme to this poem? Explain.

TOPICS FOR WRITING

1. Examine the ingredients and techniques drawn from music and folklore that make "Poppa Chicken" a special type of poem.

2. Evaluate Walker's tendency to romanticize a pimp in this poem.

Robert Lowell

Robert Lowell (1917–1977), described by John Berryman as "a talent whose ceiling is invisible," was one of the major innovators in contemporary American poetry. Born in Boston, the great-grandnephew of James Russell Lowell, he attended Harvard University and Kenyon College. Lowell converted to Catholicism in 1940, the same year that he married the first of his three wives, novelist Jean Stafford. (His other wives, Elizabeth Hardwick and Caroline Blackwood, were also writers.) He was a conscientious objector during World War II and served a prison term for violation of the Selective Service Act. Lowell's New England heritage, his personal experience, his Catholicism, his family, and his political and historical awareness were the forces that shaped his poetry. Lord Weary's Castle (1946) was awarded the Pulitzer Prize in 1947; Life Studies (1959), the National Book Award; Invitations (1961), the Bollinger Translation Prize. Each of these volumes measures Lowell's progress as an experimental poet: from formal, tightly rhymed lines; to free verse; to adaptations from poets in other languages. The selections that follow, from Lord Weary's Castle, are indicative of the power Lowell could project in formally complex religious and cultural poems.

CHILDREN OF LIGHT

Our fathers wrung their bread from stocks and stones
And fenced their gardens with the Redman's bones;
Embarking from the Nether Land of Holland,
Pilgrims unhouseled by Geneva's night,
They planted here the Serpent's seeds of light;   5
And here the pivoting searchlights probe to shock
The riotous glass houses built on rock,
And candles gutter by an empty altar,
And light is where the landless blood of Cain
Is burning, burning the unburied grain.   10

QUESTIONS

1. What, in general, is Lowell's historical view of New England in the poem? What tone emerges from this interpretation?

2. What religious allusions appear in the poem?

3. Locate the images of murder in the poem. How do they influence the theme?

4. How does "the Serpent's seeds of light" connect with the title of the poem? What does the title mean?

5. What is the effect of the past on the present in "Children of Light"?

TOPIC FOR WRITING

Analyze the colonial and Puritan heritage presented by Lowell in "Children of Light." What does this poem say about World War II and about modern times?

AFTER THE SURPRISING
CONVERSIONS

September twenty-second, Sir; today
I answer. In the latter part of May,
Hard on our Lord's Ascension, it began
To be more sensible. A gentleman
Of more than common understanding, strict   5
In morals, pious in behavior, kicked
Against our goad. A man of some renown,
An useful, honored person in the town,
He came of melancholy parents; prone
To secret spells, for years they kept alone—   10
His uncle, I believe, was killed of it:
Good people, but of too much or little wit.
I preached one Sabbath on a text from Kings;
He showed concernment for his soul. Some things
In his experience were hopeful. He   15
Would sit and watch the wind knocking a tree
And praise this countryside our Lord has made.
Once when a poor man's heifer died, he laid
A shilling on the doorsill; though a thirst
For loving shook him like a snake, he durst   20
Not entertain much hope of his estate
In heaven. Once we saw him sitting late
Behind his attic window by a light
That guttered on his Bible; through that night
He meditated terror, and he seemed   25
Beyond advice or reason, for he dreamed
That he was called to trumpet Judgment Day
To Concord. In the latter part of May
He cut his throat. And though the coroner
Judged him delirious, soon a noisome stir   30
Palsied our village. At Jehovah's nod
Satan seemed more let loose amongst us: God
Abandoned us to Satan, and he pressed
Us hard, until we thought we could not rest
Till we had done with life. Content was gone.   35
All the good work was quashed. We were undone.
The breath of God had carried out a planned

And sensible withdrawal from this land;
The multitude, once unconcerned with doubt,
Once neither callous, curious nor devout,   40
Jumped at broad noon, as though some peddler groaned
At it in its familiar twang: "My friend,
Cut your own throat. Cut your own throat. Now! Now!"
September twenty-second, Sir, the bough
Cracks with the unpicked apples, and at dawn   45
The small-mouth bass breaks water, gorged with spawn.

QUESTIONS

1. The speaker in this poem is Jonathan Edwards (1703–1758), a famous American preacher and theologian. In a monologue in the form of a letter, he describes the "great awakening," or revival of Christian faith, in his Massachusetts parish in 1734–1735, and he touches also on the suicide of his uncle, Joseph Hawley, in 1735. How do the monologue's tone and rhyme scheme echo the devices used by Robert Browning in "My Last Duchess" (page 542).

2. What is Lowell's feeling for Jonathan Edwards? Is Edwards logical? Does he sense paradoxes? Does he engage in self-analysis? Cite passages to support your interpretation.

3. How do the rhymed couplets reflect Edwards's mind and will?

4. How do the images of the "unpicked apples" and "small-mouth bass" at the end of the poem contrast with the speaker's account of the conversions?

TOPICS FOR WRITING

1. Analyze the ironic stance that Lowell takes toward his speaker, Jonathan Edwards, in this monologue.

2. Define Lowell's attitude toward religion, specifically Calvinism, in this poem and in "Children of Light."

3. Compare and contrast "After the Surprising Conversions" and "My Last Duchess" (page 542).

Lawrence Ferlinghetti

IN GOYA'S GREATEST SCENES

Lawrence Ferlinghetti (1919–   ) emerged first as a poet and publisher in the Beat scene of the 1950s in San Francisco. He founded City Lights Bookstore, which served as both focal point and publishing house for the movement. As a poet, playwright, novelist, and publisher, Ferlinghetti has been active in the struggle for control of our humanity within a society that seeks to make our behavior "normal." In his poem "Overheard Conversations," he defines his concept of poetry: "And still the whole idea of poetry being/to take control of life/out of the hand of/the terrible people." In his poetry Ferlinghetti often employs experimental and shocking language, but always strives to make it as accessible as possible to others. Looking at the poem included here, "In Goya's Greatest Scenes," we see that Ferlinghetti's use of concrete images opens both the Goya painting and the poet's vision of America to public consideration.

In Goya's greatest scenes we seem to see
                    the people of the world
          exactly at the moment when
          they first attained the title of
                    'suffering humanity'   5
          They writhe upon the page
                    in a veritable rage
                    of adversity
          Heaped up
                    groaning with babies and bayonets   10
                              under cement skies
          in an abstract landscape of blasted trees
          bent statues bats wings and beaks
                    slippery gibbets
          cadavers and carnivorous cocks   15
          and all the final hollering monsters
                    of the
                    'imagination of disaster'
          they are so bloody real
                    it is as if they really still existed   20

And they do

          Only the landscape is changed
They still are ranged along the roads
          plagued by legionaires
                    false windmills and demented roosters   25

They are the same people
                    only further from home

on freeways fifty lanes wide
on a concrete continent
spaced with bland billboards   30
illustrating imbecile illusions of happiness

The scene shows fewer tumbrils
but more maimed citizens
in painted cars
and they have strange license plates   35
and engines
that devour America

QUESTIONS

1. The first twenty lines of the poem present a verbal description of a Goya etching from a series entitled "Disasters of War." How does Ferlinghetti go about re-presenting this work? How does the description differ from the etching? What is the effect of creating a poetic interpretation of a work of art in another medium? What is the emphasis of this particular interpretation, and how does the language used reveal this emphasis?

2. How do the "landscapes" of Goya differ from the "landscapes" of today? How does the poem describe each? What is the effect of placing these different images side by side in this poem?

3. Who are the "suffering humanity" in America? What would the "imagination of disaster" be in this second "landscape"?

TOPIC FOR WRITING

This poem is arranged on the page so that the lines seem to flow one into another. Consider how this visual aspect of the poem contributes to its linguistic meaning. How do such things as line endings, line beginnings, and spacing between lines inform your reading of the poem? In what way does this layout make the poem like a painting? Is poetry a visual as well as a verbal art?

Richard Wilbur

THE DEATH OF A TOAD

Richard Wilbur (1921–   ), poet, translator, and critic, was born the son of a painter in New York City and was educated at Amherst and Harvard. In many ways, Wilbur epitomizes the tradition of academic poetry in America today. Believing that poetry need not engage social issues to have relevance, Wilbur in his verse (much of it collected in Poems of Richard Wilbur, *1963) tends toward highly formalized poetic structures and conventions. He disdains the fragmentation of existence which has become the hallmark of modern poetry in favor of a faith in the positive powers of synthesis. Wilbur typically uses traditional compositional frameworks to address the contradictions and complexities of experience. In "The Death of a Toad," Wilbur focuses on direct experience ("the only instance in which I went straight from something that happened to me to writing a poem about it . . .") in order to evoke the final contradiction between life and death.*

A toad the power mower caught,
Chewed and clipped of a leg, with a hobbling hop has got
  To the garden verge, and sanctuaried him
  Under the cineraria leaves, in the shade
    Of the ashen heartshaped leaves, in a dim,   5
      Low, and a final glade.

  The rare original heartsblood goes,
Spends on the earthen hide, in the folds and wizenings, flows
  In the gutters of the banked and staring eyes. He lies
  As still as if he would return to stone,   10
    And soundlessly attending, dies
      Toward some deep monotone,

  Toward misted and ebullient seas
And cooling shores, toward lost Amphibia's emperies.
  Day dwindles, drowning, and at length is gone   15
  In the wide and antique eyes, which still appear
    To watch, across the castrate lawn,
      The haggard daylight steer.

QUESTIONS

1. How can the poem's central image of the meshing of animal and machine be generalized? Is this a freak accident? Was it bound to happen? How does the "power mower" stand in relation to the "final glade"?

2. What is the "rare original heartsblood"? Does this "original" fluid infuse the "stone" to which the toad will return? Why is death a "monotone"?

3. The poem's last stanza presents a variety of disparate images (for example, "Amphibia's emperies," "antique eyes," "castrate lawn," and "haggard daylight"). How do these images contribute to the tone of the poem? What effect do they have on the importance you assign to the toad's death?

TOPICS FOR WRITING

1. The poem seems to adopt a tone of high seriousness in recounting the fairly mundane episode of the death of a toad. How does the poem create this serious mood? What kinds of language does it employ? How does this language organize your understanding of the poem?

2. One critic, Robert Boyers, maintains that this poem "dissolves in a kind of absurdity." Explain why you agree or disagree with this judgment.

James Dickey

THE PERFORMANCE

James Dickey (1923–   ) was born in an Atlanta, Georgia, suburb, the son of a prominent lawyer. Speaking of his poetry, he says, "I like to think the major theme, if there is one, is continuity between the self and the world and the various attempts by men to destroy this (wars and so on, heavy industry and finance and the volume turnover system). I try to say something about mankind's way or ways of protecting this sense of continuity in himself or his attempts to restore it." Dickey's poems, which draw extensively on his own history as a combat pilot, an athlete, and a hunter, seek to reach beyond the bounds of the individual ego and to generate a collective human understanding. Dickey flew as a combat pilot in the Pacific during World War II and later served as a flight instructor during the Korean War. In his poem "The Performance," Dickey draws on his wartime experience in order to evoke both a single man's humanity and the social violation of that humanity, which is war.

The last time I saw Donald Armstrong
He was staggering oddly off into the sun,
Going down, off the Philippine Islands.
I let my shovel fall, and put that hand
Above my eyes, and moved some way to one side   5
That his body might pass through the sun,

James Dickey

And I saw how well he was not
Standing there on his hands,
On his spindle-shanked forearms balanced,
Unbalanced, with his big feet looming and waving   10
In the great, untrustworthy air
He flew in each night, when it darkened.

Dust fanned in scraped puffs from the earth
Between his arms, and blood turned his face inside out,
To demonstrate its suppleness   15
Of veins, as he perfected his role.
Next day, he toppled his head off
On an island beach to the south,

And the enemy's two-handed sword
Did not fall from anyone's hands   20
At that miraculous sight,
As the head rolled over upon
Its wide-eyed face, and fell
Into the inadequate grave

He had dug for himself, under pressure.   25
Yet I put my flat hand to my eyebrows
Months later, to see him again
In the sun, when I learned how he died,
And imagined him, there,
Come, judged, before his small captors,   30

Doing all his lean tricks to amaze them—
The back somersault, the kip-up—
And at last, the stand on his hands,

Perfect, with his feet together,
His head down, evenly breathing,   35
As the sun poured up from the sea
And the headsman broke down
In a blaze of tears, in that light
Of the thin, long human frame
Upside down in its own strange joy,   40
And, if some other one had not told him,
Would have cut off the feet

Instead of the head,
And if Armstrong had not presently risen
In kingly, round-shouldered attendance,   45
And then knelt down in himself
Beside his hacked, glittering grave, having done
All things in this life that he could.

QUESTIONS

1. The poem opens with an image of Armstrong "staggering off into the sun/Going down, off the Philippine Islands." How does this association of the man with the sun inform your understanding of who he is? Is this image related to the historical connotation of the sun (the Japanese flag)?

2. The speaker says, "I saw how well he was not/Standing there. . . ." Why is this statement phrased in the negative? If he is not there, where is he?

3. Why does the image of Armstrong's "performance" organize the poem? How does the detailed physical description of his actions—the way he moves his body—evoke his character? What is the relationship between death and the body? How can the speaker "see" him "months later"?

4. The speaker describes Armstrong's last performance as his preparation for death. Is this performance essentially different from his earlier ones? Why does the poet-persona say "he toppled his head off"? Who is responsible for Armstrong's death?

TOPIC FOR WRITING

The poem builds its story of Armstrong's death through a series of concrete physical images. How are these images organized throughout the poem? How do they relate the speaker to the subject of the poem? What do the choice of images reveal to you about Armstrong? about the speaker? about the relation between them? You should consider not only the specific descriptions that are given, but also the way these modify one another.

Denise Levertov

THE ACHE OF MARRIAGE

Denise Levertov (1923–   ), whose work appears earlier in this anthology (page 386), is a committed political activist, poet, and teacher. She brings to her poetry not only a sense of concern for the world but also a sense that we can change it. Refusing to be confined by conventional definitions of how we should act, Levertov uses her poems to examine many aspects of everyday life that usually go unanalyzed because they seem so natural and familiar. In the poem presented here Levertov examines one such "natural" event—marriage—in order to ask her important question: if it is what we must do, then why does it hurt?

Denise Levertov

The ache of marriage:

thigh and tongue, beloved,
are heavy with it,
it throbs in the teeth

We look for communion   5
and are turned away, beloved,
each and each

It is leviathan and we
in its belly
looking for joy, some joy   10
not to be known outside it

two by two in the ark of
the ache of it.

QUESTIONS

1. How does the speaker first recognize the "ache of marriage"? Is this "ache" a purely physical experience? Is it a purely sexual experience?

2. The narrator claims that both she and her husband "look for communion." What does marriage as "communion" mean? Is it related to the Christian notion of marriage as sacrament? Why are they turned away?

3. What effect does it have on your reading to imagine the speaker and her husband swallowed up in marriage as if they were swallowed up by a whale? What effect does the biblical parallel to Jonah have on your understanding of what true marriage is like? of what marriage in general is like?

4. Since it was Noah's task to repopulate the world after the flood, the reference to Noah in the final two lines raises questions about future generations who will marry. Are they, too, fated to suffer the "ache of marriage"? Where does this ache come from?

TOPIC FOR WRITING

The poem uses images and metaphors drawn from different kinds of experience (physical, religious, cultural). How are all these elements united in the course of the poem? Why are they particularly appropriate to a description of the "ache of marriage"?

Carolyn Kizer

AMUSING OUR DAUGHTERS

*Carolyn Kizer (1925–   ) was born in Spokane, Washing-
ton. She received her BA from Sarah Lawrence College in
1945 and did graduate work at Columbia University and the
University of Washington. A teacher and translator, Kizer
founded* Poetry Northwest *and served as its editor from 1959
to 1965. Her collections include* The Ungrateful Garden
(1962) and Midnight Was My Cry: New and Selected Poems
*(1971). Kizer had two daughters and a son in her first
marriage. In the following poem, dedicated to another contemporary American poet and imitated from Po chū-I (T'ang
Dynasty), she seeks through these children and those of
Creeley and other "brother poets" the connectedness of
people in a potentially impersonal world.*

FOR ROBERT CREELEY

We don't lack people here on the Northern coast,
But they are people one meets, not people one cares for.
So I bundle my daughters into the car
And with my brother poets, go to visit you, brother.

Here come your guests! A swarm of strangers and children;   5
But the strangers write verses, the children are daughters like yours.
We bed down on mattresses, cots, roll up on the floor:
Outside, burly old fruit trees in mist and rain;
In every room, bundles asleep like larvae.

We waken and count our daughters. Otherwise, nothing happens.   10
You feed them sweet rolls and melon, drive them all to the zoo;
Patiently, patiently, ever the father, you answer their questions.
Later we eat again, drink, listen to poems.
Nothing occurs, though we are aware you have three daughters
Who last year had four. But even death becomes part of our ease: 15
Poems, parenthood, sorrow, all we have learned
From these, of tenderness, holds us together
In the center of life, entertaining daughters
By firelight, with cake and songs.

You, my brother, are a good and violent drinker,   20
Good at reciting short-line or long-line poems.
In time we will lose all our daughters, you and I,
Be temperate, venerable, content to stay in one place,
Sending our messages over the mountains and waters.

QUESTIONS

1. What motivates the speaker to visit her "brother" poet Robert Creeley?

2. How does Creeley receive his unexpected guests? How do the images of the fruit trees and the people sleeping "like larvae" connect in the second stanza?

3. Analyzing and entertaining children, "counting" daughters, is an idea that structures the poem. Why are the daughters important? What do they reveal about the "center of life"?

4. What portrait emerges of Robert Creeley? of the world of poets? How will the brother poets finally change?

TOPICS FOR WRITING

1. Examine the various moods that are developed in "Amusing Our Daughters" and show how mood reinforces some of the ideas that Kizer wants to project in the poem.

2. Analyze the world of poets that is described by Kizer in the poem.

Maxine Kumin

TOGETHER

Maxine Kumin (1925–   ) was born in Philadelphia and received her BA and MA degrees from Radcliffe College. She began writing children's stories and light verse while pregnant with her third child in 1953. Since that time, she has published more than a dozen books of poetry, novels, and children's fiction. She won the Pulitzer Prize for poetry in 1973 for Up Country *(1972). While noted for her close attention to objective details, Kumin has a talent for transforming her images into unique, sometimes grotesque statements about the processes of life. As in "Together," Kumin's absorption in natural phenomena serves as a way to reveal the importance of personal relationships.*

The water closing
over us and the
going down is all.
Gills are given.
We convert in a   5
town of broken hulls

and green doubloons.
O you dead pirates
hear us! There is
no salvage. All   10
you know is the color
of warm caramel. All
is salt. See how
our eyes have migrated
to the uphill side?   15
Now we are new round
mouths and no spines
letting the water cover.
It happens over
and over, me in   20
your body and you
in mine.

QUESTIONS

1. What is this poem about? At what point do you discover the subject of the poem? Is there an extended metaphor? Explain.

2. How, or in what way, do the people in this poem become absorbed in nature? Why does Kumin rely so heavily on nautical imagery to convey this absorption? What is the purpose or goal?

3. Examine each sentence in the poem. Why is it difficult to establish meanings for some of these sentences? How do the sentences connect in terms of meaning?

4. Is there a "theme" in this poem, or is the poet simply trying to transcribe the specific sensation of two human beings coming together? Explain.

TOPICS FOR WRITING

1. Explain Kumin's use of metaphorical language and imagery to depict her subject in "Together."

2. Compare and contrast this poem with Levertov's "The Ache of Marriage" (page 649).

A. R. (Archie Randolph) Ammons

THE CITY LIMITS

A. R. Ammons (1926–   ) was born in North Carolina and received a BS from Wake Forest University in 1949. Ammons's career as a poet has not followed the conventional academic route. First an elementary school principal and later an executive with a biological glass corporation, he became a lecturer and later a full professor of English at Cornell, but never entirely renounced his earlier scientific training. "The City Limits" illustrates this connection by presenting both his vital concern for the natural world and his ability to evoke the minute particularities of his experience of it. The bulk of his work appears in Selected Poems *(1968),* Collected Poems 1951–1971 *(1972), and* Selected Longer Poems *(1980). Ammons seeks in his poetry to align human creativity and potential with nature's larger works of creation.*

When you consider the radiance, that it does not withhold
itself but pours its abundance without selection into every
nook and cranny not overhung or hidden; when you consider

that birds' bones make no awful noise against the light but
lie low in the light as in a high testimony; when you consider   5
the radiance, that it will look into the guiltiest

swervings of the weaving heart and bear itself upon them,
not flinching into disguise or darkening; when you consider
the abundance of such resource as illuminates the glow-blue

bodies and gold-skeined wings of flies swarming the dumped   10
guts of a natural slaughter or the coil of shit and in no
way winces from its storms of generosity; when you consider

that air or vacuum, snow or shale, squid or wolf, rose or lichen,
each is accepted into as much light as it will take, then
the heart moves roomier, the man stands and looks about, the   15

leaf does not increase itself above the grass, and the dark
work of the deepest cells is of a tune with May bushes
and fear lit by the breadth of such calmly turns to praise.

QUESTIONS

1. Who is the "you" in the poem? What is "you" being asked to "consider"? Is there a difference between "consideration" and "observation"? How would your reading of the poem change if we substituted one for the other?

2. The poem presents five independent clauses for consideration. What is the

relationship among them? What is the effect of repeating the phrase "when you consider" in each of these? How does the syntax of the last clause differ from the earlier four?

3. How does the poem use the nature of light and illumination to orient itself?

4. Ammons uses concrete images almost exclusively in this poem. How does this attention to material existence provide a context for your reading of the poem?

TOPICS FOR WRITING

1. Look at the various images and other elements of the poem. How are they related? How does each make a particular difference? How do they contribute to the undifferentiation of the last line, where "fear lit by the breadth of such calmly turns to praise"? What is the ideal relation of humanity to the "natural world"?

2. The last "when you consider" in the poem seems to turn away from the earlier four, arguing against them but at the same time subsuming them. Analyze this clause in detail in light of the earlier ones. Does the poem "progress"? Is the poem a fruitful "consideration"?

Allen Ginsberg

A SUPERMARKET
IN CALIFORNIA

Allen Ginsberg (1926–), perhaps more than any other living American poet, has worked to integrate the activity of poetry—its reading, writing, and recitation—into the complex experience of everyday life. Born in Newark, New Jersey, where he was befriended by William Carlos Williams, Ginsberg received his BA from Columbia University before eventually moving to San Francisco. A leading figure in both the Beat movement of the 1950s and the psychedelic movement of the 1960s, Ginsberg is still in the forefront of popular cultural movements, appearing on the Clash album Combat Rock. *Aligned with the tradition of "visionary" poetry (especially Blake and Whitman), Ginsberg's poems combine images from a diversity of sources—Eastern mysticism, Western philosophy, his own experience as a homosexual, and, today, punk rock, to name only a very few—in order to address universal questions by way of his*

*own personal relationships. This emphasis on the connec-
tion between the universal and the personal, between unity
and diversity, has led Ginsberg to seek a more direct connection with his audience. He has become a premier reciter
and improviser of poetic language, thus promoting the
direct experience of poetry by collapsing the distance between poet, poem, and audience. The poem presented here is
from* Howl *(1956). "A Supermarket in California" dates from
the mid-1950s and exemplifies Ginsberg's ability to unite
cultural and experiential images in creating a vision of
American life.*

What thoughts I have of you tonight, Walt Whitman, for I walked down the
sidestreets under the trees with a headache self-conscious looking at the full
moon.

In my hungry fatigue, and shopping for images, I went into the neon fruit
supermarket, dreaming of your enumerations!

What peaches and what penumbras! Whole families shopping at night!
Aisles full of husbands! Wives in the avocados, babies in the tomatoes—and
you, García Lorca, what were you doing down by the watermelons?

I saw you, Walt Whitman, childless, lonely old grubber, poking among the
meats in the refrigerator and eyeing the grocery boys.

I heard you asking questions of each: Who killed the pork chops? What
price bananas? Are you my Angel?   5

I wandered in and out of the brilliant stacks of cans following you, and
followed in my imagination by the store detective.

We strode down the open corridors together in our solitary fancy tasting
artichokes, possessing every frozen delicacy, and never passing the cashier.

Where are we going, Walt Whitman? The doors close in an hour. Which
way does your beard point tonight?

(I touch your book and dream of our odyssey in the supermarket and feel
absurd.)

Will we walk all night through solitary streets? The trees add shade to
shade, lights out in the houses, we'll both be lonely.   10

Will we stroll dreaming of the lost America of love past blue automobiles in
driveways, home to our silent cottage?

Ah, dear father, graybeard, lonely old courage-teacher, what America did
you have when Charon quit poling his ferry and you got out on a smoking
bank and stood watching the boat disappear on the black waters of Lethe?

QUESTIONS

1. The speaker of the poem goes "shopping for images" in the "neon fruit
supermarket." What kinds of images does he "buy"? Who else is "shopping"?

2. Why is Whitman called "childless, lonely old grubber . . . eyeing the
grocery boys"? What image do you get of that man in this poem? Why is it
appropriate that he appear as a central figure in this poem?

3. What is "the lost America of love"? Where was it "found" before it was "lost"?

4. The poem closes with Whitman on the shores of the nether world of Greek mythology. Is this an appropriate final image? What does it suggest about the speaker's attitude toward America?

TOPIC FOR WRITING

The poem is written as an address to Whitman and therefore appears almost conversational in style. How does this affect your reading of the poem? How would a more formal poem treat this subject? How would it be different? Be specific in your analysis of the devices that Ginsberg uses—especially consider diction and length of lines.

W. D. (William Dewitt) Snodgrass

THE CAMPUS ON THE HILL

W. D. Snodgrass (1926–   ), Pulitzer Prize–winning poet, evolved a highly personal, confessional style that allows him to express what he sees as the poet's truth of existence —that is, "what he really thinks." Snodgrass uses his personal visions to clarify the particulars of experience, which he prefers to preserve as individual moments rather than to generalize into statements of transcendental belief. Born in Williamsburg, Pennsylvania, and raised in Beavers Falls, Snodgrass attended the University of Iowa's writers' workshops after having served in the Navy during World War II. While at Iowa, he studied with poet Robert Lowell (page 641), and together they developed a new, autobiographical, introspective mode for modern poetry. Snodgrass's poem "The Campus on the Hill" illustrates his affinity for personal contemplation and in so doing demonstrates how this personal experience is necessarily part of the larger social whole.

Up the reputable walks of old established trees
They stalk, children of the *nouveaux riches*; chimes
Of the tall Clock Tower drench their heads in blessing:
"I don't wanna play at your house;
I don't like you any more."   5
My house stands opposite, on the other hill,
Among meadows, with the orchard fences down and falling;

W. D. (William Dewitt) Snodgrass

Deer come almost to the door.
You cannot see it, even in this clearest morning.
White birds hang in the air between   10
Over the garbage landfill and those homes thereto adjacent,
Hovering slowly, turning, settling down
Like the flakes sifting imperceptibly onto the little town
In a waterball of glass.
And yet, this morning, beyond this quiet scene,   15
The floating birds, the backyards of the poor,
Beyond the shopping plaza, the dead canal, the hillside lying tilted in the
    air,
Tomorrow has broken out today:
Riot in Algeria, in Cyprus, in Alabama;   20
Aged in wrong, the empires are declining,
And China gathers, soundlessly, like evidence.
What shall I say to the young on such a morning?—
Mind is the one salvation?—also grammar?—
No; my little ones lean not toward revolt. They   25
Are the Whites, the vaguely furiously driven, who resist
Their souls with such passivity
As would make Quakers swear. All day, dear Lord, all day
They wear their godhead lightly.
They look out from their hill and say,   30
To themselves, "We have nowhere to go but down;
The great destination is to stay."
Surely the nations will be reasonable;
They look at the world—don't they?—the world's way?
The clock just now has nothing more to say.

QUESTIONS

1. What is the campus like? How do the "children of the *nouveaux riche*" fit among the "old established trees"? Who speaks through the voice of the chimes?

2. How does the speaker's house differ from the campus? How is the relation to nature different? Why is it hidden?

3. How does the image of the "waterball of glass" fit into the speaker's vision?

4. In the middle of the poem, the poet-persona's sense of time seems to break down: "Tomorrow has broken out today." Why? What is wrong with history? What is the relation between time and history? Why is the poem's final image that of a clock?

5. The children "wear their godhead lightly." What is their "godhead"? Why is "the great destination . . . to stay"? What does it mean to say that the final goal is stasis?

TOPIC FOR WRITING

In "The Wasteland," T. S. Eliot speaks of poetry as "a heap of broken images which I shore against my ruin." How does "Campus on the Hill" address this attitude? Consider what the speaker feels he can tell us students. Is "mind" enough to stave off world destruction? Is "grammar"? Is "reason"? How is the poem an answer to the chimes of the clock tower? Is this the task of poetry?

David Wagoner

A VALEDICTORY
TO STANDARD OIL OF INDIANA

David Wagoner (1926–   ), raised in an Indiana suburb of Chicago and educated at both Penn State and Indiana Universities, brings to his current home in the Pacific Northwest—where he is currently a professor of English at the University of Washington at Seattle—a knowledge and experience of the diversity of the American people. Focusing his poetry on themes of human survival, of the violation of the natural world, and of the mythic reality of Native Americans, Wagoner expresses a deep concern for the problems and possibilities of the continued survival of the human race. A novelist as well as a prolific poet, he presents in his work a thoughtful and diverse perspective on modern American life. The poem "A Valedictory to Standard Oil of Indiana" records Wagoner's experience of one facet of the American experience—the effects of industrialization on the lower middle class—in order to find "another way out."

In the darkness east of Chicago, the sky burns over the plumbers'
   nightmares
Red and blue, and my hometown lies there loaded with gasoline.
Registers ring like gas-pumps, pumps like pinballs, pinballs like broken
   alarm clocks,
And it's time for morning, but nothing's going to work.
From cat-cracker to candle-shop, from grease-works along the pipeline,   5
Over storage tanks like kings on a checkerboard ready to jump the county,
The word goes out: With refined regrets
We suggest you sleep all day in your houses shaped like lunch buckets
And don't show up at the automated gates.
Something else will tap the gauges without yawning   10
And check the valves at the feet of the cooling-towers without complaining.

David Wagoner

Standard Oil is canning my high school classmates
And the ones who fell out of junior high or slipped in the grades.
What should they do, gassed up in their Tempests and Comets, raring to go
Somewhere with their wives scowling in front and kids stuffed in the back,   15
Past drive-ins jammed like car-lots, trying to find the beaches
But blocked by freights for hours, stopped dead in their tracks
Where the rails, as thick as thieves along the lakefront,
Lower their crossing gates to shut the frontier? What can they think about
As they stare at the sides of boxcars for a sign,   20
And Lake Michigan drains slowly into Lake Huron,
The mills level the Dunes, and the eels go sailing through the trout,
And mosquitoes inherit the evening, while toads no bigger than horseflies
Hop crazily after them over the lawns and sidewalks, and the rainbows fall
Flat in the oil they came from? There are two towns now,   25
One dark, one going to be dark, divided by cyclone fences:
One pampered and cared for like pillboxes and cathedrals,
The other vanishing overnight in the dumps and swamps like a struck
    sideshow.
As the Laureate of the Class of '44—which doesn't know it has one—
I offer this poem, not from hustings or barricades   30
Or the rickety stage where George Rogers Clark stood glued to the wall,
But from another way out, like Barnum's "This Way to the Egress,"
Which moved the suckers when they'd seen enough. Get out of town.

QUESTIONS

1. In describing the coming of morning, Wagoner uses a string of mechanical images. What is the effect of describing such a "natural" phenomenon in those terms? What does it mean that "*nothing*" is going to work?

2. Using the understatement "We suggest you sleep all day . . .," the poem suggests that the workers are fired. Why is this understatement effective? Why is it significant that some*thing* else will take their place?

3. Describe the lives of the poet-persona's "canned" classmates. What kinds of images and language does he use to describe them?

4. As the motorists wait for the boxcars to pass, the natural world continues in motion. What is the nature of this movement? How is it related to the tone of the poem? Why is it important that nature impinge on this scene?

5. What are the two sides of town? How would you tell them apart? Which is closer to "nature"? How do you know? What kind of nature is this?

TOPICS FOR WRITING

1. Why is this poem a "valedictory"? Consider both the etymology and the common usage of the word. Is the poem structured as a valedictory address? How would it sound at a graduation ceremony? Who is graduating?

2. The speaker calls himself the "Laureate of the Class of '44." Does he speak for the class of '44 or is he an anomaly? What do you understand his message "get out of town" to mean in the context of the poem?

James Wright

A BLESSING

James Wright (1927–   ) was born in Martin's Ferry, Ohio, and received his BA from Kenyon College. After serving in the US Army during the occupation of Japan, he returned to complete a Ph.D. at the University of Washington and subsequently to take up teaching at Hunter College. Speaking of his own poetry, Wright has said, "I try and say how I love my country and how I despise the way it is treated. I try to speak of the beauty and again of the ugliness in lives of the poor and neglected." Seeing poetry as a form of social concern, Wright believes that "poetry [should] say something humanly important instead of just showing off the language." As a result, Wright's poetry often expresses a directness and engagement with the external world that is reminiscent of the lucid complexities of Robert Frost (see page 407), whom Wright acknowledges as one of his models. The Wright poem included in this anthology, "A Blessing," from The Branch Will Not Break *(1963), situates the poet-persona within the natural world in order to illuminate the speaker's relation to the entire world around him.*

Just off the highway to Rochester, Minnesota,
Twilight bounds softly forth on the grass.
And the eyes of those two Indian ponies
Darken with kindness.
They have come gladly out of the willows   5
To welcome my friend and me.
We step over the barbed wire into the pasture
Where they have been grazing all day, alone.
They ripple tensely, they can hardly contain their happiness
That we have come.   10
They bow shyly as wet swans. They love each other.
There is no loneliness like theirs.
At home once more,

They begin munching the young tufts of spring in the darkness.
I would like to hold the slenderer one in my arms,   15

For she has walked over to me
And nuzzled my left hand.
She is black and white,
Her mane falls wild on her forehead,
And the light breeze moves me to caress her long ear   20
That is delicate as the skin over a girl's wrist.
Suddenly I realize
That if I stepped out of my body I would break
Into blossom.

QUESTIONS

1. The first line situates the poem "Just off the highway to Rochester, Minnesota." What is the effect of locating the poem in this spot? What does it tell you about the speaker? What expectations does it establish for you as you read the rest of the poem?

2. As the speaker and his friend cross the barbed wire the ponies "ripple tensely, they can hardly contain their happiness/That we have come." Why should the animals feel this way? Is there a reciprocal experience for the speakers? Is it appropriate that this happen after the people cross the barbed wire?

3. The speaker likens the ponies to "wet swans" in love. Yet, "There is no loneliness like theirs." Explain this seeming contradiction.

4. In the last ten lines of the poem, the speaker expresses his feelings toward the "slenderer" pony. How does he describe these emotions? Are these images appropriate? How do they help explain the way the poet sees the world?

TOPICS FOR WRITING

1. The poem seems at first glance to be a very simple anecdote—a sweet story. How do the diction, poetic structure, and tone allow us to read this as "something more"? Would you understand this narrative differently if it were written as a short story? Why or why not?

2. The poet's use of "blossom" in the last line calls to mind images of fertility and sexuality. How does this image stand in relation to the rest of the poem? Does it help you understand why the poem is entitled "A Blessing"?

John Ashbery

CITY AFTERNOON

John Ashbery (1927–   ) was born in Rochester, New York, and received a BA from Harvard (1949) and an MA from Columbia before going to France on a Fulbright scholarship in 1955. He has been both a critic and an editor for a variety of journals, ranging from the New York Herald Tribune to Partisan Review, and as a result his name is now one of the hallmarks of American verse. Ashbery received the Yale Series of Younger Poets prize in 1956 for Some Trees and both the National Book Award and the Pulitzer Prize in 1976 for Self-Portrait in a Convex Mirror. His poetry has come to epitomize for many the notion that poetry does not have to mean in order to be. Ashbery writes for effect—in order to illuminate the way poetry itself is created. His poem "City Afternoon," presented here, suggests both the difficulties and subtleties which make Ashbery unique among American poets today.

A veil of haze protects this
Long-ago afternoon forgotten by everybody
In this photograph, most of them now
Sucked screaming through old age and death.

If one could seize America   5
Or at least a fine forgetfulness
That seeps into our outline
Defining our volumes with a stain
That is fleeting too
But commemorates   10
Because it does define, after all:
Gray garlands, that threesome
Waiting for the light to change,
Air lifting the hair of one
Upside down in the reflecting pool.   15

QUESTIONS

1. From what does the veil of haze protect the long-ago afternoon? How does the photographer "preserve" its image?

2. How does "Sucked screaming through old age and death" characterize the lives of the people in the photograph? Is this the speaker's vision or that of the people themselves? Does this matter?

3. What is the relationship between America and the photograph? How is it that we think of America? How do we "see" America? In what way are "we" ("our outline," "our volumes") part of a photograph of America?

4. The final four lines of the poem present a small tableau. What is this scene? Where does it come from? Why is it included in the poem?

TOPICS FOR WRITING

1. The poem is composed in two stanzas, the first seemingly a prelude to the second. Attempt to define the relationship between the two stanzas. Explore the similarities and differences in the use of image patterns, diction, tone, and subject. Is it possible to unify the poem? How does the title attempt to do this? Does it succeed?

2. Speaking of his poetry, Ashbery comments: "There are no themes or subjects in the usual sense, except the very broad one of an individual conscious-ness confronting or confronted by a world of external phenomena." How well does this commentary capture the spirit of "City Afternoon"? Why?

Anne Sexton

Before her suicide Anne Sexton (1928–1974), introduced earlier (page 408), created a body of work that was simulta-neously dark, painful, and incisive. Drawn out of her person-al life, out of her doubts and fears in her relation to her family, out of her understanding of cultural myths—in short, out of the experiences that she felt defined her as a woman— Sexton's poems present direct, often abrasive descriptions of physical existence. Poetry, she said in an interview with Patricia Marx, "should be a shock to the senses. It should almost hurt." In the two poems provided below and in an earlier selection (page 408), Sexton uses such raw physical descriptions to evoke her experience as a woman poet in a society that attempts to suppress the voices of women.

THE BLACK ART

A woman who writes feels too much,
those trances and portents!
As if cycles and children and islands
weren't enough; as if mourners and gossips
and vegetables were never enough.   5
She thinks she can warn the stars.
A writer is essentially a spy.
Dear love, I am that girl.

A man who writes knows too much,
such spells and fetiches!   10
As if erections and congresses and products
weren't enough; as if machines and galleons
and wars were never enough.

With used furniture he makes a tree.
A writer is essentially a crook.   15
Dear love, you are that man.

Never loving ourselves,
hating even our shoes and our hats,
we love each other, *precious, precious.*
Our hands are light blue and gentle.   20
Our eyes are full of terrible confessions.
But when we marry,
the children leave in disgust
There is too much food and no one left over
to eat up all the weird abundance.   25

QUESTIONS

1. What kinds of things does the woman poet "feel" that the male poet, because he "knows," can't? Are these qualitatively different ways of understanding? How can this difference be related to the different experiences that men and women have?

2. The poem's first and second stanzas have identical structures, yet the mood and tone of each are distinct. How does Sexton evoke these distinctions while using the same basic framework?

3. What is the nature of the relationship between the two persons who compose the "we" of the poem's last stanza? What does it mean to love someone when you don't love yourself? Why is their love "precious"?

4. What is the "food" in the last sentence? Why is the abundance "weird"?

TOPIC FOR WRITING

The poem is entitled "The Black Art." To what does this refer? What kind of context does it establish for your reading of the poem? What kind of expectations does it lead you to have about the poem? Are these expectations fulfilled? Why or why not? If so, how?

THE SUN

I have heard of fish
coming up for the sun
who stayed forever,
shoulder to shoulder,
avenues of fish that never got back,   5

all their proud spots and solitudes
sucked out of them.

I think of flies
who come from their foul caves
out into the arena.   10
They are transparent at first.
Then they are blue with copper wings.
They glitter on the foreheads of men.
Neither bird nor acrobat
They will dry out like small black shoes.   15

I am an identical being.
Diseased by the cold and the smell of the house
I undress under the burning magnifying glass.
My skin flattens out like sea water.
O yellow eye,   20
let me be sick with your heat,
let me be feverish and frowning.
Now I am utterly given.
I am your daughter, your sweet-meat,
your priest, your mouth and your bird   25
and I will tell them all stories of you
until I am laid away forever,
a thin gray banner.

QUESTIONS

1. The first two stanzas describe the movement of animals (fish, flies) from enclosed spaces into the open. How does the poem's narrator describe this movement? What happens as a result of this movement? Is it what you would expect?

2. What is meant by the sentence "I am an identical being"? How does this statement link the first two stanzas with the last?

3. In the last stanza the speaker turns her gaze from the external world to her own life. How do the descriptions of this life compare with the earlier descriptions? Note the use of imagery, diction, sentence patterns, and stanza structures. How do these contribute to the speaker's tone?

4. Why does the poem conclude with a list of the things the narrator feels she is? How are the elements in the list related to each other? To the images in the rest of the poem? To the narrator's view of the world?

TOPICS FOR WRITING

1. Typically in Western literature the sun is used as a symbol of illumination —of a coming to knowledge or enlightenment. How does this poem utilize this

convention? How do the poem's different descriptions of the sun organize the way we read the poem?

2. The speaker of the poem says, "I will tell them all stories of you/until I am laid away forever,/a thin gray banner." Is this poem one such story? If so, what is it the story of? What difference is there—if any—between a poem and a story? How would the narrator answer this question?

Adrienne Rich

In an essay entitled "When We Dead Awaken," Adrienne Rich (1929–   ) speaks of the purpose for poetry in terms of the collective awakening of human consciousness from the "sleep" in which most of us now exist: the sleep in which we allow ourselves to treat others as something less than fully human. For Rich (see page 347), her experience as a poet, as a teacher, as a housewife, as a mother—as woman— showed her that she would be unable to understand herself both as a woman and as a human if she allowed herself to continue as a sleepwalker, defining herself only in the terms given to her by men. In the poems presented here, "The Parting," "August," and "Peeling Onions," Rich looks at particular experiences from a personal perspective in order to draw from them a larger picture of the ways we understand the world and begin to understand how to change it.

THE PARTING: I

The ocean twanging away there
and the islands like scattered laundry—
You can feel so free, so free,
standing on the headland

where the wild rose never stands still,   5
the petals blown off

before they fall
and the chicory nodding

blue, blue, in the all-day wind.
Barbed wire, dead at your feet,   10

is a kind of dune-vine,
the only one without movement

Every knot is a knife
where two strands tangle to rust.

QUESTIONS

1. How does the poem's final image of barbed wire influence the narrator's earlier feeling of freedom?

2. In what sense is this poem a "parting"?

3. How does Rich use alliteration and dissonance to enhance the starkness of the final image?

TOPIC FOR WRITING

How does Rich's diction evoke feelings of motion and stillness? How is this related to the poem's tone?

AUGUST

Two horses in yellow light
eating windfall apples under a tree

as summer tears apart   milkweeds stagger
and grasses grow more ragged

They say there are ions in the sun   5
neutralizing magnetic fields on earth

Some way to explain
what this week has been, and the one before it!

If I am flesh sunning on rock
if I am brain burning in fluorescent light   10

if I am dream like a wire with fire
throbbing along it

if I am death to man
I have to know it

His mind is too simple, I cannot go on   15
sharing his nightmares

My own are becoming clearer, they open
into prehistory

which looks like a village lit with blood
where all the fathers are crying: *My son is mine!* 20

QUESTIONS

1. The narrator offers two different ways of explaining "what this week has been, and the week before it": her own ("Two horses in yellow light . . . grow more ragged") and theirs ("They say . . . fields on earth"). How are these descriptions related? Do they help explain each other?

2. In lines 9–14, the narrator poses questions about the possibilities of her own existence. How are these related to the explanations and descriptions in the poem's first eight lines?

3. The title of the poem situates it within a chronological frame. Why is this important for your reading of the poem?

4. In the eighth stanza, the narrator refers to "his nightmares." What are they? Why can she not go on sharing them? Why is his mind too "simple"? What might her nightmares be?

TOPIC FOR WRITING

Discuss the feelings evoked by the final vision of "prehistory." Why does this poem conclude with the exclamation "My son is mine!"?

PEELING ONIONS

Only to have a grief
equal to all these tears!

There's not a sob in my chest.
Dry-hearted as Peer Gynt

I pare away, no hero, 5
merely a cook.

Crying was labor, once
when I'd good cause.
Walking, I felt my eyes like wounds
raw in my head, 10
so postal-clerks, I thought, must stare.
A dog's look, a cat's, burnt to my brain—

yet all that stayed
stuffed in my lungs like smog.

These old tears in the chopping-bowl.   15

QUESTIONS

1. How does the poem's last line help explain what it means to "have a grief equal to all these tears"?

2. What does it mean to have "good cause" to cry? Why is this kind of crying called "labor"?

3. Why does the narrator compare the everyday activity of peeling onions to a more evocative experience of personal pain? Is one more significant than the other? How do these two different activities affect each other?

TOPIC FOR WRITING

How does Rich's use of stanzas organize the relationships between the ideas in the poem? How does it affect your reading of the poem?

Thom Gunn

ON THE MOVE

Thom Gunn (1929–   ), British born, Oxbridge trained, and American experienced, has been one of the most innovative poets in both British and American letters in recent years. Speaking of the breadth of Gunn's accomplishments, Neal Corcoran has said: "Geographically he has moved from England to America, more specifically from 1950s Cambridge to 1960s San Francisco; metrically, he has moved from highly disciplined traditional forms, through syllabics to a very loose kind of free form; and thematically, he has made use of such widely varied influences as French existentialist thought and American lysergic acid. And emotionally and sexually, Gunn has moved from poems overtly addressed to women to openly frank homosexual poems. He is, altogether, a poet difficult to get clear and difficult to get whole." "On the Move," the Gunn poem provided here, exemplifies the way he uses his diverse experience—in this case an encounter with a California motorcycle gang—in order to explain the nature of existence.

On the Move

'Man, you gotta Go!

The blue jay scuffling in the bushes follows
Some hidden purpose, and the gust of birds
That spurts across the field, the wheeling swallows,
Have nested in the trees and undergrowth.
Seeking their instinct, or their poise, or both.   5
One moves with an uncertain violence
Under the dust thrown by a baffled sense
Or the dull-thunder of approximate words.

On motorcycles, up the road, they come:
Small, black, as flies hanging in heat, the Boys,   10
Until the distance throws them forth, their hum
Bulges to thunder held by calf and thigh.
In goggles, donned impersonality,
In gleaming jackets trophied with the dust,
They strap in doubt—by hiding it, robust—   15
And almost hear a meaning in their noise.

Exact conclusion of their hardiness
Has no shape yet, but from known whereabouts
They ride, direction where the tires press.
They scare a flight of birds across the field: 20
Much that is natural, to the will must yield.
Men manufacture both machine and soul,
And use what they imperfectly control
To dare a future from the taken routes.

It is a part solution, after all.   25
One is not necessarily discord
On earth; or damned because, half animal,
One lacks direct instinct, because one wakes
Afloat on movement that divides and breaks.
One joins the movement in a valueless world,   30
Choosing it, till, both hurler and the hurled,
One moves as well, always toward, toward.

A minute holds them, who have come to go:
The self-defined, astride the created will
They burst away; the towns they travel through   35
Are home for neither bird nor holiness,
For birds and saints complete their purposes.
At worse, one is in motion; and at best,
Reaching no absolute, in which to rest,
One is always nearer by not keeping still.   40

QUESTIONS

1. The poem opens with a description of birds moving within the landscape and then moves on to a third-person, impersonal ("one") evocation of the frailty of human movement within the social and linguistic landscape ("One moves with uncertain violence . . . approximate words"). How does this juxtaposition establish the context for the poem? How does it frame your understanding of the bikers? How would your image of them be different if the poem had opened with, for example, a description of a garage or grease pit?

2. Why are the bikers called "the Boys"? What do we learn about their character from their physical description? What is meant by "donned impersonality"?

3. Why does the poem return to the initial image of "a flight of birds" in order to make the claim "Much that is natural, to the will must yield"? Do you agree with this statement? What is "natural"? What is "will"?

4. What effect does Gunn's use of the pronoun "one" to make generalizations about humanity have on the meaning of these statements? Would the substitution of "everyone" for "one" change the sense of the poem? Why or why not?

TOPICS FOR WRITING

1. The poem seems to claim that movement in and of itself is a choice and therefore an engagement with life. In this sense, the biker's life is a "part solution." To what is it a solution? What is the "movement that divides and breaks"? When is the world "aimless"? How does the poem go about framing answers to these questions?

2. What is one nearer to by not keeping still? How does the epigraph set up this question?

Gary Snyder

NOT LEAVING THE HOUSE

Gary Snyder (1930–   ) was born in San Francisco. In discussing Snyder's use of images culled from Buddhism, Native American folklore, experience of the wilderness, and his own social interactions, fellow poet Thom Gunn has said: "His [Snyder's] valuing of the primitive tribe and its relations to the earth is not a sentiment but a call for action. . . ." Snyder's poetry is rooted in his own widely varied experience. (Snyder has a BA in anthropology from Reed College; he has worked as a logger and on a Forest Service trail crew; he studied oriental languages at the University of California at Berkeley; from 1956 to 1964, he studied Buddhism in Japan; he worked on an oil tanker in the Pacific and Indian Oceans before returning to Berkeley to teach.) Snyder's poems weave a fragmented web of keen observation and profound insight into a rich tapestry on which history and nature appear as two complementary pieces of the myth of humanity. This relationship underlies Snyder's poetic project because it locates poetry at the level of experience and action—at the level of change. In a 1966 Village Voice interview, Snyder said, "I think there's a real revolution going on somewhere below or outside the level of formal politics"; and in "Not Leaving Home," we see how the birth of his son Kai affects one such personal "revolution."

When Kai is born
I quit going out

Hang around the kitchen—make cornbread
Let nobody in.
Mail is flat.   5
    Masa lies on her side, Kai sighs,
    Non washes and sweeps
We sit and watch
    Masa nurse, and drink green tea.

Navajo turquoise beads over the bed   10
A peacock tail feather at the head
A badger pelt from Nagano-ken
For a mattress; under the sheet;
A pot of yogurt setting
Under the blankets, at his feet.   15

Masa, Kai,
And Non, our friend
In the green garden light reflected in
Not leaving the house.
From dawn til late at night   20
    making a new world of ourselves
    around this life.

QUESTIONS

1. Why is the poem's first line, "When Kai is born," stated in the present tense? How does this affect the recounting of the story of his birth?

2. What is the mood of the second stanza? How does the syntax of the stanza contribute to the mood?

3. In the third stanza, we are given a list of physical objects. How do these objects relate to the mood of the second stanza? How do they extend it? What relation is there between this physical world and Kai's birth?

4. What is the "new world" of the last stanza? How is it different from the old world?

TOPIC FOR WRITING

Each of the poem's four stanzas presents a different mode of poetic expression. Examine each in detail, concentrating especially on the different uses of grammatical and symbolic structures. How do the differences contribute to your reading of the poem? How do they illuminate your understanding of the poet's "new world"?

Sylvia Plath

POINT SHIRLEY

Sylvia Plath (1932–1963), as revealed in an earlier selection in this anthology (page 371), wrote several of her most powerful poems about relationships with members of her family. "Point Shirley," written in 1959 when Plath was under the influence of Robert Lowell, is a poem in which the force of the sea shapes Plath's memory of her grandmother. Point Shirley was the home of Plath's maternal grandparents and the source of some of her warmest memories of childhood. "My childhood landscape," wrote Plath, "was not land, but the end of land—the air, salt, running hills of the Atlantic. I sometimes think that my vision of the sea is the clearest thing that I own." Here, in "Point Shirley," the destructive force of the sea creates the internal tension in the poem, as Plath attempts to find the relationship between memory and object, between that which she loves and that which is no longer here.

Point Shirley

From Water-Tower Hill to the brick prison
The shingle booms, bickering under
The sea's collapse.
Snowcakes break and welter. This year
The gritted wave leaps   5
The seawall and drops onto a bier
Of quahog chips,
Leaving a salty mash of ice to whiten

In my grandmother's sand yard. She is dead,
Whose laundry snapped and froze here, who   10
Kept house against
What the sluttish, rutted sea could do.
Squall waves once danced
Ship timbers in through the cellar window;
A thresh-tailed, lanced   15
Shark littered in the geranium bed—

Such collusion of mulish elements
She wore her broom straws to the nub.
Twenty years out
Of her hand, the house still hugs in each drab   20
Stucco socket
The purple egg-stones: from Great Head's knob
To the filled-in Gut
The sea in its cold gizzard ground those rounds.

Nobody wintering now behind   25
The planked-up windows where she set
Her wheat loaves
And apple cakes to cool. What is it
Survives, grieves
So, over this battered, obstinate spit   30
Of gravel? The waves'
Spewed relics clicker masses in the wind,

Grey waves the stub-necked elders ride.
A labor of love, and that labor lost.
Steadily the sea   35
Eats at Point Shirley. She died blessed,
And I come by
Bones, bones only, pawed and tossed,
A dog-faced sea.
The sun sinks under Boston, bloody red.   40

I would get from these dry-papped stones
The milk your love instilled in them.
The black ducks dive.
And though your graciousness might stream,

And I contrive,   45
Grandmother, stones are nothing of home
To that spumiest dove.
Against both bar and tower the black sea runs.

QUESTIONS

1. How does Plath evoke the force of the sea in the first stanza? What sound patterns convey this impression? How is the sea presented in subsequent stanzas?

2. What was the grandmother's relationship to the sea? Why is the world around her house and her life so chaotic? Was the grandmother ever able to order or subdue this world? Explain.

3. What does Plath seek in the "dry-papped stones" in stanza 6? Why does memory fail her?

4. Explain the tone of the apostrophe to Plath's grandmother in the last stanza. Why does she qualify her terms, as in "I would get" and "your graciousness might stream"?

5. State in your own words the theme of this poem.

TOPICS FOR WRITING

1. Explain the way in which the line "A labor of love, and that labor lost" captures the tensions that seem to be balanced in this poem.

2. One critic, Charles Newman, states that Plath "endows the sea with the characters of her own mind." Apply this comment to "Point Shirley."

3. Compare and contrast Plath's attitude toward her grandmother in this poem with her perception of her father in "Daddy" (page 371).

Etheridge Knight

HARD ROCK RETURNS TO PRISON FROM THE HOSPITAL FOR THE CRIMINAL INSANE

Etheridge Knight (1933–   ) discovered in prison the power of poetry to transform both personal and social life. Born in Corinth, Mississippi, Knight found himself fighting in Korea after completing only two years of high school. Sentenced to the Indiana State Prison in 1960, Knight was released in 1968. Writing of his experience on the cover of his first book of poetry, Poems from Prison *(1968), Knight says: "I died in Korea from a shrapnel wound and narcotics resurrected me. I died in 1960 from a prison sentence and poetry brought me back to life." Using his poetry to "perceive and conceptualize the collective aspirations, the collective vision of black people," Knight calls on his own experience in order to provide the material from which his evocation of the life of black Americans arises. Often witty, incisive, and sardonic, he presents characters who face the material oppression of their society in order to illustrate the way that society denies their basic human potential. The poem included here draws on his prison experience in order to illustrate the way in which white society seeks to control the "insane" actions of the black community.*

Hard Rock was "known not to take no shit
From nobody," and he had the scars to prove it:
Split purple lips, lumped ears, welts above
His yellow eyes, and one long scar that cut
Across his temple and plowed through a thick   5
Canopy of kinky hair.

The WORD was that Hard Rock wasn't a mean nigger
Anymore, that the doctors had bored a hole in his head,
Cut out part of his brain, and shot electricity
Through the rest. When they brought Hard Rock back,   10
Handcuffed and chained, he was turned loose,
Like a freshly gelded stallion, to try his new status.
And we all waited and watched, like indians at a corral,
To see if the WORD was true.

As we waited we wrapped ourselves in the cloak   15
Of his exploits: "Man, the last time, it took eight
Screws to put him in the Hole." "Yeah, remember when he
Smacked the captain with his dinner tray?" "He set
The record for time in the Hole—67 straight days!"
"Ol Hard Rock! man, that's one crazy nigger."   20
And then the jewel of a myth that Hard Rock had once bit
A screw on the thumb and poisoned him with syphilitic spit.

The testing came, to see if Hard Rock was really tame.
A hillbilly called him a black son of a bitch
And didn't lose his teeth, a screw who knew Hard Rock   25
From before shook him down and barked in his face.
And Hard Rock did *nothing*. Just grinned and looked silly,
His eyes empty like knot holes in a fence.

And even after we discovered that it took Hard Rock
Exactly 3 minutes to tell you his first name,   30
We told ourselves that he had just wised up,
Was being cool; but we could not fool ourselves for long,
And we turned away, our eyes on the ground. Crushed.
He had been our Destroyer, the doer of things
We dreamed of doing but could not bring ourselves to do,   35
The fears of years, like a biting whip,
Had cut grooves too deeply across our backs.

QUESTIONS

1. Why is Hard Rock "insane"? What does this have to do with his being "known not to take no shit from nobody"? Why is this phrase presented as a direct quotation?

2. When Hard Rock returns to prison he is turned loose "like a freshly gelded stallion." Why is he compared to a castrated horse? What is the relationship between sexuality and Hard Rock's former power?

3. What is the "WORD"? What is the effect of distinguishing this word typographically from the rest of the text?

4. Why had Hard Rock been their "Destroyer"? Why could he do things that no one else could? How is "Destroyer" different from "Savior"? Are all Destroyers-Saviors "insane"? Who decides what is insanity?

TOPICS FOR WRITING

1. Psychiatric methods have become increasingly used to deal with "troublesome elements of society" who refuse to be "normal." Given the experience of the black community within the dominant white culture, how are we to define "normality"? Can Hard Rock's actions be explained in any way other than by calling him "one crazy nigger"? Is a "mean nigger" different from a "crazy nigger"? How does the poem's use of diction influence our evaluation of what has happened to Hard Rock?

2. This poem is essentially a narrative recollection of an historical event. Try rewriting this narrative as a short story, using one paragraph for each stanza. Feel free to use the language of the poem, but do not simply fill in the "missing" information. Compare your story with the poem. How do they differ? How are they the same?

Amiri Baraka (LeRoi Jones)

IN MEMORY OF RADIO

Amiri Baraka (1934–   ), poet, playwright, novelist, and essayist, was one of the moving forces behind the cultural explosion known as the Black Arts Movement during the 1960s. Born in Newark, New Jersey, as LeRoi Jones and educated at both Howard and Columbia Universities, Baraka (the Muslim name he adopted in 1968) experienced the cultural training that was expected of both white and black intellectuals during the middle part of this century. This experience led Baraka to the realization that his own conception of who he was as a black man and who blacks as a people were within the larger white society were themselves determined by the white men's visions of the world. Using this conflict between his life as he lived it and his life as he was educated to understand it in order to examine the problems of blacks in American, Baraka comes to understand even the most mundane of daily activities in terms of the social and cultural production of the world around us. He traces this theme in Preface to a Twenty Volume Suicide Note *(1962),* Black Magic: Poetry 1961–1967 *(1967), the play* Dutchman *(1967), and other works. "In Memory of Radio" focuses on one seemingly "innocent" set of images—those from the popular radio of the 1940s and 1950s—in order to reveal the implicit message they insidiously convey.*

Who has ever stopped to think of the divinity of Lamont Cranston?
(Only Jack Kerouac, that I know of: & me.
The rest of you probably had on WCBS and Kate Smith,
Or something equally unattractive.)

What can I say?   5
It is better to have loved and lost
Than to put linoleum in your living rooms?

Am I a sage or something?
Mandrake's hypnotic gesture of the week?
(Remember, I do not have the healing powers of Oral Roberts . . .   10
I cannot, like F. J. Sheen, tell you how to get saved & *rich!*

I cannot even order you to gaschamber satori like Hitler or Goody Knight.

& Love is an evil word.
Turn it backwards/ see, see what I mean?
An evol word & besides   15
who understands it?
I certainly wouldn't like to go out on that kind of limb.

Saturday mornings we listened to *Red Lantern* & his undersea folk.
At 11, *Let's Pretend/* & we did/ & I, the poet, still do, Thank God!

What was it he used to say (after the transformation, when he was safe   20
& invisible, & the unbelievers couldn't throw stones?) "Heh, Heh, Heh,
Who knows what evil lurks in the hearts of men? The Shadow knows!"

O, yes he does
O, yes he does
An evil word it is,   25
This love.

QUESTIONS

1. Who is Lamont Cranston? Why is he "divine"? Why does no one—except
Kerouac and the speaker—think of him? What is the effect of opening the poem
with these proper names? How does the fact that these references are no longer
part of our cultural repertoire affect your reading? What kinds of expectations
does it establish for the rest of the poem?

2. Baraka uses pauses (often clichés) that could have come across the
airwaves and combines them to construct new poetic meanings. Give several
examples from the poem. How does this use of language change the way we
normally use language? How is it different from the way these words were used in
their original context?

3. Why does love enter the poem?

4. How is the poet-persona related to "The Shadow"? Why can he continue to
"pretend." What is it that "The Shadow" knows? What is it that the black man
knows?

TOPICS FOR WRITING

1. In the context of the poem, why is love an evil word?

2. Baraka's poem uses a wide variety of images and memories that seem to
have little or no connection other than the radio. How does the idea of radio
organize the poem? What are the connections among the images? Examine the
way Baraka arranges his poetic resources. Why does the poem conclude "This
love"?

Sonia Sanchez

POEM AT THIRTY

*Sonia Sanchez (1934–   ) has developed one of the most
complex and yet most direct voices to come out of the black
cultural revolution of the late 1960s (the Black Arts Movement). After growing up in Atlanta, Georgia, and then going
on to receive a BA from NYU in 1955, Sanchez found that she
could not reconcile the difference between her childhood
upbringing as a black girl in the South and her education as
an intellectual in the North. Thus she began to question
(and challenge) the systems that allow such distinctions
and disparities to exist. A committed activist, Sonia Sanchez uses her own voice and the voice of the American black
community—with its particular idioms and diction—to
evoke the personal significance of a large political situation.
In "Poem at Thirty," she selects one moment from her own
history in order to examine her relation to the social history
of black people in America.*

it is midnight
no magical bewitching
hour for me
i know only that
i am here waiting   5
remembering that
once as a child
i walked two
miles in my sleep.
did I know   10
then where i
was going?
traveling. i'm
always traveling.
i want to tell   15
you about me
about nights on a
brown couch when
i wrapped my
bones in lint and   20
refused to move.
no one touches
me anymore.
father do not
send me out   25
among strangers.
you you black man
stretching scraping
the mold from your body
here is my hand.   30
i am not afraid
of the night.

Sonia Sanchez

QUESTIONS

1. How is the poet-persona at 30 similar to and different from the child who walked two miles in her sleep? Does she know where she is going? Does it matter?

2. Why does the poem begin at midnight? Why is it not a "magical bewitching hour"? What is it instead?

3. Why does the speaker want to tell "about nights on a brown couch . . ."? What do we learn from this story?

4. The speaker asks (commands?) her father not to send her "out among strangers." Who are those "strangers"? Why would her father send her out among them? Does she need to go?

5. Will the "black man/stretching scraping/the mold from [his] body" take the hand of the poet-persona when "no one touches . . . anymore"? Why is this insistence on physical existence—on the importance of the body—part of this "Poem at Thirty"?

TOPIC FOR WRITING

At first glance this poem seems to lack what some might call the "richness" of poetic imagery; nevertheless, the poem creates a unique and moving vision of a black woman's "poetic" experience. How is this accomplished? Consider the way the poem sets out its story, the language it uses, the implied settings on which it rests. What elements do these have in common? How do they establish the tone of the poem?

June Jordan

POEM FROM
THE EMPIRE STATE

*June Jordan (1936–   ), poet, journalist, and novelist, was
born in Harlem. She attended Barnard College and the
University of Chicago and since 1975 has been a professor
at the City University of New York. Committed to what she
terms "the politics of survival and change," Jordan is a
literary figure constantly giving poetry readings at schools
and institutions around the nation, attempting to combat
"the cult of negative realism" that she says affects the
country's youth. Her poetry collections include* Some Changes *(1971),* New Days: Poems of Exile and Return *(1973), and*
Selected Poems of June Jordan: Things That I do in the Dark
*(1977). Jordan's poems are short and structurally tight,
often relying, as in the following selection, on the juxtaposition of images to capture a scene and to comment on it.*

Three of us went to the top of the city
a friend, my son, and I
on that day when winter wrote like snow
across the moonlike sky
and stood there breathing a heavy height   5
as wide as the streets to see
so poor and frozen far below
that nothing would change for you and me
that swallowing death lay wallowing still
with the wind at the bloat of piled-up swill.   10
And that was the day we conquered the air
with 100,000 tons of garbage.

*No rhyme can be said
where reason has fled.*

QUESTIONS

1. How does the "top of the city" contrast with the city "frozen far below"?
What is the relationship of the three people in the poem to this urban landscape?
What, if anything, do they conquer?

2. Identify and comment on the types of figurative language used by Jordan
in this poem.

3. Is there a rhyme scheme in this poem or simply a random set of rhymes?
What is the purpose and effect of rhyme in the poem?

4. Explain the tone and theme of the poem and the relationship of the last
two lines to the overall meaning.

TOPICS FOR WRITING

1. Classify the varieties of figurative language in the poem and the use Jordan makes of them to advance her theme.

2. This poem contains fourteen lines. Could it be considered an experimental sonnet? Why or why not?

James Welch

THE ONLY BAR IN DIXON

James Welch (1940–　　), born in Browning, Montana, and a Native American poet, brings to his verse a knowledge of the contemporary experience of Native American life that is rarely found in American poetry. Using the images and associations that derive from his cultural knowledge, Welch focuses on providing a continuity with the physical and mythic aspects of the natural world in order to decry the way in which these aspects have been devalued within modern society. "The Only Bar in Dixon" describes this process of devastation by describing the new social environment—the bar—which has replaced the natural environment as the site on which the Native American sense of identity is defined.

These Indians once imitated life.
Whatever made them warm
they called wine, song or sleep,
a lucky number on the tribal roll.

Now the stores have gone the gray   5
of this November sky. Cars
whistle by, chrome wind, knowing
something lethal in the dust.

A man could build a reputation here.
Take that redhead at the bar—   10
she knows we're thugs, killers
on a fishing trip with luck.

No luck. No room for those
sensitive enough to know they're beat.
Even the Flathead turns away,   15
A river thick with bodies,

Indians on their way to Canada.
Take the redhead—yours for just a word,
a promise that the wind will warm
and all the saints come back for laughs.   20

QUESTIONS

1. What does the statement "These Indians once imitated life" mean? How does one "imitate" life?

2. How does the world "now" differ from the world in which the Indians imitated life? How is the natural world different? the social world?

3. How does the speaker identify himself? Is this a "true" identification? Why does he have "no luck"?

TOPICS FOR WRITING

1. Analyze Welch's vision of contemporary Native American life in this poem.

2. What is the role of the "redhead" in the poem? Why is she associated with things that make one warm? Is woman envisioned as a solution to or an escape from the situation presented in the poem?

Leslie Silko

WHERE MOUNTAIN LION
LAY DOWN WITH DEER

Leslie Marmon Silko (1948–   ) was born in Albuquerque, New Mexico, of mixed ancestry—Laguna Pueblo, Mexican, and white. She grew up on the Laguna Pueblo reservation, where she lives today with her husband and two children. A widely published poet, novelist, and short story writer, Silko is preoccupied in her writing with the act, process, and ritual of storytelling as a way of celebrating tradition, preserving memory, and sustaining cultural continuity. "I

Leslie Silko

grew up with storytelling," she writes. "My earliest memories are of my grandmother telling me stories while she
watered the morning glories in her yard. Her stories were
about incidents from long ago, incidents which occurred
before she was born but which she told as certainly as if she
had been there." In the following poem, from Storyteller
(1981), Silko blends legend, nature, and personal consciousness in a tale that explore the speaker's own origins.

I climb the black rock mountain
  stepping from day to day
        silently.
I smell the wind for my ancestors
  pale blue leaves   5
  crushed wild mountain smell.
Returning
  up the gray stone cliff
  where I descended
          a thousand years ago   10
Returning to faded black stone
where mountain lion lay down with deer.
It is better to stay up here
        watching wind's reflection
        in tall yellow flowers.   15
The old ones who remember me are gone
     the old songs are all forgotten
and the story of my birth.
How I danced in snow-frost moonlight
  distant start to the end of the Earth,   20
How I swam away
      in freezing mountain water
     narrow mossy canyon tumbling down
         out of the mountain
         out of deep canyon stone   25
     down
       the memory
         spilling out
         into the world.

QUESTIONS

1. What is the speaker's relationship to nature?

2. What images suggest release and freedom? What is the speaker seeking freedom from? What is she trying to capture?

3. How does the "I" of the poem become universal and timeless in its dimensions?

4. Explain the way in which Silko develops the birth metaphor in the second half of the poem.

5. What does the title of the poem signify?

TOPICS FOR WRITING

1. Explain the way that Silko celebrates tradition, legend, and myth in "Where Mountain Lion Lay Down with Deer."

2. Analyze the mood that Silko creates in the poem and its relationship to the form of the poem and its theme.

P A R T 3

DRAMA

"All the world's a stage," wrote Shakespeare in one of the most famous lines in drama, "and all the men and women merely players." Indeed our human drama is persistent and universal, probably as old as the earliest hunters who disguised themselves and tried to act like those animals they were trying to lure into a trap and kill. The hunt and other crucial activities became ongoing dramas reflecting human conflict and the struggle for survival; and these dramas lent themselves to the creation of stories about bravery and cowardice, endurance and extinction, tragedy and comedy.

From its beginnings, drama (which Aristotle called "imitated human action"), like other forms of literature, was meant to tell the story of humankind in conflict with its world. In the acting out of events, drama often invested the most ancient and sometimes the most ordinary rituals with pomp and mystery. Western drama, in fact, grew from religious rituals; comedy derived from the Dionysian rites celebrating fertility and growth, and tragedy from the goat songs (again embedded in Dionysian rituals) that stressed the sacrificial nature of existence and the reality of death. Drama in all ages is, as William Archer stated aptly in *Play-making* (1926), "a representation of the will of man in conflict with the mysterious powers of natural forces which limit and belittle us: it is one of us thrown living upon the stage there to struggle against fatality, against social law, against one of his fellow mortals, against himself if need be, against the ambitions, the interests, the prejudices, the folly, the malevolence of those around him." There could be no drama without that universal picture, on stage, of human beings confronting physical, mental, and spiritual obstacles.

Drama differs from other forms of literature in that it demands a stage and performances. The drama critic Eric Bentley is correct when he declares that drama enjoys a double life—that it can be enjoyed by both spectator and reader. But the fact remains that most plays are written to be produced. Most critics stress this obvious but also subtle truth, that drama must be performed; in fact, performance is an element of drama. Professor J. M. Manly, for one, states that drama requires a story, told in action, by actors who impersonate the characters of the story. Similarly, Elder Olson speculates: "If we think about the things a dramatist must do, as a *minimum*, to make a play, it becomes clear that he must (1) devise some sort of action, together with characters who can appropriately carry it out, (2) contrive a scenario which shows what actions are to be enacted on the stage in what order, and (3) compose the dialog, or at least indicate roughly what sort of thing shall be said by the actors." In both definitions of drama there is, as we shall see, the relentless ghost of Aristotle dominating the various elements. Yet what is most revealing about these definitions, and all other useful explanations of the nature of drama, is that they stress the theatrical perspective.

It is the theatrical perspective that forces us to focus on drama's need for producers and directors, playwright and actors, theater and stage, audience and, alas, critics. A play, after all, is human action or human experience dramatized for stage production, and this theatrical reality offers both possibilities and constraints. Playwrights have always been aware of the special environment of theater. George Bernard Shaw, writing for the *New York Times* in 1912, listed in several paragraphs the many factors that dictate the playwright's methods. Here is a typical paragraph:

> I do not select my methods: they are imposed on me by a hundred considerations: by the physical considerations of theatrical representation, by the laws devised by the municipality to guard against fires and other accidents to which theatres are liable, by the economies of theatrical commerce, by the nature and limits of the art of acting, by the capacity of the spectators for understanding what they see and hear, and by the accidental circumstances of the particular production in hand.

Shakespeare knew about these theatrical constraints three hundred years before Shaw, just as a Broadway producer, facing a million-dollar budget, understands them more than half a century after Shaw. Theater depends on numerous art forms, and it is assuredly the most expensive of the literary arts.

The playwright, unlike the poet or fiction writer, creates for a mass audience, not for individuals. In classical times, the distinction between poet and dramatist was not so marked. In ancient Greece, playwrights were called poets, for drama was written in verse; and poets often competed in state-sponsored contests. Greek dramatic presentations (the word "drama" comes from the Greek word meaning "a thing done") were civic occasions; sometimes the performances lasted for days. Eventually, drama and poetry went their separate ways, although at times they would again merge significantly, as in works by Shakespeare, Ibsen (notably *Brand* and *Peer Gynt*), Brecht, and Archibald MacLeish. Drama can incorporate poetry while still being fiction in an imaginative sense; it shares with these major genres a telling about humankind and the world. Nevertheless, its elements ultimately contrast with those of poetry and fiction because those elements must be made visible. We go to the theater to *see*; that is its essence.

The question of exactly *what* we see has been a subject of critical debate ever since Aristotle formulated his ideas about drama, especially tragedy, in his *Poetics*. What we should see, to follow Aristotle's *Poetics*, is plot, the most important part of drama. The ancients liked to compare plot to the tying and untying of a knot. Plot should be organized, according to Aristotle, in such a way as to present the good or just hero or heroine who must suffer because of some inherent personal defect. Plot is the entire action and sequence of events in a play—all the movement arranged as an organic whole. As Aristotle explained, speaking specifically of tragedy:

> A whole is that which has a beginning, a middle, and an end. A beginning is that which does not itself follow anything by causal necessity, but after which something naturally is or comes to be. An end, on the contrary, is that which itself naturally follows some other thing, either by necessity, or as a rule, but has nothing following it. A middle is that which follows something, as some other thing follows it.

Through plot, a playwright "imitates" the cause-and-effect movement of existence, adjusting the rhythm to fit the mode of presentation, whether that mode is comedy or farce, tragedy or melodrama, tragicomedy or pantomime. Through plot, characters reach out to us in language and action, melody and spectacle (to invoke once again some key Aristotelian categories), in order to illuminate their confrontations with time and the world.

Ideally we must feel and vicariously *live* through these confrontations and the larger human experience of the play, if we are spectators, or bring an equal sensitivity to our solitary reading of the play. A playwright normally has only two to three hours to create this special magic of drama, to bring us into the theatrical universe. As the noted philosopher Susanne K. Langer states in *Feeling and Form*, drama confronts us with "the semblance of events lived and felt . . . so that they constitute a purely and completely experienced reality, a piece of *virtual life*." Perhaps we invest the characters with ourselves, sharing their pity and fear, their joy and laughter, within the enchanted context of the play. However, when it is over, we feel pleasure because our emotions have been manipulated—as we wished them to be—and we are ourselves once again. Aristotle, again referring to tragedy, termed this emotional response *catharsis*, the purging of pity and fear in the very being of an audience.

Aristotle has had such a pervasive influence on the conventions of drama that playwrights and critics have been honoring, modifying, or attempting to abandon his rules ever since they were formulated in the *Poetics*. Of course, Aristotle based his formulations about the elements of drama (for instance, the structural elements of fable, character, and thought; and the stylistic elements of language, melody, and spectacle) and about the dramatic unities of time, place, and action upon the earlier Greek drama of Sophocles, Aeschylus, Euripides, and Aristophanes. Two of these great Greek dramatists—Sophocles and Aristophanes—are represented in this anthology, including the *Oedipus Rex* of Sophocles, which Aristotle considered the perfect example of tragedy. Aristotle, in other words, based his critical theories on living drama. In *Oedipus Rex*, the perfectly

"Aristotelian" play, the characters come to destruction more from their own defects than from the wrath of the gods that Aeschylus used in an earlier time. Moreover, the plot embodied the rules of dramatic unity—that the action of the play be a unified whole, that the scene remain unchanged or be confined to a specific area, and that the action of the play be limited to 24 hours—that Aristotle esteemed.

Dramatists and critics have had to deal with Aristotle's ghost. Lost for a time, the Aristotelian concepts of drama's form and content surged back into Renaissance drama in the sixteenth century. Shakespeare, for one, modified Aristotle's conceptions of plot by creating double plots in many of his plays, notably in *King Lear;* while in *Othello*, presented in this text, there is a "violation" of the concept of unity of place. Historically, then, as drama has evolved, dramatists have questioned Aristotle's ghost. In 1663, Molière declared that "the great rule of all rules is not to please." He was not comfortable with Aristotle's influence during the neoclassical period. One of his characters in *School for Wives* (1663) echoes the wish of Molière to be free from old restraints: "When I see a play I look only whether the points strike me; and when I am well entertained, I do not ask whether I have been wrong, or whether the rules of Aristotle would forbid me to laugh." In the twentieth century, the great dramatist Bertolt Brecht would still be trying to expiate Aristotle's ghost. In his anti-Aristotelian essay, "Theatre for Pleasure or Theatre for Instruction," Brecht insists that we must not only be amused by theater and be drawn into it, but also be detached, or alienated, from the theatrical event to such an extent that we can learn from the dramatic representation on stage and feel urged to act militantly because of this detached understanding of the human drama. We can never make too much of Aristotle, but eventually we do come back to the play itself; and a play, as Thornton Wilder observed in 1941, "visibly represents pure existing."

How playwrights recreate or reproduce "pure existing" is a matter that varies from dramatist to dramatist and age to age. Shakespeare and his Elizabethan contemporaries used plot conventions that did not exist in Aristotle's time; while Brecht, in a play like *Mother Courage*, works wonders with the sort of episodic plot that Aristotle despised. Again, historical progress results in revolutions in stage-setting techniques. Devices far more complicated than those used by the Greeks were common in Renaissance drama. The Renaissance produced the modern proscenium arch, instead of the usual two or three arches, and stage setting became an art in its own right. Some playwrights, seeking maximum popularity, devised plots to utilize the spectacular: fireworks, water fountains, trapdoors, flying machines, and the like.

A play—that visible representation of pure existing—derives from the artistry of the dramatist and the values of the age. For example, Shakespeare's tragedy *Othello*, which appears in this text, is usually discussed without reference to the question of racism, but in discussions of *The Merchant of Venice* the question of anti-Semitism often arises. Was Shakespeare interested in the issue of racism in *Othello?* Textual analysis of the play and the treatment on which Shakespeare based his tragedy (see page 751) indicates that racism is an issue, adding yet another dimension to this extraordinary drama. Margaret Webster, producer of the play starring Paul Robeson and Uta Hagen, wrote: "One fact stands in sharp relief. The difference in race between Othello and every other character in the play is, indeed, the heart of the matter. This is the cause of Othello's terrible vulnerability on which Iago fastens so pitilessly; because of this, the conduct of which Desdemona is accused seems to Othello only too horribly possible; this is Iago's first and most powerful weapon, twisted to every conceivable use. . . ."

Great dramatists—Sophocles, Shakespeare, Ibsen, Miller—probe the values of their age in an effort to seek the individual's importance in the world. What William Rose Benet said of Ibsen, that he "brought the problems and ideas of his day onto the stage," is true of all significant playwrights looking for affirmations of life itself. Drama might very well have begun in imitation of life with only remembered or told events as guidelines, but today it is firmly wedded to the written word, or script. A script is composed of the dialogue and stage directions designed to set "pure existing" in motion, with the acts and scenes that structure this action—all of which, of course, are not to be found in a work of fiction or poetry as we know them today.

Fiction and poetry make us imagine, make us create paths that lead us into the writer's world. On stage, however, all is spoken or couched in movement. The sets and machinery visibly present us a place and a time that we do not have to imagine. The characters "play" before us: real, palpable, and, one hopes, as true to life or the spirit of life as the playwright wished them to be. Theme, symbol, tone, plot—indeed, all dramatic convention—unfold and evolve before us. The dramatic elements evolve from the written to the spoken word, defining and giving depth to the characters and action we see. The dramatist, like a demigod, literally *speaks* Creation into existence; and in this process the dramatist teaches the human heart, as Shelley suggested, the knowledge of itself.

Perhaps what some saw and others did not is the beginning and the essence of drama; those who had had singular experiences wished to share them, to tell a tale, to act out a story. In drama the entire process of telling stories has come full circle. The oral traditions mark our beginnings as literate peoples. Then came the signs, symbols, glyphs, and alphabets, followed by extended writing and printing. It is the combination of how well the playwright has perceived and written and how well the actor conveys the meanings of his or her words—the double utilization of language—that provides us with the most successful drama.

SUBJECT AND THEME:
MOTHERS AND SONS

A play transmits signals from the dramatist to both the actors and the audience about the nature of its subject, the range of experience that it contains, the nature and form of that experience, and what that experience ultimately means. When Maurya in John Millington Synge's *Riders to the Sea* declares at the end of the play, "No man at all can be living forever, and we must be satisfied," we see how the playwright can telegraph through one character a partial or complete theme deriving from the action of the play. We look to characters and their speeches, and to setting, action, plot, tone, mood, and figurative range of language—in short, to the total context and all the conventions of drama—in order to discover what a play means.

When we observe drama in production or read a dramatic script, we see the signs that guide us toward an appreciation and understanding of the experience being enacted. Good playwrights know the value of theme and the value of stage time, so they orchestrate their signals in order to advance action, subject, and theme in as effective and significant a manner as possible. Playwrights also know their audience. Whether it is Sophocles writing for a Greek audience more than two thousand years ago, Shakespeare writing for an Elizabethan audience, or Arthur Miller writing for us today, all great dramatists communicate what they want to say about human experience by creating, ordering, and tailoring a theatrical world in such a way that it will offer an image of the real world that we inhabit. Today we can understand the dramatic world of Sophocles and Shakespeare, because the meanings contained within the dramatic conventions that they manipulate are universal. But we can also misinterpret plays of other nations and periods. The Russians have a tendency to laugh at *Hamlet,* while we offer more sympathy in modern times to Shylock in *The Merchant of Venice* than Shakespeare probably intended. Nevertheless, we must always enter the "imaginary" world of any play, try to catch quickly the major signals (Is this going to be a comedy, a tragedy, a tragicomedy, a "problem" play, or something else?), locate other important signals, and determine finally the playwright's controlling vision of life, of human relationships, of the contours and complexities of society, and of the ultimate mysteries of the cosmos.

At times, the meaning of a play will be so baldly stated that there can be no misunderstanding, but at other times we must be prepared to bring considerable interpretative powers to bear on the drama in order to understand and appreciate it. The morality plays that were popular in Western Europe during the fourteenth to sixteenth centuries offered transparent ethical and spiritual truths. At the outset of *Everyman,* written around 1500 and the most famous English morality play, a Messenger offers the following overview of the subject and meaning of the drama.

> I pray you give all your audience
> And hear this matter with reverence
> By figure a moral play:
> The *Summoning of Everyman* called it is,
> That of our lives and ending shows
> How transitory we be all day.

The Messenger then offers a series of Christian axioms on the vanity of human pleasures, the inevitability of death, and the certainty that "our Heaven King/ Calleth Everyman to a general reckoning." The audience of the later Middle Ages and, indeed, the audience today would have little trouble in detecting in *Everyman* the highly moralistic theme of the play, for it has been spelled out.

Often the very form of a play—a morality play, a Greek tragedy, a neoclassical comedy—will alert us to possible meanings. Yet few significant plays surrender all their meaning readily, and in many instances the meaning or theme of a play can prove elusive and open to debate. Whereas Aristotle in his *Poetics* asserted that drama is the "imitation of an action," we sometimes have difficulty determining exactly *what* is being imitated and why. At times, the dramatist will provide instructions on how the subject and action of a play should be interpreted. Thus Ibsen in his notes for *A Doll's House* wrote: "A woman cannot be herself in the society of the present day, which is an exclusively masculine society, with laws framed by men and with a judicial system that judges feminine conduct from a masculine point of view." However, more typically a playwright does not provide so explicit a controlling idea for a play, thereby forcing the director to be the interpretative medium, or forcing readers themselves to be the interpreters.

Readers know that most plays work toward a clarification of some aspect of human experience. A play might concern itself with love, revenge, the fate of kings, jealousy, political or psychological oppression, and so forth. Such subjects may be universal or fairly topical. The treatment of the subjects may be tragic, farcical, fantastic, or anything in between. Above all, it is the theme of the play that lends unity and consistency to the production. For example, the general subject of the two short plays in this section, Synge's *Riders to the Sea* and Hughes's *Soul Gone Home*, is the loss of sons by their mothers. Yet what the dramatists *say* about the subject varies, as we shall see, with the vision of the playwright. Each play seeks to dramatize specific lives and to illuminate social conditions. Each play is "universal" in that it concentrates on death in the family—a subject and a reality that shall persist as long as humanity itself lasts. What is so striking about any comparative assessment of these two plays is not so much their commonality in subject as their divergence in characterization, action, tone, mood, and theme. In other words, the signals created by Synge and Hughes are different. As you read these plays, try to locate the important signals in order to discover how each work acquires from a common subject its own meaning.

John Millington Synge

RIDERS TO THE SEA

John Millington Synge (1871–1909), the son of a barrister, was born in Rathfranham, near Dublin, Ireland. His father died when Synge was 1 year old, and he was raised by an extended family consisting of his mother, grandmother, sister Annie, and various aunts. Synge entered Trinity College in 1888, his chief interests being language, history, and music. After his studies, he wandered through Europe, settling in Paris, where he met William Butler Yeats and many Irish nationalists. Synge wanted to become a critic. "Give up Paris," Yeats said. "You will never create anything by reading Racine. . . . Go to the Aran Islands. Live there as if you were one of the people themselves; express a life that has never found expression." Synge did just that, seeking creative inspiration in the peasant life of western Ireland and visiting the Aran Islands, off the Irish coast, on an annual basis. After his return to Dublin in 1903, Synge quickly became a leader in the Irish National Theatre Company and at the Abbey Theatre, which produced his plays: The Shadow of the Glen *(1903),* Riders to the Sea *(1904),* The Well of the Saints *(1905),* The Tinker's Wedding *(1907), and the controversial* Playboy of the Western World *(1907). An unfinished verse play,* Deidre of the Sorrows, *was written while Synge was dying of Hodgkin's disease.* Riders

Riders to the Sea

to the Sea is a spare, haunting play that calls to mind the Greek tragedies of Aeschylus and Sophocles. The play comes directly out of Synge's experiences in the Aran Islands. In notes that he wrote in 1904, he observed: "The loss of one man seems a slight catastrophe to all except the immediate relatives. . . . When the horses were coming down to the ship an old woman saw her son, that was drowned a while ago, riding on one of them." Riders to the Sea, one of his masterpieces and generally considered one of the greatest one-act plays of the modern theater, reveals Synge's ability to capture the intense life of the Irish people, their eloquence, their sorrows, and their stoicism in face of a harsh environment.

Characters

Maurya, an old woman
Bartley, her son
Cathleen, her daughter
Nora, a younger daughter
Men and Women

An island off the west of Ireland.

> *Cottage kitchen, with nets, oil-skins, spinning-wheel, some new boards standing by the wall, etc. Cathleen, a girl of about twenty, finishes kneading cake, and puts it down on the pot-oven by the fire; then wipes her hands, and begins to spin at the wheel. Nora, a young girl, puts her head in at the door.*

Nora *(in a low voice.)* Where is she?
Cathleen. She's lying down, God help her, and may be sleeping, if she's able.

> *Nora comes in softly, and takes a bundle from under her shawl.*

Cathleen *(spinning the wheel rapidly).* What is it you have?
Nora. The young priest is after bringing them. It's a shirt and a plain stocking were got off a drowned man in Donegal.

> *Cathleen stops her wheel with a sudden movement, and leans out to listen.*

Nora. We're to find out if it's Michael's they are, some time herself will be down looking by the sea.
Cathleen. How would they be Michael's, Nora? How would he go the length of that way to the Far North?
Nora. The young priest says he's known the like of it. "If it's Michael's they are," says he, "you can tell herself he's got a clean burial by the grace of God, and if they're not his, let no one say a word about them, for she'll be getting her death," says he, "with crying and lamenting."

> *The door which Nora half closed is blown open by a gust of wind.*

Cathleen *(looking out anxiously).* Did you ask him would he stop Bartley going this day with the horses to the Galway fair?
Nora. "I won't stop him," says he, "but let you not be afraid. Herself does be

saying prayers half through the night, and the Almighty God won't leave her destitute," says he, "with no son living."

Cathleen. Is the sea bad by the white rocks, Nora?

Nora. Middling bad, God help us. There's a great roaring in the west, and it's worse it'll be getting when the tide's turned to the wind. *(She goes over to the table with the bundle.)* Shall I open it now?

Cathleen. Maybe she'd wake up on us, and come in before we'd done. *(Coming to the table.)* It's a long time we'll be, and the two of us crying.

Nora *(goes to the inner door and listens).* She's moving about on the bed. She'll be coming in a minute.

Cathleen. Give me the ladder, and I'll put them up in the turf-loft, the way she won't know of them at all, and maybe when the tide turns she'll be going down to see would he be floating from the east.

They put the ladder against the gable of the chimney; Cathleen goes up a few steps and hides the bundle in the turf-loft. Maurya comes from the inner room.

Maurya *(looking up at Cathleen and speaking querulously).* Isn't it turf enough you have for this day and evening?

Cathleen. There's a cake baking at the fire for a short space *(throwing down the turf)* and Bartley will want it when the tide turns if he goes to Connemara.

Nora picks up the turf and puts it round the pot-oven.

Maurya *(sitting down on a stool at the fire).* He won't go this day with the wind rising from the south and west. He won't go this day, for the young priest will stop him surely.

Nora. He'll not stop him, Mother, and I heard Eamon Simon and Stephen Pheety and Colum Shawn saying he would go.

Maurya. Where is he itself?

Nora. He went down to see would there be another boat sailing in the week, and I'm thinking it won't be long till he's here now, for the tide's turning at the green head, and the hooker's tacking from the east.

Cathleen. I hear some one passing the big stones.

Nora *(looking out).* He's coming now, and he in a hurry.

Bartley *(comes in and looks round the room; speaking sadly and quietly).* Where is the bit of new rope, Cathleen, was bought in Connemara?

Cathleen *(coming down).* Give it to him, Nora; it's on a nail by the white boards. I hung it up this morning, for the pig with the black feet was eating it.

Nora *(giving him a rope).* Is that it, Bartley?

Maurya. You'd do right to leave that rope, Bartley, hanging by the boards. *(Bartley takes the rope.)* It will be wanting in this place, I'm telling you, if Michael is washed up tomorrow morning, or the next morning, or any morning in the week, for it's a deep grave we'll make him by the grace of God.

Bartley *(beginning to work with the rope).* I've no halter the way I can ride down on the mare, and I must go now quickly. This is the one boat going for two weeks or beyond it, and the fair will be a good fair for horses I heard them saying below.

Maurya. It's a hard thing they'll be saying below if the body is washed up and there's no man in it to make the coffin, and I after giving a big price for the finest white boards you'd find in Connemara. *(She looks round at the boards.)*

Bartley. How would it be washed up, and we after looking each day for nine days, and a strong wind blowing a while back from the west and south?

Maurya. If it wasn't found itself, that wind is raising the sea, and there was a star up against the moon, and it rising in the night. If it was a hundred horses, or a thousand horses you had itself, what is the price of a thousand horses against a son where there is one son only?

Bartley *(working at the halter, to Cathleen).* Let you go down each day, and see the sheep aren't jumping in on the rye, and if the jobber comes you can sell the pig with the black feet if there is a good price going.

Maurya. How would the like of her get a good price for a pig?

Bartley *(to Cathleen).* If the west wind holds with the last bit of the moon let you and Nora get up weed enough for another cock for the kelp. It's hard set we'll be from this day with no one in it but one man to work.

Maurya. It's hard set we'll be surely the day you're drownd'd with the rest. What way will I live and the girls with me, and I an old woman looking for the grave?

Bartley lays down the halter, takes off his old coat and puts on a newer one of the same flannel.

Bartley *(to Nora).* Is she coming to the pier?

Nora *(looking out).* She's passing the green head and letting fall her sails.

Bartley *(getting his purse and tobacco).* I'll have half an hour to go down, and you'll see me coming again in two days, or in three days, or maybe in four days if the wind is bad.

Maurya *(turning round to the fire, and putting her shawl over her head).* Isn't it a hard and cruel man won't hear a word from an old woman, and she holding him from the sea?

Cathleen. It's the life of a young man to be going on the sea, and who would listen to an old woman with one thing and she saying it over?

Bartley *(taking the halter).* I must go now quickly. I'll ride down on the red mare, and the gray pony'll run behind me. . . . The blessing of God on you. *(He goes out.)*

Maurya *(crying out as he is in the door).* He's gone now, God spare us, and we'll not see him again. He's gone now, and when the black night is falling I'll have no son left me in the world.

Cathleen. Why wouldn't you give him your blessing and he looking round in the door? Isn't it sorrow enough is on every one in this house without your sending him out with an unlucky word behind him, and a hard word in his ear?

Maurya takes up the tongs and begins raking the fire aimlessly without looking round.

Nora *(turning toward her).* You're taking away the turf from the cake.

Cathleen *(crying out).* The Son of God forgive us, Nora, we're after forgetting his bit of bread. *(She comes over to the fire.)*

Nora. And it's destroyed he'll be going till dark night, and he after eating nothing since the sun went up.

Cathleen (*turning the cake out of the oven*). It's destroyed he'll be, surely. There's no sense left on any person in a house where an old woman will be talking forever.

Maurya sways herself on her stool.

Cathleen (*cutting off some of the bread and rolling it in a cloth; to Maurya*). Let you go down now to the spring well and give him this and he passing. You'll see him then and the dark word will be broken, and you can say "God speed you," the way he'll be easy in his mind.

Maurya (*taking the bread*). Will I be in it as soon as himself?

Cathleen. If you go now quickly.

Maurya (*standing up unsteadily*). It's hard set I am to walk.

Cathleen (*looking at her anxiously*). Give her the stick, Nora, or maybe she'll slip on the big stones.

Nora. What stick?

Cathleen. The stick Michael brought from Connemara.

Maurya (*taking a stick Nora gives her*). In the big world the old people do be leaving things after them for their sons and children, but in this place it is the young men do be leaving things behind for them that do be old.

She goes out slowly. Nora goes over to the ladder.

Cathleen. Wait, Nora, maybe she'd turn back quickly. She's that sorry, God help her, you wouldn't know the thing she'd do.

Nora. Is she gone round by the bush?

Cathleen (*looking out*). She's gone now. Throw it down quickly, for the Lord knows when she'll be out of it again.

Nora (*getting the bundle from the loft*). The young priest said he'd be passing to-morrow, and we might go down and speak to him below if it's Michael's they are surely.

Cathleen (*taking the bundle*). Did he say what way they were found?

Nora (*coming down*). "There were two men," says he, "and they rowing round with poteen before the cocks crowed, and the oar of one of them caught the body, and they passing the black cliffs of the north."

Cathleen (*trying to open the bundle*). Give me a knife, Nora, the strings perished with the salt water, and there's a black knot on it you wouldn't loosen in a week.

Nora (*giving her a knife*). I've heard tell it was a long way to Donegal.

Cathleen (*cutting the string*). It is surely. There was a man in here a while ago—the man sold us that knife—and he said if you set off walking from the rock beyond, it would be seven days you'd be in Donegal.

Nora. And what time would a man take, and he floating?

Cathleen opens the bundle and takes out a bit of a stocking. They look at them eagerly.

Cathleen (*in a low voice*). The Lord spare us, Nora! isn't it a queer hard thing to say if it's his they are surely?

Nora. I'll get his shirt off the hook the way we can put the one flannel on the other. (*She looks through some clothes hanging in the corner.*) It's not with them, Cathleen, and where will it be?

Cathleen. I'm thinking Bartley put it on him in the morning, for his own shirt was heavy with the salt in it. *(Pointing to the corner.)* There's a bit of a sleeve was of the same stuff. Give me that and it will do.

Nora brings it to her and they compare the flannel.

Cathleen. It's the same stuff, Nora; but if it is itself aren't there great rolls of it in the shops of Galway, and isn't it many another man may have a shirt of it as well as Michael himself?

Nora *(who has taken up the stocking and counted the stiches, crying out).* It's Michael, Cathleen, it's Michael; God spare his soul, and what will herself say when she hears this story, and Bartley on the sea?

Cathleen *(taking the stocking).* It's a plain stocking.

Nora. It's the second one of the third pair I knitted, and I put up three score stiches, and I dropped four of them.

Cathleen *(counts the stitches).* It's that number is in it. *(Crying out.)* Ah, Nora, isn't it a bitter thing to think of him floating that way to the far north, and no one to keen him but the black hags that do be flying on the sea?

Nora *(swinging herself round, and throwing out her arms on the clothes).* And isn't it a pitiful thing when there is nothing left of a man who was a great rower and fisher, but a bit of an old shirt and a plain stocking?

Cathleen *(after an instant).* Tell me is herself coming, Nora? I hear a little sound on the path.

Nora *(looking out).* She is, Cathleen. She's coming up to the door.

Cathleen. Put these things away before she'll come in. Maybe it's easier she'll be after giving her blessing to Bartley, and we won't let on we've heard anything the time he's on the sea.

Nora *(helping Cathleen to close the bundle).* We'll put them here in the corner.

They put them into a hole in the chimney corner. Cathleen goes back to the spinning-wheel.

Nora. Will she see it was crying I was?

Cathleen. Keep your back to the door the way the light'll not be on you.

Nora sits down at the chimney corner, with her back to the door. Maurya comes in very slowly, without looking at the girls, and goes over to her stool at the other side of the fire. The cloth with the bread is still in her hand. The girls look at each other, and Nora points to the bundle of bread.

(After spinning for a moment.) You didn't give him his bit of bread?

Maurya begins to keen softly, without turning round.

Did you see him riding down?

Maurya goes on keening.

(A little impatient.) God forgive you; isn't it a better thing to raise your voice and tell what you seen, than to be making lamentation for a thing that's done? Did you see Bartley, I'm saying to you.

Maurya *(with a weak voice).* My heart's broken from this day.

Cathleen *(as before).* Did you see Bartley?

John Millington Synge

Maurya. I seen the fearfulest thing.

Cathleen *(leaves her wheel and looks out).* God forgive you; he's riding the mare now over the green head, and the gray pony behind him.

Maurya *(starts, so that her shawl falls back from her head and shows her white tossed hair. With a frightened voice).* The gray pony behind him.

Cathleen *(coming to the fire).* What is it ails you, at all?

Maurya *(speaking very slowly).* I've seen the fearfulest thing any person has seen, since the day Bride Dara seen the dead man with a child in his arms.

Cathleen and Nora. Uah.

They crouch down in front of the old woman at the fire.

Nora. Tell us what it is you seen.

Maurya. I went down to the spring well, and I stood there saying a prayer to myself. Then Bartley came along, and he riding on the red mare with the gray pony behind him. *(She puts up her hands, as if to hide something from her eyes.)* The Son of God spare us, Nora!

Cathleen. What is it you seen?

Maurya. I seen Michael himself.

Cathleen *(speaking softly).* You did not, Mother; it wasn't Michael you seen, for his body is after being found in the Far North, and he's got a clean burial by the grace of God.

Maurya *(a little defiantly).* I'm after seeing him this day, and he riding and galloping. Bartley came first on the red mare; and I tried to say, "God speed you," but something choked the words in my throat. He went by quickly; and "the blessing of God on you," says he, and I could say nothing. I looked up then, and I crying, at the gray pony, and there was Michael upon it—with fine clothes on him, and new shoes on his feet.

Cathleen *(begins to keen).* It's destroyed we are from this day. It's destroyed, surely.

Nora. Didn't the young priest say the Almighty God wouldn't leave her destitute with no son living?

Maurya *(in a low voice, but clearly).* It's little the like of him knows of the sea. . . . Bartley will be lost now, and let you call in Eamon and make me a good coffin out of the white boards, for I won't live after them. I've had a husband, and a husband's father, and six sons in this house—six fine men, though it was a hard birth I had with every one of them and they coming to the world—and some of them were found and some of them were not found, but they're gone now the lot of them. . . . There were Stephen, and Shawn, were lost in the great wind, and found after in the Bay of Gregory of the Golden Mouth, and carried up the two of them on the one plank, and in by that door.

She pauses for a moment, the girls start as if they heard something through the door that is half open behind them.

Nora *(in a whisper).* Did you hear that, Cathleen? Did you hear a noise in the northeast?

Cathleen *(in a whisper).* There's some one after crying out by the seashore.

Maurya *(continues without hearing anything).* There was Sheamus and his father, and his own father again, were lost in a dark night, and not a stick or

Riders to the Sea

sign was seen of them when the sun went up. There was Patch after was drowned out of a curagh that turned over. I was sitting here with Bartley, and he a baby, lying on my two knees, and I seen two women, and three women, and four women coming in, and they crossing themselves, and not saying a word. I looked out then, and there were men coming after them, and they holding a thing in the half of a red sail, and water dripping out of it—it was a dry day, Nora—and leaving a track to the door.

She pauses again with her head stretched out toward the door. It opens softly and old women begin to come in, crossing themselves on the threshold, and kneeling down in front of the stage with red petticoats over their heads.

Maurya *(half in a dream, to Cathleen).* Is it Patch or Michael, or what is it at all?

Cathleen. Michael is after being found in the Far North and when he is found there how could he be here in this place?

Maurya. There does be a power of young men floating round in the sea, and what way would they know if it was Michael they had, or another man like him, for when a man is nine days in the sea, and the wind blowing, it's hard set his own mother would be to say what man was it.

Cathleen. It's Michael, God spare him, for they're after sending us a bit of his clothes from the Far North.

She reaches out and hands Maurya the clothes that belonged to Michael. Maurya stands up slowly, and takes them in her hands. Nora looks out.

Nora. They're carrying a thing among them and there's water dripping out of it and leaving a track by the big stones.

Cathleen *(in a whisper to the women who have come in).* Is it Bartley it is?

One of the women. It is surely, God rest his soul.

Two younger women come in and pull out the table. Then men carry in the body of Bartley, laid on a plank, with a bit of a sail over it, and lay it on the table.

Cathleen *(to the women, as they are doing so).* What way was he drowned?

One of the women. The gray pony knocked him into the sea, and he was washed out where there is a great surf on the white rocks.

Maurya has gone over and knelt down at the head of the table. The women are keening softly and swaying themselves with a slow movement. Cathleen and Nora kneel at the other end of the table. The men kneel near the door.

Maurya *(raising her head and speaking as if she did not see the people around her).* They're all gone now, and there isn't anything more the sea can do to me. . . . I'll have no call now to be crying and praying when the wind breaks from the south, and you can hear the surf is in the east, and the surf is in the west, making a great stir with the two noises, and they hitting one on the other. I'll have no call now to be going down and getting Holy Water in the dark nights after Samhain, and I won't care what way the sea is when the other women will be keening. *(To Nora.)* Give me the Holy Water, Nora, there's a small sup still on the dresser.

Nora gives it to her.

Maurya *(drops Michael's clothes across Bartley's feet, and sprinkles the Holy Water over him).* It isn't that I haven't prayed for you, Bartley, to the Almighty God. It isn't that I haven't said prayers in the dark night till you wouldn't know what I'd be saying; but it's a great rest I'll have now, and it's time surely. It's a great rest I'll have now, and great sleeping in the long nights after Samhain, if it's only a bit of wet flour we do have to eat, and maybe a fish that would be stinking. *(She kneels down again, crossing herself, and saying prayers under her breath.)*

Cathleen *(to an old man).* Maybe yourself and Eamon would make a coffin when the sun rises. We have fine white boards herself bought, God help her, thinking Michael would be found, and I have a new cake you can eat while you'll be working.

The old man *(looking at the boards).* Are there nails with them?

Cathleen. There are not, Colum; we didn't think of the nails.

Another man. It's a great wonder she wouldn't think of the nails, and all the coffins she's seen made already.

Cathleen. It's getting old she is, and broken.

Maurya stands up again very slowly and spreads out the pieces of Michael's clothes beside the body, sprinkling them with the last of the Holy Water.

Nora *(in a whisper to Cathleen).* She's quiet now and easy; but the day Michael was drowned you could hear her crying out from this to the spring well. It's fonder she was of Michael, and would any one have thought that?

Cathleen *(slowly and clearly).* An old woman will be soon tired with anything she will do, and isn't it nine days herself is after crying and keening, and making great sorrow in the house?

Maurya *(puts the empty cup mouth downwards on the table, and lays her hands together on Bartley's feet).* They're all together this time, and the end is come. May the Almighty God have mercy on Bartley's soul, and on Michael's soul, and on the souls of Sheamus and Patch, and Stephen and Shawn; *(bending her head)* and may He have mercy on my soul, Nora, and on the soul of every one is left living in the world.

She pauses, and the keen rises a little more loudly from the women, then sinks away.

Michael has a clean burial in the Far North, by the grace of the Almighty God. Bartley will have a fine coffin out of the white boards, and a deep grave surely. What more can we want than that? No man at all can be living forever, and we must be satisfied.

She kneels down again and the curtain falls slowly.

QUESTIONS

1. How does the title alert us to the play's subject and theme? How is the sea described in the play? Who are the "riders" to the sea? In what way is nature the protagonist in the play?

2. Synge learned on Aran that a drowned, headless man could be identified only by his clothing. How does Synge incorporate this fact into the structure of the play? Is his method effective?

3. How does Synge present and develop the basic conflict in the play?

4. Action and dialogue are clearly dominated by women. What bearing does this have on the theme of the play? What is Bartley's function?

5. Maurya's name means "goddess of fate." What is the significance of this fact to the play's theme?

6. Why are the spinning and the baking—simple domestic tasks—significant?

7. Explain the various strengths of the dialogue in the play.

8. Some critics have charged that Maurya is too passive in her suffering at the end of this tragedy. Support or refute this assertion.

9. What is a *keen*? Synge wrote, "The keen reveals the mood of beings who feel their isolation in the face of a universe that wars on them with winds and seas." How does this statement inform the subject and theme of the play?

10. What experience does Synge ultimately want to universalize in the play?

TOPICS FOR WRITING

1. Synge once declared, "We should unite stoicism, ascetism, and ecstasy." Examine this statement in the context of *Riders to the Sea*.

2. William Butler Yeats wrote of Synge: "He loves all that has edge, all that is salt in the mouth, all that is rough in the hand, all that heightens the emotions by contest, all that stings into life the sense of tragedy." How does Yeats's observation capture the strength and brilliance of *Riders to the Sea*?

3. Establish your own definition of tragedy, and apply it to Synge's play.

4. Analyze the various patterns of color in *Riders to the Sea* and their significance.

5. Explore the world of women in the play.

Langston Hughes

SOUL GONE HOME

*James Langston Hughes (1902–1967), who appears earlier
in this text on pages 369 and 612, was born in Joplin,
Missouri, and raised in the Midwest. He attended Columbia
University, breaking off his studies to roam the world as a
seaman, visiting, among other places, Europe and Africa for
the first time. He completed his education at Lincoln University and then settled in the Harlem he came to love. In
addition to being a seaman, Hughes was also a waiter, an
editor, and a foreign correspondent. Best known for his
poetry, the earliest of which was written to accompany
blues and ballads, Hughes also wrote opera librettos, television scripts, and plays. Designated the "poet laureate of
Harlem," Hughes was a major figure of the Harlem Renaissance (1925–1929) and a seminal force of the Negritude
movement of black authors writing in French. Hughes
founded the Suitcase Theatre in Harlem, helped to establish
the Karamu House in Cleveland and the Negro Art Theatre in
Los Angeles. His plays include* Scottsboro Limited *(1932),*
Mulatto *(1935),* Tambourines to Glory *(1949), and* Simply
Heavenly *(1957). A gentle, humorous man, Hughes requested that Duke Ellington's* Do Nothing till You Hear from Me *be
played at his funeral. Hughes draws his characters and
events from the lives of black people he calls "just folks." In*
Soul Gone Home, *he merges realism and fantasy, comedy
and tragedy, into a blend of the absurd in order to create a
stark slice of urban life.*

Characters

The mother
The son
Two men

Night.

*A tenement room, bare, ugly, dirty. An unshaded electric-light bulb. In the
middle of the room a cot on which the body of a Negro youth is lying. His hands
are folded across his chest. There are pennies on his eyes. He is a soul gone
home.*

*As the curtain rises, his mother, a large, middle-aged woman in a red
sweater, kneels weeping beside the cot, loudly simulating grief.*

Mother. Oh, Gawd! Oh Lawd! Why did you take my son from me? Oh, Gawd, why
did you do it? He was all I had! Oh, Lawd, what am I gonna do? *(Looking at
the dead boy and stroking his head.)* Oh, son! Oh, Ronnie! Oh, my boy,
speak to me! Ronnie, say something to me! Son, why don't you talk to your
mother? Can't you see she's bowed down in sorrow? Son, speak to me, just a
word! Come back from the spirit-world and speak to me! Ronnie, come back
from the dead and speak to your mother!

Soul Gone Home

Son *(Lying there dead as a doornail. Speaking loudly).* I wish I wasn't dead, so I *could* speak to you. You been a hell of a mama!

Mother *(Falling back from the cot in astonishment, but still on her knees).* Ronnie! Ronnie! What's that you say? What you sayin' to your mother? *(Wild-eyed.)* Is you done opened your mouth and spoke to me?

Son. I said you a hell of a mama!

Mother *(Rising suddenly and backing away, screaming loudly).* Awo-oo-o! Ronnie, that ain't you talkin'!

Son. Yes, it is me talkin', too! I say you been a no-good mama.

Mother. What for you talkin' to me like that, Ronnie? You ain't never said nothin' like that to me before.

Son. I know it, but I'm dead now—and I can say what I want to say. *(Stirring.)* You done called on me to talk, ain't you? Lemme take these pennies off my eyes so I can see. *(He takes the coins off his eyes, throws them across the room, and sits up in bed. He is a very dark boy in a torn white shirt. He looks hard at his mother.)* Mama, you know you ain't done me right.

Mother. What you mean, I ain't done you right? *(She is rooted in horror.)* What you mean, huh?

Son. You know what I mean.

Mother. No, I don't neither. *(Trembling violently.)* What you mean comin' back to haunt your poor old mother? Ronnie, what does you mean?

Son *(Leaning forward).* I'll tell you just what I mean! You been a bad mother to me.

Mother. Shame! Shame! Shame, talkin' to your mama that away. Damn it! Shame! I'll slap your face. *(She starts toward him, but he rolls his big white eyes at her, and she backs away.)* Me, what borned you! Me, what suffered the pains o' death to bring you into this world! Me, what raised you up, what washed your dirty didies. *(Sorrowfully.)* And now I'm left here mighty nigh prostrate 'cause you gone from me! Ronnie, what you mean talkin' to *me* like that—what brought you into this world?

Son. You never did feed me good, that's what I mean! Who wants to come into the world hongry, and go out the same way?

Mother. What you mean hongry? When I had money, ain't I fed you?

Son *(Sullenly).* Most of the time you ain't had no money.

Mother. Twarn't my fault then.

Son. Twarn't *my* fault neither.

Mother *(Defensively).* You always was so weak and sickly, you couldn't earn nothin' sellin' papers.

Son. I know it.

Mother. You never was no use to me.

Son. So you just lemme grow up in the street, and I ain't had no manners nor morals, neither.

Mother. Manners and morals? Ronnie, where'd you learn all them big words?

Son. I learnt 'em just now in the spirit-world.

Mother *(Coming nearer).* But you ain't been dead no more'n an hour.

Son. That's long enough to learn a lot.

Mother. Well, what else did you find out?

Son. I found out you was a hell of a mama puttin' me out in the cold to sell papers soon as I could even walk.

Mother. What? You little liar!

Son. If I'm lyin', I'm dyin'! And lettin' me grow up all bowlegged and stunted from undernourishment.

Mother. Under-nurse-mint?

Son. Undernourishment. You heard what the doctor said last week?

Mother. Naw, what'd he say?

Son. He said I was dyin' o' undernourishment, that's what he said. He said I had TB 'cause I didn't have enough to eat never when I were a child. And he said I couldn't get well, nohow eating nothin' but beans ever since I been sick. Said I needed milk and eggs. And you said you ain't got no money for milk and eggs, which I know you ain't. *(Gently.)* We never had no money, mama, not even since you took up hustlin' on the streets.

Mother. Son, money ain't everything.

Son. Naw, but when you got TB you have to have milk and eggs.

Mother *(Advancing sentimentally).* Anyhow, I love you, Ronnie!

Son *(Rudely).* Sure you love me—but here I am dead.

Mother *(Angrily).* Well, damn your hide, you ain't even decent dead. If you was, you wouldn't be sittin' there jawin' at your mother when she's sheddin' every tear she's got for you tonight.

Son. First time you ever did cry for me, far as I know.

Mother. Tain't! You's a liar! I cried when I borned you—you was such a big child—ten pounds.

Son. Then *I* did the cryin' after that, I reckon.

Mother *(Proudly).* Sure, I could of let you die, but I didn't. Naw, I kept you with me—off and on. And I lost the chance to marry many a good man, too—if it weren't for you. No man wants to take care o' nobody else's child. *(Self-pityingly.)* You been a burden to me, Randolph.

Son *(Angrily).* What did you have me for then, in the first place?

Mother. How could I help havin' you, you little bastard? Your father ruint me—and you's the result. And I been worried with you for sixteen years. *(Disgustedly.)* Now, just when you get big enough to work and do me some good, you have to go and die.

Son. I sure am dead!

Mother. But you ain't decent dead! Here you come back to haunt your poor old mama, and spoil her cryin' spell, and spoil the mournin'. *(There is the noise of an ambulance going outside. The mother goes to the window and looks down into the street. Turns to son.)* Ronnie, lay down quick! Here comes the city's ambulance to take you to the undertaker's. Don't let them white men see you dead, sitting up here quarrelin' with your mother. Lay down and fold your hands back like I had 'em.

Son *(Passing his hand across his head).* All right, but gimme that comb yonder and my stocking cap. I don't want to go out of here with my hair standin' straight up in front, even if I is dead. *(The mother hands him a comb and his stocking cap. The son combs his hair and puts the cap on. Noise of men coming up the stairs.)*

Mother. Hurry up, Ronnie, they'll be here in no time.

Son. Aw, they got another flight to come yet. Don't rush me, ma!

Mother. Yes, but I got to put these pennies back on your eyes, boy! *(She searches in a corner for the coins as her son lies down and folds his hands, stiff in* *death. She finds the coins and puts them nervously on his eyes, watching the door meanwhile. A knock.)* Come in.

(Enter two men in the white coats of city health employees.)

Man. Somebody sent for us to get the body of Ronnie Bailey? Third floor, apartment five.

Mother. Yes, sir, here he is! *(Weeping loudly.)* He's my boy! Oh, Lawd, he's done left me! Oh, Lawdy, he's done gone home! His soul's gone home! Oh, what am I gonna do? Mister! Mister! Mister, the Lawd's done took him home! *(As the men unfold the stretchers, she continues to weep hysterically. They place the boy's thin body on the stretchers and cover it with a rubber cloth. Each man takes his end of the stretchers. Silently, they walk out the door as the mother wails.)* Oh, my son! Oh, my boy! Come back, come back, come back! Ronnie, come back! *(One loud scream as the door closes.)* Awo-ooo-o!

(As the footsteps of the men die down on the stairs, the mother becomes suddenly quiet. She goes to a broken mirror and begins to rouge and powder her face. In the street the ambulance gong sounds fainter and fainter in the distance. The mother takes down an old fur coat from a nail and puts it on. Before she leaves, she smooths back the quilts on the cot from which the dead boy has been removed. She looks into the mirror again, and once more whitens her face with powder. She dons a red hat. From a handbag she takes a cigarette, lights it, and walks slowly out the door. At the door she switches off the light. The hallway is dimly illuminated. She turns before closing the door, looks back into the room, and speaks.)

Mother. Tomorrow, Ronnie, I'll buy you some flowers—if I can pick up a dollar tonight. You was a hell of a no-good son, I swear!

Curtain.

QUESTIONS

1. Why does Hughes write in the opening stage directions that the mother should be "loudly simulating grief"? How is she portrayed throughout the play? What is her relationship to her son?

2. What does the setting of the play tell us about the lives of the characters? Compare and contrast the setting in *Soul Gone Home* with the setting in *Riders to the Sea*.

3. Why does Hughes employ comedy and fantasy to deal with a potentially tragic subject like the death of a son? How would you explain the overall tone of the play?

4. Hughes once admitted that he was a "propaganda writer; my main material is the race problem." Is there any propaganda in *Soul Gone Home*? Explain. How does the race problem influence the action?

5. Compare and contrast the facts of Irish existence as presented by Synge in *Riders to the Sea* (page 696) and black American existence as presented by Hughes in *Soul Gone Home*. Are the themes the same or different? Explain.

6. Explain the significance of the ambulance attendants at the end of the play.

TOPICS FOR WRITING

1. The playwright Loften Mitchell has stated that "the artist must seek the truth, communicate, educate, and entertain." Evaluate the success of Hughes in attaining these goals in *Soul Gone Home*.

2. Write a comparative analysis of the social commentary in *Riders to the Sea* (page 696) and *Soul Gone Home*.

3. Examine Hughes's use of dialogue to capture character, culture, and conflict in the play.

4. Assess the tragic technique of Synge and the tragicomic method of Hughes.

23

COMEDY, TRAGEDY, AND THEME: LOVE AND WAR

The two major types of dramatic composition are comedy and tragedy. There are, of course, other forms of drama: tragicomedy (which we saw in Hughes's *Soul Gone Home* in the last section), farce, allegory, melodrama, burlesque, social and political drama, and so forth. Nevertheless, tragedy is the purest form of drama that we would term "serious," while comedy is that form of drama that provokes amusement or laughter.

Pure tragedy and comedy are among our oldest dramatic forms. Aristotle defined tragedy as "the "imitation of an action that is serious, complete, and of a certain magnitude," basing his prescription largely on the classic Greek theater of the fifth century BC. Classic Greek theater—that of Aeschylus, Sophocles, and Euripides—offers some of the finest examples of tragedy. Other periods recognized for the flourishing of pure tragedy are the late Renaissance (which includes the theater of Shakespeare) and the neoclassical age of late-seventeenth-century France, which produced a great tragedian, Jean Racine. Obviously, technical and structural differences exist between the tragic dramas of different periods. For example, action in Greek tragedy develops through an alternating rhythm of dramatic scene and choral interlude, while action in a Shakespearean tragedy flows—often surges—from event to event, often ignoring the Greek obsession with the "unities" of time, place, and action. Similarly, a contemporary tragedy such as Arthur Miller's *Death of a Salesman* does not deal with the heroic and noble figures of Greek and Shakespearean tragedy but instead with ordinary men and women. Yet the sense of tragedy radiating from the great dramas of various ages remains constant, for in pure tragedy we witness individuals at war with society, the world, and themselves; caught in that universal conflict between good and evil; subjected to pain, suffering, and often death; the victims of what the Greeks termed "moira," or fate. We identify with the intense world of tragedy, sensing perhaps our own proximity to the suffering and catastrophe enacted.

In fact, it is the *experience* of tragedy that illuminates for us its essential nature. The power of tragedy lies in its ability to involve the audience in the destiny of its characters. With tragedy, we witness, typically, chief characters, or protagonists, who are immersed in suffering—not arbitrary suffering or suffering for its own sake, but suffering caused by the protagonists' painful efforts to make sense out of life and to order their destiny. These figures seek moral and spiritual certainties in a fallen world. They are noble in their quest, often grander than us in passion and purpose, but like us in their key faults, which the Greeks termed *hamartia*. As they embrace their inevitably disastrous destiny, we come to fear for their fate because we know that we could be overtaken by similar events, and to pity them for their misfortunes. Aristotle called this audience response to tragedy *catharsis*—the purging of emotion that permits a deeper wisdom to emerge. Thus we share with the tragic character a hard-earned wisdom about the inevitability of suffering and about the trials of life. But we also share with the tragic character a paradoxically affirmative insight into the potential greatness and nobility of men and women. In tragedy, Arthur Miller has written, "lies the belief—optimistic if you will—in the perfectability of man."

By contrast, the rhythm of comedy removes the audience from characters, objectifies the dramatic experience of the play, and permits us to look in a detached and often critical manner at the vices and virtues of social creatures. The world of comedy is typically a social landscape that is susceptible to order and improvement if only human beings would suppress their foibles and vices and seek to improve or reform themselves. Whereas the world of tragedy is a relatively closed universe in which an affirmative vision can emerge only after genuine suffering and loss, the world of comedy is open, joyful, often overflowing with life, and delightfully ritualistic. There is potential disaster and ruination in comedy, but comic action moves—whether farcically, amusingly, ironically, satirically, fantastically, or boisterously—toward rebirth, regeneration, and improvement.

The Greeks called comedy *komoidia*—a joyful song of celebration, a form of play that often blended the sacred, secular, and profane. The element of play is central to our enjoyment of comedy, for in the comic world we witness characters who play at being in love (or not in love) or at being warlike, who are miserly, or foolish, or pompous, or tyrannical, or villainous. These characters tend to be caricatures—simplified embodiments of specific foibles and vices. By extension, the conflicts that these ridiculous figures enmesh themselves in might be real and potentially disastrous, but we are amused by their antics and problems, rather than awed or frightened by them. At the same time, the value of comedy goes beyond our ability to laugh at characters. Comedy contains its own cathartic, or therapeutic, value, enlightening us about human weaknesses and delusions, objectifying our criticism of social and political sham and exploitation, holding the mirror of nature up to our own ridiculous behavior, and perhaps curing us of any temptation to take our problems too seriously.

In the world of comedy, fortune is a kind mediator between potential disaster and eventual triumph for individuals. Thus comedy defuses conflict, even as it offers quirky and unpredictable surprises in the advancement of the action. Despite these surprises, the comic world is known and manageable, populated with equally well known social types. Moreover, there are fairly standard plot variations in comedy, notably on the theme of love or on one's position in society or on the battle of the sexes. Governing the comic plot is the happy or favorable ending—that celebration of youth over age, goodness over wickedness, common sense over dogmatism or downright mindlessness, understanding over misunderstanding, life over death. Comedy's conclusion invokes balance, harmony, and renewal; it is an affirmation of the sheer abundance that is possible in human existence.

In this section, two of the world's greatest dramatists—Aristophanes and Shakespeare—treat the subjects of love and war from the opposing perspectives of comedy and tragedy. Aristophanes's *Lysistrata* is a boisterous, satirical, and often farcical comedy about the battle of the sexes, set against the very real backdrop of the Peloponnesian War (431–404 BC), which pitted Athens against Sparta. He ridicules and holds up for laughter what Othello calls the "Pride, pomp, and circumstance of glorious war," while exposing the farcical nature of human sexuality. By contrast, Shakespeare's *Othello* is a profound and intricate study of the destructive element that undermines the substance of love, human sexuality, life, and civilization itself. In the words of the critic Alvin Kernan, *Othello* captures through a rich symbology "those qualities of being and universal forces that are forever at war in the universe and between which tragic man is always in movement." Both plays assert their own versions of comic and tragic order at the end of the action in an attempt to show how the world should be ordered properly. Yet the divergences in these plays are equally significant. In these departures, we can discover the antithetical energies that animate comic and tragic drama.

Aristophanes

LYSISTRATA

Aristophanes (450 BC?–385 BC), generally considered the greatest classical Greek dramatic comedian, was born toward the beginning of the Age of Pericles. Under the leadership of Pericles, Greek civilization enjoyed the expansion of the city-state into an empire, the rise of democracy, and the creation of an urban culture that was highly supportive of artistic and cultural life. What little is known about Aristophanes comes largely from references to himself in his plays and allusions to him in the works of others. In Plato's Symposium, Aristophanes is referred to as a "joker and lover of jokes." We do know that he wrote drama for about forty years, that he produced at least forty plays, and that eleven of the plays written between 427 and 388 BC have survived. Nine of these plays were written during the Peloponnesian War—the struggle between Athens and Sparta that lasted from 431 to 404 BC. Thus it is understandable that this war and the conflicts it caused forms a major backdrop for Aristophanes's plays, notably The Acharians (425 BC), Peace (421 BC), and Lysistrata (411 BC). In plays such as The Wasps (422 BC), The Birds (414 BC), and The Frogs (405 BC), Aristophanes turned his comic and satiric talent toward other aspects of Greek culture—literature, philosophy, law, education, politics. Lysistrata is the finest, one of the most ribald, and assuredly the most contemporary of these comedies. In this play, the heroine, Lysistrata, urges the women on both sides of the Peloponnesian conflict to engage in a sex strike in order to subdue their warrior husbands and achieve peace. In the fantastic and zany world of Lysistrata, we see the comic impulse of Aristophanes at its best. Lysistrata, with its unique mixture of social comedy, satire, farce, sexual burlesque, and underlying seriousness, reveals Aristophanes's involvement in the life and fate of the Greek city-state.

Characters

Lysistrata
Kaloniké
Myrrhiné
Lampito
Magistrate
Attendants
Stratyllis
Women of the force in the Acropolis
Kinesias, Myrrhiné's husband
Their baby
Slave
Spartan herald
Spartan ambassadors
Athenian ambassadors
Reconciliation

Athenian youths
Porter
Athenian banquet guests
Musicians
Chorus of old men
Chorus of women
NOTE. *The Spartans speak with a Lancashire accent.*

    The scene is the slope from the Lower to the Upper City. In the background is the great gateway to the Acropolis. It is daybreak. Lysistrata is pacing up and down. She is in a flurry of impatience, and finally bursts out:

Lysistrata. If they'd been asked to attend some Bacchic beano,
    Some party for Pan, or Colias, or Aphrodite,
    You couldn't get through for the crush of revellers;
    But now, there isn't a woman in sight, not a single
    One. . . . Well, here's my neighbour coming. . . .

Enter Kaloniké

                                 Good morning,

Kaloniké.

Kaloniké. 'Morning, Lysistrata. My dear, whatever's
    The matter? You look fed to the teeth. Stop frowning!
    It doesn't suit you.
Lysistrata.   Kaloniké, I'm furious, and
    It's the women, yes *women.* We're not to be relied on—
    Don't all the men *love* to say so, and . . .
Kaloniké.   But aren't we?
Lysistrata. I *told* them all to be here; I *said* it was most important,
    And they've none of them come. They're simply hogging in bed.
Kaloniké. They'll come. You know, it's hard for a woman to get away:
    You're pottering round your husband; you're chivvying a slave,
    You're putting a baby to bed, or washing or feeding the brat. . . .
Lysistrata. But there *are* other things, like *this, far* more important.
Kaloniké. But Lysistrata, *what?* Why've you called us? What's up?
Lysistrata. Something big.
Kaloniké.   Is it really pressing?
Lysistrata.   Biggest ever.
Kaloniké. Then why on earth isn't everybody here?
Lysistrata. Oh it's not that—they'd come quick enough for *that.*
    No; it's an *idea.* Something I've *thought* of in bed,
    Alone, awake in the night, tossing and turning.
Kaloniké. It must be a teaser to keep *you* tossing and turning.
Lysistrata. It is. So simple, so all-embracing. Just that the whole salvation
    Of Greece depends on us women.
Kaloniké.   On US? Then civilization
    Hangs by a thread!
Lysistrata.   It depends on us, truly it does,
    Whether the Peloponnesians are all annihilated—
Kaloniké. Let 'em be, I say, far better if they were!

Lysistrata. And all the Boeotians—

Kaloniké. All? Oh, please not the eels;
   Surely you'd spare the *eels*?

Lysistrata. And as for the Athenians—
   I can't bring myself to say it—you must supply my meaning.
   But *if* all the women *did* come from Boeotia, the Peloponnese,
   And all of us here came, too: we could save the entire country.

Kaloniké. But women? *Us women*? Sitting as pretty as flowers
   In our saffron silks, and all made up, and moulded
   In the long folds of our gowns and our feet in dainty shoes?
   What wonders could *we* perform? What could we *do*?

Lysistrata. Just that. Those are the weapons I'm counting on to save us:
   These saffron silks and dainty shoes and scent and make-up
   And diaphanous nothings.

Kaloniké. *Save* us? *I'd* have . . . What d'you mean?

Lysistrata (*slowly and seriously*). That men shall never take spears against
   each other again . . . .

Kaloniké. I'll put on my best dress. . . .

Lysistrata. Never draw swords . . .

Kaloniké. I'll buy
   A new pair of shoes.

Lysistrata. Then wasn't it essential
   For the women to come here?

Kaloniké. Walking's far too slow;
   They ought to have flown.

Lysistrata. That's the Athenians all over:
   Do everything too late—but I'm sorry not one
   Woman's sailed up from the coast or over from Salamis.

Kaloniké. They were all manned by daybreak, too, I haven't a
   doubt.

Lysistrata. And the ones I absolutely counted on coming first,
   The girls from Acharnai—there's not a sign of them.

Kaloniké. Theagenes' wife has consulted the oracle:
   I'm afraid *she's* bound to come. . . . But look, here *are* some women,
   They're simply piling in.

   Enter Myrrhiné with a group of women.
         Hullo! (*To Lysistrata.*) Where've *they* sprung from?

Lysistrata. Anagyrus.

Kaloniké. That means we've stirred up trouble.

Myrrhiné. Are we too late, Lysistrata? . . . Well . . . say *something*!

Lysistrata. I can't say much for you, Myrrhiné, meandering up
   So late for such an occasion.

Myrrhiné. I just couldn't find
   My belt in the dark—but if this is really so urgent,
   Tell us what it's about.

Lysistrata. No, we'll wait for a bit.
   Till the Boeotians appear—and the Peloponnesians.

Myrrhiné. Yes, that's a good idea. Here's Lampito anyhow.

Enter Lampito with a group of Spartan women.

Lysistrata. Lampito, my sweet! Delighted to see you, darling,
    How pretty you look! How healthy you Spartans are!
    And my, what biceps! I believe you could throttle a bull.
Lampito. Eh, and I could that, and no mistake.
    It's the gym I do, see? Just watch me do the fling,
    And bat my bum with my heels!
Lysistrata. What magnificent breasts!
Lampito.   Prod me like that,
    And I feel like the fatted calf!
Lysistrata.   Where does *this* girl come from?
Lampito. Boeotia and she's classy!
Lysistrata.   Sweet Boeotian countryside,
    The very plain of the Cyprian . . .
Kaloniké.   And perfectly cropped and weeded.
Lysistrata. And this?
Lampito.   She's a good girl. She's from Corinth.
Lysistrata. A good girl *and* from Corinth? Well as far as I can *see* . . .
Lampito. Now tell me, who called up this gabble of girls?
Lysistrata.   I did.
Lampito. Eh, did you now? And what's it all in aid of?
Myrrhiné. Yes, Lysistrata, tell us about this "urgent business."
    What is it?
Lysistrata. Of course I'll tell you. But first, have you any objection
    If I ask one tiny question—all of you?
Myrrhiné. Ask whatever you like.
Lysistrata.   Then—don't you all crave for the fathers
    Of your children, away on service?—For I'm certain you've all got husbands
    Away at the front.
Kaloniké.   Five months in Thrace, worst luck,
    Keeping watch on Eucrates.
Myrrhiné.   Mine's seven months on Pylos.
Lampito. Mine's hardly in at the door, but he totes his equipment
    And off again . . .
Lysistrata.   Not even the ghost of a lover's
    Been left us women. So—if I find a method of stopping the war,
    Would you like it? Would you be with me?
Myrrhiné. You bet! Even if I have to pop my mantle
    And blow the proceeds on . . . well, on a party. . . .
Kaloniké. I'd cut myself in half just like a flatfish,
    And give away half for peace . . . .
Lampito.   I'd crawl to the top
    Of Taÿgetos, to see peace again, I would.
Lysistrata. All right! I'll speak then. I'll let out my great secret!
    Women! If we want to compel the men
    To make peace, we must . . . it's imperative . . .
Kaloniké. Well, go on.
Lysistrata.   Will you do it?

Kaloniké.   Die if we don't!

Lysistrata. Then —NO SLEEPING WITH THEM. Total abstinence.
Why do you turn away? Where are you going?
Why do you bite your lips and shake your heads,
Turn pale and start to snivel? Will you do it,
Or won't you? Well?

Myrrhiné.   Not me. I'll never do it.
Let the war go on!

Kaloniké.   Nor me. Let the war go on!

Lysistrata. You—and you swore you'd cut yourself in half. . . .

Kaloniké. Anything else you like—I'd go through fire
If you said I had to—but, Lysistrata, not that.
You must see, darling, not *that*: there is nothing like it.

Lysistrata. And you, Myrrhiné?

Myrrhiné.   Fire for me, too. Sorry.

Lysistrata. Women—what an utterly rotten lot
We are! It's not surprising tragedies
Are written about us, nothing but beds and cradles,
Always the same old serial, men and babies.
But Lampito—you're Spartan—if only *you'd*
Be on my side we still might pull it off:
Will you vote for me?

Lampito.   Eh, but it's tough for women,
Sleeping alone all night, waiting for the cocks to crow.
Still if we must, we must. It's peace at any price.

Lysistrata. You darling, you're the only one!

Kaloniké.   But if we *did*
Do . . . what you say (and I hope to heaven we won't
Have to) could you really *guarantee* peace that way?

Lysistrata. I'm certain of it.
Look here. We sit indoors, all tarted up,
In our most transparent things and obviously sexy,
We get the men worked up, bee-lined for bed,
And then when it comes to the point—walk out on them.
They'll make a treaty at once—you know they will.

Lampito. (Like Menelaus, coming to do her in,
Saw Helen's breasts and chucked his sword away.)

Kaloniké. But supposing they simply leave us?

Lysistrata.   We must make
The best of the next best, as the proverb says.

Kaloniké. Proverbs aren't lovers. But suppose they grab us
And drag us to bed by force?

Lysistrata.   Hang on to the door.

Kaloniké. Suppose they knock us about?

Lysistrata.   Give in and sulk.
There's not much fun in raping your wife. If you need to,
Get at them other ways. They'll soon give it up.
It's a poor lookout for a man if the woman won't play.

Kaloniké. Well, if you *really* think it'll work, I suppose
　　We'd better think so too. . . .
Lampito. Now, Spartan husbands, we can jockey them
　　Into making peace without cheating. But How about
　　Your fickle Athenian bed-bugs—how'll you get any sense
　　Out of them?
Lysistrata.　　　We'll fix *them* all right,
　　You needn't worry.
Lampito.　　　　　Not worry? While they've got
　　Their triremes ready for sea; their treasury bulging with brass?
Lysistrata. But we've provided for that. We're proposing to occupy
　　The Acropolis this morning. It's a job for the *older* girls.
　　While *we* sit here at this . . . sexplanation, *they,*
　　Pretending to sacrifice, are seizing the Treasury now.
Lampito. Got everything taped, you have—that's a bit of duff!
Lysistrata. Then come on, Lampito, let's make an oath
　　As quick as we can; then nothing can go wrong.
Lampito. Just say the words, love, I'll repeat the dose.
Lysistrata. Splendid. Who'll act as server? Don't stand there staring!
　　Set a shield hollow side up and fetch the sacrifice!
Kaloniké. Lysistrata, what *sort* of oath are we going to swear?
Lysistrata. Well, in the *Seven Against Thebes* they sacrificed a sheep.
　　Over a shield. I thought . . .
Kaloniké.　　　　　　　But Lysistrata, *dear,*
　　One would *never* swear about *peace*, over a *shield*. . . .
Lysistrata. What *shall* we do then?
Kaloniké.　　　　　　　　A white horse, would that do?
Lysistrata. A *white horse*, really, where could we get it from?
Kaloniké. What *shall* we swear on, then?
Lysistrata.　　　　　　　I know. I tell you what *I'd* like.
　　Get me a big black bowl and put it hollow side up, and—
　　We'll sacrifice a skinful, no, a jar full of Thasian WINE, and,
　　Swear not to add a drop of—WATER. How about that?
Lampito. That's a right good oath, I swear—there's more *in* that
　　than words.
Lysistrata. Then bring me the bowl and the wine-jar.
Kaloniké.　　　　　　　　My dears, just look
　　What a beautiful jar! You couldn't help being delighted
　　With emptying that.
Lysistrata.　　　　　Put down the bowl. Take hold of the victim.
　　　　　O goddess Persuasion, O loving cup,
　　　　　Accept our offering, look with favour
　　　　　Upon us women now and for ever . . . .
Kaloniké *(intoning).* "The fine red blood how bountifully it
　　flows . . . ."
Lampito *(parody).* And, by Castor, how beautiful to my nose . . . .
Myrrhine *(dreamy).* Let *me* be the first to take the oath, my
　　dears . . . .

Aristophanes

Kaloniké *(sharply)*. By the goddess, NOT unless you draw first lot!
Lysistrata *(in command)*. Now Lampito, all of you!

> Put your hands on the cup.
> Kaloniké, you be spokeswoman:
> Repeat whatever I say
> After me word for word.
> The rest of you confirm
> And abide by it faithfully.

Lysistrata. I will have no man come to me, neither lover nor husband.
Kaloniké. I will have no man come to me, neither lover nor husband.
Lysistrata. Though he comes like a battering ram. . . . Speak!
Kaloniké. Though he comes like a battering ram . . . Oh god,
    I'm weak at the knees, Lysistrata.
Lysistrata. I will live at home a virgin pure
Kaloniké. I will live at home a virgin pure
Lysistrata. In my flimsiest silk and enticingly made-up
Kaloniké. In my flimsiest silk and enticingly made-up
Lysistrata. So that my husband may particularly want me
Kaloniké. So that my husband may particularly want me
Lysistrata. But never willingly will I give myself to anyone
Kaloniké. But never willingly will I give myself to anyone
Lysistrata. And if he forces me
Kaloniké. And if he forces me
Lysistrata. I will be frigid and not respond to him.
Kaloniké. I will be frigid and not respond to him.
Lysistrata. I will not lift my legs to the ceiling
Kaloniké. I will not lift my legs to the ceiling
Lysistrata. Nor crouch like the lioness carved on the knife handle
Kaloniké. Nor crouch like the lioness carved on the knife handle
Lysistrata. Having sworn this oath may I drink from here
Kaloniké. Having sworn this oath may I drink from here
Lysistrata. But if I break it let my cup be filled with water
Kaloniké. But if I break it let my cup be filled with water.
Lysistrata. Do you all swear this?
Myrrhiné.   Oh yes, we *all* swear this.
Lysistrata. Then I'll finish the victim off!
Kaloniké. *Steady*, dear, fair shares! Let's show we're all friends
    here.

    (Female cheers and shouts off.)

Lampito. Eh, what's that hullaballoo?
Lysistrata. What I was telling you—the older women
  Have occupied the Acropolis! Now, Lampito,
  Get back to Sparta and organize things there
  (But leave your friends as hostages). We'll reinforce
  The others in the Acropolis and see
  ʹThe doors are bolted fast.

Lysistrata

Kaloniké. Won't the men come
  And attack us soon?
Lysistrata. I couldn't care less about the men.
  They can use what threats they like, they can use *fire*,
  Those doors will not be opened unless we say so,
  And only on our conditions . . . .
Kaloniké. They won't, by Aphrodite!
  If they're going to call us women insuperable and fiendish
  Let's earn the reputation!

Lampito leaves for Sparta. The rest disappear through the gates into the Acropolis. Then the chorus of old men enters staggering under the weight of great bundles of faggots and lighted charcoal braziers.

Chorus of men. Keep on, Drakés, easy does it, though you rub your shoulder
  Raw with that great olive trunk. The older I get the less I
  Know what's coming next, but I confess I never thought I'd
  Be faced with such a shocking thing—did *you*, Strymodoros?
    That these blighted sluts
    We keep and feed, worse luck
    Should maul Athene's image,
    Control the Acropolis,
    And stop us getting in
    By bolting up the gates—
  We must press on to the citadel, and be quick about it,
  And stack it thick with faggots, and, Philurgos,
  When we've ringed this persistent lot of plotters,
  We'll fire the wood with our own hands and burn the whole boiling
  (But first, that poisonous woman—Lykon's little darling).
  Agreed?
    Why, that Cleomenes, the first man to seize it,
    Did *he* get away scot-free?
    No! He surrendered to me,
    For all his Spartan spirit,
    Wearing only a clot of filthy cloth,
    Unshaven, lousy, stinking,
    Six years without a bath!
  We besieged that fellah without a break, keeping watch at the gate,
  Seventeen ranks of us sleeping at out posts . . . .
                          And as for these pests
  Whom even the gods hate (and so does Euripides)
  Shall I do nothing in face of such flagrant defiance?
  If I do, let my Marathon medals be torn from my breast!
    But as for us all
    The rest of the road
  Is a one-in-four: we strive for the citadel
    And how shall we haul
    This without a moke?
  —How sharp on my shoulders lumps this load!

But it's got to be done
And the fire kept going,
It mustn't go out before we arrive:
    So keep blowing, blowing—
    Fffff! The smoke!
    O Heracles, it's dire!
    What sparks flew up,
They bit at my brow—like a dog with rabies!
    Must be Lemnos-fire
    —And *that's* not a joke—
Or it couldn't have given me such a snap!
    But, on to the top
    Or Athene will suffer,
And when did she need help more than now,
    Laches? Keep puffing, puffing—
    Fffff! The smoke!
    Burning quite clear, thank heaven!
    So let's unload our logs here,
    Kindle a torch of vinewood,
    And burst at the door like a battering-
    Ram. And *then*, if the women
    Don't open up when we ask'em,
    Set fire to the door and smother
    The lot! Unload! Confound this
    Smoke! Will no Samian general
    Lend a hand? (My back's stopped aching.)
    Up, coal! That's *your* job, brazier—
    Fire the torch, I'll be first to brandish it!
    Now, Victory, vaunt our trophy
    Over these brazen bitches!

The chorus of women enter from the other side. For the present they do not see each other.

Chorus of women. I don't like the look of this. Am I too late to help them?
    For I hardly could get at the spring to fill my bucket
    What with the dark and the crowd, the confusion and clashing of pitchers,
        The elbowing slaves, the jostling
        Runaways; in the end
        I jumped the queue and snatched this
        Water I bring to succour
        My burning comrades.

        For I've heard those old devils saying
        They're bringing heavy enough
        Logs for a bath-furnace,
        And they're making revolting threats
        Against us women.
We're abominable, they say, they're going to burn us to ashes.

(O goddess, never never may I see it, but see us instead
Saviours of Greece and its people from war and madness.)
(Praying.)　　　　　Wherefore, O Golden-Helmet,
　　　　　　　　　Protector, we hold thy temple;
　　　　　　　　　And I entreat thine aid, Athene,
　　　　　　　　　If any set fire down there
　　　　　　　　　To bear water for us.
Wait a minute! What's this?　*(The choruses meet face to face.)*
(To chorus of old men.)　You men must be monsters—
You couldn't be anything else by the look of things.
Chorus of men. What a *remarkable* sight! Did you *ever* expect to see *this*?
A swarm of women standing guard in the gateway!
Chorus of women. What an insult! Takes *us* for a swarm!
Let me tell you you haven't seen a thousandth of our forces!
Chorus of men. Phaidrias, shall we pluck these old mocking birds,
And take a stick to their backs?
Chorus of women.　　　　　　　　Put down our pitchers, and then
　　　　　　　　　　　　　　　if they start something,
We won't be cluttered up.
Chorus of men.　　　By god, a couple of slaps like Bupalos got
And they'll shut their traps.
Chorus of women.　　　　　　　Get on then. Here I am. And I'm
　　　staying put.
　　　Nobody else is going to have the pleasure . . .
Stratyllis.　　　　　　　　　Of kicking you in the crutch!
Chorus of men. Shut up or I'll knock your old block off.
Chorus of women. Just try it! You dare lay a finger
　　　On Stratyllis . . . .
Chorus of men.　　　Suppose I give her
　　　A straight left—what'll you do?
Chorus of women.　　　　　　There won't be much *left* of you.
　　　I'll tie your lungs in a love-knot, I'll tug out your guts . . . .
Chorus of men *(mocking).* Good old Euripides, you had a line on
　　　women!
　　　There isn't a sweeter creature . . . .
Chorus of women.　　　　　　　Rhodippé, up with the jug.
Chorus of men. What's the water *for,* you god-hated women?
Chorus of women. What's the fire *for,* you old foot-in-the-grave?
Chorus of men. You'll see who's for the pyre.
Chorus of women. You'll see what the water's for!
Chorus of men. You couldn't put out a fire-fly.
Chorus of women. Couldn't I? Well, we'll see!
Chorus of men. *Why* I don't roast you, I can't imagine.
Chorus of women. Got any soap? I'll give you a bath!
Chorus of men. A bath for me, you old bitch?
Chorus of women. Yes, a bath for a bridegroom!
　　　(Cackles of derisive laughter.)
Chorus of men. What insolence—did you hear it?
Chorus of women. I can say what I like—I'm free.

Chorus of men. I'll stop your gab!
Chorus of women.   I'll take care
    You don't sit on the Bench again!
Chorus of men. Fire, set fire to her hair!
Chorus of women. Water, to your work, water!

    (They souse the old men from their pitchers.)

    The chorus of old men splutter and cough.

Chorus of women. Was it *hot* enough?
Chorus of men.   Stop it! Stop it!
    What are you doing?
Chorus of women.   Watering you!
    To make you *bloom* again—
Chorus of men. But I'm withering, shivering, shrinking . . . .
Chorus of women. You've got your fire to warm you . . . .

    Enter magistrate with his four attendants.

Magistrate. What, *another* outbreak of riot among the women?
    Oh, these little drummings and continual orgies!
    These Adonis laments from the roof-tops!
    Why, I even heard one, sitting in the Assembly:
    Demostratos—damn him—was proposing a motion
    To sail to Sicily, or some such tomfoolery,
    And there was his wife wailing "Lament for Adonis"
    And *he* roaring "We must raise a force for Zakynthos"
    And *she* yelling, half tipsy on the roof-top,
    "Weep for Adonis" and still the bellowing old blusterer
    Boring on through it all—that's a typical example
    Of this uncontrollable behaviour of women!
Chorus of men. And suppose you'd heard of their insufferable
    Effrontery today? They abused us and soused us;
    It makes us look as if we'd pissed in our tunics.
Magistrate. And serve us right, by the sea-god! We're just as blameworthy
    As *they* are. It was *we* taught them this attitude;
    We sowed the wind, we must reap the whirlwind.
    Just *look* at the way we men go on, in a shop:
      "Oh goldsmith, remember that necklace
      You made my wife—she was out dancing
      Last night, and the clasp came off and I've got to
      Run over to Salamis. If you've a *moment*,
      Could you come round tonight, and fix her
      A new clasp."
                    Well, I *ask* you.
                              And another
    Idiot goes to the cobbler, a randy bit of manhood,
    With a kit a boy couldn't handle, and says,
      "My wife's little toe is so tender;
      It's chafed by her sandal.
      Could you come round about midday and fit her

A little bit looser?"
That's what things have come to!
And now here am I, a government official,
Come to get money out the the Treasury
To pay for oars, and the gates are barricaded
Right in my face by these rampant women!
I must put a stop to this nonsense.
Fetch me crowbars! Why are you goggling
There, you slacker? Snooping about for an inn?
Crowbars! Shove these crowbars under the gates:
You, over *there*! I'll take this. Now. One—two—three—

But the gates open and there stands Lysistrata.

Lysistrata. You needn't force the gates. I'm coming out
Of my own accord—and it isn't crowbars you want,
It's common sense.
Magistrate.   Really? You . . . you—Where's my officer?
Arrest her! Tie her hands behind her back.
Lysistrata. By Artemis! The tip of a finger on me,
And public servant or not, his private service
'll be over!
Magistrate *(to his men).* Are you afraid? You there, go with him,
Tackle her round the waist, tie her up, get on with it!

Enter Kaloniké.

Kaloniké. By Hecate! A finger on *her* and I'll spread
Your guts on the road!
Magistrate.   My guts on the road, eh?
Officer! Handcuff *this* one! She talks too much.

Enter Myrrhiné.

Myrrhiné. By Phosphoros, the tip of a finger tip
On *her*, and it's two lovely black eyes . . . .
Magistrate. What's all this? Officer! *Officer!* Arrest them!
I'm warning you, we can't *have* this sort of thing.
Stratyllis *(from the chorus).* By Hecate, if he so much as makes a pass at *her*
I'll pull your hairs where it hurts most.
And you can scream your head off.
Magistrate. . . . Not an officer left. But I'll be damned
If I'll be downed by women! Scythians!
Close ranks and prepare to charge!
Lysistrata.   I'm warning *you*:
We're four companies fully armed and ready.
Magistrate. Up Scythians and at 'em!
Lysistrata.   Come on, everyone!
All you egg-sellers, greengrocers, garlic-girls,
Bread-sellers, barmaids, and all!
Sling 'em, fling 'em, bang 'em, slang 'em!
Do your worst! *(A general mêlée.)*

Aristophanes

(Lysistrata's speech continues above it.) Enough! Back there!
                          Enough! Don't strip the dead.

Magistrate *(gloomily).* A gory time for my men, and no mistake.

Lysistrata. Did you think it was *slaves* you came to fight?
    Don't you imagine women thirst for glory?

Magistrate. You *thirst* all right, if there's a bar in sight.

The two choruses face each other again.

Chorus of men *(to magistrate).* Hey, you old windbag!
    Call yourself one of our rulers?
    What's the point of negotiating
    With wild beasts?
                  Don't you know
  What sort of a wetting they gave us?

Chorus of women. Was it right to attack
    Your neighbours without a reason?
    If you do, you must take
    Whatever you get—black eyes!
    All *I* want to do
    Is to sit like a good little virgin,
    Meek and mild at home,
    Not moving a muscle, *but if you*
    Stir up a wasp's nest, be prepared for stings!

Chorus of men. O Zeus, what shall we do with these dragons?
    I can't put up with this! Let's probe
    Into this shocking affair:
    Why did they want to seize
    This Cranaan, inaccessible,
    Holy Acropolis up on the rock?
    (To magistrate.) Question them, then; take nothing for granted;
    Cross-examine them closely;
    It'd be culpable negligence not
    To get to the bottom of this!

Magistrate. Then first I want to ask: why lock us out of the citadel?

Lysistrata. To keep the money safe—so you don't go on fighting for it.

Magistrate. Is money the cause of the war?

Lysistrata.   Yes, and of every disturbance.
    Peisander—anyone—who's ever got into power:
    They always stir up trouble, then they can get at the money,
    And do what they like with it. Now, not a penny more!

Magistrate. What are you going to do?

Lysistrata.   Control the Exchequer.

Magistrate. Control the Exchequer, *you!*

Lysistrata.   Is that so funny?
    We do the housekeeping.

Magistrate.   That isn't the same.

Lysistrata.   Why isn't it?

Magistrate. This money's for *war* purposes—

Lysistrata. But that's precisely our point: No—more—war.

Magistrate. Then how shall we save the city?

Lysistrata. We'll save you!

Magistrate.   You?

Lysistrata.   That's what I said.

Magistrate.   Monstrous!

Lysistrata. Whether you like it or not.

Magistrate.   Ridiculous nonsense!

Lysistrata. *Why* get so cross? That *is* what's going to happen.

Magistrate. Preposterous!

Lysistrata.   We *must* save you.

Magistrate.   Suppose I don't *want* to be?

Lysistrata. All the more reason to.

Magistrate.   What's made you dabble
   In these matters of peace and war?

Lysistrata.   If you listen, I'll tell you.

Magistrate. You'd better be brief—or you'll catch it.

Lysistrata. Then do *listen* and try to stop clenching your fists.

Magistrate. Dammit, I *can't*! You make me so irritable!

Stratyllis *(mocking him).* You'd *better* try— or you'll catch it!

Magistrate. Be quiet, you old crow! *(To Lysistrata.) You* speak.

Lysistrata.   Thank you.
   All through the war—and what a long war—
   By controlling ourselves we managed to endure
   Somehow what you men did. We never once
   Let ourselves grumble. Not that we approved
   What you did do—simply, we understood you.
   Oh, how often at home one would hear you spouting
   Hot air about something serious! And masking
   Our misery with a smile we'd ask you gently,
   "Dear, in the Assembly today, did you decide
   Anything about peace?" And, "What's that to do with *you*,"
   You'd growl. "Shut up!" And I did.

Stratyllis.   *I never did!*

Magistrate. You'd have been sorry if you hadn't!
                   —Well . . .

Lysistrata. I held my tongue. And immediately you'd make
   Some even more crazy decision, and I'd sigh and say,
   "But how *can* you have passed this lunatic thing?"
   And you'd frown and mutter, "Stick to your spinning,
   Or you *will* have something to complain of.
   War is men's business."

Magistrate.   And quite right too!

Lysistrata. Shouldn't we try to save you from your follies?
   When we see you mooning about the streets moaning
   "Isn't there a *man left* in this country?" "Not one,"
   Says the old blimp with you. So we called a rally
   Of all the women and planned: *we* would save Greece.
   Why wait any longer? Now you must listen to *us*—
   It's our turn to talk, and *yours* to be quiet as we've been,

While *we're* busy, putting things right again.

Magistrate. You do that for *us*! Intolerab—

Lysistrata.   Silence!

Magistrate. Told to be quiet by a woman in a veil,
   I'd rather die . . . .

Lysistrata.   Oh if *that's* all it is—
   You put my veil on *your* head and be quiet! *(She puts it on him.)*

Kaloniké. And here's a spindle.   *(Forces it into his hand.)*

Myrrhiné.   And a *dear* little wool-basket.

Lysistrata. Now bundle up your skirt, card wool, and chew
   beans—
   War is women's work!

(The magistrate is reduced to impotent silence.)

Chorus of women. Come on, women, put down our pitchers and take the
   field,
      We must do our proper bit for the common cause!
                  Never shall I stop dancing,
                  Never my knees give,
                  Nothing I wouldn't dare
                  For comrades of such metal,
                  Such spirit and grace and flair,
                  Such wisdom and love of country,
                  And such entrancing *sense*!
      Born of mettlesome mothers, sharp to molest as nettles,
      Let us advance righteous, in anger, and never yield:
                  The wind stands fair!

Lysistrata *(as in prayer).* But let sweet-spirit Love, let Aphrodite breathe
                  On our breasts and thighs today
                  And enflame delight, and quicken
                  The men to desire, that we
                  May be called by all the Greeks
                        Peace-Makers.

Magistrate. Well . . . how will you do it?

Lysistrata.   First, stop the soldiers
   Sloping about the market, like morons, in battle-order.

Stratyllis. Indeed we will!

Lysistrata.   Now, you can see them slopping
   Among the stalls, the pots and vegetables, armed to the teeth,
   Like Corybantes.

Magistrate.   A soldier's a soldier anywhere:
   Esprit de corps is essential.

Lysistrata.   *Esprit de corps!*
   A soldier in full kit, *queuing to buy fish!*

Stratyllis. My word, I saw a smarty long-haired cavalry captain
   Swigging an eggnog from his helmet: bought from an old tart!
   Then there was a Thracian so petrified the shopgirl,
   Clanking his cutlery, she hopped it, and the dirty
   Cheat got his fruit *free* . . . .

Magistrate. And how do you propose
To disentangle all this and settle everybody?
Lysistrata. Easily.
Magistrate. How?
Lysistrata. Just as when wool is tangled
We untangle it, working it through
This way and that—so we'll settle the war,
Sending embassies this way and that.
Magistrate. Threads, skeins, spindles, you little fool:
What's this to do with *war*?
Lysistrata. If you had any sense you could handle
Politics as we do wool!
Magistrate. Well . . . ?
Lysistrata. Like the raw fleece in the wash tub, first
You must cleanse the city of dirt:
As *we* beat out the muck and pick out the burrs,
You must pluck out the place-seekers, sack the spongers
Out of their sinecure offices, rip off their heads—
Then the common skein of good sense:
Blend the good aliens, the allies, the strangers,
Even the debtors, into one ball;
Consider the colonies scattered threads,
Pick up their ends and gather them quick;
Make one magnificent bobbin and weave
A garment of government fit for the people!
Magistrate. It's all very well this carding and winding—women!
You haven't any idea what a war *means*.
Lysistrata (*very deliberate and serious*). We know just twice as well.
We bore the sons
You took for soldiers.
Magistrate. *Must* you recall
Such painful memories?
Lysistrata. Yes. And one's young,
And wants to be gay and enjoy one's youth—and all
The men are away. And *we* might bear it—just—
But what about the girls that've never had a man,
Growing old, alone in their beds?
Magistrate. Don't men grow old?
Lysistrata. Not like women. When a man comes home
Though he's grey as grief he can always get a girl.
There's no second spring for a woman. None.
She can't recall it, nobody wants her, however
She squanders her time on the promise of oracles,
It's no use . . . .
Magistrate (*preening himself*). Yes, if a man can still stand up for
himself . . . .
Lysistrata (*furious*). Stand up? Lie down, you dirty old dog!
And it's dead and buried I mean.
Let's get a pig and an urn,

And I'll bake you a sop
For Cerberus—and here's a garland.   *(Pours water over him.)*
Kaloniké. And *this* from me.   *(More water.)*
Myrrhiné. And this crown from me.   *(Still more water.)*
Lysistrata. What's the matter? What are you waiting for?
    The boat's afloat, and Charon's calling,
    You're keeping him from shoving off . . . .
Magistrate. This is scandalous! I'm drenched, I've had enough.
    I'll go straight to my fellow-benchers;
    They shall see what a state I'm in!
Lysistrata. Are you complaining I haven't laid you out properly?
    We'll give you your rites—all in good time! You wait!

    The women enter the citadel. The magistrate goes off fuming.

Chorus of men. No time for sitting about—come on, we're free;
                Men, we must strip for action!
Already this seems to me to stink
Of greater trouble and strife—I'm thinking
Of Hippias. There's a whiff of tyranny.
            There's no knowing whether
            Some Spartan faction
            Have put heads together
            With Cleisthenes
And inspired these ferocious females with cunning
            To seize our money—
            The actual cash
            That keeps us going!

It's abominable that *women* should boss us citizens
    With their babble and cackle of helmets and shields,
And acting on *our* behalf suck up to the Spartans
    (Men you can trust—if you trust a ravening wolf).
But what's behind it? A plot to establish a tyranny!
    Tyrannize over *me*? Not likely! I'll be on my guard,
I'll keep my sword at the ready, sheathed in myrtle,
    And post myself in the market-place beside
The statue of Aristogeiton. And just to begin with—
    I'll give this old hag a sock on the jaw!
Chorus of women. Your mother'll hardly know you—you've got
so bold!
            Girls, we must strip naked!
It's open to anyone to praise
The city and I, to the end of my days,
Shall love her for giving joy to a gentle child.
            I was only seven when I
            Carried the Sacred
            Vessels; and at ten I
            Bore the Temple Mill;
Then in yellow I acted the Little Bear at Brauron,
            And, growing taller

And lovelier, took care
Of the Holy Basket—it was heaven!
So don't you think I *want* to give my best to the city?
I was born a woman, yes, but is it my *fault*
If my advice on the present emergency is the sounder?
And I pay my share of tax—in the boys I bear.
But you, wretched old fogeys, what do *you* contribute
—Apart from contriving to squander and waste
Even the Persian Reserve built up by your fathers?
We're running the risk of ruin because of you!
What are you muttering there? You get across *me*,
And I'll take this leather slipper and bash your jaw!

Chorus of men. This is an outrage! Shall we suffer it?
—And it very much looks to me
As if there's more in the offing!
No man who *is* a man will let this go . . . .
Off with our tunics—a man should
Be Man untrammelled from top to toe.

Remember how
We comrades stood
For freedom, at Leipsydrion,
When we were young.
And now
We must take wing,
And shake old age off our bodies,
And put youth on!

Give these women an inch, they'll take an ell!
In our manly exercises they'll soon excel!
They'll build ships and sail against us with a fleet!
If they turn to riding, you can write off the knights!
A woman rides well, a gallop won't unseat her!
Look at the Amazons that Micon depicted fighting
The men, on horseback. No, we've got to check them.
Make pillories and lock them in—*by the neck*!

Chorus of women. By heaven, provoke *me*, I'll make you blubber!
—You'll see my seamy side!
I'll send you yelling to the neighbours!
I'll comb you out, you louse! Now women, up
With your cloaks: a woman should
Be Woman untrammelled from toe to top.

You go for me
In my present mood,
And garlic and beans are off your menu!
Just say the word:
You'll see,
I'll pursue you as hard
As the beetle that got the eagle's
Eggs in the end.

Aristophanes

If Lampito loves me and noble Theban Ismenia
You can go to hell, you haven't a hold on me!
Make your decrees sevenfold, you loathsome old pill!
Why, I ask my Boeotian friends for a pretty playmate
For my children on Hecate's day—a sweet little eel—
And 'Sorry we can't; it's against the law', they say.
Your stinking laws—the sort you'll always make,
Till somebody ups with your heels and *breaks your neck!*

Several days have passed. Lysistrata comes out of the gateway looking harassed.

Chorus of women. Lysistrata, why so gloomy? What's the matter?
 You, the leader of our glorious . . .
Lysistrata. Just the whole nature of women: it makes me despair!
Chorus of women. But *why?*
Lysistrata.   That's all.
Chorus of women. What ghastly thing has happened?
 We're all your friends, you can tell us.
Lysistrata.   Yes, it *is* ghastly.
 I can hardly face telling you, and yet I must.
Chorus of women. Don't bottle it up, my dear. What's the disaster?
Lysistrata. The long and the short of it is—they're mad for men!
Chorus of women. O Zeus!
Lysistrata. No, not Zeus. Men. That's the plain fact. I simply
 Can't keep them away from the men another minute.
 They just slink out.
                    Why, I caught one chipping away at
 The loophole in Pan's Cave; and another wriggling
 Down by a block and tackle; another deserting openly;
 I dragged one off a sparrow's back by the hair,
 Just taking off for Orchilochos' brothel—
 They make every sort of excuse to get home. Look!

Enter first woman.

 One's coming now. What are *you* doing?
1 Woman.   I just must
 Run home for a minute—I left my *best* Milesian
 Wool out, and the moths will positively *devour it.*
Lysistrata. You and your moths. Inside!
1 woman.   But I'll come straight back, I *promise.*
 I *only* want to spread it out on the couch.
Lysistrata. It wouldn't be wool you'd only spread. *No.*
1 woman. What, leave it all to be *ruined?*
Lysistrata.   If necessary, YES.

Enter second woman.

2 woman. I'm so *worried* about my flax,
 I left it at home unstripped . . . .
Lysistrata.   She's worried about her flax.
 Inside! And quick!

2 woman.   But I *will*
    Come back, I swear. I'll just strip it
    And come straight back.
Lysistrata.   No stripping,
    Of any sort. You begin and
    All the others'll want to, as well.

    Enter third woman.

3 woman. Oh holy goddess Eileithyia,
    Keep my pains in control,
    Till I get to some proper place!
Lysistrata. What's this?
3 woman.   My pains have begun!
Lysistrata. You weren't pregnant yesterday.
3 woman. But I am today. Oh Lysistrata,
    I must go home *at once*
    To get a midwife . . . .
Lysistrata.   Nonsense!
    What's this hard lump you've got?
3 woman *(coyly).* A little boy-baby.
Lysistrata.   Not this!   *(Tapping it.)*
    It's hollow and made of brass.
    Come off it, you little fool,
    It's the Sacred Helmet! How dare you
    Say you were pregnant?
3 woman.   But I *am!*
Lysistrata. Then what's the helmet *for?*
3 woman. If my little chick's born here,
    In the Acropolis, I'll just pop him
    Inside like a dove with its egg.
Lysistrata. Excuses and lies! It's perfectly
    Clear. You can STAY PUT
    Till the naming of your—helmet!

    Enter fourth woman and fifth woman.

4 woman. —And I can't sleep a *wink*
    Since I saw the Sacred Snake . . . .
5 woman. Nor can I. I shall die of *exhaustion.*
    These *wretched* owls—they *never* stop hooting!
Lysistrata. *You* stop lying, you devils! It's your men you want!
    Do you think they don't want *us*? What sort of nights
    Do you think *they* spend? But you've got to stick it!
    Hold out a little longer, the oracle says
    We'll win if we do—just listen to what it says.
Women. The oracle? Tell us! Tell us!
Lysistrata. Be quiet, then.

    (In a portentous voice, making it up as she goes.)

When all the Swallows gather unto One Place, eschewing the
Hoopoe-birds and their amorous pursuits, then is come the end

of all Evils, and it is ordained by Zeus the Thunderer that the
low shall be exalted over the high . . . .

Stratyllis *(from within).* Does that mean we lie on top of the men?

Lysistrata *(takes no notice).* But if the Swallows fall into dis-
sensions and fly from the Holy Temple, no longer shall they be
esteemed virtuous; but as wanton and more prone to lechery than
all the birds of the air!

1 woman *(carried away by it all).* That oracle's plain enough. O all you gods,
Let us not falter now in this extremity of craving.
Let us go back in! We would never live down the disgrace
Of betraying the oracle. Come back inside!

(The women re-enter the Acropolis.)

The two choruses face each other.

Chorus of men.   Now
Let me tell you a little story
I heard when I was a boy:
                                  How
There once was a youth called Melanion, who
Was so appalled at the prospect of women he flew
To the mountains rather than marry.
                             And he hunted hares,
                             And he set his snares,
                             With his dog there,
And never came home for anyone!
                             That was the way
                             He detested women
                             And we're no less
Wise in our ways than Melanion!

Old man *(in chorus).* Like a smacker, granny?

(Makes sound of kiss.)

Old woman *(in chorus).* You'll get one you won't like.

Old man. Like a good kick then?

Old woman. My, what hairs? What a jungle!

Old man. Myronides was black
Bow and stern (ask those who attacked him)
And so was Phormio!

Chorus of women.   Now I
Will tell you a little story
To offset your Melanion.
                                  Ti-
mon was a man with a beard so prickly
You couldn't get through to his face for the thickets.
He was savage, the son of a Fury.
                             And, to Timon, men
                             Were a terrible bane;
                             He swore like sin,
He vituperated against your vicious nature:

That was the way
He detested you,
And never ceased;

But to women he was the dearest creature.

Old woman. Like a clip on the jaw?
Old man. Try if you like . . . .
Old woman. Like a good kick then?
Old man. I'd be lost in the jungle . . . .
Old woman. What a lie you're telling!

> I may be old, but I still
> Can keep myself trim.

Lysistrata is seen above on the wall.

Lysistrata. Help! Everyone! Quick! This way!

Enter women above, with Myrrhiné.

1 woman. What's all the row about?
Lysistrata.   Look!

> A *man*! Have you ever *seen*
> A man more obviously
> In love? Aphrodite must
> Rule him with a rod of iron!

1 woman *(prays).* O Cyprian, Cytherean,

> Paphian mistress and guardian,
> Keep us to the straight and narrow . . . .
> *(Eagerly.)* *Where* is he? *Who* is he?

Lysistrata. Down by Demeter's chapel.
1 woman. So he is! Whoever is he?
Lysistrata. Does *anyone* know who he is?
Myrrhiné. Yes. My husband, Kinesias.
Lysistrata. Then it's your job, Myrrhiné,

> To lead him up the garden path:
> Love him and not love him,
> Do *everything* except the
> One thing we swore we wouldn't!

Myrrhiné *(with enthusiasm).* Trust me!
Lysistrata *(coolly).* Of course. *But* I'll stay and help you.

> We'll give him the treatment together.
> The *rest* of you, go inside!

(They all disappear but Lysistrata.)

Enter Kinesias below, followed by a slave holding a baby.

Kinesias. Oooooh, it's *torture*! I'm racked, I'm wrecked

> In a rigid spasm, I'm in agony . . . .

Lysistrata. Halt! Who goes there!
Kinesias.   I do.
Lysistrata. A man?
Kinesias.   Can't you *see* I am?
Lysistrata. Then get out!

Kinesias.   And who are you
   To throw me out?
Lysistrata.   The officer
   Of the watch.
Kinesias.   Oh heaven,
   Do fetch Myrrhiné for me . . . .
Lysistrata. Myrrhiné for *you*? Who are *you*?
Kinesias. Kinesias . . . I'm her husband.
Lysistrata. Oh, *Kinesias* . . . we know *you*!
   You're famous! your name's always
   On your wife's lips—why, she never
   Touches an egg or an apple
   But she says "To Kinesias."
Kinesias *(simpers).* Truly?
Lysistrata.   Truly . . . and if anyone
   Says a word about men, Myrrhiné
   Immediately swears they're all
   Scum but Kinesias!
Kinesias *(more overpowered).* Truly?
   Oh, *do call her!*
Lysistrata.   What'll you give me?
Kinesias. Whatever you like—whatever
   I've got. Here—all I can do . . .   *(Chink of money.)*
Lysistrata. All right. I'll go and *tell* her.

   (Exit Lysistrata.)

Kinesias. Be quick!
   Since she left, the house
   Seems horribly empty, I can't
   Go in without weeping. I'm utterly
   Depressed—I get no kick
   Out of food. It's *her* I want.
Myrrhiné *(off).* Oh yes, of course I love him,
   But he won't *let* me love him
   Don't call me out to him . . . .

   She comes out on the wall.

Kinesias. Myrrhiné, Myrrhiné darling,
   What do you mean, not love you?
   Come down to me darling . . . .
Myrrhiné.   No!
Kinesias. Not when *I* call you, Myrrhiné?
Myrrhiné. You *call*—but you don't want me!
Kinesias. Not want you? I'm dying for you.
Myrrhiné. Good-bye! *(She turns to go.)*
Kinesias *(wildly).*   But darling, *listen!*
   For our child's sake please listen
   (Sotto voce as he pinches the baby.) Here, you little—*call* your mother!

   (The baby yells.)

Kinesias. Haven't you *any* feeling?
    Aren't you at all sorry
    For our own poor little poppet,   *(Louder screams.)*
    Six days unwashed and hungry?
Myrrhiné. *I'm very* sorry for him.
    It's *you* that aren't!
Kinesias.   Then, darling,
    Do come down and take him . . . .   *(Still louder screams.)*
Myrrhiné. What it is to be a mother!
    What a life! All right, I'm coming!

(She disappears from the wall.)

Kinesias. She looks younger and even sweeter!
    When she's aloof and angry
    It just makes me want her *more* . . . .

Myrrhiné comes out of the gate and snatches the baby.

Myrrhiné. Oh my angel, my little darling,
    Come from your *horrible* daddy,
    Come to your mummy, sweetheart . . . .
Kinesias. Why treat me like this, Myrrhiné?
    We're simply hurting each other.
    It's these filthy women have got at you.
Myrrhiné. Don't *touch* me!
Kinesias.   And all our belongings
    Going to rack and ruin.
Myrrhiné.   Much I care!
Kinesias.   And your knitting
    Picked to bits by the hens?
Myrrhiné.   I
    Tell you I don't give a damn!
Kinesias. And the holy rites of marriage
    So long neglected? . . . Darling,
    Come home.
Myrrhiné.   I won't. No . . . unless you,
    And all you men, make a treaty
    To stop war.
Kinesias.   If you *want* it,
    We'll do it.
Myrrhiné.   If you want *me, do it!*
    —Then I'll come home. For the present
    I've sworn I won't.
Kinesias.   Oh darling,
    It's so long . . . . Come to me now.
Myrrhiné. No. But that isn't saying
    I don't love you . . . .
Kinesias.   If you love me,
    Why won't you—why . . .
Myrrhiné.   You idiot!
    Make love in front of the baby?

Kinesias. Take the boy home, Manes.   *(Exit slave with baby.)*
　　There! He's gone. *Now* won't you?
Myrrhiné. But where can we *go*, darling?
Kinesias. Pan's Cave. Couldn't be better.
Myrrhiné. But there's my purification,
　　Before going back to the citadel . . . .
Kinesias. Easy. The spring of Clepsydra.
Myrrhiné. But I've sworn an oath; do you want me
　　To break it?
Kinesias.　　　　I'll take the consequences.
　　Put *that* out of your head.
Myrrhiné. But we need a bed. I'll get one . . . .
Kinesias. We can lie on the ground, can't we?
Myrrhiné. *You* on the dirty ground?
　　Darling, I'd *never* let you.   *(Exit inside.)*
Kinesias *(to himself).* She loves me, oh *how* she loves me!
　　It's as plain as my pikestaff!

　　Re-enter Myrrhiné with bed.

Myrrhiné. Now hurry up and lie down.
　　I'll take off my things—*oh dear,*
　　I must go and get a mattress!
Kinesias. But I don't want a mattress!
Myrrhiné. Oh, but you do, it's beastly
　　On the bare cords.
Kinesias.　　　　　Give me
　　A kiss then?
Myrrhiné *(slaps him).* There!   *(Exit inside.)*
Kinesias. Ow! Do come back quickly!

　　Re-enter Myrrhiné with mattress.

Myrrhiné. Here's the mattress. Lie down.
　　I'll take off my things. *Oh dear,*
　　You haven't got a pillow!
Kinesias. But I don't want a pillow.
Myrrhiné. But I do!   *(Exit inside.)*
Kinesias.　　　　I'm simply starving:
　　I'm being kept waiting longer
　　Than Heracles for his dinner.

　　Re-enter Myrrhiné with pillow.

Myrrhiné. Lift up your head, darling.
Kinesias. I've got everything . . . .
Myrrhiné *(slowly).*　　　　　I wonder,
　　Have we got all we want?
Kinesias. All but you. Quick, my treasure!
Myrrhiné. I'm undoing my girdle, but remember—
　　No cheating over the treaty!
Kinesias. I'd rather die.

Myrrhiné.   But darling,
    You haven't got any blankets!
Kinesias. I don't *want* any blankets,
    I just want *you*!
Myrrhiné.   In a minute;
    I'll be as quick as I can . . . .   *(Exit inside.)*
Kinesias. She's killing me with her blankets

   Re-enter Myrrhiné with blankets.

Myrrhiné. Up a moment!
Kinesias.   I'm up, all right.
Myrrhiné. Would you like a dash of perfume?
Kinesias. No, by Apollo, I wouldn't.
Myrrhiné. By Aphrodite you would,
    Whether you like it or not.   *(Exit inside.)*
Kinesias. O Zeus, make her spill the bottle!

   Re-enter Myrrhiné with scent bottle.

Myrrhiné. Put out your hand, take it
    And rub it in.
Kinesias.   By Apollo!
    It stinks—of delay, not love!
Myrrhiné. Oh! I've brought you the wrong bottle.
    This is the cheapest Rhodian . . . .
Kinesias. All *right*, it'll do.
Myrrhiné.   Nonsense!   *(Exit inside.)*
Kinesias. Damn the man who invented scent!

   Re-enter Myrrhiné with new scent.

Myrrhiné. Just hold this bottle, will you?
Kinesias. For god's sake don't go getting
    Anything else—lie down,
    And see what I've got for you . . .
Myrrhiné. I will, darling, I will.
    There go my shoes, and Kinesias—
    You *will* vote for peace, won't you?

   (She runs through the gate. It clangs behind her.)

Kinesias. Oh, *that*, yes, I'll . . . God in heaven, she's gone!
    She's tricked me! She's left me standing!
    I've been robbed of the loveliest girl in the world!
    —But I must have *someone*!
    Or how will you ever grow up,
    My poor little hungry orphan?
    Where's Kynalopex? Quick—
    Send me a nurse, from your brothel!
Chorus of men. Poor old cock! You're in a terrible way!
    What distress of soul—I'm really sorry for you!
    These pangs of unemployment

Are more than a body can bear . . . .
Kinesias. O Zeus, what misery!
Chorus of men. And *she* did this to you!
    The utterly foul, entirely repulsive—
Kinesias. —Darling. No, she's *sweet*, utterly *sweet*!
Chorus of men. Sweet is she?
                  Sweet as muck! O Zeus, Zeus, suck
                  Her up in a whirlwind, spin
                  Her round like a ball, then let her fall
                  From a very great height
                          Right
                  On the tip of my family tree!

The chorus fall back. Enter from one side Magistrate, from the other a Spartan herald.

Herald. Heh! Can you tell me the way
    To the Senate? I've got some news.
Magistrate. News? And who may *you* be?
    A man, or Priapus in person?
Herald. A herald from Sparta, mate,
    With news of a treaty.
Magistrate.   A treaty?
    With a spear under your cloak?
Herald *(slowly).*   No . . .
    I haven't a spear . . . .
Magistrate.   Why turn
    Away? Why fiddle with your cloak then?
    Are you stiff from your journey?
Herald. The man's nuts!
Magistrate.   But *look* at you.
Herald. It's no joke!
Magistrate.   Then what is it?
Herald. A Spartan secret dispatch.
Magistrate. If *that's* a secret dispatch,
    I've got one, too.
    Come on, tell me the truth:
    How are things in Sparta?
    I know the situation.
Herald. Grim. It's all up with us.
    And all our allies.
Magistrate.   How
    Did the trouble begin? Was it Pan?
Herald. No. It was Lampito,
    Then all the blasted women,
    Kicked us out of bed.
Magistrate. And how do you like *that*?
Herald. It's a fair bastard. We creep
    About the town, bent double
    Like we were carrying lanterns

In a gale. And the women won't
Let us so much as tickle
Their fancies till we make
Peace for the whole of Greece.

Magistrate. I see the whole thing: it's a nation-
Wide plot by the women. Go quickly
And get your authorities
To send envoys with absolute powers
To make peace. I'll persuade our Council.
I can put it to them straight.

Herald. That's proper talk, mate. I'm off home. *(Exeunt.)*

Chorus of men. *Women!* There is nothing worse—not fire nor a leopard!

Chorus of women. Then why attack us when you might have had us as an
ally?

Chorus of men. *Women!* Could one *ever* cease one's hatred?

Chorus of women.   As you like it,
But seeing you all naked I don't like it—you're a figure
Of fun! Come here to me and let me put you on your tunic!

Chorus of men. Kind of you . . . I must admit I stripped it off
in anger.

Chorus of women. *Now* look a man and not a joke! *If* you'd not
annoyed me
I'd have taken out that fly that's milling in your eye now.

Chorus of men. So *that's* what has been aggravating me—the damn mosquito:
Scoop it out and show it me—it's been at me for ages.

Chorus of women. I will. But *why* must you behave so tetchily? Good heavens!
What a monster! Do you see? From the Tricorysian marshes!

Chorus of men. Bored clean through my head it has, and though you've got it
out, my
Tears keep flowing . . . .

Chorus of women. I'll wipe your eyes, although you've been so brutal,
And I'll love you . . .

Chorus of men.   No, you won't.

Chorus of women.   Say what you like, *I'll love you!*

Chorus of men. Get on with you, you flatterers! Was there ever truer saying:
"Impossible to live with you. Impossible without you."
But now I'll make a treaty, from henceforth for everlasting,
I'll never raise a finger against you, and VICE VERSA!
—Let's start the ball rolling. *You* strike up an anthem.

Chorus of women. Men! We're not prepared to
Slander anybody, but,
Quite to the con-trary,
Say and do the kindest things:
There's misery enough.
So let it be announced to
Any man or woman who
Wants a bit of money—
They can borrow it, our purses
Are simply *stuffed* (with nothing),

>   And if the peace is ratified,
>   And everybody gratified,
>   They needn't pay us back.
>   We've organized a dinner
>   For some playboys from Carystos
>   (Such *manners*)—minestrone
>   Is in the pot and sucking pig's
>   The *plat du soir*.
>   It's luscious and delicious,
>   So have an early bath and come,
>   And bring *all* your children—
>   *Just* walk in as if it were
>   Your own front door!
>   —I'm *sure* you'll never grudge it if
>   You find you cannot budge it, if
>   It's bolted in your face!

Enter the Spartan ambassadors.

Chorus of men. Look at the ambassadors from Sparta!
     Are they on crutches? They're stooping along, their beards
     Almost trailing the ground. Greetings, you Spartans!
     How are you?
1 Spartan ambassador. You can see. Do we need to answer?
Chorus of men. This disaster keeps on mounting.
1 Spartan ambassador.   True enough.
     But what can a man say? We simply *must*
     Have peace, however we get it.
Chorus of men. And here come our delegates:
     —Whatever's the matter?
     Have you got athlete's arm?

Enter the Athenian ambassador.

1 Athenian ambassador.   Can *anyone* say
     Where Lysistrata is? You can see
     What terrible shape we're in.
Chorus of men.   We're all the same.
     When d'you find it worst? When you first wake?
1 Athenian ambassador. It gets me up as much as it gets me down!
     If we don't make peace pretty soon, heaven help us,
     We'll have to fall back on Cleisthenes!
Chorus of men.   Take my advice
     And put your clothes on. Don't you remember how
     They mutilated the Hermae?
1 Athenian ambassador. Heavens yes! Thank you.
1 Spartan ambassador *(aside).* Right enough. I'll put on mine.
1 Athenian ambassador *(approaching).* Greetings, Spartans! This is a bad
     business.
1 Spartan ambassador. It is, that! *(Aside.)* Lucky they didn't see us
     A minute ago, we might have pricked their vanity.

1 Athenian ambassador. Let's get down to it at once. Why've you come?

1 Spartan ambassador. To discuss peace.

1 Athenian ambassador.   Excellent! So have we.
    Shall we send for Lysistrata? She's the only one
    Can bring us to terms.

1 Spartan ambassador. Get Lysis-whoever-you-like
    Who can settle t'matter.

1 Athenian ambassador. No need for us to call.
    She must have heard us talking and here she is.

Lysistrata comes out attended by a very pretty girl.

Chorus of men. Lysistrata! Incomparable woman!
    Now is your hour of greatness! You must
                 —Be uncompromising,
                 —Be clement,
                 —Be stern,
                 —Be conciliatory,
                 —Be wayward,
                 —Be wise,
    For you hold the leading statesman of this land
    In the palm of your beautiful hand: and we entrust you
                 With our common fate!
    It is for you to settle, for ever and finally,
                 All dispute!

Lysistrata. Not such a difficult matter (unless you take
    To taking each other to bed and I shall soon
    Know if you do!). Where's Reconciliation?

(The girl comes forward.)

Now, my dear, go and fetch those Spartans. Don't tug them
In the boorish way our husbands do with us;
Be thoroughly feminine—but if they *won't*
Give you their hands, take them and tow them, *politely*,
By their . . . life-lines. Then fetch the Athenians too,
And if *they* won't take your hand, grab hold of whatever they offer . . . .

(The ambassadors are brought to her.)

Now, you Spartans: stand near me, *here* please.
And you Athenians, *there*—and listen to me.
I may be only a woman, but I've got sense.
Partly I was born with it (and plenty of it),
Partly I listened to my father, my elders and betters
—I wasn't so ill-taught.
            So first I propose
To censure you both equally (and perfectly rightly),
You! Who have hallowed altars from one and the same ewer,
Like blood relations at Olympia—
Thermopylae—Delphi—and many another place
Will spring to your minds—and yet, I say, and yet, YET,

With a barbarian army mobilized
And ready to pounce, you have engrossed yourselves
In the destruction of your cities—
In the death of your own people!
1 Athenian ambassador. I'm dying for you, darling!
Lysistrata. Listen! Spartans, I turn to you: Pericleidas!
Does that name mean *nothing* to you?
Have you forgotten how he came here, knelt at our altars,
Pale in his purple robe, and begged for help?
—You were hard pressed by Messene; there was an earthquake
And Kimon came to your help with a force four thousand strong
And saved all Sparta!
                  —And, even so, you ravage
The land of your friends!
1 Athenian ambassador. They're wrong, Lysistrata!
1 Spartan ambassador. We're wrong, admitted we're wrong. But what a ravishing
Bottom she's got . . . .
Lysistrata. Do you think I've nothing to say to you Athenians?
You—in the livery of slaves—have you forgotten
How the Spartans came and slaughtered those Thessalians,
And how many others of Hippias' gang?
Who else was your friend that day? Who else
Restored you the cloak of freedom? Oh, don't you see?
1 Spartan ambassador. I've never seen a more desirable woman.
1 Athenian ambassador. I've never seen more clearly what I want!
Lysistrata. Bound by such mutual ties, how *can* you bear
To fight each other and bicker and squabble and scrap
And never cease? Make peace! Make peace! Why not?
1 Spartan ambassador. Give us back our breast-work and we're ready—
1 Athenian ambassador. Your—*what?*
1 Spartan ambassador.   Pylos. It's never out of our thoughts.
1 Athenian ambassador. By god, no!
Lysistrata.   Go on, give it them, why not?
1 Athenian ambassador. What trouble spot'd we have?
Lysistrata.   Ask for something *else* in exchange—
1 Athenian ambassador (illustrating his points on Lysistrata).
That's tricky. Well, suppose they give us Echinos there,
With its delta, and the Melian gulf behind and all
That's enclosed by the legs of Megara . . . .
1 Spartan ambassador.   You're mad!
You can't have everything!
Lysistrata.   Don't argue about the legs!
1 Athenian ambassador. I'd like to strip and plough my bit of land.
1 Spartan ambassador. I'd like to spread mine with dung, I would.
Lysistrata. Then come to terms and you'll be able to!
If you *really* want to, go and discuss the matter
With your allies.
1 Athenian ambassador. Why waste time? Our allies

Stand exactly where we do, all they want
Is what we want—our women!
1 Spartan ambassador. That goes for ours—
1 Athenian ambassador. And certainly the Carystians.
Lysistrata. Very well then! Go and purify yourselves
And we'll give you a banquet here
In the Acropolis tonight
On what we can rake together.
We'll make our treaty then,
And each of you can take
His wife and go home again.
1 Athenian ambassador. My dear, we'll go at once.
1 Spartan ambassador. Show me the way, brother.
1 Athenian ambassador. Quicker than light.   *(Exeunt.)*
Chorus of women. Just *anything* in my wardrobe—
   The run of my jewel-case—
  (I'm simply that sort of person),
    It's all on loan, you can choose
  For your daughter the Basket-Bearer
   Elect, or for *any* child!
It's all there for the taking,
   Nothing is so well sealed
That you can't break in and sample
   Whatever's inside—it's free!
But if you set eyes on the tiniest speck
   You've sharper eyes than me.
Are any of you starving
   With servants to support?
Or a horde of hungry children?
   I've a house full of fine wheat,
And loaves for a whole day's ration!
   If any of the poor
Will bring their sacks and baskets,
   No one can stuff in more
Than my nice young fellow, Manes . . . .
   But kindly get this right:
If you happen to come too close to my door,
   Beware of the dog. He'll bite!

 It is now evening. There is a porter on the gate. The feast is going on inside. Two Athenian youths, aged about fifteen, hammer on the door.

1 youth. Guv! Be a sport, and let us in!
Porter.   Clear off, you!
1 youth. Come on, do! Shall I tickle your arse
  With a torch? No! That'd be *vulgar*!
  I'd never do *that*—but if the audience'd *like* it . . .
  Would you?
2 youth.   'Ere, I'll 'elp.
Porter.   Hop it, you two!

Aristophanes

Or I'll pull your hair off. Git aht of it!
So these Spartans inside can go 'ome
In peace—when they done drinking.

Two Athenian banquet guests come out. They are rather drunk.

1 guest. Well, I never saw such a spread!
Folly good jellows these Spartans—
Never known you in better form,
Ol' boy, what wit, what?—'s the WINE.
2 guest. 'S it. When we're sober, we're mad.
Now, I'll give the Gov'ment a tip—
Always keep our Ambassadors tight!
Right! Why?—Go to Sparta sober,
'Mediately look for trouble.
Don't listen to a word they say
Or what they don't say—see?
Then all come back with conflic—
Conflickering reports. 'Sno good.
Now, everything's all right.
If they sing "The Minstrel Boy"   *(Does so.)*
When they ought to sing "Come Landlord fill the flowing bowl"   *(Does so.)*

Clap 'em on the back, praise 'em,
Swear they were right . . . .

(Laughter from youths.)

Porter. Blast you two kids, git aht of it, will yer!
1 youth *(going).* Not 'alf. The high-ups are comin'—they're high,
all right!   *(Exeunt youths.)*

Enter Spartan and Athenian ambassadors, with musicians.

1 Spartan ambassador *(careful of his words).* Here, lad, take the pipes
And we'll do a song and dance
In honour of the Athenians
—And ourselves, come to that.
1 Athenian Ambassador. Yes, take the pipes, boy. We'd be delighted.
Spartans *(as chorus).* Memory, awaken
The Muse of your youth! Sing
How we and the Athenians
Put paid to the bloody Persians
At Artemision—
And pounded their fleet to pulp!
Ah, we were gods then.

Leonidas was our leader
And we whetted our tusks like boars
And the sweat from our jaws ran slavering,
We were blood to the knees—the Persians
Outnumbered us ten to one.
But not by the end of the day!
Ah, we were gods then.

O woodland Artemis,
Huntress, virgin goddess,
Hither descend and bless
    Our treaty:
And by thy divine grace
May our friendship flourish
And year by year increase,
    Without deceit.
O virgin huntress
    Descend and bless!

Enter Lysistrata.

Lysistrata *(gently).* Now all is well; all is well.
    O Spartans, O Athenians, take
    Your wives. Let every man
    With his beloved dance for joy
    And bless the gods for this event—
    And may we never never make
    Wars in the world again.
Athenians *(as chorus).* Dance then, O dance for joy!
    Gather the Graces
    And Artemis and her heavenly
    Brother Apollo; bid
    Bacchus, his eyes blazing
    In a maze of Maenads; summon
    Zeus in his robe of thunder,
    His Queen serene beside him;
    Call the Holy Witnesses
    To celebrate this peace!
    The peace that Aphrodite
    The darling goddess made!
    Alalai! Lalai!
    Lift up your voices—sing
    For victory, for peace!
    Let all your voices ring
    For victory, for peace!
    Evoi! Evoi! Evoi!
Athenian voice. Spartans, *you* sing a *new* song,
    Another song, for us!
Spartans *(as chorus).* Come down, O Muse, from Taÿgetos, and praise Apollo
of Amyclai,

And the Queen of the brazen Temple
    And Castor and Pollux at play
    On the banks of Eurotas—O!
But the dance, the dance, the dance!
    Honour the city of Sparta
That loves the divine dance!
    —Whose girls on the banks of Eurotas
Fleet-foot as fillies prance,

Aristophanes

And flounce their flying hair
Like Bacchanals as they bear
Their emblems on, and there
The holy, the comely daughter
Of the Swan leads the dance!

O follow, O bind your hair,
Leap like a deer and sing
Anthem in unison:
Cheer the All-Conquering,
The Goddess, the All-Powerful,
>ATHENE! ATHENE!
>ATHENE! ATHENE!

QUESTIONS

1. The sources of classical Greek comedy were probably Greek religious rituals and festivals. In early Greek festivals, participants in processions often engaged in wild, suggestive antics, employed jokes and insults, and dressed in erotic costumes. How does Aristophanes draw on this cultural background in *Lysistrata?* Why is this ritualistic movement the reverse of tragic movement?

2. *Lysistrata* is an example of Greek "old comedy," which required a fantastic and original plot. Is the play primarily fantastic or realistic? How does Aristophanes resolve the tension?

3. A conventional element in Greek comedy is *agon*—the presence of highly formal arguments. Trace this pattern in the play.

4. What are the two main comic crises in the play?

5. How do the women remain women, even as they become warriors? How do the men become like women? What is Aristophanes saying about sexual role reversals in the play? How does he exploit role reversal for comic purposes?

6. What faults and weaknesses do the women display that they accuse the men of?

7. What is Aristophanes's attitude toward marriage and sexual life?

8. What is Aristophanes saying about the relationship of the family to the state? What connections exist among the relationships between man and woman, husband and wife, Athenian and Spartan?

9. Explain the connection that Aristophanes draws between sexual power and political power.

10. Why does Aristophanes exaggerate the sexuality of the men and women in the play?

11. Point out some of the sight gags, sexual puns, and obscenities in the play. What sort of comedy is this, and what is its purpose?

12. What is Lysistrata like? Why is she a comic character?

13. How does Kaloniké contrast with Lysistrata? What sort of comic character is she?

14. Describe Myrrhiné as a comic figure. Is she a stereotype? Explain.

15. Explain how Aristophanes lampoons or satirizes national characteristics in the play.

16. How do the Athenian Lysistrata and the Spartan Lampito relate?

17. Explain the nature of the comedy in these episodes: the prologue involving the women and their oath; the scene involving the choruses of women and old men; the conflict with the magistrate; the scene with Lysistrata and the women who want to desert the cause; the scene between Kinesias and Myrrhiné; the arrival of the ambassadors; the resolution of the play.

TOPICS FOR WRITING

1. Write an essay on the battle of the sexes as presented by Aristophanes in the play.

2. Classify the types of comedy in *Lysistrata*, and discuss examples of each type.

3. Analyze the comic conflict beween love and war in the play.

Assess Aristophanes's attitude toward nationalism, war, and peace in the play.

5. Using question 17 as a partial guide, trace the nature of comic action in the play.

William Shakespeare

OTHELLO

William Shakespeare (1564–1616) was born at Stratford-on-Avon, the eldest son of a prosperous English businessman who held many civic offices and of a gentlewoman whose own family, the Ardens, were relatively wealthy landowners. There is little factual evidence on Shakespeare's early life. He probably attended a "free," or local, grammar school, and from 1577 onward his family apparently suffered a reversal of fortunes. (It was not until the late 1590s, with Shakespeare's emerging dramatic success, that there was a restoration of the family's affluence.) In 1582, at the age of 18, Shakespeare married Anne Hathaway, a woman eight years older than her husband and pregnant. Their first child, Susanna, was baptized on May 20, 1583. Twins—Judith and Hamnet—were born two years later.

Biographers know virtually nothing about the "lost years" in Shakespeare's life, between 1585 and 1592; in 1592 a contemporary dramatic rival, Robert Greene, wrote scornfully of an "upstart crow" in London, an actor turned playwright named Shakespeare. By this time, Shakespeare was a well-established dramatist in London. By 1600, at the age of 34, he was acclaimed by many as the foremost playwright of his age, the author of fourteen plays and probably the bulk of his famous sonnets (which were not published until 1609).

Shakespeare had joined the Lord Chamberlain's Men, one of London's two leading acting companies, in 1594, and thereafter all his plays would be produced by this group, which included the great tragedian Richard Burbage and the clown Will Kempe. His early plays for the group included the histories Richard II *(1595) and* I Henry IV *(1597); the comedies* A Midsummer Night's Dream *(1595),* The Merchant of Venice *(1596), and* Much Ado about Nothing *(1598); and the tragedies* Romeo and Juliet *(1596) and* Julius Caesar *(1599). In the summer of 1599, the Lord Chamberlain's Men opened its own playhouse across the Thames in Southwick, naming it the Globe, with Shakespeare owning shares in both the company and the playhouse.* Julius Caesar *was the first play produced at the new playhouse.*

After 1600, Shakespeare devoted less time to acting and more to the writing of his greatest tragedies, Hamlet *(1602),* Othello *(1604),* King Lear *(1606),* Macbeth *(1606), and* Antony and Cleopatra *(1606), and also to such "dark" comedies as* The Tempest *(1611), his last independently written play. Shakespeare's personal fortune also increased during this period. He had inherited Stratford property upon the death of his father in 1601, and he made other profitable transactions there in 1602 and 1605. In London, he continued to reside in rented lodgings. After 1608, following a year of personal upheaval that included the deaths of an illegimate son and a younger brother, Shakespeare spent more time in Stratford. He died there on April 23, 1616, and was buried in the parish church.*

The Tragedy of Othello, the Moor of Venice, *is the most unusual of Shakespeare's later, mature tragedies. It was written by Shakespeare probably in 1602, drawn by the dramatist from a crude story in Giraldi Cinthio's* Gli Hecatommithi *(1565) and first produced in 1604. While lacking the monumental force of* King Lear, *the variety and depth of* Hamlet, *and the atmosphere of* Macbeth, Othello *is perhaps Shakespeare's finest play in terms of structure and intent.* Othello, *because of its taut plot, its taunting, premodern though subtle depiction of the effects of racism, its relatively limited number of characters, its rapid action and escalating tension, grips the audience like no other Shakespearean tragedy. Indirectly, too, it is historical, for it reminds us that for approximately 700 years the Moors from Africa ruled or shared dominions in much of southern Europe. From one perspective, the play offers a simple tale of a heroic man, Othello, poisoned in his love for his wife, Desdemona, by a pure villain, Iago, to the point where he kills her and himself. That Othello is black is a key motivating force behind Iago's deeds. But there is much more than what at first appears to be a "domestic tragedy." Othello is also a military man, a great general of the Venetian state—a basically simple, noble, courageous, and loving individual, even though an outsider, who is charged with the protection of national order and of civilization itself. We respond to his tragic fate at the personal level, and the irony here is that the civilization he is charged to protect ultimately destroys him, though he has "done the state some service." As in all his tragedies, Shakespeare offers in* Othello *a universal stage upon which unleashed evil can have the most awesome and potentially destructive impact.*

The Names of the Actors

Othello, the Moor
Brabantio, [a Venetian senator,] father to Desdemona
Cassio, an honorable lieutenant [to Othello]
Iago, [Othello's ancient,] a villain
Roderigo, a gulled gentleman
Duke of Venice
Senators [of Venice]
Montano, governor of Cyprus
Lodovico and Gratiano, [kinsmen to Brabantio,] two noble Venetians
Sailors
Clown
Desdemona, wife to Othello
Emilia, wife to Iago
Bianca, a courtesan
Messenger, herald, officers, Venetian gentlemen, musicians, attendants

Scene: *Venice and Cyprus*

William Shakespeare

Act I

Scene i

Enter Roderigo and Iago.

Roderigo.

Tush, never tell me! I take it much unkindly
That thou, Iago, who has had my purse
As if the strings were thine, shouldst know of this.   3

Iago.

'Sblood, but you'll not hear me!   4
If ever I did dream of such a matter,
Abhor me.

Roderigo.

Thou told'st me thou didst hold him in thy hate.

Iago.

Despise me if I do not. Three great ones of the city,
In personal suit to make me his lieutenant,
Off-capped to him; and, by the faith of man,   10
I know my price; I am worth no worse a place.
But he, as loving his own pride and purposes,
Evades them with a bombast circumstance.   13
Horribly stuffed with epithets of war;
[And, in conclusion,]
Nonsuits my mediators; for, "Certes," says he,   16
"I have already chose my officer."
And what was he?
Forsooth, a great arithmetician,   19
One Michael Cassio, a Florentine
(A fellow almost damned in a fair wife)   21
That never set a squadron in the field,
Nor the division of a battle knows
More than a spinster; unless the bookish theoric,
Wherein the tonguèd consuls can propose
As masterly as he. Mere prattle without practice
Is all his soldiership. But he, sir, had th' election;
And I (of whom his eyes had seen the proof
At Rhodes, at Cyprus, and on other grounds
Christian and heathen) must be belee'd and calmed   30
By debitor and creditor; this counter-caster,   31
He, in good time, must his lieutenant be,
And I—God bless the mark!—his Moorship's ancient.   33

Roderigo.

By heaven, I rather would have been his hangman.

Scene i A street in Venice **3** *this* i.e. Desdemona's elopement **4** *'Sblood* by God's blood **10**
him i.e. Othello **13** *a bombast circumstance* pompous circumlocutions **16** *Nonsuits* rejects **19**
arithmetician theoretician **21** *almost . . . wife* (an obscure allusion; Cassio is unmarried, but see
IV,i, 123) **30** *belee'd and calmed* left in the lurch **31** *counter-caster* bookkeeper **33 ancient**
ensign

Iago.
Why, there's no remedy; 'tis the curse of service.
Preferment goes by letter and affection, 36
And not by old gradation, where each second
Stood heir to th'first. Now, sir, be judge yourself,
Whether I in any just term am affined 39
To love the Moor.
Roderigo. I would not follow him then.
Iago.
O, sir, content you;
I follow him to serve my turn upon him.
We cannot all be masters, nor all masters
Cannot be truly followed. You shall mark
Many a duteous and knee-crooking knave
That, doting on his own obsequious bondage,
Wears out his time, much like his master's ass,
For naught but provender; and when he's old, cashiered. 48
Whip me such honest knaves! Others there are
Who, trimmed in forms and visages of duty, 50
Keep yet their hearts attending on themselves;
And, throwing but shows of service on their lords,
Do well thrive by them, and when they have lined their coats,
Do themselves homage. These fellows have some soul;
And such a one do I profess myself. For, sir,
It is as sure as you are Roderigo,
Were I the Moor, I would not be Iago.
In following him, I follow but myself;
Heaven is my judge, not I for love and duty,
But seeming so, for my peculiar end;
For when my outward action doth demonstrate
The native act and figure of my heart 62
In compliment extern, 'tis not long after 63
But I will wear my heart upon my sleeve
For daws to peck at; I am not what I am.
Roderigo.
What a full fortune does the thick-lips owe 66
If he can carry't thus!
Iago. Call up her father,
Rouse him. Make after him, poison his delight,
Proclaim him in the streets. Incense her kinsmen,
And though he in a fertile climate dwell,
Plague him with flies; though that his joy be joy,
Yet throw such changes of vexation on't
As it may lose some color.

---

36 *affection* favoritism   39 *affined* obliged   48 *cashiered* turned off   50 *trimmed* dressed
up   62 *The . . . heart* what I really believe and intend   63 *compliment extern* outward appearance
66 *thick-lips* (Elizabethans made no clear distinction between Moors and Negroes); *owe* own

William Shakespeare

Roderigo.
    Here is her father's house. I'll call aloud.
Iago.
    Do, with like timorous accent and dire yell   75
    As when, by night and negligence, the fire
    Is spied in populous cities.
Roderigo.
    What, ho, Brabantio! Signior Brabantio, ho!
Iago.
    Awake! What, ho, Brabantio! Thieves! thieves! thieves!
    Look to your house, your daughter, and your bags!
    Thieves! thieves!   81

    Brabantio at a window.
Brabantio *(above).*
    What is the reason of this terrible summons?
    What is the matter there?
Roderigo.
    Signior, is all your family within?
Iago.
    Are your doors locked?
Brabantio.   Why, wherefore ask you this?
Iago.
    Zounds, sir, y' are robbed! For shame, put on your gown!
    Your heart is burst; you have lost half your soul.
    Even now, now, very now, an old black ram
    Is tupping your white ewe. Arise, arise!
    Awake the snorting citizens with the bell,   90
    Or else the devil will make a grandsire of you.
    Arise, I say!
Brabantio.   What, have you lost your wits?
Roderigo.
    Most reverend signior, do you know my voice?
Brabantio.
    Not I. What are you?
Roderigo.
    My name is Roderigo.
Brabantio.   The worser welcome!
    I have charged thee not to haunt about my doors.
    In honest plainness thou hast heard me say
    My daughter is not for thee; and now, in madness,
    Being full of supper and distemp'ring draughts,
    Upon malicious knavery dost thou come
    To start my quiet.
Roderigo.
    Sir, sir, sir—
Brabantio. But thou must needs be sure

---

75 *timorous* terrifying   **81 s.d.** *Brabantio at a window* (added from quarto)   **90** *snorting*
snoring

My spirit and my place have in them power
To make this bitter to thee.

Roderigo. Patience, good sir.

Brabantio.
What tell'st thou me of robbing? This is Venice;
My house is not a grange.   106

Roderigo. Most grave Brabantio,
In simple and pure soul I come to you.

Iago. Zounds, sir, you are one of those that will not serve God if the devil
bid you. Because we come to do you service, and you think we are
ruffians, you'll have your daughter covered with a Barbary horse; you'll
have your nephews neigh to you; you'll have coursers for cousins, and   112
gennets for germans.   113

Brabantio.
What profane wretch art thou?

Iago. I am one, sir, that comes to tell you your daughter and the Moor are
now making the beast with two backs.

Brabantio.
Thou art a villain.

Iago. You are—a senator.

Brabantio.
This thou shalt answer. I know thee, Roderigo.

Roderigo.
Sir, I will answer anything. But I beseech you,
If't be your pleasure and most wise consent,
As partly I find it is, that your fair daughter,
At this odd-even and dull watch o' the' night,   123
Transported, with no worse nor better guard
But with a knave of common hire, a gondolier,
To the gross clasps of a lascivious Moor—
If this be known to you, and your allowance,   127
We then have done you bold and saucy wrongs;
But if you know not this, my manners tell me
We have your wrong rebuke. Do not believe
That, from the sense of all civility,   131
I thus would play and trifle with your reverence.
Your daughter, if you have not given her leave,
I say again, hath made a gross revolt,
Tying her duty, beauty, wit, and fortunes
In an extravagant and wheeling stranger   136
Of here and everywhere. Straight satisfy yourself.
If she be in her chamber, or your house,
Let loose on me the justice of the state
For thus deluding you.

---

106 *grange* isolated farmhouse   112 *nephews* i.e. grandsons   113 *gennets for germans*
Spanish horses for near kinsmen   123 *odd-even* between night and morning   127 *allowance*
approval   131 *from the sense* in violation   136 *extravagant and wheeling* expatriate and roving

Brabantio. Strike on the tinder, ho!
Give me a taper! Call up all my people!
This accident is not unlike my dream.   143
Belief of it oppresses me already
Light, I say! light!   *Exit (above).*
Iago. Farewell, for I must leave you.
It seems not meet, nor wholesome to my place,
To be produced—as, if I stay, I shall—
Against the Moor. For I do know the state,
However, this may gall him with some check,   149
Cannot with safety cast him; for he's embarked   150
With such loud reason to the Cyprus wars,
Which even now stand in act, that for their souls   152
Another of his fathom they have none   153
To lead their business; in which regard,
Though I do hate him as I do hell-pains,
Yet, for necessity of present life,
I must show out a flag and sign of love,
Which is indeed but sign. That you shall surely find him,
Lead to the Sagittary the raisèd search;   159
And there will I be with him. So farewell.   *Exit.* 160

Enter (below) Brabantio in his nightgown, and servants with torches.

Brabantio.
It is too true an evil. Gone she is;
And what's to come of my despisèd time
Is naught but bitterness. Now, Roderigo,
Where didst thou see her?—O unhappy girl!—
With the Moor, say'st thou?—Who would be a father?—
How didst thou know 'twas she?—O, she deceives me
Past thought!—What said she to you?—Get moe tapers!   167
Raise all my kindred!—Are they married, think you?
Roderigo.
Truly I think they are.
Brabantio.
O heaven! How got she out? O treason of the blood!
Fathers, from hence trust not your daughters' minds
By what you see them act. Is there not charms
By which the property of youth and maidhood   173
May be abused? Have you not read, Roderigo,
Of some such thing?
Roderigo. Yes, sir, I have indeed.
Brabantio.
Call up my brother.—O, would you had had her!—
Some one way, some another.—Do you know
Where we may apprehend her and the Moor?

---

143 *accident* occurrence 149 *check* reprimand 150 *cast* discharge 152 *stand in act* are
going on 153 *fathom* capacity 159 *Sagittary* an inn 160 **s.d.** *nightgown* dressing gown 167 *moe*
more 173 *property* nature

Othello

Roderigo.
> I think I can discover him, if you please
> To get good guard and go along with me.

Brabantio.
> Pray you lead on. At every house I'll call;
> I may command at most.—Get weapons, ho!
> And raise some special officers of night.—
> On, good Roderigo; I'll deserve your pains.   *Exeunt.* 185

Scene ii

Enter Othello, Iago, and attendants with torches.

Iago.
> Though in the trade of war I have slain men,
> Yet do I hold it very stuff o' th' conscience
> To do no contrived murther. I lack iniquity
> Sometimes to do me service. Nine or ten times
> I had thought t' have yerked him here under the ribs.   5

Othello.
> 'Tis better as it is.

Iago.   Nay, but he prated,
> And spoke such scurvy and provoking terms
> Against your honor
> That with the little godliness I have
> I did full hard forbear him. But I pray you, sir,
> Are you fast married? Be assured of this,   11
> That the magnifico is much beloved,   12
> And hath in his effect a voice potential   13
> As double as the Duke's. He will divorce you,   14
> Or put upon you what restraint and grievance
> The law, with all his might to enforce it on,
> Will give him cable.

Othello.   Let him do his spite.
> My services which I have done the signiory   18
> Shall out-tongue his complaints. 'Tis yet to know—   19
> Which, when I know that boasting is an honor,
> I shall promulgate—I fetch my life and being
> From men of royal siege; and my demerits   22
> May speak unbonneted to as proud a fortune   23
> As this that I have reached. For know, Iago,
> But that I love the gentle Desdemona,
> I would not my unhousèd free condition   26
> Put into circumscription and confine
> For the sea's worth. But look, what lights come yond?

185 *deserve* show gratitude for
Scene ii Before the lodgings of Othello   **5** *yerked* stabbed   **11** *fast* securely   **12** *magnifico* grandee (Brabantio)   **13** *potential* powerful   **14** *double* doubly influential   **18** *signiory* Venetian government   **19** *yet to know* still not generally known   **22** *siege* rank; *demerits* deserts   **23-24** *May speak . . . reached* are equal, I modestly assert, to those of Desdemona's family   **26** *unhoused* unrestrained

Iago.

    Those are the raisèd father and his friends.
    You were best go in.

Othello.   Not I; I must be found.

    My parts, my title, and my perfect soul   31
    Shall manifest me rightly. Is it they?

Iago.

    By Janus, I think no.

    Enter Cassio, with torches, officers.

Othello.

    The servants of the Duke, and my lieutenant.
    The goodness of the night upon you, friends!
    What is the news?

Cassio.   The Duke does greet you, general;

    And he requires your haste-post-haste appearance
    Even on the instant.

Othello.   What's the matter, think you?

Cassio.

    Something from Cyprus, as I may divine.
    It is a business of some heat. The galleys
    Have sent a dozen sequent messengers   41
    This very night at one another's heels,
    And many of the consuls, raised and met,
    Are at the Duke's already. You have been hotly called for;
    When, being not at your lodging to be found,
    The Senate hath sent about three several quests
    To search you out.

Othello.   'Tis well I am found by you.

    I will but spend a word here in the house,
    And go with you.   *Exit*

Cassio.   Ancient, what makes he here?

Iago.

    Faith, he to-night hath boarded a land carack.   50
    If it prove lawful prize, he's made for ever.

Cassio.

    I do not understand.

Iago.   He's married.

Cassio.   To who?

    Enter Othello.

Iago.

    Marry, to—Come, captain, will you go?

Othello.   Have with you.

Cassio.

    Here comes another troop to seek for you.

    Enter Brabantio, Roderigo, and others with lights and weapons.

31 *perfect soul* stainless conscience   **41** *sequent* consecutive   **50** *carack* treasure ship

Iago.
It is Brabantio. General, be advised.
He comes to bad intent.
Othello.   Holla! stand there!
Roderigo.
Signior, it is the Moor.
Brabantio.   Down with him, thief!

They draw on both sides.
Iago.
You, Roderigo! Come, sir, I am for you.
Othello.
Keep up your bright swords, for the dew will rust them.   59
Good signior, you shall more command with years
Than with your weapons.
Brabantio.
O thou foul thief, where hast thou stowed my daughter?
Damned as thou art, thou hast enchanted her!
For I'll refer me to all things of sense,
If she in chains of magic were not bound,
Whether a maid so tender, fair, and happy,
So opposite to marriage that she shunned
The wealthy curlèd darlings of our nation,
Would ever have, t'incur a general mock,
Run from her guardage to the sooty bosom
Of such a thing as thou—to fear, not to delight.
Judge me the world if 'tis not gross in sense   72
That thou hast practiced on her with foul charms,
Abused her delicate youth with drugs or minerals
That weaken motion. I'll have't disputed on;   75
'Tis probable, and palpable to thinking.
I therefore apprehend and do attach thee   77
For an abuser of the world, a practicer
Of arts inhibited and out of warrant.
Lay hold upon him. If he do resist,
Subdue him at his peril.
Othello.   Hold your hands,
Both you of my inclining and the rest.
Were it my cue to fight, I should have known it
Without a prompter. Where will you that I go
To answer this your charge?
Brabantio.   To prison, till fit time
Of law and course of direct session   86
Call thee to answer.
Othello.   What if I do obey?
How may the Duke be therewith satisfied,
Whose messengers are here about my side

59 *Keep up* i.e. sheath   72 *gross in sense* obvious   75 *motion* perception   77 *attach* arrest   86 *direct session* regular trial

Upon some present business of the state
To bring me to him?

Officer.   'Tis true, most worthy signior.
The Duke's in council, and your noble self
I am sure is sent for.

Brabantio.   How? The Duke in council?
In this time of the night? Bring him away.
Mine's not an idle cause. The Duke himself,   95
Or any of my brothers of state,
Cannot but feel this wrong as 'twere their own;
For if such actions may have passage free,
Bondslaves and pagans shall our statesmen be.   *Exeunt.*

Scene iii

Enter duke and senators, set at a table, with lights and attendants.

Duke.
There is no composition in these news   1
That gives them credit.

1 senator.   Indeed they are disporportionèd.
My letters say a hundred and seven galleys.

Duke.
And mine a hundred forty.

2 senator.   And mine two hundred.
But though they jump not on a just account—   5
As in these cases where the aim reports   6
'Tis oft with difference—yet do they all confirm
A Turkish fleet, and bearing up to Cyprus.

Duke.
Nay, it is possible enough to judgement.
I do not so secure me in the error   10
But the main article I do approve   11
In fearful sense.

Sailor *(within)*. What, ho! what, ho! what, ho!
Officer.
A messenger from the galleys.

Enter sailor

Duke.   Now, what's the business?
Sailor.
The Turkish preparation makes for Rhodes.
So was I bid report here to the state
By Signior Angelo.

Duke.
How say you by this change?

---

95 *idle* trifling
Scene iii The Venetian Senate Chamber   1 *composition* consistency   5 *jump* agree   6 *aim*
conjecture   10 *so secure me* take such comfort   11 *article* substance; *approve* accept

1 senator.   This cannot be
    By no assay of reason. 'Tis a pageant   18
    To keep us in false gaze. When we consider   19
    Th'importancy of Cyprus to the Turk,
    And let ourselves again but understand
    That, as it more concerns the Turk than Rhodes,
    So may he with more facile question bear it,   23
    For that it stands not in such warlike brace,   24
    But altogether lacks th' abilities
    That Rhodes is dressed in—if we make thought of this,
    We must not think the Turk is so unskillful
    To leave that latest which concerns him first,
    Neglecting an attempt of ease and gain
    To wake and wage a danger profitless.   30
Duke.
    Nay, in all confidence, he's not for Rhodes.
Officer.
    Here is more news.

    Enter a messenger.

Messenger.
    The Ottomites, reverend and gracious,
    Steering with due course toward the isle of Rhodes,
    Have there injointed them with an after fleet.
1 senator.
    Ay, so I thought. How many, as you guess?
Messenger.
    Of thirty sail; and now they do restem   37
    Their backward course, bearing with frank appearance
    Their purposes toward Cyprus. Signior Montano,
    Your trusty and most valiant servitor,
    With his free duty recommends you thus,
    And prays you to believe him.
Duke.
    'Tis certain then for Cyprus.
    Marcus Luccicos, is not he in town?   44
1 senator.
    He's now in Florence.
Duke.
    Write from us to him; post, post-haste dispatch.
1 senator.
    Here comes Brabantio and the valiant Moor.

    Enter Brabantio, Othello, Cassio, Iago, Roderigo, and officers.

Duke.
    Valiant Othello, we must straight employ you

18 *assay* test   **19** *in false gaze* looking the wrong way   **23** *with . . . bear* more easily
capture   **24** *brace* posture of defense   **30** *wake and wage* rouse and risk   **37** *restem* steer
again   **44** *Marcus Luccicos* (presumably a Venetian envoy)

Against the general enemy Ottoman.

(To Brabantio)

I did not see you. Welcome, gentle signior.

We lacked your counsel and your help to-night.

Brabantio.

So did I yours. Good your grace, pardon me.

Neither my place, nor aught I heard of business,

Hath raised me from my bed; nor doth the general care

Take hold on me; for my particular grief

Is of so floodgate and o'erbearing nature   56

That it engluts and swallows other sorrows,   57

And it is still itself.

Duke.   Why, what's the matter?

Brabantio.

My daughter! O, my daughter!

All.   Dead?

Brabantio.   Ay, to me.

She is abused, stol'n from me, and corrupted

By spells and medicines bought of mountebanks;

For nature so prepost'rously to err,

Being not deficient, blind, or lame of sense,   63

Sans witchcraft could not.

Duke.

Whoe'er he be that in this foul proceeding

Hath thus beguiled your daughter of herself,

And you of her, the bloody book of law

You shall yourself read in the bitter letter

After your own sense; yea, though our proper son   69

Stood in your action.   70

Brabantio.   Humbly I thank your grace.

Here is the man—this Moor, whom now, it seems,

Your special mandate for the state affairs

Hath hither brought.

All.   We are very sorry for't.

Duke. *(to Othello).*

What, in your own part, can you say to this?

Brabantio.

Nothing, but this is so.

Othello.

Most potent, grave, and reverend signiors,

My very noble, and approved good masters,   77

That I have ta'en away this old man's daughter,

It is most true; true I have married her.

The very head and front of my offending

---

56 *floodgate* torrential   **57** *engluts* devours   **63** *deficient* feeble-minded   **69** *our proper* my own   **70** *stood in your action* were accused by you   **77** *approved* tested by experience

Hath this extent, no more. Rude am I in my speech,   81
And little blessed with the soft phrase of peace;
For since these arms of mine had seven years' pith   83
Till now some nine moons wasted, they have used
Their dearest action in the tented field;
And little of this great world can I speak
More than pertains to feats of broil and battle;
And therefore little shall I grace my cause
In speaking for myself. Yet, by your gracious patience,
I will a round unvarnished tale deliver   90
Of my whole course of love—what drugs, what charms,
What conjuration, and what mighty magic
(For such proceeding am I charged withal)
I won his daughter.
Brabantio.   A maiden never bold;
Of spirit so still and quiet that her motion   95
Blushed at herself; and she—in spite of nature,
Of years, of country, credit, everything—
To fall in love with what she feared to look on!
It is a judgment maimed and most imperfect
That will confess perfection so could err
Against all rules of nature, and must be driven
To find out practices of cunning hell   102
Why this should be. I therefore vouch again   103
That with some mixtures pow'rful o'er the blood,   104
Or with some dram, conjured to this effect,
He wrought upon her.
Duke.   To vouch this is no proof,
Without more certain and more overt test
Than these thin habits and poor likelihoods   108
Of modern seeming do prefer against him.   109
1 senator.
But, Othello, speak.
Did you by indirect and forcèd courses   111
Subdue and poison this young maid's affections?
Or came it by request, and such fair question   113
As soul to soul affordeth?
Othello.   I do beseech you,
Send for the lady to the Sagittary
And let her speak of me before her father.
If you do find me foul in her report,
The trust, the office, I do hold of you

---

81 *rude* unpolished   83 *pith* strength   90 *round* plain   95–96 *her motion Blushed* her own emotions caused her to blush   102 *practices* plots   103 *vouch* assert   104 *blood* passions   108 *thin habits* slight appearances   109 *modern seeming* everyday supposition   111 *forced* violent   113 *question* conversation

Not only take away, but let your sentence
Even fall upon my life.
Duke.   Fetch Desdemona hither.
Othello.
Ancient, conduct them; you best know the place.

> *Exit Iago, with two or three Attendants.*

And still she come, as truly as to heaven
I do confess the vices of my blood,
So justly to your grave ears I'll present
How I did thrive in this fair lady's love,
And she in mine.
Duke.
Say it, Othello.
Othello.
Her father loved me, oft invited me;
Still questioned me the story of my life   129
From year to year—the battles, sieges, fortunes
That I have passed.
I ran it through, even from my boyish days
To th' very moment that he bade me tell it.
Wherin I spoke of most disastrous chances,
Of moving accidents by flood and field;
Of hairbreadth scapes i' th' imminent deadly breach;
Of being taken by the insolent foe
And sold to slavery; of my redemption thence
And portance in my travels' history;   139
Wherin of anters vast and deserts idle,   140
Rough quarries, rocks, and hills whose heads touch heaven,
It was my hint to speak—such was the process;   142
And of the Cannibals that each other eat,
The Anthropophagi, and men whose heads   144
Do grow beneath their shoulders. This to hear
Would Desdemona seriously incline;
But still the house affairs would draw her thence;
Which ever as she could with haste dispatch,
She'd come again, and with a greedy ear
Devour up my discourse. Which I observing,
Took once a pliant hour, and found good means   151
To draw from her a prayer of earnest heart
That I would all my pilgrimage dilate,   153
Whereof by parcels she had something heard,   154
But not intentively. I did consent,   155
And often did beguile her of her tears
When I did speak of some distressful stroke

---

129 *Still* continually   139 *portance* behavior   140 *anters* caves   142 *hint* occasion   **144**
Anthropophagi man-eaters   151 *pliant* propitious   153 *dilate* recount in full   154 *parcels*
portions   155 *intentively* with full attention

Othello

That my youth suffered. My story being done,
She gave me for my pains a world of sighs.
She swore, i' faith, 'twas strange, 'twas passing strange;
'Twas pitiful, 'twas wondrous pitiful.
She wished she had not heard it; yet she wished
That heaven had made her such a man. She thanked me;
And bade me, if I had a friend that loved her,
I should but teach him how to tell my story,
And that would woo her. Upon this hint I spake.   166
She loved me for the dangers I had passed,
And I loved her that she did pity them.
This only is the witchcraft I have used.
Here comes the lady. Let her witness it.

Enter Desdemona, Iago, attendants.

Duke.
I think this tale would win my daughter too.
Good Brabantio,
Take up this mangled matter at the best.
Men do their broken weapons rather use
Than their bare hands.
Brabantio.   I pray you hear her speak.
If she confess that she was half the wooer,
Destruction on my head if my bad blame
Light on the man! Come hither, gentle mistress.
Do you perceive in all this noble company
Where most you owe obedience?
Desdemona.   My noble father,
I do perceive here a divided duty.
To you I am bound for life and education;   182
My life and education both do learn me
How to respect you: you are the lord of duty;
I am hitherto your daughter. But here's my husband;
And so much duty as my mother showed
To you, preferring you before her father,
So much I challenge that I may profess   188
Due to the Moor my lord.
Brabantio.   God be with you! I have done.
Please it your grace, on to the state affairs.
I had rather to adopt a child than get it.   191
Come hither, Moor.
I here do give thee that with all my heart
Which, but thou hast already, with all my heart
I would keep from thee. For your sake, jewel,   195
I am glad at soul I have no other child;

166 *hint* opportunity   182 *education* upbringing   188 *challenge* claim the right   191 *get* beget   195 *For your sake* because of you

For thy escape would teach me tyranny, 197
To hang clogs on them. I have done, my lord.

Duke.
  Let me speak like yourself and lay a sentence 199
  Which, as a grise or step, may help these lovers 200
  Into your favor.
  When remedies are past, the griefs are ended
  By seeing the worst, which late on hopes depended.
  To mourn a mischief that is past and gone
  Is the next way to draw new mischief on.
  What cannot be preserved when fortune takes,
  Patience her injury a mock'ry makes.
  The robbed that smiles steals something from the thief;
  He robs himself that spends a bootless grief.

Brabantio.
  So let the Turk of Cyprus us beguile: 210
  We lose it not so long as we can smile.
  He bears the sentence well that nothing bears
  But the free comfort which from thence he hears;
  But he bears both the sentence and the sorrow
  That to pay grief must of poor patience borrow.
  These sentences, to sugar, or to gall,
  Being strong on both sides, are equivocal.
  But words are words. I never yet did hear
  That the bruised heart was piercèd through the ear.
  I humbly beseech you, now to the affairs of state.

Duke. The Turk with a most mighty preparation makes
  for Cyprus. Othello, the fortitude of the place is best 222
  known to you; and though we have there a substitute
  of most allowed sufficiency, yet opinion, a more sover- 224
  eign mistress of effects, throws a more safer voice on you.
  You must therefore be content to slubber the gloss of 226
  your new fortunes with this more stubborn and
  boist'rous expedition.

Othello.
  The tyrant custom, most grave senators,
  Hath made the flinty and steel couch of war
  My thrice-driven bed of down. I do agnize 231
  A natural and prompt alacrity
  I find in hardness; and do undertake
  These present wars against the Ottomites.
  Most humbly, therefore, bending to your state,
  I crave fit disposition for my wife,

---

197 *escape* escapade **199** *like yourself* as you should; *sentence* maxim **200** *grise* step   **222** *fortitude* fortification **224** *allowed* acknowledged; *opinion* public opinion **226** *slubber* sully **231–33** *agnize . . . hardness* recognize in myself a natural and easy response to hardship

Due reference of place, and exhibition,   237
With such accommodation and besort   238
As levels with her breeding.
Duke.   If you please,
Be't at her father's.
Brabantio.   I will not have it so.
Othello.
Nor I.
Desdemona. Nor I. I would not there reside,
To put my father in impatient thoughts
By being in his eye. Most gracious Duke,
To my unfolding lend your prosperous ear,   244
And let me find a charter in your voice,
T' assist my simpleness.   246
Duke.
What would you, Desdemona?
Desdemona.
That I did love the Moor to live with him,
My downright violence, and storm of fortunes,
May trumpet to the world. My heart's subdued
Even to the very quality of my lord.
I saw Othello's visage in his mind,
And to his honors and his valiant parts
Did I my soul and fortunes consecrate.
So that, dear lords, if I be left behind,
A moth of peace, and he go to the war,
The rites for which I love him are bereft me,
And I a heavy interim shall support
By his dear absence. Let me go with him.
Othello.
Let her have your voice.
Vouch with me, heaven, I therefore beg it not
To please the palate of my appetite,
Not to comply with heat—the young affects   263
In me defunct—and proper satisfaction;
But to be free and bounteous to her mind;
And heaven defend your good souls that you think
I will your serious and great business scant
When she is with me. No, when light-winged toys
Of feathered Cupid seel with wanton dullness   269
My speculative and officed instruments,   270
That my disports corrupt and taint my business,   271

---

237 *exhibition* allowance of money   **238** *besort* suitable company   **239** *levels* corresponds   **244** *prosperous* favorable   **246** *simpleness* lack of skill   **263** *heat* passions; *young affects* tendencies of youth   **269** *seel* blind   **270** *My . . . instruments* my perceptive and responsible faculties   **271** *That* so that

William Shakespeare

> Let housewives make a skillet of my helm,
> And all indign and base adversities   273
> Make head against my estimation!   274

Duke.

> Be it as you shall privately determine,
> Either for her stay or going. Th' affair cries haste,
> And speed must answer it.

1 senator.

> You must away to-night.

Othello.   With all my heart.

Duke.

> At nine i' th' morning here we'll meet again.
> Othello, leave some officer behind,
> And he shall our commission bring to you,
> With such things else of quality and respect
> As doth import you.   283

Othello.   So please your grace, my ancient;

> A man he is of honesty and trust.
> To his conveyance I assign my wife,
> With what else needful your good grace shall think
> To be sent after me.

Duke.   Let it be so.

> Good night to every one.
> *(To Brabantio)*   And, noble signior,
> If virtue no delighted beauty lack,   289
> Your son-in-law is far more fair than black

1 senator.

> Adieu, brave Moor. Use Desdemona well.

Brabantio.

> Look to her, Moor, if thou hast eyes to see:
> She has deceived her father, and may thee.
>
> > *Exeunt duke, senators, officers, etc.*

Othello.

> My life upon her faith!—Honest Iago,
> My Desdemona must I leave to thee.
> I prithee let thy wife attend on her,
> And bring them after in the best advantage.   297
> Come, Desdemona. I have but an hour
> Of love, of worldly matters and direction,
> To spend with thee. We must obey the time.
>
> > *Exit Moor and Desdemona.*

Roderigo. Iago,—

Iago. What say'st thou, noble heart?

Roderigo. What will I do, think'st thou?

Iago. Why, go to bed and sleep.

---

273 *indign* unworthy 274 *estimation* reputation 283 *import* concern 289 *delighted* delightful 297 *in the best advantage* at the best opportunity

Roderigo. I will incontinently drown myself.   305
Iago. I If thou dost, I shall never love thee after. Why, thou silly gentleman!
Roderigo. It is silliness to live when to live is torment; and then have we a
    prescription to die when death is our physician.
Iago. O villainous! I have looked upon the world for four times seven
    years; and since I could distinguish betwixt a benefit and an injury, I
    never found man that knew how to love himself. Ere I would say I would
    drown myself for the love of a guinea hen, I would change my humanity
    with a baboon.
Roderigo. What should I do? I confess it is my shame to be so fond, but it is
    not in my virtue to amend it.
Iago. Virtue? a fig! 'Tis in ourselves that we are thus or,
    thus. Our bodies are our gardens, to the which our wills
    are gardeners; so that if we will plant nettles or sow
    lettuce, set hyssop and weed up thyme, supply it with
    one gender of herbs or distract it with many—either to   320
    have it sterile with idleness or manured with industry—
    why, the power and corrigible authority of this lies in   322
    our wills. If the balance of our lives had not one scale
    of reason to poise another of sensuality, the blood and   324
    baseness of our natures would conduct us to most
    preposterous conclusions. But we have reason to cool our
    raging motions, our carnal stings, our unbitted lusts;   327
    whereof I take this that you call love to be a sect or scion.   328
Roderigo. It cannot be.
Iago. It is merely a lust of the blood and a permission of
    the will. Come, be a man! Drown thyself? Drown cats
    and blind puppies! I have professed me thy friend, and I
    confess me knit to thy deserving with cables of perdurable
    toughness. I could never better stead thee than now. Put
    money in thy purse. Follow thou the wars; defeat thy   335
    favor with an usurped beard. I say, put money in thy
    purse. It cannot be that Desdemona should long con-
    tinue her love to the Moor—put money in thy purse—nor
    he his to her. It was a violent commencement in her, and
    thou shalt see an answerable sequestration—put but   340
    money in thy purse. These Moors are changeable in their
    wills—fill thy purse with money. The food that to him
    now is as luscious as locusts shall be to him shortly as bit-
    ter as coloquintida. She must change for youth: when she   344
    is sated with his body, she will find the error of her choice.
    She must have change, she must. Therefore put money

---

305 *incontinently* forthwith   **320** *gender* species   **322** *corrigible authority* corrective
power   **324** *poise* counterbalance   **324–25** *blood and baseness* animal instincts   **327** *motions*
appetites; *unbitted* uncontrolled   **328** *sect or scion* offshoot, cutting   **335–36** *defeat thy favor* spoil
thy appearance   **340** *sequestration* estrangement   **344** *coloquintida* a medicine

in thy purse. If thou wilt needs damn thyself, do it a more
delice way than drowning. Make all the money thou   348
canst. If sanctimony and a frail vow betwixt an erring   349
barbarian and a supersubtle Venetian be not too hard for
my wits and all the tribe of hell, thou shalt enjoy her.
Therefore make money. A pox of drowning thyself! 'Tis
clean out of the way. Seek thou rather to be hanged in
compassing thy joy than to be drowned and go without
her.

Roderigo. Wilt thou be fast to my hopes, if I depend on
the issue?

Iago. Thou art sure of me. Go, make money. I have told,
thee often, and I retell thee again and again, I hate the
Moor. My cause is hearted; thine hath no less reason.   360
Let us be conjunctive in our revenge against him. If
thou canst cuckold him, thou dost thyself a pleasure, me
a sport. There are many events in the womb of time,
which will be delivered. Traverse, go, provide thy   364
money! We will have more of this to-morrow. Adieu.

Roderigo. Where shall we meet i' th' morning?

Iago. At my lodging.

Roderigo. I'll be with thee betimes.

Iago. Go to, farewell.—Do you hear, Roderigo?

Roderigo. What say you?

Iago. No more of drowning, do you hear?

Roderigo. I am changed.

Iago. Go to, farewell. Put money enough in your purse.

Roderigo. I'll sell all my land.   *Exit.*

Iago.

Thus do I ever make my fool my purse;
For I mine own gained knowledge should profane
If I would time expend with such a snipe   377
But for my sport and profit. I hate the Moor;
And it is thought abroad that 'twixt my sheets
H'as done my office. I know not if't be true;
But I, for mere suspicion in that kind,
Will do as if for surety. He holds me well;   382
The better shall my purpose work on him.
Cassio's a proper man. Let me see now:
To get his place, and to plume up my will   385
In double knavery—How, how?—Let's see:—
After some time, to abuse Othello's ears
That he is too familiar with his wife.
He hath a person and a smooth dispose   389

---

348 *Make* raise   349 *erring* wandering   360 *My cause is hearted* my heart is in it   364
Traverse forward march   377 *snipe* fool   382 *well* in high regard   385 *plume up* gratify   389
dispose manner

To be suspected—framed to make women false.
The Moor is of a free and open nature   391
That thinks men honest that but seem to be so;
And will as tenderly be led by th' nose
As asses are.
I have't! It is engend'red! Hell and night
Must bring this monstrous birth to the world's light.

Exit.

Act II
Scene i

Enter Montano and two gentlemen.

Montano.
What from the cape can you discern at sea?
1 gentleman.
Nothing at all: it is a high-wrought flood.
I cannot 'twixt the heaven and the main
Descry a sail.
Montano.
Methinks the wind hath spoke aloud at land;
A fuller blast ne'er shook our battlements.
If it hath ruffianed so upon the sea,
What ribs of oak, when mountains melt on them,
Can hold the mortise? What shall we hear of this?   9
2 gentleman
A segregation of the Turkish fleet.   10
For do but stand upon the foaming shore,
The chidden billow seems to pelt the clouds;
The wind-shaked surge, with high and monstrous mane,
Seems to cast water on the burning Bear
And quench the Guards of th' ever-fixèd pole.   15
I never did like molestation view   16
On the enchafèd flood.
Montano.   If that the Turkish fleet
Be not ensheltered and embayed, they are drowned;
It is impossible to bear it out.

Enter a third gentleman.

3 gentleman.
News, lads! Our wars are done.
The desperate tempest hath so banged the Turks
That their designment halts. A noble ship of Venice   22
Hath seen a grievous wrack and sufferance   23
On most part of their fleet.

---

391 *free* frank
Scene i An open place in Cyprus, near the harbor   **9** *hold the mortise* hold their joints
together   **10** *segregation* scattering   **15** *Guards* stars near the North Star; *pole* polestar   **16**
molestation tumult   **22** *desegment halts* plan is crippled   **23** *sufferance* disaster

Montano.
    How? Is this true?
3 gentleman.   The ship is here put in,
    A Veronesa; Michael Cassio,   26
    Lieutenant to the warlike Moor Othello,
    Is come on shore; the Moor himself at sea,
    And is in full commission here for Cyprus.
Montano.
    I am glad on't. 'Tis a worthy governor.
3 gentleman.
    But this same Cassio, though he speak of comfort
    Touching the Turkish loss, yet he looks sadly
    And prays the Moor be safe, for they were parted
    With foul and violent tempest.
Montano.   Pray heaven he be;
    For I have served him, and the man commands
    Like a full soldier. Let's to the seaside, ho!
    As well to see the vessel that's come in
    As to throw out our eyes for brave Othello,
    Even till we make the main and th' aerial blue
    An indistinct regard.   40
3 gentleman.   Come, let's do so;
    For every minute is expectancy
    Of more arrivance.

    Enter Cassio.

Cassio.
    Thanks, you the valiant of this warlike isle,
    That so approve the Moor! O, let the heavens
    Give him defense against the elements,
    For I have lost him on a dangerous sea!
Montano.
    Is he well shipped?
Cassio.
    His bark is stoutly timbered, and his pilot
    Of very expert and approved allowance;
    Therefore my hopes, not surfeited to death,   50
    Stand in bold cure.   51
    (Within.) A sail, a sail, a sail!

    Enter a messenger.

Cassio.
    What noise?
1 gentleman.
    The town is empty; on the brow o' th' sea
    Stand ranks of people, and they cry "A sail!"

---

    26 *Veronesa* ship furnished by Verona   **40** *An indistinct regard* indistinguishable   **50** *surfeited to death* over indulged   **51** *in bold cure* a good chance of fulfillment

Cassio.

My hopes do shape him for the governor.

A shot

2 gentleman.

They do discharge their shot of courtesy:
Our friends at least.

Cassio.   I pray you, sir, go forth
And give us truth who 'tis that is arrived.

2 gentleman.

I shall.   *Exit.*

Montano.

But, good lieutenant, is your general wived?

Cassio.

Most fortunately. He hath achieved a maid
That paragons description and wild fame;   62
One that excels the quirks of blazoning pens,   63
And in th' essential vesture of creation   64
Does tire the ingener.

Enter second gentleman.

                         How now? Who has put in?

2 gentleman.

'Tis one Iago, ancient to the general.

Cassio.

H'as had most favorable and happy speed:
Tempests themselves, high seas, and howling winds,
The guttered rocks and congregated sands,   69
Traitors ensteeped to clog the guiltless keel,   70
As having sense of beauty, do omit
Their mortal natures, letting go safely by   72
The divine Desdemona.

Montano.   What is she?

Cassio.

She that I spake of, our great captain's captain,
Left in the conduct of the bold Iago,
Whose footing here anticipates our thoughts   76
A se'nnight's speed. Great Jove, Othello guard,   77
And swell his sail with thine own pow'rful breath,
That he may bless this bay with his tall ship,
Make love's quick pants in Desdemona's arms,
Give renewed fire to our extincted spirits,
And bring all Cyprus comfort!

*Enter Desdemona, Iago, Roderigo, and Emilia with
attendants.*

---

62 *paragons* surpasses   63 *quirks* ingenuities; *blazoning* describing   64–65
And . . . ingener merely to describe her as God made her exhausts her praiser   69 *guttered*
jagged   70 *ensteeped* submerged   72 *mortal* deadly   76 *footing* landing   77 *sen'night's* week's

William Shakespeare

O, behold!
The riches of the ship is come on shore!
You men of Cyprus, let her have your knees.   84
Hail to thee, lady! and the grace of heaven,
Before, behind thee, and on every hand,
Enwheel thee round!
Desdemona.   I thank you, valiant Cassio.
What tidings can you tell me of my lord?
Cassio.
He is not yet arrived; nor know I aught
But that he's well and will be shortly here.
Desdemona.
O but I fear! How lost you company?
Cassio.
The great contention of the sea and skies
Parted our fellowship.
(Within.)   A sail, a sail! *(A shot.)*
                    But hark. A sail!
2 gentleman.
They give their greeting to the citadel;
This likewise is a friend.
Cassio.   See for the news.

                                              Exit gentleman.

Good ancient, you are welcome.
(To Emilia.)   Welcome, mistress.—
Let it not gall your patience, good Iago,
That I extend my manners. 'Tis my breeding
That gives me this bold show of courtesy.   99

(Kisses Emilia.)

Iago.
Sir, would she give you so much of her lips
As of her tongue she oft bestows on me,
You would have enough.
Desdemona.   Alas, she has no speech!
Iago.
In faith, too much.
I find it still when I have list to sleep.
Marry, before your ladyship, I grant,
She puts her tongue a little in her heart
And chides with thinking.
Emilia.
You have little cause to say so.
Iago.
Come on, come on! You are pictures out of doors,
Bells in your parlors, wildcats in your kitchens,

---

84 *knees* i.e. kneeling   99 **s.d.** *Kisses Emilia* (kissing was a common Elizabethan form of social courtesy)

Othello

Saints in your injuries, devils being offended,
Players in your housewifery, and housewives in your   112
    beds.
Desdemona.
    O, fie upon thee, slanderer!
Iago.
    Nay, it is true, or else I am a Turk:
    You rise to play, and go to bed to work.
Emilia.
    You shall not write my praise.
Iago.   No, let me not.
Desdemona.
    What wouldst thou write of me, if thou shouldst praise me?
Iago.
    O gentle lady, do not put me to't,
    For I am nothing if not critical.
Desdemona.
    Come on, assay.—There's one gone to the harbor?   120
Iago.
    Ay, madam.
Desdemona.
    I am not merry; but I do beguile
    The thing I am by seeming otherwise.—
    Come, how wouldst thou praise me?
Iago.
    I am about it; but indeed my invention
    Comes from my pate as birdlime does from frieze—   126
    It plucks out brains and all. But my Muse labors,
    And thus she is delivered:
    If she be fair and wise, fairness and wit—
    The one's for use, the other useth it.
Desdemona.
    Well praised! How if she be black and witty?   131
Iago.
    If she be black, and thereto have a wit,
    She'll find a white that shall her blackness fit.
Desdemona.
    Worse and worse!
Emilia.
    How if fair and foolish?
Iago.
    She never yet was foolish that was fair,
    For even her folly helped her to an heir.   137
Desdemona. These are old fond paradoxes to make fools   138
    laugh i' th' alehouse. What miserable praise hast thou
    for her that's foul and foolish?

112 *housewifery* housekeeping; *housewives* hussies **120** *assay* try **126** *birdlime* a sticky
paste; *frieze* rough cloth **131** *black* brunette **137** *folly* wantonness **138** *fond* foolish **140** *foul* ugly

Iago.

> There's none so foul, and foolish thereunto,
> But does foul pranks which fair and wise ones do.

Desdemona. O heavy ignorance! Thou praisest the worst best. But what praise couldst thou bestow on a deserving woman indeed—one that in the authority of her merit did justly put on the vouch of very malice itself? 145

Iago.

> She that was ever fair, and never proud;
> Had tongue at will, and yet was never loud;
> Never lacked gold, and yet went never gay;
> Fled from her wish, and yet said "Now I may";
> She that, being ang'red, her revenge being nigh,
> Bade her wrong stay, and her displeasure fly;
> She that in wisdom never was so frail
> To change the cod's head for the salmon's tail; 154
> She that could think, and ne'er disclose her mind;
> See suitors following, and not look behind:
> She was a wight (if ever such wight were)—

Desdemona. To do what?

Iago.

> To suckle fools and chronicle small beer. 159

Desdemona. O most lame and impotent conclusion! Do not learn of him, Emilia, though he be thy husband. How say you, Cassio? Is he not a most profane and liberal counsellor? 162

Cassio. He speaks home, madam. You may relish him more in the soldier 163 than in the scholar.

Iago *(aside).* He takes her by the palm. Ay, well said, whisper! With as little a web as this will I ensnare as great a fly as Cassio. Ay, smile upon her, do! I will gyve thee in thine own courtship.—You say true; 'tis so, 167 indeed!—If such tricks as these strip you out of your lieutenantry, it had been better you had not kissed your three fingers so oft—which now again you are most apt to play the sir in. Very good! well kissed! an 170 excellent courtesy! 'Tis so, indeed. Yet again your fingers to your lips? Would they were clyster pipes for your sake! *(Trumpet within.)* The 172 Moor! I know his trumpet.

Cassio. 'Tis truly so.

Desdemona. Let's meet him and receive him.

Cassio. Lo, where he comes.

> *Enter Othello and attendants.*

Othello.

> O my fair warrior!

Desdemona.   My dear Othello!

---

145 *put on the vouch* compel the approval   154 *To . . . tail* i.e. to exchange the good for the poor but expensive   159 *chronicle small beer* keep petty household accounts   162 *profane and liberal* wordly and licentious   163 *home* bluntly   167 *gyve . . . courtship* manacle you by means of your courtly manners   170 *sir* courtly gentleman   172 *clyster pipes* syringes

Othello.
　　　It gives me wonder great as my content
　　　To see you here before me. O my soul's joy!
　　　If after every tempest come such calms,
　　　May the winds blow till they have wakened death!
　　　And let the laboring bark climb hills of seas
　　　Olympus-high, and duck again as low
　　　As hell's from heaven! If it were now to die,
　　　'Twere now to be most happy; for I fear　　　　　　　　　185
　　　My soul hath her content so absolute
　　　That not another comfort like to this
　　　Succeeds in unknown fate.
Desdemona.　　　　　　　　　　The heavens forbid
　　　But that our loves and comforts should increase
　　　Even as our days do grow.
Othello.　　　　　　　　　　Amen to that, sweet powers!
　　　I cannot speak enough of this content;
　　　It stops me here; it is too much of joy.
　　　And this, and this, the greatest discords be
　　　(They kiss.)
　　　That e'er our hearts shall make!
Iago *(aside).*　　　　　　　　　O, you are well tuned now!
　　　But I'll set down the pegs that make this music,　　　195
　　　As honest as I am.
Othello.　　　　　Come, let us to the castle.
　　　News, friends! Our wars are done; the Turks are drowned.
　　　How does my old acquaintance of this isle?—
　　　Honey, you shall be well desired in Cyprus;　　　　　199
　　　I have found great love amongst them. O my sweet,
　　　I prattle out of fashion, and I dote
　　　In mine own comforts. I prithee, good Iago,
　　　Go to the bay and disembark my coffers.
　　　Bring thou the master to the citadel;　　　　　　　204
　　　He is a good one, and his worthiness
　　　Does challenge much respect.—Come, Desdemona,　206
　　　Once more well met at Cyprus.
　　　　　　　　Exit Othello (with all but Iago and Roderigo.)
Iago *(to an attendant, who goes out).* Do thou meet me presently at the
　　　harbor. *[to Roderigo]* Come hither. If you be'st valiant (as they say base
　　　men being in love have then a nobility in their natures more than is
　　　native to them), list me. The lieutenant to-night watches on the court of 211
　　　guard. First, I must tell thee this: Desdemona is directly in love with
　　　him.
Roderigo. With him? Why, 'tis not possible.
Iago. Lay thy finger thus, and let thy soul be instructed. Mark me with　　215

---

185 *happy* fortunate　195 *set down* loosen　199 *well desired* warmly welcomed　204 *master* ship captain　206 *challenge* deserve　211–12 *court of guard* headquarters　215 *thus* i.e. on your lips

what violence she first loved the Moor, but for bragging and telling her fantastical lies; and will she love him still for prating? Let not thy discreet heart think it. Her eye must be fed; and what delight shall she have to look on the devil? When the blood is made dull with the act of sport, there should be, again to inflame it and to give satiety a fresh appetite, loveliness in favor, sympathy in years, manners, and beauties; all which the Moor is defective in. Now for want of these required conveniences, her delicate tenderness will find itself abused, begin to   223 heave the gorge, disrelish and abhor the Moor. Very nature will instruct 224 her in it and compel her to some second choice. Now sir, this granted—as it is a most pregnant and unforced position—who stands   226 so eminent in the degree of this fortune as Cassio does? A knave very voluble; no further conscionable than in putting on the mere form of   228 civil and humane seeming for the better compassing of his salt and   229 most hidden loose affection? Why, none! why, none! A slipper and   230 subtle knave; a finder-out of occasions; that has an eye can stamp and counterfeit advantages, though true advantage never present itself; a devilish knave! Besides, the knave is handsome, young, and hath all those requisites in him that folly and green minds look after. A pestilent complete knave! and the woman hath found him already.

Roderigo. I cannot believe that in her; she's full of most blessed condition.   236

Iago. Blessed fig's-end! The wine she drinks is made of grapes. If she had been blessed, she would never have loved the Moor. Blessed pudding! Didst thou not see her paddle with the palm of his hand? Didst not mark that?

Roderigo. Yes, that I did; but that was but courtesy.

Iago. Lechery, by this hand! an index and obscure prologue to the history of lust and foul thoughts. They met so near with their lips that their breaths embraced together. Villainous thoughts, Roderigo! When these mutualities so marshal the way, hard at hand comes the master and   245 main exercise, th' incorporate conclusion. Pish! But, sir, be you ruled by 246 me: I have brought you from Venice. Watch you to-night; for the command, I'll lay't upon you. Cassio knows you not. I'll not be far from you: do you find some occasion to anger Cassio, either by speaking too loud, or tainting his discipline, or from what other course you please   250 which the time shall more favorably minister.

Roderigo. Well.

Iago. Sir, he's rash and very sudden in choler, and haply with his   253 truncheon may strike at you. Provoke him that he may; for even out of that will I cause these of Cyprus to mutiny; whose qualification shall   255 come into no true taste again but by the displanting of Cassio. So shall 256 you have a shorter journey to your desires by the means I shall then have to prefer them; and the impediment most profitably removed   258

---

223 *conveniences* compatibilities   **224** *heave the gorge* be nauseated   **226** *pregnant* evident   **228** *conscionable* conscientious   **229** *humane* polite; *salt* lecherous   **230** *slipper* slippery   **236** *condition* character   **245** *mutualities* exchanges   **246** *incorporate* carnal   **250** *tainting* discrediting   **253** *sudden in choler* violent in anger   **255** *qualification* appeasement   **256** *true taste* satisfactory state without the which there were no expectation of our prosperity.

Roderigo. I will do this if you can bring it to any opportunity.

Iago. I warrant thee. Meet me by and by at the citadel; I must fetch his
necessaries ashore. Farewell.

Roderigo. Adieu.   *Exit.*

Iago

> That Cassio loves her, I do well believe't;
> That she loves him, 'tis apt and of great credit.   265
> The Moor, howbeit that I endure him not,
> Is of a constant, loving, noble nature,
> And I dare think he'll prove to Desdemona
> A most dear husband. Now I do love her too;
> Not out of absolute lust, though peradventure
> I stand accountant for as great a sin,   271
> But partly led to diet my revenge,   272
> For that I do suspect the lusty Moor
> Hath leaped into my seat; the thought whereof
> Doth, like a poisonous mineral, gnaw my inwards;
> And nothing can or shall content my soul
> Till I am evened with him, wife for wife;
> Of failing so, yet that I put the Moor
> At least into a jealousy so strong
> That judgment cannot cure. Which think to do,
> If this poor trash of Venice, whom I trash   281
> For his quick hunting, stand the putting on,   282
> I'll have our Michael Cassio on the hip,   283
> Abuse him to the Moor in the rank garb   284
> (For I fear Cassio with my nightcap too),
> Make the Moor thank me, love me, and reward me
> For making him egregiously an ass
> And practicing upon his peace and quiet   288
> Even to madness. 'Tis here, but yet confused:
> Knavery's plain face is never seen till used.   *Exit.*

Scene ii

Enter Othello's herald, with a proclamation.

Herald. It is Othello's pleasure, our noble and valiant general, that, upon
certain tidings now arrived, importing the mere perdition of the   2
Turkish fleet, every man put himself into triumph; some to dance, some
to make bonfires, each man to what sport and revels his addiction leads
him. For, besides these beneficial news, it is the celebration of his
nuptial. So much was his pleasure should be proclaimed. All offices are   6

---

258 *prefer* advance   **265** *apt* probable   **271** *accountant* accountable   **272** *diet* feed   **281** *I trash*
I weight down (in order to keep under control)   **282** *For* in order to develop; *stand the putting on*
responds to my inciting   **283** *on the hip* at my mercy   **284** *rank barb* gross manner   **288** *practicing*
upon plotting against

    Scene ii A street in Cyprus   **2** *mere perdition* complete destruction   **6** *offices* kitchens and
storerooms

open, and there is full liberty of feasting from the present hour of five till the bell have told eleven. Heaven bless the isle of Cyprus and our noble general Othello!

Exit.

Scene iii

Enter Othello, Desdemona, Cassio, and attendants.

Othello.
Good Michael, look you to the guard to-night.
Let's teach ourselves that honorable stop,
Not to outsport discretion.

Cassio.
Iago hath direction what to do;
But not withstanding, with my personal eye
Will I look to't.

Othello. Iago is most honest.
Michael, good night. To-morrow with your earliest
Let me have speech with you.
(To Desdemona). Come, my dear love.
The purchase made, the fruits are to ensue;
That profit's yet to come 'tween me and you.—
Good night.

Exit Othello with Desdemona and attendants.

Enter Iago.

Cassio. Welcome, Iago. We must to the watch.
Iago. Not this hour, lieutenant; 'tis not yet ten o' th' clock. Our general cast 13
us thus early for the love of his Desdemona; who let us not therefore
blame. He hath not yet made wanton the night with her, and she is
sport for Jove.
Cassio. She's a most exquisite lady.
Iago. And, I'll warrant her, full of game.
Cassio. Indeed, she's a most fresh and delicate creature.
Iago. What an eye she has! Methinks it sounds a parley to provocation.
Cassio. An inviting eye; and yet methinks right modest:
Iago. And when she speaks, is it not an alarum to love?
Cassio. She is indeed perfection.
Iago. Well, happiness to their sheets! Come, lieutenant, I have a stoup of 24
wine, and here without are a brace of Cyprus gallants that would fain
have a measure to the health of black Othello.
Cassio. Not to-night, good Iago. I have very poor and unhappy brains for
drinking; I could well wish courtesy would invent some other custom of
entertainment.
Iago. O, they are our friends. But one cup! I'll drink for you.
Cassio. I have drunk but one cup to-night, and that was craftily qualified

Scene iii The Cyprian castle   13 *cast* dismissed   24 *stoup* two-quart tankard

too; and behold what innovation it makes here. I am unfortunate in the   32
infirmity and dare not task my weakness with any more.

Iago. What, man! 'Tis a night of revels: the gallants desire it.

Cassio. Where are they?

Iago. Here at the door; I pray you call them in.

Cassio. I'll do't, but it dislikes me.   *Exit.*

Iago.

> If I can fasten but one cup upon him
> With that which he hath drunk to-night already,
> He'll be as full of quarrel and offense
> As my young mistress' dog. Now my sick fool Roderigo,
> Whom love hath turned almost the wrong side out,
> To Desdemona hath to-night caroused
> Potations pottle-deep; and he's to watch.   44
> Three lads of Cyprus—noble swelling spirits,
> That hold their honors in a wary distance,   46
> The very elements of this warlike isle—   47
> Have I to-night flustered with flowing cups,
> And they watch too. Now, 'mongst this flock of drunkards
> Am I to put our Cassio in some action
> That may offend the isle.

*Enter Cassio, Montano, and gentleman servants following
with wine.*

> But here they come.
> If consequence do but approve my dream,
> My boat sails freely, both with wind and stream.

Cassio. 'Fore God, they have given me a rouse already.   54

Montano. Good faith, a little one; not past a pint, as I
am a soldier.

Iago. Some wine, ho!

> *(Sings.)*   And let me the canakin clink, clink;
>   And let me the canakin clink.
>   A soldier's a man;
>   A life's but a span,
>   Why then, let a soldier drink.

Some wine boys!

Cassio. Fore God, an excellent song!

Iago. I learned it in England, where indeed they are most potent in potting.
Your Dane, your German, and your swag-bellied Hollander—Drink,
ho!—are nothing to your English.

Cassio. Is your Englishman so expert in his drinking?

Iago. Why, he drinks you with facility your Dane dead drunk; he sweats not
to overthrow your Almain; he gives your Hollander a vomit ere the next
pottle can be filled.

Cassio. To the health of our general!

Montano. I am for it, lieutenant, and I'll do you justice.

32 qualified diluted; *innovation* disturbance   **44** *pottle-deep* bottoms up   **46**
That . . . distance very sensitive about their honor   **47** *very elements* true representatives   **54** *rouse*
bumper

Iago. O sweet England!

  (Sings.) King Stephen was a worthy peer;
     His breeches cost him but a crown;
    He held'em sixpence all too dear,
     With that he called the tailor lown.   78
    He was a wight of high renown,
     And thou art but of low degree.
    'Tis pride that pulls the country down;
     Then take thine auld cloak about thee.

  Some wine, ho!

Cassio. 'Fore God, this is a more exquisite song than the other.

Iago. Will you hear't again?

Cassio. No, for I hold him to be unworthy of his place that does those 86
  things. Well, God's above all; and there be souls must be saved, and
  there be souls must not be saved.

Iago. It's true, good lieutenant.

Cassio. For mine own part—no offense to the general,
  nor any man of quality—I hope to be saved.

Iago. And so do I too, lieutenant.

Cassio. Ay, but, by your leave, not before me. The lieutenant is to be saved before the ancient. Let's have no
  more of this; let's to our affairs.—God forgive us our
  sins!—Gentlemen, let's look to our business. Do not
  think, gentlemen, I am drunk. This is my ancient; this
  is my right hand, and this is my left. I am not drunk now.
  I can stand well enough, and I speak well enough.

All. Excellent well!

Cassio. Why, very well then. You must not think then
  that I am drunk.   *Exit.*

Montano.

  To th' platform, masters, Come, let's set the watch.

Iago.

  You see this fellow that is gone before.
  He's a soldier fit to stand by Caesar
  And give direction; and do but see his vice.
  'Tis to his virtue a just equinox,   107
  The one as long as th'other. 'Tis pity of him.
  I fear the trust Othello puts him in,
  On some odd time of his infirmity,
  Will shake this island.

Montano.   But is he often thus?

Iago.

  'Tis evermore his prologue to his sleep:
  He'll watch the horologe a double set   113
  If drink rock not his cradle.

Montano.   It were well

---

78 *lown* rascal 86–7 *does . . . things* i.e. behaves in this fashion 107 *just equinox* exact
equivalent 113 *watch . . . set* stay awake twice around the clock

The general were put in mind of it.
Perhaps he sees it not, or his good nature
Prizes the virtue that appears in Cassio
And looks not on his evils. Is not this true?

Enter Roderigo.

Iago *(aside to him).*
  How now, Roderigo?
  I pray you after the lieutenant, go!   *Exit Roderigo*
Montano.
  And 'tis great pity that the noble Moor
  Should hazard such a place as his own second
  With one of an ingraft infirmity.   123
  It were an honest action to say
  So to the Moor.
Iago.   Not I, for this fair island!
  I do love Cassio well and would do much
  To cure him of this evil.
  (Within)   Help! help!
                But hark! What noise?

Enter Cassio, driving in Roderigo.

Cassio.
  Zounds, you rogue! you rascal!
Montano.
  What's the matter, lieutenant?
Cassio.   A knave teach me my duty?
  I'll beat the knave into a twiggen bottle.   130
Roderigo.
  Beat me?
Cassio.   Dost thou prate, rogue?
  (Strikes him.)
Montano.   Nay, good lieutenant!
  (Stays him.)
  I pray you, sir, hold your hand.
Cassio.   Let me go, sir,
  Or I'll knock you o'er the mazzard.   133
Montano.   Come, come, you're drunk!
Cassio. Drunk?

  They fight.

Iago. *(aside to Roderigo)*
  Away, I say! Go out and cry a mutiny!   *Exit Roderigo.*
  Nay, good lieutenant. God's will, gentlemen!
  Help, ho!—lieutenant—sir—Montano—sir—
  Help, masters!—Here's a goodly watch indeed!

  A bell rung.

123 *ingraft* i.e. ingrained   **130** *twiggen* wicker-covered   **133** *mazzard* head

Who's that which rings the bell? Diablo, ho!
The town will rise. God's will, lieutenant, hold!   140
You'll be shamed for ever.

Enter Othello and gentlemen with weapons.

Othello.   What is the matter here?

Montano.

    Zounds, I bleed still, I am hurt to th' death.
    He dies!

Othello.

    Hold for your lives!

Iago.

    Hold, hold! Lieutenant—sir—Montano—gentlemen!
    Have you forgot all sense of place and duty?
    Hold! The general speaks to you. Hold, for shame!

Othello.

    Why, how now, ho? From whence ariseth this?
    Are we turned Turks, and to ourselves do that
    Which heaven hath forbid the Ottomites?
    For Christian shame put by this barbarous brawl!
    He that stirs next to carve for his own rage   151
    Holds his soul light; he dies upon his motion.
    Silence that dreadful bell! It frights the isle
    From her propriety. What is the matter, masters?   154
    Honest Iago, that looks dead with grieving,
    Speak. Who began this? On thy love, I charge thee.

Iago.

    I do not know. Friends, all, but now, even now,
    In quarter, and in terms like bride and groom   158
    Devesting them for bed; and then, but now—
    As if some planet had unwitted men—
    Swords out, and tilting one at other's breast
    In opposition bloody. I cannot speak
    Any beginning to this peevish odds,   163
    And would in action glorious I had lost
    Those legs that brought me to a part of it!

Othello.

    How comes it, Michael, you are thus forgot?

Cassio.

    I pray you pardon me; I cannot speak.

Othello.

    Worthy Montano, you were wont to be civil;
    The gravity and stillness of your youth
    The world hath noted, and your name is great
    In mouths of wisest censure. What's the matter   171
    That you unlace your reputation thus   172

---

140 *rise* grow riotous   151 *carve for* indulge   154 *propriety* proper self
158 *quarter* friendliness   163 *peevish odds* childish quarrel   171 *censure* judgment   172 *unlace* undo

And spend your rich opinion for the name 173
Of a night-brawler? Give me answer to it.

Montano.
Worthy Othello, I am hurt to danger.
Your officer, Iago, can inform you,
While I spare speech, which something now offends me, 177
Of all that I do know; nor know I aught
By me that's said or done amiss this night,
Unless self-charity be sometimes a vice,
And to defend ourselves it be a sin
When violence assails us.

Othello.   Now, by heaven,
My blood begins my safer guides to rule, 183
And passion, having my best judgement collied, 184
Assays to lead the way. If I once stir 185
Or do but lift this arm, the best of you
Shall sink in my rebuke. Give me to know
How this foul rout began, who set it on;
And he that is approved in this offense, 189
Though he had twinned with me, both at a birth,
Shall lose me. What! in a town of war,
Yet wild, the people's hearts brimful of fear,
To manage private and domestic quarrel? 193
In night, and on the court and guard of safety?
'Tis monstrous. Iago, who began't?

Montano.
If partially affined, or leagued in office, 196
Thou dost deliver more or less than truth,
Thou art no soldier.

Iago.   Touch me not so near.
I had rather have this tongue cut from my mouth
Than it should do offense to Michael Cassio;
Yet I persuade myself, to speak the truth
Shall nothing wrong him. This it is, general.
Montano and myself being in speech,
There comes a fellow crying out for help,
And Cassio following him with determined sword
To execute upon him. Sir, this gentleman 206
Steps in to Cassio and entreats his pause.
Myself the crying fellow did pursue,
Lest by his clamor—as it so fell out—
The town might fall in fright. He, swift of foot,
Outran my purpose; and I returned then rather
For that I heard the clink and fall of swords,
And Cassio high in oath; which till to-night 213

173 *rich opinion* high reputation 177 *offends* pains 183 *blood* passion 184 *collied*
darkened 185 *Assays* tries 189 *approved in* proved guilty of 193 *manage* carry on 196
partially . . . office prejudiced by comradeship or official relations 206 *execute* work his will 213
high in oath cursing

I ne'er might say before. When I came back—
For this was brief—I found them close together
At blow and thrust, even as again they were
When you yourself did part them.
More of this matter cannot I report;
But men are men; the best sometimes forget.
Though Cassio did some little wrong to him,
As men in rage strike those that wish them best,
Yet surely Cassio I believe received
From him that fled some strange indignity,
Which patience could not pass.   224
Othello.   I know, Iago,
Thy honesty and love doth mince this matter,
Making it light to Cassio. Cassio, I love thee;
But never more be officer of mine.

Enter Desdemona, attended.

Look if my gentle love be not raised up!
I'll make thee an example.
Desdemona.   What's the matter?
Othello.
All's well now, sweeting; come away to bed.
(To Montano.)
Sir, for your hurts, myself will be your surgeon.
Lead him off.
(Montano is led off.)
Iago, look with care about the town
And silence those whom this vile brawl distracted.   234
Come, Desdemona; 'tis the soldiers' life
To have their balmy slumbers waked with strife.
                    Exit (with all but Iago and Cassio).
Iago. What, are you hurt, lieutenant?
Cassio. Ay, past all surgery.
Iago. Marry, God forbid!
Cassio. Reputation, reputation, reputation! O, I have lost my reputation! I
    have lost the immortal part of myself, and what remains is bestial. My
    reputation, Iago, my reputation!
Iago. As I am an honest man, I thought you had received some bodily
    wound. There is more sense in that than in reputation. Reputation is an
    idle and most false imposition; oft got without merit and lost without
    deserving. You have lost no reputation at all unless you repute yourself
    such a loser. What, man! there are ways to recover the general again.   247
    You are but now cast in his mood—a punishment more in policy than in 248
    malice, even so as one would beat his offenseless dog to affright an
    imperious lion. Sue to him again, and he's yours.
Cassio. I will rather sue to be despised than to deceive so good a
    commander with so slight, so drunken, and so indiscreet an officer.

224 *pass* pass over, ignore   234 *distracted* excited   247 *recover* regain favor with   248 *cast in
his mood* dismissed because of his anger

Drunk! and speak parrot! and squabble! swagger! swear! and discourse 253
fustian with one's own shadow! O thou invisible spirit of wine, if thou 254
hast no name to be known by, let us call thee devil!

Iago. What was he that you followed with your sword? What had he done to
you?

Cassio. I know not.

Iago. Is't possible?

Cassio. I remember a mass of things, but nothing distinctly; a quarrel, but
nothing wherefore. O God, that men should put an enemy in their
mouths to steal away their brains! that we should with joy, pleasance,
revel, and applause transform ourselves into beasts! 263

Iago. Why, but you are now well enough. How came you thus recovered?

Cassio. It hath pleased the devil drunkenness to give place to the devil
wrath. One unperfectness shows me another, to make me frankly
despise myself.

Iago. Come, you are too severe a moraler. As the time, the place, and the
conditon of this country stands, I could heartily wish this had not so
befall'n; but since it is as it is, mend it for your own good.

Cassio. I will ask him for my place again: he shall tell me I am a drunkard!
Had I as many mouths as Hydra, such an answer would stop them all. 272
To be now a sensible man, by and by a fool, and presently a beast! O
strange! Every inordinate cup is unblest, and the ingredient is a devil. 274

Iago. Come, come, good wine is a good familiar creature if it be well used.
Exclaim no more against it. And, good lieutenant, I think you think I
love you.

Cassio. I have well approved it, sir. I drunk! 278

Iago. You or any man living may be drunk at some time, man. I'll tell you
what you shall do. Our general's wife is now the general. I may say so in
this respect, for that he hath devoted and given up himself to the
contemplation, mark, and denotement of her parts and graces. Confess
yourself freely to her; importune her help to put you in your place again.
She is of so free, so kind, so apt, so blessed a disposition she holds it a 284
vice in her goodness not to do more than she is requested. This broken
joint between you and her husband entreat her to splinter; and my 286
fortunes against any lay worth naming, this crack of your love shall 287
grow stronger than it was before.

Cassio. You advise me well.

Iago. I protest, in the sincerity of love and honest kindness.

Cassio. I think if freely; and betimes in the morning will I beseech the
virtuous Desdemona to undertake for me. I am desperate of my fortunes
if they check me here.

Iago. You are in the right. Good night, lieutenant; I must to the watch.

Cassio. Good night, honest Iago. *Exit Cassio.*

Iago.
And what's he then that says I play the villain,

---

253 *parrot* meaningless phrases   254 *fustian* bombastic nonsense   263 *applause* desire to
please   272 *Hydra* monster with many heads   274 *ingredient* contents   278 *approved* proved   284
free bounteous   286 *splinter* bind up with splints   287 *lay* wager

When this advice is free I give and honest,
Probal to thinking, and indeed the course   298
To win the Moor again? For 'tis most easy
Th' inclining Desdemona to subdue   300
In any honest suit; she's framed as fruitful
As the free elements. And then for her
To win the Moor—were't to renounce his baptism,
All seals and symbols of redeemèd sin—
His soul is so enfettered to her love
That she may make, unmake, do what she list,
Even as her appetite shall play the god
With his weak function. How am I then a villain
To counsel Cassio to this parallel course,   309
Directly to his good? Divinity of hell!   310
When devils will the blackest sins put on,   311
They do suggest at first with heavenly shows,
As I do now. For whiles this honest fool
Plies Desdemona to repair his fortunes,
And she for him pleads strongly to the Moor,
I'll pour this pestilence into his ear,
That she repeals him for her body's lust;   317
And by how much she strives to do him good,
She shall undo her credit with the Moor.
So will I turn her virtue into pitch,
And out of her own goodness make the net
That shall enmesh them all.
Enter Roderigo.   How, now, Roderigo?

Roderigo. I do follow here in the chase, not like a hound that hunts, but
one that fills up the cry. My money is almost spent; I have been to-night 324
exceedingly well cudgelled; and I think the issue will be—I shall have so
much experience for my pains; and so, with no money at all, and a little
more wit, return again to Venice

Iago.
How poor are they that have not patience!
What wound did ever heal but by degrees?
Thou know'st we work by wit, and not by witchcraft;
And wit depends on dilatory time.
Does't not go well? Cassio hath beaten thee,
And thou by that small hurt hast cashiered Cassio.   333
Though other things grow fair against the sun,
Yet fruits that blossom first will first be ripe.
Content thyself awhile. By the mass, 'tis morning!
Pleasure and action make the hours seem short.
Retire thee; go where thou art billeted.

---

298 *Probal* probable **300** *subdue* persuade **309** *parallel* corresponding **310** *Divinity*
theology **311** *put on* incite **317** *repeals him* seeks his recall **324** *cry* pack **333** *cashiered Cassio*
maneuvered Cassio's discharge

Away, I say! Thou shalt know more hereafter.
Nay, get thee gone!   *Exit Roderigo.*
                    Two things are to be done:
My wife must move for Cassio to her mistress;
I'll set her on;
Myself the while to draw the Moor apart
And bring him jump when he may Cassio find   344
Soliciting his wife. Ay, that's the way!
Dull not device by coldness and delay.   *Exit.*

Act III

Scene i

Enter Cassio, with musicians and the clown.

Cassio.
   Masters, play here, I will content your pains: 1
   Something that's brief; and bid "Good morrow, general."
   (They play.)
Clown. Why, masters, ha' your instruments been in Naples, that they speak   3
   i' th' nose thus?
Musician. How, sir, how?
Clown. Are these, I pray you, called wind instruments?
Musician. Ay, marry, are they, sir.
Clown. O, thereby hangs a tail.
Musician. Whereby hangs a tale, sir?
Clown. Marry, sir, by many a wind instrument that I know. But, masters,
   here's money for you; and general so likes your music that he desires
   you, for love's sake, to make no more noise with it.
Musician. Well, sir, we will not.
Clown. If you have any music that may not be heard, to't again: but, as they
   say, to hear music the general does not greatly care.
Musician. We have none such, sir.
Clown. Then put up your pipes in your bag, for I'll away.
   Go, vanish into air, away!
                      Exit musician (with his fellows).
Cassio. Dost thou hear, my honest friend?
Clown. No, I hear not your honest friend. I hear you.
Cassio. Prithee keep up thy quillets. There's a poor piece of gold for thee. If   21
   the gentlewoman that attends the general's wife be stirring, tell her there's
   one Cassio entreats her a little favor of speech. Wilt thou do this?
Clown. She is stirring sir. If she will stir hither, I shall
   seem to notify unto her.

---

344 *jump* at the exact moment
   Scene i Before the chamber of Othello and Desdemona   **1** *content* reward   **3** *Naples* (notorious
for its association with venereal disease)   **21** *quillets* quips

Cassio

    Do, good my friend.   *Exit clown.*

    Enter Igao.   In happy time, Iago.   27

Iago.

    You have not been abed then?

Cassio.

    Why, no; the day had broke

    Before we parted. I have made bold, Iago,

    To send in to your wife: my suit to her

    Is that she will to virtuous Desdemona

    Procure me some access.

Iago.   I'll send her to you presently;

    And I'll devise a mean to draw the Moor

    Out of the way, that your converse and business

    May be more free.

Cassio.

    I humbly thank you for't.   *Exit Iago.*

                        I never knew

    A Florentine more kind and honest.   38

    Enter Emilia.

Emilia.

    Good morrow, good lieutenant. I am sorry

    For your displeasure; but all will sure be well.

    The general and his wife are talking of it,

    And she speaks for you stoutly. The Moor replies

    That he you hurt is of great fame in Cyprus

    And great affinity, and that in wholesome wisdom   44

    He might not but refuse you; but he protests he loves you,

    And needs no other suitor but his likings

    To take the safest occasion by the front   47

    To bring you in again.

Cassio.   Yet I beseech you,

    If you think fit, or that it may be done,

    Give me advantage of some brief discourse

    With Desdemona alone.

Emilia.   Pray you come in.

    I will bestow you where you shall have time

    To speak your bosom freely.   53

Cassio.   I am much bound to you.

                                Exeunt.

Scene ii

    Enter Othello, Iago, and gentlemen.

    27 *In happy time* well met   **38** *Florentine* i.e. even a Florentine (like Cassio; Iago was a Venetian)   **44** *affinity* family connections   **47** *occasion* opportunity; *front* forelock   **53** *your bosom* your inmost thoughts

    Scene ii The castle

Othello.
    These letters given Iago, to the pilot
    And by him do my duties to the Senate.
    That done, I will be walking on the works;   3
    Repair there to me.
Iago.   Well, my good lord, I'll do't.
Othello.
    This fortification, gentlemen, shall we see't?
Gentlemen.
    We'll wait upon your lordship.   *Exeunt.*

Scene iii

    Enter Desdemona, Cassio, and Emilia.

Desdemona.
    Be thou assured, good Cassio, I will do
    All my abilities in thy behalf.
Emilia.
    Good madam, do. I warrant it grieves my husband
    As if the cause were his.
Desdemona.
    O, that's an honest fellow. Do not doubt, Cassio,
    But I will have my lord and you again
    As friendly as you were.
Cassio.   Bounteous madam,
    Whatever shall become of Michael Cassio,
    He's never anything but your true servant.
Desdemona.
    I know't; I thank you. You do love my lord;
    You have known him long; and be you well assured
    He shall in strangeness stand no farther off   12
    Than in a politic distance.   13
Cassio.   Ay, but, lady,
    That policy may either last so long,
    Or feed upon such nice and waterish diet,   15
    Or breed itself so out of circumstance,
    That, I being absent, and my place supplied,
    My general will forget my love and service.
Desdemona.
    Do not doubt that; before Emilia here   19
    I give thee warrant of thy place. Assure thee,
    If I do vow a friendship, I'll perform it
    To the last article. My lord shall never rest;
    I'll watch him tame and talk him out of patience;   23
    His bed shall seem a school, his board a shrift;   24

---

3 *works* fortifications
    Scene iii The castle grounds   **12** *strangeness* aloofness   **13** *Than . . . distance* than wise policy
requires   **15** *Or . . . diet* or be continued for such slight reasons   **19** *doubt* fear   **23** *watch him tame*
keep him awake until he gives in   **24** *shrift* confessional

I'll intermingle everything he does
With Cassio's suit. Therefore be merry, Cassio,
For thy solicitor shall rather die
Than give thy cause away.

Enter Othello and Iago (at a distance).

Emilia.
Madam, here comes my lord.
Cassio.
Madam, I'll take my leave.   30
Desdemona.
Why, stay, and hear me speak.
Cassio.
Madam, not now: I am very ill at ease,
Unfit for mine own purposes.
Desdemona.
Well, do your descretion.   *Exit Cassio.*
Iago.
Ha! I like not that.
Othello.   What dost thou say?
Iago.
Nothing, my lord; or if—I know not what.
Othello.
Was not that Cassio parted from my wife?
Iago.
Cassio, my lord? No, sure, I cannot think it,
That he would steal away so guilty-like,
Seeing your coming.
Othello.   I do believe 'twas he.   40
Desdemona.
How now, my lord?
I have been talking with a suitor here,
A man that languishes in your displeasure.
Othello.
Who is't you mean?
Desdemona.
Why, your lieutenant, Cassio. Good my lord,
If I have any grace or power to move you,
His present reconciliation take;   47
For if he be not one that truly loves you,
That errs in ignorance, and not in cunning,
I have no judgment in an honest face.
I prithee call him back.
Othello.   Went he hence now?
Desdemona.
Yes, faith; so humbled

47 *present* immediate

That he hath left part of his grief with me
To suffer with him. Good love, call him back.
Othello.
Not now, sweet Desdemon; some other time.
Desdemona.
But shall't be shortly?
Othello.   The sooner, sweet, for you.
Desdemona.
Shall't be to-night at supper?
Othello.   No, not to-night.
Desdemona.
To-morrow dinner then?
Othello.   I shall not dine at home;
I meet the captains at the citadel.
Desdemona.
Why, then, to-morrow night, or Tuesday morn,
On Tuesday noon or night, or Wednesday morn.
I prithee name the time, but let it not
Exceed three days. I' faith, he's penitent;
And yet his trespass, in our common reason
(Save that, they say, the wars must make examples
Out of their best), is not almost a fault   66
T'incur a private check. When shall he come?   67
Tell me, Othello. I wonder in my soul
What you could ask me that I should deny
Or stand so mamm'ring on. What? Michael Cassio,   70
That came a-wooing with you, and so many a time,
When I have spoke of you dispraisingly,
Hath ta'en your part—to have so much to do
To bring him in? By'r Lady, I could do much—
Othello.
Prithee no more. Let him come when he will!
I will deny thee nothing.
Desdemona.   Why, this is not a boon;
'Tis as I should entreat you wear your gloves,
Or feed on nourishing dishes, or keep you warm,
Or sue to you to do a peculiar profit
To your own person. Nay, when I have a suit
Wherein I mean to touch your love indeed,
It shall be full of poise and difficult weight,
And fearful to be granted.   83
Othello.   I will deny thee nothing!
Whereon I do beseech thee grant me this,
To leave me but a little to myself.
Desdemona.
Shall I deny you? No. Farewell, my lord.

66 *not almost* hardly   67 *a private check* even a private reprimand   70 *mamm'ring on*
hesitating about   83 *fearful* dangerous

Othello.

    Farewell, my Desdemon: I'll come to thee straight.

Desdemona.

    Emilia, come.—Be as your fancies teach you;

    Whate'er you be, I am obedient.   *Exit (with Emilia).*

Othello.

    Excellent wretch! Perdition catch my soul   90

    But I do love thee! and when I love thee not,

    Chaos is come again.

Iago.

    My noble lord—

Othello.   What dost thou say, Iago.?

Iago.

    Did Michael Cassio, when you wooed my lady,

    Know of your love?

Othello.

    He did, from first to last. Why dost thou ask?

Iago.

    But for a satisfaction of my thought;

    No further harm.

Othello.   Why of thy thought, Iago?

Iago.

    I did not think he had been acquainted with her.

Othello.

    O, yes, and went between us very oft.   100

Iago.

    Indeed?

Othello.

    Indeed? Ay, indeed! Discern'st thou aught in that?

    Is he not honest?

Iago.   Honest, my lord?

Othello.   Honest. Ay, honest.

Iago.

    My lord, for aught I know.

Othello.

    What dost thou think?

Iago.   Think, my lord?

Othello.   Think, my lord?

    By heaven, he echoes me,

    As if there were some monster in his thought

    Too hideous to be shown. Thou dost mean something:

    I heard thee say even now, thou lik'st not that,

    When Cassio left my wife. What didst not like?

    And when I told thee he was of my counsel

    In my whole course of wooing, thou cried'st "Indeed?"

    And didst contract and purse thy brow together,

---

90 *wretch* (a term of endearment)   **100** *went . . . us* (i.e. as messenger)

As if you then hadst shut up in thy brain
Some horrible conceit. If thou dost love me,   115
Show me thy thought.

Iago.

My lord, you know I love you.

Othello.   I think thou dost;
And, for I know thou'rt full of love and honesty
And weigh'st thy words before thou giv'st them breath,
Therefore these stops of thine fright me the more;
For such things in a false disloyal knave
Are tricks of custom; but in a man that's just
They are close dilations, working from the heart   123
That passion cannot rule.

Iago.   For Michael Cassio,
I dare be sworn I think that he is honest.

Othello.

I think so too.

Iago.   Men should be what they seem;
Or those that be not, would they might seem none!   127

Othello.

Certain, men should be what they seem.

Iago.

Why then, I think Cassio's an honest man.

Othello.

Nay, yet there's more in this.
I prithee speak to me as to thy thinkings,
As thou dost ruminate, and give thy worst of thoughts
The worst of words.

Iago.   Good my lord, pardon me:
Though I am bound to every act of duty,
I am not bound to that all slaves are free to.   135
Utter my thoughts? Why, say they are vile and false,
As where's that palace whereinto foul things
Sometimes intrude not? Who has a breast so pure
But some uncleanly apprehensions
Keep leets and law days, and in Sessions sit   140
With meditations lawful?

Othello.

Thou dost conspire against thy friend, Iago,
If thou but think'st him wronged, and mak'st his ear
A stranger to thy thoughts.

Iago.   I do beseech you—
Though I perchance am vicious in my guess

---

115 *conceit* fancy   **123–24** *close dilations . . . rule* secret emotions which well up in spite of restraint   **127** *seem none* i.e. not pretend to be men when they are really monsters   **135** *bound . . . free to* bound to tell that which even slaves are allowed to keep to themselves   **140** *leets and law days* sittings of the courts

(As I confess it is my nature's plague
To spy into abuses, and oft my jealousy   147
Shapes faults that are not), that your wisdom yet
From one that so imperfectly conjects   149
Would take no notice, nor build yourself a trouble
Out of his scattering and unsure observance.
It were not for your quiet nor your good,
Nor for my manhood, honesty, and wisdom,
To let you know my thoughts.

Othello.   What dost thou mean?

Iago.

Good name in man and woman, dear my lord,
Is the immediate jewel of their souls.   156
Who steals my purse steals trash; 'tis something, nothing;
'Twas mine, 'tis his, and has been slave to thousands;
But he that filches from me my good name
Robs me of that which not enriches him
And makes me poor indeed.

Othello.

By heaven, I'll know thy thoughts!

Iago.

You cannot, if my heart were in your hand;
Nor shall not whilst 'tis in my custody.

Othello.

Ha!

Iago. O, beware, my lord, of jealousy!
It is the green-eyed monster, which doth mock   166
The meat it feeds on. That cuckold lives in bliss
Who, certain of his fate, loves not his wronger;
But O, what damnèd minutes tells he o'er
Who dotes, yet doubts—suspects, yet strongly loves!

Othello.

O misery!

Iago.

Poor and content is rich, and rich enough;
But riches fineless is as poor as winter   173
To him that ever fears he shall be poor.
Good God, the souls of all my tribe defend
From jealousy!

Othello.   Why, why is this?
Think'st thou I'd make a life of jealousy,
To follow still the changes of the moon
With fresh suspicions? No! To be once in doubt
Is once to be resolved. Exchange me for a goat
When I shall turn the business of my soul

---

147 *jealousy* suspicion   149 *conjects* conjectures   156 *immediate* nearest the heart   166 *mock* play with, like a cat with a mouse   173 *fineless* unlimited

To such exsufflicate and blown surmises,   182
Matching this inference. 'Tis not to make me jealous
To say my wife is fair, feeds well, loves company,
Is free of speech, sings, plays, and dances;
Where virtue is, these are more virtuous.
Nor from mine own weak merits will I draw
The smallest fear or doubt of her revolt,   188
For she had eyes, and chose me. No, Iago;
I'll see before I doubt; when I doubt, prove;
And on the proof there is no more but this—
Away at once with love or jealousy!

Iago.
I am glad of this; for now I shall have reason
To show the love and duty that I bear you
With franker spirit. Therefore, as I am bound,
Receive it from me. I speak not yet of proof.
Look to your wife; observe her well with Cassio;
Wear your eyes thus, not jealous nor secure: 198
I would not have your free and noble nature,
Out of self-bounty, be abused. Look to't.   200
I know our country disposition well:
In Venice they do let God see the pranks
They dare not show their husbands; their best conscience
Is not to leav't undone, but keep't unkown.

Othello.
Dost thou say so?

Iago.
She did deceive her father, marrying you;
And when she seemed to shake and fear your looks,
She loved them most.

Othello.   And so she did.

Iago.   Why, go to then!
She that, so young, could give out such a seeming
To seel her father's eyes up close as oak—   210
He thought 'twas witchcraft—but I am much to blame.
I humbly do beseech you of your pardon
For too much loving you.

Othello.   I am bound to thee for ever.

Iago.
I see this hath a little dashed your spirits.

Othello.
Not a jot, not a jot.

Iago.   I' faith, I fear it has.
I hope you will consider what is spoke
Comes from my love. But I do see y' are moved.

---

182 *exsufflicate and blown* spat out and flyblown   **188** *revolt* unfaithfulness   **198** *secure*
overconfident   **200** *self-bounty* natural goodness   **210** *seel* close; *oak* oak grain

I am to pray you not to strain my speech
To grosser issues nor to larger reach   219
Than to suspicion.
Othello.
   I will not.
Iago.   Should you do so, my lord,
My speech should fall into such vile success   222
As my thoughts aim not at. Cassio's my worthy friend—
My lord, I see y' are moved.
Othello.   No, not much moved:
I do not think but Desdemona's honest.   225
Iago.
   Long live she so! and long live you to think so!
Othello.
   And yet, how nature erring from itself—
Iago.
   Ay, there's the point! as (to be bold with you)
Not to affect many proposèd matches
Of her own clime, complexion, and degree,
Whereto we see in all things nature tends—
Foh! one may smell in such a will most rank,
Foul disproportions, thoughts unnatural—
But pardon me—I do not in position   234
Distinctly speak of her; though I may fear
Her will, recoiling to her better judgment,   236
May fall to match you with her country forms,   237
And happily repent.   238
Othello.   Farewell, farewell!
If more thou dost perceive, let me know more.
Set on thy wife to observe. Leave me, Iago.
Iago.
   My lord, I take my leave.   *(Going.)*
Othello.
   Why did I marry? This honest creature doubtless
Sees and knows more, much more, than he unfolds.
Iago *(returns).*
   My lord, I would I might entreat your honor
To scan this thing no further: leave it to time.
Although 'tis fit that Cassio have his place,
For sure he fills it up with great ability,
Yet, if you please to hold him off awhile,
You shall by that perceive him and his means.
Note if your lady strain his entertainment   250
With any strong or vehement importunity;
Much will be seen in that. In the mean time

---

219 *To grosser issues* to mean something more monstrous   222 *vile success* evil outcome   225
honest chaste   234 *position* definite assertion   236 *recoiling* reverting   237 *fall to match* happen to
compare   238 *happily* haply, perhaps   250 *strain his entertainment* urge his recall

Let me be thought too busy in my fears   253
(As worthy cause I have to fear I am)
And hold her free, I do beseech your honor.   255

Othello.

Fear not my government.   256

Iago.

I once more take my leave.   *Exit.*

Othello.

This fellow's of exceeding honesty,
And knows all qualities, with a learned spirit   259
Of human dealings. If I do prove her haggard,   260
Though that her jesses were my dear heartstrings,   261
I'd whistle her off and let her down the wind   262
To prey at fortune. Haply, for I am black
And have not those soft parts of conversation   264
That chamberers have, or for I am declined   265
Into the vale of years—yet that's not much—
She's gone. I am abused, and my relief
Must be to loathe her. O curse of marriage,
That we can call these delicate creatures ours,
And not their appetites! I had rather be a toad
And live upon the vapor of a dungeon
Than keep a corner in the thing I love
For others' uses. Yet 'tis the plague of great ones;   273
Prerogatived are they less than the base.   274
'Tis destiny unshunnable, like death.
Even then this forkèd plague is fated to us   276
When we do quicken. Look where she comes.   277

Enter Desdemona and Emilia.

If she be false, O, then heaven mocks itself!
I'll not believe't.

Desdemona.   How now, my dear Othello?
Your dinner, and the generous islanders   280
By you invited, do attend your presence.

Othello.

I am to blame.

Desdemona.   Why do you speak so faintly?
Are you not well?

Othello.

I have a pain upon my forehead, here.

Desdemona.

Faith, that's with watching; 'twill away again.   285

253 *busy* meddlesome   255 *hold her free* consider her guiltless   256 *government*
self-control   259 *qualities* natures   259–60 *learned spirit Of* mind informed about   260 *haggard* a
wild hawk   261 *jesses* thongs for controlling a hawk   262–63 *whistle . . . fortune* turn her out and
let her take care of herself   264 *soft . . . conversation* ingratiating manners   265 *chamberers*
courtiers   273 *great ones* prominent men   274 *Prerogatived* privileged   276 *forkèd plague* i.e.
horns of a cuckold   227 *do quicken* are born   280 *generous* noble   285 *watching* working late

Let me but bind it hard, within this hour
It will be well.
Othello.   Your napkin is too little;   287
(He pushes the handkerchief from him, and it falls unnoticed.)
Let it alone. Come, I'll go in with you.   288
Desdemona.
I am very sorry that you are not well.   *Exit (with Othello).*
Emilia.
I am glad I have found this napkin;
This was her first remembrance from the Moor,
My wayward husband hath a hundred times
Wooed me to steal it; but she so loves the token
(For he conjured her she should ever keep it)
That she reserves it evermore about her
To kiss and talk to. I'll have the work ta'en out   296
And give't Iago.
What he will do with it heaven knows, not I;
I nothing but to please his fantasy.   299

    Enter Iago.

Iago.
How now? What do you here alone?
Emilia.
Do not you chide; I have a thing for you.
Iago.
A thing for me? It is a common thing—
Emilia. Ha?
Iago.
To have a foolish wife.
Emilia.
O, is that all? What will you give me now
For that same handkerchief?
Iago.   What handkerchief?
Emilia.
What handkerchief!
Why, that the Moor first gave to Desdemona;
That which so often you did bid me steal.
Iago.
Hast stol'n it from her?
Emilia.
No, faith; she let it drop by negligence,
And to th' advantage, I, being here, took't up.   312
Look, here it is.
Iago.   A good wench! Give it me.

---

287 *napkin* handkerchief **288** *it* i.e. his forehead **296** *work ta'en out* pattern copied **299**
fantasy whim **312** *to th' advantage* opportunely

Emilia.
> What will you do with't, that you have been so earnest
> To have me filch it?

Iago.   Why, what is that to you?
> *(Snatches it.)*

Emilia.
> If it be not for some purpose of import,   316
> Give't me again. Poor lady, she'll run mad
> When she shall lack it.

Iago.
> Be not acknown on't; I have use for it.   319
> Go, leave me.   *Exit Emilia.*
> I will in Cassio's lodgings lose this napkin
> And let him find it. Trifles light as air
> Are to the jealous confirmations strong
> As proofs of holy writ. This may do something.
> The Moor already changes with my poison:
> Dangerous conceits are in their natures poisons,   326
> Which at the first are scarce found to distaste,
> But with a little act upon the blood
> Burn like the mines of sulphur.
> *Enter Othello.*   I did say so.
> Look where he comes! Not poppy nor mandragora,   330
> Nor all the drowsy syrups of the world,
> Shall ever med'cine thee to that sweet sleep
> Which thou owedst yesterday.

Othello.   Ha! ha! false to me?

Iago.
> Why, how now, general? No more of that!

Othello.
> Avaunt! be gone! Thou hast set me on the rack.
> I swear 'tis better to be much abused
> Than but to know't a little.

Iago.   How now, my lord?

Othello.
> What sense had I of her stol'n hours of lust?
> I saw't not, thought it not, it harmed not me;
> I slept the next night well, fed well, was free and merry;   340
> I found not Cassio's kisses on her lips.
> He that is robbed, not wanting what is stol'n,   342
> Let him not know't, and he's not robbed at all.

Iago.
> I am sorry to hear this.

Othello.
> I had been happy if the general camp,

---

316 *import* importance   **319** *Be . . . on't* do not acknowledge it   **326** *conceits* ideas   **330** *mandragora* a narcotic   **340** *free* carefree   **342** *wanting* missing

William Shakespeare

Pioneers and all, had tasted her sweet body,   346
So I had nothing known. O, now for ever
Farewell the tranquil mind! farewell content!
Farewell the plumèd troop, and the big wars   349
That make ambition virtue! O, farewell!
Farewell the neighing steed and the shrill trump,
The spirit-stirring drum, th' ear-piercing fife,
The royal banner, and all quality,
Pride, pomp, and circumstance of glorious war!   354
And O you mortal engines whose rude throats   355
Th' immortal Jove's dread clamors counterfeit,   356
Farewell! Othello's occupation's gone!

Iago.

Is't possible, my lord?

Othello.

Villain, be sure thou prove my love a whore!
Be sure of it; give me the ocular proof;
Or, by the worth of mine eternal soul,
Thou hadst been better have been born a dog
Than answer my waked wrath!

Iago.   Is't come to this?

Othello.

Make me to see't; or at the least so prove it
That the probation bear no hinge nor loop   365
To hang a doubt on—or woe upon thy life!

Iago.

My noble lord—

Othello.

If thou dost slander her and torture me,
Never pray more; abandon all remorse;
On horror's head horrors accumulate;
Do deeds to make heaven weep, all earth amazed;
For nothing canst thou to damnation add
Greater than that.

Iago.   O grace! O heaven forgive me!
Are you a man? Have you a soul or sense?—
God b' wi' you! take mine office. O wretched fool,
That liv'st to make thine honesty a vice!
O monstrous would! Take note, take note, O world,
To be direct and honest is not safe.
I thank you for this profit; and from hence   379
I'll love no friend, sith love breeds such offense.

Othello.

Nay stay. Thou shouldst be honest.

Iago.

I should be wise; for honesty's a fool
And loses that it works for.

346 *Pioners* sappers, laborers   349 *big* stately   354 *circumstance* pageantry   355 *mortal engines* deadly artillery   356 *counterfeit* imitate   365 *probation* proof   379 *profit* profitable lesson

Othello.   By the world,
   I think my wife be honest, and think she is not;
   I think that thou art just, and think thou art not.
   I'll have some proof. Her name, that was as fresh
   As Dian's visage, is now begrimed and black
   As mine own face. If there be cords, or knives,
   Poison, or fire, or suffocating streams,
   I'll not endure it. Would I were satisfied!   390
Iago.
   I see, sir, you are eaten up with passion:
   I do repent me that I put it to you.
   You would be satisfied?
Othello.   Would? Nay, I will.
Iago.
   And may; but how? how satisfied, my lord?
   Would you, the supervisor, grossly gape on?   395
   Behold her topped?
Othello.   Death and damnation! O!
Iago.
   It were a tedious difficulty, I think,
   To bring them to that prospect. Damn them then,
   If ever mortal eyes do see them bolster   399
   More than their own! What then? How then?
   What shall I say? Where's satisfaction?
   It is impossible you should see this,
   Were they as prime as goats, as hot as monkeys,   403
   As salt as wolves in pride, and fools as gross   404
   As ignorance made drunk. But yet, I say,
   If imputation and strong circumstances
   Which lead directly to the door of truth
   Will give you satisfaction, you may have't.
Othello.
   Give me a living reason she's disloyal.
Iago.
   I do not like the office.   410
   But sith I am ent'red in this cause so far,
   Pricked to't by foolish honesty and love,
   I will go on. I lay with Cassio lately,
   And being troubled with a raging tooth,
   I could not sleep.
   There are a kind of men so loose of soul
   That in their sleeps will mutter their affairs.
   One of this kind is Cassio.
   In sleep I heard him say, "Sweet Desdemona,
   Let us be wary, let us hide our loves!"   420

   390 *satisfied* completely informed **395** *supervisor* spectator **390** *bolster* lie together **403**
prime lustful **404** *salt* lecherous; *pride* heat

And then, sir, would he gripe and wring my hand,
Cry "O sweet creature!" and then kiss me hard,
As if he plucked up kisses by the roots
That grew upon my lips; then laid his leg
Over my thigh, and sighed, and kissed, and then
Cried "Cursèd fate that gave thee to the Moor!"

Othello.

O monstrous! monstrous!

Iago.   Nay, this was but his dream.

Othello.

But this denoted a foregone conclusion: 428
'Tis a shrewd doubt, though it be but a dream.   429

Iago.

And this may help to thicken other proofs
That do demonstrate thinly.

Othello.   I'll tear her all to pieces!

Iago.

Nay, but be wise. Yet we see nothing done;
She may be honest yet. Tell me but this—
Have you not sometimes seen a handkerchief
Spotted with strawberries in your wife's hand?

Othello.

I gave her such a one; 'twas my first gift.

Iago.

I know not that; but such a handkerchief—
I am sure it was your wife's—did I to-day
See Cassio wipe his beard with.

Othello.   If it be that—

Iago.

If it be that, or any that was hers,   440
It speaks against her with the other proofs.

Othello.

O, that the slave had forty thousand lives!
One is too poor, too weak for my revenge.
Now do I see 'tis true. Look here, Iago:
All my fond love thus do I blow to heaven.
'Tis gone.
Arise, black vengeance, from the hollow hell!
Yield up, O love, thy crown and hearted throne
To tyrannous hate! Swell, bosom, with thy fraught,   449
For 'tis of aspics' tongues!   450

Iago.   Yet be content.

Othello.

O, blood, blood, blood!

Iago.

Patience, I say. Your mind perhaps may change.

---

428 *foregone conclusion* previous experience   **429** *a shrewd doubt* cursedly
suspicious   **449** *fraught* burden   **450** *aspics* deadly poisonous snakes

Othello.
Never, Iago. Like to the Pontic sea,   453
Whose icy current and compulsive course
Ne'er feels retiring ebb, but keeps due on
To the Propontic and the Hellespont,
Even so my bloody thoughts, with violent pace,
Shall ne'er look back, ne'er ebb to humble love,
Till that a capable and wide revenge   459
Swallow them up.
He kneels.   Now, by yond marble heaven,
In the due reverence of a sacred now
I here engage my words.
Iago.   Do not rise yet.

Iago kneels.

Witness, you ever-burning lights above,
You elements that clip us round about,   464
Witness that here Iago doth give up
The execution of his wit, hands, heart   466
To wronged Othello's service! Let him command,
And to obey shall be in me remorse,   468
What bloody business ever.
(They rise.)
Othello.   I greet thy love,
Not with vain thanks but with acceptance bounteous,
And will upon the instant put thee to't.
Within these three days let me hear thee say
That Cassio's not alive.
Iago.
My friend is dead; 'tis done at your request.
But let her live.
Othello.
Damn her, lewd minx! O, damn her! damn her!
Come, go with me apart. I will withdraw
To furnish me with some swift means of death
For the fair devil. Now art thou my lieutenant.
Iago.
I am your own for ever.   *Exeunt.*

Scene iv

Enter Desdemona, Emilia, and clown.
Desdemona. Do you know, sirrah, where Lieutenant
    Cassio lies?   2
Clown. I dare not say he lies anywhere.

---

    453 *Pontic sea* Black Sea   459 *capable* all-embracing   464 *clip* encompass
466 *execution* activities; *wit* mind   468 *remorse* pity
    Scene iv The environs of the castle   2 *lies* lives, lodges

Desdemona. Why, man?

Clown. He's a soldier, and for me to say a soldier lies is
  stabbing.

Desdemona. Go to. Where lodges he?

Clown. To tell you where he lodges is to tell you where I
  lie.

Desdemona. Can anything be made of this?

Clown. I know not where he lodges; and for me to devise
  a lodging, and say he lies here or he lies there, were to
  lie in mine own throat.

Desdemona. Can you enquire him out, and be edified by
  report?

Clown. I will catechize the world for him; that is, make
  questions, and by them answer.

Desdemona. Seek him, bid him come hither. Tell him I
  have moved my lord on his behalf and hope all will be   19
  well.

Clown. To do this is within the compass of man's wit,
  and therefore I'll attempt the doing of it.   *Exit.*

Desdemona.
  Where should I lose that handkerchief, Emilia?

Emilia.
  I know not, madam.

Desdemona.
  Believe me, I had rather have lost my purse
  Full of crusadoes; and but my noble Moor   26
  Is true of mind, and made of no such baseness
  As jealous creatures are, it were enough
  To put him to ill thinking.

Emilia.   Is he not jealous?

Desdemona.
  Who? he? I think the sun where he was born
  Drew all such humors from him.   31

  Enter Othello.

Emilia.   Look where he comes.

Desdemona.
  I will not leave him now till Cassio
  Be called to him.—How is't with you, my lord?

Othello.
  Well, my good lady. *(aside)* O, hardness to dissemble!—
  How do you, Desdemona?

Desdemona.   Well, my good lord.

Othello.
  Give me your hand. This hand is moist, my lady.

Desdemona.
  It yet hath felt no age nor known no sorrow.

19 *moved* made proposals 26 *crusadoes* Portuguese gold coins 31 *humors* inclinations

Othello.
> This argues fruitfulness and liberal heart.
> Hot, hot, and moist. This hand of yours requires
> A sequester from liberty, fasting and prayer,   40
> Much castigation, exercise devout;
> For here's a young and sweating devil here
> That commonly rebels. 'Tis a good hand,
> A frank one.

Desdemona. You may, indeed, say so;
> For 'twas that hand that gave away my heart.

Othello.
> A liberal hand! The hearts of old gave hands;
> But our new heraldry is hands, not hearts.   47

Desdemona.
> I cannot speak of this. Come now, your promise!

Othello.
> What promise, chuck?

Desdemona.
> I have sent to bid Cassio come speak with you.

Othello.
> I have a salt and sorry rheum offends me.   51
> Lend me thy handkerchief.

Desdemona.   Here, my lord.

Othello.
> That which I gave you.

Desdemona.   I have it not about me.

Othello.
> Not?

Desdemona. No, faith, my lord.

Othello.   That's a fault.
> That handkerchief
> Did an Egyptian to my mother give.   56
> She was a charmer, and could almost read   57
> The thoughts of people. She told her, while she kept it,
> 'Twould make her amiable and subdue my father   59
> Entirely to her love; but if she lost it
> Or made a gift of it, my father's eye
> Should hold her loathèd, and his spirits should hunt
> After new fancies. She, dying, gave it me,
> And bid me, when my fate would have me wive,
> To give it her. I did so; and take heed on't;
> Make it a darling like your precious eye.
> To lose't or give't away were such perdition   67
> As nothing else could match.

Desdemona.   Is't possible?

---

40 *sequester* removal   47 *heraldry* heraldic symbolism   51 *salt . . . rheum* distressing
head-cold   56 *Egyptian* gypsy   57 *charmer* sorceress   59 *amiable* lovable   67 *perdition* disaster

Othello.
    'Tis true. There's magic in the web of it.
    A sibyl that had numb'red in the world
    The sun to course two hundred compasses,   71
    In her prophetic fury sewed the work;
    The worms were hallowed that did breed the silk;
    And it was dyed in mummy which the skillful   74
    Conserved of maiden's hearts.
Desdemona.   I' faith? Is't true?
Othello.
    Most veritable. Therefore look to't well.
Desdemona.
    Then would to God that I had never seen't!
Othello. Ha! Wherefore?
Desdemona.
    Why do you speak so startingly and rash?
Othello.
    Is't lost? Is't gone? Speak, is it out o' th' way?
Desdemona. Heaven bless us!
Othello. Say you?
Desdemona.
    It is not lost. But what an if it were?
Othello. How?
Desdemona.
    I say it is not lost.
Othello.   Fetch't, let me see't!
Desdemona.
    Why, so I can, sir; but I will not now.
    This is a trick to put me from my suit: 87
    Pray you let Cassio be received again.
Othello.
    Fetch me the handkerchief! My mind misgives.
Desdemona.
    Come, come!
    You'll never meet a more sufficient man.
Othello.
    The handkerchief!
Desdemona.   I pray talk me of Cassio.
Othello.
    The handkerchief!
Desdemona.   A man that all his time   93
    Hath founded his good fortunes on your love,
    Shared dangers with you—
Othello.
    The handkerchief!
Desdemona.
    I' faith, you are to blame.

  71 *compasses* annual rounds   **74** *mummy* a drug made from mummies   **87** *put* divert   **93** *all . . . time* during his whole career

Othello. Zounds!   *Exit Othello.*

Emilia. Is not this man jealous?

Desdemona.

    I ne'er saw this before.

    Sure there's some wonder in this handkerchief;

    I am most unhappy in the loss of it.

Emilia.

    'Tis not a year or two shows us a man.

    They are all but stomachs, and we all but food;

    They eat us hungerly, and when they are full,

    They belch us.

Enter Iago and Cassio.

          Look you—Cassio and my husband!

Iago.

    There is no other way; 'tis she must do't.

    And lo the happiness! Go and importune her.   108

Desdemona.

    How now, good Cassio? What's the news with you?

Cassio.

    Madam, my former suit. I do beseech you

    That by your virtuous means I may again

    Exist, and be a member of his love

    Whom I with all the office of my heart

    Entirely honor. I would not be delayed.

    If my offense be of such mortal kind

    That neither service past, nor present sorrows,

    Nor purposed merit in futurity,

    Can ransom me into his love again,

    But to know so must be my benefit.

    So shall I clothe me in a forced content,

    And shut myself up in some other course,   121

    To fortune's alms.

Desdemona.   Alas, thrice-gentle Cassio!

    My advocation is not now in tune.   123

    My lord is not my lord; nor should I know him,

    Were he in favor as in humor altered.   125

    So help me every spirit sanctified

    As I have spoken for you all my best

    And stood within the blank of his displeasure   128

    For my free speech! You must awhile be patient.

    What I can do I will; and more I will

    Than for myself I dare. Let that suffice you.

Iago.

    Is my lord angry?

---

108 *happiness* good luck 121 *shut myself up in* confine myself to 123 *advocation* advocacy 125 *favor* appearance 128 *blank* bull's-eye of the target

Emilia.   He went hence but now,
    And certainly in strange unquietness.
Iago.
    Can he be angry? I have seen the cannon
    When it hath blown his ranks into the air
    And, like the devil, from his very arm
    Puffed his own brother—and is he angry?
    Something of moment then. I will go meet him.
    There's matter in't indeed if he be angry.
Desdemona.
    I prithee do so.   *Exit Iago.*
              Something sure of state,   140
    Either from Venice or some unhatched practice   141
    Made demonstrable here in Cyprus to him,
    Hath puddled his clear spirit; and in such cases   143
    Men's natures wrangle with inferior things,
    Though great ones are their object. 'Tis even so;
    For let our finger ache, and it endues   146
    Our other, healthful members even to a sense
    Of pain. Nay, we must think men are not gods,
    Nor of them look for such observancy
    As fits the bridal. Beshrew me much, Emilia,
    I was, unhandsome warrior as I am,   151
    Arraigning his unkindness with my soul;   152
    But now I find I had suborned the witness,
    And he's indicted falsely.
Emilia.
    Pray heaven it be state matters, as you think,
    And no conception nor no jealous toy   156
    Concerning you.
Desdemona.
    Alas the day! I never gave him cause.
Emilia.
    But jealous souls will not be answered so;
    They are not ever jealous for the cause,
    But jealous for they're jealous. 'Tis a monster
    Begot upon itself, born on itself.   162
Desdemona.
    Heaven keep that monster from Othello's mind!
Emilia. Lady, amen.
Desdemona.
    I will go seek him. Cassio, walk here about:
    If I do find him fit, I'll move your suit
    And seek to effect it to my uttermost.

---

    140 *state* public affairs   **141** *unhatched practice* budding plot   **143** *puddled* muddied   **146** *endues* brings   **151** *unhandsome warrior* inadequate soldier   **152** *Arraigning . . . soul* indicting his unkindness before the bar of my soul   **156** *toy* fancy   **162** *Begot . . . itself* self-engendered

Cassio.

I humbly thank your ladyship.

Exeunt Desdemona and Emilia.

Enter Bianca.

Bianca.

Save you, friend Cassio!

Cassio.   What make you from home?

How is't with you, my most fair Bianca?

I' faith, sweet love, I was coming to your house.

Bianca.

And I was going to your lodging, Cassio.

What, keep a week away? seven days and nights?

Eightscore eight hours? and lovers' absent hours,

More tedious than the dial eightscore times?   175

O weary reck'ning!

Cassio.   Pardon me, Bianca:

I have this while with leaden thoughts been pressed;

But I shall in a more continuate time   178

Strike off this score of absence. Sweet Bianca,

(Gives her Desdemona's handkerchief.)

Take me this work out.   180

Bianca.   O Cassio, whence came this?

This is some token from a newer friend.

To the felt absence now I feel a cause.

Is't come to this? Well, well.

Cassio.   Go to, woman!

Throw your vile guesses in the devil's teeth,

From whence you have them. You are jealous now

That this is from some mistress, some remembrance.

No, by my faith, Bianca.

Bianca.   Why, whose is it?

Cassio.

I know not, sweet; I found it in my chamber.

I like the work well; ere it be demanded,   189

As like enough it will, I'd have it copied.

Take it and do't, and leave me for this time.

Bianca.

Leave you? Wherefore?

Cassio.

I do attend here on the general

And think it no addition, nor my wish,

To have him see me womaned.

Bianca.   Why, I pray you?

Cassio.

Not that I love you not.

---

175 *dial* clock   178 *continuate* uninterrupted   180 *Take . . . out* copy this embroidery for me
189 *work* needlework

Bianca.   But that you do not love me!
    I pray you bring me on the way a little,
    And say if I shall see you soon at night.
Cassio.
    'Tis but a little way that I can bring you,
    For I attend here; but I'll see you soon.
Bianca.
    'Tis very good. I must be circumstanced.   *Exeunt.* 201

ACT IV

Scene i

    Enter Othello and Iago.
Iago.
    Will you think so?
Othello.   Think so, Iago?
Iago.   What,
    To kiss in private?
Othello.   An unauthorized kiss.
Iago.
    Or to be naked with her friend in bed
    An hour or more, not meaning any harm?
Othello.
    Naked in bed, Iago, and not mean harm?
    It is hypocrisy against the devil.   6
    They that mean virtuously, and yet do so,
    The devil their virtue tempts, and they tempt heaven.
Iago.
    So they do nothing, 'tis a venial slip.
    But if I give my wife a handkerchief—
Othello.
    What then?
Iago.
    Why, then 'tis hers, my lord; and being hers,
    She may, I think, bestow't on any man.
Othello.
    She is protectress of her honor too;
    May she give that?
Iago.
    Her honor is an essence that's not seen;
    They have it very oft that have it not.
    But for the handkerchief—
Othello.
    By heaven, I would most gladly have forgot it!
    Thou said'st—O, it comes o'er my memory

---

201 *circumstanced* governed by circumstances
    Scene i The environs of the castle   **6** *hyprocrisy . . . devil* i.e. feigned sin instead of feigned
virtue

As doth the raven o'er the infected house,   21
Boding to all!—he had my handkerchief.

Iago.

Ay, what of that?

Othello.   That's not so good now.

Iago.   What

If I had said I had seen him do you wrong?
Or heard him say—as knaves be such abroad
Who having, by their own importunate suit,
Or voluntary dotage of some mistress,
Convincèd or supplied them, cannot choose   28
But they must blab—

Othello.   Hath he said anything?

Iago.

He hath, my lord; but be you well assured,
No more than he'll unswear.

Othello.   What hath he said?

Iago.

Faith, that he did—I know not what he did.

Othello. What? what?

Iago.

Lie—

Othello. With her?

Iago.   With her, on her; what you will.

Othello. Lie with her? lie on her?—We say lie on her when they belie
her.—Lie with her! Zounds, that's fulsome.—Handkerchief—
confessions—handkerchief!— To confess, and be hanged for his
labor—first to be hanged, and then to confess! I tremble at it. Nature   38
would not invest herself in such shadowing passion without some
instruction. It is not words that shakes me thus.—Pish! Noses, ears,
and lips? Is't possible?—Confess?—Handkerchief?—O devil!

Falls in a trance.

Iago. Work on,
My med'cine, work! Thus credulous fools are caught,
And many worthy and chaste dames even thus,
All guiltless, meet reproach.—What, ho! my lord!
My lord, I say! Othello!

Enter Cassio.   How now, Cassio?

Cassio.

What's the matter?

Iago.

My lord is fall'n into an epilepsy.
This is his second fit; he had one yesterday.

Cassio.

Rub him about the temples.

---

21 *infected* plague-stricken   **28** *Convincèd or supplied* overcome or gratified   **38–40**
Nature . . . instruction my natural faculties would not be so overcome by passion without reason

Iago.   No, forbear.
　　The lethargy must have his quiet course.   51
　　If not, he foams at mouth, and by and by
　　Breaks out to savage madness. Look, he stirs.
　　Do you withdraw yourself a little while.
　　He will recover straight. When he is gone,
　　I would on great occasion speak with you.   *Exit Cassio.*
　　How is it, general? Have you not hurt your head?
Othello.
　　Dost thou mock me?
Iago.   I mock you? No, by heaven.
　　Would you would bear your fortune like a man!
Othello.
　　A hornèd man 's a monster and a beast.   60
Iago.
　　There's many a beast then in a populous city,
　　And many a civil monster.
Othello.
　　Did he confess it?
Iago.   Good sir, be a man.
　　Think every bearded fellow that's but yoked
　　May draw with you. There's millions now alive
　　That nightly lie in those unproper beds   66
　　Which they dare swear peculiar: your case is better.   67
　　O, 'tis the spite of hell, the fiend's arch-mock,
　　To lip a wanton in a secure couch,   69
　　And to suppose her chaste! No, let me know;
　　And knowing what I am, I know what she shall be.
Othello.
　　O, thou art wise! 'Tis certain.
Iago.   Stand you awhile apart;
　　Confine yourself but in a patient list.   73
　　Whilst you were here, o'erwhelmèd with your grief—
　　A passion most unsuiting such a man—
　　Cassio came hither. I shifted him away
　　And laid good'scuse upon your ecstasy;   77
　　Bade him anon return, and he speak with me;
　　The which he promised. Do but encave yourself   79
　　And mark the fleers, the gibes, and notable scorns
　　That dwell in every region of his face;
　　For I will make him tell the tale anew—
　　Where, how, how oft, how long ago, and when
　　He hath, and is again to cope your wife.   84
　　I say, but mark his gesture. Marry, patience!
　　Or I shall say y'are all in all in spleen,   86
　　And nothing of a man.

51 *lethargy* coma　**60** *hornèd man* cuckold　**66** *unproper* not exclusively their own　**67**
peculiar exclusively their own　**69** *secure* free from fear of rivalry　**73** *in a patient list* within the
limits of self-control　**77** *ecstasy* trance　**79** *encave* conceal　**84** *cope* meet　**86** *all in all in spleen*
wholly overcome by your passion

Othello.   Dost thou hear, Iago?
   I will be found most cunning in my patience;
   But—dost thou hear?—most bloody.
Iago.   That's not amiss;
   But yet keep time in all. Will you withdraw?
   (Othello retires)
   Now will I question Cassio of Bianca,
   A huswife that by selling her desires   92
   Buys herself bread and clothes. It is a creature
   That dotes on Cassio, as 'tis the strumpet's plague
   To beguile many and be beguiled by one.
   He, when he hears of her, cannot refrain
   From the excess of laughter. Here he comes.

   Enter Cassio.

   As he shall smile, Othello shall go mad;
   And his unbookish jealousy must conster   99
   Poor Cassio's smiles, gestures, and light behavior
   Quite in the wrong. How do you now, lieutenant?
Cassio.
   The worser that you give me the addition   102
   Whose want even kills me.
Iago.
   Ply Desdemona well, and you are sure on't.
   Now, if this suit lay in Bianca's power,
   How quickly should you speed!
Cassio.   Alas, poor caitiff!   106
Othello.
   Look how he laughs already!
Iago.
   I never knew a woman love man so.
Cassio.
   Alas, poor rogue! I think, i' faith, she loves me.
Othello.
   Now he denies it faintly, and laughs it out.
Iago.
   Do you hear, Cassio?
Othello.   Now he importunes him
   To tell it o'er. Go to! Well said, well said!
Iago.
   She gives it out that you shall marry her.
   Do you intend it?
Cassio. Ha, ha, ha!
Othello.
   Do you triumph, Roman? Do you triumph?
Cassio. I marry her? What, a customer? Prithee bear some charity to my   117
   wit; do not think it so unwholesome. Ha, ha, ha!

   92 *huswif* hussy   **99** *unbookish* uninstructed; *conster* construe, interpret   **102** *addition*
title   **106** *caitiff* wretch   **117** *customer* prostitute

Othello. So, so, so, so! They laugh that win!

Iago.

Faith, the cry goes that you shall marry her.

Cassio. Prithee say true.

Iago. I am a very villain else.

Othello. Have you scored me? Well. 123

Cassio. This is the monkey's own giving out. She is persuaded I will marry her out of her own love and flattery, not out of my promise.

Othello. Iago beckons me; now he begins the story. 126

Cassio. She was here even now; she haunts me in every place. I was t' other day talking on the sea bank with certain Venetians, and thither comes the bauble, and, by this hand, she falls me thus about my neck— 129

Othello. Crying "O dear Cassio!" as it were. His gesture imports it.

Cassio. So hangs, and lolls, and weeps upon me; so shakes and pulls me! Ha, ha, ha!

Othello. Now he tells how she plucked him to my chamber. O, I see that nose of yours, but not that dog I shall throw it to.

Cassio. Well, I must leave her company.

Enter Bianca

Iago. Before me! Look where she comes.

Cassio. 'Tis such another fitchew! marry, a perfumed one. What do you 137 mean by this haunting of me?

Bianca. Let the devil and his dam haunt you! What did you mean by that same handkerchief you gave me even now? I was a fine fool to take it. I must take out the whole work? A likely piece of work that you should find it in your chamber and know not who left it there! This is some minx's token, and I must take out the work? There! Give it your hobby-horse. Wheresoever you had it, I'll take out no work on't. 144

Cassio. How now, my sweet Bianca? How now? how now?

Othello. By heaven, that should be my handkerchief!

Bianca. An you'll come to supper to-night, you may; an you will not, come when you are next prepared for. *Exit.*

Iago. After her, after her!

Cassio. Faith, I must; she'll rail in the street else.

Iago. Will you sup there?

Cassio. Yes, I intend so.

Iago. Well, I may chance to see you; for I would very fain speak with you.

Cassio. Prithee come. Will you?

Iago. Go to! say no more. *Exit Cassio.*

Othello (comes forward) How shall I murder him, Iago,?

Iago. Did you perceive how he laughed at his vice? 158

Othello. O Iago!

Iago. And did you see the handkerchief?

Othello. Was that mine?

---

123 *scored me* settled my account (?) **126** *beckons* signals **129** *bauble* plaything **137** *fitchew* polecat (slang for whore) **144** *hobby-horse* harlot **158** *vice* i.e. vicious conduct

Iago. Yours, by this hand! And to see how he prizes the foolish woman your 162
wife! She gave it him, and he hath giv'n it his whore.

Othello. I would have him nine years a-killing!—A fine woman! a fair
woman! a sweet woman!

Iago. Nay, you must forget that.

Othello. Ay, let her rot, and perish, and be damned to-night; for she shall
not live. No, my heart is turned to stone; I strike it, and it hurts my
hand. O, the world hath not a sweeter creature! She might lie by an
emperor's side and command him tasks.

Iago. Nay, that's not your way.

Othello. Hang her! I do but say what she is. So delicate with her needle! an
admirable musician! O, she will sing the savageness out of a bear! Of so
high and plenteous wit and invention— 174

Iago. She's the worse for all this.

Othello. O, a thousand thousand times! And then, of so gentle a condition! 176

Iago. Ay, too gentle.

Othello. Nay, that's certain. But yet the pity of it, Iago! O Iago, the pity of it,
Iago!

Iago. If you are so fond over her iniquity, give her patent to offend; for if it 180
touch not you, it comes near nobody.

Othello. I will chop her into messes! Cuckold me!

Iago. O, 'tis foul in her.

Othello. With mine officer!

Iago. That's fouler.

Othello. Get me some poison, Iago, this night. I'll not
expostulate with her, lest her body and beauty un- 187
provide my mind again. This night, Iago!

Iago. Do it not with poison. Strangle her in her bed, even
the bed she hath contaminated.

Othello. Good, good! The justice of it pleases. Very good!

Iago. And for Cassio, let me be his undertaker: you shall hear more by 192
midnight.

Othello.
Excellent good!
A trumpet.   What tumpet is that same?
Iago.
I warrant something from Venice.

Enter Lodovico, Desdemona, and attendants.

'Tis Lodovico.

This comes from the Duke; and see, your wife is with him.

Lodovico.
God save you, worthy general!
Othello.   With all my heart, sir.
Lodovico.
The Duke and senators of Venice greet you.

162 *prizes* values   174 *invention* imagination   176 *condition* disposition   180 *patent*
license   187–88 *unprovide* disarm   192 *be his undertaker* undertake to deal with him

(Gives him a letter.)
Othello.
> I kiss the instrument of their pleasures.
> *(Opens the letter and reads.)*

Desdemona.
> And what's the news, good cousin Lodovico?

Iago.
> I am very glad to see you, signior.
> Welcome to Cyprus.

Lodovico.
> I thank you. How does Lieutenant Cassio?

Iago.   Lives, sir.

Desdemona.
> Cousin, there's fall'n between him and my lord
> An unkind breach; but you shall make all well.

Othello. Are you sure of that?

Desdemona. My lord?

Othello *(reads).* "This fail you not to do, as you will—"

Lodovico.
> He did not call; he's busy in the paper.
> Is there division 'twixt thy lord and Cassio?

Desdemona.
> A most unhappy one. I would do much
> T'atone them, for the love I bear to Cassio?   212

Othello.
> Fire and brimstone!

Desdemona.   My lord?

Othello.   Are you wise?

Desdemona.
> What, is he angry?

Lodovico.   May be the letter moved him;
> For, as I think, they do command him home,
> Deputing Cassio in his government.

Desdemona.
> By my troth, I am glad on't.

Othello.   Indeed?

Desdemona.   My lord?

Othello.
> I am glad to see you mad.   218

Desdemona.   Why, sweet Othello—

Othello. Devil!
> *(Strikes her)*

Desdemona. I have not deserved this.

Lodovico.
> My lord, this would not be believed in Venice,
> Though I should swear I saw't. 'Tis very much.
> Make her amends; she weeps.

212 *atone* reconcile   218 *mad* i.e. waggish

Othello. O devil, devil!
    If that the earth could teem with woman's tears,   224
    Each drop she falls would prove a crocodile.   225
    Out of my sight!
Desdemona.   I will not stay to offend you.   *(Going.)*
Lodovico.
    Truly, an obedient lady.
    I do beseech your lordship call her back.
Othello.
    Mistress!
Desdemona. My lord?
Othello.   What would you with her, sir?
Lodovico.
    Who? I, my lord?
Othello.
    Ay! You did wish that I would make her turn.
    Sir, she can turn, and turn, and yet go on
    And turn again; and she can weep, sir, weep;
    And she's obedient; as you say, obedient,
    Very obedient.—Proceed you in your tears.—
    Concerning this, sir—O well-painted passion!—   236
    I am commanded home.—Get you away;
    I'll send for you anon.—Sir, I obey the mandate
    And will return to Venice.—Hence, avaunt!

                Exit Desdemona.

    Cassio shall have my place. And, sir, to-night
    I do entreat that we may sup together.
    You are welcome, sir, to Cyprus.—Goats and monkeys!

                    Exit.

Lodovico.
    Is this the noble Moor whom our full Senate
    Call all in all sufficient? Is this the nature
    Whom passion could not shake? whose solid virtue
    The shot of accident nor dart of chance
    Could neither graze nor pierce?
Iago.   He is much changed.
Lodovico.
    Are his wits safe? Is he not light of brain?
Iago.
    He's that he is; I may not breath my censure.
    What he might be—if what he might he is not—
    I would to heaven he were!
Lodovico.   What, strike his wife?
Iago.
    Faith, that was not so well; yet would I knew
    That stroke would prove the worst!

---

  224 *teem* breed   **225** *crocodile* (crocodiles were supposed to shed hypocritical tears to lure men to destruction)   **236** *passion* grief

Lodovico.   Is it his use?   253
    Or did the letters work upon his blood
    And new-create this fault?
Iago.   Alas, alas!
    It is not honesty in me to speak.
    What I have seen and known. You shall observe him,
    And his own courses will denote him so
    That I may save my speech. Do but go after
    And mark how he continues.
Lodovico.
    I am sorry that I am deceived in him.   *Exeunt.*

Scene ii

    Enter Othello and Emilia.

Othello.
    You have seen nothing then?
Emilia.
    Nor ever heard, nor ever did suspect.
Othello.
    Yes, you have seen Cassio and she together.
Emilia.
    But then I saw no harm, and then I heard
    Each syllable that breath made up between them.
Othello.
    What, did they never whisper?
Emilia.   Never, my lord.
Othello.
    Nor send you out o' th' way?
Emilia. Never.
Othello.
    To fetch her fan, her gloves, her mask, nor nothing?
Emilia. Never, my lord.
Othello. That's strange.
Emilia.
    I durst, my lord, to wager she is honest,
    Lay down my soul as stake. If you think other,
    Remove your thought; it doth abuse your bosom.   14
    If any wretch have put this in your head,
    Let heaven requite it with the serpent's curse!   16
    For if she be not honest, chaste, and true,
    There's no man happy; the purest of their wives
    Is foul as slander.
Othello.   Bid her come hither. Go.   *Exit Emilia.*
    She says enough; yet she's a simple bawd
    That cannot say as much. This is a subtle whore,

---

253 *use* custom
    Scene ii Within the castle   14 *abuse . . . bosom* deceive your heart   16 *serpent's curse* (cf.
Genesis iii, 14)

A closet lock and key of villanous secrets;
And yet she'll kneel and pray; I have seen her do't.

Enter Desdemona and Emilia.

Desdemona.
My lord, what is you will?
Othello.   Pray, chuck, come hither.
Desdemona.
What is your pleasure?
Othello.   Let me see your eyes.
Look in my face.
Desdemona.   What horrible fancy's this?
Othello *(to Emilia).*
Some of your function, mistress.
Leave procreants alone and shut the door;   28
Cough or cry hem if anybody come.
Your mystery, your mystery! Nay, dispatch!   30

Exit Emilia.

Desdemona.
Upon my knees, what doth your speech import?
I understand a fury in your words,
[But not the words.]
Othello.
Why, what art thou?
Desdemona.   Your wife, my lord; your true
And loyal wife.
Othello.   Come, swear it, damn thyself;
Lest, being like one of heaven, the devils themselves   36
Should fear to seize thee. Therefore be double-damned—
Swear thou art honest.   38
Desdemona.   Heaven doth truly know it.
Othello.
Heaven truly knows that thou art false as hell.
Desdemona.
To whom, my lord? With whom? How am I false?
Othello.
Ah, Desdemon! away! away! away!
Desdemona.
Alas the heavy day! Why do you weep?
Am I the motive of these tears, my lord?
If haply you my father do suspect
An instrument of this your calling back,   45
Lay not your blame on me. If you have lost him,
Why, I have lost him too.
Othello.   Had it pleased heaven
To try me with affliction, had they rained

---

28 *procreants* mating couples **30** *mystery* trade, occpuation **36** *being . . . heaven* looking like
an angel **38** *honest* chaste **45** *An instrument* to be the cause

All kinds of sores and shames on my bare head,
Steeped me in poverty to the very lips,
Given to captivity me and my utmost hopes,
I should have found in some place of my soul
A drop of patience. But, alas, to make me
A fixèd figure for the time of scorn   54
To point his slow unmoving finger at!
Yet could I bear that too; well, very well.
But there where I have garnered up my heart,
Where either I must live or bear no life,
The fountain from the which my current runs
Or else dries up—to be discarded thence,
Or keep it as a cistern for fouls toads
To knot and gender in—turn thy complexion there,   62
Patience, thou young and rose-lipped cherubin!
Ay, there look grim as hell!

Desdemona.

I hope my noble lord esteems me honest.

Othello.

O, ay; as summer flies are in the shambles,   66
That quicken even with blowing. O thou weed,   67
Who art so lovely fair, and smell'st so sweet,
That the sense aches at thee, would thou hadst ne'er
    been born!

Desdemona.

Alas, what ignorant sin have I committed?

Othello.

Was this fair paper, this most goodly book,
Made to write "whore" upon? What committed?
Committed? O thou public commoner!   73
I should make very forges of my cheeks
That would to cinders burn up modesty,
Did I but speak thy deeds. What committed?
Heaven stops the nose at it, and the moon winks;   77
The bawdy wind, that kisses all it meets,
Is hushed within the hollow mine of earth
And will not hear it. What committed?
Impudent strumpet!

Desdemona.   By heaven, you do me wrong!

Othello.

Are not you a strumpet?

Desdemona.   No, as I am a Christian!

If to preserve this vessel for my lord
From any other foul unlawful touch
Be not to be a strumpet, I am none.

---

54 *time of scorn* scornful world   **62** *turn thy complexion there* change thy color at that point   **66** *shambles* slaughterhouse   **67** *quicken* come to life **73** *commoner* harlot   **77** *winks* closes her eyes

Othello.

    What, not a whore?

Desdemona.   No, as I shall be saved!

Othello. Is't possible?

Desdemona.

    O, heaven forgive us!

Othello.   I cry you mercy then.   88

    I took you for that cunning whore of Venice

    That married with Othello.—*(calling)* You, mistress,

    That have the office opposite to Saint Peter

    And keep the gate of hell!

    Enter Emilia.   You, you, ay, you!

    We have done our course; there's money for your pains:

    I pray you turn the key, and keep our counsel.   *Exit.*

Emilia.

    Alas, what does this gentleman conceive?

    How do you, madam? How do you, my good lady?

Desdemona. Faith, half asleep.   97

Emilia.

    Good madam, what's the matter with my lord?

Desdemona. With who?

Emilia. Why, with my lord, madam.

Desdemona.

    Who is thy lord?

Emilia.   He that is yours, sweet lady.

Desdemona.

    I have none. Do not talk to me, Emilia.

    I cannot weep; nor answers have I none

    But what should go by water. Prithee to-night

    Lay on my bed my wedding sheets, remember;

    And call thy husband hither.

Emilia.   Here's a change indeed!   *Exit.*

Desdemona.

    'Tis meet I should be used so, very meet.

    How have I been behaved, that he might stick

    The small'st opinion on my least misuse?   109

    Enter Iago and Emilia.

Iago.

    What is your pleasure, madam? How is't with you?

Desdemona.

    I cannot tell. Those that do teach young babes

    Do it with gentle means and easy tasks:

    He might have chid me so; for, in good faith,

    I am a child to chiding.

---

88 *cry you mercy* beg your pardon   **97** *half asleep* i.e. stunned   **109** *small'st opinion* least
suspicion; *least misuse* slightest misconduct

Iago.   What is the matter, lady?

Emilia.

Alas, Iago, my lord hath so bewhored her,
Thrown such despite and heavy terms upon her
As true hearts cannot bear.

Desdemona.

Am I that name, Iago.?

Iago.   What name, fair lady?

Desdemona.

Such as she said my lord did say I was.

Emilia.

He called her whore. A beggar in his drink
Could not have laid such terms upon his callet.   121

Iago.

Why did he so?

Desdemona.

I do not know; I am sure I am none such.

Iago.

Do not weep, do not weep. Alas the day!

Emilia.

Hath she forsook so many noble matches,
Her father and her country, and her friends,
To be called whore? Would it not make one weep?

Desdemona.

It is my wretched fortune.

Iago.   Beshrew him for't!
How comes this trick upon him?   129

Desdemona.   Nay, heaven doth know.

Emilia.

I will be hanged if some eternal villain,
Some busy and insinuating rogue,
Some cogging, cozening slave, to get some office,   132
Have not devised this slander. I'll be hanged else.

Iago.

Fie, there is no such man! It is impossible.

Desdemona.

If any such there be, heaven pardon him!

Emilia.

A halter pardon him! and hell gnaw his bones!
Why should he call her whore? Who keeps her
    company?
What place? what time? what form? what likelihood?
The Moor's abused by some most villainous knave,
Some base notorious knave, some scurvy fellow.
O heaven, that such companions thou'dst unfold,   141
And put in every honest hand a whip

---

121 *callet* whore   129 *trick* freakish behavior   132 *cogging, cozening* cheating,
defrauding   141 *companions* rogues; *unfold* expose

To lash the rascals naked through the world
Even from the east to th' west!
Iago.   Speak within door.   144
Emilia.
    O, fie upon them! Some such squire he was
    That turned your wit the seamy side without
    And made you to suspect me with the Moor.
Iago.
    You are a fool. Go to.
Desdemona.   Alas, Iago,
    What shall I do to win my lord again?
    Good friend, go to him; for, by this light of heaven,
    I know not how I lost him. Here I kneel:
    If e'er my will did trespass 'gainst his love
    Either in discourse of thought or actual deed,   153
    Or that mine eyes, mine ears, or any sense
    Delighted them in any other form,
    Or that I do not yet, and ever did,
    And ever will (though he do shake me off
    To beggarly divorcement) love him dearly,
    Comfort forswear me! Unkindness may do much;   159
    And his unkindness may defeat my life,   160
    But never taint my love. I cannot say "whore."
    It does abhor me now I speak the word;
    To do the act that might the addition earn
    Not the world's mass of vanity could make me.
Iago.
    I pray you be content. 'Tis but his humor.
    The business of the state does him offense,
    And he does chide with you.
Desdemona.
    If 'twere no other
Iago.   'Tis but so, I warrant.
    (Trumpets within.)
    Hark how these instruments summon you to supper.
    The messengers of Venice stay the meat:
    Go in, and weep not. All things shall be well.
                              Exeunt Desdemona and Emilia.

Enter Roderigo.

    How now, Roderigo?

Roderigo. I do not find that thou deal'st justly with me.
Iago. What in the contrary?
Roderigo. Every day thou daff'st me with some device, Iago, and rather, as   175
    it seems to me now, keep'st from me all conveniency than suppliest me   176

---

144 *within door* with restraint   **153** *discourse* course   **159** *Comfort forswear* happiness
forsake   **160** *defeat* destroy   **175** *thou . . . device* you put me off with some trick   **176** *conveniency*
favorable opportunities

William Shakespeare

with the least advantage of hope. I will indeed no longer endure it; nor
am I yet persuaded to put up in peace what already I have foolishly
suffered.

Iago. Will you hear me, Roderigo?

Roderigo. Faith, I have heard too much; for your words and performances
are no kin together.

Iago. You charge me most unjustly.

Roderigo. With naught but truth. I have wasted myself out of my means.
The jewels you have had from me to deliver to Desdemona would half
have corrupted a votarist. You have told me she hath received them, and 186
returned me expectations and comforts of sudden respect and   187
acquaintance; but I find none.

Iago. Well, go to; very well.

Roderigo. Very well! go to! I cannot go to, man; nor 'tis not very well. By
this hand, I say 'tis very scurvy, and begin to find myself fopped in it.   191

Iago. Very well.

Roderigo. I tell you 'tis not very well. I will make myself known to
Desdemona. If she will return me my jewels, I will give over my suit and
repent my unlawful solicitation; if not, assure yourself I will seek
satisfaction of you.

Iago. You have said now.

Roderigo. Ay, and said nothing but what I protest intendment of doing.

Iago. Why, now I see there's mettle in thee; and even from this instant do
build on thee a better opinion than ever before. Give me thy hand,
Roderigo. Thou hast taken against me a most just exception; but yet I
protest I have dealt most directly in thy affair.   202

Roderigo. It hath not appeared.

Iago. I grant indeed it hath not appeared, and your suspicion is not
without wit and judgment. But, Roderigo, if thou hast that in thee
indeed which I have greater reason to believe now than ever, I mean
purpose, courage, and valor, this night show it. If thou the next night
following enjoy not Desdemona, take me from this world with treachery
and devise engines for my life.   209

Roderigo. Well, what is it? Is it within reason and compass?

Iago. Sir, there is especial commission come from Venice to depute Cassio
in Othello's place.

Roderigo. Is that true? Why, then Othello and Desdemona return again to
Venice.

Iago. O, no; he goes into Mauritania and takes away with him the fair
Desdemona, unless his abode be lingered here by some accident;   216
wherein none can be so determinate as the removing of Cassio.   217

Roderigo. How do you mean removing of him?

Iago. Why, by making him uncapable of Othello's place—knocking out his
brains.

Roderigo. And that you would have me to do?

Iago. Ay, if you dare do yourself a profit and a right. He sups to-night with

---

186 *votarist* nun   187 *sudden respect* immediate notice   191 *fopped* duped   202 *directly*
straightforwardly   209 *engines for* plots against   216 *abode . . . here* stay here be extended   217
determinate effective

a harlotry, and thither will I go to him. He knows not yet of his
honorable fortune. If you will watch his going thence, which I will
fashion to fall out between twelve and one, you may take him at your
pleasure. I will be near to second your attempt, and he shall fall between
us. Come, stand not amazed at it, but go along with me. I will show you
such a necessity in his death that you shall think yourself bound to put
it on him. It is now high supper time, and the night grows to waste.
About it!

Roderigo. I will hear further reason for this.

Iago. And you shall be satisfied.   *Exeunt.*

Scene iii

Enter Othello, Lodovico, Desdemona, Emilia, and attendants.

Lodovico.
I do beseech you, sir, trouble yourself no further.

Othello.
O, pardon me; 'twill do me good to walk.

Lodovico.
Madam, good night, I humbly thank your ladyship.

Desdemona.
Your honor is most welcome.

Othello.   Will you walk, sir?
O, Desdemona—

Desdemona. My lord?

Othello. Get you to bed on th' instant; I will be returned forthwith. Dismiss
your attendant there. Look't be done.

Desdemona. I will, my lord.
                    Exit Othello, with Lodovico and attendants.

Emilia. How goes it now? He looks gentler than he did.

Desdemona.
He says he will return incontinent.   11
He hath commanded me to go to bed,
And bade me to dismiss you.

Emilia.   Dismiss me?

Desdemona.
It was his bidding; therefore, good Emilia,
Give me my nightly wearing, and adieu.
We must not now displease him.

Emilia. I would you had never seen him!

Desdemona.
So would not I. My love doth so approve him
That even his stubbornness, his checks, his frowns—   19
Prithee unpin me—have grace and favor in them.

Emilia. I have laid those sheets you bade me on the bed.

Desdemona.
All's one. Good faith, how foolish our minds!

Scene iii Within the castle   **11** *incontinent* at once   **19** *stubbornness* roughness; *checks*
rebukes

If I do die before thee, prithee shroud me
In one of those same sheets.
Emilia.   Come, come! You talk.
Desdemona.
My mother had a maid called Barbary.
She was in love; and he she loved proved mad   26
And did forsake her. She had a song of "Willow";
An old thing 'twas; but it expressed her fortune,
And she died singing it. That song to-night
Will not go from my mind; I have much to do
But to go hang my head all at one side
And sing it like poor Barbary. Prithee dispatch.
Emilia.
Shall I go fetch your nightgown?   33
Desdemona.   No, unpin me here.
This Lodovico is a proper man.
Emilia. A very handsome man.
Desdemona. He speaks well.
Emilia. I know a lady in Venice would have walked bare-
foot to Palestine for a touch of his nether lip.
Desdemona *(sings).*
"The poor soul sat sighing by a sycamore tree,
    Sing all a green willow;
Her hand on her bosom, her head on her knee,
    Sing willow, willow, willow.
The fresh streams ran by her and murmured her moans;
    Sing willow, willow, willow;
Her salt tears fell from her, and soft'ned the stones"—
Lay by these.
    "Sing willow, willow, willow"—
Prithee hie thee; he'll come anon.   48
    "Sing all a green willow must be my garland.
    Let nobody blame him; his scorn I approve"—
Nay, that's not next. Hark! who is't that knocks?
Emilia. It's the wind.
Desdemona *(sings).*
"I called my love false love; but what said he then?
    Sing willow, willow, willow:
If I court moe women, you'll couch with moe men."
So, get thee gone; good night. Mine eyes do itch.
Doth that bode weeping?
Emilia.   'Tis neither here nor there.
Desdemona.
I have heard it said so. O, these men, these men!
Dost thou in conscience think—tell me, Emilia—
That there be women do abuse their husbands   60
In such gross kind?

---

26 *mad* wild, faithless   **33** *nightgown* dressing gown   **48** *hie thee* hurry

Emilia.   There be some such, no question.

Desdemona.
     Wouldst thou do such a deed for all the world?

Emilia.
     Why, would not you?

Desdemona.   No, by this heavenly light!

Emilia.
     Nor I neither by this heavenly light.
     I might do't as well i' th' dark.

Desdemona.
     Wouldst thou do such as deed for all the world?

Emilia. The world's a huge thing; it is a great price for a small vice.

Desdemona.
     In troth, I think thou wouldst not.

Emilia. In troth, I think I should; and undo't when I had done it. Marry, I
     would not do such a thing for a joint-ring, nor for measures of lawn,   70
     nor for gowns, petticoats, nor caps, nor any petty exhibition; but, for all 71
     the whole world—'Ud's pity! who would not make her husband a
     cuckold to make him a monarch? I should venture purgatory for't.

Desdemona.
     Beshrew me if I would do such a wrong
     For the whole world.

Emilia. Why, the wrong is but a wrong i' th' world; and having the world for
     your labor, 'tis a wrong in your own world, and you might quickly make
     it right.

Desdemona. I do not think there is any such woman.

Emilia. Yes, a dozen; and as many to th' vantage as would store the world   80
     they played for.
     But I do think it is their husbands' faults
     If wives do fall. Say that they slack their duties
     And pour our treasures into foreign laps;
     Or else break out in peevish jealousies,   85
     Throwing restraint upon us; or say they strike us,
     Or scant our former having in despite—   87
     Why, we have galls; and though we have some grace,   88
     Yet have we some revenge. Let husbands know
     Their wives have sense like them. They see, and smell,
     And have their palates both for sweet and sour,
     As husbands have. What is it that they do
     When they change us for others? Is it sport?
     I think it is. And doth affection breed it?
     I think it doth. Is't frailty that thus errs?
     It is so too. And have not we affections,
     Desires for sport, and frailty, as men have?
     Then let them use us well; else let them know,
     The ills we do, their ills instruct us so.

---

    70 *joint-ring* ring made in separable halves   **71** *exhibition* gift   **80** *to th' vantage* besides; *store*
populate   **85** *peevish* senseless   **87** *having* allowance   **88** *galls* spirits to resent

Desdemona.

Good night, good night. God me such usage send,   100
Not to pick from bad, but by bad mend!   *Exeunt.*

ACT V

Scene i

Enter Iago and Roderigo.

Iago.

Here, stand behind this bulk; straight will he come.
Wear thy good rapier bare, and put it home.
Quick, quick! Fear nothing; I'll be at thy elbow.
It makes us, or it mars us—think on that,
And fix most firm thy resolution.

Roderigo.

Be near at hand; I may miscarry in't.

Iago.

Here, at thy hand. Be bold, and take thy stand.
(Stands aside.)

Roderigo.

I have no great devotion to the deed,
And yet he hath given me satisfying reasons.
'Tis but a man gone. Forth my sword! He dies!

Iago.

I have rubbed this young quat almost to the sense,   11
And he grows angry. Now whether he kill Cassio,
Or Cassio him, or each do kill the other,
Every way makes by gain. Live Roderigo,
He calls me to a restitution large
Of gold and jewels that I bobbed from him   16
As gifts to Desdemona.
It must not be. If Cassio do remain,
He hath a daily beauty in his life.
That makes me ugly; and besides, the Moor
May unfold me to him; there stand I in much peril.
No, he must die. Be't so! I hear him coming.

Enter Cassio.

Roderigo.

I know his gait. 'Tis he. Villain, thou diest!
(Makes a pass at Cassio.)

Cassio.

That thrust had been mine enemy indeed
But that my coat is better than thou know'st.   25

---

100 *usage* habits
Scene i A street in Cyrpus   **1** *bulk* projecting shop-front   **11** *quat* pimple; *sense* quick   **16**
bobbed swindled   **25** *coat* under-shirt of mail

I will make proof of thine.
(Draws, and wounds Roderigo.)
Roderigo.   O, I am slain!
        (Iago darts from concealment behind Cassio,
             wounds him in the leg, and exit.)

Cassio.
    I am maimed for ever. Help, ho! Murder! murder!
    (Falls.)

    Enter Othello.

Othello.
    The voice of Cassio. Iago keeps his word.
Roderigo.
    O, villain that I am!
Othello.   It is even so.
Cassio.
    O, help, ho! light! a surgeon!
Othello.
    'Tis he. O brave Iago, honest and just,
    That hast such noble sense of thy friend's wrong!
    Thou teachest me. Minion, your dear lies dead,   33
    And your unblest fate hies. Strumpet, I come.   34
    Forth or my heart those charms, thine eyes, are blotted.
    Thy bed, lust-stained, shall with lust's blood be spotted.
                                 Exit Othello.

    Enter Lodovico and Gratiano.

Cassio.
    What, ho? No watch? No passage? Murder! murder!   37
Gratiano.
    'Tis some mischance. The cry is very direful.
Cassio. O, help!
Lodovico. Hark!
Roderigo. O wretched villain!
Lodovico.
    Two or three groan. It is a heavy night.   42
    These may be counterfeits. Let's think't unsafe
    To come in to the cry without more help.
Roderigo.
    Nobody come? Then shall I bleed to death.
Lodovico. Hark!

    Enter Iago, with a light.

Gratiano.
    Here's one comes in his shirt, with light and weapons.
Iago.
    Who's there? Whose noise is this that cries on murder?   48

---

    33 *Minion* mistress   **34** *hies* hurries on   **37** *passage* passers-by   **42** *heavy* cloudy, dark   **48**
cries on raises the cry of

Lodovico.

　We do not know.

Iago.　　　　　　　Did not you hear a cry?

Cassio.

　Here, here! For heaven's sake, help me!

Iago.　　　　　　　　　　What's the matter?

Gratiano.

　This is Othello's ancient, as I take it.

Lodovico.

　The same indeed, a very valiant fellow.

Iago.

　What are you here that cry so grievously?

Cassio.

　Iago? O, I am spoiled, undone by villains!
　Give me some help.

Iago.

　O me, lieutenant! What villains have done this?

Cassio.

　I think that one of them is hereabout
　And cannot make away.　　　　　　　　　　　　58

Iago.　　　　　　　　O treacherous villains!
　(To Lodovico and Gratiano.)
　What are you there? Come in, and give some help.

Roderigo.

　O, help me here!

Cassio.

　That's one of them.

Iago.　　　　　　　O mur'drous slave! O villain!
　(Stabs Roderigo.)

Roderigo.

　O damned Iago! O inhuman dog!

Iago.

　Kill men i' th' dark?—Where be these bloody thieves?—
　How silent is this town!—Ho! murder! murder!—
　What may you be? Are you of good or evil?

Lodovico.

　As you shall prove us, praise us.

Iago. Signior Lodovico?

Lodovico. He, sir.

Iago.

　I cry you mercy. Here's Cassio hurt by villains.

Gratiano. Cassio?

Iago. How is't, brother?

Cassio.

　My leg is cut in two.

Iago.　　　　　　　Marry, heaven forbid!　　　　　72
　Light, gentleman. I'll bind it with my shirt.

58 *make* get　**72** *Marry* (from By Mary)

Enter Bianca.

Bianca.
What is the matter, ho? Who is't that cried?
Iago.
Who is't that cried?
Bianca.
O my dear Cassio! my sweet Cassio!
O Cassio, Cassio, Cassio!
Iago.
O notable strumpet!—Cassio, may you suspect
Who they should be that have thus mangled you?
Cassio. No.
Gratiano. I am sorry to find you thus. I have been to seek you.
Iago.
Lend me a garter. So. O for a chair   82
To bear him easily hence!
Bianca.
Alas, he faints! O Cassio, Cassio, Cassio!
Iago.
Gentlemen all, I do suspect this trash
To be a party in this injury.—
Patience awhile, good Cassio.—Come, come!
Lend me a light. Know we this face or no?
Alas, my friend and my dear countryman
Roderigo? No.—Yes, sure.—O heaven, Roderigo!
Gratiano. What, of Venice?
Iago.
Even he, sir. Did you know him?
Gratiano.   Know him? Ay.
Iago.
Signior Gratiano? I cry your gentle pardon.
These bloody accidents must excuse my manners
That so neglected you.
Gratiano.   I am glad to see you.
Iago.
How do you, Cassio?—O, a chair, a chair!
Gratiano. Roderigo?
Iago.
He, he, 'tis he!
(A chair brought in.) O, that's well said; the chair.   98
Some good man bear him carefully from hence.
I'll fetch the general's surgeon.
(To Bianca)   For you, mistress,
Save you your labor.—He that lies slain here, Cassio,
Was my dear friend. What malice was between you?

82 *chair* litter   **98** *well said* well done

Cassio.

None in the world; nor do I know the man.

Iago *(to Bianca).*

What, look you pale?—O, bear him out o' th' air.

(Cassio and Roderigo are borne off.)

Stay you, good gentlemen.—Look you pale, mistress?—

Do you perceive the gastness of her eye?— 106

Nay, if you stare, we shall hear more anon.

Behold her well; I pray you look upon her.

Do you see, gentlemen? Nay, guiltiness will speak,

Though tongues were out of use.

Enter Emilia

Emilia.

'Las, what's the matter? What's the matter, husband?

Iago.

Cassio hath here been set on in the dark

By Roderigo, and fellows that are scaped.

He's almost slain, and Roderigo dead.

Emilia.

Alas, good gentleman! alas, good Cassio!

Iago.

This is the fruits of whoring. Prithee, Emilia,

Go know of Cassio where he supped to-night.

(To Bianca)

What, do you shake at that?

Bianca.

He supped at my house; but I therefore shake not.

Iago.

O, did he so? I charge you go with me.

Emilia.

Fie, fie upon thee, strumpet!

Bianca.

I am no strumpet, but of life as honest 122

As you that thus abuse me.

Emilia. As I? Foh! fie upon thee!

Iago.

Kind gentlemen, let's go see poor Cassio dressed.

(To Bianca.)

Come, mistress, you must tell's another tale.

Emilia, run you to the citadel

And tell my lord and lady what hath happed.

Exit Emilia.

Will you go on afore? *Exeunt (all but Iago).*

This is the night

That either makes me or fordoes me quite. *Exit.* 129

106 *gastness* terror   122 *honest* chaste   129 *fordoes* destroys

Scene ii

Desdemona asleep in her bed. Enter Othello with a light.

Othello.
It is the cause, it is the cause, my soul.   1
Let me not name it to you, you chaste stars!
It is the cause. Yet I'll not shed her blood,
Nor scar that whiter skin of hers than snow,
And smooth as monumental alabaster.
Yet she must die, else she'll betray more men.
Put out the light, and then put out the light.
If I quench thee, thou flaming minister,   8
I can again thy former light restore,
Should I repent me; but once put out thy light,
Thou cunning'st pattern of excelling nature,
I know not where is that Promethean heat   12
That can thy light relume. When I have plucked the rose,   13
I cannot give it vital growth again;
It needs must wither. I'll smell thee on the tree.
(He kisses her.)
O balmy breath, that dost almost persuade
Justice to break her sword! One more, one more!
Be thus when thou art dead, and I will kill thee,
And love thee after. One more, and that's the last!
So sweet was ne'er so fatal. I must weep,
But they are cruel tears. This sorrow's heavenly;
It strikes where it doth love. She wakes.

Desdemona.
Who's there? Othello?

Othello.   Ay, Desdemona.

Desdemona.
Will you come to bed, my lord?

Othello.
Have you prayed to-night, Desdemon?

Desdemona.   Ay, my lord.

Othello.
If you bethink yourself of any crime   26
Unreconciled as yet to heaven and grace,
Solicit for it straight.

Desdemona.
Alack, my lord, what may you mean by that?

Othello.
Well, do it, and be brief; I will walk by.
I would not kill thy unpreparèd spirit.
No, heaven forfend! I would not kill thy soul.

Scene ii A bedchamber in the castle   **1** *cause* cause of justice   **8** *minister* servant   **12**
Promethean heat divine fire   **13** *relume* relight   **26** *crime* sin   **322** *forfend* forbid

Desdemona.

Talk you of killing?

Othello.   Ay, I do.

Desdemona.   Then heaven

Have mercy on me!

Othello.   Amen, with all my heart!

Desdemona.

If you say so, I hope you will not kill me.

Othello. Hum!

Desdemona.

And yet I fear you; for you're fatal then

When your eyes roll so. Why I should fear I know not,

Since guiltiness I know not; but yet I feel I fear.

Othello.

Think on thy sins.

Desdemona.   They are loves I bear to you.

Othello.

Ay, and for that thou diest.

Desdemona.

That death's unnatural that kills for loving.

Alas, why gnaw you so your nether lip?

Some bloody passion shakes your very frame.

These are portents; but yet I hope, I hope,   45

They do not point on me.

Othello.   Peace and be still!

Desdemona.

I will so. What's the matter?

Othello.

That handkerchief which I so loved and gave thee

Thou gav'st to Cassio.

Desdemona.   No, by my life and soul!

Send for the man and ask him.

Othello.   Sweet soul, take heed,

Take heed of perjury; thou art on thy deathbed.

Desdemona.

Ay, but not yet to die.

Othello.   Yes, presently.   52

Therefore confess thee freely of thy sin;

For to deny each article with oath

Cannot remove nor choke that strong conception   55

That I do groan withal. Thou art to die.

Desdemona.

Then Lord have mercy on me!

Othello.   I say amen.

Desdemona.

And have you mercy too! I never did

Offend you in my life; never loved Cassio   59

---

45 *portents* signs of impending violence   **52** *presently* at once   **55** *conception* belief   **59** *Offend* wrong

But with such general warranty of heaven
As I might love. I never gave him token.
Othello.
By heaven, I saw my handkerchief in's hand!
O perjured woman! thou dost stone my heart,   63
And mak'st me call what I intend to do
A murder, which I thought a sacrifice.
I saw the handkerchief.
Desdemona.   He found it then.
I never gave it him. Send for him hither.
Let him confess a truth.
Othello.   He hath confessed.
Desdemona.
What, my lord?
Othello.
That he hath used thee.
Desdemona.   How? unlawfully?
Othello.   Ay.
Desdemona.
He will not say so.
Othello.   No, his mouth is stopped.
Honest Iago hath ta'en order for't.   72
Desdemona.
O, my fear interprets. What, is he dead?
Othello.
Had all his hairs been lives, my great revenge
Had stomach for them all.
Desdemona.
Alas, he is betrayed, and I undone!
Othello.
Out, strumpet! Weep'st thou for him to my face?
Desdemona.
O, banish me, my lord, but kill me not!
Othello.
Down, strumpet!
Desdemona.
Kill me to-morrow; let me live to-night!   80
Othello.
Nay, if you strive—
Desdemona.
But half an hour!
Othello.   Being done, there is no pause.
Desdemona.
But while I say on prayer!
Othello.   It is too late.

Smothers her.

63 *stone my heart* turn my heart to stone   **72** *ta'en order* taken measures

Desdemona. O Lord, Lord, Lord!
> *Emilia at the door.*

Emilia *(calls within).*
> My lord, my lord! What, ho! my lord, my lord!

Othello.
> What noise is this? Not dead? not yet quite dead?
> I that am cruel am yet merciful;
> I would not have thee linger in thy pain.
> So, so.

Emilia *(within).*
> What, ho! my lord, my lord!

Othello.   Who's there?

Emilia *(within).*
> O, good my lord, I would speak a word with you!

Othello.
> Yes, 'tis Emilia.—By and by.—She's dead.—   92
> 'Tis like she comes to speak of Cassio's death.
> The noise was here. Ha! no more moving?
> Still as the grave.—Shall she come in? Were't good?—
> I think she stirs again. No.—What's best to do?
> If she come in, she'll sure speak to my wife.
> My wife! my wife! what wife! I have no wife.
> O, insupportable! O heavy hour!
> Methinks it should be now a huge eclipse
> Of sun and moon, and that th'affrighted globe
> Should yawn at yawn at alteration.   102

Emilia *(within).*   I do beseech you
> That I may speak with you, O good my lord!

Othello.
> I had forgot thee. O, come in, Emilia.
> Soft, by and by.—Let me the curtains draw.—
> *(Closes the bed-curtains.)*
> Where art thou?
> *(Opens the door.)*

> *Enter Emilia.*

>   What's the matter with thee now?

Emilia.
> O my good lord, yonder's foul murder done!

Othello. What? Now?

Emilia. But now, my lord.

Othello.
> It is the very error of the moon.   110
> She comes more nearer earth than she was wont
> And makes men mad.

---

92 *By and by* just a moment (addressed to Emilia)   102 *yawn* open, as in an earthquake   110 *error* straying off course

Emilia.
Cassio, my lord, hath killed a young Venetian
Called Roderigo.
Othello.   Roderigo killed?
And Cassio killed?
Emilia.   No, Cassio is not killed.
Othello.
Not Cassio killed? Then murder's out of tune,
And sweet revenge grows harsh
Desdemona.
O, falsely, falsely murdered!
Emilia.   O Lord! what cry is that?
Othello. That? What?
Emilia.
Out and alas! that was my lady's voice.
Help! help, ho! help! O lady, speak again!
Sweet Desdemona! O sweet mistress, speak!
Desdemona.
A guiltless death I die.
Emilia.
O, who hath done this deed?
Desdemona.
Nobody—I myself. Farewell.
Commend me to my kind lord. O, farewell!   126

 She dies.

Othello.
Why, how should she be murd'red?
Emilia.   Alas, who knows?
Othello.
You heard her say herself, it was not I.
Emilia.
She said so. I must needs report the truth.
Othello.
She's like a liar gone to burning hell!
'Twas I that killed her.
Emilia.   O, the more angel she,
And you the blacker devil!
Othello.
She turned to folly, and she was a whore.
Emilia.
Thou dost belie her, and thou art a devil.
Othello.
She was false as water.   135
Emilia.   Thou art rash as fire to say
That she was false. O, she was heavenly true!

126 *Commend* remember   135 *water* (which is yielding)

Othello.

 Cassio did top her. Ask thy husband else.
 O, I were damned beneath all depth in hell
 But that I did proceed upon just grounds
 To this extremity. Thy husband knew it all.

Emilia. My husband?

Othello. Thy husband.

Emilia.

 That she was false to wedlock?

Othello.

 Ay, with Cassio. Nay, had she been true,
 If heaven would make me such another world
 Of one entire and perfect chrysolite,   146
 I'd not have sold her for it.

Emilia.

 My husband?

Othello.   Ay, 'twas he that told me first.
 An honest man he is, and hates the slime
 That sticks on filthy deeds.

Emilia.   My husband?

Othello.

 What needs this iterance, woman? I say thy husband.   151

Emilia.

 O mistress, villainy hath made mocks with love!
 My husband say that she was false?

Othello.   He, woman.
 I say, thy husband. Dost understand the word?
 My friend, thy husband; honest, honest Iago.

Emilia.

 If he say so, may his pernicious soul
 Rot half a grain a day! he lies to th' heart.
 She was too fond of her most filthy bargain.

Othello. Ha!

Emilia. Do thy worst.
 This deed of thine is no more worthy heaven
 Than thou wast worthy her.

Othello.   Peace, you were best.

Emilia.

 Thou hast not half the power to do me harm
 As I have to be hurt. O gull! O dolt!   164
 As ignorant as dirt! thou hast done a deed—
 I care not for thy sword; I'll make thee known,
 Though I lost twenty lives. Help! help! Ho! help!
 The Moor hath killed my mistress! Murder! murder!

Enter Montano, Gratiano, Iago, and others.

---

146 *chrysolite* (precious topaz) 151 *iterance* repetition 164 *to be hurt* to endure hurt

Montano.

    What is the matter? How now, general?

Emilia.

    O, are you come, Iago? You have done well,   170

    That men must lay their murders on your neck.

Gratiano.

    What is the matter?

Emilia.

    Disprove this villain, if thou be'st a man.

    He says thou told'st him that his wife was false.

    I know thou didst not; thou'rt not such a villain.

    Speak, for my heart is full.

Iago.

    I told him what I thought, and told no more

    Than what he found himself was apt and true.

Emilia.

    But did you ever tell him she was false?

Iago. I did.

Emilia.

    You told a lie, an odious damnèd lie!

    Upon my soul, a lie! a wicked lie!

    She false with Cassio? Did you say with Cassio?

Iago.

    With Cassio, mistress. Go to, charm your tongue.   184

Emilia.

    I will not charm my tongue; I am bound to speak:

    My mistress here lies murdered in her bed—

All.

    O heavens forfend!

Emilia.

    And your reports have set the murder on.

Othello.

    Nay, stare not, masters. It is true indeed.

Gratiano.

    'Tis a stange truth.   190

Montano.

    O monstrous act!

Emilia.   Villainy, villainy, villainy!

    I think upon't—I think I smell't!—O villainy!

    I thought so then.—I'll kill myself for grief.—

    O villainy, villainy!

Iago.

    What, are you mad? I charge you get you home.

Emilia.

    Good gentlemen, let me have leave to speak.

184 *charm* cast a spell on

William Shakespeare

'Tis proper I obey him, but not now.
Perchance, Iago, I will ne'er go home.

Othello.

O! O! O!

Falls on the bed.

Emilia. Nay, lay thee down and roar!
For thou hast killed the sweetest innocent
That e'er lift up eye.

Othello.   O, she was foul!

(Rises.)

I scarce did know you, uncle. There lies your niece,
Whose breath, indeed, these hands have newly stopped.
I know this act shows horrible and grim.   204

Gratiano.

Poor Desdemon! I am glad thy father's dead.
Thy match was mortal to him, and pure grief
Shore his old thread in twain. Did he live now,
This sight would make him do a desperate turn;   208
Yea, curse his better angel from his side,
And fall to reprobation.   210

Othello.

'Tis pitiful; but yet Iago knows
That she with Cassio hath the act of shame
A thousand times committed. Cassio confessed it;
And she did gratify his amorous works   214
With that recognizance and pledge of love   215
Which I first gave her. I saw it in his hand.
It was a handkerchief, an antique token
My father gave my mother.

Emilia.

O God! O heavenly God!

Iago.

Zounds, hold your peace!

Emilia.   'Twill out, 'twill out! I peace?
No, I will speak as liberal as the north,   221
Let heaven and men and devils, let them all,
All, all, cry shame against me, yet I'll speak.

Iago.

Be wise, and get you home.

Emilia.   I will not.

(Iago draws and threatens Emilia.)

Gratiano.   Fie!

Your sword upon a woman?

Emilia.

O thou dull Moor, that handkerchief thou speak'st of
I found by fortune, and did give my husband;

204 *shows* appears   208 *turn* act   210 *reprobation* rejection by God, damnation   214 *gratify* reward   215 *recognizance* token   221 *liberal as the north* unchecked as the north wind blows

For often with a solemn earnestness—
More than indeed belonged to such a trifle—
He begged of me to steal't.

Iago.   Villainous whore!

Emilia.
She give it Cassio? No, alas, I found it,
And I did give't my husband.

Iago.   Filth, thou liest!

Emilia.
By heaven, I do not, I do not, gentlemen.
O murd'rous coxcomb! what should such a fool
Do with so good a wife?

Othello.   Are there no stones in heaven   235
But what serves for the thunder? Precious villain!

*The Moor runs at Iago, but is disarmed by Montano. Iago kills his
wife.*

Gratiano.
The woman falls. Sure he hath killed his wife.

Emilia.
Ay, ay. O, lay me by my misterss' side.   *Exit Iago.*

Gratiano.
He's gone, but his wife's killed.

Montano.
'Tis a notorious villain. Take you this weapon,   240
Which I have here recovered from the Moor.
Come, guard the door without. Let him not pass,
But kill him rather. I'll after that same villain,
For 'tis a damnèd slave.

                              Exit Montano, with all but Othello and Emilia.

Othello.   I am not valiant neither;
But every puny whipster gets my sword.   245
But why should honor outlive honesty?
Let it go all.

Emilia.   What did thy song bode, lady?
Hark, canst thou hear me? I will play the swan,
And die in music. *(Sings.)* "Willow, willow, willow."
Moor, she was chaste. She loved thee, cruel Moor:
So come my soul to bliss as I speak true.
So speaking as I think, alas, I die.

She dies.

Othello.
I have another weapon in this chamber;
It is a sword of Spain, the ice brook's temper.   254
O, here it is.—Uncle, I must come forth.

---

235 *stones* bolts like those used for thunderbolts   240 *notorious* notable   245 *puny whipster*
top-whipping boy   254 *ice brook's* i.e. a Spanish blade, tempered in cold running water

Gratiano *(within).*
　　If thou attempt it, it will cost thee dear.
　　Thou hast no weapon, and perforce must suffer.
Othello.
　　Look in upon me then and speak with me,
　　Or, naked as I am, I will assault thee.　　　　　　　　　　　　259

　　　Enter Gratiano.

Gratiano.
　　What is the matter?
Othello.　　　　　　　　Behold, I have a weapon;
　　A better never did itself sustain
　　Upon a soldier's thigh. I have seen the day
　　That with this little arm and this good sword
　　I have made my way through more impediments
　　Than twenty times your stop. But O vain boast!　　　　　　265
　　Who can control his fate? 'Tis not so now.
　　Be not afraid, though you do see me weaponed.
　　Here is my journey's end, here is my butt,　　　　　　　　268
　　And very seamark of my utmost sail:　　　　　　　　　　269
　　Do you go back dismayed? 'Tis a lost fear.　　　　　　　270
　　Man but a rush against Othello's breast,　　　　　　　　271
　　And he retires. Where should Othello go?
　　Now, how dost thou look now? O ill-starred wench!
　　Pale as thys mock! When we shall meet at compt,　　　　274
　　This look of thine will hurl my soul from heaven,
　　And fiends will snatch at it. Cold, cold, my girl?
　　Even like thy chastity.
　　O cursèd, cursèd slave! Whip me, ye devils,
　　From the possession of this heavenly sight!
　　Blow me about in winds! roast me in sulphur!
　　Wash me in steep-down gulfs of liquid fire!
　　Oh Desdemon! dead Desdemon! dead! Oh! Oh!

　　　Enter Lodovico, Montano, Iago (as prisoner) and officers; Cassio in a
chair.

Lodovico.
　　Where is this rash and most unfortunate man?
Othello.
　　That's he that was Othello. Here I am.
Lodovico.
　　Where is that viper? Bring the villain forth.
Othello.
　　I look down towards his feet—but that's a fable.　　　　286

---

　　259 *naked* disarmed　**265** *stop* power to stop　**268** *butt* limit　**269** *seamark* beacon,
destination　**270** *lost* wasted　**271** *Man but a rush* wield only a reed　**274** *compt* final accounting,
Last Judgment　**286** *I . . . feet* i.e. to see if they are cloven, like the Devil's

If that thou be'st a devil, I cannot kill thee.
(Wounds Iago.)

Lodovico.

Wrench his sword from him.
(Othello is disarmed.)

Iago. I bleed, sir, but not killed.

Othello.

I am not sorry neither. I'ld have thee live;
For in my sense, 'tis happiness to die.

Lodovico.

O thou Othello that wert once so good,
Fall'n in the practice of a damnèd slave, 292
What shall be said to thee?

Othello. Why, anything:

An honorable murderer, if you will;
For naught did I in hate, but all in honor.

Lodovico.

This wretch hath part confessed his villainy.
Did you and he consent in Cassio's death? 297

Othello. Ay.

Cassio.

Dear general, I never gave you cause.

Othello.

I do believe it, and I ask your pardon.
Will you, I pray, demand that demi-devil
Why he hath thus ensnared my soul and body?

Iago.

Demand me nothing. What you know, you know.
From this time forth I never will speak word.

Lodovico.

What, not to pray?

Gratiano. Torments will ope your lips.

Othello.

Well, thou dost best.

Lodovico.

Sir, you shall understand what hath befall'n,
Which, as I think, you know not. Here is a letter
Found in the pocket of the slain Roderigo;
And here another. The one of them imports 310
The death of Cassio to be undertook
By Roderigo.

Othello.

O villain!

Cassio. Most heathenish and most gross!

Lodovico.

Now here's another discontented paper

292 *practice* plot   297 *consent in* agree upon

Found in his pocket too; and this, it seems,
Roderigo meant t' have sent this damnèd villain;
But that, belike, Iago in the nick   317
Came in and satisfied him.

Othello.   O thou pernicious caitiff!—
How came you, Cassio, by that handkerchief
That was my wife's?

Cassio.   I found it in my chamber;
And he himself confessed but even now
That there he dropped it for a special purpose
Which wrought to his desire.

Othello.   O fool! fool! fool!

Cassio.
There is besides in Roderigo's letter,
How he upbraids Iago that he made him
Brave me upon the watch; whereon it came
That I was cast; and even but now he spake,   327
After long seeming dead—Iago hurt him,
Iago set him on.

Lodovico.
You must forsake this room and go with us.
Your power and your command is taken off,
And Cassio rules Cyprus. For this slave,
If there by any cunning cruelty
That can torment him much and hold him long,
It shall be his. You shall close prisoner rest
Till that the nature of your fault be known
To the Venetian state. Come, bring away.

Othello.
Soft you! a word or two before you go.
I have done the state some service, and they know't.
No more of that. I pray you, in your letters,
When you shall these unlucky deeds relate,   341
Speak of me as I am. Nothing extenuate,
Nor set down aught in malice. Then must you speak
Of one that loved not wisely, but too well;
Of one not easily jealous, but, being wrought,
Perplexed in the extreme; of one whose hand,   346
Like the base Judean, threw a pearl away   347
Richer than all his tribe; of one whose subdued eyes,   348
Albeit unusèd to the melting mood,
Drop tears as fast as the Arabian trees
Their med'cinable gum. Set you down this.
And say besides that in Aleppo once,
Where a malignant and a turbaned Turk

---

317 *nick* nick of time   327 *cast* dismissed   341 *unlucky* fatal   346 *Perplexed* distracted   347 *Judean* Judas Iscariot (?) (quarto reads "Indian")   348 *subdued* i.e. conquered by grief

Beat a Venetian and traduced the state,
I took by th' throat the circumcisèd dog
And smote him—thus.

He stabs himself.

Lodovico.
 O bloody period!   357
Gratiano.   All that's spoke is marred.
Othello.
 I kissed thee ere I killed thee. No way but this,
 Killing myself, to die upon a kiss.

He falls upon the bed and dies.

Cassio.
 This did I fear, but thought he had no weapon;
 For he was great of heart.
Lodovico(to Iago).   O Spartan dog,
 More fell than anguish, hunger, or the sea!   362
 Look on the tragic loading of this bed.
 This is thy work. The object poisons sight;
 Let it be hid. Gratiano, keep the house,   365
 And seize upon the fortunes of the Moor,   366
 For they succeed on you. To you, lord governor,
 Remains the censure of this hellish villain,   368
 The time, the place, the torture. O, enforce it!
 Myself will straight aboard, and to the state
 This heavy act with heavy heart relate.   *Exeunt.*

QUESTIONS

Act I

 1. All three scenes in Act I are set in Venice. What do we learn about the Venetian state from these scenes? What elements make up the "world" of each scene? What, especially, does the Venetian senate symbolize in terms of values?

 2. What incident first incites Iago to vengeance against Othello?

 3. Where in this act is Othello's race mentioned in a derogatory manner? What does this imply?

 4. What is Brabantio's initial reaction to the news that Othello and Desdemona are together?

 5. What conflicts emerge in Act I?

 6. We get three distinct impressions of Iago as we move through each scene in Act I. What is he like in each? Point carefully to his key speeches to support your character analysis. What composite picture of his character is formed by the end of Act I?

---

 357 *period* ending **362** *fell* cruel **365** *Let it be hid* i.e. draw the bed curtains **366** *seize upon* take legal posession of **368** *censure* judicial sentence

7. It has been noted that Othello is a dignified, noble, and heroic figure. How does this impression emerge in Act I? In this context, examine one of Othello's greatest speeches, in which he recapitulates his life (Scene iii, lines 128–170). Analyze the diction, images, and tone. Comment on Othello's growing love for Desdemona, culminating in the lines, "She loved me for the dangers I had passed/And I loved her that she did pity them."

8. Why does Shakespeare delay the entrance of Desdemona until the third scene? How does she complement Othello in her speech and behavior? How does she begin to contrast with Iago?

Act II

9. Act II opens on Cyprus, a shift in setting that Samuel Johnson objected to: "Had the scene [the play] opened in Cyprus and the preceeding incidents been occasionally related, there had been wanting to a drama of the most exact and scrupulous regularity." What is the critic objecting to here? Do you agree or disagree with Dr. Johnson's complaint? Explain.

10. Note that Venice, Cyprus, and the lands beyond the sea's horizon (symbolized in part by the invading Turkish fleet) seem to represent three different "worlds" in terms of values and levels of civilization. How does Shakespeare characterize each of these worlds? What is Othello's relationship to them?

11. Images of a turbulent sea—that "high-wrought flood," as Shakespeare describes it at the start of Act II—dominate the first scene. How does this sea imagery influence action, mood, and theme? For instance, why does Shakespeare contrive a triple landing? What does nature symbolize in the first scene? How does nature's "tempest" reflect the tempests brewing between various characters?

12. How does Cassio contrast with Iago in Act II?

13. What is Iago's conception of women, love, and sexuality in Act II?

14. Analyze the dramatic effectiveness of Othello's reunion with Desdemona (with Iago looking on) in scene i, lines 178–207.

15. What is the purpose of the herald's short proclamation in the second scene?

16. Of what new element in Othello's character do we learn from his speech in scene iii, lines 182–195?

17. Explain how Iago begins to succeed in his dark plans in the third scene of Act II. What is the significance of the fact that Othello charges that people are beginning to act like Turks (see lines 147–156)? How does the looming tragedy expand when Iago, toward the end of the act (see lines 296–322) likens himself to the devil, declaring of Desdemona, "So will I turn her virtue into pitch,/And out of her own goodness make the net/That shall enmesh them all"?

Act III

18. Why does Cassio bring musicians to play beneath Othello's window in the first scene? What is the function of this relatively lighthearted interlude? How does this action benefit Iago's ends?

19. How does Iago plant the seed of suspicion in Othello's mind?

20. Why does Shakespeare play on such words as "think" and "thought" in the exchange between Othello and Iago in the first half of the third scene? Why is Iago able to get away with his accusations against Desdemona?

21. What is Othello's state of mind in his soliloquy beginning, "This fellow's of exceeding honesty" (lines 258–277)? Why is this an unusual speech for him?

22. Contrast the relationship between Iago and Emilia in the third scene with that between Othello and Desdemona.

23. Explain how "chance," or "fate," enters into the tragedy of character in the third scene?

24. How do you interpret Iago's statement at the end of the third scene, "I am your own forever" (line 480)?

25. Trace the changes in the three meetings between Othello and Desdemona in Act III.

26. What is Bianca's function in this act?

27. Explain the progression and complication of the tragic action in *Othello* through the first three acts of the play. Has the action moved too fast? Explain.

Act IV

28. How does Iago's language change at the start of Act IV? What does this change in the tone of his language tell us about the progression of the conflict?

29. When Othello, inflamed by Iago's insinuations in the first scene, grovels at the villain's feet, is he a tragic figure or merely pathetic? Explain.

30. What new trick does Iago devise to advance Othello's jealousy in the first scene? Why does Othello fall for such an obvious deception?

31. Explain the importance of the part involving Ludovico in the first scene. Why does Othello take his leave of Ludovico muttering "Goats and monkeys" (line 242)?

32. Analyze Desdemona's character during the episode in the second scene in which Othello accuses her of being a whore. Why can't Othello perceive her essential goodness and innocence?

33. The second scene concludes with a confrontation between Roderigo and Iago. Summarize this scene and explain its importance in the advancement of the tragedy. Does Iago betray his true motives at this point or not? Explain.

34. Compare and contrast the minds of Desdemona and Emilia in the third scene. Why is Desdemona so passive?

Act V

35. Compare and contrast the two scenes in this act.

36. What tactical mistakes does Iago make in the first scene? How do these mistakes assure his own ironic fate?

37. Divide the second scene into three parts, corresponding to the major stages of the action. What happens in each episode?

38. Analyze Othello's first speech at the start of the second scene. Why must he kill Desdemona quickly, rather than listening to her pleas?

39. Describe the importance of Emilia in Act V, after Desdemona has been killed.

40. The scene before Ludovico at the end of the play resembles a trial or tribunal. Is this appropriate?

41. How does Othello regain some of his lost stature and heroic character at the end of the play?

42. In what way is order restored at the end of the tragedy?

TOPICS FOR WRITING

1. Analyze the relationship between Othello and Desdemona and the growth of tragedy in their lives.

2. It has been suggested that Othello is both a soldier and a poet. Show how Othello's inability to reconcile the soldier and the poet lends itself to the play's tragedy.

3. Evaluate Shakespeare's attitude toward race and racism in *Othello*. How does race lead to Othello's tragic downfall?

4. The noted Shakespeare scholar M. R. Ridley stated, "If I were challenged to produce a 'theme' for Othello, I should suggest 'Reason vs. Instinct.'" Write a commentary exploring this perspective on the theme of the play.

5. Write an essay on Iago as the source of evil in *Othello* and on the importance of evil to a general appreciation of tragic drama.

6. Analyze the images of women that Shakespeare offers in *Othello* and on the nature of tragedy in their lives.

7. Alvin Kernan in his introduction to an edition of *Othello* comments on the plot: "The movement of the play is from Venice to Cyprus, from *The City* to the outpost, from organized society to a condition much closer to raw nature, and from collective life to the life of the solitary individual." Comment on the tragedy in *Othello* from this perspective.

8. In his preface to *Plays Pleasant*, George Bernard Shaw wrote: "To me the tragedy and comedy of life lie in the consequences, sometimes terrible, sometimes ludicrous, of our persistent attempts to found our institutions on the ideals suggested to our imaginations by our half-satisfied passions." Apply Shaw's definition to the nature of drama in *Lysistrata* and *Othello*.

9. Define tragedy and comedy, using the plays by Aristophanes and Shakespeare as points of reference.

10. Write a comparative essay on the treatment of human sexuality by Aristophanes in *Lysistrata* and Shakespeare in *Othello*.

24

PLOT AND THEME: HUMAN DESTINY

A plot in drama, as in fiction (see pages 42–45), is a causally connected series of events arranged in such a way as to advance various conflicts and to achieve internal unity. George Santayana observed that the dramatist "allows us to see other men's minds through the medium of events." The dramatist orders events into scenes and acts, structuring elements and action according to any number of patterns. He or she ties and unties the knot of conflict in order to afford us insights not only into the human mind but also into human destiny.

Our own lives and destinies do not, of course, conform to well-defined "plots," except in the vaguest sense of the word. Dramatic plots, by contrast, impose artificial order on human actions—and typically on extremes of human action. In the spirit of Aristotle, who wrote that "the plot is the imitation of the Action," playwrights impose artistic order on existence, giving form or design to life, so that the spectator or reader can experience it intelligibly. Plot governs everything in a play, perhaps more so than in fiction. E. M. Forster acknowledges this possibility in *Aspects of the Novel* when he comments: "In the drama all human happiness and misery must take the form of action. Otherwise its existence remains unknown, and this is the great difference between the drama and the novel." If playwrights have a passion for plot, it is only because they recognize that carefully structured action is the soul of drama.

Plot asks that we remember the action and what that action implies when we finally consider what the play is "saying" to us. Plot, and there may be more than one, should quickly grip us and move us directly into the action of the drama. All plots within a single play, whether major or minor, are related, and all must be resolved to our emotional and intellectual satisfaction.

How dramatists plan their plots—their series of interrelated actions—cannot be oversimplified or rendered by a single formula. Such plot formulations as the one developed by Freytag in the nineteenth century (see the diagram on page 43) can be useful when analyzing the structures of certain types of plays. A well-built tragedy, like *Oedipus Rex* or *Hamlet*, might very well reflect the famous five-part dramatic structure outlined in our discussion of plot in fiction: the introduction or exposition; the rising action or complication; the climax or turning point; the falling action; and the resolution or catastrophe. Yet much Shakespearean and Elizabethan drama does not conform readily to this conception of plot. And with the development of modern drama by Ibsen, the many faces of dramatic plot change radically as action follows new social and psychological, as well as artistic, channels of development.

What we do look for in all dramatic plots is a series of interrelated actions that are tied together by the interplay of opposing and, typically, antagonistic forces. Without conflict, without that "itch of suspense" (as Eric Bentley terms it) fostered by clashing forces, drama would be dull indeed. In part, the function of dramatic plot is to reveal character in conflict and action. With an economy far greater than that which can be attempted by a writer of fiction, a dramatist makes every gesture, every action, every bit of dialogue advance major and minor conflicts. And through these patterned conflicts, often divided into segments defined as scenes and acts, the dramatist also uses plot to illuminate a vision of life. In *Oedipus Rex*, for example, a play containing six sections and five choral odes (a plot structure common in Greek tragedy), Sophocles structures the action so as to pile question upon question: Why have disasters overtaken Thebes? What happened when King Laius was murdered? Who murdered him and why? The answer to each question succeeds only in raising more questions, all with growing apprehension and finally horror. For all along, plot has been revealing the theme of a protagonist, or main character, in the hands of fate. Discovering this, what is Oedipus—any man or woman—to do? These are questions that force a person into psychological, physical, and ultimately spiritual conflict.

Just as Oedipus struggles with questions of destiny, or fate, seemingly written in both personal and cosmic terms (for Apollo, that ambiguous god of vengeance, penance, and prophecy, delivers to Oedipus his awful fate), the great figures of modern drama are caught in equally appropriate conflicts that define their destinies. No contemporary dramatic protagonist is more famous than Willy Loman in Arthur Miller's *Death of a Salesman*. As a caveat, we must acknowledge that the essential structure of Miller's play, with its flashbacks and rapid shifts in time, its expressionistic settings and lighting (in which the stage environment is "distorted" so that external reality reflects the internal psychological condition of the protagonist), could never have been duplicated within the plot conventions of earlier theater. Technology, the American business ethic (replacing the pantheon of Greek gods), and Freud, among other considerations, contribute to the modernity of plot in Miller's play. Nevertheless, the essence of the plots centering on Oedipus and Willy Loman are strikingly alike— confirmations in their own ways of Aristotle's dictum that plot is the "soul" of tragedy.

The questions governing plot development in *Oedipus Rex* are replaced by statements—all of which lead, as elements of plot should, to theme. Furthermore, in *Death of a Salesman*, many of the plots could have been made dramas of their own: the tension and pretension between Biff and Happy; the love-hate relationship between Biff and Willy; the obvious differences that could lead to conflict between Ben and Willy. These subplots swirl around Willy Loman, who, however, commands center stage. The tantalizing, connecting question in *Death of a Salesman* is why Biff (a reflection of his father) has become such an abominable failure. Miller supplies the answer late in Act II—but then that answer is supplied from the point of view of both father and son.

It is the burden of both Oedipus and Willy to discover the motives behind their own destinies, and for us to understand those motives through plot. Both Oedipus and Willy, victims of fate and of themselves, playthings of the material and spiritual worlds, in the end become arbiters of how the last moments of their lives will be spent. While Willy may not be the inheritor of a grand history or myth-story, it is his determination to control some aspect of his life that connects him down through the generations to Oedipus and makes us consider that despite the divergent plots, a common tragic theme is as much the domain of the pauper as it is of the prince.

Sophocles

OEDIPUS REX

Sophocles (495–405 B.C.) was born near Athens. His father was an arms manufacturer, and the family had status in the Athenian order of society. At 15, Sophocles was chosen to lead the paean sung by a chorus of boys in celebration of the victory over the Persians at the battle of Salamis (480 B.C.). For more than two centuries prior to Sophocles's birth, Greeks studied in Egypt and Egyptian colonies throughout the eastern Mediterranean. Legend says that Cadmus (Kadmos) brought the first letters of the alphabet from an Egyptian colony in Phoenicia to Greece. It was also Cadmus who founded Grecian Thebes, naming it after the even then ancient Egyptian capital at Karnak, on the Nile. The sphinx in Oedipus Rex *is a version of the original, still to be found in Ghiza in Egypt. The origin of the Oedipus story may lie in the presumed relationship between King Akhnaton, who* ruled from 1375 to 1358, and his mother, Queen Tyi who bore him a daughter, Beketan. Akhnaton possessed swollen thighs. While "Oedipus" means "swollen foot" in Greek, pous can mean "foot" or "thigh." Oedipus is mentioned in both the Iliad and the Odyssey, and thus the story was about 800 years old when Sophocles molded it into a play. He is believed to have been the author of about 150 plays, some of which were produced after his death. Oedipus Rex, Electra, and Antigone are his best-known works. Sophocles advanced Greek tragedy by extending dramatic action, by using three instead of two actors (later, he added a fourth), and by subordinating the chorus to the action on stage. Sophocles also improved costuming and set decorations. In his plays the action depends on motives that develop from the characters; this is true for both male and female figures. Other playwrights tended to concentrate more on the male characters. Sophocles's "heroes are ideal figures," wrote Harry T. Peck. While they lack the superhuman loftiness of Aeschylus's creations, they nevertheless "have a certain truth of their own. The grace peculiar to Sophocles's nature makes itself felt even in his language, the charm of which was universally praised by the ancients."

List of Characters

Oedipus
A priest
Creon
Teiresias
Iocastê
Messenger
Shepherd of Laïos
Second messenger
Chorus of Theban elders

Scene Before the palace of Oedipus, king of Thebes. A central door and two lateral doors open onto a platform which runs the length of the façade. On the platform, right and left, are altars; and three steps lead down into the "orchestra," or chorus-ground. At the beginning of the action these steps are crowded by suppliants who have brought branches and chaplets of olive leaves and who lie in various attitudes of despair. Oedipus enters.

PROLOGUE

Oedipus. My children, generations of the living
   In the line of Kadmos, nursed at his ancient hearth:
   Why have you strewn yourselves before these altars
   In supplication, with your boughs and garlands?
   The breath of incense rises from the city
   With a sound of prayer and lamentation.
                      Children,

I would not have you speak through messengers,
And therefore I have come myself to hear you—
I, Oedipus, who bear the famous name.
(To a Priest.) You, there, since you are eldest in the company,
Speak for them all, tell me what preys upon you,
Whether you come in dread, or crave some blessing:
Tell me, and never doubt that I will help you
In every way I can; I should be heartless
Were I not moved to find you suppliant here.

Priest. Great Oedipus, O powerful King of Thebes!
You see how all the ages of our people
Cling to your altar steps: here are boys
Who can barely stand alone, and here are priests
By weight of age, as I am a priest of God,
And young men chosen from those yet unmarried;
As for the others, all that multitude,
They wait with olive chaplets in the squares,
At the two shrines of Pallas, and where Apollo
Speaks in the glowing embers.
       Your own eyes
Must tell you: Thebes is in her extremity
And cannot lift her head from the surge of death.
A rust consumes the buds and fruits of the earth;
The herds are sick; children die unborn,
And labor is vain. The god of plague and pyre
Raids like detestable lightning through the city,
And all the house of Kadmos is laid waste,
All emptied, and all darkened: Death alone
Battens upon the misery of Thebes.
You are not one of the immortal gods, we know;
Yet we have come to you to make our prayer
As to the man of all men best in adversity
And wisest in the ways of God. You saved us
From the Sphinx, that flinty singer, and the tribute
We paid to her so long; yet you were never
Better informed than we, nor could we teach you:
It was some god breathed in you to set us free.

Therefore, O mighty King, we turn to you:
Find us our safety, find us a remedy,
Whether by counsel of the gods or the men.
A king of wisdom tested in the past
Can act in a time of troubles, and act well.
Noblest of men, restore
Life to your city! Think how all men call you
Liberator for your triumph long ago;
Ah, when your years of kingship are remembered,
Let them not say *We rose, but later fell—*
Keep the State from going down in the storm!

Once, years ago, with happy augury,
You brought us fortune; be the same again!
No man questions your power to rule the land:
But rule over men, not over a dead city!
Ships are only hulls, citadels are nothing,
When no life moves in the empty passageways.

Oedipus. Poor children! You may be sure I know
All that you longed for in your coming here.
I know that you are deathly sick; and yet,
Sick as you are, not one is as sick as I.
Each of you suffers in himself alone
His anguish, not another's; but my spirit
Groans for the city, for myself, for you.

I was not sleeping, you are not waking me.
No, I have been in tears for a long while
And in my restless thought walked many ways.
In all my search, I found one helpful course,
And that I have taken: I have sent Creon,
Son of Menoikeus, brother of the Queen,
To Delphi, Apollo's place of revelation,
To learn there, if he can,
What act or pledge of mine may save the city.
I have counted the days, and now, this very day,
I am troubled, for he has overstayed his time.
What is he doing? He has been gone too long.
Yet whenever he comes back, I should do ill
To scant whatever hint the god may give.

Priest. It is a timely promise. At this instant
They tell me Creon is here.

Oedipus. O Lord Apollo!
May his news be fair as his face is radiant!

Priest. It could not be otherwise: he is crowned with bay,
The chaplet is thick with berries.

Oedipus. We shall soon know;
He is near enough to hear us now.

Enter Creon.

O Prince:
Brother: son of Menoikeus:
What answer do you bring us from the god?

Creon. It is favorable. I can tell you, great afflictions
Will turn out well, if they are taken well.

Oedipus. What was the oracle? These vague words
Leave me still hanging between hope and fear.

Creon. Is it your pleasure to hear me with all these
Gathered around us? I am prepared to speak,
But should we not go in?

Oedipus.   Let them all hear it.
     It is for them I suffer, more than myself.
Creon. Then I will tell you what I heard at Delphi.

     In plain words
     The god commands us to expel from the land of Thebes
     An old defilement that it seems we shelter.
     It is a deathly thing, beyond expiation.
     We must not let it feed upon us longer.
Oedipus. What defilement? How shall we rid ourselves of it?
Creon. By exile or death, blood for blood. It was
     Murder that brought the plague-wind on the city.
Oedipus. Murder of whom? Surely the god has named him?
Creon. My lord: long ago Laïos was our king,
     Before you came to govern us.
Oedipus.   I know;
     I learned of him from others; I never saw him.
Creon. He was murdered; and Apollo commands us now
     To take revenge upon whoever killed him.
Oedipus. Upon whom? Where are they? Where shall we find a clue
     To solve that crime, after so many years?
Creon. Here in this land, he said.

                If we make enquiry,
     We may touch things that otherwise escape us.
Oedipus. Tell me: Was Laïos murdered in his house,
     Or in the fields, or in some foreign country?
Creon. He said he planned to make a pilgrimage.
     He did not come home again.
Oedipus.   And was there no one,
     No witness, no companion, to tell what happened?
Creon. They were all killed but one, and he got away
     So frightened that he could remember one thing only.
Oedipus. What was that one thing? One may be the key
     To everything, if we resolve to use it.
Creon. He said that a band of highwaymen attacked them,
     Outnumbered them, and overwhelmed the King.
Oedipus. Strange, that a highwayman should be so daring—
     Unless some faction here bribed him to do it.
Creon. We thought of that. But after Laïos' death
     New troubles arose and we had no avenger.
Oedipus. What troubles could prevent your hunting down the killers?
Creon. The riddling Sphinx's song
     Made us deaf to all mysteries but her own.
Oedipus. Then once more I must bring what is dark to light.
     It is most fitting that Apollo shows,
     As you do, this compunction for the dead.
     You shall see how I stand by you, as I should,
     To avenge the city and the city's god.

And not as though it were for some distant friend,
But for my own sake, to be rid of evil.
Whoever killed King Laïos might—who knows?—
Decide at any moment to kill me as well.
By avenging the murdered king I protect myself.
Come then, my children: leave the altar steps,
Lift up your olive boughs!
                     One of you go
And summon the people of Kadmos to gather here.
I will do all that I can; you may tell them that. *(Exit a Page.)*
So, with the help of God,
We shall be saved—or else indeed we are lost.

Priest. Let us rise, children. It was for this we came,
And now the King has promised it himself.
Phoibos has sent us an oracle; may he descend
Himself to save us and drive out the plague.

*Exeunt Oedipus and Creon into the palace by the central door. The
priest and the suppliants disperse right and left. After a short pause
the Chorus enters the orchestra.*

PÁRODOS

Strophe 1

Chorus. What is God singing in his profound
   Delphi of gold and shadow?
   What oracle for Thebes, the sunwhipped city?
   Fear unjoints me, the roots of my heart tremble.
   Now I remember, O Healer, your power, and wonder;
   Will you send doom like a sudden cloud, or weave it
   Like nightfall of the past?
   Speak, speak to us, issue of holy sound:
   Dearest to our expectancy: be tender!

Antistrophe 1

Let me pray to Athenê, the immortal daughter of Zeus,
   And to Artemis her sister
Who keeps her famous throne in the market ring,
And to Apollo, bowman at the far butts of heaven—

O gods, descend! Like three streams leap against
The fires of our grief, the fires of darkness;
Be swift to bring us rest!

As in the old time from the brilliant house
Of air you stepped to save us, come again!

Strophe 2

Now our afflictions have no end,

Oedipus Rex

Now all our stricken host lies down
And no man fights off death with his mind;

The noble plowland bears no grain,
And groaning mothers cannot bear—
See, how our lives like birds take wing,
Like sparks that fly when a fire soars,
To the shore of the god of evening.

Antistrophe 2

The plague burns on, it is pitiless,
Though pallid children laden with death
Lie unwept in the stony ways,
And old gray women by every path
Flock to the strand about the altars

There to strike their breasts and cry
Worship of Phoibos in wailing prayers:
Be kind, God's golden child!

Strophe 3

There are no swords in this attack by fire,
No shields, but we are ringed with cries.
Send the besieger plunging from our homes
Into the vast sea-room of the Atlantic
Or into the waves that foam eastward of Thrace—
For the day ravages what the night spares—

Destroy our enemy, lord of the thunder!
Let him be riven by lightning from heaven!

Antistrophe 3

Phoibos Apollo, stretch the sun's bowstring,
That golden cord, until it sing for us,
Flashing arrows in heaven!
                        Artemis, Huntress,
Race with flaring lights upon our mountains!
O scarlet god, O golden-banded brow,
O Theban Bacchos in a storm of Maenads,

Enter Oedipus, center.

Whirl upon Death, that all the Undying hate!
Come with blinding cressets, come in joy!

SCENE I

Oedipus. Is this your prayer? It may be answered. Come,
Listen to me, act as the crisis demands,
And you shall have relief from all these evils.

Sophocles

Until now I was a stranger to this tale,
As I had been a stranger to the crime.
Could I track down the murderer without a clue?
But now, friends,
As one who became a citizen after the murder,
I make this proclamation to all Thebans:
If any man knows by whose hand Laïos, son of Labdakos,
Met his death, I direct that man to tell me everything,
No matter what he fears for having so long withheld it.
Let it stand as promised that no further trouble
Will come to him, but he may leave the land in safety.

Moreover: If anyone knows the murderer to be foreign,
Let him not keep silent: he shall have his reward from me.
However, if he does conceal it; if any man
Fearing for his friend or for himself disobeys this edict,
Hear what I propose to do:

I solemnly forbid the people of this country,
Where power and throne are mine, ever to receive that man
Or speak to him, no matter who he is, or let him
Join in sacrifice, lustration, or in prayer.
I decree that he be driven from every house,

Being, as he is, corruption itself to us: the Delphic
Voice of Zeus has pronounced this revelation.
Thus I associate myself with the oracle
And take the side of the murdered king.

As for the criminal, I pray to God —
Whether it be a lurking thief, or one of a number—
I pray that that man's life be consumed in evil and wretchedness.
And as for me, this curse applies no less
If it should turn out that the culprit is my guest here,
Sharing my hearth.
                    You have heard the penalty.
I lay it on you now to attend to this
For my sake, for Apollo's, for the sick
Sterile city that heaven has abandoned.
Suppose the oracle had given you no command:
Should this defilement go uncleansed for ever?
You should have found the murderer: your king,
A noble king, had been destroyed!
                    Now I,
Having the power that he held before me,
Having his bed, begetting children there
Upon his wife, as he would have, had he lived—
Their son would have been my children's brother,
If Laïos had had luck in fatherhood!
(But surely ill luck rushed upon his reign)—
I say I take the son's part, just as though

I were his son, to press the fight for him
And see it won! I'll find the hand that brought
Death to Labdakos' and Polydoros' child,
Heir of Kadmos' and Agenor's line.
And as for those who fail me,
May the gods deny them the fruit of the earth,
Fruit of the womb, and may they rot utterly!
Let them be wretched as we are wretched, and worse!

For you, for loyal Thebans, and for all
Who find my actions right, I pray the favor
Of justice, and of all the immortal gods.
Choragos. Since I am under oath, my lord, I swear
I did not do the murder, I cannot name
The murderer. Might not the oracle
That has ordained the search tell where to find him?
Oedipus. An honest question. But no man in the world
Can make the gods do more than the gods will.
Choragos. There is one last expedient—
Oedipus.   Tell me what it is.
Though it seem slight, you must not hold it back.
Choragos. A lord clairvoyant to the lord Apollo,
As we all know, is the skilled Teiresias.
One might learn much about this from him, Oedipus.
Oedipus. I am not wasting time:
Creon spoke of this, and I have sent for him—
Twice, in fact; it is strange that he is not here.
Choragos. The other matter—that old report—seems useless.
Oedipus. Tell me. I am interested in all reports.
Choragos. The King was said to have been killed by highwaymen.
Oedipus. I know. But we have no witness to that.
Choragos. If the killer can feel a particle of dread,
Your curse will bring him out of hiding!
Oedipus.   No.
The man who dared that act will fear no curse.

Enter the blind seer Teiresias, led by a page.

Choragos. But there is one man who may detect the criminal.
This is Teiresias, this is the holy prophet
In whom, alone of all men, truth was born.
Oedipus. Teiresias: seer: student of mysteries,
Of all that's taught and all that no man tells,
Secrets of Heaven and secrets of the earth:
Blind though you are, you know the city lies
Sick with plague; and from this plague, my lord,
We find that you alone can guard or save us.

Possibly you did not hear the messengers?
Apollo, when we sent to him,
Sent us back word that this great pestilence

Would lift, but only if we established clearly
The identity of those who murdered Laïos.
They must be killed or exiled.

                Can you use
Birdflight or any art of divination
To purify yourself, and Thebes, and me
From this contagion? We are in your hands.
There is no fairer duty
Than that of helping others in distress.

Teiresias. How dreadful knowledge of the truth can be
    When there's no help in truth! I knew this well,
    But did not act on it: else I should not have come.

Oedipus. What is troubling you? Why are your eyes so cold?

Teiresias. Let me go home. Bear your own fate, and I'll
    Bear mine. It is better so: trust what I say.

Oedipus. What you say is ungracious and unhelpful
    To your native country. Do not refuse to speak.

Teiresias. When it comes to speech, your own is neither temperate
    Nor opportune. I wish to be more prudent.

Oedipus. In God's name, we all beg you—

Teiresias.   You are all ignorant.
    No; I will never tell you what I know.
    Now it is my misery; then, it would be yours.

Oedipus. What! You do know something, and will not tell us?
    You would betray us all and wreck the State?

Teiresias. I do not intend to torture myself, or you.
    Why persist in asking? You will not persuade me.

Oedipus. What a wicked old man you are! You'd try a stone's
    Patience! Out with it! Have you no feeling at all?

Teiresias. You call me unfeeling. If you could only see
    The nature of your own feelings . . .

Oedipus.   Why,
    Who would not feel as I do? Who could endure
    Your arrogance toward the city?

Teiresias.   What does it matter!
    Whether I speak or not, it is bound to come.

Oedipus. Then, if "it" is bound to come, you are bound to tell me.

Teiresias. No, I will not go on. Rage as you please.

Oedipus. Rage? Why not!
                 And I'll tell you what I think:
    You planned it, you had it done, you all but
    Killed him with your own hands: if you had eyes,
    I'd say the crime was yours and yours alone.

Teiresias. So? I charge you, then,
    Abide by the proclamation you have made:
    From this day forth
    Never speak again to these men or to me;
    You yourself are the pollution of this country.

Oedipus. You dare say that! Can you possibly think you have
    Some way of going free, after such insolence?
Teiresias. I have gone free. It is the truth sustains me.
Oedipus. Who taught you shamelessness? It was not your craft.
Teiresias. You did. You made me speak. I did not want to.
Oedipus. Speak what? Let me hear it again more clearly.
Teiresias. Was it not clear before? Are you tempting me?
Oedipus. I did not understand it. Say it again.
Teiresias. I say that you are the murderer whom you seek.
Oedipus. Now twice you have spat out infamy. You'll pay for it!
Teiresias. Would you care for more? Do you wish to be really angry?
Oedipus. Say what you will. Whatever you say is worthless.
Teiresias. I say you live in hideous shame with those
    Most dear to you. You cannot see the evil.
Oedipus. It seems you can go on mouthing like this for ever.
Teiresias. I can, if there is power in truth.
Oedipus.   There is:
    But not for you, not for you,
    You sightless, witless, senseless, mad old man!
Teiresias. You are the madman. There is no one here
    Who will not curse you soon, as you curse me.
Oedipus. You child of endless night! You cannot hurt me
    Or any other man who sees the sun.
Teiresias. True: it is not from me your fate will come.
    That lies within Apollo's competence,
    As it is his concern.
Oedipus.   Tell me:
    Are you speaking for Creon, or for yourself?
Teiresias. Creon is no threat. You weave your own doom.
Oedipus. Wealth, power, craft of statesmanship!
    Kingly position, everywhere admired!
    What savage envy is stored up against these,
    If Creon, whom I trusted, Creon my friend,
    For this great office which the city once
    Put in my hands unsought—if for this power
    Creon desires in secret to destroy me!

    He has brought this decrepit fortune-teller, this
    Collector of dirty pennies, this prophet fraud—
    Why, he is no more clairvoyant than I am!
                           Tell us:
    Has your mystic mummery ever approached the truth?
    When that hellcat the Sphinx was performing here,
    What help were you to these people?
    Her magic was not for the first man who came along:
    It demanded a real exorcist. Your birds—
    What good were they? or the gods, for the matter of that?
    But I came by,

Oedipus, the simple man, who knows nothing—
I thought it out for myself, no birds helped me!
And this is the man you think you can destroy,
That you may be close to Creon when he's king!
Well, you and your friend Creon, it seems to me,
Will suffer most. If you were not an old man,
You would have paid already for your plot.

Choragos. We cannot see that his words or yours
    Have been spoken except in anger, Oedipus,
    And of anger we have no need. How can God's will
    Be accomplished best? That is what most concerns us.

Teiresias. You are a king. But where argument's concerned
    I am your man, as much a king as you.
    I am not your servant, but Apollo's.
    I have no need of Creon to speak for me.

    Listen to me. You mock my blindness, do you?
    But I say that you, with both your eyes, are blind:
    You cannot see the wretchedness of your life,
    Nor in whose house you live, no, nor with whom.
    Who are your father and mother? Can you tell me?
    You do not even know the blind wrongs
    That you have done them, on earth and in the world below.
    But the double lash of your parents' curse will whip you
    Out of this land some day, with only night
    Upon your precious eyes.
    Your cries then—where will they not be heard?
    What fastness of Kithairon will not echo them?
    And that bridal-descant of yours—you'll know it then,
    The song they sang when you came here to Thebes
    And found your misguided berthing.
    All this, and more, that you cannot guess at now,
    Will bring you to yourself among your children.
    Be angry, then. Curse Creon. Curse my words.
    I tell you, no man that walks upon the earth
    Shall be rooted out more horribly than you.

Oedipus. Am I to bear this from him?—Damnation
    Take you! Out of this place! Out of my sight!

Teiresias. I would not have come at all if you had not asked me.

Oedipus. Could I have told that you'd talk nonsense, that
    You'd come here to make a fool of yourself, and of me?

Teiresias. A fool? Your parents thought me sane enough.

Oedipus. My parents again!—Wait: who were my parents?

Teiresias. This day will give you a father, and break your heart.

Oedipus. Your infantile riddles! Your damned abracadabra!

Teiresias. You were a great man once at solving riddles.

Oedipus. Mock me with that if you like; you will find it true.

Teiresias. It was true enough. It brought about your ruin.

Oedipus. But if it saved this town?

Oedipus Rex

Teiresias *(to the page).* Boy, give me your hand.
Oedipus. Yes, boy; lead him away.

       —While you are here
 We can do nothing. Go; leave us in peace.
Teiresias. I will go when I have said what I have to say.
 How can you hurt me? And I tell you again:
 The man you have been looking for all this time,
 The damned man, the murderer of Laïos,
 That man is in Thebes. To your mind he is foreignborn,
 But it will soon be shown that he is a Theban,
 A revelation that will fail to please.

          A blind man,
 Who has his eyes now; a penniless man, who is rich now;
 And he will go tapping the strange earth with his staff;
 To the children with whom he lives now he will be
 Brother and father—the very same; to her
 Who bore him, son and husband—the very same
 Who came to his father's bed, wet with his father's blood.

 Enough. Go think that over.
 If later you find error in what I have said,
 You may say that I have no skill in prophecy.

Exit Teiresias, led by his page. Oedipus goes into the palace.

ODE I

Strophe 1
Chorus. The Delphic stone of prophecies
 Remembers ancient regicide
 And a still bloody hand.
 That killer's hour of flight has come.
 He must be stronger than riderless
 Coursers of untiring wind,
 For the son of Zeus armed with his father's thunder
 Leaps in lightning after him;
 And the Furies follow him, the sad Furies.

Antistrophe 1
 Holy Parnossos' peak of snow
 Flashes and blinds that secret man,
 That all shall hunt him down:
 Though he may roam the forest shade
 Like a bull gone wild from pasture
 To rage through glooms of stone.
 Doom comes down on him; flight will not avail him;
 For the world's heart calls him desolate,
 And the immortal Furies follow, for ever follow.

Strophe 2

But now a wilder thing is heard
From the old man skilled at hearing Fate in the wingbeat of a bird.
Bewildered as a blown bird, my soul hovers and cannot find
Foothold in this debate, or any reason or rest of mind.
But no man ever brought—none can bring
Proof of strife between Thebes' royal house,
Labdakos' line, and the son of Polybos;
And never until now has any man brought word
Of Laïos' dark death staining Oedipus the King.

Antistrophe 2

Divine Zeus and Apollo hold
Perfect intelligence alone of all tales ever told;
And well though this diviner works, he works in his own night;
No man can judge that rough unknown or trust in second sight,
For wisdom changes hands among the wise.
Shall I believe my great lord criminal
At a raging word that a blind old man let fall?
I saw him, when the carrion woman faced him of old,
Prove his heroic mind! These evil words are lies.

SCENE II

Creon. Men of Thebes:
  I am told that heavy accusations
  Have been brought against me by King Oedipus.
  I am not the kind of man to bear this tamely.

  If in these present difficulties
  He holds me accountable for any harm to him
  Through anything I have said or done—why, then,
  I do not value life in this dishonor.
  It is not as though this rumor touched upon
  Some private indiscretion. The matter is grave.
  The fact is that I am being called disloyal
  To the State, to my fellow citizens, to my friends.
Choragos. He may have spoken in anger, not from his mind.
Creon. But did you not hear him say I was the one
  Who seduced the old prophet into lying?
Choragos. The thing was said; I do not know how seriously.
Creon. But you were watching him! Were his eyes steady?
  Did he look like a man in his right mind?
Choragos.   I do not know.
  I cannot judge the behavior of great men.
  But here is the King himself.
  Enter Oedipus.

Oedipus.   So you dared come back.
  Why? How brazen of you to come to my house,

You murderer!
                Do you think I do not know
That you plotted to kill me, plotted to steal my throne?
Tell me, in God's name: am I coward, a fool,
That you should dream you could accomplish this?
A fool who could not see your slippery game?
A coward, not to fight back when I saw it?
You are the fool, Creon, are you not? hoping
Without support or friends to get a throne?
Thrones may be won or bought: you could do neither.
Creon. Now listen to me. You have talked; let me talk, too.
    You cannot judge unless you know the facts.
Oedipus. You speak well: there is one fact; but I find it hard
    To learn from the deadliest enemy I have.
Creon. That above all I must dispute with you.
Oedipus. That above all I will not hear you deny.
Creon. If you think there is anything good in being stubborn
    Against all reason, then I say you are wrong.
Oedipus. If you think a man can sin against his own kind
    And not be punished for it, I say you are mad.
Creon. I agree. But tell me: what have I done to you?
Oedipus. You advised me to send for that wizard, did you not?
Creon. I did. I should do it again.
Oedipus.   Very well. Now tell me:
    How long has it been since Laïos—
Creon.   What of Laïos?
Oedipus. Since he vanished in that onset by the road?
Creon. It was long ago, a long time.
Oedipus.   And this prophet,
    Was he practicing here then?
Creon.   He was; and with honor, as now.
Oedipus. Did he speak of me at that time?
Creon.   He never did;
    At least, not when I was present.
Oedipus.   But . . . the enquiry?
    I suppose you held one?
Creon.   We did, but we learned nothing.
Oedipus. Why did the prophet not speak against me then?
Creon. I do not know; and I am the kind of man
    Who holds his tongue when he has no facts to go on.
Oedipus. There's one fact that you know, and you could tell it.
Creon. What fact is that? If I know it, you shall have it.
Oedipus. If he were not involved with you, he could not say
    That it was I who murdered Laïos.
Creon. If he says that, you are the one that knows it!—
    But now it is my turn to question you.
Oedipus. Put your questions. I am no murderer.
Creon. First, then: You married my sister?
Oedipus.   I married your sister.
Creon. And you rule the kingdom equally with her?

Oedipus. Everything that she wants she has from me.
Creon. And I am the third, equal to both of you?
Oedipus. That is why I call you a bad friend.
Creon. No. Reason it out, as I have done.
    Think of this first. Would any sane man prefer
    Power, with all a king's anxieties,
    To that same power and the grace of sleep?
    Certainly not I.
    I have never longed for the king's power—only his rights.
    Would any wise man differ from me in this?
    As matters stand, I have my way in everything
    With your consent, and no responsibilities.
    If I were king, I should be a slave to policy.
    How could I desire a scepter more
    Than what is now mine—untroubled influence?
    No, I have not gone mad; I need no honors,
    Except those with the perquisites I have now.
    I am welcome everywhere; every man salutes me,
    And those who want your favor seek my ear,
    Since I know how to manage what they ask.
    Should I exchange this ease for that anxiety?
    Besides, no sober mind is treasonable.
    I hate anarchy
    And never would deal with any man who likes it.

    Test what I have said. Go to the priestess
    At Delphi, ask if I quoted her correctly.
    And as for this other thing: if I am found
    Guilty of treason with Teiresias,
    Then sentence me to death! You have my word
    It is a sentence I should cast my vote for—
    But not without evidence!
                You do wrong
    When you take good men for bad, bad men for good.
    A true friend thrown aside—why, life itself
    Is not more precious!
               In time you will know this well:
    For time, and time alone, will show the just man,
    Though scoundrels are discovered in a day.
Choragos. This is well said, and a prudent man would ponder it.
    Judgments too quickly formed are dangerous.
Oedipus. But is he not quick in his duplicity?
    And shall I not be quick to parry him?
    Would you have me stand still, hold my peace, and let
    This man win everything, through my inaction?
Creon. And you want—what is it, then? To banish me?
Oedipus. No, not exile. It is your death I want,
    So that all the world may see what treason means.
Creon. You will persist, then? You will not believe me?
Oedipus. How can I believe you?

Creon.   Then you are a fool.
Oedipus. To save myself?
Creon.   In justice, think of me.
Oedipus. You are evil incarnate.
Creon.   But suppose that you are wrong?
Oedipus. Still I must rule.
Creon.   But not if you rule badly.
Oedipus. O city, city!
Creon.   It is my city, too!
Choragos. Now, my lords, be still. I see the Queen,
    Iocastê, coming from her palace chambers;
    And it is time she came, for the sake of you both.
    This dreadful quarrel can be resolved through her.

    Enter Iocastê.

Iocastê. Poor foolish men, what wicked din is this?
    With Thebes sick to death, is it not shameful
    That you should rake some private quarrel up?
    (To Oedipus.) Come into the house.
                        —And you, Creon, go now:
    Let us have no more of this tumult over nothing.
Creon. Nothing? No, sister: what your husband plans for me
    Is one of two great evils: exile or death.
Oedipus. He is right.
                    Why, woman, I have caught him squarely
    Plotting against my life.
Creon.   No! Let me die
    Accurst if ever I have wished you harm!
Iocastê. Ah, believe it, Oedipus!
    In the name of the gods, respect this oath of his
    For my sake, for the sake of these people here!

    Strophe 1
Choragos. Open your mind to her, my lord. Be ruled by her, I beg you!
Oedipus. What would you have me do?
Choragos. Respect Creon's word. He has never spoken like a fool,
    And now he has sworn an oath.
Oedipus. You know what you ask?
Choragos.   I do.
Oedipus.   Speak on, then.
Choragos. A friend so sworn should not be baited so,
    In blind malice, and without final proof.
Oedipus. You are aware, I hope, that what you say
    Means death for me, or exile at the least.

    Strophe 2
Choragos. No, I swear by Helios, first in Heaven!
    May I die friendless and accurst,
    The worst of deaths, if ever I meant that!
        It is the withering fields

Sophocles

That hurt my sick heart:
Must we bear all these ills,
And now your bad blood as well?
Oedipus. Then let him go. And let me die, if I must,
Or be driven by him in shame from the land of Thebes.
It is your unhappiness, and not his talk,
That touches me.
As for him—
Wherever he is, I will hate him as long as I live.
Creon. Ugly in yielding, as you were ugly in rage!
Natures like yours chiefly torment themselves.
Oedipus. Can you not go? Can you not leave me?
Creon. I can.
You do not know me; but the city knows me,
And in its eyes I am just, if not in yours.   *(Exit Creon.)*

Antistrophe 1
Choragos. Lady Iocastê, did you not ask the King to go to his chambers?
Iocastê. First tell me what has happened.
Choragos. There was suspicion without evidence; yet it rankled
As even false charges will.
Iocastê. On both sides?
Choragos. On both.
Iocastê. But what was said?
Choragos. Oh let it rest, let it be done with!
Have we not suffered enough?
Oedipus. You see to what your decency has brought you:
You have made difficulties where my heart saw none.

Antistrophe 2
Choragos. Oedipus, it is not once only I have told you—
You must know I should count myself unwise
To the point of madness, should I now forsake you—
You, under whose hand,
In the storm of another time,
Our dear land sailed out free.
But now stand fast at the helm!
Iocastê. In God's name, Oedipus, inform your wife as well:
Why are you so set in this hard anger?
Oedipus. I will tell you, for none of these men deserves
My confidence as you do. It is Creon's work,
His treachery, his plotting against me.
Iocastê. Go on, if you can make this clear to me.
Oedipus. He charges me with the murder of Laïos.
Iocastê. Has he some knowledge? Or does he speak from hearsay?
Oedipus. He would not commit himself to such a charge,
But he has brought in that damnable soothsayer
To tell his story.
Iocastê. Set your mind at rest.
If it is a question of soothsayers, I tell you

That you will find no man whose craft gives knowledge
Of the unknowable.
Here is my proof:

An oracle was reported to Laïos once
(I will not say from Phoibos himself, but from
His appointed ministers, at any rate)
That his doom would be death at the hands of his own son—
His son, born of his flesh and of mine!

Now, you remember the story: Laïos was killed
By marauding strangers where three highways meet;
But his child had not been three days in this world
Before the King had pierced the baby's ankles
And left him to die on a lonely mountainside.

Thus, Apollo never caused that child
To kill his father, and it was not Laïos' fate
To die at the hands of his son, as he had feared.
This is what prophets and prophecies are worth!
Have no dread of them.
It is God himself
Who can show us what he wills, in his own way.

Oedipus. How strange a shadowy memory crossed my mind,
Just now while you were speaking; it chilled my heart.

Iocastè. What do you mean? What memory do you speak of?

Oedipus. If I understand you, Laïos was killed
At a place where three roads meet.

Iocastè. So it was said;
We have no later story.

Oedipus. Where did it happen?

Iocastè. Phokis, it is called: at a place where the Theban Way
Divides into the roads towards Delphi and Daulia.

Oedipus. When?

Iocastè. We had the news not long before you came
And proved the right to your succession here.

Oedipus. Ah, what net has God been weaving for me?

Iocastè. Oedipus! Why does this trouble you?

Oedipus. Do not ask me yet.
First, tell me how Laïos looked, and tell me
How old he was.

Iocastè. He was tall, his hair just touched
With white; his form was not unlike your own.

Oedipus. I think that I myself may be accurst
By my own ignorant edict.

Iocastè. You speak strangely.
It makes me tremble to look at you, my King.

Oedipus. I am not sure that the blind man cannot see.
But I should know better if you were to tell me—

Iocaste. Anything—though I dread to hear you ask it.

Oedipus. Was the King lightly escorted, or did he ride

With a large company, as a ruler should?
Iocastè. There were five men with him in all: one was a herald;
    And a single chariot, which he was driving.
Oedipus. Alas, that makes it plain enough!
                                But who—
    Who told you how it happened?
Iocastè.   A household servant,
    The only one to escape.
Oedipus.   And is he still
    A servant of ours?
Iocastè.   No; for when he came back at last
    And found you enthroned in the place of the dead king,
    He came to me, touched my hand with his, and begged
    That I would send him away to the frontier district
    Where only the shepherds go—
    As far away from the city as I could send him.
    I granted his prayer; for although the man was a slave,
    He had earned more than this favor at my hands.
Oedipus. Can he be called back quickly?
Iocastè.   Easily.
    But why?
Oedipus.   I have taken too much upon myself
    Without enquiry; therefore I wish to consult him.
Iocastè. Then he shall come.
                  But am I not one also
    To whom you might confide these fears of yours!
Oedipus. That is your right; it will not be denied you,
    Now least of all; for I have reached a pitch
    Of wild foreboding. Is there anyone
    To whom I should sooner speak?
    Polybos of Corinth is my father.
    My mother is a Dorian: Meropê.
    I grew up chief among the men of Corinth
    Until a strange thing happened—
    Not worth my passion, it may be, but strange.

At a feast, a drunken man maundering in his cups
    Cries out that I am not my father's son!

I contained myself that night, though I felt anger
    And a sinking heart. The next day I visited
    My father and mother, and questioned them. They stormed,
    Calling it all the slanderous rant of a fool;
    And this relieved me. Yet the suspicion
    Remained always aching in my mind;
    I knew there was talk; I could not rest;
    And finally, saying nothing to my parents,
    I went to the shrine at Delphi.
    The god dismissed my question without reply;
    He spoke of other things.

Some were clear,
Full of wretchedness, dreadful, unbearable:
As, that I should lie with my own mother, breed
Children from whom all men would turn their eyes;
And that I should be my father's murderer.

I heard all this, and fled. And from that day
Corinth to me was only in the stars
Descending in that quarter of the sky,
As I wandered farther and farther on my way
To a land where I should never see the evil
Sung by the oracle. And I came to this country
Where, so you say, King Laïos was killed.
I will tell you all that happened there, my lady.

There were three highways
Coming together at a place I passed;
And there a herald came towards me, and a chariot
Drawn by horses, with a man such as you describe
Seated in it. The groom leading the horses
Forced me off the road at his lord's command;
But as this charioteer lurched over towards me
I struck him in my rage. The old man saw me
And brought his double goad down upon my head
As I came abreast.

          He was paid back, and more!
Swinging my club in this right hand I knocked him
Out of his car, and he rolled on the ground.

                      I killed him.

I killed them all.
Now if that stranger and Laïos were—kin,
Where is a man more miserable than I?
More hated by the gods? Citizen and alien alike
Must never shelter me or speak to me—
I must be shunned by all.

          And I myself
Pronounced this malediction upon myself!

Think of it: I have touched you with these hands,
These hands that killed your husband. What defilement!

Am I all evil, then? It must be so,
Since I must flee from Thebes, yet never again
See my own countrymen, my own country,
For fear of joining my mother in marriage
And killing Polybos, my father.

          Ah,
If I was created so, born to this fate,
Who could deny the savagery of God?

O holy majesty of heavenly powers!

May I never see that day! Never!
Rather let me vanish from the race of men
Than know the abomination destined me!
Choragos. We too, my lord, have felt dismay at this.
But there is hope: you have yet to hear the shepherd.
Oedipus. Indeed, I fear no other hope is left me.
Iocastè. What do you hope from him when he comes?
Oedipus.   This much:
If his account of the murder tallies with yours,
Then I am cleared.
Iocastè.   What was it that I said
Of such importance?
Oedipus.   Why, "marauders," you said,
Killed the King, according to this man's story.
If he maintains that still, if there were several,
Clearly the guilt is not mine: I was alone.
But if he says one man, singlehanded, did it,
Then the evidence all points to me.
Iocastè. You may be sure that he said there were several;
And can he call back that story now? He cannot.
The whole city heard it as plainly as I.
But suppose he alters some detail of it:
He cannot ever show that Laïos' death
Fulfilled the oracle: for Apollo said
My child was doomed to kill him; and my child—
Poor baby!—it was my child that died first.

No. From now on, where oracles are concerned,
I would not waste a second thought on any.
Oedipus. You may be right.
                      But come: let someone go
For the shepherd at once. This matter must be settled.
Iocastè. I will send for him.
I would not wish to cross you in anything,
And surely not in this.—Let us go in.

                                  Exeunt into the palace.

ODE II

Strophe 1

Chorus. Let me be reverent in the ways of right,
Lowly the paths I journey on;
Let all my words and actions keep
The laws of the pure universe
From highest Heaven handed down.
For Heaven is their bright nurse,
Those generations of the realms of light;

Oedipus Rex

Ah, never of mortal kind were they begot,
Nor are they slaves of memory, lost in sleep:
Their Father is greated than Time, and ages not.

Antistrophe 1

The tyrant is a child of Pride
Who drinks from his great sickening cup
Recklessness and vanity,
Until from his high crest headlong
He plummets to the dust of hope.
That strong man is not strong.
But let no fair ambition be denied;
May God protect the wrestler for the State
In government, in comely policy,
Who will fear God, and on His ordinance wait.

Strophe 2

Haughtiness and the high hand of disdain
Tempt and outrage God's holy law;
And any mortal who dares hold
No immortal Power in awe
Will be caught up in a net of pain:
The price for which his levity is sold.
Let each man take due earnings, then,
And keep his hands from holy things,
And from blasphemy stand apart—
Else the crackling blast of heaven
Blows on his head, and on his desperate heart;
Though fools will honor impious men,
In their cities no tragic poet sings.

Antistrophe 2

Shall we lose faith in Delphi's obscurities,
We who have heard the world's core
Discredited, and the sacred wood
Of Zeus at Elis praised no more?
The deeds and the strange prophecies
Must make a pattern yet to be understood.
Zeus, if indeed you are lord of all,
Throned in light over night and day,
Mirror this in your endless mind:
Our masters call the oracle
Words on the wind, and the Delphic vision blind!
Their hearts no longer know Apollo,
And reverence for the gods has died away.

SCENE III

Enter Iocastê.

Iocastê. Princes of Thebes, it has occurred to me
    To visit the altars of the gods, bearing
    These branches as a suppliant, and this incense.
    Our King is not himself: his noble soul
    Is overwrought with fantasies of dread,
    Else he would consider
    The new prophecies in the light of the old.
    He will listen to any voice that speaks disaster,
    And my advice goes for nothing.

She approaches the altar, right.

                                To you, then, Apollo,
    Lycean lord, since you are nearest, I turn in prayer.
    Receive these offerings, and grant us deliverance
    From defilement. Our hearts are heavy with fear
    When we see our leader distracted, as helpless sailors
    Are terrified by the confusion of their helmsman.

Enter messenger.

Messenger. Friends, no doubt you can direct me:
    Where shall I find the house of Oedipus,
    Or, better still, where is the King himself?
Choragos. It is this very place, stranger; he is inside.
    This is his wife and mother of his children.
Messenger. I wish her happiness in a happy house,
    Blest in all the fulfillment of her marriage.
Iocastê. I wish as much for you: your courtesy
    Deserves a like good fortune. But now, tell me:
    Why have you come? What have you to say to us?
Messenger. Good news, my lady, for your house and your husband.
Iocastê. What news? Who sent you here?
Messenger.   I am from Corinth.
    The news I bring ought to mean joy for you,
    Though it may be you will find some grief in it.
Iocastê. What is it? How can it touch us in both ways?
Messenger. The people of Corinth, they say,
    Intend to call Oedipus to be their king.
Iocastê. But old Polybos—is he not reigning still?
Messenger. No. Death holds him in his sepulchre.
Iocastê. What are you saying? Polybos is dead?
Messenger. If I am not telling the truth, may I die myself.
Iocastê *(to a maidservant).* Go in, go quickly; tell this to your master.

    O riddlers of God's will, where are you now!
    This was the man whom Oedipus, long ago,
    Feared so, fled so, in dread of destroying him—

But it was another fate by which he died.

Enter Oedipus, center.

Oedipus. Dearest Iocastê, why have you sent for me?
Iocastê. Listen to what this man says, and then tell me
   What has become of the solemn prophecies.
Oedipus. Who is this man? What is his news for me?
Iocastê. He has come from Corinth to announce your father's death!
Oedipus. Is it true, stranger? Tell me in your own words.
Messenger. I cannot say it more clearly: the King is dead.
Oedipus. Was it by treason? Or by an attack of illness?
Messenger. A little thing brings old men to their rest.
Oedipus. It was sickness, then?
Messenger.   Yes, and his many years.
Oedipus. Ah!
   Why should a man respect the Pythian hearth, or
   Give heed to the birds that jangle above his head?
   They prophesied that I should kill Polybos,
   Kill my own father; but he is dead and buried,
   And I am here—I never touched him, never,
   Unless he died in grief for my departure,
   And thus, in a sense, through me. No. Polybos
   Has packed the oracles off with him underground.
   They are empty words.
Iocastê.   Had I not told you so?
Oedipus. You had; it was my faint heart that betrayed me.
Iocastê. From now on never think of those things again.
Oedipus. And yet—must I not fear my mother's bed?
Iocastê. Why should anyone in this world be afraid,
   Since Fate rules us and nothing can be foreseen?
   A man should live only for the present day.
   Have no more fear of sleeping with your mother:
   How many men, in dreams, have lain with their mothers!
   No reasonable man is troubled by such things.
Oedipus. That is true; only—
   If only my mother were not still alive!
   But she is alive. I cannot help my dread.
Iocastê. Yet this news of your father's death is wonderful.
Oedipus. Wonderful. But I fear the living woman.
Messenger. Tell me, who is this woman that you fear?
Oedipus. It is Meropê, man; the wife of King Polybos.
Messenger. Meropê? Why should you be afraid of her?
Oedipus. An oracle of the gods, a dreadful saying.
Messenger. Can you tell me about it or are you sworn to silence?
Oedipus. I can tell you, and I will.
   Apollo said through his prophet that I was the man
   Who should marry his own mother, shed his father's blood
   With his own hands. And so, for all these years
   I have kept clear of Corinth, and no harm has come—

Though it would have been sweet to see my parents again.
Messenger. And is this the fear that drove you out of Corinth?
Oedipus. Would you have me kill my father?
Messenger.   As for that
You must be reassured by the news I gave you.
Oedipus. If you could reassure me, I would reward you.
Messenger. I had that in mind, I will confess: I thought
I could count on you when you returned to Corinth.
Oedipus. No: I will never go near my parents again.
Messenger. Ah, son, you still do not know what you are doing—
Oedipus. What do you mean? In the name of God tell me!
Messenger. —If these are your reasons for not going home.
Oedipus. I tell you, I fear the oracle may come true.
Messenger. And guilt may come upon you through your parents?
Oedipus. That is the dread that is always in my heart.
Messenger. Can you not see that all your fears are groundless?
Oedipus. How can you say that? They are my parents, surely?
Messenger. Polybos was not your father.
Oedipus.   Not my father?
Messenger. No more your father than the man speaking to you.
Oedipus. But you are nothing to me!
Messenger.   Neither was he.
Oedipus. Then why did he call me son?
Messenger.   I will tell you:
Long ago he had you from my hands, as a gift.
Oedipus. Then how could he love me so, if I was not his?
Messenger. He had no children, and his heart turned to you.
Oedipus. What of you? Did you buy me? Did you find me by chance?
Messenger. I came upon you in the crooked pass of Kithairon.
Oedipus. And what were you doing there?
Messenger.   Tending my flocks.
Oedipus. A wandering shepherd?
Messenger.   But your savior, son, that day.
Oedipus. From what did you save me?
Messenger. Your ankles should tell you that.
Oedipus. Ah, stranger, why do you speak of that childhood pain?
Messenger. I cut the bonds that tied your ankles together.
Oedipus. I have had the mark as long as I can remember.
Messenger. That was why you were given the name you bear.
Oedipus. God! Was it my father or my mother who did it?
Tell me!
Messenger. I do not know. The man who gave you to me
Can tell you better than I.
Oedipus. It was not you that found me, but another?
Messenger. It was another shepherd gave you to me.
Oedipus. Who was he? Can you tell me who he was?
Messenger. I think he was said to be one of Laïos' people.
Oedipus. You mean the Laïos who was king here years ago?
Messenger. Yes; King Laïos; and the man was one of his herdsmen.

Oedipus Rex

Oedipus. Is he still alive? Can I see him?
Messenger.   These men here
    Know best about such things.
Oedipus.   Does anyone here
    Know this shepherd that he is talking about?
    Have you seen him in the fields, or in the town?
    If you have, tell me. It is time things were made plain.
Choragos. I think the man he means is that same shepherd
    You have already asked to see. Iocastê perhaps
    Could tell you something.
Oedipus.   Do you know anything
    About him, Lady? Is he the man we have summoned?
    Is that the man this shepherd means?
Iocastê.   Why think of him?
    Forget this herdsman. Forget it all.
    This talk is a waste of time.
Oedipus.   How can you say that,
    When the clues to my true birth are in my hands?
Iocastê. For God's love, let us have no more questioning!
    Is your life nothing to you?
    My own is pain enough for me to bear.
Oedipus. You need not worry. Suppose my mother a slave,
    And born of slaves: no baseness can touch you.
Iocastê. Listen to me, I beg you: do not do this thing!
Oedipus. I will not listen; the truth must be made known.
Iocastê. Everything that I say is for your own good!
Oedipus.   My own good
    Snaps my patience, then: I want none of it.
Iocastê. You are fatally wrong! May you never learn who you are!
Oedipus. Go, one of you, and bring the shepherd here.
    Let us leave this woman to brag of her royal name.
Iocastê. Ah, miserable!
    That is the only word I have for you now.
    That is the only word I can ever have.

                        Exit into the palace.

Choragos. Why has she left us, Oedipus? Why has she gone
    In such a passion of sorrow? I fear this silence:
    Something dreadful may come of it.
Oedipus.   Let it come!
    However base my birth, I must know about it.
    The Queen, like a woman, is perhaps ashamed
    To think of my low origin. But I
    Am a child of luck; I cannot be dishonored.
    Luck is my mother; the passing months, my brothers,
    Have seen me rich and poor.
            If this is so,
    How could I wish that I were someone else?
    How could I not be glad to know my birth?

ODE III

Strophe

Chorus. If ever the coming time were known
    To my heart's pondering,
    Kithairon, now by Heaven I see the torches
    At the festival of the next full moon,
    And see the dance, and hear the choir sing
    A grace to your gentle shade:
    Mountain where Oedipus was found,
    O mountain guard of a noble race!
    May the god who heals us lend his aid,
    And let that glory come to pass
    For our king's cradling-ground.

Antistrophe

    Of the nymphs that flower beyond the years,
    Who bore you, royal child,
    To Pan of the hills or the timberline Apollo,
    Cold in delight where the upland clears,
    Or Hermês for whom Kyllenê's heights are piled?
    Or flushed as evening cloud,
    Great Dionysos, roamer of mountains,
    He—was it he who found you there,
    And caught you up in his own proud
    Arms from the sweet god-ravisher
    Who laughed by the Muses' fountains?

SCENE IV

Oedipus. Sirs: though I do not know the man,
    I think I see him coming, this shepherd we want:
    He is old, like our friend here, and the men
    Bringing him seem to be servants of my house.
    But you can tell, if you have ever seen him.

Enter shepherd escorted by servants.

Choragos. I know him, he was Laiïos' man. You can trust him.
Oedipus. Tell me first, you from Corinth: is this the shepherd
    We were discussing?
Messenger.   This is the very man.
Oedipus *(to shepherd).* Come here. No, look at me. You must answer
    Everything I ask.—You belonged to Laïos?
Shepherd. Yes: born his slave, brought up in his house.
Oedipus. Tell me: what kind of work did you do for him?
Shepherd. I was a shepherd of his, most of my life.

Oedipus. Where mainly did you go for pasturage?
Shepherd. Sometimes Kithairon, sometimes the hills near-by.
Oedipus. Do you remember ever seeing this man out there?
Shepherd. What would he be doing there? This man?
Oedipus. This man standing here. Have you ever seen him before?
Shepherd. No. At least, not to my recollection.
Messenger. And that is not strange, my lord, But I'll refresh
　　His memory: he must remember when we two
　　Spent three whole seasons together, March to September,
　　On Kithairon or thereabouts. He had two flocks;
　　I had one. Each autumn I'd drive mine home
　　And he would go back with his to Laïos' sheepfold. —
　　Is this not true, just as I have described it?
Shepherd. True, yes; but it was all so long ago.
Messenger. Well, then: so you remember, back in those days
　　That you gave me a baby boy to bring up as my own?
Shepherd. What if I did? What are you trying to say?
Messenger. King Oedipus was once that little child.
Shepherd. Damn you, hold your tongue!
Oedipus. 　　　　　　　　　　　　　No more of that!
　　It is your tongue needs watching, not this man's.
Shepherd. My King, my Master, what is it I have done wrong?
Oedipus. You have not answered his question about the boy.
Shepherd. He does not know . . . He is only making trouble . . .
Oedipus. Come, speak plainly, or it will go hard with you.
Shepherd. In God's name, do not torture an old man!
Oedipus. Come here, one of you; bind his arms behind him.
Shepherd. Unhappy king! What more do you wish to learn?
Oedipus. Did you give this man the child he speaks of?
Shepherd. 　　　　　　　　　　　　　　　　　I did.
　　And I would to God I had died that very day.
Oedipus. You will die now unless you speak the truth.
Shepherd. Yet if I speak the truth, I am worse than dead.
Oedipus. Very well; since you insist upon delaying —
Shepherd. No! I have told you already that I gave him the boy.
Oedipus. Where did you get him? From your house? From somewhere else?
Shepherd. Not from mine, no. A man gave him to me.
Oedipus. Is that man here? Do you know whose slave he was?
Shepherd. For God's love, my King, do not ask me
　　　　any more!
Oedipus. You are a dead man if I have to ask you again.
Shepherd. Then . . . Then the child was from the palace of Laïos?
Oedipus. A slave child? or a child of his own line?
Shepherd. Ah, I am on the brink of dreadful speech!
Oedipus. And I of dreadful hearing. Yet I must hear.

Shepherd. If you must be told, then . . .

They said it was Laïos' child,

But it is your wife who can tell you about that.

Oedipus. My wife!—Did she give it to you?

Shepherd. My lord, she did.

Oedipus. Do you know why?

Shepherd. I was told to get rid of it.

Oedipus. An unspeakable mother!

Shepherd. There had been prophecies . . .

Oedipus. Tell me.

Shepherd. It was said that the boy would kill his own father.

Oedipus. Then why did you give him over to this old man?

Shepherd. I pitied the baby, my King,

And I thought that this man would take him far away

To his own country.

He saved him—but for what a fate!

For if you are what this man says you are,

No man living is more wretched than Oedipus.

Oedipus. Ah God!

It was true!

All the prophecies!

—Now,

O Light, may I look on you for the last time!

I, Oedipus,

Oedipus, damned in his birth, in his marriage damned,

Damned in the blood he shed with his own hand!

He rushes into the palace.

ODE IV

Strophe 1

Chorus. Alas for the seed of men.

What measure shall I give these generations

That breathe on the void and are void

And exist and do not exist?

Who bears more weight of joy

Than mass of sunlight shifting in images,

Or who shall make his thought stay on

That down time drifts away?

Your splendor is all fallen.

O naked brow of wrath and tears,

O change of Oedipus!

I who saw your days call no man blest—

Your great days like ghosts gone.

Oedipus Rex

Antistrophe 1

That mind was a strong bow.
Deep, how deep you drew it then, hard archer,
At a dim fearful range,
And brought dear glory down!

You overcame the stranger—
The virgin with her hooking lion claws—
And though death sang, stood like a tower
To make pale Thebes take heart.

Fortress against our sorrow!

Divine king, giver of laws,
Majestic Oedipus!
No prince in Thebes had ever such renown,
No prince won such grace of power.

Strophe 2

And now of all men ever known
Most pitiful is this man's story:
His fortunes are most changed, his state
Fallen to a low slave's
Ground under bitter fate.

O Oedipus, most royal one!
The great door that expelled you to the light
Gave at night—ah, gave night to your glory:
As to the father, to the fathering son.

All understood too late,

How could that queen whom Laïos won,
The garden that he harrowed at his height,
Be silent when that act was done?

Antistrophe 2

But all eyes fail before time's eye,
All actions come to justice there.
Though never willed, though far down the deep past,
Your bed, your dread sirings,
Are brought to book at last.
Child by Laïos doomed to die,
Then doomed to lose that fortunate little death,
Would God you never took breath in this air
That with my wailing lips I take to cry:

For I weep the world's outcast.

I was blind, and now I can tell why:
Asleep, for you had given ease of breath
To Thebes, while the false years went by.

EXODOS

Enter, from the palace, second messenger.

Second messenger. Elders of Thebes, most honored in this land,
What horrors are yours to see and hear, what weight
Of sorrow to be endured, if, true to your birth,
You venerate the line of Labdakos!
I think neither Istros nor Phasis, those great rivers,
Could purify this place of the corruption
It shelters now, or soon must bring to light—
Evil not done unconsciously, but willed.

The greatest griefs are those we cause ourselves.
Choragos. Surely, friend, we have grief enough already;
What new sorrow do you mean?
Second messenger.   The Queen is dead.
Choragos. Iocastê? Dead? But at whose hand?
Second messenger.   Her own.
The full horror of what happened you cannot know,
For you did not see it; but I, who did, will tell you
As clearly as I can how she met her death.

When she had left us,
In passionate silence, passing through the court,
She ran to her apartment in the house,
Her hair clutched by the fingers of both hands.
She closed the doors behind her; then, by that bed
Where long ago the fatal son was conceived—
That son who should bring about his father's death—
We heard her call upon Laïos, dead so many years,
And heard her wail for the double fruit of her marriage,
A husband by her husband, children by her child.

Exactly how she died I do not know:
For Oedipus burst in moaning and would not let us
Keep vigil to the end: it was by him
As he stormed about the room that our eyes were caught.
From one to another of us he went, begging a sword,
Cursing the wife who was not his wife, the mother
Whose womb had carried his own children and himself.
I do not know: it was none of us aided him,
But surely one of the gods was in control!
For with a dreadful cry
He hurled his weight, as though wrenched out of himself,
At the twin doors: the bolts gave, and he rushed in.
And there we saw her hanging, her body swaying
From the cruel cord she had noosed about her neck.
A great sob broke from him heartbreaking to hear,
As he loosed the rope and lowered her to the ground.

I would blot out from my mind what happened next!
For the King ripped from her gown the golden brooches
That were her ornament, and raised them, and plunged them down
Straight into his own eyeballs, crying, "No more,
No more shall you look on the misery about me,
The horrors of my own doing! Too long you have known
The faces of those whom I should never have seen,
Too long been blind to those for whom I was searching!
From this hour, go in darkness!" And as he spoke,
He struck at his eyes—not once, but many times;
And the blood spattered his beard,
Bursting from his ruined sockets like red hail.

So from the unhappiness of two this evil has sprung,
A curse on the man and woman alike. The old
Happiness of the house of Labdakos
Was happiness enough: where is it today?
It is all wailing and ruin, disgrace, death—all
The misery of mankind that has a name—
And it is wholly and for ever theirs.
Choragos. Is he in agony still? Is there no rest for him?
Second messenger. He is calling for someone to lead him to the gates
  So that all the children of Kadmos may look upon
  His father's murderer, his mother's—no,
  I cannot say it!
            And then he will leave Thebes,
  Self-exiled, in order that the curse
  Which he himself pronounced may depart from the house.
  He is weak, and there is none to lead him,
  So terrible is his suffering.
                But you will see:
  Look, the doors are opening; in a moment
  You will see a thing that would crush a heart of stone.

The central door is opened; Oedipus, blinded, is led in.

Choragos. Dreadful indeed for men to see,
  Never have my own eyes
  Looked on a sight so full of fear.

  Oedipus!
  What madness came upon you, what daemon
  Leaped on your life with heavier
  Punishment than a mortal man can bear?
  No: I cannot even
  Look at you, poor ruined one.
  And I would speak, question, ponder,
  If I were able. No.
  You make me shudder.
Oedipus. God. God.

Is there a sorrow greater?
Where shall I find harbor in this world?
My voice is hurled far on a dark wind.
What has God done to me?
Choragos. Too terrible to think of, or to see.

Strophe 1
Oedipus. O cloud of night,
Never to be turned away: night coming on,
I cannot tell how: night like a shroud!
My fair winds brought me here.
         Oh God. Again
The pain of the spikes where I had sight,
The flooding pain
Of memory, never to be gouged out.
Choragos. This is not strange.
You suffer it all twice over, remorse in pain,
Pain in remorse.

Antistrophe 1
Oedipus. Ah dear friend
Are you faithful even yet, you alone?
Are you still standing near me, will you stay here,
Patient, to care for the blind?
        The blind man!
Yet even blind I know who it is attends me,
By the voice's tone—
Though my new darkness hide the comforter.
Choragos. O fearful act!
What god was it drove you to rake black
Night across your eyes?
Oedipus. Apollo. Apollo. Dear
Children, the god was Apollo.
He brought my sick, sick fate upon me.
But the blinding hand was my own!
How could I bear to see
When all my sight was horror everywhere?
Choragos. Everywhere; that is true.
Oedipus. And now what is left?
Images? Love? A greeting even,
Sweet to the senses? Is there anything?
Ah, no, friends: lead me away.
Lead me away from Thebes.
       Lead the great wreck
And hell of Oedipus, whom the gods hate.
Choragos. Your fate is clear, you are not blind to that.
Would God you had never found it out!

Oedipus Rex

Antistrophe 2

Oedipus. Death take the man who unbound
   My feet on that hillside
   And delivered me from death to life! What life?
   If only I had died,
   This weight of monstrous doom
   Could not have dragged me and my darlings down.
Choragos. I would have wished the same.
Oedipus. Oh never to have come here
   With my father's blood upon me! Never
   To have been the man they call his mother's husband!
   Oh accurst! Oh child of evil,
   To have entered that wretched bed—
                          the selfsame one!
   More primal than sin itself, this fell to me.
Choragos. I do not know how I can answer you.
   You were better dead than alive and blind.
Oedipus. Do not counsel me any more. This punishment
   That I have laid upon myself is just.
   If I had eyes,
   I do not know how I could bear the sight
   Of my father, when I came to the house of Death,
   Or my mother: for I have sinned against them both
   So vilely that I could not make my peace
   By strangling my own life.
                  Or do you think my children,
   Born as they were born, would be sweet to my eyes?
   Ah never, never! Nor this town with its high walls,
   Nor the holy images of the gods.
              For I,
   Thrice miserable—Oedipus, noblest of all the line
   Of Kadmos, have condemned myself to enjoy
   These things no more, by my own malediction
   Expelling that man whom the gods declared
   To be a defilement in the house of Laïos.
   After exposing the rankness of my own guilt,
   How could I look men frankly in the eyes?
   No, I swear it,
   If I could have stifled my hearing at its source,
   I would have done it and made all this body
   A tight cell of misery, blank to light and sound:
   So I should have been safe in a dark agony
   Beyond all recollection.
              Ah Kithairon!
   Why did you shelter me? When I was cast upon you,
   Why did I not die? Then I should never
   Have shown the world my execrable birth.

Ah Polybos! Corinth, city that I believed
The ancient seat of my ancestors: how fair
I seemed, your child! And all the while this evil
Was cancerous within me!
                    For I am sick
In my daily life, sick in my origin.

O three roads, dark ravine, woodland and way
Where three roads met: you, drinking my father's blood,
My own blood, spilled by my own hand: can you remember
The unspeakable things I did there, and the things
I went on from there to do?
                  O marriage, marriage!
The act that engendered me, and again the act
Performed by the son in the same bed—
                        Ah, the net
Of incest, mingling fathers, brothers, sons,
With brides, wives, mothers: the last evil
That can be known by men: no tongue can say
How evil!
        No. For the love of God, conceal me
Somewhere far from Thebes; or kill me; or hurl me
Into the sea, away from men's eyes for ever.
Come, lead me. You need not fear to touch me.
Of all men, I alone can bear this guilt.

Enter Creon.

Choragos. We are not the ones to decide; but Creon here
    May fitly judge of what you ask. He only
    Is left to protect the city in your place.
Oedipus. Alas, how can I speak to him? What right have I
    To beg his courtesy whom I have deeply wronged?
Creon. I have not come to mock you, Oedipus,
    Or to reproach you, either.
    (To attendants.)   —You, standing there:
    If you have lost all respect for man's dignity,
    At least respect the flame of Lord Helios:
    Do not allow this pollution to show itself
    Openly here, an affront to the earth
    And Heaven's rain and the light of day. No, take him
    Into the house as quickly as you can.
    For it is proper
    That only the close kindred see his grief.
Oedipus. I pray you in God's name, since your courtesy
    Ignores my dark expectation, visiting
    With mercy this man of all men most execrable:
    Give me what I ask—for your good, not for mine.
Creon. And what is it that you would have me do?

Oedipus. Drive me out of this country as quickly as may be
    To a place where no human voice can ever greet me.
Creon. I should have done that before now—only,
    God's will had not been wholly revealed to me.
Oedipus. But his command is plain: the parricide
    Must be destroyed. I am that evil man.
Creon. That is the sense of it, yes; but as things are,
    We had best discover clearly what is to be done.
Oedipus. You would learn more about a man like me?
Creon. You are ready now to listen to the god.
Oedipus. I will listen. But it is to you
    That I must turn for help. I beg you, hear me.

    The woman in there—
    Give her whatever funeral you think proper:
    She is your sister.
               —But let me go, Creon!
    Let me purge my father's Thebes of the pollution
    Of my living here, and go out to the wild hills,
    To Kithairon, that has won such fame with me,
    The tomb my mother and father appointed for me,
    And let me die there, as they willed I should.
    And yet I know
    Death will not ever come to me through sickness
    Or in any natural way: I have been preserved
    For some unthinkable fate. But let that be.
    As for my sons, you need not care for them.
    They are men, they will find some way to live.
    But my poor daughters, who have shared my table,
    Who never before have been parted from their father—
    Take care of them, Creon; do this for me.
    And will you let me touch them with my hands
    A last time, and let us weep together?
    Be kind, my lord,
    Great prince, be kind!
               Could I but touch them,
    They would be mine again, as when I had my eyes.

Enter Antigonê and Ismenê, attended.

    Ah, God!
    Is it my dearest children I hear weeping?
    Has Creon pitied me and sent my daughters?
Creon. Yes, Oedipus: I knew that they were dear to you
    In the old days, and know you must love them still.
Oedipus. May God bless you for this—and be a friendlier
    Guardian to you than he has been to me!

    Children, where are you?
    Come quickly to my hands: they are your brother's—

Hands that have brought your father's once clear eyes
To this way of seeing—
                    Ah dearest ones,
I had neither sight nor knowledge then, your father
By the woman who was the source of his own life!
And I weep for you—having no strength to see you—,
I weep for you when I think of the bitterness
That men will visit upon you all your lives.
What homes, what festivals can you attend
Without being forced to depart again in tears?
And when you come to marriageable age,
Where is the man, my daughters, who would dare
Risk the bane that lies on all my children?
Is there any evil wanting? Your father killed
His father; sowed the womb of her who bore him;
Engendered you at the fount of his own existence!
That is what they will say of you.
                         Then, whom
Can you ever marry? There are no bridegrooms for you,
And your lives must wither away in sterile dreaming.
O Creon, son of Menoikeus!
You are the only father my daughters have,
Since we, their parents, are both of us gone for ever.
They are your own blood: you will not let them
Fall into beggary and loneliness;
You will keep them from the miseries that are mine!
Take pity on them; see, they are only children,
Friendless except for you. Promise me this,
Great Prince, and give me your hand in token of it.

Creon clasps his right hand.

Children:
I could say much, if you could understand me,
But as it is, I have only this prayer for you:
Live where you can, be as happy as you can—
Happier, please God, than God has made your father!
Creon. Enough. You have wept enough. Now go within.
Oedipus. I must; but it is hard.
Creon.   Time eases all things.
Oedipus. But you must promise—
Creon.   Say what you desire.
Oedipus. Send me from Thebes!
Creon.   God grant that I may!
Oedipus. But since God hates me . . .
Creon.   No, he will grant your wish.
Oedipus. You promise?
Creon.   I cannot speak beyond my knowledge.
Oedipus. Then lead me in.
Creon.   Come now, and leave your children.

Oedipus. No! Do not take them from me!
Creon. Think no longer
That you are in command here, but rather think
How, when you were, you served your own destruction.

*Exeunt into the house all but the Chorus; the Choragos chants
directly to the audience.*

Choragos. Men of Thebes: look upon Oedipus.
This is the king who solved the famous riddle
And towered up, most powerful of men.
No mortal eyes but looked on him with envy,
Yet in the end ruin swept over him.
Let every man in mankind's frailty
Consider his last day; and let none
Presume on his good fortune until he find
Life, at his death, a memory without pain.

QUESTIONS

1. What kind of ruler does Oedipus seem to be when we first meet him? Why does he address his people as children?

2. What incidents have happened in this country? Why has Oedipus sent Creon to Delphi?

3. What *is* Delphi? Can it be related to a modern institution?

4. Why is revenge such a political-philosophical imperative? Which Old Testament saying supports revenge?

5. What function does the Chorus serve in the play? What is the relation of the choral odes to the scenes? How do they help to advance the plot?

6. In *Oedipus* how has kindness developed into evil, and what is the message in this development?

7. How does Oedipus's own power entrap him?

8. Explain how Sophocles has observed the unities of time, place, and action in *Oedipus*. How could you apply the Freytag formula (see page 43 and page 852) to the play?

9. Describe the ironic elements in the play.

10. What does Sophocles say, ultimately, about fate and human nature in this play?

TOPICS FOR WRITING

1. What are the plot elements that make *Oedipus* a classical tragedy? Explore the reasons why we feel sympathy for the king at the play's end. Also examine the reasons why he does not, cannot, revoke the curses he has uttered.

2. Is Oedipus a hero or a victim? Develop both possibilities, defining both terms.

3. Why does Oedipus feel that blindness is worse than death? What does his self-inflicted blindness symbolize?

4. Has catharsis (the purging of pity and fear) been achieved at the end? Is there present a sense of satisfaction? Why or why not? What other emotions might prevail at the end of the play?

Arthur Miller

DEATH OF A SALESMAN

Arthur Miller, born in New York in 1915, decided that he wanted to be a writer while working in a warehouse after graduating from high school. He read The Brothers Kara-mazov *during his lunch breaks, and that reading convinced him to enroll at the University of Michigan, where he began his playwriting career. He had some success at Ann Arbor and then returned to New York, where he wrote a novel,* Focus *(1945), whose subject was racism. His first major success was the play* All My Sons *(1947), which was fol-lowed two years later by the Pulitzer Prize–winning play* Death of a Salesman. *Miller continued his success with* The Crucible *(1953) and with* A View *from the Bridge (1955). From one of his short stories, the film* The Misfits *(1961) was made, starring his wife Marilyn Monroe, who also figured, it is believed, in Miller's 1964 play,* After the Fall. I Don't Need You Anymore *(1967) and* The Creation of the World and Other Businesses *(1972) are story collections.* Death of a Sales-man, *wrote William Rose Benet, "exemplified Miller's conten-tion that tragedy is possible in modern theatre and that its proper hero is the common man."*

List of Characters

Willy Loman
Linda
Biff
Happy
Bernard
The Woman
Charley
Uncle Ben
Howard Wagner
Jenny
Stanley
Miss Forsythe
Letta

Death of a Salesman

Scene *The action takes place in Willy Loman's house and yard and in various places he visits in the New York and Boston of today.*

ACT I

Scene *A melody is heard, played upon a flute. It is small and fine, telling of grass and trees and the horizon. The curtain rises.*

Before us is the Salesman's house. We are aware of towering, angular shapes behind it, surrounding it on all sides. Only the blue light of the sky falls upon the house and forestage; the surrounding area shows an angry glow of orange. As more light appears, we see a solid vault of apartment houses around the small, fragile-seeming home. An air of the dream clings to the place, a dream rising out of reality. The kitchen at center seems actual enough, for there is a kitchen table with three chairs, and a refrigerator. But no other fixtures are seen. At the back of the kitchen there is a draped entrance, which leads to the living room. To the right of the kitchen, on a level raised two feet, is a bedroom furnished only with a brass bedstead and a straight chair. On a shelf over the bed a silver athletic trophy stands. A window opens onto the apartment house at the side.

Behind the kitchen, on a level raised six and a half feet, is the boys' bedroom, at present barely visible. Two beds are dimly seen, and at the back of the room a dormer window. (This bedroom is above the unseen living room.) At the left a stairway curves up to it from the kitchen.

The entire setting is wholly or, in some places, partially transparent. The roof-line of the house is one-dimensional; under and over it we see the apartment buildings. Before the house lies an apron, curving beyond the forestage into the orchestra. This forward area serves as the back yard as well as the locale of all Willy's imaginings and of his city scenes. Whenever the action is in the present the actors observe the imaginary wall-lines, entering the house only through its door at the left. But in the scenes of the past these boundaries are broken, and characters enter or leave a room by stepping "through" a wall onto the forestage.

From the right, Willy Loman, the Salesman, enters, carrying two large sample cases. The flute plays on. He hears but is not aware of it. He is past sixty years of age, dressed quietly. Even as he crosses the stage to the doorway of the house, his exhaustion is apparent. He unlocks the door, comes into the kitchen, and thankfully lets his burden down, feeling the soreness of his palms. A word-sigh escapes his lips—it might be "Oh, boy, oh, boy." He closes the door, then carries his cases out into the living room, through the draped kitchen doorway.

Linda, his wife, has stirred in her bed at the right. She gets out and puts on a robe, listening. Most often jovial, she has developed an iron repression of her exceptions to Willy's behavior—she more than loves him, she admires him, as though his mercurial nature, his temper, his massive dreams and little cruelties, served her only as sharp reminders of the turbulent longings within him, longings which she shares but lacks the temperament to utter and follow to their end.

Linda *(hearing Willy outside the bedroom, calls with some trepidation).* Willy!

Willy. It's all right. I came back.

Linda. Why? What happened? *(Slight pause.)* Did something happen, Willy?

Willy. No, nothing happened.

Linda. You didn't smash the car, did you?

Willy *(with casual irritation).* I said nothing happened. Didn't you hear me?

Linda. Don't you feel well?

Willy. I'm tired to the death. *(The flute has faded away. He sits on the bed beside her, a little numb.)* I couldn't make it. I just couldn't make it, Linda.

Linda *(very carefully, delicately).* Where were you all day? You look terrible.

Willy. I got as far as a little above Yonkers. I stopped for a cup of coffee. Maybe it was the coffee.

Linda. What?

Willy *(after a pause).* I suddenly couldn't drive any more. The car kept going off onto the shoulder, y'know?

Linda *(helpfully).* Oh. Maybe it was the steering again. I don't think Angelo knows the Studebaker.

Willy. No, it's me, it's me. Suddenly I realize I'm goin' sixty miles an hour and I don't remember the last five minutes. I'm—I can't seem to—keep my mind to it.

Linda. Maybe it's your glasses. You never went for your new glasses.

Willy. No, I see everything. I came back ten miles an hour. It took me nearly four hours from Yonkers.

Linda *(resigned).* Well, you'll just have to take a rest, Willy, you can't continue this way.

Willy. I just got back from Florida.

Linda. But you didn't rest your mind. Your mind is overactive, and the mind is what counts, dear.

Willy. I'll start out in the morning. Maybe I'll feel better in the morning. *(She is taking off his shoes.)* These goddam arch supports are killing me.

Linda. Take an aspirin. Should I get you an aspirin? It'll soothe you.

Willy *(with wonder).* I was driving along, you understand? And I was fine. I was even observing the scenery. You can imagine, me looking at scenery, on the road every week of my life. But it's so beautiful up there, Linda, the trees are so thick, and the sun is warm. I opened the windshield and just let the warm air bathe over me. And then all of a sudden I'm goin' off the road! I'm tellin' ya, I absolutely forgot I was driving. If I'd've gone the other way over the white line I might've killed somebody. So I went on again—and five minutes later I'm dreamin' again, and I nearly . . . *(He presses two fingers against his eyes.)* I have such thoughts, I have such strange thoughts.

Linda. Willy, dear. Talk to them again. There's no reason why you can't work in New York.

Willy. They don't need me in New York. I'm the New England man. I'm vital in New England.

Linda. But you're sixty years old. They can't expect you to keep traveling every week.

Willy. I'll have to send a wire to Portland. I'm supposed to see Brown and Morrison tomorrow morning at ten o'clock to show the line. Goddammit, I could sell them! *(He starts putting on his jacket.)*

Linda *(taking the jacket from him).* Why don't you go down to the place tomorrow and tell Howard you've simply got to work in New York? You're too accommodating, dear.

Willy. If old man Wagner was alive I'd a been in charge of New York now! That man was a prince, he was a masterful man. But that boy of his, that Howard, he don't appreciate. When I went north the first time, the Wagner Company didn't know where New England was!

Linda. Why don't you tell those things to Howard, dear?

Willy *(encouraged).* I will, I definitely will. Is there any cheese?

Linda. I'll make you a sandwich.

Willy. No, go to sleep. I'll take some milk. I'll be up right away. The boys in?

Linda. They're sleeping. Happy took Biff on a date tonight.

Willy *(interested).* That so?

Linda. It was so nice to see them shaving together, one behind the other, in the bathroom. And going out together. You notice? The whole house smells of shaving lotion.

Willy. Figure it out. Work a lifetime to pay off a house. You finally own it, and there's nobody to live in it.

Linda. Well, dear, life is a casting off. It's always that way.

Willy. No, no, some people—some people accomplish something. Did Biff say anything after I went this morning?

Linda. You shouldn't have criticized him, Willy, especially after he just got off the train. You mustn't lose your temper with him.

Willy. When the hell did I lose my temper? I simply asked him if he was making any money. Is that a criticism?

Linda. But, dear, how could he make any money?

Willy *(worried and angered).* There's such an undercurrent in him. He became a moody man. Did he apologize when I left this morning?

Linda. He was crestfallen, Willy. You know how he admires you. I think if he finds himself, then you'll both be happier and not fight any more.

Willy. How can he find himself on a farm? Is that a life? A farmhand? In the beginning, when he was young, I thought, well, a young man, it's good for him to tramp around, take a lot of different jobs. But it's more than ten years now and he has yet to make thirty-five dollars a week!

Linda. He's finding himself, Willy.

Willy. Not finding yourself at the age of thirty-four is a disgrace!

Linda. Shh!

Willy. The trouble is he's lazy, ·goddammit!

Linda. Willy, please!

Willy. Biff is a lazy bum!

Linda. They're sleeping. Get something to eat. Go on down.

Willy. Why did he come home? I would like to know what brought him home.

Linda. I don't know. I think he's still lost, Willy. I think he's very lost.

Willy. Biff Loman is lost. In the greatest country in the world a young man with such—personal attractiveness, gets lost. And such a hard worker. There's one thing about Biff—he's not lazy.

Linda. Never.

Willy *(with pity and resolve).* I'll see him in the morning; I'll have a nice talk with him. I'll get him a job selling. He could be big in no time. My God! Remember how they used to follow him around in high school? When he smiled at one of them their faces lit up. When he walked down the street . . . *(He loses himself in reminiscences.)*

Linda *(trying to bring him out of it).* Willy, dear, I got a new kind of American-type cheese today. It's whipped.

Willy. Why do you get American when I like Swiss?

Linda. I just thought you'd like a change . . .

Willy. I don't want a change! I want Swiss cheese. Why am I always being contradicted?

Linda *(with a covering laugh).* I thought it would be a surprise.

Willy. Why don't you open a window in here, for God's sake?

Linda *(with infinite patience).* They're all open, dear.

Willy. The way they boxed us in here. Bricks and windows, windows and bricks.

Linda. We should've bought the land next door.

Willy. The street is lined with cars. There's not a breath of fresh air in the neighborhood. The grass don't grow any more, you can't raise a carrot in the back yard. They should've had a law against apartment houses. Remember those two beautiful elm trees out there? When I and Biff hung the swing between them?

Linda. Yeah, like being a million miles from the city.

Willy. They should've arrested the builder for cutting those down. They massacred the neighborhood. *(Lost.)* More and more I think of those days, Linda. This time of year it was lilac and wisteria. And then the peonies would come out, and the daffodils. What fragrance in this room!

Linda. Well, after all, people had to move somewhere.

Willy. No, there's more people now.

Linda. I don't think there's more people. I think . . .

Willy. There's more people! That's what's ruining this country! Population is getting out of control. The competition is maddening! Smell the stink from that apartment house! And another one on the other side . . . How can they whip cheese?

On Willy's last line, Biff and Happy raise themselves up in their beds, listening.

Linda. Go down, try it. And be quiet.

Willy *(turning to Linda, guiltily).* You're not worried about me, are you, sweetheart?

Biff. What's the matter?

Happy. Listen!

Linda. You've got too much on the ball to worry about.

Willy. You're my foundation and my support, Linda.

Linda. Just try to relax, dear. You make mountains out of molehills.

Willy. I won't fight with him any more. If he wants to go back to Texas, let him go.

Linda. He'll find his way.

Willy. Sure. Certain men just don't get started till later in life. Like Thomas Edison, I think. Or B. F. Goodrich. One of them was deaf. *(He starts for the bedroom doorway.)* I'll put my money on Biff.

Linda. And Willy—if it's warm Sunday we'll drive in the country. And we'll open the windshield, and take lunch.

Willy. No, the windshields don't open on the new cars.

Linda. But you opened it today.

Willy. Me? I didn't. *(He stops.)* Now isn't that peculiar! Isn't that a remarkable
. . . *(He breaks off in amazement and fright as the flute is heard distantly.)*

Linda. What, darling?

Willy. That is the most remarkable thing.

Linda. What, dear?

Willy. I was thinking of the Chevvy. *(Slight pause.)* Nineteen twenty-eight . . .
when I had that red Chevvy . . . *(Breaks off.)* That funny? I coulda sworn I
was driving that Chevvy today.

Linda. Well, that's nothing. Something must've reminded you.

Willy. Remarkable. Ts. Remember those days? The way Biff used to simonize that
car? The dealer refused to believe there was eighty thousand miles on it. *(He
shakes his head.)* Heh! *(To Linda.)* Close your eyes, I'll be right up. *(He
walks out of the bedroom.)*

Happy *(to Biff).* Jesus, maybe he smashed up the car again!

Linda *(calling after Willy).* Be careful on the stairs, dear! The cheese is on the
middle shelf. *(She turns, goes over to the bed, takes his jacket, and goes out
of the bedroom.)*

*Light has risen on the boys' room. Unseen, Willy is heard talking to himself,
"Eighty thousand miles," and a little laugh. Biff gets out of bed, comes
downstage a bit, and stands attentively. Biff is two years older than his brother
Happy, well built, but in these days bears a worn air and seems less
self-assured. He has succeeded less, and his dreams are stronger and less
acceptable than Happy's. Happy is tall, powerfully made. Sexuality is like a
visible color on him, or a scent that many women have discovered. He, like his
brother, is lost, but in a different way, for he has never allowed himself to turn
his face toward defeat and is thus more confused and hard-skinned, although
seemingly more content.*

Happy *(getting out of bed).* He's going to get his license taken away if he keeps
that up. I'm getting nervous about him, y'know, Biff?

Biff. His eyes are going.

Happy. I've driven with him. He sees all right. He just doesn't keep his mind on it.
I drove into the city with him last week. He stops at a green light and then it
turns red and he goes. *(He laughs.)*

Biff. Maybe he's color-blind.

Happy. Pop? Why he's got the finest eye for color in the business. You know that.

Biff *(sitting down on his bed).* I'm going to sleep.

Happy. You're not still sour on Dad, are you, Biff?

Biff. He's all right, I guess.

Willy *(underneath them, in the living room).* Yes, sir, eighty thousand miles—
eighty-two thousand!

Biff. You smoking?

Happy *(holding out a pack of cigarettes).* Want one?

Biff *(taking a cigarette).* I can never sleep when I smell it.

Willy. What a simonizing job, heh?

Happy *(with deep sentiment).* Funny, Biff, y'know? Us sleeping in here again?

The old beds. *(He pats his bed affectionately.)* All the talk that went across those two beds, huh? Our whole lives.

Biff. Yeah. Lotta dreams and plans.

Happy *(with a deep and masculine laugh).* About five hundred women would like to know what was said in this room. *(They share a soft laugh.)*

Biff. Remember that big Betsy something—what the hell was her name—over on Bushwick Avenue?

Happy *(combing his hair).* With the collie dog!

Biff. That's the one. I got you in there, remember?

Happy. Yeah, that was my first time—I think. Boy, there was a pig. *(They laugh, almost crudely.)* You taught me everything I know about women. Don't forget that.

Biff. I bet you forgot how bashful you used to be. Especially with girls.

Happy. Oh, I still am, Biff.

Biff. Oh, go on.

Happy. I just control it, that's all. I think I got less bashful and you got more so. What happened, Biff? Where's the old humor, the old confidence? *(He shakes Biff's knee. Biff gets up and moves restlessly about the room.)* What's the matter?

Biff. Why does Dad mock me all the time?

Happy. He's not mocking you, he . . .

Biff. Everything I say there's a twist of mockery on his face. I can't get near him.

Happy. He just wants you to make good, that's all. I wanted to talk to you about Dad for a long time, Biff. Something's—happening to him. He—talks to himself.

Biff. I noticed that this morning. But he always mumbled.

Happy. But not so noticeable. It got so embarrassing I sent him to Florida. And you know something? Most of the time he's talking to you.

Biff. What's he say about me?

Happy. I can't make it out.

Biff. What's he say about me?

Happy. I think the fact that you're not settled, that you're still kind of up in the air . . .

Biff. There's one or two other things depressing him, Happy.

Happy. What do you mean?

Biff. Never mind. Just don't lay it all to me.

Happy. But I think if you just got started—I mean—is there any future for you out there?

Biff. I tell ya, Hap, I don't know what the future is. I don't know—what I'm supposed to want.

Happy. What do you mean?

Biff. Well, I spent six or seven years after high school trying to work myself up. Shipping clerk, salesman, business of one kind or another. And it's a measly manner of existence. To get on that subway on the hot mornings in summer. To devote your whole life to keeping stock, or making phone calls, or selling or buying. To suffer fifty weeks of the year for the sake of a two-week vacation, when all you really desire is to be outdoors, with your shirt off. And always to have to get ahead of the next fella. And still—that's how you build a future.

Happy. Well, you really enjoy it on a farm? Are you content out there?

Biff *(with rising agitation).* Hap, I've had twenty or thirty different kinds of jobs since I left home before the war, and it always turns out the same. I just realized it lately. In Nebraska when I herded cattle, and the Dakotas, and Arizona, and now in Texas. It's why I came home now, I guess, because I realized it. This farm I work on, it's spring there now, see? And they've got about fifteen new colts. There's nothing more inspiring or—beautiful than the sight of a mare and a new colt. And it's cool there now, see? Texas is cool now, and it's spring. And whenever spring comes to where I am, I suddenly get the feeling, my God, I'm not gettin' anywhere! What the hell am I doing, playing around with horses, twenty-eight dollars a week! I'm thirty-four years old, I oughta be makin' my future. That's when I come running home. And now, I get here, and I don't know what to do with myself. *(After a pause.)* I've always made a point of not wasting my life, and everytime I come back here I know that all I've done is to waste my life.

Happy. You're a poet, you know that, Biff? You're a—you're an idealist!

Biff. No, I'm mixed up very bad. Maybe I oughta get married. Maybe I oughta get stuck into something. Maybe that's my trouble. I'm like a boy. I'm not married, I'm not in business, I just—I'm like a boy. Are you content, Hap? You're a success, aren't you? Are you content?

Happy. Hell, no!

Biff. Why? You're making money, aren't you?

Happy *(moving about with energy, expressiveness).* All I can do now is wait for the merchandise manager to die. And suppose I get to be merchandise manager? He's a good friend of mine, and he just built a terrific estate on Long Island. And he lived there about two months and sold it, and how he's building another one. He can't enjoy it once it's finished. And I know that's just what I would do. I don't know what the hell I'm workin' for. Sometimes I sit in my apartment—all alone. And I think of the rent I'm paying. And it's crazy. But then, it's what I always wanted. My own apartment, a car, and plenty of women. And still, goddammit, I'm lonely.

Biff *(with enthusiasm).* Listen, why don't you come out West with me?

Happy. You and I, heh?

Biff. Sure, maybe we could buy a ranch. Raise cattle, use our muscles. Men built like we are should be working out in the open.

Happy *(avidly).* The Loman Brothers, heh?

Biff *(with vast affection).* Sure, we'd be known all over the counties!

Happy *(enthralled).* That's what I dream about, Biff. Sometimes I want to just rip my clothes off in the middle of the store and outbox that goddam merchandise manager. I mean I can outbox, outrun, and outlift anybody in that store, and I have to take orders from those common, petty sons-of-bitches till I can't stand it any more.

Biff. I'm tellin' you, kid, if you were with me I'd be happy out there.

Happy *(enthused).* See, Biff, everybody around me is so false that I'm constantly lowering my ideals . . .

Biff. Baby, together we'd stand up for one another, we'd have someone to trust.

Happy. If I were around you . . .

Biff. Hap, the trouble is we weren't brought up to grub for money. I don't know how to do it.

Happy. Neither can I!

Biff. Then let's go!

Happy. The only thing is—what can you make out there?

Biff. But look at your friend. Builds an estate and then hasn't the peace of mind to live in it.

Happy. Yeah, but when he walks into the store the waves part in front of him. That's fifty-two thousand dollars a year coming through the revolving door, and I got more in my pinky finger than he's got in his head.

Biff. Yeah, but you just said . . .

Happy. I gotta show some of those pompous, self-important executives over there that Hap Loman can make the grade. I want to walk into the store the way he walks in. Then I'll go with you, Biff. We'll be together yet, I swear. But take those two we had tonight. Now weren't they gorgeous creatures?

Biff. Yeah, yeah, most gorgeous I've had in years.

Happy. I get that any time I want, Biff. Whenever I feel disgusted. The only trouble is, it gets like bowling or something. I just keep knockin' them over and it doesn't mean anything. You still run around a lot?

Biff. Naa. I'd like to find a girl—steady, somebody with substance.

Happy. That's what I long for.

Biff. Go on! You'd never come home.

Happy. I would! Somebody with character, with resistance! Like Mom, y'know? You're gonna call me a bastard when I tell you this. That girl Charlotte I was with tonight is engaged to be married in five weeks. *(He tries on his new hat.)*

Biff. No kiddin'!

Happy. Sure, the guy's in line for the vice-presidency of the store. I don't know what gets into me, maybe I just have an overdeveloped sense of competition or something, but I went and ruined her, and furthermore I can't get rid of her. And he's the third executive I've done that to. Isn't that a crummy characteristic? And to top it all, I go to their weddings! *(Indignantly, but laughing.)* Like I'm not supposed to take bribes. Manufacturers offer me a hundred-dollar bill now and then to throw an order their way. You know how honest I am, but it's like this girl, see. I hate myself for it. Because I don't want the girl, and still, I take it and—I love it!

Biff. Let's go to sleep.

Happy. I guess we didn't settle anything, heh?

Biff. I just got one idea that I think I'm going to try.

Happy. What's that?

Biff. Remember Bill Oliver?

Happy. Sure, Oliver is very big now. You want to work for him again?

Biff. No, but when I quit he said something to me. He put his arm on my shoulder, and he said, "Biff, if you ever need anything, come to me."

Happy. I remember that. That sounds good.

Biff. I think I'll go to see him. If I could get ten thousand or even seven or eight thousand dollars I could buy a beautiful ranch.

Happy. I bet he'd back you. 'Cause he thought highly of you, Biff. I mean, they all do. You're well liked, Biff. That's why I say to come back here, and we both have the apartment. And I'm tellin' you, Biff, any babe you want . . .

Biff. No, with a ranch I could do the work I like and still be something. I just wonder though. I wonder if Oliver still thinks I stole that carton of basketballs.

Death of a Salesman

Happy. Oh, he probably forgot that long ago. It's almost ten years. You're too sensitive. Anyway, he didn't really fire you.

Biff. Well, I think he was going to. I think that's why I quit. I was never sure whether he knew or not. I know he thought the world of me, though. I was the only one he'd let lock up the place.

Willy *(below).* You gonna wash the engine, Biff?

Happy. Shh!

Biff looks at Happy, who is gazing down, listening. Willy is mumbling in the parlor.

Happy. You hear that?

They listen. Willy laughs warmly.

Biff *(growing angry).* Doesn't he know Mom can hear that?

Willy. Don't get your sweater dirty, Biff!

A look of pain crosses Biff's face.

Happy. Isn't that terrible? Don't leave again, will you? You'll find a job here. You gotta stick around. I don't know what to do about him, it's getting embarrassing.

Willy. What a simonizing job!

Biff. Mom's hearing that!

Willy. No kiddin', Biff, you got a date? Wonderful!

Happy. Go on to sleep. But talk to him in the morning, will you?

Biff *(reluctantly getting into bed).* With her in the house. Brother!

Happy *(getting into bed).* I wish you'd have a good talk with him.

The light on their room begins to fade.

Biff *(to himself in bed).* That selfish, stupid . . .

Happy. Sh . . . Sleep, Biff.

Their light is out. Well before they have finished speaking, Willy's form is dimly seen below in the darkened kitchen. He opens the refrigerator, searches in there, and takes out a bottle of milk. The apartment houses are fading out, and the entire house and surroundings become covered with leaves. Music insinuates itself as the leaves appear.

Willy. Just wanna be careful with those girls, Biff, that's all. Don't make any promises. No promises of any kind. Because a girl, y'know, they always believe what you tell 'em, and you're very young, Biff, you're too young to be talking seriously to girls.

Light rises on the kitchen. Willy, talking, shuts the refrigerator door and comes downstage to the kitchen table. He pours milk into a glass. He is totally immersed in himself, smiling faintly.

Willy. Too young entirely, Biff. You want to watch your schooling first. Then when you're all set, there'll be plenty of girls for a boy like you. *(He smiles broadly at a kitchen chair.)* That so? The girls pay for you? *(He laughs)* Boy, you must really be makin' a hit.

Willy is gradually addressing—physically—a point offstage, speaking through the wall of the kitchen, and his voice has been rising in volume to that of a normal conversation.

Willy. I been wondering why you polish the car so careful. Ha! Don't leave the hubcaps, boys. Get the chamois to the hubcaps. Happy, use newspaper on the windows, it's the easiest thing. Show him how to do it Biff! You see, Happy? Pad it up, use it like a pad. That's it, that's it, good work. You're doin' all right, Hap. *(He pauses, then nods in approbation for a few seconds, then looks upward.)* Biff, first thing we gotta do when we get time is clip that big branch over the house. Afraid it's gonna fall in a storm and hit the roof. Tell you what. We get a rope and sling her around, and then we climb up there with a couple of saws and take her down. Soon as you finish the car, boys, I wanna see ya. I got a surprise for you, boys.

Biff *(offstage).* Whatta ya got, Dad?

Willy. No, you finish first. Never leave a job till you're finished—remember that. *(Looking toward the "big trees.")* Biff, up in Albany I saw a beautiful hammock. I think I'll buy it next trip, and we'll hang it right between those two elms. Wouldn't that be something? Just swingin' there under those branches. Boy, that would be . . .

Young Biff and Young Happy appear from the direction Willy was addressing. Happy carries rags and a pail of water. Biff, wearing a sweater with a block "S," carries a football.

Biff *(pointing in the direction of the car offstage).* How's that, Pop, professional?

Willy. Terrific. Terrific job, boys. Good work, Biff.

Happy. Where's the surprise, Pop?

Willy. In the back seat of the car.

Happy. Boy! *(He runs off.)*

Biff. What is it, Dad? Tell me, what'd you buy?

Willy *(laughing, cuffs him).* Never mind, something I want you to have.

Biff *(turns and starts off).* What is it, Hap?

Happy *(offstage).* It's a punching bag!

Biff. Oh, Pop!

Willy. It's got Gene Tunney's signature on it!

Happy runs onstage with a punching bag.

Biff. Gee, how'd you know we wanted a punching bag?

Willy. Well, it's the finest thing for the timing.

Happy *(lies down on his back and pedals with his feet).* I'm losing weight, you notice, Pop?

Willy *(to Happy).* Jumping rope is good too.

Biff. Did you see the new football I got?

Willy *(examining the ball).* Where'd you get a new ball?

Biff. The coach told me to practice my passing.

Willy. That so? And he gave you the ball, heh?

Biff. Well, I borrowed it from the locker room. *(He laughs confidentially.)*

Willy *(laughing with him at the theft).* I want you to return that.

Happy. I told you he wouldn't like it!

Biff *(angrily)*. Well, I'm bringing it back!

Willy *(stopping the incipient argument, to Happy)*. Sure, he's gotta practice with a regulation ball, doesn't he? *(To Biff.)* Coach'll probably congratulate you on your initiative!

Biff. Oh, he keeps congratulating my initiative all the time, Pop.

Willy. That's because he likes you. If somebody else took that ball there'd be an uproar. So what's the report, boys, what's the report?

Biff. Where'd you go this time, Dad? Gee we were lonesome for you.

Willy *(pleased, puts an arm around each boy and they come down to the apron)*. Lonesome, heh?

Biff. Missed you every minute.

Willy. Don't say? Tell you a secret, boys. Don't breathe it to a soul. Someday I'll have my own business, and I'll never have to leave home any more.

Happy. Like Uncle Charley, heh?

Willy. Bigger than Uncle Charley! Because Charley is not—liked. He's liked, but he's not—well liked.

Biff. Where'd you go this time, Dad?

Willy. Well, I got on the road, and I went north to Providence. Met the Mayor.

Biff. The Mayor of Providence!

Willy. He was sitting in the hotel lobby.

Biff. What'd he say?

Willy. He said, "Morning!" And I said, "You got a fine city here, Mayor." And then he had coffee with me. And then I went to Waterbury. Waterbury is a fine city. Big clock city, the famous Waterbury clock. Sold a nice bill there. And then Boston—Boston is the cradle of the Revolution. A fine city. And a couple of other towns in Mass., and on to Portland and Bangor and straight home!

Biff. Gee, I'd love to go with you sometime, Dad.

Willy. Soon as summer comes.

Happy. Promise?

Willy. You and Hap and I, and I'll show you all the towns. America is full of beautiful towns and fine, upstanding people. And they know me, boys, they know me up and down New England. The finest people. And when I bring you fellas up, there'll be open sesame for all of us, 'cause one thing, boys: I have friends. I can park my car in any street in New England, and the cops protect it like their own. This summer, heh?

Biff and Happy *(together)*. Yeah! You bet!

Willy. We'll take our bathing suits.

Happy. We'll carry your bags, Pop!

Willy. Oh, won't that be something! Me comin' into the Boston stores with you boys carryin' my bags. What a sensation!

Biff is prancing around, practicing passing the ball.

Willy. You nervous, Biff, about the game?

Biff. Not if you're gonna be there.

Willy. What do they say about you in school, now that they made you captain?

Happy. There's a crowd of girls behind him everytime the classes change.

Biff *(taking Willy's hand)*. This Saturday, Pop, this Saturday—just for you, I'm going to break through for a touchdown.

Happy. You're supposed to pass.

Biff. I'm takin' one play for Pop. You watch me, Pop, and when I take off my helmet, that means I'm breakin' out. Then you watch me crash through that line!

Willy *(kisses Biff).* Oh, wait'll I tell this in Boston!

Bernard enters in knickers. He is younger than Biff, earnest and loyal, a worried boy.

Bernard. Biff, where are you? You're supposed to study with me today.

Willy. Hey, looka Bernard. What're you lookin' so anemic about, Bernard?

Bernard. He's gotta study, Uncle Willy. He's got Regents next week.

Happy *(tauntingly, spinning Bernard around).* Let's box, Bernard!

Bernard. Biff! *(He gets away from Happy.)* Listen, Biff, I heard Mr. Birnbaum say that if you don't start studyin' math he's gonna flunk you, and you won't graduate. I heard him!

Willy. You better study with him, Biff. Go ahead now.

Bernard. I heard him!

Biff. Oh, Pop, you didn't see my sneakers! *(He holds up a foot for Willy to look at.)*

Willy. Hey, that's a beautiful job of printing!

Bernard *(wiping his glasses).* Just because he printed University of Virginia on his sneakers doesn't mean they've got to graduate him. Uncle Willy!

Willy *(angrily).* What're you talking about? With scholarships to three universities they're gonna flunk him?

Bernard. But I heard Mr. Birnbaum say . . .

Willy. Don't be a pest, Bernard! *(To his boys.)* What an anemic!

Bernard. Okay, I'm waiting for you in my house, Biff.

Bernard goes off. The Lomans laugh.

Willy. Bernard is not well liked, is he?

Biff. He's liked, but he's not well liked.

Happy. That's right, Pop.

Willy. That's just what I mean. Bernard can get the best marks in school, y'understand, but when he gets out in the business world, y'understand, you are going to be five times ahead of him. That's why I thank Almighty God you're both built like Adonises. Because the man who makes an appearance in the business world, the man who creates personal interest, is the man who gets ahead. Be liked and you will never want. You take me, for instance. I never have to wait in line to see a buyer. "Willy Loman is here!" That's all they have to know, and I go right through.

Biff. Did you knock them dead, Pop?

Willy. Knocked 'em cold in Providence, slaughtered 'em in Boston.

Happy *(on his back, pedaling again).* I'm losing weight, you notice, Pop?

Linda enters as of old, a ribbon in her hair, carrying a basket of washing.

Linda *(with youthful energy).* Hello, dear!

Willy. Sweetheart!

Linda. How'd the Chevvy run?

Willy. Chevrolet, Linda, is the greatest car ever built. *(To the boys.)* Since when do you let your mother carry wash up the stairs?

Biff. Grab hold there, boy!

Happy. Where to, Mom?

Linda. Hang them up on the line. And you better go down to your friends, Biff. The cellar is full of boys. They don't know what to do with themselves.

Biff. Ah, when Pop comes home they can wait!

Willy (laughs appreciatively). You better go down and tell them what to do, Biff.

Biff. I think I'll have them sweep out the furnace room.

Willy. Good work, Biff.

Biff (goes through wall-line of kitchen to doorway at back and calls down). Fellas! Everybody sweep out the furnace room! I'll be right down!

Voices. All right! Okay, Biff.

Biff. George and Sam and Frank, come out back! We're hangin' up the wash! Come on, Hap, on the double! *(He and Happy carry out the basket.)*

Linda. The way they obey him!

Willy. Well, that's training, the training. I'm tellin' you, I was sellin' thousands and thousands, but I had to come home.

Linda. Oh, the whole block'll be at that game. Did you sell anything?

Willy. I did five hundred gross in Providence and seven hundred gross in Boston.

Linda. No! Wait a minute, I've got a pencil. *(She pulls pencil and paper out of her apron pocket.)* That makes your commission . . . Two hundred . . . my God! Two hundred and twelve dollars!

Willy. Well, I didn't figure it yet, but . . .

Linda. How much did you do?

Willy. Well, I—I did—about a hundred and eighty gross in Providence. Well, no—it came to—roughly two hundred gross on the whole trip.

Linda (without hesitation). Two hundred gross. That's . . . *(She figures.)*

Willy. The trouble was that three of the stores were half-closed for inventory in Boston. Otherwise I woulda broke records.

Linda. Well, it makes seventy dollars and some pennies. That's very good.

Willy. What do we owe?

Linda. Well, on the first there's sixteen dollars on the refrigerator . . .¢

Willy. Why sixteen?

Linda. Well, the fan belt broke, so it was a dollar eighty.

Willy. But it's brand new.

Linda. Well, the man said that's the way it is. Till they work themselves in, y'know.

They move through the wall-line into the kitchen.

Willy. I hope we didn't get stuck on that machine.

Linda. They got the biggest ads of any of them!

Willy. I know, it's a fine machine. What else?

Linda. Well, there's nine-sixty for the washing machine. And for the vacuum cleaner there's three and a half due on the fifteenth. Then the roof, you got twenty-one dollars remaining.

Willy. It don't leak, does it?

Linda. No, they did a wonderful job. Then you owe Frank for the carburetor.

Willy. I'm not going to pay that man! That goddam Chevrolet, they ought to prohibit the manufacture of that car!

Linda. Well, you owe him three and a half. And odds and ends, comes to around a hundred and twenty dollars by the fifteenth.

Willy. A hundred and twenty dollars! My God, if business don't pick up I don't know what I'm gonna do!

Linda. Well, next week you'll do better.

Willy. Oh, I'll knock 'em dead next week. I'll go to Hartford. I'm very well liked in Hartford. You know, the trouble is, Linda, people don't seem to take to me.

They move onto the forestage.

Linda. Oh, don't be foolish.

Willy. I know it when I walk in. They seem to laugh at me.

Linda. Why? Why would they laugh at you? Don't talk that way, Willy.

Willy moves to the edge of the stage. Linda goes into the kitchen and starts to darn stockings.

Willy. I don't know the reason for it, but they just pass me by. I'm not noticed.

Linda. But you're doing wonderful, dear. You're making seventy to a hundred dollars a week.

Willy. But I gotta be at it ten, twelve hours a day. Other men—I don't know—they do it easier. I don't know why—I can't stop myself—I talk too much. A man oughta come in with a few words. One thing about Charley. He's a man of few words, and they respect him.

Linda. You don't talk too much, you're just lively.

Willy *(smiling).* Well, I figure, what the hell, life is short, a couple of jokes. *(To himself.)* I joke too much! *(The smile goes.)*

Linda. Why? You're . . .

Willy. I'm fat. I'm very—foolish to look at, Linda. I didn't tell you, but Christmas time I happened to be calling on F. H. Stewarts, and a salesman I know, as I was going in to see the buyer I heard him say something about—walrus. And I—I cracked him right across the face. I won't take that. I simply will not take that. But they do laugh at me. I know that.

Linda. Darling . . .

Willy. I gotta overcome it. I know I gotta overcome it. I'm not dressing to advantage, maybe.

Linda. Willy, darling, you're the handsomest man in the world . . .

Willy. Oh, no, Linda.

Linda. To me you are. *(Slight pause.)* The handsomest.

From the darkness is heard the laughter of a woman. Willy doesn't turn to it, but it continues through Linda's lines.

Linda. And the boys, Willy. Few men are idolized by their children the way you are.

Music is heard as behind a scrim, to the left of the house; The Woman, dimly seen, is dressing.

Willy *(with great feeling).* You're the best there is, Linda, you're a pal, you know that? On the road—on the road I want to grab you sometimes and just kiss the life outa you.

The laughter is loud now, and he moves into a brightening area at the left, where The Woman has come from behind the scrim and is standing, putting on her hat, looking into a "mirror" and laughing.

Willy. Cause I get so lonely—especially when business is bad and there's nobody to talk to. I get the feeling that I'll never sell anything again, that I won't make a living for you, or a business, a business for the boys. *(He talks through The Woman's subsiding laughter; The Woman primps at the "mirror.")* There's so much I want to make for . . .

The Woman. Me? You didn't make me, Willy. I picked you.

Willy *(pleased).* You picked me?

The Woman *(who is quite proper-looking, Willy's age).* I did. I've been sitting at that desk watching all the salesmen go by, day in, day out. But you've got such a sense of humor, and we do have such a good time together, don't we?

Willy. Sure, sure. *(He takes her in his arms.)* Why do you have to go now?

The Woman. It's two o'clock . . .

Willy. No, come on in! *(He pulls her.)*

The Woman. . . . my sisters 'll be scandalized. When'll you be back?

Willy. Oh, two weeks about. Will you come up again?

The Woman. Sure thing. You do make me laugh. It's good for me. *(She squeezes his arm, kisses him.)* And I think you're a wonderful man.

Willy. You picked me, heh?

The Woman. Sure. Because you're so sweet. And such a kidder.

Willy. Well, I'll see you next time I'm in Boston.

The Woman. I'll put you right through to the buyers.

Willy *(slapping her bottom).* Right. Well, bottoms up!

The Woman *(slaps him gently and laughs).* You just kill me.

Willy *(He suddenly grabs her and kisses her roughly.)* You kill me. And thanks for the stockings. I love a lot of stockings. Well, good night.

Willy. Good night. And keep your pores open!

The Woman. Oh, Willy!

The Woman bursts out laughing, and Linda's laughter blends in. The Woman disappears into the dark. Now the area at the kitchen table brightens. Linda is sitting where she was at the kitchen table, but now is mending a pair of her silk stockings.

Linda. You are, Willy. The handsomest man. You've got no reason to feel that . . .

Willy *(coming out of The Woman's dimming area and going over to Linda).* I'll make it all up to you, Linda, I'll . . .

Linda. There's nothing to make up, dear. You're doing fine, better than . . .

Willy *(noticing her mending).* What's that?

Linda. Just mending my stockings. They're so expensive . . .

Willy *(angrily, taking them from her).* I won't have you mending stockings in this house! Now throw them out!

Linda puts the stockings in her pocket.

Bernard *(entering on the run).* Where is he? If he doesn't study!

Willy *(moving to the forestage, with great agitation).* You'll give him the answers!

Bernard. I do, but I can't on a Regents! That's a state exam! They're liable to arrest me!

Willy. Where is he? I'll whip him, I'll whip him!

Linda. And he'd better give back that football, Willy, it's not nice.

Willy. Biff! Where is he? Why is he taking everything?

Linda. He's too rough with the girls, Willy. All the mothers are afraid of him!

Willy. I'll whip him!

Bernard. He's driving the car without a license!

The Woman's laugh is heard.

Willy. Shut up!

Linda. All the mothers . . .

Willy. Shut up!

Bernard *(backing quietly away and out).* Mr. Birnbaum says he's stuck up.

Willy. Get outa here!

Bernard. If he doesn't buckle down he'll flunk math! *(He goes off.)*

Linda. He's right, Willy, you've gotta . . .

Willy *(exploding at her).* There's nothing the matter with him! You want him to be a worm like Bernard? He's got spirit, personality . . .

As he speaks, Linda, almost in tears, exits into the living room. Willy is alone in the kitchen, wilting and staring. The leaves are gone. It is night again, and the apartment houses look down from behind.

Willy. Loaded with it. Loaded! What is he stealing? He's giving it back, isn't he? Why is he stealing? What did I tell him? I never in my life told him anything but decent things.

Happy in pajamas has come down the stairs; Willy suddenly becomes aware of Happy's presence.

Happy. Let's go now, come on.

Willy *(sitting down at the kitchen table).* Huh! Why did she have to wax the floors herself? Everytime she waxes the floors she keels over. She knows that!

Happy. Shh! Take it easy. What brought you back tonight?

Willy. I got an awful scare. Nearly hit a kid in Yonkers. God! Why didn't I go to Alaska with my brother Ben that time! Ben! That man was a genius, that man was success incarnate! What a mistake! He begged me to go.

Happy. Well, there's no use in . . .

Willy. You guys! There was a man started with the clothes on his back and ended up with diamond mines!

Happy. Boy, someday I'd like to know how he did it.

Willy. What's the mystery? The man knew what he wanted and went out and got it! Walked into a jungle, and comes out, the age of twenty-one, and he's rich! The world is an oyster, but you don't crack it open on a mattress!

Happy. Pop, I told you I'm gonna retire you for life.

Willy. You'll retire me for life on seventy goddam dollars a week? And your women and your car and your apartment, and you'll retire me for life! Christ's sake, I couldn't get past Yonkers today! Where are you guys, where are you? The woods are burning! I can't drive a car!

Charley has appeared in the doorway. He is a large man, slow of speech, laconic, immovable. In all he says, despite what he says, there is pity, and, now, trepidation. He has a robe over pajamas, slippers on his feet. He enters the kitchen.

Charley. Everything all right?

Happy. Yeah, Charley, everything's . . .

Willy. What's the matter?

Charley. I heard some noise. I thought something happened. Can't we do something about the walls? You sneeze in here, and in my house hats blow off.

Happy. Let's go to bed, Dad. Come on.

Charley signals to Happy to go.

Willy. You go ahead, I'm not tired at the moment.

Happy *(to Willy).* Take it easy, huh? *(He exits.)*

Willy. What're you doin' up?

Charley *(sitting down at the kitchen table opposite Willy).* Couldn't sleep good. I had a heartburn.

Willy. Well, you don't know how to eat.

Charley. I eat with my mouth.

Willy. No, you're ignorant. You gotta know about vitamins and things like that.

Charley. Come on, let's shoot. Tire you out a little.

Willy *(hesitantly).* All right. You got cards?

Charley *(taking a deck from his pocket).* Yeah, I got them. Someplace. What is it with those vitamins?

Willy *(dealing).* They build up your bones. Chemistry.

Charley. Yeah, but there's no bones in a heartburn.

Willy. What are you talkin' about? Do you know the first thing about it?

Charley. Don't get insulted.

Willy. Don't talk about something you don't know anything about.

They are playing. Pause.

Charley. What're you doin' home?

Willy. A little trouble with the car.

Charley. Oh. *(Pause.)* I'd like to take a trip to California.

Willy. Don't say.

Charley. You want a job?

Willy. I got a job, I told you that. *(After a slight pause.)* What the hell are you offering me a job for?

Charley. Don't get insulted.

Willy. Don't insult me.

Charley. I don't see no sense in it. You don't have to go on this way.

Willy. I got a good job. *(Slight pause.)* What do you keep comin' in here for?

Charley. You want me to go?

Willy *(after a pause, withering).* I can't understand it. He's going back to Texas again. What the hell is that?

Charley. Let him go.

Willy. I got nothin' to give him, Charley, I'm clean, I'm clean.

Charley. He won't starve. None a them starve. Forget about him.

Willy. Then what have I got to remember?

Charley. You take it too hard. To hell with it. When a deposit bottle is broken you
    don't get your nickel back.
Willy. That's easy enough for you to say.
Charley. That ain't easy for me to say.
Willy. Did you see the ceiling I put up in the living room?
Charley. Yeah, that's a piece of work. To put up a ceiling is a mystery to me. How
    do you do it?
Willy. What's the difference?
Charley. Well, talk about it.
Willy. You gonna put up a ceiling?
Charley. How could I put up a ceiling?
Willy. Then what the hell are you bothering me for?
Charley. You're insulted again.
Willy. A man who can't handle tools is not a man. You're disgusting.
Charley. Don't call me disgusting, Willy.

    *Uncle Ben, carrying a valise and an umbrella, enters the forestage from
around the right corner of the house. He is a stolid man, in his sixties, with a
mustache and an authoritative air. He is utterly certain of his destiny, and
there is an aura of far places about him. He enters exactly as Willy speaks.*

Willy. I'm getting awfully tired, Ben.

    Ben's music is heard. Ben looks around at everything.

Charley. Good, keep playing; you'll sleep better. Did you call me Ben?

    Ben looks at his watch.

Willy. That's funny. For a second there you reminded me of my brother Ben.
Ben. I only have a few minutes. (*He strolls, inspecting the place. Willy and
    Charley continue playing.*)
Charley. You never heard from him again, heh? Since that time?
Willy. Didn't Linda tell you? Couple of weeks ago we got a letter from his wife in
    Africa. He died.
Charley. That so.
Ben (*chuckling*). So this is Brooklyn, eh?
Charley. Maybe you're in for some of his money.
Willy. Naa, he had seven sons. There's just one opportunity I had with that
    man . . .
Ben. I must make a train, William. There are several properties I'm looking at in
    Alaska.
Willy. Sure, sure! If I'd gone with him to Alaska that time, everything would've
    been totally different.
Charley. Go on, you'd froze to death up there.
Willy. What're you talking about?
Ben. Opportunity is tremendous in Alaska, William. Surprised you're not up
    there.
Willy. Sure, tremendous.
Charley. Heh?
Willy. There was the only man I ever met who knew the answers.

Charley. Who?

Ben. How are you all?

Willy *(taking a pot, smiling).* Fine, fine.

Charley. Pretty sharp tonight.

Ben. Is Mother living with you?

Willy. No, she died a long time ago.

Charley. Who?

Ben. That's too bad. Fine specimen of a lady, Mother.

Willy *(to Charley).* Heh?

Ben. I'd hoped to see the old girl.

Charley. Who died?

Ben. Heard anything from Father, have you?

Willy *(unnerved).* What do you mean, who died?

Charley *(taking a pot).* What're you talkin' about?

Ben *(looking at his watch).* William, it's half-past eight!

Willy *(as though to dispel his confusion he angrily stops Charley's hand).* That's my build!

Charley. I put the ace . . .

Willy. If you don't know how to play the game I'm not gonna throw my money away on you!

Charley *(rising).* It was my ace, for God's sake!

Willy. I'm through, I'm through!

Ben. When did Mother die?

Willy. Long ago. Since the beginning you never knew how to play cards.

Charley *(picks up the cards and goes to the door).* All right! Next time I'll bring a deck with five aces.

Willy. I don't play that kind of game!

Charley *(turning to him).* You ought to be ashamed of yourself!

Willy. Yeah?

Charley. Yeah! *(He goes out.)*

Willy *(slamming the door after him).* Ignoramus!

Ben *(as Willy comes toward him through the wall-line of the kitchen).* So you're William.

Willy *(shaking Ben's hand).* Ben! I've been waiting for you so long! What's the answer? How did you do it?

Ben. Oh, there's a story in that.

Linda enters the forestage, as of old, carrying the wash basket.

Linda. Is this Ben?

Ben *(gallantly).* How do you do, my dear.

Linda. Where've you been all these years? Willy's always wondered why you . . .

Willy *(pulling Ben away from her impatiently).* Where is Dad? Didn't you follow him? How did you get started?

Ben. Well, I don't know how much you remember.

Willy. Well, I was just a baby, of course, only three or four years old . . .

Ben. Three years and eleven months.

Willy. What a memory, Ben!

Ben. I have many enterprises, William, and I have never kept books.

Willy. I remember I was sitting under the wagon in—was it Nebraska?

Ben. It was South Dakota, and I gave you a bunch of wild flowers.

Willy. I remember you walking away down some open road.

Ben *(laughing).* I was going to find Father in Alaska.

Willy. Where is he?

Ben. At that age I had a very faulty view of geography, William. I discovered after a few days that I was heading due south, so instead of Alaska, I ended up in Africa.

Linda. Africa!

Willy. The Gold Coast!

Ben. Principally diamond mines.

Linda. Diamond mines!

Ben. Yes, my dear. But I've only a few minutes . . .

Willy. No! Boys! Boys! *(Young Biff and Happy appear.)* Listen to this. This is your Uncle Ben, a great man! Tell my boys, Ben!

Ben. Why, boys, when I was seventeen I walked into the jungle, and when I was twenty-one I walked out. *(He laughs.)* And by God I was rich.

Willy *(to the boys).* You see what I been talking about? The greatest things can happen!

Ben *(glancing at his watch).* I have an appointment in Ketchikan Tuesday week.

Willy. No, Ben! Please tell about Dad. I want my boys to hear. I want them to know the kind of stock they spring from. All I remember is a man with a big beard, and I was in Mamma's lap, sitting around a fire, and some kind of high music.

Ben. His flute. He played the flute.

Willy. Sure, the flute, that's right!

New music is heard, a high, rollicking tune.

Ben. Father was a very great and a very wild-hearted man. We would start in Boston, and he'd toss the whole family into the wagon, and then he'd drive the team right across the country; through Ohio, and Indiana, Michigan, Illinois, and all the Western states. And we'd stop in the towns and sell the flutes that he'd made on the way. Great inventor, Father. With one gadget he made more in a week than a man like you could make in a lifetime.

Willy. That's just the way I'm bringing them up, Ben—rugged, well liked, all-around.

Ben. Yeah? *(To Biff.)* Hit that, boy—hard as you can. *(He pounds his stomach.)*

Biff. Oh, no, sir!

Ben *(taking boxing stance).* Come on, get to me! *(He laughs.)*

Willy. Go to it, Biff! Go ahead, show him!

Biff. Okay! *(He cocks his fists and starts in.)*

Linda *(to Willy).* Why must he fight, dear?

Ben *(sparring with Biff).* Good boy! Good boy!

Willy. How's that, Ben, heh?

Happy. Give him the left, Biff!

Linda. Why are you fighting?

Ben. Good boy! *(Suddenly comes in, trips Biff, and stands over him, the point of his umbrella poised over Biff's eye.)*

Linda. Look out, Biff!

Biff. Gee!

Ben *(Patting Biff's knee).* Never fight fair with a stranger, boy. You'll never get out of the jungle that way. *(Taking Linda's hand and bowing.)* It was an honor and a pleasure to meet you, Linda.

Linda *(withdrawing her hand coldly, frightened).* Have a nice—trip.

Ben *(to Willy).* And good luck with your—what do you do?

Willy. Selling.

Ben. Yes. Well . . . *(He raises his hand in farewell to all.)*

Willy. No, Ben, I don't want you to think . . . *(He takes Ben's arm to show him.)* It's Brooklyn, I know, but we hunt too.

Ben. Really, now.

Willy. Oh, sure, there's snakes and rabbits and—that's why I moved out here. Why Biff can fell any one of these trees in no time! Boys! Go right over to where they're building the apartment house and get some sand. We're gonna rebuild the entire front stoop right now! Watch this, Ben!

Biff. Yes, sir! On the double, Hap!

Happy *(as he and Biff run off).* I lost weight, Pop, you notice?

Charley enters in knickers, even before the boys are gone.

Charley. Listen, if they steal any more from that building the watchman'll put the cops on them!

Linda *(to Willy).* Don't let Biff . . .

Ben laughs lustily.

Willy. You shoulda seen the lumber they brought home last week. At least a dozen six-by-tens worth all kinds a money.

Charley. Listen, if that watchman . . .

Willy. I gave them hell, understand. But I got a couple of fearless characters there.

Charley. Willy, the jails are full of fearless characters.

Ben *(clapping Willy on the back, with a laugh at Charley).* And the stock exchange, friend!

Willy *(joining in Ben's laughter).* Where are the rest of your pants?

Charley. My wife bought them.

Willy. Now all you need is a golf club and you can go upstairs and go to sleep. *(To Ben.)* Great athlete! Between him and his son Bernard they can't hammer a nail!

Bernard *(rushing in).* The watchman's chasing Biff!

Willy *(angrily).* Shut up! He's not stealing anything!

Linda *(alarmed, hurrying off left).* Where is he? Biff, dear! *(She exits.)*

Willy *(moving toward the left, away from Ben).* There's nothing wrong. What's the matter with you?

Ben. Nervy boy. Good!

Willy *(laughing).* Oh, nerves of iron, that Biff!

Charley. Don't know what it is. My New England man comes back and he's bleedin', they murdered him up there.

Willy. It's contacts, Charley, I got important contacts!

Charley *(sarcastically).* Glad to hear it, Willy. Come in later, we'll shoot a little casino. I'll take some of your Portland money. *(He laughs at Willy and exits.)*

Willy *(turning to Ben).* Business is bad, it's murderous. But not for me, of course.

Ben. I'll stop by on my way back to Africa.

Willy *(longingly).* Can't you stay a few days? You're just what I need, Ben, because I—I have a fine position here, but I—well, Dad left when I was such a baby and I never had a chance to talk to him and I still feel—kind of temporary about myself.

Ben. I'll be late for my train.

They are at opposite ends of the stage:

Willy. Ben, my boys—can't we talk? They'd go into the jaws of hell for me, see, but I . . .

Ben. William, you're being first-rate with your boys. Outstanding, manly chaps!

Willy *(hanging on to his words).* Oh, Ben, that's good to hear! Because sometimes I'm afraid that I'm not teaching them the right kind of—Ben, how should I teach them?

Ben *(giving great weight to each word, and with a certain vicious audacity).* William, when I walked into the jungle, I was seventeen. When I walked out I was twenty-one. And, by God, I was rich! *(He goes off into darkness around the right corner of the house.)*

Willy. . . . was rich! That's just the spirit I want to imbue them with! To walk into a jungle! I was right! I was right! I was right!

Ben is gone, but Willy is still speaking to him as Linda, in nightgown and robe, enters the kitchen, glances around for Willy, then goes to the door of the house, looks out and sees him. Comes down to his left. He looks at her.

Linda. Willy, dear? Willy?

Willy. I was right!

Linda. Did you have some cheese? *(He can't answer.)* It's very late, darling. Come to bed, heh?

Willy *(looking straight up).* Gotta break your neck to see a star in this yard.

Linda. You coming in?

Willy. Whatever happened to that diamond watch fob? Remember? When Ben came from Africa that time? Didn't he give me a watch fob with a diamond in it?

Linda. You pawned it, dear. Twelve, thirteen years ago. For Biff's radio correspondence course.

Willy. Gee, that was a beautiful thing. I'll take a walk.

Linda. But you're in your slippers.

Willy *(starting to go around the house at the left).* I was right! I was! *(Half to Linda, as he goes, shaking his head.)* What a man! There was a man worth talking to. I was right!

Linda *(calling after Willy).* But in your slippers, Willy!

Willy is almost gone when Biff, in his pajamas, comes down the stairs and enters the kitchen.

Biff. What is he doing out there?

Linda. Sh!

Biff. God Almighty, Mom, how long has he been doing this?

Linda. Don't, he'll hear you.

Biff. What the hell is the matter with him?

Linda. It'll pass by morning.

Biff. Shouldn't we do anything?

Linda. Oh, my dear, you should do a lot of things, but there's nothing to do, so go to sleep.

Happy comes down the stair and sits on the steps.

Happy. I never heard him so loud, Mom.

Linda. Well, come around more often; you'll hear him. *(She sits down at the table and mends the lining of Willy's jacket.)*

Biff. Why didn't you ever write me about this, Mom?

Linda. How would I write to you? For over three months you had no address.

Biff. I was on the move. But you know I thought of you all the time. You know that, don't you, pal?

Linda. I know, dear, I know. But he likes to have a letter. Just to know that there's still a possibility for better things.

Biff. He's not like this all the time, is he?

Linda. It's when you come home he's always the worst.

Biff. When I come home?

Linda. When you write you're coming, he's all smiles, and talks about the future, and—he's just wonderful. And then the closer you seem to come, the more shaky he gets, and then, by the time you get here, he's arguing, and he seems angry at you. I think it's just that maybe he can't bring himself to—to open up to you. Why are you so hateful to each other? Why is that?

Biff *(evasively)*. I'm not hateful, Mom.

Linda. But you no sooner come in the door than you're fighting!

Biff. I don't know why. I mean to change. I'm tryin', Mom, you understand?

Linda. Are you home to stay now?

Biff. I don't know. I want to look around, see what's doin'.

Linda. Biff, you can't look around all your life, can you?

Biff. I just can't take hold, Mom. I can't take hold of some kind of a life.

Linda. Biff, a man is not a bird, to come and go with the springtime.

Biff. Your hair . . . *(He touches her hair.)* Your hair got so gray.

Linda. Oh, it's been gray since you were in high school. I just stopped dyeing it, that's all.

Biff. Dye it again, will ya? I don't want my pal looking old. *(He smiles.)*

Linda. You're such a boy! You think you can go away for a year and . . . You've got to get it into your head now that one day you'll knock on this door and there'll be strange people here . . .

Biff. What are you talking about? You're not even sixty, Mom.

Linda. But what about your father?

Biff *(lamely)*. Well, I meant him too.

Happy. He admires Pop.

Linda. Biff, dear, if you don't have any feeling for him, then you can't have any feeling for me.

Biff. Sure I can, Mom.

Linda. No. You can't just come to see me, because I love him. *(With a threat, but only a threat, of tears.)* He's the dearest man in the world to me, and I won't have anyone making him feel unwanted and low and blue. You've got to make up your mind now, darling, there's no leeway any more. Either he's your father and you pay him that respect, or else you're not to come here. I know he's not easy to get along with—nobody knows that better than me—but . . .

Willy *(from the left, with a laugh)*. Hey, hey, Biffo!

Biff *(starting to go out after Willy).* What the hell is the matter with him? *(Happy stops him.)*

Linda. Don't—don't go near him!

Biff. Stop making excuses for him! He always, always wiped the floor with you. Never had an ounce of respect for you.

Happy. He's always had respect for . . .

Biff. What the hell do you know about it?

Happy *(surlily).* Just don't call him crazy!

Biff. He's got no character—Charley wouldn't do this. Not in his own house— spewing out that vomit from his mind.

Happy. Charley never had to cope with what he's got to.

Biff. People are worse off than Willy Loman. Believe me, I've seen them!

Linda. Then make Charley your father, Biff. You can't do that, can you? I don't say he's a great man. Willy Loman never made a lot of money. His name was never in the paper. He's not the finest character that ever lived. But he's a human being, and a terrible thing is happening to him. So attention must be paid. He's not to be allowed to fall into his grave like an old dog. Attention, attention must be finally paid to such a person. You called him crazy . . .

Biff. I didn't mean . . .

Linda. No, a lot of people think he's lost his—balance. But you don't have to be very smart to know what his trouble is. The man is exhausted.

Happy. Sure!

Linda. A small man can be just as exhausted as a great man. He works for a company thirty-six years this March, opens up unheard-of territories to their trademark, and now in his old age they take his salary away.

Happy *(indignantly).* I didn't know that, Mom.

Linda. You never asked, my dear! Now that you get your spending money someplace else you don't trouble your mind with him.

Happy. But I gave you money last . . .

Linda. Christmas time, fifty dollars! To fix the hot water it cost ninety-seven fifty! For five weeks he's been on straight commission, like a beginner, an unknown!

Biff. Those ungrateful bastards!

Linda. Are they any worse than his sons? When he brought them business, when he was young, they were glad to see him. But now his old friends, the old buyers that loved him so and always found some order to hand him in a pinch—they're all dead, retired. He used to be able to make six, seven calls a day in Boston. Now he takes his valises out of the car and puts them back and takes them out again and he's exhausted. Instead of walking he talks now. He drives seven hundred miles, and when he gets there no one knows him any more, no one welcomes him. And what goes through a man's mind, driving seven hundred miles home without having earned a cent? Why shouldn't he talk to himself? Why? When he has to go to Charley and borrow fifty dollars a week and pretend to me that it's his pay? How long can that go on? How long? You see what I'm sitting here and waiting for? And you tell me he has no character? The man who never worked a day but for your benefit? When does he get the medal for that? Is this his reward—to turn around at the age of sixty-three and find his sons, who he loved better than his life, one a philandering bum . . .

Happy. Mom!

Linda. That's all you are, my baby! *(To Biff.)* And you! What happened to the love you had for him? You were such pals! How you used to talk to him on the phone every night! How lonely he was till he could come home to you!

Biff. All right, Mom. I'll live here in my room, and I'll get a job. I'll keep away from him, that's all.

Linda. No, Biff. You can't stay here and fight all the time.

Biff. He threw me out of this house, remember that.

Linda. Why did he do that? I never knew why.

Biff. Because I know he's a fake and he doesn't like anybody around who knows!

Linda. Why a fake? In what way? What do you mean?

Biff. Just don't lay it all at my feet. It's between me and him—that's all I have to say. I'll chip in from now on. He'll settle for half my pay check. He'll be all right. I'm going to bed. *(He starts for the stairs.)*

Linda. He won't be all right.

Biff (turning on the stairs, furiously). I hate this city and I'll stay here. Now what do you want?

Linda. He's dying, Biff.

Happy turns quickly to her, shocked.

Biff (after a pause). Why is he dying?

Linda. He's been trying to kill himself.

Biff (with great horror). How?

Linda. I live from day to day.

Biff. What're you talking about?

Linda. Remember I wrote you that he smashed up the car again? In February?

Biff. Well?

Linda. The insurance inspector came. He said that they have evidence. That all these accidents in the last year—weren't—weren't—accidents.

Happy. How can they tell that? That's a lie.

Linda. It seems there's a woman . . . *(She takes a breath as:)*

 Biff (sharply but contained). What woman?

 Linda (simultaneously). . . . and this woman . . .

Linda. What?

Biff. Nothing. Go ahead.

Linda. What did you say?

Biff. Nothing, I just said what woman?

Happy. What about her?

Linda. Well, it seems she was walking down the road and saw his car. She says that he wasn't driving fast at all, and that he didn't skid. She says he came to that little bridge, and then deliberately smashed into the railing, and it was only the shallowness of the water that saved him.

Biff. Oh, no, he probably just fell asleep again.

Linda. I don't think he fell asleep.

Biff. Why not?

Linda. Last month . . . *(With great difficulty.)* Oh, boys, it's so hard to say a thing like this! He's just a big stupid man to you, but I tell you there's more good in him than in many other people. *(She chokes, wipes her eyes.)* I was looking for a fuse. The lights blew out, and I went down the cellar. And behind the fuse box—it happened to fall out—was a length of rubber pipe—just short.

Happy. No kidding!

Linda. There's a little attachment on the end of it. I knew right away. And sure enough, on the bottom of the water heater there's a new little nipple on the gas pipe.

Happy *(angrily).* That—jerk.

Biff. Did you have it taken off?

Linda. I'm—I'm ashamed to . How can I mention it to him? Every day I go down and take away that little rubber pipe. But, when he comes home, I put it back where it was. How can I insult him that way? I don't know what to do. I live from day to day, boys. I tell you, I know every thought in his mind. It sounds so old-fashioned and silly, but I tell you he put his whole life into you and you've turned your backs on him. *(She is bent over in the chair, weeping, her face in her hands.)* Biff, I swear to God! Biff, his life is in your hands!

Happy *(to Biff).* How do you like that damned fool!

Biff *(kissing her).* All right, pal, all right. It's all settled now. I've been remiss. I know that, Mom. But now I'll stay, and I swear to you, I'll apply myself. *(Kneeling in front of her, in a fever of self-reproach.)* It's just—you see, Mom, I don't fit in business. Not that I won't try. I'll try, and I'll make good.

Happy. Sure you will. The trouble with you in business was you never tried to please people.

Biff. I know, I . . .

Happy. Like when you worked for Harrison's. Bob Harrison said you were tops, and then you go and do some damn fool thing like whistling whole songs in the elevator like a comedian.

Biff *(against Happy).* So what? I like to whistle sometimes.

Happy. You don't raise a guy to a responsible job who whistles in the elevator!

Linda. Well, don't argue about it now.

Happy. Like when you'd go off and swim in the middle of the day instead of taking the line around.

Biff *(his resentment rising).* Well, don't you run off? You take off sometimes, don't you? On a nice summer day?

Happy. Yeah, but I cover myself!

Linda. Boys!

Happy. If I'm going to take a fade the boss can call any number where I'm supposed to be and they'll swear to him that I just left. I'll tell you something that I hate to say, Biff, but in the business world some of them think you're crazy.

Biff *(angered).* Screw the business world!

Happy. All right, screw it! Great, but cover yourself!

Linda. Hap, Hap!

Biff. I don't care what they think! They've laughed at Dad for years, and you know why? Because we don't belong in this nuthouse of a city! We should be mixing cement on some open plain or—or carpenters. A carpenter is allowed to whistle!

Willy walks in from the entrance of the house, at left.

Willy. Even your grandfather was better than a carpenter. *(Pause. They watch* *him.)* You never grew up. Bernard does not whistle in the elevator, I assure you.

Biff *(as though to laugh Willy out of it).* Yeah, but you do, Pop.

Willy. I never in my life whistled in an elevator! And who in the business world thinks I'm crazy?

Biff. I didn't mean it like that, Pop. Now don't make a whole thing out of it, will ya?

Willy. Go back to the West! Be a carpenter, a cowboy, enjoy yourself!

Linda. Willy, he was just saying . . .

Willy. I heard what he said!

Happy *(trying to quiet Willy).* Hey, Pop, come on now . . .

Willy *(continuing over Happy's line).* They laugh at me, heh? Go to Filene's, go to the Hub, go to Slattery's, Boston. Call out the name Willy Loman and see what happens! Big shot!

Biff. All right, Pop.

Willy. Big!

Biff. All right!

Willy. Why do you always insult me?

Biff. I didn't say a word. *(To Linda.)* Did I say a word?

Linda. He didn't say anything, Willy.

Willy *(going to the doorway of the living room).* All right, good night, good night.

Linda. Willy, dear, he just decided . . .

Willy *(to Biff).* If you get tired hanging around tomorrow, paint the ceiling I put up in the living room.

Biff. I'm leaving early tomorrow.

Happy. He's going to see Bill Oliver, Pop.

Willy *(interestedly).* Oliver? For what?

Biff *(with reserve, but trying, trying).* He always said he'd stake me. I'd like to go into business, so maybe I can take him up on it.

Linda. Isn't that wonderful?

Willy. Don't interrupt. What's wonderful about it? There's fifty men in the City of New York who'd stake him. *(To Biff.)* Sporting goods?

Biff. I guess so. I know something about it and . . .

Willy. He knows something about it! You know sporting goods better than Spalding, for God's sake! How much is he giving you?

Biff. I don't know, I didn't even see him yet, but . . .

Willy. Then what're you talkin' about?

Biff *(getting angry).* Well, all I said was I'm gonna see him, that's all!

Willy *(turning away).* Ah, you're counting your chickens again.

Biff *(starting left for the stairs).* Oh, Jesus, I'm going to sleep!

Willy *(calling after him).* Don't curse in this house!

Biff *(turning).* Since when did you get so clean?

Happy *(trying to stop them).* Wait a . . .

Willy. Don't use that language to me! I won't have it!

Happy *(grabbing Biff, shouts).* Wait a minute! I got an idea. I got a feasible idea. Come here, Biff, let's talk this over now, let's talk some sense here. When I was down in Florida last time, I thought of a great idea to sell sporting goods. It just came back to me. You and I, Biff—we have a line, the Loman Line. We train a couple of weeks, and put on a couple of exhibitions, see?

Willy. That's an idea!

Happy. Wait! We form two basketball teams, see? Two water-polo teams. We play each other. It's a million dollars' worth of publicity. Two brothers, see? The Loman Brothers. Displays in the Royal Palms—all the hotels. And banners over the ring and the basketball court: "Loman Brothers." Baby, we could sell sporting goods!

Willy. That is a one-million-dollar idea!

Linda. Marvelous!

Biff. I'm in great shape as far as that's concerned.

Happy. And the beauty of it is, Biff, it wouldn't be like a business. We'd be out playin' ball again . . .

Biff *(enthused).* Yeah, that's . . .

Willy. Million-dollar . . .

Happy. And you wouldn't get fed up with it, Biff. It'd be the family again. There'd be the old honor, and comradeship, and if you wanted to go off for a swim or somethin'—well, you'd do it! Without some smart cooky gettin' up ahead of you!

Willy. Lick the world! You guys together could absolutely lick the civilized world.

Biff. I'll see Oliver tomorrow. Hap, if we could work that out . . .

Linda. Maybe things are beginning to . . .

Willy *(wildly enthused, to Linda).* Stop interrupting! *(To Biff.)* But don't wear sport jacket and slacks when you see Oliver.

Biff. No, I'll . . .

Willy. A business suit, and talk as little as possible, and don't crack any jokes.

Biff. He did like me. Always liked me.

Linda. He loved you!

Willy *(to Linda).* Will you stop! *(To Biff.)* Walk in very serious. You are not applying for a boy's job. Money is to pass. Be quiet, fine, and serious. Everybody likes a kidder, but nobody lends him money.

Happy. I'll try to get some myself, Biff. I'm sure I can.

Willy. I see great things for you kids, I think your troubles are over. But remember, start big and you'll end big. Ask for fifteen. How much you gonna ask for?

Biff. Gee, I don't know . . .

Willy. And don't say "Gee." "Gee" is a boy's word. A man walking in for fifteen thousand dollars does not say "Gee!"

Biff. Ten, I think, would be top though.

Willy. Don't be so modest. You always started too low. Walk in with a big laugh. Don't look worried. Start off with a couple of your good stories to lighten things up. It's not what you say, it's how you say it—because personality always wins the day.

Linda. Oliver always thought the highest of him . . .

Willy. Will you let me talk?

Biff. Don't yell at her, Pop, will ya?

Willy *(angrily).* I was talking, wasn't I?

Biff. I don't like you yelling at her all the time, and I'm tellin' you, that's all.

Willy. What're you, takin' over this house?

Linda. Willy . . .

Willy *(turning to her)*. Don't take his side all the time, goddammit!

Biff *(furiously)*. Stop yelling at her!

Willy *(suddenly pulling on his cheek, beaten down, guilt ridden)*. Give my best to Bill Oliver—he may remember me. *(He exits through the living room doorway.)*

Linda *(her voice subdued)*. What'd you have to start that for? *(Biff turns away.)* You see how sweet he was as soon as you talked hopefully? *(She goes over to Biff.)* Come up and say good night to him. Don't let him go to bed that way.

Happy. Come on, Biff, let's buck him up.

Linda. Please, dear. Just say good night. It takes so little to make him happy. Come. *(She goes through the living room doorway, calling upstairs from within the living room.)* Your pajamas are hanging in the bathroom, Willy!

Happy *(looking toward where Linda went out)*. What a woman! They broke the mold when they made her. You know that, Biff?

Biff. He's off salary. My God, working on commission!

Happy. Well, let's face it: he's no hot-shot selling man. Except that sometimes, you have to admit, he's a sweet personality.

Biff *(deciding)*. Lend me ten bucks, will ya? I want to buy some new ties.

Happy. I'll take you to a place I know. Beautiful stuff. Wear one of my striped shirts tomorrow.

Biff. She got gray. Mom got awful old. Gee, I'm gonna go in to Oliver tomorrow and knock him for a . . .

Happy. Come on up. Tell that to Dad. Let's give him a whirl. Come on.

Biff *(steamed up)*. You know, with ten thousand bucks, boy!

Happy *(as they go into the living room)*. That's the talk, Biff, that's the first time I've heard the old confidence out of you! *(From within the living room, fading off.)* You're gonna live with me, kid, and any babe you want just say the word . . . *(The last lines are hardly heard. They are mounting the stairs to their parents' bedroom.)*

Linda *(entering her bedroom and addressing Willy, who is in the bathroom. She is straightening the bed for him)*. Can you do anything about the shower? It drips.

Willy *(from the bathroom)*. All of a sudden everything falls to pieces. Goddam plumbing, oughta be sued, those people. I hardly finished putting it in and the thing . . . *(His words rumble off.)*

Linda. I'm just wondering if Oliver will remember him. You think he might?

Willy *(coming out of the bathroom in his pajamas)*. Remember him? What's the matter with you, you crazy? If he'd've stayed with Oliver he'd be on top by now! Wait'll Oliver gets a look at him. You don't know the average caliber any more. The average young man today—*(he is getting into bed)*—is got a caliber of zero. Greatest thing in the world for him was to bum around.

Biff and Happy enter the bedroom. Slight pause.

Willy *(stops short, looking at Biff)*. Glad to hear it, boy.

Happy. He wanted to say good night to you, sport.

Willy *(to Biff)*. Yeah. Knock him dead, boy. What'd you want to tell me?

Biff. Just take it easy, Pop. Good night. *(He turns to go.)*

Willy *(unable to resist)*. And if anything falls off the desk while you're talking to him—like a package or something—don't you pick it up. They have office boys for that.

Linda. I'll make a big breakfast . . .

Willy. Will you let me finish? *(To Biff.)* Tell him you were in the business in the West. Not farm work.

Biff. All right, Dad.

Linda. I think everything . . .

Willy *(going right through her speech).* And don't undersell yourself. No less than fifteen thousand dollars.

Biff *(unable to bear him).* Okay. Good night, Mom. *(He starts moving.)*

Willy. Because you got a greatness in you, Biff, remember that. You got all kinds a greatness . . . *(He lies back, exhausted. Biff walks out.)*

Linda *(calling after Biff).* Sleep well, darling!

Happy. I'm gonna get married, Mom. I wanted to tell you.

Linda. Go to sleep, dear.

Happy *(going).* I just wanted to tell you.

Willy. Keep up the good work. *(Happy exits.)* God . . . remember that Ebbets Field game? The championship of the city?

Linda. Just rest. Should I sing to you?

Willy. Yeah. Sing to me. *(Linda hums a soft lullaby.)* When that team came out—he was the tallest, remember?

Linda. Oh, yes. And in gold.

Biff enters the darkened kitchen, takes a cigarette, and leaves the house. He comes downstage into a golden pool of light. He smokes, staring at the night.

Willy. Like a young god. Hercules—something like that. And the sun, the sun all around him. Remember how he waved to me? Right up from the field, with the representatives of three colleges standing by? And the buyers I brought, and the cheers when he came out—Loman, Loman, Loman! God Almighty, he'll be great yet. A star like that, magnificent, can never really fade away!

The light on Willy is fading. The gas heater begins to glow through the kitchen wall, near the stairs, a blue flame beneath red coils.

Linda *(timidly).* Willy dear, what has he got against you?

Willy. I'm so tired. Don't talk any more.

Biff slowly returns to the kitchen. He stops, stares toward the heater.

Linda. Will you ask Howard to let you work in New York?

Willy. First thing in the morning. Everything'll be all right.

Biff reaches behind the heater and draws out a length of rubber tubing. He is horrified and turns his head toward Willy's room, still dimly lit, from which the strains of Linda's desperate but monotonous humming rise.

Willy *(staring through the window into the moonlight).* Gee, look at the moon moving between the buildings!

Biff wraps the tubing around his hand and quickly goes up the stairs.

ACT II

Scene Music is heard, gay and bright. The curtain rises as the music fades away. Willy, in shirt sleeves, is sitting at the kitchen table, sipping coffee, his hat in his lap. Linda is filling his cup when she can.

Willy. Wonderful coffee. Meal in itself.

Linda. Can I make you some eggs?

Willy. No. Take a breath.

Linda. You look so rested, dear.

Willy. I slept like a dead one. First time in months. Imagine, sleeping till ten on a Tuesday morning. Boys left nice and early, heh?

Linda. They were out of here by eight o'clock.

Willy. Good work!

Linda. It was so thrilling to see them leaving together. I can't get over the shaving lotion in this house!

Willy *(smiling)*. Mmm . . .

Linda. Biff was very changed this morning. His whole attitude seemed to be hopeful. He couldn't wait to get downtown to see Oliver.

Willy. He's heading for a change. There's no question, there simply are certain men that take longer to get—solidified. How did he dress?

Linda. His blue suit. He's so handsome in that suit. He could be a—anything in that suit!

Willy gets up from the table. Linda holds his jacket for him.

Willy. There's no question, no question at all. Gee, on the way home tonight I'd like to buy some seeds.

Linda *(laughing)*. That'd be wonderful. But not enough sun gets back there. Nothing'll grow any more.

Willy. You wait, kid, before it's all over we're gonna get a little place out in the country, and I'll raise some vegetables, a couple of chickens . . .

Linda. You'll do it yet, dear.

Willy walks out of his jacket. Linda follows him.

Willy. And they'll get married, and come for a weekend. I'd build a little guest house. 'Cause I got so many fine tools, all I'd need would be a little lumber and some peace of mind.

Linda *(joyfully)*. I sewed the lining . . .

Willy. I could build two guest houses, so they'd both come. Did he decide how much he's going to ask Oliver for?

Linda *(getting him into the jacket)*. He didn't mention it, but I imagine ten or fifteen thousand. You going to talk to Howard today?

Willy. Yeah. I'll put it to him straight and simple. He'll just have to take me off the road.

Linda. And Willy, don't forget to ask for a little advance, because we've got the insurance premium. It's the grace period now.

Willy. That's a hundred . . .?

Linda. A hundred and eight, sixty-eight. Because we're a little short again.

Willy. Why are we short?

Linda. Well, you had the motor job on the car . . .

Willy. That goddam Studebaker!

Linda. And you got one more payment on the refrigerator . . .

Willy. But it just broke again!

Linda. Well, it's old, dear.

Willy. I told you we should've bought a well-advertised machine. Charley bought a General Electric and it's twenty years old and it's still good, that son-of-a-bitch.

Linda. But, Willy . . .

Willy. Whoever heard of a Hastings refrigerator? Once in my life I would like to own something outright before it's broken! I'm always in a race with the junkyard! I just finished paying for the car and it's on its last legs. The refrigerator consumes belts like a goddam maniac. They time those things. They time them so when you finally paid for them, they're used up.

Linda (*buttoning up his jacket as he unbuttons it*). All told, about two hundred dollars would carry us, dear. But that includes the last payment on the mortgage. After this payment, Willy, the house belongs to us.

Willy. It's twenty-five years!

Linda. Biff was nine years old when we bought it.

Willy. Well, that's a great thing. To weather a twenty-five year mortgage is . . .

Linda. It's an accomplishment.

Willy. All the cement, the lumber, the reconstruction I put in this house! There ain't a crack to be found in it any more.

Linda. Well, it served its purpose.

Willy. What purpose? Some stranger'll come along, move in, and that's that. If only Biff would take this house, and raise a family . . . (*He starts to go.*) Good-by, I'm late.

Linda (*suddenly remembering*). Oh, I forgot! You're supposed to meet them for dinner.

Willy. Me?

Linda. At Frank's Chop House on Forty-eighth near Sixth Avenue.

Willy. Is that so! How about you?

Linda. No, just the three of you. They're gonna blow you to a big meal!

Willy. Don't say! Who thought of that?

Linda. Biff came to me this morning, Willy, and he said, "Tell Dad, we want to blow him to a big meal." Be there six o'clock. You and your two boys are going to have dinner.

Willy. Gee whiz! That's really somethin'. I'm gonna knock Howard for a loop, kid. I'll get an advance, and I'll come home with a New York job. Goddammit, now I'm gonna do it!

Linda. Oh, that's the spirit, Willy!

Willy. I will never get behind a wheel the rest of my life!

Linda. It's changing, Willy, I can feel it changing!

Willy. Beyond a question. G'by, I'm late. (*He starts to go again.*)

Linda (*calling after him as she runs to the kitchen table for a handkerchief*). You got your glasses?

Willy (*feels for them, then comes back in*). Yeah, yeah, got my glasses.

Linda (*giving him the handkerchief*). And a handkerchief.

Willy. Yeah, handkerchief.

Linda. And your saccharine?
Willy. Yeah, my saccharine.
Linda. Be careful on the subway stairs.

She kisses him, and a silk stocking is seen hanging from her hand. Willy notices it.

Willy. Will you stop mending stockings? At least while I'm in the house. It gets me nervous. I can't tell you. Please.

Linda hides the stocking in her hand as she follows Willy across the forestage in front of the house.

Linda. Remember, Frank's Chop House.
Willy *(passing the apron).* Maybe beets would grow out there.
Linda *(laughing).* But you tried so many times.
Willy. Yeah. Well, don't work hard today. *(He disappears around the right corner of the house.)*
Linda. Be careful!

As Willy vanishes, Linda waves to him. Suddenly the phone rings. She runs across the stage and into the kitchen and lifts it.

Linda. Hello? Oh, Biff! I'm so glad you called, I just . . . Yes, sure, I just told him. Yes, he'll be there for dinner at six o'clock, I didn't forget. Listen, I was just dying to tell you. You know that little rubber pipe I told you about? That he connected to the gas heater? I finally decided to go down the cellar this morning and take it away and destroy it. But it's gone! Imagine? He took it away himself, it isn't there! *(She listens.)* When? Oh, then you took it. Oh—nothing, it's just that I'd hoped he'd taken it away himself. Oh, I'm not worried, darling, because this morning he left in such high spirits, it was like the old days! I'm not afraid any more. Did Mr. Oliver see you? . . . Well, you wait there then. And make a nice impression on him, darling. Just don't perspire too much before you see him. And have a nice time with Dad. He may have big news too! . . . That's right, a New York job. And be sweet to him tonight, dear. Be loving to him. Because he's only a little boat looking for a harbor. *(She is trembling with sorrow and joy.)* Oh, that's wonderful, Biff, you'll save his life. Thanks, darling. Just put your arm around him when he comes into the restaurant. Give him a smile. That's the boy . . . Good-by, dear . . . You got your comb? . . . That's fine. Good-by, Biff dear.

In the middle of her speech, Howard Wagner, thirty-six, wheels on a small typewriter table on which is a wire-recording machine and proceeds to plug it in. This is on the left forestage. Light slowly fades on Linda as it rises on Howard. Howard is intent on threading the machine and only glances over his shoulder as Willy appears.

Willy. Pst! Pst!
Howard. Hello, Willy, come in.
Willy. Like to have a little talk with you, Howard.
Howard. Sorry to keep you waiting. I'll be with you in a minute.
Willy. What's that, Howard?
Howard. Didn't you ever see one of these? Wire recorder.

Willy. Oh. Can we talk a minute?

Howard. Records things. Just got delivery yesterday. Been driving me crazy, the most terrific machine I ever saw in my life. I was up all night with it.

Willy. What do you do with it?

Howard. I bought it for dictation, but you can do anything with it. Listen to this. I had it home last night. Listen to what I picked up. The first one is my daughter. Get this. *(He flicks the switch and "Roll out the Barrel" is heard being whistled.)* Listen to that kid whistle.

Willy. That is lifelike, isn't it?

Howard. Seven years old. Get that tone.

Willy. Ts, ts. Like to ask a little favor if you . . .

The whistling breaks off, and the voice of Howard's daughter is heard.

His Daughter. "Now you, Daddy."

Howard. She's crazy for me! *(Again the same song is whistled.)* That's me! Ha! *(He winks.)*

Willy. You're very good!

The whistling breaks off again. The machine runs silent for a moment.

Howard. Sh! Get this now, this is my son.

His Son. "The capital of Alabama is Montgomery; the capital of Arizona is Phoenix; the capital of Arkansas is Little Rock; the capital of California is Sacramento . . . " *(and on, and on.)*

Howard *(holding up five fingers).* Five years old, Willy!

Willy. He'll make an announcer some day!

His Son *(continuing).* "The capital . . ."

Howard. Get that—alphabetical order! *(The machine breaks off suddenly.)* Wait a minute. The maid kicked the plug out.

Willy. It certainly is a . . .

Howard. Sh, for God's sake!

His Son. "It's nine o'clock, Bulova watch time. So I have to go to sleep."

Willy. That really is . . .

Howard. Wait a minute! The next is my wife.

They wait.

Howard's Voice. "Go on, say something." *(Pause.)* "Well, you gonna talk?"

His Wife. "I can't think of anything."

Howard's Voice. "Well, talk—it's turning."

His Wife *(shyly, beaten).* "Hello." *(Silence.)* "Oh, Howard, I can't talk into this . . ."

Howard *(snapping the machine off).* That was my wife.

Willy. That is a wonderful machine. Can we . . .

Howard. I tell you, Willy, I'm gonna take my camera, and my bandsaw, and all my hobbies, and out they go. This is the most fascinating relaxation I ever found.

Willy. I think I'll get one myself.

Howard. Sure, they're only a hundred and a half. You can't do without it. Supposing you wanna hear Jack Benny, see? But you can't be at home at that hour. So you tell the maid to turn the radio on when Jack Benny comes on, and this automatically goes on with the radio . . .

Death of a Salesman

Willy. And when you come home you . . .

Howard. You can come home twelve o'clock, one o'clock, any time you like, and you get yourself a Coke and sit yourself down, throw the switch, and there's Jack Benny's program in the middle of the night!

Willy. I'm definitely going to get one. Because lots of times I'm on the road, and I think to myself, what I must be missing on the radio!

Howard. Don't you have a radio in the car?

Willy. Well, yeah, but who ever thinks of turning it on?

Howard. Say, aren't you supposed to be in Boston?

Willy. That's what I want to talk to you about, Howard. You got a minute? *(He draws a chair in from the wing.)*

Howard. What happened? What're you doing here?

Willy. Well . . .

Howard. You didn't crack up again, did you?

Willy. Oh, no. No . . .

Howard. Geez, you had me worried there for a minute. What's the trouble?

Willy. Well, tell you the truth, Howard. I've come to the decision that I'd rather not travel any more.

Howard. Not travel! Well, what'll you do?

Willy. Remember, Christmas time, when you had the party here? You said you'd try to think of some spot for me here in town.

Howard. With us?

Willy. Well, sure.

Howard. Oh, yeah, yeah. I remember. Well, I couldn't think of anything for you, Willy.

Willy. I tell ya, Howard. The kids are all grown up, y'know. I don't need much any more. If I could take home—well, sixty-five dollars a week, I could swing it.

Howard. Yeah, but Willy, see I . . .

Willy. I tell ya why, Howard. Speaking frankly and between the two of us, y'know—I'm just a little tired.

Howard. Oh, I could understand that, Willy. But you're a road man, Willy, and we do a road business. We've only got a half-dozen salesmen on the floor here.

Willy. God knows, Howard. I never asked a favor of any man. But I was with the firm when your father used to carry you in here in his arms.

Howard. I know that, Willy, but . . .

Willy. Your father came to me the day you were born and asked me what I thought of the name of Howard, may he rest in peace.

Howard. I appreciate that, Willy, but there just is no spot here for you. If I had a spot I'd slam you right in, but I just don't have a single solitary spot.

He looks for his lighter. Willy has picked it up and gives it to him. Pause.

Willy *(with increasing anger).* Howard, all I need to set my table is fifty dollars a week.

Howard. But where am I going to put you, kid?

Willy. Look, it isn't a question of whether I can sell merchandise, is it?

Howard. No, but it's a business, kid, and everybody's gotta pull his own weight.

Willy *(desperately).* Just let me tell you a story, Howard . . .

Howard. 'Cause you gotta admit, business is business.

Willy *(angrily).* Business is definitely business, but just listen for a minute. You don't understand this. When I was a boy—eighteen, nineteen—I was already on the road. And there was a question in my mind as to whether selling had a future for me. Because in those days I had a yearning to go to Alaska. See, there were three gold strikes in one month in Alaska, and I felt like going out. Just for the ride, you might say.

Howard *(barely interested).* Don't say.

Willy. Oh, yeah, my father lived many years in Alaska. He was an adventurous man. We've got quite a little streak of self-reliance in our family. I thought I'd go out with my older brother and try to locate him, and maybe settle in the North with the old man. And I was almost decided to go, when I met a salesman in the Parker House. His name was Dave Singleman. And he was eighty-four years old, and he'd drummed merchandise in thirty-one states. And old Dave, he'd go up to his room, y'understand, put on his green velvet slippers—I'll never forget—and pick up his phone and call the buyers, and without ever leaving his room, at the age of eighty-four, he made his living. And when I saw that, I realized that selling was the greatest career a man could want. 'Cause what could be more satisfying than to be able to go, at the age of eighty-four, into twenty or thirty different cities, and pick up a phone, and be remembered and loved and helped by so many different people? Do you know? when he died—and by the way he died the death of a salesman, in his green velvet slippers in the smoker of the New York, New Haven and Hartford, going into Boston—when he died, hundreds of salesmen and buyers were at his funeral. Things were sad on a lotta trains for months after that. *(He stands up. Howard has not looked at him.)* In those days there was personality in it, Howard. There was respect, and comradeship, and gratitude in it. Today, it's all cut and dried, and there's no chance for bringing friendship to bear—or personality. You see what I mean? They don't know me any more.

Howard *(moving away, to the right).* That's just the thing, Willy.

Willy. If I had forty dollars a week—that's all I'd need. Forty dollars, Howard.

Howard. Kid, I can't take blood from a stone, I . . .

Willy *(desperation is on him now).* Howard, the year Al Smith was nominated, you father came to me and . . .

Howard *(starting to go off).* I've got to see some people, kid.

Willy *(stopping him).* I'm talking about your father! There were promises made across this desk! You mustn't tell me you've got people to see—I put thirty-four years into this firm, Howard, and now I can't pay my insurance! You can't eat the orange and throw the peel away—a man is not a piece of fruit! *(After a pause.)* Now pay attention. Your father—in 1928 I had a big year. I averaged a hundred and seventy dollars a week in commissions.

Howard *(impatiently).* Now, Willy, you never averaged . . .

Willy *(banging his hand on the desk).* I averaged a hundred and seventy dollars a week in the year of 1928! And your father came to me—or rather, I was in the office here—it was right over this desk—and he put his hand on my shoulder . . .

Howard *(getting up).* You'll have to excuse me, Willy, I gotta see some people. Pull yourself together. *(Going out.)* I'll be back in a little while.

On Howard's exit, the light on his chair grows very bright and strange.

Death of a Salesman

Willy. Pull myself together! What the hell did I say to him? My God, I was yelling at him! How could I? *(Willy breaks off, staring at the light, which occupies the chair, animating it. He approaches this chair, standing across the desk from it.)* Frank, Frank, don't you remember what you told me that time? How you put your hand on my shoulder, and Frank . . . *(He leans on the desk and as he speaks the dead man's name he accidentally switches on the recorder, and instantly)*

Howard's Son. ". . . of New York is Albany. The capital of Ohio is Cincinnati, the capital of Rhode Island is . . ." *(The recitation continues.)*

Willy *(leaping away with fright, shouting).* Ha! Howard! Howard! Howard!

Howard *(rushing in).* What happened?

Willy *(pointing at the machine, which continues nasally, childishly, with the capital cities).* Shut it off! Shut it off!

Howard *(pulling the plug out).* Look, Willy . . .

Willy *(pressing his hands to his eyes).* I gotta get myself some coffee. I'll get some coffee . . .

Willy starts to walk out. Howard stops him.

Howard *(rolling up the cord).* Willy, look . . .

Willy. I'll go to Boston.

Howard. Willy, you can't go to Boston for us.

Willy. Why can't I go?

Howard. I don't want you to represent us. I've been meaning to tell you for a long time now.

Willy. Howard, are you firing me?

Howard. I think you need a good long rest, Willy.

Willy. Howard . . .

Howard. And when you feel better, come back, and we'll see if we can work something out.

Willy. But I gotta earn money, Howard. I'm in no position to . . .

Howard. Where are your sons? Why don't your sons give you a hand?

Willy. They're working on a very big deal.

Howard. This is no time for false pride, Willy. You go to your sons and you tell them that you're tired. You've got two great boys, haven't you?

Willy. Oh, no question, no question, but in the meantime . . .

Howard. Then that's that, heh?

Willy. All right, I'll go to Boston tomorrow.

Howard. No, no.

Willy. I can't throw myself on my sons. I'm not a cripple!

Howard. Look, kid, I'm busy this morning.

Willy *(grasping Howard's arm).* Howard, you've got to let me go to Boston!

Howard *(hard, keeping himself under control).* I've got a line of people to see this morning. Sit down, take five minutes, and pull yourself together, and then go home, will ya? I need the office, Willy. *(He starts to go, turns, remembering the recorder, starts to push off the table holding the recorder.)* Oh, yeah. Whenever you can this week, stop by and drop off the samples. You'll feel better, Willy, and then come back and we'll talk. Pull yourself together, kid, there's people outside.

Howard exits, pushing the table off left. Willy stares into space, exhausted. Now the music is heard—Ben's music—first distantly, then closer, closer. As Willy speaks, Ben enters from the right. He carries valise and umbrella.

Willy. Oh, Ben, how did you do it? What is the answer? Did you wind up the Alaska deal already?

Ben. Doesn't take much time if you know what you're doing. Just a short business trip. Boarding ship in an hour. Wanted to say good-by.

Willy. Ben, I've got to talk to you.

Ben (*glancing at his watch*). Haven't the time, William.

Willy (*crossing the apron to Ben*). Ben, nothing's working out. I don't know what to do.

Ben. Now, look here, William. I've bought timberland in Alaska and I need a man to look after things for me.

Willy. God, timberland! Me and my boys in those grand outdoors!

Ben. You've a new continent at your doorstep, William. Get out of these cities, they're full of talk and time payments and courts of law. Screw on your fists and you can fight for a fortune up there.

Willy. Yes, yes! Linda, Linda!

Linda enters as of old, with the wash.

Linda. Oh, you're back?

Ben. I haven't much time.

Willy. No, wait! Linda, he's got a proposition for me in Alaska.

Linda. But you've got . . . (*To Ben.*) He's got a beautiful job here.

Willy. But in Alaska, kid, I could . . .

Linda. You're doing well enough, Willy!

Ben (*to Linda*). Enough for what, my dear?

Linda (*frightened of Ben and angry at him*). Don't say those things to him! Enough to be happy right here, right now. (*To Willy, while Ben laughs.*) Why must everybody conquer the world? You're well liked, and the boys love you, and someday—(*To Ben*)—why, old man Wagner told him just the other day that if he keeps it up he'll be a member of the firm, didn't he, Willy?

Willy. Sure, sure. I am building something with this firm, Ben, and if a man is building something he must be on the right track, mustn't he?

Ben. What are you building? Lay your hand on it. Where is it?

Willy (*hesitantly*). That's true, Linda, there's nothing.

Linda. Why? (*To Ben.*) There's a man eighty-four years old—

Willy. That's right, Ben, that's right. When I look at that man I say, what is there to worry about?

Ben. Bah!

Willy. It's true, Ben. All he has to do is go into any city, pick up the phone, and he's making his living and you know why?

Ben (*picking up his valise*). I've got to go.

Willy (*holding Ben back*). Look at this boy!

Biff, in his high school sweater, enters carrying suitcase. Happy carries Biff's shoulder guards, gold helmet, and football pants.

Willy. Without a penny to his name, three great universities are begging for him,

Death of a Salesman

and from there the sky's the limit, because it's not what you do, Ben. It's who you know and the smile on your face! It's contacts, Ben, contacts! The whole wealth of Alaska passes over the lunch table at the Commodore Hotel, and that's the wonder, the wonder of this country, that a man can end with diamonds here on the basis of being liked! *(He turns to Biff.)* And that's why when you get out on that field today it's important. Because thousands of people will be rooting for you and loving you. *(To Ben, who has again begun to leave.)* And Ben! when he walks into a business office his name will sound out like a bell and all the doors will open to him! I've seen it, Ben, I've seen it a thousand times! You can't feel it with your hand like timber, but it's there!

Ben. Good-by, William.

Willy. Ben, am I right? Don't you think I'm right? I value your advice.

Ben. There's a new continent at your doorstep, William. You could walk out rich. Rich! *(He is gone.)*

Willy. We'll do it here, Ben! You hear me? We're gonna do it here!

Young Bernard rushes in. The gay music of the Boys is heard.

Bernard. Oh, gee, I was afraid you left already!

Willy. Why? What time is it?

Bernard. It's half-past one!

Willy. Well, come on, everybody! Ebbets Field next stop! Where's the pennants? *(He rushes through the wall-line of the kitchen and out into the living room.)*

Linda *(to Biff).* Did you pack fresh underwear?

Biff *(who has been limbering up).* I want to go!

Bernard. Biff, I'm carrying your helmet, ain't I?

Happy. No, I'm carrying the helmet.

Bernard. Oh, Biff, you promised me.

Happy. I'm carrying the helmet.

Bernard. How am I going to get in the locker room?

Linda. Let him carry the shoulder guards. *(She puts her coat and hat on in the kitchen.)*

Bernard. Can I, Biff? 'Cause I told everybody I'm going to be in the locker room.

Happy. In Ebbets Field it's the clubhouse.

Bernard. I meant the clubhouse. Biff!

Happy. Biff!

Biff *(grandly, after a slight pause).* Let him carry the shoulder guards.

Happy *(as he gives Bernard the shoulder guards).* Stay close to us now.

Willy rushes in with the pennants.

Willy *(handing them out).* Everybody wave when Biff comes out on the field. *(Happy and Bernard run off.)* You set now, boy?

The music has died away.

Biff. Ready to go, Pop. Every muscle is ready.

Willy *(at the edge of the apron).* You realize what this means?

Biff. That's right, Pop.

Willy *(feeling Biff's muscles).* You're comin' home this afternoon captain of the All-Scholastic Championship Team of the City of New York.

Biff. I got it, Pop. And remember, pal, when I take off my helmet, that touchdown is for you.

Willy. Let's go! *(He is starting out, with his arm around Biff, when Charley enters, as of old, in knickers.)* I got no room for you, Charley.

Charley. Room? For what?

Willy. In the car.

Charley. You goin' for a ride? I wanted to shoot some casino.

Willy *(furiously).* Casino! *(Incredulously.)* Don't you realize what today is?

Linda. Oh, he knows, Willy. He's just kidding you.

Willy. That's nothing to kid about!

Charley. No, Linda, what's goin on?

Linda. He's playing in Ebbets Field.

Charley. Baseball in this weather?

Willy. Don't talk to him. Come on, come on! *(He is pushing them out.)*

Charley. Wait a minute, didn't you hear the news?

Willy. What?

Charley. Don't you listen to the radio? Ebbets Field just blew up.

Willy. You go to hell! *(Charley laughs. Pushing them out.)* Come on, come on! We're late.

Charley *(as they go).* Knock a homer, Biff, knock a homer!

Willy *(the last to leave, turning to Charley).* I don't think that was funny, Charley. This is the greatest day of his life.

Charley. Willy, when are you going to grow up?

Willy. Yeah, heh? When this game is over, Charley, you'll be laughing out of the other side of your face. They'll be calling him another Red Grange. Twenty-five thousand a year.

Charley *(kidding).* Is that so?

Willy. Yeah, that's so.

Charley. Well, then, I'm sorry, Willy. But tell me something.

Willy. What?

Charley. Who is Red Grange?

Willy. Put up your hands. Goddam you, put up your hands!

Charley, chuckling, shakes his head and walks away, around the left corner of the stage. Willy follows him. The music rises to a mocking frenzy.

Willy. Who the hell do you think you are, better than everybody else? You don't know everything, you big, ignorant, stupid . . . Put up your hands!

Light rises, on the right side of the forestage, on a small table in the reception room of Charley's office. Traffic sounds are heard. Bernard, now mature, sits whistling to himself. A pair of tennis rackets and an overnight bag are on the floor beside him.

Willy *(offstage).* What are you walking away for? Don't walk away! If you're going to say something say it to my face! I know you laugh at me behind my back. You'll laugh out of the other side of your goddam face after this game. Touchdown! Touchdown! Eighty thousand people! Touchdown! Right between the goal posts.

Bernard is a quiet, earnest, but self-assured young man. Willy's voice is coming from right upstage now. Bernard lowers his feet off the table and listens. Jenny, his father's secretary, enters.

Jenny *(distressed).* Say, Bernard, will you go out in the hall?

Bernard. What is that noise? Who is it?

Jenny. Mr. Loman. He just got off the elevator.

Bernard *(getting up).* Who's he arguing with?

Jenny. Nobody. There's nobody with him. I can't deal with him any more, and your father gets all upset everytime he comes. I've got a lot of typing to do, and your father's waiting to sign it. Will you see him?

Willy *(entering).* Touchdown! Touch—*(He sees Jenny.)* Jenny, Jenny, good to see you. How're ya? Workin'? Or still honest?

Jenny. Fine. How've you been feeling?

Willy. Not much any more, Jenny. Ha, ha! *(He is surprised to see the rackets.)*

Bernard. Hello, Uncle Willy.

Willy *(almost shocked).* Bernard! Well, look who's here! *(He comes quickly, guiltily, to Bernard and warmly shakes his hand.)*

Bernard. How are you? Good to see you.

Willy. What are you doing here?

Bernard. Oh, just stopped by to see Pop. Get off my feet till my train leaves. I'm going to Washington in a few minutes.

Willy. Is he in?

Bernard. Yes, he's in his office with the accountant. Sit down.

Willy *(sitting down).* What're you going to do in Washington?

Bernard. Oh, just a case I've got there, Willy.

Willy. That so? *(Indicating the rackets.)* You going to play tennis there?

Bernard. I'm staying with a friend who's got a court.

Willy. Don't say. His own tennis court. Must be fine people, I bet.

Bernard. They are, very nice. Dad tells me Biff's in town.

Willy *(with a big smile).* Yeah, Biff's in. Working on a very big deal, Bernard.

Bernard. What's Biff doing?

Willy. Well, he's been doing very big things in the West. But he decided to establish himself here. Very big. We're having dinner. Did I hear your wife had a boy?

Bernard. That's right. Our second.

Willy. Two boys! What do you know!

Bernard. What kind of a deal has Biff got?

Willy. Well, Bill Oliver—very big sporting-goods man—he wants Biff very badly. Called him in from the West. Long distance, carte blanche, special deliveries. Your friends have their own private tennis court?

Bernard. You still with the old firm, Willy?

Willy *(after a pause).* I'm—I'm overjoyed to see how you made the grade, Bernard, overjoyed. It's encouraging thing to see a young man really—really . . . Looks very good for Biff—very . . . *(He breaks off, then.)* Bernard . . . *(He is so full of emotion, he breaks off again.)*

Bernard. What is it, Willy?

Willy *(small and alone).* What—what's the secret?

Bernard. What secret?

Willy. How—how did you? Why didn't he ever catch on?

Bernard. I wouldn't know that, Willy.

Willy *(confidentially, desperately).* You were his friend, his boyhood friend. There's something I don't understand about it. His life ended after that Ebbets Field game. From the age of seventeen nothing good ever happened to him.

Bernard. He never trained himself for anything.

Willy. But he did, he did. After high school he took so many correspondence courses. Radio mechanics; television; God knows what, and never made the slightest mark.

Bernard *(taking off his glasses).* Willy, do you want to talk candidly?

Willy *(rising, faces Bernard).* I regard you as a very brilliant man, Bernard. I value your advice.

Bernard. Oh, the hell with the advice, Willy. I couldn't advise you. There's just one thing I've always wanted to ask you. When he was supposed to graduate, and the math teacher flunked him . . .

Willy. Oh, that son-of-a-bitch ruined his life.

Bernard. Yeah, but, Willy, all he had to do was go to summer school and make up that subject.

Willy. That's right, that's right.

Bernard. Did you tell him not to go to summer school?

Willy. Me? I begged him to go. I ordered him to go!

Bernard. Then why wouldn't he go?

Willy. Why? Why! Bernard, that question has been trailing me like a ghost for the last fifteen years. He flunked the subject, and laid down and died like a hammer hit him!

Bernard. Take it easy, kid.

Willy. Let me talk to you—I got nobody to talk to. Bernard, Bernard, was it my fault? Y'see? It keeps going around in my mind, maybe I did something to him. I got nothing to give him.

Bernard. Don't take it so hard.

Willy. Why did he lay down? What is the story there? You were his friend!

Bernard. Willy, I remember, it was June, and our grades came out. And he'd flunked math.

Willy. That son-of-a-bitch!

Bernard. No, it wasn't right then. Biff just got very angry, I remember, and he was ready to enroll in summer school.

Willy *(surprised).* He was?

Bernard. He wasn't beaten by it at all. But then, Willy, he disappeared from the block for almost a month. And I got the idea that he'd gone up to New England to see you. Did he have a talk with you then?

Willy stares in silence.

Bernard. Willy?

Willy *(with a strong edge of resentment in his voice).* Yeah, he came to Boston. What about it?

Bernard. Well, just that when he came back—I'll never forget this, it always mystifies me. Because I'd thought so well of Biff, even though he'd always taken advantage of me. I loved him, Willy, y'know? And he came back after that month and took his sneakers—remember those sneakers with "University of Virginia" printed on them? He was so proud of those, wore them every day. And he took them down in the cellar, and burned them up in the furnace. We had a fist fight. It lasted at least half an hour. Just the two of us, punching each other down the cellar, and crying right through it. I've often thought of how strange it was that I knew he'd given up his life. What happened in Boston, Willy?

Willy looks at him as at an intruder.

Bernard. I just bring it up because you asked me.
Willy (*angrily*). Nothing. What do you mean, "What happened?" What's that got to do with anything?
Bernard. Well, don't get sore.
Willy. What are you trying to do, blame it on me? If a boy lays down is that my fault?
Bernard. Now, Willy, don't get . . .
Willy. Well, don't—don't talk to me that way! What does that mean, "What happened?"

Charley enters. He is in his vest, and he carries a bottle of bourbon.

Charley. Hey; you're going to miss that train. (*He waves the bottle.*)
Bernard. Yeah, I'm going. (*He takes the bottle.*) Thanks, Pop. (*He picks up his rackets and bag.*) Good-by, Willy, and don't worry about it. You know, "If at first you don't succeed . . ."
Willy. Yes, I believe in that.
Bernard. But sometimes, Willy, it's better for a man just to walk away.
Willy. Walk away?
Bernard. That's right.
Willy. But if you can't walk away?
Bernard (*after a slight pause*). I guess that's when it's tough. (*Extending his hand.*) Good-by, Willy.
Willy (*shaking Bernard's hand*). Good-by, boy.
Charley (*an arm on Bernard's shoulder*). How do you like this kid? Gonna argue a case in front of the Supreme Court.
Bernard (*protesting*). Pop!
Willy (*genuinely shocked, pained, and happy*). No! The Supreme Court!
Bernard. I gotta run. 'By, Dad!
Charley. Knock 'em dead, Bernard!

Bernard goes off.

Willy (*as Charley takes out his wallet*). The Supreme Court! And he didn't even mention it!
Charley (*counting out money on the desk*). He don't have to—he's gonna do it.
Willy. And you never told him what to do, did you? You never took any interest in him.
Charley. My salvation is that I never took any interest in anything. There's some money—fifty dollars. I got an accountant inside.
Willy. Charley, look . . . (*With difficulty.*) I got my insurance to pay. If you can manage it—I need a hundred and ten dollars.

Charley doesn't reply for a moment; merely stops moving.

Willy. I'd draw it from my bank but Linda would know, and I . . .

Charley. Sit down, Willy.

Willy *(moving toward the chair).* I'm keeping an account of everything, remember. I'll pay every penny back. *(He sits.)*

Charley. Now listen to me, Willy.

Willy. I want you to know I appreciate . . .

Charley *(sitting down on the table).* Willy, what're you doin'? What the hell is going on in your head?

Willy. Why? I'm simply . . .

Charley. I offered you a job. You make fifty dollars a week, and I won't send you on the road.

Willy. I've got a job.

Charley. Without pay? What kind of a job is a job without pay? *(He rises.)* Now, look, kid, enough is enough. I'm no genius but I know when I'm being insulted.

Willy. Insulted!

Charley. Why don't you want to work for me?

Willy. What's the matter with you? I've got a job.

Charley. Then what're you walkin' in here every week for?

Willy *(getting up).* Well, if you don't want me to walk in here. . . .

Charley. I'm offering you a job.

Willy. I don't want your goddam job!

Charley. When the hell are you going to grow up?

Willy *(furiously).* You big ignoramus, if you say that to me again I'll rap you one! I don't care how big you are! *(He's ready to fight.)*

Pause.

Charley *(kindly, going to him).* How much do you need, Willy?

Willy. Charley, I'm strapped. I'm strapped. I don't know what to do. I was just fired.

Charley. Howard fired you?

Willy. That snotnose. Imagine that? I named him. I named him Howard.

Charley. Willy, when're you gonna realize that them things don't mean anything? You named him Howard, but you can't sell that. The only thing you got in this world is what you can sell. And the funny thing is that you're a salesman, and you don't know that.

Willy. I've always tried to think otherwise, I guess. I always felt that if a man was impressive, and well liked, that nothing . . .

Charley. Why must everybody like you? Who liked J. P. Morgan? Was he impressive? In a Turkish bath he'd look like a butcher. But with his pockets on he was very well liked. Now listen, Willy, I know you don't like me, and nobody can say I'm in love with you, but I'll give you a job because—just for the hell of it, put it that way. Now what do you say?

Willy. I—I just can't work for you, Charley.

Charley. What're you, jealous of me?

Willy. I can't work for you, that's all, don't ask me why.

Charley *(angered, takes out more bills).* You been jealous of me all your life, you damned fool! Here, pay your insurance. *(He puts the money in Willy's hand.)*

Willy. I'm keeping strict accounts.

Charley. I've got some work to do. Take care of yourself. And pay your insurance.

Willy *(moving to the right)*. Funny, y'know? After all the highways, and the trains, and the appointments, and the years, you end up worth more dead than alive.

Charley. Willy, nobody's worth nothin' dead. *(After a slight pause.)* Did you hear what I said?

Willy stands still, dreaming.

Charley. Willy!

Willy. Apologize to Bernard for me when you see him. I didn't mean to argue with him. He's a fine boy. They're all fine boys, and they'll end up big—all of them. Someday they'll all play tennis together. Wish me luck, Charley. He saw Bill Oliver today.

Charley. Good luck.

Willy *(on the verge of tears)*. Charley, you're the only friend I got. Isn't that a remarkable thing? *(He goes out.)*

Charley. Jesus!

Charley stares after him a moment and follows. All light blacks out. Suddenly raucous music is heard, and a red glow rises behind the screen at right. Stanley, a young waiter, appears, carrying a table, followed by Happy, who is carrying two chairs.

Stanley *(putting the table down)*. That's all right, Mr. Loman, I can handle it myself. *(He turns and takes the chairs from Happy and places them at the table.)*

Happy *(glancing around)*. Oh, this is better.

Stanley. Sure, in the front there you're in the middle of all kinds of noise. Whenever you got a party, Mr. Loman, you just tell me and I'll put you back here. Y'know, there's a lotta people they don't like it private, because when they go out they like to see a lotta action around them because they're sick and tired to stay in the house by theirself. But I know you, you ain't from Hackensack. You know what I mean?

Happy *(sitting down)*. So how's it coming, Stanley?

Stanley. Ah, it's a dog's life. I only wish during the war they'd a took me in the Army. I coulda been dead by now.

Happy. My brother's back, Stanley.

Stanley. Oh, he come back, heh? From the Far West.

Happy. Yeah, big cattle man, my brother, so treat him right. And my father's coming too.

Stanley. Oh, your father too!

Happy. You got a couple of nice lobsters?

Stanley. Hundred per cent, big.

Happy. I want them with the claws.

Stanley. Don't worry, I don't give you no mice. *(Happy laughs.)* How about some wine? It'll put a head on the meal.

Happy. No. You remember, Stanley, that recipe I brought you from overseas? With the champagne in it?

Stanley. Oh, yeah, sure. I still got it tacked up yet in the kitchen. But that'll have to cost a buck apiece anyways.

Happy. That's all right.

Stanley. What'd you, hit a number or somethin'?

Happy. No, it's a little celebration. My brother is—I think he pulled off a big deal today. I think we're going into business together.

Stanley. Great! That's the best for you. Because a family business, you know what I mean?—that's the best.

Happy. That's what I think.

Stanley. 'Cause what's the difference? Somebody steals? It's in the family. Know what I mean? *(Sotto voce.)* Like this bartender here. The boss is goin' crazy what kinda leak he's got in the cash register. You put it in but it don't come out.

Happy *(raising his head).* Sh!

Stanley. What?

Happy. You notice I wasn't lookin' right or left, was I?

Stanley. No.

Happy. And my eyes are closed.

Stanley. So what's the . . .?

Happy. Strudel's comin'.

Stanley *(catching on, looks around).* Ah, no, there's no . . .

He breaks off as a furred, lavishly dressed girl enters and sits at the next table. Both follow her with their eyes.

Stanley. Geez, how'd ya know?

Happy. I got radar or something. *(Staring directly at her profile.)* Oooooooo . . . Stanley.

Stanley. I think that's for you, Mr. Loman.

Happy. Look at that mouth. Oh, God. And the binoculars.

Stanley. Geez, you got a life, Mr. Loman.

Happy. Wait on her.

Stanley *(going to the Girl's table).* Would you like a menu, ma'am?

Girl. I'm expecting someone, but I'd like a . . .

Happy. Why don't you bring her—excuse me, miss, do you mind? I sell champagne, and I'd like you to try my brand. Bring her a champagne, Stanley.

Girl. That's awfully nice of you.

Happy. Don't mention it. It's all company money. *(He laughs.)*

Girl. That's a charming product to be selling, isn't it?

Happy. Oh, gets to be like everything else. Selling is selling, y'know.

Girl. I suppose.

Happy. You don't happen to sell, do you?

Girl. No, I don't sell.

Happy. Would you object to a compliment from a stranger? You ought to be on a magazine cover.

Girl *(looking at him a little archly).* I have been.

Stanley comes in with a glass of champagne.

Happy. What'd I say before, Stanley? You see? She's a cover girl.

Stanley. Oh, I could see, I could see.

Happy *(to the Girl).* What magazine?

Girl. Oh, a lot of them. *(She takes the drink.)* Thank you.

Happy. You know what they say in France, don't you? "Champagne is the drink of the complexion"—Hya, Biff!

Biff has entered and sits with Happy.

Biff. Hello, kid. Sorry I'm late.

Happy. I just got here. Uh, Miss . . .?

Girl. Forsythe.

Happy. Miss Forsythe, this is my brother.

Biff. Is Dad here?

Happy. His name is Biff. You might've heard of him. Great football player.

Girl. Really? What team?

Happy. Are you familiar with football?

Girl. No, I'm afraid I'm not.

Happy. Biff is quarterback with the New York Giants.

Girl. Well, that is nice, isn't it? *(She drinks.)*

Happy. Good health.

Girl. I'm happy to meet you.

Happy. That's my name. Hap. It's really Harold, but at West Point they called me Happy.

Girl (now really impressed). Oh, I see. How do you do? *(She turns her profile.)*

Biff. Isn't Dad coming?

Happy. You want her?

Biff. Oh, I could never make that.

Happy. I remember the time that idea would never come into your head. Where's the old confidence, Biff?

Biff. I just saw Oliver . . .

Happy. Wait a minute. I've got to see that old confidence again. Do you want her? She's on call.

Biff. Oh, no. *(He turns to look at the Girl.)*

Happy. I'm telling you. Watch this. *(Turning to the Girl.)* Honey? *(She turns to him.)* Are you busy?

Girl. Well, I am . . . but I could make a phone call.

Happy. Do that, will you, honey? And see if you can get a friend. We'll be here for a while. Biff is one of the greatest football players in the country.

Girl (standing up). Well, I'm certainly happy to meet you.

Happy. Come back soon.

Girl. I'll try.

Happy. Don't try, honey, try hard.

The Girl exits. Stanley follows, shaking his head in bewildered admiration.

Happy. Isn't that a shame now? A beautiful girl like that? That's why I can't get married. There's not a good woman in a thousand. New York is loaded with them, kid!

Biff. Hap, look . . .

Happy. I told you she was on call!

Biff (strangely unnerved). Cut it out, will ya? I want to say something to you.

Happy. Did you see Oliver?

Biff. I saw him all right. Now look, I want to tell Dad a couple of things and I want you to help me.

Happy. What? Is he going to back you?

Biff. Are you crazy? You're out of your goddam head, you know that?

Happy. Why? What happened?

Biff *(breathlessly).* I did a terrible thing today, Hap. It's been the strangest day I ever went through. I'm all numb, I swear.

Happy. You mean he wouldn't see you?

Biff. Well, I waited six hours for him, see? All day. Kept sending my name in. Even tried to date his secretary so she'd get me to him, but no soap.

Happy. Because you're not showin' the old confidence, Biff. He remembered you, didn't he?

Biff *(stopping Happy with a gesture).* Finally, about five o'clock, he comes out. Didn't remember who I was or anything. I felt like such an idiot, Hap.

Happy. Did you tell him my Florida idea?

Biff. He walked away. I saw him for one minute. I got so mad I could've torn the walls down! How the hell did I ever get the idea I was a salesman there? I even believed myself that I'd been a salesman for him! And then he gave me one look and—I realized what a ridiculous lie my whole life has been! We've been talking in a dream for fifteen years. I was a shipping clerk.

Happy. What'd you do?

Biff *(with great tension and wonder).* Well, he left, see. And the secretary went out. I was all alone in the waiting room. I don't know what came over me, Hap. The next thing I know I'm in his office—paneled walls, everything. I can't explain it. I—Hap, I took his fountain pen.

Happy. Geez, did he catch you?

Biff. I ran out. I ran down all eleven flights. I ran and ran and ran.

Happy. That was an awful dumb—what'd you do that for?

Biff *(agonized).* I don't know, I just—wanted to take something, I don't know. You gotta help me, Hap, I'm gonna tell Pop.

Happy. You crazy? What for?

Biff. Hap, he's got to understand that I'm not the man somebody lends that kind of money to. He thinks I've been spiting him all these years and it's eating him up.

Happy. That's just it. You tell him something nice.

Biff. I can't.

Happy. Say you got a lunch date with Oliver tomorrow.

Biff. So what do I do tomorrow?

Happy. You leave the house tomorrow and come back at night and say Oliver is thinking it over. And he thinks it over for a couple of weeks, and gradually it fades away and nobody's the worse.

Biff. But it'll go on forever!

Happy. Dad is never so happy as when he's looking forward to something!

Willy enters.

Happy. Hello, scout!

Willy. Gee, I haven't been here in years!

Stanley has followed Willy in and sets a chair for him. Stanley starts off but Happy stops him.

Happy. Stanley!

Stanley stands by, waiting for an order.

Biff *(going to Willy with guilt, as to an invalid).* Sit down, Pop. You want a drink?

Willy. Sure, I don't mind.

Biff. Let's get a load on.

Willy. You look worried.

Biff. N-no. *(To Stanley.)* Scotch all around. Make it doubles.

Stanley. Doubles, right. *(He goes.)*

Willy. You had a couple already, didn't you?

Biff. Just a couple, yeah.

Willy. Well, what happened, boy? *(Nodding affirmatively, with a smile.)* Everything go all right?

Biff *(takes a breath, then reaches out and grasps Willy's hand).* Pal . . . *(He is smiling bravely, and Willy is smiling too.)* I had an experience today.

Happy. Terrific, Pop.

Willy. That so? What happened?

Biff *(high, slightly alcoholic, above the earth).* I'm going to tell you everything from first to last. It's been a strange day. *(Silence. He looks around, composes himself as best he can, but his breath keeps breaking the rhythm of his voice.)* I had to wait quite a while for him, and . . .

Willy. Oliver?

Biff. Yeah, Oliver. All day, as a matter of cold fact. And a lot of—instances—facts, Pop, facts about my life came back to me. Who was it, Pop? Who ever said I was a salesman with Oliver?

Willy. Well, you were.

Biff. No, Dad, I was shipping clerk.

Willy. But you were practically . . .

Biff *(with determination).* Dad, I don't know who said it first, but I was never a salesman for Bill Oliver.

Willy. What're you talking about?

Biff. Let's hold on to the facts tonight, Pop. We're not going to get anywhere bullin' around. I was a shipping clerk.

Willy *(angrily).* All right, now listen to me . . .

Biff. Why don't you let me finish?

Willy. I'm not interested in stories about the past or any crap of that kind because the woods are burning, boys, you understand? There's a big blaze going on all around. I was fired today.

Biff *(shocked).* How could you be?

Willy. I was fired, and I'm looking for a little good news to tell your mother, because the woman has waited and the woman has suffered. The gist of it is that I haven't got a story left in my head, Biff. So don't give me a lecture about facts and aspects. I am not interested. Now what've you got to say to me?

Stanley enters with three drinks. They wait until he leaves.

Willy. Did you see Oliver?

Biff. Jesus, Dad!

Willy. You mean you didn't go up there?

Happy. Sure he went up there.

Biff. I did. I—saw him. How could they fire you?

Willy *(on the edge of his chair).* What kind of a welcome did he give you?

Biff. He won't even let you work on commission?

Willy. I'm out! *(Driving.)* So tell me, he gave you a warm welcome?

Happy. Sure, Pop, sure!

Biff *(driven).* Well, it was kind of . . .

Willy. I was wondering if he'd remember you. *(To Happy.)* Imagine, man doesn't see him for ten, twelve years and gives him that kind of a welcome!

Happy. Damn right!

Biff *(trying to return to the offensive).* Pop, look . . .

Willy. You know why he remembered you, don't you? Because you impressed him in those days.

Biff. Let's talk quietly and get this down to the facts, huh?

Willy *(as though Biff had been interrupting).* Well, what happened? It's great news, Biff. Did he take you into his office or'd you talk in the waiting room?

Biff. Well, he came in, see, and . . .

Willy *(with a big smile).* What'd he say? Betcha he threw his arm around you.

Biff. Well, he kinda . . .

Willy. He's a fine man. *(To Happy.)* Very hard man to see, y'know.

Happy *(agreeing).* Oh, I know.

Willy *(to Biff).* Is that where you had the drinks?

Biff. Yeah, he gave me a couple of—no, no!

Happy *(cutting in).* He told him my Florida idea.

Willy. Don't interrupt. *(To Biff.)* How'd he react to the Florida idea?

Biff. Dad, will you give me a minute to explain?

Willy. I've been waiting for you to explain since I sat down here! What happened? He took you into his office and what?

Biff. Well—I talked. And—and he listened, see.

Willy. Famous for the way he listens, y'know. What was his answer?

Biff. His answer was—*(He breaks off, suddenly angry.)* Dad, you're not letting me tell you what I want to tell you!

Willy *(accusing, angered).* You didn't see him, did you?

Biff. I did see him!

Willy. What'd you insult him or something? You insulted him, didn't you?

Biff. Listen, will you let me out of it, will you just let me out of it!

Happy. What the hell!

Willy. Tell me what happened!

Biff *(to Happy).* I can't talk to him!

A single trumpet note jars the ear. The light of green leaves stains the house, which holds the air of night and a dream. Young Bernard enters and knocks on the door of the house.

Young Bernard *(frantically).* Mrs. Loman, Mrs. Loman!

Happy. Tell him what happened!

Death of a Salesman

Biff *(to Happy).* Shut up and leave me alone!
Willy. No, no! You had to go and flunk math!
Biff. What math? What're you talking about?
Young Bernard. Mrs. Loman, Mrs. Loman!

 Linda appears in the house, as of old.

Willy *(wildly).* Math, math, math!
Biff. Take it easy, Pop!
Young Bernard. Mrs. Loman!
Willy *(furiously).* If you hadn't flunked you'd've been set by now!
Biff. Now, look, I'm gonna tell you what happened, and you're going to listen to me.
Young Bernard. Mrs. Loman!
Biff. I waited six hours . . .
Happy. What the hell are you saying?
Biff. I kept sending in my name but he wouldn't see me. So finally he . . . ¢ *(He continues unheard as light fades low on the restaurant.)*
Young Bernard. Biff flunked math!
Linda. No!
Young Bernard. Birnbaum flunked him! They won't graduate him!
Linda. But they have to. He's gotta go to the university. Where is he? Biff! Biff!
Young Bernard. No, he left. He went to Grand Central.
Linda. Grand—You mean he went to Boston!
Young Bernard. Is Uncle Willy in Boston?
Linda. Oh, maybe Willy can talk to the teacher. Oh, the poor, poor boy!

 Light on house area snaps out.

Biff *(at the table, now audible, holding up a gold fountain pen).* . . .so I'm washed up with Oliver, you understand? Are you listening to me?
Willy *(at a loss).* Yeah, sure. If you hadn't flunked . . .
Biff. Flunked what? What're you talking about?
Willy. Don't blame everything on me! I didn't flunk math—you did! What pen?
Happy. That was awful dumb, Biff, a pen like that is worth—
Willy *(seeing the pen for the first time).* You took Oliver's pen?
Biff *(weakening).* Dad, I just explained it to you.
Willy. You stole Bill Oliver's fountain pen!
Biff. I didn't exactly steal it! That's just what I've been explaining to you!
Happy. He had it in his hand and just then Oliver walked in, so he got nervous and stuck it in his pocket!
Willy. My God, Biff!
Biff. I never intended to do it, Dad!
Operator's Voice. Standish Arms, good evening!
Willy *(shouting).* I'm not in my room!
Biff *(frightened).* Dad, what's the matter? *(He and Happy stand up.)*
Operator. Ringing Mr. Loman for you!
Willy. I'm not there, stop it!
Biff *(horrified, gets down on one knee before Willy).* Dad, I'll make good, I'll make good. *(Willy tries to get to his feet. Biff holds him down.)* Sit down now.

Willy. No, you're no good, you're no good for anything.

Biff. I am, Dad, I'll find something else, you understand? Now don't worry about anything. *(He holds up Willy's face.)* Talk to me, Dad.

Operator. Mr. Loman does not answer. Shall I page him?

Willy *(attempting to stand, as though to rush and silence the Operator).* No, no, no!

Happy. He'll strike something, Pop.

Willy. No, no . . .

Biff *(desperately, standing over Willy).* Pop, listen! Listen to me! I'm telling you something good. Oliver talked to his partner about the Florida idea. You listening? He—he talked to his partner, and he came to me . . . I'm going to be all right, you hear? Dad, listen to me, he said it was just a question of the amount!

Willy. Then you . . . got it?

Happy. He's gonna be terrific, Pop!

Willy *(trying to stand).* Then you got it, haven't you? You got it! You got it!

Biff *(agonized, holds Willy down).* No, no. Look, Pop. I'm supposed to have lunch with them tomorrow. I'm just telling you this so you'll know that I can still make an impression, Pop. And I'll make good somewhere, but I can't go tomorrow, see?

Willy. Why not? You simply . . .

Biff. But the pen, Pop!

Willy. You give it to him and tell him it was an oversight!

Happy. Sure, have lunch tomorrow!

Biff. I can't say that . . .

Willy. You were doing a crossword puzzle and accidentally used his pen!

Biff. Listen, kid, I took those balls years ago, now I walk in with his fountain pen? That clinches it, don't you see? I can't face him like that! I'll try elsewhere.

Page's Voice. Paging Mr. Loman!

Willy. Don't you want to be anything?

Biff. Pop, how can I go back?

Willy. You don't want to be anything, is that what's behind it?

Biff *(now angry at Willy for not crediting his sympathy).* Don't take it that way! You think it was easy walking into that office after what I'd done to him? A team of horses couldn't have dragged me back to Bill Oliver!

Willy. Then why'd you go?

Biff. Why did I go? Why did I go! Look at you! Look at what's become of you!

Off left, The Woman laughs.

Willy. Biff, you're going to go to that lunch tomorrow, or . . .

Biff. I can't go. I've got no appointment!

Happy. Biff, for . . .!

Willy. Are you spiting me?

Biff. Don't take it that way! Goddammit!

Willy *(strikes Biff and falters away from the table).* You rotten little louse! Are you spiting me?

The Woman. Someone's at the door, Willy!

Death of a Salesman

Biff. I'm no good, can't you see what I am?

Happy (separating them). Hey, you're in a restaurant! Now cut it out, both of you! *(The girls enter.)* Hello, girls, sit down.

The Woman laughs, off left.

Miss Forsythe. I guess we might as well. This is Letta.

The Woman. Willy, are you going to wake up?

Biff (ignoring Willy). How're ya, miss, sit down. What do you drink?

Miss Forsythe. Letta might not be able to stay long.

Letta. I gotta get up very early tomorrow. I got jury duty. I'm so excited! Were you fellows ever on a jury?

Biff. No, but I been in front of them! *(The girls laugh.)* This is my father.

Letta. Isn't he cute? Sit down with us, Pop.

Happy. Sit him down, Biff!

Biff (going to him). Come on, slugger, drink us under the table. To hell with it! Come on, sit down, pal.

On Biff's last insistence, Willy is about to sit.

The Woman (now urgently). Willy, are you going to answer the door!

The Woman's call pulls Willy back. He starts right, befuddled.

Biff. Hey, where are you going?

Willy. Open the door.

Biff. The door?

Willy. The washroom . . . the door . . . where's the door?

Biff (leading Willy to the left). Just go straight down.

Willy moves left.

The Woman. Willy, Willy, are you going to get up, get up, get up, get up?

Willy exits left.

Letta. I think it's sweet you bring your daddy along.

Miss Forsythe. Oh, he isn't really your father!

Biff (at left, turning to her resentfully). Miss Forsythe, you've just seen a prince walk by. A fine, troubled prince. A hard-working, unappreciated prince. A pal, you understand? A good companion. Always for his boys.

Letta. That's so sweet.

Happy. Well, girls, what's the program? We're wasting time. Come on, Biff. Gather round. Where would you like to go?

Biff. Why don't you do something for him?

Happy. Me!

Biff. Don't you give a damn for him, Hap?

Happy. What're you talking about? I'm the one who—

Biff. I sense it, you don't give a good goddam about him. *(He takes the rolled-up hose from his pocket and puts it on the table in front of Happy.)* Look what I found in the cellar, for Christ's sake. How can you bear to let it go on?

Happy. Me? Who goes away? Who runs off and—

Biff. Yeah, but he doesn't mean anything to you. You could help him—I can't! Don't you understand what I'm talking about? He's going to kill himself, don't you know that?

Happy. Don't I know it! Me!

Biff. Hap, help him! Jesus . . . help him . . . Help me, help me, I can't bear to look at his face! *(Ready to weep, he hurries out, up right.)*

Happy *(starting after him).* Where are you going?

Miss Forsythe. What's he so mad about?

Happy. Come on, girls, we'll catch up with him.

Miss Forsythe *(as Happy pushes her out).* Say, I don't like that temper of his!

Happy. He's just a little overstrung, he'll be all right!

Willy *(off left, as The Woman laughs).* Don't answer! Don't answer!

Letta. Don't you want to tell your father . . .

Happy. No, that's not my father. He's just a guy. Come on, we'll catch Biff, and, honey, we're going to paint this town! Stanley, where's the check! Hey, Stanley!

They exit. Stanley looks toward left.

Stanley *(calling to Happy indignantly).* Mr. Loman! Mr. Loman!

Stanley picks up a chair and follows them off. Knocking is heard off left. The Woman enters, laughing. Willy follows her. She is in a black slip; he is buttoning his shirt. Raw, sensuous music accompanies their speech:

Willy. Will you stop laughing? Will you stop?

The Woman. Aren't you going to answer the door? He'll wake the whole hotel.

Willy. I'm not expecting anybody.

The Woman. Whyn't you have another drink, honey, and stop being so damn self-centered?

Willy. I'm so lonely.

The Woman. You know you ruined me, Willy? From now on, whenever you come to the office, I'll see that you go right through to the buyers. No waiting at my desk anymore, Willy. You ruined me.

Willy. That's nice of you to say that.

The Woman. Gee, you are self-centered! Why so sad? You are the saddest, self-centeredest soul I ever did see-saw. *(She laughs. He kisses her.)* Come on inside, drummer boy. It's silly to be dressing in the middle of the night. *(As knocking is heard.)* Aren't you going to answer the door?

Willy. They're knocking on the wrong door.

The Woman. But I felt the knocking. And he heard us talking in here. Maybe the hotel's on fire!

Willy *(his terror rising).* It's a mistake.

The Woman. Then tell him to go away!

Willy. There's nobody there.

The Woman. It's getting on my nerves, Willy. There's somebody standing out there and it's getting on my nerves!

Willy *(pushing her away from him).* All right, stay in the bathroom here, and don't come out. I think there's a law in Massachusetts about it, so don't come out. It may be that new room clerk. He looked very mean. So don't come out. It's a mistake, there's no fire.

The knocking is heard again. He takes a few steps away from her, and she vanishes into the wing. The light follows him, and now he is facing Young Biff, who carries a suitcase. Biff steps toward him. The music is gone.

Biff. Why didn't you answer?

Willy. Biff! What are you doing in Boston?

Biff. Why didn't you answer? I've been knocking for five minutes, I called you on the phone . . .

Willy. I just heard you. I was in the bathroom and had the door shut. Did anything happen home?

Biff. Dad—I let you down.

Willy. What do you mean?

Biff. Dad . . .

Willy. Biffo, what's this about? *(Putting his arm around Biff.)* Come on, let's go downstairs and get you a malted.

Biff. Dad, I flunked math.

Willy. Not for the term?

Biff. The term. I haven't got enough credits to graduate.

Willy. You mean to say Bernard wouldn't give you the answers?

Biff. He did, he tried, but I only got a sixty-one.

Willy. And they wouldn't give you four points?

Biff. Birnbaum refused absolutely. I begged him, Pop, but he won't give me those points. You gotta talk to him before they close the school. Because if he saw the kind of man you are, and you just talked to him in your way, I'm sure he'd come through for me. The class came right before practice, see, and I didn't go enough. Would you talk to him? He's like you, Pop. You know the way you could talk.

Willy. You're on. We'll drive right back.

Biff. Oh, Dad, good work! I'm sure he'll change it for you!

Willy. Go downstairs and tell the clerk I'm checkin' out. Go right down.

Biff. Yes, sir! See, the reason he hates me, Pop—one day he was late for class so I got up at the blackboard and imitated him. I crossed my eyes and talked with a lithp.

Willy *(laughing).* You did? The kids like it?

Biff. They nearly died laughing!

Willy. Yeah? What'd you do?

Biff. The thquare root of thixthy twee is . . . *(Willy bursts out laughing; Biff joins.)* And in the middle of it he walked in!

Willy laughs and The Woman joins in offstage.

Willy *(without hesitation).* Hurry downstairs and . . .

Biff. Somebody in there?

Willy. No, that was next door.

The Woman laughs offstage.

Biff. Somebody got in your bathroom!

Willy. No, it's the next room, there's a party—

The Woman *(enters, laughing; she lisps this).* Can I come in? There's something in the bathtub, Willy, and it's moving!

Willy looks at Biff, who is staring open-mouthed and horrified at The Woman.

Willy. Ah—you better go back to your room. They must be finished painting by now. They're painting her room so I let her take a shower here. Go back, go back . . . *(He pushes her.)*

The Woman *(resisting).* But I've got to get dressed, Willy, I can't—

Willy. Get out of here! Go back, go back . . . *(Suddenly striving for the ordinary.)* This is Miss Francis, Biff, she's a buyer. They're painting her room. Go back, Miss Francis, go back . . .

The Woman. But my clothes, I can't go out naked in the hall!

Willy *(pushing her offstage).* Get outa here! Go back, go back!

Biff slowly sits down on his suitcase as the argument continues offstage.

The Woman. Where's my stockings? You promised me stockings, Willy!

Willy. I have no stockings here!

The Woman. You had two boxes of size nine sheers for me, and I want them!

Willy. Here, for God's sake, will you get outa here!

The Woman *(enters holding a box of stockings).* I just hope there's nobody in the hall. That's all I hope. *(To Biff.)* Are you football or baseball?

Biff. Football.

The Woman *(angry, humiliated).* That's me too. G'night. *(She snatches her clothes from Willy, and walks out.)*

Willy *(after a pause).* Well, better get going. I want to get to the school first thing in the morning. Get my suits out of the closet. I'll get my valise. *(Biff doesn't move.)* What's the matter! *(Biff remains motionless, tears falling.)* She's a buyer. Buys for J. H. Simmons. She lives down the hall—they're painting. You don't imagine—*(He breaks off. After a pause.)* Now listen, pal, she's just a buyer. She sees merchandise in her room and they have to keep it looking just so . . . *(Pause. Assuming command.)* All right, get my suits. *(Biff doesn't move.)* Now stop crying and do as I say. I gave you an order. Biff, I gave you an order! Is that what you do when I give you an order? How dare you cry! *(Putting his arm around Biff.)* Now look, Biff, when you grow up you'll understand about these things. You mustn't—you mustn't overemphasize a thing like this. I'll see Birnbaum first thing in the morning.

Biff. Never mind.

Willy *(getting down beside Biff).* Never mind! He's going to give you those points. I'll see to it.

Biff. He wouldn't listen to you.

Willy. He certainly will listen to me. You need those points for the U. of Virginia.

Biff. I'm not going there.

Willy. Heh? If I can't get him to change that mark you'll make it up in summer school. You've got all summer to—

Biff *(his weeping breaking from him).* Dad . . .

Willy *(infected by it).* Oh, my boy . . .

Biff. Dad . . .

Willy. She's nothing to me, Biff. I was lonely, I was terribly lonely.

Biff. You—you gave her Mama's stockings! *(His tears break through and he rises to go.)*

Death of a Salesman

Willy *(grabbing for Biff)*. I gave you an order!

Biff. Don't touch me, you—liar!

Willy. Apologize for that!

Biff. You fake! You phony little fake! You fake! *(Overcome, he turns quickly and weeping fully goes out with his suitcase. Willy is left on the floor on his knees.)*

Willy. I gave you an order! Biff, come back here or I'll beat you! Come back here! I'll whip you!

Stanley comes quickly in from the right and stands in front of Willy.

Willy *(shouts at Stanley)*. I gave you an order . . .

Stanley. Hey, let's pick it up, pick it up, Mr. Loman. *(He helps Willy to his feet.)* Your boys left with the chippies. They said they'll see you home.

A second waiter watches some distance away.

Willy. But we were supposed to have dinner together.

Music is heard, Willy's theme.

Stanley. Can you make it?

Willy. I'll—sure, I can make it. *(Suddenly concerned about his clothes.)* Do I—I look all right?

Stanley. Sure, you look all right. *(He flicks a speck off Willy's lapel.)*

Willy. Here—here's a dollar.

Stanley. Oh, your son paid me. It's all right.

Willy *(putting it in Stanley's hand)*. No, take it. You're a good boy.

Stanley. Oh, no, you don't have to . . .

Willy. Here—here's some more, I don't need it any more *(After a slight pause)* Tell me—is there a seed store in the neighborhood?

Stanley. Seeds? You mean like to plant?

As Willy turns, Stanley slips the money back into his jacket pocket.

Willy. Yes. Carrots, peas . . .

Stanley. Well, there's hardware stores on Sixth Avenue, but it may be too late now.

Willy *(anxiously)*. Oh, I'd better hurry. I've got to get some seeds. *(He starts off to the right.)* I've got to get some seeds, right away. Nothing's planted. I don't have a thing in the ground.

Willy hurries out as the light goes down. Stanley moves over to the right after him, watches him off. The other waiter has been staring at Willy.

Stanley *(to the waiter)*. Well, whatta you looking at?

The waiter picks up the chairs and moves off right. Stanley takes the table and follows him. The light fades on this area. There is a long pause, the sound of the flute coming over. The light gradually rises on the kitchen, which is empty. Happy appears at the door of the house, followed by Biff. Happy is carrying a large bunch of long-stemmed roses. He enters the kitchen, looks around for Linda. Not seeing her, he turns to Biff, who is just outside the house door, and makes a gesture with his hands, indicating "Not here, I guess." He looks into the living room and freezes. Inside, Linda, unseen is seated, Willy's coat on her lap. She rises ominously and quietly and moves toward Happy, who backs up into the kitchen, afraid.

Happy. Hey, what're you doing up? *(Linda says nothing but moves toward him implacably.)* Where's Pop? *(He keeps backing to the right and now Linda is in full view in the doorway to the living room.)* Is he sleeping?

Linda. Where were you?

Happy *(trying to laugh it off).* We met two girls, Mom, very fine types. Here, we brought you some flowers. *(Offering them to her.)* Put them in your room, Ma.

She knocks them to the floor at Biff's feet. He has now come inside and closed the door behind him. She stares at Biff, silent.

Happy. Now what'd you do that for? Mom, I want you to have some flowers . . .

Linda *(cutting Happy off, violently to Biff).* Don't you care whether he lives or dies?

Happy *(going to the stairs).* Come upstairs, Biff.

Biff *(with a flare of disgust, to Happy).* Go away from me! *(To Linda.)* What do you mean, lives or dies? Nobody's dying around here, pal.

Linda. Get out of my sight! Get out of here!

Biff. I wanna see the boss.

Linda. You're not going near him!

Biff. Where is he? *(He moves into the living room and Linda follows.)*

Linda *(shouting after Biff).* You invite him for dinner. He looks forward to it all day—*(Biff appears in his parents' bedroom, looks around, and exits)*—and then you desert him there. There's no stranger you'd do that to!

Happy. Why? He had a swell time with us. Listen, when I—*(Linda comes back into the kitchen)*—desert him I hope I don't outlive the day!

Linda. Get out of here!

Happy. Now look, Mom . . .

Linda. Did you have to go to women tonight? You and your lousy rotten whores!

Biff re-enters the kitchen.

Happy. Mom, all we did was follow Biff around trying to cheer him up! *(To Biff.)* Boy, what a night you gave me!

Linda. Get out of here, both of you, and don't come back! I don't want you tormenting him any more. Go on now, get your things together! *(To Biff.)* You can sleep in his apartment. *(She starts to pick up the flowers and stops herself.)* Pick up this stuff, I'm not your maid any more. Pick it up, you bum, you!

Happy turns his back to her in refusal. Biff slowly moves over and gets down on his knees, picking up the flowers.

Linda. You're a pair of animals! Not one, not another living soul would have had the cruelty to walk out on the man in a restaurant!

Biff *(not looking at her).* Is that what he said?

Death of a Salesman

Linda. He didn't have to say anything. He was so humiliated he nearly limped when he came in.

Happy. But, Mom, he had a great time with us . . .

Biff *(cutting him off violently).* Shut up!

Without another word, Happy goes upstairs.

Linda. You! You didn't even go in to see if he was all right!

Biff *(still on the floor in front of Linda, the flowers in his hand; with self-loathing).* No. Didn't. Didn't do a damned thing. How do you like that, heh? Left him babbling in a toilet.

Linda. You louse. You . . .

Biff. Now you hit it on the nose! *(He gets up, throws the flowers in the wastebasket.)* The scum of the earth, and you're looking at him!

Linda. Get out of here!

Biff. I gotta talk to the boss, Mom. Where is he?

Linda. You're not going near him. Get out of this house!

Biff *(with absolute assurance, determination).* No. We're gonna have an abrupt conversation, him and me.

Linda. You're not talking to him.

Hammering is heard from outside the house, off right. Biff turns toward the noise.

Linda *(suddenly pleading).* Will you please leave him alone?

Biff. What's he doing out there?

Linda. He's planting the garden!

Biff *(quietly).* Now? Oh, my God!

Biff moves outside, Linda following. The light dies down on them and comes up on the center of the apron as Willy walks into it. He is carrying a flashlight, a hoe, and a handful of seed packets. He raps the top of the hoe sharply to fix it firmly, and then moves to the left, measuring off the distance with his foot. He holds the flashlight to look at the seed packets, reading off the instructions. He is in the blue of night.

Willy. Carrots . . . quarter-inch apart. Rows . . . one-foot rows. *(He measures it off.)* One foot. *(He puts down a package and measures off.)* Beets. *(He puts down another package and measures again.)* Lettuce. *(He reads the package, puts it down.)* One foot—*(He breaks off as Ben appears at the right and moves slowly down to him.)* What a proposition, ts,ts. Terrific, terrific. 'Cause she's suffered, Ben, the woman has suffered. You understand me? A man can't go out the way, he came in, Ben, a man has got to add up to something. You can't, you can't—*(Ben moves toward him as though to interrupt.)* You gotta consider, now. Don't answer so quick. Remember, it's a guaranteed twenty-thousand-dollar proposition. Now look, Ben, I want you to go through the ins and outs of this thing with me. I've got nobody to talk to, Ben, and the woman has suffered, you hear me?

Ben *(standing still, considering).* What's the proposition?

Willy. It's twenty thousand dollars on the barrelhead. Guaranteed, gilt-edged, you understand?

Ben. You don't want to make a fool of yourself. They might not honor the policy.

Willy. How can they dare refuse? Didn't I work like a coolie to meet every premium on the nose? And now they don't pay off? Impossible!

Ben. It's called a cowardly thing, William.

Willy. Why? Does it take more guts to stand here the rest of my life ringing up a zero?

Ben *(yielding).* That's a point, William. *(He moves, thinking, turns.)* And twenty thousand—that is something one can feel with the hand, it is there.

Willy *(now assured, with rising power).* Oh, Ben, that's the whole beauty of it! I see it like a diamond, shining in the dark, hard and rough, that I can pick up and touch in my hand. Not like—like an appointment! This would not be another damned-fool appointment, Ben, and it changes all the aspects. Because he thinks I'm nothing, see, and so he spites me. But the funeral . . . *(Straightening up.)* Ben, that funeral will be massive! They'll come from Maine, Massachusetts, Vermont, New Hampshire! All the oldtimers with the strange license plates—that boy will be thunderstruck, Ben, because he never realized—I am known! Rhode Island, New York, New Jersey—I am known, Ben, and he'll see it with his eyes once and for all. He'll see what I am, Ben! He's in for a shock, that boy!

Ben *(coming down to the edge of the garden).* He'll call you a coward.

Willy *(suddenly fearful).* No, that would be terrible.

Ben. Yes. And a damned fool.

Willy. No, no, he mustn't, I won't have that! *(He is broken and desperate.)*

Ben. He'll hate you, William.

The gay music of the Boys is heard.

Willy. Oh, Ben, how do we get back to all the great times? Used to be so full of light, and comradeship, the sleigh-riding in winter, and the ruddiness on his cheeks. And always some kind of good news coming up, always something nice coming up ahead. And never even let me carry the valises in the house, and simonizing, simonizing that little red car! Why, why can't I give him something and not have him hate me?

Ben. Let me think about it. *(He glances at his watch.)* I still have a little time. Remarkable proposition, but you've got to be sure you're not making a fool of yourself.

Ben drifts off upstage and goes out of sight. Biff comes down from the left.

Willy *(suddenly conscious of Biff, turns and looks up at him, then begins picking up the packages of seeds in confusion.)* Where the hell is that seed? *(Indignantly.)* You can't see nothing out here! They boxed in the whole goddam neighborhood!

Biff. There are people all around here. Don't you realize that?

Willy. I'm busy. Don't bother me.

Biff *(taking the hoe from Willy).* I'm saying good-by to you, Pop. *(Willy looks at him, silent, unable to move.)* I'm not coming back any more.

Willy. You're not going to see Oliver tomorrow?

Biff. I've got no appointment, Dad.

Death of a Salesman

Willy. He put his arm around you, and you've got no appointment?

Biff. Pop, get this now, will you? Everytime I've left it's been a fight that sent me out of here. Today I realized something about myself and I tried to explain it to you and I—I think I'm just not smart enough to make any sense out of it for you. To hell with whose fault it is or anything like that. *(He takes Willy's arm.)* Let's just wrap it up, heh? Come on in, we'll tell Mom. *(He gently tries to pull Willy to left.)*

Willy *(frozen, immobile, with guilt in his voice).* No, I don't want to see her.

Biff. Come on! *(He pulls again, and Willy tries to pull away.)*

Willy *(highly nervous).* No, no, I don't want to see her.

Biff *(tries to look into Willy's face, as if to find the answer there).* Why don't you want to see her?

Willy *(more harshly now).* Don't bother me, will you?

Biff. What do you mean, you don't want to see her? You don't want them calling you yellow, do you? This isn't your fault; it's me, I'm a bum. Now come inside! *(Willy strains to get away.)* Did you hear what I said to you?

Willy pulls away and quickly goes by himself into the house. Biff follows.

Linda *(to Willy).* Did you plant, dear?

Biff *(at the door, to Linda).* All right, we had it out. I'm going and I'm not writing any more.

Linda *(going to Willy in the kitchen).* I think that's the best way, dear. 'Cause there's no use drawing it out, you'll just never get along.

Willy doesn't respond.

Biff. People ask where I am and what I'm doing, you don't know, and you don't care. That way it'll be off your mind and you can start brightening up again. All right? That clears it, doesn't it? *(Willy is silent, and Biff goes to him.)* You gonna wish me luck, scout? *(He extends his hand.)* What do you say?

Linda. Shake his hand, Willy.

Willy *(turning to her, seething with hurt).* There's no necessity to mention the pen at all, y'know.

Biff *(gently).* I've got no appointment, Dad.

Willy *(erupting fiercely).* He put his arm around . . .?

Biff. Dad, you're never going to see what I am, so what's the use of arguing? If I strike oil I'll send you a check. Meantime forget I'm alive.

Willy *(to Linda).* Spite, see?

Biff. Shake hands, Dad.

Willy. Not my hand.

Biff. I was hoping not to go this way.

Willy. Well, this is the way you're going. Good-by.

Biff looks at him a moment, then turns sharply and goes to the stairs.

Willy *(stops him with).* May you rot in hell if you leave this house!

Biff *(turning).* Exactly what is it that you want from me?

Willy. I want you to know, on the train, in the mountains, in the valleys, wherever you go, that you cut down your life for spite!

Biff. No, no.

Willy. Spite, spite, is the word of your undoing! And when you're down and out, remember what did it. When you're rotting somewhere beside the railroad tracks, remember, and don't you dare blame it on me!

Biff. I'm not blaming it on you!

Willy. I won't take the rap for this, you hear?

Happy comes down the stairs and stands on the bottom step, watching.

Biff. That's just what I'm telling you!

Willy *(sinking into a chair at a table, with full accusation).* You're trying to put a knife in me—don't think I don't know what you're doing!

Biff. All right, phony! Then let's lay it on the line. *(He whips the rubber tube out of his pocket and puts it on the table.)*

Happy. You crazy . . .

Linda. Biff! *(She moves to grab the hose, but Biff holds it down with his hand.)*

Biff. Leave it there! Don't move it!

Willy *(not looking at it).* What is that?

Biff. You know goddam well what that is.

Willy *(caged, wanting to escape).* I never saw that.

Biff. You saw it. The mice didn't bring it into the cellar! What is this supposed to do, make a hero out of you? This supposed to make me sorry for you?

Willy. Never heard of it.

Biff. There'll be no pity for you, you hear it? No pity!

Willy *(to Linda).* You hear the spite!

Biff. No, you're going to hear the truth—what you are and what I am!

Linda. Stop it!

Willy. Spite!

Happy *(coming down toward Biff).* You cut it now!

Biff *(to Happy).* The man don't know who we are! The man is gonna know! *(To Willy.)* We never told the truth for ten minutes in this house!

Happy. We always told the truth!

Biff *(turning on him).* You big blow, are you the assistant buyer? You're one of the two assistants to the assistant, aren't you?

Happy. Well, I'm practically—

Biff. You're practically full of it! We all are! And I'm through with it *(to Willy.)* Now hear this, Willy, this is me.

Willy. I know you!

Biff. You know why I had no address for three months? I stole a suit in Kansas City and I was in jail. *(To Linda, who is sobbing.)* Stop crying. I'm through with it.

Linda turns away from them, her hands covering her face.

Willy. I suppose that's my fault!

Biff. I stole myself out of every good job since high school!

Willy. And whose fault is that?

Biff. And I never got anywhere because you blew me so full of hot air I could never stand taking orders from anybody! That's whose fault it is!

Willy. I hear that!

Linda. Don't, Biff!

Biff. It's goddam time you heard that! I had to be boss big shot in two weeks, and I'm through with it!

Willy. Then hang yourself! For spite, hang yourself!

Biff. No! Nobody's hanging himself, Willy! I ran down eleven flights with a pen in my hand today. And suddenly I stopped, you hear me? And in the middle of that office building, do you hear this? I stopped in the middle of that building and I saw—the sky. I saw the things that I love in this world. The work and the food and time to sit and smoke. And I looked at the pen and said to myself, what the hell am I grabbing this for? Why am I trying to become what I don't want to be? What am I doing in an office, making a contemptuous, begging fool of myself, when all I want is out there, waiting for me the minute I say I know who I am! Why can't I say that, Willy? *(He tries to make Willy face him, but Willy pulls away and moves to the left.)*

Willy *(with hatred, threateningly).* The door of your life is wide open!

Biff. Pop! I'm a dime a dozen, and so are you!

Willy *(turning on him now in an uncontrolled outburst).* I am not a dime a dozen! I am Willy Loman, and you are Biff Loman!

Biff starts for Willy, but is blocked by Happy. In his fury, Biff seems on the verge of attacking his father.

Biff. I am not a leader of men, Willy, and neither are you. You were never anything but a hard-working drummer who landed in the ash can like all the rest of them! I'm one dollar an hour, Willy I tried seven states and couldn't raise it. A buck an hour! Do you gather my meaning? I'm not bringing home any prizes any more, and you're going to stop waiting for me to bring them home!

Willy *(directly to Biff).* You vengeful, spiteful mut!

Biff breaks from Happy. Willy, in fright, starts up the stairs. Biff grabs him.

Biff *(at the peak of his fury).* Pop, I'm nothing! I'm nothing, Pop. Can't you understand that? There's no spite in it any more. I'm just what I am, that's all.

Biff's fury has spent itself, and he breaks down, sobbing, holding on to Willy, who dumbly fumbles for Biff's face.

Willy *(astonished).* What're you doing? What're you doing? *(To Linda.)* Why is he crying?

Biff *(crying, broken).* Will you let me go, for Christ's sake? Will you take that phony dream and burn it before something happens? *(Struggling to contain himself, he pulls away and moves to the stairs.)* I'll go in the morning. Put him—put him to bed. *(Exhausted, Biff moves up the stairs to his room.)*

Willy *(after a long pause, astonished, elevated).* Isn't that—isn't that remarkable? Biff—he likes me!

Linda. He loves you, Willy!

Happy *(deeply moved).* Always did, Pop.

Willy. Oh, Biff! *(staring wildly.)* He cried! Cried to me. *(He is choking with his love, and now cries out his promise.)* That boy—that boy is going to be magnificent!

Ben appears in the light just outside the kitchen.

Ben. Yes, outstanding, with twenty thousand behind him.

Linda *(sensing the racing of his mind, fearfully, carefully).* Now come to bed, Willy. It's all settled now.

Willy *(finding it difficult not to rush out of the house).* Yes, we'll sleep. Come on. Go to sleep, Hap.

Ben. And it does take a great kind of a man to crack the jungle.

In accents of dread, Ben's idyllic music starts up.

Happy *(his arm around Linda).* I'm getting married, Pop, don't forget it. I'm changing everything. I'm gonna run that department before the year is up. You'll see, Mom. *(He kisses her.)*

B^n. The jungle is dark but full of diamonds, Willy.

Willy turns, moves, listening to Ben.

Linda. Be good. You're both good boys, just act that way, that's all.

Happy. 'Night, Pop. *(He goes upstairs.)*

Linda *(to Willy).* Come, dear.

Ben *(with greater force).* One must go in to fetch a diamond out.

Willy *(to Linda, as he moves slowly along the edge of kitchen, toward the door).* I just want to get settled down, Linda. Let me sit alone for a little.

Linda *(almost uttering her fear).* I want you upstairs.

Willy *(taking her in his arms).* In a few minutes, Linda. I couldn't sleep right now. Go on, you look awful tired. *(He kisses her.)*

Ben. Not like an appointment at all. A diamond is rough and hard to the touch.

Willy. Go on now. I'll be right up.

Linda. I think this is the only way, Willy.

Willy. Sure, it's the best thing.

Ben. Best thing!

Willy. The only way. Everything is gonna be—go on, kid, get to bed. You look so tired.

Linda. Come right up.

Willy. Two minutes.

Linda goes into the living room, then reappears in her bedroom. Willy moves just outside the kitchen door.

Willy. Loves me. *(Wonderingly.)* Always loved me. Isn't that a remarkable thing? Ben, he'll worship me for it!

Ben *(with promise).* It's dark there, but full of diamonds.

Willy. Can you imagine that magnificence with twenty thousand dollars in his pocket?

Linda *(calling from her room).* Willy! Come up!

Willy *(calling into the kitchen).* Yes! yes. Coming! It's very smart, you realize that, don't you, sweetheart? Even Ben sees it. I gotta go, baby. 'By! 'By! *(Going over to Ben, almost dancing.)* Imagine? When the mail comes he'll be ahead of Bernard again!

Ben. A perfect proposition all around.

Willy. Did you see how he cried to me? Oh, if I could kiss him, Ben!

Ben. Time, William, time!

Willy. Oh, Ben, I always knew one way or another we were gonna make it, Biff and I!

Ben *(looking at his watch).* The boat. We'll be late. *(He moves slowly off into the darkness.)*

Willy *(elegiacally, turning to the house).* Now when you kick off, boy, I want a seventy-yard boot, and get right down the field under the ball, and when you hit, hit low and hit hard, because it's important, boy. *(He swings around and faces the audience.)* There's all kinds of important people in the stands, and the first thing you know . . . *(Suddenly realizing he is alone.)* Ben! Ben, where do I . . . ?*(He makes a sudden movement of search.)* Ben, how do I . . .?

Linda *(calling).* Willy, you coming up?

Willy *(uttering a gasp of fear, whirling about as if to quiet her).* Sh! *(He turns around as if to find his way; sounds, faces, voices, seem to be swarming in upon him and he flicks at them, crying.)* Sh! Sh! *(Suddenly music, faint and high, stops him. It rises in intensity, almost to an unbearable scream. He goes up and down on his toes, and rushes off around the house.)* Shhh!

Linda. Willy?

There is no answer. Linda waits. Biff gets up off his bed. He is still in his clothes. Happy sits up. Biff stands listening.

Linda *(with real fear).* Willy, answer me! Willy!

There is the sound of a car starting and moving away at full speed.

Linda. No!

Biff *(rushing down the stairs).* Pop!

As the car speeds off, the music crashes down in a frenzy of sound, which becomes the soft pulsation of a single cello string. Biff slowly returns to his bedroom. He and Happy gravely don their jackets. Linda slowly walks out of her room. The music has developed into a dead march. The leaves of day are appearing over everything. Charley and Bernard, somberly dressed, appear and knock on the kitchen door. Biff and Happy slowly descend the stairs to the kitchen as Charley and Bernard enter. All stop a moment when Linda, in clothes of mourning, bearing a little bunch of roses, comes through the draped doorway into the kitchen. She goes to Charley and takes his arm. Now all move toward the audience, through the wall-line of the kitchen. At the limit of the apron, Linda lays down the flowers, kneels, and sits back on her heels. All stare down at the grave.

REQUIEM

Charley. It's getting dark, Linda.

Linda doesn't react. She stares at the grave.

Biff. How about it, Mom? Better get some rest, heh? They'll be closing the gate soon.

Linda makes no move. Pause.

Happy *(deeply angered).* He had no right to do that. There was no necessity for it. We would've helped him.

Charley *(grunting).* Hmmm.

Biff. Come along, Mom.

Linda. Why didn't anybody come?

Charley. It was a very nice funeral.

Linda. But where are all the people he knew? Maybe they blame him.

Charley. Naa. It's a rough world, Linda. They wouldn't blame him.

Linda. I can't understand it. At this time especially. First time in thirty-five years we were just about free and clear. He only needed a little salary. He was even finished with the dentist.

Charley. No man only needs a little salary.

Linda. I can't understand it.

Biff. There were a lot of nice days. When he'd come home from a trip; or on Sundays, making the stoop; finishing the cellar; putting on the new porch; when he built the extra bathroom; and put up the garage. You know something, Charley, there's more of him in that front stoop than in all the sales he ever made.

Charley. Yeah. He was a happy man with a batch of cement.

Linda. He was so wonderful with his hands.

Biff. He had the wrong dreams. All, all, wrong.

Happy *(almost ready to fight Biff).* Don't say that!

Biff. He never knew who he was.

Charley *(stopping Happy's movement and reply. To Biff).* Nobody dast blame this man. You don't understand: Willy was a salesman. And for a salesman, there is no rock bottom to the life. He don't put a bolt to a nut, he don't tell you the law or give you medicine. He's a man way out there in the blue, riding on a smile and a shoeshine. And when they start not smiling back—that's an earthquake. And then you get yourself a couple of spots on your hat, and you're finished. Nobody dast blame this man. A salesman is got to dream, boy. It comes with the territory.

Biff. Charley, the man didn't know who he was.

Happy *(infuriated).* Don't say that!

Biff. Why don't you come with me, Happy?

Happy. I'm not licked that easily. I'm staying right in this city, and I'm gonna beat this racket! *(He looks at Biff, his chin set.)* The Loman Brothers!

Biff. I know who I am, kid.

Happy. All right, boy. I'm gonna show you and everybody else that Willy Loman did not die in vain. He had a good dream. It's the only dream you can have—to come out number-one man. He fought it out here, and this is where I'm gonna win it for him.

Biff *(with a hopeless glance at Happy, bends toward his mother).* Let's go, Mom.

Linda. I'll be with you in a minute. Go on, Charley. *(He hesitates.)* I want to, just for a minute. I never had a chance say good-by.

Charley moves away, followed by Happy. Biff remains a slight distance up and left of Linda. She sits there, summoning herself. The flute begins, not far away, playing behind her speech.

Linda. Forgive me, dear. I can't cry. I don't know what it is, I can't cry. I don't understand it. Why did you ever do that? Help me Willy, I can't cry. It seems to me that you're just on another trip. I keep expecting you. Willy, dear, I can't cry. Why did you do it? I search and search and I search, and I can't understand it, Willy. I made the last payment on the house today. Today, dear. And there'll be nobody home. *(A sob rises in her throat.)* We're free and clear. *(Sobbing more fully, released.)* We're free. *(Biff comes slowly toward her.)* We're free . . . We're free . . .

Biff lifts her to her feet and moves out up right with her in his arms. Linda sobs quietly. Bernard and Charley come together and follow them, followed by Happy. Only the music of the flute is left on the darkening stage as over the house the hard towers of the apartment buildings rise into sharp focus, and the curtain falls.

QUESTIONS

Act I

1. What is unusual about the staging of *Death of a Salesman*? What is the function of such staging?

2. Why does Linda offer an excuse for Willy after he has driven off the road?

3. How does Miller point us toward coming conflicts with the Wagner company, with Biff, and with the environment? What does the environment symbolize?

4. Describe the impasse that confronts Biff and Happy. Why has it developed?

5. Miller has established graphic contrasts. Which ones stand out most vividly?

6. How does the secondary theme of planned obsolescence of material goods apply to Willy Loman?

7. Discuss Willy's faith in things: cars, refrigerators, advertised products. Why do they all seem to be worthless, betrayers of his confidence? How does this motif help to structure the plot?

8. Why does Willy get angry when Linda mends her stockings?

9. What does Ben, Willy's brother, represent?

10. Why do Biff and Happy not really like each other?

11. Linda knows that Willy's not earning, but borrowing money from Charlie. Why does she remain silent?

12. What does it say about Willy that he hasn't left the Wagner company on his own? Relate this to his failure to use the rubber tubing.

Act II and Requiem

13. This part of the play opens with rising action, filled with optimism. Explain why.

14. Describe how revelations about Willy and the business deepen the plot of the play.

15. Willy implies in conversation with Howard that a deeper relationship should exist between the individual and the company for which he works. How does this relate to events occurring in the United States during the last decade.

16. Explain how Biff is a reflection of Willy and why that intensifies the hostility between them.

17. Why does Biff take or steal things of no consequence?

18. We do not know what Willy sells. Explain why this does not seem to be important.

19. What does the Requiem contribute to plot and theme?

TOPICS FOR WRITING

1. How has Miller managed the flashbacks so adroitly, with a bare minimum of set changes? The laughter of the Woman is both flashback and flashforward. Explain fully why this is so.

2. One of the ingredients of tragedy is that the protagonist himself is instrumental in the misadventures that befall him. How is this true of both Oedipus and Willy Loman?

3. We feel different kinds of sympathy for Oedipus and Willy. Why? Oedipus begins as a king and ends a blind man leaving his country, his wife a suicide. Willy has only dreamed of being on top. He kills himself while his wife lives. Where are the similarities in their lives? the differences?

4. Compare and contrast how Sophocles and Miller have observed the Aristotelian unities. How does Miller manage to escape them while preserving them?

5. "You cut down your life for spite!" Willy yells at Biff. Define spite, and relate it to question 4.

6. Why does Miller use a requiem in this play? What is deposited in the Requiem and by whom? What challenge is accepted here and by whom? Explain how something of Willy Loman will continue.

7. There are several ironic elements in *Death of a Salesman*, and they are underlined by Linda's final words. Find the ironic elements and describe them.

8. Explain how the theme of human destiny or fate is revealed and advanced through the plots of *Oedipus Rex* and *Death of a Salesman*.

25

CHARACTER AND THEME: WOMEN AND REBELLION

When the stage opens before us—either as spectators or readers—we are confronted first and immediately with characters in the world of the play. We want to know about these characters: What are they like? What motivates them? What are their problems and conflicts? What are their destinies? As participants in the dramatic experience, we seem to be interested first and foremost in the people set in motion by the play.

Aristotle might have been correct in terming plot the "soul" of drama, yet it is equally true that there could be no "soul" in drama without character. Character is revealed through plot, the total structure of the play. As Santayana states in *The Sense of Beauty:* "Plot is the synthesis of actions, and is a reproduction of those experiences from which our notion of things is originally derived; for character can never be observed in the world except as manifested in action." Yet it is character that looms out of that plotted action. Through our interest in the characters on the stage, we learn about human nature, the characters' relationship to the world, and the dramatist's vision of the world. Put simply, as playwright and novelist Arnold Bennett once did, the foundation of both drama and fiction is "character creating and nothing else."

Unlike fiction and poetry, drama gives us *living* images of people on stage. Characterization in fiction (see pages 72–75) can create memorable figures, but it is clear that playwrights have other stylistic and technical resources, as well as formal constraints, to deal with in their "invention" of human figures. A dramatist, preoccupied with stage time, does not have the leisure of the novelist in developing character. He or she must get us to "see" and "hear" characters from the outset of a script. We understand the characters' motives through what they say and do and through the responses of other characters to them. Othello would not be the tragic figure we know without Iago's view of him or without Iago's reaction to him. We know something about Maurya's pain before we see her through Cathleen and Nora in *Riders to the Sea.*

Playwrights use many techniques and conventions to make their dramatic characters stand out on the stage. Characters do not just talk idly, as we do in common speech. Their dialogues and monologues are rooted in *thought,* as in Hamlet's famous "To be or not to be." Making thought the basis of a dramatic figure's speech is a common technique of character development. With drama, we are also interested in the very rhythms of the characters' speech. Again, Shakespeare affords a brilliant example of rhythmic dialogue in Macbeth's lines,

> Tomorrow, and tomorrow, and tomorrow
> Creeps in this petty pace from day to day
> To the last syllable of recorded time,

This is pure poetry transmuted into spoken lines. Closely related to this procedure of establishing rhythmic patterns for dialogue is the playwright's revelation of character through imagery (see pages 388–390 in the poetry section); another technique is the vivid reproduction of sense experience. Iago's fondness for lacing his speech with violent and distasteful animal imagery reveals much about himself, his motives, and the world of *Othello.*

At an equally basic theatrical level, character is a composite of the physical appearance, the voices, the gestures, the clothing and costumes, the setting—all created by the playwright, director, designers and technicians, and the actors themselves. The crooked, humpbacked figure of the protagonist in Shakespeare's *Richard III* is a vivid reflection of Richard's twisted character. Willy Loman's fondness for gardens, and his own sterile garden "prop" (indeed all the stage props that comprise setting in *Death of a Salesman*), reveals his dreams and inner conflicts. The costumes in *A Doll's House* and *Wine in the Wilderness,* the two plays presented in this section, help to make visible the characters' essence and their lives. We get to "know" characters through a broad range of theatrical conventions.

Yet determining exactly how a great playwright "discovers" a character is a more difficult task than recognizing the dramatic methods involved in the creation of character. Ibsen tells us as much as any modern dramatist about the art of character invention:

> Before I write down one word I have to have the character in mind through and through. I must penetrate to the last wrinkle of his soul. I always proceed from the

individual. The stage setting, the dramatic ensemble, all *that* comes naturally and does not cause me any worry, as soon as I am certain of the individual in every aspect of his humanity. I have to have his exterior in mind also, down to the last button, how he stands and walks, his behavior, what his voice sounds like.

A character must come to life in the author's imagination. Then, as William Faulkner once said of his characters, the writer must pursue his or her character down the road and into the action or field of conflict and existence.

It would be difficult for great drama—any drama—to exist without tension and conflict. These elements arise through the use of characters who tend to be opposites (e.g., good and bad) or through the use of protagonists and antagonists. Sometimes characters are rounded, or strongly drawn; sometimes, as in most comedy, they are flat "types"; sometimes characters may possess a bit of both the rogue and the hero; and sometimes, as in Ibsen's *The Wild Duck* (1855), it may be difficult to find a protagonist. Characters in classical tragedies are three dimensional and monumental, but their sense of "doom" makes them ultimately a little mysterious and elusive in their characterization. In modern drama, character can defy all theatrical norms; a modern play such as Hecht and MacArthur's *The Front Page* (1928), a comedy, utilizes heroes with somewhat unsavory characteristics and villains with rather likeable characteristics. Frequently in contemporary drama, the antagonist is not another character at all, but society and its systems.

In the modern era of drama, no one has had a greater impact on the revelation of character against both social and psychological backdrops than Henrik Ibsen. In *A Doll's House*, there is clear dramatic tension between the characters Nora and Helmer; she is the protagonist, and he the antagonist. This tension between the sexes engages us today as much as it was involved in the works of Aristophanes and Shakespeare. Moreover, in the Ibsen play multiple tensions are brewing between the characters: Nora and Krogstad; Krogstad and Mrs. Linde (apparently); Helmer and Krogstad. With each confrontation, the characters take on new dimensions for us, until the theme begins to emerge, arising as it must directly out of the actions of each of the characters.

The best drama is created upon those themes that endure through human experience and are revealed through human nature. Location, dialogue, and even society may change, but somehow the conditions that perpetuate universal themes continue. *Wine in the Wilderness*, by Alice Childress, set in another time and place and among a particular American people, uses in dialogue the vernacular of those people and the streets from which some of them have come. In Ibsen's play, the major characters come from the same struggling middle class. In Childress's play, there is a meeting of two classes—the artistic and professional black middle class and the street-talking black underclass.

Here there are two levels of dramatic tension: the riot outside that brought all the characters together, and the tension of class differences. However, because all the characters are Afro-American, one might conclude that somehow they're all alike. In fact, the play suggests that at some point in their lives they have all had similar experiences and that the superficial class differences that exist between them should therefore be abandoned in favor of "goin back to the nitty-gritty crowd, where the talk is we-ness and us-ness."

In both plays, women dominate the action and carry forward the theme. Nora grows in strength; Tommy grows in wisdom. Tommy is perceptive from the beginning, and Nora displays an early cunning that we are meant to sense will later be troublesome. A theme present in both is that if society is going to be changed for the better, women will change it since men don't seem to have noticed that there is anything wrong. The women in these plays are characters who accomplish their ends and realize their destinies. Childress would agree with Ibsen, who wrote of his characters: "I finally stand at the limit of knowledge: I know my people from close and long association—they are my intimate friends, they will not disappoint me, I shall always see them as I do now."

Henrik Ibsen

A DOLL'S HOUSE

Henrik Ibsen (1828–1906) was born in the little seaport town of Skien on the picturesque southern coast of Norway. His father was a successful merchant until 1836, when the family fortune was lost and the Ibsens had to retire to a small farm. At 15 Ibsen became an apothecary's assistant in Grimstad, where during that time he tried writing without success. In 1850, however, through the influence of Ole Bull, the famous violinist, Ibsen was appointed a "theater poet" at the Bergen Theater. Here he served his apprenticeship as reader, stage manager, playwright, and director. (His first play, Love's Comedy, *was staged there in 1862.) Ibsen married Susannah Thoresen, who was devoted to furthering his career. A government stipend allowed them to move to Rome and later, to Dresden. Recognition came to Ibsen when* Brand *(1866) was staged, followed the next year by* Peer Gynt. *Both were written in verse. However, by the time* A Doll's House *was staged (1879), poetry had given way to prose, and Ibsen had become a "social dramatist" and the "father of modern drama."* Ghosts *(1881) and* An Enemy of the People *(1882) were frontal assaults on marriage and convention, as were the rest of Ibsen's plays. Ibsen simplified dramatic technique, gaining greater compactness of plot; he discarded monologues and asides and episodic movement. Wrote Ibsen: "I look upon it as my appointed task to use the talents God has given me in rousing my countrymen from their lethargy and making them see the import of the great life problems."*

"When we speak of Ibsen," wrote Helge Krog, "there comes a mental picture of a small man, faultlessly dressed, looking very formal and reserved; a cold expression and a manner a bit gruff and grouchy making him seem quite unapproachable. That is the picture the world has pre-

*served of the famous playwright. But his contemporaries
remembered a very different picture—a vivid picture of a gay
Bohemian youth, carelessly dressed, fond of drinking, talkative and full of anecdotes, defiant, exuberantly mocking. . . .
Ibsen was not a reformer, but a revolutionary: 'The State
must go!' he wrote in a letter. 'That revolution I agree to.
Undermine the idea of a state, set up free will and spiritual
kinship as the one condition for union—that is the beginning of a freedom worth something.' If Ibsen had not belonged to his time, he would not have belonged to any time
at all."*

List of Characters

Torvald Helmer, a lawyer
Nora, his wife
Dr. Rank
Mrs. Linde
Krogstad
The Helmers' three small children
Anne-Marie, the children's nurse
A housemaid
A porter

Scene *The Helmers' living room*

ACT I

*A pleasant, tastefully but not expensively furnished, living room. A door on the
rear wall, right, leads to the front hall, another door, left, to Helmer's study.
Between the two doors a piano. A third door in the middle of the left wall;
further front a window. Near the window a round table and a small couch.
Towards the rear of the right wall a fourth door; further front a tile stove with a
rocking chair and a couple of armchairs in front of it. Between the stove and the
door a small table. Copperplate etchings on the walls. A whatnot with porcelain
figurines and other small objects. A small bookcase with de luxe editions. A rug
on the floor; fire in the stove. Winter day.*

    *The doorbell rings, then the sound of the front door opening. Nora, dressed
for outdoors, enters, humming cheerfully. She carries several packages, which
she puts down on the table, right. She leaves the door to the front hall open;
there a porter is seen holding a Christmas tree and a basket. He gives them to
the Maid, who has let them in.*

Nora. Be sure to hide the Christmas tree, Helene. The children mustn't see it
before tonight when we've trimmed it. (*Opens her purse; to the porter.*) How
much?
Porter. Fifty ore.
Nora. Here's a crown. No, keep the change. (*The porter thanks her, leaves. Nora
closes the door. She keeps laughing quietly to herself as she takes off her*

coat, etc. She takes a bag of macaroons from her pocket and eats a couple. She walks cautiously over to the door to the study and listens. Yes, he's home. *(Resumes her humming, walks over to the table, right.)*

Helmer *(in his study).* Is that my little lark twittering out there?

Nora *(opening some of the packages).* That's right.

Helmer. My squirrel bustling about?

Nora. Yes.

Helmer. When did squirrel come home?

Nora. Just now. *(Puts the bag of macaroons back in her pocket, wipes her mouth.)* Come out here, Torvald. I want to show you what I've bought.

Helmer. I'm busy! *(After a little while he opens the door and looks in, pen in hand.)* Bought, eh? All that? So little wastrel has been throwing money around again?

Nora. Oh but Torvald, this Christmas we can be a little extravagant, can't we? It's the first Christmas we don't have to scrimp.

Helmer. I don't know about that. We certainly don't have money to waste.

Nora. Yes, Torvald, we do. A little, anyway. Just a tiny little bit? Now that you're going to get that big salary and make lots and lots of money.

Helmer. Starting at New Year's, yes. But payday isn't till the end of the quarter.

Nora. That doesn't matter. We can always borrow.

Helmer. Nora! *(Goes over to her and playfully pulls her ear.)* There you go being irresponsible again. Suppose I borrowed a thousand crowns today and you spent it all for Christmas and on New Year's Eve a tile hit me in the head and laid me out cold.

Nora *(putting her hand over his mouth).* I won't have you say such horrid things.

Helmer. But suppose it happened. Then what?

Nora. If it did, I wouldn't care whether we owed money or not.

Helmer. But what about the people I had borrowed from?

Nora. Who cares about them! They are strangers.

Helmer. Nora, Nora, you *are* a woman. No, really! You know how I feel about that. No debts! A home in debt isn't a free home, and if it isn't free it isn't beautiful. We've managed nicely so far, you and I, and that's the way we'll go on. It won't be for much longer.

Nora *(walks over toward the stove).* All right, Torvald. Whatever you say.

Helmer *(follows her).* Come, come, my little songbird mustn't droop her wings. What's this? Can't have a pouty squirrel in the house, you know. *(Takes out his wallet.)* Nora, what do you think I have here?

Nora *(turns around quickly).* Money!

Helmer. Here. *(Gives her some bills.)* Don't you think I know Christmas is expensive?

Nora *(counting).* Ten—twenty—thirty—forty. Thank you, thank you, Torvald. This helps a lot.

Helmer. I certainly hope so.

Nora. It does, it does. But I want to show you what I got. It was cheap, too. Look. New clothes for Ivar. And a sword. And a horse and trumpet for Bob. And a doll and a little bed for Emmy. It isn't any good, but it wouldn't last, anyway. And here's some dress material and scarves for the maids. I feel bad about old Anne-Marie, though. She really should be getting much more.

Helmer. And what's in here?

Nora *(cries).* Not till tonight!

Helmer. I see. But now what does my little prodigal have in mind for herself?

Nora. Oh, nothing. I really don't care.

Helmer. Of course you do. Tell me what you'd like. Within reason.

Nora. Oh, I don't know. Really, I don't. The only thing—

Helmer. Well?

Nora *(fiddling with the buttons without looking at him).* If you really want to give me something, you might—you could—

Helmer. All right, let's have it.

Nora *(quickly).* Some money, Torvald. Just as much as you think you can spare. Then I'll buy myself something one of these days.

Helmer. No, really Nora—

Nora. Oh yes, please, Torvald. Please? I'll wrap the money in pretty gold paper and hang it on the tree. Won't that be nice?

Helmer. What's the name for little birds that are always spending money?

Nora. Wastrels, I know. But please let's do it my way, Torvald. Then I'll have time to decide what I need most. Now that's sensible, isn't it?

Helmer *(smiling).* Oh, very sensible. That is, if you really bought yourself something you could use. But it all disappears in the household expenses or you buy things you don't need. And then you come back to me for more.

Nora. Oh, but Torvald—

Helmer. That's the truth, dear little Nora, and you know it. *(Puts his arm around her.)* My wastrel is a little sweetheart, but she *does* go through an awful lot of money awfully fast. You've no idea how expensive it is for a man to keep a wastrel.

Nora. That's not fair, Torvald. I really save all I can.

Helmer *(laughs).* Oh, I believe that. All you can. Meaning, exactly nothing!

Nora *(hums, smiles mysteriously).* You don't know all the things we songbirds and squirrels need money for, Torvald.

Helmer. You know, you're funny. Just like your father. You're always looking for ways to get money, but as soon as you do it runs through your fingers and you can never say what you spent it for. Well, I guess I'll just have to take you the way you are. It's in your blood. Yes, that sort of thing is hereditary, Nora.

Nora. In that case, I wish I had inherited many of Daddy's qualities.

Helmer. And I don't want you any different from just what you are—my own sweet little songbird. Hey!—I think I just noticed something. Aren't you looking what's the word?—a little—sly—?

Nora. I am?

Helmer. You definitely are. Look at me.

Nora *(looks at him).* Well?

Helmer *(wagging a finger).* Little sweet-tooth hasn't by any chance been on a rampage today, has she?

Nora. Of course not. Whatever makes you think that?

Helmer. A little detour by the pastryshop maybe?

Nora. No, I assure you, Torvald—

Helmer. Nibbled a little jam?

Nora. Certainly not!

Helmer. Munched a macaroon or two?

Nora. No, really, Torvald, I honestly—

Helmer. All right. Of course I was only joking.

Nora *(walks toward the table, right).* You know I wouldn't do anything to displease you.

Helmer. I know. And I have your promise. *(Over to her.)* All right, keep your little Christmas secrets to yourself, Nora darling. They'll all come out tonight, I suppose, when we light the tree.

Nora. Did you remember to invite Rank?

Helmer. No, but there's no need to. He knows he'll have dinner with us. Anyway, I'll see him later this morning. I'll ask him then. I did order some good wine. Oh Nora, you've no idea how much I'm looking forward to tonight!

Nora. Me too. And the children, Torvald! They'll have such a good time!

Helmer. You know, it *is* nice to have a good, safe job and a comfortable income. Feels good just thinking about it. Don't you agree?

Nora. Oh, it's wonderful!

Helmer. Remember last Christmas? For three whole weeks you shut yourself up every evening till long after midnight, making ornaments for the Christmas tree and I don't know what else. Some big surprise for all of us, anyway. I'll be damned if I've ever been so bored in my whole life!

Nora. I wasn't bored at all.

Helmer *(smiling).* But you've got to admit you didn't have much to show for it in the end.

Nora. Oh, don't tease me again about that! Could I help it that the cat got in and tore up everything?

Helmer. Of course you couldn't, my poor little Nora. You just wanted to please the rest of us, and that's the important thing. But I *am* glad the hard times are behind us. Aren't you?

Nora. Oh yes. I think it's just wonderful.

Helmer. This year I won't be bored and lonely. And you won't have to strain your dear eyes and your delicate little hands—

Nora *(claps her hands).* No I won't, will I, Torvald? Oh, how wonderful, how lovely, to hear you say that! *(Puts her arm under his.)* Let me tell you how I think we should arrange things, Torvald. Soon as Christmas is over—*(The doorbell rings.)* Someone's at the door. *(Straightens things up a bit.)* A caller, I suppose. Bother!

Helmer. Remember, I'm not home for visitors.

Maid *(in the door to the front hall).* Ma'am, there's a lady here—

Nora. All right. Ask her to come in.

Maid *(to Helmer).* And the Doctor just arrived.

Helmer. Is he in the study?

Maid. Yes, sir.

Helmer exits into his study. The maid shows Mrs. Linde in and closes the door behind her as she leaves. Mrs. Linde is in travel dress.

Mrs. Linde *(timid and a little hesitant).* Good morning, Nora.

Nora *(uncertainly).* Good morning.

Mrs. Linde. I don't believe you know who I am.

Nora. No—I'm not sure—Though I know I should—Of course! Kristine! It's you!

Mrs. Linde. Yes, it's me.

Nora. And I didn't even recognize you! I had no idea! (*In a lower voice.*) You've changed, Kristine.

Mrs. Linde. I'm sure I have. It's been nine or ten long years.

Nora. Has it really been that long? Yes, you're right. I've been so happy these last eight years. And now you're here. Such a long trip in the middle of winter. How brave!

Mrs. Linde. I got in on the steamer this morning.

Nora. To have some fun over the holidays, of course. That's lovely. For we *are* going to have fun. But take off your coat! You aren't cold, are you? (*Helps her.*) There, now! Let's sit down here by the fire and just relax and talk. No, you sit there. I want the rocking chair. (*Takes her hands.*) And now you've got your old face back. It was just for a minute, right at first—Though you are a little more pale, Kristine. And maybe a little thinner.

Mrs. Linde. And much, much older, Nora.

Nora. Maybe a little older. Just a teeny-weeny bit, not much. (*Interrupts herself, serious.*) Oh, but how thoughtless of me, chatting away like this! Sweet, good Kristine, can you forgive me?

Mrs. Linde. Forgive you what, Nora?

Nora (*in a low voice*). You poor dear, you lost your husband, didn't you?

Mrs. Linde. Three years ago, yes.

Nora. I know. I saw it in the paper. Oh please believe me, Kristine. I really meant to write you, but I never got around to it. Something was always coming up.

Mrs. Linde. Of course, Nora. I understand.

Nora. No, that wasn't very nice of me. You poor thing, all you must have been through. And he didn't leave you much, either, did he?

Mrs. Linde. No.

Nora. And no children?

Mrs. Linde. No.

Nora. Nothing at all, in other words?

Mrs. Linde. Not so much as a sense of loss—a grief to live on—

Nora (*incredulous*). But Kristine, how can that *be*?

Mrs. Linde (*with a sad smile, strokes Nora's hair*). That's the way it sometimes is, Nora.

Nora. All alone. How awful for you. I have three darling children. You can't see them right now, though; they're out with their nurse. But now you must tell me everything—

Mrs. Linde. No, no; I'd rather listen to you.

Nora. No, you begin. Today I won't be selfish. Today I'll think only of you. Except there's one thing I've just got to tell you first. Something marvelous that's happened to us just these last few days. You haven't heard, have you?

Mrs. Linde. No; tell me.

Nora. Just think. My husband's been made manager of the Mutual Bank.

Mrs. Linde. Your husband—! Oh, I'm so glad!

Nora. Yes, isn't that great? You see, private law practice is so uncertain, especially when you won't have anything to do with cases that aren't—you know—quite nice. And of course Torvald won't do that, and I quite agree with him. Oh, you've no idea how delighted we are! He takes over at New Year's, and he'll be getting a big salary and all sorts of extras. From now on we'll be able to live in quite a different way—exactly as we like. Oh, Kristine! I feel so carefree and happy! It's lovely to have lots and lots of money and not have to worry about a thing! Don't you agree?

Mrs. Linde. It would be nice to have enough, at any rate.

Nora. No, I don't mean just enough. I mean lots and lots!

Mrs. Linde *(smiles).* Nora, Nora, when are you going to be sensible? In school you spent a great deal of money.

Nora *(quietly laughing).* Yes, and Torvald says I still do. *(Raises her finger at Mrs. Linde.)* But "Nora, Nora" isn't so crazy as you all think. Believe me, we've had nothing to be extravagant with. We've both had to work.

Mrs. Linde. You too?

Nora. Yes. Oh, it's been little things mostly—sewing, crocheting, embroidery— that sort of thing. *(Casually.)* And other things too. You know, of course, that Torvald left government service when we got married? There was no chance of promotion in his department, and of course he had to make more money than he had been making. So for the first few years he worked altogether too hard. He had to take jobs on the side and work night and day. It turned out to be too much for him. He became seriously ill. The doctors told him he needed to go south.

Mrs. Linde. That's right; you spent a year in Italy, didn't you?

Nora. Yes, we did. But you won't believe how hard it was to get away. Ivar had just been born. But of course we had to go. Oh, it was a wonderful trip. And it saved Torvald's life. But it took a lot of money, Kristine.

Mrs. Linde. I'm sure it did.

Nora. Twelve hundred specie dollars. Four thousand eight hundred crowns. That's a lot of money.

Mrs. Linde. Yes. So it's lucky you have it when something like that happens.

Nora. Well, actually we got the money from Daddy.

Mrs. Linde. I see. That was about the time your father died, I believe.

Nora. Yes, just about then. And I couldn't even go and take care of him. I was expecting little Ivar any day. And I had poor Torvald to look after, desperately sick and all. My dear, good Daddy! I never saw him again, Kristine. That's the saddest thing that's happened to me since I got married.

Mrs. Linde. I know you were very fond of him. But then you went to Italy?

Nora. Yes, for now we had the money, and the doctors urged us to go. So we left about a month later.

Mrs. Linde. And when you came back your husband was well again?

Nora. Healthy as a horse!

Mrs. Linde. But—the doctor?

Nora. What do you mean?

Mrs. Linde. I thought the maid said it was the doctor, that gentleman who came the same time I did.

Nora. Oh, that's Dr. Rank. He doesn't come as a doctor. He's our closest friend. He looks in at least once every day. No, Torvald hasn't been sick once since then. And the children are strong and healthy, too, and so am I. *(Jumps up and claps her hands.)* Oh God, Kristine! Isn't it wonderful to be alive and happy! Isn't it just lovely!—But now I'm being mean again, talking only about myself and my things. *(Sits down on a footstool close to Mrs. Linde and puts* *her arms on her lap.*) Please, don't be angry with me! Tell me, is it really true that you didn't care for your husband? Then why did you marry him?

Mrs. Linde. Mother was still alive then, but she was bedridden and helpless. And I had my two younger brothers to look after. I didn't think I had the right to turn him down.

Nora. No, I suppose not. So he had money then?

Mrs. Linde. He was quite well off, I think. But it was an uncertain business, Nora. When he died, the whole thing collapsed and there was nothing left.

Nora. And then—?

Mrs. Linde. Well, I had to manage as best I could. With a little store and a little school and anything else I could think of. The last three years have been one long work day for me, Nora, without any rest. But now it's over. My poor mother doesn't need me any more. She passed away. And the boys are on their own too. They've both got jobs and support themselves.

Nora. What a relief for you—

Mrs. Linde. No, not relief. Just a great emptiness. Nobody to live for any more. (*Gets up, restlessly.*) That's why I couldn't stand it any longer in that little hole. Here in town it has to be easier to find something to keep me busy and occupy my thoughts. With a little luck I should be able to find a permanent job, something in an office—

Nora. Oh but Kristine, that's exhausting work, and you look worn out already. It would be much better for you to go to a resort.

Mrs. Linde (*walks over to the window*). I don't have a Daddy who can give me the money, Nora.

Nora (*getting up*). Oh, don't be angry with me.

Mrs. Linde (*over to her*). Dear Nora, don't *you* be angry with *me*. That's the worst thing about my kind of situation: you become so bitter. You've nobody to work for, and yet you have to look out for yourself, somehow. You've got to keep on living, and so you become selfish. Do you know—when you told me about your husband's new position I was delighted not so much for your sake as for my own.

Nora. Why was that? Oh, I see. You think maybe Torvald can give you a job?

Mrs. Linde. That's what I had in mind.

Nora. And he will too, Kristine. Just leave it to me. I'll be ever so subtle about it. I'll think of something nice to tell him, something he'll like. Oh I so much want to help you.

Mrs. Linde. That's very good of you, Nora—making an effort like that for me. Especially since you've known so little trouble and hardship in your own life.

Nora. I—?—have known so little—?

Mrs. Linde (*smiling*). Oh well, a little sewing or whatever it was. You're still a child, Nora.

Nora (*with a toss of her head, walks away*). You shouldn't sound so superior.

Mrs. Linde. I shouldn't?

Nora. You're just like all the others. None of you think I'm good for anything really serious.

Mrs. Linde. Well, now—

Nora. That I've never been through anything difficult.

Mrs. Linde. But Nora! You just told me all your troubles!

Nora. That's nothing (*Lowers her voice.*) I haven't told you about *it*.

Mrs. Linde. It? What's that? What do you mean?

Nora. You patronize me, Kristine, and that's not fair. You're proud that you worked so long and so hard for your mother.

Mrs. Linde. I don't think I patronize anyone. But it *is* true that I'm both proud and happy that I could make mother's last years comparatively easy.

Nora. And you're proud of all you did for your brothers.

Mrs. Linde. I think I have the right to be.

Nora. And so do I. But now I want to tell you something, Kristine. I have something to be proud and happy about too.

Mrs. Linde. I don't doubt that for a moment. But what exactly do you mean?

Nora. Not so loud! Torvald mustn't hear—not for anything in the world. Nobody must know about this, Kristine. Nobody but you.

Mrs. Linde. But what is it?

Nora. Come here. (*Pulls her down on the couch beside her.*) You see, I *do* have something to be proud and happy about. I've saved Torvald's life.

Mrs. Linde. Saved—? How do you mean—"saved"?

Nora. I told you about our trip to Italy. Torvald would have died if he hadn't gone.

Mrs. Linde. I understand that. And so your father gave you the money you needed.

Nora (*smiles*). Yes, that's what Torvald and all the others think. But—

Mrs. Linde. But what?

Nora. Daddy didn't give us a penny. *I* raised that money.

Mrs. Linde. *You* did? That whole big amount?

Nora. Twelve hundred specie dollars. Four thousand eight hundred crowns. *Now* what do you say?

Mrs. Linde. But Nora, how could you? Did you win in the state lottery?

Nora (*contemptuously*). State lottery! (*Snorts.*) What is so great about that?

Mrs. Linde. Where did it come from then?

Nora (*humming and smiling, enjoying her secret*). Hmmm. Tra-la-la-la-la!

Mrs. Linde. You certainly couldn't have borrowed it.

Nora. Oh? And why not?

Mrs. Linde. A wife can't borrow money without her husband's consent.

Nora (*with a toss of her head*). Oh, I don't know—take a wife with a little bit of a head for business—a wife who knows how to manage things—

Mrs. Linde. But Nora, I don't understand at all—

Nora. You don't have to. I didn't say I borrowed the money, did I? I could have gotten it some other way. (*Leans back.*) An admirer may have given it to me. When you're as tolerably goodlooking as I am—

Mrs. Linde. Oh, you're crazy.

Nora. I think you're dying from curiosity, Kristine.

Mrs. Linde. I'm beginning to think you've done something very foolish, Nora.

Nora (*sits up*). Is it foolish to save your husband's life?

Mrs. Linde. I say it's foolish to act behind his back.

Nora. But don't you see: he couldn't be told! You're missing the whole point, Kristine. We couldn't even let him know how seriously ill he was. The doctors came to *me* and told me his life was in danger, that nothing could save him but a stay in the south. Don't you think I tried to work on him? I told him how lovely it would be if I could go abroad like other young wives. I cried and begged. I said he'd better remember what condition I was in, that he had to be nice to me and do what I wanted. I even hinted he could borrow the money. But that almost made him angry with me. He told me I was being irresponsible and that it was his duty as my husband not to give in to my moods and whims—I think that's what he called it. All right, I said to myself, you've got to be saved somehow, and so I found a way—

Mrs. Linde. And your husband never learned from your father that the money didn't come from him?

Nora. Never. Daddy died that same week. I thought of telling him all about it and ask him not to say anything. But since he was so sick—It turned out I didn't have to—

Mrs. Linde. And you've never told your husband?

Nora. Of course not! Good heavens, how could I? He, with his strict principles! Besides, you know how men are. Torvald would find it embarrassing and humiliating to learn that he owed me anything. It would upset our whole relationship. Our happy, beautiful home would no longer be what it is.

Mrs. Linde. Aren't you ever going to tell him?

Nora (*reflectively, half smiling*). Yes—one day, maybe. Many, many years from now, when I'm no longer young and pretty. Don't laugh! I mean when Torvald no longer feels about me the way he does now, when he no longer thinks it's fun when I dance for him and put on costumes and recite for him. Then it will be good to have something in reserve—(*Interrupts herself.*) Oh, I'm just being silly! That day will never come.—Well, now, Kristine, what do you think of my great secret? Don't you think I'm good for something too?—By the way, you wouldn't believe all the worry I've had because of it. It's been very hard to meet my obligations on schedule. You see, in business there's something called quarterly interest and something called installments on the principal, and those are terribly hard to come up with. I've had to save a little here and a little there, whenever I could. I couldn't use much of the housekeeping money, for Torvald has to eat well. And I couldn't use what I got for clothes for the children. They have to look nice, and I didn't think it would be right to spend less than I got—the sweet little things!

Mrs. Linde. Poor Nora! So you had to take it from your own allowance?

Nora. Yes, of course. After all, it was my affair. Every time Torvald gave me money for a new dress and things like that, I never used more than half of it. I always bought the cheapest, simplest things for myself. Thank God, everything looks good on me, so Torvald never noticed. But it was hard many times, Kristine, for it's fun to have pretty clothes. Don't you think?

Mrs. Linde. Certainly.

Nora. Anyway, I had other ways of making money too. Last winter I was lucky enough to get some copying work. So I locked the door and sat up writing every night till quite late. God! I often got so tired—! But it was great fun, too, working and making money. It was almost like being a man.

Mrs. Linde. But how much have you been able to pay off this way?

Nora. I couldn't tell you exactly. You see, it's very difficult to keep track of business like that. All I know is I have been paying off as much as I've been able to scrape together. Many times I just didn't know what to do. (*Smiles.*) Then I used to imagine a rich old gentleman had fallen in love with me—

Mrs. Linde. What! What old gentleman?

Nora. Phooey! And now he was dead and they were reading his will, and there it said in big letters, "All my money is to be paid in cash immediately to the charming Mrs. Nora Helmer."

Mrs. Linde. But dearest Nora—who *was* this old gentleman?

Nora. For heaven's sake, Kristine, don't you see! There *was* no old gentleman. He was just somebody I made up when I couldn't think of any way to raise the money. But never mind him. The old bore can be anyone he likes to for all I care. I have no use for him or his last will, for now I don't have a single worry in the world. (*Jumps up.*) Dear God, what a lovely thought that is! To be able to play and have fun with the children, to have everything nice and pretty in the house, just the way Torvald likes it! Not a care! And soon spring will be here, and the air will be blue and high. Maybe we can travel again. Maybe I'll see the ocean again! Oh, yes, yes!—it's wonderful to be alive and happy! *The doorbell rings.*

Mrs. Linde (*getting up*). There's the doorbell. Maybe I better be going.

Nora. No, please stay. I'm sure it's just someone for Torvald—

Maid (*in the hall door*). Excuse me, ma'am. There's a gentleman here who'd like to see Mr. Helmer.

Nora. You mean the bank manager.

Maid. Sorry, ma'am; the bank manager. But I didn't know—since the Doctor is with him—

Nora. Who is the gentleman?

Krogstad (*appearing in the door*). It's just me, Mrs. Helmer.

Mrs. Linde starts, looks, turns away toward the window.

Nora (*takes a step toward him, tense, in a low voice*). You? What do you want? What do you want with my husband?

Krogstad. Bank business—in a way. I have a small job in the Mutual, and I understand your husband is going to be our new boss—

Nora. So it's just—

Krogstad. Just routine business, ma'am. Nothing else.

Nora. All right. In that case, why don't you go through the door to the office.

Dismisses him casually as she closes the door. Walks over to the stove and tends the fire.

Mrs. Linde. Nora—who was that man?

Nora. His name's Krogstad. He's a lawyer.

Mrs. Linde. So it *was* him.

Nora. Do you know him?

Mrs. Linde. I used to—many years ago. For a while he clerked in our part of the country.

Nora. Right. He did.

Mrs. Linde. He has changed a great deal.

Nora. I believe he had a very unhappy marriage.

Mrs. Linde. And now he's a widower, isn't he?

Nora. With many children. There now; it's burning nicely again. (*Closes the stove and moves the rocking chair a little to the side.*)

Mrs. Linde. They say he's into all sorts of business.

A Doll's House

Nora. Really? Maybe so. I wouldn't know. But let's not think about business. It's such a bore.

Dr. Rank (*appears in the door to Helmer's study*). No, I don't want to be in the way. I'd rather talk to your wife a bit. (*Closes the door and notices Mrs. Linde.*) Oh, I beg your pardon. I believe I'm in the way here too.

Nora. No, not at all. (*Introduces them.*) Dr. Rank. Mrs. Linde.

Rank. Aha. A name often heard in this house. I believe I passed you on the stairs coming up.

Mrs. Linde. Yes. I'm afraid I climb stairs very slowly. They aren't good for me.

Rank. I see. A slight case of inner decay, perhaps?

Mrs. Linde. Overwork, rather.

Rank. Oh, is that all? And now you've come to town to relax at all the parties?

Mrs. Linde. I have come to look for a job.

Rank. A proven cure for overwork, I take it?

Mrs. Linde. One has to live, Doctor.

Rank. Yes, that seems to be the common opinion.

Nora. Come on, Dr. Rank—you want to live just as much as the rest of us.

Rank. Of course I do. Miserable as I am, I prefer to go on being tortured as long as possible. All my patients feel the same way. And that's true of the moral invalids too. Helmer is talking with a specimen right this minute.

Mrs. Linde (*in a low voice*). Ah!

Nora. What do you mean?

Rank. Oh, this lawyer, Krogstad. You don't know him. The roots of his character are decayed. But even he began by saying something about having to *live*—as if it were a matter of the highest importance.

Nora. Oh? What did he want with Torvald?

Rank. I don't really know. All I heard was something about the bank.

Nora. I didn't know that Krog—that this Krogstad had anything to do with the Mutual Bank.

Rank. Yes, he seems to have some kind of job there. (*To Mrs. Linde.*) I don't know if you are familiar in your part of the country with the kind of person who is always running around trying to sniff out cases of moral decrepitude and as soon as he finds one puts the individual under observation in some excellent position or other. All the healthy ones are left out in the cold.

Mrs. Linde. I should think it's the sick who need looking after the most.

Rank (*shrugs his shoulders*). There we are. That's the attitude that turns society into a hospital.

Nora, absorbed in her own thoughts, suddenly starts giggling and clapping her hands.

Rank. What's so funny about that? Do you even know what society is?

Nora. What do I care about your stupid society! I laughed at something entirely different—something terribly amusing. Tell me, Dr. Rank—all the employees in the Mutual Bank, from now on they'll all be dependent on Torvald, right?

Rank. Is that what you find so enormously amusing?

Nora (*smiles and hums*). That's my business, that's my business! (*Walks around.*) Yes, I do think it's fun that we—that Torvald is going to have so much influence on so many people's lives. (*Brings out the bag of macaroons.*) Have a macaroon, Dr. Rank.

Rank. Well, well—macaroons. I thought they were banned around here.

Nora. Yes, but these were some that Kristine gave me.

Mrs. Linde. What! I?

Nora. That's all right. Don't look so scared. You couldn't know that Torvald won't let me have them. He's afraid they'll ruin my teeth. But who cares! Just once in a while—! Right, Dr. Rank? Have one! (*Puts a macaroon into his mouth.*) You too, Kristine. And one for me. A very small one. Or at most two. (*Walks around again.*) Yes, I really feel very, very happy. Now there's just one thing I'm dying to do.

Rank. Oh? And what's that?

Nora. Something I'm dying to say so Torvald could hear.

Rank. And why can't you?

Nora. I don't dare to, for it's not nice.

Mrs. Linde. Not nice?

Rank. In that case, I guess you'd better not. But surely to the two of us—? What is it you'd like to say for Helmer to hear?

Nora. I want to say, "Goddammit!"

Rank. Are you out of your mind!

Mrs. Linde. For heaven's sake, Nora!

Rank. Say it. Here he comes.

Nora (*hiding the macaroons*). Shhh!

Helmer enters from his study, carrying his hat and overcoat.

Nora (*going to him*). Well, dear, did you get rid of him?

Helmer. Yes, he just left.

Nora. Torvald, I want you to meet Kristine. She's just come to town.

Helmer. Kristine—? I'm sorry; I don't think—

Nora. Mrs. Linde, Torvald dear. Mrs. Kristine Linde.

Helmer. Ah, yes. A childhood friend of my wife's, I suppose.

Mrs. Linde. Yes, we've known each other for a long time.

Nora. Just think; she has come all this way just to see you.

Helmer. I'm not sure I understand—

Mrs. Linde. Well, not really—

Nora. You see, Kristine is an absolutely fantastic secretary, and she would so much like to work for a competent executive and learn more than she knows already—

Helmer. Very sensible, I'm sure, Mrs. Linde.

Nora. So when she heard about your appointment—there was a wire—she came here as fast as she could. How about it, Torvald? Couldn't you do something for Kristine? For my sake. Please?

Helmer. Quite possibly. I take it you're a widow, Mrs. Linde?

Mrs. Linde. Yes.

Helmer. And you've had office experience?

Mrs. Linde. Some—yes.

Helmer. In that case I think it's quite likely that I'll be able to find you a position.

Nora (*claps her hands*). I knew it! I knew it!

Helmer. You've arrived at a most opportune time, Mrs. Linde.

A Doll's House

Mrs. Linde. Oh, how can I ever thank you—

Helmer. Not at all, not at all. (*Puts his coat on.*) But today you'll have to excuse me—

Rank. Wait a minute; I'll come with you. (*Gets his fur coat from the front hall, warms it by the stove.*)

Nora. Don't be long, Torvald.

Helmer. An hour or so; no more.

Nora. Are you leaving, too, Kristine?

Mrs. Linde (*putting on her things*). Yes, I'd better go and find a place to stay.

Helmer. Good. Then we'll be going the same way.

Nora (*helping her*). I'm sorry this place is so small, but I don't think we very well could—

Mrs. Linde. Of course! Don't be silly, Nora. Goodbye, and thank you for everything.

Nora. Goodbye. We'll see you soon. You'll be back this evening, of course. And you too, Dr. Rank; right? If you feel well enough? Of course you will. Just wrap yourself up.

General small talk as all exit into the hall. Children's voices are heard on the stairs.

Nora. There they are! There they are! (*She runs and opens the door. The nurse Anne-Marie enters with the children.*)

Nora. Come in! Come in! (*Bends over and kisses them.*) Oh, you sweet, sweet darlings! Look at them, Kristine! Aren't they beautiful?

Rank. No standing around in the draft!

Helmer. Come along, Mrs. Linde. This place isn't fit for anyone but mothers right now.

Dr. Rank, Helmer, and Mrs. Linde go down the stairs. The Nurse enters the living room with the children. Nora follows, closing the door behind her.

Nora. My, how nice you all look! Such red cheeks! Like apples and roses. (*The children all talk at the same time.*) You've had so much fun? I bet you have. Oh, isn't that nice! You pulled both Emmy and Bob on your sleigh? Both at the same time? That's very good, Ivar. Oh, let me hold her for a minute, Anne-Marie. My sweet little doll baby! (*Takes the smallest of the children from the Nurse and dances with her.*) Yes, yes, of course; Mama'll dance with you too, Bob. What? You threw snowballs? Oh, I wish I'd been there! No, no; I want to take their clothes off, Anne-Marie. Please let me; I think it's so much fun. You go on in. You look frozen. There's hot coffee on the stove.

The Nurse exits into the room to the left. Nora takes the children's wraps off and throws them all around. They all keep telling her things at the same time.

Nora. Oh, really? A big dog ran after you? But it didn't bite you. Of course not. Dogs don't bite sweet little doll babies. Don't peek at the packages, Ivar! What's in them? Wouldn't you like to know! No, no; that's something terrible! Play? You want to play? What do you want to play? Okay, let's play hide-and-seek. Bob hides first. You want *me* to? All right. I'll go first.

Laughing and shouting, Nora and the children play in the living room and in the adjacent room, right. Finally, Nora hides herself under the table; the children rush in, look for her, can't find her. They hear her low giggle, run to the table, lift the rug that covers it, see her. General hilarity. She crawls out, pretends to scare them. New delight. In the meantime there has been a knock on the door between the living room and the front hall, but nobody has noticed. Now the door is opened halfway; Krogstad appears. He waits a little. The play goes on.

Krogstad. Pardon me, Mrs. Helmer—

Nora *(with a muted cry turns around, jumps up).* Ah! What do you want?

Krogstad. I'm sorry. The front door was open. Somebody must have forgotten to close it—

Nora *(standing up).* My husband isn't here, Mr. Krogstad.

Krogstad. I know.

Nora. So what do you want?

Krogstad. I'd like a word with you.

Nora. With—? *(To the children.)* Go in to Anne-Marie. What? No, the strange man won't do anything bad to Mama. When he's gone we'll play some more.

She takes the children into the room to the left and closes the door.

Nora *(tense, troubled).* You want to speak with me?

Krogstad. Yes I do.

Nora. Today—? It isn't the first of the month yet.

Krogstad. No, it's Christmas Eve. It's up to you what kind of holiday you'll have.

Nora. What do you want? I can't possibly—

Krogstad. Let's not talk about that just yet. There's something else. You do have a few minutes, don't you?

Nora. Yes. Yes, of course. That is,—

Krogstad. Good. I was sitting in Olsen's restaurant when I saw your husband go by.

Nora. Yes—?

Krogstad. —with a lady.

Nora. What of it?

Krogstad. May I be so free as to ask: wasn't that lady Mrs. Linde?

Nora. Yes.

Krogstad. Just arrived in town?

Nora. Yes, today.

Krogstad. She's a good friend of yours, I understand?

Nora. Yes, she is. But I fail to see—

Krogstad. I used to know her myself.

Nora. I know that.

Krogstad. So you know about that. I thought as much. In that case, let me ask you a simple question. Is Mrs. Linde going to be employed in the bank?

Nora. What makes you think you have the right to cross-examine me like this, Mr. Krogstad—you, one of my husband's employees? But since you ask, I'll tell you. Yes, Mrs. Linde is going to be working in the bank. And it was I who recommended her, Mr. Krogstad. Now you know.

Krogstad. So I was right.

Nora *(walks up and down).* After all, one does have a little influence, you know. Just because you're a woman, it doesn't mean that—Really, Mr. Krogstad, people in a subordinate position should be careful not to offend someone who—oh well—

Krogstad. —has influence?

Nora. Exactly.

Krogstad *(changing his tone).* Mrs. Helmer, I must ask you to be good enough to use your influence on my behalf.

Nora. What do you mean?

Krogstad. I want you to make sure that I am going to keep my subordinate position in the bank.

Nora. I don't understand. Who is going to take your position away from you?

Krogstad. There's no point in playing ignorant with me, Mrs. Helmer. I can very well appreciate that your friend would find it unpleasant to run into me. So now I know who I can thank for my dismissal.

Nora. But I assure you—

Krogstad. Never mind. Just want to say you still have time. I advise you to use your influence to prevent it.

Nora. But Mr. Krogstad, I don't have any influence—none at all.

Krogstad. No? I thought you just said—

Nora. Of course I didn't mean it that way. I! Whatever makes you think that I have any influence of that kind on my husband?

Krogstad. I went to law school with your husband. I have no reason to think that the bank manager is less susceptible than other husbands.

Nora. If you're going to insult my husband, I'll ask you to leave.

Krogstad. You're brave, Mrs. Helmer.

Nora. I'm not afraid of you any more. After New Year's I'll be out of this thing with you.

Krogstad *(more controlled).* Listen, Mrs. Helmer. If necessary, I'll fight as for my life to keep my little job in the bank.

Nora. So it seems.

Krogstad. It isn't just the money; that's really the smallest part of it. There is something else—Well, I guess I might as well tell you. It's like this. I'm sure you know, like everybody else, that some years ago I committed—an impropriety.

Nora. I believe I've heard it mentioned.

Krogstad. The case never came to court, but from that moment all doors were closed to me. So I took up the kind of business you know about. I had to do something, and I think I can say about myself that I have not been among the worst. But now I want to get out of all that. My sons are growing up. For their sake I must get back as much of my good name as I can. This job in the bank was like the first rung on the ladder. And now your husband wants to kick me down and leave me back in the mud again.

Nora. But I swear to you, Mr. Krogstad; it's not at all in my power to help you.

Krogstad. That's because you don't want to. But I have the means to force you.

Nora. You don't mean you're going to tell my husband I owe you money?

Krogstad. And if I did?

Nora. That would be a mean thing to do. *(Almost crying.)* That secret, which is my joy and my pride—for him to learn about it in such a coarse and ugly manner—to learn it from *you*—! It would be terribly unpleasant for me.

Krogstad. Just unpleasant?

Nora (heatedly). But go ahead! Do it! It will be worse for you than for me. When my husband realizes what a bad person you are, you'll be sure to lose your job.

Krogstad. I asked you if it was just domestic unpleasantness you were afraid of?

Nora. When my husband finds out, of course he'll pay off the loan, and then we won't have anything more to do with you.

Krogstad (stepping closer). Listen, Mrs. Helmer—either you have a very bad memory, or you don't know much about business. I think I had better straighten you out on a few things.

Nora. What do you mean?

Krogstad. When your husband was ill, you came to me to borrow twelve hundred dollars.

Nora. I knew nobody else.

Krogstad. I promised to get you the money—

Nora. And you did.

Krogstad. I promised to get you the money on certain conditions. At the time you were so anxious about your husband's health and so set on getting him away that I doubt very much that you paid much attention to the details of our transaction. That's why I remind you of them now. Anyway, I promised to get you the money if you would sign an I.O.U., which I drafted.

Nora. And which I signed.

Krogstad. Good. But below your signature I added a few lines, making your father security for the loan. Your father was supposed to put his signature to those lines.

Nora. Supposed to—? He did.

Krogstad. I had left the date blank. That is, your father was to date his own signature. You recall that, don't you, Mrs. Helmer?

Nora. I guess so—

Krogstad. I gave the note to you. You were to mail it to your father. Am I correct?

Nora. Yes.

Krogstad. And of course you did so right away, for no more than five or six days later you brought the paper back to me, signed by your father. Then I paid you the money.

Nora. Well? And haven't I been keeping up with the payments?

Krogstad. Fairly well, yes. But to get back to what we were talking about—those were difficult days for you, weren't they, Mrs. Helmer?

Nora. Yes, they were.

Krogstad. Your father was quite ill, I believe.

Nora. He was dying.

Krogstad. And died shortly afterwards?

Nora. That's right.

Krogstad. Tell me, Mrs. Helmer; do you happen to remember the date of your father's death? I mean the exact day of the month?

Nora. Daddy died on September 29.

Krogstad. Quite correct. I have ascertained that fact. That's why there is something peculiar about this (*takes out a piece of paper*), which I can't account for.

Nora. Peculiar? How? I don't understand—

Krogstad. It seems very peculiar, Mrs. Helmer, that your father signed this promissory note three days after his death.

Nora. How so? I don't see what—

Krogstad. Your father died on September 29. Now look. He has dated his signature October 2. Isn't that odd?

Nora remains silent.

Krogstad. Can you explain it?

Nora is still silent.

Krogstad. I also find it striking that the date and the month and the year are not in your father's handwriting but in a hand I think I recognize. Well, that might be explained. Your father may have forgotten to date his signature and somebody else may have done it here, guessing at the date before he had learned of your father's death. That's all right. It's only the signature itself that matters. And that is genuine, isn't it, Mrs. Helmer? You father *did* put his name to this note?

Nora (after a brief silence tosses her head back and looks defiantly at him). No, he didn't. I wrote Daddy's name.

Krogstad. Mrs. Helmer—do you realize what a dangerous admission you just made?

Nora. Why? You'll get your money soon.

Krogstad. Let me ask you something. Why didn't you mail this note to your father?

Nora. Because it was impossible. Daddy was sick—you know that. If I had asked him to sign it, I would have had to tell him what the money was for. But I couldn't tell him, as sick as he was, that my husband's life was in danger. That was impossible. Surely you can see that.

Krogstad. Then it would have been better for you if you had given up your trip abroad.

Nora. No, that was impossible! That trip was to save my husband's life. I couldn't give it up.

Krogstad. But didn't you realize that what you did amounted to fraud against me?

Nora. I couldn't let that make any difference. I didn't care about you at all. I hated the way you made all those difficulties for me, even though you knew the danger my husband was in. I thought you were cold and unfeeling.

Krogstad. Mrs. Helmer, obviously you have no clear idea of what you have done. Let me tell you that what I did that time was no more and no worse. And it ruined my name and reputation.

Nora. You! Are you trying to tell me that you did something brave once in order to save your wife's life?

Krogstad. The law doesn't ask about motives.

Nora. Then it's a bad law.

Krogstad. Bad or not—if I produce this note in court you'll be judged according to the law.

Nora. I refuse to believe you. A daughter shouldn't have the right to spare her dying old father worry and anxiety? A wife shouldn't have the right to save her husband's life? I don't know the laws very well, but I'm sure that somewhere they make allowance for cases like that. And you, a lawyer, don't know that? I think you must be a bad lawyer, Mr. Krogstad.

Krogstad. That may be. But business—the kind of business you and I have with one another—don't you think I know something about that? Very well. Do what you like. But let me tell you this: if I'm going to be kicked out again, you'll keep me company. (*He bows and exits through the front hall.*)

Nora (*pauses thoughtfully; then, with a defiant toss of her head*). Oh, nonsense! Trying to scare me like that! I'm not all that silly. (*Starts picking up the children's clothes; soon stops.*) But—? No! That's impossible! I did it for love!

Children (*in the door to the left*). Mama, the strange man just left. We saw him.

Nora. Yes, yes; I know. But don't tell anybody about the strange man. Do you hear? Not even Daddy.

Children. We won't. But now you'll play with us again, won't you, Mama?

Nora. No, not right now.

Children. But Mama—you promised.

Nora. I know, but I can't just now. Go to your own room. I've so much to do. Be nice now, my little darlings. Do as I say. (*She nudges them gently into the other room and closes the door. She sits down on the couch, picks up a piece of embroidery, makes a few stitches, then stops.*) No! (*Throws the embroidery down, goes to the hall door and calls out.*) Helene! Bring the Christmas tree in here, please! (*Goes to the table, left, opens the drawer, halts.*) No—that's impossible!

Maid (*with the Christmas tree*). Where do you want it, ma'am?

Nora. There. The middle of the floor.

Maid. You want anything else?

Nora. No, thanks. I have everything I need. (*The maid goes out. Nora starts trimming the tree.*) I want candles—and flowers—That awful man! Oh, nonsense! There's nothing wrong. This will be a lovely tree. I'll do everything you want me to, Torvald. I'll sing for you—dance for you—

Helmer, a bundle of papers under his arm, enters from outside.

Nora. Ah—you're back already?

Helmer. Yes. Has anybody been here?

Nora. Here? No.

Helmer. That's funny. I saw Krogstad leaving just now.

Nora. Oh? Oh yes, that's right. Krogstad was here for just a moment.

Helmer. I can tell from your face that he came to ask you to put in a word for him.

Nora. Yes.

Helmer. And it was supposed to be your own idea, wasn't it? You were not to tell me he'd been here. He asked you that too, didn't he?

Nora. Yes, Torvald, but—

Helmer. Nora, Nora, how could you! Talk to a man like that and make him promises! And lying to me about it afterwards—!

Nora. Lying—?

Helmer. Didn't you say nobody had been here? (*Shakes his finger at her.*) My little songbird must never do that again. Songbirds are supposed to have clean beaks to chirp with—no false notes. (*Puts his arm around her waist.*) Isn't that so? Of course it is. (*Lets her go.*) And that's enough about that. (*Sits down in front of the fireplace.*) Ah, it's nice and warm in here. (*Begins to leaf through his papers.*)

Nora (*busy with the tree; after a brief pause*). Torvald.

Helmer. Yes.

Nora. I'm looking forward so much to the Stenborgs' costume party day after tomorrow.

Helmer. And I can't wait to find out what you're going to surprise me with.

Nora. Oh, that silly idea!

Helmer. Oh?

Nora. I can't think of anything. It all seems so foolish and pointless.

Helmer. Ah, my little Nora admits that?

Nora (*behind his chair, her arms on the back of the chair*). Are you very busy, Torvald?

Helmer. Well—

Nora. What are all those papers?

Helmer. Bank business.

Nora. Already?

Helmer. I've asked the board to give me the authority to make certain changes in organization and personnel. That's what I'll be doing over the holidays. I want it all settled before New Year's.

Nora. So that's why this poor Krogstad—

Helmer. Hm.

Nora (*leisurely playing with the hair on his neck*). If you weren't so busy, Torvald, I'd ask you for a great big favor.

Helmer. Let's hear it, anyway.

Nora. I don't know anyone with better taste than you, and I want so much to look nice at the party. Couldn't you sort of take charge of me, Torvald, and decide what I'll wear—Help me with my costume?

Helmer. Aha! Little Lady Obstinate is looking for someone to rescue her?

Nora. Yes, Torvald. I won't get anywhere without your help.

Helmer. All right. I'll think about it. We'll come up with something.

Nora. Oh, you *are* nice! (*Goes back to the Christmas tree. A pause.*) Those red flowers look so pretty.—Tell me, was it really all that bad what this Krogstad fellow did?

Helmer. He forged signatures. Do you have any idea what that means?

Nora. Couldn't it have been because he felt he had to?

Helmer. Yes, or like so many others he may simply have been thoughtless. I'm not so heartless as to condemn a man absolutely because of a single imprudent act.

Nora. Of course not, Torvald!

Helmer. People like him can redeem themselves morally by openly confessing their crime and taking their punishment.

Nora. Punishment—?

Helmer. But that was not the way Krogstad chose. He got out of it with tricks and evasions. That's what has corrupted him.

Nora. So you think that if—?

Helmer. Can't you imagine how a guilty person like that has to lie and fake and dissemble wherever he goes—putting on a mask before everybody he's close to, even his own wife and children. It's this thing with the children that's the worst part of it, Nora.

Nora. Why is that?

Helmer. Because when a man lives inside such a circle of stinking lies he brings infection into his own home and contaminates his whole family. With every breath of air his children inhale the germs of something ugly.

Nora *(moving closer behind him).* Are you so sure of that?

Helmer. Of course I am. I have seen enough examples of that in my work. Nearly all young criminals have had mothers who lied.

Nora. Why mothers—particularly?

Helmer. Most often mothers. But of course fathers tend to have the same influence. Every lawyer knows that. And yet, for years this Krogstad has been poisoning his own children in an atmosphere of lies and deceit. That's why I call him a lost soul morally. *(Reaches out for her hands.)* And that's why my sweet little Nora must promise me never to take his side again. Let's shake on that.—What? What's this? Give me your hand. There! Now that's settled. I assure you, I would find it impossible to work in the same room with that man. I feel literally sick when I'm around people like that.

Nora *(withdraws her hand and goes to the other side of the Christmas tree).* It's so hot in here. And I have so much to do.

Helmer *(gets up and collects his papers).* Yes, and I really should try to get some of this reading done before dinner. I must think about your costume too. And maybe just possibly I'll have something to wrap in gilt paper and hang on the Christmas tree. *(Puts his hand on her head.)* Oh my adorable little songbird! *(Enters his study and closes the door.)*

Nora *(after a pause, in a low voice).* It's all a lot of nonsense. It's not that way at all. It's impossible. It has to be impossible.

Nurse *(in the door, left).* The little ones are asking ever so nicely if they can't come in and be with their mama.

Nora. No, no, no! Don't let them in here! You stay with them, Anne-Marie.

Nurse. If you say so, ma'am. *(Closes the door.)*

Nora *(pale with terror).* Corrupt my little children—! Poison my home—? *(Brief pause; she lifts her head.)* That's not true. Never. Never in a million years.

ACT II

The same room. The Christmas tree is in the corner by the piano, stripped, shabby-looking, with burnt-down candles. Nora's outside clothes are on the couch. Nora is alone. She walks around restlessly. She stops by the couch and picks up her coat.

Nora *(drops the coat again).* There's somebody now! *(Goes to the door, listens.)* No. Nobody. Of course not—not on Christmas. And not tomorrow either.— But perhaps—*(Opens the door and looks.)* No, nothing in the mailbox. All empty. *(Comes forward.)* How silly I am! Of course he isn't serious. Nothing like that could happen. After all, I have three small children.

The nurse enters from the room, left, carrying a big carton.

Nurse. Well, at last I found it—the box with your costume.

Nora. Thanks. Just put it on the table.

Nurse *(does so)*. But it's all a big mess, I'm afraid.

Nora. Oh, I wish I could tear the whole thing to little pieces!

Nurse. Heavens! It's not as bad as all that. It can be fixed all right. All it takes is a little patience.

Nora. I'll go over and get Mrs. Linde to help me.

Nurse. Going out again? In this awful weather? You'll catch a cold.

Nora. That might not be such a bad thing. How are the children?

Nurse. The poor little dears are playing with their presents, but—

Nora. Do they keep asking for me?

Nurse. Well, you know; they're used to being with their mamma.

Nora. I know. But Anne-Marie, from now on I can't be with them as much as before.

Nurse. Oh well. Little children get used to everything.

Nora. You think so? Do you think they'll forget their mamma if I were gone altogether?

Nurse. Goodness me—gone altogether?

Nora. Listen, Anne-Marie—something I've wondered about. How could you bring yourself to leave your child with strangers?

Nurse. But I had to, if I were to nurse you.

Nora. Yes, but how could you *want* to?

Nurse. When I could get such a nice place? When something like that happens to a poor young girl, she'd better be grateful for whatever she gets. For *he* didn't do a thing for me—the louse!

Nora. But your daughter has forgotten all about you, hasn't she?

Nurse. Oh no! Not at all! She wrote to me both when she was confirmed and when she got married.

Nora *(putting her arms around her neck)*. You dear old thing—you were a good mother to me when I was little.

Nurse. Poor little Nora had no one else, you know.

Nora. And if my little ones didn't, I know you'd—oh, I'm being silly! *(Opens the carton.)* Go in to them, please. I really should—. Tomorrow you'll see how pretty I'll be.

Nurse. I know. There won't be anybody at that party half as pretty as you, ma'am. *(Goes out, left.)*

Nora *(begins to take clothes out of the carton; in a moment she throws it all down)*. If only I dared to go out. If only I knew nobody would come. That nothing would happen while I was gone.—How silly! Nobody'll come. Just don't think about it. Brush the muff. Beautiful gloves. Beautiful gloves. Forget it. Forget it. One, two, three, four, five, six—*(Cries out.)* There they are! *(Moves toward the door, stops irresolutely.)*

Mrs. Linde enters from the hall. She has already taken off her coat.

Nora. Oh, it's you, Kristine. There's no one else out there, is there? I'm so glad you're here.

Mrs. Linde. They told me you'd asked for me.

Nora. I just happened to walk by. I need your help with something—badly. Let's sit here on the couch. Look. Torvald and I are going to a costume party tomorrow night—at Consul Stenborg's upstairs—and Torvald wants me to go as a Neapolitan fisher girl and dance the tarantella. I learned it when we were on Capri.

Mrs. Linde. Well, well! So you'll be putting on a whole show?

Nora. Yes. Torvald thinks I should. Look, here's the costume. Torvald had it made for me while we were there. But it's all so torn and everything. I just don't know—

Mrs. Linde. Oh, that can be fixed. It's not that much. The trimmings have come loose in a few places. Do you have needle and thread? Oh, here we are. All set.

Nora. I really appreciate it, Kristine.

Mrs. Linde (sewing). So you'll be in disguise tomorrow night, eh? You know—I may come by for just a moment, just to look at you.—Oh dear. I haven't even thanked you for the nice evening last night.

Nora (gets up, moves around). Oh, I don't know. I don't think last night was as nice as it usually is.—You should have come to town a little earlier, Kristine.— Yes, Torvald knows how to make it nice and pretty around here.

Mrs. Linde. You too, I should think. After all, you're your father's daughter. By the way, is Dr. Rank always as depressed as he was last night?

Nora. No, last night was unusual. He's a very sick man, you know—very sick. Poor Rank, his spine is rotting away. Tuberculosis, I think. You see, his father was a nasty old man with mistresses and all that sort of thing. Rank has been sickly ever since he was a little boy.

Mrs. Linde (dropping her sewing to her lap). But dearest Nora, where have you learned about things like that?

Nora (still walking about). Oh, you know—with three children you sometimes get to talk with—other wives. Some of them know quite a bit about medicine. So you pick up a few things.

Mrs. Linde (resumes her sewing; after a brief pause). Does Dr. Rank come here every day?

Nora. Every single day. He's Torvald's oldest and best friend, after all. And my friend too, for that matter. He's part of the family, almost.

Mrs. Linde. But tell me, is he quite sincere? I mean, isn't he the kind of man who likes to say nice things to people?

Nora. No, not at all. Rather the opposite, in fact. What makes you say that?

Mrs. Linde. When you introduced us yesterday, he told me he'd often heard my name mentioned in this house. But later on it was quite obvious that your husband really had no idea who I was. So how could Dr. Rank—?

Nora. You're right, Kristine, but I can explain that. You see, Torvald loves me so very much that he wants me all to himself. That's what he says. When we were first married he got almost jealous when I as much as mentioned anybody from back home that I was fond of. So of course I soon stopped doing that. But with Dr. Rank I often talk about home. You see, he likes to listen to me.

Mrs. Linde. Look here, Nora. In many ways you're still a child. After all, I'm quite a bit older than you and have had more experience. I want to give you a piece of advice. I think you should get out of this thing with Dr. Rank.

Nora. Get out of what thing?

Mrs. Linde. Several things in fact, if you want my opinion. Yesterday you said something about a rich admirer who was going to give you money—

Nora. One who doesn't exist, unfortunately. What of it?

Mrs. Linde. Does Dr. Rank have money?

Nora. Yes, he does.

Mrs. Linde. And no dependents?

Nora. No. But—?

Mrs. Linde. And he comes here every day?

Nora. Yes, I told you that already.

Mrs. Linde. But how can that sensitive man be so tactless?

Nora. I haven't the slightest idea what you're talking about.

Mrs. Linde. Don't play games with me, Nora. Don't you think I know who you borrowed the twelve hundred dollars from?

Nora. Are you out of your mind! The very idea—! A friend of both of us who sees us every day—! What a dreadfully uncomfortable position that would be!

Mrs. Linde. So it really isn't Dr. Rank?

Nora. Most certainly not! I would never have dreamed of asking him—not for a moment. Anyway, he didn't have any money then. He inherited it afterwards.

Mrs. Linde. Well, I still think it may have been lucky for you, Nora dear.

Nora. The idea! It would never have occurred to me to ask Dr. Rank—. Though I'm sure that if I *did* ask him—

Mrs. Linde. But of course you wouldn't.

Nora. Of course not. I can't imagine that that would ever be necessary. But I am quite sure that if I told Dr. Rank—

Mrs. Linde. Behind your husband's back?

Nora. I must get out of—this other thing. That's also behind his back. I *must* get out of it.

Mrs. Linde. That's what I told you yesterday. But—

Nora (*walking up and down*). A man manages these things so much better than a woman—

Mrs. Linde. One's husband, yes.

Nora. Silly, silly! (*Stops.*) When you've paid off all you owe, you get your I.O.U. back; right?

Mrs. Linde. Yes, of course.

Nora. And you can tear it into a hundred thousand little pieces and burn it—that dirty, filthy, paper!

Mrs. Linde (*looks hard at her, puts down her sewing, rises slowly*). Nora— you're hiding something from me.

Nora. Can you tell?

Mrs. Linde. Something's happened to you, Nora, since yesterday morning. What is it?

Nora (*going to her*). Kristine! (*Listens.*) Shhh. Torvald just came back. Listen. Why don't you go in to the children for a while. Torvald can't stand having sewing around. Get Anne-Marie to help you.

Mrs. Linde (*gathers some of the sewing things together*). All right, but I'm not leaving here till you and I have talked.

She goes out left, just as Helmer enters from the front hall.

Nora (towards him). I have been waiting and waiting for you, Torvald.

Helmer. Was that the dressmaker?

Nora. No, it was Kristine. She's helping me with my costume. Oh Torvald, just wait till you see how nice I'll look!

Helmer. I told you. Pretty good idea I had, wasn't it?

Nora. Lovely! And wasn't it nice of me to go along with it?

Helmer *(his hand under her chin).* Nice? To do what your husband tells you? All right, you little rascal; I know you didn't mean it that way. But don't let me interrupt you. I suppose you want to try it on.

Nora. And you'll be working?

Helmer. Yes. *(Shows her a pile of papers.)* Look. I've been down to the bank. *(Is about to enter his study.)*

Nora. Torvald.

Helmer *(halts).* Yes?

Nora. What if your little squirrel asked you ever so nicely—

Helmer. For what?

Nora. Would you do it?

Helmer. Depends on what it is.

Nora. Squirrel would run around and do all sorts of fun tricks if you'd be nice and agreeable.

Helmer. All right. What is it?

Nora. Lark would chirp and twitter in all the rooms, up and down—

Helmer. So what? Lark does that anyway.

Nora. I'll be your elfmaid and dance for you in the moonlight, Torvald.

Helmer. Nora, don't tell me it's the same thing you mentioned this morning?

Nora (closer to him). Yes, Torvald. I beg you!

Helmer. You really have the nerve to bring that up again?

Nora. Yes. You've just got to do as I say. You *must* let Krogstad keep his job.

Helmer. My dear Nora. It's his job I intend to give to Mrs. Linde.

Nora. I know. And that's ever so nice of you. But can't you just fire somebody else?

Helmer. This is incredible! You just don't give up, do you? Because you make some foolish promise, I am supposed to—!

Nora. That's not the reason, Torvald. It's for your own sake. That man writes for the worst newspapers. You've said so yourself. There's no telling what he may do to you. I'm scared to death of him.

Helmer. Ah, I understand. You're afraid because of what happened before.

Nora. What do you mean?

Helmer. You're thinking of your father, of course.

Nora. Yes. Yes, you're right. Remember the awful things they wrote about Daddy in the newspapers. I really think they might have forced him to resign if the ministry hadn't sent you to look into the charges and if you hadn't been so helpful and understanding.

Helmer. My dear little Nora, there is a world of difference between your father and me. Your father's official conduct was not above reproach. Mine is, and I intend for it to remain that way as long as I hold my position.

Nora. Oh, but you don't know what vicious people like that may think of. Oh, Torvald! Now all of us could be so happy together here in our own home, peaceful and carefree. Such a good life, Torvald, for you and me and the children! That's why I implore you—

Helmer. And it's exactly because you plead for him that you make it impossible for me to keep him. It's already common knowledge in the bank that I intend to let Krogstad go. If it gets out that the new manager has changed his mind because of his wife—

Nora. Yes? What then?

Helmer. No, of course, that wouldn't matter at all as long as little Mrs. Pighead here got her way! Do you want me to make myself look ridiculous before my whole staff—make people think I can be swayed by just anybody—by outsiders? Believe me, I would soon enough find out what the consequences would be! Besides, there's another thing that makes it absolutely impossible for Krogstad to stay on in the bank now that I'm in charge.

Nora. What's that?

Helmer. I suppose in a pinch I could overlook his moral shortcomings—

Nora. Yes, you could; couldn't you, Torvald?

Helmer. And I understand he's quite a good worker, too. But we've known each other for a long time. It's one of those imprudent relationships you get into when you're young that embarrass you for the rest of your life. I guess I might as well be frank with you: he and I are on a first name basis. And that tactless fellow never hides the fact even when other people are around. Rather, he seems to think it entitles him to be familiar with me. Every chance he gets he comes out with his damn "Torvald, Torvald." I'm telling you, I find it most awkward. He would make my position in the bank intolerable.

Nora. You don't really mean any of this, Torvald.

Helmer. Oh? I don't? And why not?

Nora. No, for it's all so petty.

Helmer. What! Petty? You think I'm being petty!

Nora. No, I *don't* think you are petty, Torvald dear. That's exactly why I—

Helmer. Never mind. You think my reasons are petty, so it follows that I must be petty too. Petty! Indeed! By God, I'll put an end to this right now! (*Opens the door to the front hall and calls out.*) Helene!

Nora. What are you doing?

Helmer (*searching among his papers*). Making a decision. (*The maid enters.*) Here. Take this letter. Go out with it right away. Find somebody to deliver it. But quick. The address is on the envelope. Wait. Here's money.

Maid. Very good, sir. (*She takes the letter and goes out.*)

Helmer (*collecting his papers*). There now, little Mrs. Obstinate!

Nora (*breathless*). Torvald—what was that letter?

Helmer. Krogstad's dismissal.

Nora. Call it back, Torvald! There's still time! Oh Torvald, please—call it back! For my sake, for your own sake, for the sake of the children! Listen to me, Torvald! Do it! You don't know what you're doing to all of us!

Helmer. Too late.

Nora. Yes. Too late.

Helmer. Dear Nora, I forgive you this fear you're in, although it really is an insult to me. Yes, it is! It's an insult to think that I am scared of a shabby scrivener's revenge. But I forgive you, for it's such a beautiful proof how much you love me. (*Takes her in his arms.*) And that's the way it should be, my sweet darling. Whatever happens, you'll see that when things get really rough I have both strength and courage. You'll find out that I am man enough to shoulder the whole burden.

Nora (*terrified*). What do you mean by that?

Helmer. All of it, I tell you—

Nora (*composed*). You'll never have to do that.

Helmer. Good. Then we'll share the burden, Nora—like husband and wife, the way it ought to be. (*Caresses her.*) Now are you satisfied? There, there, there. Not that look in your eyes—like a frightened dove. It's all your own foolish imagination.—Why don't you practice the tarantella—and your tambourine, too. I'll be in the inner office and close both doors, so I won't hear you. You can make as much noise as you like. (*Turning in the doorway.*) And when Rank comes, tell him where to find me. (*He nods to her, enters his study carrying his papers, and closes the door.*)

Nora (*transfixed by terror, whispers*). He would do it. He'll do it. He'll do it in spite of the whole world.—No, this mustn't happen. Anything rather than that! There must be a way—! (*The doorbell rings.*) Dr. Rank! Anything rather than that! Anything—anything at all!

She passes her hand over her face, pulls herself together, and opens the door to the hall. Dr. Rank is out there, hanging up his coat. Darkness begins to fall during the following scene.

Nora. Hello there, Dr. Rank. I recognized your ringing. Don't go in to Torvald yet. I think he's busy.

Rank. And you?

Nora (*as he enters and she closes the door behind him*). You know I always have time for you.

Rank. Thanks. I'll make use of that as long as I can.

Nora. What do you mean by that—As long as you can?

Rank. Does that frighten you?

Nora. Well, it's a funny expression. As if something was going to happen.

Rank. Something is going to happen that I've long been expecting. But I admit I hadn't thought it would come quite so soon.

Nora (*seizes his arm*). What is it you've found out? Dr. Rank—tell me!

Rank (*sits down by the stove*). I'm going downhill fast. There's nothing to do about that.

Nora (*with audible relief*). So it's you—

Rank. Who else? No point in lying to myself. I'm in worse shape than any of my other patients, Mrs. Helmer. These last few days I've been making up my inner status. Bankrupt. Chances are that within a month I'll be rotting up in the cemetery.

Nora. Shame on you! Talking that horrid way!

Rank. The thing itself is horrid—damn horrid. The worst of it, though, is all that other horror that comes first. There is only one more test I need to make. After that I'll have a pretty good idea when I'll start coming apart. There is something I want to say to you. Helmer's refined nature can't stand anything hideous. I don't want him in my sick room.

Nora. Oh, but Dr. Rank—

Rank. I don't want him there. Under no circumstance. I'll close my door to him. As soon as I have full certainty that the worst is about to begin I'll give you my card with a black cross on it. Then you'll know the last horror of destruction has started.

Nora. Today you're really quite impossible. And I had hoped you'd be in a particularly good mood.

Rank. With death on my hands? Paying for someone else's sins? Is there justice in that? And yet there isn't a single family that isn't ruled by that same law of ruthless retribution, in one way or another.

Nora (puts her hands over her ears). Poppycock! Be fun! Be fun!

Rank. Well, yes. You may just as well laugh at the whole thing. My poor, innocent spine is suffering for my father's frolics as a young lieutenant.

Nora (over by the table, left). Right. He was addicted to asparagus and goose liver paté, wasn't he?

Rank. And truffles.

Nora. Of course. Truffles. And oysters too, I think.

Rank. And oysters. Obviously.

Nora. And all the port and champagne that go with it. It's really too bad that goodies like that ruin your backbone.

Rank. Particularly an unfortunate backbone that never enjoyed any of it.

Nora. Ah yes, that's the saddest part of it all.

Rank (looks searchingly at her). Hm—

Nora (after a brief pause). Why did you smile just then?

Rank. No, it was you that laughed.

Nora. No, it was you that smiled, Dr. Rank!

Rank (gets up). You're more of a mischief-maker than I thought.

Nora. I feel in the mood for mischief today.

Rank. So it seems.

Nora (with both her hands on his shoulders). Dear, dear Dr. Rank, don't you go and die and leave Torvald and me.

Rank. Oh, you won't miss me for very long. Those who go away are soon forgotten.

Nora (with an anxious look). Do you believe that?

Rank. You'll make new friends, and then—

Nora. Who'll make new friends?

Rank. Both you and Helmer, once I'm gone. You yourself seem to have made a good start already. What was this Mrs. Linde doing here last night?

Nora. Aha—Don't tell me you're jealous of poor Kristine?

Rank. Yes, I am. She'll be my successor in this house. As soon as I have made my excuses, that woman is likely to—

Nora. Shh—not so loud. She's in there.

Rank. Today too? There you are!

Nora. She's mending my costume. My God, you really *are* unreasonable. (*Sits down on the couch.*) Now be nice, Dr. Rank. Tomorrow you'll see how beautifully I'll dance, and then you are to pretend I'm dancing just for you—and for Torvald too, of course. (*Takes several items out of the carton.*) Sit down, Dr. Rank; I want to show you something.

Rank (sitting down). What?

Nora. Look.

Rank. Silk stockings.

Nora. Flesh-colored. Aren't they lovely? Now it's getting dark in here, but tomorrow—No, no. You only get to see the foot. Oh well, you might as well see all of it.

Rank. Hmm.

Nora. Why do you look so critical? Don't you think they'll fit?

Rank. That's something I can't possibly have a reasoned opinion about.

Nora (looks at him for a moment). Shame on you. (*Slaps his ear lightly with the stocking.*) That's what you get. (*Puts the things back in the carton.*)

Rank. And what other treasures are you going to show me?

Nora. Nothing at all, because you're naughty. (*She hums a little and rummages in the carton.*)

Rank (after a brief silence). When I sit here like this, talking confidently with you, I can't imagine—I can't possibly imagine what would have become of me if I hadn't had you and Helmer.

Nora (smiles). Well, yes—I do believe you like being with us.

Rank (in a lower voice, lost in thought). And then to have to go away from it all—

Nora. Nonsense. You are not going anywhere.

Rank (as before). —and not to leave behind as much as a poor little token of gratitude, hardly a brief memory of someone missed, nothing but a vacant place that anyone can fill.

Nora. And what if I were to ask you—? No—

Rank. Ask me what?

Nora. For a great proof of your friendship—

Rank. Yes, yes—?

Nora. No, I mean—for an enormous favor—

Rank. Would you really for once make me as happy as all that?

Nora. But you don't even know what it is.

Rank. Well, then; tell me.

Nora. Oh, but I can't, Dr. Rank. It's altogether too much to ask—It's advice and help and a favor—

Rank. So much the better. I can't even begin to guess what it is you have in mind. So for heaven's sake tell me! Don't you trust me?

Nora. Yes, I trust you more than anyone else I know. You are my best and most faithful friend. I know that. So I will tell you. All right, Dr. Rank. There is something you can help me prevent. You know how much Torvald loves me—beyond all words. Never for a moment would he hesitate to give his life for me.

Rank (leaning over to her). Nora—do you really think he's the only one—?

Nora (with a slight start). Who—?

Rank. —would gladly give his life for you.

Nora (heavily). I see.

Rank. I have sworn an oath to myself to tell you before I go. I'll never find a better occasion.—All right, Nora; now you know. And now you also know that you can confide in me more than in anyone else.

Nora (gets up; in a calm, steady voice). Let me get by.

Rank (makes room for her but remains seated). Nora—

Nora (in the door to the front hall). Helene, bring the lamp in here, please. *(Walks over to the stove.)* Oh, dear Dr. Rank. That really wasn't very nice of you.

Rank (gets up). That I have loved you as much as anybody—was that not nice?

Nora. No, not that. But that you told me. There was no need for that.

Rank. What do you mean? Have you known—?

The maid enters with the lamp, puts it on the table, and goes out.

Rank. Nora—Mrs. Helmer—I'm asking you: did you know?

Nora. Oh, how can I tell what I knew and didn't know! I really can't say—But that you could be so awkward, Dr. Rank! Just when everything was so comfortable.

Rank. Well, anyway, now you know that I'm at your service with my life and soul. And now you must speak.

Nora (looks at him). After what just happened?

Rank. I beg of you—let me know what it is.

Nora. There is nothing I can tell you now.

Rank. Yes, yes. You mustn't punish me this way. Please let me do for you whatever anyone *can* do.

Nora. Now there is nothing you can do. Besides, I don't think I really need any help, anyway. It's probably just my imagination. Of course that's all it is. I'm sure of it! *(Sits down in the rocking chair, looks at him, smiles.)* Well, well, well, Dr. Rank! What a fine gentleman you turned out to be! Aren't you ashamed of yourself, now that we have light?

Rank. No, not really. But perhaps I ought to leave—and not come back?

Nora. Don't be silly; of course not! You'll come here exactly as you have been doing. You know perfectly well that Torvald can't do without you.

Rank. Yes, but what about you?

Nora. Oh, I always think it's perfectly delightful when you come.

Rank. That's the very thing that misled me. You are a riddle to me. It has often seemed to me that you'd just as soon be with me as with Helmer.

Nora. Well, you see, there are people you love, and then there are other people you'd almost rather be with.

Rank. Yes, there is something in that.

Nora. When I lived at home with Daddy, of course I loved him most. But I always thought it was so much fun to sneak off down to the maids' room, for they never gave me good advice and they always talked about such fun things.

Rank. Aha! So it's *their* place I have taken.

Nora (jumps up and goes over to him). Oh dear, kind Dr. Rank, you know very well I didn't mean it that way. Can't you see that with Torvald it is the way it used to be with Daddy?

The maid enters from the front hall.

Maid. Ma'am! *(Whispers to her and gives her a caller's card.)*

Nora (glances at the card). Ah! *(Puts it in her pocket.)*

Rank. Anything wrong?

Nora. No, no; not at all. It's nothing—just my new costume—

Rank. But your costume is lying right there!

Nora. Oh yes, that one. But this is another one. I ordered it. Torvald mustn't know—

Rank. Aha. So that's the great secret.

Nora. That's it. Why don't you go in to him, please. He's in the inner office. And keep him there for a while—

Rank. Don't worry. He won't get away. (*Enters Helmer's study.*)

Nora (to the maid). You say he's waiting in the kitchen?

Maid. Yes. He came up the back stairs.

Nora. But didn't you tell him there was somebody with me?

Maid. Yes, but he wouldn't listen.

Nora. He won't leave?

Maid. No, not till he's had a word with you, ma'am.

Nora. All right. But try not to make any noise. And, Helene—don't tell anyone he's here. It's supposed to be a surprise for my husband.

Maid. I understand, ma'am—(*She leaves.*)

Nora. The terrible is happening. It's happening, after all. No, no, no. It can't happen. It won't happen. (*She bolts the study door.*)

The maid opens the front hall door for Krogstad and closes the door behind him. He wears a fur coat for traveling, boots, and a fur hat.

Nora (toward him). Keep your voice down. My husband's home.

Krogstad. That's all right.

Nora. What do you want?

Krogstad. To find out something.

Nora. Be quick, then. What is it?

Krogstad. I expect you know I've been fired.

Nora. I couldn't prevent it, Mr. Krogstad. I fought for you as long and as hard as I could, but it didn't do any good.

Krogstad. Your husband doesn't love you any more than that? He knows what I can do to you, and yet he runs the risk—

Nora. Surely you didn't think I'd tell him?

Krogstad. No, I really didn't. It wouldn't be like Torvald Helmer to show that kind of guts—

Nora. Mr. Krogstad, I insist that you show respect for my husband.

Krogstad. By all means. All due respect. But since you're so anxious to keep this a secret, may I assume that you are a little better informed than yesterday about exactly what you have done?

Nora. Better than *you* could ever teach me.

Krogstad. Of course. Such a bad lawyer as I am—

Nora. What do you want of me?

Krogstad. I just wanted to find out how you are, Mrs. Helmer. I've been thinking about you all day. You see, even a bill collector, a pen pusher, a—anyway, someone like me—even he has a little of what they call a heart.

Nora. Then show it. Think of my little children.

Krogstad. Have you and your husband thought of mine? Never mind. All I want to tell you is that you don't need to take this business too seriously. I have no intention of bringing charges right away.

Nora. Oh no, you wouldn't; would you? I knew you wouldn't.

Krogstad. The whole thing can be settled quite amiably. Nobody else needs to know anything. It will be between the three of us.

Nora. My husband must never find out about this.

Krogstad. How are you going to prevent that? Maybe you can pay me the balance on the loan?

Nora. No, not right now.

Krogstad. Or do you have a way of raising the money one of these next few days?

Nora. None I intend to make use of.

Krogstad. It wouldn't do you any good, anyway. Even if you had the cash in your hand right this minute, I wouldn't give you your note back. It wouldn't make any difference *how* much money you offered me.

Nora. Then you'll have to tell me what you plan to use the note *for*.

Krogstad. Just keep it; that's all. Have it on hand, so to speak. I won't say a word to anybody else. So if you've been thinking about doing something desperate—

Nora. I have.

Krogstad. —like leaving house and home—

Nora. I have!

Krogstad. —or even something worse—

Nora. How did you know?

Krogstad. —then: don't.

Nora. How did you know I was thinking of *that*?

Krogstad. Most of us do, right at first. I did, too, but when it came down to it I didn't have the courage—

Nora (tonelessly). Nor do I.

Krogstad (relieved). See what I mean? I thought so. You don't either.

Nora. I don't. I don't.

Krogstad. Besides, it would be very silly of you. Once that first domestic blow-up is behind you—. Here in my pocket is a letter for your husband.

Nora. Telling him everything?

Krogstad. As delicately as possible.

Nora (quickly). He mustn't get that letter. Tear it up. I'll get you the money somehow.

Krogstad. Excuse me, Mrs. Helmer. I thought I just told you—

Nora. I'm not talking about the money I owe you. Just let me know how much money you want from my husband, and I'll get it for you.

Krogstad. I want no money from your husband.

Nora. Then, what *do* you want?

Krogstad. I'll tell you, Mrs. Helmer. I want to rehabilitate myself; I want to get up in the world; and your husband is going to help me. For a year and a half I haven't done anything disreputable. All that time I have been struggling with the most miserable circumstances. I was content to work my way up step by step. Now I've been kicked out, and I'm no longer satisfied just getting my old job back. I want more than that; I want to get to the top. I'm being quite serious. I want the bank to take me back but in a higher position. I want your husband to create a new job for me—

Nora. He'll never do that!

Krogstad. He will. I know him. He won't dare not to. And once I'm back inside and he and I are working together, you'll see! Within a year I'll be the manager's right hand. It will be Nils Krogstad and not Torvald Helmer who'll be running the Mutual Bank!

Nora. You'll never see that happen!

Krogstad. Are you thinking of—?

Nora. Now I *do* have the courage.

Krogstad. You can't scare me. A fine, spoiled lady like you—

Nora. You'll see, you'll see!

Krogstad. Under the ice, perhaps? Down into that cold, black water? Then spring comes, and you float up again—hideous, can't be identified, hair all gone—

Nora. You don't frighten me.

Krogstad. Nor you me. One doesn't do that sort of thing, Mrs. Helmer. Besides, what good would it do? He'd still be in my power.

Nora. Afterwards? When I'm no longer—?

Krogstad. Aren't you forgetting that your reputation would be in my hands?

Nora stares at him, speechless.

Krogstad. All right; now I've told you what to expect. So don't do anything foolish. When Helmer gets my letter I expect to hear from him. And don't you forget that it's your husband himself who forces me to use such means again. That I'll never forgive him. Goodbye, Mrs. Helmer. (*Goes out through the hall.*)

Nora (*at the door, opens it a little, listens*). He's going. And no letter. Of course not! That would be impossible! (*Opens the door more.*) What's he doing? He's still there. Doesn't go down. Having second thoughts—? Will he—?

The sound of a letter dropping into the mailbox. Then Krogstad's steps are heard going down the stairs, gradually dying away.

Nora (*with a muted cry runs forward to the table by the couch; brief pause*). In the mailbox. (*Tiptoes back to the door to the front hall.*) There it is. Torvald, Torvald—now we're lost!

Mrs. Linde (*enters from the left, carrying Nora's Capri costume*). There now. I think it's all fixed. Why don't we try it on you—

Nora (*in a low, hoarse voice*). Kristine, come here.

Mrs. Linde. What's wrong with you? You look quite beside yourself.

Nora. Come over here. Do you see that letter? There, look—through the glass in the mailbox.

Mrs. Linde. Yes, yes; I see it.

Nora. That letter is from Krogstad.

Mrs. Linde. Nora—it was Krogstad who lent you the money!

Nora. Yes, and now Torvald will find out about it.

Mrs. Linde. Oh believe me, Nora. That's the best thing for both of you.

Nora. There's more to it than you know. I forged a signature—

Mrs. Linde. Oh my God—!

Nora. I just want to tell you this, Kristine, that you must be my witness.

Mrs. Linde. Witness? How? Witness to what?

Nora. If I lose my mind—and that could very well happen—

Mrs. Linde. Nora!

Nora. —or if something were to happen to me—something that made it impossible for me to be here—

Mrs. Linde. Nora, Nora! You're not yourself!

Nora. —and if someone were to take all the blame, assume the whole responsibility—Do you understand—?

Mrs. Linde. Yes, yes; but how can you think—!

Nora. —then you are to witness that that's not so, Kristine. I am not beside myself. I am perfectly rational, and what I'm telling you is that nobody else has known about this. I've done it all by myself, the whole thing. Just remember that.

Mrs. Linde. I will. But I don't understand any of it.

Nora. Oh, how could you! For it's the wonderful that's about to happen.

Mrs. Linde. The wonderful?

Nora. Yes, the wonderful. But it's so terrible, Kristine. It mustn't happen for anything in the whole world!

Mrs. Linde. I'm going over to talk to Krogstad right now.

Nora. No, don't. Don't go to him. He'll do something bad to you.

Mrs. Linde. There was a time when he would have done anything for me.

Nora. He!

Mrs. Linde. Where does he live?

Nora. Oh, I don't know—Yes, wait a minute—*(Reaches into her pocket.)* here's his card.—But the letter, the letter—!

Helmer *(in his study, knocks on the door).* Nora!

Nora *(cries out in fear).* Oh, what is it? What do you want?

Helmer. That's all right. Nothing to be scared about. We're not coming in. For one thing, you've bolted the door, you know. Are you modeling your costume?

Nora. Yes, yes; I am. I'm going to be so pretty, Torvald.

Mrs. Linde *(having looked at the card).* He lives just around the corner.

Nora. Yes, but it's no use. Nothing can save us now. The letter is in the mailbox.

Mrs. Linde. And your husband has the key?

Nora. Yes. He always keeps it with him.

Mrs. Linde. Krogstad must ask for his letter back, unread. He's got to think up some pretext or other—

Nora. But this is just the time of day when Torvald—

Mrs. Linde. Delay him. Go in to him. I'll be back as soon as I can.

(*She hurries out through the hall door.*)

Nora *(walks over to Helmer's door, opens it, and peeks in).* Torvald!

Helmer *(still offstage).* Well, well! So now one's allowed in one's own living room again. Come on, Rank. Now we'll see—(*In the doorway.*) But what's this?

Nora. What, Torvald dear?

Helmer. Rank prepared me for a splendid metamorphosis.

Rank *(in the doorway).* That's how I understood it. Evidently I was mistaken.

Nora. Nobody gets to admire me in my costume before tomorrow.

Helmer. But, dearest Nora—you look all done in. Have you been practicing too hard?

Nora. No, I haven't practiced at all.

Helmer. But you'll have to, you know.

Nora. I know it, Torvald. I simply must. But I can't do a thing unless you help me. I have forgotten everything.

Helmer. Oh it will all come back. We'll work on it.

Nora. Oh yes, please, Torvald. You just have to help me. Promise? I am so nervous. That big party—. You mustn't do anything else tonight. Not a bit of business. Don't even touch a pen. Will you promise, Torvald?

Helmer. I promise. Tonight I'll be entirely at your service—you helpless little thing.—Just a moment, though. First I want to—(*Goes to the door to the front hall.*)

Nora. What are you doing out there?

Helmer. Just looking to see if there's any mail.

Nora. No, no! Don't, Torvald!

Helmer. Why not?

Nora. Torvald, I beg you. There is no mail.

Helmer. Let me just look, anyway. (*Is about to go out.*)

> *Nora by the piano, plays the first bars of the tarantella dance.*

Helmer (*halts at the door*). Aha!

Nora. I won't be able to dance tomorrow if I don't get to practice with you.

Helmer (*goes to her*). Are you really all that scared, Nora dear?

Nora. Yes, so terribly scared. Let's try it right now. There's still time before we eat. Oh please, sit down and play for me, Torvald. Teach me, coach me, the way you always do.

Helmer. Of course I will, my darling, if that's what you want. (*Sits down at the piano.*)

> *Nora takes the tambourine out of the carton, as well as a long, many-colored shawl. She quickly drapes the shawl around herself, then leaps into the middle of the floor.*

Nora. Play for me! I want to dance!

> *Helmer plays and Nora dances. Dr. Rank stands by the piano behind Helmer and watches.*

Helmer (*playing*). Slow down, slow down!

Nora. Can't!

Helmer. Not so violent, Nora!

Nora. It has to be this way.

Helmer (*stops playing*). No, no. This won't do at all.

Nora (*laughing, swinging her tambourine*). What did I tell you?

Rank. Why don't you let me play?

Helmer (*getting up*). Good idea. Then I can direct her better.

> *Rank sits down at the piano and starts playing. Nora dances more and more wildly. Helmer stands over by the stove, repeatedly correcting her. She doesn't seem to hear. Her hair comes loose and falls down over her shoulders. She doesn't notice but keeps on dancing. Mrs. Linde enters.*

Mrs. Linde (*stops by the door, dumbfounded*). Ah—!

Nora (*dancing*). We're having such fun, Kristine!

Helmer. My dearest Nora, you're dancing as if it were a matter of life and death!

Nora. It is! It is!

Helmer. Rank, stop. This is sheer madness. Stop, I say!

A Doll's House

    Rank stops playing; Nora suddenly stops dancing.

Helmer *(goes over to her).* If I hadn't seen it I wouldn't have believed it. You've forgotten every single thing I ever taught you.

Nora *(tosses away the tambourine).* See? I told you.

Helmer. Well! You certainly need coaching.

Nora. Didn't I tell you I did? Now you've seen for yourself. I'll need your help till the very minute we're leaving for the party. Will you promise, Torvald?

Helmer. You can count on it.

Nora. You're not to think of anything except me—not tonight and not tomorrow. You're not to read any letters—not to look in the mailbox—

Helmer. Ah, I see. You're still afraid of that man.

Nora. Yes—yes, that too.

Helmer. Nora, I can tell from looking at you. There's a letter from him out there.

Nora. I don't know. I think so. But you're not to read it now. I don't want anything ugly to come between us before it's all over.

Rank *(to Helmer in a low voice).* Better not argue with her.

Helmer *(throws his arm around her).* The child shall have her way. But tomorrow night, when you've done your dance—

Nora. Then you'll be free.

Maid *(in the door, right).* Dinner can be served any time, ma'am.

Nora. We want champagne, Helene.

Maid. Very good, ma'am. *(Goes out.)*

Helmer. Aha! Having a party, eh?

Nora. Champagne from now till sunrise! *(Calls out.)* And some macaroons, Helene. Lots!—just this once.

Helmer *(taking her hands).* There, there—I don't like this wild—frenzy—Be my own sweet little lark again, the way you always are.

Nora. Oh, I will. But you go on in. You too, Dr. Rank. Kristine, please help me put up my hair.

Rank *(in a low voice to Helmer as they go out).* You don't think she is—you know—expecting—?

Helmer. Oh no. Nothing like that. It's just this childish fear I was telling you about. *(They go out, right.)*

Nora. Well?

Mrs. Linde. Left town.

Nora. I saw it in your face.

Mrs. Linde. He'll be back tomorrow night. I left him a note.

Nora. You shouldn't have. I don't want you to try to stop anything. You see, it's a kind of ecstasy, too, this waiting for the wonderful.

Mrs. Linde. But what is it you're waiting *for*?

Nora. You wouldn't understand. Why don't you go in to the others. I'll be there in a minute.

    Mrs. Linde enters the dining room, right.

Nora *(stands still for a little while, as if collecting herself; she looks at her watch).* Five o'clock. Seven hours till midnight. Twenty-four more hours till next midnight. Then the tarantella is over. Twenty-four plus seven—thirty-one more hours to live.

Helmer *(in the door, right).* What's happening to my little lark?
Nora *(to him, with open arms).* Here's your lark!

ACT III

The same room. The table by the couch and the chairs around it have been moved to the middle of the floor. A lighted lamp is on the table. The door to the front hall is open. Dance music is heard from upstairs.

 Mrs. Linde is seated by the table, idly leafing through the pages of a book. She tries to read but seems unable to concentrate. Once or twice she turns her head in the direction of the door, anxiously listening.

Mrs. Linde *(looks at her watch).* Not yet. It's almost too late. If only he hasn't—(*Listens again.*) Ah! There he is. (*She goes to the hall and opens the front door carefully. Quiet footsteps on the stairs. She whispers.*) Come in. There's nobody here.

Krogstad *(in the door).* I found your note when I got home. What's this all about?

Mrs. Linde. I've got to talk to you.

Krogstad. Oh? And it has to be here?

Mrs. Linde. It couldn't be at my place. My room doesn't have a separate entrance.

 Come in. We're quite alone. The maid is asleep and the Helmers are at a party upstairs.

Krogstad *(entering).* Really? The Helmers are dancing tonight, are they?

Mrs. Linde. And why not?

Krogstad. You're right. Why not, indeed.

Mrs. Linde. All right, Krogstad. Let's talk, you and I.

Krogstad. I didn't know we had anything to talk about.

Mrs. Linde. We have much to talk about.

Krogstad. I didn't think so.

Mrs. Linde. No, because you've never really understood me.

Krogstad. What was there to understand? What happened was perfectly commonplace. A heartless woman jilts a man when she gets a more attractive offer.

Mrs. Linde. Do you think I'm all that heartless? And do you think it was easy for me to break with you?

Krogstad. No?

Mrs. Linde. You really thought it was?

Krogstad. If it wasn't, why did you write the way you did that time?

Mrs. Linde. What else could I do? If I had to make a break, I also had the duty to destroy whatever feelings you had for me.

Krogstad *(clenching his hands).* So that's the way it was. And you did—that—just for money!

Mrs. Linde. Don't forget I had a helpless mother and two small brothers. We couldn't wait for you, Krogstad. You know yourself how uncertain your prospects were then.

Krogstad. All right. But you still didn't have the right to throw me over for somebody else.

Mrs. Linde. I don't know. I have asked myself that question many times. Did I have that right?

Krogstad *(in a lower voice).* When I lost you I lost my footing. Look at me now. A shipwrecked man on a raft.

Mrs. Linde. Rescue may be near.

Krogstad. It *was* near. Then you came between.

Mrs. Linde. I didn't know that, Krogstad. Only today did I find out it's your job I'm taking over in the bank.

Krogstad. I believe you when you say so. But now that you *do* know, aren't you going to step aside?

Mrs. Linde. No, for it wouldn't do you any good.

Krogstad. Whether it would or not—*I* would do it.

Mrs. Linde. I have learned common sense. Life and hard necessity have taught me that.

Krogstad. And life has taught me not to believe in pretty speeches.

Mrs. Linde. Then life has taught you a very sensible thing. But you do believe in actions, don't you?

Krogstad. How do you mean?

Mrs. Linde. You referred to yourself just now as a shipwrecked man.

Krogstad. It seems to me I had every reason to do so.

Mrs. Linde. And I am a shipwrecked woman. No one to grieve for, no one to care for.

Krogstad. You made your choice.

Mrs. Linde. I had no other choice that time.

Krogstad. Let's say you didn't. What then?

Mrs. Linde. Krogstad, how would it be if we two shipwrecked people got together?

Krogstad. What's this!

Mrs. Linde. Two on one wreck are better off than each on his own.

Krogstad. Kristine!

Mrs. Linde. Why do you think I came to town?

Krogstad. Surely not because of me?

Mrs. Linde. If I'm going to live at all I must work. All my life, for as long as I can remember, I have worked. That's been my one and only pleasure. But now that I'm all alone in the world I feel nothing but this terrible emptiness and desolation. There is no joy in working just for yourself. Krogstad—give me someone and something to work for.

Krogstad. I don't believe this. Only hysterical females go in for that kind of high-minded self-sacrifice.

Mrs. Linde. Did you ever know me to be hysterical?

Krogstad. You really could do this? Listen—do you know about my past? All of it?

Mrs. Linde. Yes, I do.

Krogstad. Do you also know what people think of me around here?

Mrs. Linde. A little while ago you sounded as if you thought that together with me you might have become a different person.

Krogstad. I'm sure of it.

Mrs. Linde. Couldn't that still be?

Krogstad. Kristine—do you know what you are doing? Yes, I see you do. And you think you have the courage—?

Mrs. Linde. I need someone to be a mother to, and your children need a mother. You and I need one another. Nils, I believe in you—in the real you. Together with you I dare to do anything.

Krogstad (*seizes her hands*). Thanks, thanks, Kristine—now I know I'll raise myself in the eyes of others.—Ah, but I forget—!

Mrs. Linde (*listening*). Shh!—There's the tarantella. You must go; hurry!

Krogstad. Why? What is it?

Mrs. Linde. Do you hear what they're playing up there? When that dance is over they'll be down.

Krogstad. All right. I'm leaving. The whole thing is pointless, anyway. Of course you don't know what I'm doing to the Helmers.

Mrs. Linde. Yes, Krogstad; I do know.

Krogstad. Still, you're brave enough—?

Mrs. Linde. I very well understand to what extremes despair can drive a man like you.

Krogstad. If only it could be undone!

Mrs. Linde. It could, for your letter is still out there in the mailbox.

Krogstad. Are you sure?

Mrs. Linde. Quite sure. But—

Krogstad (*looks searchingly at her*). Maybe I'm beginning to understand. You want to save your friend at any cost. Be honest with me. That's it, isn't it?

Mrs. Linde. Krogstad, you may sell yourself once for somebody else's sake, but you don't do it twice.

Krogstad. I'll demand my letter back.

Mrs. Linde. No, no.

Krogstad. Yes, of course. I'll wait here till Helmer comes down. Then I'll ask him for my letter. I'll tell him it's just about my dismissal—that he shouldn't read it.

Mrs. Linde. No, Krogstad. You are not to ask for that letter back.

Krogstad. But tell me—wasn't that the real reason you wanted to meet me here?

Mrs. Linde. At first it was, because I was so frightened. But that was yesterday. Since then I have seen the most incredible things going on in this house. Helmer must learn the whole truth. This miserable secret must come out in the open; those two must come to a full understanding. They simply can't continue with all this concealment and evasion.

Krogstad. All right; if you want to take that chance. But there is one thing I *can* do, and I'll do that right now.

Mrs. Linde (*listening*). But hurry! Go! The dance is over. We aren't safe another minute.

Krogstad. I'll be waiting for you downstairs.

Mrs. Linde. Yes, do. You must see me home.

Krogstad. I've never been so happy in my whole life. (*He leaves through the front door. The door between the living room and the front hall remains open.*)

Mrs. Linde (*straightens up the room a little and gets her things ready*). What a change! Oh yes!—what a change! People to work for—to live for—a home to bring happiness to. I can't wait to get to work—! If only they'd come soon—(*Listens.*) Ah, there they are. Get my coat on—(*Puts on her coat and hat.*)

Helmer's and Nora's voices are heard outside. A key is turned in the lock, and Helmer almost forces Nora into the hall. She is dressed in her Italian costume, with a big black shawl over her shoulders. He is in evening dress under an open black cloak.

Nora (*in the door, still resisting*). No, no, no! I don't want to! I want to go back upstairs. I don't want to leave so early.

Helmer. But dearest Nora—

Nora. Oh please, Torvald—please! I'm asking you as nicely as I can—just another hour!

Helmer. Not another minute, sweet. You know we agreed. There now. Get inside. You'll catch a cold out here. (*She still resists, but he guides her gently into the room.*)

Mrs. Linde. Good evening.

Nora. Kristine!

Helmer. Ah, Mrs. Linde. Still here?

Mrs. Linde. I know. I really should apologize, but I so much wanted to see Nora in her costume.

Nora. You've been waiting up for me?

Mrs. Linde. Yes, unfortunately I didn't get here in time. You were already upstairs, but I just didn't feel like leaving till I had seen you.

Helmer (*removing Nora's shawl*). Yes, do take a good look at her, Mrs. Linde. I think I may say she's worth looking at. Isn't she lovely?

Mrs. Linde. She certainly is—

Helmer. Isn't she a miracle of loveliness, though? That was the general opinion at the party, too. But dreadfully obstinate—that she is, the sweet little thing. What can we do about that? Will you believe it—I practically had to use force to get her away.

Nora. Oh Torvald, you're going to be sorry you didn't give me even half an hour more.

Helmer. See what I mean, Mrs. Linde? She dances the tarantella—she is a tremendous success—quite deservedly so, though perhaps her performance was a little too natural—I mean, more than could be reconciled with the rules of art. But all right! The point is: she's a success, a tremendous success. So should I let her stay after that? Weaken the effect? Of course not. So I take my lovely little Capri girl—I might say, my capricious little Capri girl—under my arm—a quick turn around the room—a graceful bow in all directions, and—as they say in the novels—the beautiful apparition is gone. A finale should always be done for effect, Mrs. Linde, but there doesn't seem to be any way of getting that into Nora's head. Poooh—! It's hot in here. (*Throws his cloak down on a chair and opens the door to his room.*) Why, it's dark in here! Of course. Excuse me—(*Goes inside and lights a couple of candles.*)

Nora (*in a hurried, breathless whisper*). Well?

Mrs. Linde (*in a low voice*). I have talked to him.

Nora. And—?

Mrs. Linde. Nora—you've got to tell your husband everything.

Nora (no expression in her voice). I knew it.

Mrs. Linde. You have nothing to fear from Krogstad. But you must speak.

Nora. I'll say nothing.

Mrs. Linde. Then the letter will.

Nora. Thank you, Kristine. Now I know what I have to do. Shh!

Helmer (returning). Well, Mrs. Linde, have you looked your fill?

Mrs. Linde. Yes. And now I'll say goodnight.

Helmer. So soon? Is that your knitting?

Mrs. Linde (takes it). Yes, thank you. I almost forgot.

Helmer. So you knit, do you?

Mrs. Linde. Oh yes.

Helmer. You know—you ought to take up embroidery instead.

Mrs. Linde. Oh? Why?

Helmer. Because it's so much more beautiful. Look. You hold the embroidery
so—in your left hand. Then with your right you move the needle—like
this—in an easy, elongated arc—you see?

Mrs. Linde. Maybe you're right—

Helmer. Knitting, on the other hand, can never be anything but ugly. Look here:
arms pressed close to the sides—the needles going up and down—there's
something Chinese about it somehow—. That really was an excellent champagne they served us tonight.

Mrs. Linde. Well, goodnight, Nora. And don't be obstinate any more.

Helmer. Well said, Mrs. Linde!

Mrs. Linde. Goodnight, sir.

Helmer (sees her to the front door). Goodnight, goodnight. I hope you'll get home
all right? I'd be very glad to—but of course you don't have far to walk, do you?
Goodnight, goodnight. *(She leaves. He closes the door behind her and
returns to the living room.)* There! At last we got rid of her. She really is an
incredible bore, that woman.

Nora. Aren't you very tired, Torvald?

Helmer. No, not in the least.

Nora. Not sleepy either?

Helmer. Not at all. Quite the opposite. I feel enormously—animated. How about
you? Yes, you do look tired and sleepy.

Nora. Yes, I am very tired. Soon I'll be asleep.

Helmer. What did I tell you? I was right, wasn't I? Good thing I didn't let you stay
any longer.

Nora. Everything you do is right.

Helmer (kissing her forehead). Now my little lark is talking like a human being.
But did you notice what splendid spirits Rank was in tonight?

Nora. Was he? I didn't notice. I didn't get to talk with him.

Helmer. Nor did I—hardly. But I haven't seen him in such a good mood for a long
time. *(Looks at her, comes closer to her.)* Ah! It does feel good to be back in
our own home again, to be quite alone with you—my young, lovely, ravishing
woman!

Nora. Don't look at me like that, Torvald!

Helmer. Am I not to look at my most precious possession? All that loveliness that
is mine, nobody's but mine, all of it mine.

Nora *(walks to the other side of the table).* I won't have you talk to me like that tonight.

Helmer *(follows her).* The tarantella is still in your blood. I can tell. That only makes you all the more alluring. Listen! The guests are beginning to leave. *(Softly.)* Nora—soon the whole house will be quiet.

Nora. Yes, I hope so.

Helmer. Yes, don't you, my darling? Do you know—when I'm at a party with you, like tonight—do you know why I hardly ever talk to you, why I keep away from you, only look at you once in a while—a few stolen glances—do you know why I do that? It's because I pretend that you are my secret love, my young, secret bride-to-be, and nobody has the slightest suspicion that there is anything between us.

Nora. Yes, I know. All your thoughts are with me.

Helmer. Then when we're leaving and I lay your shawl around your delicate young shoulders—around that wonderful curve of your neck—then I imagine you're my young bride, that we're coming away from the wedding, that I am taking you to my home for the first time—that I am alone with you for the first time—quite alone with you, you young, trembling beauty! I have desired you all evening—there hasn't been a longing in me that hasn't been for you. When you were dancing the tarantella, chasing, inviting—my blood was on fire; I couldn't stand it any longer—that's why I brought you down so early—

Nora. Leave me now, Torvald. Please! I don't want all this.

Helmer. What do you mean? You're only playing your little teasing bird game with me; aren't you, Nora? Don't want to? I'm your husband, aren't I?

There is a knock on the front door.

Nora *(with a start).* Did you hear that—?

Helmer *(on his way to the hall).* Who is it?

Rank *(outside).* It's me. May I come in for a moment?

Helmer *(in a low voice, annoyed).* Oh, what does he want now? *(Aloud.)* Just a minute. *(Opens the door.)* Well! How good of you not to pass by our door.

Rank. I thought I heard your voice, so I felt like saying hello. *(Looks around.)* Ah yes—this dear, familiar room. What a cozy, comfortable place you have here, you two.

Helmer. Looked to me as if you were quite comfortable upstairs too.

Rank. I certainly was. Why not? Why not enjoy all you can in this world? As much as you can for as long as you can, anyway. Excellent wine.

Helmer. The champagne, particularly.

Rank. You noticed that too? Incredible how much I managed to put away.

Nora. Torvald drank a lot of champagne tonight, too.

Rank. Did he?

Nora. Yes, he did, and then he's always so much fun afterwards.

Rank. Well, why not have some fun in the evening after a well spent day?

Helmer. Well spent? I'm afraid I can't claim that.

Rank *(slapping him lightly on the shoulder).* But you see, I can!

Nora. Dr. Rank, I believe you must have been conducting a scientific test today.

Rank. Exactly.

Helmer. What do you know—little Nora talking about scientific tests!

Nora. May I congratulate you on the result?

Rank. You may indeed.

Nora. It was a good one?

Rank. The best possible for both doctor and patient—certainty.

Nora (a quick query). Certainty?

Rank. Absolute certainty. So why shouldn't I have myself an enjoyable evening afterwards?

Nora. I quite agree with you, Dr. Rank. You should.

Helmer. And so do I. If only you don't pay for it tomorrow.

Rank. Oh well—you get nothing for nothing in this world.

Nora. Dr. Rank—you are fond of costume parties, aren't you?

Rank. Yes, particularly when there is a reasonable number of amusing disguises.

Nora. Listen—what are the two of us going to be the next time?

Helmer. You frivolous little thing! Already thinking about the next party!

Rank. You and I? That's easy. You'll be Fortune's Child.

Helmer. Yes, but what is a fitting costume for that?

Rank. Let your wife appear just the way she always is.

Helmer. Beautiful. Very good indeed. But how about yourself? Don't you know what you'll go as?

Rank. Yes, my friend. I know precisely what I'll be.

Helmer. Yes?

Rank. At the next masquerade I'll be invisible.

Helmer. That's a funny idea.

Rank. There's a certain black hat—you've heard about the hat that makes you invisible, haven't you? You put that on, and nobody can see you.

Helmer (suppressing a smile). I guess that's right.

Rank. But I'm forgetting what I came for. Helmer, give me a cigar—one of your dark Havanas.

Helmer. With the greatest pleasure. *(Offers him his case.)*

Rank (takes one and cuts off the tip). Thanks.

Nora (striking a match). Let me give you a light.

Rank. Thanks. *(She holds the match; he lights his cigar.)* And now goodbye!

Helmer. Goodbye, goodbye, my friend.

Nora. Sleep well, Dr. Rank.

Rank. I thank you.

Nora. Wish me the same.

Rank. You? Well, if you really want me to——. Sleep well. And thanks for the light. *(He nods to both of them and goes out.)*

Helmer (in a low voice). He had had quite a bit to drink.

Nora (absently). Maybe so.

Helmer takes out his keys and goes out into the hall.

Nora. Torvald—what are you doing out there?

Helmer. Emptying the mailbox. It is quite full. There wouldn't be room for the newspapers in the morning—

Nora. Are you going to work tonight?

Helmer. You know very well I won't.—Say! What's this? Somebody's been at the lock.

Nora. The lock—?

Helmer. Yes. Why, I wonder. I hate to think that any of the maids—. Here's a broken hairpin. It's one of yours. Nora.

Nora (*quickly*). Then it must be one of the children.

Helmer. You better make damn sure they stop that. Hm, hm.—There! I got it open, finally. (*Gathers up the mail, calls out to the kitchen.*) Helene?—Oh Helene—turn out the light here in the hall, will you? (*He comes back into the living room and closes the door.*) Look how it's been piling up. (*Shows her the bundle of letters. Starts leafing through it.*) What's this?

Nora (*by the window*). The letter! Oh no, no, Torvald!

Helmer. Two calling cards—from Rank.

Nora. From Dr. Rank?

Helmer (*looking at them*). "Doctor medicinae Rank." They were on top. He must have put them there when he left just now.

Nora. Anything written on them?

Helmer. A black cross above the name. What a macabre idea. Like announcing his own death.

Nora. That's what it is.

Helmer. Hm? You know about this? Has he said anything to you?

Nora. That card means he has said goodbye to us. He'll lock himself up to die.

Helmer. My poor friend. I knew of course he wouldn't be with me very long. But so soon—. And hiding himself away like a wounded animal—

Nora. When it has to be, it's better it happens without words. Don't you think so, Torvald?

Helmer (*walking up and down*). He'd grown so close to us. I find it hard to think of him as gone. With his suffering and loneliness he was like a clouded background for our happy sunshine. Well, it may be better this way. For him, at any rate. (*Stops.*) And perhaps for us, too, Nora. For now we have nobody but each other. (*Embraces her.*) Oh you—my beloved wife! I feel I just can't hold you close enough. Do you know, Nora—many times I have wished some great danger threatened you, so I could risk my life and blood and everything —everything, for your sake.

Nora (*frees herself and says in a strong and firm voice*). I think you should go and read your letters now, Torvald.

Helmer. No, no—not tonight. I want to be with you, my darling.

Nora. With the thought of your dying friend—?

Helmer. You are right. This has shaken both of us. Something not beautiful has come between us. Thoughts of death and dissolution. We must try to get over it—out of it. Till then—we'll each go to our own room.

Nora (*her arms around his neck*). Torvald—goodnight! Goodnight!

Helmer (*kisses her forehead*). Goodnight, my little songbird. Sleep well, Nora. Now I'll read my letters. (*He goes into his room, carrying the mail. Closes the door.*)

Nora (*her eyes desperate, her hands groping, finds Helmer's black cloak and throws it around her; she whispers, quickly, brokenly, hoarsely*). Never see him again. Never. Never. Never. (*Puts her shawl over her head.*) And never see the children again, either. Never; never.—The black, icy water— fathomless—this—! If only it was all over.—Now he has it. Now he's reading it. No, no; not yet. Torvald—goodbye—you—the children—

Henrik Ibsen

She is about to hurry through the hall, when Helmer flings open the door to his room and stands there with an open letter in his hand.

Helmer. Nora!

Nora (cries out). Ah—!

Helmer. What is it? You know what's in this letter?

Nora. Yes, I do! Let me go! Let me out!

Helmer *(holds her back).* Where do you think you're going?

Nora (trying to tear herself loose from him). I won't let you save me, Torvald!

Helmer *(tumbles back).* True! Is it true what he writes? Oh my God! No, no—this can't possibly be true.

Nora. It is true. I have loved you more than anything else in the whole world.

Helmer. Oh, don't give me any silly excuses.

Nora (taking a step towards him). Torvald—!

Helmer. You wretch! What have you done!

Nora. Let me go. You are not to sacrifice yourself for me. You are not to take the blame.

Helmer. No more playacting. (*Locks the door to the front hall.*) You'll stay here and answer me. Do you understand what you have done? Answer me! Do you understand?

Nora (gazes steadily at him with an increasingly frozen expression). Yes. Now I'm beginning to understand.

Helmer *(walking up and down).* What a dreadful awakening. All these years—all these eight years—she, my pride and my joy—a hypocrite, a liar—oh worse! worse!—a criminal! Oh, the bottomless ugliness in all this! Damn! Damn! Damn!

Nora, silent, keeps gazing at him.

Helmer *(stops in front of her).* I ought to have guessed that something like this would happen. I should have expected it. All your father's loose principles— Silence! You have inherited every one of your father's loose principles. No religion, no morals, no sense of duty—. Now I am being punished for my leniency with him. I did it for your sake, and this is how you pay me back.

Nora. Yes. This is how.

Helmer. You have ruined all my happiness. My whole future—that's what you have destroyed. Oh, it's terrible to think about. I am at the mercy of an unscrupulous man. He can do with me whatever he likes, demand anything of me, command me and dispose of me just as he pleases—I dare not say a word! To go down so miserably, to be destroyed—all because of an irresponsible woman!

Nora. When I am gone from the world, you'll be free.

Helmer. No noble gestures, please. Your father was always full of such phrases too. What good would it do me if you were gone from the world, as you put it? Not the slightest good at all. He could still make the whole thing public, and if he did, people would be likely to think I had been your accomplice. They might even think it was my idea—that it was I who urged you to do it! And for all this I have you to thank—you, whom I've borne on my hands through all the years of our marriage. *Now* do you understand what you've done to me?

Nora (with cold calm). Yes.

Helmer. I just can't get it into my head that this is happening; it's all so incredible. But we have to come to terms with it somehow. Take your shawl off. Take it off, I say! I have to satisfy him one way or another. The whole affair must be kept quiet at whatever cost.—And as far as you and I are concerned, nothing must seem to have changed. I'm talking about appearances, of course. You'll go on living here; that goes without saying. But I won't let you bring up the children; I dare not trust you with them.—Oh! Having to say this to one I have loved so much, and whom I still—! But all that is past. It's not a question of happiness any more but of hanging on to what can be salvaged— pieces, appearances—*(The doorbell rings.)*

Helmer *(jumps.)* What's that? So late. Is the worst—? Has he—! Hide, Nora! Say you're sick.

Nora doesn't move. Helmer opens the door to the hall.

Maid *(half dressed, out in the hall).* A letter for your wife, sir.

Helmer. Give it to me. *(Takes the letter and closes the door.)* Yes, it's from him. But I won't let you have it. I'll read it myself.

Nora. Yes—you read it.

Helmer *(by the lamp).* I hardly dare. Perhaps we're lost, both you and I. No; I've got to know. *(Tears the letter open, glances through it, looks at an enclosure; a cry of joy.)* Nora!

Nora looks at him with a question in her eyes.

Helmer. Nora!—No, I must read it again.—Yes, yes; it is so! I'm saved! Nora, I'm saved!

Nora. And I?

Helmer. You too, of course; we're both saved, both you and I. Look! He's returning your note. He writes that he's sorry, he regrets, a happy turn in his life—oh, it doesn't matter what he writes. We're saved, Nora! Nobody can do anything to you now. Oh Nora, Nora—. No, I want to get rid of this disgusting thing first. Let me see—*(Looks at the signature.)* No, I don't want to see it. I don't want it to be more than a bad dream, the whole thing. *(Tears up the note and both letters, throws the pieces in the stove, and watches them burn.)* There! Now it's gone.—He wrote that ever since Christmas Eve—. Good God, Nora, these must have been three terrible days for you.

Nora. I have fought a hard fight these last three days.

Helmer. And been in agony and seen no other way out than—. No, we won't think of all that ugliness. We'll just rejoice and tell ourselves it's over, it's all over! Oh, listen to me, Nora. You don't seem to understand. It's over. What *is* it? Why do you look like that—that frozen expression on your face? Oh my poor little Nora, don't you think I know what it is? You can't make yourself believe that I have forgiven you. But I have, Nora; I swear to you, I have forgiven you for everything. Of course I know that what you did was for love of me.

Nora. That is true.

Helmer. You have loved me the way a wife ought to love her husband. You just didn't have the wisdom to judge the means. But do you think I love you any less because you don't know how to act on your own? Of course not. Just lean on me. I'll advise you; I'll guide you. I wouldn't be a man if I didn't find you twice as attractive because of your womanly helplessness. You mustn't pay any attention to the hard words I said to you right at first. It was just that first shock when I thought everything was collapsing all around me. I have forgiven you, Nora. I swear to you—I really have forgiven you.

Nora. I thank you for your forgiveness. (*She goes out through the door, right.*)

Helmer. No, stay—(*Looks into the room she entered.*) What are you doing in there?

Nora (within). Getting out of my costume.

Helmer (by the open door). Good, good. Try to calm down and compose yourself, my poor little frightened songbird. Rest safely; I have broad wings to cover you with. (*Walks around near the door.*) What a nice and cozy home we have, Nora. Here's shelter for you. Here I'll keep you safe like a hunted dove I have rescued from the hawk's talons. Believe me: I'll know how to quiet your beating heart. It will happen by and by, Nora; you'll see. Why, tomorrow you'll look at all this in quite a different light. And soon everything will be just the way it was before. I won't need to keep reassuring you that I have forgiven you; you'll feel it yourself. Did you really think I could have abandoned you, or even reproached you? Oh, you don't know a real man's heart, Nora. There is something unspeakably sweet and satisfactory for a man to know deep in himself that he has forgiven his wife—forgiven her in all the fullness of his honest heart. You see, that way she becomes his very own all over again—in a double sense, you might say. He has, so to speak, given her a second birth; it is as if she had become his wife and his child, both. From now on that's what you'll be to me, you lost and helpless creature. Don't worry about a thing, Nora. Only be frank with me, and I'll be your will and your conscience.— What's this? You're not in bed? You've changed your dress—!

Nora (in an everyday dress). Yes, Torvald. I have changed my dress.

Helmer. But why—now—this late—?

Nora. I'm not going to sleep tonight.

Helmer. But my dear Nora—

Nora (looks at her watch). It isn't all that late. Sit down here with me, Torvald. You and I have much to talk about. (*Sits down at the table.*)

Helmer. Nora—what is this all about? That rigid face—

Nora. Sit down. This will take a while. I have much to say to you.

Helmer (sits down, facing her across the table). You worry me, Nora. I don't understand you.

Nora. No, that's just it. You don't understand me. And I have never understood you—not till tonight. No, don't interrupt me. Just listen to what I have to say.—This is a settling of accounts, Torvald.

Helmer. What do you mean by that?

Nora (after a brief silence). Doesn't one thing strike you, now that we are sitting together like this?

Helmer. What would that be?

Nora. We have been married for eight years. Doesn't it occur to you that this is the first time that you and I, husband and wife, are having a serious talk?

Helmer. Well—serious—. What do you mean by that?

Nora. For eight whole years—longer, in fact—ever since we first met, we have never talked seriously to each other about a single serious thing.

Helmer. You mean I should forever have been telling you about worries you couldn't have helped me with anyway?

Nora. I am not talking about worries. I'm saying we have never tried seriously to get to the bottom of anything together.

Helmer. But dearest Nora, I hardly think that would have been something *you*—

Nora. That's the whole point. You have never understood me. Great wrong has been done to me, Torvald. First by Daddy and then by you.

Helmer. What! By us two? We who have loved you more deeply than anyone else?

Nora *(shakes her head)*. You never loved me—neither Daddy nor you. You only thought it was fun to be in love with me.

Helmer. But, Nora—what an expression to use!

Nora. That's the way it has been, Torvald. When I was home with Daddy, he told me all his opinions, and so they became my opinions too. If I disagreed with him I kept it to myself, for he wouldn't have liked that. He called me his little doll baby, and he played with me the way I played with my dolls. Then I came to your house—

Helmer. What a way to talk about our marriage!

Nora *(imperturbably)*. I mean that I passed from Daddy's hands into yours. You arranged everything according to your taste, and so I came to share it—or I pretended to; I'm not sure which. I think it was a little of both, now one and now the other. When I look back on it now, it seems to me I've been living here like a pauper—had a hand-to-mouth kind of existence. I have earned my keep by doing tricks for you, Torvald. But that's the way you wanted it. You have great sins against me to answer for, Daddy and you. It's your fault that nothing has become of me.

Helmer. Nora, you're being both unreasonable and ungrateful. Haven't you been happy here?

Nora. No, never. I thought I was, but I wasn't.

Helmer. Not—not happy!

Nora. No; just having fun. And you have always been very good to me. But our home has never been more than a playroom. I have been your doll wife here, just the way I used to be Daddy's doll child. And the children have been my dolls. I thought it was fun when you played with me, just as they thought it was fun when I played with them. That's been our marriage, Torvald.

Helmer. There is something in what you are saying—exaggerated and hysterical though it is. But from now on things will be different. Playtime is over; it's time for growing up.

Nora. Whose growing up—mine or the children's?

Helmer. Both yours and the children's, Nora darling.

Nora. Oh Torvald, you're not the man to bring me up to be the right kind of wife for you.

Helmer. How can you say that?

Nora. And I—? What qualifications do I have for bringing up the children?

Helmer. Nora!

Nora. You said so yourself a minute ago—that you didn't dare to trust me with them.

Helmer. In the first flush of anger, yes. Surely, you're not going to count that.

Nora. But you were quite right. I am *not* qualified. Something else has to come first. Somehow I have to grow up myself. And you are not the man to help me do that. That's a job I have to do by myself. And that's why I'm leaving you.

Helmer (jumps up). What did you say!

Nora. I have to be by myself if I am to find out about myself and about all the other things too. So I can't stay here with you any longer.

Helmer. Nora, Nora!

Nora. I'm leaving now. I'm sure Kristine will put me up for tonight.

Helmer. You're out of your mind! I won't let you! I forbid you!

Nora. You can't forbid me anything any more; it won't do any good. I'm taking my own things with me. I won't accept anything from you, either now or later.

Helmer. But this is madness!

Nora. Tomorrow I'm going home—I mean back to my old hometown. It will be easier for me to find some kind of job there.

Helmer. Oh, you blind, inexperienced creature—!

Nora. I must see to it that I get experience, Torvald.

Helmer. Leaving your home, your husband, your children! Not a thought of what people will say!

Nora. I can't worry about that. All I know is that I have to leave.

Helmer. Oh, this is shocking! Betraying your most sacred duties like this!

Nora. And what do you consider my most sacred duties?

Helmer. Do I need to tell you that? They are your duties to your husband and your children.

Nora. I have other duties equally sacred.

Helmer. You do not. What duties would they be?

Nora. My duties to myself.

Helmer. You are a wife and a mother before you are anything else.

Nora. I don't believe that any more. I believe I am first of all a human being, just as much as you—or at any rate that I must try to become one. Oh, I know very well that most people agree with you, Torvald, and that it says something like that in all the books. But what people say and what the books say is no longer enough for me. I have to think about these things myself and see if I can't find the answers.

Helmer. You mean to tell me you don't know what your proper place in your own home is? Don't you have a reliable guide in such matters? Don't you have religion?

Nora. Oh but Torvald—I don't really know what religion is.

Helmer. What are you saying!

Nora. All I know is what the Reverend Hansen told me when he prepared me for confirmation. He said that religion was *this* and it was *that.* When I get by myself, away from here, I'll have to look into that, too. I have to decide if what the Reverend Hansen said was right, or anyway if it is right for *me.*

Helmer. Oh, this is unheard of in a young woman! If religion can't guide you, let me appeal to your conscience. For surely you have moral feelings? Or— answer me—maybe you don't?

Nora. Well, you see, Torvald, I don't really know what to say. I just don't know. I am confused about these things. All I know is that my ideas are quite different from yours. I have just found out that the laws are different from what I thought they were, but in no way can I get it into my head that those laws are right. A woman shouldn't have the right to spare her dying old father or save her husband's life! I just can't believe that.

Helmer. You speak like a child. You don't understand the society you live in.

Nora. No, I don't. But I want to find out about it. I have to make up my mind who is right, society or I.

Helmer. You are sick, Nora; you have a fever. I really don't think you are in your right mind.

Nora. I have never felt so clearheaded and sure of myself as I do tonight.

Helmer. And clearheaded and sure of yourself you're leaving your husband and children?

Nora. Yes.

Helmer. Then there is only one possible explanation.

Nora. What?

Helmer. You don't love me any more.

Nora. No, that's just it.

Helmer. Nora! Can you say that?

Nora. I am sorry, Torvald, for you have always been so good to me. But I can't help it. I don't love you any more.

Helmer (*with forced composure*). And this too is a clear and sure conviction?

Nora. Completely clear and sure. That's why I don't want to stay here any more.

Helmer. And are you ready to explain to me how I came to forfeit your love?

Nora. Certainly I am. It was tonight, when the wonderful didn't happen. That was when I realized you were not the man I thought you were.

Helmer. You have to explain. I don't understand.

Nora. I have waited patiently for eight years, for I wasn't such a fool that I thought the wonderful is something that happens any old day. Then this—thing —came crashing in on me, and then there wasn't a doubt in my mind that now—now comes the wonderful. When Krogstad's letter was in that mailbox, never for a moment did it even occur to me that you would submit to his conditions. I was so absolutely certain that you would say to him: make the whole thing public—tell everybody. And when that had happened—

Helmer. Yes, then what? When I had surrendered my wife to shame and disgrace—!

Nora. When that had happened, I was absolutely certain that you would stand up and take the blame and say, "I'm the guilty one."

Helmer. Nora!

Nora. You mean I never would have accepted such a sacrifice from you? Of course not. But what would my protests have counted against yours? *That* was the wonderful I was hoping for in terror. And to prevent that I was going to kill myself.

Helmer. I'd gladly work nights and days for you, Nora—endure sorrow and want for your sake. But nobody sacrifices his *honor* for his love.

Nora. A hundred thousand women have done so.

Helmer. Oh, you think and talk like a silly child.

Nora. All right. But you don't think and talk like the man I can live with. When you had gotten over your fright—not because of what threatened *me* but because of the risk to *you*—and the whole danger was past, then you acted as if nothing at all had happened. Once again I was your little songbird, your doll, just as before, only now you had to handle her even more carefully, because she was so frail and weak. (*Rises.*) Torvald—that moment I realized that I had been living here for eight years with a stranger and had borne him three children—Oh, I can't stand thinking about it! I feel like tearing myself to pieces!

Helmer *(heavily).* I see it, I see it. An abyss has opened up between us.—Oh but Nora—surely it can be filled?

Nora. The way I am now I am no wife for you.

Helmer. I have it in me to change.

Nora. Perhaps—if your doll is taken from you.

Helmer. To part—to part from you! No, no, Nora! I can't grasp that thought!

Nora *(goes out, right).* All the more reason why it has to be. (*She returns with her outdoor clothes and a small bag, which she sets down on the chair by the table.*)

Helmer. Nora, Nora! Not now! Wait till tomorrow.

Nora *(putting on her coat).* I can't spend the night in a stranger's rooms.

Helmer. But couldn't we live here together like brother and sister—?

Nora *(tying on her hat).* You know very well that wouldn't last long—. (*Wraps her shawl around her.*) Goodbye, Torvald. I don't want to see the children. I know I leave them in better hands than mine. The way I am now I can't be anything to them.

Helmer. But some day, Nora—some day—?

Nora. How can I tell? I have no idea what's going to become of me.

Helmer. But you're still my wife, both as you are now and as you will be.

Nora. Listen, Torvald—when a wife leaves her husband's house, the way I am doing now, I have heard he has no more legal responsibilities for her. At any rate, I now release you from all responsibility. You are not to feel yourself obliged to me for anything, and I have no obligations to you. There has to be full freedom on both sides. Here is your ring back. Now give me mine.

Helmer. Even this?

Nora. Even this.

Helmer. Here it is.

Nora. There. So now it's over. I'm putting the keys here. The maids know everything about the house—better than I. Tomorrow, after I'm gone, Kristine will come over and pack my things from home. I want them sent after me.

Helmer. Over! It's all over! Nora, will you never think of me?

Nora. I'm sure I'll often think of you and the children and this house.

Helmer. May I write to you, Nora?

Nora. No—never. I won't have that.

Helmer. But send you things—? You must let me.

Nora. Nothing, nothing.

Helmer. —help you, when you need help—

Nora. I told you, no; I won't have it. I'll accept nothing from strangers.

Helmer. Nora—can I never again be more to you than a stranger?

Nora *(picks up her bag).* Oh Torvald—then the most wonderful of all would have to happen—

Helmer. Tell me what that would be—!

Nora. For that to happen, both you and I would have to change so that—Oh Torvald, I no longer believe in the wonderful.

Helmer. But I *will* believe. Tell me! Change, so that—?

Nora. So that our living together would become a true marriage. Goodbye. (*She goes out through the hall.*)

Helmer (*sinks down on a chair near the door and covers his face with his hands*). Nora! Nora! (*Looks around him and gets up.*) All empty. She's gone. (*With sudden hope.*) The most wonderful—?!

From downstairs comes the sound of a heavy door slamming shut.

QUESTIONS

Act I

1. Describe Nora's behavior during her first appearance.

2. How does this contrast to Helmer's behavior during his first appearance?

3. What is the initial, overriding concern of both Nora and Helmer very early in the play?

4. What behavior of Nora's indicates a latent rebelliousness? What else does this behavior indicate?

5. Explain why Mrs. Linde doesn't feel even "a grief to live on" (page 969). Why would this be so?

6. Describe the similarities in the lives of Nora and Mrs. Linde, and tell what this mutual situation symbolizes.

7. What in Mrs. Linde's statements makes Nora reveal some information about how she got the money to take Helmer to Italy when he was sick? What is Nora trying to prove?

8. What are we allowed to believe she had done to earn the money?

9. Why would Helmer be embarrassed and humiliated to learn that he owed his wife anything? Why does Nora feel that she must have something, if only a secret?

10. What dramatic devices does Ibsen use to heighten tension?

11. Krogstad says, "what I did that time was no more and no worse" than the fraud Nora has committed (page 981). In light of what's happened to Krogstad, what does this imply about Ibsen's society? Is sex discrimination the only issue?

Act II

1. What irony is revealed in this act, and who is involved?

2. How does Helmer's behavior here relate to question 9? How does his behavior, like Oedipus's, entrap him? Draw a comparison.

3. What does Nora reveal during the scene with Rank that for the first time relates to the title of the play?

4. What manner of person does Rank seem to be?

5. What does Krogstad ultimately contribute to Nora's rebirth? What does Rank contribute?

6. From what disease, more fully developed in a later play by Ibsen, is Rank really dying? What is meant by his remark, "my poor innocent spine is suffering for my father's frolics as a young lieutenant"?

7. How does this belief square with Helmer's that certain behavioral traits are also transmitted from generation to generation?

8. Does Rank's impending death influence Nora's decision to leave? Explain.

Act III

1. Does Mrs. Linde's initiative with Krogstad deepen her as a character? How?

2. How does Mrs. Linde's previous situation with her family and late husband compare to Nora's crisis with Helmer's illness and her father's death?

3. With Krogstad is Mrs. Linde being "hysterical" or realistic?

4. Why does Mrs. Linde insist that the "concealment and evasion" of Nora and Helmer be brought to an end?

5. In earlier times the tarantella dance was believed to be a remedy for tarantism, which results from the bite of a tarantula. Explain the symbolism of the spider. Who or what would be the spider, and who would have been bitten?

6. What mood does talk of the dance and the dance itself evoke in Nora? in Rank? in Helmer?

7. What is the symbolism behind Helmer's talk of knitting versus embroidery?

8. At what point in this act does Nora truly perceive Helmer's self-centered concern for convention?

TOPICS FOR WRITING

1. In Act II Rank says, ". . . there isn't a single family that isn't ruled by that same law of ruthless retribution, in one way or the other." Relate the "crime" and the retribution theme as it appears in *Oedipus, Death of a Salesman,* and *A Doll's House.*

2. What circumstances might have made it fun for Helmer to be in love with Nora? What did Nora contribute to such a relationship that made it fun? In what ways has Nora's relationship with Helmer been similar to her relationship with her father?

3. Seventy years passed between the initial performances of *A Doll's House* and *Death of a Salesman,* yet there are reasons enough to draw a comparison between Linda and Nora. Do so, eliminating the time differences, and *contrast* the husbands, Helmer and Willy.

4. Detail the contrasting characteristics of the three men in *A Doll's House,* evaluating their strengths and weaknesses. What does "convention" seem to mean to each of them?

5. Describe how Mrs. Linde becomes a model for Nora's behavior, taking into account the encumbrances of each.

Alice Childress

WINE IN THE WILDERNESS

Alice Childress (1920–   ) was born in Charleston, South Carolina. She is an actor, playwright, and director. Her first role was in Anna Lucasta *in New York during World War II. She also played in* The Candy Story *and* The Emperor's Clothes. *Childress collaborated with Langston Hughes on his musical* Simply Heavenly *(1957); earlier, she had written the plays* Florence *(1949) and* Gold through the Trees *(1952). After spending most of her time in theater with the American Negro Theater, Childress won the 1956 Obie (off-Broadway award) with* Trouble in Mind. Wedding Band *(1966) was produced at Arthur Miller's university, Michigan.* Wine in the Wilderness *(1969) was first presented on television in Boston. Childress also is the editor of* Black Scenes *(1971), a collection of scenes from plays by black playwrights.* Wine in the Wilderness, *set against violent action, poses internal questions for the characters, whose dilemmas are universally those of "Third World enclaves" within the societies that dominate them. The same questions might be asked by the Irish, the Palestinians, the East Indians of Canada, and various groups within the Soviet Union.*

Characters

Bill Jameson, an artist aged thirty-three
Oldtimer, an old roustabout character in his sixties
Sonny-man, a writer aged twenty-seven
Cynthia, a social worker aged twenty-five, Sonny-man's wife.
Tommy, a woman factory worker aged thirty

Time: The summer of 1964. Night of a riot.

Place: Harlem, New York City, New York, U.S.A.

Alice Childress

    Scene: *A one room apartment in a Harlem Tenement. It used to be a three room apartment but the tenant has broken out walls and is half finished with a redecorating job. The place is now only partly reminiscent of its past tawdry days, plaster broken away and lathing exposed right next to a new brick-faced portion of wall. The kitchen is now a part of the room. There is a three-quarter bed covered with an African throw, a screen is placed at the foot of the bed to insure privacy when needed. The room is obviously black dominated, pieces of sculpture, wall hangings, paintings. An artist's easel is standing with a drapery thrown across it so the empty canvas beneath it is hidden. Two other canvases the same size are next to it, they too are covered and conceal paintings. The place is in a beautiful, rather artistic state of disorder. The room also reflects an interest in other darker peoples of the world . . . A Chinese incense-burner Buddha, an American Indian feathered war helmet, a Mexican serape, a Japanese fan, a West Indian travel poster. There is a kitchen table, chairs, floor cushions, a couple of box crates, books, bookcases, plenty of artist's materials. There is a small raised platform for model posing. On the platform is a backless chair. The tail end of a riot is going on out in the street. Noise and screaming can be heard in the distance. . . . running feet, voices shouting over loudspeakers.*

Offstage voices. Offa the street! Into your homes! Clear the street! (*The whine of a bullet is heard.*) Cover that roof! It's from the roof! (*Bill is seated on the floor with his back to the wall, drawing on a large sketch pad with charcoal pencil. He is very absorbed in his task but flinches as he hears the bullet sound, ducks and shields his head with upraised hand. . . . then resumes sketching. The telephone rings, he reaches for phone with caution, pulls it toward him by the cord in order to avoid going near window or standing up.*)

Bill. Hello? Yeah, my phone is on. How the hell I'm gonna be talkin' to you if it's not on? (*Sound of glass breaking in the distance.*) I could lose my damn life answerin' the phone. Sonny-man, what the hell you callin' me up for! I thought you and Cynthia might be downstairs dead. I banged on the floor and hollered down the air-shaft, no answer. No stuff! Thought yall was dead. I'm sittin' here drawin' a picture in your memory. In a bar! Yall sittin' in a bar? See there, you done blew the picture that's in your memory . . . No kiddin', they wouldn't let you in the block? Man, they can't keep you outta your own house. Found? You found who? Model? What model? Yeah, yeah, thanks, . . . but I like to find my own models. No! Don't bring nobody up here in the middle of a riot . . . Hey, Sonny-man! Hey! (*Sound of yelling and rushing footsteps in the hall.*)

Woman's voice (*offstage*). Damnit, Bernice! The riot is over! What you hidin' in the hall for? I'm in the house, your father's in the house, . . . and you out here hidin' in the hall!

Girl's voice (*offstage*). The house might burn down!

Bill. Sonny-man, I can't hear you!

Woman's voice (*offstage*). If it do burn down, what the hell you gon' do, run off and leave us to burn up by ourself? The riot is over. The police say it's over! Get back in the house!

(*Sound of running feet and a knock on the door.*)

Bill. They say it's over. Man, they oughta let you on your own block, in your own house . . . Yeah, we still standin', this seventy year old house got guts. Thank you, yeah, thanks but I like to pick my own models. You drunk? Can't you hear when I say not to . . . Okay, all right, bring her . . . *(Frantic knocking at the door.)* I gotta go. Yeah, yeah, bring her. I gotta go . . . *(Hangs up phone and opens the door for Oldtimer. The old man is carrying a haul of loot . . . two or three bottles of liquor, a ham, a salami and a suit with price tags attached.)* What's this! Oh, no, no, no, Oldtimer, not here . . . *(Faint sound of a police whistle.)* The police after you? What you bring that stuff in here for?

Oldtimer *(Runs past Bill to center as he looks for a place to hide the loot).* No, no, they not really after me but ˙. . . I was in the basement so I could stash this stuff, . . . but a fella told me they pokin' round down there . . . in the back yard pokin' round . . . the police doin' a lotta pokin' round.

Bill. If the cops are searchin' why you wanna dump your troubles on me?

Oldtimer. I don't wanta go to jail. I'm too old to go to jail. What we gonna do?

Bill. We can throw it the hell outta the window. Didn't you think of just throwin it away and not worry 'bout jail?

Oldtimer. I can't do it. It's like . . . I'm Oldtimer but my hands and arms is somebody else that I don' know-a-tall. *(Bill pulls stuff out of Oldtimer's arms and places loot on the kitchen table. Oldtimer's arms fall to his sides.)* Thank you, son.

Bill. Stealin' ain't worth a bullet through your brain, is it? You wanna get shot down and drown in your own blood, . . . for what? A suit, a bottle of whiskey? Gonna throw your life away for a damn ham?

Oldtimer. But I ain' really stole nothin', Bill, cause I ain' no thief. Them others, . . . they smash the windows, they run in the stores and grab and all. Me, I pick up what they left scatter in the street. Things they drop . . . things they trample underfoot. What's in the street ain' like stealin'. This is leavin's. What I'm gon' do if the police come?

Bill *(starts to gather the things in the tablecloth that is on the table).* I'll throw it out the air-shaft window.

Oldtimer *(places himself squarely in front of the air-shaft window).* I be damn. Uh-uh, can't let you do it, Bill-Boy. *(Grabs the liquor and holds on.)*

Bill *(wraps the suit, the ham and the salami in the tablecloth and ties the ends together in a knot).* Just for now, then you can go down and get it later.

Oldtimer *(getting belligerent).* I say I ain' gon' let you do it.

Bill. Sonny-man calls this "The people's revolution." A revolution should not be looting and stealing. Revolutions are for liberation. *(Oldtimer won't budge from before the window.)* Okay, man, you win, it's all yours. *(Walks away from Oldtimer and prepares his easel for sketching.)*

Oldtimer. Don't be mad with me, Bill-Boy, I couldn' help myself.

Bill *(at peace with the old man).* No hard feelin's.

Oldtimer *(as he uncorks bottle).* I don't blame you for bein' fed up with us, . . . fella like you oughta be fed up with your people sometime. Hey, Billy, let's you and me have a little taste together.

Bill. Yeah, why not.

Oldtimer *(at table pouring drinks).* You mustn't be too hard on me. You see, you talented, you got somethin' on the ball, you gonna make it on past these white folk, . . . but not me, Billy-boy, it's too late in the day for that. Time, time, time, . . . time done put me down. Father Time is a bad white cat. Whatcha been paintin' and drawin' lately? You can paint me again if you wanta, . . . no charge. Paint me 'cause that might be the only way I get to stay in the world after I'm dead and gone. Somebody'll look up at your paintin' and say, . . . "Who's that?" And you say, . . . "That's Oldtimer." *(Bill joins Oldtimer at table and takes one of the drinks.)* Well, here's lookin' at you and goin' down me. *(Gulps drink down.)*

Bill *(raising his glass).* Your health, Oldtimer.

Oldtimer. My day we didn't have all this grants and scholarship like now. Whatcha been doin'?

Bill. I'm working on the third part of a triptych.

Oldtimer. A what tick?

Bill. A triptych.

Oldtimer. Hot-damn, that call for another drink. Here's to the trip-tick. Down the hatch. What is one-a-those?

Bill. It's three paintings that make one work . . . three paintings that make one subject.

Oldtimer. Goes together like a new outfit . . . hat, shoes and suit.

Bill. Right. The title of my triptych is . . . "Wine in the Wilderness" . . . Three canvases on black womanhood. . . .

Oldtimer *(eyes light up).* Are they naked pitchers?

Bill *(crosses to paintings).* No, all fully clothed.

Oldtimer *(wishing it was a naked picture).* Man, ain' nothin' dirty 'bout naked pitchers. That's art. What you call artistic.

Bill. Right, right, right, but these are with clothes. That can be artistic too. *(Uncovers one of the canvases and reveals painting of a charming little girl in Sunday dress and hair ribbon.)* I call her . . . "Black girlhood."

Oldtimer. Awwwww, that's innocence! Don't know what it's all about. Ain't that the little child that live right down the street? Yeah. That call for another drink.

Bill. Slow down, Oldtimer, wait till you see this. *(Covers the painting of the little girl, then uncovers another canvas and reveals a beautiful woman, deep mahogany complexion, she is cold but utter perfection, draped in startling colors of African material, very "Vogue" looking. She wears a golden head-dress sparkling with brilliants and sequins applied over the paint.)* There she is. . . "Wine In The Wilderness" . . . Mother Africa, regal, black womanhood in her noblest form.

Oldtimer. Hot damn. I'd die for her, no stuff, . . . oh, man. "Wine In The Wilderness."

Bill. Once, a long time ago, a poet named Omar told us what a paradise life could be if a man had a loaf of bread, a jug of wine and . . . a woman singing to him in the wilderness. She is the woman, she is the bread, she is the wine, she is the singing. This Abyssinian maiden is paradise, . . . perfect black womanhood.

Oldtimer *(pours for Bill and himself).* To our Abyssinian maiden.

Bill. She's the Sudan, the Congo River, the Egyptian Pyramids . . . Her thighs are African Mahogany . . . she speaks and her words pour forth sparkling clear as the waters . . . Victoria Falls.

Oldtimer. Ow! Victoria Falls! She got a pretty name.

Bill *(covers her up again).* Victoria Falls is a waterfall not her name. Now, here's the one that calls for a drink. *(Snatches cover from the empty canvas.)*

Oldtimer *(stunned by the empty canvas).* Your . . . your pitcher is gone.

Bill. Not gone . . . she's not painted yet. This will be the third part of the triptych. This is the unfinished third of "Wine In The Wilderness." She's gonna be the kinda chick that is grass roots, . . . no, not grass roots, . . . I mean she's underneath the grass roots. The lost woman, . . . what the society has made out of our women. She's as far from my African queen as a woman can get and still be female, she's as close to the bottom as you can get without crackin' up . . . she's ignorant, unfeminine, coarse, rude . . . vulgar . . . a poor, dumb chick that's had her behind kicked until it's numb . . . and the sad part is . . . she ain't together, you know . . . there's no hope for her.

Oldtimer. Oh, man, you talkin' 'bout my first wife.

Bill. A chick that ain' fit for nothin' but to . . . to . . . just pass her by.

Oldtimer. Yeah, later for her. When you see her, cross over to the other side of the street.

Bill. If you had to sum her up in one word it would be nothin'!

Oldtimer *(roars with laughter).* That call for a double!

Bill *(beginning to slightly feel the drinks. He covers the canvas again).* Yeah, that's a double! The kinda woman that grates on your damn nerves. And Sonny-man just called to say he found her runnin' round in the middle-a this riot, Sonny-man say she's the real thing from underneath them grass roots. A back-country chick right outta the wilds of Mississippi, . . . but she ain' never been near there. Born in Harlem, raised right here in Harlem, . . . but back country. Got the picture?

Oldtimer *(full of laughter).* When . . . when . . . when she get here let's us stomp her to death.

Bill. Not till after I paint her. Gonna put her right here on this canvas. *(Pats the canvas, walks in a strut around the table.)* When she gets put down on canvas, . . . then triptych will be finished.

Oldtimer *(joins him in the strut).* Trip-tick will be finish . . . trip-tick will be finish . . .

Bill. Then "Wine In The Wilderness" will go up against the wall to improve the view of some post office . . . or some library . . . or maybe a bank . . . and I'll win a prize . . . and the queen, my black queen will look down from the wall so the messed up chicks in the neighborhood can see what a woman oughta be . . . and the innocent child on one side of her and the messed up chick on the other side of her . . . MY STATEMENT.

Oldtimer *(turning the strut into a dance).* Wine in the wilderness . . . up against the wall . . . wine in the wilderness . . . up against the wall . . .

Woman from upstairs apt *(offstage).* What's the matter! The house on fire?

Bill *(calls upstairs through the air-shaft window).* No, baby! We down here paintin' pictures! *(Sound of police siren in distance.)*

Woman from upstairs apt *(offstage).* So much-a damn noise! Cut out the noise! *(To her husband hysterically.)* Percy! Percy! You hear a police siren! Percy! That a fire engine?!

Bill. Another messed up chick. *(Gets a rope and ties it to Oldtimer's bundle.)* Got an idea. We'll tie the rope to the bundle, . . . then . . . *(Lowers bundle out of window.)* lower the bundle outta the window . . . and tie it to this nail here behind the curtain. Now! Nobody can find it except you and me . . . Cops come, there's no loot. *(Ties rope to nail under curtain.)*

Oldtimer. Yeah, yeah, loot long gone 'til I want it. *(Makes sure window knot is secure.)* It'll be swingin' in the breeze free and easy. *(There is knocking on the door.)*

Sonny-man. Open up! Open up! Sonny-man and company.

Bill *(putting finishing touches on securing knot to nail).* Wait, wait, hold on. . . .

Sonny-man. And-a here we come! *(Pushes the door open. Enters room with his wife Cynthia and Tommy. Sonny-man is in high spirits. He is in his late twenties, his wife Cynthia is a bit younger. She wears her hair in a natural style, her clothing is tweedy and in good, quiet taste. Sonny-man is wearing slacks and a dashiki over a shirt. Tommy is dressed in a mis-matched skirt and sweater, wearing a wig that is not comical, but is wiggy looking. She has the habit of smoothing it every once in a while, patting to make sure it's in place. She wears sneakers and bobby sox, carries a brown paper sack.)*

Cynthia. You didn't think it was locked, did you?

Bill. Door not locked? *(Looking over Tommy.)*

Tommy. You oughta run him outta town, pushin' open people's door.

Bill. Come right on in.

Sonny-man *(standing behind Tommy and pointing down at her to draw Bill's attention).* Yes, sireeeeee.

Cynthia. Bill, meet a friend-a ours . . . This is Miss Tommy Fields. Tommy, meet a friend-a ours . . . this is Bill, Jameson . . . Bill, Tommy.

Bill. Tommy, if I may call you that . . .

Tommy *(likes him very much).* Help yourself, Bill. It's a pleasure. Bill Jameson, well, all right.

Bill. The pleasure is all mine. Another friend-a ours, Oldtimer.

Tommy *(with respect and warmth).* How are you, Mr. Timer?

Bill *(laughs along with others, Oldtimer included).* What you call him, baby?

Tommy. Mr. Timer, . . . ain't that what you say? *(They all laugh expansively.)*

Bill. No, sugar pie, that's not his name, . . . we just say . . . "Oldtimer," that's what everybody call him. . . .

Oldtimer. Yeah, they all call me that . . . everybody say that . . . Oldtimer.

Tommy. That's cute, . . . but what's your name?

Bill. His name is . . . er . . . er . . . What is your name?

Sonny-man. Dog-bite, what's your name, man? *(There is a significant moment of self-consciousness as Cynthia, Sonny and Bill realize they don't know Oldtimer's name.)*

Oldtimer. Well, it's . . . Edmond L. Matthews.

Tommy. Edmond *L.* Matthews. What's the L for?

Oldtimer. Lorenzo, . . . Edmond Lorenzo Matthews.

Bill and Sonny-man. Edmond Lorenzo Matthews.

Tommy. Pleased to meetcha, Mr. Matthews.

Oldtimer. Nobody call me that in a long, long time.

Tommy. I'll call you Oldtimer like the rest but I like to know who I'm meetin'. *(Oldtimer gives her a chair.)* There you go. He's a gentleman too. Bet you can tell my feet hurt. I got one corn, . . . and that one is enough. Oh, it'll ask you for somethin'. *(General laughter. Bill indicates to Sonny-man that Tommy seems right. Cynthia and Oldtimer take seats near Tommy.)*

Bill. You rest yourself, baby, er . . . er . . . Tommy. You did say Tommy.

Tommy. I cut it to Tommy . . . Tommy-Marie, I use both of 'em sometime.

Bill. How 'bout some refreshment?

Sonny-man. Yeah, how 'bout that. *(Pouring drinks.)*

Tommy. Don't yall carry me too fast, now.

Bill *(indicating liquor bottles).* I got what you see and also some wine . . . couple-a cans-a beer.

Tommy. I'll take the wine.

Bill. Yeah, I knew it.

Tommy. Don't wanta start nothin' I can't keep up. *(Oldtimer slaps his thigh with pleasure.)*

Bill. That's all right, baby, you just a wine-o.

Tommy. You the one that's got the wine, not me.

Bill. I use this for cookin'.

Tommy. You like to get loaded while you cook? *(Oldtimer is having a ball.)*

Bill *(as he pours wine for Tommy).* Oh, baby, you too much.

Oldtimer *(admiring Tommy).* Oh, Lord, I wish, I wish, I wish I was young again.

Tommy *(flirtatiously).* Lively as you are, . . . I don't know what we'd do with you if you got any younger.

Oldtimer. Oh, hush now!

Sonny-man *(whispering to Bill and pouring drinks).* Didn't I tell you! Know what I'm talkin' about. You dig? All the elements, man.

Tommy *(worried about what the whispering means).* Let's get somethin' straight. I didn't come bustin' in on the party . . . I was asked. If you married and any wives or girl-friends round here . . . I'm innocent. Don't wanta get shot at, or jumped on. Cause I wasn't doin' a thing but mindin' my business! . . . *(Saying the last in loud tones to be heard in other rooms.)*

Oldtimer. Jus' us here, that's all.

Bill. I'm single, baby. Nobody wants a poor artist.

Cynthia. Oh, honey, we wouldn't walk you into a jealous wife or girl friend.

Tommy. You paint all-a these pitchers? *(Bill and Sonny-man hand out drinks.)*

Bill. Just about. Your health, baby, to you.

Tommy *(lifts her wine glass).* All right, and I got one for you. . . . Like my grampaw used-ta say, . . . Here's to the men's collars and the women's skirts, . . . may they never meet. *(General laughter.)*

Oldtimer. But they ain't got far to go before they do.

Tommy *(suddenly remembers her troubles).* Niggers, niggers . . . niggers, . . . I'm sick-a niggers, ain't you? A nigger will mess up everytime . . . Lemmie tell you what the niggers done . . .

Bill. Tommy, baby, we don't use that word around here. We can talk about each other a little better than that.

Cynthia. Oh, she doesn't mean it.

Tommy. What must I say?

Bill. Try Afro-Americans.

Tommy. Well, . . . the Afro-Americans burnt down my house.

Oldtimer. Oh, no they didn't!

Tommy. Oh, yes they did . . . it's almost burn down. Then the firemen nailed up my door . . . the door to my room, nailed up shut tight with all I got in the world.

Oldtimer. Shame, what a shame.

Tommy. A *damn* shame. My clothes . . . Everything gone. This riot blew my life. All I got is gone like it never was.

Oldtimer. I know it.

Tommy. My transistor radio . . . that's gone.

Cynthia. Ah, gee.

Tommy. The transistor . . . and a brand new pair-a shoes I never had on one time . . . *(Raises her right hand.)* If I never move, that's the truth . . . new shoes gone.

Oldtimer. Child, when hard luck fall it just keep fallin'.

Tommy. And in my top dresser drawer I got a my-on-ase jar with forty-one dollars in it. The fireman would not let me in to get it . . . And it was a Afro-American fireman, don'tcha know.

Oldtimer. And you ain't got no place to stay. *(Bill is studying her for portrait possibilities.)*

Tommy *(rises and walks around room).* That's a lie. I always got some place to go. I don't wanta boast but I ain't never been no place that I can't go back the second time. Woman I use to work for say . . . "Tommy, any time, any time you want a sleep-in place you come right here to me." . . . And that's Park Avenue, my own private bath and T.V. set. . . . But I don't want that . . . so I make it on out here to the dress factory. I got friends . . . not a lot of 'em . . . but a few *good* ones. I call my friend—girl and her mother . . . they say . . . "Tommy, you come here, bring yourself over here." So Tommy got a roof with no sweat. *(Looks at torn walls.)* Looks like the Afro-Americans got to you too. Breakin' up, breakin' down, . . . that's all they know.

Bill. No, Tommy, . . . I'm re-decorating the place . . .

Tommy. You mean you did this to yourself?

Cynthia. It's gonna be wild . . . brick-face walls . . . wall to wall carpet.

Sonny-man. She was breakin' up everybody in the bar . . . had us all laughin' . . . crackin' us up. In the middle of a riot . . . she's gassin' everybody!

Tommy. No need to cry, it's sad enough. They hollerin' whitey, whitey . . . but who they burn out? Me.

Bill. The brothers and sisters are tired, weary of the endless get-no-where struggle.

Tommy. I'm standin' there in the bar . . . tellin' like it is . . . next thing I know they talkin' bout bringin' me to meet you. But you know what I say? Can't nobody pick nobody for nobody else. It don't work. And I'm standin' there in a mis-match skirt and top and these sneaker-shoes. I just went to put my dresses in the cleaner . . . Oh, Lord, wonder if they burn down the cleaner. Well, no matter, when I got back it was all over . . . They went in the grocery store, rip out the shelves, pull out all the groceries . . . the hams . . . the . . . the . . . the can goods . . . everything . . . and then set fire . . . Now who you think live over the grocery? Me, that's who. I don't even go to the store lookin' this way . . . but this would be the time, when . . . folks got a fella they want me to meet.

Bill *(suddenly self-conscious).* Tommy, they thought . . . they thought I'd like to paint you . . . that's why they asked you over.

Tommy *(pleased by the thought but she can't understand it).* Paint me? For what? If he was gonna paint somebody seems to me it'd be one of the pretty girls they show in the beer ads. They even got colored on television now, . . . brushin' their teeth and smokin' cigarettes, . . . some of the prettiest girls in the world. He could get them, . . . couldn't you?

Bill. Sonny-man and Cynthia were right. I want to paint you.

Tommy *(suspiciously).* Naked, with no clothes on?

Bill. No, baby, dressed just as you are now.

Oldtimer. Wearin' clothes is also art.

Tommy. In the cleaner I got a white dress with a orlon sweater to match it, maybe I can get it out tomorrow and pose in that. *(Cynthia, Oldtimer and Sonny-man are eager for her to agree.)*

Bill. No, I will paint you today, Tommy, just as you are, holding your brown paper bag.

Tommy. Mmmmmm, me holdin' the damn bag, I don't know 'bout that.

Bill. Look at it this way, tonight has been a tragedy.

Tommy. Sure in hell has.

Bill. And so I must paint you tonight, . . . Tommy in her moment of tragedy.

Tommy. I'm tired.

Bill. Damn, baby, all you have to do is sit there and rest.

Tommy. I'm hungry.

Sonny-man. While you're posin' Cynthia can run down to our house and fix you some eggs.

Cynthia *(gives her husband a weary look).* Oh, Sonny, that's such a lovely idea.

Sonny-man. Thank you, darlin', I'm in there, . . . on the beam.

Tommy *(ill at ease about posing).* I don't want no eggs. I'm goin' to find me some Chinee food.

Bill. I'll go. If you promise to stay here and let me paint you, . . . I'll get you anything you want.

Tommy *(brightening up).* Anything I want. Now, how he sound? All right, you comin' on mighty strong there. "Anything you want." When last you heard somebody say that? . . . I'm warnin' you, now, . . . I'm free, single and disengage, . . . so you better watch yourself.

Bill *(keeping her away from ideas of romance).* Now this is the way the program will go down. First I'll feed you, then I'll paint you.

Tommy. Okay, I'm game, I'm a good sport. First off, I want me some Chinee food.

Cynthia. Order up, Tommy, the treat's on him.

Tommy. How come it is you never been married? All these girls runnin' round Harlem lookin' for husbands. *(To Cynthia.)* I don't blame 'em, 'cause I'm lookin' for somebody myself.

Bill. I've been married, married and divorced, she divorced me, Tommy, so maybe I'm not much of a catch.

Tommy. Look at it this-a-way. Some folks got bad taste. That woman had bad taste. *(All laugh except Bill who pours another drink.)* Watch it, Bill, you gonna rust the linin' of your stomach. Ain't this a shame? The riot done wipe me out and I'm sittin' here havin' me a ball. Sittin' here ballin'! *(As Bill refills her glass.)* Hold it, that's enough. Likker ain' my problem.

Oldtimer. I'm havin' me a good time.

Tommy. Know what I say 'bout divorce. *(Slaps her hands together in a final gesture.)* Anybody don' wantcha, . . . later, let 'em go. That's bad taste for you.

Bill. Tommy, I don't wanta ever get married again. It's me and my work. I'm not gettin' serious about anybody. . . .

Tommy. He's spellin' at me, now. Nigger, . . . I mean Afro-American . . . I ain' ask you nothin'. You hinkty, I'm hinkty too. I'm independent as a hog on ice, . . . and a hog on ice is dead, cold, well-preserved . . . and don't need a mother-grabbin' thing. *(All laugh heartily except Bill and Cynthia.)* I know models get paid. I ain' no square but this is a special night and so this one'll be on the house. Show you my heart's in the right place.

Bill. I'll be glad to pay you, baby.

Tommy. You don't really like me, do you? That's all right, sometime it happen that way. You can't pick for *nobody.* Friends get to matchin' up friends and they mess up everytime. Cynthia and Sonny-man done messed up.

Bill. I like you just fine and I'm glad and grateful that you came.

Tommy. Good enough. *(Extends her hand. They slap hands together.)* You 'n me friends?

Bill. Friends, baby, friends. *(Putting rock record on.)*

Tommy *(trying out the model stand).* Okay, Dad! Let's see 'bout this *anything I want* jive. Want me a bucket-a Egg Foo Yong, and you get you a shrimp-fry rice, we split that and each have some-a both. Make him give you the soy souce, the hot mustard and the duck sauce too.

Bill. Anything else, baby?

Tommy. Since you ask, yes. If your money hold out, get me a double order egg roll. And a half order of the sweet and sour spare ribs.

Bill *(to Oldtimer and Sonny-man).* Come on, come on. I need some strong men to help me bring back your order, baby.

Tommy *(going into her dance . . . simply standing and going through some boo-ga-loo motions).* Better go get it 'fore I think up some more to go 'long with it. *(The men laugh and vanish out of the door. Steps heard descending stairs.)* Turn that off. *(Cynthia turns off record player.)* How could I forget your name, good as you been to me this day. Thank you, Cynthia, thank you. I *like* him. Oh, I *like* him. But I don't wanta push him too fast. Oh, I got to play these cards right.

Cynthia *(a bit uncomfortable).* Oh, Honey, . . . Tommy, you don't want a poor artist.

Tommy. Tommy's not lookin' for a meal ticket. I been doin' for myself all my life. It takes two to make it in this high-price world. A black man see a hard way to go. The both of you gotta pull together. That way you accomplish.

Cynthia. I'm a social worker . . . and I see so many broken homes. Some of these men! Tommy, don't be in a rush about the marriage thing.

Tommy. Keep it to yourself, . . . but I was thirty my last birthday and haven't ever been married. I coulda been. Oh, yes, indeed, coulda been. But I don't want any and everybody. What I want with a no-good piece-a nothin'? I'll never forget what the Reverend Martin Luther King said . . . "I have a dream." I liked him sayin' it 'cause truer words have never been spoke. *(Straightening the room.)* I have a dream, too. Mine is to find a man who'll treat me just half-way decent . . . just to meet me half-way is all I ask, to smile, be kind to me. Somebody in my corner. Not to wake up by myself in the mornin' and face this world all alone.

Cynthia. About Bill, it's best not to ever count on anything, anything at all, Tommy.

Tommy *(this remark bothers her for a split second but she shakes it off)*. Of course, Cynthia, that's one of the foremost rules of life. Don't count on *nothin'!*

Cynthia. Right, don't be too quick to put your trust in these men.

Tommy. You put your trust in one and got yourself a husband.

Cynthia. Well, yes, but what I mean is . . . Oh, you know. A man is a man and Bill is also an artist and his work comes before all else and there are other factors . . .

Tommy *(sits facing Cynthia)*. What's wrong with me?

Cynthia. I don't know what you mean.

Tommy. Yes you do. You tryin' to tell me I'm aimin' too high by lookin' at Bill.

Cynthia. Oh, no, my dear.

Tommy. Out there in the street, in the bar, you and your husband were so sure that he'd *like* me and want to paint my picture.

Cynthia. But he does want to paint you, he's very eager to . . .

Tommy. But why? Somethin' don't fit right.

Cynthia *(feeling sorry for Tommy)*. If you don't want to do it, just leave and that'll be that.

Tommy. Walk out while he's buyin' me what I ask for, spendin' his money on me? That'd be too dirty. *(Looks at books. Takes one from shelf.)* Books, books, books everywhere. "Afro-American History." I like that. What's wrong with me, Cynthia? Tell me, I won't get mad with you, I swear. If there's somethin' wrong that I can change, I'm ready to do it. Eighth grade, that's all I had of school. You a social worker, I know that mean college. I come from poor people. *(Examining the book in her hand.)* Talkin' 'bout poverty this and poverty that and studyin' it. When you in it you don' be studyin' 'bout it. Cynthia, I remember my mother tyin' up her stockin's with strips-a rag 'cause she didn't have no garters. When I get home from school she'd say, . . . "Nothin' much here to eat." Nothin' much might be grits, or bread and coffee. I got sick-a all that, got me a job. Later for school.

Cynthia. The Matriarchal Society.

Tommy. What's that?

Cynthia. A Matriarchal Society is one in which the women rule . . . the women have the power. . . . the women head the house.

Tommy. We didn't have nothin' to rule over, not a pot nor a window. And my papa picked hisself up and run off with some finger-poppin' woman and we never hear another word 'til ten, twelve years later when a undertaker call up and ask if Mama wanta come claim his body. And don'cha know, mama went on over and claim it. A woman need a man to claim, even if it's a dead one. What's wrong with me? Be honest.

Cynthia. You're a fine person . . .

Tommy. Go on, I can take it.

Cynthia. You're too brash. You're too used to looking out for yourself. It makes us lose our femininity . . . It makes us hard . . . it makes us seem very hard. We do for ourselves too much.

Tommy. If I don't, who's gonna do for me?

Cynthia. You have to let the black man have his manhood again. You have to give it back, Tommy.

Tommy. I didn't take it from him, how I'm gonna give it back? What else is the matter with me? You had school, I didn't. I respect that.

Cynthia. Yes, I've had it, the degree and the whole bit. For a time I thought I was about to move into another world, the so-called "integrated" world, a place where knowledge and know-how could set you free and open all the doors, but that's a lie. I turned away from that idea. The first thing I did was give up dating white fellas.

Tommy. I never had none to give up. I'm not soundin' on you. White folks nothin' happens when I look at 'em. I don't hate 'em, don't love 'em . . . just nothin' shakes a-tall. The dullest people in the world. The way they talk . . . "Oh, hotty, hooty, hoo" . . . Break it down for me to A, B, C's. That Bill . . . I like him, with his black, uppity, high-handed ways. What do you do to get a man you want? A social worker oughta tell you things like that.

Cynthia. Don't chase him . . . at least don't let it look that way. Let him pursue you.

Tommy. What if he won't? Men don't chase me much, not the kind I like.

Cynthia *(rattles off instructions glibly).* Let him do the talking. Learn to listen. Stay in the background a little. Ask his opinion . . . "What do you think, Bill?"

Tommy. Mmmmm, "Oh, hooty, hooty, hoo."

Cynthia. But why count on him? There are lots of other nice guys.

Tommy. You don't think he'd go for me, do you?

Cynthia *(trying to be diplomatic).* Perhaps you're not really his type.

Tommy. Maybe not, but he's mine. I'm so lonesome . . . I'm *lonesome* . . . I want somebody to love. Somebody to say . . . "That's all right," when the World treats me mean.

Cynthia. Tommy, I think you're too good for Bill.

Tommy. I don't wanta hear that. The last man that told me I was too good for him . . . was tryin' to get away. He's good enough for me. *(Straightening room.)*

Cynthia. Leave the room alone. What we need is a little more sex appeal and a little less washing, cooking and ironing. *(Tommy puts down the room straightening.)* One more thing . . . do you have to wear that wig?

Tommy *(a little sensitive).* I like how your hair looks. But some of the naturals I don't like. Can see all the lint caught up in the hair like it hasn't been combed since know not when. You a Muslim?

Cynthia. No.

Tommy. I'm just sick-a hair, hair, hair. Do it this way, don't do it, leave it natural, straighten it, process, no process. I get sick-a hair and talkin' 'bout it and foolin' with it. That's why I wear the wig.

Cynthia. I'm sure your own must be just as nice or nicer than that.

Tommy. It oughta be. I only paid nineteen ninety five for this.

Cynthia. You ought to go back to usin' your own.

Tommy *(tensely).* I'll be givin' that some thought.

Cynthia. You're pretty nice people just as you are. Soften up, Tommy. You might surprise yourself.

Tommy. I'm listenin'.

Cynthia. Expect more. Learn to let men open doors for you . . .

Tommy. What if I'm standin' there and they don't open it?

Cynthia *(trying to level with her)*. You're a fine person. He wants to paint you, that's all. He's doing a kind of mural thing and we thought he would enjoy painting you. I'd hate to see you expecting more out of the situation than what's there.

Tommy. Forget it, sweetie-pie, don' nothin' happen that's not suppose to. *(Sound of laughter in the hall. Bill, Oldtimer and Sonny-man enter.)*

Bill. No Chinese restaurant left, baby! It's wiped out. Gone with the revolution.

Sonny-man *(to Cynthia)*. Baby, let's move, split the scene, get on with it, time for home.

Bill. The revolution is here. Whatta you do with her? You paint her!

Sonny-man. You write her . . . you write the revolution. I'm gonna write the revolution into a novel nine hundred pages long.

Bill. Dance it! Sing it! "Down in the cornfield Hear dat mournful sound . . . *(Sonny-man and Oldtimer harmonize.)* Dear old Massa am-a sleepin' A-sleepin' in the cold, cold ground." Now for "Wine In The Wilderness!" Triptych will be finished.

Cynthia *(in Bill's face)*. "Wine In The Wilderness," huh? Exploitation!

Sonny-man. Upstairs, all out, come on, Oldtimer. Folks can't create in a crowd. Cynthia, move it, baby.

Oldtimer *(starting toward the window)*. My things! I got a package.

Sonny-man *(heads him off)*. Up and out. You don't have to go home, but you have to get outta here. Happy paintin', yall. *(One backward look and they are all gone.)*

Bill. Whatta night, whatta night, whatta night, baby. It will be painted, written, sung and discussed for generations.

Tommy *(notices nothing that looks like Chinese food; he is carrying a small bag and a container)*. Where's the Foo-Yong?

Bill. They blew the restaurant, baby. All I could get was a couple-a franks and a orange drink from the stand.

Tommy *(tersely)*. You brought me a frank-footer? That's what you think-a me, a frank-footer?

Bill. Nothin' to do with what I think. Place is closed.

Tommy *(quietly surly)*. This is the damn City-a New York, any hour on the clock they sellin' the chicken in the basket, barbecue ribs, pizza pie, hot pastrami samitches; and you brought me a frank-footer?

Bill. Baby, don't break bad over somethin' to eat. The smart set, the jet, the beautiful people, kings and queens eat frankfurters.

Tommy. If a queen sent you out to buy her a bucket-a Foo-yung, you wouldn't come back with no lonely-ass frank-footer.

Bill. Kill me 'bout it, baby! Go 'head and shoot me six times. That's the trouble with our women, yall always got your mind on food.

Tommy. Is that our trouble? *(Laughs.)* Maybe you right. Only two things to do. Either eat the frankfooter or walk on outta here. You got any mustard?

Bill *(gets mustard from the refrigerator)*. Let's face it, our folks are not together. The brothers and sisters have busted up Harlem, . . . no plan, no nothin'.

There's your black revolution, heads whipped, hospital full and we still in the same old bag.

Tommy *(seated at the kitchen table)*. Maybe what everybody need is somebody like you, who know how things oughta go, to get on out there and start some action.

Bill. You still mad about the frankfurter?

Tommy. No. I keep seein' pitchers of what was in my room and how it all must be spoiled now. *(Sips the orange drink.)* A orange never been near this. Well, it's cold. *(Looking at an incense burner.)* What's that?

Bill. An incense burner, was given to me by the Chinese guy, Richard Lee. I'm sorry they blew his restaurant.

Tommy. Does it help you to catch the number?

Bill. No, baby, I just burn incense sometime.

Tommy. For what?

Bill. Just 'cause I feel like it. Baby, ain't you used to nothin'?

Tommy. Ain't used to burnin' incent for nothin'.

Bill *(laughs)*. Burnin' what?

Tommy. That stuff.

Bill. What did you call it?

Tommy. Incent.

Bill. It's not incent, baby. It's incense.

Tommy. Like the sense you got in your head. In-sense. Thank you. You're a very correctable person, ain't you?

Bill. Let's put you on canvas.

Tommy *(stubbornly)*. I have to eat first.

Bill. That's another thing 'bout black women, they wanta eat 'fore they do anything else. Tommy, . . . Tommy, . . . I bet your name is Thomasina. You look like a Thomasina.

Tommy. You could sit there and guess til your eyes pop out and you never would guess my first name. You might could guess the middle name but not the first one.

Bill. Tell it to me.

Tommy. My name is Tomorrow.

Bill. How's that?

Tommy. Tomorrow, . . . like yesterday and *tomorrow*, and the middle name is just plain Marie. That's what my father name me, Tomorrow Marie. My mother say he thought it had a pretty sound.

Bill. Crazy! I never met a girl named Tomorrow.

Tommy. They got to callin' me Tommy for short, so I stick with that. Tomorrow Marie, . . . Sound like a promise that can never happen.

Bill *(straightens chair on stand; he is very eager to start painting)*. That's what Shakespeare said, . . . "Tomorrow and tomorrow and tomorrow." Tomorrow, you will be on this canvas.

Tommy *(still uneasy about being painted)*. What's the hurry? Rome wasn't built in a day, . . . that's another saying.

Bill. If I finish in time, I'll enter you in the exhibition.

Tommy *(loses interest in the food. Examines the room. Looks at portrait on the wall)*. He looks like somebody I know or maybe saw before.

Bill. That's Frederick Douglass. A man who used to be a slave. He escaped and spent his life trying to make us all free. He was a great man.

Tommy. Thank you, Mr. Douglass. Who's the light colored man? *(Indicates a frame next to the Douglass.)*

Bill. He's white. That's John Brown. They killed him for tryin' to shoot the country outta the slavery bag. He dug us, you know. Old John said, "Hell no, slavery must go."

Tommy. I heard all about him. Some folks say he was crazy.

Bill. If he had been shootin' at *us* they wouldn't have called him a nut.

Tommy. School wasn't a great part-a my life.

Bill. If it was you wouldn't-a found out too much 'bout black history cause the books full-a nothin' but whitey, . . . all except the white ones who dug us, . . . they not there either. Tell me, . . . who was Elijah Lovejoy?

Tommy. Elijah Lovejoy, . . . Mmmmmmm. I don't know. Have to do with the Bible?

Bill. No, that's another white fella, . . . Elijah had a printin' press and the main thing he printed was "Slavery got to go." Well the man moved in on him, smashed his press time after time . . . but he kept puttin' it back together and doin' his thing. So, one final day, they came in a mob and burned him to death.

Tommy *(blows her nose with sympathy as she fights tears).* That's dirty.

Bill *(as Tommy glances at titles in book case).* Who was Monroe Trotter?

Tommy. Was he white?

Bill. No, soul brother. Spent his years tryin' to make it all right. Who was Harriet Tubman?

Tommy. I heard-a her. But don't put me through no test, Billy. *(Moving around studying pictures and books.)* This room is full-a things I don' know nothin' about. How'll I get to know?

Bill. Read, go to the library, book stores, ask somebody.

Tommy. Okay, I'm askin'. Teach me things.

Bill. Aw, baby, why torment yourself? Trouble with our women, . . . they all wanta be great brains. Leave somethin' for a man to do.

Tommy *(eager to impress him).* What you think-a Martin Luther King?

Bill. A great guy. But it's too late in the day for the singin' and prayin' now.

Tommy. What about Malcolm X?

Bill. Great cat . . . but there again . . . Where's the program?

Tommy. What about Adam Powell? I voted for him. That's one thing bout me. I vote. Maybe if everybody vote for the right people . . .

Bill. The ballot box. It would take me all my life to straighten you on that hype.

Tommy. I got the time.

Bill. You gonna wind up with a king size headache. The Matriarchy gotta go. Yall throw them suppers together, keep your husband happy, raise the kids.

Tommy. I don't have a husband. Course, that could be fixed. *(Leaving the unspoken proposal hanging in the air.)*

Bill. You know the greatest thing you could do for your people? Sit up there and let me put you down on canvas.

Tommy. Bein' married and havin' a family might be good for your people as a race, but I was thinkin' bout myself a little.

Bill. Forget yourself sometime, sugar. On that canvas you'll be givin' and givin' and givin' . . . That's where you can do you thing best. What you stallin' for?

Tommy *(returns to table and sits in chair).* I . . . I don't want to pose in this outfit.

Bill *(patience is wearing thin).* Why, baby, why?

Tommy. I don't feel proud-a myself in this.

Bill. Art, baby, we talkin' art. Whatcha want ˙. . . Ribbons? Lace? False eyelashes?

Tommy. No, just my white dress with the orlon sweater, . . . or anything but this what I'm wearin'. You oughta see me in that dress with my pink linen shoes. Oh, hell, the shoes are gone. I forgot 'bout the fire . . .

Bill. Oh, stop fightin' me! Another thing . . . our women don't know a damn thing bout bein' feminine. *Give in* sometime. It won't kill you. You tellin' me how to paint? Maybe you oughta hang out your shingle and give art lessons! You too damn opinionated. You gonna pose or you not gonna pose? Say somethin'!

Tommy. You makin' me nervous! Hollerin' at me. My mama never holler at me. Hollerin'.

Bill. I'll soon be too tired to pick up the brush, baby.

Tommy *(eye catches picture of white woman on the wall).* That's a white woman! Bet you never hollered at her and I bet she's your girlfriend . . . too, and when she posed for her pitcher I bet yall was laughin' . . . and you didn't buy her no frankfooter!

Bill *(feels a bit smug about his male prowess).* Awww, come on, cut that out, baby. That's a little blonde, blue-eyed chick who used to pose for me. That ain't where it's at. This is a new day, the deal is goin' down different. This is the black moment, doll. Black, black, black is bee-yoo-tee-full. Got it? *Black is beautiful.*

Tommy. Then how come it is that I don't *feel* beautiful when you *talk* to me?!!

Bill. That's your hang-up, not mine. You supposed to stretch forth your wings like Ethiopia, shake off them chains that been holdin' you down. Langston Hughes said let 'em see how beautiful you are. But you determined not to ever be beautiful. Okay, that's what makes you Tommy.

Tommy. Do you have a girl friend? And who is she?

Bill *(now enjoying himself to the utmost).* Naw, naw, naw, doll. I *know* people, but none-a this "tie-you-up-and-I-own-you" jive. I ain't mistreatin' nobody and there's enough-a me to go around. That's another thing with our women, . . . they wanta *latch* on. Learn to play it by ear, roll with the punches, cut down on some-a this "got-you-to-the-grave" kinda relationship. Was today all right? Good, be glad, . . . take what's at hand because tomorrow never comes, it's always today. *(She begins to cry.)* Awwww, I didn't mean it that way . . . I forgot your name. *(He brushes her tears away.)* You act like I belong to you. You're jealous of a picture?

Tommy. That's how women are, always studyin' each other and wonderin' how they look up 'gainst the next person.

Bill *(a bit smug).* That's human nature. Whatcha call healthy competition.

Tommy. You think she's pretty?

Bill. She was, perhaps still is. Long, silky hair. She could sit on her hair.

Tommy *(with bitter arrogance).* Doesn't *everybody?*

Bill. You got a head like a rock and gonna have the last word if it kills you. Baby, I bet you could knock out Mohamud Ali in the first round, then rare back and scream like Tarzan . . . "Now, I am the greatest!" *He is very close to her and is amazed to feel a great sense of physical attraction.)* What we arguin' bout? *(Looks her over as she looks away. He suddenly wants to put the conversation on a more intimate level. His eye is on the bed.)* Maybe tomorrow would be a better time for paintin'. Wanna freshen up, take a bath, baby? Water's nice n' hot.

Tommy *(knows the sound and turns to check on the look; notices him watching the bed; starts weeping).* No, I don't! Nigger!

Bill. Was that nice? What the hell, let's paint the picture. Or are you gonna hold that back too?

Tommy. I'm posin'. Shall I take off the wig?

Bill. No, it's a part of your image, ain't it? You must have a reason for wearin' it. *(Tommy snatches up her orange drink and sits in the model's chair.)*

Tommy *(with defiance).* Yes, I wear it cause you and those like you go for long, silky hair, and this is the only way I can have some without burnin' my mother-grabbin' brains out. Got it? *(She accidentally knocks over container of orange drink into her lap.)* Hell, I can't wear this. I'm soaked through. I'm not gonna catch no double pneumonia sittin' up here wringin' wet while you paint and holler at me.

Bill. Bitch!

Tommy. You must be talkin' bout your mama!

Bill. Shut up! Aw, shut-up! *(Phone rings. He finds an African throw-cloth and hands it to her.)* Put this on. Relax, don't go way mad, and all the rest-a that jazz. Change, will you? I apologize. I'm sorry. *(He picks up phone.)* Hello, survivor of a riot speaking. Who's calling? *(Tommy retires behind the screen with the throw. During the conversation she undresses and wraps the throw around her. We see Tommy and Bill, but they can't see each other.)* Sure, told you not to worry. I'll be ready for the exhibit. If you don't dig it, don't show it. Not time for you to see it yet. Yeah, yeah, next week. You just make sure your exhibition room is big enough to hold the crowds that's gonna congregate to see this fine chick I got here. *(This perks Tommy's ears up.)* You oughta see her. The finest black woman in the world . . . No, . . . the finest *any* woman in the world . . . This gorgeous satin chick is . . . is . . . black velvet moonlight . . . an ebony queen of the universe . . . *(Tommy can hardly believe her ears.)* One look at her and you go back to Spice Islands . . . She's Mother Africa . . . You flip, double flip. She has come through everything that has been put on her . . . *(He unveils the gorgeous woman he has painted . . . "Wine In The Wilderness." Tommy believes he is talking about her.)* Regal . . . grand . . . magnificent, fantastic . . . You would vote her the woman you'd most like to meet on a desert island, or around the corner from anywhere. She's here with me now . . . and I don't know if I want to show her to you or anybody else . . . I'm beginnin' to have this deep attachment . . . She sparkles, man, Harriet Tubman, Queen of the Nile . . . sweetheart, wife, mother, sister, friend . . . The night . . . a black diamond . . . A dark, beautiful dream . . . A cloud with a silvery lining . . . Her wrath is a storm over the Bahamas. "Wine In The Wilderness" . . . The memory of Africa . . . The *now* of things . . . but best of all and most important . . . She's tomorrow . . . she's my tomorrow . . . *(Tommy is dressed in the African wrap. She is suddenly awakened to the feeling of being loved and admired. She removes the wig and fluffs her hair. Her hair under the wig must not be an accurate, well-cut Afro . . . but should be rather attractive natural hair. She studies herself in a mirror. We see her taller, more relaxed and sure of herself. Perhaps braided hair will go well with Afro robe.)*Aw, man, later. You don't believe in nothin'! *(He covers "Wine In The Wilderness." Is now in a glowing mood.)* Baby, whenever you ready. *(She emerges from behind the screen. Dressed in the wrap, sans wig. He is astounded.)* Baby, what . . .? Where . . . where's the wig?

Tommy. I don't think I want to wear it, Bill.

Bill. That is very becoming . . . the drape thing.

Tommy. Thank you.

Bill. I don't know what to say.

Tommy. It's time to paint. *(Steps up on the model stand and sits in the chair. She is now a queen, relaxed and smiling her appreciation for his past speech to the art dealer. Her feet are bare.)*

Bill *(mystified by the change in her; tries to do a charcoal sketch).* It is quite late.

Tommy. Makes me no difference if it's all right with you.

Bill *(wants to create the other image).* Could you put the wig back on?

Tommy. You don't really like wigs, do you?

Bill. Well, no.

Tommy. Then let's have things the way you like.

Bill *(has no answer for this. He makes a haphazard line or two as he tries to remember the other image).* Tell me something about yourself, . . . anything.

Tommy *(now on sure ground).* I was born in Baltimore, Maryland and raised here in Harlem. My favorite flower is " Four O'clocks," that's a bush flower. My wearin' flower, corsage flower, is pink roses. My mama raised me, mostly by herself, God rest the dead. Mama belonged to "The Eastern Star." Her father was a "Mason." If a man in the family is a "Mason" any woman related to him can be an "Eastern Star." My grandfather was a member of "The Prince Hall Lodge." I had a uncle who was an "Elk," . . . a member of "The Improved Benevolent Protective Order of Elks of the World": "The Henry Lincoln Johnson Lodge." You know, the white "Elks" are called "The Benevolent Protective Order of Elks" but the black "Elks" are called "The *Improved* Benevolent Protective Order of Elks of the World." That's because the black "Elks" got the copyright first but the white "Elks" took us to court about it to keep us from usin' the name. Over fifteen hundred black folk went to jail for wearin' the "Elk" emblem on their coat lapel. Years ago, . . . that's what you call history.

Bill. I didn't know about that.

Tommy. Oh, it's understandable. Only way I heard bout John Brown was because the black "Elks" bought his farmhouse where he trained his men to attack the government.

Bill. The black "Elks" bought the John Brown Farm? What did they do with it?

Tommy. They built a outdoor theatre and put a perpetual light in his memory,

. . . and they buildin' cottages there, one named for each state in the union and . . .

Bill. How do you know about it?

Tommy. Well, our "Elks" helped my cousin go through school with a scholarship. She won a speaking contest and wrote a composition titled "Onward and Upward, O, My Race." That's how she won the scholarship. Coreen knows all that Elk history.

Bill *(seeing her with new eyes).* Tell me some more about you, Tomorrow Marie. I bet you go to church.

Tommy. Not much as I used to. Early in life I pledged myself in the A.M.E. Zion Church.

Bill *(studying her face, seeing her for the first time).* A.M.E.

Tommy. A.M.E. That's African Methodist Episcopal. We split off from the white Methodist Episcopal and started our own in the year Seventeen hundred and ninety six. We built our first buildin' in the year 1800. How bout that?

Bill. That right?

Tommy. Oh, I'm just showin' off. I taught Sunday School for two years and you had to know the history of A.M.E. Zion . . . or else you couldn't teach. My great, great grandparents was slaves.

Bill. Guess everybody's was.

Tommy. Mine was slaves in a place called Sweetwater Springs, Virginia. We tried to look it up one time but somebody at Church told us that Sweetwater Springs had become a part of Norfolk . . . so we didn't carry it any further . . . As it would be a expense to have a lawyer trace your people.

Bill *(throws charcoal pencil across room).* No good! It won't work! I can't work anymore.

Tommy. Take a rest. Tell me about you.

Bill *(sits on bed).* Everybody in my family worked for the Post Office. They bought a home in Jamaica, Long Island. Everybody on that block bought an aluminum screen door with a duck on it, . . . or was it a swan? I guess that makes my favorite flower crab grass and hedges. I have a lot of bad dreams. *(Tommy massages his temples and the back of his neck.)* A dream like suffocating, dying of suffocation. The worst kinda dream. People are standing in a weird looking art gallery, they're looking and laughing at everything I've ever done. My work begins to fade off the canvas, right before my eyes. Everything I've ever done is laughed away.

Tommy. Don't be so hard on yourself. If I was smart as you I'd wake up singin' every mornin'. *(There is the sound of thunder. He kisses her.)* When it thunders that's the angels in heaven playin' with their hoops, rollin' their hoops and bicycle wheels in the rain. My Mama told me that.

Bill. I'm glad you're here. Black is beautiful, you're beautiful, A.M.E. Zion, Elks, pink roses, bush flower, . . . blooming out of the slavery of Sweetwater Springs, Virginia.

Tommy. I'm gonna take a bath and let the riot and the hell of living go down the drain with the bath water.

Bill. Tommy, Tommy, Tomorrow Marie, let's save each other, let's be kind and good to each other while it rains and the angels roll those hoops and bicycle wheels. *(They embrace. The sound of rain.)*

(Music in as lights come down. As lights fade down to darkness, music

comes in louder. There is a flash of lightning. We see Tommy and Bill in each other's arms. It is very dark. Music up louder, then softer and down to very soft. Music is mixed with the sound of rain beating against the window. Music slowly fades as gray light of dawn shows at window. Lights go up gradually. The bed is rumpled and empty. Bill is in the bathroom. Tommy is at the stove turning off the coffee pot. She sets table with cups and saucers, spoons. Tommy's hair is natural, she wears another throw draped around her. She sings and hums a snatch of a joyous spiritual.)

Tommy. "Great day, Great day, the world's on fire, Great day . . . " *(Calling out to Bill who is in bath.)* Honey, I found the coffee, and it's ready. Nothin' here to go with it but a cucumber and a Uneeda biscuit.

Bill *(offstage; joyous yell from offstage).* Tomorrow and tomorrow and tomorrow! Good mornin', Tomorrow!

Tommy *(more to herself than to Bill).* "Tomorrow and tomorrow." That's Shakespeare. *(Calls to Bill.)* You say that was Shakespeare?

Bill *(offstage).* Right, baby, right!

Tommy. I bet Shakespeare was black! You know how we love poetry. That's what give him away. I bet he was passin'. *(Laughs.)*

Bill *(offstage).* Just you wait, one hundred years from now all the honkys gonna claim our poets just like they stole our blues. They gonna try to steal Paul Laurence Dunbar and LeRoi and Margaret Walker.

Tommy *(to herself).* God moves in a mysterious way, even in the middle of a riot. *(A knock on the door.)* Great day, great day the world's on fire . . . *(Opens the door. Oldtimer enters. He is soaking wet. He does not recognize her right away.)*

Oldtimer. 'Scuse me, I must be in the wrong place.

Tommy *(patting her hair).* This is me. Come on in, Edmond Lorenzo Matthews. I took off my hair-piece. This is me.

Oldtimer *(very distracted and worried).* Well, howdy-do and good mornin'. *(He has had a hard night of drinking and sleeplessness.)* Where Bill-boy? It pourin' down some rain out there. *(Makes his way to the window.)*

Tommy. What's the matter?

Oldtimer *(raises the window and starts pulling in the cord, the cord is weightless and he realizes there is nothing on the end of it).* No, no, it can't be. Where is it? It's gone! *(Looks out the window.)*

Tommy. You gonna catch your death. You wringin' wet.

Oldtimer. Yall take my things in? It was a bag-a loot. A suit and some odds and ends. It was my loot. Yall took it in?

Tommy. No. *(Realizes his desperation. She calls to Bill through the closed bathroom door.)* Did you take in any loot that was outside the window?

Bill *(offstage).* No.

Tommy. He said "no."

Oldtimer *(yells out window).* Thieves, . . . dirty thieves . . . lotta good it'll do you . . .

Tommy *(leads him to a chair, dries his head with a towel).* Get outta the wet things. You smell just like a whiskey still. Why don't you take care of yourself. *(Dries off his hands.)*

Oldtimer. Drinkin' with the boys. Likker was everywhere all night long.

Tommy. You got to be better than this.

Oldtimer. Everything I ever put my hand and mind to do, it turn out wrong, . . . Nothin' but mistakes . . . When you don' know, you don' know. I don' know nothin'. I'm ignorant.

Tommy. Hush that talk . . . You know lotsa things, everybody does. *(Helps him remove wet coat.)*

Oldtimer. Thanks. How's the trip-tick?

Tommy. The what?

Oldtimer. *Trip-tick.* That's a paintin'.

Tommy. See there, you know more about art than I do. What's a trip-tick? Have some coffee and explain me a trip-tick.

Oldtimer *(proud of his knowledge).* Well, I tell you, . . . a trip-tick is a paintin' that's in three parts . . . but they all belong together to be looked at all at once. Now . . . this is the first one . . . a little innocent girl . . . *(Unveils picture.)*

Tommy. She's sweet.

Oldtimer. And this is "Wine In The Wilderness" . . . The Queen of the Universe . . . the finest chick in the world.

Tommy *(Tommy is thoughtful as he unveils the second picture).* That's not me.

Oldtimer. No, you gonna be this here last one. The worst gal in town. A messed-up chick that—that—*(He unveils the third canvas and is face to face with the almost blank canvas, then realizes what he has said. He turns to see the stricken look on Tommy's face.)*

Tommy. The messed-up chick, *that's* why they brought me here, ain't it? That's why he wanted to paint me! Say it!

Oldtimer. No, I'm lyin', I didn't mean it. It's the society that messed her up. Awwwwww, Tommy, don't look that-a-way. It's art, . . . it's only art . . . He couldn't mean you . . . it's art . . . *(The door opens. Cynthia and Sonny-man enter.)*

Sonny-man. Any body want a ride down . . . down . . . down . . . downtown? What's wrong? Excuse me . . . *(Starts back out.)*

Tommy *(blocking the exit to Cynthia and Sonny-man).* No, come on in. Stay with it . . . "Brother" . . . "Sister." Tell 'em what a trip-tick is, Oldtimer.

Cynthia *(very ashamed).* Oh, no.

Tommy. You don't have to tell 'em. They already know. The messed-up chick! How come you didn't pose for that, my sister? The messed-up chick lost her home last night, . . . burnt out with no place to go. You and Sonny-man gave me comfort, you cheered me up and took me in, . . . *took me in!*

Cynthia. Tommy, we didn't know you, we didn't mean . . .

Tommy. It's all right! I was lost but now I'm found! Yeah, the blind can see! *She dashes behind the screen and puts on her clothing, sweater, skirt etc.)*

Oldtimer *(goes to bathroom door).* Billy, come out!

Sonny-man. Billy, step out here, please! *(Bill enters shirtless, wearing dungarees.)* Oldtimer let it out 'bout the triptych.

Bill. The rest of you move on.

Tommy *(looking out from behind screen).* No, don't go a step. You brought me here, see me out!

Bill. Tommy, let me explain it to you.

Tommy *(coming out from behind screen).* I gotta check out my apartment, and my clothes and money. Cynthia, . . . I can't wait for anybody to open the door or look out for me and all that kinda crap you talk. A bunch-a liars!

Bill. Oldtimer, why you . . .

Tommy. Leave him the hell alone. He ain't said nothin' that ain' so!

Sonny-man. Explain to the sister that some mistakes have been made.

Bill. Mistakes have been made, baby. The mistakes were yesterday, this is today . . .

Tommy. Yeah, and I'm Tomorrow, remember? Trouble is I was Tommin' to you, to all of you, . . . "Oh, maybe they gon' like me." . . . I was your fool, thinkin' writers and painters know moren' me, that maybe a little bit of you would rub off on me.

Cynthia. We are wrong. I knew it yesterday. Tommy, I told you not to expect anything out of this . . . this arrangement.

Bill. This is a relationship, not an arrangement.

Sonny-man. Cynthia, I tell you all the time, keep outta other people's business. What the hell you got to do with who's gonna get what outta what? You and Oldtimer, yakkin' and yakkin'. *(To Oldtimer.)* Man, your mouth gonna kill you.

Bill. It's me and Tommy. Clear the room.

Tommy. Better not. I'll kill him! The "black people" this and the "Afro-American" . . . that . . . You ain' got no use for none-a us. Oldtimer, you their fool too. 'Til I got here they didn't even know your damn name. There's something inside-a me that says I ain' suppose to let *nobody* play me cheap. Don't care how much they know! *(She sweeps some of the books to the floor.)*

Bill. Don't you have any forgiveness in you? Would I be beggin' you if I didn't care? Can't you be generous enough . . .

Tommy. Nigger, I been too damn generous with you, already. All-a these people know I wasn't down here all night posin' for no pitcher, nigger!

Bill. Cut that out, Tommy, and you not going anywhere!

Tommy. You wanna bet? Nigger!

Bill. Okay, you called it, baby, I did act like a low, degraded person . . .

Tommy *(combing out her wig with her fingers while holding it).* Didn't call you no low, degraded person. Nigger! *(To Cynthia who is handing her a comb.)* "Do you have to wear a wig?" Yes! To soften the blow when yall go up side-a my head with a baseball bat. *(Going back to taunting Bill and ignoring Cynthia's comb.)* Nigger!

Bill. That's enough-a that. You right and you're wrong too.

Tommy. Ain't a-one-a us you like that's alive and walkin' by you on the street . . . you don't like flesh and blood niggers.

Bill. Call me that, baby, but don't call yourself. That what you think of yourself?

Tommy. If a black somebody is in a history book, or printed on a pitcher, or drawed on a paintin', . . . or if they're a statue, . . . dead, and outta the way, and can't talk back, then you dig 'em and full-a so much-a damn admiration and talk 'bout *"our"* history. But when you run into us livin' and breathin' ones, with the life's blood still pumpin' through us, . . . then you comin' on 'bout how we ain' never together. You hate us, that's what! *You hate black me!*

Bill *(stung to the heart, confused and saddened by the half truth which applies to himself).* I never hated you, I never will, no matter what you or any of the rest of you do to *make* me hate you. I won't! Hell, woman, why do you say that! Why would I hate you?

Tommy. Maybe I look too much like the mother that give birth to you. Like the Ma and Pa that worked in the post office to buy you a house and a screen door with a damn duck on it. And you so ungrateful you didn't even like it.

Bill. No, I didn't, baby. I don't like screen doors with ducks on 'em.

Tommy. You didn't like who was livin' behind them screen doors. Phoney Nigger!

Bill. That's all! Damnit! don't go there no more!

Tommy. Hit me, so I can tear this place down and scream bloody murder.

Bill *(somewhere between laughter and tears).* Looka here, baby, I'm willin' to say I'm wrong, even in fronta the room fulla people . . .

Tommy *(through clenched teeth).* Nigger.

Sonny-man. The sister is upset.

Tommy. And you stop callin' me "the" sister, . . . if you feelin' so brotherly why don't you say "my" sister? Ain't no we-ness in your talk. "The" Afro-American, "the" black man, there's no we-ness in you. Who you think you are?

Sonny-man. I was talkin' in general er . . . *my* sister, 'bout the masses.

Tommy. There he go again. "The" masses. Tryin' to make out like we pitiful and you got it made. You the masses your damn self and don't even know it. *(Another angry look at Bill.)* Nigger.

Bill *(pulls dictionary from shelf).* Let's get this ignorant "nigger" talk squared away. You can stand some education.

Tommy. You *treat* me like a nigger, that's what. I'd rather be called one than treated that way.

Bill *(questions Tommy).* What is a nigger? *(Talks as he is trying to find word.)* A nigger is a low, degraded person, *any* low degraded person. I learned that from my teacher in the fifth grade.

Tommy. Fifth grade is a liar! Don't pull that dictionary crap on me.

Bill *(pointing to the book).* Webster's New World Dictionary of The American Language, College Edition.

Tommy. I don't need to find out what no college white folks say nigger is.

Bill. I'm tellin' you it's a low, degraded person. Listen. *(Reads from the book.)* Nigger, N-i-g-g-e-r, . . . A Negro . . . A member of any dark-skinned people . . . Damn. *(Amazed by dictionary description.)*

Sonny-man. Brother Malcolm *said* that's what they meant, . . . nigger is a Negro, Negro is a nigger.

Bill *(slowly finishing his reading).* A vulgar, offensive term of hostility and contempt. Well, so much for the fifth grade teacher.

Sonny-man. No, they do not call low, degraded white folks niggers. Come to think of it, did you ever hear whitey call Hitler a nigger? Now if some whitey digs us, . . . the others might call him a nigger-*lover*, but they don't call him no nigger.

Oldtimer. No, they don't.

Tommy *(near tears).* When they say "nigger," just dry-long-so, they mean educated you and uneducated me. They hate you and call you "nigger," I called you "nigger" but I love you. *(There is dead silence in the room for a split second.)*

Sonny-man *(trying to establish peace).* There you go. There you go.

Cynthia *(cautioning Sonny-man)*. Now is not the time to talk, darlin'.

Bill. You love me? Tommy, that's the greatest compliment you could . . .

Tommy *(sorry she said it)*. You must be runnin' a fever, nigger, I ain' said nothin' 'bout lovin' you.

Bill *(in a great mood)*. You did, yes, you did.

Tommy. Well, you didn't say it to *me*.

Bill. Oh, Tommy, . . .

Tommy *(cuts him off abruptly)*. And don't you dare say it now. I'm tellin' you, . . . it ain't to be said now. *Checks through her paper bag to see if she has everything. Starts to put on the wig, changes her mind, holds it to end of scene. Turns to the others in the room)* Oldtimer, . . . my brothers and my sister.

Oldtimer. I wish I was a thousand miles away, I'm so sorry. *(He sits at the foot of the model stand.)*

Tommy. I don't stay mad, it's here today and gone tomorrow. I'm sorry your feelin's got hurt, . . . but when I'm hurt I turn and hurt back. Somewhere, in the middle of last night, I thought the old me was gone, . . . lost forever, and gladly. But today was flippin' time, so back I flipped. Now it's "turn the other cheek" time. If I can go through life other-cheekin' the white folk, . . . guess yall can be other-cheeked too. But I'm goin' back to the nitty-gritty crowd, where the talk is we-ness and us-ness. I hate to do it but I have to thank you cause I'm walkin' out with much more than I brought in. *(Goes over and looks at the queen in the "Wine In The Wilderness" painting.)* Tomorrow-Marie had such a lovely yesterday. *(Bill takes her hand, she gently removes it from his grasp.)* Bill, I don't have to wait for anybody's by-your-leave to be a "Wine In The Wilderness" woman. I can be it if I wanta, . . . and I *am.* I am. I am. I'm not the one you made up and painted, the very pretty lady who can't talk back, . . . but I'm "Wine In The Wilderness" . . . alive and kickin', me . . . Tomorrow-Marie, cussin' and fightin' and lookin' out for my damn self cause ain' nobody else 'round to do it, dontcha know. And, Cynthia, if my hair is straight, or if it's natural, or if I wear a wig, or take it off, . . . that's all right; because wigs . . . shoes . . . hats . . . bags . . . and even this . . . *(She picks up the African throw she wore a few moments before . . . fingers it.)* They're just what you call . . . access . . . *(Fishing for the word.)* . . . like what you wear with your Easter outfit . . .

Cynthia. Accessories.

Tommy. Thank you, my sister. Accessories. Somethin' you add on or take off. The real thing is takin' place on the inside . . . that's where the action is. That's "Wine In The Wilderness," . . . a woman that's a real one and a good one. And yall just better believe I'm it. *(She proceeds to the door.)*

Bill. Tommy. *(She turns. He takes the beautiful queen, "Wine In The Wilderness" from the easel.)* She's not it at all, Tommy. This chick on the canvas, . . . nothin' but accessories, a dream. I drummed up outta the junk room of my mind. *(Places the "queen" to one side.)* You are and . . . *(Points to Oldtimer.)* . . . Edmund Lorenzo Matthews . . . the real beautiful people, . . . Cynthia . . .

Cynthia *(bewildered and unbelieving)*. Who? Me?

Bill. Yeah, honey, you and Sonny-man, don't know how beautiful you are. *(Indicates the other side of model stand.)* Sit there.

Sonny-man *(places cushions on the floor at the foot of the model stand)*. Just sit here and be my beautiful self. *(To Cynthia.)* Turn on, baby, we gonna get our picture took. *(Cynthia smiles.)*

Bill. Now there's Oldtimer, the guy who was here before there were scholarships and grants and stuff like that, the guy they kept outta the schools, the man the factories wouldn't hire, the union wouldn't let him join . . .

Sonny-man. Yeah, yeah, rap to me. Where you goin' with it, man? Rap on.

Bill. I'm makin' a triptych.

Sonny-man. Make it, man.

Bill *(indicating Cynthia and Sonny-man).* On the other side, Young Man and Woman, workin' together to do our thing.

Tommy *(quietly).* I'm goin' now.

Bill. But you belong up there in the center, "Wine In The Wilderness" . . . that's who you are. *(Moves the canvas of "the little girl" and places a sketch pad on the easel.)* The nightmare, about all that I've done disappearing before my eyes. It was a good nightmare. I was painting in the dark, all head and no heart. I couldn't see until you came, baby. *(To Cynthia, Sonny-man and Oldtimer.)* Look at Tomorrow. She came through the biggest riot of all, . . . somethin' called "Slavery," and she's even comin' through the "now" scene, . . . folks laughin' at her, even her own folks laughin' at her. And look *how* . . . with her head high like she's poppin' her fingers at the world. *(Takes up charcoal pencil and tears old page off sketch pad so he can make a fresh drawing.)* Aw, let me put it down, Tommy. "Wine In The Wilderness," you gotta let me put it down so all the little boys and girls can look up and see you on the wall. And you know what they're gonna say? "Hey, don't she look like somebody we know?" *(Tommy slowly returns and takes her seat on the stand. Tommy is holding the wig in her lap. Her hands are very graceful looking against the texture of the wig.)* And they'll be right, you're somebody they know . . . *(He is sketching hastily. There is a sound of thunder and the patter of rain.)* Yeah, roll them hoops and bicycle wheels. *(Music in low. Music up higher as Bill continues to sketch.)*

Curtain.

QUESTIONS

1. What is symbolized by the fact that, while a riot is occurring outside, in Bill's apartment very little reference is made to it?

2. The creative artists, Bill the painter and Sonny-man the writer, are isolated in different places during the riot when the play opens. What might this symbolize?

3. Why does Tommy like Oldtimer right away? What does he recognize and like in her?

4. What does the name Tomorrow symbolize?

5. What is intended by the author at the point where everyone realizes that they do not know Oldtimer's real name?

6. Some of the advice Cynthia gives Tommy echoes the way Nora behaves in *A Doll's House.* Explain.

7. Bill, like Helmer, has a definite conception of women. In Bill's case, however, this extends only to "street" women. Draw a comparison between the conceptions of both men.

8. Why does Bill's inability to paint Tommy coincide with her recitation of a part of history he does not know?

TOPICS FOR WRITING

1. The *confidant* in a drama is a character to whom information is supplied. That information helps the audience to understand what a third character does not. Who are the *confidants* in *A Doll's House* and *Wine in the Wilderness*? What dimension do they add to the plays?

2. Aside from race and time, which differences exist between Tommy and Nora? In which ways are they similar?

3. Evidences of class differences are present in *A Doll's House* and in *Wine in the Wilderness*. Who or what defines these differences? What does Cynthia contribute to this alignment? Krogstad?

4. Although Childress uses the language of the street, and Ibsen uses the language of seventy years ago, how do the problems, aspirations, and personalities of Nora and Tommy find common ground?

5. What symbolism may be attached to the fact that Sonny-man and Cynthia lead Tommy to Bill's, but it is Oldtimer who reveals to her what she initially represented to them?

GLOSSARY OF
LITERARY TERMS

Act A major division of a play.

Affective fallacy The fallacy of wrongly evaluating a literary work by emphasizing only its emotional impact.

Allegory A narrative whose characters, symbols, and situations represent elements outside the text. For example, the character Christian in the allegory *Pilgrim's Progress* represents the Everyman who is a Christian.

Alliteration The repetition of consonant or vowel sounds at the beginning of words.

Allusion An indirect reference to some literary or historical figure or event. For example, the line in T. S. Eliot's *Love Song of J. Alfred Prufrock*, "No! I am not Prince Hamlet, nor was meant to be," is an allusion.

Ambiguity A literary device in which an author uses words with more than one meaning, deliberately leaving the reader uncertain.

Analogy A comparison of two different things on the basis of their similarity.

Anapest A metrical foot consisting of two unaccented syllables followed by an accented one (⌣ ⌣ /), as in the phrase "on the ship."

Antagonist A competitor or opponent of the main character (protagonist) in a work of literature.

Antihero A protagonist in a modern literary work who has none of the noble qualities associated with a traditional hero.

Antistrophe In a Greek play, the portion of the Chorus that responds to the comments made by the first part of the Chorus, the Strophe.

Antithesis A phrase that contains words whose meanings harshly contrast with each other and are in rhetorical balance. For example, Alexander Pope's "Man proposes, God disposes" is an antithesis.

Aphorism A terse, sharp statement of a large principle or idea. Thomas Hobbes's "The life of man, solitary, poor, nasty, brutish, and short" is an aphorism.

Apostrophe A direct, emotional address to an absent character or quality, as it if were present.

Archetype An image or character representative of some greater, more common element that recurs constantly and variously in literature.

Aside Lines in a play that are delivered not to another character but to the audience or to the speaker himself or herself.

Assonance The use of similar vowel sounds in adjacent or closeby words (for example, *slide* and *mind*).

Avant garde A term used to describe writing that is strikingly different from the dominant writing of the age—in its form, style, content, and attitude.

Ballad A poem originally sung or singable, recounting some domestic or heroic story, usually within a four-line stanza alternating three-beat and four-beat lines.

Bathos An unsuccessful attempt to arouse great emotion, becoming not grand but absurd or silly.

Blank verse Unrhymed lines of iambic pentameter.

Caesura A pause within a line of poetry, often created through punctuation.

Canto A division of certain long poems, such as Dante's *Divine Comedy* and Byron's *Don Juan.*

Carpe diem Latin for "seize the day," used in literature to describe poetry that examines temporary human pleasures against the backdrop of eternity—as in Marvell's "To His Coy Mistress."

Catharsis Exhaustion and cleansing of an audience member's emotions through participation in the events of a tragedy.

Character A person created by an author for use in a work of fiction, poetry, or drama.

Chorus A group of singers or actors who comment on and respond to the action in a play of classical Greece; also, a refrain in a song or poem.

Classicism A term deriving from the era of the ancient Greeks and Romans, used in English literature to describe the outlook of the eighteenth century, where writers celebrated the "classical" values of restraint, order, and stylistic elegance.

Cliché A phrase so overused that it has lost its original punch (for example, "beating a dead horse").

Climax A point at which the events in a play or story reach their crisis, where the maximum emotional reaction of the reader is created.

Coda A closing section of some literary works, occurring after the main action has been resolved.

Colloquialism A term used in speech but not acceptable in formal writing.

Colloquy A debate or conversation among characters.

Comedy A work of literature, often a play, whose first intention is to amuse and that ordinarily has a happy ending.

Comic relief A light, amusing section of a play or story that relieves tension and often comments by its humor on the surrounding serious action.

Complication A part of a plot in which the conflict among characters or forces is engaged.

Conceit A metaphor extended to great lengths in a poem (for example, Donne's "The Flea").

Conflict A struggle among opposing forces or characters in fiction, poetry, or drama.

Connotation Implications of words or sentences, beyond their literal, or denotative, meanings.

Consonance Repetition of consonant sounds within words.

Couplet Two lines of verse that have unity within themselves, often because they rhyme.

Cue In a play, words or action from one character that signal the start of another character's words or action.

Dactyl A metrical foot containing an accented syllable followed by two unaccented syllables (/ ⏑ ⏑), as in the word "craziness."

Denotation Literal meaning of a word or of sentences.

Denouement The final action of a plot, in which the conflict is resolved; the outcome.

Deus ex machina Literally, "God from a machine"—the improbable intervention of an outside force that arbitrarily resolves a conflict.

Dialogue Conversation between two people in fiction, drama, or poetry.

Diction The use of words; good diction is accurate and appropriate to the subject.

Dimeter A line of poetry composed of two metrical feet.

Dionysian A term referring to the ancient Greek values embraced by the god Dionysius and his worshipers—faith in the irrational and in the primacy of human emotions; often a descriptive term in literature.

Dramatic irony A term used to describe the effect of words of a character in a play that have more significance than they appear to have.

Dramatic monologue A poem spoken by a character other than the author (for example, Browning's "My Last Duchess").

Elegy A poetic meditation on death, often occasioned by the death of a specific individual.

End-stopped lines Lines of poetry completed with the pause of punctuation.

Enjambment Lines of poetry whose sense and grammar continue without a pause from one line into the next.

Epic A long poem, usually narrative, recounting the trials and victories of a great hero, a hero usually important to an entire nation or people.

Epigram A sharp, witty saying, such as Oscar Wilde's "I can resist everything but temptation."

Epigraph A short inscription at the start of a literary work.

Epilogue A concluding portion of a literary work, occurring after the main action has been completed.

Epithet A descriptive word or phrase pointing out a specific quality—as when Shakespeare is referred to as "the Bard." The word is often used to describe terms of contempt.

Epode The third portion of the comments of the Chorus in a classical Greek play, following the strophe and the antistrophe.

Essay Literally, "attempt"—any short piece of nonfiction prose that makes specific points and statements about a limited topic.

Euphemism A word or phrase substituting indirect for direct statement (for example, "passed away" in place of "died").

Euphony A use of words to pleasant musical effect.

Exposition A portion of a narrative or dramatic work that establishes the tone, setting, and basic situation.

Fable A short tale that presents a specific moral and whose characters are often animals.

Fantasy A work that takes place in a world that does not exist.

Farce A broadly comic play relying for its humor on unlikely situations and characters.

Feminine ending An additional syllable at the end of a line that has no metrical stress.

Figurative language Language that deliberately departs from everyday phrasing, with dramatic and imagistic effects that move the reader into a fresh mode of perception.

Foot A metrical unit of a line of poetry that contains at least one stressed syllable and one or more unstressed syllables.

Foreshadowing In a plot, an indication of something yet to happen.

Form The structure and organization of a work of art; form expresses its content.

Free verse Poetry that relies more on rhythm than on regular meter for its effectiveness.

Genre A distinct kind of writing, such as mystery, gothic, farce, or black comedy.

Gothic fiction Novels, often historical, in which weird, grotesque activity takes place; Mary Shelley's *Frankenstein* is an example of gothic fiction.

Haiku A form of Japanese poetry now also practiced by Westerners, which in three lines of five, seven, and then five syllables presents a sharp picture and a corresponding emotion or insight.

Heptameter A line of poetry composed of seven metrical feet.

Heroic couplet Two lines of rhyming iambic pentameter.

Hero (or heroine) The central character of a literary work; he or she often has great virtues and faults, and his or her trials and successes form the main action of the plot.

Hexameter A line of poetry containing six metrical feet.

Hubris Overbearing or insolent pride; in Greek drama, the arrogance toward the gods that leads to a character's downfall.

Humours The four Renaissance divisions of human temperament, corresponding to the liquids of the human body—blood, yellow bile, black bile, and phlegm—which are often associated with the personalities of dramatic characters.

Hyperbole Deliberately overstated, exaggerated figurative language, used either for comic or great emotional effect.

Iamb A metrical foot composed of one unaccented syllable followed by one stressed syllable (˘ ⁄), as in the word "undone."

Iambic pentameter A line containing five iambic feet, the most widely used meter in English-language poetry.

Illusion A false belief or perception.

Image, imagism A concrete expression of something perceived by the senses, using simile, metaphor, and figurative language.

Internal rhyme Rhyme that occurs within a single line of poetry.

Irony An effect associated with statements or situations in which something said or done is at odds with how things truly are.

Line The fundamental element of a poem—a set of words that ends at a specific point on the page and has a unity independent of what goes before and after.

Lyric A short, personal poem marked by strong feeling, musicality, and vivid language.

Masculine ending The last stressed syllable in a line of poetry.

Meditative poetry Verse with a strong and personal expression of religious feeling, especially as practiced by John Donne and others in the seventeenth century; also, a form of poetry in which the poet muses quietly and personally on a particular scene or emotion.

Metafiction A contemporary form of fiction in which an author makes the process of writing fiction part of his or her subject.

Metaphor An implicit comparison of an object or feeling with another unlike it, as when Eliot's "Prufrock" says, "I have measured out my life with coffee spoons."

Metaphysical poetry Thoughtful, often religious, intellectually vigorous poetry, as practiced by John Donne and others in the seventeenth century.

Meter A rhythmic pattern in a poem created by the regular alternation of stressed and unstressed syllables.

Metonymy A figure of speech in which an object or person is not mentioned directly but suggested by an object associated with it, as when a reference to "the White House" means "the President."

Mock heroic A form of long poem in which the structures and values of the epic are used to burlesque a trivial subject (for example, Pope's "The Rape of the Lock").

Monometer A line of poetry composed of only one metrical foot.

Mood The emotional tone or outlook an author brings to a subject.

Muse Originally any one of nine Greek goddesses presiding over the arts; "the muse" usually refers to an abstract being that inspires poets to write.

Myth Ancient stories of unknown origin involving the supernatural; myths have provided cultures and writers with interpretations of the world's events.

Narrative A story that consists of an account of a sequence of events.

Naturalism Literature in which the author attempts to represent the world in a realistic and often harsh and hopeless way.

Novel A long fictional narrative that represents human events, characters, and actions.

Novella A short novel or tale.

Octameter A line of poetry composed of eight metrical feet.

Octave An eight-line stanza of poetry, often part of a sonnet.

Ode A lyric meditation, usually in elevated figurative language, upon some specific object, event, or theme.

Off rhyme A form of rhyme employing not-quite-identical sounds, such as "slip" and "slap."

Omniscient narrator A speaker or implied speaker of a work of fiction who can tell the story, shift into the minds of one or more characters, be in various places, and comment on the meaning of what is happening in the story.

Onomatopoeia An effect in which a word or phrase sounds like its sense (for example, Tennysons's "murmuring of innumerable bees").

Ottava rima An eight-line stanza whose end-words usually rhyme in an *abababcc* pattern; used by many English poets (for example, Byron in *Don Juan*).

Pacing Narrative or linguistic devices that keep literary works moving and interesting.

Parable A story illustrating a moral, in which every detail parallels the moral situation.

Paradox A statement that seems contradictory but actually points out a truth (for example, Wordsworth's line, "The Child is father of the Man").

Parody A literary work that deliberately makes fun of another literary work or of a social situation.

Pathetic fallacy The fallacy of attaching human feelings to nature.

Pathos The qualities in a work of art that arouse pity or sadness, especially the helpless feeling caused by undeserved bad luck.

Persona The mask through which a writer gives expression to his or her own feelings or participates in the action of a story, poem, or play.

Personification A literary strategy giving nonhuman things human characters or attitudes, as in Aesop's fables or Keats's poem "To Autumn."

Plot The sequence of events in a story, poem, or play; the events build upon each other toward a convincing conclusion.

Poetry A form of writing in which the author writes in lines, with either a metrical pattern or a free-verse rhythm.

Point of view The angle from which a writer tells a story. Point of view can be either omniscient, limited, or through the eyes of one or more characters.

Prologue A preface or introduction setting the scene for what is to follow.

Prose Any form of writing that does not have the rhythmic patterns of metrical verse or free verse. Good prose is characterized by tightness, specificity, and a sense of style.

Protagonist The leading character; the protagonist engages the main concern of readers or audience.

Proverb A statement putting forth a great truth (for example, the Biblical proverb "Go to the ant, thou sluggard; consider his ways and be wise").

Pun A form of word play, often serious, that relies on the double meaning of words or sounds for its effect (for example, the dying Mercutio's words to Romeo, "ask for me tomorrow and you shall find me a grave man").

Quatrain A four-line stanza.

Realism An approach to writing that emphasizes recording everyday experience.

Refrain A line or group of lines repeated several times in a poem.

Resolution The dramatic action occurring after the climax of a play, before the events themselves are played out.

Rhetoric The study and practice of language in action—presenting ideas and opinions in the most effective way.

Rhyme Similarity of sound between words.

Rhythm In poetry, the regular recurrence of stressed syllables; in literature in general, the overall flow of language, having a sensory effect on the reader.

Romance Any work of fiction that takes place in an extravagent world remote from daily life.

Romanticism A powerful literary movement beginning in the late eighteenth century; it shook off classical forms and attitudes, embracing instead the power, promise, and political dignity of the imaginative individual.

Satire A literary work using wit, irony, anger, and parody to criticize human foibles and social instutitions.

Scansion The act of counting out the meter of a poem.

Scene A portion of a drama, poem, or work of fiction that occurs within one time and setting.

Science fiction Fantasy in which scientific facts and advances fuel the plot.

Sestet A six-line stanza of poetry, often part of a sonnet.

Setting The background of a literary work—the time, the place, the era, the geography, and the overall culture.

Short story A brief fictional narrative.

Simile A comparison of two things via the word "like" or "as."

Situational irony The contrast between what a character wants and what he or she receives, arising not through the character's fault but from other circumstances.

Soliloquy A speech by a character who is alone on stage, talking to himself or herself or to the audience.

Sonnet A poem of fourteen lines using some kind of metrical form and rhyme scheme and always unified with a concentrated expression of a large subject.

Sound In literature, the combination of sensations perceived by the ear or the mind's ear.

Spondee A metrical foot containing two stressed syllables, as in the phrase "time out."

Sprung rhythm A form of meter defined by the poet Gerard Manley Hopkins that emphasizes only the number of stresses in a line, thus making a kind of tense meter of accentual irregularity.

Stanza A portion of a poem set off by blank space before and after; more formally, a stanza may have rhyme and metrical regularity matching that of stanzas before and after.

Stereotype Widely believed and oversimplified attitudes toward a person, an issue, a style, and so on.

Stream of consciousness Writing that attempts to imitate and follow a character's thought processes.

Stress The emphasis a syllable or word naturally receives within a line of poetry, or in human speech.

Strophe In an ancient Greek play, the comments of that portion of the Chorus speaking first during a scene.

Style The property of writing that gives form, expression, and individuality to the content.

Subject The person, place, idea, situation, or thing with which some piece of literature most immediately concerns itself.

Subplot A complication within a play or piece of fiction that is not part of the main action but often complements it.

Subtext Significant communication, especially in dialogue, that gives motivation for the words being said.

Surrealism Art that values and expresses the unconscious imagination by altering what is commonly seen as reality.

Suspense Those literary qualities that leave a reader breathlessly awaiting further developments with no clear idea of what those developments will be.

Symbol Something that represents something else, the way a flag represents a country or a rose may stand for love—implying not only another physical thing but an associated meaning.

Synecdoche A kind of metaphor in which the mention of a part stands for the whole (for example, "head" refers not only to the heads of cattle but to each animal as a whole).

Synesthesia A subjective sensation or image (as of color) that is felt in terms of another sense (as of sound).

Synopsis A summary of the main points of a plot.

Syntax The arrangement of words to form sentences.

Tercet A three-line stanza, often one in which each line ends with the same rhyme.

Terza rima A series of three-line stanzas that rhyme *aba, bcb, cdc, ded*, and so on; used by Dante in the *Divine Comedy* and by Shelley, among others.

Tetrameter A line of verse composed of four metrical feet.

Theater of the absurd Avant-garde, post–World War II drama representing the hopelessness of the human condition by abandoning realistic characters, language, and plot.

Theme The main idea of a literary work created by its treatment of its immediate subject.

Tone The expression of a writer's attitudes toward a subject; the mood the author has chosen for a piece.

Tour de force A display of literary skill that is very impressive, but often empty.

Tragedy A literary work, usually a play, where the main characters participate in events that lead to their destruction.

Tragicomedy A work of literature, usually a play, that deals with potentially tragic events that are finally avoided, leading to a happy ending.

Trimeter A line of poetry containing three metrical feet.

Trochee A metrical foot consisting of an accented syllable followed by an unaccented one (/ ‿), as in the word "salty."

Understatement A passage that deliberately and ironically states or implies that something is less than it really is.

Utopia An ideal social and political state created by an author (for example, Plato, Thomas More, H. G. Wells, and Paul Goodman wrote utopias).

Verbal irony The discrepancy between things as they are stated and as they really are.

Verse A unit of poetry, usually a line or stanza; in general, any kind of literary work written in lines.

Wit Originally a word that meant "intelligence," "wit" now refers to a facility for quick, deft writing that usually employs humor to make its point.

ACKNOWLEDGMENTS

Ammons, A. R., "The City Limits" is reprinted from *Collected Poems, 1951–1971*, by A. R. Ammons, by permission of W. W. Norton and Company, Inc. Copyright © by A. R. Ammons

Anderson, Sherwood, "Hands" from *Winesburg, Ohio* by Sherwood Anderson. Copyright 1919 by B. W. Huebsch. Copyright renewed 1947 by Eleanor Copenhaven Anderson. Reprinted by permission of Viking Penguin, Inc.

Aristophanes, "Lysistrata" from *Aristophanes Plays: 2* translated by Patrik Dickinson, © Oxford University Press 1957, 1970. Reprinted by permission of Oxford University Press.

Ashbery, John, "City Afternoon" from *Self-Portrait in a Convex Mirror* by John Ashbery. Reprinted by permission of Viking Penguin, Inc.

Atwood, Margaret, "The City Planners," copyright 1966 © by Margaret Atwood from *The Circle Game* (Toronto: House of Anansi Press). Reprinted by permission of the publisher.

Auden, W. H., "Musée des Beaux Arts." Copyright 1940 and renewed 1968 by W. H. Auden. Reprinted from *W. H. Auden: Collected Poems*, by W. H. Auden, edited by Edward Mendelson, by permission of Random House, Inc., and Faber and Faber, Ltd.

Auden, W. H., "The Unknown Citizen," copyright 1940 and renewed 1968 by W. H. Auden. Reprinted from *W. H. Auden: Collected Poems*, by W. H. Auden, edited by Edward Mendelson, by permission of Random House, Inc., and Faber and Faber, Ltd.

Baldwin, James, "The Man Child" from *Going to Meet the Man* by James Baldwin. Copyright © 1948, 1951, 1957, 1958, 1960, 1965 by James Baldwin. A Dial Press book reprinted by permission of Doubleday and Co., Inc.

Baraka, Amiri, "In Memory of Radio" from *Preface to a 20 Volume Suicide Note* by LeRoi Jones (aka Amiri Baraka). Reprinted by permission of The Sterling Lord Agency, Inc. Copyright © 1961 by LeRoi Jones.

Berryman, John, "The Ball Poem" from *Short Poems* by John Berryman. Copyright 1948 by John Berryman. Copyright © renewed 1976 by Kate Berryman. Reprinted by permission of Farrar, Strauss and Giroux, Inc.

Bishop, Elizabeth, "Filling Station" from *The Complete Poems 1927–1979* by Elizabeth Bishop. Copyright © 1955, 1969 by Elizabeth Bishop. Copyright © 1983 by Alice Helen Methfessel. Reprinted by permission of Farrar. Straus and Giroux, Inc.

Bogan, Louise, "Cassandra" from *The Blue Estuaries* by Louise Bogan. Copyright 1923, 1968 by Louise Bogan. Reprinted by permission of Farrar, Straus and Giroux, Inc.

Bontemps, Arna, "A Summer Tragedy," reprinted by permission of Dodd, Mead and Company, Inc., from *The Old South* by Arna Bontemps. Copyright 1933 by Arna Bontemps. Copyright © renewed 1961 by Arna Bontemps. Copyright © 1973 by Alberta Bontemps, Executrix.

Borges, Jorge Luis, "The South" from *Ficciones*. Reprinted by permission of Grove Press, Inc. Copyright © 1962.

Boyle, Kay, "Astronomer's Wife." Reprinted by permission of A. Watkins, Inc. as agents for Kay Boyle.

Boyle, Kay, "For Marianne Moore's Birthday." Reprinted by permission of *Cumberlands*.

Bradbury, Ray, "August 2026: There Will Come Soft Rains." Copyright © 1950 by Ray Bradbury, copyright renewed 1978. Reprinted by permission of Harold Matson Co., Inc.

Brooks, Gwendolyn, "A Song in the Front

Yard" from *The World of Gwendolyn Brooks* by Gwendolyn Brooks. Copyright 1945 by Gwendolyn Brooks Blakely. By permission of Harper & Row, Publishers, Inc.

Brooks, Gwendolyn, "God Works in a Mysterious Way" and "firstly inclined to take what it is told" from *The World of Gwendolyn Brooks*. Copyright 1945 by Gwendolyn Brooks Blakely. By permission of Harper & Row, Publishers, Inc.

Brown, Sterling, "Southern Road" from *Collected Poems* published by Harcourt Brace Jovanovich, Inc.

Chekhov, Anton, "The Bet" from *The Schoolmistress and Other Stories* translated by Constance Garnett. Reprinted by permission of The Estate of Constance Garnett and Chatto & Windus, Ltd.

Childress, Alice, *Wine in the Wilderness* is reprinted by permission of the Dramatists Play Service, Inc. The use of the play in its present form must be confined to study and reference. Attention in particular is called to the fact that this play, being duly copyrighted, may not be publically read or performed or otherwise used without permission. All inquiries should be addressed to the Dramatists Play Service, Inc., 440 Park Avenue South, New York, N.Y. 10016.

Conrad, Joseph, "The Lagoon" from *Tales of Unrest* by Joseph Conrad. Reprinted by permission of Doubleday and Company, Inc.

Cruz, Victor Hernandez, "Today Is a Day of Great Joy" from *Snaps*, by Victor Hernandez Cruz. Copyright © 1968, 1969 by Victor Hernandez Cruz. Reprinted by permission of Random House, Inc.

Cullen, Countee, "Yet Do I Marvel" and "Incident," copyright 1925 by Harper & Row, Publishers, Inc. Renewed 1953 by Ida M. Cullen. By permission of Harper & Row, Publishers, Inc.

Cummings, E. E., "in Just—" is reprinted from *Tulips and Chimneys* by E. E. Cummings, by permission of Liveright Publishing Corporation. Copyright 1923, 1925 and renewed 1951, 1953 by E. E. Cummings. Copyright © 1973, 1976 by George James Firmage.

Cummings, E. E., "next to of course America, I" reprinted from *IS5*, poems by E. E. Cummings, by permission of Liveright Publishing Corporation. Copyright 1926 by Horace Liveright. Copyright renewed 1953 by E. E. Cummings.

Cummings, E. E., "pity this busy monster, manunkind," copyright 1944 by E. E. Cummings, renewed 1972 by Nancy T. Andrews. Reprinted from *Complete Poems 1913–1962* by E. E. Cummings by permission of Harcourt Brace Jovanovich, Inc.

Deutsch, Babette, "Disasters of War: Goya at the Museum." Reprinted by permission of Curtis Brown, Ltd.

Deutsch, Babette, "Natural Law." Reprinted by permission of Curtis Brown, Ltd.

Dickinson, Emily, "A Light Exists in Spring." Reprinted by permission of the publishers and the Trustees of Amherst College from *The Poems of Emily Dickinson*, edited by Thomas H. Johnson, Cambridge, Mass.: The Belknap Press of Harvard University Press, copyright © 1951, 1955, 1979 by The President and Fellows of Harvard College.

Dickinson, Emily, "Because I Could Not Stop for Death." Reprinted by permission of the publishers and the Trustees of Amherst College from *The Poems of Emily Dickinson*, edited by Thomas H. Johnson, Cambridge, Mass.: The Belknap Press of Harvard University Press, copyright © 1951, 1955, 1979 by The President and Fellows of Harvard College.

Dickinson, Emily, "I Like to See It Lap the Miles." Reprinted by permission of the publishers and the Trustees of Amherst College from *The Poems of Emily Dickinson*, edited by Thomas H. Johnson, Cambridge, Mass.: The Belknap Press of Harvard University Press, copyright © 1951, 1955, 1979 by The President and Fellows of Harvard College.

Dickinson, Emily, "She Rose to His Requirement." Reprinted by permission of the publishers and the Trustees of Amherst College from *The Poems of Emily Dickinson*, edited by Thomas H. Johnson, Cambridge, Mass.: The Belknap Press of Harvard University Press, copyright © 1951, 1955, 1979 by The President and Fellows of Harvard College.

Dickinson, Emily, "There's a Certain Slant of Light." Reprinted by permission of the publishers and the Trustees of Amherst College from *The Poems of Emily Dickinson*, edited by Thomas H. Johnson, Cambridge, Mass.: The Belknap Press of Harvard University Press, copyright © 1951, 1955, 1979 by The President and Fellows of Harvard College.

Dickinson, Emily, "Wild Nights, Wild Nights." Reprinted by permission of the publishers and the Trustees of Amherst College from *The Poems of Emily Dickinson*, edited by Thomas H. Johnson, Cambridge, Mass.: The Belknap Press of Harvard University Press, copyright © 1951, 1955, 1979 by The President and Fellows of Harvard College.

Dickey, James, "The Performance." Copyright © 1960 by James Dickey. Reprinted from *Poems 1957–1967* by permission of Wesleyan University Press. This poem first appeared in *Into the Stone*.

Doolittle, Hilda, "Pear Tree" from *Collected Poems, 1912–1914*. Copyright © 1982 by the estate of Hilda Doolittle. Reprinted by permission of New Directions Publishing Corporation.

Eliot, T. S., "The Love Song of J. Alfred Prufrock." *From Collected Poems 1909–1962* by T. S. Eliot, copyright 1936 by Harcourt Brace and Jovanovich, Inc.; copyright © 1963, 1964 by T. S. Eliot. Reprinted by permission of the publisher.

Ellison, Ralph, "King of the Bingo Game." Reprinted by permission of William Morris Agency,

ers." Copyright 1926 by Alfred A. Knopf, Inc. and renewed 1954 by Langston Hughes. Reprinted from *Selected Poems of Langston Hughes*, by Langston Hughes, by permission of Alfred A. Knopf, Inc.

Hughes, Langston, "Without Benefit of Declaration" from *The Panther and the Lash*, by Langston Hughes. Copyright © 1967 by Langston Hughes. Reprinted by permission of Alfred A. Knopf, Inc.

Ibsen, Henrik, *A Doll's House* by Henrik Ibsen, translated by Otto Reinert. Copyright © 1977 by Otto Reinert. Reprinted from *Thirteen Plays: An Introduction Anthology*, edited by Otto Reinert and Peter Arnott, by permission of Little, Brown and Company.

Jackson, Shirley, "The Lottery" from *The Lottery* by Shirley Jackson. Copyright 1948, 1949 by Shirley Jackson. Copyright © renewed 1976, 1977 by Laurence Hyman, Barry Hyman, Mrs. Sarah Webster, and Mrs. Joanne Schnurer. "The Lottery" originally appeared in *The New Yorker*. Reprinted by permission of Farrar, Straus and Giroux, Inc.

Jarrell, Randall, "The Death of the Ball Turret Gunner" from *The Complete Poems* by Randall Jarrell. Copyright 1945, 1969 by Mrs. Randall Jarrell. Copyright © renewed 1973 by Mrs. Randall Jarrell. Reprinted by permission of Farrar, Straus and Giroux, Inc.

Jeffers, Robinson, "Hurt Hawks." Copyright 1928 and renewed 1956 by Robinson Jeffers. Reprinted from *The Selected Poetry of Robinson Jeffers*, by Robinson Jeffers, by permission of Random House, Inc.

Jordon, June, "Poem from The Emprie State." Reprinted by permission of the author.

Joyce, James, "Araby" from *Dubliners* by James Joyce. Originally published in 1916 by B. W. Huebsch. Definitive text copyright © 1967 by The Estate of James Joyce. Reprinted by permission of Viking Penguin, Inc.

Kafka, Franz, "A Hunger Artist." Reprinted by permission of Schocken Books, Inc., from *The Penal Colony* by Franz Kafka, translated by Willa and Edwin Muir. Copyright © 1948, 1976 by Schocken Books, Inc.

Kizer, Caroline, "Amusing Our Daughters." Reprinted by permission of the author.

Knight, Etheridge, "Hard Rock Returns to Prison from the Hospital for the Criminal Insane." Reprinted by permission of the author.

Kumin, Maxine, "Together" from *The Nightmare Factory*. Copyright © 1970 by Maxine Kumin. Reprinted by permission of Curtis Brown, Ltd.

Lawrence, D. H., "Piano" from *The Complete Poems of D. H. Lawrence*. Collected and edited by Vivian de Sola Pinto and F. Warren Roberts. Copyright © 1964, 1971 by Angelo Ravagli and C. M. Weekley, Executors of the Estate of Frieda Lawrence Ravagli. Reprinted by permission of Viking Penguin Inc.'

Lawrence, D. H., "The Rocking-Horse Winner" from *The Collected Short Stories of D. H. Lawrence*. Reprinted by permission of Lawrence Pollinger, Ltd., and The Estate of Frieda Lawrence Ravagli, and Viking Penguin, Inc.

LeGuin, Ursula K., "A Trip to the Head" from *The Wind's Twelve Quarters* by Ursula K. LeGuin. Copyright © 1970, 1975 by Ursula K. LeGuin; reprinted by permission of the author and the author's agent, Virginia Kidd.

Lessing, Doris, "Flight" from *The Habit of Loving* by Doris Lessing (Thomas Y. Crowell, Publishers). Copyright © 1957 by Doris Lessing. Reprinted by permission of Harper & Row Publishers, Inc., and by permission of Curtis Brown, Ltd., London, on behalf of Doris Lessing.

Levertov, Denise, "The Ache of Marriage" from Denise Levertov, *Taste and See*. Copyright © 1964 by Denise Levertov Goodman. Reprinted by permission of New Directions Publishing Corporation.

Levertov, Denise, "The Victors" from Denise Levertov, *O Taste and See*. Copyright © 1964 by Denise Levertov Goodman. Reprinted by permission of New Directions Publishing Corporation.

Levertov, Denise, "What Were They Like?" from Denise Levertov, *The Sorrow Dance*. Copyright © 1966 by Denise Levertov Goodman. Reprinted by permission of New Directions Publishing Corporation.

Lowell, Amy, "The Taxi" from *The Complete Poetical Works of Amy Lowell*. Copyright © 1955 by Houghton Mifflin Company. Reprinted by permission of the publisher.

Lowell, Robert, "After the Surprising Conversions" and "Children of Light" from *Lord Weary's Castle*, copyright 1946, 1974 by Robert Lowell. Reprinted by permission of Harcourt Brace Jovanovich, Inc.

MacLeish, Archibald, "Ars Poetica" from *New and Collected Poems* 1917–1976 by Archibald MacLeish. Reprinted by permission of Houghton Mifflin Company.

Malamud, Bernard, "The Magic Barrel" from *The Magic Barrel* by Bernard Malamud. Copyright © 1954, 1958 by Bernard Malamud. Reprinted by permission of Farrar, Straus, and Giroux, Inc.

Mansfield, Katherine, "Miss Brill" from *The Short Stories of Katherine Mansfield*. Copyright 1937 and renewed 1965 by Alfred A. Knopf, Inc. Reprinted by permission of the publisher.

McCullers, Carson, "The Jockey" from *The Ballad of the Sad Cafe and Collected Short Stories* by Carson McCullers. Copyright © 1955 by Carson McCullers. Reprinted by permission of Houghton Mifflin Company.

McGinley, Phyllis, "Portrait of Girl with Comic Book" from *Times Three* by Phyllis McGinley.

Roethke, Theodore, "Root Cellar." Copyright 1954 by Theodore Roethke and copyright 1943 by Modern Poetry Associates, Inc. from the book *The Collected Poems of Theodore Roethke.* Reprinted by permission of Doubleday and Company, Inc.

Rukeyser, Muriel, "The Lost Romans." Reprinted by permission of International Creative Management. Copyright © 1976 by Muriel Rukeyser.

Sanchez, Sonia, "Poem at Thirty." Reprinted by permission of the author.

Sandburg, Carl, "The Harbor." From *Chicago Poems* by Carl Sandburg, copyright 1916 by Holt, Rinehart and Winston, Inc., copyright 1944 by Carl Sandburg. Reprinted by permission of Harcourt Brace Jovanovich, Inc.

Sexton, Anne, "The Black Art" from *All My Pretty Ones* by Anne Sexton. Copyright © 1961, 1962 by Anne Sexton. Reprinted by permission of Houghton Mifflin Co.

Sexton, Anne, "The Fury of Flowers and Worms" from *The Death Notebooks* by Anne Sexton. Copyright © 1974 by Anne Sexton. Reprinted by permission of Houghton Mifflin Company.

Sexton, Anne, "The Sun" from *All My Pretty Ones* by Anne Sexton. Copyright © 1961, 1962 by Anne Sexton. Reprinted by permission of Houghton Mifflin Company.

Shakespeare, William, *Othello.* Introduction and notes by Gerald Eades Bentley. Copyright © 1958 and 1970 by Penguin Books, Inc. Reprinted by permission of Penguin Books, Inc.

Silko, Leslie, "Where Mountain Lion Lay Down with Deer." Copyright © 1981 by Leslie Marmon Silko. Reprinted from *Storyteller* by Leslie Marmon Silko, published by Seaver Books, New York, 1981.

Singer, Isaac Bashevis, "Old Love." From *Passions and Other Stories* by Isaac Bashevis Singer. Copyright © 1975 by Isaac Bashevis Singer. "Old Love" originally appeared in *The New Yorker.* Reprinted by permission of Farrar, Straus and Giroux, Inc.

Sitwell, Edith, "Trio for Two Cats and a Trombone" from *Collected Poems* by Edith Sitwell. Reprinted by permission of David Higham Associates, Limited.

Smith, Stevie, "The Weak Monk" from *Selected Poems of Stevie Smith.* Copyright © 1964 by Stevie Smith. Reprinted by permission of New Directions Publishing Corporation, and by James MacGibbon.

Snodgrass, W. D., "The Campus on the Hill." Copyright © 1958 by W. D. Snodgrass. Reprinted from *Heart's Needle,* by W. D. Snodgrass, by permission of the publisher.

Snyder, Gary, "Not Leaving the House" from *Regarding Wave.* Copyright © 1970 by Gary Snyder. Reprinted by permission of New Directions Publishing Corporation.

Sophocles, *Oedipus Rex. The Oedipus Rex of Sophocles: An English Version* by Dudley Fitts and Robert Fitzgerald, copyright 1949 by Harcourt Brace Jovanovich, Inc.; renewed 1977 by Cornelia Fitts and Robert Fitzgerald. Reprinted by permission of the publisher. Caution: All rights, including professional, amateur, motion picture, recitation, lecturing, public reading, radio broadcasting, and television are strictly reserved. Inquiries on all rights should be addressed to Harcourt Brace Jovanovich, Inc., Permissions Department, 757 Third Avenue, New York, N.Y. 10017.

Spender, Stephen, "An Elementary School Classroom in a Slum." Copyright 1942 and renewed 1970 by Stephen Spender. Reprinted from *Collected Poems 1928–1953,* by Stephen Spender, by permission of Random House, Inc., and Faber and Faber, Ltd.

Stanford, Ann, "The Blackberry Thicket" from *The Weathercock* by Ann Stanford. Copyright 1955 by Ann Stanford. Reprinted by permission of Viking Penguin, Inc.

Steinbeck, John, "The Chrysanthemums" from *The Long Valley* by John Steinbeck. Copyright 1938 by John Steinbeck. Copyright renewed 1966 by John Steinbeck. Reprinted by permission of Viking Penguin, Inc.

Stevens, Wallace, "Anecdote of the Jar." Copyright 1923 and renewed 1951 by Wallace Stevens. Reprinted from *The Collected Poems of Wallace Stevens,* by Wallace Stevens, by permission of Alfred A. Knopf, Inc.

Stevens, Wallace, "Sunday Morning." Copyright 1923 and renewed 1951 by Wallace Stevens. Reprinted from *The Collected Poems of Wallace Stevens,* by Wallace Stevens, by permission of Alfred A. Knopf, Inc.

Stevens, Wallace, "The Snow Man." Copyright 1923 and renewed 1951 by Wallace Stevens. Reprinted from *The Collected Poems of Wallace Stevens* by permission of Alfred A. Knopf, Inc.

Swenson, May, "Analysis of Baseball" from *New and Selected Things Taking Place* by May Swenson. Copyright © 1971 by May Swenson. By permission of Little, Brown and Company in association with the Atlantic Monthly Press.

Swenson, May, "Hearing the Wind at Night." Reprinted by permission of the author, copyright' © 1967 in *Half Sun Half Asleep* (Scribner's).

Teasdale, Sara, "Barter." Reprinted with permission of Macmillan Publishing Co., Inc., from *Collected Poems* by Sara Teasdale. Copyright 1917 by Macmillan Publishing Co., Inc., renewed 1945 by Mamie T. Wheless.

Tellez, Hernando, "Just Lather, That's All." Reprinted by permission of Donald Yates and Beatriz Tellez.

Thomas, Dylan, "Fern Hill" from *Collected Poems* by Dylan Thomas. Copyright 1945 by the Trustees for the Copyrights of Dylan Thomas.

Reprinted by permission of New Directions Publishing Corporation, and J. M. Dent.

Thurber, James, "The Catbird Seat." Copyright 1945 by James Thurber. Copyright © 1973 by Helen W. Thurber and Rosemary T. Sawyers. From *The Thurber Carnival*, published by Harper & Row.

Tolson, Melvin B., "A Legend of Versailles" from *Harlem Gallery* by Melvin B. Tolson. Copyright © 1965 by Twayne Publishers, Inc., and reprinted with the permission of Twayne Publishers, a division of G. K. Hall and Co., Boston.

Tolstoy, Leo, "God Sees the Truth, but Waits" from *Twenty-three Tales* by Leo Tolstoy, translated by Louise and Aylmer Maude (1906). Reprinted by permission of Oxford University Press.

Toomer, Jean, "Georgia Dusk." "Georgia Dusk" is reprinted from *Cane* by Jean Toomer, by permission of Liveright Publishing Corporation. Copyright 1923 by Boni and Liveright. Copyright renewed 1951 by Jean Toomer.

Wagoner, David, "A Valedictory to Standard Oil of Indiana" from *Collected Poems 1956–1976*, by David Wagoner, copyright © 1976 by Indiana University Press. Reprinted by permission of the publishers.

Walcott, Derek, "Nearing La Guaira." From *Selected Poems* by Derek Walcott. Copyright © 1962, 1963, 1964 by Derek Walcott. Reprinted by permission of Farrar, Straus and Giroux, Inc.

Walker, Margaret, "Poppa Chicken" from *For My People*. Published by Yale University Press, 1942. Reprinted by permission of Margaret Walker Alexander.

Walsh, Chad, "Port Authority Tunnel: 9 a.m. Monday." From *The End of Nature* by Chad Walsh. Reprinted by permission of Ohio University Press.

Welch, James, "The Only Bar in Dixon." From *Riding the Earthboy 40* by James Welch. Copyright © 1970 by James Welch. First published in *The New Yorker*. Reprinted by permission of Harper & Row, Publishers, Inc.

Welty, Eudora, "A Worn Path." Copyright 1941, 1969 by Eudora Welty. Reprinted from her volume *A Curtain of Green and Other Stories* by permission of Harcourt Brace Jovanovich, Inc.

Welty, Eudora, "Powerhouse." Copyright 1941, 1969 by Eudora Welty. Reprinted from her volume *A Curtain of Green and Other Stories* by permission of Harcourt Brace Jovanovich, Inc.

Wilbur, Richard, "The Death of a Toad." Copyright 1950, 1978 by Richard Wilbur. Reprinted from his volume *Ceremony and other Poems* by permission of Harcourt Brace Jovanovich, Inc.

Williams, William Carlos, "The Red Wheelbarrow" from *Collected Earlier Poems*. Copyright 1938 by New Directions Publishing Corporation. Reprinted by permission of New Directions Publishing Corporation.

Williams, William Carlos, "Spring and All" from *Collected Earlier Poems*. Copyright 1938 by New Directions Publishing Corporation. Reprinted by permission of New Directions Publishing Corporation.

Williams, William Carlos, "This Is Just to Say" from *Collected Earlier Poems*. Copyright 1938 by New Directions Publishing Corporation. Reprinted by permission of New Directions Publishing Corporation.

Williams, William Carlos, "To Waken an Old Lady" from *Collected Earlier Poems*. Copyright 1938 by New Directions Publishing Corporation. Reprinted by permission of New Directions Publishing Corporation.

Wright, James, "A Blessing." Copyright © 1961 by James Wright. Reprinted from *The Branch Will Not Break* by permission of Wesleyan University Press. This poem first appeared in *Poetry*.

Wright, Judith, "Extinct Birds" from *Birds* is reproduced with the permission of Angus and Robertson (UK) Ltd. and Houghton Mifflin Company.

Wright, Judith, "The Surfer" from *Collected Poems 1942–1970* is reproduced with the permission of Angus and Robertson (UK) Ltd.

Wright, Richard, "The Man Who Was Almost a Man" from *Eight Men* by Richard Wright (J. Y. Crowell). Copyright 1940, 1961 by Richard Wright. Reprinted by permission of Harper & Row, Publishers, Inc.

Wylie, Elinor, "Puritan Sonnet." Copyright 1921 by Alfred A. Knopf, Inc., and renewed 1949 by William Rose Benet. Reprinted from *Collected Poems of Elinor Wylie*, by Elinor Wylie, by permission of Alfred A. Knopf, Inc.

Yeats, William Butler, "Leda and the Swan." Reprinted with the permission of Macmillan Publishing Co., Inc. and A. P. Watt, Ltd., from *Collected Poems* by William B. Yeats. Copyright 1928 by Macmillan Publishing Co., Inc. Renewed 1956 by Georgie Yeats.

Yeats, William Butler, "Sailing to Byzantium." Copyright 1928 by Macmillan Publishing Co., Inc., renewed 1956 by Georgie Yeats. Reprinted with permission of Macmillan Publishing Co. and A. P. Watt, Ltd.

INDEX OF AUTHORS AND TITLES

Ache of Marriage, The, 649
After the Surprising Conversions, 642
Against Love, 506
America, 425
AMMONS, A. R. (Archie Randolph)
    The City Limits, 654
Amusing Our Daughters, 651
Analysis of Baseball, 442
ANDERSON, SHERWOOD
    Hands, 233
Anecdote of the Jar, 570
Anthem for Doomed Youth, 601
Araby, 112
ARISTOPHANES
    Lysistrata, 714
ARNOLD, MATTHEW
    Dover Beach, 451
    To Marguerite—Continued, 548
Ars Poetica, 416
ASHBERY, JOHN
    City Afternoon, 663
Astronomer's Wife, 180
ATWOOD, MARGARET
    The City Planners, 477
AUDEN, W. H.
    Musée des Beaux Arts, 620
    The Unknown Citizen, 428
August, 668
August 2026: There Will Come Soft Rains,
    159
Author to Her Book, The, 414

Bait, The, 435
BALDWIN, JAMES
    The Man Child, 315

Ball Poem, The, 634
BARAKA, AMIRI (LeRoi Jones)
    In Memory of Radio, 679
Barter, 577
Because I could not stop for Death, 551
Before the Birth of One of Her Children,
    505
BEHN, APHRA
    The Defiance, 353
    Song: A Thousand Martyrs I Have Made,
    509
Bermudas, 447
BERRYMAN, JOHN
    The Ball Poem, 634
Bet, The, 14
BISHOP, ELIZABETH
    Filling Station, 626
Black Art, The, 664
Black Cat, The, 185
Blackberry Thicket, The, 398
BLAKE, WILLIAM
    The Garden of Love, 518
    The Lamb, 516
    London, 472
    The Tyger, 517
Blessing, A, 661
BOGAN, LOUISE
    Cassandra, 607
BONTEMPS, ARNA
    A Summer Tragedy, 135
BORGES, JORGE LUIS
    The South, 265
BOYLE, KAY
    Astronomer's Wife, 180
    For Marianne Moore's Birthday, 617

BRADBURY, RAY
August 2026: There Will Come Soft
Rains, 159
BRADSTREET, ANNE
The Author to Her Book, 414
Before the Birth of One of Her Children,
505
In Memory of My Dear Grand-Child, 503
To My Dear and Loving Husband, 342
Bredon Hill, 559
Bride Comes to Yellow Sky, The, 45
Bright Star, 536
BRONTË, EMILY
Remembrance, 544
BROOKS, GWENDOLYN
Firstly Inclined to Take What It Is Told,
465
God Works in a Mysterious Way, 465
Song in the Front Yard, A, 357
BROWN, STERLING A.
Southern Road, 610
BROWNING, ELIZABETH BARRETT
Consolation, 462
If thou must love me, let it be for naught,
354
When our two souls stand up erect and
strong, 537
BROWNING, ROBERT
My Last Duchess, 542
BURNS, ROBERT
Green Grow the Rashes, O, 519
My Heart's in the Highlands, 437
BYRON, GEORGE GORDON, LORD
On This Day I Complete My Thirty-Sixth
Year, 526
She Walks in Beauty, 525

CAMPION, THOMAS
There is a Garden in Her Face, 489
Campus on the Hill, The, 657
Captain Carpenter, 596
Cask of Amontillado, The, 8
Cassandra, 607
Catbird Seat, The, 258
Cavalry Crossing a Ford, 547
Change of Heart, A, 201
Channel Firing, 556
CHEKHOV, ANTON
The Bet, 14
Gooseberries, 225
CHESNUTT, CHARLES WADDELL
How Dasdy Came Through, 221
Children of Light, 641
CHILDRESS, ALICE
Wine in the Wilderness, 1017

CHOPIN, KATE
A Respectable Woman, 207
Chrysanthemums, The, 171
Church-Monuments, 403
City Afternoon, 663
City Limits, The, 654
City Planners, The, 477
COLERIDGE, SAMUEL TAYLOR
Kubla Khan, 523
Composed Upon Westminster Bridge,
September 3, 1802, 520
CONRAD, JOSEPH
The Lagoon, 211
Consolation, 462
Conversation with My Father, A, 311
CRANE, STEPHEN
The Bride Comes to Yellow Sky, 45
CRUZ, VICTOR HERNANDEZ
Today is a Day of Great Joy, 419
CULLEN, COUNTEE
Incident, 616
Yet Do I Marvel, 463
CUMMINGS, E. E.
in Just—, 602
next to of course god, 426
pity this busy monster, manunkind, 603

Daddy, 371
Dalliance of the Eagles, The, 548
Darkling Thrush, The, 555
DAUDET, ALPHONSE
The Last Lesson, 197
Death of a Salesman, 892
Death of a Toad, The, 646
Death of the Ball Turret Gunner, The, 636
Defiance, The, 353
Delight in Disorder, 499
Description of a City Shower, A, 469
DEUTSCH, BABETTE
Disasters of War: Goya at the Museum,
367
Natural Law, 606
DICKEY, JAMES
The Performance, 647
DICKINSON, EMILY
Because I could not stop for Death, 551
A Light exists in Spring, 552
I like to see it lap the miles, 550
She rose to His Requirement, 356
There's a certain slant of light, 406
Wild Nights—Wild Nights! 346
Disasters of War: Goya at the Museum, 367
Doll's House, A, 964
DONNE, JOHN
The Bait, 435

DONNE, JOHN (*Cont.*):
  Holy Sonnet 7 (At the round earth's imagined corners), 492
  Holy Sonnet 14 (Batter my heart, three-personed God), 459
  Song: Go and catch a falling star, 491
Dover Beach, 451
Dry September, 126
DRYDEN, JOHN
  Why Should a Foolish Marriage Vow, 507
Dulce et Decorum Est, 366

Elementary School Classroom in a Slum, An, 624
ELIOT, T. S.
  The Love Song of J. Alfred Prufrock, 591
ELLISON, RALPH
  King of the Bingo Game, 27
Evenin' Air Blues, 612
Extinct Birds, 637

FAULKNER, WILLIAM
  Dry September, 126
FERLINGHETTI, LAWRENCE
  In Goya's Greatest Scenes, 644
Fern Hill, 632
Filling Station, 626
FINCH, ANNE
  Trail All Your Pikes, 510
Firstly Inclined to Take What It Is Told, 465
Flight, 67
For Marianne Moore's Birthday, 617
FROST, ROBERT
  Once by the Pacific, 568
  The Oven Bird, 569
  The Road Not Taken, 567
  Stopping by Woods on a Snowy Evening, 407
  Tree at My Window, 382
Fury of Flowers and Worms, The, 409

Garden of Love, The, 518
Georgia Dusk, 605
GINSBERG, ALLEN
  A Supermarket in California, 655
GIOVANNI, NIKKI
  Mothers, 359
  Poetry, 417
Go and catch a falling star (Song), 491
God Sees the Truth, but Waits, 75
God Works in a Mysterious Way, 465
Good Man is Hard to Find, A, 86

Gooseberries, 225
Green Grow the Rashes, O, 519
GUNN, THOM
  On the Move, 670

H. D. (Hilda Doolittle)
  Pear Tree, 584
Hands, 233
Harbor, The, 575
Hard Rock Returns to Prison from the Hospital for the Criminal Insane, 677
HARDY, THOMAS
  Channel Firing, 556
  The Darkling Thrush, 555
Harlem, 614
HAWTHORNE, NATHANIEL
  Young Goodman Brown, 102
HAYDEN, ROBERT
  Those Winter Sundays, 629
Hearing the Wind at Night, 384
HEMINGWAY, ERNEST
  The Killers, 270
HERBERT, GEORGE
  Church-Monuments, 403
HERRICK, ROBERT
  Delight in Disorder, 499
  To the Virgins, to Make Much of Time, 497
Holy Sonnet 7 (At the round earth's imagined corners), 492
Holy Sonnet 14 (Batter my heart, three-personed God), 459
HOPKINS, GERARD MANLEY
  Pied Beauty, 558
Housewife, 628
HOUSMAN, A. E.
  Bredon Hill, 559
  To an Athlete Dying Young, 438
How Dasdy Came Through, 221
How soon hath Time, 500
HOWARD, HENRY
  To His Lady, 481
HUGHES, LANGSTON
  Evenin' Air Blues, 612
  Harlem, 614
  The Negro Speaks of Rivers, 613
  Soul Gone Home, 706
  Without Benefit of Declaration, 369
Hunger Artist, A, 20
Hurt Hawks, 585

I come home from you, 347
I Knew a Woman, 623
I like to see it lap the miles, 550

I Saw in Louisiana a Live-Oak Growing,
    380
IBSEN, HENRIK
  A Doll's House, 964
If thou must love me, let it be for naught,
    354
In a Station of the Metro, 473
In an Artist's Studio, 553
In Answer to a Lady Who Advised Retire-
    ment, 512
In Goya's Greatest Scenes, 644
in Just—, 602
In Memory of My Dear Grand-Child, 503
In Memory of Radio, 679
Incident, 616
It is a Beauteous Evening, 522

JACKSON, SHIRLEY
  The Lottery, 34
JARRELL, RANDALL
  The Death of the Ball Turret Gunner, 636
JEFFERS, ROBINSON
  Hurt Hawks, 585
JEWETT, SARAH ORNE
  A Change of Heart, 201
Jockey, The, 307
JOHNSON, BEN
  On My First Daughter, 495
  On My First Son, 495
  Still to be neat, 496
  To Celia, 494
JORDAN, JUNE
  Poem from the Empire State, 683
JOYCE, JAMES
  Araby, 112
Just Lather, That's All, 155

KAFKA, FRANZ
  A Hunger Artist, 20
KEATS, JOHN
  Bright Star, 536
  Ode on a Grecian Urn, 534
  To Autumn, 392
  Written in Disgust of Vulgar Supersti-
    tion, 405
Killers, The, 270
King of the Bingo Game, 27
KIZER, CAROLYN
  Amusing Our Daughters, 651
KNIGHT, ETHERIDGE
  Hard Rock Returns to Prison from the
    Hospital for the Criminal Insane, 677
Kubla Khan, 523
KUMIN, MAXINE
  Together, 652

Lagoon, The, 211
Lamb, The, 516
Last Lesson, The, 197
LAWRENCE, D. H.
  Piano, 580
  The Rocking-Horse Winner, 238
Leda and the Swan, 562
Legend of Versailles, A, 609
LE GUIN, URSULA K.
  A Trip to the Head, 328
LESSING, DORIS
  Flight, 67
Let me not to the marriage of true minds,
    341
LEVERTOV, DENISE
  The Ache of Marriage, 649
  The Victors, 386
  What Were They Like? 430
Light exists in Spring, A, 552
London, 472
Lost Romans, The, 630
Lottery, The, 34
Love Song of J. Alfred Prufrock, The, 591
LOVELACE, RICHARD
  To Lucasta, Going to the Wars, 364
LOWELL, AMY
  The Taxi, 566
LOWELL, ROBERT
  After the Surprising Conversions, 642
  Children of Light, 641
Lysistrata, 714

McCULLERS, CARSON
  The Jockey, 307
McGINLEY, PHYLLIS
  Portrait of Girl With Comic Book, 618
  Reflections Outside of a Gymnasium, 440
McKAY, CLAUDE
  America, 425
  Outcast, 598
MacLEISH, ARCHIBALD
  Ars Poetica, 416
Magic Barrel, The, 54
MALAMUD, BERNARD
  The Magic Barrel, 54
Man Child, The, 315
Man Who Was Almost a Man, The, 288
MANSFIELD, KATHERINE
  Miss Brill, 249
MARLOWE, CHRISTOPHER
  The Passionate Shepherd to His Love,
    486
MARVELL, ANDREW
  Bermudas, 447
  To His Coy Mistress, 343

MAUPASSANT, GUY DE
  The Piece of String, 81
MILES, JOSEPHINE
  Housewife, 628
MILLAY, EDNA ST. VINCENT
  Wild Swans, 600
MILLER, ARTHUR
  Death of a Salesman, 892
MILTON, JOHN
  How soon hath Time, 500
  On the Late Massacre in Piedmont, 501
  When I consider how my light is spent, 460
Miss Brill, 249
MONTAGUE, LADY MARY WORTLEY
  In Answer to a Lady Who Advised Retirement, 512
MOORE, MARIANNE
  Poetry, 587
Mothers, 359
Musée des Beaux Arts, 620
My Heart's in the Highlands, 437
My Last Duchess, 542

Natural Law, 606
Near Dover, 449
Nearing La Guaira, 454
Negro Speaks of Rivers, The, 613
next to of course god, 426
Noiseless Patient Spider, A, 546
Not Leaving the House, 673
Notorious Jumping Frog of Calaveras County, The, 192
Nymph's Reply to the Shepherd, The, 483

Oak, The, 378
OATES, JOYCE CAROL
  Stalking, 117
O'CONNOR, FLANNERY
  A Good Man is Hard to Find, 86
Ode on a Grecian Urn, 534
Oedipus Rex, 853
Old Love, 278
On a Certain Lady at Court, 511
On My First Daughter, 495
On My First Son, 495
On the Late Massacre in Piedmont, 501
On the Move, 670
On This Day I Complete My Thirty-Sixth Year, 525
Once by the Pacific, 568
Only Bar in Dixon, The, 684
Othello, 750
Outcast, 598

Oven Bird, The, 569
OWEN, WILFRED
  Anthem for Doomed Youth, 601
  Dulce et Decorum Est, 366
Ozymandias, 424

PALEY, GRACE
  A Conversation with My Father, 311
PARKER, DOROTHY
  The Standard of Living, 253
Parting, The: I, 667
Passionate Shepherd to His Love, The, 486
Pear Tree, 584
Peeling Onions, 669
Performance, The, 647
PHILIPS, KATHERINE
  Against Love, 506
Piano, 580
Piece of String, The, 81
Pied Beauty, 558
PIRANDELLO, LUIGI
  War, 152
pity this busy monster, manunkind, 603
PLATH, SYLVIA
  Daddy, 371
  Point Shirley, 674
POE, EDGAR ALLAN
  The Black Cat, 185
  The Cask of Amontillado, 8
  To Helen, 538
Poem at Thirty, 681
Poem from the Empire State, 683
Poetry (Giovanni), 417
Poetry (Moore), 587
Point Shirley, 674
POPE, ALEXANDER
  On a Certain Lady at Court, 511
Poppa Chicken, 638
Port Authority Terminal: 9 A.M. Monday, 475
PORTER, KATHERINE ANNE
  Rope, 166
Portrait of Girl With Comic Book, 618
POUND, EZRA
  In a Station of the Metro, 473
  The River-Merchant's Wife: A Letter, 582
  A Virginal, 582
Powerhouse, 298
Puritan Sonnet, 579

RALEIGH, SIR WALTER
  The Nymph's Reply to the Shepherd, 483
RANSOM, JOHN CROWE
  Captain Carpenter, 596

Reflections Outside of a Gymnasium, 440
Remembrance, 544
Respectable Woman, A, 207
RICH, ADRIENNE
    August, 668
    I come home from you, 347
    The Parting: I, 667
    Peeling Onions, 669
Richard Cory, 564
Riders to the Sea, 696
River-Merchant's Wife: A Letter, The, 582
Road Not Taken, The, 567
ROBINSON, E. A.
    Richard Cory, 564
Rocking-Horse Winner, The, 238
ROETHKE, THEODORE
    I Knew a Woman, 623
    Root Cellar, 622
Root Cellar, 622
Rope, 166
ROSSETTI, CHRISTINA
    In an Artist's Studio, 553
RUKEYSER, MURIEL
    The Lost Romans, 630

Sailing to Byzantium, 563
SANCHEZ, SONIA
    Poem at Thirty, 681
SANDBURG, CARL
    The Harbor, 575
SEXTON, ANNE
    The Black Art, 664
    The Fury of Flowers and Worms, 409
    The Sun, 665
SHAKESPEARE, WILLIAM
    Let me not to the marriage of true minds
        (sonnet 116), 341
    Othello, 750
    Shall I compare thee to a summer's day?
        487
    Since brass, nor stone, nor earth, nor
        boundless sea, 413
    That time of year thou mayst in me be-
        hold, 488
    Winter, 391
Shall I compare thee to a summer's day?
    487
She rose to His Requirement, 356
She Walks in Beauty, 525
SHELLEY, PERCY BYSSHE
    Ozymandias, 424
    Stanzas Written in Dejection, Near Na-
        ples, 528
    To a Skylark, 530

SIDNEY, SIR PHILIP
    With how sad steps, O Moon, 485
SILKO, LESLIE
    Where Mountain Lion Lay Down with
        Deer, 685
Since brass, nor stone, nor earth, nor
    boundless sea, 413
SINGER, ISAAC BASHEVIS
    Old Love, 278
SITWELL, EDITH
    Trio for Two Cats and a Trombone, 589
SMITH, STEVIE
    The Weak Monk, 615
SNODGRASS, W. D. (William Dewitt)
    The Campus on the Hill, 657
Snow Man, The, 394
SNYDER, GARY
    Not Leaving the House, 673
Song: Go and catch a falling star, 491
Song: A Thousand Martyrs I Have Made,
    509
Song: Why so pale and wan, fond lover?
    502
Song in the Front Yard, A, 357
Sonnet 75: One day I wrote her name upon
    the strand, 482
SOPHOCLES
    Oedipus Rex, 853
Soul Gone Home, 706
South, The, 265
Southern Road, 610
SPENDER, STEPHEN
    An Elementary School Classroom in a
        Slum, 624
SPENSER, EDMUND
    Sonnet 75: One day I wrote her name
        upon the strand, 482
Spring and All, 396
Stalking, 117
Standard of Living, The, 253
STANFORD, ANN
    The Blackberry Thicket, 398
Stanzas Written in Dejection, Near Naples,
    528
STEINBECK, JOHN
    The Chrysanthemums, 171
STEVENS, WALLACE
    Anecdote of the Jar, 570
    The Snow Man, 394
    Sunday Morning, 571
Still to be neat, 496
Stopping by Woods on a Snowy Evening,
    407
SUCKLING, SIR JOHN
    Song: Why so pale and wan, fond lover?
        502

Summer Tragedy, A, 135
Sun, The, 665
Sunday Morning, 571
Supermarket in California, A, 655
Surfer, The, 453
SWENSON, MAY
　Analysis of Baseball, 442
　Hearing the Wind at Night, 384
SWIFT, JONATHAN
　A Description of a City Shower, 469
SYNGE, JOHN MILLINGTON
　Riders to the Sea, 696

Taxi, The, 566
TEASDALE, SARA
　Barter, 577
TÉLLEZ, HERNANDO
　Just Lather, That's All, 155
TENNYSON, ALFRED LORD
　The Oak, 378
　Ulysses, 539
That time of year thou mayest in me be-
　hold, 488
There Is a Garden in Her Face, 489
There's a certain slant of light, 406
They flee from me, 479
This Is Just to Say, 577
THOMAS, DYLAN
　Fern Hill, 632
Those Winter Sundays, 629
THURBER, JAMES
　The Catbird Seat, 258
To a Skylark, 530
To an Athlete Dying Young, 438
To Autumn, 392
To Celia, 494
To Helen, 538
To His Coy Mistress, 343
To His Lady, 481
To Lucasta, Going to the Wars, 364
To Marguerite—Continued, 548
To My Dear and Loving Husband, 342
To the Right Honorable William, Earl of
　Dartmouth, 514
To the Virgins, to Make Much of Time, 497
To Waken an Old Lady, 576
Today is a Day of Great Joy, 419
Together, 652
TOLSON, MELVIN B.
　A Legend of Versailles, 609
TOLSTOY, LEO
　God Sees the Truth, but Waits, 75
TOOMER, JEAN
　Georgia Dusk, 605

Trail All Your Pikes, 510
Tree at My Window, 382
Trio for Two Cats and a Trombone, 589
Trip to the Head, A, 328
TWAIN, MARK
　The Notorious Jumping Frog of Calaveras
　　County, 192
Tyger, The, 517

Ulysses, 539
Unknown Citizen, The, 428

Valedictory to Standard Oil of Indiana, A,
　659
Victors, The, 386
Virginal, A, 582

WAGONER, DAVID
　A Valedictory to Standard Oil of Indiana,
　　659
WALCOTT, DEREK
　Nearing La Guaira, 454
WALKER, MARGARET
　Poppa Chicken, 638
WALSH, CHAD
　Port Authority Terminal: 9 A.M. Monday,
　　475
War, 152
Weak Monk, The, 615
WELCH, JAMES
　The Only Bar in Dixon, 684
WELTY, EUDORA
　Powerhouse, 298
　A Worn Path, 143
What Were They Like? 430
WHEATLEY, PHILLIS
　To the Right Honorable William, Earl of
　　Dartmouth, 514
When I consider how my light is spent, 460
When our two souls stand up erect and
　strong, 537
Where Mountain Lion Lay Down with Deer,
　685
WHITMAN, WALT
　Cavalry Crossing a Ford, 547
　The Dalliance of the Eagles, 548
　I Saw in Louisiana a Live-Oak Growing,
　　380
　A Noiseless Patient Spider, 546
Why Should a Foolish Marriage Vow, 507
WILBUR, RICHARD
　The Death of a Toad, 646
Wild Nights—Wild Nights! 346

Wild Swans, 600
WILLIAM CARLOS WILLIAMS
    Spring and All, 396
    This Is Just to Say, 577
    To Waken an Old Lady, 576
Wine in the Wilderness, 1017
Winter, 391
With how sad steps, O Moon, 485
Without Benefit of Declaration, 369
WORDSWORTH, WILLIAM
    Composed Upon Westminster Bridge,
        September 3, 1802, 520
    It is a Beauteous Evening, 522
    Near Dover, 449
Worn Path, A, 143
WRIGHT, JAMES
    A Blessing, 661
WRIGHT, JUDITH
    Extinct Birds, 637

WRIGHT, JUDITH (Cont.):
    , The Surfer, 453
WRIGHT, RICHARD
    The Man Who Was Almost a Man, 288
Written in Disgust of Vulgar Superstition,
    405
WYATT, SIR THOMAS
    They flee from me, 479
WYLIE, ELINOR
    Puritan Sonnet, 579

YEATS, WILLIAM BUTLER
    Leda and the Swan, 562
    Sailing to Byzantium, 563
Yet Do I Marvel, 463
Young Goodman Brown, 102

INDEX OF LITERARY METHODS AND TECHNIQUES

Alliteration, 433
Allusion, 368, 402
Anapest, 446
Antithesis, 481
Apostrophe, 377–378
Assonance, 433
Atmosphere, 124–125

Caricature, 713
Catharsis, 691, 712
Character, 72–75, 961–964
Comedy, 711–713
Conflict, 44
Connotation, 350–352
Content, 6–8

Dactyl, 446
Denotation, 350–352
Dissonance, 433
Drama, 659–663
Dramatic irony, 151

Epiphany, 101

Fiction, 1–5
Figures of speech, 362
Flashback, 45
Foreshadowing, 45
Form, 6

Haiku, 389–390
Hamartia, 712
Hyperbole, 422

Iamb, 446–447
Imagery, 388–390
Irony, 150–152, 421–423

Metaphor, 165, 362–364
Metapoetic, 638
Meter, 445–447
Metonomy, 365
Metrical foot, 446
Mood, 124–126
Motif, 8

Novel, 4–5

Onomatopoeia, 433
Oxymoron, 499, 564

Paradox, 151, 421–423
Personification, 375–378
Plot, 42–45, 851–853
Poetic structure, 467–469
Poetry, 335–338
Point of view, 99–102

Refrain, 433
Rhyme, 433
Rhythm, 444–447

Satire, 151, 421–423
Scansion, 446
Short story, 4–8
Simile, 363
Sonnet, 457–459
Sound, 432–435
Spondee, 446
Subject, 6–8, 339–340, 694–696

Symbolism, 164–166, 400–403
Synethesia, 530

Theme, 6–8, 339–340, 694–696
Tone, 150–152, 411–412
Tragedy, 711–713
Trochee, 446

Understatement, 151

Verbal irony, 151